PHAIDON Dictionary of Twentieth-Century Art

PHAIDON

Dictionary of
Twentieth - Century Art

PHAIDON

Phaidon Press Limited
Littlegate House, St. Ebbe's Street, Oxford

Published in the United States of America by
E. P. Dutton, New York

First published 1973
© 1973 by Phaidon Press Limited

Second impression 1975
Second edition (paperback) 1977

ISBN 0 7148 1822 4
Library of Congress Catalog Card Number 77–81957

Printed in Great Britain by Butler and Tanner Limited Frome and London

Contributors

Morton C. Abromson

Fritz Baumgart

Oto Bihalji-Merin

Joachim Buchner

Herma Buse

Stephen Chaplin

Alexandre Cirici-Pellicer

Jurgen Claus

Sybille Claus

Elisabeth Decker

Jean Dypreau

Dimitris A. Fatouros

Yona Fischer

Teruo Fujieda

Karl Gutbrod

Werner Haftmann

Douglas Hall

Robert Haycraft

Dietrich Helms

R. H. Hubbard

Elisabeth Ingles

Michael McLeod

Duncan McMillan

Julio E. Payro

Eric Peskett

Hans Platte

Mieczyslaw Porebsky

Nancy Reynolds

Keith Roberts

Jurgen Schultze

H. L. Swart

Karin Thomas

Yoshiaki Tono

Eduard Trier

Peter Vergo

Bitite Vinklers

Paul Vogt

Nicholas Wadley

Emily Wassermann

Simon Wilson

Foreword

'Twentieth-century art' falls within certain limits; to fix these limits is not the simple task it may appear. This dictionary covers fully all those artists whose major creative phases fall within this century, including those active at the present time. There are no entries on young painters and sculptors who are only now beginning to gain recognition, since it is not yet possible to say whether they will live up to their promise or whether, like many an acclaimed newcomer before them, they will sink rapidly into obscurity. It was felt that this was a reasonable limitation. Every work of this kind must be to some extent subjective in scope; it is hoped that the reader will understand and accept this basic premise.

Deciding where to begin also presented difficulties. The giants of the late nineteenth century have, properly speaking, no place in a dictionary of twentieth-century art; yet it was felt that without mention of the innovators who gave a new direction to art, any discussion of the style and development of their successors would be meaningless. The most influential figures from the great decades at the end of the last century have accordingly been included.

The writers who have contributed to this book are of many nationalities, and their views naturally differ widely. Articles on artists of the same school written by different authors may therefore contain inconsistencies. It was thought that the views of each author should be respected and that it was unnecessary and undesirable to demand consistency in this respect.

Much of the material here presented was originally written in German, and Mr. Gerald Onn undertook the difficult task of translating it.

Cross-references have been inserted in the text where necessary; names such as de Chirico and van Gogh are found under C and G respectively and are not cross-referenced under D or V.

A

Aaltonen, Wäinö. Finnish sculptor, b. 1894; d. 1966. Aaltonen's work includes busts and full-length figures. His style is classical and his forms mature.

Abstract art. All art is an abstraction and a lot of abstract art inevitably registers figurative associations in the spectator's eye and mind. The twentieth-century concept 'abstract art' is of an art devoid of figurative images which does not seek to represent other visual experiences: it commands its own auto-nomous terms of reference. Many of its protagonists have spoken of achieving a greater 'reality' (devoid of imitation) and have justified their art in terms of its relevance to the contemporary environment, particularly in its new spiritual, philosophical or scientific experiences. The first abstract paintings made in full consciousness of their implications were probably by Kandinsky, 1910–13. The chief prece-dents and motives behind his initiative lie in late nineteenth-century art.

A major aspect of nineteenth-century art was the demise of traditional subject matter, replaced by nature and particularly the landscape. Impressionism, exclusively perceptual, reduced subject matter to something as abstract as light. In reacting to its limitations (also perhaps to the competition of the camera as an eye) the Post-Impressionists resorted to symbolic means of representation. Gauguin spoke against painting things seen, and for the vision of the 'inner eye' (the soul). Following his lead, and the emphasis of marks-on-canvas thrown up by Im-pressionism, Maurice Denis wrote his famous defini-tion of a painting: before all else, it is 'a flat surface covered by colours assembled in a certain order' (1891).

In the great wave of flat, decorative painting sur-rounding *art nouveau*, these ideas became common currency throughout Europe, as did comparisons between art and the pure condition of music. The innate expressive properties of lines, colours, shapes and rhythms became the prime concern of theorists, artists and designers. The close contact between fine and applied arts at this point encouraged artists to use materials freely, uninhibited by traditions of easel painting, etc. Brancusi's early near-abstract carvings relate to this rapport.

Kandinsky said later that a Monet painting re-vealed to him how the expressive power of colour was obstructed by subject matter, but he was also fully conversant with *art nouveau* and its theory in Russia and Germany. His *Improvisations* and *Compositions* (1910–14 on) were conscious experi-ments in an Abstract Expressionism (see his essay *Concerning the Spiritual in Art*, 1912).

For the other pioneers of abstract art—Mondrian (Neo-Plasticism), Malevich (Suprematism), Delaunay (Orphism), Gabo and the Russian Constructivists—the crucial transition was via Cubism, and led to a more formalist, geometric idiom. To Mondrian the only logical conclusion to Analytical Cubism was a wholly autonomous abstract art. Throughout Europe the same conclusion prompted many excur-sions into experimental abstract art (Léger, Picabia, Larionov, Severini, Balla, Lewis, Bomberg, etc.). For Mondrian it was the start of a monumental series of austere, geometric paintings (1917 on) that lasted over twenty years. He saw his art and the whole *de Stijl* movement in Holland as the aesthetic expres-sion of an ideal sense of order, almost an ideal social blueprint.

The major Russian contributions to abstract art were all conceived within the political ferment sur-rounding the 1917 Revolution, and their manifestos also express aspirations for a new sense of order. Malevich's archetypal *Black Square on White* (c. 1915) was an extreme example. He described Suprematism as 'the primacy of pure sensation in the visual arts'. The geometric asymmetry of his later work was highly influential. The Constructivists (Tatlin, Gabo, Pevsner, El Lissitzky, Rodchenko), starting from Cubist collage-constructions but rejecting in principle all traces of Cubist representation, created the frame-work for most later twentieth-century abstract sculpture. They wrote in terms of a modern Realism, the reality of space, the reality of new materials, which were neither modelled nor carved but con-structed. Carving has survived (Arp, Brancusi, etc.), but Constructivism has remained the dominant principle even when its purist aesthetic is rejected (Calder, David Smith).

Apart from the great influence of abstract art on modern architecture and design (especially through the Bauhaus), the only new development between the wars was that of the so-called 'automatic' abstract paintings and drawings of Surrealism (Miró, Masson, Lam). Revived post-war interest in abstract art started from these. Paintings in America (Pollock, Tobey, early Rothko, de Kooning) and Europe (Mathieu, Wols, Davie) were informal, often gestural and Expressionist (hence 'Abstract Expressionism', 'Action Painting'). This was sustained in a more controlled form in later Rothko, Motherwell, Kline, Gottlieb, de Staël, Poliakoff, etc. The subjectivity of this activity has revived an art-for-art's-sake, 'High Art' aura around much abstract art. The flatter 'Post-Painterly Abstraction' of the Americans (New-man, Reinhardt, Kelly, Noland, Olitski); Frank Stella's shaped canvases; the exploitation of kinetic effects (Vasarély, Poons, Riley): all these have fed from each other in an inbred process absent from earlier developments. Inbred criticism has en-couraged it.

Some recent sculpture has been heavily influenced by painting and colour used extensively. The range of media used in three-dimensional art still grows, including light and sound devices. 'Minimal sculpture' (Robert Morris, Judd) has questioned the Cubist-Constructivist tradition of unit or planar construction. 'Earth works' or 'land art' have taken the activity away from the studio artefact and perhaps the most abstract art of all is that of the conceptual artist, since the object need not materialize at all, remaining in the mind of the artist or at most on the printed page.

In the first half-century of its history abstract art has sustained most of its terms of reference, with its old masters securely placed, its principles obviously now part of a longer tradition and its influence clearly felt outside the confines of fine art.

Sidney Janis. *Abstract and Surrealist Art in America*, New York 1944.
Marcel Brion. *Art abstrait*, Paris 1956.
Michel Seuphor. *Dictionary of Abstract Painting, Preceded by a History of Abstract Painting*, London and New York 1958; *Abstract Painting*, London and New York 1962.

Abstract Expressionism. The term 'Abstract Expressionism' in American art was applied to the strongly original and influential development of American painting occurring from the early 1940s to the late 1950s, often also described as 'Action Painting' or 'The New York School'. The major painters, working in highly individualistic and diverse styles, included Arshile Gorky, Jackson Pollock, Robert Motherwell, Hans Hofmann, Mark Rothko, Clyfford Still, Willem de Kooning, Franz Kline and Philip Guston.

After a period of initial hostility by the public to these painters, in the 1950s Abstract Expressionism spread over the United States and became an international development. An important supporter and exponent of the American Abstract Expressionist artists was the critic Clement Greenberg, who suggested in 1948 that the future of western art depended on this phase of American painting.

Harold Rosenberg. 'The American Action Painters', *Art News* LI, December 1952.
Exhibition catalogue, *American Abstract Expressionists and Imagists*, Solomon R. Guggenheim Museum, New York 1961.
Artforum IV, No. 1, September 1965. Special issue on Abstract Expressionism.
Exhibition catalogue, *The New York School: The First Generation; Paintings of the 1940s and 1950s*, ed. Maurice Tuchman, Los Angeles County Museum of Art, Los Angeles 1965.
Irving Sandler. *Abstract Expressionism: The Triumph of American Painting*, London and New York 1970.

Abstraction-Création. In Paris in 1931 a large number of abstract artists combined to form the artists' association known as the *Abstraction-Création*. Their aim was to promote non-objective art by mounting communal exhibitions. This association, which was led by August Herbin and Vantongerloo, was open to artists of all nationalities and at one stage had a membership of 400. In fact, it became a rallying point for artists of the most diverse trends,

from Constructivism to Neo-Plasticism, from Lyrical Abstraction to Expressionism. Its most important members were: Gabo, Pevsner, Mondrian, Doesburg, Lissitzky, Kandinsky, Arp, Kupka, Magnelli, Baumeister, Herbin and Vantongerloo. But, although the *Abstraction-Création* was a heterogeneous body which embraced a wide range of styles and personalities, its members were all abstract artists and to this extent they shared a common attitude to art. Because of this and because of the influence brought to bear by the Neo-Plasticists—who were the strongest single element in the group—the *Abstraction-Création* revealed a general trend towards a Constructivist and concrete art form, in which formal factors took precedence over considerations of colour.

Up to 1936 regular exhibitions were held, which contributed greatly to the breakthrough of modern art. From 1932 to 1936 the group also published an illustrated annual under the title *Abstraction-Création, Art non-figuratif*.

Abstraction Lyrique (Lyrical Abstraction). Between 1947 and the late 1950s a new and completely unconscious art form was evolved, which is frequently referred to as *Abstraction Lyrique*. Other, virtually identical, names for this development are Action Painting, Informal Art and *Tachisme*. The joint exhibition of works by Camille Bryen and Georges Mathieu, which was staged in 1947 under the title *L'Imaginaire*, was originally supposed to have been called *Vers l'Abstraction Lyrique*, and it was only at the very last moment that the name was changed. The concept *Abstraction Lyrique* was evolved in the first instance as a polemical device with which to combat the exponents of 'geometrical abstraction', although it should be pointed out that some of the artists in this new movement felt that the phrase 'psychic abstraction' would have furnished a more precise statement of their objectives. But in the event *Abstraction Lyrique* won the day and came to represent a type of painting in which no significance was attached to objective factors or connotations, these being replaced by a dynamic and, above all, rhythmical form of self-portrayal. The established forms of abstract art gave way to completely spontaneous compositions, in which painterly gesture predominates.

P. Restany. *Lyrisme et Abstraction*, Milan 1960.
G. Mathieu. *Au-delà du Tachisme*, Paris 1963.

Académie Carrière. In 1898 Eugène Carrière opened his academy in Paris. This school of painting, which lasted for only a few years, is remembered more for its pupils than its founder. In 1899 Henri Matisse, Derain, Puy, Laprade and Chabaud, who were later to form the nucleus of the Fauvist movement, all studied at the Académie Carrière. Carrière himself understood little or nothing of their revolutionary ideas, but he was a capable teacher who helped his pupils to develop their individual talents.

Académie Julian. The Académie Julian, which was founded in 1860 by Rodolphe Julian, soon became one of the best-known private schools of art in Paris. It was strictly academic in its approach and subscribed to a literary and sentimental form of naturalism. Its most famous teacher was Bouguereau. In 1888 Sérusier, Bonnard, Vuillard, Ranson, Vallotton, Roussel and Ibels were students at the Académie Julian and, shortly after leaving the school, these artists combined to form the *Nabis* group. It is to this circumstance that the Académie Julian owes its reputation as an early proving ground. Other important students were Corinth (1884), Matisse (1892), Nolde (1899), De La Fresnaye (1903), Derain and Léger (1904) and—later—Marcel Duchamp and Bazaine.

Académie Ranson. In 1908 the *Nabis* painter Paul Ranson opened a private academy in Paris in order to further the cause of *synthétisme*. The venture was highly successful and, when Ranson died, his wife continued to run the school aided by a few of the *Nabis*. Sérusier, Maurice Denis and Roussel all taught at the Académie Ranson, which remained an artistic centre up to the present day and attracted many students from abroad. In the mid-1930s a group of young students, including Manessier, Le Moal, Vieira da Silva and Bertholle, were introduced to Klee's doctrines at the Académie Ranson by Bissière, who taught there from 1925 to 1938 and was the first Frenchman to give serious consideration to Klee's artistic theories. Following the liberation in 1945 Bissière's former students contributed greatly to the revival of the *École de Paris*.

Accardi, Carla. Italian painter, b. 1924 in Traponi, Italy. After studying at the Academy in Palermo Accardi became a founder member of the *Forma* group. She produces automatic script, usually on a monochrome ground, which is reminiscent of Tobey's 'White Writings'.

Achiam, Israel. Israeli sculptor, b. 1916 in Bet-Gan, Palestine. Achiam is a farmer's son who first began to sculpt in a British camp after being interned for opposing the mandatory regime in Palestine. When he was released he spent several years working in a quarry and now sculpts exclusively in stone, chiefly basalt. In 1947 he settled in Paris.

In his works Achiam depicts the human figure in powerful, abstract shapes. The surfaces of his sculptures are invariably coarse-grained.

Acht, René-Charles. Swiss painter, b. 1920 in Basle, Switzerland. Acht studied painting and sculpture at the Academy in Basle. The dark, expressive paintings of his early period (1941–3) were clearly influenced by H. von Marées. In his second period (1945–7), when he was living in Geneva and Stockholm, he produced geometric compositions that are reminiscent of the work of M. Bill. In 1956 he again changed his style and now paints Tachist pictures, in which the structural elements are particularly pronounced. At present he is living in Basle.

Ackermann, Max. German painter, b. 1887 in Berlin. Ackermann studied in Weimar (under van de Velde), Dresden and Munich and—from 1912— Stuttgart (under A. Hölzel). He is an exponent of 'absolute painting', in which the composition follows musical laws. Ackermann is now living in Stuttgart.

Max Ackermann, Societätsverlag, Frankfurt 1965.

Action Painting. Action Painting is one of a group of concepts used to describe what was probably the dominant style of painting between 1945 and 1955. It has one great advantage over expressions such as *Abstraction Lyrique*, Informal Art and *Tachisme* in that it is self-explanatory. Action Painting is quite literally an action performed by a painter, one which involves no objective associations and which produces a permanent record of a dynamic process carried out within a specific period of time. The expression gained general currency after it was used in an article by the American writer Harold Rosenberg in 1952. Jackson Pollock has described what is involved by Action Painting. The canvas, he said, becomes an 'arena', in which the painting is unfolded as if it were part of the painter's life. Other artists who have worked and are still working in this style are Robert Motherwell, Franz Kline, Mathieu, Emilio Vedova, Sonderborg, Helen Frankenthaler, Jean-Paul Riopelle and K. O. Götz.

H. Rosenberg. 'The American Action Painters', *Art News* 1952; *The Tradition of the New*, New York 1959.
N. Ponente. *Zeitgenössische Strömungen*, Geneva 1960.
M. Tuchman (ed.). Catalogue, *The New York School: The First Generation; Paintings of the 1940s and 1950s*, Los Angeles County Museum of Art, Los Angeles 1965.

Adam, Henri-Georges. French sculptor, b. 1904 in Paris; d. 1967 in Perros-Guirec, Brittany. Adam began his career as a painter, draughtsman and graphic artist and in 1938 was awarded the Blumenthal Prize for his etchings. It was not until 1939– 40 that he turned to sculpture. He quickly made his mark in the new medium and in 1943 his carving, *Gisant*, aroused the interest of Picasso, who invited him to come and stay with him. From 1946 onwards Adam was also engaged on tapestry work, producing black and white abstract designs with a strong graphic line. Between 1947 and 1949 he made a series of illustrations for Gérard de Nerval's *Chimères* and in 1955 created a concrete monument

22 metres wide for the port of Le Havre. From 1959 onwards, when he was living in Ville-du-Bois, Seine-et-Oise, he gave sculpture classes at the Paris Academy.

Adam worked in more or less equal measure as a sculptor, a graphic artist and a tapestry designer. His early sculptures are mythically inspired figure compositions, in which the figures have been reduced to their monumental components after the manner of Brancusi. Later he produced abstract works, many of them covered with graphic designs based on geometric shapes.

Catalogue, *Henri-Georges Adam*, Stedelijk Museum, Amsterdam 1955.
Catalogue, *Henri-Georges Adam*, Los Angeles County Museum of Art, Los Angeles 1955.

Adami, Valerio. Italian painter, b. 1935 in Bologna. After studying at the Brera Academy in Milan from 1953 to 1957 Adami worked in London from 1961 to 1962 and in Paris from 1962 to 1964. He is now living in Milan.

In his pictures, which are composed of pure colours framed by comic-strip type drawings, Adami depicts man against the background of posters, adverts and television, which constitutes his 'ready-made world'. His work reveals the influence of Pop Art, Matta and Bacon.

Adams, Robert. British sculptor, b. 1917 in Northampton, England. Adams studied sculpture in Northampton but later moved to London, where he obtained a teaching post at the Central School of Art in 1949. Up to 1954 he worked primarily in wood and stone but has since incorporated bronze, steel and concrete into his range of materials. In 1959 he created a large relief in reinforced concrete for the Municipal Theatre in Gelsenkirchen. His sculptures fall into two main categories: relief-like structures consisting of arrangements of clearly defined cubes and free-standing constructions incorporating flat areas of metal interspersed with rods, the latter exercising a linear function. In 1962 there was a special exhibition of his works at the Biennale in Venice. Adams is now living in London.

Adler, Jankel. Polish painter, b. 1895 in Tuszin, near Lodz; d. 1949 in Aldbourne, England. Adler was born into an orthodox Jewish family. From 1914 to 1918 he studied art in Barmen and in 1922 went to live in Düsseldorf, where he joined the Rhenish Secession. In his early pictures, most of which are portrayals of Jews and the Jewish environment, he successfully integrated the most diverse influences —from Chagall and Cubism to Léger, Max Ernst and Picasso—and so created a highly personal, poetic style. But from 1931 onwards, as a result of his contact with Klee, he developed a looser, more abstract type of pictorial composition. After emigra-

ting to Paris in 1933 he worked in Atelier 17 with Hayter. Later, in the South of France, he received a powerful stimulus from Picasso and turned to pure abstracts. In 1939 he went to Scotland with the Free Polish Army before moving to London in 1943. His late figure compositions are highly abstract works, which were strongly influenced by Picasso and which themselves influenced Colquhoun, MacBryde and Le Brocquy.

A. Klapheck. *Jankel Adler*, Recklinghausen 1966.

Adrian-Nilsson, Gösta. Swedish painter, b. 1884 in Lund. After attending the Zahrtmann-Rhode School in Copenhagen Adrian-Nilsson made a thorough study of Futurism and Cubism. In 1914 he went to Berlin, where he developed a preference for dark luminous colours and evolved a decorative and dynamic semi-abstract style which reveals the influence of Wassily Kandinsky and Franz Marc. By 1919 Adrian-Nilsson was producing completely non-objective works and was the first Swedish artist to do so. In the 1920s he painted stylized figures based on geometrical forms that are reminiscent of Léger. These were followed by surrealist works in the 1930s, after which Adrian-Nilsson reverted to pure abstract compositions with a powerful emotional component. Adrian-Nilsson gave considerable impetus to the Swedish 'Halmstad group'.

Aeropittura. In this movement the whole of the Futurist programme was reduced to a single theme: the sensations induced by the technical phenomena of modern life, especially flying. The first attempts to portray these sensations were made in 1926. Three years later, in 1929, Marinetti published a manifesto entitled *Aeropittura*. In 1931 the first *Aeropittura* exhibition was staged and included works by Dottori, Filla, B. Marinetti, Tato and Munari. This was followed by further exhibitions in Paris (1932) and Berlin (1934), where the *Aeropittura* artists enjoyed the patronage of Goebbels. The movement began to fall apart following the death of Marinetti in 1944 and broke down completely when Fascism collapsed in 1945.

The artists of the *Aeropittura* association used Neo-Impressionist techniques to portray the sensation of aircraft speed and its dynamic lines of force.

Aeschbacher, Hans. Swiss sculptor, b. 1906 in Zürich. Aeschbacher comes from peasant stock. After serving an apprenticeship as a printer and finding that he had little liking for his trade he decided to train as a book illustrator. In 1926 he went to Rome, where he combined his artistic activities with a wide variety of temporary occupations. Then, in 1936, he suddenly turned to sculpture, carving extremely sensuous human figures. Over the years, however, his work grew progressively less representational and in 1956 he produced his first monolithic stele. Since then he has created endless variations on the same basic theme of the architectonic, harmoniously proportioned stele or menhir. He himself often refers to these works, which are carved in stone (usually lava, granite or marble), as 'figures'. Aeschbacher is now living in Zürich.

Hans Aeschbacher, Neuchâtel 1959.

Afro (Afro Basaldella). Italian painter, b. 1912 in Udine. Afro is the son of a painter and decorator and the brother of Mirko and Dino Basaldella, the sculptors. He trained at the Academies in Florence and Rome, completing his studies in 1931. After a short stay in Paris he eventually settled in Rome in 1937. From 1940 to 1944, when he was serving with the Italian forces, he gave occasional classes at the Venice Academy. In 1947 he aligned himself with the *Fronte Nuovo delle Arti* and in 1950 visited the USA. Two years later he exhibited with the *Gruppo degli Otto*. In 1954–5 he produced his first murals and in 1956 won the First Prize for Italian Painting at the Biennale in Venice. In 1958 he taught at Mills College in Oakland, California, and executed a mural for the UNESCO Building in Paris. He is now living in Rome and teaches at the Rome Academy.

Afro is a post-Cubist painter who transforms natural experiences into abstract images. His flickering colours and illusionist use of space place him in the company of the Abstract Impressionists.

L. Venturi. *Afro*, Rome 1954.
Afro (with a preface by J. J. Sweeney), Rome 1961.

Agam, Yaacov. Israeli kinetic artist, b. 1928 in Rishon-le-Zion, Israel. After completing his studies at the Bezalel School of Art in Jerusalem Agam attended the School of Arts and Crafts in Zurich from 1949 to 1951. He then settled in Paris, where he is still living today. Agam produces variable paintings and reliefs. In his early works in this genre the variability depended on the angle from which the works were viewed, that is, the pictures moved when the viewer moved. Later, however, Agam went on to create variable tableaux, in which the viewer is able to rearrange the component elements and thus plays an active part in the creative process. These variables are linked with acoustic and lighting effects. In 1964 Agam won the Grand Prix at the Bienal in São Paulo. He has also produced wall paintings and is interested in the multi-dimensional theatre.

Y. Agam. *Y. Agam*, Neuchâtel 1962 (a collection of Agam's writings).
Jasia Reichardt. *Y. Agam*, London 1966.
Exhibition catalogue, *Lumière et Mouvement*, Paris 1967.

Agar, Eileen. British painter and constructivist, b. 1904 in Buenos Aires. She now lives in London, having been educated and trained in England. She participated in Surrealist exhibitions in London (1936), New York and Tokyo (1937) and Amsterdam (1938), and is represented in the Tate Gallery. Her work is typical of the British interpretation of Surrealism, exploiting the unexpected conjunction of forms and objects, but avoiding the literary, political and psychological connections of the movement.

Agostini, Peter. American sculptor, b. 1913 in New York City. He studied for one year at the Leonardo da Vinci School of Art, New York, and at the University of Mexico (1948) while also studying mural painting at San Miguel de Allende. In 1949 he studied at the Atelier Fernand Léger, Paris. An artist who emerged along with the second generation of Abstract Expressionists, he works mainly in plaster over various armatures. In *Christmas Package* (1963, plaster, New York, Stephen Radich Gallery) his use of plaster over drapery and balloon-like spheres anticipates Pop imagery, while in *Hurricane* (1962, aluminium and plaster, New York, Stephen Radich Gallery) his sweeping form soaring to an apex emphasizes a sense of movement and freedom. In 1964 he received a Brandeis University Creative Arts Award and in the same year exhibited at the Whitney Annual and the São Paulo Bienal.

E. A. Navaretta. 'Agostini Makes a Sculpture', *Art News* LXI, May 1962.

Ahlers-Hestermann, Friedrich. German painter, b. 1883 in Hamburg. Ahlers-Hestermann associated with the members of the German Matisse school in Paris. He was also influenced by Cézanne and evolved a cultured style of painting based on a modified form of Cubism. He is now living in Berlin.

F. Ahlers-Hestermann. *Pause vor dem dritten Akt* (Memoirs), Berlin 1949.

Ajmone, Giuseppe. Italian painter, b. 1923 in Carpignano, Italy. Since studying at the Brera Academy in Milan Ajmone has developed a lyrical style of painting, in which he transforms natural experiences into abstract images. He is now living in Milan.

M. Valsecchi. *Giuseppe Ajmone*, Milan 1958.

Akasegawa, Genpei. Japanese painter, b. 1937 in Yokohama. He studied at Musashino Art University, Tokyo, and later was a founding member of the Neo-Dada Organizer group. Under the influence of Surrealism, he made packed objects. In 1963 he fabricated counterfeit money, for which he was prosecuted and judged guilty. He now lives in Tokyo.

Albers, Josef. American painter and designer, b. 1888 in Germany; d. 1976. His first lithographs and woodcuts (1916–19) were done in Essen, Germany, in the Expressionist tradition of Erich Heckel and Karl Schmidt-Rottluff. While at the Munich Art Academy during the following years, he studied with Franz von Stuck, who had been the teacher of Kandinsky and Klee. At the age of 32 Albers entered the Bauhaus school in Weimar, first as a student and later as a teacher. There, during the early 1920s, he was occupied by the creation of stained-glass windows, and also began a series of glass paintings that gave the first evidence of his use of the square as a distinct form. These were didactic, exhaustive and carefully gauged investigations into relationships of line, shape, colour, transparency and opacity. They demonstrate Albers' striving for the permanent and austere, which is reflected in his subsequent use of materials in paintings, prints or architectural projects. He also designed furniture, using these same principles of smooth surface, uniform texture and hard, durable substances, creating the first bent laminated chair intended for mass production. Albers' theoretical precision was always equalled by a precision of craft, and his avowed aesthetic was that 'in producing art I please myself and educate others to see'.

In 1933, upon the closing of the Bauhaus, Albers was one of the first of its teachers to emigrate to the United States, where he became one of the most influential propagators of Bauhaus ideas on design reform and methods. At Black Mountain College in North Carolina, where he taught from 1933 to 1949, he opened a textile class; from 1938 to 1948 he worked on masonite, evolving geometric forms, with the square finally emerging as his dominant theme. Moving on to Yale University in 1950, where he became chairman of the department of architecture and design, he began his renowned series of paintings and lithographs, which have been given the generic title *Homage to the Square*. Albers reduced that shape to a basic concentric arrangement, which anticipated the reductive, structural direction art was to take in the 1960s (*Homage to the Square: Ascending*, 1953, New York, Whitney Museum). His exploitation of the fact that chromatically proximate colours can produce the illusion of a third colour also made him a precursor of the Op artists who experiment with visual perception. Although Albers preferred to speak of the 'interaction' of colours rather than to use the term 'vibration', there is usually in his paintings a sense of receding or advancing movement of coloured planes within the pictorial space, as well as a contraction and expansion of their contours on the picture surface.

François Bucher. *Josef Albers: Despite Straight Lines; An Analysis of his Graphic Constructions*, London and New Haven (Conn.) 1961.
Josef Albers. *Interaction of Color*, London and New Haven (Conn.) 1963.
Los Angeles County Museum of Art. *Josef Albers: White Line Squares*, Los Angeles 1966.

Albert, Calvin. American sculptor, b. 1918 in Grand Rapids, Michigan. He studied in Chicago, and moved to New York in 1947. In 1953 he won an ICA competition. He developed his own metal alloy, which he used to produce Abstract Expressionist work. In 1960 there was a retrospective show of his work at the Jewish Museum, New York.

Albiker, Karl. German sculptor, b. 1878 in Ühlingen, Black Forest; d. 1961 in Ettlingen. After studying at the Academy in Karlsruhe and the Académie Julian in Paris (1898 onwards), Albiker spent two years in Rome (1904–6). He also became friendly with Hermann Haller. From 1919 onwards he taught at the Technical School of Art and the Academy in Dresden. In 1945 he settled in Ettlingen.

Albiker was influenced by Rodin, Maillol and early Greek sculpture. Like Kolbe, he evolved an heroic, monumental human type, which owed much to Nietzsche's Superman concept.

Karl Albiker. *Das Problem der Kunst*, Frankfurt 1962.

Albright, Ivan Le Lorraine. American painter, b. 1897 in North Harvey, Illinois. Before the First World War he studied architecture at Northwestern University and at the University of Illinois; during the war he was attached to a medical unit and made surgical drawings whose clinical precision was echoed in his later paintings. Afterwards he enrolled at the École des Beaux-Arts in Nantes, and from 1919 to 1923 studied at the Art Institute of Chicago. In the early 1920s Albright began to achieve notoriety for his morbidly meticulous renderings of reality. His painting *That Which I Should Have Done I Did Not Do* (1931–41, Chicago, Art Institute) won a medal as the best entry in the 1942 Artists for Victory Exhibition held at the Metropolitan Museum in New York. In it one sees a gnarled door, a funeral wreath, and a sepulchral hand enshrouded in an aura of decay and horror. This almost surrealistic painting, with its wealth of minuscule textural details, took ten years to complete. Sometimes Albright spent many years on his initial charcoal sketches, and then gently applied glazes, working perhaps for a week on a single square inch of the canvas.

Like his contemporary Hyman Bloom or the group of painters known as the Magic Realists, Albright was interested in revealing that each particle of life—even if depicted as withering flesh—is shimmeringly alive. For the most part, however, the viewing public was repulsed by his preoccupation with putrescent themes, while still impressed by the artist's technical abilities in recording them. Major retrospectives of Albright's work were held at the Art Institute of Chicago in 1964 and in New York at the Whitney Museum of American Art in 1965.

Exhibition catalogue: *Ivan Albright: A Retrospective Exhibition*, Art Institute of Chicago 1964. Text by Frederick A. Sweet.

Alcopley, Lewin. German-American painter, b. 1910 in Germany. He received some early art training in Dresden but is mainly self-taught. He resided in Switzerland for two years (1935–7) and has lived in the United States since 1937. Between 1945 and 1947 he was a member of Stanley William Hayter's Atelier 17 in New York, and was one of the twelve founders of 'The Club' in 1949, a New York meeting ground for artists. He was given his first one-man show in 1946 at the Ashley Gallery, New York. Alcopley was also a member of the American Abstract Artists and the *Groupe Espace* in Paris, where he lived from 1952 to 1959. During this European period he spent time in London and Germany, executing a 50-foot mural at the University of Freiburg in 1958 and initiating the exhibition *L'Encre de Chine dans la Calligraphie et l'Art Japonais Contemporain* which was first shown in 1955 at the Stedelijk Museum, Amsterdam. He is primarily a painter of movement, rhythm and colour. Though avoiding the literal, many of his series of works are thematic, such as the themes of New York or his series entitled *Spiritus ubi vult spirat* ('the spirit bloweth where it listeth') which has a decidedly Japanese flavour of delicate stroke, sense of space and planned voids (*Spiritus ubi vult spirat xxv*, 1960–2, New York, Louis Alexander Gallery). Also a practising research specialist in the biological and medical sciences, the artist is married to the Icelandic painter Nina Tryggvadottir.

Kenneth B. Sawyer. Exhibition catalogue, *Lewin Alcopley*, Louis Alexander Gallery, New York, 6–24 March 1962.

Alechinsky, Pierre. Belgian painter and graphic artist, b. 1927 in Brussels. After studying at the École supérieure d'Architecture et d'Art décoratif in Brussels Alechinsky joined the *Jeune Peinture belge* association in 1947. In 1949 he also joined the *Cobra* group but disassociated himself from it in 1951. He then moved to Paris where he studied drawing with Hayter at Atelier 17 in 1952. Soon afterwards he made contact with a number of Japanese calligraphers, including Shiryu Morita. In 1955 he travelled in the Far East and made a film in Japan entitled *Calligraphie Japonaise*. From 1960 onwards he travelled in the USA and Mexico. He is now living in Paris.

In his early phase Alechinsky worked in a post-Cubist style, which was influenced by Picasso. He next moved towards Ensor and then—when he was in contact with the *Cobra* group, especially Asger Jorn—towards a kind of Nordic Expressionism, painting ghostly visions in an ecstatic style with swirling strokes of the brush. Alechinsky's work, which reveals the influence of eastern calligraphy, includes a large number of graphic designs.

Jacques Putman. *Pierre Alechinsky*, Paris 1967.
Catalogue of Graphic Works. Gal. van de Loo, Munich 1967.

Alex, Kosta. American painter and sculptor, b. 1925 in Elizabeth, New Jersey. After training as a carpenter Alex first worked as a painter before finally turning to sculpture. He has been living in Paris since 1947.

With very few exceptions Alex's sculptures deal with one of two themes: heads and hands. His favourite materials are clay, wood and bronze. Some of his works are modelled or carved in bas-relief and painted in a primitive style, others are free-standing, severely abstract structures, which are reminiscent of ritual idols. The overall impression created by his work is one of great naïveté and almost manic obsession.

Alliance of Youth. This group, an *avant-garde* artists' association formed in St. Petersburg in 1909, was similar to the *Bubonovgi Valet* association, which was founded in Moscow in the following year, in that it too was western- and, more particularly, Munich-oriented. At the first Alliance of Youth exhibition in 1910 all the pictures shown were by St. Petersburg artists, the most important of whom were Pavel Filinov and Olga Rosanova. But at the second exhibition staged later the same year at the Vladimir Izdebskiy Gallery in Odessa pictures by Moscow artists such as Larionov, Gontcharova and the brothers Burljuk were also exhibited. So too were works by various members of the Munich school, including Kandinsky (who showed fifty-two pictures), Jawlensky and Gabriele Münter. It was in Odessa that Kandinsky first made contact with the Moscow group. The Alliance of Youth also became a focal point of Russian Futurism. In November 1913 it staged its last exhibition, which was followed in December 1913 by a large-scale Futuristic theatrical presentation in the Luna Park Theatre.

Allied Artists' Association. This group was formed in 1908 by a group of progressive French-oriented artists led by Walter Sickert in order to oppose the reactionary attitude of the Royal Academy and organize communal exhibitions after the manner of the Salon des Indépendants. Their artistic aims, as defined by the art critic Frank Rutter, were simplicity, sincerity and expression. Their models were Gauguin, Cézanne and van Gogh. Apart from Sickert, the members of the association were Harold Gilman, Spencer Gore, Augustus John, Lucien Pissarro, Henry Lamb, Robert Bevan, Walter Bayes, Charles Ginner and J. B. Manson. Their first exhibition was staged as early as 1908 in the Royal Albert Hall. Others followed. The influential Camden Town Group evolved from the Association in 1911.

All-over Painting. The term 'all-over painting' was first associated in American art with the large, Abstract Expressionist drip paintings of Jackson Pollock, which appeared at times to have no distinct top or bottom and to imply possible extension beyond the canvas. The concept was suggested by the seemingly random, overall treatment of the canvas, which Pollock often laid on the floor, working on it from all sides or even from within the canvas itself. Later, the same term could also be applied to the paintings of other artists which had an overall design of almost identical elements or a nearly uniform colour-field.

Altherr, Heinrich. Swiss painter, b. 1878 in Basle; d. 1947 in Zürich. After studying in Munich (under Knirr), Rome, and Basle Altherr taught at the Academy in Stuttgart from 1913 onwards. In 1939 he returned to Switzerland.

Apart from his mosaics and stained-glass windows Altherr also produced many murals. In his sombre, highly expressive paintings, which are reminiscent of Daumier, he portrayed the darker aspects of human existence.

W. Überwasser and W. Braun. *Der Maler Heinrich Altherr. Sein Weg und Werk*, Zürich 1938.

Alva. German painter, b. 1901 in Berlin. After spending his childhood and youth in Galicia Alva began to paint in Paris in 1928. He went to Palestine in 1934, moving on to England in the following year and remaining there until 1955. He then returned to Paris, where he is now living.

Alva's paintings are lyrical abstracts.

Herbert Read. *Alva*, London 1951.

Alvermann, Hans Peter. German sculptor, b. 1931 in Düsseldorf. Alvermann studied at the Academy of Art in Düsseldorf from 1954 to 1958. His early works are combinations of ready-made, collage and painting. For him art is a vehicle of contemporary social criticism. Not surprisingly, therefore, he has veered more and more towards the conception of 'Art as a sociogram', as a form of propaganda. The significance of his works lies in the provocative, ironical and parodistic juxtaposition of functional objects.

Alviani, Getulio. Italian sculptor and designer, b. 1939 in Udine. Alviani first began to analyse the problems of visual art in 1959; in 1960 he worked on polyvalent and monochrome pictures and variable living units; in 1961 he programmed groups of dynamic optical structures, carried out an investigation into light vibrations and turned out mass-produced sculptural objects. He has also made numerous optical designs for clothing materials. Alviani's favourite material is aluminium. He is a member of the international movement 'New Trends'.

Amaral, Tarsila do. Brazilian painter, sculptress and authoress, b. 1900 in São Paulo, Brazil. After studying in São Paulo from 1917 onwards Amaral came to Europe in 1921, where she first began to paint in an impressionistic manner. She then met Lhôte, Léger and Gleizes and was influenced by them. In 1925 Amaral returned to Brazil, where she became a member of the *avant-garde* and joined the *Antropofágico* group in São Paulo. On a visit to Minas Gerais she was deeply impressed by the local folk art and subsequently incorporated its strong decorative colours and primitive forms into her own pictures. Of recent years Amaral has been producing sombre and socially committed pictures, which reflect her political sympathies.

Sergio Milliet. *Tarsila do Amaral*, São Paulo 1953.

American Abstract Artists. The American Abstract Artists became a formal group of American painters and sculptors in 1936, with Balcomb Greene the first president. The organization developed from informal artists' discussions in New York, during a period when American abstract art was generally ignored in favour of painting depicting the American scene. The American Abstract Artists resolved to form independent exhibitions and defined their purpose as uniting American abstract artists, exhibiting their work, and providing an opportunity for them to exchange ideas. The founding members included Josef Albers, Ilya Bolotowsky and Ibram Lassaw; over the next thirty years the organization attracted a total of about two hundred artists. The first exhibition opened in April 1937 and was followed by annual exhibitions, held primarily in New York but occasionally also sent elsewhere in the United States and abroad (a European tour was organized in 1950 and a Japanese exhibition in 1955). Other activities included the publication of books, lecture series, and in 1940, a public demonstration against the policies of the Museum of Modern Art as too conservative. The original purpose of establishing acceptance of American abstract art was largely achieved by 1944, and several members advocated dissolving the organization; it experienced a period of internal dissension and a decline in activity due to the war, but in the 1950s it again increased in membership and activity.

Catalogue, *Geometric Abstraction in America*, Whitney Museum of American Art, New York 1962.

American Association of Painters and Sculptors, Inc. The major accomplishment, although originally not the only purpose, of the American Association of Painters and Sculptors was the organization of the 1913 Armory Show in New York. Formed as a gesture of dissatisfaction with the rigid and narrow exhibition standards of the National Academy of Design, the Association was to hold exhibitions, on a non-jury basis, of the best available modern art from both Europe and America. The first official meeting of the organization, initiated by four young artists, Henry Fitch Taylor, Jerome Myers, Elmer MacRae and Walt Kuhn, was held on 19 December

1911. At this meeting the following officers were elected: J. Alden Weir, president; Gutzon Borglum, vice-president; Walt Kuhn, secretary; and Elmer MacRae, treasurer. Eventually the group numbered twenty-five and represented a considerable diversity of outlook; many of the members had been associated with earlier American *avant-garde* groups, such as The Eight (all of whom accepted membership except Everett Shinn) and the Independent Artists, who had organized an exhibition in 1910, but there were also a number of prominent and widely respected artists such as Weir, Borglum and Arthur Davies, and even some who belonged to the Academy. The anti-Academy spirit of the Association prevailed, however, and was further emphasized by the press, which provided enthusiastic and favourable coverage, so that Weir, an Academician, felt compelled to resign his presidency as early as January 1912. The new president was Davies, who revealed himself as a strongly independent leader but also as an indispensable, energetic and excellent organizer and the major financial supporter of the entire undertaking. His major assistants were Walt Kuhn and Walter Pach, while the other members of the Association participated in various specialized organizational committees. The form of the first, and only, exhibition planned by the Association, which became known as the Armory Show, was that of a large international exhibition, inspired by the Cologne Sonderbund show in Germany in 1912. It finally included approximately 1,300 works, about one-third of which were American; many of the European works represented the most modernistic European artists, most of whom had never before been seen in the United States. Exhibited in New York, Chicago and Boston, the Armory Show was accompanied by publicity on a tremendously large scale, which included postcards, catalogues and monographs.

Although the Association had been envisaged as a long-term organization, as is evident from its carefully constructed constitution, at the end of the Armory Show it virtually ceased its activity. The group was effectively dissolved at the membership meeting of 18 May 1914, when most of the members resigned, even though on paper it continued to exist until 23 August 1916, the date of the last entry in the financial records. The dissolution of the Association was essentially the result of disenchantment with the lack of measurable gain and profit from the Armory Show and, perhaps even more, of the increasingly strong and significant division between two factions in American art: one group, such as The Eight, favouring the interests of American art *per se* and another, including Davies and his circle, supporting primarily the modernistic trends of European art.

American Association of Painters and Sculptors, Inc. *For and Against: Views on the International Exhibition Held in New York and Chicago*, ed. Frederick J. Gregg, New York 1913.

Arthur B. Davies. 'Explanatory Statement: The Aim of the American Association of Painters and Sculptors', *Arts and Decoration* III, March 1913. Special issue on the Armory Show.
Milton Brown. *The Story of the Armory Show*, Greenwich (Conn.) 1963.

American Scene Painting. A strong movement of American scene painting developed in the mid-1920s and culminated in the 1930s as part of the general American isolationist and nationalistic trend following the First World War. In art, the reaction was against the modernist wave of the preceding decade towards realistic art with social content. Although partly a revival of a realistic depiction of contemporary American life as established by The Eight and others of the early twentieth century, the American scene painting of the 1920s and 1930s differed in being more nationalistic and in having rural or small-town, rather than urban, subject matter; contemporary literary parallels existed in the work of such writers as Sherwood Anderson and Sinclair Lewis. The first major painters of the American scene in the twenties were Charles Burchfield and Edward Hopper, both of whom worked in a generally realistic style (although Burchfield tended also towards the fantastic), choosing motifs of bleakness and loneliness in American life. A much more extreme manifestation of American scene painting was represented in the 1930s by Thomas Benton, John Steuart Curry and Grant Wood, who showed a stronger regionalism that was centred in the rural Midwest.

Milton W. Brown. 'The Early Realism of Hopper and Burchfield', *College Art Journal* VII, Autumn, 1947; *American Painting from the Armory Show to the Depression*, Princeton 1955.
John I. H. Baur. *Revolution and Tradition in Modern American Art*, Cambridge (Mass.) 1951.

Amiet, Cuno. Swiss painter, b. 1868 in Solothurn; d. 1961 in Oschwand, Switzerland. From 1884–6 Amiet was a pupil of Frank Buchser, from 1886–8 he studied at the Academy of Art in Munich and from 1888–91 at the Académie Julian in Paris (under Bouguereau). He then made contact with Vallotton, Sérusier and Maurice Denis, spent some time painting in Brittany and in 1892, when he was in Pont-Aven, met Émile Bernard and Armand Séguin, who introduced him to the artistic ideas evolved by the Gauguin school. Later the same year he returned to Switzerland. There he became friendly with Hodler, who shared an exhibition with him and Giovanni Giacometti (who was also a friend of Amiet's) in Zürich in 1898. In the same year Amiet went to live on the Oschwand and spent the rest of his life there, surrounded by numerous students, including Morgenthaler. In 1904 he and Hodler again exhibited together, this time at the Vienna *Sezession*. In 1906 he was invited to join the *Brücke*, which he did for a short time. In 1918 he began to sculpt as well as paint and in the immediate postwar period also produced a large number of frescoes (Züricher Kunsthaus, Kunstmuseum, Berne, etc.). In 1931 fifty of his early works were destroyed when the Munich Glaspalast was burnt down. Up to 1939 he made regular visits to Paris.

Amiet and his friend, Hodler, were the two foremost exponents of *Jugendstil* in Switzerland. Amiet's highly luminous style of painting, which was based on a simplified colour scheme, was the fruit of his encounter with the symbolism of the *Nabis* and with the school of Pont-Aven. During his early period he was influenced primarily by van Gogh, Gauguin and Hodler. Subsequently, however, he also took a lively interest in the ideas evolved by the Fauves and the German Expressionists, successfully resolving the problems which these posed for his own development.

A. Baur. *Cuno Amiet*, Basle 1943.
A. Tatarinoff. *Cuno Amiet*, Solothurn 1958.

Anderlecht, Englebert van. Belgian painter, b. 1918 in Schaerbeck, Belgium; d. 1961. After a hard childhood and youth Anderlecht studied painting at evening classes at the Academy of St. Josse ten Noode. He won the *Prix de Rome* and a scholarship. He was a member of the *G 58* group and one of the founder members of the *Hessenkreis* in Antwerp. From 1950 onwards he suffered from chronic illness.

Anderlecht painted in an Abstract Expressionist mode. His works, which are highly dramatic, are reminiscent of Vedova and Gérard Schneider.

Englebert van Anderlecht, Solothurn 1962.

Andersson, Torsten. Swedish painter, b. 1926. When he started to paint in 1955 Andersson produced geometrical abstracts after the manner of Dewasne. From this geometrical style he subsequently evolved a type of Abstract Expressionism. Andersson has held a professorial post at the College of Art in Stockholm since 1960.

Andreou, Constantin. Greek sculptor, b. 1917 in São Paulo, Brazil. Andreou was born in Brazil of Greek parents, who took him to Athens in 1924, when he was seven. Later he attended the Industrial School of Art in Athens, winning a travelling scholarship in 1945. This brought him to Paris, where he has been living ever since.

Andreou models abstract bronzes inspired by animal forms.

Andrews, Michael. British painter, b. 1928 in Norwich. He was trained at the Slade School of Art, and was a Rome Scholar in 1953. He is represented in the Tate Gallery and the Arts Council collection. Andrews is a figurative painter influenced by Bacon and, through the Slade School, the Euston Road School tradition. He now lives in London.

Andriessen, Mari Silvester. Dutch sculptor, b. 1897 in Haarlem. Andriessen studied at the Technical School of Art in Haarlem and the Academies in Amsterdam and Munich (under Blecker). After an early period, in which he carved realistic sculptures under the influence of the Gothic and Romanesque traditions, he moved towards a modified form of Expressionism. Andriessen has created numerous monuments. He is now living in Haarlem.

Marius van Beek. *Mari Andriessen*, Amsterdam 1964.

Angeli, Franco. Italian painter, b. 1935 in Rome. Angeli is one of the artists who have developed a 'new figuration', i.e. a new type of figurative composition, from informal art. In his works he incorporates texts, fragments of texts and political and economic symbols (dollar notes, ciphers, swastikas). Angeli is now living in Rome.

Angeli, Radovani Kosta. Yugoslav sculptor, b. 1916 in London. Angeli completed his studies at the Accademia di Brera in Milan in 1938 and had his first exhibition in 1940 in Zagreb. The principal features of his works—which include portraits, nudes and figurative compositions—are their block-like simplification and their vital expression. The inner tensions are resolved without fragmentation. Angeli's anthropomorphic female figures are both primitive and transfigured at one and the same time. Their solid materials transcend the natural sphere and pass over into an eternal inorganic realm: the flesh appears both as an incarnation of fertility and as a tangible symbol of an intellectual form of sensitivity. The subject matter of Angeli's extremely powerful graphic works ranges from prehistoric matriarchal idols to the contrapuntal designs of modern art.

O. Bihalji-Merin. *Abenteuer der modernen Kunst*, Cologne 1962.
Jure Kastelan. *Introduction to the Catalogue for the Gallery of Contemporary Art*, Zagreb 1965.

Annenkopf, Georges (Yuri Annenkov). Russian painter, b. 1894 in Petropavlovsk, Kamchatka. Annenkopf studied in St. Petersburg and Paris. Upon his return to Russia in 1913 he joined the Russian Cubo-Futurists. His principal works during this period—which were all executed in the Cubo-Futurist mode—were collages and stage-sets. Since 1924 Annenkopf has lived and worked in Paris.

Anquetin, Louis. French painter, b. 1861 in Entrepagny, Eure; d. 1932 in Paris. After meeting Émile Bernard and Toulouse-Lautrec in the Atelier Cormon Anquetin joined with them and van Gogh in founding the *Groupe du Petit Boulevard* in 1886–7. He was also introduced to the painters of Pont-Aven and to the *Nabis* by Bernard, who was doubtless the inspiration for the experimental Pointillist and Cloisonnist work which Anquetin produced at this time. In 1889 he was represented at the exhibition staged by the *Groupe Synthétiste* in the Café Volpini. His figure compositions, which are enlivened by decorative *motifs*, were influenced by Gauguin and van Gogh.

Antes, Horst. German painter, sculptor and graphic artist, b. 1936 in Heppenheim, Germany. After studying under H. A. P. Grieshaber at the Karlsruhe Academy from 1957 to 1959 Antes returned there in 1965 to join the teaching staff. He is now living in Wolfartsweier near Karlsruhe.

When he first began to paint in the late 1950s Antes took his orientation partly from German Expressionism and partly from his former teacher Grieshaber, producing powerfully coloured works which were a variant of the 'New Figuration'. From these he went on to develop his 'Gnome' pictures: profile views of magical, gnome-like figures spread out rather like Egyptian reliefs and consisting of head, legs and arms, often with the eyes set one above the other. Since Antes visited Italy in 1962–3 his pictorial structures have become much clearer and in many of his works the figures and the pictorial space are completely fused. In his painting, in which he appears to be pursuing a path of development midway between Beckmann and Léger, Antes has depicted individual figures, pairs, groups of three and—from the mid-1960s onwards—single heads, which are frequently offset by simple object or animal forms of a symbolic nature such as a letter, a dove, a cock's comb. Antes has also produced sculptures and graphic works.

Anthoons, Willy. Belgian sculptor, b. 1911 in Malines. Anthoons studied both architecture and sculpture. In 1933 he was a pupil of Oscar Jespers. In 1945, when the *Jeune Peinture belge* association was set up, he was the only sculptor to become a founder member. From 1948 onwards he has lived in Paris.

During his early period Anthoons was an academic sculptor but subsequently, due to the influence of Laurens and Vitullo, he began to carve abstract works in wood and stone. These later pieces with their simple, clearly defined structures are reminiscent of stelae.

Michel Seuphor. *Willy Anthoons*, Antwerp 1954.

Anuskiewicz, Richard. American painter, b. 1930 in Erie, Pennsylvania. Anuskiewicz studied at the Cleveland Institute of Art and at Yale under Josef Albers. He works on abstract combinations of colours in geometrical shapes which dazzle the spectator and produce curious optical effects.

Apollinaire, Guillaume (Wilhelm Apollinaris de Krostowitski). French poet and author, b. 1880 in Rome; d. 1918 in Paris. Apollinaire was the son of a Polish noblewoman and an Italian officer. He first came to Paris in 1898 and, apart from visits to Holland, Bavaria and Bohemia, spent the next three years in the French capital, where he led a Bohemian existence. In 1901, when he was 21 years of age, he became house tutor to a noble Rhenish family but relinquished the post in the following year to return to Paris, where he worked as author and publisher of erotic literature and contributed to newspapers and literary journals. From 1913 onwards he was the central figure in a group of young poets in Paris. During this period he wrote novels, short stories, essays and critical works, e.g. *Les Peintres Cubistes* of 1913. His most important works were his lyrics. *Le Bestiaire ou Cortège d'Orphée* ('The Bestiary or the Retinue of Orpheus') of 1911 was followed by *Alcools* of 1913 and *Calligrammes* of 1918. In this last work the poet's and the painter's arts are merged, for Apollinaire used typographical techniques to produce optical effects, a device that is still being used in contemporary art. As a lyricist he initiated experimental writing as a literary mode and mediated between Symbolism and Surrealism, whilst as an *avant-garde* critic he wrote about Matisse, Picasso and Braque, proclaimed the Futurist movement and espoused the cause of Cubism, whose theoretical basis he himself had evolved. At the same time he developed an experimental form of poetry, which corresponded to Cubism in so far as it reflected the same kind of world, one in which perspective was replaced by the simultaneity of different views and different events. It was Apollinaire who invented the term Orphism to denote the colour Cubism developed by Delaunay. He also coined the word Surrealism, in the subtitle of his farce *Les Mamelles de Tirésias* ('The Breasts of Tiresias') of 1917, and must be regarded as a precursor of this movement, for Breton, Soupault and—above all—Cocteau were all strongly influenced by his lyrical works. Apollinaire was one of the principal architects of our modern period, one of the real sources of twentieth-century thought. This has now been proved beyond doubt by the evidence of his posthumous papers.

Appel, Karel. Dutch painter, b. 1921 in Amsterdam. Appel studied at the Academy of Art in Amsterdam from 1940 to 1943. Subsequently he became a founder member of the International Association for Experimental Art and of the *Cobra* group (1948). In 1950 he moved to Paris, where he is still living today. In 1960 he won the International Guggenheim Prize.

Appel is a member of the Nordic School of Abstract Expressionists, who paint in a style derived from Jorn and de Kooning. Appel himself produces ghostly fantasy pieces, using strong, vital colours. Like many of the *Cobra* artists he is fascinated by the art forms of primitive peoples and his female nudes often reveal a fetishistic quality. Appel has also been influenced by the Dutch Expressionists, although he is far more revolutionary in his disregard of formal structures. Not infrequently he applies his paint straight from the tube, building up an interlacing and multi-layered network of colour. For a while he incorporated objects (e.g. puppets) into his pictures but soon abandoned the practice in favour of two-dimensional compositions. Appel is also a sculptor and has produced occasional works in this medium throughout the whole of his career. His large, coloured genealogical pieces are typical.

Hugo Claus. *Karel Appel: Painter*, Amsterdam 1962.
Catalogue, *Karel Appel*, Stedelijk Museum, Amsterdam 1965.
Catalogue, *Karel Appel*, Martha Jackson Gallery, New York 1967.

Appleby, Theodore. American painter, b. 1923 in Long Branch, N.J. He studied graphics in Japan, 1945–6, and then collaborated with Siqueiros on the murals of the former convent of Santa Rosa in San Miguel de Allende, Mexico (1948–9). In the early 1950s he moved to Paris where he studied under F. Léger. Here he participated in the Salons des Réalités Nouvelles, 1950–2, and had his first one-man show at Studio Facchetti (1956). The following year he had his first American one-man show at the Martha Jackson Gallery. Mainly concerned with colour, his paint is delicately applied to the canvas, giving one a wide range of impressions, from a starry night to a profusion of autumn foliage to the intricacy of a stained-glass window (*Composition*, 1957, Chicago, Art Institute; *Painting*, 1958, Brussels, Coll. Paul Pechère).

Jérôme Mellquist. 'Theodore Appleby', *Quadrum* No. 8, 1960, pp. 144–5.

Arakawa, Shusaku. Japanese artist, b. 1936 in Nagoya. In 1958 in Tokyo he organized a Neo-Dada group, and produced series of *Boxes*. In 1961 he left for New York. His main works are series of large *Diagrams*. These began around 1963 with a systematic arrangement of silhouettes and precise drawings of such objects as combs, tennis rackets, footprints and refrigerators. Gradually even the diagrammatic representation of objects began to disappear, to be replaced by words. 'I am attempting to pictorialize the state before the imagination begins to work,' he said. His work is a kind of 'pregnant vacuum', out of which a number of possible pictures may arise between the canvas and the viewer. His recent works go even further than his previous attempts to illustrate and point out the mechanism of the imagination, so that now he has become involved in a unique way with both the spacing and embodiment of consciousness and its possibilities of finding (trapping?) itself through its systematic investigation of languages. He has also made a two-hour film entitled *Why Not (Serenade of Eschatological Ecology)*, 1969.

Archambault, Louis. Canadian sculptor, b. 1915 in Montreal. He began by studying ceramics at the École des Beaux-Arts, Montreal, but won sculpture prizes in the *Concours Artistiques* of the Province of Quebec in 1948 and 1950. His first work to achieve recognition was the *Iron Bird* (1950, Ottawa, National Gallery of Canada), exhibited at the Festival of Britain sculpture exhibition in Battersea Park, London; it was the subject of a cartoon by David Low. In 1953–4 he worked in Paris and at Vence and in 1956 was commissioned to make a ceramic wall, *La Vie canadienne* (now Ottawa, National Gallery of Canada), for the Canadian Pavilion of the Brussels Exhibition, 1958. He has carried out numerous commissions for public buildings across Canada. He teaches at the École des Beaux-Arts, Montreal, and lives at Saint-Lambert, Quebec.

Exhibition catalogue, *Louis Archambault*, Laing Galleries, Toronto 1966.

Archipenko, Alexander. Russian-American sculptor, b. 1887 in Kiev; d. 1964 in New York. At first Archipenko studied in Kiev and in Moscow from 1903 onwards. Then, in 1908, he moved to Paris, where he studied archaic sculptures, especially those of Ancient Egypt and Central America. In Paris he also established friendly relations with the Cubists and took part in their exhibitions. It was then that he began to apply Cubist ideas in the field of sculpture. In 1912 he introduced concave structures and so translated space into a sculptural element. In his *Circus Medrano* he broke down the individual figures —which are composed of wood, metal, glass, etc., and are reminiscent of the *Manichini* of de Chirico and Carrà—into geometrical shapes: cones, globes and hollow forms. By this time his sculptures were the talk of the international art world and in 1913 he had comprehensive exhibitions in the Osthaus-Museum in Hagen and the Sturm-Galerie in Berlin and was also represented at the Armory Show in New York. In 1914 he evolved his *Sculpto-Peinture*, which, as the name implies, was a synthesis of sculpture and painting. In 1921 he went to live in Berlin, where he started an art school, severed his connections with Cubism and moved towards Constructivism. Then, in 1923, he emigrated to the USA. In the following year he invented his *Archipentura*, a sort of 'moving picture', which was intended to create a synthesis between painting, space and time. In 1928 he acquired American citizenship. From 1935–6 he taught at Washington University and in 1937 at the New Bauhaus. In 1937 he also opened his own school in Chicago and, two years later, a school of sculpture in New York. From 1946 onwards he made his 'light modulators', which were Plexiglass sculptures illuminated from within. He continued to teach at various universities in the USA and at his own school in New York up to his death in 1964.

Archipenko's influence on the development of sculpture between 1910 and 1920 was considerable.

The Cubists had freed painting from its naturalistic setting. He recognized their achievement and applied it to sculpture. Although he never abandoned human figures entirely he now began to construct them from independent sculptural elements, creating architectonic structures which were far removed from the unitary modelled shapes produced by his predecessors. This movement away from solid mass was further reinforced by the introduction of non-sculptural materials (glass, wood and metal) and techniques (painting). All this, of course, was adaptation. But Archipenko was also an innovator. The revolutionary idea of using concave shapes as sculptural components—which has since been put to good effect by a wide variety of sculptors ranging from González to Belling, Lipchitz and Moore—stemmed from him.

Alexander Archipenko. *Alexander Archipenko. Fifty Creative Years*, New York 1960
Catalogue, *Alexander Archipenko*, University of California at Los Angeles Art Galleries, Los Angeles 1967.

Ardizzone, Edward. British painter and illustrator, b. 1900 in Haiphong. He is represented in the Tate Gallery (principally by drawings which he did as official War Artist, 1940–5). He is famous as a book-illustrator, humorous draughtsman and writer for children; his style evokes a Dickensian cosiness or idyllic innocence.

Ardon, Mordecai (formerly **Bronstein**). Israeli painter, b. 1896 in Tuchow, Poland. He studied with Klee, Kandinsky and Itten, and later taught at Itten's art school in Berlin. He emigrated to Palestine in 1933 and taught at the Bezalel Art School in Jerusalem, becoming director of the school in 1940. In 1952, he became art adviser to the Israeli Ministry of Education. After gaining a local reputation, he emerged in the 1950s as an important painter, with exhibitions in European and American museums and galleries. He is a remarkable colourist who combines formal brilliance with a powerful oneiric fantasy. Monumental triptychs can be seen at the Amsterdam Stedelijk, and his *Missa Dura* at the Tate Gallery in London is of special interest.

Arico, Rodolfo. Italian painter and sculptor, b. 1930 in Milan. Arico studied architecture at the Milan Polytechnic and painting at the Accademia di Brera. He is now living in Milan.

In his 'picture-objects', which frequently serve a didactic purpose, Arico tries to integrate irrational components into a rational schema. Basically, his compositions are derived from the alienation technique developed by Bacon and Matta and the colour refraction of Delaunay.

Arikha, Avigdor. Israeli painter, b. 1929 in Radautzi, Rumania. Arikha went to Palestine in 1944 and studied under Ardon. After creating illustrations for books by Rilke and Becket he gradually moved towards abstract art, developing a highly mystical style of painting.

Arman (Armand Fernandez). French painter and sculptor, b. 1928 in Nice. Arman studied at the École des Arts Décoratifs and the École du Louvre in Paris. He now lives partly in Nice, partly in New York.

In the mid-1950s Arman created his first *Cachets* (imprints). In 1959 he went on to his *Allures*. These are a variant of the *Cachets* and consist of impressions made on canvas with a variety of functional objects previously dipped in paint. In the same year he began to produce his *Colères* (arrangements of broken objects, especially musical instruments) and his *Accumulations* (accumulations of refuse or consumer objects). Arman is in fact a typical representative of the New Realist movement. In 1966 he won the Marzotto prize.

P. Restany. *Arman Exhibition Catalogue*, Galleria Schwarz, Milan 1968.

Armfield, Maxwell. British painter and writer, b. 1882 in Ringwood, Hants; d. 1972. He trained in Birmingham and later in Paris and Italy. He exhibited frequently at the Venice Biennale, the New English Art Club and in America. He worked in tempera, producing flower studies and landscapes; he also illustrated many books, including his own and his wife's.

Armitage, Kenneth. British sculptor, b. 1916 in Leeds, Yorks. Armitage studied at the Leeds College of Art and then spent two years at the Slade School. At the end of the war he became head of the sculpture department of Bath Academy of Art. He had his first one-man exhibition in London in 1952, at the Gimpel Fils Gallery. In 1958 he won a prize at the Fifth International Exhibition of Drawings and Engravings in Lugano. He also won an award at the Venice Biennale the same year. Armitage has exhibited regularly in London and New York. In 1959 the Whitechapel Gallery in London put on a retrospective show of his work, which consists mainly of single figures and groups.

Armory Show. Properly called the International Exhibition of Modern Art, the show was held at the 69th Regiment Armory in New York City from 17 February to 15 March 1913. The idea for this now famous exhibition originated with the 1910 Independents Show in New York, which was an unjuried exhibition of American painting that attempted to provide a showcase for native artists who were being neglected by an art market still limited to the Old Masters and to certain established American and foreign painters. In 1911 the artists Walt Kuhn,

Jerome Myers and Elmer Livingston MacRae (1875–1955) began discussing the possibility of a large invitational exhibition with their dealer, the landscape painter Henry Fitch Taylor (1853–1925). Later that year the idea was realized with the formation of the American Association of Painters and Sculptors, an organization whose original members included both conservative academicians and realists as well as radically oriented artists. As its president, the society chose J. Alden Weir—a noted Impressionist and a staunch member of the National Academy—but when he discovered that the avowed purpose of the group was to exhibit anti-academic artists, he declined the position and was replaced by Arthur B. Davies, who was familiar with both European and American modernist tendencies. Walt Kuhn became the group's publicist, and thus the association had two leaders committed to a programme that would guarantee an exhibition with an international scope and liberal leanings. Kuhn defined the Armory Show as 'the starting point of the new spirit in art, at least as far as America is concerned'. The show did, in fact, create an artistic revolution by confronting conservative critics with modernist trends and by shocking a complacent public.

The Armory Show was actually two exhibitions in one. The American section included works by the organizers of the show (who were America's younger and more 'radical' artists, but who still remained unaffected by modern European art), as well as paintings by some of the more conservative native painters. John Sloan's *Sunday, Women Drying Their Hair* (1912, Andover, Mass., Addison Gallery of American Art, Phillips Academy), William Glackens' *Family Group* (1911, Washington, D.C., Coll. Mr. and Mrs. Ira Glackens), and Alfred Maurer's *Autumn* (before 1913, Coll. Mr. and Mrs. Ira Glackens) were among some of the more notable of the American entries. The European section was meant to demonstrate that the nineteenth-century French tradition of J. A. D. Ingres, Pierre Puvis de Chavannes, Eugène Delacroix and Jean-Baptiste Camille Corot was the evolutionary foundation for contemporary modernist developments, and the works exhibited clearly indicated that the Europeans were far more advanced than their American colleagues. Works by Henri Matisse, Odilon Redon, Paul Cézanne, Georges Braque, Pablo Picasso, Wassily Kandinsky and Marcel Duchamp's *Nude Descending a Staircase, No. 2* (1912, Philadelphia, Museum of Art) were major attractions. Davies attempted to classify the European artists in three categories—classicists, realists and romantics—but in actuality many different schools were represented, including Impressionism, Post-Impressionism, Neo-Impressionism, Fauvism and Cubism. The European section was predominantly French; German Expressionism was almost completely neglected, other omissions being Italian Futurism and Orphic Cubism. Sculpture was also poorly chosen, although pieces by Auguste Rodin, Aristide Maillol, Constantin Brancusi and Wilhelm Lehmbruck were included. Thus the show provided a somewhat incomplete panorama of modernist developments.

Critical and public response to the Armory Show was inflammatory and outraged. Academic artists such as William Merritt Chase echoed the journalistic diatribes, and only the critic Frederick James Gregg called for an open mind, sensing the import of something he himself was slow to grasp. At a time when American art needed—and its youngest practitioners wanted—to assimilate European modernism, the country was experiencing a great migration from the Continent, and the defensive position in respect to art was closely allied to the general sense of threat concerning foreign invasion. The underdevelopment of American art revealed the cultural and aesthetic gap between the two continents.

The ultimate effect of the exhibition was to force American artists to come to terms with a living tradition and to discard academicism in favour of a new and independent formal order; contemporary art could no longer be neglected and ridiculed in America. Although the museums still largely ignored modernism (in spite of the fact that the Metropolitan Museum, New York, purchased its first Cézanne—*View of the Domaine St-Joseph, c.* 1895—at the Armory Show), and the colleges and art schools did not update their curricula, the Armory Show did educate the public, and helped to stimulate and expand the art market. In the year immediately following, new galleries opened in rapid succession and American collecting expanded. Before the mid-twentieth century most of these collections were institutionalized or opened for viewing, making available a permanent showcase for modernism to a once outraged public.

Arts and Decoration III, March 1913. Special issue on the Armory Show.
Milton W. Brown. *The Story of the Armory Show*, Greenwich (Conn.) 1963.

Armstrong, John. British painter, b. 1893 in Hastings, Sussex. He is represented at the Tate Gallery. A member of Unit One in 1933, Armstrong subscribed to its architectonic ideals, but his whole work shows more of fantasy and owes something to Surrealism and the sharp-focus school. He has painted murals and designed for the theatre and films. He is now living in London.

Arnal, François. French painter, b. 1924 in La Valette. Arnal began to paint in 1944 and went to live in Paris in 1948. He paints in an informal style, creating works based in part on the serial organization of microforms and microstructures. He is also well known for his tapestry designs.

Aroch, Arie. Russian-Israeli painter, b. 1908 in Kharkov. Aroch settled in Jerusalem in 1924. After working as an Expressionist up to 1960 he evolved a kind of archaic imagery based on the associative value of printed words and of Jewish and other signs and *motifs*.

Arp, Jean *or* Hans. French sculptor, b. 1887 in Strasbourg; d. 1966 in Basle. He studied at Strasbourg, Weimar and Paris. Discouraged by conventional art teaching, he turned to poetry, and withdrew for a period of isolation. Born a German subject in Alsace, his allegiance was to France; he went to Switzerland in 1909, and was in Zürich at the formation of the original Dada group in 1916. Arp could claim that he was present when the group was christened with its inconsequent-seeming, but actually appropriate name. He was the most serious visual artist connected with the Zürich Dada group.

In 1915 Arp met Sophie Taeuber and together they experimented with reliefs, constructions and collages in unconventional media which are among the earlier abstractions. These had elements that continued through Arp's whole work. Their forms were organic rather than of the geometric or mechanical types used by most early Abstractionists. They were made with an elegance that was impersonal because Arp did not attach importance to his own manual style. They were often inspired by an innocent-seeming wit and play on ideas, not unlike the wit of Klee if somewhat blander.

From these beginnings Arp gradually turned towards full three-dimensional sculpture. By about 1930, when this transformation was complete, Arp had settled in Paris and Dada had passed into history, and had merged into Surrealism, a name given both to a partisan group of intellectuals and to a far-reaching current of thought. Arp remained friendly with the Surrealists, but his sculpture deals only distantly with Surrealist imagery. Of the enduring characteristics mentioned earlier, the most important to his later work was organicism. Arp is naturally compared to Brancusi. They are linked by their love of polished surfaces and sensuous curves. But if their works sometimes appear similar, they were approached from different sides. Brancusi refined down a natural form whereas it was cardinal to Arp to create organically from the beginning. This difference is reflected in Arp's much greater output, although this is partly because Arp employed assistants in the later stages of his works.

The idea of spontaneous generation of form is a very fundamental one in modern art with mystical overtones and connections with Surrealism, Automatism and more recent developments. The later work of Arp is probably the finest sculptural expression of this doctrine which he himself interpreted in one of the most succinct definitions ever written: *art is a fruit that grows in man*.

Through holding this belief Arp came to reject the term 'abstract' as applied to his work and preferred to call it 'concrete', since to him nothing could be more concrete than a piece of sculpture without imitation or symbolism. Future art historians will surely follow him in applying the term 'concrete' to a whole range of what is now called abstract.

Art Autre (Other Art). This concept was formulated by Michel Tapié, who published a book under this title in 1952; it is largely synonymous with Informal Art and *Tachisme*. Although Tapié's account is undoubtedly subjective, it none the less provides a psychological and historical derivation of Informal Art, which clearly distinguishes this new development from other art forms, e.g. geometric art. In his book Tapié cites, amongst others, Dubuffet, Fautrier, Mathieu, Matta and Wols as exponents of *Art Autre*, which he regards as a 'total adventure', as a process in which reality is discovered anew and which finds expression in new procedures. Tapié considers that *Art Autre* possesses the same sort of historical significance as Dada. In 1960 Tapié published his *Morphologie Autre*.

M. Tapié. *Un art autre*, Paris 1952.

Art Brut. *Art Brut* is the concept used by the painter Jean Dubuffet to describe the kind of art forms found in the work of psychotics, children and amateur painters, which emerge spontaneously from the unconscious mind. In so far as they are diametrically opposed to the highly conscious, intentional style of the professional artist it would, in fact, be more appropriate—from a traditional point of view —to describe these spontaneous art forms as 'anti-art forms'. Dubuffet, however, insists that, on the contrary, they are the really creative components of true art and he has quite consciously introduced them into his own work. Subsequently many other artists followed his lead. Dubuffet's interest in *Art Brut* dates from an early stage in his career and he has made a systematic collection of the artistic products of psychotics, children and amateur painters. In 1947 he showed this collection at an exhibition in the Galerie René Drouin in Paris. In June 1948 he founded a society for the promotion of *Art Brut* (*Compagnie de l'art brut*) which was liquidated in 1951 for lack of funds. Up to 1962 Dubuffet's collection was kept in the USA, in the house of the painter Ossorio. But then the society was re-founded —by Dubuffet, Asger Jorn, Raymond Queneau and others—and the collection, which now contains some five thousand works, was moved to a private museum in Paris, where it can be seen by arrangement.

Jean Dubuffet. *Écrits de Jean Dubuffet*, Paris 1967; contains a copy of the *Cahiers de la Compagnie de l'art brut*.
Exhibition catalogue, *Art Brut*, Musée des arts décoratifs, Paris 1967.

Art nouveau. A widespread, revolutionary and extremely complex movement in western architecture and design, beginning in the second half of the nineteenth century and ending with the outbreak of the First World War. It was the forerunner of the Modern Movement. There are two major styles within *art nouveau*: one is characterized by a sinuous, organic asymmetrical linearity (e.g. a drawing by Aubrey Beardsley or a vase by Louis Comfort Tiffany); the other by a severe geometry and reductive ornamentation (e.g. architecture and furniture by Charles Rennie Mackintosh or the Viennese architect J. M. Olbrich). The two are not necessarily incompatible and indeed often appear together: what matters in all *art nouveau* is the basic design philosophy: the object, whatever it may be, from a skyscraper to a candlestick, is conceived as an organic whole in which structure and ornament are unified as never before. *Art nouveau* is also characterized by a strong element of fantasy and a strong latent erotic content. It was a totally original style although intensely eclectic, drawing on many sources: the Byzantine, the Celtic, the Egyptian, the Gothic, the Japanese, the Baroque, the Rococo, the Symbolist painters of the 1880s and 1890s and certain major individual artists, notably William Blake, D. G. Rossetti and Edward Burne-Jones in England and Paul Gauguin in France. *Art nouveau* is the accepted name for the movement, but it was also known as *Style Moderne* (in France), *Jugendstil* (in Germany), *Sezessionsstil* (in Austria), *Stile Liberty* (in Italy) and *Modernista* (in Spain). Its origins lie in the reaction in England and France to the abysmal standards of design and manufacture revealed by the 1851 Great Exhibition at the Crystal Palace. In France in the 1850s numerous bodies were established to promote new standards of design, and in England the Department of Science and Art was created in 1852 and the Victoria and Albert Museum was founded in the same year. Nine years later, in 1861, William Morris started the London firm of Morris & Co., and began to produce furniture, textiles, carpets, tapestries, wallpapers and stained glass to unprecedentedly high standards of design and craftsmanship. This was the start of the Arts and Crafts Movement, which soon developed into *art nouveau*. The movement gathered pace through the 1880s with the foundation of the Century Guild in 1882 by the architect Arthur Mackmurdo, who in the same year designed his famous chair which is the first example of *art nouveau* in the applied arts (Morris Museum, Walthamstow, London). In 1884 Walter Crane, who made a vital contribution to *art nouveau* in the field of book design, formed the Art Workers' Guild and in 1888 the Arts and Crafts Exhibition Society held the first of the annual exhibitions which over the next decade were to become a showcase for English and foreign *art nouveau* of every kind, from ashtrays and bookbindings to complete interior schemes and architectural projects. In April 1893 a new magazine, *The Studio*, appeared. It quickly achieved an international circulation and was a major factor in spreading abroad the gospel of the English movement and the influence of English designers such as Christopher Dresser, C. R. Ashbee, C. A. Voysey and the illustrator and graphic artist Aubrey Beardsley, whose black-and-white drawings and designs for books are perhaps the most characteristic and genial products of English *art nouveau*.

From this moment *art nouveau* became an international movement. It appeared first in Belgium, where it took on its most sinuous form in the work of Victor Horta and Henry van de Velde. In France *art nouveau* was similarly sinuous and reached its apogee in the extraordinary entrances for the Paris Métro designed by Hector Guimard in 1899 and in the posters of Alphonse Mucha. In Spain the movement was dominated by Antonio Gaudí, who began as a neo-Gothic architect but by the end of the 1890s had evolved an *art nouveau* style of his own which can be seen in the cathedral of the Sagrada Familia and other buildings in Barcelona. In the USA the leading figure was Louis Comfort Tiffany, who by the early 1890s was producing his famous fantastically shaped iridescent glass objects as well as jewellery, stained glass, lamps and interior designs. In Scotland in 1897 Charles Rennie Mackintosh built one of the great masterpieces of *art nouveau* architecture, the Glasgow School of Art. The severity of Mackintosh's style had a considerable influence on the development of the Vienna Secession, and in the work of the Viennese architects Josef Hoffmann and Joseph Maria Olbrich *art nouveau* is taken to its extreme limits of purity and abstraction.

Stephen Tschudi Madsen. *Sources of Art Nouveau*, New York 1956; *Art Nouveau*, London and New York 1967.
P. Selz and M. Constantine (eds.). *Art Nouveau: Art and Design at the Turn of the Century*, London and New York 1960.
Robert Schmutzler. *Art Nouveau*, London and New York 1964.
Mario Amaya. *Art Nouveau*, London and New York 1966.

Artymowski, Roman. Polish painter, b. 1919 in Lwow. Artymowski studied at the Academy of Art in Cracow. From 1962 to 1967 he held a professorial post at the Academy of Fine Arts in Baghdad. He is now living in Warsaw.

Artymowski is an abstract painter whose work is remarkable for the extreme sophistication of its colouring. He has also produced experimental works incorporating colour projections and materials that are sensitive to light.

Ashcan School—*see* **The Eight**

Assemblage—*see* **Collage**

Atlan, Jean. French painter, b. 1913 in Constantine, Algeria; d. 1960 in Paris. Atlan was a Berber and an orthodox Jew. In 1930 he moved to Paris, where he studied philosophy and wrote experimental poetry before becoming a painter in 1941. During the German occupation he was locked up in the lunatic asylum of Sainte-Anne. Later, in 1944, he published his first book of poems, *Le Sang profond*, and had his first Paris exhibition, at which Gertrude Stein bought up every single picture. Like Hartung, Soulages, Schneider, etc., Atlan was one of a group of artists at the *École de Paris* who established their reputation after the Second World War. His semi-abstract, magical paintings with their dark totemistic signs and their gleaming colours are reminiscent of pre-Columbian and Negro art.

A. Verdet. *Atlan*, Paris 1956.

Auberjonois, René. Swiss painter, b. 1872 in Montagny, near Yverdon; d. 1957 in Lausanne. Auberjonois came from Swiss peasant stock. After spending a brief period at the Technical Schools of Art in Dresden and Vienna he went to London in 1896, where he studied at the School of Art in Kensington. In 1897 he was a pupil at the Academy in Paris and in Whistler's studio. In 1900 he visited Italy, making copies of works by Uccello and Fra Angelico. From 1901 to 1914 he lived in Paris, where he made contact with the Cubists and formed a friendship with the poet Charles Ferdinand Ramuz, for whom he subsequently made numerous illustrations. From the wide variety of influences to which he was exposed—Neo-Impressionism, *Nabis*, Cézanne, Renoir, Rousseau, the early Cubism of Picasso and Braque, Derain, Bonnard and Modigliani—Auberjonois gradually evolved a highly personal, poetic style. In 1914 he returned to Switzerland and settled in Lausanne, where he lived in complete seclusion for the rest of his life, paying no attention whatsoever to subsequent artistic developments. Instead, he concentrated on integrating the experiences of his Paris period. Later, from 1940 onwards, he produced a large number of graphic works. His paintings, which are executed in warm, strong colours, are very simple and devoid of all pathos. The unsophisticated brushwork gives an air of gentleness to these works, most of which depict the human figure. The most enduring influence in this branch of Auberjonois's work was exerted by Bonnard and Modigliani.

C. R. Ramuz. *René Auberjonois*, Lausanne 1943.
H. L. Mermod. *René Auberjonois. Dessins, Textes, Photographies,* Lausanne 1958.

Auerbach, Frank. British painter, b. 1931 in Berlin. Auerbach came to England in 1939, and trained at St. Martin's School of Art and the RCA. He is represented at the Tate Gallery and in many public collections. He is one of a group of figurative painters influenced by David Bomberg, using paint thickly and heavily as a means of expression both chromatic and sculptural.

Ault, George C. American painter, b. 1891 in Cleveland, Ohio; d. 1948 in Woodstock, New York. He moved to London with his family in 1899 and later attended the Slade School of Fine Art and the St. John's Wood Art School there. He returned to the United States in 1911, living in New York and New Jersey before moving, due to his poor health, to Woodstock. He first exhibited at the Society of Independents in 1921 and was given a one-man show five years later at the Downtown Gallery, New York. *The Pianist* (1923, New York, Zabriskie Gallery), with its sharply defined patterns and deep sense of mystery, anticipates the works of many of the Immaculate and Cubist-Realist painters with whom he is identified. Usually recording the environment in which he lived, his paintings of the 1920s and 1930s deal chiefly with the New York cityscape, while the works from the last decade of his life depict the area around Woodstock (*Road to Stony Cove, Woodstock*, New York, Zabriskie Gallery).

Hilton Kramer. 'Art: Adapting Cubist Style to American Subjects', *New York Times*, 15 February 1969.

Auricoste, Emmanuel. French sculptor, b. 1908 in Paris. Auricoste studied under Bourdelle and Despiau. His early portrait busts and figures were modelled in clay and then cast in plaster or bronze. Later he preferred to work with iron or lead.

Auricoste has been described as an exponent of 'Expressionist Realism'. Together with F. Gruber and G. Richier he helped promote the Paris 'May Salon'. He also taught at the École des Arts Décoratifs in Paris and the Académie de la Grande-Chaumière and the École des Beaux-Arts in Orléans.

Automatism. Breton uses the well-known phrase 'pure psychic automatism' in his Surrealist manifesto of 1924, relating the expression to the state of the dream, the real functioning of the mind, the absence of control by reason or preoccupation with moral or aesthetic criteria. However, from 1916 Jean Arp and Sophie Taeuber-Arp had experimented with repeated drawings of shapes to produce variations 'automatically', and with the tearing of coloured papers which then fell to produce configurations of shapes. From 1919 date Breton's and Soupault's automatic texts, published in *Littérature* under the title 'Les Champs Magnétiques'. Here an attempt was made to transcribe into written words the free flow of thought. This had previously been practised by the Dadaists in Zurich: also Arp had known of the Cubists' *papiers collés*. Yet another source was Breton's knowledge of Freud, dating from the war years. To many free association seemed more effective in the verbal than in the visual sphere. However, Ernst thought he had discovered the true equivalent to automatic writing on 10 August 1925, when he began the random placing of paper on, for example, scrubbed floorboards, thereby producing rubbings (*frottages*). Ernst knew of Leonardo's staring at stained walls to provoke images. André Masson, because he could not find liberation in oil painting, allowed his pen simply to travel upon the paper; figures emerged under his hand, as in *Furious Suns*, 1924. However, during the 1930s European Surrealists turned from Automatism to the creation of objects; there were contacts between them and American painters *c.* 1940, which proved of great importance to the development of art in America (Action Painting, Abstract Expressionism). The precise contribution has yet to be established, but Pollock's dripping technique has been described as an 'automatic splash and trickle' and Rosenberg's theory of action painting may be seen as a development of the ideas of Arp, Ernst and Masson. Both movements stress the unconscious, but it must be emphasized that American writers do not often use the word 'automatic' and that the dominant characteristics of American art lie beyond Surrealist and Dada ideas.

M. Jean. *Geschichte des Surrealismus*, Cologne 1961.
A. Breton. *Manifestes du Surréalisme*, Paris 1962.
J. Claus. *Theorien zeitgenössischer Malerei*, Reinbek 1963.

Avery, Milton. American painter, b. 1893 in Altmar, New York; d. 1965 in New York. His only formal training was a class in life drawing and painting at the Connecticut League of Art in Hartford in 1905. Beginning in 1930, Avery demonstrated a marked Fauvist influence in his work (*Mother and Child*, 1944, New York, Grace Borgenicht Gallery), although he always retained a personal style that was seemingly naïve and childlike in its outlook. It is partly through Avery that American painters assimilated Henri Matisse's teachings concerning space and flat patterns of decorative colours of equal value, despite the latter's negligible influence in the 1940s on the École de Paris artists. Cubism did not play an important part in Avery's development, unlike many other American artists of his generation.

Avery contributed to the progress of twentieth-century American painting, his works heralding the radical streamlining of form that was employed in the 1950s by New York's Abstract Expressionist painters. His ability to eliminate detail and to organize the canvas into transparent, closely keyed zones of colour found favour with such younger artists as Adolph Gottlieb and Mark Rothko. Many of his paintings are bold, stark seascapes reminiscent of those of Albert Pinkham Ryder and John Marin. In *Green Sea* (1954, New York, Metropolitan Museum), Avery used remarkably simple geometric forms that foreshadow the hard-edge style in abstract painting of the late 1960s. His earlier *Evening at Home* (1940, New York, Coll. Curt Valentin), like most of his paintings, is a small canvas that becomes curiously monumental, with its bizarre, hulking shapes suggesting an enormity of space beyond their own scale. Retrospective exhibitions of Avery's works were held at the Baltimore Museum of Art (1952) and at the Whitney Museum, New York (1960).

Adelyn Breeskin. *Milton Avery*, American Federation of Arts, New York 1960.
Hilton Kramer. *Milton Avery: Paintings, 1930–1960*, New York 1962.

Avramidis, Joannis. Greek sculptor, b. 1922 in Batum, USSR. Avramidis is the son of Greek parents, who emigrated to Russia from Turkey. From 1937 to 1939 he studied art in Batum but left Russia when his father died, and settled in Athens. In 1943 he was brought to Vienna as a foreign worker. Following the Nazi capitulation in 1945 he attended the Academy of Arts in Vienna, where he first joined a painting class and subsequently—from 1953 to 1956—studied under Wotruba, who influenced him considerably. From 1965 to 1966 he was given charge of a life class at the Viennese Academy and from 1966 to 1967 was visiting lecturer at the Hamburg Academy. He is now living in Vienna.

In his sculptures Avramidis is trying to establish sculptural criteria similar to those governing the early Greek phase of Classical Antiquity and the Early Italian Renaissance. His figures, groups of figures and heads are highly abstract, columniform works, many of which are rhythmically structured by means of parallel rims. Avramidis's art is closely akin to that of Brancusi and—above all—Schlemmer.

Catalogue, *Avramidis*, Kestner-Gesellschaft, Hanover 1967.

Ayres, Gillian. British painter, b. 1930 in Barnes, London. After studying at the Camberwell School of Art from 1946 to 1950, Ayres had her first exhibition in 1957 with the Tachist group of British artists. In the early 1960s she was painting informal spatial colour compositions but has since created a more settled decorative style, which incorporates vegetable forms and certain elements of *art nouveau*. Ayres is now living in Barnes.

Ayrton, Michael. British painter and sculptor, b. 1921 in London. Ayrton studied in London, at the Heatherley and St. John's Wood Schools of Art, and in Paris. He had a retrospective exhibition at the Whitechapel Gallery, London, in 1955. He has also written and illustrated a number of books.

Azuma, Kengiro. Japanese sculptor and painter, b. 1926 in Yamagata, Japan. After studying at the Tokyo Academy and the Accademia di Brera in Milan Azuma settled in Milan in 1956. Since then he has produced stele- and block-shaped sculptures, some of them pierced, all of them smoothly textured. His neo-concrete pictures, which are virtually monochromes, reveal a similar uniform texture.

B

Baargeld, Johannes Theodor (Alfred Grünwald). German painter and poet, date of birth unknown; d. 1927. Baargeld was politically the most committed member of the Cologne Dada group, which he founded in 1919 together with Max Ernst and Hans Arp. He was editor of the *Ventilator*, the successful pro-Communist magazine which was banned soon after it appeared, and also of the Dada magazine *Schammade*. His paintings, some of which were executed in collaboration with Max Ernst, consist of collages, montages and assemblages in the Dadaist manner. In 1921 Baargeld gave up painting.

Bacon, Francis. British painter, b. 1909 in Dublin. Bacon is a descendant of his Elizabethan namesake. Virtually self-taught, he engaged exclusively in painting from the age of about 35. He spent two years in Berlin and Paris, where he was influenced by the Picasso exhibition, 1926; he went to London in 1928, and there made furniture, rugs, etc., as an interior designer. He painted intermittently throughout the 1930s, not unnoticed—a *Crucifixion* (1933) being reproduced in Herbert Read's *Art Now*. Some of his works in a Lefevre Gallery mixed exhibition (1945) included *Three Studies for Figures at the Base of a Crucifixion* (1944, now in the Tate). Bacon is quoted as saying: 'I began with this picture.' He lived in Monte Carlo until 1950 and thereafter mainly in London, with a year (1959–60) in St. Ives.

He has affinities with Grünewald, Rembrandt and Daumier, but Bacon's painting is peculiarly isolated and individual. His employment of, for example, Velasquez's *Pope Innocent X* (from reproductions) is little distinguished from his use of magazine and newspaper photographs. Images such as van Gogh's *Self-Portrait on the Road to Tarascon* or the still of the screaming nurse from Eisenstein's film *The Battleship Potemkin* equally become the core for a projection of Bacon's existential type of awareness—like that of Sartre's Roquentin in *La Nausée* (who experienced the reality of a tree as a moist excretion from the soil, viscosity, an odour). With this criterion future opinion may agree that 'he is one of the greatest painters of the twentieth century' (Robert Melville), though, without paradox, dismissing some of his horrific content as 'creaking melodrama' (Lawrence Alloway).

Bacon's images refer to reality. Often deeply ambiguous and on the fringe of experience for many, they are seldom incredible. They are generalized, not specific images: not—*this individual*, but—*a concentration of raw meat*; not—*this particular room*, but —*a claustrophobic sense of enclosure*. ('Art is a method of opening up areas of feeling.')

Bacon accepts the artistic consequences of his pessimistic philosophy: 'Man now realizes that he is an accident, that he is a completely futile being, that he has to play the game without reason . . . all art has become a game by which man distracts himself . . . in my case all painting—and the older I get the more it becomes so—is an accident.' Of Matthew Smith, but by inference of himself, he says: 'Real painting is a mysterious and continuous struggle with chance. Mysterious because the very substance of the paint . . . can make such a direct assault upon the nervous system; continuous because the medium is so fluid and subtle that every change that is made loses whatever is there in the hope of making a fresh gain.'

Despite his own destruction of much of his output Bacon has exhibited very widely over the last twenty years: 1949–59—eight Hanover Gallery exhibitions; 1959—5th São Paulo Bienal; 1960–7—four Marlborough Gallery exhibitions; 1962—a Tate retrospective; 1963—an exhibition at the Guggenheim Gallery, New York; and subsequently in Hamburg, Stockholm, Paris, Rome and Turin. Many of his works are to be seen in the Tate, the New York Museum of Modern Art, and other important galleries throughout the world.

R. Alley and J. Rothenstein. *Francis Bacon*, London 1964.
M. Leiris. Catalogue, *Maeght and Marlborough Exhibition*, London 1967.
A. Bowness. *Recent British Painting*, London 1968.

Badii, Libero. Italian sculptor, b. 1916 in Arezzo, Italy. When he was eleven Badii went to live in Buenos Aires, where he later studied at the Academy of Art. After an early phase based on a nativistic form of naturalism he turned to figurative abstraction and subsequently to geometrical abstracts containing symbolic allusions. Badii is now living in Buenos Aires.

Baenninger, Otto-Charles. Swiss sculptor, b. 1897 in Zürich. After being apprenticed to a local sculptor in Zürich from 1914 to 1918 Baenninger attended the Académie de la Grande Chaumière in Paris from 1920 to 1921. For the next eight years he collaborated with Bourdelle. During the 1920s and 1930s he lived partly in Paris, partly in Zürich, but in 1939 he settled permanently in his home town. In 1941 he won the first prize at the Biennale in Venice.

Baenninger's sculptures include nudes, portraits and monumental works. They are basically classical and reveal the influence of both Rodin and Maillol. He has cast a set of bronze doors for the Minster in Schaffhausen.

Baertling, Olle. Swedish painter and sculptor, b. 1911 in Halmstad, Sweden. Baertling is a non-objective artist of the Mondrian school. In his early period the rigid construction of his neoplastic paintings was dominated by rectangular forms. Later these

were superseded by diagonal wedge shapes. Baertling's hard metallic colours, mostly red and black,
produce a highly dynamic, three-dimensional effect.
We find the same dynamism in his sculptures, which
he first began to make in 1954 from welded and
painted iron and which are remarkable for their
delicate linear construction. Baertling became a
founder member of the Parisian *Groupe Espace* in
1952.

T. Brunius. *Baertling: Discoverer of Open Form*, Rosa Fried Gallery,
New York 1965.

Baizerman, Saul. American sculptor, b. 1889 in
Vitebsk, Russia; d. 1957 in New York. In Russia,
Baizerman briefly attended the Imperial Art School
in Odessa. In 1910 he emigrated to New York and
studied for a year at the National Academy of
Design and, until 1920, at the Beaux-Arts Institute
of Design, under the sponsorship of the architect
Lloyd Eliot Warren (1868–1922).

Until the mid-1920s, Baizerman worked primarily
with small sculptures, based on the observation of
ordinary people, as in the series *The City and the
People* (1920–5). This series initiated Baizerman's
work in hammered metal, which became the distinctive mark of his style and resulted in his major
oeuvre of hammered copper reliefs. His technique
was slow and exacting, as he worked from both sides
of the metal, simultaneously modulating both
surfaces so that, in his own words, his sculptures 'go
backward as well as forward and rightly should be
seen from both sides'. His primary subject became
the nude human figure on a heroic scale, ranging
from single images to group *motifs* recalling Classical
friezes, which he called 'sculptural symphonies'
(*March of the Innocents*, 1931–9; *Exuberance*, 1940–
9). The musical titles he often chose indicate the
lyrical, subtle and harmonious quality of his work,
which attains a universality through frequent references to Classical motifs and through the anonymity
of the figures, rarely particularized with faces or
detailed limbs.

Baizerman's first exhibition of his large copper
sculpture was in 1938, followed by several one-man
shows, primarily in New York, with retrospectives
in 1953, 1958 and 1961; his awards include a
Guggenheim Fellowship in 1952.

Julius S. Held. Exhibition catalogue, *Saul Baizerman*, Walker Art
Center, Minneapolis 1953.

Baj, Enrico. Italian painter, sculptor and graphic
artist, b. 1924 in Milan. Baj studied art at the
Accademia di Brera in Milan while reading for a law
degree. In 1951 he became a founder member of
the Movimento Nucleare. In 1953 he and Asger
Jorn founded the *Mouvement International pour une
Bauhaus Imaginiste* at the Hochschule für Gestaltung
in Ulm, against the wishes of Max Bill, the school's
director. In 1955, in conjunction with Dangelo and

Jaguer, he launched the magazine *Il Gesto*. It was
about then that he first began to use the collage
technique in his Neo-Figurative paintings. The principal features of these works are their grotesque
appearance and the artist's obvious virtuosity in his
use of a wide range of materials (carpets, cords,
metals and various kinds of timber). In the 1960s
Baj began to construct sculptures from children's
bricks. He is now living partly in Milan, partly in Paris.

Exhibition catalogue, *Omaggio a Baj*, in *Alternative Attuali/2*,
1965, containing a selection of articles on Baj.

Bakić, Vojin. Yugoslav sculptor, b. 1915 in Bjelovar,
Croatia. Bakić completed his studies at the Academy
of Fine Arts in Zagreb in 1939. In the small format
figures and heads, which formed the major part of
his output during the war years, he was already
moving towards the sculptural simplification which
is the hallmark of his later works. In 1947 he
created a statue of a resistance fighter to commemorate the deeds of the partisans during the
occupation. Then, from 1950 onwards, he produced
a series of organic abstracts after the manner of
Brancusi and Arp, in which he sought to establish a
pure and concentrated sculptural form. The smooth
forms and 'unfurled' surfaces of the late 1950s testify
to Bakić's preoccupation with space and internal
form. Since 1963 he has been producing mirror
surfaces, which resemble discuses and seem to
radiate rhythm and light into the surrounding space.
His determined advocacy of pure abstraction and his
exploitation of form and light have exerted a
crucial influence on the younger generations of
sculptors in Yugoslavia.

O. Bihalji-Merin. *Twentieth Century Sculpture*, Belgrade 1955.
Vera Horvat-Pintarić. *Vojin Bakić Exhibition Catalogue: Salon of
the Modern Gallery*, Belgrade 1965.

Bakst, Léon. Russian painter and stage designer,
b. 1866 in St. Petersburg; d. 1924 in Paris. Bakst
first studied at the Art Academies in Moscow and
then, from 1893 onwards, in Paris. In 1900 he returned to St. Petersburg, where he joined Diaghilev's
circle and the *Mir Iskusstva* (World of Art) association. In 1902 he designed his first stage sets and
theatrical costumes and shortly afterwards worked
for the St. Petersburg theatre. Later, in 1908, he also
designed a number of ballet sets for Fokine. It was
in 1909, when he moved to Paris, that he embarked
on his period of collaboration with Diaghilev and the
Russian Ballet, producing designs for *Cléopatra*,
Schéhérazade, *L'Après-midi d'un Faune*, etc. From
1922 onwards he created designs for Petipa and
Serge Lifar and also worked as a producer.

Bakst's contribution to scenic design, especially
during his Diaghilev period, was significant. His
highly imaginative décors and costume designs with
their perfect blending of colours were delightfully
sophisticated and extremely artful. In Debussy's

Jeux, for example, only three colours were used: blue, green and white. It may be noted in passing that Bakst exerted a crucial influence on the young Chagall in St. Petersburg prior to 1908.

André Levinson. *The Story of Léon Bakst's Life*, London and New York 1922.
C. Einstein. *Léon Bakst*, Berlin 1927.

Balla, Giacomo. Italian painter, sculptor and interior decorator, b. 1871 in Turin; d. 1958 in Rome. After attending the Accademia Albertina in Turin for a short while Balla settled in Rome in 1895 and remained there for the rest of his life. In 1900 he visited Paris for a period of seven months and whilst there became acquainted with the system of optical mixtures developed by the French Neo-Impressionists. In 1910 he signed the first manifestos issued by the Futurist painters. He also worked in sculpture and décor, designed furniture and carried out interior decoration.

After his return from Paris in 1900 Balla acquired a number of pupils, including Umberto Boccioni and Gino Severini, whom he introduced to the Neo-Impressionist technique of optical mixtures. This divisionist system made it possible to handle colour in a more abstract way and so provided a point of departure for the first Futurist experiments. Boccioni and Severini employed it as a means of breaking down the pictorial object and, by the abstract use of form and colour, discovered new ways of expressing movement and speed, which they regarded as the real characteristics of modern civilization. They involved Balla in their investigations and introduced him to Marinetti, the leader of the Futurist movement, and to the painters Carrà and Russolo. As a result Balla signed the *Technical Manifesto of Futuristic Painting* on 11 April 1910, and later his name was added to the list of signatures on the earlier *Manifesto of Futuristic Painters* (11 February 1910). Both of these manifestos dealt with the application of the Futuristic idea to painting. Two years later, in 1912, Balla painted his first Futuristic picture, in which he portrayed a dog running. Without actually deforming the dog he contrived to break down the sequence of movement into component phases, which he depicted simultaneously. However, he soon abandoned this naturalistic approach and began to express movement, speed and dynamism by means of signs, which were built up from coloured forms and were almost completely abstract. But, although his pictures are perfect examples of Futuristic painting, they lack the vitality and inventiveness of Boccioni's work. In about 1930 Balla reverted to objective painting and did not produce any further experimental abstract works until the closing years of his life.

Archivi del Futurismo, Rome, I 1958; II 1962.
'G. Balla' in *Italian Painting from Futurism to the Present Day*, Museum of Modern Art, New York 1961.

Exhibition catalogue, *Giacomo Balla*, Galleria d'Arte Moderna, Turin 1963.
C. Baumgarth. *Geschichte des Futurismus*, Reinbek 1966.

Ballets Russes. This ballet troupe of the impresario Serge Diaghilev, which dazzled western audiences at its première in Paris in 1909, continued to attract devotees of the *avant-garde* in the capitals of Europe until its mentor's death in 1929, which marked the collapse of the company. Diaghilev, a former staff member of the Imperial Theatre, St. Petersburg, and a founder of the *Mir Iskusstva* (World of Art) magazine, and the movement of that name, was a ceaseless innovator of exacting tastes, seeking out not only the finest in choreographers (Fokine, Balanchine, Massine) but in composers (Stravinsky, Milhaud) and designers as well.

In costume and scenic design, two strains were nurtured by the *Ballets Russes*. Diaghilev's resident designers, Léon Bakst (*Schéhérazade*, 1910) and Alexandre Benois (*Petrushka*, 1911), created a lush, aristocratic world of exotic colours and romantic imagery derived from Russian roots—including folkloric and Oriental *motifs*—which was, however, independent of any style produced in Russia itself. Their beautiful but retardataire art was essentially self-consuming, although echoes of their vision appear in Georges Rouault's décor for *The Prodigal Son* (1929). At the same time, Diaghilev was commissioning designs from noted experimental painters in some of the most advanced art styles of the day. These included Picasso's Cubist décor for *Parade*, 1917; the Fauvist *La Boutique Fantasque* (1919) by André Derain; the Constructivist *La Chatte* (1927) by Naum Gabo and Antoine Pevsner; and designs by Nathalie Gontcharova (*Les Noces*, 1923); Marie Laurencin (*Les Biches*, 1924); Henri Matisse (*Le Chant du Rossignol*, 1926); Giorgio de Chirico (*Le Bal*, 1929); Joan Miró; Georges Braque; and Mikhail Larionov.

Camilla Gray. *The Great Experiment: Russian Art 1863–1922*, London and New York 1962.
Council of Europe. Catalogue, *Les Ballets Russes de Serge Diaghilev*, Strasbourg 1968.

Balmford, Mary—*see* **Martin,** Mary

Balthus (Balthasar Klossowski de Rola). French painter, b. 1908 in Paris. When he was still only a boy Balthus was urged both by his father (the Polish painter and author E. Klossowski) and by Bonnard and Derain to devote himself to painting. A little later Rilke also encouraged this young prodigy. After spending his childhood in Switzerland Balthus lived and worked in complete seclusion in the vicinity of Paris until 1961, when he was appointed Director of the Villa Medici at Malraux's instigation.

In Balthus's early street scenes and interiors, which are both magical and realistic at one and the same time, a variety of influences—Bonnard, Derain,

Braque, the Early Italian Renaissance and Surrealism —are successfully integrated. His later paintings— which are all interiors—are quite different. In these works Balthus portrays adolescent girls sleeping, daydreaming, reading or looking pensively out of the window in rooms which seem part of a twilight world and in which there is no hint of movement. The mood of these interior scenes is unmistakably erotic. The other change which has taken place over the years concerns Balthus's choice of colours. In his early phase these were dull and earthy but later he brightened his palette quite considerably, producing pale, almost transparent effects. Balthus has also painted remarkable landscapes.

A. Camus. *Balthus*, New York 1949.

Exhibition catalogue, *Balthus*, Musée des Arts Décoratifs, Paris 1966.

John Russell. *Balthus*, Tate Gallery, London 1968.

Bandeira, Antonio. Brazilian painter, b. 1922 in Fortaleza, Brazil. After first studying in Rio de Janeiro Bandeira continued his training in Paris at the Académie and Atelier de la Grande Chaumière. He then returned briefly to Brazil before settling permanently in Paris, where he became friendly with Wols and Bryen. Bandeira is a lyrical abstract painter.

Baranoff-Rossiné, Vladimir. Russo-French painter and sculptor, b. 1888 in Kherson, Russia; d. 1942. After studying art in St. Petersburg Baranoff-Rossiné went to Paris in 1910. He returned to Russia four years later and was given a professorial post at the Moscow Academy. In 1930 he again left Russia to settle permanently in Paris.

Baranoff-Rossiné became known both for his 'polytechnic' sculptures, which he constructed from pieces of gutter pipe, bedsprings and such like, and— above all—for his 'colour piano', with which he gave a number of 'colour concerts' in Moscow and Paris. After starting as a Post-Impressionist he passed through a Cubist phase before going over to abstract art.

Bargheer, Eduard. German painter, b. 1901 in Hamburg-Finkenwerder, Germany. Bargheer is a self-taught painter. In 1938 he left Germany for Italy, settling on Ischia, where he associated with Gilles, Levy, Heldt, etc. After passing through an early Expressionist phase he turned to landscapes, painting Mediterranean scenes in a crystalline, hermetic style, which he had derived from Orphism and from Klee. Bargheer now lives partly in Forio d'Ischia, partly in Hamburg.

F. Baumgart. *Der Maler Eduard Bargheer*, Stuttgart 1955.

Barlach, Ernst. German sculptor, poet and graphic artist, b. 1870 in Wedel, nr. Hamburg; d. 1938 in Rostock. After attending the School of Arts and Crafts in Hamburg from 1888 to 1891 Barlach studied at the Dresden Academy in Robert Diez's 'masters' class' until 1895. Like many of his contemporaries he spent one year of his four-year course at the Académie Julian in Paris. Although the sculptures which Barlach carved for the Rathaus in Nuremberg between 1897 and 1899 give no indication of an individual style, the drawings which he executed for the *Jugend* magazine at the turn of the century certainly do. Here we see the first signs of the *Jugendstil* that was to form the basis of his work, certainly during his early period. And the qualities which are hinted at in the sweeping contours of these drawings emerge more clearly in the pottery designs which he made between 1901 and 1904: simplification and adaptation of the form so as to do justice to the material in accordance with the craftsmanship ethic of the *Jugendstil*. During his visit to Russia in 1906 Barlach discovered new *motifs* (such as the *Beggar Woman*) and his Italian journey in 1909— during which he met Theodor Däubler, the classical exponent of expressionist poetry—strengthened his interest in such themes. In 1910 Barlach settled in Güstrow in Mecklenburg, where he wrote his first poems. But his really important period as a poet did not begin until the 1920s, by which time he had become a member of the Berlin Academy of Art (1919). In the 1920s and early 1930s he also produced his major works of sculpture: the monuments for Güstrow Cathedral (1927) and Magdeburg Cathedral (1930), the celebrated *Frieze of the Listeners* (1931) and, subsequently, the sculptures for St. Catherine's Church in Lübeck, in which Barlach demonstrated his ability to assimilate the craft ethic of the medieval masons, which was closely allied to his own. In 1933, despite the fact that he had been made a Knight of the Order 'Pour Le Mérite', he was proscribed by the National Socialists, and 381 of his works were confiscated by the state. Like Nolde and Käthe Kollwitz, Barlach was one of the individualists of the German Expressionist movement. His extensive oeuvre, which embraces a large body of poetry, sculptures—most of them carved in wood—and extremely powerful graphic works, has two principal characteristics: expressiveness and commitment. His techniques, which were already fully developed by 1907 and scarcely changed from then onwards, owed little to contemporary trends. They were derived partly from the folk art of primitive cultures and, more especially, from the late Gothic woodcarvings of Northern Europe. With their flowing drapery, their ecstatic gestures and their compressed, block-like forms his heavy, earthy figures express elemental feelings. Barlach himself has told us what he tried to depict: 'humanity enlarged to gigantic proportions, shaken by fate or beside itself from self-forgetfulness'.

F. Dross. *Ernst Barlach: Das Leben und Werk in seinen Briefen*, Munich 1952.

C. D. Carls. *Ernst Barlach*, Berlin 1954.
F. Schalt. *Ernst Barlach: Das graphische Werk*, with a catalogue of works, Hamburg 1957; *Ernst Barlach: Das plastische Werk*, with a catalogue of works, Hamburg 1959.

Barnard, George Grey. American sculptor, b. 1863 in Bellefonte, Pennsylvania; d. 1938 in New York. Barnard studied in Chicago and later in Paris, where he won a gold medal. He returned to the USA in 1896, and had a number of pieces in the Armory Show (1913). He worked mainly in marble, and many of his sculptures are figure groups.

Barradas, Rafael Pérez. Uruguayan painter, b. 1890 in Montevideo; d. 1929 in Montevideo. Barradas started his career as a caricaturist in Montevideo, where he was a well-known figure in artistic and literary circles. Then, in 1912, he went to Europe and remained there for the next sixteen years. He made contact with the Futurists and Cubists in Italy and France before settling in Spain, where he joined the *avant-garde* and became friendly with Torres Garcia. From Futurism Barradas developed a highly personal pictorial style, which he called 'vibrationism' and which drew its inspiration from the dynamism that he found in the streets of Madrid and the harbour of Barcelona. Whilst in Spain Barradas painted harbour and inn scenes, townscapes, landscapes and, later, religious works. After returning to Montevideo in 1928 he produced his large format watercolours, which he called 'Pictures of Montevideo'. In these works, some of which reveal traces of *simultanéisme*, Barradas painted his childhood memories of Montevideo with delicate humour and a hint of melancholy. He also designed stage sets and illustrated books.

J. J. Casal. *Rafael Barradas*, Buenos Aires 1949.
J. P. Argul. *Les artes plasticas del Uruguay*, Montevideo 1966.

Barraud, Maurice. Swiss painter, b. 1889 in Geneva; d. 1954 in Geneva. After serving an apprenticeship as a graphic artist Barraud took drawing lessons and then started a commercial enterprise, producing posters, etc., for advertising purposes. It was not until 1913, when he was 24, that he became a full-time painter. From 1938 onwards he lived partly in Cassis-sur-Mer.

Barraud produced murals, frescoes (including one for Lucerne Railway Station), landscapes, nudes, figures and portraits. His works, which are painted in pastel shades, reveal the influence of Renoir, Degas and Matisse.

Adrien Bovey. *Maurice Barraud*, Lausanne 1940.
P. Cailler and H. Dardel. *Catalogue illustré de l'oeuvre gravé et lithographié de Maurice Barraud*, Geneva 1944.

Bartolini, Luigi. Italian painter and poet, b. 1892 in Cupramontana, Ancona. Bartolini studied medicine, literature and the natural sciences at the universities in Rome, Siena and Florence. He began to etch in 1914 but was subsequently forced to break off his artistic activities because of the outbreak of war. He has been a writer since 1927. He now lives and works in Rome.

Bartolini is generally regarded as one of Italy's leading Expressionists, and he is undoubtedly one of her most accomplished etchers. In his graphic works he uses simplified forms which create an impression of immediacy. The draughtsmanship and chiaroscuro in his etchings are quite masterly.

Basaldúa, Héctor. Argentinian painter, illustrator and stage designer, b. 1895 in Pergamino, Argentina. Basaldúa studied from 1923 to 1930, first at the Academy in Buenos Aires, then in Paris. He paints landscapes, figurative compositions and still lifes which vacillate between objectivity and abstraction and in which highly sensitive draughtsmanship is combined with delicate colouring. Like Figari, he takes his themes from childhood memories. For many years Basaldúa was stage designer for the Teatro Colón, the great opera house in Buenos Aires.

Baschlakow, Alexei Iljitsch. Russo-German painter, b. 1936 in Slaboda, Russia. During the war Baschlakow was uprooted from his home and in 1945 found himself in Germany. In 1948, when he was 12, he began to paint and in 1954 won a Henry Ford art scholarship. He then served a three-year apprenticeship from 1954 to 1957 and attended the Werkkunstschule in Hanover from 1958 to 1959. In 1962 he visited Florence. He is now living in Hanover.

In his pictures, which are firmly rooted in Constructivism, Baschlakow builds up relief-like structures from geometrical components, which he paints in rich colours. Abstract heraldic shapes thrust forward into the picture space, where they link up to form composite designs.

Exhibition catalogue, *A. Baschlakow*, Brusberg Galerie, Hanover 1965.

Baskin, Leonard. American sculptor and printmaker, b. 1922 in New Brunswick, New Jersey. Baskin's art education began with the Rumanian-born sculptor Maurice Glickman (b. 1906), from 1937 to 1939, and continued at Yale University in New Haven, Connecticut, the New School for Social Research in New York (BA, 1949), the Académie de la Grande Chaumière in Paris, and the Academy of Fine Arts in Florence. Thereafter he became a teacher of printmaking at the School of the Worcester Art Museum, Worcester, Massachusetts, and a professor at Smith College, Northampton, Massachusetts. He had numerous one-man shows from 1939 on, and was awarded an Honourable Mention for the Prix de Rome, an L. C. Tiffany Fellowship, and a Guggenheim Foundation Fellowship for print-making.

Baskin was preoccupied in his art with both physical death and spiritual decay; in 1959 he wrote: 'Man has made of Arden a landscape of death. In this garden I dwell, and in limning its horror, the degradation and the filth, I hold the cracked mirror up to man.' The artist's role, he believed, should be the communication of moral ideas, especially through the human image. Baskin took up the theme of mortality in 1950, after seeing the sculptured tombs of the past in Europe, in this way fusing traditional art with contemporary ideas, a synthesis that he considered highly important. Working in stone, wood or bronze, he created a series of massive, ponderous human figures that are either physically or spiritually dead. His effigies of the dead, such as *Dead Poet*, a portrayal of John Donne in a winding sheet (1955, Newton Center, Mass., Coll. Mr. and Mrs. Arthur Vershbow) or *The Great Dead Man* (limestone, 1956), suggest death as the natural state of man. Other images, however, including *Poet Laureate* (bronze, 1956) and *The Guardian* (limestone, 1956), show a decadent smugness through suggestive physical characteristics: small, pig-like eyes, an obese and awkward nude body and weak, tapering legs. At the same time they express authority with their arms crossed over the chest. Baskin frequently also used symbolic animal images, particularly birds, either in combination with the men, or in direct fusion with their bodies (*Birdman*, 1961, New York, Grace Borgenicht Gallery).

Bowdoin College Museum of Art. Catalogue, *Leonard Baskin*, Brunswick (Maine) 1962.
Alfred Werner. 'Leonard Baskin: Art for Life's Sake', *American Artist* XXVIII, November 1964.

Batlle Planas, Juan. Spanish-Argentinian painter and art theorist, b. 1911 in Torroella de Montgri, Catalonia; d. 1966 in Buenos Aires. Batlle Planas was taken to Argentina in 1913 whilst still a small child and subsequently received his training there from his uncle José Planas Casas. In 1939 he mounted his first exhibition of collages, which he called *paranoid X-ray pictures*. Batlle Planas was a Surrealist. But, although he used a technique that was both arbitrary and automatistic, his works invariably reveal a high degree of structural cohesion. Batlle Planas is one of the leading personalities in the Argentinian art world. Apart from working as a painter and book illustrator, he is active as a publicist and has also founded a private research institute, where he has trained numerous pupils.

Battke, Heinz. German painter, b. 1900 in Berlin; d. 1966 in Frankfurt am Main. Battke studied at the Berlin Academy under Karl Hofer from 1921 to 1925. In 1935 he emigrated to Florence. From 1956 onwards he taught at the College of Fine Arts in Frankfurt am Main.

Battke was an abstract painter who transformed his impressions of nature into poetic images after the manner of Klee. In his later years his output consisted largely of drawings, which reveal a high degree of technical precision and are notable for their irrational perspectives.

O. Stelzer. *Heinz Battke: Zeichnungen*, Baden-Baden 1955.

Batz, Eugen. German painter, b. 1905 in Velbert, Rhineland. Batz studied at the Bauhaus in Dessau under Klee and Kandinsky from 1929 to 1931 and in Klee's 'Masters' Class' at the Düsseldorf Academy from 1931 to 1933. He is now living in Neviges in the Rhineland.

Batz transforms his poetic impressions of nature into hermetic, abstract images. Up to 1945 the major part of his output consisted of watercolours and graphic works. Since then he has also painted in oils.

Exhibition catalogue, *Eugen Batz*, Kunst- und Museumsverein, Wuppertal 1965.

Bauchant, André. French painter, b. 1873 in Châteaurenault, Indre-et-Loire; d. 1958 in Montoire, Loire-et-Cher. Together with Rousseau, Bombois, Vivin and Séraphine, Bauchant belonged to the group of five 'naïve painters', who were introduced to the art public by the German critic Wilhelm Uhde in a joint exhibition staged in the Galerie Quatre Chemins in Paris in 1928. These five, who were presented as the *Painters of the Sacred Heart*, were the pioneers of modern primitive art. In 1937–8 they again showed their works in a joint exhibition entitled *Maîtres populaires de la Réalité*, which was put on in Paris, Zürich and New York.

Like his father before him Bauchant worked as a gardener throughout his entire life apart from the period of the First World War, when he served as a soldier at the Dardanelles and in Greece. During his military service he began to make sketches from nature and in 1917 his skill as a draughtsman brought him a posting as an army land surveyor. When he was demobilized he also began to paint, using dry but heightened earth colours with a little pink, pale blue, grey and white, which were applied with irregular strokes of the brush to produce gentle contrasts of light and shade. He preferred large-scale works and his favourite subjects were historical or mythological scenes taken from the Ancient Greek world. The Greeks and their gods are depicted in these paintings with Hellenistic drapery fluttering about their contoured forms. Bauchant also produced paintings of peasant life in Touraine, floral studies and modern landscapes. But, although he himself liked to think of these works as realistic, his view of reality was so coloured by his poetic vision that they actually have more in common with the idyllic world of fable than with twentieth-century France. In 1920 his paintings attracted the attention of Ozenfant, Le Corbusier and Jeanne Bucher, and in 1921 he had his first exhibition in the Salon d'Automne. In 1927 Diaghilev commissioned him to produce the stage sets for Stravinsky's ballet *Apollon Musagète*. In 1949 he had a retrospective exhibition—at which 250 of his pictures were on show—in the Galerie Charpentier in Paris.

M. Gauthier. *André Bauchant*, Paris 1943.

Bauer, Rudolph. German-American painter, b. 1889 in Lindenwald, Germany; d. 1954 near New York. At the age of 12 he began working as a cartoonist, and continued in this vein working as a designer of humorous publications and gaining a reputation as a caricaturist after his brief study at the Academy of Fine Arts, Berlin (1905). Progressing through a sequence of Academic, Impressionist, Expressionist and Cubist phases he finally arrived at a 'futuristic art of non-objectivity'. As early as 1915 he exhibited as a member of the *Sturm* at the Glaspalast, Berlin and later founded a private museum of Non-Objectivity, the Geistreich, in Berlin. In the 1920s and 1930s he was the author of several books, among them such works as *Manifest der Malerei* (Berlin, 1921), *Das Geistreich* (Berlin, 1931) and *Eppur si muove* (Berlin, 1935). By the time he came to the United States shortly before the Second World War, his paintings and those of Kandinsky formed the basis of the Solomon R. Guggenheim Collection of Non-Objective Paintings. The completely formal painting from that collection entitled *Spiritual Pleasures*, which lacks any identifiable subject, is representative of his style. Though it is an arrangement of circles, cones and triangles rendered in pure, bright, local colours set in a flat, two-dimensional space, the modulation of tone gives the viewer some sense of a space into which the geometric forms are placed.

Art of Tomorrow, catalogue of the Solomon R. Guggenheim Collection of Non-Objective Paintings, New York 1939.

Bauhaus. The Bauhaus school of design, craftsmanship and architecture was founded by Walter Gropius at Weimar in 1919. Gropius established a 'Council of Masters', consisting of Itten, Marcks and Feininger, and invited many of the leading artists of his day, including Klee, Kandinsky, Schlemmer and Moholy-Nagy, to come to Weimar as 'masters of form', i.e. artistic directors. The curriculum provided for both theoretical and practical work in various departments, each of which was run by an artistic and a technical director. All students undertook a six-month introductory course, in which they were acquainted with form, colour and the nature of material. In 1925–6 the Bauhaus moved to Dessau, where several of the early students—such as

Albers, Bayer and Breuer—were appointed to the teaching staff. At the end of 1926 Gropius' new building was completed. It had three principal wings, which were occupied by the technical institutes, the laboratory workshops and the *Atelier* house. In Dessau the dual system of instruction was abandoned. Instead of having both an artistic and a technical director, each department was placed in charge of a single director, who undertook both functions. In 1926 Gropius left the Bauhaus in the face of growing difficulties and personal attacks. He was accompanied by Breuer, Moholy-Nagy and Bayer. The architect Hannes Meyer then ran the Bauhaus until the summer of 1930, when he was succeeded by Mies van der Rohe. In 1932 the institute moved to Berlin, where it was dissolved in the following year due to political pressure. But even after the Bauhaus had been closed down its methods and ideas continued to exert widespread influence. They were brought to America by Moholy-Nagy, who opened the New Bauhaus (later the Institute of Design) in Chicago, and by Josef Albers, who joined the staff of Black Mountain College in North Carolina. The architectural faculty of Harvard University also adopted Bauhaus methods, as did the Hochschule für Gestaltung (College of Design) in Ulm. The whole essence of the Bauhaus was contained in its revolutionary teaching method, in which the traditional view of education based on the 'teacher–student relationship' was replaced by the new conception of a community of artists working to the same end. The Bauhaus did not regard itself as an institution set apart from society but rather as an intrinsic part of the social process. It looked upon art as the visual symbol of a new social order and wanted to remove it from the isolation to which it had been subjected by the philosophy of 'art for art's sake' and lead it back into daily life. It is quite evident from the name which Gropius gave to his institute—*Bauhaus* (Building House)—that he was intent on establishing a link with the *Bauhütten* (masonic guilds) which were responsible for the erection of the medieval German cathedrals and in which art and craftsmanship were still indissolubly fused. In the Bauhaus manifesto of April 1919 Gropius exhorted his collaborators to join him in creating 'the building of the future, which will be all things in the one form—and which will one day rise up to heaven as a crystalline symbol of a new, coming faith'. Initially the Bauhaus style was determined primarily by the Expressionists of the *Sturm* and the *Blauer Reiter* but, when the Constructivist Moholy-Nagy was invited to join the staff in 1923, the institute entered on its 'functionalist' phase, in which it investigated the utilitarian aspect of art and moved towards industrial design. The *de Stijl* movement, which had been expounded to the Bauhaus community by van Doesburg on lecture visits, also contributed to this development. The artistic stimuli which emanated from the Bauhaus were quite exceptional and continue to influence western art to this day. The publication of the 'Bauhaus Books'—which included Klee's *Pedagogical Sketchbook*, Kandinsky's *Point and Line to Plane* and Mondrian's *New Design*—helped to propagate these new ideas.

H. Bayer, W. Gropius and Ilse Gropius. *Bauhaus 1919–28*, Museum of Modern Art, New York 1938.
H. M. Wingler. *Das Bauhaus 1919–1933*, Cologne 1962.
Will Grohmann. Catalogue, *Painters of the Bauhaus*, Marlborough Fine Art Ltd., London 1962.
Bauhaus Exhibition Catalogue, Stuttgart 1968.
Gillian Naylor. *The Bauhaus*, London 1968.

Baum, Otto. German sculptor, b. 1900 in Leonberg, Württemberg. After serving an apprenticeship as a mechanic Baum studied sculpture at the Academy in Stuttgart. He became a member of the Academy staff in 1946 and is still teaching there today.

Baum carves block-like sculptures, in which the organic element is reduced to simple elemental forms. His works, which he executes in wood or stone, reveal the influence of Brancusi and Arp.

Franz Roh. *Otto Baum*, Tübingen 1950.

Baumeister, Willi. German painter, b. 1889 in Stuttgart; d. 1955 in Stuttgart. Baumeister has a place as an important progenitor of the abstract school in German painting. His work covers the period from 1912 to 1955, encompassing that fermenting period of new, anti-traditionalist ideas of the first half of the twentieth century.

In his formative years he was influenced by Cézanne and Post-Impressionism, later developing a sympathy for the work of Fernand Léger. Through him Baumeister became associated with Ozenfant and the French Purist school, producing at this time architecturally oriented work of a formal, geometric nature.

He was a close friend of Oskar Schlemmer, but was not a member of the Bauhaus group. His work became more personal and free, leading to the abstract form which he developed during the 1930s. Baumeister is important in that he was among the first to realize that a painting could be its own subject. It needed no visible object as starting-point for portrayal or abstractionist presentation. A painting could be conceived as belonging more to the world of the string quartet than of the illustrated book.

In the the early 1920s he experimented with the idea, which became almost commonplace later in the century, of the identity of picture and wall. He produced 'wall-reliefs', using sand and modelling pastes as additives to the paint. His subsequent work remains in the traditionalist format of easel-painting.

Baumeister was much concerned with the philosophy of art, believing that freely imagined forms provide images relating to the deeper, primitive roots of humanity. His thinking along these and similar lines was published in 1947 in a book written by himself, *Das Unbekannte in der Kunst* ('The Unknown in Art').

Every painting has some reason for its existence, and the near-infinite freedom of purpose which Baumeister's kind of abstraction allowed the forms would be dependent on the artist's predilection at that time. Thus his *Eidos* series of 1939 shows cell-like organisms of marine biology. His *African Pictures* of 1943 are like ideograms of implied interpretive meaning. Later, he produced areas of bold flat silhouetted shapes, map-like *Territories*. Though spurning 'representation', he shows by his titles and the style of his images that his work is not intended as subjectless, but as representations of 'other' realities. Deemed to have serious meaning, they are a kind of abstract Surrealism.

In common with many of the best German artists of the time Baumeister was disowned by the National Socialists, and labelled degenerate in 1933. Unlike the majority of artists similarly affected he remained in Germany, working in obscurity in Stuttgart. He was reinstated after the war, and became Director of the Stuttgart Academy. He died in 1955, late enough to see the general acceptance of much that he had helped to pioneer in his early career.

Bawden, Edward. British painter, b. 1903 in Braintree, Essex. He studied in Cambridge and at the Royal College of Art. He produced decorations for Morley College, as well as designing ships' interiors and big general exhibitions. His first one-man show was at Zwemmer's Gallery in 1934. He was a member of the Seven and Five Society from 1932 to 1934. During the Second World War he was an official war artist. He has also taught at the Royal College of Art. He was elected an RA in 1956.

Bayer, Herbert. Austrian-American painter and graphic artist, b. 1900 in Haag, Austria. After studying with the architect Professor Schnidthammer in Linz in 1919, he worked with the architect Emanuel Margold in Darmstadt for a year and then took up studies in 1921 at the Bauhaus in Weimar. Here he studied under Kandinsky and himself became a teacher of advertising layout and typography (1925–8). For the next ten years he worked in Berlin doing exhibition planning, paintings, typography and advertising work. It was soon after his first one-man show in Paris in 1929 that he took an active interest in photography, producing Surrealist photo-montages which formally relate to the paintings of Miró. When he moved to New York in 1938 he worked mainly in advertising and design for John Wanamaker's and J. Walter Thompson. In the same year he published a book entitled *Bauhaus 1919–1928*. Though active as a painter, his ideas and aesthetic are best studied in his book jackets, posters and magazine covers. His Bauhaus affiliations are evident in his poster for the exhibition of the German Werkbund, Paris, 1930, while a more personal expression is revealed in the booklet he designed for the exhibition *Das Wunder des Lebens* (Berlin, 1934).

Alexander Dorner. *The Way Beyond 'Art'—The Work of Herbert Bayer*, New York 1947.

Bazaine, Jean. French painter, b. 1904 in Paris. He began by studying sculpture, but his interest was gradually drawn to painting, and he first exhibited his pictures in 1932. His approach was to probe beneath the ordinary surface of objects and to open them up, to separate their component parts so that they were enabled to harmonize with their background.

Over a period of some fifteen years his work became progressively more non-figurative, until by about 1947 the natural objects he used in his paintings were unrecognizable as such. He drew his inspiration from the world about him which he interpreted in his own rhythmic bold style, with its emphasis on line, in such pictures as *Sea Wind*, 1949, or *Child and Night*, 1949. He strove to overcome the physical limitations of the canvas by making his rhythmical line appear to spill over the edge, giving the impression that his compositions were contained only with difficulty. After some years the accent of his paintings shifted from line to colour, and he experimented with blends and unusual combinations of pure colours. The rich subtlety of these shimmered from the surface of his seascapes and snow paintings.

This awareness of the richness of colour is also revealed in his stained-glass windows and his mosaics, both of which media are eminently suited to his style. Examples of his work are to be seen in the church at Andincourt and in the UNESCO headquarters in Paris.

A. Maeght. *Jean Bazaine*, Paris 1953.

Baziotes, William. American painter, b. 1912 in Pittsburgh; d. 1963 in New York. He came to New York in 1933, and studied at the National Academy of Design with Leon Kroll (b. 1884). During the next few years (1936–41) he worked for the WPA Federal Art Project, both as a teacher and painter. In 1948, along with Robert Motherwell, Barnett Newman and Mark Rothko, he was the co-founder of a school called 'The Subject of the Artist'. Out of this grew 'The Club', which held weekly meetings and discussions among New York's *avant-garde* artists. Baziotes worked in relative obscurity until 1944, when his work was shown at Peggy Guggenheim's important gallery, Art of This Century.

Painting for Baziotes meant a looking inward to discover the magical nature of inspiration and the mystery of the painting as the artist's own mirror. In his works he aimed for a stillness and a slow, haunting possession that would take hold of the viewer. Baziotes' art was linked to an interest current among several New York artists at the time, namely the universal basis of primitive forms and mythological themes as a valid content for their works. He was also particularly interested in the essential nature of aesthetic inspiration. Despite a high degree of abstraction in his later work, he remained deeply involved with subject matter, although content was not always explicit or obvious, even when recognizable forms emerged. He favoured amoeba-like biomorphic shapes, which could be traced back to the creations of Arp, Miró, and the psychic automatism of the Surrealists. Baziotes never developed the bravado Expressionism or painterly style of his contemporaries, and throughout the development of his mature style, he flattened forms into decorative patterns, floating them in a misty atmosphere (*Red Landscape*, 1957, Minneapolis, Institute of Arts). *Primeval Landscape* (1953, Philadelphia, Museum of Art) and *Pompeii* (1956, New York, Museum of Modern Art) are characteristic of his exceptional gifts as a subtle colourist, and indicate his method of conjuring up amorphous configurations.

Catalogue, *William Baziotes: A Memorial Exhibition*, Solomon R. Guggenheim Museum, New York 1965.

Beardsley, Aubrey. English illustrator and graphic designer, b. 1872; d. 1898. His drawings have always symbolized the Decadence of the 1890s, but although his working life was scarcely more than five years and his work virtually entirely black and white he was also one of the most original artists of his generation. He was educated in Brighton and then worked as a clerk in a London office. He was an admirer of Burne-Jones and of Whistler, and the Peacock Room was, with Burne-Jones' *Briar Rose* series (exhibited 1890), an important source of inspiration for him. This is apparent in drawings of 1890 and 1891 (*Tannhäuser* and *Dante in Exile*) which also show a debt to artists like Mantegna and Blake.

In 1892 he visited Paris (he returned there in 1896) and it was later in that year that his professional career really began. John Dent commissioned him to illustrate the *Morte d'Arthur*, which was published in 1894. In April of 1893 the first number of *Studio*, for which he had designed the cover, contained an article on Beardsley by Joseph Pennell that launched him internationally. It was here that the first version of one of his most famous drawings appeared, *J'ai baisé ta bouche, Jokanaan*, from Wilde's *Salome*. This led directly to a commission from John Lane to illustrate *Salome* (published in 1894). Beardsley already knew Wilde, but the public identification with him through these illustrations proved disastrous. In April 1895, on Wilde's arrest, public hostility turned also against Beardsley and the *Yellow Book* of which he had been made art editor at its foundation in January 1894 by John Lane. Pressure was put on Lane, and Beardsley was sacked. He had up to then designed and illustrated the first four numbers of the *Yellow Book*.

Where the *Salome* drawings are tense and linear, with some Japanese inspiration, some of the *Yellow Book* drawings (*Garçons de Café*, *Wagnerites*, for example) are more open with a bold simplification of light and shade, perhaps bringing him closer to his French contemporaries like Bonnard and Toulouse-Lautrec. After leaving the *Yellow Book* he was taken up by Leonard Smithers, who started a new magazine, the *Savoy*, and made him its chief illustrator. It ran for eight numbers throughout 1896. Smithers also published, among other works by Beardsley, his illustrations to the *Rape of the Lock* (1896), to Aristophanes' *Lysistrata* (1896), which contained some of his most notorious drawings, and to Ernest Dowson's *Pierrot of the Minute* (1897). The *Savoy* drawings, especially those for Beardsley's own erotic novel *Under the Hill* that was in part published there, and the illustrations to the *Rape of the Lock* are in a kind of fantastic eighteenth-century idiom. In them the stipple and hatching that he uses (abandoning simple black and white for the first time) and the decorative details of furniture and costume multiply and spread so that the total effect is a dense, flat, almost abstract pattern. In the *Lysistrata*, on the other hand, the drawing is clear and simple. The organization and the use of line and stipple recall the engravings by Piroli and Blake after Flaxman.

His drawings for the *Pierrot of the Minute* are inspired by Watteau. They show a new interest in space and chiaroscuro and a perfect balance of depth and surface. They are among the most delicate and simply poetic of all his work. In the last year of his life he extended this interest in depth, solidity, and tone, and attained new monumentality through a boldness of pictorial invention that anticipates Picasso and Matisse (*The Lady at the Dressing-Table*, and *The Lady with the Rose*, illustrations to Gautier's *Mademoiselle de Maupin* published by Smithers in 1898). The last project that he undertook but which was never completed was the illustration of Ben Jonson's *Volpone*. The illuminated capitals are drawings carefully modelled in tone. They have a classical solidity that gives them a new authority and seriousness, a solemn ferocity and an ominous power that would convince us if nothing else did that Beardsley's was not merely a talent for the perverse but a true poetic gift—though the poetry was, like its author, *maudite*. He was a victim of tuberculosis, and after 1895 his health declined rapidly. In March 1897 he became a Roman Catholic. He left England for the last time in November of that year and died at Menton the following March at the age of 25.

The Early Work of Aubrey Beardsley, London 1899.
The Later Work of Aubrey Beardsley, London 1901.
Last Letters of Beardsley, ed. J. Gray, London 1904.
Letters of Beardsley to Smithers, ed. R. A. Walker, London 1937.
Victoria and Albert Museum catalogue, *Beardsley Exhibition*, 1967.
Brian Reade, *Aubrey Beardsley*, 1969.

Beaudin, André. French painter, illustrator and sculptor, b. 1895 in Mennecy, Seine-et-Oise. Beaudin studied at the École des Arts Décoratifs in Paris from 1911 to 1915. His acquaintance with Juan Gris, which dates from 1922, was an important factor in his artistic development. He is now living in Paris.

After coming to terms with Derain, Picasso (in his late Cubist phase) and the Surrealist Masson Beaudin evolved a delicate style of painting with refined colours and clear, orderly Cubist structures that is reminiscent of Villon and Nicholson. His block-like sculptures are also derived from Cubism.

Georges Limbour. *André Beaudin*, Paris 1961.

Bechteler, Theodor. German sculptor, b. 1903 in Immenstadt, Allgau. After serving an apprenticeship in Oberammergau Bechteler studied sculpture in Berlin. He is now living in Augsburg.

Bechteler produces wooden, stone and bronze sculptures, the last by the *cire perdu* process. By combining open areas with frame constructions he creates rooms, houses and streets which serve as settings for human figures.

Beckmann, Max. German painter, b. 1884 in Leipzig; d. 1950 in New York. After studying at the Weimar Academy from 1899 to 1903 Beckmann visited Paris, Geneva, Florence and Jutland before settling in Berlin in 1907. There he made contact with the members of the Berlin *Sezession* and joined their movement in 1910, only to leave it again in the following year. In 1914–15 he served as a medical orderly in East Prussia, then went to live in Frankfurt, where he remained until 1933. In 1921 he wrote four stage plays, none of which was ever performed. In 1925 he was appointed Professor at the Städelschule in Frankfurt but was dismissed when the National Socialists came to power in 1933. He then returned to Berlin, where he lived for four years before emigrating, first to Paris and subsequently to Amsterdam. In 1947 he left Holland and, after visiting Nice and Paris, settled in the USA and taught at the University of St. Louis. In 1949 he moved to New York, where he was given a professorial post at the Brooklyn Museum and won the Carnegie Prize. In 1950 he was awarded an honorary doctorate by the University of St. Louis and won a prize for painting at the Biennale.

During his early Berlin period Beckmann was regarded as one of the brightest prospects of the Impressionist-oriented *Sezession*. But he soon tired of *plein-air* painting. In order to do justice to the kind of reality with which he found himself confronted—especially after his wartime service—he sought a completely unacademic and non-virtuoso style, which he found in a new kind of expressive realism. The early work of this period reveals a close affinity to the later Corinth although the visionary scenes which followed have more in common with the psychological art of the Norwegian Edvard Munch. But, above all, Beckmann concentrated on figurative compositions and he is now regarded as one of the most important portraitists of his day. Certainly his portraits and, more especially, his self-portraits dominate his oeuvre. Only very few German painters have put so much of themselves into their art. But then Beckmann was always an individualist. His work is not so easy to grasp and is not so directly related to contemporary events as that of other artists. Many of his paintings are to be understood as allegories reflecting the *comédie humaine*. Certain objects—candles, masks, musical instruments—constantly recur and provide the key to a second and deeper level of reality underlying the surface reality of his compositions. Beckmann's triptychs constitute an important facet of his oeuvre and afford the clearest example of the 'transcendental realism' that is one of the chief characteristics of his style. Beckmann used monumental and highly simplified forms which are so powerful that they threaten to destroy the composition. Many critics have bemoaned the harshness, the brutality and the cruelty of much of his work, failing to realize that, although many of these pictures were painted at times when he was suffering from severe depressions, his sole object in executing them was to create a fusion of symbol and object, of dream and reality. This harsh realism belongs primarily to Beckmann's middle period. Towards the end of his life he was able to recapture the lighter tones of his early years. Beckmann also produced a large and highly significant body of graphic works consisting primarily of etchings but also including a number of woodcuts.

E. Göpel. *Max Beckmann*, Munich 1957.
B. Reifenburg and W. Hausenstein. *Max Beckmann*, Feldafing 1959.
G. Busch. *Max Beckmann*, Munich 1960.
P. Selz. *Max Beckmann*, New York 1964.

Beerbohm, Sir Max. British caricaturist and writer, b. 1872 in London; d. 1956 in Rapallo. A prominent dandy at the turn of the century, Beerbohm survived to be a broadcaster in the Second World War. He is best known for his novel *Zuleika Dobson*, and his numerous satirical drawings and captions. In these he treats with gentle irony the aesthetes of his own and the previous two generations, especially *Rossetti*

and his Circle (1916–17). The originals of this series are in the Tate Gallery.

Bell, Graham. British painter, b. 1910 in South Africa; d. 1943. Bell studied at the Durban Art School, and came to England in 1931. He was influenced by the work of Geoffrey Tibble and William Coldstream; he showed non-representational works at the *Objective Abstractions* exhibition, 1934. From then until 1937 he practised journalism, but returned to painting as a member of the Euston Road School, 1937. He is represented in the Tate Gallery.

Bell, Vanessa. British painter and designer, b. 1879 in London; d. 1961 in Sussex. Born Vanessa Stephen, she married Clive Bell in 1907; her sister was Virginia Woolf. The Bells' house in Gordon Square, London, was a centre of the 'Bloomsbury Group'. Vanessa Bell worked with Roger Fry in his Omega Workshops, 1913–19, and collaborated with Duncan Grant in many schemes of decoration between 1914 and 1946. At her boldest, around 1914–15, she showed a creative understanding of Matisse and Derain; her later work was more *intimiste* or decorative. She is represented in the Tate Gallery.

Bellegarde, Claude. French painter, b. 1927 in Paris. Bellegarde began to paint in 1947. From then until 1952 he produced figurative works, from 1953 to 1957 he was a Tachist and from 1958 to 1961 an Abstract Expressionist. Two years later, in 1963, he began to produce his 'Typograms', in which he is trying to analyse the psychological and cosmic ramifications of pure colour. Bellegarde is now living in Paris.

Belling, Rudolf. German sculptor, b. 1886 in Berlin. Belling studied at the Berlin Academy from 1911 to 1912. In 1918 he became a founder member of the *Novembergruppe* and from 1920 onwards maintained close contact with Archipenko. In 1937 Poelzig obtained a teaching post for him at the Academy in Istanbul, where he remained until 1966. He then settled in Krailling near Munich. From 1951 onwards he had been making regular visits to Europe.

During the 1920s Belling was an important figure in the artistic life of Berlin, where he introduced the new sculptural ideas which had emerged from Cubism (Archipenko) and Futurism (Boccioni). Archipenko influenced him considerably at that time and Belling constructed a number of figurative sculptures based on Cubist structures, in which negative forms acquired a positive sculptural significance. Shortly afterwards he began to use Constructivist techniques but without abandoning the figurative element. (His *Head* of 1923 illustrates this development.) But he also produced pure abstract works during this period, e.g. his *Triad* of 1919. Later Belling's love of stylization and lively decorative effects often brought him dangerously close to the sphere of 'arts and crafts'. In Turkey he produced conventional work but is now continuing with his earlier experimental sculptures.

Catalogue, *Rudolf Belling*, Galerie Ketterer, Munich 1967 (with a catalogue of works and a bibliography).

Bellmer, Hans. Polish-French painter, graphic artist and sculptor, b. 1902 in Kattowitz, Upper Silesia. Bellmer attended the Berlin Technical School of Art in 1923 and began to work as a graphic artist in the following year. In 1924–5 he was in Paris. In 1934–5 he made contact with the Paris Surrealists and in 1938 left Berlin to settle in Paris, where—apart from the war and immediate postwar years—he has lived ever since.

It was not until the second half of the 1960s that Bellmer began to reach a wider public. The central theme of his work is the female body, whose inner and outer forms have proved a constant source of fascination to this erotically fixated artist. Commenting on these motifs, Bellmer once said: 'I believe that the various means of expression—posture, movement, gesture, action, tone, speech, graphic quality and pictorial composition—arise out of one and the same mechanism.' Although Bellmer's drawings—which reveal a predilection for *art nouveau* arabesques—have sometimes degenerated into occasional works of modish elegance, for the most part they are executed with a degree of technical precision more readily associated with classical draughtsmanship. Bellmer's *Doll*, a mobile sculpture which he executed in various versions from 1933 onwards, acquired a certain renown even before the Second World War. He has also published numerous books, ranging from *The Doll* of 1934 to *Mode d'emploi* of 1967.

Exhibition catalogue, *Hans Bellmer*, Kestner Gesellschaft, Hanover 1967.

Bellows, George Wesley. American painter, b. 1882 in Columbus, Ohio; d. 1925 in New York. Excelling in sports while attending Ohio State University and encouraged to pursue a career as a professional baseball player, he left the university during his last year (1904) to study art in New York. Almost immediately he became a student of Robert Henri and closely associated with The Eight. Like his colleagues, he was fascinated with America and particularly New York; the earliest cityscapes painted in that metropolis reveal his love of this genre (*Forty-Two Kids*, 1907, oil, Washington, D.C., Corcoran Gallery of Art). He was an immediate success, securing a prize at the National Academy in 1908 and becoming an associate member of the Academy at the age of 27 (1909), the youngest man to receive such an honour. In the same year he painted the *Stag at Sharky's* (oil, Cleveland Museum of Art), representing an illegal boxing match. Executed in broad, bold strokes, he captures the excitement of the event through the

placement of figures and the handling of light and shade rather than by means of colour. His propensity towards monochrome is echoed in the 195 lithographs he produced between 1916 and 1925. These, like his paintings, depict scenes of a purely American nature—prize fights, street scenes and social commentary (slums, prayer meetings, political events). It was not until his last five years that he became more interested in colour. These were also the years of his finest portraits. Curiously, colour is not usually used to dazzle the eye but is handled in a subtly graded manner to reveal the character of his sitter, as in the rarefied and compelling 1920 portrait of *Aunt Fanny* (oil, Des Moines, Iowa, Des Moines Art Center). While his portraits reveal the compassion and humanity of the artist, the boisterous scenes of Americana express his hearty spirit and convivial demeanour.

Emma S. Bellows. *The Paintings of George Bellows*, New York 1929.
Peyton Boswell Jr. *George Bellows*, New York 1942.
Charles H. Morgan. *George Bellows, Painter of America*, New York 1965.

Beneš, Vincenc. Czech painter, b. 1883. Beneš was a member of the Group of Avant-Garde Artists, formed in Prague in 1911 by Emil Filla and Antonín Procházka. This was influenced largely by Cubism and also by German Expressionism, and linked the two in an original art which brought Czechoslovakia into the mainstream of the *avant-garde*.

Benner, Gerrit. Dutch painter, b. 1897 in Leeuwarden, Friesland. Benner is a self-taught artist who first began to paint in 1939. In 1953 he moved into K. Appel's studio in Amsterdam. He has lived in Amsterdam ever since.

During the early part of his career Benner was influenced by the Dutch Expressionists. Later he moved towards the *Cobra* style. Essentially, however, he is an extremely individual artist with a strong meditative bent. His oeuvre is made up of simple, abstract compositions executed in powerful colours and with a certain primitive quality that is reminiscent of natural forms.

Exhibition catalogue, *Gerrit Benner*, Städtische Kunstgalerie, Bochum 1960–1.

Benois, Alexandre. Russian painter, stage designer and writer on art, b. 1870 in St. Petersburg; d. 1960 in Paris. Benois was a self-taught painter who made his name with the stage sets which he created for Diaghilev. He was one of the founders of the *Mir Iskusstva* (World of Art) movement, which developed into the Russian focus for the *avant-garde*, and he produced the sets for some of Diaghilev's most famous ballets (*Le Pavillon d'Armide*, 1909; *Petrushka*, 1911). In his work for the *Ballets Russes* he turned away from traditional theatre design, constructing his sets as if they were pictures, i.e. treating décor and costumes as interrelating elements of a single corporate design. He used just a few luminous colours and his style, in which arabesques were an important feature, was a development of *art nouveau*. From 1938 onwards Benois worked for La Scala in Milan. He designed his last stage sets in 1950.

Benton, Thomas Hart. American painter, b. 1889 in Missouri; d. 1975. A descendant of Missouri politicians, Thomas Hart Benton showed an early preference for art rather than law, and at the age of 17 worked as a cartoonist for a newspaper in Joplin, Missouri. He attended Western Military Academy in Alton, Illinois, in 1906, and the next year studied at the Art Institute in Chicago. For three years Benton lived in Paris, and from 1912 to 1918 he lived in New York. These were years of struggle and discouragement as he tried to achieve a satisfactory painting style. Later he wrote indignantly of his experience in both New York and Paris, insisting that the great cities and the 'life of art' had failed him. After serving briefly in the Navy in Norfolk, Virginia, where he worked as an architectural draughtsman, he returned to New York. There, he turned his back upon his earlier experiments with Cubism and Synchromism and began painting 'subject pictures' dealing with the American scene. While teaching at the Art Students' League, Benton made annual trips into the heartland of America to discover themes for his painting. As a result of his painting and ideas, he soon became a leader of the burgeoning Regionalist movement. In 1935 he left New York and returned to his native Missouri.

Thomas Hart Benton is one of America's most prolific muralists. His murals include the painting entitled *American Life* for the New School for Social Research in New York (1930–1), paintings for the old Whitney Museum now installed at the Art Museum of the New Britain Institute of American Art, in Connecticut, and other works for the state capitol building in Jefferson City, Missouri (1935), the Power Authority installation at Massena, New York (1956–7), and the Truman Library in Independence, Missouri (1961).

Rural and small-town America, especially of the South and Midwest, furnished Benton with much of the subject matter for his smaller canvases, such as *Boom Town* (1928, Rochester, N.Y., Rochester Memorial Art Gallery), *Weighing Cotton* (1938, Washington, D.C., Private Coll.) and *Roasting Ears* (1938–9, New York, Metropolitan Museum). As in his murals, there is in these works an emphasis on balanced composition and on surface rhythms within a controlled arrangement of pictorial elements. These rhythms were to exert an influence on the work of Jackson Pollock, Benton's most famous student.

Although Benton's paintings lack the visual acuteness of a Wyeth or the melancholic moods of a Hopper, they possess a sureness of form and richness of colour that place them among the finest works of the American realist tradition in this century.

Thomas Hart Benton: A Descriptive Catalogue, with an examination of the artist and his work by Thomas Craven, New York 1939.
Lloyd Goodrich and John Baur. *American Art of Our Century*, New York 1961.
Barbara Rose. *American Art since 1900; A Critical History*, New York 1967.
Thomas Hart Benton, *An Artist in America*, Columbia (Missouri) 1968.

Béothy, Étienne. Hungarian sculptor, b. 1897 in Heves, Hungary. After completing his architectural studies Béothy made the acquaintance of Moholy-Nagy and established contact with the *M.A.* group. He then trained as a sculptor at the Academy in Budapest from 1920 to 1924. In the following year he toured Europe before settling in Paris. In 1932 he became a founder member of the *Abstraction-Création* association. In 1939 he published a treatise entitled *La Série d'Or*, in which he analysed the relationship between art and mathematics. He became a founder member and the vice-president of the *Salon des Réalités Nouvelles* in 1946 and of the *Espace* association in 1951. He is now living in Paris.

Béothy started as a Constructivist. Then, in 1929, he began to carve his slender, elongated wooden sculptures, whose elegance and technical perfection are based on mathematical calculations. Many of these pieces look just like tongues of flame. Their basic structures—which are used in endless variations—are the spiral and the parabola. Béothy's artistic aims are akin to those of Max Bill.

M. Seuphor. *Béothy*, Paris 1956.

Bérard, Christian. French painter and designer, b. 1902 in Paris; d. 1949 in Paris. He studied under Vuillard at the Académie Ranson and to begin with concentrated on painting and drawing. Later he turned to designing scenery and created sets for plays, ballets and films.

Beres, Jerzy. Polish sculptor, b. 1930 in Novy Sacz. Beres studied at the Academy of Art in Cracow, where he is still living today.

Beres's sculptures, which are roughly carved in wood, are inspired by traditional household articles.

Berghe, Frits van den. Belgian painter, b. 1883 in Ghent; d. 1939 in Ghent. In 1905, after completing his studies at the Academy in Ghent, van den Berghe went to live in the artists' colony in Laethem-Saint-Martin, where he joined with Permeke and the brothers Gustave and Léon de Smet in forming the 'Second Laethem Group'. In 1907 he was given a professorial post at the Academy in Ghent and in 1913 he visited the USA. He spent the war years in Holland in the company of Gustave de Smet. There he met Le Fauconnier and was greatly impressed by the German Expressionists, especially Franz Marc and Campendonk. In 1922 he returned to Belgium, where he lived in Ostend and Laethem before settling in Ghent in 1925. Around 1926 he began moving towards Surrealism and from 1929 onwards contributed drawings to the Socialist newspaper *Vooruit*. He was a member of *Les Neuf, Art vivant* and *Art contemporain*.

Van den Berghe is generally regarded as the spiritual head of the 'Second Laethem Group' and later he became one of the foremost Flemish Expressionists. From 1926–7 onwards he worked in a Surrealist mode, producing fantastic compositions after the manner of Bosch and—more especially—Ensor. In these works he depicts a nightmare world which is completely divorced from external reality and in which vegetable and mineral shapes are transformed into monstrous creations with both human and animal characteristics. The major part of van den Berghe's output consists of gouaches and drawings.

P. G. van Hecke. *Frits van den Berghe*, Antwerp 1948.
E. Langui. *Frits van den Berghe*, Brussels 1966.

Bergmann, Anna-Eva. Norwegian-French painter, b. 1909 in Stockholm. Bergmann is of Norwegian extraction. She studied painting in Oslo, Vienna and Paris from 1926 onwards and is now living in Paris as the wife of Hans Hartung the painter.

In 1947 Bergmann began to paint her cool, mystical pictures, whose flat, metallic, abstract forms are reminiscent of Arctic landscapes.

D. Aubier. *Anna-Eva Bergmann*, Paris 1964.

Berke, Hubert. German painter, b. 1908 in Buer, Westphalia. After completing a course in philosophy Berke attended the Academy of Art in Königsberg before joining Paul Klee's class at the Düsseldorf Academy (1932–3). He became a member of the Zen group. In 1960 he was made a Professor at the College of Art in Aachen and is now living in Rodenkirchen near Cologne.

Although Berke is an abstract artist most of his paintings have objective connotations. He works in a wide variety of styles, ranging from that of Klee to *Tachisme* and *Art brut*.

Catalogue, *Hubert Berke*, Gesellschaft für Kunst, Mainz 1962.

Berlewi, Henryk. Polish painter, b. 1894 in Warsaw; d. 1967 in Paris. Berlewi studied at the Academies in Warsaw, Antwerp and Paris. In 1921 he made the acquaintance of El Lissitzky and in 1922–3, when he was staying in Berlin, he established contact with van Doesburg, Richter, Eggeling and Moholy-Nagy. In 1924 he published the manifesto for his *Mechano-Faktur* in *Der Sturm*. In 1928 he went to live in Paris.

Berlewi was a Constructivist painter, who evolved his own particular form of Constructivism from Suprematism and *de Stijl*.

Exhibition catalogue, *Henryk Berlewi*, Maison de France, Berlin 1964 (with a bibliography).

Berlin Secession—*see* **Secession**

Berman, Eugene. Russian-American painter and designer, b. 1899 in St. Petersburg; d. 1972. His first schooling was in his native Russia where his teacher was S. Grosenberg, an architect with strong roots in the Palladian tradition. He fled with his family to Paris in 1918 during the Revolution. In Paris he studied painting at the Académie Ranson under Vuillard and M. Denis, and became friendly with Christian Bérard, Pavel Tchelitchew and others of similar artistic views. He and his friends joined together in a conscious effort to re-establish figurative painting. All of their works from this period are mournful, dreamlike pictures inspired by Picasso's Blue and Rose periods. After the exhibition they held in 1927, they were known as the Neo-Romantics. In 1935 he went to the United States where he gained an international reputation as a painter of imaginary landscapes. Such works as *Memories of Verona* (1931, New York, Coll. Thomas F. Howard) with its exaggerated architectural perspective and *Desolate Landscape* (1936, New York, Coll. Julien Levy) whose miserable figures are placed in an expansive, debris-strewn desert setting are typical of his work in the 1930s. When in the United States he began executing set designs and costumes for such productions as *Threepenny Opera* for the Théâtre de l'Étoile, Paris, *Romeo and Juliet* for the Ballet Theatre, New York, and *The Island God* for the Metropolitan Opera, New York. It was especially during the years 1951–7 that he created many designs for the latter company. He retired from theatrical work in 1957 and moved to Rome where he lived until 1962. He came out of retirement in that year to do sets and costumes for the Metropolitan Opera's production of *Otello*. His late paintings and especially his scenic designs often combine the chiaroscuro quality of Polidoro da Caravaggio (*Death in Venice*, 1945–6, Portland, Oregon, Coll. John Yeon), the imaginary landscapes of Pannini and Hubert Robert and the weird daemonic fervour of Callot (sets for the Ballet Theatre's production of *Giselle*, 1946). A book of his drawings was published in 1956 under the title *Imaginary Promenades in Italy*.

Exhibition catalogue, *Eugene Berman*, Boston Institute of Contemporary Art, Boston 1941.

Bernard, Émile. French painter, b. 1868 in Lille; d. 1941 in Paris. After studying in F. Cormon's *atelier* in Paris from 1884 to 1886 Bernard spent two years in Brittany and Normandy, where he met Gauguin and the painters of Pont-Aven. In 1891 he was back in Paris. There, together with Gauguin

Laval, Moret, Anquetin, Schuffenecker and de Montfreid, he joined the *Groupe Synthétiste*, which was formed in order to oppose Impressionism. Later the same year Bernard, Hodler, Jan Toorop and O. Redon joined the Rosicrucians. Meanwhile, in 1890, Bernard had embarked on his literary career with articles on van Gogh and Cézanne. In 1893, after publishing van Gogh's letters, he travelled via Constantinople and Samos to Egypt, where he remained for the next eight years. In 1901 he went to Venice. In 1904 he paid his first visit to Cézanne and in 1905 his last. From 1921 to 1928 Bernard lived almost exclusively in Venice, where he devoted himself to his writing. In 1939 he visited the artists' colony in Pont-Aven.

After early Impressionist and Neo-Impressionist phases Bernard moved towards Cloisonnism and Symbolism largely as a result of his friendship with van Gogh, whom he did his best to help. In his Cloisonnist works Bernard evolved a highly simplified type of composition based on powerful forms and painted in strong flat colours which are separated from one another by dark contours. Although they lacked van Gogh's dramatic force his works exerted a considerable influence on the *Nabis*. Bernard also made an important contribution to the history of art as a publicist. He founded the magazine *La Rénovation esthétique* and he collected and published critical and autobiographical statements by his painter friends.

Catalogue, *É. Bernard and Pont-Aven*, Hirschl and Adler Galleries Inc., New York 1957.
P. Mornand. *É. Bernard et ses amis*, Geneva 1957.
M. Chesneau and J. Cheyron. *Hommage de la ville de Pont-Aven à Émile Bernard*, Pont-Aven 1960.
Exhibition catalogue, *Émile Bernard*, Kunsthalle, Bremen 1967.

Berni, Antonio. Argentinian painter, b. 1905 in Rosario, Argentina. Berni trained in Rosario and subsequently, from 1925 to 1931, in Paris (under André Lhôte and Émil-Othon Friesz). In 1932 he returned to Argentina. After a brief early phase, in which he was attracted to *pittura metafisica*, Berni was influenced by contemporary Mexican artists and turned to Social Realism. In 1932 in Buenos Aires he collaborated with Siqueiros on a number of wall paintings. In 1941 he visited Bolivia, Peru, Mexico and the USA. In 1959 he produced a series of collages (*Juanito Laguna*) and a series of graphic works (*Ramona*) which were executed in a completely new style and reveal a strong sense of social commitment. In 1962 Berni received an international prize for drawing and graphic art at the Venice Biennale. About three years later he began to produce his highly original 'Monsters' (*Hypocrisy* and *Gluttony*) which have a certain affinity to *nouveau réalisme* and Pop Art.

Revista Ars, special issue, Buenos Aires.
Roger Plá. *Antonio Berni*, Buenos Aires 1945.

Bernik, Janez. Yugoslav painter and graphic artist, b. 1933 in Ljubljana. Bernik studied at the Academy of Art in Ljubljana. In his early phase he delved more and more deeply into the structure of the material world, with the result that he gradually dispensed with the human figure and focused his attention on physical phenomena, e.g. scarred walls, mountain rocks and desolate, prehistoric landscapes. The only human elements in these works are the barely legible symbols taken from Old Slavonic and other archaic scripts, which are inscribed here and there in the weathered stones. With his highly intuitive powers of perception Bernik is able to penetrate the dividing line between time and space and he experiences the inner structure of matter as a concrete reality. In his latest phase he has introduced human figures, which are conceived with hallucinatory intensity, into the dark sphere of his abstract landscapes, where they bear witness to the life process.

O. Bihalji-Merin. Introduction to the catalogue *L'Art contemporain en Yougoslavie*, published by the Musée Nationale d'Art Moderne, Paris 1961–2.
Zoran Kržišnik. *Janez Bernik*, Založba Obzorja, Maribor 1966.

Berrocal, Miguel. Spanish sculptor, b. 1933 in Algaidas, near Málaga. After studying architecture and sculpture at the San Fernando School of Fine Arts and at the School of Arts and Crafts and School of Graphic Art in Madrid, Berrocal lived in Italy from 1952 to 1957. Today he spends part of his time at his foundry near Verona and part in Paris.

Berrocal is trying to analyse and break down sculptural volume. In order to achieve this objective he constructs his sculptures from a variety of components, which not only possess intrinsic sculptural value but which also unite to create composite structures. Although Berrocal uses a mixture of geometrical, organic and realistic elements he always depicts the same subject: the human torso. His favourite material is bronze, which he polishes to a high finish.

Exhibition catalogue, *Berrocal*, Kestner-Gesellschaft, Hanover 1969.

Bertholle, Jean. French painter, b. 1909 in Dijon; d. 1970. He studied at the academies in Saint-Étienne and Lyons. Subsequently he formed a lasting friendship with Roger Bissière.

Bertholle worked in a painterly style after the manner of the *École de Paris*. He was a member of the *Témoignage* group.

Bertholo, René. Portuguese painter and sculptor, b. 1935 in Alhandra, Portugal. In 1951 Bertholo joined the Academy of Art in Lisbon. In 1958 he moved to Paris and, before the year was out, began publishing the magazine *KWY* in conjunction with L. Castro,

Voss and Pinheiro. In 1959 he was awarded a one-year scholarship by the Gulbenkian Foundation. In 1966 he began to sculpt whilst still continuing with his paintings. He is now living in Paris.

Bertholo's work falls within the category of *figuration narrative*. There is often a hint of irony and sometimes of ridicule in the situations presented in his paintings and sculptures. He also has frequent recourse to *motifs* taken from children's books.

Bertini, Gianni. Italian painter, b. 1922 in Pisa. Together with Enrico Baj and Dangelo, Bertini founded the Tachist group *Arte Nucleare* in 1951. From 1954 onwards he incorporated mechanical allusions into his pictures. Today he uses slide-projections, which appear on specially prepared canvases. Bertini lives in Milan and Paris.

Bertoia, Harry. American sculptor, b. 1915 in San Lorenzo, Italy. He went to the United States in 1930, and studied art at the Detroit Society of Arts and Crafts and at the Cranbrook Academy of Art in Bloomfield Hills, Michigan, where he also taught (1937–41). Bertoia established a reputation not only as a sculptor, but also as an interior designer, furniture designer and graphic artist, for he considered all these disciplines to be related. While working as a sculptor-designer for Knoll Associates in New York City during the early 1950s, Bertoia designed a wire chair; due to his particular interest in the integration of sculpture and architecture, he created much architectural sculpture for public buildings, of which one of the most successful examples is the 70-foot metal screen commissioned by Skidmore, Owings and Merrill for the Fifth Avenue branch of the Manufacturers Trust Company, New York (1954).

Bertoia's sculptural technique is flow welding of brass, bronze, and nickel-silver alloys over metal constructions, leaving a molten metal surface; in this respect his work is related to that of Herbert Ferber, Ibram Lassaw, Seymour Lipton, Theodore Roszak and Calvin Albert. The forms of Bertoia's sculpture are essentially abstract, yet they retain a basis in natural forms and phenomena, such as plant leaves, stars or clouds, and often suggest naturalistic growth or clustering processes.

'Pure Design Research', *Architectural Forum* XCVII, September 1952.
J. Langsner. 'Harry Bertoia', *Arts and Architecture* LXX, January 1953.
'Twenty-Five: Year of Appraisal; Interview', *Interiors* CXXV, November 1965.

Bertoni, Wander. Italian sculptor, b. 1925 in Codisotto, Emilia.

Bertoni was transported to Vienna in 1943 as a foreign worker. After the Nazi capitulation in 1945 he began to train as a sculptor at the Vienna Academy under Wotruba. In 1953 he won the Sculp-

ture Prize at the Second Bienal in São Paulo. He is now living in Vienna.

Up to 1950 Bertoni carved elegant and highly decorative figures. He then went over to abstract sculpture and has since produced 'open form' structures built up from wedge-shaped components arranged in centrifugal patterns. Occasionally these abstract constructions are reminiscent of figure compositions. Bertoni works in metal, stone and wood.

Exhibition catalogue, *Wander Bertoni, Sculptures 1945 to 1959*, Kapfenberg 1959 (lists all works up to 1959).

Bertrand, Gaston. Belgian painter, b. 1910 in Wonck, Belgium. After studying at the Academies in Brussels and Saint Josse Bertrand paid a brief visit to Paris. From 1941 to 1946 he contributed to the annual exhibitions of the *Apport*. In 1945 he became a founder member of the *Jeune Peinture belge* association. At this time he was painting in a 'Neo-Expressionist' style derived from Permeke. Subsequently— due to the influence of Manessier, Singier and Herbin of the *École de Paris*—he began to move away from objective art altogether and by 1949 was producing geometrical abstracts. In these works, in which the geometrical shapes are boldly outlined and painted in bright, transparent colours, he has been experimenting with the spatial aspects of painting. Bertrand is now living in Brussels.

R.-L. Delevoy. *Gaston Bertrand*, Antwerp 1953; Paris 1955.

Beuys, Joseph. German sculptor and organizer of happenings, b. 1921 in Cleves, Germany. Beuys studied at the Academy of Art in Düsseldorf, where he joined the teaching staff in 1961. He is now living in Düsseldorf.

Beuys constructs his sculptures from junk, from refuse, from discarded objects of all kinds. In the 1960s he organized a number of happenings by arranging such objects in a room, then changing the arrangement at set intervals before finally restoring it to its original condition. Beuys's favourite materials are felt and fat, and his favourite colour is rust brown. In his works he depicts human situations by arranging his material in Existential contexts. He is indebted for many of his ideas to the Symbolists of the turn of the century.

Ströher Collection Exhibition Catalogue, Munich 1968 (and elsewhere).

Bevan, Robert. British painter, b. 1865 in Hove, Sussex; d. 1925 in London. He is represented at the Tate Gallery, and his works are mainly horses, landscapes and street scenes. A member of the Camden Town and London groups, Bevan together with Gilman, Ginner and Gore stands for a well-defined English Post-Impressionism. He knew Gauguin at Pont-Aven, and was the truest British representative of Synthetism.

Biasi, Guido. Italian painter, b. 1933 in Naples. Biasi studied at the Academy of Art in Naples and later became a founder member of *Gruppo 58*. In 1959 he settled in Paris, where he is still living today and where he has been an active member of the *Phases* group.

In his paintings, which reveal the influence of Surrealism, Biasi depicts unidentifiable organic creatures in an imaginary architectonic setting.

Biederman, Charles Joseph. American painter, sculptor and theorist, b. 1906 in Cleveland, Ohio. When he had completed an apprenticeship in a commercial art studio (1922–6) he attended the School of the Art Institute of Chicago (1926–9), studying under John Norton, Frederic Poole and Laura van Pappelendam. His early paintings of 1929–34 show first and most strongly an influence of Cézanne as well as Post-Impressionism, Cubism and Abstraction. Soon after moving to New York in 1934 he created his first wholly abstract work, influenced by Gris, Léger, Miró and Mondrian. In 1935–6 he began building three-dimensional equivalents of Mondrian's works and paintings of brightly coloured shapes with a biomorphic limpness suspended against monochrome backgrounds (*Painting. 1/30/1936,* Coll. of artist), reminiscent of Miró. After his first one-man show at the Pierre Matisse Gallery, New York, in 1936, he spent a year in Paris, where he concentrated on Constructivism and *de Stijl* and was strongly influenced by the works of Mondrian, as well as by the writings of and meeting with Pevsner which led to his constant Constructivist thinking in the years to come. In 1938, a year after he returned to the United States, he attended lectures by Alfred Korzybski, the founder of the General Semantics Institute. This experience fostered an interest in applying Korzybski's philosophy to the history of world art, a desire which came to fruition ten years later with the publication of his book *Art as the Evolution of Visual Knowledge* (Red Wing, Minnesota, 1948). In the 1940s he revised his adherence to Neo-Plasticist principles. His interest in scientific models and his acceptance of the novel methods and materials of the Constructivists served as the impetus for a number of over-sized relief constructions (*Relief Construction. New York No. 9, 7/1940,* painted wood, glass and fluorescent tubes, Red Wing, Minn., Coll. Mrs. Raymond F. Hedin). In 1951 he published *Letters on the New Art* based on correspondence with Joan Saugrain. From 1952 on, Biederman rejected Constructivism and termed his 'new art' Structurism —three-dimensional constructions in which small single-coloured rectangles are placed on a solid coloured background, at right angles to the background and to each other. At this time too, his previous book found strong sympathizers in Victor Pasmore, Kenneth and Mary Martin and Anthony Hill, which led to a revival in Constructivist interest in

England. In 1958 he published *The New Cézanne,* challenging the contribution to the understanding of Cézanne's influence on contemporary art in general and on Structurist art in particular. Biederman's late works such as *Structurist Relief. Red Wing No. 6, 9/1957–1963* (painted aluminium, Minneapolis, Minn., Walker Art Center) exhibit a further elaboration of his Structurist theory, handled in a freer, more advanced organization of planes.

Charles Biederman: The Structurist Relief 1935–1964, Minneapolis 1965.

Bigatti, Alfredo. Argentinian painter, b. 1898 in Buenos Aires; d. 1964 in Buenos Aires. Bigatti trained in Buenos Aires and in Paris (under Antoine Bourdelle). He has created numerous monumental works (his monument to General Bartolomé Mitre in La Plata, 1940, is a typical example). In 1937 Bigatti was awarded the Grand Prix for Sculpture at the International Exhibition in Paris. He was a member of the National Academy of the Fine Arts in Argentina.

Bigge, John A. S. British painter, b. 1892 in Oxford. He was a classical scholar at Winchester and later Oxford. He went to the Slade in 1914, but enlisted the same year. His autobiographical note in Herbert Read's *Unit One,* of which Bigge was a member, is indicative of English modernism in the early 1930s— he was influenced by *art non-figuratif* elements in the *École de Paris.* His rationale for abstraction includes the 'very consistent relationship between beauty of form and efficiency of function'. Bigge also exhibited with the Surrealists in 1936.

Bijelić, Jovan. Yugoslav painter, b. 1886 in Kolunic; d. 1964 in Belgrade. He studied in Cracow and Prague, and worked in Paris. His Expressionist art produced nudes, landscapes and still lifes.

Bill, Max. Swiss painter, sculptor and architect, b. 1908 in Winterthur, Switzerland. After studying at the Industrial School of Art in Zürich from 1924 to 1927 and the Bauhaus in Dessau from 1927 to 1929, Bill embarked on his multiple career, in which he has worked as architect, painter, sculptor, publicist and product designer. The concept of 'function' lies at the heart of all his practical and theoretical work. Having acquired this idea at the Bauhaus, where it was taught primarily in terms of architecture, Bill extended it to the fine arts, i.e. to painting and sculpture. His ultimate objective was to establish a condition of unity between the individual branches of the fine arts. He once defined art as the 'sum of all functions in harmonious unity'.

From 1932 to 1936 Bill belonged to the *Abstraction-Création* association in Paris. In 1937 he joined *Allianz,* the association of modern Swiss artists, and in 1941 founded the Allianz Press. In 1944 he organized an international exhibition in Basle entitled *Concrete Art*, and in 1960 staged a retrospective exhibition in Zürich under the same name, which reviewed the achievements of modern art from 1910 onwards. Meanwhile—in 1944—Bill was asked to teach design at the Technische Hochschule in Zürich. This was the beginning of his activities as a product designer. In 1947 he founded the Institute for Progressive Culture and from 1951 to 1956 was rector and lecturer at the Hochschule für Gestaltung in Ulm, which he then developed along his own lines. Bill designed the Swiss pavilion at the Triennale in Milan in 1936 and 1951, receiving the *Grand Prix* on the second occasion. He also contributed to the 1964 Expo in Lausanne.

Bill's painting is based on precise design systems and frequently features geometrical elements, which are integrated into rhythmical sequences within the composition. The organization of these pictorial rhythms depends to a considerable extent on colour values, Bill's range of colours being extremely wide, extending as it does from the strongly contrasting, poster-type shades (which he uses for large pictorial areas) at one end of the scale to dematerialized colours at the other.

In the sphere of sculpture Bill carried out experimental work with a view to resolving the problem of the endless loop. He made his first attempt in 1935, although it was not until 1953 that he finally found a satisfactory solution. In many of his sculptures he also anticipated the so-called *primary structures*. But, although he has had constant recourse to mathematical formulae, he has never regarded them in the light of a final arbiter: for him they are simply a necessary tool. Bill was awarded the *Grand Prix* for sculpture at the Bienal in São Paulo in 1951.

T. Maldonado. *Max Bill*, Buenos Aires 1955.

Bille, Ejler. Danish painter, sculptor and writer on art, b. 1910 in Odder, Denmark. After a brief period as a Surrealist Bille began to paint decorative and imaginative abstracts, which he executes in sophisticated and personal colours. His animal sculptures are more naturalistic.

Bionda, Mario. Italian painter, b. 1913 in Turin. Bionda studied in F. Casorati's studio from 1927 to 1932. After serving as a soldier in the Second World War he first worked as a toy manufacturer. Then, in 1957, he began to paint his *Wall Pictures*, which are informal works. Bionda is now living in Milan.

A. Lucia. *Mario Bionda: 12 Opere*, Milan 1960.

Birolli, Renato. Italian painter, b. 1906 in Verona; d. 1959 in Milan. After studying for a brief period at the Accademia Cignaroli in Verona, Birolli moved to Milan, where he met Carrà, Manzù and Sassu. In 1938 he joined with Cassinari, Guttuso and others in founding the anti-Fascist artists' association *Corrente*. In 1946—along with Cassinari, Guttuso, Santomaso, Vedova, etc.—he became a founder member of the *Nuova Secessione Artistica Italiana*, from which the *Fronte Nuovo delle Arti* subsequently emerged. Six years later, in 1952, Birolli and five other members of the *Fronte Nuovo*, including Corpora, Santomaso and Vedova, acted on a suggestion made by Lionello Venturi and founded the *Gruppo degli Otto Pittori Italiani*. Both as a painter and as a political thinker and writer Birolli exerted a very active influence on contemporary Italian artists, especially those grouped around the *Corrente* and the *Fronte Nuovo*. He was represented at the Biennale in Venice on a number of occasions, the first being in 1948. He also had a large retrospective exhibition in 1960.

Following an early phase, in which he painted after the manner of van Gogh, Birolli came under the influence of Picasso (especially his *Guernica*) and also of Pignon and Gischia. As a result he developed a more abstract style, in which he incorporated prismatic structures, although the objective world continued to furnish the subject matter for his paintings. Later, when he had come to terms with Orphism and the new conceptions emanating from the *École de Paris* (under Bazaine and Manessier), he evolved a form of Abstract Impressionism based on lively colour designs. But even then objective factors still made their presence felt.

Sandro Bini. *Renato Birolli*, Milan 1941.
A. Tullier. *Birolli*, Milan 1951.
Renato Birolli. *Taccuini* (with an introduction by E. Emmanuelli), Turin 1960.

Bischoff, Elmer. American painter, b. 1916 in Berkeley, California. After receiving a BA and MA (1938 and 1939) from the University of California, Berkeley, he served in the 8th Air Force in England (1942–6). Soon after he began teaching at the California School of Fine Arts he had his first one-man show at the California Palace of the Legion of Honor, San Francisco (1947). In 1953 he was head of the Art Department at Yuba College, Marysville, California, and then became Chairman of the Graduate Program, San Francisco Art Institute. Bischoff has since taught at his *alma mater*. His figurative style uses sharp colour applied with a great freedom of stroke. *Two Bathers* (1960, New York, Staempfli Gallery) with its lack of interest in spatial considerations and in its handling of pigment seems strongly influenced by the works of Cézanne. The mood of his paintings is often one of solitude which is counterbalanced and dispelled through the vibrancy of colour and bravura of brushstroke (*Lavender Curtain*, 1963, New York, Staempfli Gallery).

Eleanor C. Munro. 'Figures to the Fore', *Horizon* II, No. 6, July 1960, pp. 16–24 ff.

Bishop, Isabel. American painter and graphic artist, b. 1902 in Cincinnati, Ohio. She studied at the New York School of Applied Design (1918–20) and then at the Art Students' League under Kenneth Hayes Miller and Guy Pène du Bois. Her early works show a certain relation to 'modern' painting, with their emphasis on geometricized forms (*Nude, c.* 1925, etching). Her strongest stylistic connection, however, is with the Ashcan School, and she has a special affinity with the spirit of the works of Reginald Marsh. This style, which continued throughout the 1950s, can be seen as early as 1934 in etchings such as *On the Street.* Here a straightforward unromanticized expression of New York city life contrasts in execution and subject with both her graphic works of the 1960s and the drawings of her entire career. A greater economy and variety of line, an increased interest in light and a more forceful relationship of the figure to its space occurs in the 1963 *Nude* (etching and aquatint). The small size and variety of surface recalls Dutch Old Masters, while *Waiting* (1935, ink, wash and pencil, New York, Whitney Museum of American Art), with its rapid stroke, economy of line and intense juxtapositions of light and dark, recalls seventeenth-century Italian drawings. The artist joined Hayter's Atelier 17 at the New School for Social Research, New York, in 1941 and has taught at the Skowhegan (Maine) School of Painting and Sculpture.

U. Johnson and J. Miller. *Isabel Bishop. Prints and Drawings 1925–1964*, Brooklyn Museum, New York 1964.

Bissier, Julius. German painter, b. 1893 in Freiburg-im-Breisgau, Germany; d. 1965 in Ascona, Switzerland. After studying for a short while at the Academy in Karlsruhe Bissier joined the German forces in 1914. In 1918, when hostilities ceased, he went back to painting but taught himself. In 1927 he became friendly with the Freiburg sinologue Ernst Grosse, who introduced him to Chinese culture. Shortly afterwards, due partly to his friendship with Baumeister and partly to his meeting with Brancusi at Paris in 1930, Bissier went over to abstract art. Between 1933 and 1945 he was in close contact with Oskar Schlemmer. Between 1935 and 1938 he made several visits to Italy. In 1939 he went to live in Hagnau on Lake Constance and remained there until 1961, when he settled in Ascona. He was a member of the Zen group.

After an initial period, in which he was influenced by the Old Masters and worked in a style that owed much to the *Neue Sachlichkeit*, Bissier turned abstract in the early 1930s. His subsequent development was largely determined by his encounter with Brancusi, whose sculptural forms deeply impressed him by their archaic simplicity, and—more especially—by his intensive study of Eastern culture and art. As a result of his preoccupation with the Far East he evolved a new calligraphic style,

whose symbolic signs give expression to the essential polarity of man's experience in terms of 'male and female', 'empty and full', 'life and death'. Bissier himself referred to these signs as 'signs of bipolar life'. After 1945 Bissier evolved a free painterly style, producing small format monotypes, which reveal a great wealth of colour combinations and are executed with the kind of precision normally reserved for miniatures. These were followed in 1951–2 by small format watercolours and from 1956 onwards by the 'miniatures', which brought Bissier widespread recognition during his late period. These miniatures are painted in egg tempera finished with an oil glaze on pieces of canvas cut or torn to give an irregular shape. With their transparent colouring and their poetic, meditative quality the simple symbolic forms in these works create a whole world in miniature.

W. Schmalenbach. *Bissier*, Stuttgart 1963.
Catalogue, *Julius Bissier: 70th Year Retrospective*, Institute of Contemporary Art, Boston 1963.

Bissière, Roger. French painter, b. 1888 in Villeréal, Lot-et-Garonne; d. 1964 in Boissierette, Lot. After studying at the Academy of Art in Bordeaux Bissière went to Paris in 1910. He then worked as a journalist for the next four years. From 1911 to 1918 he lived in North Africa. In 1918 he met André Lhôte and in 1921 Georges Braque. During this period he came to terms with Cubism, which he tried to 'humanize'. In the early 1920s he published articles on Ingres, Seurat and Corot in *Esprit Nouveau*. From 1925 to 1938 he taught at the Académie Ranson, where his pupils included Manessier, Le Moal, Bertholle and Vieira da Silva. In 1939 Bissière contracted an eye complaint which seriously impaired his sight. He then retired to a family property in Boissierette, where he lived the life of a farmer. Whilst there he carved several totemistic wooden sculptures and also collaborated with his wife on a number of very beautiful tapestries, which consist of pieces of cloth joined together by needlework. In 1945 he began to paint again and in 1948 underwent an operation which partially restored his vision. In 1952 he was awarded the *Grand Prix National des Arts*. From 1957 onwards he produced stained-glass windows (e.g. for Metz Cathedral, 1960–1). At this time he was still living his secluded life in Boissierette and continued to do so until he died.

In conjunction with his friends and former students, such as Manessier, Le Moal, Bertholle, Vieira da Silva, Bazaine, Estève and Singier, Bissière played a crucial part in the development of the *École de Paris* after 1945, when it began moving towards Abstract Impressionism. He was also one of the first painters in France to recognize the importance of Paul Klee, both as an artist and an art theorist, and introduced his students to Klee's methods in the 1930s. During his early period

Bissière painted lyrical Cubist works after the manner of Braque, but, as a result of his eye complaint, which left him virtually blind, he acquired a more contemplative, poetic view of the objective world. In his paintings, most of which are small format works, Bissière translated his visual and mental impressions of nature into poetic compositions which are based on tapestry designs and incorporate abstract signs to denote human beings, birds, stars, church spires, flags, etc. He used warm, rich shades of gold, brown, purple and pale green.

M. P. Fouchet. *Bissière*, Paris 1955.

Exhibition catalogue, *Bissière*, Musée des Arts Décoratifs, Paris 1966.

Blake, Peter. British painter, b. 1932 in Dartford, Kent. Blake studied at Gravesend Art School and the Royal College of Art. His work is represented in the Tate Gallery. He is one of the first painters to whose work the term Pop Art was applied; he used sharp-focus or *trompe-l'oeil* to depict popular imagery such as badges and buttons or magazine clippings.

Blanchard, Maria. Spanish-French painter, b. 1881 in Santander, Spain; d. 1932 in Paris. Maria Blanchard, the crippled child of a Spanish father and a Franco-Polish mother, came to Paris in 1906, where André Lhôte introduced her into Cubist circles. In 1913 she went back to Spain but three years later settled permanently in Paris, where she established close contact with Juan Gris, Lipchitz, Rivera and Metzinger. But, although Blanchard's name is always associated with Cubism, she was not one of its more extreme exponents. She never adopted a purely intellectual approach. On the contrary, her works faithfully reflect their emotional and figurative origins. From 1919 onwards she became more realistic, although her paintings still retained their Cubist structure. Blanchard used her profound understanding of the human condition to portray men and women in scenes from their daily lives. Her pictures of sad, solitary children are particularly impressive.

Blanchet, Alexandre. Swiss painter, b. 1882 in Pforzheim, Germany; d. 1961 in Geneva. Blanchet, a Swiss citizen by descent, grew up in Geneva and attended the local academy, completing his studies there in 1903. Between 1905 and 1914 he lived in Paris, Florence and Rome. In 1918 he turned to sculpture for a brief period. From 1930 to 1942 he taught at the École des Beaux-Arts in Geneva.

Blanchet evolved a highly simplified pictorial style, which reveals the influence of Munch and, more especially, Cézanne, and which he combined with fresco-like colours. He painted nudes, still lifes, landscapes and religious works, and also produced frescoes and mosaics.

H. Fosca. *Alexandre Blanchet*, Lausanne 1929.

Exhibition catalogue, *Alexandre Blanchet*, Kunstmuseum, Winterthur 1963.

Blauer Reiter. On 12 December 1911 a number of artists, including Kandinsky, Marc and Münter, seceded from the New Artists' Association and shortly afterwards staged a joint exhibition, which they called *Der Blaue Reiter* (Blue Rider). This name, which Kandinsky had first used for a picture painted in 1903, was then adopted by the new group both as a general designation and as a title for the *Almanach*, which it published from 1912 onwards. Macke and Klee were both closely associated with the group whilst Jawlensky and Werefkin became members in 1912. Although the *Blauer Reiter* was always a very loose association and had no clearly defined programme it was based on a general conception of form which Macke once described as a 'mystical and inward construction' and which, according to Marc, was to be employed for the artistic representation of 'mysterious forces'. (Such ideas were of course closely linked with the development of Orphism and Fauvism from 1912 onwards.) The principal influences at work within the group were the mystical pathos and sharp intelligence of Kandinsky, the romantic-cum-pantheistic beliefs of Marc, the visual poetry of Macke, the Russian mysticism of Jawlensky and the artistic sensitivity of Klee. The interaction of these diverse forces led—under Kandinsky's supervision—to a form of non-objective painting which, although entirely novel, was in fact a logical consequence of the fundamentally Expressionist attitude shared by the members of the group. Although it is true that these artists depicted recognizable objects in their paintings the objects were not important in themselves. What mattered were the artistic impressions and compositions which they triggered. At the first *Blauer Reiter* Exhibition 43 works were shown by the following artists: Albert Bloch, David and Vladimir Burljuk, Heinrich Campendonk, Eugen Kahler, Kandinsky, Macke, Marc, Münter, Jean Bloé Niestlé, Arnold Schoenberg, Henri Rousseau, Robert Delaunay and Elisabeth Epstein. The broad, international basis of the *Blauer Reiter* group, which distinguishes it from the *Brücke*, was extended still further in 1912 when its theoretical premises were expounded in the *Almanach*. The editors of this publication—Kandinsky, Marc, Burljuk, Macke and Schoenberg—sought to establish new paths of development for a new era. Apart from reproductions of works by Kandinsky and his friends and by Cézanne, Rousseau and Delaunay the *Almanach* published examples of primitive and folk art, children's drawings, Asiatic and Egyptian works and medieval woodcuts and sculptures. Franz Marc wrote on the 'German Fauves', i.e. the members of the *Brücke*, on the New Secession, which had been founded in Berlin under the leadership of Pechstein, and on the New Artists' Association and the influence exerted on it by the Russians and French. Burljuk reported on the Russian *avant-garde*. Cubism and Delaunay's Orphic Cubism came up for discussion, and Matisse and Picasso were singled out as the leading exponents of this new art form. Kandinsky, whose book *Über das Geistige in der Kunst* (*Concerning the Spiritual in Art*) had also appeared in 1912, wrote an article in the *Almanach* entitled 'On the Question of Form'. In this article he spoke of two poles that open up two paths, 'which eventually lead to the same goal'. He called one of these paths the path of 'Great Realism', quoting Rousseau's lapidary style of object presentation as an example, and the other the path of 'Great Abstraction'. A further important concept for the *Blauer Reiter* was that of the 'correspondence between different art forms'. This was discussed in the *Almanach* in connection with Skriabin's *Prometheus*, which constituted an attempt to treat music and coloured lighting as parallel phenomena. Kandinsky attached great importance to the operas of Richard Wagner, which he regarded as 'total works of art'. This conception was manifested in his stage play *Der gelbe Klang* (*The Yellow Sound*), which was published in the *Almanach* and which incorporated dance, mime, coloured lighting and music. New developments in music were discussed in the *Almanach* by Schoenberg and von Hartmann. There were also special musical supplements, in which scores by Schoenberg, Berg and Webern were printed. With the outbreak of war in 1914 the *Blauer Reiter* group was disbanded: Kandinsky and the other Russians were then obliged to leave Germany, Macke fell in 1914 and Marc in 1916. But the ideas developed by the *Blauer Reiter* artists before the war provided a point of departure for postwar developments. Kandinsky, Klee and Feininger (who had been invited to exhibit with the *Blauer Reiter* artists in the First German Autumn Salon in 1913) all became masters at the Bauhaus.

Ludwig Grote. *Der Blaue Reiter: München und die Kunst des 20. Jahrhunderts*, Munich 1949.
H. M. Wingler. *Der Blaue Reiter*, Feldafing (Germany) 1954.
L. G. Buchheim. *Der Blaue Reiter und die Neue Künstlervereinigung München*, Feldafing 1959.
Catalogue, *The Blue Rider Group*, Royal Scottish Academy, Edinburgh 1960.
Catalogue, *Vor 50 Jahren: Neue Künstlervereinigung; Der Blaue Reiter*, Galerie Stangl, Munich 1962.

Blaue Vier. The *Blaue Vier* (Blue Four) was an artists' association consisting of just four painters: Feininger, Jawlensky, Kandinsky and Klee. Galka Scheier was the driving force behind the group. She proposed its formation and also suggested its name, which is clearly derived from the *Blauer Reiter*. On 31 March 1924 an agreement was drawn up authorizing Scheier to act on behalf of all four artists with a view to publicizing their paintings and their artistic ideas overseas. In May of the same year she set sail for the USA, taking with her a representative collection of their works. The first exhibition was held in San Francisco. Then, in the autumn of 1926,

Scheier organized a travelling exhibition, which toured the major centres of the West (starting in Oakland, California) and was staged in conjunction with a series of lectures.

Bloc, André. French painter, sculptor and author, b. 1896 in Algiers; d. 1966 in New Delhi. After spending his childhood and youth in Paris Bloc took an engineering degree and became editor of a technical journal. During this period he met Le Corbusier and launched a new magazine entitled *Architecture aujourd'hui*. In 1940, when he was in the South of France, he began to sculpt and was influenced by Laurens. In 1945 he returned to Paris and in 1949 produced his first abstract sculptures. Two years later he joined with Béothy, del Marle and others in founding the *Groupe Espace* and launching the magazine *Art aujourd'hui*.

As editor, exhibition organizer, art theorist and experimental artist Bloc has contributed many stimulating ideas to the Paris art world. In his efforts to find a synthesis between architecture and art he has employed a wide variety of techniques (stained glass, weaving, mosaics) and materials (cement, iron, Plexiglass, corrugated iron, etc.). His works range from harmonious stone sculptures carved in the round, which are reminiscent of Laurens, Arp and Brancusi, to constructions of metal rods, which are more in line with Pevsner.

Ch. Delloye. *André Bloc*, Paris 1959.

Blok. This was the name taken by the first Polish abstract artists' association which was formed in 1924 as a result of Constructivist and Suprematist influences. Its aims were essentially the same as those pursued by the *de Stijl* group: the de-individualization of art and the evolution of general criteria to cover all spheres of artistic activity including architecture, industrial design and town planning. The most important members of the association were Vladislav Strzeminski, Henryk Stázewski and the sculptor Katazyna Kobro. The *Blok*—which issued a quarterly magazine under its own name and also published various individual works such as Strzeminski's *Unism in Painting*—was later enlarged to include architects as well as artists. It was then known as the *Praesens* association.

Bloom, Hyman. American painter, b. 1913 in Latvia. He emigrated to the United States in 1920 and settled in Boston, where he was encouraged by the art educator Harold Zimmerman to study the works of Michelangelo, Tintoretto and Tiepolo. A visit to the Museum of Modern Art in New York gave Bloom and the painter Jack Levine, then a fellow art student in Boston, the opportunity of discovering the Expressionist paintings of Georges Rouault and Chaim Soutine. After working for the WPA Federal

Art Project during the Depression, Bloom had his first major show at the Museum of Modern Art's *Americans 1942* exhibition. His preoccupation with his Jewish origins was revealed in *Synagogue* (1940, New York, Museum of Modern Art) and in later series of paintings on Jewish themes. All these works, interpreted in an Expressionist style, employed surfaces encrusted with jewel-like colours, and portrayed a painted world both luminous and mystical. In 1945 Bloom began his so-called *Corpse* series, strongly influenced by Soutine's violently distorted representations of slaughtered oxen. *Female Corpse, Back View* (1947, New York, Durlacher Brothers) created a controversy when it was exhibited at the Virginia Museum Biennial of American Painting, due to its bold display of a visceral, morbid subject. Bloom's works from the 1950s onwards continued to dwell on the theme of decay and mortality (*Autopsy*, 1953; and the *Anatomist*, 1953; both New York, Whitney Museum). In later scenes of dissection this sense of horror is still largely present. Bloom's subsequent style evokes Rembrandt and the Baroque masters he had examined as a student, as well as the sweeping brushstrokes and brilliantly impasted colouration of Théodore Géricault.

Institute of Contemporary Art Catalogue, *Hyman Bloom*, Boston 1954 (with text by Lloyd Goodrich).
Brian O'Doherty. 'Hyman Bloom: A Portrait', *Art in America* XLIX, No. 3, 1961. Based on an interview with the artist.

Blow, Sandra. British painter, b. 1925 in London. She studied at the St. Martin's School of Art and the Royal Academy Schools. Her work is represented in the Tate Gallery. She is prominent among the first postwar generation of abstract painters for the consistent assurance and elegance of her gestural and colour-field paintings, of which texture is usually an important part.

Bluemner, Oscar. American painter, b. 1867 in Hanover, Germany; d. 1938 in South Braintree, Massachusetts. He was trained as an architect and portrait painter in Germany, and after emigrating to America in 1892 maintained an architectural office in New York. His original plans for the Bronx Borough Courthouse were stolen from him by his partner, and only after ten years were lawsuits settled in his favour. The money thus won allowed him to devote his life to painting. Bluemner exhibited in the 1913 Armory Show, was a member of Alfred Stieglitz's influential 291 Gallery, and participated in the Forum Exhibition of 1916.

Bluemner is known particularly for his expressionistic and irrational use of colour. Although influenced by the Cubists, he worked in an independent vein, and unlike them was concerned with a simplification of reality rather than a complex dissection and rearrangement of forms. As a colour theorist, he derived his concepts as much from Byzantine mosaics,

medieval stained glass and illuminations, or Oriental painting, as from the ideas of Robert Delaunay and the American Synchromists. However, Bluemner differed from these colourists in that he chose to reject pure abstraction. Inner emotion and a mystical romanticism motivated his art, and his working aim was to find some symbolic-realistic form for his daring use of colour. This he sought in a geometricized version of landscape, in which sharp contrasts of light and shade define his characteristically cubic forms (*Old Canal Port*, 1914, New York, Whitney Museum). Bluemner's almost exclusive concentration on the landscape genre tended to limit his repertory of forms; but this often allowed for a bold intensification of colour moods and surprising configurations within a dense and compact visual fabric.

Bluemner's compositions usually consist of two or three tones, with the added dramatic impact of unconventional 'stage-set' illumination. When he verged on abstraction—as in the visionary watercolour *Moonrise* (1928) or the strident 1929 oil painting *Red Glare* (also called *An American Night*), both of which are in the Graham Gallery in New York—Bluemner endowed colour with some of its most original and luminous effects.

The Forum Exhibition of Modern American Painters . . . On View at the Anderson Galleries, New York, New York 1916 (with a statement by the artist).

Bluhm, Norman. American painter, b. 1920 in Chicago. He studied architecture with Mies van der Rohe both before and after his service in the United States Air Force (1941–5). When he completed his studies he moved to Europe where he took up painting. During his years in Paris (1947–56) he practised a delicate lyrical mode created through patterns of opalescent shapes brought about by veils of colour and coalesced drops of pigment. The year he returned to New York he was given his first one-man show at the Leo Castelli Gallery, and two years later was included in Documenta II in Kassel, Germany (1959). In October 1960 he collaborated with the poet Frank O'Hara on poem paintings based on the seasons. These works, such as *It's raining and I'm thinking* . . . are now on permanent loan to New York University. When Bluhm returned to Paris after ten years in New York, his style took on a decidedly vigorous quality as opposed to his earlier works. The triptych *BC* (1964, New York, Coll. Douglas McElvy) with its simple, open, frank shapes, illusion of depth, sense of movement and sensual pigment betrays a strong debt to the Abstract Expressionists working in New York in the late 1950s.

Pierre Schneider. Exhibition catalogue, *Norman Bluhm*, Stadler Galerie, Paris 1968.

Blume, Peter. American painter, b. 1906 in Russia. He was brought to America when he was five, and

received his early training in New York at the Art
Students' League and the Beaux-Arts Institute of
Design. Blume's first major works were based on the
lessons of Cubism, but in the early 1930s he turned
towards Surrealism, achieving widespread recognition when his painting *South of Scranton* (1931, New
York, Metropolitan Museum) won first prize at the
Carnegie International Competition of 1934. Here
one sees for the first time the artist's use of floating,
mystical figures frozen in motion against skies
painted like theatrical backdrops.

In 1932 and 1936 Blume was in Italy on Guggenheim Fellowships. It was during this period that he
began his most famous work, the *Eternal City* (1934–
7, New York, Museum of Modern Art). In this
canvas Blume undertook a social statement against
Fascism, using complex symbolism and a highly
polished technique aimed at capturing the smallest
details. Amid Roman ruins that include shattered
fragments of antique statues of embracing lovers, a
ludicrous papier-mâché head of the dictator Mussolini snakes out of the rubble in the form of a monstrous jack-in-the-box. Satirical references, ranging
from parodies of financial profiteers to false images
of Christ, are also present. Satire is seen too in *Light
of the World* (1932, New York, Whitney Museum),
in which the artist comments on the awestruck
neighbours who stand in the back yards of a typical
rural town, compulsively viewing some miraculous
modern contraption. His later works are a faithfully
detailed transcription of reality.

Blume has been termed a Magic Realist because of
his frequent combination of factual, prosaic scenes
with incongruous or surreal images and spacing. He
considered the communication of ideas to be one of
the primary functions of the plastic arts, and was
convinced of the value of literary, or narrative, content in his paintings.

Robert U. Godsoe. 'Peter Blume, A New Vision', *Creative Art* XI,
    September 1932.
Currier Gallery of Art catalogue, *Peter Blume: Paintings and
    Drawings in Retrospect, 1925–1964*, Manchester (N.H.) 1964.
Kennedy Galleries, Inc. Catalogue, *Peter Blume*, New York 1968
    (with text by Frank Getlein).

Blumenthal, Hermann. German sculptor, b. 1905 in
Essen; d. 1942 in Russia. He studied sculpture in
Essen and then moved to Berlin, where he worked
under Wilhelm Gerstel and Edwin Scharff. He won a
prize at the Prussian Academy of Art, and spent a
year in Rome (1931–2), eventually returning to
Berlin. He had two exhibitions in 1936—one at
Edinburgh, and the other at the Buchholz Galerie,
Berlin. He made another trip to Italy that year, and
in 1937 gained the Cornelius Prize in Düsseldorf.

His work is largely figure sculpture, showing
clearly his connection with the working class, and
the pieces are done with restraint in a style not unlike that of Gerhard Marcks and Ludwig Kaspar—

based on the Neoclassical tradition, but with an
attempt at a new form of expression.

Christian Adolf Isermeyer. *Der Bildhauer Hermann Blumenthal*,
    Berlin 1947.

Bluth, Manfred. German painter, b. 1926 in Berlin.
Bluth studied at the Academies in Berlin and
Munich (under Willi Geiger). He is now living in
Berlin.

Bluth has successfully integrated the influences
exerted on him by Altdorfer, C. D. Friedrich, Ensor
and Max Ernst into a sort of romantic Surrealism.
Although basically poetic, his landscapes possess an
ironic quality, which gives them an 'alienation effect'.

Boccioni, Umberto. Italian painter and sculptor, b.
1882 in Reggio-Calabria; d. 1916 in Sorte, near
Verona. Boccioni spent his youth in Forlì, Genoa,
Padua and Catania. He wanted to become a journalist
and in 1900 went to live in Rome, where he began
to paint. Together with Severini he was introduced
to Neo-Impressionism by Balla. In 1906 he visited
Paris and subsequently Russia, returning to Italy at
the end of the year. He then lived in Padua and
studied at the Academy of Art in Venice. In 1907 he
moved to Milan, where he earned his living as a
commercial artist. In Milan he met F. T. Marinetti,
who later became the spokesman for the Futurists,
and joined the *Famiglia Artistica* association, which
also numbered Carlo Carrà and Luigi Russolo among
its members. Together with them he signed the first
two manifestos of Futurist painting (the two important ones) in 1910. In the autumn of the same
year he accompanied Marinetti, Carrà and Russolo
to Paris, where he made friends with Apollinaire and
the French *avant-garde* painters. Boccioni took part
in all the large Futurist assemblies held between
1910 and 1915. From 1912 onwards he was also
evolving a Futurist form of sculpture. Following the
outbreak of war in 1914 he and many other Futurists
volunteered for active service. He was killed on the
North Italian front in 1916.

Boccioni, a widely read and highly intelligent
artist, was the guiding spirit behind the Futurist
group of painters. He wrote the *Technical Manifesto
of Futuristic Painting* of April 1910, the introduction
for the exhibition catalogues of 1912 and the *Manifesto of Futuristic Sculpture* of April 1912. From 1913
onwards he published a number of articles on
pictorial dynamism in *Lacerba*. In the following year
he adapted these articles for his book, *Pittura-
Scultura Futurista*, which still remains the most
important theoretical account of Futurism. In his
theory Boccioni took up Marinetti's revolutionary
demand, namely that artists should burn all the
bridges linking them with the past and surrender
themselves up to the sensations of modern technical
civilization, and applied it to the sphere of painting.
He urged his fellow painters to seize hold of modern

life with all its dynamism, vitality and speed. According to Boccioni, even stationary objects had to be conceived in dynamic terms. In other words they had to be broken down into lines of force so that a sense of movement could be conveyed by the portrayal on the canvas of various stages of a single kinetic sequence. It would be possible to do this, he suggested, by reproducing abstract signs, which had been evolved from that sequence and which created an impression of movement.

Boccioni consistently applied Futurist theory in his artistic works, and paintings such as his *Street Noises Penetrate into the House* (1911) and *Elasticity* (1912) or sculptures such as his *Bottle in Space* (1912) and *Forms of Continuity in Space* (1913) demonstrate the great stylistic potential of the moving object. In these works a whole complex of impressions and associated sensations is presented simultaneously. Boccioni abandoned normal perspective and the naturalistic reproduction of objects. Instead he employed a fluid system of perspective involving the simultaneous use of several vanishing points and an abstract method of object presentation based on the kinetic properties of the objects concerned. His painting technique was a development of the optical mixtures introduced by the Neo-Impressionists: shivers of complementary colours are built up into a highly dynamic and vibrant prismatic network, which transforms and reflects the original motif.

F. T. Marinetti. *Umberto Boccioni. Opera Completa*, Foligno 1927.
G. C. Argan. *Umberto Boccioni*, Rome 1953.
J. C. Taylor. Catalogue, *The Graphic Work of Umberto Boccioni*, Museum of Modern Art, New York 1961.
R. de Grada. *Boccioni*, Milan 1962.
C. Baumgarth. *Geschichte des Futurismus*, Reinbek 1966.

Böckstiegel, Peter August. German painter, b. 1889 in Arrode-Werther, Westphalia; d. 1951 in Arrode-Werther. Böckstiegel was apprenticed to a painter in Bielefeld, where he also attended the local school of arts and crafts. Subsequently he studied at the Academy in Dresden. He lived in Dresden and Arrode.

Like his friend Felix Müller, Böckstiegel belonged to the second generation of Expressionists. His works reveal the influence of the *Brücke* and of Nolde and Rohlf.

Das graphische Werk Peter August Böckstiegels, Bielefelder Kunstverein, Bielefeld 1932.
Exhibition catalogue, *Peter August Böckstiegel*, Münster (Westphalia) 1956.

Bodmer, Walter. Swiss painter and sculptor, b. 1903 in Basle. After studying painting at the School of Arts and Crafts in Basle Bodmer spent some time in France and Spain. He had his first exhibition in 1928, when he was still working in a Post-Impressionist style. From 1933 onwards he carried out abstract experiments, producing a series of colour compositions which became progressively more in-

formal. In 1936 he made his first wire constructions. Since 1939 he has been teaching at the Technical School in Basle and of recent years has pursued geological and palaeontological studies. He is now living in Basle.

Like Bill and Lohse Bodmer belongs to the first generation of Abstract-Constructivist artists in Switzerland. He made his name with his wire sculptures and his wire constructions in space. During the early stages of his abstract period Bodmer's linear designs still contained gentle allusions to objective and spatial factors, but subsequently they grew more and more abstract until eventually they developed into informal arrangements of dynamic lines of force, which are characterized by their harmony and elegance.

W. J. Moeschlin. *Walter Bodmer*, Basle 1951–2 (with a portfolio of prints).

Boeckl, Herbert. Austrian painter, b. 1894 in Klagenfurt, Austria. After studying architecture under Adolf Loos at the Technical College in Vienna from 1912 onwards Boeckl taught himself to paint. Between 1921 and 1924 he visited Paris, Berlin and Palermo. In 1935 he joined the staff of the Academy of Art in Vienna.

Boeckl belonged to the same generation as Kokoschka, Kolig and Wiegele, although he was a little younger. His affinity with these painters is particularly evident in his early works which, although originally inspired by Cézanne, resemble Kokoschka's Dresden pictures in their lively handling and expressive colouring. During that period Boeckl was generally regarded as one of Austria's leading colourists. Later his works were to lose their freshness. Under Picasso's influence his composition grew more deliberate. At the same time he became more and more interested in religious themes or themes involving the power of fate. A particularly fine example of his late work is to be found in the frescoes which he painted for the Engelskapelle in Seckau in 1952.

C. Pack. *Der Maler Herbert Boeckl*, Vienna 1964 (with a catalogue of works).

Boezem, Marinus Lambertus van den. Dutch painter, b. 1934. Boezem trained at the French Artibus Academy in Utrecht and the Free Academy in The Hague. Since then he has worked as a painter and etcher, and he has also created pictorial objects. He made his name with his *gonflables* (inflatable objects). His work has been classified as '*art sensorial*'.

Boezem. *Boezem Air Objects*, Gorinchem 1966.

Bogart, Bram. Dutch painter, b. 1921 in Delft. After spending ten years in Paris—from 1951 to 1961—Bogart settled in Brussels, where he is still living today.

Bogart is an Abstract Expressionist, whose work is chiefly remarkable for its tactility: the colour is heavily impasted and resembles solidified lava. Unlike the Tachists, however, Bogart uses his colour shapes as constructive elements.

Bolotowsky, Ilya. American painter, film-maker, playwright and translator, b. 1907 in St. Petersburg. Educated in Russia and the College of St. Joseph, Istanbul, he arrived in the United States in 1923 and studied at the National Academy of Design with Ivan Olinsky. He was given his first one-man show in New York in 1930. Since 1933 his works have shown a constant debt to Mondrian, attempting to create a perfect harmony through the use of neutral elements. While working on mural projects for the WPA (Williamsburg Housing Project, Brooklyn, N.Y., 1936) he and Ibram Lassaw, George L. K. Morris and Ad Reinhardt were instrumental in founding the American Abstract Artists. He has taught at Black Mountain College, N.C. (1946–8), the University of Wyoming (1948–57) and is at present head of the Art Department at Southampton College, N.Y. Among his plays are *The Neurotic Lion* and *Darling, Poor Darling.* In 1962 he compiled the *Russian–English Dictionary of Painting and Sculpture,* a lexicon of art terminology in the two languages.

American Abstract Artists Yearbook, 1939.
The Pinacoteca, New York, November 1947.

Bomberg, David. British painter, b. 1890 in Birmingham; d. 1957 in London. The son of a Polish immigrant, he moved to London at the age of four. He was first apprenticed to a lithographer, then studied painting part-time; finally he was helped by the Jewish Educational Aid Society to attend the Slade School full-time, 1911–13. Between 1912 and 1914 Bomberg's forceful modernism compelled serious attention and he was able to go straight to the centre of *avant-garde* activity not only in London but in Paris. His disillusionment began with the rejection of his first design for a Canadian War Memorial picture in 1918 and the failure of his postwar exhibitions. The financial troubles that followed were to continue, easing only briefly in the early 1930s, until his death. Bomberg was never associated with any tight group after 1915 until he became the inspirer of the Borough Group of younger artists (cf. Frank Auerbach) during his teaching years at the Borough Polytechnic (1946–53). His isolation was increased by the English dislike of Expressionism, towards which his art began to turn after about 1929. Only after his death has the revaluation of Expressionism permitted Bomberg's work to find its true level.

Bomberg's impact before 1914 rested on four large compositions which have been called Cubist. Unlike classical Cubist works *The Mud Bath* (Tate Gallery) is a straightforward rendering of figures in crisp geometric forms. It had more in common with Matisse or Léger than with Picasso or Braque. Prevented from realizing his war picture in this style, Bomberg never returned to it. His retreat from geometricism was abrupt. In 1923–7 he was in Palestine, and in 1924 made some meticulous paintings at Petra. His conversion to expressive brush-strokes is seen in paintings executed in Spain in 1929. At first the strokes were mainly short and disconnected; later, especially in the Cornish landscapes of 1947, they grew longer, broader and more sinuous. These brush-strokes and the colours they carry are literally the medium between Bomberg and nature. They serve to define both the form of the subject and his mood while painting it, and, in the best examples of this type, unite them indissolubly.

Bombois, Camille. French painter, b. 1883 in Vénary-les-Laumes (Côte d'Or); d. 1970. After spending his childhood on board cargo boats Bombois became a circus wrestler in 1903. Four years later he settled in Paris, where he worked on the Métro and as a porter in various newspaper presses. In 1922, when he took part in a street exhibition in Montmartre, he received favourable press notices and was encouraged to continue with his painting by the journalist Noel Bureau and the art dealers Mathot and Wilhelm Uhde. In 1928 he was represented at Uhde's exhibition *Painters of the Sacred Heart,* which also included works by Rousseau, Bauchant, Séraphine and Vivin, and in 1937–8 he contributed to the *Maîtres populaires de la Réalité Nouvelle,* an international exhibition that was staged in Paris, Zürich and New York.

Bombois first started to paint when he was sixteen years old, despite the fact that he was then engaged on extremely arduous physical work. Most of his pictures deal with the circus, which he represented as an exciting and glamorous but basically false world. The acrobats and clowns, who form the central *motif* in these works, are seen against a backcloth of fairground booths, whose mysterious and grotesque activities lend a tragic dimension to these essentially heroic figures. In order to portray such popular themes Bombois evolved an extremely imaginative and colourful style, in which distorted forms combine with luminous, Romantic colours to produce a naïve and highly expressive form of realism. The precise definition of the individual pictorial objects in his work is offset by the use of powerful chiaroscuro, perspective and glaring colours similar to those used in cheap prints. Bombois's paintings are a combination of self-portrait and psychic landscape: his central figures, who seem extremely powerful when considered in isolation, are alienated from the world of reality by their Surrealistic fairground environment. Against this colourful background these athletic but melancholy circus artists symbolize the painter's personal longing.

W. Uhde. *Five Primitive Masters*, New York 1949.
B. H. Bing. *Camille Bombois*, Paris 1951.

Bonalumi, Agostino. Italian painter and sculptor, b. 1935 in Milan. After training as a technical draughtsman Bonalumi began to sculpt in 1958 and for the next two years was in close contact with Manzoni and Castellani. In 1946 he began work on his 'picture reliefs', in which a monochrome canvas is stretched on a wooden skeleton. Bonalumi is now living in Milan.

Bonhomme, Léon. French painter, b. 1870 in St-Denis; d. 1924 in Paris. He was a pupil of Gustave Moreau. From 1888 he had work exhibited in the Salon of the Société des Artistes Français. His work consisted mainly of portraits and figures.

Bonnard, Pierre. French painter, b. 1867 in Fontenay-aux-Roses; d. 1947 in Le Cannet. From about 1885 to 1888 he studied law in Paris: he failed the examination in 1888. He then studied at the École des Beaux-Arts and at the Académie Julian, where he met Denis, Sérusier, Vuillard and Ranson: together this group formed the Nabis. In 1889 Bonnard's first poster design was sold. From 1889 to 1890 he did his military service. Returning to Paris in 1890, he shared a studio with Denis and Vuillard. In 1891 he exhibited at the Salon des Indépendants. From 1891 to 1905 he was very active as a decorator, graphic artist and designer. He made screens and posters; lithographs for *La Revue Blanche*, *L'Escarmouche*; theatre designs for the Théâtre d'Art, Théâtre de l'Oeuvre, Théâtre des Pantins, and illustrations including *Quelques Aspects de la Vie de Paris* (1895), *Parallèlement* (1900), *Daphnis and Chloë* (1902) for Vollard, and Jules Renard's *Histoires Naturelles* (1904). In 1896 he had his first one-man show of paintings at Durand-Ruel's gallery. Around 1899 he signed a contract with the dealer Bernheim-Jeune. From about 1905 he concentrated increasingly on painting, and gained the admiration of Redon and Monet. From 1910 on he started to divide his time between Paris and the south of France (St-Tropez, Le Cannet). In 1925 he married Maria Boursin, his mistress and model since about 1895 (she died in 1940). In 1926 he was a pall-bearer at Monet's funeral. From the 1920s on he lived a settled, quiet existence as a painter, with occasional commissions as an illustrator. He exhibited regularly in Paris and extensively throughout Europe and America. He was awarded medals at the Carnegie International Exhibition, Pittsburgh, in 1923 and 1936. Large one-man exhibitions of his work were held in Paris, 1924, 1937, 1947; New York, 1928, 1934; Stockholm, 1939. Bonnard's contemporaries in the 1890s were con-cerned with the Post-Impressionist revival of Symbolism led by Gauguin. He did not share their literary and intellectual pretensions: his only real link with the Nabis lay in his brilliance as a designer-decorator. Inspired by Japanese art and by Toulouse-Lautrec (the respect here was mutual), his work of the 1890s combined a shrewd eye for anecdotal incident with a natural instinct for two-dimensional design. The poster *La Revue Blanche* (1894, Bibliothèque Nationale, Paris) exemplifies his decorative use of silhouettes and textures, his wit and his facility as a draughtsman. His prolific ability matched a sudden demand in the fields of graphic art and design.

His career as a painter started with decorative panels and screens and the heavily textured *intimiste* interiors which, with Vuillard's, did much to popularize Post-Impressionist painting throughout Europe. After 1905–10 his painting became less decorative and took on a more serious appraisal of the late work of Monet. He deliberately forsook the finesse of execution and the artful colour taste of his earlier work in paintings that were more exclusively based on things seen, and the stylishness disappeared from his work (see *Pont de la Concorde*, 1913, London, Tate Gallery). The landscapes, townscapes and interiors of this date were in direct descent from the Impressionism of Monet, Renoir and Degas, and bore little explicit relationship to current *avant-garde* art.

In the 1920s and 1930s his acute perception of appearances continued to dominate his painting, but was increasingly reconciled to a sense of structure. The great series of nudes and bath scenes (*Baignoire*, 1925, London, Tate Gallery; *Nu dans le Bain*, 1935, Paris, Petit Palais) contain precise observation of light values, faithfully recorded. At the same time, through simplicity of composition, the rich variety of pattern and paint texture across the surface and the sensuality of sumptuous colour relationships, the paintings resume something of the quality of decoration of his early oeuvre. In his late work the allover surface quality intensified; it was stressed by cut images, framing devices and unusual viewpoints, as in *Breakfast Room*, 1930–1 (New York, Museum of Modern Art); *Coin de Table*, c. 1935 (Paris, Musée d'Art Moderne). Some of the canvases appear highly abstract, the surface treated as an arena for rich, painterly colour relationships.

Bonnard was a rather conservative figure by some twentieth-century standards, in view of his subject matter and of his continued endorsement of the activity of painting on canvas. His reputation among younger painters stood, like Matisse's, considerably higher in the mid-twentieth century than during his lifetime.

John Rewald. Catalogue, *Pierre Bonnard*, Museum of Modern Art, New York 1948.
Antoine Terrasse. *Bonnard: Biographical and Critical Study*, Geneva 1964.

Jean and Henri Dauberville. *Bonnard: Catalogue raisonné de l'oeuvre peint*, 2 vols., Paris 1965.
Annette Vaillant. *Bonnard*, London and New York 1966.

Bonnet, Anne. Belgian painter, b. 1908 in Brussels; d. 1960 in Brussels. Bonnet studied at the Académies in Brussels and Saint-Josse. She was a founder member of *La Route Libre* (artists' association, 1939), *Apport* (salon, 1941), *Jeune Peinture belge* (artists' association, 1945) and *Art actuel* (salon, 1958). From 1950 onwards she painted abstract pictures which were prompted by impressions of nature and executed in harmonious colours.

P. Davay. *Anne Bonnet*, Antwerp 1954.

Bonnier, Olle. Swedish painter, b. 1925. He was an abstract painter, and with Olof Rohde (b. 1916) and Karl Axel Pehrson, formed a group who called themselves the 'Men of 1947'.

Bontecou, Lee. American sculptress, b. 1931 in Providence, Rhode Island. Bontecou studied with William Zorach and John Hovannes (b. 1900) at the Art Students' League in New York from 1952 to 1955, then worked in Rome from 1957 to 1958 on a Fulbright Fellowship, and in 1959 received an L. C. Tiffany Grant. Bontecou's early sculpture, of the mid-fifties, included birds, animals and human figures in terra-cotta and metal; the human images in particular were formed by slightly separated, armour-like plates revealing dark cavities beneath. These sculptures were the forerunners of Bontecou's canvas constructions, characterized by faceted planes punctured by large dark orifices, which she began making in 1959. Most of these constructions are wall reliefs—although some are freestanding—and constitute some of the earliest and most successful examples in American art of the shaped canvas. Greyish, generally monochromatic tarpaulin, cut into abstract and irregular geometric shapes, is fastened on to the frame with wires that protrude as sharp, dangerous barbs. These geometric planes converge towards one or more black, gaping holes that are sometimes equipped with jagged, toothlike elements or with bars, creating a surrealistic contrast to the otherwise rather severely formal conception. The inscrutable and seemingly infinite openings become the focal points of the constructions and function as equivocal images, simultaneously inviting and menacing the viewer.

Dorothy C. Miller (ed.). Catalogue *Americans 1963*, Museum of Modern Art, New York 1963 (with statements by the artists).
Donald Judd. 'Lee Bontecou', *Arts Magazine* XXXIX, April 1965.

Borduas, Paul-Émile. Canadian painter, b. 1905 in St. Hilaire, Quebec; d. 1960 in Paris. After receiving his art training in Montreal Borduas went to live in Paris in 1928 and worked in the Atelier d'Art sacré under Maurice Denis. He returned to Montreal in 1930, where he taught in various institutes. In 1940 he went over to abstracts and in 1942 became a rallying point for a group of young painters, which included Riopelle and from which *Les Automatistes* later emerged. In 1953 Borduas moved to New York, where he made contact with de Kooning and Motherwell and found a friend in Franz Kline; in 1955 he moved to Paris; in 1960 he was posthumously awarded the Guggenheim National Prize.

Borduas was the mentor and—apart from Riopelle —the foremost representative of modern Canadian art. After passing through early Cubist, Fauvist and Surrealist phases he went abstract in 1942, producing lyrical, automatistic works which reveal the influence of Gorky and Bram van Velde. Later, by using the spatula technique which he had acquired from Franz Kline and de Staël and by reducing his scale of colours virtually to black and white, he created an impression of stark simplicity, which is extremely effective.

Robert Élie. *Paul-Émile Borduas*, Montreal 1943.
Exhibition catalogue, *Paul-Émile Borduas*, the Montreal Museum of Fine Arts, 1960.

Borès, Francisco. Spanish painter, b. 1898 in Madrid. After training in Madrid Borès joined the *avant-garde* group *Ultraiste*, before moving to Paris in 1923. There he met Juan Gris, Picabia, Miró and Matisse. Due above all to Gris' influence he began to paint in the Cubist mode but soon broke away when he found the severity of Cubist composition uncongenial. After a brief flirtation with Surrealism he evolved a more vital and more naturalistic style of his own, in which the Cubist line of the preliminary sketch simply serves as a point of departure for his basically two-dimensional pastel-coloured compositions. Borès is now living in Paris.

J. Grenier. *Borès*, Paris 1961.

Boriani, Davide. Italian experimental and kinetic artist, b. 1936 in Milan. Boriani is a member of the *Gruppo T*, which was founded in Milan in 1959, the year in which he produced his first 'cine-visual and programmed objects', on which metal shavings form changing patterns due to the action of rotating magnets mounted out of sight of the viewer. Boriani is now living in Milan.

Boshier, Derek. British painter, b. 1937 in Portsmouth. He was at the Royal College of Art from 1959 to 1962, and had his early successes in *Young Contemporaries* exhibitions. He was first associated with Pop imagery, and became a leading English *avant-garde* painter of the mid-sixties, producing large canvases combining the optical dazzle of stripes of primary colours with a bold pseudo-perspective effect that sometimes required a shaped canvas. Boshier now lives in London.

Botelho, Carlos Antonio. Portuguese painter and decorative artist, b. 1899 in Lisbon. He was a pupil of Condeixa in Lisbon at the art school, and later studied in Paris. He has won many prizes, including the first prize of the Watson Foundation at the International Exhibition in San Francisco, 1939, and the Grand Prix at the 1937 Paris International Exhibition. He has been responsible for the decoration of the Portuguese pavilions in several large exhibitions: Paris, 1931, 1937; New York, 1939; San Francisco, 1939; and the Portuguese World Exhibition in 1940. He paints mainly landscapes, and is also a stage designer.

Botero, Fernando. Colombian painter, b. 1932 in Bogotá. In his highly sophisticated paintings Botero portrays gross, primitive, grotesque creatures in the lush consumer territory of New York City, which he visited in 1955. These monstrous figures, and the rotting fruits on which they gorge themselves, are executed with the technical skill of the Spanish Renaissance masters Goya and Velasquez, and constitute a blasphemous indictment of a degenerate colonial bourgeoisie.

Boto, Marta Segunda. Argentinian painter, b. 1925 in Buenos Aires. Boto studied at the National Schools of Art in Buenos Aires up to 1947. In 1958 she became a founder member of the *ANFA* abstract group. Three years later, in 1961, she settled in Paris. Since then she has carried out research into the apparent movement of structures induced by lighting and optical effects and has created a kind of 'hydraulic sculpture'.

Bott, Francis. German painter and graphic artist, b. 1904 in Frankfurt am Main. Bott moved to Paris in 1937 and has lived there ever since. At first he joined the French Surrealists but later evolved an abstract form of composition, in which the different areas of colour interlock to form angular patterns. In 1953 Bott designed the stained-glass windows for the chapel at the Castle of Reux in Calvados.

Bouché, Louis. American painter, b. 1896 in New York City. He first studied in Paris at the Académie Colarossi, the Académie de la Grande Chaumière and the École des Beaux-Arts under L. Simon, J. P. Laurens and R. Miller, and then at the Art Students' League with L. Mora and O. Linde. He was the recipient of a Guggenheim Fellowship in 1933 and since 1934 has taught at the Art Students' League. Bouché is best known for his murals of the 1930s which include a large work for Radio City Music Hall, Rockefeller Center, New York, and wall paintings for the Attorney General's Office, Department of Justice Building, Washington, D.C., the Auditorium of the Department of the Interior Building, Washington, D.C., and the Home Building Center

at the 1939 New York World's Fair which he completed with Allen Saalburg and Everett Henry. His canvases are often in the style of G. Luks and Guy Pène du Bois, representing scenes from daily American life (*Shooting Gallery*, n.d., Pennsylvania Academy of Fine Arts).

Philip Rhys Adams and Robert Morris Coffin. *An American Show*, Cincinnati Art Museum, 1948.

Bourdelle, Antoine. French sculptor, painter and designer, b. 1861 in Montauban, Ille-et-Vilaine; d. 1929 in Le Vésinet, Seine-et-Oise. Bourdelle started his career studying in Paris, first with Jules Dalou and Alexandre Falguière, then moving into Rodin's studio. It was Rodin who was to have the greatest influence on Bourdelle, and it could be seen right up to the end of his life. His early works reveal both his Romantic leanings and his search for the expression of power and force. This is evident in the many representations of Beethoven which he created throughout his life—the character of the composer made him an ideal subject for the sculptor's aspirations.

His works show traces of other influences—for instance, the Romanesque style is evident in his *Vierge d'Alsace* which stands at the highest point of the Vosges mountains. His rather flamboyant style is manifest in the exaggerated poses of his powerful figures, although he can curb this where necessary, and a modicum of restraint produces more successful works, such as the bas-reliefs he was asked to do for the Théâtre des Champs-Élysées, Paris, in 1912, or the *Monument to General Alvear*, the Argentinian hero, a group which consists of an equestrian statue surrounded by Liberty, Victory, Strength and Eloquence.

Bourdelle is well known for his portrait busts, but sculpture is not his only means of expression, and works in other media, such as painting and ceramics, form part of the collection kept in his studio in Paris and now called the Musée Bourdelle.

Ionel Jianou and Michel Dufet. *Émile Antoine Bourdelle*, London 1965.

Bourgeois, Louise. American sculptress, b. 1911 in Paris. Her education included studies in Paris at the Sorbonne, the École du Louvre, the Académie des Beaux-Arts, and a number of private studios, including that of the painter Fernand Léger; in New York City, where she moved in 1938, she studied at the Art Students' League. She taught at the Louvre and the Académie de la Grande Chaumière in Paris and at Brooklyn College in New York. Bourgeois is best known for her sculpture, although she has also exhibited drawings. She emerged as an important modernist sculptor in the early 1950s with her wood constructions, usually uniformly painted in either black or white. Around 1949, she experimented with images that represented tall and thin, abstract, anonymous personages, related to the sculpture of David Smith and Isamu Noguchi, and meant to be grouped around the viewer; works from this period include *The Blind Leading the Blind* (painted wood, 1949). A few years later Bourgeois organized her forms into compositions suggesting landscape or architecture, as in *Garden at Night* (painted wood, 1953). These black or white wooden assemblages preceded those of Louise Nevelson, and contributed a new sort of elegance and austerity to modern American sculpture, while retaining a romantic quality. In the 1960s, Bourgeois turned away from constructions to modelling forms in plaster, intended for casting in metal.

Daniel Robbins. 'Sculpture by Louise Bourgeois', *Art International* VIII, Zürich, October 1964.
Wayne V. Andersen. 'American Sculpture: The Situation in the Fifties', *Artforum* V, June 1967.

Boussingault, Jean-Louis. French painter, b. 1883 in Paris; d. 1944 in Paris. Boussingault was a grandson of the famous chemist. While still a young man he met Dunoyer de Segonzac, L. A. Moreau, La Fresnaye and, subsequently, Laprade and Desvallières. Through these artists Boussingault established contact with the *Grande Revue*, which published a number of his early drawings. From 1911 onwards he designed models and created decorations for Paul Poiret. From the early 1920s he exhibited with the Indépendants. For his portraits, figure compositions, landscapes and still lifes he used agitated brushwork and sophisticated colouring. Following a visit to England in 1929 Boussingault also worked as a graphic artist, and produced some impressive works in this genre. In the early 1940s he painted a number of large murals, and produced cartoons for tapestries.

Boyd, Arthur. Australian painter and sculptor, b. 1920 in Victoria, Australia. He was born into a family of artists. In 1943 he started a commercial pottery, and later made ceramic paintings and sculpture. He went to England in 1959, and with Nolan and others forms the expatriate Australian school in London. Boyd combines a romantic sensuous symbolism with images of early, rural Australia.

Bradley, Martin. British painter, b. 1931 in Richmond, Surrey. After three years as a cabin-boy, Bradley taught himself to paint. His work is influenced by Klee, Tobey and Chinese and Japanese calligraphy. He does not abstract from reality but constructs his works from ideographs, sometimes calligraphic, sometimes incised with a more deliberate, totemic quality. He is represented in the Museum of Modern Art, New York.

Brancusi, Constantin. Rumanian-French sculptor, b. 1876 in Hobitza, Rumania; d. 1957 in Paris. He

was born into a large family of peasant stock in a rural district with a tradition of woodworking. He attended the School of Arts and Crafts at Craiova, 1895–8, then the School of Fine Arts at Bucharest for three years.

He arrived in Paris in 1904. He worked briefly for Rodin, about 1906–7, but was established as an independent innovatory artist from 1907–8. One of the most seminal artists of the whole modern movement, Brancusi exerted a profound influence on the modern concept of form in the fine arts and also in the design of manufactured objects. Much of his work went to the USA. He bequeathed his studio to the French nation; it has been reconstructed in the Musée National d'Art Moderne with many finished and unfinished wood carvings, plasters and some finished marbles and bronze casts. There are other important collections of his work in American museums, and in Rumania (mostly early works).

On his first arrival in Paris Brancusi practised modelling and experimented with fragmentation after the manner of Rodin (e.g. certain heads half emerging from a surrounding mass) and Impressionism in the manner of Medardo Rosso. One piece (*Torment*, 1906–7) is even derived from Dalou. Brancusi's innovations between 1907 and 1910 belong with the first break with Impressionist sculpture also achieved by Epstein and Gaudier-Brzeska, which was founded on an appreciation of archaic sculpture stopping short of the full-blown primitivism of Picasso in his painting of 1907–8, and as yet unconnected with Cubism; also on direct carving. The life-size kneeling nude *Prayer* (1907–9) also suggests that Brancusi admired the renovated Classicism of Maillol. In 1910 Brancusi produced two works of special importance. The stone carving *The Kiss* (Montparnasse Cemetery, Paris) is the work in which direct carving produced Brancusi's most perfect fusion between the stone forms and the forms required by the subject. It sets a standard for all succeeding modern sculpture that laid claim to 'truth to materials'. *Sleeping Muse*, a detached head lying on its cheek, begins the sequence of reductive steps by which Brancusi refined down an organic shape to one so perfect and unblemished that it can only represent a conceptual image of the original.

The highly polished works in marble and bronze have a calming effect on their surroundings derived from their condensed perfectionism. The accounts of visitors to Brancusi's studio witness that he tried constantly to surround himself with calm. However, the wood carvings display another aspect of the matter. They have a robust vitality and show the strength of Brancusi's links with his native culture. Wood was the chosen medium for certain works of a fetishistic incantatory character. Finally it was in wood that Brancusi first developed the repeated form of his various versions of the *Endless Column*, which goes beyond the calming effect of the polished sculptures to reach the more primitively soothing, almost drugging effect of unvaried repetition many times over. Brancusi also explored this effect in the stone *Gate of the Kiss* and a few other pieces.

Brancusi is the most important of the foreign artists in Paris during the formative period of modern art who put, not just a temperament or an imagery, but a deep-rooted traditional art form at the service of the new purposes. His sensuous involvement with wood, stone and polished surfaces was a necessary corrective to the more cerebral aspect of modern art. Brancusi and Gabo were the earliest, in their entirely different ways, to define an attitude to modern sculpture dependent on material considerations and independent of theories of representation, such as still concerned the early Cubist or Futurist sculptors.

Brangwyn, Sir Frank. British painter, b. 1867 in Bruges; d. 1956 in Sussex. Self-taught as a painter, Brangwyn achieved a great reputation and many honours: he was knighted in 1941. His hot colour and grandiose semi-realism owe more to Belgian than British example, and are still out of favour. He executed many mural schemes, including one for the House of Lords that was rejected in 1930 and is now at Swansea.

Braque, Georges. French painter, b. 1882 in Argenteuil-sur-Seine; d. 1963 in Paris. He lived in Le Havre from about 1890 to 1900, and from then on lived and worked in Paris. He was craftsman-trained as an apprentice in both Le Havre and Paris until his military service in 1901. From 1902 to 1904 he studied painting at the Académie Humbert and (briefly) at the École des Beaux-Arts in the *atelier* of Léon Bonnat. In 1904 he set up his own studio. In 1905 he came under the influence of Fauvism. He exhibited at the Salon d'Automne in 1906. In 1907 he signed a contract with the dealer Daniel-Henri Kahnweiler. He saw the Cézanne memorial exhibition, and met Apollinaire, Matisse and Picasso in that year. In 1909 his paintings at the Salon d'Automne were criticized as 'cubist'. He married in 1912. In 1914 he enlisted in the army; he received severe head wounds in 1915 and was discharged the following year. He returned to Paris, where he contributed to the *Section d'Or* exhibitions in 1920 and 1925. In later life he also worked in graphic media, sculpture, ceramics, theatre design, stained glass and illustration. He undertook several major public commissions, including the ceiling decoration for the Salle Henri II at the Louvre. Major retrospective exhibitions of his work were mounted in Basle, 1933, Brussels, 1936, America, 1939–40 and 1948–9, Berne and Zürich, 1953, and London, 1956. In 1948 he published his *Cahiers*, and was awarded the Grand Prix at the Venice Biennale.

After a peripheral involvement with late Fauvism in 1905–6, Braque rapidly assumed a leading role in Parisian *avant-garde* painting. He saw his Fauvist paintings as his 'first creative works': most of his earlier work was destroyed. His meeting with Picasso and their subsequent close working relationship (1907–14) provided both the context of and the major initiatives behind Cubism. Although primacy of ideas between them has been the subject of much partisan discussion, it is not an important issue. It was the very different nature of ideas and outlook that each contributed which made the partnership so important and so fertile.

Braque's own contribution was anticipated by his earlier works. Drawn into Fauvism by his friendship with two Le Havre painters, Dufy and Friesz, his seascapes of Antwerp, Le Havre, L'Estaque and Le Ciotat, 1905–7 (e.g. *Jetty at l'Estaque*, 1906, Paris, Musée d'Art Moderne), showed him steeped in the traditions of French Post-Impressionist art. Still in the wake of Impressionist landscapes, their strong colour, separated loose brushmarks and heavy tonal pattern combine in reconciling atmospheric perceptual painting with a flatly structured picture surface. This educated allegiance to a Parisian tradition of *belle peinture* remained with him, strengthened in 1907 by the influence of Cézanne.

La Grande Nue, 1907–8 (Paris, Cuttoli Coll.), showed his reaction to Picasso's primitivist influence, tempered by his own painterly instincts and by a systematic Cézannesque technique of reduced colour and ordered brushwork. His Analytical Cubist paintings—e.g. *Houses at l'Estaque*, 1908 (Berne, Kunstmuseum), *Still Life with Violin and Pitcher*, 1909–10 (Basle, Kunstmuseum)—saw a steady progress away from naturalism.

The new attitudes to representing reality in art were clear in the new technical means of 1910–12: stencilled letters, *faux-bois* (an imitation wood-graining technique acquired during his Le Havre apprenticeship), and *papier collé* (pasted paper). All of these devices were drawn from outside traditional fine art, all were direct, non-illusionistic references to reality and all emphasized the flat reality of the picture surface—*Le Portugais*, 1911 (Basle, Kunstmuseum), *Composition with Ace of Clubs*, 1913 (Paris, Musée d'Art Moderne). His collages, unlike Picasso's, were simple, spacious, almost classical (*Guitar*, 1913–14, New York, Museum of Modern Art). Although he did make experimental paper reliefs and constructions (now lost) he pursued the new spatial concepts of collage principally through painting (*Music*, 1914, Washington, Phillips Coll.).

His mature work remained within the terms of Cubist easel painting. The famous series of *Atelier* paintings (1948 on) are typical in their modest, domestic subject matter, their sensuous use of colour and paint and in the occasional inclusion of enigmatic poetic symbols (the white bird, etc.).

Although a relatively traditional European painter

seen in the whole context of twentieth-century *avant-garde* art, Braque remained a respected and influential artist until his death. Picasso described him as 'one of the two great incomprehensibles whom everyone can understand' (the other being James Joyce).

Henry Radford Hope. Catalogue, *Georges Braque*, Museum of Modern Art, New York 1949.
Maurice G. Gieure. *Braque*, New York 1956.
John Russell. *Braque*, London and New York 1959.
John Richardson. *G. Braque*, London and New York 1961.

Bratby, John. British painter, b. 1928 in Wimbledon. He studied at Kingston College of Art and the Royal College of Art. In 1954 he won an Italian Government scholarship to Italy. In 1956 he won the Guggenheim Award in the British section of the Venice Biennale. He won it again jointly with Ben Nicholson in 1959. In 1958 he did the paintings for the film of Joyce Carey's *The Horse's Mouth*. His style, bold and painterly, is influenced by van Gogh and the Expressionists in handling. During the fifties he was a pioneer in the use of popular imagery and subject matter.

Brauer, Erich. Austrian painter, b. 1929 in Vienna. After studying under Gütersloh at the Vienna Academy Brauer joined the Viennese School of Fantastic Realism. He now lives in Vienna, Paris and Israel.

Brauer's visionary landscapes, which are painted in bright, cheerful colours, are reminiscent of Bruegel and Bosch.

W. Schmied. *Malerei des Phantastischen Realismus—Die Wiener Schule*, Vienna 1964.

Brauner, Victor. Rumanian-French painter, b. 1903 in Pietra Naemtz, Rumania; d. 1966 in Paris. Victor Brauner was brought up in Bucharest where he spent a stormy, rebellious adolescence. He studied at the Bucharest School of Fine Arts, which he left in 1924. In this year he had his first exhibition. These paintings remain in Rumania, but among the titles *The Factory Girl* and *Christ in the Dance Hall* perhaps give some idea of their content. In 1924, too, he painted sets for a production of Oscar Wilde's Symbolist play *Salomé*, and founded, together with the poet Ilarie Voronca, a review called *75 HP*—a title reminiscent of that of the Dada periodical *291* founded in 1915. *75 HP* was Dadaist in spirit, as was *UNU*, another *avant-garde* periodical Brauner contributed to at this time. In *75 HP* he published a manifesto called 'Pictopoetry', a term which he defined thus: 'Pictopoetry is not poetry. Pictopoetry is not painting. Pictopoetry is Pictopoetry.' He was clearly aligning himself with the Surrealist movement which at this exact moment was emerging in Paris from the ashes of Dada. Brauner visited Paris in 1925 and finally settled there in 1930, spending some time working with his fellow countryman, the sculptor Brancusi, before making friends with the painter Yves Tanguy and being introduced by him into the Surrealist group. André Breton, the founder of Surrealism, welcomed him and wrote an enthusiastic introduction for the catalogue of Brauner's one-man exhibition at the Galerie Pierre in 1934. Following this he returned to Rumania, where he remained until 1938. In these years he painted a series of small panel pictures showing various mutilations of the eye. These proved prophetic since he lost his left eye in a studio brawl after his return to Paris in 1938. He spent the war as a refugee in the Hautes Alpes. In 1948 he broke with the Surrealists after a phase of making what he called 'magic drawings' and turned to painting cycles of pictures with titles like *Depolarization of Consciousness* and *Memory of Present Unreality*.

Victor Brauner was an immensely gifted artist who seems never to have managed to create a style of his own. His early work is strongly influenced by de Chirico, Miró, Max Ernst, André Masson and Paul Klee; many of his 'magic drawings' of the 1940s are pastiches of Picasso and the cycles of the 1950s are in the manner of Roberto Matta. He is probably best remembered for the 'Mr. K.' paintings (inspired by Alfred Jarry's *Ubu Roi*), shown at his 1934 exhibition and for his *Self-Portrait with Extracted Eye* and the mutilated eye pictures which followed it.

A. Jouffroy, *Victor Brauner*, Paris 1959.
Catalogue, *Victor Brauner*, Alexander Tolas Gallery, New York 1963.

Breitner, George Hendrik. Dutch painter, b. 1857 in Rotterdam; d. 1923 in Amsterdam. After studying in Rotterdam under C. Neuerdenburg and C. Rochussen in 1875, Breitner attended the Academy in The Hague from 1875 to 1882. He made contact with W. Maris in 1880 and later with J. Maris. From 1886 to 1887 he attended the classes given by A. Allenbé at the Academy in Amsterdam. Breitner was one of the foremost Dutch Impressionists. At a relatively early stage in his career he developed a highly personal style, applying the paint with broad strokes of his brush and working almost exclusively in dark colours. Since this style remained virtually unchanged, Breitner's works can be conveniently dated by their themes. His favourite *motifs* were people and animals, and he made numerous studies of horses, mounted hussars and artillery scenes. Later, after visiting Paris in 1884, he also painted many townscapes, mostly views of the old inner city of Amsterdam. In addition to paintings, Breitner produced etchings, watercolours and photographs.

Catalogue, *Breitner en Amsterdam*, Stedelijk Museum, Amsterdam 1947.
P. H. Hefting and C. C. G. Quarles van Ufford, *Breitner als Photograph*, Rotterdam 1966.
P. H. Hefting, *George Hendrik Breitner*, Amsterdam 1968.

Brianchon, Maurice. French painter, b. 1899 in Fresnay-sur-Sarthe, France. Brianchon studied in Bordeaux and later, from 1917 onwards, in Paris. He was given a professorial post at the Academy of Art in Paris in 1949.

Brianchon was influenced by Manet and, subsequently, by Bonnard. The major part of his output consists of landscapes, interiors and female portraits in the Bonnard tradition. He has also produced designs for stage sets.

R. Heyd. *Brianchon*, Neuchâtel 1954.

Brignoni, Serge. Swiss painter and sculptor, b. 1903 in Chiasso. Brignoni trained as a painter in Berne and Berlin. He took up sculpture in 1927. Since 1940 he has been living in Berne.

Brignoni is a Surrealist. His work has been influenced by de Chirico and Max Ernst.

Brizzi, Ary. Argentinian painter and sculptor, b. 1930 in Avellaneda, Argentina. After training at the National Schools of Art in Buenos Aires Brizzi completed his studies by visiting Chile, Bolivia, Peru and Brazil between 1951 and 1955. In 1959 he designed the Argentinian Pavilion for the International Exhibition in New York. He also contributed to the 'Beyond Geometry' exhibition in New York.

Brook, Alexander. American painter, b. 1898 in Brooklyn, N.Y. He received his first painting instruction as a child while ill with infantile paralysis. After a short period at Pratt Institute, Brooklyn, he studied at the Art Students' League (1915) under Kenneth Hayes Miller. He first exhibited with his wife Peggy Bacon in 1923. To supplement his income he became assistant director of the Whitney Studio Club, a position he held from 1924 to 1927. For similar reasons he taught periodically at the Art Students' League and elsewhere. While so employed, he also occupied himself writing articles, which included studies of the works of Toulouse-Lautrec, A. Dasburg, Y. Kuniyoshi and others. He is best known for his portraits, such as *Biddy and Sandy* (1928, Dayton, Ohio, Coll. Mrs. Howell Howard). This work is typical of his close, direct approach to portraiture, casting aside any unnecessary detail and seizing on the mass and bulk of the figures. Rather than attempting a strong personal confrontation between sitter and viewer, he creates a sense of the sitter's mood. Though portraits were his forte, Brook has also painted landscapes, still lifes and studio nudes.

Alexander Brook. American Artists Group, New York 1945.

Brooker, Bertram. Canadian painter, b. 1888 in Croydon, Surrey; d. 1955 in Toronto. He went to Portage la Prairie, Manitoba, in 1905. With no formal art training, he developed an early interest in the art of Kandinsky and in film. In early life he worked in the advertising and editorial departments of newspapers in western Canada; in Winnipeg he met L. L. FitzGerald and began to paint the local scene. After moving to Toronto he began to paint abstractions and was in touch with Lawren Harris. While painting (*Alleluia*, 1929, Ottawa, National Gallery of Canada), he wrote books on advertising art, art criticism for Canadian newspapers, and two editions (1928–9 and 1936) of the *Yearbook of the Arts in Canada*. His novel *Think of the Earth* won the Governor General's Medal for the best fiction of 1936. He also illustrated several books.

J. R. Harper. *Painting in Canada*, Toronto 1966, pp. 352–8.

Brooks, James. American painter, b. 1906 in St. Louis, Mo. From 1923 to 1925 he attended Southern Methodist University, where he majored in art, and in the following academic year studied under Martha Simkins (a student of William M. Chase) at the Dallas Art Institute. He moved to New York in 1926 and enrolled at the Art Students' League, where he worked under Boardman Robinson and Kimon Nicolaides. In the 1930s his subjects related to the areas in which he grew up—Oklahoma, Texas, Colorado—rendered in a manner close to that of the Social Realists. It was in this decade, too, that he worked as a muralist for the WPA (*The Acquisition of Long Island*, 1938, Queens, N.Y., Woodside Library) and while working for this federal agency met J. Pollock and P. Guston. In 1939–42 he produced a mural entitled *Flight* for the rotunda of the Marine Air Terminal Building, La Guardia Airport, Queens, N.Y. The brightly coloured symbols and abstract shapes which presage the chromaticism of his later abstract paintings are interspersed with stiff, bulky, monumental figures creating a counterpoint of weighty figurative elements and delicate free-form abstractions. The work was thoughtlessly painted out in 1954–5. After serving in the United States Army 1942–5 he began experimentations with pure abstraction. The influence of Picasso's and Braque's synthetic Cubism and the atmospheric Cubism of B. W. Tomlin is coupled with the vivid tonalities of his earlier style in his 1947 *Dialogue* (coll. of artist). In the late 1940s a fluidity and sense of motion enters his work, revealing a strong influence of the automatism of his friend Pollock (*Number 41*, 1949, coll. of artist). He received his first one-man show at this time (Peridot Gallery, N.Y.) and continued such exhibitions through 1953. His style of 1952–9 exhibits a composition of two alternating colours, as the red and green of *R* (1953, New York, Coll. Chase Manhattan Bank). This bold, assertive style is a strong contrast to his works of the early 1950s which are characterized by a poetic, diaphanous, fragile quality achieved through the thin application of pigment and an almost Oriental colour refinement and spacing of masses. From 1959 his forms become stiffer and even more solidly constructed. This new rigidity in the large shapes produces a sullen grandeur in such works as the red, white and black *Rasalus* (1959, New York, Whitney Museum of American Art) and the 1962 *Burwak* (New York, Coll. Edward J. Mathews). Brooks has taught at Columbia University (1946–8) and Pratt Institute, Brooklyn, N.Y. (1948–59), and has served as visiting critic of advanced painting at Yale University.

Sam Hunter. *James Brooks*, New York 1963.

Brown, Frederick. British painter, b. 1851 in Chelmsford; d. 1941 in Richmond, Surrey. He studied at the Royal College of Art and in Paris. He taught at the Westminster School of Art from 1877 to 1892, then became Slade Professor. He was a founder member of the New English Art Club in 1886.

Bruce, Patrick Henry. American painter, b. 1880 in Virginia; d. 1937. He first studied with Robert Henri and then he went to Paris in 1907 with P. Matisse. Here he became an unofficial Synchromist and worked under his friend R. Delaunay from 1912 to 1914. He was a member of the New Society of American Artists, Paris, and exhibited in the Salon d'Automne, the Salon des Indépendants (1914), was one of the few American modernists to exhibit in the Armory Show and from 1920 on took part in the exhibitions of the *Société Anonyme*. His geometric still lifes of the 1920s have little to do with his earlier preoccupation with Synchromism. He most often confined himself to pastel-coloured solid forms placed against dark backgrounds, with little or no use of line (*Still Life*, c. 1929–30, New York, Coll. Benjamin Garber). Because of the lack of interest taken in his work, he destroyed all but fifteen of his canvases in 1932, gave the surviving works to Henri Pierre Roché and moved to the relative seclusion of Versailles. After a brief trip to the United States in 1936 he took his own life.

William C. Agee. Exhibition catalogue, *Synchromism and Color Principles in American Painting*, M. Knoedler & Co., New York 1965.

Brücke, die. The *Brücke* (Bridge) artists' association, which was formed in Dresden in 1905 by Ernst Ludwig Kirchner, Fritz Bleyl, Erich Heckel and Karl Schmidt-Rottluff, was one of the focal points of German Expressionism. With the exception of Kirchner, who had spent one semester at the school of art run by W. Debschütz and H. Obrist in Munich in 1903–4, these four were all self-taught. They met while studying architecture at the Dresden Technical College and between them evolved an aggressive and archaic style of painting which was diametrically opposed to the bourgeois taste of their day and made a direct appeal to the sense of mission felt by the younger generation. In their work they drew on the

colour compositions of the Neo-Impressionists, the woodcuts of Vallotton, the graphic art of Munch, the lithographs of Toulouse-Lautrec and the paintings of Bonnard, Vuillard and Denis. In 1904 Kirchner had seen an exhibition of sculptures from the South Sea Islands in the Ethnological Museum in Dresden and recognized their artistic quality. (This discovery of his coincided with similar discoveries by Derain, Vlaminck, Picasso and Matisse.) Other sources of inspiration for the *Brücke* were provided by the Late Gothic woodcut and the works of medieval German masters such as Beham and Cranach. By 1907–8 the *Brücke* artists were working in a completely individual manner. After coming to terms with the *Nabis* and the *Jugendstil* they had developed a trenchant style based on simplified natural forms and an expressive use of line which lent itself particularly well to graphic work. In their early phase they had employed the optical mixtures of the Neo-Impressionists, but later they abandoned these in favour of large areas of luminous colour. It is primarily the exuberance and vitality of the *Brücke* colouring which distinguishes this group from the Munich New Artists' Association and the *Blauer Reiter*. Stylization was completely alien to the *Brücke* artists. Nor did they try to create an esoteric pictorial world. Their hieroglyphs were not secret symbols but expressive emblems of the new reality with which they were confronted. But although, initially at least, the members of the *Brücke* undoubtedly shared in a group-style, they also had quite specific individual characteristics. Kirchner was an extremely sensitive, almost visionary artist. Schmidt-Rottluff, on the other hand, was better known for the power and boldness of his composition, whilst Heckel's principal quality was his lyrical temperament. As early as 1906 Cuno Amiet, L. Zyl, Axel Gallen-Kallela and Emil Nolde joined the *Brücke* and in the same year Kirchner formulated the group's programme, which attracted a number of associate members, who paid an annual subscription in return for a portfolio containing three or four art prints. In October 1906 the group held its first exhibition of paintings, which was staged in Dresden-Löbtau on the premises of the Seifert lamp firm. This was followed by an exhibition of graphic art which ran from December 1906 to January 1907. Later in 1907 a travelling exhibition was organized. In the same year Nolde left the group and in the following year Kees van Dongen and Franz Nölken joined it for a brief period. Subsequently Pechstein moved to Berlin and was joined there in 1911 by Kirchner, Heckel and Schmidt-Rottluff. Kirchner and Pechstein then founded the MUIM—*Moderner Unterricht im Malen* (Modern Training in Painting) Institute, which marked the beginning of the real struggle with Liebermann and the Impressionists of the Berlin *Sezession*. Meanwhile, in 1910 (the year in which Otto Müller became a member of the *Brücke*), the whole group had joined the New Secession, which had just been founded under Pechstein's leadership. In 1911 Bohumil Kubišta, a Czech artist and a member of the *Manes* artists' association in Prague, also joined the *Brücke*. But this was an isolated case. In general the *Brücke*—unlike the *Blauer Reiter*—was not an international body. The last occasion on which the *Brücke* artists appeared as a group was at the 1912 *Sonderbund* exhibition in Cologne. In the following year, due apparently to the dissension sparked off by Kirchner's *Brücke* chronicle, the group was disbanded. In point of fact, however, the members of the *Brücke* had been following divergent paths for some considerable time and the group-style had long since disappeared.

H. Bollinger and E. W. Kornfeld. *Ausstellung Künstlergruppe Brücke: Jahresmappen 1906–1912*, Berne 1958.
Catalogue, *Brücke, 1905–1913: Eine Künstlergemeinschaft des Expressionismus*, Folkwang Museum, Essen 1958.
H. Wentzel. *Bildnisse der Brücke-Künstler voneinander*, Stuttgart 1961.
W. Grohmann. *Painters of the Brücke*, Tate Gallery, London 1964.
Le Fauvisme français et les débuts de l'Expressionisme allemand, Musée National d'Art Moderne, Paris 1966.

Brüning, Peter. German painter and sculptor, b. 1929 in Düsseldorf. Brüning studied at the Academy of Art in Stuttgart under Willi Baumeister from 1950 to 1952. He then came under the influence of Cy Twombly. Up to 1964 he drew freely on a wide variety of pictorial forms but has since restricted his range to a specific category of forms based on cartographic and related signs, which are intended to present the modern environment—especially the industrial landscape—in a new light. In 1964 he received an Honourable Award at the Third International Biennale for Young Artists in Tokyo. Brüning is now living in Ratingen, near Düsseldorf.

Brunori, Enzo. Italian painter, b. 1924 in Perugia. Brunori studied at the Academy of Art in Perugia. After an early Neo-Cubist phase he entered into a loose association with the *Gruppo degli Otto Pittori Italiani*. Since then his paintings have been executed in powerful, luminous colours; their surfaces are structured by the brushwork, acquiring a sculptural appearance which heightens the rhythm of the interlacing colours. Brunori is now a concrete painter.

Brusse, Mark. Dutch sculptor, b. 1937 in Alkmaar, Holland. After training at the Academy of Art in Arnheim from 1956 to 1960 Brusse became a member of the *Nada* group. In 1961 he went to live in Paris, where he made contact with the artists of the *nouveau réalisme* movement centred on Spoerri. Brusse constructs sculptural objects from chains and pieces of wood which are reminiscent of agricultural implements. Since 1965 he has lived in New York.

Brusselmans, Jan. Belgian painter, b. 1884 in Brussels; d. 1953 in Dilbeck. After his studies at the Brussels Academy, he was drawn to Fauvism and Impressionism; at the beginning of the twenties he opted for Constructivist Expressionism. Although he turned away from the outside world, yet he continually evoked it; a picture was for him above all a composition of forms whose regularity and rigour belong more to geometry than to the world of objects. His style is not without rigidity or schematism, especially as the colour, which can be as brilliant as on a poster, is sometimes as harsh as the line. For all that, Brusselmans is not unaware of the subtlety of halftones; it is just that he is not bothered about charm or attraction: his concern is to coax every plastic element into its rightful place, in his vigorous and strictly regulated work.

Bryen, Camille. French painter, poet and writer, b. 1907 in Nantes. In 1926 Bryen settled in Paris, where his first volume of poems was published in the same year under the title *Opoponax*. This was followed by further volumes in 1932 (*Experiences*) and 1934 (*Les Quadrupèdes de la Chasse*). In 1934 he also began to exhibit his 'automatic drawings'. Later he developed his 'spot and sign mosaics', which were amongst the earliest products of Informal Art. Although—like Wols, Mathieu, Hartung and Riopelle—he became an exponent of 'new painting' after the war, he was essentially a follower of this trend and not one of its leaders. As a painter he espoused a poetic, meditative and organic style, whilst as a poet and writer he used a form of language evolved from Dada and Surrealism and remarkable for its sound associations, its word-plays and its sudden contrasts.

C. Bryen and J. Audiberti. *L'Oeuvre-Boîte*, Paris 1952.
R. V. Gindertael. *Bryen*, Paris 1960.

Brzozowski, Tadeusz. Polish painter, b. 1918 in Lwow. Brzozowski studied at the Academy of Art in Cracow and later became a professor at the College of Fine Arts in Poznan. He now lives in Poznan and Zakopane.

The expressive qualities of late medieval and provincial icon painting have been a source of constant fascination to Brzozowski and his detailed knowledge of these ancient techniques has been one of the major factors in his artistic development. At a later stage in his career, when he came under the influence of Surrealism and Informal Art, he began to deform and transpose his figurative *motifs*. This practice, which has not infrequently produced grotesque results, has become more and more pronounced over the years, although Brzozowski has never completely abandoned objective forms, for his works are still suffused by an emotional quality which stems from an original objective *motif*.

Bubenik, Gernot. German painter, b. 1942 in Troppau. Bubenik trained at the Academy in Stuttgart and the College of Fine Arts in Berlin. Natural objects, technological products (transistors, generators, etc.), physical formulae and manufacturers' instructions are all featured in his pictures, which are symmetrical compositions painted in glaring colours. In 1965 Bubenik began to produce his visual diagrams and his conceptual pictures. From 1967 onwards he has produced visual diagrams with slide-projections. Bubenik is now living in Berlin.

Bubonovgi Valet. The *Bubonovgi Valet* (Jack of Diamonds) was a Moscow-based group of progressive, western-oriented Russian artists who staged their first exhibition in Moscow in 1911. The Russian contributors to this exhibition included Larionov, Gontcharova, Malevich and the Burljuk brothers. But in order to emphasize their solidarity with the West the organizers also invited contributions from foreign and expatriate Russian artists, namely Le Fauconnier, Gleizes and Lhôte, Jawlensky and Kandinsky. At subsequent exhibitions works were shown by the members of the *Blauer Reiter* and *Brücke* associations and also by leading French artists such as Picasso, Matisse and Léger. Initially the group was influenced chiefly by Cézanne and the early Cubists, but it subsequently became the focal point of Russian Futurism, whose principal spokesmen were David Burljuk and the poet Mayakovsky, a late recruit to the *Bubonovgi Valet*. With this change of direction the literary side of the group's activities came more to the fore and in 1912 it staged its first Futurist operetta and drama. Despite their attachment to western art the members of the *Bubonovgi Valet* insisted absolutely on the independent character of Russian Futurism, so much so that they gave offence to Marinetti when he came to Russia in 1914. In 1916 the *Bubonovgi Valet* had its sixth exhibition, to which Malevich, Chagall, Ventulov and Rosanova all contributed. In 1917 it had its seventh. Larionov and Gontcharova took no part in the later exhibitions. They had left the *Bubonovgi Valet* shortly after its foundation in protest against its western 'eclecticism', and went on to develop Rayonnism.

Camilla Gray. *The Great Experiment: Russian Art 1863–1922*, London and New York 1962.

Buchheister, Carl. German painter, b. 1890 in Hanover; d. 1964 in Hanover. Buchheister was a self-taught painter. His first pictures date from 1919 and are painted in the style of the *Neue Sachlichkeit*. In 1921 he established friendly relations with Schwitters and the Constructivists and, due to their influence, went over to abstract art. From 1928 to 1933 he was a member of the Hanover Abstracts and from 1933 to 1936 of the *Abstraction-Création* associ-

ation. Subsequently he reverted to objectivity for a period but from 1945 onwards produced abstract collages, in which Constructivist and lyrical components are successfully blended with elements of Dada and *Art brut*.

R. Lange. *Carl Buchheister*, Göttingen 1964.

Buchholz, Erich. German painter and sculptor, b. 1891 in Bromberg, West Prussia. From 1918 to 1925 Buchholz belonged to the Constructivist circle in Berlin. He was on friendly terms with El Lissitzky and was a member of the *Novembergruppe*. His pictures, reliefs and constructions are all geometric abstracts based on Suprematism and *de Stijl*. He was already using glass as a component material in 1921. He is now living in Berlin.

Buffet, Bernard. French painter, b. 1928 in Paris. Buffet began drawing in 1943 and entered the École des Beaux-Arts in the following year. He first became known when he won the 'Prix de la Critique'. He is a member of *L'homme Témoin* and lives in Paris.

In his early period Buffet was influenced by Utrillo's Post-Impressionism. Then, from 1948 onwards, he produced harshly realistic portraits, still lifes and townscapes, which provided an almost programmatic account of J. P. Sartre's existential philosophy. With his pale grey, melancholy tones and his hard, sharp and black linear composition Buffet depicted the desolation and misery of modern man, isolated and crucified in an unrelated world. But, having made his name, Buffet was inundated with highly paid commissions and his work quickly deteriorated. His pictures are now purely decorative.

P. Bergé. *B. Buffet*, Geneva 1958.

Burchfield, Charles. American painter, b. 1893 in Ashtabula Harbor, Ohio; d. 1967 in New York. In 1912 he attended the Cleveland School of Art, but in 1918 his studies were interrupted by his induction into the Army. After serving in the First World War, he designed wallpaper until 1929, when he was able to concentrate his attention on painting. As early as 1917, in a series of watercolours that the artist called 'conventions for abstract thought', Burchfield had worked out a set of archetypal pictographs for basic states of mind (fascination with evil, dangerous brooding, fear, etc.), which he was to use extensively in his later, more truly representational paintings. In *Church Bells Ringing* (1917, Cleveland, Museum of Art) Burchfield presents his deepest childhood fears —a black rain falls across drooping shapes of houses, while an ominous sound of bells is felt, swirling around a daemonic steeple. Another watercolour, the *Night Wind* (1918, New York, priv. coll.), is also typical of his Romantic visions of strange phantoms, and of his surrender to moods of melancholic nostalgia or terror.

Burchfield's style from 1920 to 1940 tended to be rather conservative, although the emotional emphasis was still on the sinister, as he recorded the gloomy and oppressive mood of small Ohio towns (*Six O'Clock*, 1936, Syracuse, Museum of Fine Arts). In this period his work relates to that of Edward Hopper, who was similarly concerned with the barren loneliness in America's cities and rural towns. Their interest in the American scene was to develop later into the Regionalist movement of the early 1930s and the Social Realism of the 1940s.

After 1940 Burchfield attempted to return to his earlier style, even reworking paintings he had done in that period. His paintings were no longer inspired directly by buildings, and he turned increasingly towards nature in order to reveal its mysterious, basic forms. *An April Mood* (1955, New York, Whitney Museum) is typical of this late landscape style.

John I. H. Baur. *Charles Burchfield*, New York 1965.
Charles Burchfield. *The Drawings of Charles Burchfield*, ed. Edith H. Jones, New York 1968.

Burckhardt, Carl. Swiss sculptor and painter, b. 1878 in Lindau, near Zürich. After training as a painter, first in Basle, then in Munich (1896–7 under Knirr), Burckhardt visited Rome in 1899. There he was influenced by Böcklin, Klinger and Marées. Between 1900 and 1904 he lived in Rome and Capri and produced his first sculptures. In 1909 he was in Florence and in the following year, when he created his polychrome statue of *Venus* from a variety of coloured stones including marble and onyx, he finally abandoned painting in order to devote himself entirely to sculpture. From 1914 to 1920 he lived in Basle, where he worked on the colossal figures for the fountain *Wiese und Rhein* facing the Badischer Bahnhof. In 1921 he settled in Ligornetto and spent the rest of his life there.

Burckhardt was one of the most important figurative sculptors in Switzerland at the beginning of the twentieth century. His highly simplified, monumental figures, which were strongly influenced by archaic Greek sculpture, also reveal traces of Maillol and Cubism. Burckhardt created numerous public monuments in Switzerland.

W. Barth. *Carl Burckhardt: Der Bildhauer und Maler*, Zürich and Leipzig 1936.

Buri, Max. Swiss painter, b. 1868 in Burgdorf; d. 1915 in Interlaken. He studied in Munich and at the Académie Julian in Paris. Like Ferdinand Hodler, who influenced him and who also became a personal friend, Buri was one of the most striking *Jugendstil* painters working in Switzerland at the turn of the century. His favourite *motifs* were the peasants and landscapes of the Bernese Oberland. For his figures he used extremely bold outlines.

Burlin, Paul. American painter, b. 1886 in New York City; d. 1969. Brought up in New York and London, he first worked as an illustrator in 1903 for *Delineator* when Theodore Dreiser was its editor. After exhibiting in the Armory Show of 1913 he moved to Santa Fé, New Mexico, and married Natalie Curtis, a musician and ethnologist who wrote *The Indian Book*, a study of Indian music and folklore. While living in the South West he exhibited periodically at the Daniel Gallery, N.Y. Such canvases as *Negro* (1921, coll. of artist), which owes much to the contemporary Parisian Cubism of Braque, Picasso and Gris, are representative of his style at this time. From 1921 to 1932 he lived, worked and exhibited in Paris and travelled through Europe and North Africa. While abroad he collaborated with Adolph Bohm on a series of stage decorations for an Indian ballet to be presented in New York. The artist has described the years following his return to the United States as 'the most tortuous, the most searching' of his life. In the 1940s he experimented with Surrealism (*Tiger, Tiger, Burning Bright*, 1941–2, Northfield, Minn., Carleton College) as well as with the type of grotesque cubistic abstractions which Picasso painted in the late 1930s (*Young Man Alone with His Face*, 1944, New York, Whitney Museum of American Art). Dissolution of recognizable forms increases in the late 1950s and 1960s. In these works, such as *It Is* (coll. of artist), he uses bright, vibrant colour, and a highly painterly surface reminiscent of de Kooning. From 1949 to 1954 he was artist in residence at Washington University, St. Louis, Mo., and founded the Art Department at Union College, Schenectady, N.Y. (1954–5).

Exhibition catalogue, *Paul Burlin*, Boston University Art Gallery, Boston 1964.

Burljuk, David. Russian-American painter, b. 1882 in Kharkov, Russia; d. 1967 in New York. After studying art in Kazan, Odessa, Munich and Paris Burljuk settled in Moscow in 1907. Like Larionov and Gontcharova he joined the Blue Rose Group and, from 1910 to 1913, attended the Moscow Academy. He then became friendly with Mayakovsky and during the war years these two formed the focal point of the Futurist movement in Moscow. Burljuk also joined the *Bubonovgi Valet* group. Earlier, in 1910, Burljuk had met Kandinsky and in 1911 had become a founder member of the *Blauer Reiter*. In the years that followed he was represented in various of the exhibitions staged by the *Sturm*. Then, in 1918, he left Russia and, after visiting China and Japan, arrived in New York in 1922. In 1930 he acquired American citizenship. Whilst in the USA he edited the magazine *Color and Rhyme*.

After an early period as a Russian 'primitive' Burljuk went over to Futurism in 1910 and was one of the first representatives of the movement in Russia. In the West he was best known as a member of the *Blauer Reiter*.

K. Dreier. *David Burljuk*, New York 1944.
Camilla Gray. *The Great Experiment: Russian Art 1863–1922*, London and New York 1962.

Burljuk, Vladimir. Russian painter, b. 1886 in Russia; d. 1917. Together with his brother David Burljuk, Larionov and Gontcharova, Burljuk—who studied in Odessa and Munich (under Azbe)—belonged to the inner cadre of the Russian *avant-garde*. He played an active part in the Russian Futurist movement and exhibited with the *Bubonovgi Valet* and the *Blauer Reiter* groups. Burljuk, who was highly esteemed as a painter by Kandinsky, died on active service in 1917.

Camilla Gray. *The Great Experiment: Russian Art 1863–1922*, London and New York 1962.

Burra, Edward. British painter, b. 1905 in London. After early satiric work somewhat in the manner of Georg Grosz, Burra became one of the minority of surrealistically inclined English artists who joined Unit One in 1933. He exhibited with the English Surrealists in 1936 and 1938. He works entirely in watercolour, often on a large scale. His work is marked by a Mannerist extremism of style and of subject, which is usually directly or indirectly sinister. He is represented in the Tate Gallery.

Burri, Alberto. Italian painter, b. 1915 in Città di Castello, Italy. After studying medicine from 1934 to 1940 Burri served as a medical officer with the Italian forces in North Africa. He was taken prisoner in 1944 and spent the next two years in a prisoner-of-war camp in Texas. There he began to paint. After returning to Italy in 1946 he settled in Rome, gave up medicine and became a full-time painter. He has had regular exhibitions in Rome since 1947 and in various international art centres since 1950. From 1950 to 1952 he was a member of the *Origine* group in Rome, to which Capogrossi also belonged. In 1959 Burri was awarded the *Premio dell'Ariete* in Milan and the *Premio del AICA* at the 30th Biennale in Venice. In 1963 he produced a ballet for the Scala in Milan. He is now living in Grottarossa, outside Rome.

Burri's highly personal form of artistic expression is a direct result of his tragic experiences in the field hospitals of the Second World War. This is particularly true of his *Sacchi*, a group of collages consisting of bits of charred sackcloth and blood-stained remnants of cloth coarsely stitched together and superimposed on a black or dark red ground, which can be seen through the tears and burn holes in the material. This pictorial representation of blood seeping through bandages symbolizes man's complete vulnerability. Burri has produced a large number of collages, using linen, jute, wood, metal and artificial packaging materials. They include his *Gobbi* (1950), *Sacchi* (from 1952), *Legni* (1955–9), *Ferri* (1958–9), *Combustioni* (from 1957) and *Plastichi* (from 1961). Burri first damages the component materials in order to give them an expressive quality, then forms them into fantastic designs. Many of these are distinctly menacing, others are delicate reliefs with a vaguely melancholy beauty. Although technically they are derivatives of Picasso's Cubist montages, Schwitters' compositions and Dadaist experiments, Burri's collages are unique and perfect works both because of their size and because of their highly personal, expressive power.

J. J. Sweeney. Catalogue, *Alberto Burri*, Museum of Fine Arts, Houston 1963.
C. Brandi. *Burri*, Rome 1963.
Exhibition catalogue, *Alberto Burri*, Kunstverein, Darmstadt 1967.

Burssens, Jan. Belgian painter, b. 1925 in Malines, Belgium. Burssens studied from 1943 to 1945 at the Academy in Ghent. He then joined the purist group, *Art abstrait*, but shortly afterwards went over to a dramatic and 'deforming' type of Abstract Expressionism, which subsequently received a powerful boost from the new American school of action painting (Jackson Pollock: mid-1950s). Burssens is now living in Ghent.

Bury, Pol. French painter and sculptor, b. 1922 in Haine St. Pierre. Bury first began to play an active part in the artistic life of La Louvière, where he lived and worked for several years, when he was only seventeen years old. He studied at the Academy of Art in Mons from 1938 to 1939, and produced his first pictures in the wake of the Surrealist movement. After belonging to the *Tendances contemporaines* association in La Louvière, he went on to become a member of the *Jeune Peinture belge* and also joined in the activities of the *Cobra* and *Art abstrait* groups. In the spring of 1953 Bury put away his easel and produced his first mobiles: 10 '*plans mobiles*', i.e. movable compositions, which can be rotated at will, thus creating different combinations and inviting viewer participation in the creative process. In 1955 Bury took part in the *Le Mouvement* exhibition which was held in the Galerie Denise René in Paris. Bury reached an important stage in his development when he decided to incorporate small motors, first into his '*plans mobiles*', and subsequently into his '*multiplans*'. He called these motors 'form mixers'. During this period Bury progressed via various intermediary stages—such as his '*ponctuations pneumatiques*' and his '*entités érectiles*' and '*rétractiles*'—from reliefs to sculptures. As he did so he was able to diversify and consolidate his conception. For his '*cinétisations*' Bury reverted to flat surfaces. Unlike Jean Tinguely's mobiles, which are invariably violent and in some cases self-destructive, Bury's works in this genre are extremely gentle. Their movements are so slow as to be almost imperceptible, and they create an impression that is both humorous and significant at one and the same time.

Butler, Horacio. Argentinian painter, b. 1897 in Buenos Aires. After training in Buenos Aires Butler went to Europe in 1922, where he worked, first in Worpswede and, subsequently, in Paris (in the Atelier run by André Lhôte and Émile-Othon Friesz). In 1932 he returned to Buenos Aires. During his main period Butler painted landscapes and still lifes in a highly decorative style. He also produced book illustrations and tapestry and stage designs. Of recent years his work has become more abstract and more structured but still retains an innate figurative quality.

Julio E. Payró. *Horacio Butler*, Buenos Aires 1954.
Horacio Butler. *La pintura y mi tiempo*, Buenos Aires 1966.

Butler, Reg. British sculptor, b. 1913 in Buntingford. After training as an architect from 1932 to 1937 Butler taught at the Architectural Association School until 1939. He then spent twelve months as an engineer before going to work in a smithy in Sussex (as a conscientious objector). Although he began to sculpt in 1944, architecture remained his principal occupation and from 1946 to 1950 he worked as an editor for various architectural journals. In 1950, however, he opted for sculpture, which he then studied at Leeds University. In 1953 he won the first prize in the international competition for a monument to *The Unknown Political Prisoner*. Meanwhile, in 1952, he had taken part in the Venice Biennale and started work as a teacher at Hatfield in Hertfordshire, later transferring to the Slade School in London. In 1954 he again contributed to the Biennale. He is now living in Berkhamstead, Hertfordshire.

Like Chadwick and Armitage Butler belongs to the first generation of English metal sculptors. The works of his early period, which were influenced by González and Calder, were all Constructivist, but subsequently he returned to figurative work, fashioning hybrid creatures—half human, half insect—in wire. Recently he has been producing human figures, most of them girls, which he frequently places in a Constructivist framework of metal bars after the manner of Germaine Richier and Giacometti. In this sort of setting the girls appear as victims of oppression—and yet their anxiety and apparent helplessness is offset by a rich sensuality, which has been the hallmark of Butler's latest work.

R. Butler. *Creative Development*, London 1962.
Catalogue, *Reg Butler*, Pierre Matisse Gallery, New York 1962.

C

Cabaret Voltaire. The *Cabaret Voltaire* was one of the original sources of the Dada movement. It was founded in February 1916 in Zürich, Spiegelgasse 1, by Hugo Ball and was used as a centre for widely varying activities which included exhibitions, bruitism (or noise music), simultaneous readings and dances. Ball's object in founding the *Cabaret Voltaire*, as he himself said in 1916, was to draw attention to the small minority of people who had transcended 'the war and the fatherlands' and who lived their own lives, in which they pursued 'quite different ideals'. He was backed in this undertaking by his wife Emmy Hennings, by Richard Huelsenbeck, Marcel Janco, Tristan Tzara and many others. In June 1916 a brochure, edited by Ball, was published under the title *Cabaret Voltaire*. There were no further publications and at the beginning of 1917 the *Cabaret Voltaire* was closed down, its activities being transferred to the Galerie Dada in Zürich.

W. Verkauf (ed.). *Dada: Monograph of a Movement*, London and New York 1957.

Cadmus, Paul. American painter, b. 1904 in New York. Cadmus took an interest in art while still a youth, since his father was a commercial lithographer and watercolourist and his mother an illustrator. He studied at the National Academy of Design and then at the Art Students' League, both in New York. At first he worked with etchings, then from 1928 to 1931 he did layouts for an advertising agency; between 1934 and 1937 he executed murals for the WPA Federal Art Project and the US Treasury Department.

Cadmus developed a delicately detailed style, but his graphic portrayals of sex or horror often shocked viewers. Like Reginald Marsh, who painted New York's Skid Row and its amusement areas, Cadmus successfully captured the emotional tone of the Second World War years in America. Because he combined a perverse vision of everyday life—as in *Fantasia on a Theme by Dr. S.* (1946, New York, Whitney Museum of American Art), which takes place at a seaside resort—with a precise technical manner, Cadmus was characterized as one of the Magic Realists, a group that included such diverse painters as Ivan Albright and Peter Blume. In *Sailors and Floozies* (Whitney Museum), he preserved a nostalgic and gentle spirit, along with this rowdy hedonism.

Childe Reece. 'Paul Cadmus, Etcher', *Magazine of Art* XXX, November 1937.
Lee Nordness (ed.). *Art: USA: Now* I, New York 1963.

Caesar, Doris Porter. American sculptress, b. 1892 in Brooklyn, N.Y. In 1909 she entered the Art Students' League while still attending the Spence School. She studied there until her marriage in

1913, working especially under Bridgman. For the next twelve years she was little occupied with art, but in 1925 she entered Alexander Archipenko's school and studied with him for five years. Although this was her first adventure in sculpture, there is little discernible influence of teacher on student. Few of her works of the 1920s and 1930s, executed in the realistic vein of Rodin, survive. She was given her first one-man show in 1931 at the Montross Gallery and, from 1935 on, a long series of exhibitions at the Weyhe Gallery. Through her relationship with this gallery she became interested in the works of Lehmbruck, Barlach, Belling, Nolde and Kollwitz. *Laughing Couple* (1933, Wallingford, Conn., Coll. John F. Joseph) betrays the influence of Barlach in its mass, weight and density, while the variety of surface texture gives the work the quality of a sketch. By the 1950s she abandoned the male figure, portraiture, story-telling groups and facial expression for the single theme of the female nude. Only in the late 1950s is variety of surface neglected in favour of a greater emphasis on the structure of muscle and bone. The 1953 *Torso* (New York, Whitney Museum of American Art) still shows evidence of interest in the material used, although the elongation (which was first in evidence about 1934) has increased and the power of muscle and the strength and vitality of movement stretching upwards are the salient features. By 1957, all surface interest is gone. The emphasis is on the smooth body with its sense of soaring stressed through the sleekness of the form and the radical reduction of the size of the head (*Ascent*, New York, Weyhe Gallery).

J. Baur and L. Goodrich. Exhibition catalogue, *Four American Expressionists*, Whitney Museum of American Art, New York 1959.

Cagli, Corrado. Italian painter, b. 1910 in Ancona. Cagli studied at the Academy of Art in Rome. In 1938 he settled in Paris and in 1940 in New York. In the following year he joined the forces, serving as a soldier until 1945, when he returned to New York. Three years later, in 1948, he returned to Rome, where he is still living today.

Cagli has passed through a number of strongly contrasting phases in the course of his career. In the early 1930s he painted figurative works, including numerous murals. Later he was influenced, first by Picasso, then by the Rome Expressionists (Mafai and Scipione) and finally by the Surrealists. After the war he turned to abstract painting, producing both geometrical and lyrical compositions. These were followed in the late 1950s by *trompe l'oeil* pictures, which were followed in their turn, from about 1965 onwards, by ornamental linear abstracts.

Exhibition catalogue, *Sei Pittori Italiani*, Istituto Italo-Latino Americano, Rome 1967.

Caille, Pierre. French ceramic artist, b. 1912 in Tournai. After training at the École Nationale Supérieure des Arts Décoratifs Caille worked as a painter, but subsequently turned to pottery and became a professor of ceramics in 1949. His inventiveness, his eclecticism and his occasional boldness have been a source of inspiration for his students. As a potter Caille is far more than a mere artisan; he is an authentic artist, a sculptor with a marked lyrical talent, who has succeeded in preserving his own individual style despite the numerous influences to which he has been exposed.

Calder, Alexander. American sculptor, b. 1898 in Philadelphia; d. 1976. Despite the environment in which he was raised (his father was the sculptor A. Sterling Calder and his mother a painter), Calder's early interests were in the field of engineering, which he studied at the Stevens Institute of Technology (1915–19). Not until 1923 was he drawn to art. He enrolled at the School of the Art Students' League, studying with Luks, Du Bois and Sloan. During a stay in Paris (1926–7) he became keenly interested in the circus; he created animals, figures and circus apparatus of wire and string and gave performances in his room. From these fanciful objects sprang his first wire sculptures (*Helen Wills*, 1928, wire, coll. of artist). He produced his first animal sculptures when he returned to the US. Back in Paris, he met Miró and Pascin and later Arp and Léger. These *avant-garde* artists surely had an aesthetic influence on the first abstract stabiles (1930), which also owe much to the rectilinear designs of Mondrian. From these works developed the manual and motor mobiles (*Dancing Torpedo Shape*, 1932, wood, iron, wire and aluminium, Pittsfield, Mass., Berkshire Museum) which set Mondrian's rectangles into an oscillating movement. These sculptures created a constantly changing relationship of the solid objects to the space around them. The natural development from the motorized mobile was the wind mobile, which allowed complete freedom of movement in a wholly unpredictable and natural manner (*Lobster Trap and Fish Tail*, 1939, steel wire and sheet aluminium, New York, Museum of Modern Art). He was almost exclusively occupied with the creation of mobiles (the expression coined by Duchamp) and stabiles (term invented by Arp) for the next twenty years. In the 1940s the components of his works remained basically the same—wire and metal discs painted in primary colours or black—but he often combined both the mobile and stabile into a single unit (*Red Petals*, 1942, Chicago, The Arts Club). The 1950s saw a larger number of stabiles, often having a psychologically sinister quality in their spiny forms (*Black Widow*, 1959, New York, Museum of Modern Art). His largest sculpture, the 60 foot high *Teodelapio*, created in 1962 as a gateway to the city of Spoleto, stems directly from the biomorphic pieces of the preceding decade. He began to exhibit his gouaches in the 1960s; they are related to his sculptures in colour (black, white, red, yellow, blue) and form (circles, triangles, spirals and ellipses) as well as to the amoeba-like forms of Miró and Arp.

J. J. Sweeney. *Alexander Calder*, Museum of Modern Art, New York 1951.
H. H. Arnason. *Calder*, Princeton (N. J.) 1966.

Calderara, Antonio. Italian painter, b. 1903 in Abbiategrasso, Italy. After training as an engineer Calderara taught himself to paint in 1924. He produces concrete pictures which are virtually monochromes. He is now living in Milan.

M. Mendes. *Calderara: Pitture da 1925 al 1965*, Milan 1965.

California Painters and Sculptors. The work of the so-called Pacific artists Mark Tobey and Robert Graves during the 1940s, with its common ties to Oriental art, is perhaps the earliest tendency that can be isolated in West Coast art. In the mid-1950s, a more clearly recognizable, though still local, school, that of the Bay Area Figurativists, who applied an Abstract Expressionist use of paint to realistic subject matter, centred around Richard Diebenkorn and included such painters as Nathan Oliveira, David Park, and Elmer Bischoff.

The Assemblage movement, beginning around 1957 and extending into the 1960s, of which Edward Kienholz was a major practitioner and Wallace Berman an important precursor, put California on the map in a national sense; and with Pop Art (with its chief exponents Billy Al Bengstrom, Edward Ruscha, Joe Goode, Wayne Thiebaud and Mel Ramos), California may be said to have joined the mainstream.

Developments of more limited interest during the 1960s were San Francisco funk art—mostly sculpture—whose anti-intellectual stance tied it to Pop, and the hard-edge 'fetish finish' sculpture of Southern California. Individual figures active during this period were the Expressionist painter John Altoon and the sculptor Peter Voulkos, who experimented in bronze.

As on the East Coast, working in Plexiglass became popular in the mid-1960s, as seen in the elegant designs of Craig Kaufmann and the pristine boxes of Larry Bell, and, later, in the sculpture of Norman Zammitt and DeWayne Valentine. Light artists (all from the north of California) included James Turrell and Doug Wheeler (both of whom were active in other fields as well), while Minimalist sculpture was represented by the work of John McCracken, Clark Murray, David Gray and Tony DeLap. The early 1970s saw the environmentalist works of painter-theoretician Robert Irwin and others, as well as a good deal of activity in the sphere of technological art.

J. Livingston. 'Two Generations in Los Angeles', *Art in America* LVII, January 1969.

Callahan, Kenneth. American painter, b. 1906 in Spokane, Washington. Largely self-taught and having no university degrees, he received some training during his two years at the University of Washington and from his travels to London, Paris, Florence and Mexico (1926–8). He was given his first one-man show just before this trip abroad in 1926 at the Schwabacher-Frey Galleries, San Francisco. In the 1930s he worked for the mural division of the WPA and at the same time was Assistant Director of the Seattle Art Museum, a position he held for twenty years (1933–53). His murals of the 1930s include works in three post offices: at Centralia, Washington (1935), Anacortes, Washington (1936), and Rugby, North Dakota (1937). He took an active interest in mural painting again in the 1960s, executing decorations at the Washington State Library, Olympia, Washington (1960), Syracuse University, Syracuse, New York (1964), and the Seattle Civic Theatre, Seattle, Washington (1966). In addition to his creative and administrative activities, he has led a productive teaching career, holding positions between 1954 and 1966 at the University of Southern California, Washington State, Pennsylvania State, Syracuse and Boston Universities. His canvases are most often non-representational, yet with a strong relationship to nature, building living forms from the microcosm and macrocosm in nature (*Totem Drift*, 1955, New York, Coll. Mr. and Mrs. Burgess Meredith). Mountains, cliffs, waterfalls, clouds, trees and rocks are his subjects, handled in a painterly, yet often curiously brittle manner with a palette which often tends towards the monochromatic (*Quest*, Eugene, Oregon, Coll. University of Oregon).

An Exhibition of Paintings and Drawings by Kenneth Callahan from the Collection of Emily Winthrop Miles, New York 1960.

Callery, Mary. American sculptress, b. 1903 in New York. She graduated from the Spence School, New York, in 1921 and then studied for four years with Edward McCartan at the Art Students' League. In 1930 she left for Paris where she worked in the *atelier* of the Russian-French sculptor Jacques Loutchansky and came under the influence of Maillol. Her years in Paris were also influenced by friendships with Picasso, A. Ozenfant, H. Laurens and the art critic C. Zervos. Returning to the United States in 1940, she had her first one-man show in 1944 at the Buchholz Gallery. Her works during this time are of elongated figures with a certain rubbery quality, whose twisted appendages create a variety of spatial relationships within the figure and with the figures' environment (*Reclining Figure*, 1944, Huntington, N.Y., Coll. Mr. and Mrs. Robert Leonhardt). These same forms appear in the works of 1943 and 1949 which she executed in collaboration with Léger (*Mural Composition*, 1949, painted plaster, Biot, Alpes Maritimes, Musée Léger). In the 1950s these agile forms became more angularized (*A Summer's Afternoon II*, 1953, New York, Coll. Mr. and Mrs. E. J. Mathews), developing in the late

1950s into pure abstractions concerned with the relationships of circular discs and rectangular forms to each other and to the space they inhabit (*Joust*, 1957, copper, steel and brass, coll. of artist). The interest in strict geometricity wanes in the 1960s with a greater concern for complicated surface textures and curvilinear forms (*Composition 8*, steel and brass, coll. of artist).

Mary Callery, Sculpture, intro. by Philip R. Adams, and essay by Christian Zervos, New York 1961.

Calo, Aldo. Italian sculptor, b. 1910 in San Cesario di Lecce, Italy. Calo studied at the School of Art in Lecce and the Istituto d'Arte in Florence. He is now living in Volterra.

After an early phase, in which he moved towards Surrealism, Calo turned abstract. His favourite materials are wood and iron, which he frequently combines to produce fetishistic forms.

Camargo, Iberé. Brazilian painter and graphic artist, b. 1914 in Restinga Seca. Camargo studied under Salvador Parlagreco at the Santa Maria Art School in Rio Grande do Sul. He then won a scholarship and went to Rio de Janeiro, where he continued his studies as a pupil of Alberto da Veiga Guignard. In his pictures Camargo portrays scenes from Brazilian life, using techniques similar to those developed in Mexico.

Jorge Romero Brest. *La pintura brasileña contemporánea*, Buenos Aires 1945.

Camargo, Sergio de. Brazilian sculptor, b. 1930 in Rio de Janeiro. Camargo trained under Emilio Pettoruti and Lucio Fontana in Buenos Aires. In 1948 he made his first visit to Paris, where he studied the work of Brancusi and Arp. He returned to Paris in 1951, and remained there until 1953. In 1954 he visited China. In 1961 he settled in Paris. In 1963 he won the international prize for sculpture at the Paris Biennale.

Camargo creates wooden reliefs composed of small, highly dynamic elements. These works, which are painted white, produce interesting chiaroscuro effects. Camargo has also created an important wall decoration for the Brazilian Foreign Ministry building in Brasília.

G. Brett. *Camargo*, London 1966.

Camaro, Alexander. German painter, b. 1901 in Breslau. Camaro trained as a painter under Otto Mueller in Breslau from 1920 onwards. At the same time, however, he also trained as a ballet dancer and in 1928 joined Mary Wigman in Dresden. Nearly twenty years were to elapse before he showed his first pictures to the public: in 1946 he exhibited a series of nineteen oil paintings under the title *Wooden Theatre*. He has been teaching at the Academy of Art in Berlin since 1951.

Camaro's pictures are lyrical pieces. Working from sketches, which reveal a delicate, hovering line, he paints imaginary subjects on a transparent ground. Since 1950 he has been moving away from objective art.

Exhibition catalogue, *Alexander Camaro*, Kunstverein, Wolfsburg 1961.

Camden Town Group. An English group that was formed in 1911 as the formal expression of a loose association of artists who had in common an interest in French Post-Impressionist painting and who had been in the habit of meeting informally at Sickert's studio, 19 Fitzroy Street, London. One of the main purposes of formalizing the association was in order to arrange exhibitions, and in fact between June 1911 and January 1913 four exhibitions were held, the last being in Brighton. After the latter date the function of the Group was taken over by the newly founded London Group. After the foundation of the Camden Town Group, it was decided to limit membership to sixteen. The original members were F. Spencer Gore who was president, J. B. Manson, secretary, Walter Bayes, Robert Bevan, Harold Gilman, Charles Ginner, Malcolm Drummond, J. D. Innes, Augustus John, Henry Lamb, Wyndham Lewis, R. G. Lightfoot, Lucien Pissarro, William Ratcliffe, D. Turner and Walter Sickert. Duncan Grant replaced Lightfoot on the latter's death in 1911. This list contained some very diverse personalities, and if the Group was supposed to represent the influence of French Post-Impressionism in Britain this is really only true of a central core of its members. Lucien Pissarro and Sickert were very influential, but their own styles were already formed by 1911, and the painters who best represent a Camden Town style are Gilman, Gore, Bevan and Ginner. They have subject matter in common and also a sensitive understanding of the colour and structure of the Post-Impressionists. They created a style that was adopted by a great many inferior imitators in Britain throughout the next forty or so years.

Arts Council exhibition catalogue, *The Camden Town Group*, London 1951, 1953.
Arts Council exhibition catalogue, *Drawings of the Camden Town Group*, London 1961.

Cameron, Sir David Young. Scottish painter and etcher, b. 1865 in Glasgow; d. 1945. He began studying art at night school in Glasgow and then in 1885 went to the Royal Institution in Edinburgh, where he first took up etching. In the 1890s he was one of the Glasgow Boys, the school of painters specializing in landscape, and to some extent reflecting French influence that flourished in Glasgow at the end of the last century. His style as a painter was formed at this time. He used in landscape the rather flat simplified areas of colour that derive ultimately from Gauguin. As an etcher he was perhaps inspired by Meryon and he always used a harder and more definite line than that made fashionable by Whistler. He illustrated a number of books, and it was through his etchings that he was best known. In 1917 he was commissioned as a war artist by the Canadian Government. In 1918 he was made an RSA, and in 1920 an RA. In 1924 he was knighted and in 1933 was made King's Limner for Scotland.

Camoin, Charles. French painter, b. 1879 in Marseilles; d. 1965 in Paris. Camoin studied with Matisse, Marquet, Rouault and Manguin in the *atelier* of Gustave Moreau at the Paris Academy. He then joined the Fauves and contributed to the famous 1905 exhibition held in the Salon d'Automne, from which this group acquired its name. In 1912–13 he accompanied Matisse and Marquet to Morocco. In the course of the next few years he met Renoir in Cagnes and was deeply impressed by him. From then on his works—Mediterranean landscapes, nudes and interiors—were painted in a late Impressionist style, which reveals the influence of both Renoir and Bonnard.

J. Leymarie. *Fauvisme*, Geneva 1959.

Campendonk, Heinrich. German painter, b. 1889 in Krefeld; d. 1957 in Amsterdam. Campendonk first studied art in Krefeld under Jan Thorn Prikker. He moved to Sindelsdorf, Bavaria, in 1911 to join Franz Marc, and exhibited that year with the *Blauer Reiter* in Munich. He made a visit to Italy (1920) before joining the staff at the Essen Industrial School of Art in 1923; in 1925 he moved to the Düsseldorf Academy. Declared a degenerate artist by the Nazis, he moved to Belgium and then Holland, where he taught at the Rijksacademie virtually until he died. He is well known for his stained-glass windows, for which he won an award at the Paris International Exhibition in 1937.

Georg Bermann. *Heinrich Campendonk*, Leipzig 1921.
P. Wember. *Heinrich Campendonk*, Krefeld 1960.

Campigli, Massimo. Italian painter, b. 1895 in Florence; d. 1971. From 1907 to 1915 he worked as a journalist in Milan, where he became acquainted with the Futurists. He then joined the Italian forces, serving as a soldier before being taken prisoner. In 1919, after returning from a prisoner-of-war camp, he began to paint. From 1919 to 1923 he lived in Paris, where he was influenced by Léger and Picasso and also by Ancient Egyptian and Cretan art. In 1939 he went to live in Milan and remained there for a period of ten years, during which time he received several commissions for frescoes. He then visited New York before settling in Paris, where he lived till the end of his life.

An exhibition of Etruscan works which he saw in the Villa Giulia in Rome in 1928 transformed Campigli's whole attitude to art. He immediately abandoned the use of perspective and the plastic representation of pictorial objects and from then onwards produced two-dimensional silhouettes. In the paintings of this second period the figures are simply placed side by side or one above the other, the relationship between them being expressed by exaggerated mimic gestures. The pale, earthy colours are applied with a rough finish and there is no attempt to produce contrasting effects by means of light and shade. The statuesque quality and the transparent beauty of this image of modern man, which here assumes the form of a hovering idol, remind us of Campigli's affinity with the artists of early archaic times.

F. Russoli. *Campigli Pittore*, Milan 1965.

Campoli, Cosmo Pietro. American sculptor, b. 1922 in South Bend, Indiana. He studied in Chicago, and later taught there. He sculpts human and animal figures, and works largely in lead, bronze and reinforced concrete.

Caniaris, Vlassis. Greek painter, b. 1928 in Athens. He first studied medicine, then art; he spent some time in Rome and now lives in Paris. He creates an art which is somewhere between painting and sculpture. He uses rags, scarecrows and garments, thus trying to express a way of life through an aesthetic sensibility. Tragic experiences are expressed with honesty and give a sense of dignity to his work.

Canogar, Rafael. Spanish painter, b. 1934. Canogar was a member of the *El Paso* group which was founded in Madrid in 1957, together with Millares, Feitó and Saura. This group was hostile to the Franco regime and made its attitude clear by its exhibitions and the review of the same name which survived until 1960. Its members were exponents of Informal Art.

Cantatore, Domenico. Italian painter, b. 1906 in Rivo di Puglia. Cantatore is a self-taught artist. In 1920 he went to live in Rome before settling in Milan in 1929. In 1932–3 he visited Paris. He is now living in Milan, where he teaches at the Accademia di Brera.

After coming to terms with the influences exerted on him in Paris (Cézanne, Picasso, Modigliani) Cantatore turned to the works of Carrà and the *Novecento*. He then began to produce simple, figurative paintings, landscapes and still lifes in an archaic and sometimes monumental style. The colours are applied by a *pastosa* technique, which not only makes the pictorial objects appear three-dimensional but the diffused lighting as well. The melancholy, magical quality of these paintings is heightened by the pure, compact colour values, which range from shaded grey to brown.

A. Gatto. *Domenico Cantatore*, Milan 1934.
R. Carrière. *Cantatore*, Milan 1955.

Čapek, Josef. Czech painter, b. 1887; d. 1945. With Beneš, Gutfreund and Špála he joined the *Group of Avant-Garde Artists*, founded in Prague in 1911 by Emil Filla and Antonín Procházka. They were exposed to various forms of modern art, and their group approach to style embraced Cubism and German Expressionism. The result was an original Czech contribution to modern art in Europe.

Capogrossi, Giuseppe. Italian painter, b. 1900 in Rome. Capogrossi began to paint in 1930 after completing his legal studies. In 1927 he had gone to live in Paris and remained there until 1933 when he returned to Italy and became a founder member of the *Gruppo Romano*. In 1951 he joined the *Origine* association. He is now living in Rome.

After an early phase, in which he was influenced by the Cubists, Capogrossi embraced the illustrative technique of the *Gruppo Romano*. Later—in 1949—he withdrew from this group and developed a highly individual pictorial style, which was adopted by the *Movimento Arte Concreta*, an Italian artists' association that had been formed in the previous year. When he evolved this personal style Capogrossi invented a new sign, which looks rather like a comb and consists of a curved back to which a number of teeth are attached. Usually this calligraphic image is executed with broad, clear strokes of the brush, which tend to thin out towards the open end. Although its basic schema remains constant in all cases, its colour, size, extension and pictorial organization are all subject to variation. By overlapping or linking the individual signs Capogrossi allows them to spread out over the picture surface in various directions, thus creating a sort of *leitmotiv*. These *Superficies* paintings have no individual titles to indicate the nature of their subject matter. They are simply numbered. In fact, these pictures do two things: they present a systematic account of Capogrossi's pictorial consciousness and they create a two-dimensional structure which is organized as a subject for meditation. Capogrossi is a concrete painter.

G. C. Argan and M. Fagiolo. *Capogrossi*, Rome 1968.

Cappello, Carmelo. Italian sculptor, b. 1912 in Ragusa, Italy. Cappello trained in Monza. Since 1947 he has exhibited on several occasions at the Biennale in Venice and had a special show there in 1958. He now lives in Milan.

Cappello's sculptures are abstract linear constructions made from polished metals. Their graceful and frequently concentric line and their technical perfection are reminiscent of the work of Max Bill.

Carena, Felice. Italian painter, b. 1880 in Turin. Carena trained at the Academy of Art in Turin under G. Grosso. In 1925 he obtained a professorial post at the Academy of Art in Florence. He is now living in Venice.

During his early period, when he was vacillating between a variety of styles, Carena took his lead from such diverse painters as Carrière, Whistler, Cézanne, Bellini, Titian and Rubens. He next embarked on a Futurist phase before finding in the *Novecento* a style that suited his particular temperament. He then produced large format, veristic figure compositions and landscapes. Carena's brushwork during this period remained very tight for some considerable time, but eventually he evolved a more fluid technique which he derived from the Impressionists.

A. Maraini. *Felice Carena*, Milan 1930.

Carles, Arthur Beecher. American painter, b. 1882 in Philadelphia; d. 1952 in Philadelphia. Carles studied at the Pennsylvania Academy of the Fine Arts in Philadelphia intermittently between 1901 and 1907. During his travels to Europe in 1905 and 1907 he became acquainted with several of the important young painters in Paris—Matisse, Picasso, Robert Delaunay, Hans Hofmann and the American John Marin. Several years later, Carles exhibited his own works at Alfred Stieglitz's Photo-Secession Gallery, and also in the 1913 Armory Show in New York. During the 1920s and 1930s, however, he ceased to exhibit publicly, and only friends viewed his work. In this period he evolved a decorative yet representational style that became increasingly abstract, providing an alternative to Cubism, but still within a Modernist context. Throughout his development, Carles made very personal use of chromatic relationships, based on an appreciation of the plastic potentialities of colour; in certain of his works the picture surface and its images contain literally hundreds of hues. One of his earliest works, *L'Église* (c. 1910, New York, Metropolitan Museum of Art), reveals a clear Fauvist influence in its organization of clearly delineated areas of saturated colour. Between 1937 and 1941, when he finally stopped painting, Carles created works, often on a mural scale, whose spontaneously brushed surfaces and violent rhythms anticipate the Abstract Expressionism of American painting in the 1950s.

Exhibition catalogue, *A Memorial Exhibition of Arthur B. Carles*, Pennsylvania Academy of the Fine Arts and Philadelphia Museum of Art, Philadelphia 1953.

Carlstedt, Birger. Finnish painter, b. 1907 in Helsinki. Carlstedt studied in Helsinki and Paris. After an early period in which he experimented with Cubism and Surrealism, Carlstedt developed a monumental style of painting, using rich colours and synthetic simplification. Between 1947 and 1950 he executed wall-paintings for the factory in Kauttua. Later he turned to abstract paintings, producing extremely dynamic compositions executed in powerful colours.

Caro, Anthony. British sculptor, b. 1924 in London. After reading engineering at Cambridge (1942–4), Caro attended the Royal Academy Schools (1947–52). From 1951 to 1953 he worked as an assistant to Henry Moore, then taught at the St. Martin's School of Art in London and, subsequently (1963–4), at Bennington College, Vermont, USA. He now lives in London and New York.

Following a visit to the USA in 1959, Caro abandoned the traditional modelling technique which he had been using until then and evolved a new syntactical method based on simple structures. For this new method he used prefabricated sections of riveted and welded metal, which he painted in strong colours. Consequently—because of the inherent expressiveness both of these open-form structures and the colour—his work transcends the pure Constructivist idiom. Writing of Caro's sculptures in the catalogue for the Venice Biennale of 1966, D. Thompson said: 'They define a gesture, a mood, an experience, but use their scale and their material presence to make such things as real as a table in a room, and to involve the spectator in a kind of open dialogue within the space they both occupy.' Both as a teacher and as a practising artist Caro has exerted a crucial influence on the younger English sculptors.

C. Greenberg. Exhibition catalogue, *Paolozzi and Caro*, Rijksmuseum Kröller-Müller, Otterlo 1967.

Carr, Emily. Canadian painter, b. 1871 in Victoria, British Columbia; d. 1945 in Victoria. She studied first at the San Francisco School of Art (1889–c. 1895), then at the Westminster School of Art in London (c. 1899–1904), returning to Canada occasionally to teach painting and to paint the Indian villages of the British Columbia coast. During the years 1910–11 she was in Europe, studying at the Académie Colarossi in Paris, sketching in Brittany and travelling in Sweden. At this time she almost certainly met Frances Hodgkins (1871–1947), the New Zealand painter teaching in France. After her return to Victoria, Carr held her first exhibition and began to paint in a Fauvist style. She experienced difficult times, and to support herself she made carpets and pottery with Indian designs. Encouraged by Mark Tobey and Lawren Harris, she began her most characteristic work in the late 1920s (*Blunden Harbor*, 1929, Ottawa, National Gallery of Canada). In the 1930s and 1940s, she evolved her style into a personal and powerful expression of nature, using spiralling forms and intense colours (*Rushing Sea of Undergrowth*, 1936, Vancouver, Art Gallery).

Emily Carr. *Growing Pains; The Autobiography of Emily Carr*, Toronto 1946; *Hundreds and Thousands; The Journals of Emily Carr*, Toronto 1966.

Carrà, Carlo. Italian painter, b. 1881 in Quargnento, Piedmont; d. 1966 in Milan. In 1893, when he was twelve, Carrà was apprenticed to a decorative painter. Seven years later, in 1900, he exhibited at the International Exhibition in Paris, and subsequently visited London. In 1906 he enrolled at the Brera in Milan, where he met R. Romani, A. Bonzagni, U. Boccioni, L. Russolo and the Futurists in Marinetti's circle. In February 1910 he signed the *Manifesto of Futurist Painting* and on 11 April 1910 the *Technical Manifesto of Futurist Painting*. In 1913 he published his own manifesto, in which he called for a 'painting of tones, noises and smells'. Meanwhile, he had met Picasso and Braque in Paris in 1911, and Apollinaire in 1912. He contributed to *Lacerba*, and made close contact with the Florentine Futurists, especially those grouped around A. Soffici. In 1915 he published his Futurist writings under the title *Guerra pittura*. Up to 1915 he played an active part in the Futurist movement. He also served in the Italian forces, and in 1916 met G. de Chirico in the army hospital in Ferrara, where they founded the *Pittura Metafisica*. From 1919 to 1922 Carrà contributed to the *Valori Plastici* magazine and later made contact with the *Novecento*. Ever since 1911 Carrà had taken a profound interest in Giotto, Masaccio and the whole field of Quattrocento art, and he also published several studies on this period. He also wrote about contemporary artists, and from 1922 onwards worked as art critic for the Milan magazine *L'Ambrosiano*. Later, from 1941 to 1952, he was Professor of Painting at the Brera in Milan.

Carrà was inevitably influenced by Giotto and Masaccio, whose works provided him with critical and objective guide lines in every phase of his artistic development. The restless energy that was the hallmark of Carrà's early Futurist period was brought under firm control after he had come to terms with the new pictorial ideas advanced by the modern French artists. He regarded Cézanne as the great exemplar, but it was Picasso and Braque who taught him (in 1912) that objects must be reduced to their basic Cubist forms. From the simplified, large-format, flat compositions developed by Seurat Carrà evolved a type of composition that was extremely precise and was remarkable for its luminous, Neo-Impressionist colouring. Carrà's Futurist paintings are most impressive and reveal a wealth of interrelating and intersecting forms that is almost Baroque. But the pictures which he produced during the ensuing period, when he came under the influence of the French Cubists, possess these qualities to a much higher degree. However, it was not until he had joined with de Chirico in founding the *Pittura Metafisica* that he was able really to perfect his style. In the paintings of this period the pictorial objects were reduced to just a few recurring *motifs*: animals, people, landscapes, streets. These *motifs*, which are of archaic simplicity, are depicted in a completely static condition so that they acquire a kind of still-life quality. With their warm, fresco-like colours these simple three-dimensional works express a metaphysical view of life. Between 1922 and 1926 Carrà turned towards the *Valori Plastici* with the result that his pictorial objects became more clearly defined. From then until the end of the decade his landscapes were composed of large, still volumes bathed in a gentle light. But from c. 1930 onwards his pictorial forms were less precise, and his work acquired a new painterly quality. He also adopted a brighter and more varied palette, and so turned away from the quiet, earthy colours of his metaphysical period. At the same time, the clear outlines of the pictorial objects in his landscapes, still lifes and figure compositions were replaced by soft contours, which blended with the background in an Impressionistic *sfumato* manner.

C. Carrà. *Guerrapittura*, Milan 1915; *Pittura Metafisica*, Florence and Milan 1945; *La mia vita*, Rome 1945; *Segreto professionale*, Florence 1962.
Alberto Lorenzi. Exhibition catalogue, *Carlo Carrà*, Palazzo Reale, Milan 1962.
Massimo Carrà. *Carrà: tutta l'opera pittorica*, Milan 1967/8.

Cascella, Andrea. Italian sculptor, b. 1920 in Pescara, Italy. Cascella is the brother of Pietro Cascella. During his early period he was influenced both by Cubist sculptors and by Hans Arp. His works are composed of closed Classical forms, which combine, often in an articulatory manner, to produce organic structures, many of which are extremely elegant. Cascella is now living in Milan.

Cascella, Pietro. Italian sculptor, b. 1921 in Pescara, Italy. Cascella is the brother of Andrea Cascella. He has been influenced by both primitive art and European abstract art. His monumental, abstract sculptures, which he usually carves in stone, are remarkable for their archaic simplicity and power. Cascella is now living in Rome.

Casorati, Felice. Italian painter, b. 1883 in Novara, Italy; d. 1963 in Turin. After first studying law, Casorati attended the Academies in Padua, Naples (1908–11) and Verona (1911–14). He then served in the Italian army until 1918, when he settled in Turin and obtained a teaching post at the local Academy. He subsequently exerted a crucial influence on the Turin school. Pre-Raphaelitism and *Jugendstil* were the hallmarks of Casorati's early period. But in c. 1920 the linear ornamentation and the hard colours which had characterized his work until then were modified under the influence of the *Valori Plastici*. Unlike Carrà and de Chirico, however, Casorati fashioned his figures from minute particles of paint and placed them in a picture space which he created in strict accordance with the rules of perspective. His pictorial objects are alienated by a restless, ghostly light, which destroys any sensuous quality they might otherwise have had and transforms them into rigid, metaphysical symbols. Later, c. 1930, Casorati abandoned his harsh chiaroscuro and began

to use a bright and powerful palette. At the same time he reduced his pictorial objects to little more than rhythmically structured, linear arabesques, which he organized in accordance with decorative principles.

A. Galvano. *Felice Casorati*, Milan 1947.
Exhibition catalogue, *Casorati*, Turin 1964.
L. Carluccio. *Felice Casorati*, Milan 1964.

Cassinari, Bruno. Italian painter, b. 1912 in Piacenza. After serving an apprenticeship as a goldsmith, Cassinari studied painting and sculpture at the Academy in Piacenza from 1926 to 1929. He then transferred to the Brera in Milan, which he attended until 1938. In 1940 he joined the *Corrente* and in 1946 became a member of the Venetian *Nuova Secessione Italiana* and the *Fronte Nuovo delle Arti*. In 1950 he met Picasso in Antibes. He is now living in Milan.

After an early phase, in which he was influenced by Modigliani and European Expressionism, Cassinari turned to Cubist forms but did not use extreme foreshortening. The powerful luminous colours and the prismatic organization of his compositions provide the structural framework for poetic *motifs* which are derived from nature.

Castellani, Enrico. Italian painter, b. 1930 in Castelmassa, Italy. After studying at the Academy of Art in Brussels from 1952 to 1956, Castellani joined with Manzoni in 1959 in founding the *avant-garde* journal *Azimuth*. He is now living in Milan.

Castellani makes 'picture reliefs'; these consist of monochrome canvases—usually white or pastel shades—which are stretched on reliefs made with nails. The indented surfaces then produce a continuous interplay of light and shade.

Castillo, Jorge. Spanish painter, b. 1933 in Pontevedra, Spain. Castillo was taken to Buenos Aires as a child but returned to Spain in 1955. In 1969 he studied in Berlin on an exchange scholarship. He is now living in Loano.

After an early phase, in which he was influenced by Cubism and—above all—by Picasso's *Guernica*, Castillo began to paint in a Surrealist style. In the works of this period he places clear-cut and rather grotesque figure compositions against smoky and delicately coloured three-dimensional grounds.

Castro, Sergio Fernández de. Argentinian painter and musician, b. 1922 in Buenos Aires. Castro started out life as a musician. After studying in Switzerland and Uruguay, he worked as assistant to Manuel de Falla in Cordoba, Argentina, in 1945–6. Meanwhile, he had started to paint in 1939 and studied under Torres García from 1941 to 1942 in Montevideo. In 1949 he settled in Paris and, whilst there, gave up music in order to concentrate on painting. Although he has not completely freed himself from the Constructivist principles instilled in him by Torres García, his works are none the less extremely personal. Castro has produced series of constellations, pillars, *papiers teints* and structured still lifes. Since 1966, he has also been working on various large stained-glass windows for religious buildings in France and Germany.

Denys Sutton. *Sergio de Castro*, Paris 1964.
M. Strub and A. Chastel. *Sergio de Castro*, Museum für Kunst und Kunstgeschichte, Freiburg 1966.

Caulfield, Patrick. English painter, b. 1936 in London. From 1957 to 1960 he studied at the Chelsea School of Art and from 1960 to 1963 at the Royal College of Art. He now teaches at the Chelsea School of Art. He held his first one-man show in 1965. Influenced by American painters like Roy Lichtenstein, his work is based on popular illustration, but exploited for its pictorial value rather than any literary content.

Cavallon, Giorgio. Italian-American painter, b. 1904 in Sorio, Vicenza, Italy. He went to the United States in 1920 and began studying at the National Academy of Design in 1925. He attended the Academy until he left for Italy in 1930. He returned to the United States in 1933 and two years later was again studying, now at the Hans Hofmann School of Art. It was while he was in Italy that he received his first one-man show, at the Bottega d'Arte in Vicenza (1932). In the 1930s he assisted A. Gorky on his mural projects and was a founder member of the American Abstract Artists. This association and his connections with Gorky and Hofmann indicate his early penchant for abstraction. Such a canvas as the 1950 *Abstraction* (New York, Egan Gallery) is typical of his style. The two-dimensional rectangular forms, often with slightly slanted sides, are statically contained within the picture frame. Unlike many artists using geometric elements, his approach is rather painterly, with fuzzy edges to the forms which produce a sense of overlapping. Among the important exhibitions in which he has been included are *Abstract Painting and Sculpture in America* (1944, New York, Museum of Modern Art) and *Documenta II* (1959, Kassel, Germany).

Čelebonović, Marko. Yugoslav painter, b. 1902 in Belgrade. Čelebonović read law at Oxford and Paris but then gave up his legal career in order to become an artist. After working under Bourdelle as a student sculptor he turned to painting in 1923. He remained in France, living in Paris and St. Tropez, and during the German occupation played an active part in the Resistance movement. From 1949 to 1952 he was a diplomat on the staff of the Yugoslav Embassy in Paris. In 1960 he received a professorial post at the Academy of Fine Art in Belgrade. He now lives partly in Paris, partly in Belgrade.

After starting as a poetic Realist Čelebonović quickly developed a personal style, in which he successfully combined a primitive modelling technique with a highly cultivated palette. The paintings of this early period, which were on show as early as 1925 when Čelebonović had his first exhibition at the Salon des Tuileries in Paris, are intimate works, in which the gentle tonality of the colours lends transparency to the subject, heightening its psychological impact. From 1933 onwards he used a *sfumato* technique, creating a green patina effect, in which light and shade are perfectly blended. The works of this second period may be regarded as the incunabula of modern Yugoslav art, for they have exerted a lasting influence on later generations of artists. Since 1950, Čelebonović has been striving for greater simplicity. This has led to a reduction in the expressive use of colour and a greater reliance on linear form. His subjects have also become more simple; he now frequently paints such things as bottles, fruits and loaves. Like Morandi, who also favours such themes, Čelebonović has revealed little interest in the spirit of the age. Essentially he anthropomorphizes natural forms, depicting them as living creatures within an existential setting. For him human faces, the fruits of the earth and the products of fantasy are all equally valid phenomena.

Jean Bouret. 'Un des Piliers de l'École de Paris: Marko', *Arts*, Paris, 15 February 1952.
Miodrag B. Protic. *Introduction to the Catalogue of the Čelebonović Retrospective Exhibition*, Museum of Contemporary Art, Belgrade.
O. Bihalji-Merin. *Introduction to the Catalogue for the IVth Bienal*, São Paulo 1957.

Ćelić, Stojan. Yugoslav painter, graphic artist and art historian, b. 1925 in Bosanski Novi, Yugoslavia. After studying at the Academy of Art in Belgrade, Ćelić subsequently obtained a teaching post there. He also became editor of the *Umetnost* (Art) magazine. Ćelić translates his impressions of nature into rhythmical, abstract, two-dimensional landscapes. What interests him in nature is the secret, inner life of plants and minerals. He expresses this process of hidden growth by means of calligraphic techniques and bold handling, which emphasize both the form and the essence of his paintings.

J. Denegri. *Introduction to the Catalogue for the 32nd Biennale*, Venice 1964.
A. Čelebonović. *Painting in Yugoslavia*, Belgrade 1965.

Cercle et Carré. A group and a periodical founded in Paris in 1929 by Michel Seuphor (Ferdinand Berckelaers) and Joaquín Torres-García. Seuphor was a fervent apologist for new developments in abstract art, a writer, a critic and an artist. He had a great admiration for Mondrian and has written a monograph on his work. Torres-García was first influenced by Puvis de Chavannes, then by Klee and Mondrian: he was in Paris from 1924 to 1932 and then continued publication of *Circle and Square* in Montevideo. He believed that in abstraction one could escape from sensuality and the impedimenta of learning and attain a state of being in the full sense. This movement shows an attempt tinged with mysticism to confirm and publicize abstract art in Paris. In 1931, however, the *Abstraction-Création* movement was founded; this drew abstract tendencies more firmly together and formed the centre for non-representational art for some years.

Ceroli, Mario. Italian sculptor, b. 1938 in Castelfrentano, Chieti, Italy. Ceroli trained at the Istituto d'Arte in Rome from 1949 to 1955. In 1964 he began to execute sculptures using the rough timber from wooden boxes as material. At first he made enlarged versions of functional artefacts, such as telephones, and, subsequently, human silhouettes. Since 1967 he has been constructing cage-like sculptures, which can be viewed from inside as well as outside. Ceroli is now living in Rome.

César (César Baldachini). French sculptor, b. 1921 in Marseilles. After a long academic training at the École des Beaux-Arts in Marseilles (1935–9) and the École des Beaux-Arts in Paris (from 1943 onwards), César began to make his way as an artist in the immediate postwar period. This way was to lead him far from the Classical canon of academic sculpture. In 1954 he had his first one-man show at Lucien Durand's gallery in Paris. This was quickly followed by exhibitions in Venice, Amsterdam, São Paulo, London and other big cities, with the result that by 1965 César had already acquired an international reputation. Since 1958 he has had regular exhibitions at Claude Bernard's gallery in Paris, where he is now living.

Most of César's works are in iron, although recently he has also had occasional recourse to synthetic components. He finds his materials on refuse dumps and in breakers' yards. In the mid-1950s he used these *objets trouvés* to compose figurative works such as seated nudes and animals. Gradually, as he himself developed, these were transformed into fantastic hybrid creatures, e.g. *La Grande Duchesse*, *Valentin* and *L'Homme de Draguignan*. Since 1960, he has also been producing his *compressions dirigées*: metal objects with interesting surface structures which César makes by crushing car bodies and engine parts with a hydraulic press. His love of experiment, his sure instinct for sculptural values and his gift for witty, pointed compositions have enabled him to produce a wide range of highly inventive figurative and abstract works, which testify to both his versatility and his integrity.

Douglas Cooper. *César*, Amriswil 1960.

Cesetti, Giuseppe. Italian painter, b. 1902 in Viterbo, Tuscany. Cesetti is a self-taught painter. He is now teaching at the Academy in Venice. Although at first sight Cesetti's pictures appear to be typical examples of primitive art, they are actually based on a detailed study of Italian Quattrocento painting, especially that of Piero della Francesca and Paolo Uccello. At a later stage in his career Cesetti also produced numerous works which reveal the influence of H. Rousseau, E. Munch and F. Marc. His theme is invariably the Tuscan landscape, which he portrays —without recourse to legend—in a lyrical and poetic style. His tightly structured compositions reveal no trace of chiaroscuro. In his earlier works he used soft colours, which blend harmoniously and are linked by a uniform light. Of recent years his palette has become stronger.

C. Cardazzo. *Giuseppe Cesetti*, Venice 1934.

Cézanne, Paul. French painter, draughtsman and watercolourist, b. 1839 in Aix-en-Provence; d. 1906 in Aix. The son of a prosperous bank manager, Cézanne was originally destined, like Degas, for a career in the law, but in 1861 he abandoned his studies for art. While at the Collège Bourbon in Aix, he had become a close friend of the future writer, Émile Zola, whose glowing reports of Paris encouraged Cézanne to study in the capital, which he did from 1861 onwards. In his first year there, he met Camille Pissarro at the Atelier Suisse. In 1863 he exhibited at the notorious Salon des Refusés, while in the following year, his work was rejected by the official Salon (this was to be a regular occurrence). Cézanne was praised by Zola in the newspaper *L'Événement* in 1866; in 1867–8 he was on the fringe of the Café Guerbois circle, which included Renoir and Manet.

In 1870, on the outbreak of the Franco-Prussian War, Cézanne avoided military service by going to live (and work) at L'Estaque, where he secretly set up house with his mistress, Hortense Fiquet. In 1872 Hortense bore him a son, and although the relationship was made more difficult by the initial hostility of his father, who discovered the liaison in 1878, Cézanne and Hortense were finally married in 1886. Meanwhile Cézanne had been working with Pissarro (Pontoise, 1872); become friendly with Dr. Gachet, one of the earliest patrons of Impressionism (1873), and contributed to the character of Claude Lantier in Zola's *Le Ventre de Paris* (1873); and he had shown three paintings at the first Impressionist Exhibition (1874) and sixteen at the third (1877).

Although Cézanne is probably the most widely admired of all nineteenth-century French artists, by critics and collectors alike, his artistic beginnings were humble in the extreme. He had almost no facility and early paintings such as the *Portrait of M. Cézanne Reading* (London, National Gallery) are clumsy and inept. At the same time, many of these early works, with their passionate feeling transmuted into thick surfaces of paint often worked with the palette knife, already reveal the directness and solidity of his vision. This preference for strong, ordered effects was perhaps the main reason for Cézanne's qualms about the 'instantaneousness' of Impressionism, which he felt was always in danger of becoming trivial: he once said that he wanted to make of Impressionism something solid and durable, like the art of the museums. At the same time, he was committed to the characteristically Impressionist doctrine of making a direct observation of nature the basis of art. When Cézanne made his famous, oft-quoted remark that he wanted to 'do Poussin over again, from nature', he was expressing with some precision the central aim of his life, which was to reconcile ordered pictorial form with a strict record of natural appearance.

Cézanne's method, which was subject to a complex development that is impossible to summarize, was—very broadly speaking—to break down whatever he was painting—a human figure, an apple or a landscape—into a series of facets, for each of which there was an equivalent stroke of paint. Each stroke had to express the colour of the object and the manner in which it might be affected by light and shade, and it also had to define the changes in direction in the modelling that would create an effect of three-dimensional solidity. Each stroke, moreover, had to contribute to an underlying, fundamentally abstract structure that he also wanted in each painting, to provide that subliminal architecture that he associated with ordered form. It was this underlying, abstract element, which became stronger in his later work, that so appealed to the *avant-garde* painters of the early twentieth century; and, indeed, it is easy to see that it is but a short step from a picture such as the late *Bathers* in the National Gallery, London, to the works of Matisse and the early Cubism of Picasso and Braque.

Cézanne was never interested in the illusionism of representation, in any conventional sense of the term; and this left him freer than most painters when it came to subject matter. Cézanne is probably the only major artist who has ever succeeded equally well with landscape, portraiture and still life, which he depicted with as great a mastery in watercolours as in oils.

After the early 1880s Cézanne's career became more conventionally successful. In 1882 he had a portrait in the Salon; while at the Paris World Fair in 1889 he showed a landscape. In 1895 Vollard organized Cézanne's first one-man show, which created a great impression among forward-looking artists and connoisseurs. There were, however, personal set-backs. The friendship with Zola, one of the most important relationships of his life, ended in 1886 after the publication of *L'Oeuvre*, a novel in

which Zola had again used Cézanne's career, but this time in a less sympathetic way.

Cézanne had always laid great stress on painting landscape out of doors, straight from the *motif*. And it was while walking home from the site, in the autumn of 1906, that he was caught in a storm; he collapsed and died on 22 October.

Lionello Venturi. *Cézanne: Son Art, Son Oeuvre*, Paris 1936.
John Rewald. *The Ordeal of Paul Cézanne*, London and New York 1950.
Kurt Badt. *The Art of Cézanne*, London and Berkeley (Calif.) 1965.

Chabaud, Auguste. French painter, b. 1882 in Nîmes; d. 1955 in Graveson. He painted circus and café scenes in a Fauvist style. Later he depicted the Provençal landscapes around his home.

Chadwick, Lynn. British sculptor, b. 1914 in London. After studying architecture at Merchant Taylors' in London and serving as a pilot in the Second World War, Chadwick worked as an architectural and furniture designer up to 1946. In the following year he moved to Gloucestershire, where he produced his first mobiles and constructions. These works, which are made of metal or metal and coloured glass, reveal the influence of Calder and González. From 1953 onwards Chadwick developed a more individual style which involved the use of reinforcement techniques: he first constructed a steel skeleton, which he then covered with a skin of plaster reinforced with iron filings before casting it in bronze. In 1956 he won the *Grand Prix* at the Biennale in Venice. He is now living in Stroud, Gloucestershire.

Like Butler and Armitage, Chadwick belongs to the distinguished group of English metal sculptors which appeared on the artistic scene after the Second World War. Although an abstract artist, his sharp, angular sculptures have definite human or animal connotations. With their aggressive appearance and daemonic power they call to mind strange armour- or spine-clad creatures, which are not unlike certain species of insects, birds, fishes and crustaceans.

J. P. Hodin. *Lynn Chadwick*, London 1961.
Catalogue, *Lynn Chadwick*, Marlborough Fine Art Ltd., London 1961.

Chagall, Marc. Russian-French painter, b. 1889 at Vitebsk. He came of a poor Jewish family. He studied painting first at Vitebsk (1907), then (1907–10) in St. Petersburg, working part-time as a sign painter. In about 1910 he studied under Léon Bakst, and gained his first knowledge of modern European art. From 1910 to 1914 he lived in Paris; the trip was financed by a Russian patron, Vinaver. He met Modigliani, Soutine and the artists of Cubist circles; he developed a friendship with Delaunay, Cendrars, Apollinaire and Canudo, and exhibited at the Salon des Indépendants. In 1914 he made a visit to Berlin, where he exhibited at the Sturm Gallery (the catalogue introduction was written by Apollinaire). He then returned to Vitebsk for a holiday: he was detained there by the outbreak of war. He contributed to *avant-garde* exhibitions in Moscow. In 1915 he married Bella Rosenfeld, the subject of many of his paintings. He was called up for army service in St. Petersburg. After the outbreak of the October Revolution in 1917, he was appointed Minister of Fine Arts for Vitebsk. In 1918 he set up an Art Academy at Vitebsk, but after disagreements with Malevich resigned in 1919 and left for Moscow. From 1919 to 1922 he created mural decorations and set designs for the Jewish State Theatre, Moscow. In 1922 he went to Berlin, and also made his first etchings. In 1923 he went to Paris at Vollard's invitation to illustrate Gogol's *Dead Souls*. This was followed by further commissions, including illustrations to La Fontaine and the Bible, until Vollard's death in 1939. In 1930 his autobiography *Ma Vie* was published in France. During the 1930s he travelled widely in Europe and the Middle East. His first major retrospective exhibition was held in Basle in 1933. In 1939 he moved out of Paris to Gordes, Marseilles.

From 1941 to 1947 he lived in America, where he designed the sets and costumes for Massine's ballet *Aleko*. In 1944 his wife Bella died. He designed the sets and costumes for Stravinsky's *Firebird* at the Metropolitan Opera, New York, in 1945. In 1947 he returned to Paris, and two years later moved to Vence, where he lived until 1966. His first ceramics appeared in 1950, his first sculptures in 1951. From 1955 to 1966 he worked on his *Message Biblique* series of paintings, which were shown at the Louvre in 1967. In 1956 he produced the *Circus* series of lithographs.

Since then he has been given many public commissions for stained glass (Plateau d'Assy, France, 1957; Metz Cathedral, 1958–68; Hadassah Synagogue, Jerusalem, 1960–2; UN Building in New York, 1964; Tudeley, Kent, 1967); for murals (Frankfurt, 1959; L'Opéra, Paris, 1963–4; Tokyo, 1964–5; Metropolitan Opera House and Lincoln Art Center, New York, both 1965); for mosaics and tapestries (Parliament Building, Jerusalem, 1966–9; Nice University, 1968), as well as further theatre designs and illustrations. He has travelled widely, including many trips to Israel. He has received many honorary doctorates and awards and has been the subject of major exhibitions in 1959 (Paris, Munich, Hamburg), 1963 (Tokyo), 1967 (Zürich, Cologne), 1968 (New York), 1969–70 (Paris). In 1966 he moved to St-Paul, where he still lives.

Chagall's early work set the tone of his oeuvre: personal, often autobiographical in content and with strong echoes of his Russian origins and a respect for Jewish traditions and symbols. The influences of Parisian colour, of the fragmented dislocations of

Cubism, and his contact with *avant-garde* poets like Apollinaire and Cendrars, 1910–14, gave him new resources. Liberated from the concept of naturalism in either colour, form or imagery, he now felt free to organize images poetically. The stylistic influence of Cubism is very apparent at first (*I and the Village*, 1911, New York, Museum of Modern Art), but gave way to a more open painterly style, often exuberant in colour (*The Poet Reclining*, 1915, London, Tate Gallery; *The Birthday*, 1915–23, New York, Guggenheim Museum). Once found, this Romantic allegorical language remained an adequate framework for his whole career and did not undergo any major transformation. Changes in mood more often than not reflect events in his personal life. In many works (e.g. *Time is a River without Banks*, 1930–9, New York, Museum of Modern Art) the content seems too personal to be anything but a poetic enigma: this is what the Surrealists admired in him.

In general the attitude of other artists to Chagall's work has been respect, but at a distance, and he remains an isolated figure in twentieth-century art history. Since the Second World War he has enjoyed growing public recognition and a remarkably successful public career.

Franz Meyer. *Chagall*, London and New York 1964.
Jean Cassou. *Chagall*, London and New York 1965.
Walter Erben. *Marc Chagall*, London and New York 1966.

Chamberlain, John. American sculptor, b. 1927 in Rochester, Indiana. Chamberlain was trained in Chicago. His early sculpture, influenced by David Smith, was linear and open, constructed largely from iron pipes. Later, developing the possibilities of twisted metal sheets, he emerged as an important sculptor in the late 1950s and early 1960s with assemblages made from the discarded metal of wrecked automobiles (*Johnnybird*, 1959). The past associations of his chosen material are not directly important to Chamberlain's work, however, and his purpose is not social commentary or irony; rather, he exploited his materials for their colour and abstract formal qualities. The grand scale and the suggestions of violence and energy in his work also could be compared with action painting, but Chamberlain's approach differs in its dependence for materials on the environment, specifically the environment of the discarded and the damaged; in this way he resembles several other artists of his period, especially Richard Stankiewicz, Mark di Suvero and Robert Rauschenberg. Around the mid-1960s Chamberlain also began working with other materials, such as fibreglass or urethane foam and plastic, which he crumpled in similar fashion to the metal.

Beginning in 1960, Chamberlain had numerous one-man shows in New York, on the West Coast and in Europe.

Barbara Rose. 'How to Look at John Chamberlain's Sculpture', *Art International* VII, January 1964.
Exhibition catalogue, *American Sculpture of the Sixties*, Los Angeles County Museum of Art, Los Angeles 1967.

Chapoval, Jules. Russian-French painter, b. 1919 in Kiev; d. 1951 in Paris. Chapoval went to Paris whilst still quite young. He had intended to become a doctor but gave up his medical studies to attend the École des Beaux-Arts in Marseilles and later Toulouse. He began to paint in 1940, and during his early period produced objective works. Later he evolved a geometrical abstract style, painting pictures in which he investigated the relationship between pictorial objects and pictorial space. During his late period he was completely preoccupied with this one problem. In 1947 Chapoval won the prize awarded by the *Jeune Peinture* association in Paris.

Charchoune, Serge. Russian painter, b. 1888 in Buruguslan, Russia. In 1912, after completing his training in Moscow, Charchoune went to live in Paris, where he painted Cubist pictures until he joined the Dada movement in 1921–2. In 1922 he also visited Berlin and had an exhibition in the Sturm Gallery. He contributed articles to various magazines at this time including *Merz, Mecano* and *Revue 391.* In 1935 he began to analyse the relationship between art and music, which has been the inspiration for the delicate monochrome abstracts of his mature period. Charchoune is now living in Paris.

Chastel, Roger. French painter, b. 1897 in Paris. From 1912 to 1914 Chastel attended the Académie Julian and the École des Beaux-Arts in Paris. After the war he worked as a caricaturist and also designed theatrical costumes. In 1928 he settled in Saint-Germain-en-Laye, where he is still living today. In 1940 he met P. Bonnard.

Although he came into contact with the Cubists and Fauvists Chastel was not influenced by them. During his early period he painted portraits, landscapes and still lifes, using fully modelled forms. Then, in c. 1950, he turned to abstract painting.

Exhibition catalogue, *R. Chastel*, Aix-en-Provence 1968.

Chighine, Alfredo. Italian painter and sculptor, b. 1914 in Milan. Chighine studied painting at the Istituto Superiore d'Arte Decorativa in Monza and sculpture at the Accademia di Brera in Milan. He is now living in Milan.

After an initial neo-Cubist phase, Chighine began to paint informal pictures. In these large-scale works the strongly coloured grounds are broken down into smaller, rhythmically organized areas by the dynamics of the superimposed linear design.

Chillida, Eduardo. Spanish sculptor, b. 1924. Chillida studied in Paris for three years (1948–51).

He then started to make sculptures in the Spanish wrought-iron tradition, turning out his pieces with the great craftsmanship and finish typical of his native district (San Sebastian). In this sense his works derive from Julio González and the painter Antonio Tapiès. At the same time he is intellectually attached to the advanced experimental sculpture typified by David Smith and Anthony Caro, both of whom have their roots in technology.

His work has progressed from jagged or twisted ribbons of metal, in the fifties, to more solid, block-like forms. It is always austere, pared down to the bare minimum. Whereas before he left his spaces free and unrestrained, he now encloses them and uses them as an element in the complete structure.

Chirico, Giorgio de. Italian painter, b. 1888 in Volo, Greece. De Chirico had already embarked on an engineering course when he decided to become a painter. He then trained at the Academies in Athens and Munich before going to Paris in 1911, where he associated with Apollinaire and his circle but without embracing their Cubist aesthetic. In fact, he was far more impressed by Henri Rousseau's primitive view of the world. In 1915 de Chirico returned to Italy and was called up for military service. Two years later, in 1917, he met Carlo Carrà and his brother Savinio in the military hospital in Ferrara and it was as a result of this meeting that the *Pittura Metafisica* movement was founded. In 1918–19 de Chirico lived in Florence and Rome, where he collaborated with the *Valori Plastici* group. From 1924 onwards he again spent a number of years in Paris and during the early part of his stay there associated with the Surrealists and contributed to their exhibitions. In 1929 he published his novel, *Hebdomeros*, and in 1930 created the décor for Krenek's *Orestes* in the Krolloper in Berlin. From 1935 to 1938 he again made Paris his principal centre. Since then he has lived in Milan, Paris, Florence and Rome.

De Chirico was influenced by various painters—Böcklin with his all-embracing art, Klinger with his Symbolism, Uccello, Masaccio and Piero della Francesca with their Classical clarity and grandeur—and also by Nietzsche with his novel philosophical conceptions. De Chirico first began to make a name for himself in 1911 with a series of townscapes depicting an anguished dream world, in which deserted squares are hemmed in by arcades and houses. These scenes are built up in stark perspective like a theatrical set, the solid mass presented by the blocks of houses standing in marked contrast to the absolute void of the open spaces. Because of this juxtapositioning of contrasting elements and because of the distortion produced by the monuments, the absurd towers and the wide range of framelike structures, which de Chirico has introduced into these scenes, they all assume a ghostly character. In the dead light the pictorial objects acquire an aura of timelessness, so that they look like monuments to themselves. From c. 1915 but more especially from 1917, the year of the *Pittura Metafisica*, the deserted squares in de Chirico's phantom townscapes are peopled by '*Manichini*', the faceless figures which he constructed from a weird assortment of objects (biscuits, fragments of maps, etc.). These 'displaced' figures with their air of melancholy evoke mythical characters: Hector and Andromache, metaphysicians and troubadours. The sense of threat, the nihilism and the pathos which inform these works are derived from the philosophy of Nietzsche. Kafka and Proust are kindred spirits.

De Chirico rejected the traditional method of perception employed by the naturalistic painters and evolved a new psychological method, in which objects are seen as isolated phenomena. This innovation, which was enthusiastically propagated by Apollinaire during de Chirico's first stay in Paris, gave a vital impetus to Dadaism and the incipient Surrealist movement before 1918. Max Ernst and, subsequently, Tanguy, Magritte and Delvaux all drew on de Chirico's stylistic discoveries in their early periods.

In c. 1918, however, i.e. shortly after the theoretical formulation of the aesthetics of the *Pittura Metafisica*, de Chirico again changed his style. The great Classical works of the Renaissance began to fire his imagination and from 1919 onwards he moved away from his disconcerting dream world, producing Classical landscapes, paintings of Roman villas and figure compositions with sad groups of horses. These works are more in line with visible reality and consequently more representational. During his second long stay in Paris (from 1924 onwards) de Chirico, prompted by the current success of his early pictures amongst the up and coming Surrealists, reverted to his 'metaphysical' themes. But by then his style had become more pictorial and more florid and was less amenable to the harsh reality of an object world. The luminosity of Renoir, the pathos of Delacroix and Géricault and the vigorous realism of Courbet concerned him more deeply than the pictorial definition of his own experiences in terms of inanimate objects. In the end de Chirico opted for the past, developing an historicizing style which has become more and more academic. Although his late works are quite excellent in their own way, they lack the poetic quality which distinguishes his early metaphysical paintings.

J. T. Soby. *Giorgio de Chirico*, New York 1955.
Giorgio de Chirico. *Memorie della mia Vita*, Milan 1962.

Christo, Jachareff. Bulgarian sculptor, b. 1935 in Gabrova, Bulgaria. After training at the Academies in Sofia and Vienna from 1955 to 1957 Christo went to Paris in 1958. There he joined the *Nouveaux Réalistes* and, together with Bertholo, Castro, Pinheiro and Voss, became a founder member of the *KWY*. He is now living in New York. Christo first made a name for himself with his assemblages of oil casks (Cologne, June 1961; Paris, Rue Visconti, June 1962) and his *empaquetages*, in which mundane objects are arranged in transparent packages. Since 1964–5, he has been designing store fronts, i.e. shop windows hung with cloth.

Chryssa (Chryssa Vardea Mavromichali). Greek-American sculptress, b. 1933 in Athens. She studied at the Académie de la Grande Chaumière, Paris, 1953–4, and the California School of Fine Arts, San Francisco, 1954–5. Her early works were metal reliefs (*Cycladic Book* series, 1955–6), and blocks with the background cut away from raised images, as in printer's type, which revealed her continuing interest in communication symbols—letters of the alphabet, books, journals, arrows and other directional signals. She moved to the USA in 1957.

She first used neon—which has figured prominently in all her subsequent work—in 1962 (*Times Square Sky*); here, neon letters are cut out, detached from the monolithic backgrounds of her tablet period. The largest work of this type is *The Gates to Times Square* (1966), a series of eight structures in stainless steel and neon through which the spectator can walk. *Analysis of the Letter Y* (1967, neon and Plexiglass) includes a rheostat, allowing the spectator to control the light intensity.

Diane Waldman. *Chryssa: Selected Works 1955–1967*. Pace Gallery, New York 1968.

Chwistek, Leon. Polish painter and art theorist, b. 1884 in Zakopane; d. 1944 in Berwisze, near Moscow. Chwistek was Professor of Logic at the University of Lemberg, a mathematician and philosopher and the author of an original doctrine which he called 'The Multiplicity of Realities'. He also belonged to the 'Formists', an artists' association which existed from 1917 to 1922. As the leading theorist of this association he insisted on the primacy of form and of the imagination over external reality. With their deliberate, rhythmical construction Chwistek's Formist pictures reveal the influence of both Futurism and Cubism. A characteristic feature of his paintings is the reproduction of identical elements in contrasting structural and colour zones. It was on the basis of this technique that he formulated the principle of Strefism, which he advanced in c. 1925 in order to give a new direction to the Formist movement. Subsequently, this approach brought him into conflict with Strzeminski, who advocated an opposite approach based on 'unism'. But it was well received by the young Polish artists of the 1930s.

Cierici, Fabricio. Italian painter, b. 1913 in Milan. Cierici trained as an architect and obtained his diploma at the Architectural College in Rome in 1937. As a student he was deeply impressed by the artistic and architectural monuments of the Renaissance, Mannerist and Baroque periods which he encountered in Rome. Like his friendship with the Surrealist Alberto Savinio, which dates from 1936, they were to exert a crucial influence on his subsequent development. In the paintings which he produced after the Second World War fantastic, magical visions are incorporated into a rigorous, architectonic framework. The unreality of these works, many of which are arranged as cycles, is heightened by their cool, pale blue and green colouring. Cierici is also an important book illustrator and has designed theatre costumes and décors.

Exhibition catalogue, *Fabricio Cierici*, Berlin 1968.

Cimiotti, Emil. German sculptor, b. 1927 in Göttingen, Germany. After serving his apprenticeship as a stonemason from 1946 to 1948, Cimiotti trained as a sculptor (first in Stuttgart and then under Hartung in Berlin) from 1949 to 1953. Subsequently he became a pupil of Zadkine in Paris. Since 1963 he has been teaching at the Academy in Brunswick. Cimiotti produces abstract bronze sculptures of natural scenes (mountains, clouds, etc.), which appear to hover in mid-air.

H. Wille. *Emil Cimiotti*, Göttingen 1966.

Ciucurencu, Alexandru. Rumanian painter, b. 1903 in Tulcea. He studied in Bucharest and Paris (with André Lhôte). He has exhibited in the Venice Biennale in 1954 and 1956. His art is richly coloured and full of light, with a lyrical quality.

Ciurlionis, Mykolas Konstantas. Lithuanian painter and musician, b. 1875 in Varena, Lithuania; d. 1911 in Warsaw. After studying music in Leipzig and Warsaw, Ciurlionis painted his first pastels in 1902, when he was under the influence of Odilon Redon. In 1905 he enrolled at the Academy of Art in Warsaw. He then made contact with the Rosicrucians but shortly afterwards had a complete mental breakdown and died in a sanatorium without recovering his sanity. Ciurlionis, who had been looked upon as an infant prodigy, had synaesthetic responses. Partly as a result of this gift, partly as a result of his strong inclination to mysticism, he surrendered himself up to the old Romantic notion of the affinity between music and painting, one which had been revived in his day by the Symbolists and *Jugendstil* artists. He wanted to 'paint music' and his pictures, which he called 'Fugues' or 'Sea Sonatas', were composed in accordance with musical laws. Melody was expressed by linear factors, pitch by nuances of colour, and musical tempi (andante, scherzo) by long curves or short zigzag lines. Although Ciurlionis still used objective forms in his early period, he soon developed a preference for more abstract components. In his later work, *Jugendstil* arabesques, circular forms, rhythmical gradations and abstract ornaments evoke 'universal landscapes' or cosmic visions. Although these paintings are not abstract in the full sense of the word, Ciurlionis must none the less be regarded as a precursor of modern abstract art.

N. Worobiew. *M. K. Ciurlionis: der Litauische Maler und Musiker*, Leipzig 1938.

Clará Ayats, Josep. Spanish sculptor, b. 1878 in Olot, Catalonia; d. 1958. During his early period Clará Ayats created Symbolist sculptures which reveal the influence of Rodin and betray a preoccupation with visual and atmospheric values. But from 1900 onwards he moved towards a Mediterranean style similar to that evolved by the French Catalan artist Maillol, producing works of greater formal precision which depend for their effect on the disposition of sculptural volumes in space. The poise, the physical and mental balance, the Olympic indifference of Clará Ayats' mature work are clearly seen in his *Goddess*, which stands in the Plaça de Catalunya in Barcelona, in his seated *Serenity*, and in numerous female nudes. In 1969 Clará Ayats' former studio on Calatrava Street in Barcelona was opened as the Clará Museum.

Claret, Joan. Spanish painter, b. 1929 in Barcelona. Claret is undoubtedly the most consistent of the Catalan school of geometrical abstract painters. Basically, his pictures are *grisailles* built up on white grounds from networks of lines and areas of grey which he superimposes one on top of the other to produce an impression of depth and transparency.

Clark, Lygia. Brazilian painter, b. 1921 in Minas Gerais, Brazil. Clark studied under Roberto Burle Marx in Brazil and Fernand Léger and Arpad Szenes in Paris. She had her first exhibition in Paris in 1951 and has since contributed works to the São Paulo Bienal and the Venice Biennale. Clark paints concrete pictures with bold, flat geometrical designs.

Lygia Clark, Rio de Janeiro 1958.

Clarke, Geoffrey. British sculptor, b. 1924. He excels in numerous techniques: sculpture, stained glass—some of his work was incorporated into Basil Spence's Coventry Cathedral—and enamel work. His sculpture can be seen in the Tate Gallery, London.

Clatworthy, Robert. British sculptor, b. 1928 in Bridgwater, Somerset. Clatworthy attended the Slade School, among others, from 1951 to 1954, and had his first exhibition in 1955. He has recently been teaching at the Chelsea and St. Martin's Schools of Art, London.

Claus, Jürgen. German painter, b. 1935 in Berlin. Claus undertook a course of study at Munich University in 1955 but withdrew in 1960 to become a full-time painter. He is now living in Munich. Claus makes artistic arrangements consisting of what he calls *Hochbilder* (literally 'raised pictures', i.e. reliefs) and tablets of pure colour. This process, which is basically architectural, depends for its effect on an 'open form' conception and on variable components. Claus also writes on art.

Clausen, Franciska. Danish painter, b. 1899 in Apenrade, Denmark. After studying under Moholy-Nagy and Archipenko in Germany from 1922 to 1924, Clausen continued to study under Léger for a further nine years. She then turned to neo-Plasticism, which she tried hard to promote in her native Denmark. She was Mondrian's most faithful disciple.

Clavé, Antoni. Spanish painter and designer, b. 1913 in Barcelona. He moved to Paris in 1939, and there produced many exciting sets for the theatre—plays, ballet and opera. Some of his most successful were done for Roland Petit's ballet company. His figurative paintings are richly and boldly coloured; he also does still lifes, and has produced lithographs for book illustrations.

Clough, Prunella. British painter, b. 1919 in London. In 1938–9 she studied at the Chelsea School of Art, where she has also since taught. She was given a retrospective exhibition at the Whitechapel Art Gallery in 1960 and is represented at the Tate Gallery. Clough first began to work against the background of wartime and postwar Neo-Romanticism, in which she shared for a time. In the 1950s she evolved a more objective, semi-abstract treatment of industrial landscapes and workers. Since then, she has tended towards a more abstract imagery, but this is balanced by a tightly knit material construction and a formal language of great individuality and variety.

Cobbaert, Jan. Belgian painter, b. 1909 in Héverlée-les-Louvain. After a protracted early period, in which he painted in a somewhat dramatic style, Cobbaert has recently begun to produce fantasy works, which testify to both his imaginative powers and his powers of observation. At one point in his career Cobbaert flirted briefly with abstract art.

Cobra. This was the name given to an international artists' association that existed in Europe from 1948 to 1951. It was founded in Paris by Karel Appel, Constant, Corneille, Christian Dotremont, Asger Jorn and Noiret and constituted an extension of the activities and manifestations of the Danish *Spiralen* group, the Belgian *Bureau International de Surréalisme Révolutionnaire* (which was founded in Brussels in 1947 by Jorn, Dotremont and others) and the Dutch

Experimental Group with its magazine *Reflex* (both of which were founded by Constant in 1948). The name *Cobra* was made up from the initials of the cities of Copenhagen, Brussels and Amsterdam, in which the original members of the association were living. Later other artists—such as Atlan, Piene, Alechinsky and K. O. Götz—also joined. Eight issues of a *Cobra Revue* and fifteen monographs were published by the association, which also staged various joint exhibitions: *Hoest* (Copenhagen 1948) and the first and second *Exposition Internationale d'Art Experimental-Cobra* (Amsterdam 1949 and Liège 1951). Both the *Cobra Revue* and the exhibitions testify to the interest of the *Cobra* artists in folk and primitive art and in spontaneous expression. The *Cobra* movement, which owed much to the enterprise of Jorn, paved the way in Europe for the development of a type of informal art with highly expressive features. The social, philosophical and urban commitment of the *Cobra* artists continued to make itself felt in the *Mouvement International pour un Bauhaus Imaginiste* (1953–7) and the Internationale of the Situationists (1957 onwards), to which a number of them also belonged.

Ch. Dotremont, 'Cobra', *L'Oeil*, No. 96, December 1962.
Catalogue, *Cobra 1949–51*, Stedelijk Museum, Amsterdam 1962.
Bert Schierbeek. *The Experimentalists*, Amsterdam (n.d.).

Cocteau, Jean. French novelist, dramatist, critic and draughtsman, b. 1889 in Maisons-Lafitte; d. 1963 in Milly-la-Foèt. In 1908 Cocteau gave his first poetry reading in the Théâtre Fémine in Paris, and met various French writers including Lucien Daudet, Marcel Proust and Edmond Rostand. In 1910 he met Igor Stravinsky and Serge Diaghilev, and saw the Russian Ballet, which inspired him to write a ballet of his own—*Le Dieu Bleu*—which was produced in the Théâtre du Chatelet in 1912. He then took up flying, following the example of his friend Roland Garros, who was a fully trained pilot. In 1916 Cocteau established close contact with the poets and painters of Montparnasse: Blaise Cendrars, Guillaume Apollinaire, Max Jacob, André Salmon, Amedeo Modigliani and Pablo Picasso. The year 1917 brought the first choreographic performance of his *Parade*, and from 1918 onwards he concentrated on work for the theatre. This led to collaboration with composers and painters, and Cocteau joined with Stravinsky in publishing the musical manifesto *Le Coq et l'Arlequin*. He also became the spokesman for the *Société des Nouveaux Jeunes* and *Les Six*. In 1920, 1921 and 1922 Cocteau had three successive premières: *Le Boeuf sur le toît* (music by Darius Milhaud); *Les Mariées de la tour Eiffel*; and *Antigone* (music by A. Honegger, stage sets and costumes by P. Picasso). In 1926 Cocteau produced book illustrations. But in the previous year he had become addicted to narcotics, and for the next five years was completely dependent on opium. This phase of his life came to an end in 1930, the year in which his first film—*Le Sang d'un poète*—was released. There then followed a fruitful period, in which Cocteau produced numerous book illustrations and worked extensively for the theatre. From 1938 onwards he also wrote novels. In 1942 Cocteau pleaded in court for the writer Jean Giono, and obtained his release from Fresne prison. During the closing years of the war Cocteau found it virtually impossible to engage in creative activity, but in the immediate postwar period he wrote various film scripts and created his own famous series of films: *La Belle et la Bête* in 1946, *L'Aigle à deux Têtes* in 1947, *Les Parents terribles* in 1949, *Orphée* in 1950 and—after a serious illness—*Le Testament d'Orphée*. Between 1945 and 1963 he also wrote more than half of his poetical works. He was in the USA in 1948, and later visited Egypt, Palestine, Istanbul and Athens. During his late period Cocteau produced a large number of paintings, drawings and pottery articles, and also created theatrical designs. In his painting and draughtsmanship Cocteau was influenced by Picasso. He dealt with a wide range of themes, but Harlequin—the theatrical figure *par excellence*—and Orpheus—the personification of the poet—were his favourite *motifs*.

Friedrich Hagen. *Zwischen Stern und Spiegel: Jean Cocteau als Zeichner,* Munich 1956.
J.-J. Kihm. *Cocteau,* Paris 1960.
Exhibition catalogue, *Jean Cocteau,* Hamburg 1966.

Coetzee, Christo. South African painter, b. 1930 in Johannesburg. After studying at the Slade School in London Coetzee made his name with pictures and reliefs which might best be described as Neo-Baroque. They are chiefly remarkable for their physical texture. Although abstract, they none the less evoke organic or natural forms.

Cohen, Bernard. British painter, b. 1933 in London. Cohen is the younger brother of Harold Cohen. He attended the St. Martin's School of Art for a year in 1950–1; he then studied at the Slade School from 1951 to 1954. His first one-man exhibition took place at the Midland Group Gallery, Nottingham, in 1958. He was a teacher at Ealing Art School, London, from 1961 to 1964. Cohen adopted the hard-edge style of painting that developed in the USA through the work of Barnett Newman, Mark Rothko and Ad Reinhardt. His work now, with its partly improvised, partly controlled line, is close to semantic painting.

Cohen, Harold. British painter, b. 1928 in London. Cohen is Bernard Cohen's brother. He studied at the Slade School in London from 1948 to 1952 and has been teaching there since 1962. He is now living in London. Up to c. 1964, Cohen's paintings were composed of bands of colour. K. Hoffmann has described

these works in the following terms: 'Simple sequences alternate with narrow bands and bulges; the individual bands either disintegrate or form serpentine designs; like muscle fibres they encircle organic openings ... and intertwine to form independent organisms.' Since 1966, Cohen has been covering his picture surfaces with dots of paint so that they look as if they were studded with stars. Wavy lines now run across the canvas, the structure of the work appears involuted and the ornamental character, which was a feature of his earlier paintings, is far less pronounced.

Coldstream, Sir William. British painter and administrator, b. 1908 in Belford, Northumberland. Coldstream trained at the Slade School from 1926 to 1929. He had an early association with the London Group and, after working in documentary films from 1934 to 1937, with Claude Rogers and Victor Pasmore he founded the Euston Road School in 1938. He lives in London and, since 1949, he has been Slade Professor of Fine Art at London University. Sometime Trustee of both the National Gallery and the Tate Gallery, he has been Chairman of the National Advisory Council on Art Education since 1958.

On resuming painting in 1937, Coldstream devoted himself exclusively to the study of exact representation, avoiding conventions evolved in the past. His output, chiefly of portraits, has been small and not often exhibited, although he was given an exhibition at the South London Art Gallery in 1962 and is represented at the Tate Gallery.

Coleman, Glenn O. American painter, b. 1887 in Springfield, Ohio; d. 1932 in Long Beach, Long Island, N.Y. He spent his youth in Indianapolis, where he received some preliminary art training. In 1905 he moved to New York where he studied with R. Henri and E. Shinn and first exhibited in a group show with members of the Henri circle—R. Kent, G. Pène du Bois, G. Bellows and others. His early paintings and lithographs are decidedly figurative, with a pervading sense of nostalgic sorrow. *Minetta Lane, Night* (1910, lithograph) reveals a brooding quality, a sense of terrifying night streets and imminent danger. After 1927, the figure becomes less important and architecture dominates. The greater impersonality and structural emphasis of composition is usually executed in lively colours and with a bolder painterliness than his previous works. The preoccupation with structure can be seen in the 1927 *By the Bridge* (Clinton, N.Y., Hamilton College, Coll. E. W. Root) where the weight and density of the architecture pushing out into and receding from the viewers' space is the artist's main concern. He was given an important one-man show at the Downtown Gallery, N.Y., in 1930, two years before his death. His oeuvre deals with the life and scenes of New

York, except for three 'arrangements', a few pictures done on a holiday in Cuba and some very late works depicting Long Island.

C. A. Glassgold. *Glenn O. Coleman*, New York 1932.

Colla, Ettore. Italian painter and sculptor, b. 1899 in Parma; d. 1968. In 1926 Colla settled in Rome and lived there all his life. After working as a painter he turned to sculpture in 1947. In 1951, along with Burri and Capogrossi, he became a founder member of the *Origine* group, which was to play such an important part in the development of Italian art, and in 1952 he helped launch the magazine *Arti Visive*. Since 1953–4, he has been composing sculptures from ready-made, iron objects. The poetry of iron and the poetry of the *objet trouvé* are in fact the two major and co-ordinate qualities of his static, linear works, in which he reveals a preference for emblematic or heraldic subjects.

Exhibition catalogue, *Lo Spazio dell'Imagine*, Foligno 1967.

Collage. The collage, which was foreshadowed by certain aspects of *trompe l'oeil* and folk art, is one of the most important of all twentieth-century art forms. The first artists to make systematic use of the collage (from the French *coller*=to stick) were Picasso and Braque. From 1912 onwards they incorporated newspaper articles, newspaper titles and pre-printed patterns into their paintings and drawings. Thus, a piece of reality—which usually reflected some aspect of the 'civilized' world—entered into the work of art, where it fulfilled a dual function: on the one hand it existed in its own right as a representative element of the real world, whilst on the other hand it was used as a formal element within the total composition. But the essential quality of the collage—and this is true in all cases—was its tendency to break the bounds of the traditional two-dimensional painting, thus creating a spatial or environmental painting or sculpture. Over and above this, of course, the collage technique enabled the artist to introduce elements of social criticism and to make direct statements on the current political situation. This process of selection and 'acquisition' (see 'Ready-mades') is, of course, capable of infinite extension since the artist has the whole of his environment to choose from. For this reason the collage technique has been expanded to assemblage and now includes *décollage* (unsticking), *découpage* (cutting), *brûlage* (burning) and *déchirage* (tearing). ('The collage constantly provokes the discovery of new techniques for the distortion, alienation, integration and destruction of its material' —F. Mon.) The principal application of the collage technique has been in the sphere of painting, where it has been adopted by representatives of virtually every major art movement of the twentieth century, including Futurism (Carrà and Severini), Dada

(Schwitters, Hausmann and Man Ray), Surrealism (Ernst and Miró), Constructivism (El Lissitzky and Moholy-Nagy), Informal Art (Dubuffet, Motherwell, Klein and Burri), *Nouveau Réalisme* (Hains, Rotella, Arman and Spoerri) and Pop Art (Hamilton, Dine and Oldenburg). For a number of artists—such as Schwitters, Heartfield, Nevelson and Marca-Relli— the collage constitutes the central feature of their entire oeuvre.

W. Seitz. Exhibition catalogue, *The Art of Assemblage*, Museum of Modern Art, New York 1961.
Allan Kaprow. *Assemblage, Environment, and Happenings*, New York 1966.
H. Janis and R. Blesh. *Collage*, New York 1967.
H. Wescher, *Collage*, Cologne 1968.

Collignon, Georges. Belgian painter, b. 1923 in Liège. After training at the Academy of Art in Liège Collignon turned abstract from 1949 onwards. He joined the *Jeune Peinture belge* and *Cobra* associations, and won the 'Prix de la Jeune Peinture' in 1950. In 1951 he settled in Paris, where he collaborated with the architects of the EGAU group. Collignon has successfully reconciled constructive and Baroque elements.

Cologne Sonderbund Exhibition. The Cologne *Sonderbund* Exhibition, which was held in the municipal exhibition rooms in Cologne in 1912, was the first one to provide a really comprehensive survey of modern developments in European art. Van Gogh, Cézanne and Munch each had a separate room, while a smaller room was devoted to pictures by El Greco. In an article published in the *Blauer Reiter Almanach* in 1912 Franz Marc wrote: 'Cézanne and El Greco are kindred spirits. Today the works of both these artists stand at the threshold of a new epoch of painting. Both sensed the intrinsically mystical construction inherent in man's attitude to the world, which poses a major problem for the present generation.' This was the kernel of the Cologne *Sonderbund* Exhibition, and around it the organizers arranged works by Gauguin, Signac, Picasso and the new French, Swiss, English and Dutch artists. The *Brücke* artists came from Berlin, the *Blauer Reiter* artists from Munich. E. L. Kirchner and E. Heckel decorated the chapel, whose stained-glass windows were designed by Thorn-Prikker. The Cologne *Sonderbund* Exhibition was an important exhibition which effectively demonstrated the range of the new anti-naturalistic movement in European art.

Sonderbund: Internationaler Ausstellungskatalog, Ausstellungshalle der Stadt Köln am Aachener Tor, Cologne 1912.

Colquhoun, Robert. British painter, b. 1914 in Kilmarnock, Scotland; d. 1962 in London. Colquhoun studied at the Glasgow School of Art and settled in London in 1941. With his friends John

Minton and Robert MacBryde, he contributed greatly to the tense, angular romanticism of wartime and postwar British art. He is represented at the Tate Gallery and also designed for the theatre, including *King Lear* (Stratford, 1953).

Colville, Alex. Canadian painter, b. 1920 in Toronto. Growing up at St. Catherines, Ontario, and Amherst, Nova Scotia, he studied at the art school of Mount Allison University, Sackville, New Brunswick, from 1938 to 1942. His first significant work as a painter was as an Official War Artist with the Canadian Army, 1944–6, in the Mediterranean and North European areas. During his teaching at Mount Allison University, 1946–63, he developed a 'Magic Realist' style in the painting of familiar subjects; it shows a high degree of precision in execution and a formal purity of style (*Hound in a Field*, 1958, Ottawa, National Gallery of Canada). He has painted murals for public buildings; designed the Canadian Centennial coinage (1967); and executed serigraphs. He was appointed to the Canada Council in 1966 and the Order of Canada (Service Medal) in 1967. He lives at Sackville and exhibits regularly in New York and London.

Patrick Hutchings. 'The Celebrative Realism of Alex Colville', *Westerly* No. 2, Univ. of Western Australia Press, August 1965.

Colvin, Marta. Chilean sculptress, b. 1917 in Chillán. She studied in Santiago, and visited Europe in 1948, where she learned from Henry Moore, Ossip Zadkine and Henri Laurens. Eventually she moved to France and settled there permanently. Here she was able to give expression in her work to the awesome strength of the Chilean mountains and the mystery of Chile's legends, which were at the root of her inspiration.

Combine Painting. In concept an extension of the collage, Combine Painting involves the use of any flat or three-dimensional materials, in addition to paint, that are usually still attached to a canvas or other surface related to the wall. In American art the term 'combine' was originated by Robert Rauschenberg, who used, in combination with a bold painting style, not only paper, wood, rubber, metal and cloth materials, but also stuffed animals and electrical apparatus such as operating radios, fans and light bulbs. Rauschenberg's combines date from 1953 to the early 1960s and reflect the prevalent use of discarded 'junk' materials in the art of the 1950s and the growing trends towards a fusion of painterly and sculptural concepts and environmental art.

William C. Seitz. *The Art of Assemblage*, Museum of Modern Art, New York 1961.
Alan Solomon. *Robert Rauschenberg*, New York 1963.

Comic strip (Comics, *Bande dessinée*). Although it had a number of precursors, the comic strip as such is an invention of the late nineteenth century. 'Funnies', 'cartoons' or 'comic strips' have been featured in the Sunday supplements of North American newspapers since 1895. They appear in serial form and depend for their continuity, not on a story line, but on a 'grotesque' figure. They are published purely for their entertainment value and today the comic strip is one of the most popular of all visual media. (The number of comic strip readers in the USA alone is said to be 90 million.) R. Hiepe has suggested that the popularity and wide circulation of the comic strip is due to its stereotype simplification, for in this medium normally complex pictures are reduced to a standard pattern and broken down into component panels. The comic strip artists utilize every conceivable *motif*, from animal stories to space travel, and of recent years have attached growing importance to political themes. Although the comic strip was once influenced by artists like William Hogarth (1697–1764) and Honoré Daumier (1808–79), of recent years it is the artists who have been influenced by the comic strip. Some twentieth-century artists began their careers as commercial artists and one of these—Lyonel Feininger—produced two comic strip series as early as 1906. But it was in the mid-1950s, when artists began to take such an active interest in the trivia of modern life, that the comic strip really came into its own. Like advertisements and posters, it has been incorporated into the works of many contemporary painters. Some of these have simply used the comic strip as an occasional *motif*, others have dealt at length with both its formal and its thematic aspects. The Californian Jess Collins, who constructed collages between 1953 and 1959, is an example of the first type of artist, whilst Öyvind Fahlström, whose entire output since 1958 has been based on the comic strip, is typical of the second. The incorporation of comic strip features has enabled contemporary artists to formalize and so reduce the emotional content of their work (Roy Lichtenstein and Valerio Adami), to break down the picture surface into component sequences (Hervé Télémaque and Bernard Rancillac) and to use undifferentiated, flat colours (Allan d'Arcangelo and Otman Alt). The development of the comic strip is linked with that of Pop Art and Science Fiction.

H. Politzer. *The Funnies: An American Idiom*, New York 1967.
The Penguin Book of Comics, Middlesex 1967.
Exhibition catalogue, *Bande Dessinée et Figuration Narrative*, Musée des Arts Décoratifs, Paris 1967.
'Comics', *Tendenzen*, September 1968.

Computer art. The concept of producing works of art by mechanical means is not new, but it is only in the last twenty years or so that these simple mechanical methods have been superseded by the development of sophisticated computers capable of being programmed in the most complex ways. Since the introduction of computers into science and industry, artists have explored the possibility of using them for aesthetic purposes; and from about 1965–6, when the term 'computer art' became current, the results obtained have often been beautiful and highly original.

Artists using computers to produce graphics, poetry, music, etc., need at least a basic knowledge of the technical processes involved; many computer artists started out as technicians and have become absorbed in the aesthetically interesting results which have sometimes emerged from their work. The American designer William A. Fetter is an example of this—his computer drawings made to find the most efficient arrangement for an aeroplane cockpit have won various art awards.

Computer art is hard to define in terms of style, since there is enormous variation in the works produced and no one variation can be called typical. Kenneth C. Knowlton (USA) and Manfred R. Schroeder (Germany) have made graphics based on photographs of the human face and figure; while the Germans Georg Nees and Frieder Nake have worked out geometric patterns based on a few simple sign elements. Nees also produces computer sculpture, as does the Spanish artist J. L. Alexanco. Other important computer artists and groups include Jack P. Citron, John Whitney—who makes computer films—and A. Michael Noll in the USA; Herbert W. Franke in Germany; the Computer Technique Group, Japan (which disbanded in 1969); the *ars intermedia* group in Vienna, led by Otto Beckmann; and Alan Sutcliffe in Britain. There is a programme of collaboration between artists and mathematicians at Madrid University, and centres of computer art activity in Buenos Aires, Amsterdam, Germany and Italy. The major exhibition in this field was *Cybernetic Serendipity*, organized by Jasia Reichardt and held at the Institute of Contemporary Arts, London, in 1968. Käthe Schröder has organized a travelling exhibition, *Computer Art—on the Eve of Tomorrow*, which was first shown in Hanover in 1969 and moved to Munich, Hamburg, Oslo, Brussels, Rome and Tokyo. There was also a section devoted to computer graphics at the 1970 Venice Biennale. Exhibitions in the US have included *World Exhibition of Computer Graphics*, at the Howard Wise Gallery, New York, 1965; the 1965 Fall Joint Computer Conference at Las Vegas; and a travelling show organized by the Western Association of Art Museums and first put on at Dartmouth College, Hanover, New Hampshire, in 1966.

Traditional criteria cannot be applied to computer-produced art. The fact that very often it needs no manual skill has proved a great stumbling-block to some critics, who refuse to accept it as art. Nevertheless, work produced by computers and intended to have some aesthetic value will be a tremendous influence on the opinions and attitudes of the art-loving public in the future—not least because it brings together in a unique way the 'two cultures' of the humanities and the sciences. In the words of Herbert W. Franke, it 'has elucidated the interaction between art, technology and science as no medium has ever done before'.

Jasia Reichardt. Catalogue, *Cybernetic Serendipity*, ICA, London 1968; *The Computer in Art*, London and New York 1971.
Lloyd Sumner. *Computer Art and Human Response*, Charlottesville (Va.) 1968.
Georg Nees. *Generative computergraphik*, Munich 1969.
Herbert W. Franke. *Computer Graphics—Computer Art*, London and New York 1971.

Concrete art. The most important early examples of concrete art, which were produced by artists like Kandinsky, Kupka, Mondrian and Malevich, date from the 1920s. The actual concept was formulated in 1930 when the *Manifesto of Concrete Art* was published in the first and only issue of the magazine *Art Concret* by Theo van Doesburg. In this manifesto van Doesburg called for a type of abstract art in which the pictorial elements would not be based on natural phenomena and would not serve lyrical or symbolic ends. On the contrary, they were to be simple, technically precise and purely visual forms, which would be completely self-sufficient. Van Doesburg died in the following year, but his ideas were taken up and further developed by the *Abstraction-Création* association between 1931 and 1936. The five annuals published by the association provide an important and authentic commentary on the early evolution of concrete art. Later Max Bill became the spokesman for this movement. In 1944 he organized the first international exhibition of concrete art in Basle and founded the magazine *Abstrakt/Konkret*. By 1960, the year in which Bill staged a comprehensive exhibition in Zürich under the title *Concrete Art: Fifty Years of Development*, concrete art was firmly established as a new artistic movement with numerous publications to its credit and with groups in many different countries, the most important being those in Switzerland, Italy and South America. Many more recent groups, such as the Italian *Gruppo T* and *Gruppo N*, have also been influenced by the theories and works of concrete art. So too have hard edge, Op Art, Primary Structures and many other contemporary movements. Concrete art has often been represented as an essentially geometrical art form. This is a completely mistaken view, as has been pointed out by Margit Staber: 'It [concrete art] is linked with the concept of structure, which is here understood as the conscious organizing principle or, to be more precise, the controlled and controllable organizing schema in the creative process. Ungeometric, amorphous formations are just as likely to be found there as precise, geometric elements . . .' According to Max Bill the aim of those engaged in concrete art is 'to objectify things which did not previously exist in a visible or tangible form . . . to represent abstract thoughts in a sensuous and tangible form . . .'

Exhibition catalogue, *Konkrete Kunst*, Zürich 1960.
Margit Staber. *Konkrete Kunst*, St. Gallen 1966.

Concrete poetry. The work of the international Concretist movement, which uses words as a graphic medium, is related to the typographical experiments of Dada and Futurism. The poet/artist makes patterns and pictures out of words which bear some relationship to each other and together have some meaning; their sense is echoed by the form in which they are displayed. The words themselves can be printed in different colours and mixtures of type-faces; or one word can be used over and over again to make a pattern which may produce overtones suggestive of other thoughts and ideas conjured up by the word. Each work determines its own shape and the amount of space it will require. It may be, in the words of the Scots poet Ian Hamilton Finlay, a case of 'separating the letters of an individual word in order to disclose new decorative and semantic possibilities'.

Finlay is the best-known concrete poet in Britain. He runs a publishing company, the Wild Hawthorn Press, which produces prints and cards with his highly individual stamp. He also edits the magazine *Poor. Old. Tired. Horse.* Other leading figures are Dom Sylvester Houédard, Pierre Garnier, the Austrian Ernst Jandl and the Brazilian Pedro Xisto.

Conder, Charles. British painter, b. 1868 in London; d. 1909 in Virginia Water, Surrey. He went to Australia in 1884 and studied in Sydney and Melbourne; from there he moved to Paris. He had an exhibition with William Rothenstein in Paris in 1891. In 1893 he became a member of the New English Art Club. He settled in London in 1897, and had his first British show in 1899 at the Carfax Gallery. A memorial exhibition of his work was held at the Tate Gallery in 1927.

Condopoulos, Alecos. Greek painter, b. 1905 in Lamia. He trained in Athens and spent two years in Paris, 1931–3. He is a forerunner of abstract painting in Greece. His work is consistently geometrical; it is richly varied and vividly coloured.

Consagra, Pietro. Italian sculptor, b. 1920 in Mazara del Vallo, Sicily. Consagra studied from 1938 onwards at the Academy of Art in Palermo. In 1944 he went to Rome, where he formed a friendship with Guttuso and entered into close contact with the New Realists. But in 1947 he joined the non-objective movement and became a founder member of the *Forma 1* group together with Dorazio, Turcato, Perilli, etc. He then came under the influence of the French abstract artists, especially Magnelli. In 1960 he won the International Sculpture Award at the Biennale in Venice. In the following year he joined the *Continuità* group and in 1966 created a large fountain for the Palazzo Farnesina in Rome, where he is now living.

Consagra's first sculptures were carved in the Neo-Expressionist style developed by the Roman school. From 1947 onwards he produced abstract metal constructions and by 1950 had evolved his own personal style. The constructions of this period consist of multi-layered metal walls, whose component sections were first cut from a single large sheet of metal with the aid of a template and then arranged in an overlapping pattern to form a relief structure. Over the years the depth of projection of Consagra's reliefs has gradually diminished and recently he has been constructing metal surfaces which are very nearly flat. These *Ferri trasparenti*, as he calls them, are all painted in a uniform, luminous colour and, with their indented edges and jagged holes, they look rather like silhouettes of tree trunks. Consagra usually works in bronze but occasionally uses charred timber.

U. Apollonio. *Pietro Consagra*, Rome 1957.
G. C. Argan. *Pietro Consagra*, Neuchâtel 1962.
Catalogue, *Pietro Consagra: Recent Sculpture*, Marlborough-Gerson Gallery, New York 1967–8.

Constant (Constant A. Nieuwenhys). Dutch painter, sculptor and architect, b. 1920 in Amsterdam. Constant studied at the Academy of Art in Amsterdam. In 1945 he painted his first 'experimental' pictures, which helped prepare the ground for the *Cobra* style. Then, in 1948, he joined the Experimental Group, from which the international *Cobra* movement subsequently emerged. But since 1952 his interest in painting has been largely replaced by a growing preoccupation with spatial and architectural problems. In 1953 he created his first sculptural constructions. Since 1956 he has been producing designs and models for his ideal urban project, *New Babylon*. Commenting on this scheme, he said that 'the world of *homo ludens*, i.e. the *New Babylon*, will be created by a concerted effort on the part of the masses; for it to be realized, the enormous creative potential which is lying unused in the masses will have to be activated'. Constant is now living in Amsterdam.

H. van Haaren. *Constant*, Amsterdam 1966.

Constructivism. An international style in painting, architecture and design; in painting, Constructivism may be seen as the logical conclusion of the Suprematist experiments of Malevich, the reduction of painting to abstract, geometrical essentials, and of the Post-Cubist work of artists such as Tatlin, Exter and Popova. Constructivism emerged as the dominant style in Russian art during the course of 1921, the point at which the first true consolidation of artistic policy in post-Revolutionary Russia was attempted. The establishment of the Institute of Art Culture (*Inkhuk*, founded in 1920), the rejection of Kandinsky's proposed course of instruction for the Institute, and the triumph of the Constructivist group (which included Rodchenko, Tatlin, Stepanova and others) was to lead to a mass exodus of Russian artists during the early twenties (Kandinsky,

Chagall, Gabo, Pevsner), and to the increasing isolation of those who, like Malevich, while remaining in Russia, refused to associate themselves with the Constructivist movement.

Tatlin's phrase 'the culture of materials' was to become the watchword of the new movement. There soon arose, however, two groups within Constructivism: those who, while announcing the 'death of easel painting', still envisaged the continuation of what was termed 'laboratory art'; and those who, like Tatlin, dreamed of the 'artist-engineer' and saw the primary role of Constructivism as fulfilling social needs. (The latter group may be termed 'Productivists'.) The devaluation of pure painting resulted, in any case, in Constructivism manifesting itself most strongly in the 'applied' fields of architecture and typography, and also in the theatre, where lively experiments by designers such as Popova, Stepanova and others continued for most of the twenties. The often extremely interesting projects by the most gifted of the Constructivist architects, men like Melnikov or the Vesnin brothers, fared less happily, remaining frequently no more than projects, due to the acute shortage of money and materials. In the field of printing and typography, one may point to the work of Rodchenko and Lissitzky, although the latter's work continued to show, at times, the marked influence of Suprematism; Camilla Gray has referred to the 'horizontal, static, heavy machine-rhythm of the Constructivists, as opposed to the diagonal, dynamic and spatial play of Lissitzky's Suprematist-derived work, with its far more subtle contrasts in scale and plane'.

J. L. Martin, B. Nicholson and N. Gabo (eds.). *Circle: International Survey of Constructive Art*, London and Toronto 1937.
Camilla Gray. *The Great Experiment: Russian Art 1863–1922*, London and New York 1962.
George Rickey. *Constructivism: Origins and Evolution*, New York 1967.

Conti, Primo. Italian painter, draughtsman and stage designer, b. 1900 in Florence. Conti is self-taught; his talent revealed itself early. His first works were done in an Impressionist manner, but he turned to Futurism, 1917–19. Later he allied himself with the ideas of the *Novecento*. His painting is notable for its finely blended colours, restrained figure composition and graphic exactness. It also reveals the artist's feeling of a close communion with nature.

Continuità Group. The *Continuità* group was formed in Rome in 1961 by Consagra, Dorazio, Perilli and Turcato, who had all been members of the *Forma* group. Later they were joined by Novelli, Bemporad, Fontana, G. and A. Pomodoro and Tancredi. Their spokesman was A. G. Argan. The *Continuità* group was strongly opposed to 'informal art'. It called for a reappraisal of Italian art, in

which formal qualities had always played an important role, and wanted to see the development of a modern Italian art form that would represent a natural extension of this tradition.

Cook, Roger. British painter, b. 1940 in London. From 1958 to 1963 he studied at the Slade, and in 1964 he won the Gulbenkian Purchase award. He exhibited in the New Generation Exhibition, and at that time his painting was a thoughtful and tasteful response to the American preoccupation with surface and the object quality of the canvas. His pictures were composed of several canvases joined together with plain colour surfaces balancing the colour against the shape of the composition.

Corinth, Lovis. German painter, b. 1858 in Tatiau, Germany; d. 1925 in Zandvoort, Holland. Corinth, the son of an East Prussian craftsman, studied in Königsberg (1876–80), Munich (1880–4), Antwerp (summer of 1884) and at the Académie Julian in Paris (1884–7). In 1891 he settled in Munich, where he associated with Leibl and Trübner and also came under the influence of the *Jugendstil* artists, Eckmann and Leistikov. In 1891 he also produced his first etchings and in 1894 his first lithographs. In 1900 he followed his friend Leistikov to Berlin and it was there that he made his mark as an artist. Acting on the advice of Max Liebermann, who helped to advance him, he joined the Berlin *Sezession*. In 1902 he was elected to the Committee of the *Sezession* and in 1911–12 and 1915 was its director. Although he visited the Tyrol and Italy after recovering from a serious illness in 1911–12 and paid regular visits to Urfeld-am-Walchensee from 1918 onwards, Berlin remained his principal residence. In 1903 he married the painter and writer Charlotte Behrend.

Corinth is the only painter of note to have come from East Prussia. After freeing himself from Courbet's influence and coming to terms with the works of Leibl and, more especially, Trübner (who was a personal friend), Corinth gradually evolved his own highly individual style. His early period was dominated by figure compositions, genre pictures and biblical scenes. Later, in Munich, his preoccupation with these media was superseded by a growing interest in landscape painting, which came to maturity in Berlin, when he associated with the Berlin landscapists. In Liebermann's circle Corinth's brushwork underwent a change: he overcame the last vestiges of his long academic training and developed a powerful, fiery and highly expressive style. His painting was anything but French. Indeed, there was even a touch of carelessness in the way he handled his materials and applied his paint. Grey was the dominant colour in his palette, just as it was in Liebermann's. Corinth's approach to his subjects was never rigid. On the contrary, his pictures are almost always anecdotal and in the portrayal of these anecdotes he did not fight shy of ugliness or cruelty. For example, he painted many slaughterhouse scenes featuring butchers and limbs of animals, in which he drew on memories of early childhood. But, although Corinth continued to paint figure compositions throughout his life, the sphere in which he acquired the greatest degree of artistic freedom was the landscape. With his impulsive nature Corinth often painted straight on to the canvas without making studies or preliminary sketches. His unusually fiery brushwork, which can be positively frightening, was often remarkably similar to that of the German Expressionists, especially in his final period.

Corinth's fertile early period in Berlin ended in 1911–12 with a serious illness, which left him debilitated for life. From then onwards every picture was a struggle; he literally had to force his hand to work. In these late paintings, in which the sensuous beauty of his earlier work was complemented by a deep spiritual quality, Corinth came very close indeed to the masters of German Expressionism. His pictures of Walchensee, which became a second home to him in the closing years of his life, are amongst his best-known pieces.

Robert Bertrand. *Lovis Corinth*, Paris 1940.
Gert von der Osten. *Lovis Corinth*, Munich 1955.
Charlotte Behrend-Corinth. *Die Gemälde von Lovis Corinth*, Munich 1958.
Catalogue, *Lovis Corinth*, Gallery of Modern Art, New York 1964.

Corneille (Cornelis van Beverloo). Belgian painter, b. 1922 in Liège. Corneille is of Dutch descent. After studying drawing at the Rijksakademie in Amsterdam he taught himself to paint. Then, in 1948, he became a founder member of the Dutch 'Experimental Group' and, subsequently, of the *Cobra* group. In 1953 he studied graphic techniques with Hayter in Atelier 17 in Paris. In 1954 he produced pottery. In 1956 he was awarded the Guggenheim National Prize. From 1962 to 1966 he spent the summer months in Cadaques, where he painted gouaches. He is now living in Paris.

At first Corneille painted evocative landscapes in strong colours, which reveal the influence of Picasso and Miró. Later he changed his palette, using dark, warm colours (chiefly red, green and blue), and also shifted his viewpoint, painting landscapes from above and producing a sort of ground-plan effect, rather like an aerial view. Recently he has changed his style yet again. He now uses brighter colours—usually on a pale ground—and has introduced a more fluid type of composition, painting luminous red or blue forms interspersed with linear or ornamental forms, e.g. circles, scrolls, wheels or latticework. This combination produces a distinctly cheerful effect.

Exhibition catalogue, *Corneille*, Stedelijk Museum, Amsterdam 1966.

Cornell, Joseph. American sculptor, b. 1903 in Nyack, New York; d. 1973. He began painting, without any formal training, during the Depression and had his first exhibition in New York in 1932; he continued to have one-man shows in the United States, including a major retrospective in 1967 (New York, Guggenheim Museum).

Cornell is best known for his enclosed constructions assembled of various objects and clippings within picture-frame boxes; the unexpected juxtapositions of the materials seem surrealistic, yet the constructions are. controlled by a remarkable precision, order and a sense of stillness (even in those instances when the boxes are meant to be handled to activate certain mobile parts). There is a remote and nostalgic quality about Cornell's boxes, with their allusions to both geographical and temporal distances, achieved through historical references (*Medici Slot Machine*, 1942; *Taglioni's Jewel Casket*, 1940) or through cosmological elements, as in the *Sun Box* and *Eclipse Series* of the early 1960s. The world of Cornell's constructions is also unreachably distant and hermetic in visual terms, for the objects are placed behind a glass pane and are often even further removed by being individually encased in glass jars or drinking glasses; furthermore, through the use of mirrors, there is frequently an illusion of depth and multiplicity, and thus an ambiguous orientation, in the physically shallow box. In a number of ways Cornell utilized theatre and film conventions, with which he was familiar through his own experiments in film-making. His work marks a stage in the development of collage and assemblage in the twentieth century between Dadaism (although lacking the same kind of irony and criticism) and later large-scale assemblages, such as Robert Rauschenberg's combines.

William Seitz. Exhibition catalogue, *The Art of Assemblage*, Museum of Modern Art, New York 1961.
Diane Waldman. Retrospective exhibition catalogue, *Joseph Cornell*, Solomon R. Guggenheim Museum, New York 1967.

Corpora, Antonio. Italian painter, b. 1909 in Tunis. Corpora studied under A. Vergeaud at the École des Beaux-Arts in Tunis. In 1929 he was in Paris and, after returning to Tunis for a brief period, visited a number of Italian cities before settling in Rome in 1930. In 1945–6 he belonged to the Italian Neo-Cubist association, in 1947 he became a founder member of the *Fronte Nuovo delle Arti* and in 1948 joined the *Otto Pittori Italiani*. He is now living in Rome.

Corpora's art is grounded in French Neo-Impressionism, Fauvism and Cubism. In 1937 he produced his first semi-abstract painting and between 1949 and 1952 evolved a completely abstract style, which was essentially the same as that developed by the French painters grouped around Bazaine. The works of this period are extremely dynamic compositions, in which the colour and lighting are integrated in a rhythmical relationship. In 1953–4 Corpora began to paint colour compositions, i.e. he no longer attempted to create formal associations with the objective world. The expressiveness of the colours in these works is toned down by the use of rich, uniform lighting. Since 1960, Corpora has been producing free interpretations of informal art.

Guido Ballo. *Corpora: Opere 1951–1956*, Rome 1956.
Christian Zervos. *Corpora: Oeuvres 1951–1957*, Paris 1957.

Corrente. This association was founded in Milan by R. Birolli in 1938. Cassinari, Sassu and R. Guttuso were founder members; Santomaso, Mafai, Afro, Fazzini, Mirko and Pirandello joined later. A public platform was provided by the *Vita Giovanile*, a magazine for literature, art and politics which was edited by E. Treccani, who later renamed it *Corrente di Vita Giovanile*. The contributors to this magazine included artists such as Birolli, Migneco, Guttuso and Manzù, and writers and critics such as R. de Grada, Carlo Bo and Quasimodo. In March 1939 the *Corrente* association had its first exhibition, which was restricted to Milanese artists of diverse schools. In the following year the association was banned by the state, but its activities were continued by the Bottega Gallery (later renamed Galleria della Spiga e Corrente). By 1943, however, the movement had lost its momentum and two years later, when the war was over, it came to a complete standstill.

Apart from its declared opposition to Fascist and, more particularly, *Novecento* art, the *Corrente* association had no fixed programme. Its members included artists of widely differing temperament and artistic persuasion. But, despite these personal and professional differences, they were all agreed on the one fundamental principle, namely that art imposes, not only an aesthetic, but also a moral obligation. This they endeavoured to fulfil by defending the modern movement, i.e. Surrealism, Expressionism, etc., against the charge of 'degenerate art'.

Coubine, Othon. Czech painter and graphic artist, b. 1883 in Boskovice. After studying at the School of Sculpture in Horice from 1898 to 1900 Coubine attended the Prague Academy from 1900 to 1905, and subsequently the École des Beaux-Arts in Paris. He made educational journeys to Italy, France, Belgium, Holland and Provence before settling in Paris in 1913. He now lives and works in Prague. During his early period Coubine was influenced, first by the French Impressionists, and subsequently by van Gogh, the Fauvists and the Cubists. On his lengthy journeys he was able to study the work of Giotto, Piero della Francesca, Verrocchio, Holbein, David, Watteau and Manet in considerable detail. But Coubine was also a keen student of nature, which he was always careful to observe at first hand, and consequently he managed to free himself from

the influence exerted on him by these old masters and evolve an independent style. The sense of ecstasy conveyed by his landscapes is kept within bounds by the Classical rhythm of the composition and the cool, muted colours. We find the same harmonic organization in Coubine's still lifes and figure compositions, where the objective representation of the different *motifs* is offset by the clear lighting and smooth brushwork.

Charles Kunstler. *Coubine*, Paris 1929.

Coulentianos, Costas. Greek sculptor, b. 1918 in Athens. He studied in Athens and moved to Paris in 1945. He has worked extensively in the field of murals. He is a post-Cubist whose personal contribution lies in a strong awareness of spatial organization.

Cousins, Harold. American sculptor, b. 1916 in Washington. Although he pursued Classical studies at university, his predilection for craft dates back to his childhood days of making little mechanical engines. These early interests were taken up years later when he studied at the Art Students' League under William Zorach. An exhibition in 1946 of the works of González awakened his interest in the possibilities of forged iron. Soon after he moved to Paris and joined Zadkine's studio in 1949, he relinquished working in stone and turned to metal. His early works are largely figurative, most often animals and mythological subjects. He soon turned to the use of metal rods, in which the solder becomes a decorative element. This can be seen in his *Forest* series of 1954–5. The evocative power of the stems is increased by the shadows projected against the supporting wall, producing an animated relief. In the late 1950s and 1960s he combined the linearity of the rods with more compact elements of iron, bronze or nickel. In *Winter Plaiton* (1959, Brussels, Coll. B. Goldschmidt) the stems support rectangular plaques with tendrils rising above. The verticality thus produced is carried further in his later works where metal stems are clustered together, creating a density and at the same time a lightness due to the flamboyant Gothic ornamentality and the spatial voids which puncture the clusters—as in *Gothic Plaiton (Orpheus)*, c. 1961, Paris, Galerie Karl Flinker.

Georges Boudaille. 'Harold Cousins', *Cimaise* VIII, 1961.

Coutaud, Lucien. French painter and stage designer, b. 1904 in Meynes, near Nîmes. Coutaud served an apprenticeship as a goldsmith and studied painting in Nîmes and Paris. Since 1926 he has worked primarily as a stage designer. He was a founder member of the Salon de Mai. He is now living in Paris.

Coutaud is best known as a stage designer. His fantastic Surrealist sets—in which Manichino-like figures are positioned in front of a background of sea and strand—were influenced by Max Ernst, de Chirico and Dali. Coutaud has also produced murals, tapestries and a large number of drawings.

P. Mazars. *Lucien Coutaud*, Geneva 1964.

Couturier, Robert. French sculptor, b. 1905 in Angoulême. After meeting Maillol for the first time in 1928, he became a friend and one of his favourite disciples. The influence of the master is evident even in works such as *Mediterranean* (1942) or *Leda* (1944), which, however, have the stamp of Couturier's own personality. Soon afterwards, the artist rejected neo-Classical canons and abandoned stone for plaster with its greater flexibility and ease of handling. From then on, his shapes grew thinner and longer (*Adam and Eve*, 1945; *Monument to Étienne Dolet*, 1947), eventually giving rise to gaunt, angular sculptures, almost linear in form: the *Shepherd* (1950), *Little Girl Skipping* (1951), the series of *Fauns* (1959). In 1964 he was made professor at the École Nationale des Beaux-Arts in Paris.

Couzijn, Wessel. Dutch sculptor, b. 1912 in Amsterdam. Couzijn lived in New York from 1915 to 1929 and from 1931 to 1932. From 1941 to 1946 he lived partly in New York and partly in New Orleans and Alabama. In between these protracted visits to the USA he pursued his studies in Amsterdam and made visits to Rome, Paris and Perpignan. His most celebrated work is his *Corporate Entity*, which was produced in 1962 and is now in Rotterdam. In 1967 Couzijn won the Dutch national prize for sculpture.

Couzijn is one of the most important Dutch bronze sculptors. After an early period, in which he produced monumental and highly simplified figurative sculptures in bronze and stone, Couzijn came under Lipchitz's influence in the early 1950s and gradually moved away from solid structures. His sculptural forms became more abstract and more disrupted and began to extend into space, thus creating a sculptural parallel to the Abstract Expressionism which was then emerging in the sphere of painting. During the 1960s Couzijn's forms have grown more restful and more 'mechanical'. He has also incorporated ready-made components, such as pieces of piping, fire-screens and bed-frames, into his works. He now appears to be evolving a new science-fiction-type figuration.

K. E. Schnurman. *Wessel Couzijn*, Amsterdam 1967.
Exhibition catalogue, *Wessel Couzijn*, Stedelijk Museum, Amsterdam 1968.

Cox, Jan. Belgian painter, b. 1919 in The Hague. Although both his parents were Belgian, Cox did not live in Belgium until he was seventeen, when he settled, first in Antwerp, and subsequently in Brussels. He became a founder member of the *Jeune Peinture belge* association, but differed from the majority of his fellow members by continuing to paint in a figurative style which, although essentially a derivation of Flemish Expressionism, also owed much to Kandinsky. In 1956 Cox went to live in Boston, where he now teaches. In Boston his palette has been influenced by conditions of light which are very different from those obtaining in his native Europe. Cox's painting has been described by some critics as Surrealist. But although Cox readily concedes that the world of dreams and fantasy is a factor in his work, he has rejected this classification.

Cracow Group (*Grupa Krakowska*). The Cracow Group, an *avant-garde* artists' association founded in Cracow in 1930, is still an active force in present-day Poland. The most important of its earlier members were Maria Jarema, Jonasz Stern and the sculptor Wicinski. The fresh impetus which it received after the war was due primarily to Tadeusz Kantor.

Craig, (Edward Henry) Gordon. British theatre designer, b. 1872 in Stevenage; d. 1966 in Vence. Craig was the son of the actress Ellen Terry and the architect and stage designer E. W. Godwin, and he himself acted for eight years. However, by 1900 he was experimenting with wood-engraving and watercolour, and he was influenced by James Pryde and William Nicholson (the 'Beggarstaff Brothers'). Stephen Haweis taught him etching (Florence, 1907). Craig, who drew for the British Press for thirty years, recognized the vigour of the newer US periodicals—*Harper's Monthly, The Century, Scribner's*—and was also inspired by the Quattrocento Italians and by architectural theorists such as Serlio.

Craig's first productions in England emphasized English authorship—*Dido* (Purcell), *A Masque* (Purcell), *Acis* (Handel and Gay)—but his most positive support came from abroad. Count Kessler, Otto Brahm (of the Lessing Theatre) and Max Reinhardt drew Craig to Germany. His two-year liaison with Isadora Duncan (who bore him a daughter) is significant at this point. Craig conceived theatre as expressible through an abstract synthesis of movement, sound and light.

A true precursor of recent Kinetic art, he experimented with moving geometric blocks under static light, and static blocks under moving light. The closure of his 'school' (Arena Goldoni, Florence) by the war—where such ideas were conceived—was a tragedy. His true genius, however, was expressed in the composite art of the theatre, from which his graphics, having their *raison d'être* and often their subject matter, should not arbitrarily be dissociated. His son's biography indicates this totality and Craig's considerable international significance.

Gordon Craig. *Index to the Story of My Days*, London 1957.
Ferruccio Marotti. *Gordon Craig*, Bologna 1961.
Denis Bablet. *Edward Gordon Craig*, Paris 1962.
Edward Anthony Craig. *Gordon Craig*, London 1968.

Crawford, Ralston. American-Canadian painter and photographer, b. 1906 in St. Catharines, Ontario. He received his art training at the Otis Art Institute, Los Angeles, after having lived in Buffalo, N.Y., since 1910. While studying in Los Angeles he was also working at Walt Disney's studio. From 1927 to 1930 he studied at the Pennsylvania Academy, Philadelphia, and the Barnes Foundation, Merion, Pa. He then spent two years in New York before going to Paris, where he studied at the Académie Colarossi and Académie Scandinave (1932–3). His first one-man show came in 1934 at the Maryland Institute of Art, Baltimore, during which time he was painting in Chadds Ford and Exton, Pa.

The works of the first half of his career are concerned with the beauty and vitality of familiar images of modern industrial architecture (bridges, grain elevators, factories, steel mills, etc.). In *Watertank* (1938, Montclair, N.J., Coll. Mr. and Mrs. Howard Hennington) he places all the emphasis on shape, form and silhouette, reducing all elements, including shadows, to an essential structural quality—an approach strongly reminiscent of C. Sheeler. Like Sheeler, he became intensely interested in photography (c. 1937–8). After the war, his style grew steadily more abstract, reducing his subjects to their elemental geometric shapes. As in *Factory Interior* (1946, New Rochelle, N.Y., Coll. Mr. and Mrs. Charles Friedman) the content is not always immediately recognizable, but rather merely suggestive of the industry and strength, simplicity and force of a modern age. Since 1940 Crawford has also led an active teaching career at the Art Academy of Cincinnati (1940–1), the School of Fine Arts, Buffalo, N.Y. (1942), the Brooklyn Museum School (1948–9), Louisiana State University (1949–50) and the New School for Social Research, N.Y. (since 1951).

R. B. Freeman. *Ralston Crawford*, University of Alabama 1953.

Craxton, John. British painter, b. 1922 in London. Craxton studied at Goldsmith's College of Art, London. He held his first one-man show at the Leicester Galleries in 1944. In his early work he was very much influenced by the English Surrealists. Since 1946 he has lived and worked a great deal in Greece, and that country and its landscape have played a large part in his inspiration.

Exhibition catalogue, *John Craxton*, Leicester Galleries, London 1944, 1951.

Creeft, José de. American sculptor, b. 1884 in Guadalajara, Spain. De Creeft's experience with sculpture began at a very young age: at twelve he worked as an apprentice in a bronze foundry; at sixteen he became an apprentice in Madrid to Don Agustín Querol (1863–1909), the official government sculptor; and at twenty-one he was in Paris, studying at the Académie Julian. The academic approach to sculpture dissatisfied him, however, especially the customary practice of having the sculpture carved by professional stonecutters. In 1911 he went to work as a craftsman in a stonecutters' workshop in order to learn carving himself. This training enabled him to copy his own plaster casts in stone, but in 1915 he abandoned this process and began direct carving. From then on, the underlying principle of his sculpture was fidelity to the material, whether he worked in stone (his usual medium), wood or lead. His contribution to American sculpture, after his arrival in the United States in 1929, was his strong position in the renewal of direct carving, which became prominent in America in the 1920s and 1930s through the work of such sculptors as William Zorach and John Flannagan.

When De Creeft began direct carving, he made an intense study of Oriental philosophy and sculpture as general models for his own work; his female heads and figures, which constitute his most typical subject matter, have the strong, rounded, and sensuous forms of Eastern, and sometimes pre-Columbian, sculpture. De Creeft's work tends towards the monolithic and the monumental, and usually shows an interest in texture. Polished and rough surfaces are frequently juxtaposed so that the smooth forms often appear to be enveloped by or emerging from a rough background. Characteristic examples of his stylistically rather uniform oeuvre are *Maya* (black Belgian granite, 1935) and *Emerveillement* (serpentine, 1941); less typical but sometimes more remarkable are his experiments with hammered lead, such as the portrait head of *Sergei Rachmaninoff* (1943).

Jules Campos. *José de Creeft*, New York 1945.
Charlotte Devree. *José de Creeft*. American Federation of Arts, New York 1960.

Cremonini, Leonardo. Italian painter, b. 1925 in Bologna. After studying at the Schools of Art in Bologna and Rome, Cremonini went to Paris in 1951. Since then he has made protracted visits to Ischia. He now lives in Rome and Paris. After an early landscape phase Cremonini developed a type of figurative composition, in which he portrays man in his existential relationship to the world around him. His pictorial objects acquire a bright, ethereal quality from his use of transparent colours which he applies in a thin film.

Exhibition catalogue, *Leonardo Cremonini*, Palais des Beaux-Arts, Brussels 1969.

Crippa, Roberto. Italian painter and sculptor, b. 1921 in Monza, Italy. Crippa studied under Funi and Carrà at the Accademia di Brera in Milan, where he was a contemporary of Carpi, until 1940. In 1948 he joined the *Movimento Spaziale*. He now lives and works in Milan. During the early, formative phase of his career, Crippa was influenced by the Surrealist R. E. Matta. As a result he evolved an Abstract

Expressionist style, depicting objects hovering in space, which consist of groups of intersecting spirals lying in different planes. In 1956 Crippa began to sculpt. He produces relief collages, in which he explores the artistic potential of *art brut*. Crippa is an informal artist.

G. Giani. *Crippa*, Venice 1954.
A. Jouffroy. *Crippa*, Milan 1962.
Exhibition catalogue, *Roberto Crippa*, Kunsthalle, Mannheim 1965.

Cross, Henri-Edmond. French painter, b. 1856 in Douai; d. 1910 in St-Clair. Cross was born in Douai of French parents, by name Delacroix, which he subsequently changed to the English form to avoid obvious confusion when he became a painter. He was closely associated with Seurat and Signac, discovering his identity with them at the formation of the Salon des Indépendants in 1884, of which he, like them, was a founder member. From this association the so-called Neo-Impressionist movement developed.

Cross shared with Seurat the attitude that painting is not a matter of intuitive impulse. They preferred to use a kind of scientific purpose of picture-making, with plans well laid, and pre-thought even to the methodical use of the brush itself. In the planning period, however, Cross, like Seurat, did produce sketches and drawings of fine quality with much more freedom of approach.

With this common purpose Cross eagerly adopted Seurat's interest and research into the growing science of optics, particularly in relation to perception of colour and space. He was himself possessed of a fine colour sense, particularly for bright, pure colour. This last distinguishes him from Seurat and their friend Signac, and is probably one reason why Matisse, whom he came to know in 1904, had great respect for his influence.

The particular optical theories of the time led to a demand for a visual mixing of reflected light rather than the mixing of pigments. Cross helped to develop a technique to allow this. Briefly, it involved the building of coloured areas with methodically placed dots of primary colours, pre-mixed with black or white. Viewed at the proper distance these dots fused visually to give the right effect of tone and colour. This technique came to be styled 'Pointillism'.

After Seurat's untimely death in 1891 Cross and Signac continued to support his theory and method. Cross, however, had great respect for the freedom of the imagination; his work broadened in technique, and his colour became more intuitional, bright as against the Pointillist greys. His subject matter was largely landscape, in which his predilection for logic and order move close to abstract painting. He also anticipated twentieth-century ideas in believing that painting could be conceived as 'chromatic harmonies completely invented and established so to speak without reference to nature as a point of departure'.

Of the Neo-Impressionists, Cross is not so well remembered as Signac; but in his ideas, especially through Matisse, he most probably had the deeper influence on subsequent developments in painting.

Cruxent, José María. Spanish sculptor, b. 1911 in Barcelona. After coming to terms with Expressionism, Surrealism, collages and Informal Painting Cruxent turned to kinetic art. Recently he has been investigating the dynamic effect of light and shade by enclosing lengths of fibre or cord in box-like constructions.

Cruz-Diez, Carlos. Venezuelan painter, b. 1923 in Caracas. After training at the School of Fine Arts in Caracas from 1940 to 1945 Cruz-Diez worked as artistic director of an advertising firm and as an illustrator for the newspaper *El Nacional* from 1946 to 1951. He then taught graphic art at the Central University of Venezuela. In 1955 he visited Barcelona, but returned home the following year to become Director of the School of Fine Arts. In 1960 he went to live in Paris, where he began work on his series of *Polychromes*. He has also produced kinetic pictorial objects. Most of these consist of coloured, perpendicular, relief-like structures arranged in parallel, which create an impression of movement due to the fluctuation in the interplay of light and colour set up by the viewer's movements. In 1966 Cruz-Diez was awarded the Grand Prix at the American Biennale in Cordoba, Argentina.

Csaky, Joseph. Hungarian-French sculptor, b. 1888 in Szeged, Hungary. After studying in Budapest from 1904 to 1905, Csaky moved to Paris in 1908. Three years later he joined the Cubists and Cubism has remained the strongest single factor in his work, although since 1932 it has been accompanied by a trend towards greater objectivity. Csaky is now living in Paris.

W. George. *Csaky*, Paris n.d.

Cubism. Among the proliferation of modern art movements since the end of the nineteenth century, Cubism was probably the most fertile watershed, compared by many to the Italian Renaissance. Its stated objective was a greater reality in art and its enormous influence lies in the many new propositions and concepts of 'the real' that it threw up. Its late nineteenth-century heritages, first in the new Post-Impressionist emphasis on the flat picture surface, and second in the oblique anti-naturalistic representations of the Symbolists, provided very strong incentives for a redefinition of Realism. Contemporary ideas in other arts, philosophy, science and engineering also stimulated the quest for new languages. Finally it was the abstracted visual analysis of Cézanne's late painting (the memorial exhibition in 1907) and Picasso's discovery of an anti-naturalistic approach to representation in African tribal masks that were the catalysts. A bizarre but fertile fusion of these two concepts can be seen in Picasso's *Demoiselles d'Avignon* (1906–7, New York, Museum of Modern Art), usually recognized as the birth of Cubism. The name 'Cubist' was given derisively to some geometric landscape paintings by Braque of 1908–9.

The first phase of Cubism based itself closely on the structured language of Cézanne's art, but without his passionate commitment to the *motif*. From 1902 to 1912 (Analytical Cubism), Picasso and Braque together explored means of representing the 'idea' of the object seen (still lifes, landscapes, portraits). They wanted to be free from the artifice of traditional illusionistic painting, which was tied to a fixed moment of time and a fixed viewpoint. The fragmented, crystalline structures of early Cubist paintings carry explicit references to the *motif* and strong sensations of light, form and space, without compromising the integrity of the flat surface. The effect is of a more total experience, combining different aspects and viewpoints of the *motif* which are assembled on the surface. By 1911–12, Picasso's experimental toying with the ambiguities of picture-making was so involved that the subject was scarcely recognizable. It was this phase of Cubism that was so influential for abstract art (e.g. Mondrian, Delaunay).

Having established the autonomy of the painting, later (Synthetic) Cubism did not start from analysis of a particular *motif*, but from materials which were put together to create a *motif*. The picture surface was no longer the transparent window onto an illusion, but the flat arena on which this assemblage took place. The new means used in paintings and collages—printed words; pasted papers, objects and materials; ready-made pictorial devices like illusionistic wallpapers, reproductions or photographs—were real in themselves and the *motif* made from them was in no sense an imitation of anything else. Many of the objects used were everyday, disposable trivia—newspaper, matchboxes, etc.—bringing art closer to the informal commonplace reality of life. For Picasso art had become the making of relationships, whether between images, or materials, or both. Almost all later art, figurative and abstract, two- and three-dimensional, random or hieratic, was conditioned in some way by these new dimensions of reality.

Picasso and Braque were the chief originators of Cubism, but did not contribute to the group exhibitions (1910–11 on) by which the movement became known. Juan Gris joined them around 1910 and made an original contribution to collage. Few of the other Cubists understood the full implications of Cubism.

The other major painters associated with the movement were Léger, whose concept of a modern Realism had as much to do with subject matter as technique, and Delaunay, who moved away from Cubist concepts (around 1912) into an abstract art of colour (Orphism). Marcel Duchamp's later importance was an extreme conceptualization of elements implicit in Cubism. All three of them played a major role in group exhibitions, meetings, etc., such as the foundation of the *Section d'Or* group which held an inaugural exhibition in 1912. (The name reflects the Duchamps' interest at the time in mathematics and little else.) Other painters involved were Gleizes, Metzinger, Le Fauconnier, Marcoussis, Gris, La Fresnaye, Lhôte, Picabia, Villon and Kupka. It was primarily through their work that Cubism rapidly spread its influence across Europe and America. Some sculptors (Archipenko, Duchamp-Villon, Laurens, Lipchitz) also joined the movement, but it was outside France (by Boccioni in Italy, the Constructivists in Russia) that Cubism's implications for sculpture were realized. Throughout its life, the active interest in Cubism of contemporary writers (especially Apollinaire, author of *Les Peintres Cubistes*, Paris, 1913) sustained its intellectual vitality and supported its public appearances. The movement was split up by the outbreak of war, and although further *Section d'Or* exhibitions were organized (1920, 1925), 1914 was in effect the terminal date.

Alfred H. Barr Jr. (ed.). Catalogue, *Cubism and Abstract Art*, Museum of Modern Art, New York 1936.
Guillaume Apollinaire. *The Cubist Painters: Aesthetic Meditations*, New York 1944.
Bernard Dorival. Catalogue, *Le Cubisme*, Musée National d'Art Moderne, Paris 1953.
John Golding. *Cubism: A History and an Analysis, 1907–1914*, London and New York 1959.
Guy Habasque. *Cubism: Biographical and Critical Study*, New York and Paris 1959.
Robert Rosenblum. *Cubism and Twentieth-Century Art*, London and New York 1961.
Douglas Cooper. *The Cubist Epoch*, London, New York and Los Angeles 1970.

Cubo-Futurism. This concept describes a specific phase in the development of Russian art in the years immediately prior to the outbreak of the First World War. Cubist and Futurist elements were then combined in a composite style, which bore a certain resemblance to Léger's early curvilinear Cubism. The principal representative of this new style was Malevich who, together with Burljuk and Funi, showed a number of typical Cubo-Futurist pictures at the celebrated *Target* exhibition in 1913. In these works the pictorial objects are broken down into gleaming, cylindrical components which set up a jagged, almost mechanical rhythm. Cubo-Futurism was the transitional style which preceded the pure abstraction of Suprematism and Constructivism.

Cuevas, José Luis. Mexican draughtsman and painter, b. 1933 in Mexico City. Cuevas attended the La Esmeralda School of Art for a brief period in 1947. But this was the only formal training he received, and he is virtually a self-taught artist. Since 1947 he has worked as an illustrator for Mexican newspapers and magazines. He has also illustrated books by Kafka. His drawings are chiefly remarkable for their originality and dramatic intensity. Cuevas teaches at the School of Art attached to the Latin American University of Mexico.

Justina Fernández. *Antología de pintores mexicanos del siglo XX*, Mexico 1958.

Cuixart, Modesto. Spanish painter, b. 1925. Cuixart joined the *Dau al Set* group when it was founded in 1948 by Antonio Tàpies and others. After a Surrealist stage he moved back to a richly coloured informalism about 1956. From 1965 his work has taken on a medieval aspect, with its magical or sadistic subjects.

Curatella Manes, Pablo. Argentinian sculptor, b. 1891 in La Plata; d. 1962 in Buenos Aires. Curatella Manes was trained by Arturo Dresco and Lucio Correa Morales in Buenos Aires. From 1911 to 1917 he visited Italy, Spain and France on a travelling scholarship and in 1920 settled in Paris, where he held a diplomatic post until 1947. During his early period, when he was in close contact with Bourdelle, Lhôte, Juan Gris, Gargallo and Laurens, Curatella Manes developed a form of sculpture which was based on the artistic principles underlying synthetic Cubism and which is often reminiscent of Zadkine and Lipchitz. Later he turned to pure abstracts. From 1945 onwards he produced *structures in space*, using Plexiglass and metal components, and voluminous, abstract sculptures in stone and bronze. Curatella Manes and Antonio Sibellino were the founders of modern sculpture in Argentina.

O. Svanascini. *Curatella Manes*, Buenos Aires 1963.
J. M. Taverna Irigoyen. *Escultura argentina de este siglo*, Santa Fé 1967.

Curry, John Steuart. American painter and muralist, b. 1897 in Dunavant, Kansas; d. 1946 in Madison, Wisconsin. Curry was born and raised on a Kansas stock farm. His mother urged him to draw, and he later studied at the Art Institute in Kansas City, Missouri, and at the Art Institute of Chicago. After five years as an illustrator, he went to work in Paris for a year. His realistic study of an American subject, *Baptism in Kansas* (1928, New York, Whitney Museum of American Art), focused national attention on him. The painting depicts a radiant moment as Plains people perform their simple religious rites. This was followed by other popular scenes of Mid-Western farm life, including *Hogs Killing a Rattlesnake* (1930, Chicago, Art Institute). By the 1930s Curry had become the leading figure among the American regionalist painters, who also included Thomas Hart Benton and Grant Wood. From 1936 until his death, he was Professor of Art at the University of Wisconsin, where he promoted not only regionalism but also a social consciousness and individualism that he believed were at the root of all art. His most powerful achievements are the murals he painted (1938–40) for the state capitol in Topeka, Kansas. One depicts the lonely expanse of Kansas prairie lands. Another is dominated by the turbulent figure of the abolitionist John Brown, flanked by Union and Confederate soldiers; on the outer edges dynamic pillars, formed by a tornado and a buffalo hunter, surround the frenzied scene. Although this mural is executed with the bold, broad brushwork necessary to the theme, certain areas—such as the wild flowers in the corners—are still painted as delicately as in an easel painting.

Laurence Schmeckebier. 'John Steuart Curry: Retrospective Exhibition at the Joe and Emily Lowe Art Center, Syracuse University', *College Art Journal* XVII, No. 1, Autumn 1957; *John Steuart Curry's Pageant of America*, New York 1943.

Czyzewski, Tytus. Polish painter and poet, b. 1880 in Berdychow; d. 1945 in Cracow. Czyzewski studied at the Academy of Art in Cracow. From 1907 to 1909 and from 1911 to 1912 he was in Paris, where he became interested in Neo-Impressionism and Cubism. In 1917 he became a founder member of the Formist artists' association in Cracow, which came into being largely at his instigation. In his early works Czyzewski combined Neo-Impressionist handling with decorative, naïve structures, producing effects that are reminiscent of *verre eglomisée*. In his constructive period, which lasted from 1917 to 1922 and in which he tried to establish new spatial relationships, Czyzewski produced multi-dimensional pictures, using prismatic elements which projected from the picture surface. Later—after touring Italy, Spain and France in 1925—he turned his attention to colour compositions. In 1930 he moved to Warsaw, where he spent the rest of his life. As a poet Czyzewski participated in the festivals organized by the Polish Futurists. He also had close links with the Dada movement, for he insisted on the 'anarchy of the word' and called for a-logical poetry.

D

Dacosta, Milton. Brazilian painter, b. 1915 in Niterbi, Brazil. Originally Dacosta had intended to become a lawyer but broke off his legal studies to train as a painter at the National School of Fine Arts in Rio de Janeiro. Later he made contact with Candido Portinari, who introduced him to modern artistic structures. In 1944 Dacosta became interested in the European school of geometrical abstract painting and began to work in this medium. He is now living in Rio de Janeiro.

Jorge Romero Brest. *La pintura brasilena contemporanea*, Buenos Aires 1945.

Dacre, Winifred—see **Nicholson,** Winifred

Dada (Hobbyhorse). This was an international movement, whose principal activities fell within the seven-year period 1916–23. Various etymological derivations have been advanced for this word, which was picked on in a French dictionary in 1916 and enthusiastically adopted by the followers of the movement as a general name to cover all their activities. Dada appeared at first in two main centres. It was developed in New York from 1915 onwards by Alfred Stieglitz and his associates (Arensberg, Picabia, Ray, de Zayas), who were able to publicize their ideas through the magazine *291*. Marcel Duchamp, who made his first visit to New York in 1915, also made an important contribution. Meanwhile, the European centre of Dada was in Zürich, where it was launched, also in 1915, by an international group of artists, who had sought refuge from the First World War in Switzerland. In 1916, when the Independent Exhibition was being prepared in New York and the Parisian magazine *Sic* was beginning to adopt a Dadaist line, Hugo Ball founded the *Cabaret Voltaire* in Zürich. The first Dada manifestations in Zürich were organized by Jean Arp, Hugo Ball, Richard Huelsenbeck, Marcel Janco and Tristan Tzara. For the most part, these took the form of group activities, magazine articles, pamphlets and exhibitions. Writing on this period in 1925 Arp stated: 'Dadaism fell upon the fine arts . . . Dadaism carried assent and dissent *ad absurdum*. In order to achieve indifference, it was destructive.' And Duchamp, writing in 1946, observed: 'Dada was . . . a way of discarding a certain mental attitude and ensuring that we were not influenced, either by our immediate environment or by the past: [it was a way] of ridding ourselves of clichés, of freeing ourselves.' In 1917 Ball and Tzara opened the Galerie Dada in Zürich, Duchamp published the magazines *The Blind Man* and *Wrong-Wrong* in New York, whilst Picabia brought out the first issue of the magazine *391* in Barcelona. In 1918 the Dada movement caught on in Berlin, where it displayed strong socio-critical and political characteristics. In 1919 Dada artists gathered around Kurt Schwitters in Hanover, and around Arp, Max Ernst and Johannes Baargeld in Cologne. Subsequently, Paris became the principal centre for Dadaist literary and artistic activities, and a Dada group was formed around the magazine *Littérature*, which was edited by Aragon, Breton and Soupault. The first big Dada festival was held in the Salon des Indépendants in 1920, and the Dada bulletin was also published in Paris from then onwards. From Paris the movement spread to other countries such as Italy and Holland, where Dada magazines were launched (*Bleu* in Italy, *Mecano* in Holland). In 1922 the Paris Dada group broke up into smaller factions.

The influence of Dada made itself felt in numerous spheres including typography, films, music, the theatre and architecture. Surrealism also owed much to this movement. The early works of Rauschenberg, Johns and kindred artists, which appeared in the late 1950s, were promptly dubbed 'Neo-Dada', although in point of fact this label would apply only to certain formal aspects of their paintings. Both Pop Art and *Nouveau Réalisme* were also intimately concerned, from the very outset, with the contemporary environment, with the folklore of the industrial age, with advertising and mass production.

R. Motherwell (ed.). *The Dada Painters and Poets*, New York 1951.
W. Verkauf (ed.). *Dada: Monograph of a Movement*, London and New York 1957.
Hans Richter. *Dada: Art and Anti-Art*, London and New York 1965.
William S. Rubin. Catalogue, *Dada, Surrealism and their Heritage*, Museum of Modern Art, New York 1968.

Daeye, Hippolyte. Belgian painter, b. 1873 in Ghent; d. 1952 in Antwerp. Daeye studied in Ghent and Antwerp. From 1914 to 1920 he lived in England, where he met Permeke, Tytgat and van de Woestyne. He was deeply impressed by Modigliani. In 1920 Daeye returned to Antwerp and subsequently became a member of *Les Neuf, Les Compagnons de l'Art* and various other groups.

The major part of Daeye's output consists of pictures of young girls executed in delicate colours. These reveal the influence of the Laethem School and of Modigliani.

A. Corbet. *Hippolyte Daeye*, Antwerp 1949.

Dahmen, Karl Fred. German painter, b. 1917 in Stolberg, nr. Aachen. Dahmen studied at the School of Art and Crafts in Aachen from 1931 to 1933. In 1952 he visited Paris. From 1956 onwards he has associated with the Tachist Group centred on *Galerie 22* in Düsseldorf. In 1967 he joined the staff of the Munich Academy.

Dahmen is an informal artist. His early works consisted of relief-like 'wall pictures', which are painted in a *pastosa* technique, and 'terrestrial formations', which are torn and indented and are executed in hard layers of paint compounded of brown, ochre, red and grey. Since 1958 he has been producing collages, and since 1963 montages composed of canvas, wood, metal and *objets trouvés*.

Exhibition catalogue, *Karl Fred Dahmen*, Kölnischer Kunstverein, Cologne 1965.

Dali, Salvador. Spanish painter, b. 1904 in Figueras. Dali is one of the best known of all twentieth-century painters, partly because of his talent for self-advertisement, but more because of the genuinely hallucinatory quality of his painting. This derives from his remarkable ability to impose his own fantasies on the world of appearances, from the subject matter of those fantasies: sexuality, death, metamorphosis and the infinite, and from his style of painting—in his own words, his works are 'hand-made photographs'.

According to Dali (in *My Secret Life*, published 1942), his childhood was violent and marked by fits of hysteria. The megalomania that he considers one of his major creative assets also appeared early in life. Dali's origins are very much reflected in his work: as well as the Spanish obsession with death and the particularly Catalan love of fantasy (Dali greatly admires the *art nouveau* architect Antonio Gaudí), the bleak landscape backgrounds of many of his paintings are unmistakably Spanish.

In adolescence Dali explored most of the current *avant-garde* styles from Impressionism to Cubism, but admired nineteenth-century genre painters for their precise and detailed depiction of reality. He later focused this admiration on the outstanding practitioner of this type of painting, the Frenchman Meissonier. The English Pre-Raphaelites were also important to him, as were Vermeer and Velasquez. In 1921 he went to the Madrid School of Fine Arts and in 1923 came under the influence of the Italian metaphysical painters, Giorgio de Chirico and Carlo Carrà, whose work was well known in *avant-garde* circles in Spain at this time. This influence was crucial to his development as a painter: eventually it led him to reject abstract art ('that model mental debility' as he later called it). For the moment, however, while he painted mysterious still lifes in the manner of de Chirico and Carrà, he continued to paint Cubist-influenced abstractions and straightforward naturalistic works. In 1924 Dali was suspended from the art school for a year on a charge of inciting the students to insurrection and he was also briefly imprisoned by the government for subversive activity. He was expelled permanently from the school in 1926 for extravagant personal behaviour. He began to exhibit with the Sociedad de Artistos Ibericos in Madrid and at the Gallery Dalmau in Barcelona, and became known as the leading Catalan painter of the younger generation. In 1928 Dali made two visits to Paris, on the first of which he met Picasso, and on the second, Miró. He also signed a contract for an exhibition at the Goemans Gallery and returned home to prepare for it. In the next few months the influence of Miró became paramount in Dali's work, but this phase was the last time he was to be concerned with abstract painting and by the summer of 1929 he was painting in his mature style. When the paintings arrived in Paris it was apparent that his work was Surrealist in character, and André Breton appointed him an official Surrealist and wrote a catalogue introduction for his exhibition. Dali soon became one of the most spectacular members of the Surrealist group. His approach to the problems of Surrealist painting was both personal and original. In his book *La Femme Visible* published in 1930 he wrote, 'I believe the moment is at hand when, by a paranoiac and active advance of the mind, it will be possible (simultaneously with automatism and other passive states) to systematize confusion and thus to help discredit completely the world of reality'. He changed Surrealist inspirational activity from a passive to an active process. This process he called the paranoiac-critical method and it involved the active elaboration of his own fantasies and their substitution for, or imposition on, the world of external appearances. He declared that his art sprang from an hallucinatory energy and that he proposed to paint like a madman. This programme led to some of the most extraordinary images in the history of art: works like *Autumn Cannibalism* (1936) or the *Spectre of Sex Appeal* (1934) are totally convincing as visual messages from the human subconscious mind—the Id—as described by Freud. Dali of course read Freud (whose influence on him and on the whole Surrealist movement was fundamental) and announced that he was determined to document the workings of the subconscious: this is the basic aim of his painting and indeed of all Surrealist art. In 1929 he collaborated with Luis Bunuel on the film *Un Chien Andalou* and again in 1931 on *L'Age d'Or*; both have become classics. In 1938 he was expelled from the Surrealist group by Breton and in 1940 settled in the USA. In 1955, he returned to live in Spain, at Cadaques, as a supporter of the Franco regime.

Salvador Dali. *Diary of a Genius*, New York 1965; London 1966.
A. Reynolds Morse. *Salvador Dali, 1910–1965*, Greenwich (Conn.) 1966.
Max Gerard. *Dali*, London and New York 1968.

Dalwood, Hubert. British sculptor, b. 1924 in Bristol. After apprenticeship to the Bristol Aeroplane Co. and service in the Navy, Dalwood studied at the Bath Academy, Corsham, from 1946 to 1949. He was a Gregory Fellow at Leeds University, 1955–8. He is represented in the Tate Gallery. Dalwood was prominent among the younger sculptors who broke with the anxiety-expressive wrought and welded manner which dominated the fifties. He opposed to this a more volumetric sculpture strangely combining straight-sided forms, ribbed and edged, with more fluid ones. Aluminium, cast and partly polished, was the most favoured medium and gave these pieces a bland and disconcerting presence.

Damian, Horia. Rumanian painter, b. 1922 in Bucharest. After studying in Bucharest Damian went to Paris in 1946, where he worked in André Lhôte's *atelier* from 1946 to 1947 and in Fernand Léger's *atelier* from 1948 to 1949. In 1949 he came under the influence of Mondrian and turned to abstract art. In 1951 he met Herbin. Since then he has exhibited in the Salon des Réalités Nouvelles. Damian now lives in Paris.

Damnjanovic (Damnjan, Radomir). Yugoslav painter and graphic artist, b. 1936 in Mostar. Damnjanovic trained at the Academy of Art in Belgrade, where he is now living. By simplifying the formal elements in his works, Damnjanovic translates real objects into mysterious emblems, which have their habitat midway between the spheres of fantasy and geometry.

J. Denegri. *Introduction to the Damnjanovic Exhibition Catalogue*, Belgrade 1968.

Dangelo, Sergio. Italian painter, b. 1931 in Milan. In 1949–50 Dangelo visited Paris and Brussels as a student and made contact with the *Cobra* group. In 1952, together with Enrico Baj, he signed the first manifesto of the *Movimento d'Arte Nucleare*. Subsequently he contributed to three magazines: *Phases*, *Temps Mêlées* and *Phantomas*. He is now living in Milan.

After coming to terms with the *Cobra* movement, Dangelo evolved a Romantic form of concrete painting.

Danziger, Ytshak. German-Israeli sculptor, b. 1916 in Berlin. Danziger went to live in Palestine in 1923. After an early period in which he produced figurative works such as his *Nimrod* of 1938, he began to design monuments in a style that is both abstract and meaningful at one and the same time. The thematic concept underlying these late works is that of integration into city or country life.

Dardel, Nils von. Swedish painter and draughtsman, b. 1888; d. 1943. Von Dardel studied in Paris from 1910 to 1912, where he came to terms with Seurat, Rousseau, Matisse and the Cubists. In 1917 he visited Japan and subsequently produced paintings with fussy contours and clearly defined pictorial forms which were based on Japanese woodcuts and Persian miniatures. Von Dardel's colours are often rather venomous, and his *motifs* reveal a preoccupation with the morbid and decadent aspects of life. The dreamlike Surrealistic world of his paintings in this period is inhabited by grotesque figures with the kind of features found on Oriental masks, by youths and young girls, by dogs, horses and peacocks. His painting *Visit hos excentrisk dam* (*Visit to an Eccentric Lady*, 1921, National Museum, Stockholm) is typical. So too are the stage sets which he designed for the Swedish ballet *Dårhuset* (*The Lunatic Asylum*, 1920). In the 1920s and 1930s von Dardel tended to concentrate on portraits, which he executed in a more realistic style. But his best Realistic works were the watercolours which he painted on a visit to Mexico and Guatemala towards the end of his life. Both as an artist and as a human being von Dardel played the part of the eccentric dandy; as a sensitive and imaginative person he felt compelled to conceal his vulnerability behind a façade of artificiality and sarcasm.

K. Asplund. *Nils von Dardel*, 2 vols., Stockholm 1957, 1958.

Dau al Set (Dice with Seven). The *Dau al Set* was an artists' association, which existed in Barcelona from 1948 to 1953. It published a magazine under the same name and included amongst its members the poet Joan Brossa, the philosopher Arnauld Puig and the artists Modesto Cuixart, Joan Ponc, Antonio Tàpies and Joan J. Tharrats. Although basically Surrealist, the *Dau al Set* also revealed certain Expressionist tendencies. Together with *Escuela de Altamira* (founded in 1948), the *October Salon*, *Club 49*, *Grupo R* (also Barcelona), *Grupo Espacio* (founded in 1954 in Cordova) and the *El Paso* group (founded in 1957 in Madrid), the *Dau al Set* played an important part in the promotion of 'new art' in Spain.

Davie, Alan. British painter and lithographer, b. 1920 in Grangemouth, Scotland. Davie trained at the Edinburgh College of Art, 1938–40. Army service followed from 1941 to 1946. His first one-man exhibition was held in Edinburgh in 1946. He took up a travelling scholarship, 1948–9, and saw works by Jackson Pollock in Venice. He then taught jewellery design at the Central School of Art, London, and held one-man exhibitions at Gimpel Fils from 1950. He was a Gregory Fellow at Leeds University, 1957–9, and gained many other prizes and distinctions. As a student Davie absorbed the colour characteristics of the Edinburgh school of painters, but his aim was to liberate both that colour and himself from their influence. His discovery of Pollock, his experience as a jazz musician and his experiments with jewellery helped him to assert colour as a quality of freedom and a sensuous expression of life akin to rhythm and inseparable from the action of painting.

Davie's solid reputation abroad, which places him in the highest rank of British painters, is perhaps due to this non-British physical *élan* and at the same time an athletic, disciplined assurance in the handling of paint and knowledge of its properties. By an odd paradox, American painting was the catalyst which enabled this immensely gifted Scot to break away from Scots or English parochialism and integrate himself with the European tradition to which he securely belongs. His early paintings with larger forms and gestures owed more to the New York school, but he soon developed his highly individual forms and dense skeins of brush-strokes. His later pictures also show a highly developed sense of space considered as an attribute of colour.

Davies, Arthur Bowen. American painter, b. 1862 in Utica, New York; d. 1928 in Florence. Before moving to Chicago with his family in 1878, he saw the works of George Inness and Winslow Homer at the Utica Art Association; in Chicago he studied part-time at the Academy of Design. In 1880 Davies went to Mexico as an engineering draughtsman. Upon his return to the United States, he studied at the Art Institute of Chicago, but by 1886 he had shifted his attention to New York, where he enrolled at the Gotham School and the Art Students' League. Davies then settled in Congers, New York, painting and doing magazine illustrations to earn a living. In 1893 the art dealer William Macbeth persuaded the philanthropist Benjamin Altman to finance a European trip for the young Davies; as a consequence, he came under the influence of the Venetian painters, the German Romantics, the English Pre-Raphaelites, J. A. M. Whistler and Puvis de Chavannes.

The early works of Davies are pastoral scenes, using rich colour and heavy impasto, but by 1903 he had formulated a more characteristic style, as seen in the *Unicorns* (1906, New York, Metropolitan Museum) and *Crescendo* (1910, New York, Whitney Museum). In these idyllic paintings the landscapes project an almost mystical calm, which is also reflected in the artist's favourite figures of enigmatic and ethereal female nudes. Davies' mysterious *Dream* (c. 1908, Metropolitan Museum) is akin to the elusive mythological and visionary subjects of Odilon Redon.

While Davies' poetic themes had little to do with the realism of New York's Ashcan School, his painterly style and his attitudes concerning the artist's independence seem to have had something in common with this group, and he exhibited with them in a show held at the Macbeth Gallery in New York. In 1913 Davies was elected president of the Association of American Painters and Sculptors, and was also chosen to play a major role in the organizing of the Armory Show, along with the painter Walt Kuhn. The works he helped to assemble for this exhibition prompted Davies to try several modernist-formalist experiments of his own (*Intermezzo*, c. 1913, New York, Graham Gallery), but it is primarily for his earlier romantic reveries that he is remembered.

Metropolitan Museum of Art. *Arthur B. Davies: Catalogue of a Memorial Exhibition*, New York 1930 (with an introduction by Bryson Burroughs).

Bennard B. Perlman. 'The Armory Show: The Years Before', *Art in America* LI, February 1963.

Davis, John Warren. English sculptor, b. 1919 in Pembrokeshire. He attended the Westminster School of Art but then went directly into war service. On his return to sculpture, he began working in a figurative style, but in this the forms of the figure began to be more and more identified with the forms of landscape, until the two tended to fuse, as in Henry Moore's work of roughly the same period. In the later fifties and in the sixties these figures were replaced by elemental forms, often of rough-hewn wood. These are sometimes painted, giving them the appearance of primitive symbols or totem figures.

Davis, Stuart. American painter, b. 1894 in Philadelphia, Pennsylvania; d. 1964 in New York City. A student of Robert Henri and friend of many of the important realists of the Ashcan School, Stuart Davis painted, throughout his career, the world that he found around him, the world of the city. The flashing neon lights, the garish billboards, the tempo and noise of street traffic, the beat of jazz, and all the other cacophonous, albeit vital, sensations of modern urban life determined to a great extent the content of his paintings. Davis' style, however, was derived from the Fauvist and, especially, Cubist traditions. He became acquainted with the works of the Post-Impressionists, Fauvists and Cubists at the Armory Show in 1913 (at which he exhibited five watercolours). Davis writes of this show as being 'the greatest shock to me—the greatest single influence I have experienced in my work'.

In the early 1920s, Davis began experimenting with Cubist-inspired *collages*, which led directly to the illusionistic paintings of cigarette packages (*Lucky Strike*, 1921, New York, Museum of Modern Art). In these works he combined the simple, flat designs of the packages themselves with words and other inscriptions.

In 1927 Davis set up a still-life arrangement consisting of an egg beater, electric fan and rubber glove, which he painted over and over again for about a year. In the process he reduced the still life to a grouping of receding and interconnecting planes (*Eggbeater No. 2*, 1927, New York, Whitney Museum). His paintings of Paris streets, executed while he was in Paris from 1928 to 1929, reveal a comparable treatment of planes. Illusionistic elements reappear, however, in the form of architectural details rendered in a fine, taut line, as in *Place Pasdeloup* (1928, Whitney Museum).

During the 1930s, Davis expanded his imagery to fit the requirements of mural painting. He executed his first mural, *Men Without Women*, for Radio City Music Hall in 1932. Later he painted two murals under the auspices of the WPA, one of which, the *WNYC Mural*, completed in 1939 for the Municipal Broadcasting Company of New York, recalls the style of Fernand Léger with its stark and simple design.

In the 1940s Davis employed bright, vivid colours combined with flat patterns and rich surface textures in his paintings (*Hot Still Life in Six Colors*, 1940, Coll. Halpert). Jazz had an impact on *motifs* (as in the *WNYC Mural*) and on compositions and even on titles (*The Mellow Pad*, 1945–51, Coll.

Lowenthal; *Rapt at Rappaport's*, 1952, Joseph H. Hirshhorn Foundation).

Davis' paintings took on greater monumentality and simplicity during the 1950s as he began to concentrate on large, bold compositions (*Little Giant Still Life*, 1950, Richmond, Virginia Museum of Art). He returned to a more complex treatment of the painting surface, however, in *The Paris Bit* (1959, Whitney Museum), in which he juxtaposed positive and negative images to create the impression of strong lights and deep shadows.

Stuart Davis Memorial Exhibition, with an introduction by H. H. Arnason, Washington (D.C.) 1965.
E. C. Goossen. *Stuart Davis*, New York 1966.

Davring(hausen), Heinrich. German painter, b. 1894 in Aachen, Germany. Davring is a self-taught painter. After starting as an Expressionist he went over to the *Neue Sachlichkeit* and, during this second phase of his career, produced a body of veristic works with harsh Surrealistic lighting effects, which were intended as acts of social criticism.

Décollage. In the strict sense this concept refers to those processes involving the separation or removal of any layer of gummed material (*décoller* = to unstick). Consequently, although it has been used to describe a variety of art forms—either by the artists themselves or by their interpreters—it is most readily applicable to the work of the *affichistes* or poster artists. Wolf Vostell has stated that his whole oeuvre is based on *décollage*, which he regards as an artistic method in its own right, one based on the principle of destruction, which may manifest itself both in an intentional and a spontaneous form (e.g. torn posters, blurred TV programmes, happenings). Vostell has been editing a magazine entitled *Décollage* since 1962.

J. Becker and W. Vostell. *Happenings*, Reinbek 1965.

Degas, Edgar. French painter, draughtsman and sculptor, b. 1834 in Paris; d. 1917 in Paris. His name was originally de Gas, but was later contracted by the artist. The eldest of five children, he was at first intended for the law; but his father, a banker of cultivated taste, raised no objections when Degas announced that he wanted to paint. He studied under F. J. Barrias and with one of Ingres' disciples, Louis Lamothe. Copying in the Louvre and studying the prints of Dürer, Mantegna, Goya and Rembrandt were also part of his regime.

Until the mid-1860s, Degas, a superlative draughtsman with a very strong sense of artistic tradition, concentrated on historical subjects—of which *The Young Spartans* (c. 1860, London, National Gallery) is probably the most successful—and portraits. But after that, partly under the influence of Manet and Duranty, he became more and more interested in scenes from modern life, and often those in which figures could display professional skill: the ballet, the race-track, the laundry, the circus and the milliner's shop. To this list he later added the female nude in domestic surroundings; he also continued to paint portraits.

The question of Degas' role in the history of Impressionism is complex, turning as it does on the definition of that ambiguous movement. What remains certain, however, is that Degas contributed to seven of the eight group exhibitions mounted by the Impressionists between 1874 and 1886, and that his work embodies many of the principles in which other members of the movement—Manet, Renoir, Monet, Pissarro *et al.*—also believed. Degas' everyday subject matter is comparable (though he was not very interested in landscape), and so are some of his pictorial devices, such as the oblique perspective and the 'interruption' of a figure by the edge of the frame, both of which reveal the influence of photography and Japanese colour prints. The cardinal importance that Degas attached to the role of drawing, both in the preparation of a picture and in its execution, prevented him from going so far as some of his colleagues in the rendering of light and the way in which it appears to soften and blur forms seen at a distance.

In the 1880s, Degas' eyesight, never good after an illness contracted during the Franco-Prussian War (1870–1), began to deteriorate; in the 1890s matters became worse; and in 1908 he more or less gave up working altogether. At first, he had alleviated the problem by resorting to pastel, a medium that was easier to work in, and one which allowed him to retain colour without sacrificing line. But here, too, he was ultimately defeated. His work after the mid-1880s became increasingly uneven in quality; and the dispersal of many inferior paintings, pastels and drawings at the Studio Sales in 1918 has not helped his reputation. His activities as a sculptor, on the other hand, which continued well into the present century, but which were largely unknown to the public during his lifetime (he only exhibited one piece, at the Impressionist Exhibition of 1881—*The Little Dancer of Fourteen Years*), were very successful. Seventy-four models found in his studio after his death were cast in bronze through the *cire perdue* process by A. A. Hébrard.

The best of Degas' paintings, drawings, monotypes and sculptures entitle him to be ranked among the greatest masters of the nineteenth century. The incisiveness of his observation was matched by the delicacy of his touch; the ingenuity and brilliance of his compositions were equalled by the subtle beauty of his colouring. He created unforgettable images of unmemorable facts. And it was the tone of his imagery, as much as the novelty of his style, that was to make him an important influence on late nineteenth- and early twentieth-century art. Greatly respected by his contemporaries, and by the younger generation, Degas influenced both Toulouse-Lautrec and Gauguin. His style and subject matter made an unforgettable impact on Forain and Sickert, and on the young Picasso. In a less direct way, Degas' deliberate concentration on a few, restricted themes —often of a highly artificial kind—as a basis for artistic achievement anticipates movements like Cubism.

Paul-André Lemoisne. *Degas: Son Oeuvre*, 4 vols., Paris 1946–9.
John Rewald. *Degas' Sculpture*, London and New York 1957.
Jean Sutherland Boggs. *Portraits by Degas*, Berkeley (Calif.) 1962.

Degenerate Art (*Entartete Kunst*). The expression Degenerate Art was used as a slogan by the National Socialist ideologists in the Third Reich, and was also the name of an exhibition staged in the Hofgarten buildings in Munich in 1937 and subsequently in other German towns. Degenerate Art was the antithesis to 'German Art' (*Deutsche Kunst*), i.e. the type of art which was advocated by Hitler in *Mein Kampf* and Rosenberg in *Der Mythos des 20. Jahrhunderts*, and which was displayed in the exhibitions held in the Haus der Kunst in Munich between 1937 and 1945. Both formally and thematically Degenerate Art was a negation of the propagandistic art prescribed by the National Socialist Party. In their racial theory and in their moral teachings the National Socialists rejected Degenerate Art as an inferior and dangerous phenomenon. From 1937 onwards all modern German works of art were officially classified as 'degenerate' or 'Judo-Bolshevist'. The same classification was applied to foreign works of art (from Impressionism onwards), although this was not adopted as official policy until 1938. A special commission was set up with powers to confiscate any examples of Degenerate Art found in German museums. As a result some irreplaceable works of art were destroyed, a few were sold to private collectors, and a significant number were auctioned in Lucerne in 1938 in order to obtain foreign currency. In this way works by some of the great masters of twentieth-century art found their way into foreign collections.

Degottex, Jean. French painter, b. 1918 in Sathonay. Degottex moved to Paris in 1933 and has lived mainly there ever since. During his early period he was influenced by Fauvism, but in 1949 he began to paint in an abstract style, which subsequently became progressively more informal. He has made an intensive study of Eastern writings, which he has analysed both formally and symbolically. His objective is: 'Purposeless, the void (in the sense of Quidditas), gestural trance, a state of great spiritual freedom.'

Dekkers, Adrian. Dutch artist, b. 1938 in Nieuwpoort; d. 1974. Dekkers trained in the Department of Commercial Design at the Academy of Fine Arts in Rotterdam from 1954 to 1958. The major part of his oeuvre consisted of reliefs made from synthetic materials—mostly polyester—and executed almost exclusively in white. He worked with geometrical figures, exploring their design potential by creating different views of one and the same figure. Lighting plays an important part in his work. So too do texture and depth of colouring.

A. Dekkers. 'Statement on my Work', *Struktur* 6/2, 1964.

Delahaut, Jo. Belgian painter and sculptor, b. 1911 in Vottem-lez-Liège. Delahaut holds a doctorate in the History of Art. In 1940 he began to paint pictures in a near Fauvist style and in 1945 progressed to geometrical abstracts. He was a founder member of the *Art Abstrait, Formes*, and *Art Construit* associations. He has produced mobiles (1956) and reliefs in space, and has often worked in collaboration with architects, especially those of the EGAU group.

Delaunay, Robert. French painter, b. 1885 in Paris; d. 1941 in Montpellier. After training as a decorative painter, Delaunay became a full-time artist in 1904. In 1906 he completed his military service in Laon and then, in the course of the next two years, came to terms with Neo-Impressionism and Chevreul's colour theories. In 1909 he created his first important series (*St. Séverin*), which was a pointer to his future development. Then, from 1910 onwards, he produced compositions based on a new conception of optical and rhythmical laws, including *La Tour Eiffel* (destructive period or period of transition from Cézanne to Cubism) and *Les Fenêtres simultanées prismatiques* (beginning of the constructive period). In 1910 Delaunay married the painter Sonia Terk. In 1911 he made contact with the members of the *Blauer Reiter* and began to contribute to their exhibitions, exerting considerable influence on Marc, Macke and Klee. In 1912 he evolved his *Disques* and his *Formes circulaires cosmiques*, in which he finally turned his back on natural forms. Between 1915 and 1917 Delaunay visited Spain and Portugal and in 1918 he designed stage sets for the Russian Ballet. In 1921 he returned to Paris, where he completed his second *Tour Eiffel* series and started *Les Coureurs* (a series of pictures of footballers) in 1924. Between 1930 and 1935 he produced his *Jeu de disques multicolores* and started work on his *Rhythmes* and his plaster reliefs. In 1937 he created murals for the Palais des Chemins de Fer and the Palais de l'Air at the International Exhibition in Paris. In 1939 he helped to organize the first exhibition at the Salon des Réalités Nouvelles. In 1940 he fled, first to the Auvergne and then to Mougins near Cannes, where he contracted a serious illness, to which he succumbed in the following year in a clinic in Montpellier.

As a result of his intensive preoccupation with

Neo-Impressionism and with Chevreul's colour theories Delaunay was able to establish a new conception of the rhythmical effects of colour early on in his career. In his series of interior views of the Church of St. Séverin in Paris he was still painting in a basically Cubist style, restricting his use of colour in order to emphasize the plasticity of his composition. But when he came to paint his Eiffel Tower series in 1910 he made colour the dominant feature and this, coupled with the realization—which he first demonstrated in his 'Window Pictures'—that light and colour are identical, led to the development of the inimitable style to which Delaunay's friend Apollinaire gave the name 'Orphic Cubism'. Delaunay's ideas on light—which he discussed in an article in Walden's *Sturm* in 1913—also helped him in his approach to the problem of simultaneity, which was then occupying the Futurists. Delaunay's *Fenêtres simultanées prismatiques*, which are pure colour compositions, were one of the fruits of his investigations into the contrasts between simultaneous colours. From then onwards he largely dispensed with visual impressions and objective *motifs* in order to concentrate on coloured abstractions, as in *Les Disques* and *Les Formes circulaires cosmiques*. These early ventures into 'pure painting' set the tone for the whole of Delaunay's subsequent work, although he did have occasional recourse to simplified objective forms, as in *Les Coureurs*. His last important works were the huge murals which he painted for the International Exhibition in Paris in 1937. Delaunay's constructive ideas, such as his conception of movement as a product of colour contrasts (harmonious colours produce slow movement; discordant colours produce fast movement), and the rhythmical interplay of coloured pictorial forms to which these give rise, exerted a considerable influence on European art. His use of purely optical phenomena as pictorial elements also made a great impact. The *Blauer Reiter* would scarcely have been conceivable but for Delaunay, whose art has remained a source of inspiration right down to our day.

F. Gilles de la Tourette. *Robert Delaunay*, Paris 1950.
R. Delaunay. *Du Cubisme à l'art abstrait: Documents inédits*, Paris 1957.
G. Schmidt. *Robert Delaunay*, Baden-Baden 1964.
G. Vriessen and M. Imdahl. *Robert Delaunay: Licht und Farbe*, Cologne 1967.

Delaunay-Terk, Sonia. Russian-French painter, b. 1885 in the Ukraine. Delaunay-Terk spent her childhood in St. Petersburg. She studied in Karlsruhe from 1903 to 1905 and subsequently at the Académie de la Palette in Paris, where she met Ozenfant and Dunoyer de Segonzac, and was influenced by van Gogh, Gauguin and the Fauves. Following her marriage to Robert Delaunay in 1910 she came to terms with Orphism and *Simultanéisme*, incorporating 'simultaneous contrasts' into designs for fabrics, costumes and book covers. She also created costumes for Diaghilev's presentation of the opera *Cleopatra*. From 1922 onwards she worked as a fashion designer, and the hand-printed 'simultaneous' fabrics, which she produced in 1924, exerted a considerable influence on the international fashion world for a number of years. In 1930 she became a member of the *Abstraction-Création* association. In 1939 she helped to organize the first *Réalités Nouvelles* exhibition (together with R. Delaunay, Doesburg, etc.). From 1940 to 1944 she was in the South of France, where she lost her husband in 1941. After the war, in 1946, she helped to re-establish the *Salon des Réalités Nouvelles*. Since then she has continued working on her 'simultaneous experiments', using designs which have grown more severe and more two-dimensional.

André Lhôte. *Sonia Delaunay-Terk: Ses peintures, ses tissus simultanées, ses modes*, Paris 1925.
Robert and Sonia Delaunay Exhibition Catalogue, Galerie Nationale du Canada, Ottawa 1965.
Catalogue, *Retrospective Sonia Delaunay*, Musée Nationale d'Art Moderne, Paris 1967–8.

Del Marle, Félix. French painter, b. 1889 in Pont-sur-Sambre, Nord; d. 1952. He studied in Lille, Brussels and Paris. In about 1913 he embraced Futurism. From 1920 on he was an associate of Kupka and Mondrian. He became attached to the Neo-Plastic movement, then turned to representational painting. In about 1943 he returned to a geometrical style.

Del Pezzo, Lucio. Italian painter and sculptor, b. 1933 in Naples. In 1958 Del Pezzo and a number of his friends founded the *Gruppo 58* and launched the magazine *Documento Sud*. In 1962 he ended his Dadaist phase and began to depict the kind of pictorial objects first introduced into modern art by the *Pittura Metafisica*. In the harmonious and economical compositions of this late period he uses colour as a means of emphasis. Del Pezzo settled in Milan in 1960. He now lives in Milan and Paris.

Del Prete, Juan. Argentinian painter, b. 1897 in Vasto, Italy. Del Prete has lived in Buenos Aires since early childhood. After teaching himself to paint he began to produce pictures in a Fauvist style. In 1929 he went to Paris, where he became interested in lyrical abstraction and joined the *Abstraction-Création* association. Four years later, when he returned to Argentina, Del Prete staged an exhibition of collages and abstract paintings. In the following year, 1934, he showed abstract wire constructions and plaster sculptures. Del Prete, who was one of Argentina's first abstract artists, subsequently moved towards a figurative form of Abstract Expressionism.

Joan Merli. *Juan del Prete*, Buenos Aires 1946.
Salvador Presta. *Arte argentino actual*, Buenos Aires 1960.

Delvaux, Paul. Belgian painter, b. 1897 in Antheit, Belgium. It was only after a protracted development that Delvaux, who is essentially a Classical artist, discovered the strange, magical and timeless pictorial world of his maturity, a world in which contemporary *motifs* appear in conjunction with *motifs* taken from history or legend. During his early period Delvaux painted in a Realistic style, modelling his work on Frans Courtens. He then became interested in the colour theories of the Neo-Impressionists but subsequently turned his attention to Expressionism. Vlaminck, Degreef, Ensor, Permeke and Gustave de Smet were his first true mentors. But even before he discovered his personal world Delvaux painted a number of pictures which gave a hint of things to come. One such is his painting of the female plaster figures in the Musée Spitzner, which dates from 1932. In fact, most of the *motifs* which, from 1936 onwards, combined to create the sense of alienation that characterized Delvaux's paintings at that time are to be found in earlier works, where, however, they appear in isolation. These *motifs* include: small sad railway stations, empty trams or trains, deserted suburbs, and even the lamps which later served to distinguish different spatial and temporal spheres. It was Delvaux's encounter with Surrealism that liberated him from his obsessional preoccupation with such *motifs* by enabling him to incorporate them into fully integrated works of the imagination. Although he was deeply impressed by the work of Magritte, it was the paintings of Giorgio de Chirico, which he saw in an exhibition at the Palais des Beaux-Arts in Brussels, that provided the crucial impetus. From then onwards, even though he did not actually belong to the Surrealist movement, and did not subscribe to its moral and political aims, 'the great artery of the dream sent the Surrealist sap through his canvases' (Breton). This new vision was reinforced by the wonders and terrors of childhood memories: the antique palaces and temples reflected the feelings of puberty, of initiation into manhood, just as the trains and railway stations reflected the various stages of dreams. Although Delvaux constantly invokes sensuality with his 'great motionless woman' (Éluard), he does so in a rational manner; these female nudes are like a phase in a ceremony, one that is perhaps dedicated to the kind of non-communication evoked by his skeletons and distracted savants. Delvaux's heightened sense of space, his sophisticated colour contrasts, the disturbing precision of his pictorial structures, his hallucinatory and compelling eroticism, and his predilection for nocturnal scenes are reminiscent of certain eighteenth-century Mannerists, whose works are not always sufficiently appreciated. But the modernity of Delvaux's oeuvre, its growing power to fascinate, is equally undeniable.

R. Gaffé. *Paul Delvaux ou les rêves éveillés*, Brussels 1945.
P. A. de Bock. *Paul Delvaux*, Hamburg 1965.

Demarco, Hugo Rodolfo. Argentinian painter, b. 1932 in Buenos Aires. Demarco studied at the Academy in Buenos Aires, where he was a contemporary of Garcia-Rossi, Sobrino and Le Parc. In 1960 he joined with them in founding the *Groupe de Recherche d'Art Visuel*, but withdrew from the group shortly afterwards. In 1962 he won a French government scholarship and went to Paris, where he experimented with coloured optical vibrations and used ultraviolet rays to show the sequence of movements made by small objects in dark rooms. He is now living in Buenos Aires, where he teaches painting and graphic art.

Demuth, Charles. American painter, b. 1883 in Lancaster, Pa.; d. 1935 in Lancaster. Because of his ill-health and the artistic leanings of relatives, Demuth's well-to-do family encouraged him to pursue painting rather than join the family business. He first studied at the School of Industrial Art in Philadelphia and then at the Pennsylvania Academy of Fine Arts under Thomas Anschutz, the latter training interrupted by a trip to Paris (1907–8). In 1912–14 he was back in Paris studying at the Académie Colarossi and Académie Julian. His early works, mostly watercolours, betray the influence of Marin and the Fauves (particularly Matisse). During his best years, 1915–1920, his subjects were confined mainly to acrobatic and vaudeville scenes, café and bar scenes and flower pieces. The Armory Show and the Stieglitz group encouraged him to use greater variety of colour and texture. Emphasized by the whiteness of the paper and the shimmering of lights and shadows playing over petals, *Daisies* (1918, watercolour, New York, Whitney Museum of American Art) captures the very form and character of the flowers. His figural works are in direct psychological opposition to the idyllic quality of the still lifes. Though stylistically similar in the use of superimposed colour and handling of light, the subjects themselves have a decidedly decadent and sexually degenerate character, e.g. his illustrations for Zola's *Nana* and James' *The Turn of the Screw*. Contemporary with these works is an alliance with Cubism through his friend Marcel Duchamp. *Bermuda, No. 2 (The Schooner)* (1917, watercolour, New York, Metropolitan Museum of Art) is close to the style of Feininger, Metzinger and Gleizes, with its emphasis on diagonal lines and shafts of lights and darks. His oils of the same period seem slightly laboured in comparison, but the medium lends itself to the greater weight and density of his architectonic subjects (*Paquebot Paris*, 1921/2, oil, Columbus, Ohio, Gallery of Fine Arts). His late 'poster portraits', usually oil on board, incorporate the Cubists' use of words, letters and numerals as pre-fabricated formal elements.

A. E. Gallatin. *Charles Demuth*, New York 1927.
Andrew C. Ritchie. *Charles Demuth*, New York 1950.

Denis, Maurice. French painter, b. 1870 in Granville; d. 1943 in Paris. After completing his studies at the Lycée Condorcet, which he attended from 1881 to 1887, Denis enrolled at the Académie Julian, where he met Émile Bernard, Pierre Bonnard, Gabriel Ibels, Paul Ranson and, subsequently, Paul Sérusier. In 1889 he became a founder member of the *Nabis* association; in 1891 he produced illustrations for Paul Verlaine's *Sagesses*; and in 1893 he married Marthe Meurier. Shortly afterwards he painted a series of vignettes for André Gide's *Le Voyage d'Urien*. In 1899 Ambroise Vollard showed his series of coloured lithographs *Amour*. Next Denis executed wall paintings for the Chapel of Sainte Croix in Le Vésinet, and in 1901 painted his *Hommage à Cézanne*. In 1901 and 1902 he contributed to the magazine *L'Imitation de Jésus-Christ*; in 1904 he had his first one-man show (at Druet's in Paris), and a second Paris exhibition (with Bernheim-Jeune) in 1907. In 1908, when the Académie Ranson was founded, Denis joined the staff, and continued to teach there until 1919. In 1917 he painted frescoes for the Church of St. Paul's in Geneva, and in 1919, the year in which his wife died, he founded the *Ateliers d'art sacré*. In 1921 Denis visited Algeria and Tunisia, and published his *Nouvelles Théories*. In 1922 he married Élisabeth Graterolle. In 1924 the Musée des Arts Décoratifs in Paris staged a retrospective exhibition of his work; and in 1932 he became a member of the Académie des Beaux-Arts in Paris. In 1939 he published his *Sérusier: sa vie, son oeuvre.*

Denis' oeuvre reflected the many different but interrelating trends within Symbolism, Mysticism and Catholicism. He was a man of profound erudition, who combined a passionate interest in philosophy with a Pre-Raphaelite sense of purity, a refined sensitivity and immense enthusiasm. The publication of Denis' revolutionary article in *Art et Critique* (1890) made him the spokesman for the anti-naturalistic movement. In this article he said: 'Remember that a picture, before being a horse, a nude or some kind of anecdote, is essentially a flat surface covered with colours assembled in a certain order.' The theoretical aims of Symbolistic, decorative, primitive and ideational art, which had been formulated as a result of both the similarity and the antithesis between a whole range of different ideas and models, were all embraced by this statement. Denis was one of those *Nabis* who never tired of analysing, discussing and proclaiming their ideas. In his early period Denis' works were chiefly remarkable for their delicacy, their clarity and brightness, their sensitivity and their balanced composition. In his ideal landscapes, which are above all painterly works, he achieved a genuine synthesis, in which the world of dreams and the world of consciousness interact in perfect harmony.

Fr. Fosca. *Maurice Denis*, Paris 1924.

M. Brillant. *Maurice Denis*, Paris 1930.
M. Denis. *Journal: 1884–1943*, Paris 1959.
Catalogue, *Exposition Maurice Denis*, Musée Toulouse-Lautrec, Albi 1963.
M. Denis. *Du Symbolisme au Classicisme: Théories*, Paris 1964.

Denny, Robyn. British painter, b. 1930 in Abinger, Surrey. After studying at the St. Martin's School of Art and the Royal College of Art in London, Denny taught in various English institutes and schools of art, including the Slade School in London. In 1959 he began painting murals and mosaics. He is now living in London.

Denny was one of the artists presented to the English public in 1960 by L. Alloway in a comprehensive exhibition of recent English abstract art entitled *Situation*. In Denny's paintings, the majority of which are large-scale works, rectilinear forms are symmetrically organized to form ornamental compositions. The colouring is subtle and beautiful.

D. Thompson. *Robyn Denny Exhibition Catalogue*, Venice Biennale No. 33, 1966.

Derain, André. French painter and sculptor, b. 1880 in Chaton, near Paris; d. 1954 in Chaton. From 1898 to 1899 Derain studied at the Académie Carrière in Paris, where he met Matisse. Two years later he saw a van Gogh exhibition at the Bernheim-Jeune Gallery. This was the turning point in his artistic development, and from then onwards he maintained close contact with the Paris *avant-garde*. In conjunction with his friend Vlaminck, with whom he shared a studio, and subsequently with Matisse he began to treat colour as an independent decorative element, and so contributed to the emergence of the Fauvist movement. In 1905 he took part in the famous exhibition staged by the Fauves in the Salon d'Automne. Around 1908 he espoused the Cubist theories of Picasso and Braque. Two years later, in 1910, he painted with Picasso in Cadaques (Spain) and in the South of France. In 1911, however, he moved away from Cubism and embarked on his 'Gothic period', in which he was influenced by the masters of the Early Italian and French Renaissance, some of whose works he had already copied on earlier occasions in the Louvre. From 1914 to 1918 he worked on décors for the *Ballets Russes* and from 1920 onwards made numerous lengthy visits to Italy and the South of France. Between 1920 and 1940 he was a prominent member of the *École de Paris*.

Derain was highly versatile. He worked as a painter, a sculptor and a potter; he designed theatre sets and costumes and he illustrated books. His importance for the history of art lies in the major contribution which he made to the development of Fauvism. Between 1905 and 1907 he painted a large number of portraits, figure compositions, landscapes and street scenes, including the celebrated series of London views of 1906. The works of this period are composed of contrasting areas of strong, luminous colours. These produce an effect which functions quite independently of the actual objects, whose contours are treated with little reverence. At this point in his career Derain looked upon tubes of colour as 'sticks of dynamite' which discharged light. In his subsequent Cubist phase his use of colour was far more restrained. Then his principal concern was to depict the inner architecture of simple things after the manner of Cézanne. But Derain's Cubist pictures were never as extreme as those painted by Picasso or Braque at that time. He did not introduce completely abstract geometrical shapes, nor did he attempt to co-ordinate the constituent planes to the same degree. And, of course, Derain did not remain a Cubist for long. During his 'Gothic period', which lasted for ten years, he produced a body of work which was far more traditional and entirely figurative. These paintings are characterized by solidity and Classical simplicity. Subsequently Derain developed his own brand of Classical Realism, which was very much in tune with the objective aspirations of the 1920s and exerted a considerable influence on them. By then he had completely abandoned the Impressionist-cum-Fauvist colour schemes and the Cubist structures which had dominated his early work. Later still he embraced an academic style of painting, which drew its inspiration from the nineteenth-century French masters, especially Corot.

Derain's sculptures are more akin to the artistic products of ancient and non-European cultures than to the works of his contemporaries. He made his first stone carvings as early as 1905, at a time when his paintings were still completely Fauvist. These early pieces were strictly geometrical and resembled caryatids. But then painting gained the upper hand again, and it was not until 1914–18 that Derain returned to sculpture. During this second phase he fashioned a wide range of masks from granite shells. Over twenty years later, in 1939, Derain embarked on his third and final phase as a sculptor, when he produced a series of highly expressive heads, masks, figurines and reliefs, which were cast in bronze after his death. The primitive archaism of these pieces is reminiscent both of Romanesque sculpture and of the Benin Bronzes.

G. Duthuit. *Les Fauves*, Geneva 1949.
André Derain. *Lettres à Vlaminck*, Paris 1955.
D. Sutton. *André Derain*, London 1959; New York 1960.
Gaston Diehl. *Derain*, New York 1964.
P. Cailler. *Catalogue of André Derain's Sculptures*, Lausanne 1965.

Derkovits, Gyula. Hungarian painter, b. 1894 in Szombathely; d. 1934 in Budapest. After fighting in the First World War he took up the study of art in Budapest, and moved to Vienna in 1923. There he became involved with socialist groups, and his commitment to reform was reflected in his violently Expressionist painting.

Desnoyer, François. French painter and sculptor, b. 1894 in Montauban; d. 1972. His style lay somewhere between Cubism and Fauvism, in which the influence of Cézanne is evident. His sculptures are sensual forms created by a warm, joyous personality who cared more for the delights of the physical than the somewhat dry discipline of the academic. He also did watercolours, murals, landscapes and figures.

Despiau, Charles. French sculptor, b. 1874 in Mont-de-Marsan (Landes); d. 1946 in Paris. Despiau went to Paris when he was seventeen to study at the École des Arts Décoratifs under Hector Lemaire (who had been a pupil of Carpeaux) and, subsequently, at the École des Beaux-Arts under Barrias. Like many of his contemporaries, Despiau was quick to realize the great cultural value of the Louvre and the collection of plaster casts in the Musée de Sculpture Comparée. From 1901 onwards he exhibited at the Société Nationale des Beaux Arts and, later, in the Salon d'Automne. During this initial phase he came to terms with the great Rodin, for whom he worked for a number of years. But like Brancusi, who also made contact with Rodin at that time, Despiau felt the need to get away from this powerful figure and go his own way. As a result he turned away from the 'literary' style and, at a relatively early stage in his career, discovered his niche in portraiture. He also created a number of statues—such as his *Eve* of 1925, *Assia* of 1937 and *Apollo* of 1946—which clearly demonstrate his allegiance to the formal canon of early Classical antiquity but which account for only a minor portion of his oeuvre. His splendid series of portrait busts began in 1904 with the *Petite Fille des Landes I* and ended in 1943 with the bust of *M. Portalès*. In these works Despiau tried to strike a balance between complete naturalism and structural simplification. In his constant quest for psychological truth, he steered his course between the two extremes of abstraction based on fundamental sculptural forms (such as R. Duchamp-Villon tried to achieve in his portraits) and photographic Realism. Two outstanding examples of his extraordinary facility in capturing the inner life of his subjects are his *Mme. de Waroquier* of 1927 and his *Portrait of the Painter Dunoyer de Segonzac*. Apart from his sculptures—most of which were cast in bronze—Despiau also produced numerous working sketches and illustrations for books, including Baudelaire's *Les Fleurs du Mal*.

Léon Deshairs. *Charles Despiau*, Paris 1930.
Waldemar George. *Despiau*, New York 1959.

De Stijl—*see* **Stijl, de**

Desvallières, Georges. French painter and designer of stained glass, b. 1861 in Paris; d. 1950 in Paris. To begin with he was influenced by Gustave Moreau, and later by the Synthetists. He made a great many decorations with religious themes, and produced murals and stained glass for churches all over Europe and the USA. His work is marked by its expressive colours, decorative form and often ecstatic mood. He has also illustrated books, including the poetry of Musset.

Dewasne, Jean. French painter and sculptor, b. 1921 in Lille. After studying at the Academy of Art in Paris, Dewasne spent two years training as a sculptor. He has been painting abstracts since 1943. In c. 1950 he was associated with the Salon des Réalités Nouvelles and was in contact with abstract artists such as Mortensen, Hartung, Poliakoff and Vasarély. In 1950 he founded the *Atelier d'Art abstrait* and in 1968 was represented at the Biennale in Venice.

In his early period Dewasne painted the kind of abstract pictures with interlocking, coloured geometrical forms that were typical of the postwar *École de Paris.* But in the early 1950s he developed a more personal style: his geometrical forms became more 'meaningful', more symbolic, and set up dramatic tensions within the total composition. As a result they came to serve as emblems for the technological world. At the same time Dewasne began to construct his *Antisculptures,* using parts of motorcar bodies, which he then painted so as to produce a sense of formal alienation. Subsequently he abandoned easel and brush in favour of a spray-gun technique, for which he employed enamel paint and masking tape. In purely technical terms Dewasne's composition—his method of arranging geometrical shapes in series and clusters—is derived from Herbin. Unlike Herbin, however, he uses forms to reflect aspects of reality, which he takes from the world of sport, the cinema and technology.

P. Descargue. *Jean Dewasne,* Paris 1952.

Dewing, Thomas Wilmer. American painter, b. 1851 in Boston; d. 1938 in New York. He studied at the École des Beaux-Arts, Paris, in 1876, and in 1895 was a founder member of The Ten, who included J. Alden Weir and John Twachtman.

Dexel, Walter. German painter and writer on art, b. 1890 in Munich. After studying art in Munich, Dexel made contact with Theo van Doesburg and the Bauhaus artists. From 1936 to 1942 he was Professor of the Theory of Art and Design at the Hochschule für Kunsterziehung (College for Art Education) in Berlin. He is now living in Brunswick.

Prior to 1933 Dexel was one of the pioneers of concrete art in Germany.

Exhibition catalogue, *Walter Dexel,* Wilhelm Lehmbruck Museum, Duisburg 1966.

Deyrolle, Jean Jacques. French painter, b. 1911 in Nogent-sur-Marne; d. 1967 in Toulon. Deyrolle studied in Paris at the École d'Art et de Publicité (School of Art and Publicity). During his early period his work was influenced, first by Sérusier, then by Braque and, finally, by the Cubists. Much later, in 1943, he entered on his second, abstract period, largely as the result of Domela's influence. He then associated with the concrete artists grouped around the Salon des Réalités Nouvelles and the Galerie Denise René. From 1959 up to his death he taught at the Munich Academy.

Deyrolle produced his best work during his late period, when he was painting geometric abstracts. These reveal some lyrical elements.

Dias, Cicero. Brazilian painter, b. 1908 in Pernambuco. He studied architecture in Rio de Janeiro, then went to Paris in 1937 as an attaché with the Brazilian embassy. His first one-man show in Paris was held in 1938 at the Jeanne Castel Gallery. Since about 1943 he has been an abstract artist.

Dibbets, Gerardus Johannes Maria (Jan). Dutch painter, b. 1941 in Weert. Dibbets trained at the Academy of Fine Arts in Tilburg under J. Gregor. Since then he has worked as a painter and draughtsman, created pictorial objects, and designed various environmental works, a number of which have been realized. He has also produced multiples, and carried out research into perception. His work has been classified as 'conceptual art'.

J. Dibbets. 'Teile eines Gesprächs', *Galerie Swart Catalogue,* Amsterdam 1968.

Dickinson, Edwin. American painter, b. 1897 in Seneca Falls, New York. Dickinson studied with William Merritt Chase and Charles Hawthorne (1872–1930) and first exhibited in 1916. *Villa la Mouette* (New York, Metropolitan Museum), painted at Sanary-sur-Mer, France, in 1938, reflects in its airy spontaneity his Provincetown, Massachusetts, training with Hawthorne. Dickinson painted many other small atmospheric works, including views of Cape Cod sand dunes, although it is for his monumental paintings that he is better known. The ambitious *Ruin at Daphne* (1943–53, Metropolitan Museum) reveals his interest in Roman architecture, with its fantasy of columns, aqueduct arches and illogically combined fragments of ruins. Steps spiralling out of vague, unfinished areas reach to mysterious heights. Amid these reminiscences of ancient splendour, mythical and symbolical details are embedded. The painting represents a kind of summation of the sophisticated Romantic imaginings that characterize much of Dickinson's work throughout his career. He constantly reworked themes, often on the same canvas, which gives his paintings an evocative intensity that links him in spirit to nineteenth-century Romantics.

Lloyd Goodrich. *The Drawings of Edwin Dickinson,* New Haven (Conn.) 1963.

Dickinson, Preston. American painter, b. 1891 in New York; d. 1930 in Spain. Dickinson, who was an artist of somewhat limited technical means, is noted mainly as a pioneer of Cubism in America. His early study was at the Art Students' League in New York, and then, between 1910 and 1915, at the École du Louvre in Paris. Influenced by the 1913 Armory Show in New York, Dickinson also relied on Japanese prints and later on Cézanne for his pictorial inspiration. His personal translation of Cézanne's methods, in which he used the discordance of Fauvist colour to enliven his compositions, was Expressionistic rather than structural. His *Old Quarter, Quebec* (1927, Washington, D.C., Phillips Gallery) has all the jagged violence of the German Expressionist Ernst Ludwig Kirchner, with a touch of the storminess of Maurice de Vlaminck. Practising a Cubist-Realist simplification of form (called Precisionism in America), Dickinson produced a number of lively though fragile pictures of industrial and urban sites (*Industry*, before 1924; New York, Whitney Museum), still, however, relying on Oriental design.

In his *Still Life with Yellow-Green Chair* (1928, Columbus, Ohio, Gallery of Fine Arts), Dickinson is perhaps at his most original. Although the arrangement of objects recalls the work of the Spanish painter Joan Miró, he created a colossal, ponderous space, coupled with an unusual disposition of ordinary objects. A frequent traveller to Europe, Dickinson was in Spain, in a small town near the French border, when he died. The exact location is not known.

S. M. Kootz. 'Preston Dickinson', *Creative Art* VIII, May 1931.
Milton W. Brown. *Cubist-Realism: An American Style*, New York 1943–5.

Diebenkorn, Richard. American painter, b. 1922 in Portland, Oregon. Diebenkorn studied at Stanford University and the University of California from 1940 to 1943. During the Second World War, while stationed in Washington, D.C., he frequented the Phillips Collection, which included the work of such modern French painters as Matisse, Picasso, Braque and Bonnard; this exposure had a decisive influence on his early artistic vision. In 1946 Diebenkorn enrolled in the California School of Fine Arts in San Francisco, where he taught from 1947 to 1950, along with Clyfford Still, Mark Rothko and others who offered him encouragement. His earliest work consisted of still lifes, interiors and figurative paintings; but, after some contact with American painting of the mid to late 1940s in New York, he began to work in a non-objective, action-charged style. He made a rapid transition from geometric abstraction to a freer, expressionistic style, looking to Willem de Kooning for a use of vigorous, calligraphic line (*Albuquerque*, 1951, Albuquerque, N.M., University of New Mexico Art Gallery).

Until 1955, Diebenkorn's work remained abstract; then, encouraged by his friend, the painter David Park (b. 1911), he began to experiment with representational painting again, distrusting the hyperemotionalism of his previous canvases. He turned slowly to figures, landscapes and still lifes, attempting to organize Abstract Expressionist brushwork into the recognizable forms of representational art (*Man and Woman in Room*, 1957, New York, Coll. Joseph H. Hirshhorn). Nevertheless, Diebenkorn retained certain lessons from his middle period, and continued to form areas with blocks or masses of colour rather than by line. He showed particular interest in asymmetrical compositions (*Corner of Studio—Sink*, 1963, New York, Poindexter Gallery; and *Girl Smoking*, 1963, San Francisco, Coll. Mr. and Mrs. Peter A. Salz), and in an organization of pictorial space into negative, open areas, balanced by a positive concentration of incidents in smaller sections of the canvas. Showing a greater concern for the necessities of the subject, he grew increasingly independent of the discoveries he made through Abstract Expressionism. Diebenkorn's development from non-objective painting back to a figurative style is contrary to the main directions in twentieth-century art, but it suggests a special alternative to the abstract trend.

Hilton Kramer. 'Pure and Impure Diebenkorn', *Arts* XXXVIII, December 1963.
Gerald Nordland. Retrospective exhibition catalogue, *Richard Diebenkorn*, Gallery of Modern Art, Washington (D.C.) 1964.

Dienst, Rolf-Günter. German painter and author, b. 1939 in Kiel. Dienst has edited the magazine *Das Kunstwerk* since 1964. After an early informal phase he evolved a new style of painting incorporating ornamental structures which serve as signs.

R.-G. Dienst. *Positionen*, Cologne 1968.
R.-G. Dienst. *Deutsche Kunst: Eine Neue Generation*, Cologne 1970.

Dietrich, Adolph. Swiss amateur painter, b. 1877 in Berlingen, Switzerland; d. 1957 in Berlingen. Dietrich is the best known of the Swiss amateur painters. His draughtsmanship aroused favourable comment when he was still only a child, but as a poor farmer's son he was unable to study. Instead he worked in a knitting factory, as a lumberman and as a casual labourer until his father's death, when he took over the family farm. He painted his first picture in 1905, but it was not until 1926 that he was able to devote the major part of his time to his art. He had a big exhibition in the Mannheim Kunsthalle as early as 1922 and a second in the Museum of Modern Art in 1937.

Dietrich's still lifes, landscapes, portraits, flower pieces and animal paintings, which are extremely sensitive and poetical works, testify to his close observation of nature and his loving care for detail. The precision of his draughtsmanship and his mastery of painting techniques are quite astonishing and call to mind the Italian Quattrocento and German Romanticism.

K. Hoenn. *Adolph Dietrich*, Zürich 1942.

Diller, Burgoyne. American painter and sculptor, b. 1906 in New York; d. 1965 in New York. He received his first training at Michigan State College and later studied at the Art Students' League and with Hans Hofmann in New York. Piet Mondrian was to become his major influence. In the late 1930s, Diller belonged to the American Abstract Artists group, which included Fritz Glarner, Ilya Bolotowsky (b. 1907), Lee Krasner (b. 1911), Willem de Kooning, Josef Albers, David Smith and other artists who generally worked within the conventions of Neo-Plasticism or based their style on that of Picasso's studio interiors of the late 1920s. From 1935 to 1940 Diller was head of the mural division of the New York Federal Art Project, a position that made it possible for him to help many young painters—such as Jackson Pollock, Adolph Gottlieb, Mark Rothko and Ad Reinhardt—to continue painting during the Depression years. In 1940–1 he was assistant technical director of the New York Works Progress Art Project.

In the late 1940s, Diller began to activate his canvas with complex, ladder-like configurations consisting of narrow, intersecting horizontal and vertical bars. He described these paintings, such as the *Third Theme* (1946–8, New York, Galerie Chalette), as 'elements submerged in activity'. The influence of Mondrian's New York paintings (1944) can be seen in these syncopated compositions. In his later works, Diller turned to simpler arrangements in which a few rectangles are suspended freely on the coloured grounds that characterized an earlier manner. Also dating from this later period is a series of blocky formica structures, such as the lustrous black *Project for Granite, No. 6* (New York, Coll. Noah Goldowsky and Richard Bellamy), which, despite its comparatively small dimensions, evokes the mystery and monumentality of an Egyptian pylon.

Lawrence Campbell. 'The Rule that Measures Emotion', *Art News* LX, May 1961.
Sidney Tillim. 'Exhibition at the Galerie Chalette', *Arts* XXXV, May/June 1961.

Dine, James (Jim). American painter, b. 1935 in Cincinnati, Ohio. Dine studied at the Boston Museum School and Ohio University. He began painting in the 1950s and first exhibited in New York in 1960, at which time he had also been involved for some years in the phenomena known as Environments and Happenings. He produced four of these during 1959–60—*Smiling Workman, Jim Dine's Vaudeville, Car Crash* and the *Shining Bed*. Considering them an extension of his life, he participated in several of his Happenings himself, using paint, words and other sounds, familiar actions, costumes, odours, and theatrical and illogical acts and motions. Dine was close in spirit to Claes Oldenburg, and for a time they worked jointly on their Happenings. After 1960 he returned to painting. He is considered by some critics a Pop artist.

Dine owed a great deal to the climate created by Robert Rauschenberg and Jasper Johns, who raised the problem of combining objects and painting into a single entity. New York Dada, particularly the work of Marcel Duchamp, is also considered an important influence in his development. He was concerned with what is permissible aesthetically in a work of art, and, testing the limits, he consistently included real objects (such as bathrobes, ties, hair and household appliances) in his paintings, displaced and dissociated from their everyday context in a theatrical manner that is sophisticated in its frivolity (*Two Palettes in Black with Stovepipe*, 1963, New York, Sidney Janis Gallery; *Shoes Walking on My Brain*, 1960, New York, Coll. Dr. A. Solomon). Most of his creations make their initial impact as visual puns or parodies, with all kinds of juxtapositions and combinations of elements and images. His is an elusive 'entertainment psychology', in the words of the critic Max Kozloff. In the mid-1960s Dine enclosed objects, such as garments, within glass boxes, cast life-size feet, boots and hands (*Double Right-Handed Doorway*, 1965, Sidney Janis Gallery), made plywood hearts and executed collages.

Max Kozloff. 'The Honest Elusiveness of James Dine', *Artforum* III, No. 3, December 1964.
Michael Kirby. *Happenings: An Illustrated Anthology*, New York 1965.

Dix, Otto. German painter, b. 1891 in Unternhaus, Gera; d. 1969 in Hemmenhofen, Lake Constance. After serving an apprenticeship with a painter and decorative artist in Gera from 1905 to 1909, Dix attended the School of Art in Dresden from 1909 to 1914. After this he completed four years' military service before going on to study at the Academy of Art in Düsseldorf from 1919 to 1922. The central theme of Dix's work was social criticism, which was directed against the horrors of war and the injustices of the postwar world. Around 1923 he moved towards the *Neue Sachlichkeit* and in the following year was represented at the exhibition staged by this association in Mannheim. From the verism of his early period, he proceeded to evolve a style based on the works of the old German masters. In 1925 he moved to Berlin, and in 1927 he was given a professorial post at the Dresden Academy but was dismissed in 1933 at the behest of the National Socialists. He then went to live in Randegg, near Siegen, where he began to paint landscapes. In 1934 he was forbidden to exhibit, and in 1936 he settled in Hemmenhofen. In 1937 eight of Dix's paintings were included in the National Socialist 'Exhibition of Degenerate Art' and within the year 260 of his works were removed from German museums and confiscated by the state. In 1945 Dix served with the *Volkssturm* (German Home Guard) and was taken prisoner by the French. After his release he returned to Hemmenhofen, where he lived in seclusion until his death in 1969.

Dix was one of those artists whose reputations are bound up with a specific historical period. In his case this was the period immediately following the First World War, in which he painted his scenes of life in the trenches and his vicious pictures and Dadaist collages of disabled ex-servicemen, of black marketeers and prostitutes in a pitilessly realistic style. Dix also made extensive use of the graphic media at that time. Examples are his *Dance of Death, anno '17* and his *Trenches*. But by 1923–4 the pseudo-romantic traits which had always been present in his work came to the fore, and he adopted a new style derived from the sixteenth-century German and Netherlandish masters. By introducing precise linear structures, transparent colouring and modelled forms, Dix created an exaggerated, Mannerist type of Realism, which grew progressively more congenial from the early 1930s onwards. The central feature of Dix's oeuvre is his portraits. During the early 1920s especially these probing psychological studies, some of which border on caricature, were quite pitiless. But after the Second World War Dix's work underwent a complete transformation. In place of his traditionalist compositions, he began to produce large-format works executed in a style that was essentially, but not excessively, expressive. The religious pictures and allegorical studies, the still lifes and portraits which he produced in his final period reveal Late Expressionist traits.

O. Conzelmann (ed.). *Otto Dix*, Hanover 1959.
Fritz Löffler. *Otto Dix*, Vienna and Munich 1967.

Dobson, Frank. English sculptor, b. 1886 in London; d. 1963. From 1900 until 1902 Dobson attended Leyton School of Art. In 1902 he served as apprentice to the decorative sculptor, Sir William Reynolds Stephens. Then, from 1906 to 1910, he was a scholar at Hospitalfields, Arbroath, Scotland. Returning to London he was deeply impressed by the two Post-Impressionist exhibitions, and it was after this that he began to experiment with direct carving, then a very unconventional method for a sculptor to follow. In 1914, after working in Cornwall, he had his first exhibition of paintings and drawings in London. In the same year he met Wyndham Lewis, and after serving in the war he was again associated with Lewis in Group X in 1920 as the only sculptor. With Group X he showed *Pigeon Boy* and *Concertina Man*, both showing the influence of Cubism and Brancusi. In 1922 he joined the London Group, of which he was President, 1924–8. Roger Fry was closely involved with the group at this time, and he took up Dobson enthusiastically. Per-

haps as a consequence of this, the first important public recognition of his work came in 1931 when his large bronze figure of Truth (1930) was presented to the nation by the Contemporary Art Society (London, Tate Gallery). He was for a time Professor of Sculpture at the Royal College, retiring in 1953. The main subject of Dobson's work was always the female nude, simplified and monumentalized, but rarely abstracted. Portraiture was, however, also important in his work (Asquith, T. E. Lawrence, Osbert Sitwell). Though less adventurous than that of the younger Henry Moore, remaining untouched by Surrealism, Dobson's work has a dignity and consistency that establishes him as one of the most important English sculptors of this century, as well as being one of the pioneers of modern sculpture in Britain.

Dodeigne, Eugène. Belgian sculptor of French origin, b. 1923 in Rouvreaux. Apprenticed to his father as a stonecutter, he studied modelling at the Beaux-Arts School at Tourcoing, then about 1943 went to stay in Paris, where he was a frequent visitor to galleries and museums. In 1949 he discovered Vézelay, and a year later decided to settle in the north, built a house, and began to sculpt in Soignies stone. From the beginning his sculpture had a dramatic quality with its smooth sensuous masses. His exploitation of the stone surface carried the risk of leading to formalism, and in order to avoid this, around 1960 he started to bring out an explosive element in his forms. Proceeding from reality, Dodeigne works a rough and monumental image of man in contact with the land.

Doesburg, Theo van (Christian Emil Marie Küpper). Dutch painter and art publicist, b. 1883 in Utrecht; d. 1931 in Davos. Van Doesburg was a self-taught artist. He had his first exhibition in 1908 and published his first articles in 1912. In 1915 he met Mondrian and in 1916 collaborated with the architects J. J. Oud and Jan Wils. It was in 1916 that van Doesburg and Mondrian first conceived the idea of the *de Stijl* movement and in the following year, largely on van Doesburg's initiative, the *de Stijl* magazine was launched. This was followed in November 1918 by the first *de Stijl* manifesto. Subsequently van Doesburg made contact with Mies van der Rohe, Mendelssohn and Gropius, and visited the Bauhaus in Weimar. In 1922 he became friendly with Schwitters and participated in the Dada movement in Holland. Van Doesburg gave lectures in Prague, Vienna and Brünn on the aesthetics of the *de Stijl* movement before evolving his 'Elementalism', a variant of Neo-Plasticism based on the use of diagonals, which led to a rift with Mondrian. In 1926 he published the manifesto of Elementalism. Then, from 1926 to 1928, he collaborated with Arp and Sophie Taeuber-Arp on the decoration of the L'Aubette restaurant in Strasbourg. In 1931 he became a founder member of the Parisian *Abstraction-Création* association. He was also co-editor, with Hélion, of the magazine *Art Concret*. Apart from Mondrian van Doesburg was the most important member of the *de Stijl* or Neo-Plastic movement. Although he was not a particularly gifted painter he was a lively and highly intelligent polemicist and was largely responsible for the propagation of the concept of 'concrete form' or *forme esprit*. It was van Doesburg who said that there was nothing more concrete or more real than a line, a colour or a plane. The ideas which he helped to formulate exerted a considerable influence on both the Bauhaus and the *Abstraction-Création* association.

Theo van Doesburg. *Grundbegriffe der neuen gestaltenden Kunst*, Bauhausbuch 25; contributions to various magazines such as *de Stijl, Mecanoa, Art Concret* and *Valori Plastici*.
J. J. Sweeney. *Theo van Doesburg, Retrospective Exhibition*, Art of This Century Gallery, New York 1947.
Exhibition catalogue, *Theo van Doesburg*, Van Abbe Museum, Eindhoven 1968.

Domela, César. Dutch painter, b. 1900. An abstract artist, Domela was a member of the *de Stijl* movement.

Dominguez, Oscar. Spanish painter and sculptor, b. 1906 in Tenerife, Canary Islands; d. 1958 in Paris. Dominguez taught himself to paint in 1924. In 1927 he paid his first visit to Paris and in 1934 settled there permanently. In the following year he met Breton and Éluard. He then joined the Surrealist movement, remaining a member until 1945.

After painting Surrealist-cum-Veristic pictures after the manner of Dali Dominguez began to produce his automatic paintings in 1935, using the *Decalcomanie* process ('*sans objet préconçu*', i.e. automatic) which he is said to have invented. The works of this period were fantastic rock, grotto and jungle landscapes. Later, under the influence of Picasso and Lam, he created a more objective pictorial world, in which technological products—telephones, typewriters, etc.—were projected into a fantasy environment. Unlike the earlier landscapes, however, this environment was no longer charged with magical power. Dominguez also constructed Surrealist sculptures, in which he utilized ready-mades.

Domoto, Hisao. Japanese painter and sculptor, b. 1928 in Kyoto. Domoto attended the Kyoto Academy, completing his studies there in 1949. In 1955 he settled in Paris, where he first worked in a lyrical, informal style. Later, in the early 1960s, he began to strengthen his composition, producing serried structures, which he has also executed in aluminium from 1963 onwards.

Donaldson, Antony. English painter, b. 1939 at Godalming, Surrey. Donaldson studied at the Slade School, 1958–62, exhibiting annually in the *Young Contemporaries* exhibitions at the same time. He held his first one-man exhibition in 1963, at which a picture was bought by the Tate Gallery. Donaldson is one of a group of very young artists who came into sudden prominence in the early sixties. The Anglo-American style then current tended towards Pop imagery or towards large colour fields or repeated units of form. Donaldson combined both by using, for example, silhouettes of nude photographs as intersecting or interlocking units.

Donati, Enrico. American painter and sculptor, b. 1909 in Milan, Italy. After studying at the University of Pavia, Italy, Donati moved to the United States in 1934 and pursued his studies at the New School for Social Research and the Art Students' League. From 1942 to 1950 he belonged to the Surrealist group with André Breton, Marcel Duchamp, Max Ernst, Matta and others. His works of the mid-1940s reflect this association—roots, undersea fauna, birds, butterflies, fantastic clouds and whirling organic arabesques are placed in open voids as in *St. Elmo's Fire* (1944, New York, Museum of Modern Art). In the late 1940s he replaced his jewel-like biomorphic forms with linear Constructivist compositions such as *Chambre à pression osmotique* (1947, coll. of artist). This style was quickly forfeited for a mode of personal calligraphy executed in melted tar (*Letter to a Friend*, 1949, coll. of artist). It was at this point that Donati became interested in texture. By 1950, when he exhibited in the Venice Biennale, he was working with thickly grained materials, using chemically treated dirt from a vacuum cleaner combined with pigment to produce an opaque woolly texture, as in *Black and Three Whites—Moonscape Series* (1953, Brussels, Musées Royaux des Beaux-Arts de Belgique). His most noteworthy use of colour comes in his late fossil series, as in *Red-Yellow Fossil* (1964, Miami and Detroit, Coll. Mr. and Mrs. Lee Hills) where colour and texture each reinforce the other. In 1961 Donati was given a major retrospective exhibition at the Palais des Beaux-Arts, Brussels.

Peter Selz. *Enrico Donati*, Paris 1965.

Dongen, Kees van. Dutch painter, sculptor and potter, b. 1877 in Delfshaven/Rotterdam; d. 1968. After visiting the USA in 1895 van Dongen worked as a draughtsman for the Rotterdam *Nieuwsblad* until 1897, when he settled in Paris. Between 1900 and 1907 he made frequent visits to the Netherlands, and when in Paris he worked as a porter and housepainter. In 1910 he visited Spain, Morocco and Italy and in 1913 Egypt. From 1913 to 1914 he worked for the *Folle Époque*. From 1932 he lived and worked in Paris and Monaco.

In c. 1897 van Dongen abandoned the heavy, ponderous compositions of his early period and progressed via Monet-style Impressionism to Fauvism, which he completely mastered by 1905. With their luminous, impasted colours and their forceful linear arabesques the paintings which he produced in this period are extremely dynamic. Meanwhile his graphic work revealed the influence of Steinlen, Forain and Toulouse-Lautrec. But in 1913 van Dongen's work began to lose its dynamism, and by 1918 he had become the mundane portraitist of the *Folle Époque*. He then portrayed the actors and financiers, the industrial magnates and politicians, the artists, the *femmes du monde* and the *demi-monde* of his day in decorative and elegant poses. This was the beginning of a uniform period, in which van Dongen tended to make concessions to public taste and in which he established the character of his sitters chiefly by means of dress and décor. In the 1920s and 1930s van Dongen's portraits acquired a sort of monumental elegance. By then he had become the chronicler of a hedonistic era, portraitist to the *beau-monde*, which found its fulfilment in gambling casinos and dance halls.

L. Chaumeuil. *Van Dongen: L'homme et l'artiste. La vie et l'oeuvre*, Geneva 1967.
G. Diehl. *Van Dongen*, Munich 1969.

Donkey's Tail. The *Donkey's Tail* was an artists' association formed under the leadership of Larionov and Gontcharova in Moscow in 1911 by a group of artists who had seceded from the *Bubonovgi Valet* (Jack of Diamonds) association because they objected to its western orientation. The first *Donkey's Tail* exhibition was staged in Moscow on 11 March 1922 and contained works by Larionov, Gontcharova, Malevich, Tatlin and many lesser-known Russian artists. Chagall, who sent a picture from Paris, was also represented. The principal aim of the association was to free Russian art from its dependence on western models by drawing attention to traditional Russian art forms, namely icon painting and peasant art. Although the western influence continued to assert itself and actually increased following the introduction of Futurism, which swept the whole of Russia and pervaded both the *Donkey's Tail* and the *Bubonovgi Valet*, the members of both these associations still insisted on the independent character of Russian art in general and of Russian Futurism in particular.

Dorazio, Piero. Italian painter, b. 1927 in Rome. After studying architecture in 1945–6 Dorazio made contact with the members of the *Arte Sociale* movement and began to paint Social Realist pictures. But in the following year he joined the *Forma I* abstract group and, together with Consagra, Turcato, Perilli, Accardi and others, signed the manifesto opposing Social Realism. In 1947–8 Dorazio visited Prague and Paris and in 1949–50 Austria and Germany. In 1950 he became a founder member of the *Age d'Or* group, which had galleries in Rome, Florence and

Milan. In 1953 he visited the USA. In 1960 he taught at the School of Fine Arts attached to the University of Pennsylvania and from 1963 to 1967 at the University of Pennsylvania proper. In 1968 he spent six months in Berlin. He now lives partly in Rome and partly in Philadelphia. In the mid-1950s following an early Futurist and Constructivist period Dorazio began to produce magical compositions based on coloured squares, which he called *Kasimir* pictures. Then, in 1958, after a brief and superficial contact with Informal Art, Dorazio went on to paint finely structured colour compositions, whose net-like structures are capable of infinite extension. In the following year he produced the first of his screen-processed compositions. During the 1960s these were repeatedly modified and eventually led to the development of his most recent works, which are based on large, powerfully coloured, horizontal bands. Dorazio's pictures are charged with colour and light; he is extremely sensitive to the changing values and gradations of his colour scale, to the quality of spatial movement and to the intrinsic nature of linear and two-dimensional components.

Exhibition catalogue, *P. Dorazio*, Marlborough Gallery, Rome 1969.

D'Orgeix, Christian. French painter, b. 1927 in Foix/Ariège. In 1946 D'Orgeix moved to Paris, where he worked for a theatrical scene painter and an advertising agency. Whilst in Paris he met Wols and saw exhibitions of works by Klee and Kandinsky. In 1949 he visited London, and was impressed by William Blake and the Pre-Raphaelites. In 1950 he visited Spain, and produced his first drawings. In 1951 he returned to Paris, where he created pictorial objects. In 1953 he had his first exhibition (in the Salon des Surindépendants in Paris). In 1955 he visited R. Oelze in Worpswede. In 1961 he won a prize at the Second Biennale in Paris. He now lives partly in Paris and partly in St. Étienne Vallée Française, Lozère.

Catalogue, *Christian d'Orgeix*, Kunsthalle, Düsseldorf 1967.

Dottori, Gherardo. Italian painter, b. 1888 in Perugia. After studying at the Academy of Art in Perugia, Dottori became a Futurist in 1912 and subsequently joined the *Aeropittura* movement together with Tato, Munari, Depero and Filla. In 1922 he left the Futurist camp and evolved an individual style, in which he combined Umbrian tradition with certain aspects of modern art.

P. T. Marinetti. *Dottori pittore perugino*, Perugia 1959.
Dottori: Opere futuriste, Milan 1963 (with a bibliography).

Dova, Gianni. Italian painter, b. 1925 in Rome. Dova studied at the Accademia di Brera, where he was a contemporary of Carrà, Funi and Carpi. Later he met Vantongerloo and Max Bill. He is now living in Milan.

In the composition of his early works, in which he portrayed fantastic and—not infrequently—Baroque themes, Dova was influenced, first by Picasso, and subsequently by the Paris Surrealists. Later, after he had seen works by Mondrian and the *de Stijl* painters, he modified his pictorial conception. In about 1950 Dova evolved a Tachist style based on Chinese ink drawings.

Dove, Arthur Garfield. American painter, b. 1880 in Canadaigua, New York; d. 1946 in Centerport, New York. After attending Hobart College and graduating from Cornell University in 1903, Dove began a career as a commercial illustrator of popular magazines, continuing with this occupation as his means of support until about 1930. During an extended visit to Europe (1907–9) he became friendly with the painters Alfred Maurer and Arthur B. Carles and through the former was introduced to the photographer Alfred Stieglitz, who exhibited his works in 1910 at the 291 Gallery. Dove's *Abstractions* of 1910 clearly place him among the most progressive painters of the time and link his name with that of Kandinsky. Stieglitz gave him a one-man show, again at 291, two years later, where his pastels (a medium in which he worked extensively from 1912 until 1920) were particularly successful. In the mid-twenties Dove experimented with collage in a vein of Dada satire (*Goin' Fishin'*, collage, 1925, Washington, D.C., Phillips Collection). His works of the thirties, while remaining non-figurative, are alive with an electric linearity and suggestive of nature in a metaphysical rather than a literal sense (*Rise of the Full Moon*, oil, 1937, Phillips Collection). Less specificity of subject and greater dependence on rectilinear geometry characterize his output of the 1940s, which includes such works as *Parabola* (1943, oil, New York, Downtown Gallery).

Catalogue, *Arthur G. Dove, 1880–1946, A Retrospective Exhibition*, Andrew Dickson White Museum of Art, Cornell University, Ithaca (N.Y.) 1954.
Frederick S. Wight. *Arthur G. Dove*, University of California Press, Berkeley and Los Angeles 1958.

Drip Painting. This is a painting technique in which, instead of being applied with a brush, spatula or similar tool, the paint is dripped (or poured) on to the canvas. Although this technique was occasionally used by early twentieth-century artists such as Max Ernst, it only really came to the fore in the 1940s when the Action Painters, especially Jackson Pollock, created an entirely new pictorial style by this means. The Drip Painting technique, as employed by Pollock from 1947 onwards, was admirably suited to the representation of action and of calligraphic movement, which was the very essence of his work. In Action Painting the canvas is laid on the floor so that the artist is able to drip his paint on with great accuracy, creating what are virtually diagrammatic lines of force. Although Drip Painting has much in common with Automatism, it differs from it in so far as its principal objective is the development of formal factors and not the exploration of the subconscious.

Du Bois, Guy Pène. American painter, b. 1884 in Brooklyn, New York; d. 1958 in Boston, Mass. The son of Henri Pène du Bois, a critic and writer on art, literature and music, he received his art training at the New York School of Art (1899–1905) under Carrol Beckwith, William M. Chase, Frank V. Du Mond, Robert Henri and Kenneth H. Miller. He went to Europe in 1905 where he studied with T. Steinlen at the Académie de la Grande Chaumière and first exhibited at the 1906 Salon des Beaux-Arts. When he returned to the United States in 1906 he worked as a reporter and then an art critic on the *New York American* and later on the *New York Tribune* and *New York Evening Post*. For seven years he was editor of *Arts and Decorations*, for which he wrote many articles. During his years of teaching at the Art Students' League (1920–4) he had his first one-man show at the Kraushaar Galleries. His early work, such as *Waiter!* (1912, Passaic, New Jersey, Coll. William F. Laporte), reflects the tutelage of Henri with its loose, painterly stroke, suppression of detail, genre subject and directness of confrontation between figures and spectator. He went to Europe again from 1924 to 1930, where he developed a style of great simplicity. *Opera Box* (1926, New York, Whitney Museum of American Art), with its large single form and simple severe outline of a light figure silhouetted against a dark background, is typical of the period. When he returned to the United States he again taught at the League. By this time his wooden, manikin-like figures, seemingly suspended in space and placed against simple backgrounds, had become permanent fixtures in the history of American painting. Du Bois was also the author of several monographs published by the Whitney Museum of American Art, which include *Edward Hopper* (1931), *George B. Luks* (1931), *John Sloan* (1931), *William J. Glackens* (1931) and *Ernest Lawson* (1932) as well as the 1940 publication *Artists Say the Silliest Things*.

Royal Cortissoz. *Guy Pène du Bois*, New York 1938.
Richard Carl Medford. *Guy Pène du Bois*, Washington County Museum of Fine Arts, Hagerstown (Md.) 1940.

Dubuffet, Jean. French painter, b. 1901 in Le Havre. Dubuffet moved to Paris in 1918. After attending the Académie Julian for a brief period he began to concern himself with literature, music, philosophy and languages. In 1919 he met Max Jacob. During this period he produced only occasional pictures and in 1924 gave up painting altogether. In the following year he took over his father's wine business in Le Havre. Later he went to Buenos Aires as an industrial designer but was dissatisfied with the work and returned to France within a few months. In 1930 he opened a wine wholesale business. He also started to paint again but did not become a full-time painter until 1942. In 1944 he had his first exhibition at René Dronin's gallery in Paris, which was followed by a New York exhibition staged by Pierre Matisse in 1947. Between 1947 and 1949 he made repeated visits to the Sahara, which exerted a considerable influence on his work. In 1961 he had an exhibition in the Museum of Modern Art in New York. Dubuffet is now living in Venice and Paris.

Dubuffet is one of the most original and most uncompromising of contemporary artists. Ever since 1951, when the Studio Facchetti in Paris presented works by Dubuffet, Fautrier, Michaux, Mathieu, Riopelle and Serpan as *Signifiants de l'Informe*, Dubuffet has been regarded as the driving force behind informal art. The richness and versatility of his oeuvre are quite astonishing. So too is the ease with which he has mastered his materials, his technique and his composition. Dubuffet took an early interest in the artistic products of psychotics and amateurs. He collected many of their works and, from 1947 onwards, showed them to the public and even founded a special company to promote this type of art (*Compagnie de l'art brut*). He himself coined the expression 'art brut' to denote the spontaneous, unconscious and 'anti-artistic' quality of such works, many of whose stylistic qualities he incorporated into his own paintings. In his advocacy of 'anti-art' Dubuffet has been the most consistent of all the Dadaist disciples. The direct influence of children's drawings (and of Paul Klee) is to be found primarily in his figurative compositions, such as his Paris *wall pictures* (1942–3), his grotesque series *Corps de Dames* (1950–1) and his *Beardman* (1959). In Dubuffet's art the evocative force of the material plays a very special part. At his exhibition *Microbolus, Macadam & Cie, Hautes Pâtes* of 1946 he showed pictures, whose surfaces consist of a malleable substance made up of plaster, glue, putty and asphalt, which he kneaded, scratched and scribbled on to create the mysterious worn texture of walls that are 'pregnant with experience'. Since 1951 Dubuffet has been producing his *Sols et Terrains* and *Terres Radieuses*. In these pictures of the earth the pictorial ground is modelled so as to represent geological structures, which reveal imprints of vegetable forms, microcosmic concentrations of cellular creatures and traces of tellural events. Both thematically and stylistically these works have much in common with Max Ernst's *Histoire Naturelle*. From 1956 onwards Dubuffet evolved a new and extremely poetic technique. From painted canvases he cut small star-shaped, circular and rhomboid sections and stuck these together—often combining them with dried flowers and leaves and pieces of tinfoil—to form a kind of jigsaw pattern. The uninhibited way in which Dubuffet treats his materials,

that enables him to give free rein to his artistic imagination, has led to the emergence of a completely new conception of painting, for which Michel Tapié has coined the phrase 'art autre'. It is this experimental approach that has made Dubuffet one of the most stimulating artists of the postwar period.

G. Limbourg. *Tableau bon levain à vous de coire la pâte: l'art brut de Jean Dubuffet*, Paris 1953.
P. Selz. Catalogue, *The Work of Jean Dubuffet*, Museum of Modern Art, New York 1962.
M. Loreau. *Catalogue des Travaux de Jean Dubuffet*, Lausanne 1966.
Jean Dubuffet. *Écrits de Jean Dubuffet*, Paris 1967.

Duchamp, Marcel. French painter and art theorist, b. 1887 in Blainville; d. 1968 in Neuilly. Duchamp was the son of a notary, four of whose six children became well-known artists: the painter Jacques Villon, the sculptor Duchamp-Villon, the painter Suzanne Duchamp and Duchamp himself.

After training as a librarian in Geneviève Duchamp worked as a draughtsman and illustrator for the *Courrier Français*. Between 1908 and 1910 he painted a number of Impressionist pictures in order to acquaint himself with the techniques of painting. In 1911 he joined the *Section d'Or* group, and in its exhibition in 1912 exhibited his *Nude Descending a Staircase*, which was to provide the point of departure for a new type of precision painting. In the same year Duchamp completed his pamphlet *Journey around Painting in Eight Months*, and turned his back on conventional art. In 1913 he exhibited his *Nude Descending a Staircase* in the Armory Show in New York where it sparked off a violent controversy. During this period Duchamp earned his living by giving French lessons. In 1913 he made various versions of the *Chocolate Grater*, which anticipated the ready-mades of 1914 onwards. In his ready-mades Duchamp tried to obtain fresh pictorial insights from commonplace objects, thus establishing a new aesthetic medium. According to H. P. Roché, 'Ready-mades are objects which one takes as they are, because one finds them pleasing or displeasing, or which one changes slightly in order to change their original significance.'

In 1914 Duchamp met Francis Picabia who, like him, became one of the mentors of the Dada and Surrealist movements. In 1915 Duchamp went to the USA, where he exerted a considerable influence on Stieglitz and his associates, who had launched an American anti-art movement that ran parallel to the European Dada movement. Between 1915 and 1923 Duchamp worked on his monumental wire and glass construction *The Bride stripped bare by her Bachelors, Even* (*La Mariée mise à nu par ses célibataires, même*). In 1917 he edited two magazines: *The Blind Man* and *Wrong-Wrong*, and in 1920 made experimental abstract films. In 1926 he organized a large exhibition of modern art in New York, and in 1934 published a portfolio entitled *La Mariée mise à nu*. During this period he also produced his *Rotoreliefs*. In 1941 he organized the big Surrealist exhibition in New York, and became co-editor (with André Breton and Max Ernst) of the New York magazine *VVV*. In 1947 he played a leading part in the international Surrealist exhibition in Paris. Duchamp was also a gifted critic and theorist. He wrote in a terse style and had considerable powers of discernment.

Robert Lebel. *Marcel Duchamp*, New York 1959; London 1969.
Catalogue, *The Almost Complete Works of Marcel Duchamp*, Tate Gallery, London 1966.
Calvin Tompkins. *The World of Marcel Duchamp*, New York 1966.

Duchamp-Villon, Raymond (Pierre-Maurice-Raymond Duchamp). French sculptor, b. 1876 in Rouen; d. 1918 in Cannes. He was the son of a lawyer, and the brother of Jacques Villon and Marcel Duchamp. (They agreed to use different surnames around 1901.) From 1894 to 1898 he was a medical student at Paris University: his studies were curtailed through illness. In about 1899 or 1900 he took up sculpture during his convalescence. In 1901 he settled in Paris, and married in 1903. From 1905 on he exhibited annually at the Salon d'Automne. In 1906 he had a one-man show in Prague. In 1907 he moved to the suburb of Puteaux, where he was a neighbour of Villon and Kupka. In 1910 he was appointed vice-president of the jury of the Salon d'Automne and in 1911 was instrumental in organizing a group hanging of Cubist paintings there. He became a central figure in Cubist circles. In 1912 he contributed to the *Section d'Or* exhibition in Paris, and in 1913 to the Armory Show in New York. In 1914 he enlisted in the Medical Corps, and was stationed at St-Germain. He was transferred to the front in 1915, and a year later contracted typhoid fever while stationed in Champagne. He spent the years 1917–18 in military hospitals at Mourmelon and Cannes, where he died on 7 October 1918. The following year a memorial retrospective exhibition was held at the Salon d'Automne in Paris. It is particularly difficult to estimate what was lost by Duchamp-Villon's early death. Most of his small oeuvre is that of an intelligent, educated, but slightly academic *avant-gardiste* and only one or two works hold hints of a major potential.

His early terra-cottas were *art nouveau* in character, but after the relative naturalism of *Torso*, 1907 (Paris, Musée d'Art Moderne), his work became more angularly simplified. The bronze bust of *Baudelaire*, 1911 (New York, Museum of Modern Art), is the most impressive and original of his works at this point. The consciously abstracted *The Lovers*, a plaster relief of 1912 (New York, Museum of Modern Art), and the architectural maquette *Maison Cubiste*, 1912 (now lost), are a sort of academic modernism, with superficial stylistic affinities to Cubism. His most famous work, *Horse*, bronze, 1914 (New York, Museum of Modern Art), grew from similarly stylized

drawings into a self-consciously machine-age image, close to Futurism and possibly influenced by Boccioni's sculpture, which was shown in Paris in 1913. The last work—*Portrait of Professor Gosset*, bronze, 1917–18 (Buffalo, Albright-Knox Art Gallery)—is the most abstract.

Walter Pach. *Raymond Duchamp-Villon*, Paris 1924.
G. H. Hamilton. Catalogue, *Raymond Duchamp-Villon*, Knoedler & Co., New York 1967.

Dudant, Roger. Belgian painter, b. 1929 in Laplaigne. Dudant trained at the Institut de la Cambre under Paul Delvaux. Although he has always concentrated on the structural aspects of painting, in his earlier period Dudant's works invariably contained figurative *motifs*, most of which were taken from the factories and installations of the Hennuyer industrial district. Of recent years, however, his preoccupation with the use of line and the distribution of colour has led to the production of rhythmically organized colour compositions that have grown progressively more abstract.

Dufrêne, François. French affichiste, b. 1930 in Paris. Between 1954 and 1959 Dufrêne belonged to the Parisian group of Letterists. Then, in 1960, he became a founder member of the association of *Nouveaux Réalistes*. He is now living in Paris.

Dufrêne made his name with his *Dessous d'affiches*. These consist of the lower layers of posters, which he tries to interpret as one would interpret a palimpsest. Unlike other poster artists, e.g. Hain, Dufrêne attaches considerable importance to the aesthetic appeal of colour and tone values.

Dufresne, Charles. French painter, b. 1876 in Millemont, Seine-et-Oise; d. 1938 in Seyne-sur-Mer. After training in the sculptors' studio at the École des Beaux-Arts in Paris, Dufresne began to paint in a naturalistic style. Later he attached primary importance to the use of colour, producing works in which Fauvist, Cubist and Post-Cubist elements combined to form a new artistic synthesis. Dufresne's choice of colours was strongly influenced by Delacroix, whilst his composition and brushwork were modelled on Cézanne. Dufresne was a close friend of Dunoyer de Segonzac. From 1899 onwards his work was regularly hung in the Paris Salon; between 1900 and 1905 he also exhibited in the Salon des Indépendants and from 1923 onwards in the Salon des Tuileries. Dufresne's paintings include portraits, landscapes and religious works. He also produced a large body of etchings.

Dufy, Raoul. French painter, b. 1877 in Le Havre; d. 1953 in Forcalquier. After attending evening classes at the École des Beaux-Arts in Le Havre, where he met Othon Friesz and Georges Braque, Dufy continued his studies at the Academy in Paris, which he joined in 1900 and where he renewed his acquaintance with Friesz. In 1903 he had his first show in the Salon des Indépendants, which continued to exhibit his works up to 1936. In 1905 he met Matisse and joined the Fauves. From 1907 onwards he was associated with the Salon d'Automne. In 1908 he stayed with Braque in L'Estaque and came under the influence of Cézanne. In the following year he and Friesz visited Munich together. His friendship with Apollinaire and the fashion designer Poiret also dated from this period. It was Poiret who interested him in textile design and from 1912 onwards, when he worked as a designer for the Lyons silk manufacturer Bianchini-Férier, he exerted considerable influence on the fashion world. In 1913 Dufy visited Hyères, in 1920 Venice and between 1922 and 1923 Florence, Rome and Sicily. In 1925 he accompanied Poiret to Morocco and when the Exposition Internationale des Arts Décoratifs was staged he executed fourteen tapestries for Poiret. In 1930 he won the Carnegie Prize. In 1936–7 he created the décor for the Pavillon de l'Electricité and, later, for the monkey house in the Jardin des Plantes and for the theatre in the Palais de Chaillot (in collaboration with Friesz). During the Second World War Dufy lived in the South of France and in 1950 visited the USA for an operation on his hands, which were partially paralysed. In 1952 he won the International Grand Prix for painting at the Biennale in Venice. He then settled in Forcalquier and remained there for the rest of his life.

Up to 1905 Dufy painted Impressionist works which revealed the influence of van Gogh. He then met Matisse and was overwhelmed by his picture *Luxe, Calme et Volupté.* With its free, flat use of pure colour, its total lack of atmosphere and its rejection of modelled forms, this painting taught him how to heighten his artistic effects, which was what he was looking for at that time. But Dufy's Fauvism was more restrained and decorative than that of Vlaminck or Derain, and the conscious use of colour dissonances, which is such a feature of Matisse's work, did not appeal to him. Although in the early townscapes which he painted between 1905 and 1907 —e.g. *Old Houses in Honfleur* and *Streets with Flags* —he used this powerful, intensive palette of the Fauves, the individual areas of colour are enclosed by powerful contours, which are themselves coloured. This ornamental combination of coloured outlines and areas of pure colour remained the principal characteristic of Dufy's composition. By 1908 his work had also been influenced by Cézanne's constructive view of pictorial form and, when he accompanied Braque to l'Estaque, he produced landscapes and still lifes which reveal the subdued colours, the crystalline structures and the hatching of the Cubists. But Dufy soon abandoned these techniques. By 1910, due no doubt in part to this new-found interest in textile design, his palette had again become brighter and his brushwork lighter and more rhythmical. He then discovered a whole host of new themes in the elegant world of the gambling casinos, the racetracks and the regattas. During this period he used a lively, decorative line which transformed his pictorial objects into arabesques. About 1947 Dufy abandoned multipartite structures and colour contrasts. His *Hommage à Mozart* and his *Red Violin* of 1948 are virtually monochromes. In these works, in which the large, elegantly contoured objects emerge from areas of red, blue or yellow colour, Dufy found a completely individual and highly aesthetic solution to the problems posed by the powerful palette of the Fauves.

J. Lassaigne. *Dufy*, Geneva 1954.
A. Roudinesco. *Dessins de Raoul Dufy*, Lausanne 1958.
M. Brion. *Raoul Dufy*, Paris 1959.
R. Cogniat. *Raoul Dufy*, New York 1962.

Dumitresco, Natalia. Rumanian-French painter, b. 1915 in Bucharest. Dumitresco completed her studies at the Bucharest Academy in 1939 and settled in Paris in 1947. She is married to the painter Alexandre Istrati.

Dumitresco paints lyrical abstract works after the manner of the postwar *École de Paris.*

Dunikowski, Xavery. Polish sculptor, b. 1875 in Cracow; d. 1964 in Warsaw. Dunikowski studied at the Warsaw School of Fine Arts, where he later held a professorial post (1904–9). From 1913 to 1923 he lived in London and Paris, then returned to Poland to take up a teaching post at the Cracow Academy of Art, which he held until 1939. From 1940 to 1945 he was an inmate of Auschwitz Concentration Camp. After the Second World War he taught in Cracow, Warsaw (from 1955) and Wroclaw (from 1959).

After an early Expressionistic and Symbolist phase Dunikowski evolved an individual style, in which he combined decorative forms with a strong sense of objective reality. His oeuvre includes portraits, architectonic sculptures and monuments. The principal feature of his last works (such as *Gora sw Anny* and *Olsztyn*) is their monumental form.

Exhibition catalogues, *Xavery Dunikowski*, Muzeum Nar. Warsaw 1958 and 1961; Muzeum 'Krolikarnia', Warsaw 1968.

Dunoyer de Segonzac, André. French painter, b. 1884 in Boussy-St-Antoine; d. 1974. After studying at the École des Beaux-Arts, Paris, under L. O. Merson from 1901 to 1902 and subsequently under J. P. Laurens and J. E. Blanche, Dunoyer de Segonzac left the school in 1906, and completed his studies independently. In 1908 he became a member of the Société du Salon d'Automne, and in 1909 exhibited with the Indépendants. From 1914 to 1918 he served with the French forces. In 1919 he became a member of the Société Nationale des Beaux-Arts.

In the course of his development Dunoyer de

Segonzac was influenced by various schools of French art. As a student he took his lead from Daumier, Delacroix and Courbet, but between 1906 and 1908 he turned away from the solid composition and dark colours of this early style, and moved towards Impressionism. After his encounter with Cubism Dunoyer de Segonzac simplified his pictorial objects and paid closer attention to the use of perspective, thus producing clearer compositions; after studying Cézanne he brightened his palette and began to use colour as a means of modelling. Having thus equipped himself, he was able to evolve a personal style from c. 1920 onwards, which found expression in portraits of women, landscapes, interiors and still lifes. This style was, and has always remained, an Impressionist style. Throughout his life Dunoyer de Segonzac has recorded his impressions of natural figures and objects in richly coloured and highly differentiated compositions. Not surprisingly, he has tended to favour the watercolour technique, which is particularly well suited to the rapid reproduction of momentary impressions.

C. Roger-Marx. *Dunoyer de Segonzac*, Geneva 1951.
B. Dorival. *Dunoyer de Segonzac*, Geneva 1956.
M. Genevoix. *Dunoyer de Segonzac*, Paris 1960.

Dvijenie (Movement Association). This is an artists' association which was founded in Moscow in 1962 and whose theoretical premises were derived from Constructivism and Suprematism. The pure geometric compositions produced by the members of this association, most of which feature linear screens and kinetic Op Art effects, are all based on the principle of axial symmetry. In 1963 the *Dvijenie* artists also began to produce three-dimensional kinetic objects, which have now been supplemented by kinetic presentations with programmed light projection, electronic music, mime, ballet and recitations. The intellectual leader of the *Dvijenie* association is Lev Nusberg. His ultimate objective is to incorporate the viewer into the artistic process as an active participant. His *Kyber Theatre* is an example of this experimental approach. Originally the *Dvijenie* association consisted of just five painters. Today it also includes musicians, actors, scientists and scholars.

Dvijenie Catalogue, Nuremberg Biennale 1969 (constructive art).

Džamonja, Dušan. Yugoslav sculptor, b. 1928 in Strumica, Macedonia. Džamonja studied at the Academy of Art in Zagreb. From 1954 to 1957 he produced 'geometrical skeletons', i.e. transparent constructions in space, whose symbolic import is subject to the static laws of volume. Since 1957 he has been making block-like, crystalline figures in wood, glass and metal. These fundamentally lyrical structures, which are partly carved, partly chased, and in some cases fitted with glass intestines, are covered with countless tiny spikes and treated with a coat of lead that shines like silver. Although at first sight their pregnant forms are reminiscent of nature in bud, in actual fact they are so different from vegetable and organic structures that they really constitute a rejection of nature. These solemn, festive figures form a link between the human and the creatureless spheres of astral bodies and crystals.

O. Bihalji-Merin. Introduction to the Catalogue for the 30th Biennale, Venice 1960.
Heinz Fuchs. Exhibition catalogue, *Džamonja*, Kunsthalle, Mannheim 1967.

E

Eardley, Joan. British painter, b. 1921 in Sussex; d. 1963 at Killearn, Stirlingshire. Eardley trained at the Glasgow School of Art, 1940–3, and later, after three years as a builder's labourer, at Hospitalfield, Arbroath. She worked in Glasgow and at Catterline on the north-east coast of Scotland. Joan Eardley's intense dedication was balanced by the humanity that led her to live among working people and restricted her subjects to those of the most general significance in her society: the harvest field, the harsh coast, the hearths, tenements and children of the poor. She painted these with a controlled Expressionism that never lost sight of their essential importance.

Eardley first attracted wide notice by her pastels of Glasgow children. At Catterline she devoted much time and energy to her endeavours to paint the sea, though her inland landscapes may be judged even more consistently successful. Since these majestic paintings are still not well-known outside Scotland, her full recognition has been delayed. A representation of her work is in the Scottish National Gallery of Modern Art.

École de Paris. A phrase loosely applied to the artistic life of Paris during the years just before the Great War and between the World Wars, when the city offered the freest opportunity for discussion and exhibition anywhere in Europe and consequently formed the focal point of artistic activity. It is also used to describe a formal, non-Expressionist, figurative (or semi-abstract) style of painting, and even to indicate the painterly Expressionism of the '*peintres maudits*'—misery, alcohol, drugs, poverty and an art of high emotional charge. By the turn of the century the art of the Impressionists, the Post-Impressionists, Rodin and the *Nabis* was internationally known; the museums, the life of the cafés, the private art institutions and studios as well as the presence of masters of the *avant-garde* drew artists from abroad. During the nineteenth century Paris had been a centre for French art, but from around 1905 to 1940 the city provided a home for artists from all over Europe. Picasso settled permanently in Paris in 1904; Gris in 1906; Pascin in 1903; Archipenko and Lipchitz (from Russia) in 1909; Modigliani (from Italy) in 1906; Chagall (from Russia) in 1910–14; Brancusi (from Rumania) by 1904. After the war the movement of artists to Paris continued: Miró came from Spain in 1920, Mondrian 1920–38, Kandinsky 1933–44; Pevsner and Gabo came in 1923 and 1932 respectively. Visits (some extended) by Macdonald Wright, Morgan Russell, Hans Hartung, Matthew Smith and Alexander Calder should also be noted. The *Cercle et Carré*, *Art Concret*, and *Abstraction-Création* movements gave impetus to abstraction, and Paris was also the centre of Surrealism (Breton, Miró, Masson). The freedom of the French capital may be seen in contradistinction to other parts of Europe, e.g. Russia and Germany, in terms of race, creed, politics and artistic styles. Before the Second World War there were exhibitions which drew attention to the paramount importance of Paris as an art centre. In 1949 the Royal Academy held an exhibition entitled *L'École de Paris* in London. The term was revived in the 1950s as the *Nouvelle École de Paris*, which formed the basis for the first *Biennale de Paris*. It is noticeable that many of the innovations of modern art have seminal associations with Paris. However, during the later 1950s, with the international recognition of American abstract painting, New York took the place of Paris.

Eggeling, Viking. Swedish painter and film-maker, b. 1880 in Lund, Sweden; d. 1925 in Berlin. After studying painting in Milan, Eggeling went to live in Paris in 1911. In 1915, shortly after his meeting with Jean Arp, he left Paris for Switzerland, where he met Tristan Tzara. He then established contact with the Dada movement and became a close friend of Hans Richter, with whom he collaborated between 1919 and 1921 on the latter's family estate outside Berlin. Together they evolved their 'scroll pictures' and made the first ever abstract film—*Diagonalsymphonie*—which had its world première in Berlin in 1922. It was largely due to his work on this film that Eggeling made his name.

In his paintings Eggeling tried to construct systematic designs according to the principles of musical composition.

Exhibition catalogue, *Viking Eggeling*, Swedish National Museum, Stockholm 1950.

Egger-Lienz, Albin. Austrian painter, b. 1868 in Stribach, Lienz; d. 1925 in Rentsch, Bolzano. Egger-Lienz was the son of Georg Egger, the church painter. In 1885 he enrolled at the Munich Academy, where he studied under Raupp, Hackl and Lindenschmidt. In 1899 he went to live in Vienna. From 1911 to 1921 he taught at the School of Art in Weimar.

In his early period Egger-Lienz was influenced, first by Defregger, and subsequently by Millet and Hodler. During the First World War he served as an infantryman on the South Tyrolean front, and began to paint monumental pictures, in which war was presented in an heroic light. In these stimulating works the movements and forms were simplified, and there was only one colour: a mixture of red and brown, which was broken down into light and dark areas. A typical example is the fresco in the military chapel in Lienz, which dates from 1925. After the war Egger-Lienz abandoned the linear style that he had used until then, and developed a painterly style. During this period he produced a series of peasant pictures, and also created new versions of earlier paintings (*The Sower* and *The Sower and the Devil* of 1921, and *Totentanz* of 1921). Later he painted ideational pictures, in which he dealt with religious or philosophical themes. In 1925 the University of Innsbruck conferred an honorary doctorate on Egger-Lienz.

H. Hammer. *Albin Egger-Lienz*, Innsbruck 1929.

Egry, József. Hungarian painter, b. 1883; d. 1951. He painted landscapes, including many of Lake Balaton, in which he expressed a loneliness that was almost painful.

Eight, The. The group of New York painters later known as 'The Eight' formed in 1907 to protest at the restrictive exhibition policies of the National Academy of Design, especially in regard to its rejection that year of a painting by George Luks. The group included Robert Henri, previously a jury member of the Academy, who became the leader of the group, John Sloan, William Glackens, George Luks, Everett Shinn, Arthur Davies, Maurice Prendergast and Ernest Lawson. The eight artists exhibited together as an independent group in February 1908 at the Macbeth Galleries, New York, and despite some negative criticism, the show was a great success—it attracted large crowds, publicity from the press and several sales, and later toured eight other cities, mainly in the Mid-West. Although the artists originally planned to hold other exhibitions, which would also have included European artists, this idea was never carried out. The unity and importance of The Eight lay primarily in their purpose to break away from the Academy and to emphasize the validity of the depiction of the contemporary American scene, especially urban life, in both its happy and less pleasant forms; in this respect the artists paralleled the contemporary American literary movement of the naturalistic novel, e.g. the work of Theodore Dreiser. The styles of The Eight differed, although they reflected European influences, and a realistic style predominated; their frequently dark palettes provoked such epithets as the 'Black Gang' and the 'Black Revolutionists', and in the 1930s the rather misleading term 'Ashcan School' became associated with them. The Eight furthered the American artists' freedom and precipitated later independent exhibitions such as the Exhibition of Independent Artists of 1910 and the Armory Show of 1913, in both of which they were well represented.

Walter Pach. 'The Eight Then and Now', *Art News* XLII, January 1944.
Van Wyck Brooks. 'The Eight's Battle for US Art', *Art News* LIII, November 1954.
Sam Hunter. '"The Eight"—Insurgent Realists', *Art in America* XLIV, Fall 1956.

Eikaas, Ludvig. Norwegian painter, b. 1920. After training at the Oslo Industrial School of Art and the Oslo Academy of Art (under Jean Heiberg) Eikaas continued his studies on journeys to Denmark, Spain, France, Holland and Italy. In 1950 he collaborated with Gundersen on the decorations for the Kemiske Fabrik Norden and the façade of the Kunstnärsförbundet House in Oslo, and between 1959 and 1961 joined with Synnøve Aurdal and Sigrun Berg in producing textile designs for the Haakonshalle in Bergen. Eikaas has created a body of important graphic work, primarily woodcuts, and has also produced some splendid watercolours and oil paintings. He is one of the few modern artists with a real gift for portraiture, and his work in this sphere is remarkable for its subtlety. He likes to play with the visual world and often breaks down objective forms, but has never completely discarded them. The conscious irony with which he regards both his environment and himself is reminiscent of the great caricaturists of the interwar years.

Eilshemius, Louis Michel. American painter, b. 1864 in Newark, New Jersey; d. 1941 in New York. Of Dutch descent, he was educated in Geneva and Dresden. After his return to the United States in 1881, he studied book-keeping and agriculture at Cornell University, but soon after took up the study of academic painting at New York's Art Students' League (1884) and at the Académie Julian in Paris under William Bouguereau (1886). His early work is Impressionistic in its focus, but later a more personalized fantasy takes over. In 1908 Eilshemius met Albert Pinkham Ryder, whose visionary paintings became the prime influence on his own often naïvelooking art. For twenty years he travelled throughout the world, to such places as Morocco and Samoa, which proved a great inspiration to his work.

Although a prolific painter, Eilshemius received little recognition until he was acclaimed by Marcel Duchamp and other American artists at the Independents show of 1917; this was followed by his first one-man show in 1920 at the newly formed gallery of the Société Anonyme. However, few collectors purchased his work, and his haunting landscapes and moonlit urban scenes (*New York at Night*, c. 1917, New York, Metropolitan Musuem) remained unknown to the general public. In *Jealousy* (1915, formerly New York, Curt Valentin Gallery) one sees the artist's tortured forms at their most typical: ghostly shapes of women sprawl threateningly in a room whose mood is filled with evil portents. The round painted corners of the canvas, which Eilshemius frequently used to create an illusionistic frame around his pictures, give this work a strikingly theatrical effect. In *Afternoon Wind* (1899, New York, Museum of Modern Art) female nudes float dreamily through a silvery landscape, joined together in erotic, hybrid shapes.

William Schack. *And He Sat Among the Ashes*, New York 1939.
Catalogue, *Masterpieces of Eilshemius*, Artists' Gallery, New York 1959 (with an introduction by Hugh Stix).

Ekeland, Arne. Norwegian painter, b. 1908. During his early period, when he was influenced by the Surrealists, Per Krohg and the German Expressionists, Ekeland developed a socially and politically committed art form. His oeuvre includes numerous paintings in which pale, ghostly figures are set against barren landscapes or working-class townscapes, scenes of battle and insurrections, and visionary works depicting a Utopian future. Since 1948 his painting has become more Realistic.

El Paso. This was a Spanish artists' association which was formed in Madrid in 1957. It was inspired by the Catalonian *Dau al Set* association, and its founder members were the painters Millares, Saura, Feito and Canogar, and the writers Manuel Condé and José Ayllón. In 1958 the painters Manuel Viola and Manuel Rivera and the sculptor Chirino also joined *El Paso*, which continued to stage group exhibitions up to 1960. Its members were exponents of Informal Art, and they exerted a significant influence on the development of modern art in Spain.

Enckell, Magnus. Finnish painter, b. 1870 in Frederikshamm; d. 1925 in Stockholm. Enckell made various working visits to Paris in the 1890s. In 1914 he became a founder member of the *Septem* group. He was the first artist in Finland to offer serious opposition to the Naturalist tradition. After his early Symbolist phase Enckell came under the influence of Renoir, Cézanne and Bonnard in c. 1908 and evolved a decorative form of monumental painting, in which colour was the dominant feature and which had a considerable effect on the development of modern Finnish painting. His *Nyland's Nation*, which he executed in Helsinki in 1913, is a characteristic work.

Ende, Edgar. German painter, b. 1901 in Hamburg-Altona, Germany; d. 1965 near Munich. After serving an apprenticeship as a house painter and then attending the College of Art in Hamburg-Altona, Ende moved to Munich in 1931 and remained either in the city of Munich or its environs for the rest of his life. Together with Schlichter and Geitlinger he became a founder member of the *Neue Gruppe* in 1947 and was represented at the Biennale in Venice in 1954.

Ende is a Surrealist artist. He paints figurative works with mythical and literary overtones after the manner of Dali.

Engelmann, Martin. Dutch painter, b. 1924 in Hoenkoop, Holland. After studying at the School of Graphic Art in Amsterdam and the Industrial School of Art in St. Gallen, Engelmann settled in Paris in 1948. Since then he has painted Surrealist pictures which are peopled by fantasy creatures—half human and half animal—and which appear to have been derived from Sutherland and Bacon.

Engels, Pieter Gerardus Maria (Pieter). Dutch painter, b. 1938 in Rosmalen. Engels trained at the Academy of Art and Design in 's Hertogenbosch and the State Academy of Art in Amsterdam. He worked as a painter until 1962, and has also produced projects, prose writings, poems, short films, etc. He founded the *Engels Products Organization* (EPO), the *Engels New Interment Organization* (ENIO) and the *Engels Third Institute for Research in Subcultural Brambuilding*. Engels' work falls into the category of conceptual and process art.

Catalogue 455, P. G. M. Engels, *The Self-Portrait of this Century*, Stedelijk Museum, Amsterdam.

Engonopoulos, Nicos. Greek painter and poet, b. 1910 in Athens. He spent about five years in Paris and returned to Athens to study art. From 1967 he has been Professor of Painting at the School of Architecture, National Technical University, Athens. He is an eminent Surrealist poet and has produced excellent work in stage scenery and costumes. He is a pure Surrealist. He uses elements inspired by the Mediterranean landscape and the tradition of Greek Classical and folk art.

Engström, Leander. Swedish painter, b. 1886; d. 1927. Engström belonged to the generation which pioneered modern painting in Sweden. In 1907 he entered the school run by the Konstnärsförbundet (The Swedish Artists' Association) in Stockholm, but left in the following year to go to Paris, where he studied under Matisse and was deeply impressed by Cézanne. Cézanne's influence is clearly discernible in his early paintings, which are chiefly remarkable for their gentle atmosphere and delicate colouring. Engström's most original works were inspired by a visit to Lapland and the Lofoten islands. His *Andjägaren* (*Duck Hunter*, 1918), a decorative composition executed in bright, clear colours, is typical. When Engström visited Italy in the early 1920s he was deeply impressed by the monumental paintings of the Early Renaissance and upon his return produced Realistic pictures of the woods and waterfalls of northern Sweden. Of recent years his work has acquired a new dramatic quality.

N. Palmgren. *Leander Engström*, Stockholm 1939.

Ensor, Baron James. Belgian painter, etcher and draughtsman, b. 1860 in Ostend; d. 1949 in Ostend. He made a major contribution to the Symbolist movement in the 1880s and 1890s and is an important forerunner of Expressionism.

James Ensor lived all his life in Ostend except for a brief period in Brussels. His parents kept a souvenir shop selling seashells, fans, porcelain, puppets and carnival masks: objects which appear frequently in Ensor's painting. His childhood was unhappy and he resented the domination of his sensitive artistic father by his mother, a hard-headed businesswoman. His father died of alcoholism in 1887. This background provides part of the explanation for the depressive nature of much of Ensor's work.

For commercial reasons Madame Ensor encouraged him to paint and in 1877 he was sent to the Brussels Academy where he spent three years. From his last year at the Academy dates the precocious drawing *Mystic Death of a Theologian*. Here he establishes his practice of making major statements in this medium (the *Mystic Death* measures 47×41 inches), using a dramatic chiaroscuro technique derived from Rembrandt. Here, too, his sense of the grotesque and his sour humour are already apparent. In painting at this time he was doing still lifes and figures in the Realist tradition of Millet and Courbet. His palette rapidly lightened and in 1881 and 1882 he produced a remarkably original group of interior scenes which anticipate by over a decade the *Intimiste* works of Vuillard and Bonnard. These works brought him his first success: in 1881 he exhibited with the *avant-garde* groups La Chrysalide and L'Essor and at the Brussels Salon. In 1882 two works were accepted by the Paris Salon, but this triumph was soured when the Antwerp Academy rejected his major painting *Woman Eating Oysters* of 1882. Worse was to follow: in 1883 the same picture was rejected by the supposedly *avant-garde* L'Essor and in 1884 his whole entry was turned down by the Brussels Salon. In 1883 Ensor had joined *Les Vingt*, an important exhibiting group which played a major role in the development of Post-Impressionism, but even *Les Vingt* were to reject Ensor's work from time to time.

It seems that the paranoia induced by the critical attacks upon him combined with his unhappy childhood memories to inspire the bitterness and horror of much of his painting over the next fifteen years.

A new phase in his art had already been heralded in 1883 by the painting *Scandalized Masks* in which a man sits drinking at a table while a grotesquely ugly crone carrying a cudgel confronts him in the doorway. Her face is indeed mask-like and in Ensor's paintings of the 1880s and 1890s human faces are replaced by horrific carnival masks. It is largely through this device of the mask that Ensor expressed his *angst*-ridden vision. In 1888 he painted his most famous canvas, the enormous $(8 \times 14$ feet approx.) *Entry of Christ into Brussels*, a carnival vision of Christ in procession in the city streets surrounded by hundreds of mocking masked faces. This painting relates to a group of drawings and etchings by Ensor of scenes from the life of Christ and there is no doubt that he identified himself with Christ: he too was mocked and persecuted. This is made quite clear by a drawing of 1886, *Calvary*, in which the usual inscription INRI is replaced by the word ENSOR. The *Entry of Christ* is freely painted in raw colour and is no doubt Ensor's masterpiece. *Les Vingt* refused to exhibit it.

As well as the masks Ensor was painting still lifes and even landscapes in a colourful, delicate, intensely luminous manner, which he continued to use to the end of his life. About 1900 the visionary quality vanished from his art, although after this date he often tried to recapture it by painting replicas of earlier works. It is ironic that from this time also dates the fame which was to lead to his barony in 1929.

Libby Tannenbaum. *James Ensor*, Museum of Modern Art, New York 1951.

Paul Haesaerts. *James Ensor*, London and New York 1959.

Environments. Environmental art in the United States became especially prominent in the 1960s, as the traditional concept of art as an object notably declined, with trends towards the involvement or participation of the viewer and towards the integration not only of painting, sculpture and architecture, but also of the visual arts with the other art forms. The concept of sculpture as environment, which the viewer can enter, has been exemplified by such artists as Herbert Ferber, who created a room, *Sculpture as Environment*, in 1961, and Mark di Suvero, building huge constructions from junk materials that often invite the viewer to climb on to them or move them. Environmental rooms with fused sculptural and architectural ideas include the work of Frederick Kiesler and, later, Harold Paris. In Pop Art, a certain kind of environmental art was created by life-size tableaux—for example, by George Segal, Edward Kienholz and Claes Oldenburg, some of which the spectator can enter (e.g. Kienholz's *Beanery*

of 1965, a recreation of an actual eating-place of that name). Among the most prominent figures in developing and promoting the integration of the arts in the form of environments and happenings, which may be indoors or outdoors, was Allan Kaprow. In his conception, the environment is closely related to the happening and is often more like an event. Other artists creating environment and happenings in a similar way include Claes Oldenburg and Jim Dine. In addition, the idea of environmental art has come to include the use of aspects of the existing outdoor environment, such as weather or plant and animal life. An example of this is the systems art of Hans Haacke.

Allan Kaprow. *Assemblage, Environments, and Happenings*, New York 1966.

Epstein, Sir Jacob. American-British sculptor, b. 1880 in New York; d. 1959 in London. Epstein was the son of Russian Jewish emigrants. In 1901 he started work in a bronze foundry and attended evening classes in drawing at the Art Students' League in New York. His first teacher was the sculptor George C. Barnard. In 1902 he went to Paris, where he studied at the École des Beaux Arts and, subsequently, at the Académie Julian. Whilst in Paris he travelled to Florence to see the works of Donatello and Michelangelo. He also visited the Louvre, where the Egyptian and ancient Oriental sculptures made a deep impression on him. In 1905 he moved to London and in 1907 became a British citizen. 1907 also saw the completion of the *Strand Statues*, the first of many public commissions to cause a furore. In 1908–9 Epstein produced his first portraits. His tombstone for the grave of Oscar Wilde (d. 1900) evoked a violent reaction both on account of the subject matter and on account of its treatment. In 1912 when Epstein exhibited in Paris, he met Brancusi, Modigliani and Picasso. Then, in 1913, he joined with the sculptor H. Gaudier-Brzeska and a number of painters in founding *The Vortex*, an *avant-garde* group which survived for only two years. During this experimental period, Epstein gravitated towards abstract art: in some of his sculptures he moved towards Brancusi whilst in his *Rock Drill* he reflected the widespread interest generated by the hard, dynamic forms of the new machine age. His reputation was based primarily on the numerous portraits of members of his family, friends, people in high society and famous men and women of his day, which he modelled in an Impressionist style with great psychological insight and a virtuoso technique. But his monumental works, most of which were carved in stone, remained genuinely experimental. They reveal a marked predilection for archaic and primitive forms and a definite interest in Symbolist values that is reminiscent of Blake. Epstein, who had numerous exhibitions and was commissioned to execute works for various public bodies, was knighted for his services in 1954. He exercised great authority in the British art world but, because of the dual nature of his work, he remained a highly controversial figure to the day of his death.

Richard Buckle. *Jacob Epstein: Sculptor*, London and New York 1963.
Epstein, Sir Jacob. *Epstein, An Autobiography*, London and New York 1963.

Equipo 57. The *Equipo 57* is a group of Spanish artists from Córdoba who broke away from the *Grupo Espacio* in 1957. Its members are José Duarte (b. 1928), Juan Serrano (b. 1929), Ángel Duart (b. 1930), Augustín Ibbarola (b. 1930) and Juan Cuenca (b. 1934). Their work, which is systematically organized in the Constructivist mode, is grounded in the theoretical premises of Pevsner, Gabo and Vasarély.

Erbslöh, Adolf. German painter, b. 1881 in New York; d. 1947 in Irschenhausen, Upper Bavaria. Erbslöh studied in Karlsruhe and Munich. He then settled in Munich in 1904 and spent the rest of his life there. In 1909 he became a founder member of the New Artists' Association, which broke up two years later due to differences of opinion between those artists who followed Erbslöh and Kanoldt and a second group of artists who subsequently founded the *Blauer Reiter* association. From 1916 to 1920 Erbslöh was a member of the *New Secession*.

In his early work, which was strongly influenced by the Fauvist paintings of Jawlensky and—to a lesser extent—Kandinsky, Erbslöh combined linear composition with an expressive use of colour. Later he adopted a traditional style, producing purely decorative landscapes and portraits.

Exhibition catalogue, *Adolf Erbslöh*, Kunst- und Museumsverein, Wuppertal 1967 (with a complete catalogue of works and a bibliography).

Erichsen, Thorvald. Norwegian painter, b. 1868 in Trondheim; d. 1939 in Oslo. He lived in Paris for a while (1893) and was influenced by the Impressionists, particularly Monet and Bonnard. However, he used light in a Realist rather than an Impressionist manner. He did not align himself with any particular school but worked to a great extent in isolation.

Eriksson, Elis. Swedish sculptor, b. 1906. During his early period Eriksson created works which reflect a great love of fairy tales. Later, he abandoned this imaginative approach in favour of a constructive style of sculpture, producing semi-abstract polychrome plaster reliefs, tile mosaics and collage-like reliefs composed of sawn-out plywood shapes. In 1956 Eriksson created a relief for the façade of the grammar school in the Blackeberg district of Stockholm.

Erixson, Sven. Swedish painter, b. 1899 in Botkyrka, Sweden. During his early period Erixson worked as a craftsman and decorative artist and as a teacher of drawing. Later, in the 1930s, he became the leading representative of the Primitivist-Expressionist faction within the *Färg och Form* (Colour and Form) group. From 1943 to 1953 he held a professorial post at the Stockholm College of Art.

For his paintings of scenes from everyday life, Erixson evolved his own highly personal palette, beginning with dark, earthy colours and progressing to exuberant and incandescent hues. His decorative talent brought him numerous commissions for monumental works. He also created designs for tapestries, stained-glass windows and, above all, stage sets, which made a significant contribution to the development of Swedish theatrical art.

Erni, Hans. Swiss painter, b. 1909 in Lucerne. He visited Paris and joined the *Abstraction-Création*. He produced murals and posters and illustrated books, as well as painting in various styles. He also wrote art criticism.

Ernst, Jimmy (Ulrich). American painter, b. 1920 in Bruehl, near Cologne, Germany. The son of the Surrealist painter Max Ernst and the art critic and journalist Louise Amalia Straus, he attended the Lindenthal Real-Gymnasium, Cologne (1932–6), and then a craft school in Altona, Germany. He went to the United States in 1938 just before the outbreak of the Second World War and began his artistic career in New York in 1940, without having had any formal training. His early works show a strong influence of Surrealism but his serene organic abstractions are closer to the works of Matta than to those of his father. This influence and a high degree of technical ability in the handling of intricate detail can be seen in the early *Flying Dutchman* (1942, New York, Museum of Modern Art). A few years after his first one-man show (1943), entitled *Reflections of the Inner Eye*, at the Norlyst Gallery, N.Y., he entered the second phase of his development, the Jazz period. This new theme of 1946–9 was in evidence at another exhibition at the Norlyst Gallery under the title *Black Music*. From 1949 to 1956 he entered his White and Black period. *Silent Moment* (1954, Utica, N.Y., Munson-Williams-Proctor Institute) is comprised of rectangles of irregular dimensions interspersed with a few sudden bursts of abstract stars. The hardened forms, complicated geometric configurations and formalized composition are representative of the period. His lack of colour at this time perhaps stems from his association with members of *Studio 35* which included Pollock, de Kooning and Motherwell. He was included in the 1956 Venice Biennale and the following year entered his Rococo period, which was quickly usurped by his rock paintings of 1960, in which he reintroduced vibrant colour (*Rim Rock*, coll. of artist). 1961 saw the emergence of his Gothic period. *Here and Now* (1963, New York, Grace Borgenicht Gallery) continues the density of form seen in his Rococo period (1957–9). The emphasis is on straight lines and a decided verticality superimposed over minute subdivisions of the surface which gives the canvas the quality of a mosaic or stained-glass window. Ernst has taught at Brooklyn College since 1950, and among his scholarly articles is 'The Artist as Humanist' (*College Art Journal*, 1955).

Robert D. Kinsman. *The Art of Jimmy Ernst*, Institute of Arts, Detroit 1963–4.

Ernst, Max. German-French painter, sculptor, collagist and inventor of Surrealist techniques, b. 1891 in Germany; d. 1976. Ernst was one of the most influential and best loved of the Surrealists. His own account of his birth is typical of the vein of poetic fantasy which permeates his work: 'On 2 April at 9.45 a.m. Max Ernst hatched from the egg which his mother had laid in an eagle's nest and over which the bird had brooded for seven years.' (From *An Informal Life of Max Ernst*, written by Ernst mostly in the third person, and first published in the catalogue of the retrospective exhibition held at the Museum of Modern Art, New York, 1961.) Childhood memories play an important role in his art. He remembers the 'enchantment and terror' he felt the first time his father (an amateur painter) took him into the forest (strong echoes of this feeling can be found in his *Forest* paintings). He remembers, too, the death of a sister after which, he said, 'the feeling of nothingness and the powers of destruction were utmost in his mind, his behaviour and later in his work', and the death of his pet cockatoo which coincided with the birth of another sister and is no doubt responsible for his later obsession with birds (Ernst in fact identified himself with 'Loplop, Bird Superior' who appears in many of his paintings and drawings).

Under pressure from his parents he enrolled at Bonn University in 1909 but neglected his studies to paint. He was fascinated by the art of the insane which he discovered at this time. In 1911 he met Macke and through him came into contact with the *avant-garde Blauer Reiter* group. He began exhibiting and in 1913 took part in the Erste Deutsche Herbstsalon (First German Autumn Salon) in Berlin organized by Macke and Kandinsky. He made his first visit to Paris in this year. He spent the war as an artillery engineer and later wrote, 'On 1 August 1914 Max Ernst died. He was resurrected on 11 November 1918 as a young man who aspired to find the myths of his time.' He also wrote, 'How to overcome the disgust and fatal boredom that military life and the horrors of war create? Howl? Blaspheme? Vomit?'

After the war Ernst became a leading figure in the Cologne branch of Dada, working under the *nom de guerre* of Dadamax. In 1919 he composed his first collages. Collage had been used by the Cubists as a formal device, but Ernst uses it to record 'a faithful and fixed image of my hallucination'. Used in both these ways it has become one of the most fruitful techniques in twentieth-century art. In 1922 he settled in Paris and the following year painted *Les Hommes n'en sauront rien* (now in the Tate Gallery, London), one of the first masterpieces of Surrealist painting. Made a year before the publication of the First Surrealist Manifesto, it is dedicated to André Breton, the founder of Surrealism. It already has all the characteristic elements of Surrealist painting: the dreamlike atmosphere, the irrational juxtaposition of images of widely different associations, the diagrams of celestial phenomena, the desert landscape and the central eroticism. In 1925 he developed another crucial technique—*frottage*: 'At random I drop pieces of paper on the floor and then rub them with black lead.' The images and textures thus obtained could be freely combined into drawings. Ernst later adapted the technique to painting where, in, for example, the *Forest* series, it had the crucial effect of freeing him from the basically traditional figurative technique he had so far been using.

The first *frottage* drawings were published in 1925 as a book, *Histoire Naturelle*, and in 1929 he produced his first collage book, *La Femme Cent Têtes*. This was followed in 1934 by his masterpiece in this genre, *Une Semaine de Bonté*. In 1938 Ernst quarrelled with Breton and left the Surrealist group. In 1941 he settled in New York and married Peggy Guggenheim. The following year he exhibited a painting, *Man Intrigued by the Flight of a Non-Euclidean Fly*, partly executed by allowing paint to drip from the can. Since the early 1950s his painting has become richly coloured, intensely lyrical and more or less abstract. In 1954 he won first prize at the Venice Biennale and since then has had major retrospective exhibitions at Berne (1956), Paris (1959), New York (1961) and London (1961). Latterly he lived in France.

Escher, Maurits Cornelis. Dutch graphic artist, b. 1898 in Leeuwarden; d. 1972. He trained at the Technical School of Art in Haarlem from 1919 to 1922. He has been living in Baarn (Netherlands) since 1941. Escher's works are based on a Constructivist and mathematical premise. He tries to express concepts such as 'time' and 'infinity' in pictorial terms, although he is well aware that for a graphic artist, who is obliged to work within a two-dimensional framework, such an undertaking is ultimately illusory. Escher's compositions have been used as illustrations in mathematical textbooks for middle-grade students. In 1964 an exhibition of his works was staged at the International Mathematical Congress in Amsterdam, and in 1965 a book by Professor MacGillvray entitled *Symmetry Aspects of M. C. Escher's Periodic Drawings* was published under the auspices of the International Union of Crystallography. A large part of Escher's oeuvre is made up of lithographs, woodcuts and mezzotints.

Catalogue, *M. C. Escher*, Gemeentemuseum, The Hague.
The Graphic Work of M. C. Escher, London 1967.

Estève, Maurice. French painter, b. 1904 in Culan. Estève moved to Paris in 1913. In 1923 he went to Barcelona to work as a draughtsman in a textile factory, but returned to Paris in the following year and attended the Académie Colarossi. From 1930 onwards he exhibited in the Salon des Surindépendants and from 1941 in the Salon d'Automne. He is now living in Paris.

After an early period, in which he painted Realistic and Impressionistic pictures, Estève investigated the curvilinear Cubism of F. Léger in c. 1928. Then, after a brief Surrealist phase, he discovered Cézanne, whose paintings exerted a crucial influence on the whole of his subsequent development. Thus, the precise constructive figure compositions, interiors and still lifes of the 1920s underwent a crucial change in the course of the 1930s, when they acquired a marked painterly quality. Finally, in the 1940s Estève evolved a new form of free abstract art, and from 1945 onwards made a major contribution to the development of the *École de Paris*. Of recent years he has been producing extremely compact compositions executed in deep colours.

P. Francastel. *Maurice Estève*, Paris, 1958.
Catalogue, *Maurice Estève*, Kunsthalle, Düsseldorf 1961.

Etchells, Frederick. English painter and architect, b. 1886; d. 1973. He studied at the Royal College and became a member of Fry's Omega Workshop, but in 1913 he broke away with Wyndham Lewis to found the Rebel Art Centre, and became a member of the Vorticist Group. After the war he was again associated with Lewis in Group X. He was also a founder member of the London Group. Later he turned to architecture.

Étienne-Martin (Martin Étienne). French sculptor, b. 1913 in Loriol, Drôme. After training at the École des Beaux-Arts in Lyons from 1929 to 1933 Étienne-Martin moved to Paris, where he is still living today. Until 1939 he worked at the Académie Ranson, which was run by Malfray and Maillol. Although he won several prizes between 1938 and 1949, including the Prix Blumenthal, Étienne-Martin long remained the most celebrated *inconnu* in the *École de Paris*. His work was considered to be esoteric and hermetic; because of its biographical connotations and enigmatic contents, it could not be assessed in purely visual or tactile terms. It was not until he took part in the 'Vitalità nell'arte' exhibition in Venice in 1959 and had a one-man show in the Galerie Breteau in Paris in 1960 that Étienne-Martin began to acquire an international reputation. In 1966 he won the Grand Prix for sculpture at the Venice Biennale. Even Étienne-Martin's early works—wood carvings and bronzes that are often reminiscent of Henri Laurens—illustrate the great range of his thought, which embraces such diverse themes as *Meetings, Couples, Habitations (Demeures)* and *Games*. As a 'traditional sculptor with revolutionary ideas' (Ammann) Étienne-Martin was able to indicate several new paths of development in his multifaceted oeuvre, which acquires its inner coherence from the artist's mythological and cabbalistic *Weltanschauung*. His cave-like *Demeures* have made a major contribution to the fusion of sculptural and architectonic elements. In its capacity as a magical object his *Demeure Nr. 5 (Le Manteau)*, which dates from 1962, anticipated the trends developed at a later date by artists such as Oldenburg and Beuys. With its Baroque vitality and its often highly expressive forms Étienne-Martin's oeuvre embraces figurative, abstract and non-objective tendencies, which are essentially divisive and are held together only by the strong personality of this 'sculptor-alchemist' (P. Guégen).

Catalogue, *Étienne-Martin*, Stedelijk Museum, Amsterdam 1963–4.
Jean-Christophe Ammann. 'Der Bildhauer Étienne-Martin', *Werk*, 1967.

Euston Road School. The name of a school of drawing and painting founded in 1937 and which ran until 1939. It was established by a group of painters who came to be known as the Euston Road Group. The most important of these were Claude Rogers, Graham Bell (who was killed in the war), Victor Pasmore and William Coldstream. Their common aim and their aim in founding the school was to assert the value of an objective relation of the artist to nature as a reaction from and as a positive alternative to the overwhelming influence of contemporary European abstract art. Pasmore and Graham Bell had been involved in a somewhat similar attempt in the Objective Abstraction Group of 1934. The painters naturally turned for inspiration to Sickert and the Camden Town Group and the Euston Road label given them by Clive Bell, suggesting proximity to Camden Town, deliberately suggests this. In their approach to nature the painters emphasized structure above all, still therefore following Cézanne. With William Coldstream structure has remained the chief preoccupation. Claude Rogers, too, has remained faithful to the Euston Road tenets, but Pasmore turned back to abstraction in 1949. The Euston Road painters also provided inspiration for a number of younger artists, but in the end their experiment had little sequel and was cut short by the war. Some painters, such as Medley and Moynihan, exhibited with the group without being members of the school.

R. S. Lambert (ed.). *Art in England*, London 1938.
Arts Council exhibition, London 1948.

Evans, Merlyn. British painter, b. 1910; d. 1973. He was brought up in Scotland. In 1927 he went to the Glasgow School of Art and in 1930, as a scholar, to the Royal College. In the same year he travelled in Europe on a Haldane scholarship. In the 1930s, working in London, he was in contact with the London Surrealists. His work developed in the thirties and forties from a kind of Post-Cubist abstraction towards a more Surrealist attitude to form. From this in the sixties he has turned to compositions of very simple abstract shapes which are entirely non-figurative.

Catalogues, Leicester Art Galleries, London 1949–55, 1958; Whitechapel Gallery, London 1956.

Evenepoel, Henri. Belgian painter, b. 1872 in Nice; d. 1899 in Paris. After some preliminary training in Brussels, Evenepoel migrated to Paris, where he eventually became a pupil of Gustave Moreau. The works of Manet, however, with their rich and painterly handling and rather non-committal, un-literary approach to subject matter, were to be of greater influence on Evenepoel's development. His chosen subject matter was the everyday life of Paris: the parks, bistros and markets, and the ordinary people of the city. The tone of his paintings is still Impressionist, even if many of his stylistic devices, including a sense of pattern derived from Toulouse-Lautrec's posters, were influenced by the Post-Impressionists. Evenepoel was a talented, and at his best a distinguished painter, but his premature death at the age of 27 makes evaluation extremely difficult. His best-known picture is probably the *Spaniard in Paris* (1899, Ghent, Museum of Fine Arts). He also designed posters.

F. Hellens. *Henri Evenepoel*, Antwerp 1947.

Evergood, Philip. American painter, b. 1901 in New York. Educated in England at Eton and Cambridge at the insistence of his parents, Evergood was later drawn to painting. His studies with George Luks at the Art Students' League in 1923 encouraged him to pursue an artistic career. He painted for a short while at the Académie Julian in Paris, but he was disappointed with the teaching methods there, and began a long period of self-training. He returned to America in 1926, yet remained there only three years before travelling to Europe again. He went back to the United States in 1931 during the depths of the Depression, which had much to do with the turn his painting took shortly afterwards. In 1933 he enrolled in the Federal Public Works of Art Project, and in

the next few years he produced his most militant social protest paintings. These works also relate him to the Social Realist trend that was characteristic of American painting during the 1930s (*New Lazarus*, 1927–54, New York, Whitney Museum).

Evergood was always concerned with democratic ideals, and a deep devotion to the resolution of human suffering and social injustice permeates all his work. His propagandistic style was tempered in time, and he eventually returned to his earlier themes of bizarre fantasy. Yet even in a gay and seemingly innocent work such as *Lily and the Sparrows* (1939, New York, Whitney Museum), his preoccupation with the sordid conditions of life remains evident. Despite Evergood's aim to surcharge his paintings with universal meaning—often creating unexpected relationships between the subjects and forms—his palette retained the vivid freshness of children's art.

John I. H. Baur. Catalogue, *Philip Evergood*, Whitney Museum of American Art, New York 1960.
Lucy Lippard. *The Graphic Work of Philip Evergood: Selected Drawings and Complete Prints*, New York 1966.

Expressionism. This concept appears to have been coined by Herwarth Walden, the editor of the *Sturm* magazine, in 1911. In its original form it embraced all progressive movements from Fauvism and Cubism to Futurism and the early abstract trends. Today, however, Expressionism generally refers to one specific artistic movement, which reached its peak in the early part of the twentieth century and was concentrated primarily in Germany. This movement developed as a reaction to Impressionism, which had been concerned with the representation of external appearances; it was remarkable in the first instance for its complete lack of illusionist devices. These were replaced by pictorial forms calculated to express the artist's innermost feelings, which were often prompted by religious zeal, by a sense of social commitment, by a keen awareness of psychological factors or by fervent visions of a golden age. The artists working in this sphere turned away from nature and towards the spirit. For them physical reality was simply a trigger mechanism, a device for sparking off inner experiences. In order to give expression to these experiences they created a simple, powerful and direct pictorial style based on large areas of unbroken colour, dramatic brushwork and a type of structural deformation that often verged on caricature and greatly enhanced the expressiveness of their work. It was van Gogh and Gauguin who paved the way for Expressionism. Van Gogh took the brighter colours evolved by the Impressionists and Pointillists and, by heightening them, produced an expressive technique capable of rendering his own inner feelings, whilst Gauguin created new rhythmical structures by incorporating ornamental forms. This new style, which first appeared in France in the form of Émile Bernard's *Cloisonnisme*, was introduced into

Germany partly by the *Nabis* and partly as a result of the growing interest in the work of Toulouse-Lautrec. The *Nabis* also exerted considerable influence on Edvard Munch, who subsequently made a great impact in Germany. Two other foreign artists who contributed to the development of Expressionism in Germany were Ensor and Hodler. A further important factor was the reappraisal at that time of various unrealistic or naïve art forms, which had been neglected by earlier generations: medieval art, the masks and cult objects of primitive tribes and the colourful, simple designs of folk art. The most extreme form of German Expressionism was evolved by the ecstatic visionaries of the *Brücke*. Further artists who adopted this style included Nolde, Otto Müller, Kokoschka, Beckmann and Rohlfs. The other Expressionist-oriented group in Germany in the 1910s was the *Blauer Reiter*, which developed out of the New Artists' Association. But the members of the *Blauer Reiter*—who were influenced by their contacts with Russian art and with the French Fauvist and Orphist movements—were considerably more restrained than the *Brücke* artists; they incorporated Romantic elements into their work whilst at the same time attaching far greater importance to structural values. Expressionism also led to a resurgence of graphic art, and the prints and drawings produced by the German Expressionists are of a very high order. The most important Expressionist sculptors were Lehmbruck and Barlach. There were, however, virtually no Expressionist architects, for Expressionism did not lend itself to this medium. Although typically German, Expressionism was not restricted to Germany. There were Expressionist movements in nearly all European countries, the most important being French Fauvism. But by and large the Fauves were less concerned with their personal thoughts and feelings than with the artistic problems posed by 'pure painting'. The one exception to this general rule was Rouault, whose religious and satirical painting were certainly inner-directed, although it must be said that today these are seldom classified as Fauvist works. The paintings of Soutine, who was born in Russia and came to Paris as a young man, provide the most extreme examples of Expressionist deformation in French art. As a typical *Sturm und Drang* phenomenon Expressionism did not lend itself to further development. This posed a considerable problem for the postwar generation of German artists and, although Beckmann was able to resolve the dilemma, most could not. Some, like Kandinsky and Jawlensky, sought a solution in abstract art, which led to the evolution—during and after the Second World War—of the international movement known as Abstract Expressionism.

Bernard Myers. *The German Expressionists: A Generation in Revolt*, New York 1957.
Peter Selz. *German Expressionist Painting*, Berkeley (Calif.) 1957.
Carl Zigrosser. *The Expressionists: A Survey of their Graphic Art*, New York 1957.
L. G. Buchheim. *The Graphic Art of German Expressionism*, New York 1960.
Catalogue, *Le Fauvisme français et les débuts de l'Expressionisme allemand*, Paris 1966.

F

Faaberg, Finn. Norwegian painter, b. 1902. Faaberg attended the Oslo School of Arts and Crafts and the Oslo Academy of Art (where he studied under Axel Revold). Since 1946 he has taught at the Oslo School of Arts and Crafts. During his early period Faaberg painted desolate Norwegian landscapes, in which he combined bold, simple compositions with a palette composed of cool blue tints. Later he produced numerous interiors with figures, which reveal a strong sense of social commitment. Many of these depict scenes observed in hospitals, waiting rooms and air raid shelters during the Second World War. After 1945 Faaberg painted views of the Norwegian coast, for which he also used a blue palette.

Fabri, Agenore. Italian sculptor, b. 1911 in Barba, Pistoia. After studying in Pistoia Fabri went to Albissola in Liguria in 1925, where he first worked as an assistant in Tullio Mazzotti's pottery. He now lives and works in Milan.

After an early naturalistic period Fabri came under the influence of A. Martini, M. Marini and the primitive sculptors. His strangely expressive fantasy creations are executed in coloured terra-cotta.

Fahlström, Öyvind. Swedish painter, b. 1928 in São Paulo, Brazil. After spending his early childhood in Brazil, Fahlström lived in Sweden from 1939 to 1961, when he settled in New York. As a student he read archaeology and the history of art, and has since written theatre plays and poems and worked as a journalist. It was in 1952, when he was working with the Fries Opera, that he first began to paint composite pictures incorporating the movement and the narrative development of a whole sequence of scenes. Then, in 1962, he produced his first variable pictures. These works are composed of two or more basic elements and usually have one dominant colour. They presuppose the presence of an observer, who actively participates in the artistic process by arranging the individual *Gestalts* in a composite pattern. Thus the composition is determined by 'character form'. Frequently the individual sections of these pictures are fitted with magnets to facilitate rearrangement. In 1966 Fahlström began making variable multiples. Political, scientific and day-to-day events all feature in his pictures, which reveal the influence of the comic strip.

Faistauer, Anton. Austrian painter, b. 1887 in St. Martin, nr. Lofer, Austria; d. 1930 in Vienna. Faistauer studied at the Academy of Art in Vienna from 1906 to 1909, when he became a founder member of the anti-academic New Art Group of Vienna. In 1926 he painted murals for the Festspielhaus in Salzburg, which were later removed.

Faistauer was a spirited colourist, who painted still-life and figurative compositions. These works, which were influenced by van Gogh, Cézanne, Gauguin and Matisse, occasionally reveal Symbolistic and Naturalistic traits.

A. Roessler. *Der Maler Anton Faistauer*, Vienna 1947.

Falkenstein, Claire. American sculptress and painter, b. 1909 in Coos Bay, Oregon. After receiving a BA degree from the University of California, Berkeley, she taught at Mills College, Oakland, California, and the California School of Fine Arts, San Francisco. Her first interest was painting, but from 1942 she turned increasingly to sculpture. She first used stone and wood and later bronze, synthetic stone and plastics. With these materials, her production was mainly confined to idealized portraiture and then monumental abstractions. In the late 1940s she executed fountains and other quasi-architectural works. This sphere of production continued after she left for Europe in 1950, producing a portal for the villa of Principessa Pignatelli at Santa Marinella near Rome and gates for the garden entrance to Peggy Guggenheim's Palazzo Venier dei Leoni on the Grand Canal, Venice (1962). In Paris she developed her mature style, employing the direct-metal techniques of welding, soldering and brazing. Using sheet iron, brass, copper, iron and silver often fused with glass, she creates lively open forms which, through their intricacy and balance, never seem weak or unstructural. Working in the United States again in the 1960s, she has continued her preoccupation with architecturally oriented sculpture, as in her brazed copper and Venetian glass *Suspended Fountain* of 1962 (Long Beach, California, Dr. and Mrs. Robert Buffum).

M. Tapié. *Claire Falkenstein*, New York 1958.

Fassbender, Joseph. German painter and graphic artist, b. 1903 in Cologne. He studied under R. Seewald at the Cologne Werkschule. In 1929 he won the Villa Romana prize. He is one of those artists whose work goes beyond the Realistic representation of nature and draws freely on its forms and colours. Fassbender now lives in Bornheim.

Fautrier, Jean. French painter, b. 1898 in Paris; d. 1964 in Paris. In 1909 when he was eleven years old, Fautrier was brought to England, where he subsequently studied at the Royal Academy of Fine Arts and the Slade School of Art in London. In 1917 he returned to France and made friends with a number of writers, including Malraux, Ungaretti, Paulhan and Ponge. In 1928 he created a series of lithographs for a luxury edition of Dante's *Inferno*, which are now thought to have anticipated certain aspects of Informal Painting. In 1942 he produced the first of his series of *Otages* (Hostages), creating the *pastosa* texture which has since become so characteristic of his work and which he achieves by applying layer upon layer of very thick, usually whitish-coloured paint with a palette knife. From this mass of paint he fashions the heads, nudes, objects and landscapes which form the subject matter of his pictures and which he frequently arranges in cycles. But the objective significance of these subjects is not immediately apparent: they are presented in the form of signs and hieroglyphs, which the viewer has to decipher. In his choice of colours Fautrier is considered to have been a traditionalist and a comparison has been made between him and Chardin in this respect. Fautrier also tackled the problem of *Originaux Multiples*. He issued these from 1950 onwards but with little initial success. Palma Bucarelli has reported four or five instances of pictures which were executed in editions of 300 copies.

P. Bucarelli. *Jean Fautrier*, Milan 1960.

Fauvism. The term Fauvism does not describe a clearly definable movement, nor any very specific set of commonly shared objectives. There were no manifestos, no theoretical statements. It was coined when the critic Louis Vauxcelles, at the Salon d'Automne, Paris, in 1905, described a restrained sculpture in a room of paintings by Matisse, Rouault, Derain, Vlaminck and others as '*un Donatello parmi les fauves*' (i.e. a genuine artist among the wild beasts). The wildness lay essentially in the violent execution and experimental colour of the paintings. It may also have referred to the subject matter (mainly prostitutes) of Rouault's current paintings, which drew the heaviest criticism. The independence of Rouault's art from any common identity measures the disparateness of Fauve painting. For some, like Vlaminck, a self-styled anarchist, it was a bravado last fling of Post-Impressionism; for Matisse it was a crucial moment of educated decision-making.

Matisse's leadership and influence on the younger painters around him (he was 35) was the dominating aspect of the phenomenon. Most of them had studied alongside him previously: Marquet (at the Petit École, 1891); Rouault, Manguin, Camoin, Flandrin, Guérin, Piot (in the studio of Gustave Moreau, a gifted teacher, 1892–8); Derain, Biette, Chabaud, Laprade, Puy (in Carrière's studio, 1899). He met Derain's friend Vlaminck in 1901. Two Le Havre painters, Friesz and Dufy, exhibited with them in 1905 and were joined by a third, Braque, in a second group show at the 1906 Salon d'Automne. Valtat and van Dongen were also associated with the Fauves.

Fauvism's extra dimension of ruthlessness is attributable in part to the growing interest in primitive arts (Derain and Vlaminck bought a negro mask around 1904/5) and in part to a reaction against the precious narcissism of *fin-de-siècle* Symbolism and *art nouveau*. (In this respect it is comparable to early Expressionism in Germany, Russia, etc., which it influenced extensively.)

This apart, the experimental nature of Fauve painting had obvious roots in the ideas of the great Post-Impressionists, Cézanne, Seurat, van Gogh and Gauguin, all of whose work was widely exhibited in Paris in the 1900s. The use of pure colour in an expressive rather than a naturalistic role; the emphatically separated brushmarks; formal distortions and simplifications; a rhythmic, curvilinear surface organization—all these concerns had been precipitated by the 1880s generation.

The Fauves' overriding preoccupation with the structural and expressive properties of colour was relatively short-lived. Around 1907, Picasso's more formal, sculptural and anti-decorative concerns turned the direction of Parisian painting away from colour towards a more systematic and monochromatic art. This was reflected in the subsequent work of Braque, Derain, Dufy, Vlaminck and others among the Fauves.

For Matisse, Fauvism was an isolated but necessary moment of aggression. He wrote later that 'although I knew I had found my true path, . . . I took fright, realizing that I could not turn back. So I charged head down . . . urged forward by I know not what—a force that I see today is quite alien to my normal life as a man' (1952). In a sense all of Fauvism was symptomatic of its time in this way: a primitive and raw self-assertion of the twentieth-century artist that was almost compulsive. The quality of violence was not sustained by any of the artists concerned.

Jean Leymarie. *Fauvism: Biographical and Critical Study*, London and New York 1959.
Jean Paul Crespelle. *The Fauves*, Greenwich (Conn.) 1962; London 1963.
Charles Chassé. *Les Fauves et leur temps*, Lausanne 1963.
Joseph-Émile Muller. *Fauvism*, London and New York, 1967.

Fazzini, Pericle. Italian sculptor, b. 1913 in Grottamare. After training as a sculptor in Rome, Fazzini accompanied Despiau and de Segonzac on a visit to Paris in 1934. He is now living in Rome.

Fazzini's work revolves around the human figure, which he fashions in strict accordance with the *contrapposto* technique of Classical Italian sculpture. The firm modelling of his figures combines with the sensuous, and in many cases wanton, charm of their attitudes. The natural movement of the limbs, which swing freely in space, is accentuated by the differentiated treatment of the surfaces.

R. Palluchini. *Pericle Fazzini*, Rome 1965.

Feeley, Paul. American painter, b. 1910 in Des Moines, Iowa; d. 1966 in New York City. He was brought up and began his art studies in Palo Alto, California. He completed his training in New York City at the Art Students' League with Thomas Hart Benton and at the Beaux-Arts Institute of Design. In 1954, Feeley's paintings, along with the work of such other then unknowns as Kenneth Noland and Robert Morris, were selected by the critic Clement Greenberg for inclusion in a group exhibition at the Kootz Gallery, New York City, entitled *Emerging Talent* and devoted to the most promising artists of the post-Abstract Expressionist generation.

His work is characterized by a concern with simple abstract shapes, lucid colouring and a feeling of emotional repose. This almost Classical disengagement contrasts with the Expressionistic tendencies of many of his contemporaries. In his later years, Feeley began to experiment with sculpture, a logical extension of his concern with form. He was also highly influential as a teacher and organized the first major exhibitions of the work of the sculptor David Smith and the painters Jackson Pollock and Hans Hoffman. The painter Helen Frankenthaler was one of his pupils.

Catalogue, *Paul Feeley: Memorial Exhibition*, Solomon R. Guggenheim Museum, New York 1968.

Fehrenbach, Gerson. German sculptor, b. 1932 in Villingen, Black Forest. Fehrenbach trained in Berlin under Karl Hartung at the College of Fine Arts from 1954 onwards. In his sculptures he combines vegetal and mineral structures with a sense of proportion based on the human form.

Feininger, Lyonel. American painter, b. 1871 in New York; d. 1956 in New York. Feininger's parents were musicians who emigrated to New York from Germany. Feininger was also a gifted musician. He took violin lessons from the age of twelve, and in 1887 set out for Hamburg to study music. But on the way he decided to become a painter instead and, upon arrival, enrolled at the Industrial School of Art in Hamburg, going on from there to the Berlin Academy in the autumn of 1888. In Berlin he studied under Hancke, Schlabitz and Woldemar Friedrich, who helped him develop his outstanding draughtsmanship. Between 1890 and 1906 Feininger produced illustrations and humorous drawings for *Ulk* and *Lustige Blätter* in Berlin. In 1890 he attended the Jesuit College in Liège, and in 1892–3 studied at the Académie Colarossi in Paris before returning to Berlin. In 1906, the year in which he signed a contract with the Chicago *Sunday Tribune*, he visited Weimar. From there he went on to Paris, where he made contact with the German painters in Matisse's circle in the Café du Dôme. He also became friendly with Jules Pascin and Richard Goetz, and was introduced by the latter to the colour theories of Georges Seurat. In 1906 he had his first meeting with Robert Delaunay, and from 1907 onwards concentrated exclusively on painting. In 1910 Feininger exhibited with the Berlin *Sezession*, in 1911 he contributed to the Salon des Indépendants and in 1913 to the First German Autumn Salon. In 1917 he had his first one-man show, which was staged by H. Walden in the Sturm Gallery in Berlin, and in 1919 W. Gropius invited him to join the staff of the Bauhaus in Weimar. He accepted, and remained in Weimar until 1924 as a 'master of form' and artistic director of the printing shop. In 1924 Feininger joined the *Blaue Vier*. From 1925 to 1933 his permanent residence was in Dessau, but the two years from 1929 to 1931 he spent in Halle. In 1936 he returned to the USA, his work having been proscribed in Germany by the Nazis. In 1939 he painted murals for the International Exhibition in New York.

During his early period Feininger was full of self-doubt, and found it difficult to make his way. It is widely held that R. Delaunay, the French Cubists and the German Expressionists were the principal influences in his artistic development. In point of fact, however, Caspar David Friedrich and J. M. W. Turner, van Gogh and Cézanne were just as important. Feininger's principal *motif* was architecture, which he depicted in Cubist terms, using clearly recognizable and extremely precise linear structures. The rigidity of these basic forms, which appear quite uniform, is relieved by patches of rich colour built up in the Neo-Impressionist manner, which ebb and flow according to a completely illogical pattern and exert a highly dynamic effect. Thus, the corporeality of the pictorial objects is greatly reduced, and these architectural *motifs* acquire an unreal quality, like objects in a dream world. In addition to his architectural pictures, Feininger painted a series of seascapes (the Baltic) and pictures of sailing ships. During his Weimar period he painted views of Thuringian villages and towns (such as Gelmerode, of which he did thirteen separate versions, Zirchow, Mönchroda and Erfurt) and pictures of bridges and viaducts. Then, when he moved to Dessau, he painted his views of Lüneburg, whilst the townscapes of Halle date from the two years he spent in that city. After his return to the USA Feininger produced further architectural paintings. His Manhattan series of 1939 is typical.

Dorothy Miller. *Lyonel Feininger*, New York 1944.
Hans Hess. *Lyonel Feininger*, London and New York 1961.
Catalogue, *Lyonel Feininger*, Kunstverein, Hamburg 1961.
Ernst Scheyer. *Lyonel Feininger: Caricature and Fantasy*, Detroit 1964.
Theodore L. Feininger. *Lyonel Feininger: City at the Edge of the World*, London and New York 1965.

Feitó, Luis. Spanish painter, b. 1929. With Saura, Canogar and Millares he helped to form the anti-government *El Paso* group in Madrid, 1957. His painting suggests vast reaches of space with great delicacy. He now paints in a flat style.

Fekete, Esteban. Hungarian-Argentinian graphic artist and painter, b. 1924 in Cinkota, Hungary. Fekete trained as an engineer but gave up his professional career to become a painter. He lived in Turkey, Hungary, Italy and France before settling in Argentina in 1948, where he later became a naturalized Argentinian. In his paintings, which are executed in oils and tempera, he treats *motifs* taken partly from real life and partly from his imagination. He has also illustrated various books and published a series of portfolios of coloured woodcuts. Since 1964 he has been living in Gundernhausen, near Darmstadt.

Julio E. Payró. *Litografías de Esteban Fekete*, Buenos Aires 1959.

Felixmüller, Conrad. German painter and graphic artist, b. 1897 in Dresden. Felixmüller studied in Dresden. In 1916 he had an exhibition in the Sturm Gallery in Berlin. Subsequently he joined the Dresden Secession and the *Novembergruppe*. After the First World War, when he produced a large number of graphic works, he became one of the best-known exponents of *Brücke*-style Expressionism. Later his art became more and more Naturalistic. He is now living in Berlin.

Exhibition catalogue No. 34, *Conrad Felixmüller*, Galerie Ketterer, Munich 1966.

Fell, Sheila. British landscape painter, b. 1931 in Cumberland. Fell studied at the Carlisle School of Art and at St. Martin's School, London. She had her first one-man show at the Beaux-Arts Gallery in 1955. Her pictures, always straight landscapes, frequently of Cumberland, have developed from the slightly patterned heavy drawing of the fifties to the freer and more atmospheric handling of her work at the present time.

Catalogues, Beaux-Arts Gallery, 1955, 1958, 1960, 1962, 1964; Arts Council, 1959.

Fenosa, Apeles. Spanish sculptor, b. 1899. Like many of his fellow-countrymen—Picasso, Gris, Dali and Miró among them—he was involved with the developments in art that took place in Paris in the first half of the twentieth century. His bronzes are lyrical and delicate in style, vegetal in form and sometimes flamboyant.

Ferat, Serge (Gastrebzoff). French painter of Russian origin, b. 1881 in Moscow; d. 1958 in Paris. Ferat went to Paris in 1901. After meeting Picasso and Apollinaire in 1910 he became a faithful disciple of Cubism. In 1913 he bought the *Soirée de Paris* and turned it into an *avant-garde* journal. Later he withdrew from public life an impoverished and embittered man and destroyed a large number of his works.

Ferber, Herbert. American sculptor, b. 1906 in New York. While studying dentistry at Columbia University, New York (DDS, 1930), Ferber studied sculpture at night at the Beaux-Arts Institute of Design (1927–30), and subsequently maintained both careers. His first one-man exhibition was held in 1937, and thereafter he exhibited widely both in the United States and Europe. He received numerous public commissions and the following awards: the Beaux-Arts Institute, New York, Paris prize, 1929; L. C. Tiffany Grant, 1930; Museum of Modern Art, Artists for Victory prize, 1942; International Unknown Political Prisoner competition, Honourable Mention, 1953.

Ferber's sculpture shows a long line of development from closed to open form—from sculpture as object to sculpture as environment. His early work, from the 1930s, is generally massive, and carved in wood or stone. In 1940 he made his first open-wood sculpture, and through the forties worked for greater openness, partly influenced by Henry Moore. At the same time, Ferber's sculpture became strongly vertical, often resting on a single point (*Flame*, lead and brass rods, 1949). Corresponding to this development of form, Ferber's subject matter became increasingly abstract, moving from the human figure, through abstracted organic forms, to the abstract 'roofed sculptures' and 'cages' after 1954, which were based on the concept of sculpture within a limited space; these were paralleled in full scale by the room commissioned in 1961 by the Whitney Museum of American Art, New York, called *Sculpture as Environment, Interior,* consisting of a room-size construction through which the spectator could move, thus participating in the spaces of the sculpture. This construction was the first environmental sculpture to be defined by the limits of a room, and exemplified a 'sculpture of extension', in which space is not displaced, but is pierced and held in tension, a concept that Ferber considered to be the essential innovation of contemporary sculpture. In the 1960s his work became increasingly simplified and formal, best seen in the series of *Calligraphs.*

Ferber also showed notable originality in technique; as he sought more open and abstract forms, he was almost inevitably led away from carved and cast sculpture to direct-metal processes. Around 1945 he began soldering repoussé sheets of lead together at their edges to create hollow forms, and later used copper and brass, which required a natural change to welding in 1950. In addition to using these techniques for constructing his sculpture, Ferber also used them to texture the surfaces with molten metal, another important innovation in contemporary sculpture, which he shared with such sculptors as Ibram Lassaw, Seymour Lipton and Theodore Roszak.

Herbert Ferber. 'On Sculpture', *Art in America* XLII, No. 4, Winter 1954.
Wayne V. Andersen. Retrospective exhibition catalogue, *The Sculpture of Herbert Ferber*, Walker Art Center, Minneapolis 1962.

Fernández Muro, José Antonio. Argentinian painter of Spanish origin, b. 1920 in Madrid. Fernández Muro is a naturalized Argentinian. He first started to paint when he settled in Buenos Aires in 1937 and during his early period worked in a Spanish Expressionist style that is reminiscent of Gutiérrez Solana. Later he turned strictly abstract and joined the Group of Concrete Artists, which had been founded in 1952 and to which his wife Sarah Grilo and Tomás Maldonado also belonged. In 1957 Fernández Muro exhibited with the other members of this group in the Stedelijk Museum in Amsterdam. In 1957–8 he visited Europe and the USA before settling in New York. In 1958 he won the Gold Medal at the International Exhibition in Brussels and in 1960 was awarded the Guggenheim Prize.

C. Cordova Iturburu. *La pintura argentina del siglo XX*, Buenos Aires 1960.

Ferrant, Angel. Spanish sculptor, b. 1891 in Madrid; d. 1961. Like Julio González, Ferrant worked to free himself of the traditional style of sculpture, and moved towards abstraction. In this he was influenced by developments in France, though he did not spend much time outside Spain himself. He has produced mobiles and montages which the spectator can alter himself.

Festa, Tano. Italian painter, b. 1938 in Rome. Festa's early works were influenced by M. Rothko's light walls. In 1960 he went on to monochrome relief collages, which operated at different levels due to the use of linear elements. In 1962–3 he produced 'object paintings' after the manner of M. Duchamp. He then came under the influence of American Op Art and in 1965 began to work in an *aeropittura* style, painting pictures which produce a visual impression of the experience of flight.

Figari, Pedro. Uruguayan painter, b. 1861 in Montevideo; d. 1938 in Montevideo. Figari was a self-taught artist, but he was also a lawyer and politician. Consequently, although he had begun to paint as a young man, it was not until he had retired from professional life at the age of sixty that he was able to paint full time. In 1914 he was made an honorary member of the Society of Uruguayan Artists. In 1921, when he retired, he went to live in Buenos Aires for four years, then moved on to Paris for the next ten years. In his brightly coloured and completely uninhibited paintings, which are reminiscent of the *intimisme* of Vuillard and Bonnard, Figari treated folk *motifs* culled from the Uruguayan urban and rural life of his childhood. In 1935 he returned to Montevideo, where he continued to maintain close contacts with Argentina until his death.

G. Pillement. *Pedro Figari*, Paris 1930.
C. A. Herrera Maclean. *Figari*, Buenos Aires 1943.

Filinov, Pavel. Russian painter, b. 1883 in Moscow. In 1896 Filinov went to St. Petersburg as an orphan. He began to draw at an early age and in 1902, 1908 and 1910 attended classes at the St. Petersburg Academy of Art. In 1910 he also became a founder member of the St. Petersburg artists' association, 'Union of Youth'. In 1914 he created stage sets and illustrations for Mayakovsky's plays. Filinov has never left Russia.

During his early period Filinov was influenced by the Italian Futurists, and produced highly dynamic compositions featuring flat monumental figures. But in 1915 he turned away from Futurism, and began to paint in a less dynamic style based on the principles of Analytical Cubism. The pictures of this later period are delicate and extremely sensitive colour compositions.

Filla, Emil. Czech painter, b. 1882 in Chropyne, Moravia; d. 1953 in Prague. Filla trained under Fr. Thiele and V. Bukovac at the Prague Academy from 1903 to 1906, and from 1907 to 1914 made repeated visits to France, Italy and Germany, where he continued his studies. He spent the whole of the First World War in Holland. During the Second World War he was interned in Buchenwald Concentration Camp as a political prisoner. After the war he taught at the Industrial School of Art in Prague.

Filla was one of the earliest and, from 1946 onwards, one of the most consistent representatives of Cubism in Bohemia. After an early period, in which he painted expressive pictures in a style derived from E. Munch, he was influenced by Georges Braque and, more especially, Pablo Picasso. The figure compositions and still lifes of his maturity are extremely cultured works. Filla also published a book in which he discussed the theories underlying his art (*Kunst und Wirklichkeit: Erwägungen eines Malers*, Prague 1936). Filla was a founder member of the *Osma* group, a member of the *Manes* association, and editor of the *Volné Smery* magazine. He also produced a large graphic oeuvre. As a result of his experiences in Buchenwald he gradually developed a realistic attitude to the object world.

A. Matajcek. *Emil Filla*, Prague 1938.

Film (Experimental Film, Underground Film). Creative artists began to exploit the film medium almost as soon as it was discovered. In 1914 in Russia Michel Larionov made the first Futurist film, *Drama in the Futurist Cabaret No. 13*. This was followed in 1916 by two Italian films: *Futurist Document* and *Il perfido incanto*. By then the Futurist manifesto had been published, and its authors called for a broadly based film technique, which would incorporate elements of all the artistic media. The art films made after 1916 can be divided into three rough categories: (1) abstract films; (2) films prompted by, and representing, real objects; (3) films with a narrative content. Early abstract films were produced by Viking Eggerling (*Diagonalsymphonie* of 1921), Hans Richter (*Rhythmus 21* and *Rhythmus 23*) and Marcel Duchamp (*Anémique Cinéma* of 1925–6); the object film was established by Fernand Léger (*Mechanical Ballet* of 1924) and Man Ray (*Return to Reason* of 1923 and *Emak Bakia* of 1926), whilst films with a narrative content were largely the province of the Surrealists (the most famous of these being the Dali-Bunuel film *Le Chien Andalou* of 1929). Today artists of every school are to be found working in this medium, and many of them have produced outstanding work within the framework of the underground film. One completely new development is the mixed-media presentation, which has led to the combination of film and television techniques (by Nam June Paik, Aldo Tambellini and Wolf Vostell) and also to the emergence of the computer-controlled film (John Whitney's *Permutations* of 1968 and Stan Vanderbeek's *When in the Course of* of 1966–7). Other well-known artist film-makers are: Andy Warhol, Robert Breer, Len Lye, Harry Kramer, Luca Patella, Raymond Hains, Bruce Connor and Robert Nelson.

J. Claus. *Kunst Heute*, Munich 1965.
S. Renan. *The American Underground Film*, New York 1967.
G. Battcock (ed.). *The New American Cinema*, New York 1967.

Finch, Willy. British-Finnish painter, b. 1854 in Brussels; d. 1930 in Helsinki. He studied in Belgium and Paris and joined *Les Vingt*, the Belgian Symbolist group. He met Seurat in 1890; in 1897 he moved to Helsinki and turned to decorative work. Eight years later, when he started painting again, his Neo-Impressionist pictures of the countryside brought a new style to Finland.

Fini, Leonor. Italian-Argentinian painter and designer, b. 1908 in Buenos Aires. Fini is self-taught. In Milan she came under the influence of Carrà, Funi and Tosi. Since 1933 she has been living in Paris. Her work has affinities with Surrealism, in its feeling for the magic world of dreams and fantasies. She has designed for the theatre (mainly ballet) and for films, and has painted portraits of many well-known figures, among them Jean Genet.

Fiori, Ernesto di. Italian sculptor, b. 1884 in Rome; d. 1945 in São Paulo, Brazil. Fiori started his career as a painter and, as a young man, was influenced by F. Hodler. In 1903 he visited Munich, returning to Rome in the following year. In 1908–9 he visited London and Munich. From 1911 to 1914 he lived in Paris, where he was so impressed by the works of A. Maillol and E. Degas that he began to sculpt. In 1916–17 he fought in the war on the German side. From 1917 to 1920 he trained as a sculptor under H. Haller. He then settled in Paris, remaining there until 1936, when he emigrated to Brazil to escape from the National Socialist menace.

Fiori belonged to a generation of sculptors which occupied an intermediate position between two extremes: although it had resolutely turned away from the bourgeois, monumental style of the turn of the century, it was not prepared to go all the way with abstract art. Fiori himself found his artistic niche in the sphere of the nude human figure, which he portrayed in plain and simple terms without recourse to the Classical ideal of beauty or to the Naturalist creed of faithful reproduction. After producing a number of youthful works, which were charged with pathos and full of movement, he displayed a passing interest in the new formal aesthetic of Cubism. But then, between 1910 and 1920, he evolved a completely personal style, in which he fashioned sculptures in wood, bronze and terra-cotta. In these works the attitudes struck by the individual figures and their direction are brought into a state of harmony by means of simple movement *motifs* whilst their form is offset and enhanced by the profound expression of sincerity which illumines their features. The severity and, in many cases, the angularity of the relaxed limbs is mitigated by the treatment of the sculptural surface, which is virtually Impressionistic. The surface texture is never smooth. On the contrary, it invariably reveals traces of the chisel or spatula. The austere reserve of Fiori's nudes stands in marked contrast to the passionate expressiveness that characterizes so many of his portraits and portrait busts.

First German Autumn Salon. The First German Autumn Salon was the biggest and most important of the exhibitions staged by Herwarth Walden in the Sturm Gallery in Berlin prior to the First World War. It was held in 1913 and was inspired by the Parisian Salon d'Automne. The 360 works which Walden showed at this exhibition came from ninety different artists and provided a comprehensive survey of the *avant-garde* art of the day. The contributors included the members of the *Blauer Reiter* and their Russian associates, the members of the *Brücke*, Kokoschka, Kubin, Rohlfs, Nolde, Feininger, Baumeister, the Italian Futurists and the French Orphists (Delaunay, Léger, Gleizes, Metzinger and Picabia). Russia and Eastern Europe were represented by

Chagall, Archipenko, Brancusi, Epstein, Larionov, Gutfreund and Filla. Mondrian, Max Ernst and Arp also took part. But, in addition to contemporary works, Walden also exhibited examples of folk art, Chinese silk paintings and Oriental miniatures, which was of course in keeping with the Expressionist quest for new sources. Henri Rousseau was accorded a place of honour at the exhibition, where no less than twenty of his works were on show.

Fjell, Kai. Norwegian painter, b. 1907 in Skøger, Norway. Fjell studied at the Academy of Art in Oslo. He is now living in Oslo.

In his early works, which were strongly influenced by Munch, Fjell depicted sombre and often macabre themes, using dark and powerful colours. Subsequently he received a fresh stimulus from folk art with the result that his colours became richer and brighter and his pictorial forms more rhythmical and decorative. The principal *motif* in these lyrical works is the madonna or mother. Fjell has also created stage sets and wall paintings.

Flandrin, Jules. French painter and lithographer, b. 1871 in Corenc (Isère); d. 1947 in Paris. He was a pupil of Moreau. He joined the Société Nationale des Beaux-Arts, and also exhibited with the Indépendants and the Salon d'Automne from 1905. Later (from 1923) he also showed work at the Salon des Tuileries. His work consists mainly of decorative figure compositions in a somewhat similar style to those of Maurice Denis, as well as landscapes and townscapes.

Flannagan, John Bernard. American sculptor, b. 1895 in Fargo, North Dakota; d. 1942 in New York. Flannagan's artistic development began with painting; from 1914 to 1917 he studied painting at the Minnesota Institute of Arts, and in the early 1920s painted in a wax technique he learned from Arthur B. Davies. During these years he also began to carve, at first in wood, but after 1928, only in stone.

Flannagan was acutely sensitive to the artistic process: he felt that the image resided within the rock and that the sculptor's creative act merely freed it; in line with this, he wanted to preserve the identity of the original rock so that it would seem free, simple and barely carved at all. For these reasons, he chose to use field stone, and usually preserved a rough, unfinished texture to emphasize its tactility. Flannagan shared this loyalty to the properties of the material with a number of American sculptors of the 1920s and 1930s, even though they worked in divergent styles and different materials.

Flannagan's subject matter, mainly animal images, likewise reflects his desire for the natural and the objective. In fact, he usually preferred animals to 'the narcissistic human figure', as he wanted to avoid the projection of the artist's personality into his work;

to him the material and the sculpture were of the highest importance, with the artist functioning mainly as a means to an end. At the same time, Flannagan's carve-direct sculpture, with no intermediary process between the artist's touch and the final result, remains personal and intimate, especially considering its small scale; he always shunned the monumental. The recurrent *motif* in his work is birth or development, as in *Triumph of the Egg* (granite, 1937), *Jonah and the Whale: Rebirth Motif* (bronze, 1937) and a number of mother and child images. Yet, contrary to this emphasis on growth, an outwardly unfolding process, Flannagan's solid forms turn in on themselves in a circular, self-contained manner, as if towards death or in eternal flux.

Flannagan's first one-man show in New York was in 1927, and was followed by others on a regular basis. In the early 1930s he spent two years in Ireland, the second time on a Guggenheim Fellowship. After 1939, when he suffered a near-fatal accident, he had to give up the strenuous work of carving, and thus turned to cast sculpture, drawings and watercolours. His life, however, had been almost constantly extremely difficult and tragic, and in 1942 he died by suicide, even though by that time his work was beginning to receive recognition.

John B. Flannagan. *Letters of John B. Flannagan*, New York 1942 (with an introduction by W. R. Valentiner; assembled by Margherita Flannagan).
Dorothy C. Miller (ed.). Catalogue, *The Sculpture of John B. Flannagan*, Museum of Modern Art, New York 1942.

Flavin, Dan. American light artist, b. 1933 in Jamaica, N.Y. Flavin had little formal training; he did not pursue art seriously until 1959. In 1961 he began a series of 'icons', which he described as 'blank, almost featureless square-fronted constructions with obvious electric lights'. With his 1963 *Diagonal of Personal Ecstasy*, consisting of a single fluorescent light tube, for the first time without an accompanying 'construction', he sought to dissolve and reform walls, corners and ceilings, restructuring spatial volumes by the placing of his lights. He is considered an outstanding exponent of Minimalist tendencies in light art.

Catalogue, *Dan Flavin: Fluorescent Light, Etc., from Dan Flavin*, National Gallery of Canada, Ottawa 1969.

Fleischmann, Adolf Richard. German painter, b. 1892 in Esslingen, Germany. He studied at the Königliche Kunstgewerbeschule and the Königliche Kunstakademie in Stuttgart where Robert von Haug, Friedrich von Keller, Robert Poetzelberger, Adolf Hölzel and Christian Speyer were among his teachers. He later worked under Karl Caspar at the Kunstakademie in Munich. His career was interrupted by the First World War, during which he was severely injured (1917). After convalescence in Switzerland, he took part in the 1922 *Neue Sezession* exhibition in Munich. While he was living in Germany, Spain and Italy in the 1920s and 1930s, his production of abstract paintings was sporadic, but after 1937, when he settled in France, he restricted himself entirely to this idiom. He lived under various assumed French names during the Second World War and worked in the underground movement in various French cities. Nearly all his paintings were either destroyed during the war or lost during the German Occupation. In France after the war, he was a founder of the *Espace* group and had several one-man shows. He moved to the United States in 1952, where he was a member of the American Abstract Artists. His non-representational style proceeded from one of curved to straight lines and, like Mondrian, he developed a mode confined to horizontals and verticals, though often arranged in an oval format (*1954, No. 20*, Basle, Switzerland, Galerie d'Art Moderne).

Albert Schulze Vellinghausen. *Adolf Fleischmann*, Stuttgart 1966.

Fluxus. This concept, named from the Latin word meaning flowing, disintegrating, describes a new movement which embraces artists from many different countries. It was defined by George Maciunas, one of its promoters, in 1964: 'By and large it would be true to say that *Fluxus* is opposed to serious art and culture and their institutions, it is opposed to Europeanism. It is also opposed to professionalism in art . . . and to every form of art which promotes the artistic ego.' The members of the *Fluxus* movement include: George Brecht, Ay-O, Willem de Ridder, Dick Higgins, Alison Knowles, George Maciunas, Ben Patterson, Ben Vantier, Robert Watts, Emmett Williams and La Monte Young. *Fluxus* festivals were held from 1962 onwards in Wiesbaden, Copenhagen, Paris, Düsseldorf, New York and various other cities. The central feature of all these festivals was the happening, which incorporated elements of the theatre, of music, literature and the more popular entertainment media such as the circus and vaudeville. *Fluxus* is closely related to the happening.

Fluxus Magazine 1–4.
J. Becker and W. Vostell. *Happenings*, Reinbek 1965.

Fontana, Lucio. Italian painter, sculptor and potter, b. 1899 in Rosario di Santa Fé, Argentina; d. 1968 in Varese, Italy. Fontana's parents, who were both Italian, brought him to Milan in 1905 when he was still a child. From 1927 to 1929 he studied at the Accademia di Brera under A. Wildt. In 1930 he began producing abstract sculpture and in 1936 pottery. Meanwhile, in 1934, he had started to contribute to the exhibitions staged by the *Abstraction-Création* association. From 1939 to 1946 he was in Argentina, where he joined with a group of local art students in issuing the *Manifesto Blanco* (1946).

Following his return to Milan he founded the *Movimento Spaziale* or *Spazialismo* association, which embraced artists, critics and art lovers. Fontana then created a number of works, including his luminous ceiling for the Galleria del Naviglio in Milan (1949), in which he embodied the basic spatialist conception underlying this new movement. At that time—in fact, from 1948 onwards—he was active as a potter and also began working on various projects in collaboration with architects. One such joint scheme was the entrance hall for the Ninth International Fair in Milan (1952), for which Fontana produced a sculpture constructed from neon lights. In the preceding year (1951) he had published his *Technical Manifesto*. In 1966 he won the Prize for Italian Artists at the Biennale in Venice.

Fontana's conception of a total art form—one that would also contain a spatial dimension—is dealt with in both of his manifestos (1946 and 1951). He was striving for an integral art, in which 'the human being functions and is made manifest as a total entity'. He conceived this entity as 'a synthesis of physical elements: colour, sound, movement, time and space, which bring about a psycho-physical unity. Colour (the element of space), sound (the element of time) and motion (which develops in time and space) are the fundamental forms of the new art' (1946). In his creative works, especially from the mid-1940s onwards, Fontana transcended the bounds of the orthodox disciplines, i.e. painting and sculpture. This was due partly to his experiments with electric light, partly to the cuts and cracks which he introduced into his paintings and sculptures. Although it is possible to distinguish a dominant stylistic feature in Fontana's output— namely, the opening of plane and space—it is not possible to place his entire output in any one stylistic category. His range extends from Neo-Baroque creations via informal abstracts to monochrome and 'programmed' work. Even his palette has undergone a marked development, his colours having grown progressively more clear—even garish —from the 1950s onwards. Both as an artist and as a human being Fontana exerted a crucial influence on many of his more youthful contemporaries, including the former members of the *Zero* group (e.g. Piero Manzoni).

A. Pica. *Fontana e 20 Spazialismo*, Venice 1953.
Manifesto Blanco (revised edition), Milan 1966.
Exhibition catalogue, *Lucio Fontana*, Kestner Gesellschaft, Hanover 1968 (and elsewhere).

Forain, Jean-Louis. French painter, etcher, lithographer and draughtsman, b. 1852 in Rheims; d. 1931 in La Chesnay, near Versailles. After studying with J. de la Chevreuse; under Gérôme at the École des Beaux-Arts; and with Jean-Baptiste Carpeaux, Forain began to paint in 1870 in the studio of André Gill. He first made his name, however, with drawings of the Parisian scene—done to scrape together a living—that he contributed to various journals. Many of these combined the biting satire of Daumier with the purely visual qualities of Degas. Forain produced a long series of illustrations for magazines such as *Rire*, *La Vie Parisienne*, *Figaro*, *L'Écho de Paris* and *La Vie Moderne*, and also for albums such as *Nous, Vous, Eux* (1893) and *Deux Pays* (1897).

Forain was on friendly terms with Manet, Degas and Desboutin, and he contributed to four of the Impressionist exhibitions, between 1879 and 1886. As a painter, he was also influenced by Degas and Manet. The curious composition of *Le Pêcheur* (Southampton Art Gallery) is pure Degas, and so are many of his other subjects—the scenes of backstage life, with the dancers limbering up or receiving the attentions of elderly admirers. In other paintings, the modelling and colours recall Manet. Although a very uneven artist, Forain, at his best, was able to blend these influences into a distinctive and pleasing personal style. Many of his later pictures and drawings were of courtroom scenes (e.g. *Le Tribunal*, c. 1893–5; *Le Prétoire*, 1908; both in London, Tate Gallery), which derive from Daumier but usually lack his sense of moral seriousness.

In 1898, Forain founded—with Caran d'Ache— the journal *Psst*, and later he was a founder member of the society, *Les Humoristes*. A Chevalier of the Legion of Honour, Forain became a member of the Institut, President of the Société Nationale and, in 1930, an Honorary RA. In the early 1920s, he gave up graphic work to concentrate on oil painting.

Campbell Dodgson. *Forain*, New York 1936.
J. Pujet. *La Vie extraordinaire de Forain*, Paris 1957.

Forner, Raquel. Argentinian painter, b. 1902 in Buenos Aires. Forner is married to the sculptor Bigatti. After training at the Academy in Buenos Aires, she went to Paris, where she completed her studies under Émile-Othon Friesz. In 1932 she returned to Buenos Aires, where she joined with her husband and others in founding the 'Free Art Courses'. In her powerful pictures, which are painted in violent colours and combine objective and abstract forms, Forner reveals a preference for dramatic *motifs*. Characteristic of this tendency are *Spain* (1937) and *The Apocalypse* (1954–6). Since 1957 Forner has drawn her inspiration from space travel and superterrestrial creatures.

J. Merli. *Raquel Forner*, Buenos Aires 1952.
G. Giani. *Raquel Forner*, Milan 1960.

Forrester, John. New Zealand painter, b. 1922. He started painting in 1938, but his career was interrupted by war service from 1939 to 1945. He held his first one-man show in New Zealand in 1946. In 1953 he moved to St. Ives in Cornwall, later to Italy, then in 1960 to Paris. Between 1954 and 1958 he was connected with the Parkhill project in Sheffield. His work is non-figurative and in it he shows a great interest in the pictorial qualities of texture.

Foujita, Tsugouharu. Japanese-French painter and graphic artist, b. 1886 in Tokyo; d. 1968. He studied at the Tokyo Academy of Art from 1906 to 1910 then visited Korea and China in 1911 and London in 1912. The following year he went to Paris, where—apart from the period of the Second World War—he decided to settle. Foujita soon made a name for himself in Paris and joined the circle centred on Chagall, Soutine and Modigliani. After an early period, in which he painted in the European manner, Foujita reverted to a more Japonic art form from about 1925 onwards. His oeuvre includes animal paintings, landscapes, self-portraits and nudes. He has also illustrated many books.

P. Morand. *Foujita*, Paris 1928.
G. Bauer and R. Rey. *Foujita*, Paris 1958.

'Four Bossots'. This is a group organized and named by the critic Yoshiaki Tono. The four exhibited for the first time as a group at the Paris Biennale in 1969. 'Bossot' is the Japanese term for 'without expression' or 'just there'. The group consists of Jiro Takamatsu, Shintaro Tanaka, Nobuo Sekine and Katsuhiko Narita. Their works have these factors in common: the use of basic elements of 'nature' (water, fire, soil, etc.); the proposal of a clearly defined plan; deliberate dependence on natural processes for the plan's implementation.

Franchina, Nino. Italian sculptor, b. 1912 in Palermo. After completing his studies in Palermo in 1935, Franchina went to live in Milan in the following year. In 1936-7 he joined the *Corrente* association in Milan. In 1939 he moved to Rome. In 1947 he became a member of the *Fronte nuovo delle Arti*. He is now living in Rome.

After an early period, in which he was influenced by the Classical art of Maillol and Despiau, Franchina went over to archaic style in 1947. But it was when he began to use abstract forms that he really came into his own. His best works are the coloured metal sheets which he created in the early 1950s. These highly expressive constructions, which he welded together from parts of car bodies and finished in stove enamel, were followed from 1955 onwards by thin, ethereal sculptures, which set up extremely powerful spatial tensions.

Francis, Sam. American painter, b. 1923 in San Mateo, California. After initial study in medicine and psychology at the University of California, Berkeley (1941-3), Francis studied painting with David Parks at the California School of Fine Arts in San Francisco and continued his artistic education at Berkeley (1948-50), receiving both BA and MA degrees. In 1950 he went to Paris where he was friendly with the Canadian painter Jean-Paul Riopelle. He was given his first one-man show in Paris in 1952 and from that time on has been exhibiting steadily in both the United States and in Europe. In the early 1950s his colours were light in tone, owing to the Impressionists, Cézanne and the environment of Paris (*Large Yellow*, 1952, Tokyo, Coll. Sazo Idemitsu). By 1954 his canvases reveal a new boldness in tonality and form as seen in *Red and Black* (New York, Solomon R. Guggenheim Museum) where three areas of colour are inhabited by abstract patterns which bleed into adjacent areas. His world trip in 1957, with long stops in New York, Mexico and Japan, was perhaps the major influence on his future career. The cool palette and compression of elements into segments of the canvas rather than the previous filling of the surface seen in *Japan Line* (1957, coll. of artist) is perhaps suggestive of the *haboku* or 'flung ink' style. The thin texture of the pigment and the delicate drips recall Japanese calligraphy just as the asymmetry and potently empty spaces seem rooted in Japanese tradition. Francis was included in both the 1959 Bienal de São Paulo (Brazil) and Documenta II (Kassel, Germany) of the same year. In the early 1960s he executed his *Blue Balls* series and became increasingly interested in lithography. His work of the mid-1960s has a continued Oriental sensibility with a simplicity of form and composition closely allied to contemporary Minimalist trends (*Mako*, 1966, coll. of artist). A retrospective exhibition of the artist's work was held jointly by the Museum of Fine Arts, Houston, Texas, and the University Art Museum, University of California, Berkeley, in 1967.

J. H. Sweeney. Exhibition catalogue, *Sam Francis*, Museum of Fine Arts, Houston (Texas) 1967.

Francken, Ruth. French painter of Czech origin, b. 1924 in Prague. Francken left Czechoslovakia and settled in Vienna. Later she went to Paris, then from Paris to England, where she studied under Arthur Segall in Oxford. In 1942 she went to New York and attended evening classes at the Art Students' League. In 1950 she visited Italy. In 1952 she settled in Paris, where she is still living today.

Francken draws and paints in an expressive style. Her subject is the human figure, but there is a definite trace of informal influences in her work.

Frankenthaler, Helen. American painter, b. 1928 in New York City. She studied art with the Mexican painter Rufino Tamayo in high school (the Dalton Schools, New York) and, after considerable Cubist training and exercise with Paul Feeley at Bennington College, was led to her own style of Abstract Expressionism through the work of Arshile Gorky and early paintings of Kandinsky. In 1950 Frankenthaler worked with Hans Hofmann, consolidating her already evident talents. She saw Jackson Pollock's work in 1951, at which point she was also looking at Willem de Kooning's paintings. She soon began to recognize more possibilities for herself in Pollock's vocabulary than in the de Kooning-Gorky idiom, which so many young painters were imitating at the time. She responded particularly to a certain surreal element in Pollock—the understated image that was present beneath his webs of interlaced lines. Frankenthaler was also interested in Matisse, and especially Miró, in whom she discovered the same associative qualities that attracted her to Pollock's paintings. In 1958 she married the Abstract Expressionist painter Robert Motherwell.

The initial step in a painting by Helen Frankenthaler is the exploration of various colour combinations, although these may change midway through the work. Her paintings show a preoccupation with small areas of colour on a large canvas, and with ways in which edges meet and accidents are controlled. Her lyrical and sensitive approach to colour allowed a unique interpretation of Pollock's methods. After having used much blank canvas in order to allow a picture to 'breathe', she progressively covered the canvas with washes of colour drawing in paint and not with line. From 1962 Frankenthaler used predominantly acrylic paints, which tend to have less density and opacity than oils. In 1952 she painted *Mountains and Sea* (New York, Metropolitan Museum), whose fragile blues and pinks defined a new approach to the staining of unsized, unprimed canvas with thin liquid pigment, a technique derived from Pollock's method of dripping and staining into raw canvas. In 1953 this painting attracted the attention of the painters Morris Louis and Kenneth Noland, who were soon converted to Frankenthaler's working methods, which they saw as a means to achieve a maximum opticality in their own work. The colour is soaked into the canvas, so as literally to identify painted configuration with actual surface, creating a purely optical, rather than a three-dimensional or illusionistic pocket of space. Frankenthaler subsequently used stronger, although no less original colouration, in more solid-looking shapes than her earlier diaphanous trails and pools.

Frank O'Hara. Catalogue, *Helen Frankenthaler*, Solomon R. Guggenheim Museum, New York 1960.
E. C. Goossen. 'Helen Frankenthaler', *Art International* V, October 1961.

Freddie (Frederik Wilhelm Carlsen). Danish painter and graphic artist, b. 1909 in Copenhagen. He attended the graphic school of the academy in Copenhagen, though as a painter he is self-taught. He has visited France, Germany, Belgium and Sweden, and is one of the leading exponents of Surrealism in Denmark. He has had many exhibitions in Denmark and Sweden.

French, Daniel Chester. American sculptor, b. 1850 in Exeter, New Hampshire; d. 1931 in Stockbridge, Massachusetts. He was self-taught, and worked mainly in bronze and marble. Many of his subjects are portraits of both historical and contemporary figures. He won the Medal of Honour at the Paris Exposition in 1900, and became a member of the American National Academy in 1902.

Fresnaye, Roger de la—*see* **La Fresnaye,** Roger de

Freud, Lucian. German-British painter, b. 1922 in Berlin. The grandson of Sigmund Freud, Lucian Freud came to England in 1932 and was naturalized a British subject in 1939. He studied at the Central School and at Goldsmiths' College. His first one-man show was held in 1944. He is represented at the Tate Gallery. Freud reacted to the Neo-Romanticism of wartime English painting with an art of meticulous detail and pitiless observation. In his later paintings the brushwork is no longer concealed but becomes the vehicle for a sculptural study of faces and bodies. Dramatic lighting and posing is now used instead of the weird ordinariness of his earlier subjects.

Freundlich, Otto. German sculptor, painter and graphic artist, b. 1878 in Stolp, Pomerania; d. 1943 in Lublin. He studied art history under Wölfflin before turning to the practice of art. During the period 1909–14 he visited Paris, where he was Picasso's neighbour at the Bateau-Lavoir. Early on he began to make sculptures; his work of these years reveals the merest flirtation with Cubism. He exhibited at the Cologne *Sonderbund* exhibition of 1912, and in 1919 with the *Novembergruppe*; in 1924 the Graphische Kabinett Nierendorf held an important exhibition of Freundlich's work. From 1924, he was again resident in Paris; these were the years of the influence of Constructivism and primitive art—and, in his pictorial work, of increasing abstraction. Seuphor refers to his 'pure colours, heart in hand, simply juxtaposed in small rectangles, of so candid a freshness that one would vainly seek in them the shadow of a shadow'. From 1932 onwards he became identified with the *Abstraction-Création* group. In 1938 the Galerie Jeanne Bucher in Paris held a retrospective exhibition to mark Freundlich's sixtieth birthday. His art was, however, banned in his own country by the Nazi regime, and was shown at the notorious exhibition of Degenerate Art, held in Munich in 1937 (Freundlich's sculpture *Der neue Mensch* is reproduced as the cover of the catalogue of this exhibition). Arrested in the Pyrenees, where he had made his home, in February 1943, Freundlich died in a Nazi concentration camp.

C. Giedion-Welcker. *Contemporary Sculpture*, New York 1955.
M. Seuphor. *Sculpture of this Century*, London 1959.

Friedlaender, Johnny. German graphic artist and illustrator, b. 1912 in Pless, Silesia. Between 1928 and 1930 Friedlaender studied graphic techniques in Breslau, first under Otto Müller and subsequently under Karl Mensel. From 1930 to 1932 he was in Dresden but fled the country in the following year, proceeding via Czechoslovakia, Switzerland, Austria, France and Belgium to Holland. From 1939 to 1945 he was interned. In 1945 he went to Paris, where he is still living today.

Friedlaender's rhythmical use of line and contour lends a diffuse, visionary quality to his illustrations. Up to 1948 he worked only in black and white, but since then he has also produced coloured illustrations.

Friesz, Othon. French painter, b. 1879 in Le Havre; d. 1949 in Paris. At the age of 12 he went to the local art school where he was taught by the painter Lhuillier, an enlightened man who recommended Delacroix, Géricault, Corot and Chardin as masters he could learn from. Georges Braque and Raoul Dufy also attended this school and Dufy and Friesz became friends. By this time he was painting coastal scenes and views of the port of Le Havre.

In 1899 the town council awarded him a scholarship. He settled in Paris on the Quai St. Michel and attended the studio of Bonnat. Next door was the studio of Gustave Moreau where Matisse and Rouault were students, and they soon became friends. By 1904, Friesz had developed an intensely luminous style, and in 1905 he exhibited at the Salon d'Automne with his fellow townsmen, Braque and Dufy. Together they formed a Le Havre contingent within the Fauve group led by Matisse, which created a sensation at the Salon that year with their intensely coloured, freely painted canvases. Fauvism was the first major movement in modern art, and for the next three years Friesz was one of the most vigorous exponents of the style.

In 1908 the Fauve group broke up. In Friesz the fires of Fauvism were soon extinguished and he spent the rest of his life painting in a relatively conservative manner.

M. Gauthier. *Othon Friesz*, Geneva 1957.

Frink, Elisabeth. British sculptress, b. 1930 in Suffolk. She held her first one-man show at the Beaux-Arts Gallery in London in 1951. She works mostly in bronze. Her work is semi-representational of animals and birds, heavily modelled, suggestive and vaguely menacing, and it is fairly typical of British sculpture of the 1950s. She is influenced perhaps by Giacometti. She has received a great many public commissions both in Britain and abroad.

Catalogues, Beaux-Arts Gallery, London 1952; Whitworth Gallery, Manchester 1962; Arnolfini Gallery, Bristol 1962; Waddington Gallery, London 1968.

Frost, Arthur Burdett. American painter, b. 1887 in Philadelphia; d. 1917 in New York. He was in contact early on with the Synchromists (led by Stanton Macdonald-Wright) and with Robert Henri. He studied in Philadelphia and, in 1905, in New York with William Merritt Chase. In 1906 he went to Paris and came to know the work of the Impressionists. He experimented with theories of colour, learning from Matisse and Delaunay in this respect.

Frost, Terry. British painter, b. 1915 in Leamington. After years of part-time painting, Frost was helped to professional status from 1946 by association with the St. Ives Group, with whom he has remained in contact. He was at the Camberwell School of Art, 1947–9, and taught at the Bath Academy, Corsham, in 1952; he was a Gregory Fellow at Leeds University, 1954–6. Frost is prominent with the St. Ives Group, William Scott and others, in the school of painterly abstraction which came to dominate modern English art in the 1950s, and which depends on intuitive arrangements of form and colour evoking sensations digested from visual experience.

Fruhtrunk, Günther. German painter, b. 1923 in Munich. Before turning to painting Fruhtrunk studied architecture. He then became a pupil in the Atelier Fernand Léger in 1952 and settled in Paris in 1954. In 1967 he obtained a professorial post at the Academy of Art in Munich. Fruhtrunk is a concrete painter.

Fry, Roger. British painter, scholar and critic, b. 1866 in Highgate, London; d. 1934 in London. At Cambridge, Fry obtained a first-class degree in natural science before turning to the study of art. With Fry, painting and the study of art history proceeded together, but he considered himself a painter first. He worked on the *Athenaeum* and the *Burlington Magazine*, on the latter as editor. From 1905 to 1910 he directed the Metropolitan Museum of Art in New York. In 1910 he organized an exhibition at the Grafton Galleries in London, *Manet and the Post-Impressionists*, from which he became known as the champion of the modern French school. He was responsible for the foundation in 1913 of the Omega Workshops, which produced items of furniture, decoration, etc., of beauty and value. He was also closely associated with the London Group, and played a large part in its activities during the height of its achievement in the twenties.

His admiration of the Post-Impressionists, his writings and lectures outweighed his painting in his own time and since. All his writings promoted a clear understanding of the formal basis of expression; he strove for this, sometimes laboriously, in his painting also.

Roger Fry. *Reflections on British Painting*, London 1934; *Last Lectures*, London 1939.
V. Woolf. *Roger Fry*, London 1940.
Q. C. S. Bell. *Roger Fry*, London 1964.

Fuchs, Ernst. Austrian painter, b. 1930 in Vienna. Fuchs studied at the Vienna Academy under Gütersloh from 1946 to 1950. He now lives in Vienna and Paris.

Fuchs is a member of the Viennese School of Fantastic Realism. His mystical, Mannerist portrayals of biblical scenes are inspired by Dürer, Grünewald and Gustave Moreau. Fuchs has also produced a large number of drawings.

W. Schmied. *Malerei des Phantastischen Realismus—Die Wiener Schule*, Vienna 1964.

Fuhr, Xaver. German painter, b. 1898 in Meckarau, near Mannheim, Germany. Fuhr is a self-taught painter. From 1935 to 1945 he was forbidden to work by the Nazis. From 1946 to 1966 he held a professorial post at the Academy of Art in Munich. He has been living in Regensburg since 1950.

Fuhr belongs to the generation of Post-Expressionist painters who have tried to forge a new link between abstract art and objective reality. The works of Cézanne, Chagall and the Cubists constituted the principal points of departure for his paintings, most of which are townscapes. In these works the graphic design, which is built up of a network of completely straight lines, stands out from the multi-coloured ground.

C. Linfert. *Xaver Fuhr*, Berlin 1949.
Exhibition catalogue, *Xaver Fuhr*, Berlin 1968.

Fukushima, Noriaki. Japanese sculptor, b. 1940 in Tottori. He graduated from Kyoto University of Arts and stayed in the United States from 1965 to 1966. After returning to Japan he became concerned with colour in sculpture, but soon after tried to get rid of its visuality, to make defocused work. He used the floor directly, where round plates were scattered at the one-man show of Gallerie 16, Kyoto, in 1966. He has shown in many exhibitions, including the 5th Guggenheim International Exhibition in 1967. He now lives in Kyoto.

Funi, Achille. Italian painter, b. 1890 in Ferrara. Funi trained at the Dosso Dossi Academy in Ferrara and, subsequently (1906–10), at the Accademia di Brera in Milan. From 1914 to 1918 he served with the Italian forces. In 1922 he became a founder member of the *Novecento* and from 1926 onwards helped to organize its exhibitions. Since 1938 he has been Professor of Fresco Painting at the Brera in Milan.

After an early Cubist phase Funi became a Futurist painter. Then, in c. 1920, he joined Derain and the Paris Neo-Classicists. Between 1934 and 1937 he created the frescoes in the conference room of the Palazzo Comunale in Ferrara. After executing this commission he gradually went over to a decorative and sometimes magical form of Realism, which was doubtless inspired by his contact with the Ferrarese Quattrocento school.

G. de Chirico. *Achille Funi*, Milan 1940.

Futurism. This movement was founded by the writer F. T. Marinetti. It was a general movement embracing literature, painting, sculpture, architecture and music. Marinetti published his first Futurist manifesto in an article in *Le Figaro* on 20 February 1909, which called for a new form of art that would reflect contemporary living conditions. This was followed in February 1910 by the 'Manifesto of Futurist Painting', which was signed by C. Carrà, U. Boccioni, G. Balla and G. Severini, who appealed to their fellow artists to develop a Futurist style of painting. In April 1910 a 'Technical Manifesto of Futurist Painting' appeared, and was followed in 1912 and 1914 by two further manifestos, the first on sculpture and the second on architecture. Like the 'Technical Manifesto', these contained practical programmes for the implementation of the Futurist principle of universal dynamism. Futurism brought about a complete break with the aesthetic tradition of the nineteenth century, which had advocated the Classicistic conception of a harmonious and essentially passive art form. The Futurist aesthetic was completely different. It glorified the twin phenomena of movement and speed, the hallmarks of twentieth-century reality, which even in the first decade of the twentieth century was dominated by the development of high-speed transportation and so called for a new visual approach based on psychoanalytical insights and capable of registering simultaneous events. The Futurists expressed the psychological impact of dynamism by introducing new colour qualities and vibrant arabesques. In this way they hoped to create a synthesis embracing time, place, form and colour. By using a Pointillist technique to produce vibrant patches of colour and highly expressive lines of force, the early Futurists were able to 'dematerialize' their pictorial objects. Subsequently, from 1912 onwards, Futurist painting gradually turned non-objective, due to the influence of French Analytical Cubism. Employing Cubist techniques, the Futurists painted pictures in which they portrayed subjective and objective sequences as simultaneous, interlacing movements, thus producing dynamic spatial compositions based on linear structures. In 1912 Boccioni turned to sculpture, creating objects in space, in which the temporal element was represented as a further dimension of movement by the introduction of convex and concave forms which interacted to produce abstract patterns. Italian

Futurism exerted a considerable influence on Dadaism, on Delaunay's Orphic Cubism and on the Russian Rayonnist and Suprematist movements. In Moscow the Burljuk brothers formed a Russian Futurist movement, which was closely allied to Russian abstract Constructivism. The general attitude of the Italian Futurists to social and political questions was strangely ambivalent. Thus, whilst subscribing to the concept of an artistic and political élite—which led them to support the Italian Fascist movement in 1919—they were none the less deeply committed to the eradication of social injustice. They were also a revolutionary group in so far as their futuristic and interdisciplinary conceptions paved the way for the incorporation into the artistic process of modern industrial techniques.

G. C. Argan. *Mostra nazionale della pittura e scultura futurista*, Bologna 1951.
Guido Ballo. Catalogue, *Preistoria del Futurismo*, Milan 1960.
C. Bruni and M. Drudi Gambillo (eds.). *After Boccioni: Futurist Paintings and Documents from 1915 to 1919*, Rome 1961.
Joshua C. Taylor. *Futurism*, New York and Toronto 1961.
R. Carrieri. *Futurism*, Milan 1963.
Marianne W. Martin. *Futurist Art and Theory, 1909–1915*, London and New York 1968.

G

Gabo, Naum. Russian-American sculptor, b. 1890 in Briansk, Russia. Gabo is the brother of A. Pevsner. His real name is Naum Neemia Pevsner. In 1910, in compliance with his father's wishes, Gabo began to study medicine and the natural sciences at the University in Munich, where he also attended a course of lectures by Wölfflin on the history of art and took classes at the Polytechnic. As a result of these extramural activities he became more and more interested in the fine arts. In 1912 he went to Italy to see the art treasures. In 1913 and 1914 he visited his brother Antoine, who was then living in Paris as a painter and who introduced him to Cubism and Orphism. Following the declaration of war Gabo travelled via Copenhagen to Oslo, where his brother joined him in 1915. By then Gabo had created his first constructions (1915), which he signed Gabo. In 1917 he returned to Russia, where he and his brother issued their '*Realistic Manifesto*', in which they proclaimed the Constructivist programme, in 1920. In 1922, by which time it was clear that revolutionary Russia was not interested in abstract art, Gabo left Moscow and settled in Berlin, where he remained for the next ten years. His exhibitions and lectures in Germany and Holland and his contacts with the Bauhaus, the *de Stijl* group and the new architectural movements were all devoted to the propagation of the Constructivist idea, which embraced not only the fine arts but architecture and the social order as well. In 1930 he had his first one-man show entitled *Konstruktive Plastik* in the gallery of the Kestner Gesellschaft in Hanover. Two years later he left Germany, which had been crippled by financial crises, and settled in Paris, where he played a leading part in the affairs of the *Abstraction-Création* association. Soon he was attracted by the activities of the new English artists and art critics and in 1935 he moved to London. There, in conjunction with D. Nicholson and L. Martin, he edited the *Circle* magazine, in which many of his theoretical writings on the artistic and social aspects of Constructivism were subsequently published. In 1938 he made his first visit to the USA in connection with a commission which he had received for the International Exhibition. He also visited the exhibition of his own works which was staged there in the same year. In 1946 he settled in the USA permanently and acquired American citizenship in 1952. He is now living in Middlebury, Connecticut. Gabo created a construction for the Museum in Baltimore in 1951–2 and a relief for the Rockefeller Center in New York in 1956; in 1957 he completed his *Rotterdam Construction*, which now stands in front of the Bijenkorf department store. By now Gabo's Constructivist works have been shown in numerous exhibitions around the world. But this is not the only way in which he has tried to spread the Constructivist idea, which—according to H. Read—appeared to him as 'a vision of transcendental order'. He has often addressed himself to the public, especially the younger generation, in articles in which he has dealt with the different aspects of Constructivism. Moreover, in 1953–4, he was visiting professor at Harvard University, where he was also able to expound his theory.

During his first Constructivist phase Gabo produced figurative works. These consisted of heads and busts constructed along Cubist lines from metal discs, a method that has a parallel in the technological process of cell formation. But as early as 1923 he made his first non-figurative, kinetic sculptures, in which the moving parts were driven by electromotors. He then began to make extensive use of transparent material such as Plexiglass and—a little later—bronze and steel, which he incorporated into his curving and apparently weightless constructions in space. Gabo does not regard his works as an antithesis to nature but as a part of the whole complex of nature. In his view the Constructivist Idea is 'neither a technical schema for an artistic method nor a rebellious demonstration on the part of an artistic sect'. On the contrary, it is 'a general view of the world, an ideology that is grounded in life'.

Catalogue, *Naum Gabo, Antoine Pevsner*, Museum of Modern Art, New York 1948.

Herbert Read and Leslie Martin. *Naum Gabo*, London and Cambridge (Mass.) 1957.
Naum Gabo—Bauten Skulptur Malerei Zeichnungen Grafik (with essays by H. Read and L. Martin), Neuchâtel 1961.

Gaïtis, Yannis. Greek painter, b. 1923 in Athens. He studied in Athens, and from 1954 has been living mainly in Paris. His work is mainly influenced by the informal technique, whether on a canvas or on objects. The human figure appears as a caricature. He very often retains some of the manner of children's drawings.

Gallén-Kallela, Akseli. Finnish painter, b. 1865 in Pori, Finland; d. 1931. Apart from E. Munch, Gallén-Kallela was the most important Scandinavian *Jugendstil* painter. He studied in Helsinki from 1881 to 1883 and in Paris from 1884 to 1890 (under Bouguereau and Bastien-Lepage). After returning home he concentrated primarily on the theme of the Finnish national epic *Kalevala,* for which he produced a series of book illustrations in 1922. For a while Gallén-Kallela was a member of the *Brücke.* He painted numerous frescoes for public buildings and also produced a large graphic oeuvre. His designs for fabrics, jewellery and stained glass gave a powerful impetus to the Finnish craft industry.

After an early Naturalistic phase Gallén-Kallela progressed via French Symbolism and Synthetism to a flat, decorative and stylized form of painting, into which he incorporated elements of Early Renaissance art following a visit to Italy. His Symbolistic art, which was based on a powerful and original feeling for nature and a romantic sense of patriotism, exerted an influence in Finland that went far beyond the borders of the fine arts.

O. Okkonen. *Akseli Gallén-Kallela*, Helsinki 1949.

Garcia-Rossi, Horacio. Argentinian kinetic artist, b. 1929 in Buenos Aires. Garcia-Rossi was a founder member of the *Groupe de Recherche d'Art Visuel* in Paris. In his 'light boxes' the light is constantly refracted either in a transparent filter or in groups of translucent Plexiglass rods. The viewer is able to change both the *motif* and the coloured lights. Garcia-Rossi is now living in Paris.

Garelli, Franco. Italian sculptor, painter and doctor, b. 1909 in Diano d'Alba, Italy. Garelli's principal occupation is surgery. He taught himself to paint and had his first exhibition in Turin in 1936. Since 1948 he has been represented at the Biennale in Venice on various occasions. His sculptures are metal constructions. Their jagged edges and sharp gashes give them an aggressive appearance, which—although basically abstract—is none the less reminiscent of the human figure. Garelli is now living in Milan.

Sculture di Garelli, Milan 1958.

Gargallo, Pablo. Spanish sculptor, b. 1891 in Maella, Aragon; d. 1934 in Reus, near Tarragona. Gargallo went to Paris in 1911 and was attracted by Cubism. His style, under the influence of Picasso, became 'modern', though he was not to neglect the tradition from which he sprang. His first metal sculptures were done in 1911, and they mainly consisted of masks of iron, lead or copper. Later he began to produce complete figures in an expressive style. The powerful *Prophet* in the Musée National d'Art Moderne, Paris, is one of his last works (1933).

Gatch, Lee. American painter, b. 1902 in Baltimore, Maryland; d. 1968 in Trenton, New Jersey. Gatch first studied art with Leon Kroll (b. 1884) and John Sloan at the Maryland Institute of Fine Arts in Baltimore (1920–4). He continued his training in France (1924–5) at the American School in Fontainebleau and at the Académie Moderne, Paris, where his teacher was the Cubist painter André Lhôte. During his stay in France, Gatch came to know and admire the *Nabis* painters and these later influenced his own style. Returning to New York in 1925, he held his first one-man exhibition in 1927 at J. B. Neumann's New Art Circle, New York. The later exhibitions of his work include entries in the Venice Biennale (1950, 1956) and a retrospective exhibition at the Whitney Museum of American Art in New York (1960).

Gatch's paintings are abstractions from nature that reveal his strong interest in formal relationships, texture and Symbolism. His early works in the 1920s were oriented towards Cubism, reflecting his training in Paris. In the 1930s and 1940s he developed a more personal style, employing the figure in abstract compositions and experimenting with paintings based on variations of a single colour (*Pleasure Garden*, 1945, New York, Coll. Mr. and Mrs. Lionel Bauman). Gatch's compositional devices often included sweeping circular shapes and large rectangular elements placed diagonally within the picture frame, especially as his designs increased in simplicity and freedom (*Night Gothic*, 1957, Boston, Museum of Fine Arts). The surface texture, however, increased in richness and in contrasts between thin, translucent passages and thick, matt areas of paint. The use of symbols, often with religious connotations, is also prevalent in Gatch's later work (*The Lamb*, 1954, New York, Coll. Joseph H. Hirschhorn).

Martica Sawin. 'Paintings of Lee Gatch', *Arts* XXXII, New York, May 1958.
Perry T. Rathbone. *Lee Gatch*, American Federation of Arts, New York 1960.

Gaudí, Antonio. Spanish architect, b. 1852 in Reus, Tarragona; d. 1926 in Barcelona. From 1873 to 1878 Gaudí studied architecture and trained as a metalsmith. He was a well-read man, whose interests ranged from the history of art to modern building technology and the social problems of his day; he admired Viollet-le-Duc and Ruskin on the one hand, and medieval Catalan and Arabian art on the other. He executed his first work—a monumental fountain in Barcelona—between 1877 and 1882. He then began to work for Count Guell, who later became his most important patron. The buildings which he designed for the Count include the Casa Guell (1885–9), in which he appears to have anticipated *art nouveau*, and dwellings for factory workers. Meanwhile, in 1884, Gaudí had been placed in charge of the work on the enormous neo-Gothic Church of the Sagrada Familia in Barcelona. Later, between 1891 and 1900, he created a large number of decorative sculptures for this project and, from 1914 until his death in 1928, worked on it exclusively. Other important architectural works, in which Gaudí demonstrated his sculptural bent, were the Casa Milá (1905–10) and the Guell Park (from 1900 onwards).

Essentially Gaudí was a constructive architect who sought to establish a contemporary Gothic style with a distinctly Mediterranean character. Examples of his constructive methods are to be found in the designs which he made for the Church of the Sagrada Familia and the Guell Park, where he employed transverse supports. In his Casa Milá he created a modelled structure, which is thought, amongst other things, to have been a forerunner of Le Corbusier's designs. Gaudí wanted to create a style of architecture which would incorporate all the other arts. After trying to achieve this by adding rich ornamentation to his early buildings, he eventually produced a genuine fusion of the two major artistic disciplines by creating buildings which themselves possessed sculptural and pictorial qualities.

José L. Sert and James J. Sweeney. *Antoni Gaudí*, London and New York 1960.
George R. Collins. *Antonio Gaudí*, London and New York 1960.
E. Casanelles. *Antonio Gaudí: A Reappraisal*, Greenwich (Conn.) and London 1968.

Gaudier-Brzeska, Henri. French sculptor, b. 1891 in St-Jean-de Braye; d. 1915 in Neuville St-Vaast. His name was originally Henri Gaudier. He went to England to study commerce, but turned to sculpture around 1910/11 and settled in London with Sophie Brzeska, where they both adopted the combined name. He was a friend of Wyndham Lewis, and contributed statements on Vorticist sculpture to Lewis's magazine *Blast*. In 1913 he met Roger Fry and Ezra Pound, and exhibited his first sculptures. In 1914 he enlisted in the French Army: during this time he made wood carvings in the trenches and continued to exhibit in London. A year later he was killed at the front. In 1918 a memorial exhibition of his work was held at the Leicester Gallery, London.

During his short working life Gaudier-Brzeska ran the gamut of available *avant-garde* idioms and entered fully into the rather confused spirit of the London art world. His early drawings, gouaches and pastels, richly coloured and textured, reveal the impact of Fry's exhibitions of Matisse and the Post-Impressionists. After 1913 his sculpture developed away from a Rodin-based modelling towards a more personal style of carving. The best late examples are the *Red Stone Dancer* and *Imp*, in veined alabaster (both 1914, London, Tate Gallery). These show some of the influence of Brancusi and Epstein. They have an energetic primitivism and a sense of the modern 'truth to materials' dictum: Henry Moore admired them. All of his sculpture is highly experimental and never developed beyond the stage of a gifted but eclectic artistic adolescence.

H. Brodzky. *Henri Gaudier-Brzeska, 1891–1915*, London 1933.
Mervyn Levey. *Gaudier-Brzeska: Drawings and Sculpture*, London and New York 1965.

Gauguin, Paul. French painter, b. 1848 in Paris; d. 1903 in Atuana, Marquesas Islands. In 1851 his family emigrated to Peru (Lima); his father, a journalist, died on the voyage. In 1855 he returned to France: he lived and was educated at Orléans and then, 1860–5, at a Paris boarding school. From 1865 to 1867 he served as a seaman in the merchant navy on routes to Rio de Janeiro and Valparaiso. In 1867 his mother died. From 1868 to 1871 he served in the French Navy. Back in Paris in 1871, he entered a stockbroker's office. He took evening classes in drawing and started painting. In 1873 he married Mette-Sophie Gad, a Danish girl: they had five children between 1874 and 1883. He was increasingly successful in business and started collecting paintings. Around 1875 he met Pissarro. The following year he exhibited a landscape at the Paris Salon. By 1877 he owned a considerable collection of Barbizon and Impressionist paintings. He started to learn carving and modelling at around this time and from 1879 on frequently spent summers painting with Pissarro. From 1880 to 1886 he contributed to the last four Impressionist exhibitions. In 1883 he gave up work to devote all of his time to painting. In 1884 he went to Rouen for a year, hoping (vainly) to find patrons, and in Denmark, 1884–5, suffered the same experience. In 1885 he returned to Paris, leaving his family in Copenhagen. In 1886 he met van Gogh and, on a first trip to Pont-Aven in Brittany, Émile Bernard. In 1887 he made his first bid for a more exotic environment: he travelled first to Panama, where he worked as a labourer on the canal to raise funds, and then to Martinique. After a severe bout of dysentery he was repatriated. In 1888 he returned to work at Pont-Aven and then (October–December) joined van Gogh at Arles. Back in Paris in 1889, he was impressed by Javanese and Indonesian art at the World's Fair. He exhibited with the French Symbolists at the Café Volpini and with *Les Vingt* in Brussels. In the summer he returned to Brittany (Pont-Aven and Le Pouldu) and grew determined to leave Europe. By 1890 he was a leading figure in Symbolist circles and met the writers Morice, Moréas, Mallarmé and Mirbeau. In 1891 he organized a fund-raising sale of his work. Mallarmé presided at a farewell banquet before his departure on April 4 for Tahiti. The years 1891–3 were spent in Tahiti, first at Papeete and then inland at Mataiea, living among natives. He studied books on Tahitian lore and started writing his own *Ancien Culte Maorie*. He was seldom out of debt or in health and was repatriated in 1893. From then until 1895 he divided his time between Paris and Brittany. He exhibited his Tahitian paintings and started writing *Noa Noa*. He also contracted syphilis. In 1895 he returned to Tahiti (Punavia), and again lived as a native. Increasingly demoralized by ill-health and non-payment of promised funds from Paris, he broke off his correspondence with Mette and, in 1897, attempted suicide by poison. Recovered, he took part-time work in Papeete in 1898 and at the same time Vollard started buying his work in Paris. By 1899 he was regularly publishing satirical attacks on the colonial government in his pamphlet *Le Sourire*. In 1900 he made a contract with Vollard as his dealer and received a monthly allowance. Next year he moved to La Dominique on the Marquesas Islands. Here he wrote his autobiographical *Racontars d'un Rapin* and *Avant et Après*. He continued to conduct campaigns against colonial taxation and injustice and was imprisoned for libel in March 1903. He died at Atuana on 8 May of that year.

Gauguin was one of the major Post-Impressionist painters. His historical importance lies in his leadership of the anti-naturalist Symbolist movement in painting and in the new and positive artistic impulse that he gave to the traditional romance of the 'noble savage'.

After his early rapid assimilation of Impressionist techniques (*Pont d'Iéna*, 1875, Louvre, Paris), his admiration of primitive, medieval and popular arts and his romantic yearning for primitive cultures found sympathy with widely felt social and artistic discontents. He quickly became the focus of a like-minded circle of poets, critics and artists who fed him with ideas and confidence. An aggressive extrovert, he attracted a large following among the younger painters and the reluctant admiration of elders like Pissarro.

Cézanne, Manet and Degas were important early influences, but he was more attracted to Japanese prints, woodcut book illustrations and applied art techniques. The flatly coloured silhouettes and heavy contours of the *Synthétiste* or *Cloisonniste* style of 1888–9 marked the first radical break with Impressionism (*Jacob Wrestling with the Angel*, 1888, Edinburgh, National Gallery). Claims to invention of the style were later hotly disputed by Émile Bernard. For Gauguin it was an important, self-conscious

theoretical shift, renouncing the European tradition of naturalism as decadent. He wrote that painting should not describe, but suggest 'as music does' and warned followers against copying nature—'Art is an abstraction'. These were key issues in his arguments with van Gogh.

In Brittany he wrote of wanting to achieve in his painting something like 'the muffled, heavy and powerful note' of his wooden clogs on the granite soil; in Tahiti of striving for 'a barbaric splendour'. He went to Tahiti hoping to find a world of primitive superstition and, disillusioned by the degree of European influence, reconstructed such a world in his painting and writing. His subject matter comprises oblique questioning allegories of life and death, drawing reference freely from both pagan and Christian arts and traditions. *Where do we come from? What are we? Where are we going?* 1897 (Boston, Museum of Fine Art)—an intended last statement before suicide—sets an Adam and Eve image beside a primitive idol. The figures in his paintings are usually inert and brooding (*Nevermore*, 1897, London, Courtauld Institute Gallery) and the abstract patterns and coloured shapes—he called them 'the musical part'—contribute to the mood of exotic mystery and ambivalence.

He made carvings and woodcuts of the same sort of subject, often executed with a primitive, artless aggression. Both aspects of his art were enormously influential for North European Expressionism and early abstract art theory. The late works, such as *The Call*, 1902 (Cleveland, Museum of Art), were more rapturously idyllic and luxuriant in colour. Their stimulus to the European escapist dream has been reflected in all the arts, fine and popular.

Robert Goldwater. *Paul Gauguin*, New York 1957.

G. Wildenstein. *Gauguin*, Paris 1964.

Bengt Danielsson. *Gauguin in the South Seas*, London and New York 1965.

Catalogue, *Gauguin and the Pont-Aven Group*, Tate Gallery, London 1966.

Gaul, August. German sculptor, b. 1869 in Gross-Anheim; d. 1921 in Berlin. He trained in Hanau and Berlin, and for four years (1893–7) was assistant to the sculptor Reinhold Begas. He spent some time in Italy (1897–8), where he met Adolf von Hildebrand and Hans von Marées. His bronze *Lioness* (1899) and *Lion* (1906) were well received, and he is considered one of the best animal sculptors of his period.

Gaul, Winfred. German painter, b. 1928 in Düsseldorf. Gaul studied from 1950 to 1953 at the Academy of Art in Stuttgart, where Willi Baumeister was one of his teachers. Between 1955 and 1961 he painted informal pictures, many of which he himself has described as 'imaginary landscapes'. Then, in 1961, he made a protracted visit to Rome and, whilst there, developed an interest in the big city. Above all, he concerned himself with traffic signs and signals, which soon became the principal elements of his new pictorial world. Since 1962 he has had several exhibitions of *Traffic Signs and Signals*, of which the artist said: 'Their aesthetics are grounded in the garish colours and gigantic forms which are the new dimension of city life; they constitute an art form which has its habitat amongst the skyscrapers and the new industrial buildings, amongst the lines of traffic at the intersections on the motorways.' Gaul now lives in Antwerp and Düsseldorf.

Exhibition catalogue, *Winfred Gaul. Signaux, Signalen*, Palais des Beaux-Arts, Brussels 1967.

Gear, William. British painter, b. 1915 at Methil, Scotland. Gear trained at the Edinburgh College of Art from 1932 to 1937. He won a travelling scholarship, 1937–8, and studied under Léger. During his war service, 1940–7, he was given his first exhibition in Italy, 1944. He lived in Paris from 1947 to 1950 and was Curator of the Tower Art Gallery, Eastbourne, from 1958 to 1964, when he was appointed Head of Fine Art at Birmingham Art College. He now lives in Birmingham. Examples of his work are in the Tate Gallery.

A member of the School of Paris before New York began to challenge its position, Gear adopted an expressive abstract calligraphy combined with a Scottish colour sense. In c. 1951 he developed a system of interlocking forked diagonal bands of colour to create complex spatial relationships, and since then he has painted consistently in this manner.

Gecelli, Johannes. German painter, b. 1925 in Königsberg. Gecelli studied at the Academy of Art in Düsseldorf from 1947 to 1951. In 1965 he was given a professorial post at the College of Fine Arts in Berlin, which he still holds. Since 1958 Gecelli has been painting monochromes, in which the human body appears in the form of a silhouette executed in a series of interrelating shades.

Geiger, Rupprecht. German architect and painter, b. 1908 in Munich. Geiger is the son of the painter Willi Geiger. Up to 1939 he worked as an architect and did not begin to paint until 1945. He became a member of the *Zen 49* group in 1949 and has been teaching at the Academy of Art in Düsseldorf since 1965. Geiger's meditative compositions, most of which are either monochromes or two-colour works, are closely related to Malevich's Suprematism. Both the ground and the superimposed forms—circles or squares—are painted in carefully graduated, luminous poster colours.

Exhibition catalogue, *Rupprecht Geiger*, Kestner Gesellschaft, Hanover 1967.

Geiger, Willi. German painter and graphic artist, b. 1878 in Schönbrunn, near Landshut. Geiger was a pupil of Stuck. He taught at the Academy of Art in Leipzig from 1928 to 1933 and at the Munich Academy from 1945 to 1951. He is now living in Munich. By using a mixture of reds, blues and violets Geiger creates diffuse and luminous colour effects that are well suited to his Surrealist, visionary paintings of flowers and masks. He has also produced an impressive body of drawings.

W. Petzet. *Willi Geiger*, Munich 1960.

Geiser, Karl. Swiss sculptor, b. 1889 in Berne; d. 1957 in Zürich. Geiser was self-taught. He moved to Zürich in 1922 and began to make groups and single-figure sculptures. He worked very slowly and with great thoroughness. His early period, when his subjects were mainly young boys, contrasts with the period before he died in which he produced solidly curving female figures, executed with warm sensuality.

Geitlinger, Ernst. German painter, b. 1895 in Frankfurt am Main. Geitlinger studied in America and Munich. During the early part of his career he worked as a scenic artist. In 1947 he became a founder member of the *Neue Gruppe* in Munich and from 1951 to 1964 he taught at the Munich Academy. He is now living in Munich, where he runs a private school of art. After painting figurative works, which reveal the influence of Klee, Geitlinger turned to abstract art in 1951.

Generalić, Ivan. Yugoslav painter, b. 1914 in Hlebine, Croatia. During his childhood and early youth, which were spent in a peasant community in the heart of the countryside, Generalić taught himself to draw and, subsequently, to paint. When he was fifteen years old the well-known Yugoslav painter, Krsto Hegedušić, was impressed by his talent and gave him drawing lessons. Two years later, in 1931, he exhibited with the *Zemlja* (Earth) group. In his paintings he depicts the natural processes of growth, which he knows so well, using a completely primitive technique that makes the pictorial objects stand out in bold relief. Although the precision and intimate detail of his narrative art hint at psychological tensions, these are raised from a personal to a mythological level by the colouring, which is entirely positive. Imagination blends with memory in perfect harmony. In his works Generalić has revived the nameless forces which are the inspiration of all folk art and which are threatened by our modern civilization. He is the leading representative, not only of the *Hlebine* school of peasant art, but of all primitive art in Yugoslavia.

O. Bihalji-Merin. *Ivan Generalić: Yugoslav Pastorals*, Baden-Baden 1961.

Genovés, Juan. Spanish painter, b. 1930 in Valencia, Spain. Genovés studied at the Academy in Valencia until 1950. He is now living in Madrid. He paints aerial views of great crowds of antlike human beings packed together in a solid mass, or fleeing in terror in all directions, or taking part in demonstrations. He uses distorted perspective to create an irrational setting.

Exhibition catalogue, *Juan Genovés*, Marlborough Gallery, London 1967.

Gentilini, Franco. Italian painter, b. 1909 in Faenza, Italy. After training at the Academy in Bologna, Gentilini worked in a factory as a potter from 1921 to 1925. He has lived in Rome since 1929. Once he had integrated the Cubist and Expressionist influences of his early period Gentilini evolved a simple form of still-life composition. The individual objects depicted in his works, which are sharply distinguished from one another by firm contours, are modulated by the use of soft colours. The uniform light in Gentilini's paintings intensifies and raises them to a metaphysical and Surrealistic level.

A. Moravia. *Gentilini*, Venice 1952.

Gentils, Victor A. Belgian sculptor, b. 1919 in Ilfracombe, Devonshire. After studying at the Academy of Art in Antwerp, 1934–42, Gentils became a founder member of *Gruppe 58* and of the 'New Flemish School'. He is well represented in Belgian and Dutch public collections and he exhibited at the Tokyo Biennale in 1963, at the Venice Biennale in 1964 and the following year at the Fifth Biennale at San Marino, where he won first prize. He was also given exhibitions at the Galeria Bonino, New York, and the Kunsthalle, Basle, in 1966, and at the Hamilton Galleries, London, in 1967. He is now living in Antwerp.

Early Expressionistic landscapes were followed by a phase of Neo-Surrealism and Abstraction. In the mid-1950s, Gentils evolved the creative assemblages of diverse materials and objects for which he is best known. He uses ready-made wooden components such as pieces of furniture and musical instruments, which he first dismantles and then rearranges in new structural sequences (*Hommage à Mozart*, 1962, used old piano keys).

A. Juda. Exhibition catalogue, *Vic Gentils*, Hamilton Galleries, London 1967.

Georgiadis, Nicholas. Greek painter and theatrical designer, b. 1925 in Athens. After training as an architect in Athens and New York Georgiadis studied painting at the Slade School in London.

Georgiadis paints abstract pictures in which geometrical shapes interact to create complex and strictly formal compositions. He has produced numerous stage sets, including many for the choreographer Kenneth Macmillan at the Royal Ballet, Covent Garden (*Romeo and Juliet*, 1965).

German Artists' Association. The German Artists' Association, which was founded in Weimar in 1903, was a genuine national association and represented the interests of all German artists irrespective of their artistic allegiance. Its founder members included Franz von Stuck, Lovis Corinth and Henry van de Velde. With the exception of wartime and periods of national emergency, the German Artists' Association staged annual exhibitions, a different city being chosen each year. In 1936 the association was dissolved by the National Socialists. It was revived in 1950.

Gerstein, Noemi. Argentinian sculptress, b. 1908 in Buenos Aires. Gerstein trained under Bigatti. During her early period she worked in the Bourdelle tradition. But during a visit to Paris in 1950–1 Zadkine introduced her to a more abstract conception of sculptural form. She received a prize for her entry in the competition for a *Monument to the Unknown Political Prisoner* (London, 1954). Four years later she stopped working in marble and bronze and began to make iron structures. With her later constructions, in which she has combined iron tubes, sheet metal, aluminium and polystyrene, Gerstein has produced quite remarkable dynamic effects.

Osvaldo Svanascini. *Noemi Gerstein*, Buenos Aires 1963.

Gerstner, Karl. Swiss painter and designer, b. 1930 in Basle. Gerstner was trained in an advertising office and now owns an advertising agency in Basle. In his artistic work he pursues a policy of 'programming', in accordance with the theories advanced in his book *Programme Entwerfen* (1964). In other words, he reproduces his works in quantity. But he does more than this. For not only is the original work reproduced, it is also capable of modification within itself. Since 1964, Gerstner and Daniel Spoerri have been editing a publication in which they deal with this process: *Edition MAT* (*Multiplication d'Art Transformable*). Gerstner now lives in Basle and Düsseldorf.

Gertler, Mark. British painter, b. 1891 in Spitalfields, London; d. 1939 in Highgate, London. Of Polish-Jewish parentage, Gertler was brought up in a close Yiddish-speaking community. In 1907 he was employed in a glass-painter's workshop; in 1908, on the advice of William Rothenstein, the Jewish Educational Society sent him to the Slade, where he was an outstandingly brilliant student.

Gertler's early work is directly drawn from the community he came from. When he lost touch with it, his art was less immediately inspired and, as he was not imaginative, he relied heavily on still life. He suffered increasingly from doubts about the final status of his art and eventually committed suicide. He is represented at the Tate Gallery.

Gestel, Leendert (Leo). Dutch painter and graphic artist, b. 1881 in Wouden; d. 1941 in Hilversum. After receiving his initial training from his father, W. Gestel, Gestel studied at the Teachers' Training College in Amsterdam from 1900 to 1903, and during this period attended evening classes at the State Academy of Art under A. Allabé and N. van der Waay. In his early phase Gestel produced paintings, lithographs, etchings, watercolours, gouaches and numerous drawings. Like Jan Sluyters and Mondrian, he was influenced by Cubism at this stage in his career. Later, however, he became preoccupied with the representation of light, and incorporated various features of Flemish Expressionism into his work. He is, in fact, normally classified as a member of the Bergen school.

Ghermandi, Quinto. Italian sculptor, b. 1916 in Crevalcore, near Bologna. Ghermandi studied at the Academy in Bologna. He is now living in Verona. His bronze sculptures, which reveal abstract Surrealist traits and create Illusionist effects by means of light refraction, are full of Baroque movement. Despite the extreme simplification of the sculptural forms, the most striking feature of these abstract works is their Mannerist elegance.

Ghika, Nickolas (Nickolas Chadjikyriakos-Ghika). Greek painter, b. 1906 in Athens. He studied in Athens and worked in Paris with Bissière. From 1942 to 1960 he was Professor of Painting at the School of Architecture, National Technical University, Athens (now professor emeritus). He has done excellent and extensive work in stage scenery and costumes. From 1960 he has been living in London and Paris with periodic stays in Greece. He is the most important pathfinder of contemporary art in Greece, with a profound philosophical outlook. His painting has a Post-Cubist style, and echoes of Oriental art with a strong sensual feeling of the Mediterranean landscape. In his recent work the geometrical elements are diminishing and persist only as calligraphic signs.

Giacometti, Alberto. Swiss painter, sculptor and draughtsman, b. 1901 in Stampa (Grisons); d. 1966 in Chur. Giacometti received his initial training from his father Giovanni, who was himself a painter, and produced his first sculptures and paintings whilst still a young boy. From 1919 to 1920 he attended the École des Arts et Métiers in Geneva, and subsequently travelled extensively in Italy. In 1922 he went to live in Paris, where he worked in Antoine Bourdelle's *atelier* for three years. Whilst there he was influenced by Cubism and the Cycladic idols and began to develop an independent style. In 1929 he made contact with Breton's Surrealist group but broke away again in 1935. Although Giacometti normally devoted practically as much time to paint-ing as to sculpture, during this particular period, in which he first began to form his highly personal conception of the human figure, there was a marked decline in his output of paintings. Thus, his style was evolved within the sculptural sphere. Giacometti passed the war years in Geneva. In 1945 he returned to Paris, and—apart from lengthy summer holidays which he spent in his native Stampa—remained there for the rest of his life. In 1962 he was awarded the Grand Prix at the Venice Biennale, and in 1964 the Guggenheim Prize for Painting.

Giacometti's sculptures and paintings, and his brilliant drawings, are all based on a specific conception of the human figure, which reflects the vulnerability and fragility of twentieth-century man. Giacometti might be aptly described as an Existentialist artist, for agoraphobia is a major constituent of his work. In the preface to the catalogue of the 1948 Giacometti Exhibition in the Pierre Matisse Gallery in New York—which laid the foundations for Giacometti's international reputation—J. P. Sartre defined the two basic components of his art as absolute freedom and existential fear. According to Sartre, Giacometti lived on the edge of an abyss. And his analysis was borne out by Giacometti himself: 'I make pictures and sculptures in order to attack reality, in order to defend myself, to resist death, and be as free as possible'. As a sculptor, Giacometti passed through an early Impressionist phase, in which he was influenced by Rodin and Bourdelle. Then, in 1925, he began to experiment with Cubist structures, but abandoned these two years later and produced sculptural figures reminiscent of idols. However, it was not long before these works, which vacillated between figurative and non-figurative forms, gave way to anthropomorphous or magical 'objects' of Surrealist provenance. The *Palace at 4 am*, which dates from 1932 and consists of a ghostly ensemble of objects set in a transparent 'space cage' made of wire, is the best-known example of this phase of Giacometti's work. In the following year Giacometti reverted to more Realistic figures and more solid forms. Then, in 1937, his work underwent a remarkable transformation. The heads and bodies of his sculptural figures became still more Realistic but were reduced to a minute format and consequently appeared far less substantial. But it was not until 1947 that Giacometti finally evolved a sculptural form that gave perfect expression to his conception of man. Working with plaster of Paris on a wire foundation, he created elongated, emaciated figures which are so insubstantial that the coarse-grained plaster seems to hang on the wire frame like an empty skin and the figures themselves are like apparitions. By combining such forms Giacometti was able to produce a number of highly poetical compositions: lonely figures walking across bridges or through strange rooms, figures walking past one another or standing in silent groups on public squares. From 1960 onwards Giacometti's figures were bigger, more powerful and better defined, but they still retained their sense of quiet dignity and their visionary quality. Most of Giacometti's paintings are either portraits of friends or relations, or still lifes which he executed in his studio. But although their subject matter is more personal and consequently more realistic, their agitated brushwork and their grey, earthy colouring are quite unnatural, and so create the same visionary quality that is one of the principal features of his sculptures. Giacometti's splendid drawings are more spontaneous, although their structure reveals the same careful execution that Giacometti so greatly admired in Cézanne.

Palma Bucarelli. *Giacometti*, Rome 1962.
Jacques Dupin. *Alberto Giacometti*, Paris 1963.
Catalogue, *Alberto Giacometti*, Museum of Modern Art, New York 1965.
Franz Meyer. *Alberto Giacometti*, Stuttgart 1968.

Giacometti, Augusto. Swiss painter, b. 1887 in Stampa, Grisons; d. 1947 in Zürich. Giacometti studied at the Technical School of Art in Zürich from 1894 and under the *Jugendstil* artist Eugen Grasset from 1897. From 1902 to 1915 he lived in Berlin. His principal concern throughout the whole of his career was with colour. He had already experimented with abstract colour designs before the turn of the century and in the period prior to 1920 he produced a large number of compositions of this kind. Using a landscape, a still life or a picture by an old master (e.g. Fra Angelico) as a model, he would create a Pointillist, abstract design which expressed, in terms of colour and tone values, his own impression of the original. Thus colour came to symbolize experience. Although Giacometti's paintings became more objective from 1920 onwards, his preoccupation with colour remained. He also produced a large body of mosaics, frescoes and stained-glass windows.

E. Poeschel. *Augusto Giacometti*, Zürich and Leipzig 1928.
A. M. Zendralli. *Augusto Giacometti*, Zürich 1936.

Giacometti, Giovanni. Swiss painter, b. 1868 in Stampa, Grisons; d. 1933 in Glion, Switzerland. Giacometti was a cousin of Augusto and the father of Alberto Giacometti. In 1886–7 he studied under Knirr in Munich, and from 1888 to 1891 under Bouguereau and T. Robert-Fleury at the Académie Julian in Paris, where he was a contemporary of C. Amiet. But despite his long apprenticeship Giacometti was essentially a self-taught artist. In 1883 he was in Rome and Naples. From 1894 onwards he frequently visited Maloja with Giovanni Segantini. But his permanent residence was always in Stampa.

During his early period Giacometti was influenced by Cézanne and van Gogh. Later, he took his lead from his friend Amiet and from Segantini, who continued to exert a powerful influence on him throughout his life. Giacometti was an Impressionist and *plein-air* painter. He also produced a large number of graphic works with soft and flowing forms.

Catalogue, *Giovanni Giacometti*, Kunsthaus, Zürich 1934.
C. Amiet. *Giovanni Giacometti: Ein Jugendbild*, Zürich 1936.

Gibson, Charles Dana. American illustrator and painter, b. 1867 in Roxbury, Massachusetts; d. 1944 in New York. He trained in New York at the Art Students' League, and in Paris at the Académie Julian. On returning to the US he produced magazine illustrations and cartoons, and his 'Gibson Girl' became world-famous.

Gierowski, Stefan. Polish painter, b. 1925 in Czestochowa. Gierowski studied at the Academy of Art in Cracow. Later he became a lecturer at the Warsaw Academy. Since 1956 Gierowski has been painting non-objective pictures which have something of the quality of Op art. By reducing contrast to a minimum he obtains a smooth, painterly effect with just a hint of movement.

Giersing, Harald. Danish painter, b. 1881 in Copenhagen; d. 1927 in Valdal. After studying in Copenhagen from 1901 onwards, Giersing visited Paris in 1906–7, where he was influenced by the colour techniques of Bonnard, Vuillard and Matisse. The principal characteristics of his early work were his predilection for flat, simplified shapes and his use of rhythmical contours. Subsequently, between c. 1918 and 1920, his composition became more disciplined, due to Cubist influences. The school of painting which Giersing founded played a significant part in the development of modern Danish art.

L. Swane. *Harald Giersing*, Copenhagen 1931.
S. Rindholt. *Harald Giersing*, Copenhagen 1937.

Gilbert, Sir Alfred. British sculptor, b. 1854 in London; d. 1934 in London. He studied in London and Paris, and spent six years in Rome. He became a full member of the Royal Academy in 1892. He worked on portraits including a seated figure of Queen Victoria (1887) at Winchester. His most famous piece is the Eros fountain in Piccadilly, London (finished 1893).

Gilbert, Stephen. British painter and sculptor, b. 1910 in Scotland. In 1930 he turned from architecture to study painting at the Slade. His early works are paintings in an Impressionist and Post-Impressionist style. He spent the war years in Dublin, and in 1945 moved to Paris where he worked until 1965. In 1954 he changed from abstract painting to making constructions. These were originally coloured and formal, but he turned gradually to the highly polished curvilinear sheet-metal constructions now typical of his work.

Gilioli, Emile. Italian sculptor, b. 1911 in Paris. Gilioli spent his childhood in Italy. Until 1928, when he became a student at the École des Beaux-Arts in Nice, he worked in a smithy. In 1931 he went to Paris to continue his studies in the *atelier* of J. Bouché. In 1940 he settled in Grenoble. He then met A. Farcy and the painter Closon and subsequently—after his return to Paris—Deyrolle and Dewasne. In 1947 he joined the 'Abstracts', a group centred on the Galerie Denise René in Paris. Since 1949 he has been associated with the Salon de la Jeune Sculpture in Paris, where he is now living.

The major influences revealed by Gilioli's abstract works stem from Brancusi, Laurens, Picasso, Romanesque cathedral carvings and primitive art. The directional and tensile force set up by the asymmetrical structures in his bronze and stone sculptures is offset by meticulous care in the treatment of the external surfaces.

Exhibition catalogue, *Emile Gilioli*, Paris 1962.

Gill, Eric. British sculptor, engraver and typographer, b. 1882 in Brighton; d. 1940 in Uxbridge, Middlesex. He attended Chichester Art School and was then apprenticed to an architect in London, 1900–3. At the same time he studied at the Central School of Art under typographer Edward Johnson, and after 1903 he earned his living as a typecutter. He became a Roman Catholic in 1913 and was commissioned to carve the *Stations of the Cross* for Westminster Cathedral (1913–18). In the 1920s he worked extensively for the Golden Cockerel Press and also designed several new typefaces, including Perpetua (1927) and Gill Sans-Serif (1928). From 1929 to 1931 he executed the monumental sculpture on London's Broadcasting House. In 1937 he was elected an ARA. Amongst his best-known book designs are *The Canterbury Tales*, 1927, and the *Four Gospels*, 1931. He was a major figure in the revival of book design and the reform of typography as well as in sculpture. The latter, in its simplified forms, reflects Brancusi, and he was one of the first artists in Britain to return to the practice of direct carving.

Eric Gill. *Autobiography*, London 1940.
Exhibition catalogue, *The Engraved Work of Eric Gill*, Victoria and Albert Museum, London 1963.
R. Speaight. *The Life of Gill*, London 1966.

Gilles, Werner. German painter, b. 1894 in Reydt; d. 1961 in Essen. In 1914 he enrolled at the Academy of Art in Kassel, but had to go into the army. At the end of the war he went to the Bauhaus at Weimar, and studied under Lyonel Feininger from 1919 to 1921; after a year spent in Italy he returned to Weimar, this time to study with Oskar Schlemmer. He moved to Rome in 1931, and spent most of the next ten years there. Thereafter he lived in Munich and Ischia.

His sojourn in Ischia inspired symbolic compositions in brilliant colours, depicting the gods and myths of ancient Italy and Greece. He also drew inspiration from the poetry of Hölderlin, Rimbaud and Rilke, and from the Bible. His best-known works are the cycles on the Orpheus legend, done in 1947 and 1949.

Alfred Hentzen. *Werner Gilles*, Cologne 1960.
Karl Ruhrberg. *Werner Gilles*, Recklinghausen 1962.

Gillet, Roger Edgard. French painter, b. 1924 in Paris. Gillet studied at the École Boulle from 1939 to 1944 and the École des Arts Décoratifs in Paris from 1944 to 1946. From 1946 to 1948 he held a professorial post at the Académie Julian. He is now living in Paris. After an early phase, in which he came to grips with informal art, Gillet turned to abstract painting. Since then he has been producing works in which block-like forms painted in red, black and ochre are integrated into rhythmical compositions, where they are offset by impasted, relief-like textures.

Gilman, Harold. British painter, b. 1876 in Rode, Somerset; d. 1919 in London. After studying at the Slade School in London from 1897 to 1901, Gilman began painting after the manner of Velasquez. But from 1906 onwards, due primarily to the influence of Lucien Pissarro, he became interested in Impressionism. In 1911, he joined with Walter Sickert, Charles Ginner and Spencer Gore in founding the Post-Impressionist Camden Town Group. Two years later, when the London Group was formed, he became its first president. His output consists of landscapes, portraits and interiors with figures, all executed in bright colours.

W. Lewis and L. F. Ferguson. *Harold Gilman: An Appreciation*, London 1919.
Exhibition catalogue, *Harold Gilman*, Tate Gallery, London 1954.

Gimmi, Wilhelm. Swiss painter, b. 1886 in Zürich; d. 1965 in Chexbres. He studied at the Académie Julian in Paris, and was influenced by Cézanne. He painted café scenes and landscapes, portraits and murals. In 1962 he gained the Zürich Grand Prix.

Ginner, Charles. British painter, b. 1878 in Cannes; d. 1952 in London. From 1899 to 1908 Ginner studied architecture and painting in Paris. He settled in London in 1910 and, with Sickert, Spencer Gore and Harold Gilman, founded the Camden Town Group in 1911. After the death of Gore and Gilman, he continued to paint according to the same principles which, in 1914, Ginner defined as 'Neo-Realism'. He knew and admired the Post-Impressionists, especially van Gogh, but disliked Symbolism and its derivatives. His Neo-Realism involved an even, meticulous low-toned rendering of the scene, anchored to the picture surface by a careful masonry of small units of paint. A representative group of Ginner's works, including his *Café Royal* (1911), is in the Tate Gallery, London.

Exhibition catalogue, *Charles Ginner: Paintings and Drawings*, Arts Council of Great Britain, London 1953.

Giorgi, Bruno. Brazilian sculptor, b. 1908 in Rio de Janeiro. Giorgi lived in Italy and Paris for a number of years and studied under Maillol at the Grande Chaumière. In 1939 he received the first prize for sculpture at the Second Bienal in São Paulo. Giorgi entered into close contact with Brazil's modern architects and has collaborated with them on various public buildings. Amongst other things he created the war memorial at Brasilia. He is now living in Carrara.

Omeba (ed.). *Enciclopedia del Arte en América*, Buenos Aires 1969.

Girola, Claudio. Argentinian sculptor, b. 1923 in Rosario, Argentina. Girola is a brother of the sculptor Iommi and one of the founder members of the *Arte Concreto-Invención* group. In 1953 he took part in a group exhibition in the Stedelijk Museum in Amsterdam, to which other abstract artists such as Maldonado, Fernández Muro, Ocampo and Iommi also contributed. Girola makes metal constructions which create delicate linear patterns.

Salvador Presta. *Arte Argentino Actual*, Buenos Aires 1960.

Gischia, Léon. French painter, b. 1903 in Dax, Landes. After studying the history of literature and art Gischia began to paint in 1923. He was a pupil of O. Friesz and F. Léger. In 1927 he went to the USA for three years and, whilst there, gave up painting. But in 1936, encouraged by Léger and Beaudin, he started again and in the following year collaborated with Léger and Le Corbusier on the decorations for the French Pavilion (*Temps Nouveaux*) at the International Exhibition in Paris. In 1941, together with Bazaine, Manessier, Pignon and others, he took part in the exhibition *Jeunes Peintres de la Tradition Française*. After the war Gischia created numerous excellent stage sets for Jean Vilar's Théâtre National Populaire. He belonged to the generation of Pignon, Marchand, Estève and Bazaine, who worked within the field of force set up by Picasso and whose development extended from Neo-Cubism to partial abstraction. But Gischia's bold composition and his use of decorative colours stem primarily from Léger.

Léon Gischia *et al. Les Arts Primitifs Français*, Paris 1953.

Glackens, William. American painter, b. 1870 in Philadelphia; d. 1938 in New York. Glackens began his studies at the Pennsylvania Academy of the Fine Arts in Philadelphia. In 1891, he met Robert Henri, who persuaded him to take up painting and who remained a major influence in Glackens' career.

Henri encouraged the young student to aim for a kind of Realism that would capture the character and actuality of daily life. At this time Glackens was illustrating for the Philadelphia *Press*, together with George Luks, John Sloan and Everett Shinn. All of these artists ultimately gained recognition for their portrayal of American life in paintings devoid of Victorian prudery and aesthetic pretensions. In 1895 Glackens worked in Paris, where he exhibited at the Salon. In the years following his return he continued to work as an illustrator for the New York *Herald* and the New York *World* newspapers, as well as for *McClure's Magazine*, where his work drew critical acclaim for its freshness and immediacy. By 1900 all of his Philadelphia friends had gathered in New York where, eight years later, they organized an exhibition at the Macbeth Gallery, calling themselves The Eight. This show grew out of their failure, in spite of Robert Henri's position as judge, to gain admission to the National Academy. Glackens, Sloan and Henri brought together this now-famous exhibition that declared their artistic, if not stylistic, independence from the academic establishment.

Glackens' range of subject matter included portraits, still lifes and scenes of middle-class life—boating, bathing, parks and cityscapes. Even in his portraits, however, he usually took a disinterested point of view, preferring the typical rather than the individual qualities of his sitters. In *Chez Mouquin* (1905, Chicago, Art Institute)—the title referring to a restaurant where The Eight frequently met—Glackens paid homage both to Édouard Manet's *Bar at the Folies-Bergère* (1881–2, London, Courtauld Institute), and to Renoir, whose manner especially influenced his later works. For many years Glackens was art consultant to Dr. Albert C. Barnes in Merion, Pennsylvania, and was responsible for the acquisition of most of the works by Renoir, Cézanne and other Impressionist masters in Barnes' extraordinary collection. The predominance of paintings by Renoir is certainly due to Glackens' predilection for the charming nudes and female portraits that are found in his own production. His *Nude with Apple* (1910, New York, Brooklyn Museum), with its radiant flesh and pale, tinted blushes, is clear evidence of this preference. The rosy tints and everyday subjects of his paintings executed from 1914 until 1930 continue to show the influence of Renoir.

Guy Pène du Bois. Memorial exhibition catalogue, *William Glackens*, Whitney Museum of American Art, New York 1938.
Ira Glackens. *William Glackens and the Ashcan Group: The Emergence of Realism in American Art*, New York 1957.

Glarner, Fritz. Swiss-American painter, b. 1899 in Zürich. As a child the artist lived in Paris, Chartres and various Italian cities. He began his training at the Royal Institute of Fine Arts in Naples during the First World War and continued his studies at the Académie Colarossi in Paris, 1924–6. His first one-man show was held in Paris in 1928. Since that time he has concerned himself with bringing about 'a purer and closer interrelationship between form and space'. In Paris he was active in the *Abstraction-Création* and *Surindépendants* groups of the early 1930s. When he went to New York in 1936, his previous interest in the form-symbol with its memory of an object in space ceased to exist. In its place he concerned himself solely with form and space. He accepted two major assumptions of his friend and teacher Piet Mondrian: first, that painting must be an abstract two-dimensional experience, and second, that equilibrium is established through opposition. The works of the early 1940s are characterized by dominant diagonal and rectangular shapes with sloping sides (*Dynamid Balance*, 1942, Coll. Mr. and Mrs. Wallace K. Harrison). After the Second World War his goal was to totally eliminate the implication of the background. This late phase of his oeuvre the artist terms 'Relational Painting'. Using red, yellow, blue, black, white and grey he weds form and space, a phenomenon which depends heavily on his use of grey, sometimes acting as positive form, sometimes as shadow, to activate the surface. From 1945 onwards, the tondo became a favourite format in which to explore these compositional and formal problems (*Tondo 34*, 1954–5, Paris, Galerie Louis Carré).

Dore Ashton. 'Fritz Glarner', *Art International* VII, Zürich, January 1963.

Glasgow School, The.

In its Victorian heyday Glasgow had many connections with Europe and America, and French *plein-air* painting found a ready sale. The painters loosely grouped as the 'Glasgow School' found support in such painting for their own revolt against academic conventionality. Many trained in Paris, and the best brought to still life and landscape a naturalism and *brio* that won them a wide reputation abroad. Out of more than twenty associated painters, the best known today are probably Sir D. Y. Cameron (1865–1945), Joseph Crawhall (1861–1913), E. A. Hornel (1869–1933), W. Y. McGregor (1855–1923) and E. A. Walton (1860–1922). Sir John Lavery (1856–1941) has also been grouped with them.

Initiated in the 1850s and 1860s, the group came to a peak before 1900, and dispersed with the decline of Glasgow after 1918, although some of their attributes passed to younger painters.

Exhibition catalogue, *The Glasgow Boys*, The Scottish Arts Council, 1968.

Gleichmann, Otto.

German painter, b. 1887 in Mainz; d. 1963 in Hanover. After studying at the Academies in Düsseldorf, Breslau and Weimar from 1906 to 1910, Gleichmann lived primarily in Hanover until 1919. During his early period Gleich-

mann was influenced by the artists of the Berlin *Sturm*. Later he modified the expressive quality of his work in favour of a more lyrical and objective style of painting. His oeuvre consists of landscapes and portraits.

R. Lange. 'Otto Gleichmann', *Niedersächsische Künstler der Gegenwart* I, Göttingen 1963.

Gleizes, Albert.

French painter and writer on art, b. 1881 in Paris; d. 1953 in St-Remy. He worked at first as an industrial designer, and started painting in the early 1900s. In 1906 he met Alexandre Mercereau and, through him, around 1909–10, the Cubist painters—Le Fauconnier, Metzinger, Delaunay, Picasso. In 1910 and 1911 he exhibited with the Cubists at the Salon des Indépendants. In 1911 he wrote an article on Metzinger. In 1911 and 1912 he held weekly meetings of Cubist artists in his Courbevoie studio. In 1912 his essay *Du Cubisme* (written with Metzinger) was published. He was a founder member of the *Section d'Or* group. He was represented in the 1913 Armory Show in New York. He did his military service in 1914–15, after which he went to America and exhibited in New York and elsewhere; he then went to Spain and Portugal until 1919, when he returned to Paris. In 1920 he was instrumental in reviving the *Section d'Or* exhibition, in Paris and then in Rome, and again in 1925. He was represented in a succession of group Cubist exhibitions throughout Europe and America. In the 1930s he was active as a mural painter. In 1939 he moved to St-Rémy, Provence. His memoirs, *Souvenirs. Le Cubisme 1908–14*, were published in 1957.

Gleizes was one of the best-known public figures of Cubism during the movement's lifetime, but as an artist contributed relatively little to it. Like most of his generation, he abandoned an early Impressionist manner for a more formalist painting under the influence of Cézanne, 1907. The post-Cézanne style of painting that he adopted in 1909–11 was little more than traditional concepts wearing modern geometrical dress. In a sense this still applies to his later Cubist paintings, where the style is more developed and more informed by the influence of Picasso, Braque and Gris (*Harvest Threshing*, 1912, New York, Guggenheim Museum). In his works of 1913–14, influenced by the synthetic Cubism of the major artists, conventions of perspective and tonal modelling were limited in a flatter, more decorative style (*Woman at the Piano*, 1914, Philadelphia, Museum of Art). The subject matter of his painting was inspired more by the romantic modernism of Léger and Delaunay than the fixed reality of Picasso's still lifes. In the same spirit he responded to the prevalent Futurist dynamism in New York (*Broadway*, 1915, New York, Altschul Coll.). His later work returned to a colouristic decorative manner. His response to Cubism was that of a sensitive minor artist, and his historical importance was as a disseminator of Cubism as a style both in Paris and abroad.

J. Chevalier. *Albert Gleizes et le Cubisme*, Basle 1962.

Gliha, Oton. Yugoslav painter, b. 1914 in Crnomely, Yugoslavia. After studying at the Academy of Fine Arts in Zagreb from 1933 to 1937, Gliha went to live in Paris. In his paintings, which are based on Post-Impressionist and Fauvist techniques, he tries to capture the essential quality of his native land, more particularly of the islands off the Dalmatian coast. Since 1945 he has concentrated on the structural forms of this limestone terrain, producing a body of work in which the colours became progressively purer and the composition more precise, until in the end his paintings lost their last tangible links with the objective world and Gliha entered the sphere of abstract art. In his late works the sky, the sea and the earth are transformed into a quintessence of creation. By his persistent analysis of line and plane he has succeeded in building up an architectonic structure, in which the diagonals provide a firm counterbalance to the wide-ranging tonal values.

Boris Vižintin. *Oton Gliha*, Zagreb 1958.
Vera Horvat-Pintarić. *Introduction to the Yugoslav Catalogue for the XXXIst Biennale in Venice*, 1962.

Gnoli, Domenico. Italian painter, b. 1933 in Rome; d. 1970 in New York. Gnoli was a self-taught artist. Between 1953 and 1959 he designed stage sets and theatrical costumes, and from 1962 to 1965 produced illustrations for various magazines. In the early 1960s he also began to paint, and after an early phase, in which he responded to the aesthetic appeal of informal art, he worked his way towards a new objective style, encouraged by the Paris Surrealists and, more especially, by his friend Hundertwasser. In this final period Gnoli took his lead from the objectivity and formal precision of *Nouveau Réalisme* and American Pop Art.

Catalogue, *Domenico Gnoli*, Kestner Gesellschaft, Hanover 1968.

Goepfert, Hermann. German sculptor, b. 1926 in Bad Nauheim, Germany. Goepfert studied at the Städelschule in Frankfurt from 1951 to 1957. Since then he has executed numerous commissions for murals, stained-glass windows and sculptures. He also constructs kinetic assemblages, in which he is trying to demonstrate the aesthetic quality of light by indicating both its volume and its colour content. In his *Optophonium*, electrical frequencies are rendered audible by means of a loudspeaker and made visible by means of lights. Goepfert is now living in Frankfurt am Main.

Goerg, Édouard. French painter, b. 1893 in Sydney, Australia. Goerg went to Paris in 1900, where he later studied at the Académie Ranson under Maurice Denis and Sérusier. In the course of his career he associated with other objective artists such as Laboureur, Gromaire, Pignon, Gruber and Fougeron. Goerg paints romantic and somewhat sentimental pictures of women and girls in a slightly Surrealistic style that has scarcely changed over the years. His work is an amalgam of Renoir, Chagall and Gromaire. Goerg's book illustrations, especially those for *Les Fleurs du Mal*, have enjoyed great popularity.

W. George. *Édouard Goerg*, Geneva 1965.

Goeritz, Mathias. Mexican sculptor, architect, painter and author, b. 1915 in Danzig, Germany. Goeritz studied philosophy and art in Berlin, where he steeped himself in the Expressionist, Dadaist and Constructivist ideas which had determined the artistic climate of that city in the 1920s and which have influenced his work ever since. When war broke out in 1939, he went to live in Tetuan in Spanish Morocco and in 1945 moved on to Spain. There he founded the 'Abstract School of Altamira', which exerted considerable influence on the younger generation of Spanish painters. During this Spanish period he was in contact with Miró, Tàpies and the artists of the *Dau al Set* group. In 1949 Goeritz was offered a teaching post at the University of Guadalajara. He accepted and has lived in Mexico ever since. Whilst there he has concentrated on sculpture and architecture. In 1952–3 he built the El Eco Museum of Experimental Art, in 1954 he became a lecturer at the University of Mexico, where he carried out research into optical processes, and in 1957 he opened a School of Industrial Design, the first of its kind in Mexico. Goeritz's modern experimental ideas brought him into conflict with the revolutionary painters (such as Rivera and Siqueiros). In the five triangular towers which he built near Mexico City, he tried to give practical effect to his theory of 'emotional architecture'.

O. Zúñiga. *Mathias Goeritz*, Mexico 1963.

Goesch, Roland. Austrian sculptor, b. 1932 in Salzburg. After studying at the Academy of Art in Vienna from 1956 to 1960 Goesch became a pupil and subsequently, from 1963 onwards, an assistant of Wotruba. Goesch works in bronze and wood. Initially the great majority of his sculptures dealt with the standing human figure. Those executed in wood were coloured. Today all his sculptures are coloured and all are completely non-objective. Instead of taking their orientation from the human figure they are now related to environmental objects.

Gogh, Vincent van. Dutch painter, b. 1853 at Groot-Zundert (Brabant); d. 1890 in Auvers-sur-

Oise, France. He was the son of a pastor and nephew of three art dealers. From 1869 to 1876 he worked for Goupil & Co., art dealers, at The Hague (1869–73), London (1873–5) and Paris (1875–6) until dismissed. In 1875 he started serious study of the Bible and in the same year began his lifelong correspondence with his brother Theo. In 1876 he worked in England as a teaching assistant in schools at Ramsgate and Isleworth. In 1877 he studied at a theological college in Amsterdam and then, 1877–8, at an evangelical school in Brussels. Failure here was followed by a period working as a voluntary lay preacher in the Borinage mining district of Southern Belgium. Dismissed by the Church authorities for 'over-zealous' conduct, he decided in 1880 to become an artist. He had drawn since early childhood, but now went to Brussels and took lessons in anatomy and perspective. He spent a disturbed year (1881) living with his parents in Etten: there were heated arguments with his father over religion. From 1881 to 1883 he lived in The Hague in independent poverty; he set up house with a prostitute, Christine (Sien), model for many of his drawings. He was tutored occasionally by Anton Mauve. His uncle commissioned twelve views of The Hague from him. In 1883, after a short period at Drenthe, he returned to his parents for two years at Nuenen. His financial dependence on Theo began at this point. The death of his father occurred in 1885.

From 1885 to 1886 he spent three months in Antwerp painting and life-drawing at the Academy. He discovered Japanese prints and the art of Rubens. From 1886 to 1888 he lived with Theo in Paris, studying at the Louvre and the École des Beaux-Arts, in the atelier of Cormon. He met Toulouse-Lautrec, Gauguin, Bernard, Signac, Pissarro, and admired the work of Seurat, Degas and Monet.

In 1888 he moved to Arles, Provence; he rented 'The Yellow House' and set up home and studio there, making painting and drawing excursions in the surrounding district (Saintes-Maries, Montmajour, etc.). From October to December Gauguin came to stay at his invitation. Their heated disagreement ended in Vincent's first breakdown (a form of mental epilepsy was hereditary in his family) and self-mutilation. He spent a month in hospital.

In 1889 he voluntarily entered an asylum at St-Rémy, Provence. Here he suffered four more serious seizures, the last followed by a suicide attempt. The birth of Theo's son Vincent in January 1890 increased his guilt about dependence on Theo. In 1890 van Gogh exhibited with Les Vingt in Brussels and at the Salon des Indépendants in Paris. Aurier published an article on his painting in the Mercure de France. In May 1890 he discharged himself from the asylum and went via Paris to live in Auvers-sur-Oise under the care of Dr. Gachet, a friend of Cézanne and Pissarro. After increasing depression,

van Gogh shot himself on 27 July 1890 and died two days later. Theo died mentally disturbed in 1891.

A memorial exhibition of van Gogh's work was held at the 1891 Salon des Indépendants. The two major collections of his paintings and drawings are in Holland: the Rijksmuseum Kröller-Müller, Otterlo, and the newly established van Gogh Foundation, Amsterdam.

After a succession of ill-fated early careers, van Gogh devoted himself to art and in the space of ten years produced the prolific oeuvre on which his reputation stands. Disillusioned with the Church, he entered art in 1880 with a missionary zeal and ambitions to become 'a draughtsman of the people'. This was fostered by his admiration of Victorian graphic artists seen during his years in England and particularly by Millet, his life-long idol. It is expressed in the social conscience of all his early subject matter. For most of this time he lived and worked among working people—miners and peasants.

His energy was shared between a sense of identity with them and an extraordinary, often naïve ambition for art education—do-it-yourself books, reading, evening classes and the academies of Brussels, Antwerp and Paris. The first high-point was in the drawings of Christine at The Hague, taut, strong and expressive (Sorrow, 1882, London, private collection), and his early career culminated in the great series of peasant drawings at Nuenen, 1883–5. These were followed by his first ambitious painting, The Potato Eaters, 1885 (van Gogh Foundation).

In Antwerp, the discovery of Japanese prints and his admiration of Rubens precipitated a new interest in colour: in Paris, the impact on him of Impressionist and Post-Impressionist painting resolved it. When he withdrew to seclusion in Arles, he was a painter and a spectacular colourist. He developed the Impressionists' broken brushwork into a controlled system of coloured marks, educating himself all the time in the expressive and structural properties of paint and colour. Concurrently he evolved an elaborate calligraphic drawing style using a range of Japanese reed pens. These absorptions with intricate textures and refined colour-mixing were a major cause for disagreement with Gauguin: the other was van Gogh's insistence on working from nature. Their main common ground was a concern with Symbolism.

In his early Arles paintings (The Night Café, etc.), van Gogh experimented with a literal use of colour, but this gave way to a more abstract, pantheistic colour-symbolism. His later work combined a Monet-like insistence on acute perception with a personal vocabulary of symbolic images (the sower, sunflowers, the sun, yellow; the reaper, cypress trees, crows, blue, etc). His symbolism is nature-based, and from his intense, literate letters it seems clear that he actually saw nature in heightened terms. After the northern climate he was used to, the hard brilliant light of Provence must have come as something of a revelation.

When confined to his room in St-Rémy he either painted from his window or made copies from his own work and that of other artists (Delacroix, Doré, Millet, etc.).

The compulsive rhythms of late works like *Starry Night*, 1889 (New York, Metropolitan Museum), are intricately related to his decorative drawing style and are not uncontrolled. Throughout his career he was highly educated, well-read and articulate in his attitudes: during bouts of illness he seldom worked. A prototype for many Expressionist painters as well as for Romantic artist-images, van Gogh consciously developed each phase of his art, assimilating ideas and techniques from widespread sources with discrimination. His work exerted considerable influence on turn-of-the-century painters (Munch, *art nouveau*, German Expressionism, early Picasso and Matisse, etc.).

Julius Meier-Graefe. *Vincent van Gogh: A Biographical Study*, New York 1933; London 1936.
Meyer Schapiro. *Vincent van Gogh*, New York 1950; London 1951.
Frank Elgar. *Van Gogh: A Study of His Life and Work*, London and New York 1958.
Pierre Cabanne. *Van Gogh*, London and New York 1963.

Goldberg, Michael. American painter, b. 1924 in New York. As with many of his contemporaries, his artistic training was interrupted by service in the armed forces during the Second World War. Both before and after his service in the United States Army (1942–6), he studied at the Art Students' League with José de Creeft (1938–42 and 1946), at the College of the City of New York (1940–2 and 1946–7) and the Hans Hofmann School of Art (1941–2 and 1948–50). He had his first one-man show at the Tibor de Nagy Gallery, New York, in 1953 and in 1959 was included in both the fifth São Paulo Bienal and Documenta II, Kassel, Germany. Active in painting as well as in collage, he sometimes combines these two modes of expression, cutting up oil paintings and re-combining the parts with cut papers as in *Murder, Inc.* (1960, New York, Martha Jackson Gallery). Goldberg taught at the University of California, 1961–2.

W. Berkson. 'Michael Goldberg Paints a Picture', *Art News* LXII, New York, January 1964.

Golden Section—*see* **Section d'Or**

Goller, Bruno. German painter, b. 1901 in Gummersbach, Germany. Goller is a self-taught painter. At first he belonged to the circle of the *Mutter Ey*. Then, in 1928, he became a founder member of the Rhenish Secession. From 1949 to 1964 he taught at the Academy of Art in Düsseldorf, where he is now living. Goller paints isolated trivial objects—for example, a hat, an umbrella, a coffee grinder—in a sort of ornamental Pop Art style, which contains elements of Magic Realism, Surrealism (Max Ernst) and Primitive painting. He has also been influenced by Braque. Goller exerted a powerful influence on his pupils, one of whom was Klapheck.

A. Klapheck. *Bruno Goller*, Recklinghausen 1958.

Golovin, Alexander. Russian painter, b. 1863 in Moscow; d. 1930 in Leningrad. He was a member of the *Mir Iskusstva* and designed sets for Diaghilev's *Ballets Russes*.

Golub, Leon. American painter, b. 1922 in Chicago. He received a BA degree at the University of Chicago in 1942 and, after serving in the United States Army (1943–6), he returned to Chicago where he studied at the Art Institute, earning both BFA (1949) and MFA (1950) degrees. His first one-man show was held in 1950 at the Contemporary Gallery. His work of the late 1950s reflects his stay in Italy, 1956–7. The *Fallen Warrior* (1958, New York, Allan Frumkin Gallery) is directly inspired by a reproduction of one of the fragmentary Aegina pediment figures, while other works owe something to late Roman sculpture, with their rude concentration on anatomy, often representing figures without heads. The figures do not have the balance and proportion of his Classical prototypes, however, emphasizing the supported members of the body rather than the supportive ones. His working method involves the application of thick layers of lacquer which are then scraped and gouged with carving tools. This layer is then covered with a clear lacquer and lastly rubbed with pumice. This technique creates a tremendous activity in the surface, enlivening his palette of browns, greens, blacks, reds and ivories. After teaching for two years at Indiana University (1957–9), he moved to Paris (1959–64). It was during this time that he was included in the Bienal at São Paulo, Brazil (1961), and Documenta III at Kassel, Germany (1964). When he returned to the United States, a retrospective exhibition was held at Temple University, Philadelphia.

Robert Pincus-Witten. 'A Note on Golub', *Artforum* VI, San Francisco 1968.

Gontcharova, Natalia. Russian sculptress and painter, b. 1881 in Tula, Russia; d. 1962 in Paris. Gontcharova joined the Moscow Academy as a student of sculpture in 1898. Two years later, while still a student, she met the painter Mikhail Larionov, whom she subsequently married and with whom she frequently collaborated. It was then that she first became interested in painting. Later she joined the *Bubonovgi Valet* but left it, together with Larionov, in 1911 in order to form the *Donkey's Tail* group. In 1912 Gontcharova was represented at the second exhibition staged by the *Blauer Reiter* and in 1913 she signed the Rayonnist and Futurist manifesto and also produced her first stage sets for Diaghilev's *Ballets Russes*. In 1914 Gontcharova visited Paris. In the following year she and Larionov left Russia for good and settled permanently in Paris, where Gontcharova worked for the Russian Ballet.

Like Larionov, Gontcharova was a leading member of the Russian *avant-garde* up to 1915. Prior to 1911—in her 'primitive' period—she had produced flat and extremely colourful compositions based on religious and peasant *motifs*, in which she had tried to reconcile contemporary western trends with the traditional values of Russian folk art and icon painting. But she was best known as a member of Larionov's Rayonnist movement, to which she made an important contribution, and for the numerous décors which she created for Diaghilev's *Ballets Russes*. One of her most celebrated stage sets was that produced for Rimsky-Korsakov's *Le Coq d'Or*.

Waldemar George. *Nathalie Gontcharova, Oeuvres Anciennes et Récentes*, Paris 1956.
Catalogue, *Retrospective Exhibition: Larionov and Goncharova*, Arts Council, London 1961.
Camilla Gray. *The Great Experiment: Russian Art 1863–1922*, London and New York 1962.
Russian Stage and Costume Designs . . ., loan exhibition, New York 1967.

González, Julio. Spanish painter and sculptor, b. 1876 in Barcelona; d. 1942 in Arcueil, near Paris. After he and his brother Joan had learnt the goldsmith's trade in their father's workshop, González attended evening classes in drawing and painting at the Barcelona School of Fine Arts. In 1900 the whole of the González family moved to Paris, where the two brothers made contact with their fellow countryman Picasso and his circle of friends. But they did not become Cubist painters. The delicate use of light and shade to indicate volume in the chased metal groups and masks which they produced at that time is in fact reminiscent of an Impressionist view of the world. Soon afterwards, in 1908, Joan González died. This was a bitter blow to González, for he had felt very close to his brother, both as a human being and as an artist. For many long years he lived in almost total seclusion, his only contacts being with Picasso and Brancusi. Then in 1927—when he was 50—he finally resolved his inner problem, gave up painting and reverted to metal sculptures. His earlier experiences of Cubism now served as a base for new experiments, in which he gradually penetrated into uncharted territory. At first he forged metal masks which are reminiscent of negro sculptures. In these works González was actually reformulating in extremely penetrating terms the statement which Picasso had made in 1910 in his Cubist bronze *Head of a Woman*. Subsequently González moved away from this Cubist model and both the rigidity of his iron masks—which look very much like still lifes—

and their figurative quality gradually disappeared. He then set himself a dual task: to transform iron—a rigid material—into a viable artistic medium and to create signs in space. His solution of this problem is to be found in his *Personnages*—weird, skeleton-like structures, which were forged from iron or pure metals and were intended to function as dynamic and expressive signs in space. Next González constructed Surrealist figures by welding metal pipes and pieces of sheet metal. But, despite their Constructivist origin, these figures are decidedly anti-technical and non-functional. Picasso will almost certainly have contributed to this splendid artistic development. Between 1930 and 1933 González had helped Picasso in the technical production of his iron sculptures and will doubtless have been stimulated by these bold and imaginative works. González had his own ideas about the use of iron. He wanted to give it a new function and so destroy its previous identity as a 'murderer or the mere instrument of an over-mechanized science'. In this connection he once said: 'Today the way is clear for this material to be forged and hammered by the peaceful hands of an artist.' This reforming zeal went hand in hand with his formal conception of 'drawing in space', that is, using space as a part of sculpture, as if it were 'a discovered material'. In a number of his iron sculptures, like *Maternity*, *The Prayer* and *Dancer with Flying Hair* (1931–3), he reduced the volume and strengthened the linear elements, thus creating dynamic and expressive signs in space. In c. 1935, however, he reverted to compact volumes. He then produced lyrical or dramatic figures in an abstract style (e.g. *Woman Dressing Her Hair*, 1936) and realistic statues (e.g. *La Montserrat*, a work symbolizing the suffering of the Spanish people in the civil war, which was shown at the 1937 International Exhibition in Paris). In 1939–40 he created his *Cactus People*: abstract, spine-clad figures, whose defensive gestures seem to have hinted at the violence which was about to engulf Europe. Following the outbreak of the Second World War González left Paris to live in the *Département* of Lot, but in the autumn of 1941 he returned to the capital, where he started work on a large realistic figure, which was conceived as a second *Montserrat*.

Catalogue, *Julio González, Sculptures*, Musée National d'Art Moderne, Paris 1952.
Michel Seuphor. *The Sculpture of this Century*, London and New York 1960.
Leon Degand. *González*, Amsterdam 1964.

Gordin, Sidney. Russian-American sculptor, b. 1918 in Chelyabinsk, Siberia. He started out as a painter, but turned to sculpture in the forties. His work is abstract, and was at first somewhat geometrical, but later became more organic in form. He has had exhibitions at the Metropolitan Museum, the Museum of Modern Art and the Whitney Museum in New York, and has taught at the University of California at Berkeley.

Gore, Spencer Frederick. British painter, b. 1878 in Epsom, Surrey; d. 1914 in Richmond, Surrey. He began his studies at the Slade, 1896–9. In 1904 he met Sickert in Dieppe and thus established an important connection with French painting. He spent six months in France in 1906 and, under the influence of Sickert, he began a series of music-hall and ballet subjects. At the same time, and up until 1910, he produced a series of Impressionist landscapes which owe some debt to both Pissarros (father and son), but which are very personally seen. In 1911 he was important in the founding of the Camden Town Group, of which he was made president. Stimulated by the Post-Impressionist exhibitions of 1910 and 1912, he was gradually assimilating their influence and the London pictures of this period are a perfect balance of Impressionist and Post-Impressionist elements (e.g. *Mornington Crescent*, 1911, London, Tate Gallery). In a series of landscapes painted in 1912, however, his interest in form and structure becomes increasingly apparent. During the last year of his life, in the views of Richmond and Richmond Park, the influence of Cézanne is uppermost, but in no way disrupts his innate sense of the mood and unity of a landscape. Gore's painting is perhaps the freshest and most original of all that produced in Britain under the immediate influence of Post-Impressionism, although the importance of his achievement was perhaps obscured by his tragically early death.

J. W. Palmer. Exhibition catalogue, *Spencer Frederick Gore, 1878–1914*, Arts Council, London 1955.

Gorin, Jean. French painter and sculptor, b. 1899 in St. Emilion-Blain. Gorin studied at the Académie de la Grande Chaumière in Paris and the Academy in Nantes from 1916 onwards. In 1927 he became friendly with Mondrian. In 1930 he joined the *Cercle et Carré* group and in 1932 the *Abstraction-Création* association. In 1946 he became a founder member of the Salon des Réalités Nouvelles and in 1953 signed the manifesto of the *Groupe Espace*. He is now living in Meudonval-Fleuri near Paris. Gorin has been a Neo-Plasticist throughout his career. In his pictures and constructions, in which verticals and horizontals predominate, he is seeking to establish a synthesis between sculpture and painting.

Exhibition catalogue, *Jean Gorin*, Stedelijk Museum, Amsterdam 1967.

Gorky, Arshile (Vosdanig Manoog Adoian). American painter, b. 1905 in Hayotz Dzore, Turkish Armenia; d. 1948 in Sherman, Connecticut. He arrived at Ellis Island from Eastern Europe (where he had learned English at an American missionary school) on 1 March 1920. His early years were spent in New England, studying at the Rhode Island School of Design. He moved to New York c. 1925, becoming first a pupil and then a teacher at the Grand Central School of Art. Always interested in the old masters, *The Artist and His Mother* (c. 1926–9, oil, New York, Whitney Museum of American Art) shows a certain relationship to the art of Uccello, with its large simple planes, clear delineation of form and lack of depth; his use of colour, however, is confined to earth tones. By the 1930s, when he abandoned teaching, the influence of Cézanne and especially of the early works of Picasso is discernible, as in *Portrait of Vartoosh* (c. 1933, oil, New York, Coll. Joseph H. Hirshhorn). Here Picasso's bland colourism (blues and browns) and Cubistic primitivism are joined with the earlier use of clear outlines and an emphasized two-dimensionality; but a far greater freedom of brushstroke provides a foretaste of his later style. He was given his first one-man show in 1934 (Philadelphia, Mellon Galleries) and the following year joined the WPA Federal Art Project, working on a mural for Newark Airport: *Aviation: Evolution of Forms under Aerodynamic Limitations*. He began his last phase c. 1942, painting thinly with brightly coloured washes and tints, coupled with vividly active calligraphic strokes of black; the whole effect was one of fluidity and flux. André Breton, whom the artist met in 1944, used the term 'hybrid' to describe these late, rather visceral works (e.g. *The Liver is the Cock's Comb*, 1944, Buffalo, Albright-Knox Art Gallery).

Ethel K. Schwabacher. *Arshile Gorky*, New York 1957.
Harold Rosenberg. *Arshile Gorky: The Man, the Time, the Idea*, New York 1962.
William C. Seitz. Catalogue, *Arshile Gorky, Paintings, Drawings, Studies*, Museum of Modern Art, New York 1962.
Julien Levy. *Arshile Gorky*, New York 1968.

Gostomski, Zbigniev. Polish painter, b. 1932 in Bydogoszcz, Poland. Gostomski studied at the Academy of Art in Warsaw, where he is now a member of the teaching staff. In 1962 Gostomski began to produce relief compositions consisting of modelled surfaces executed in black and white. In 1967 he turned to 'environments' and spatial constructions.

Exhibition catalogue, *Constructive Art: Elements and Principles*, Nuremberg Biennale, 1969.
Peinture moderne Polonnaise: Sources et Recherches, Musée Galliera, Paris 1969.

Gotsch, Friedrich Karl. German painter, b. 1900 in Pries, near Kiel. After studying under Kokoschka at the Dresden Academy of Art from 1920 to 1923, Gotsch lived in various countries before settling in St. Peter, Schleswig-Holstein, in 1950. Gotsch belongs to the second generation of German Expressionists. With their sketch-like forms and their highly expressive colouring, his pictures are firmly rooted in the Kokoschka tradition.

Gottlieb, Adolph. American painter, b. 1903 in New York; d. 1973. He received his initial training in 1920 at the Art Students' League, New York, under John Sloan and Robert Henri. Later he worked in Paris at the Académie de la Grande Chaumière, travelled through Europe and then returned to New York, where he attended the Parsons School of Design, Cooper Union, and the Educational Alliance Art School. By 1930 his first exhibition of Expressionistic figures and landscapes had been held at the Dudensing Gallery in New York, and in 1935 he again travelled to Europe. Gottlieb was one of the founder members of The Ten, a group that also included Lee Gatch, Mark Rothko and Ilya Bolowtowsky (b. 1907), painters dedicated to an abstract and Expressionist style of painting. In 1936 Gottlieb worked as an easel painter for the WPA Federal Art Project, painting in a representational style influenced by Milton Avery's soft colouristic manner. About this time he also began to collect primitive sculpture, an interest that was to parallel a dimension of his painting during the 1940s and early 1950s. In 1937 Gottlieb lived in the Arizona desert area; his early style, whether manifested in still lifes, figure paintings, sea- or landscapes, contained Surrealistic overtones derived from Salvador Dali, and irrationally circumscribed spaces that caught the effects of this new setting. Ovoids, discs and horizon-like divisions formed a new pictorial vocabulary that became a consistent feature of Gottlieb's work throughout his later career.

In 1941 Gottlieb's mature style began to evolve with a feeling of rebellion against American provincial Realism and European geometric Abstraction. Along with other Abstract Expressionists—Mark Rothko, Jackson Pollock, Clyfford Still, Theodoros Stamos—Gottlieb came into contact with the European expatriate Surrealists in New York during the Second World War. He was especially interested in their use of the unconscious as a source for contemporary subject matter. Freudian psychology and long-standing association with primitive and Indian art of the North-west Coast also helped form the basis for his series of *Pictographs*, sustained from 1941 until 1951. These paintings are characteristically divided into grid-like compartments containing literal, cryptic and suggestively Freudian images (*Voyager's Return*, 1946, New York, Museum of Modern Art), while their titles often refer to antique mythological concepts (*Rape of Persephone*, 1943, New York, Coll. Barnett Newman). Gottlieb did not intend to illustrate such themes, however, and for him the pictographic process was one of free association, in which he could explore the ambiguity and irrationality of the symbols in order to generate a significant and revitalized formal whole. The more overt allusions to Freudian psychology (masks, blind eyes, fragmented faces) were later transformed into abstract signs and themes in which the grid still

functioned as a working skeleton (*Romanesque Façade*, 1949, Urbana, Ill., University of Illinois, Krannert Art Museum). The years 1951–6 marked a departure into the *Imaginary Landscape* series, whose obvious horizontal divisions between a 'sky' zone punctuated with frozen suns or astral forms, and a loosely brushed 'ground' area, were later eliminated and dissolved in the fluid fields of the *Burst* series, begun in 1957. Large in format, these paintings mark the ultimate reduction and modification of Gottlieb's art, although they are still consistent with the qualities of painterly subjectivism, universal iconography and repetitive pictorial format that distinguished his earlier work. Solar orbs are suspended in hovering tension above exploding earth masses painted in rich contrasts of scarlet and black against buff or white fields, or in soft, close-valued pastels (*Expanding*, 1962, Chicago, Art Institute). In 1968 a large retrospective exhibition of Gottlieb's work was held jointly at the Whitney and Guggenheim Museums in New York.

Adolph Gottlieb. 'The Artist and the Public', *Art in America* XLII, December 1954.
Martin Friedman. Exhibition catalogue, *Adolph Gottlieb*, Walker Art Center, Minneapolis 1963.
R. Doty and D. Waldman. Catalogue, *Adolph Gottlieb*, Whitney Museum of American Art, New York 1968.

Götz, Karl Otto. German painter, b. 1914 in Aachen, Germany. Götz first began to paint in 1932. Between 1933 and 1934 he came to terms with Cubism (Juan Gris) and from 1935 to 1937 produced photographic montages and pictures based on a spray technique. In 1941 he was conscripted for military service and posted to Norway, where he had access to radar installations and was able to carry out experiments into electronic picture sequences. In 1948 he founded the magazine *Meta*, which continued to appear up to 1953. In 1949 he made contact with the *Cobra* group.

Götz is one of the best-known representatives of Action Painting in Germany. His works are executed in three distinct stages. In the first of these he writes with dark colours on a light ground until the design and the ground are no longer clearly distinguishable. In the second stage he works on the paint, while it is still wet, with a rubber scraper, producing an interlacing pattern of light and dark areas. In the third and final stage he again writes with the brush. Götz is also carrying out fundamental research into the reproduction of electronic picture sequences. His first experiments with abstract films, in which he has been trying to reformulate the structural processes of painting in logical and material terms, go back to 1935.

Karl Otto Götz, Edizione dell'Attico, Rome 1962.

Graevenitz, Gerhard von. German kinetic artist, b. 1934 in Schilde, Mark Brandenburg. Graevenitz studied at the Academy of Art in Munich from 1957 to 1961. During this time he was joint editor of the magazine *Nota* (1959–60, four editions). After producing white reliefs in his early period (1958), Graevenitz moved on to kinetic assemblages (1961) and light objects (since 1963). He is now living in Munich.

Grandma Moses—*see* **Moses,** Anna

Grant, Duncan. British painter, b. 1885 in Rothiemurchus, Inverness-shire. Born into a Scottish landed family, Grant attended the Westminster and Slade Schools and studied with J. E. Blanche. He was formed aesthetically by journeys to Europe and the Near East and by his friendship with the Bloomsbury Group. Like Vanessa Bell, he was briefly influenced by Post-Impressionism, c. 1912–14, before adapting his style to the contingencies of their many joint decorative schemes.

Raymond Mortimer. *Duncan Grant*, Harmondsworth (Middx.) 1948.

Graubner, Gotthard. German painter, b. 1930 in Erlbach, Vogtland. After studying at the Academies in Berlin, Dresden and Düsseldorf, Graubner began to produce Constructivist pictures in 1955. Since then he has gradually reduced the structural definition of his delicately shaded monochromes. Recently he has built up his canvases with layers of foam rubber and polyester so that they look like cushions. Graubner is now living in Düsseldorf.

Graves, Morris. American painter, b. 1910 in Fox Valley, Oregon. He grew up in the Pacific North-West, and worked as a seaman on mail ships headed for the Orient (he made three trips to the Far East) before turning to art. He first gained recognition when he was awarded a prize from the Seattle Art Museum in 1933; this was followed by a one-man show three years later. Like many other American artists, Graves was supported during the Depression by the WPA Federal Art Project.

Oriental art, and the manner in which the West Coast painter Mark Tobey used it, influenced Graves early in his career, as did his interest in Zen Buddhist and Vedanta (Indian) philosophy. Around 1937 he gave up using oil to work with tempera, wax, ink and gouache on thin papers, employing methods and techniques that were related to Japanese and Chinese scrollwork. In 1942 he received critical acclaim for some of his first works in this manner with a show at the Museum of Modern Art, New York. In 1946 Graves planned to work in Japan, but the outbreak of hostilities between the United States and that country during the Second World War forced him to paint in Honolulu instead. The images of blind birds, pine trees and waves bounded

by lines of white tracery—reminiscent of Tobey's calligraphic 'white writing'—are common in Graves' paintings. The *Little Known Bird of the Inner Eye* (1941, New York, Museum of Modern Art) evokes his mystical attitude towards nature, and while it does not imitate Oriental art *per se*, the delicacy of its colours and definition reveals Graves' interest in the Far East.

Kenneth Rexroth. 'The Visionary Painting of Morris Graves', *Perspectives U.S.A.* No. 10, 1955.
Frederick S. Wight. *Morris Graves*, Berkeley and Los Angeles 1956.

Greaves, Derrick. British painter, b. 1927 in Sheffield. Greaves studied at the Royal College of Art from 1948 to 1952. He has exhibited in London since 1953. His earlier work recalls Dubuffet, combining an interest in child imagery with a sophisticated handling of texture. In the 1960s his paintings became entirely non-figurative, composed of large simple areas of colour. He is represented in the major public collections in England.

Greco, Emilio. Italian sculptor, b. 1913 in Catania, Sicily. When he was thirteen Greco was apprenticed to a stonemason, who worked in marble. Later he attended the Academy of Art in Palermo. In 1948 he obtained a teaching appointment as assistant to the sculptor Q. Ruggeri at the Liceo Artistico in Rome.

Greco has concentrated primarily on portraits and female nudes. His style combines Italian Mannerist features with certain archaicizing Classical tendencies. The texture of his work is reminiscent of G. Manzù whilst the build-up of his sculptural forms reveals a certain similarity with M. Marini.

Bernhard Degenhart. *Emilio Greco*, Berlin and Mainz 1960.
Fortunato Bellonzi. *Emilio Greco*, Rome 1962.

Greene, Balcomb. American painter, b. 1904 in Niagara Falls, New York. He presents something of an anomaly in the history of modern American painting, for his oeuvre develops from pure geometric abstractions (he was a founder member of the American Abstract Artists) towards an increasingly representational style. After graduating from Syracuse University with a degree in philosophy (1926), he spent a post-graduate year at the University of Vienna, attending lectures in psychology. He returned to the United States in 1927 and attended Columbia University, New York, as a Master's degree candidate in English. During his Instructorship in English at Dartmouth College, Hanover, New Hampshire (1928–31), he wrote four novels and many short stories, all unpublished. Greene left for Paris in 1931 intending to be an artist, although he had had no training. The major influence in this venture was his wife Gertrude Glass, a sculptress and painter. He began working independently at the Académie de la Grande Chaumière and held his first one-man show in Paris that same year. On his return to New York in 1933, he supported himself by writing for two publications: *Broadway Brevities* and *Graft*. Art as a vocation only came with his work in the mural division of the WPA (1936–9), executing murals at the Williamsburg Housing Project, Brooklyn, N.Y., and at the Federal Hall of Medicine at the 1939 New York World's Fair. Most of the geometric abstractions which he produced in the 1930s were destroyed in a 1941 fire at his studio, although some collages, used as studies for these paintings, do survive—for example *Collage* (1937, coll. of artist) with its crisp linear patterns and tilted planes. He attended New York University where he received an MA degree in art history in 1943, for which he wrote a thesis entitled *Mechanistic Tendencies in Painting, 1901–1908*. His figurative style began in the first half of the 1940s. *Black Angels* (1946, coll. of artist) has a vaguely Surrealistic quality, with its rather fragmented figures placed against a geometric background which harks back to his earlier style. His mature style dates from 1947, the year of his first American one-man show at J. B. Neumann's New Art Circle—a period when he was teaching art history at the Carnegie Institute of Technology, Pittsburg, Pa. (a position he held 1942–59). His figures are now less fragmented, sometimes emerging clearly as in *Interior* (1948, coll. artist), at other times glimpsed through blinding light and deep shadow as in *Olympia* (1951, coll. of artist). The play with chiaroscuro and the interest in the eroticism of the nude are also reflected in his photographic work, a field which has interested him since the early 1940s. Since about 1955 his figures have become more physically specific, often engaged in some sort of action, and placed into a specific setting (*Joan By the Sea*, 1959, New York, Bertha Schaefer Gallery). These factors are all counter to his earlier use of ambiguous, immobile figures placed against an abstract background.

Exhibition catalogue, *Balcomb Greene*, Whitney Museum of American Art, New York 1961.

Greis, Otto. German painter, b. 1913 in Frankfurt am Main, Germany. Greis first studied engineering. He did not begin his art training until 1938 (in Frankfurt), although he actually started painting in 1933. During his early period he was influenced by Braque, Gris and Klee. It was not until 1952, when he joined the *Quadriga* group, that he produced his first Tachist pictures. His works are lyrical abstract impressions executed in pale pastel shades. He has been living in La Frette sur Seine, near Paris, since 1956.

Otto Greis. *Imaginationen*, Baden-Baden 1960.

Grieshaber, Helmut. German graphic artist, b. 1909 in Rot. He studied in London and Paris, and

travelled in the Middle East before settling in Reutlingen in 1947. He taught at the Academy in Karlsruhe, 1955–60. He first started making woodcuts in 1932, and thereafter used this technique for his most important works, including some of mural size (*Elysium*, 1953).

Grimond, Marcel-Antoine. French sculptor, b. 1894 in Tournon, Ardèche; d. 1961 in Nogent-sur-Marne. His first sculptures were monumental, derived from the influence of Maillol, under whom he studied, but he later turned to making portrait busts.

Grippe, Peter. American sculptor, b. 1912 in Buffalo, New York. Grippe studied art at the Albright Art School and the Art Institute, both in Buffalo. He taught sculpture and other art subjects at Black Mountain College in North Carolina (1948); Pratt Institute, Brooklyn, New York (1949–1950); Smith College, Northampton, Massachusetts (1951–2); and Brandeis University, Waltham, Massachusetts (from 1952). He was also director of Atelier 17, an etching and engraving workshop in New York. Grippe received numerous awards for his work, which is represented in New York at the Museum of Modern Art, the Metropolitan Museum and the Whitney Museum of American Art (*Three Furies, II*, 1955–6, bronze), as well as in the Philadelphia Museum and many other public and private collections.

Grippe's stylistic development is rooted in the series of terra-cotta *Cities* that he began in 1939. In these he fused the images of the figures and the buildings (by treating the figure and background as one) to express movement and to show man's relationship to his environment. During the early 1940s this series changed direction, as Grippe reduced the detail, separated the figures from their background and aimed at transparent, open sculpture. Named *Space Figures* by the artist, these sculptures, together with Ibram Lassaw's constructions, formed the first American examples of cage-like sculpture. Seeking a clearer articulation of space than was possible with terra-cotta, which had been his primary medium until 1944, Grippe began to explore the lost-wax process of bronze casting, a technique he perfected until his intricately interwoven forms could be cast in one piece. Major new influences on his work resulted from a re-reading of the classics around 1952 and a visit to Europe in 1953, when he was particularly impressed by Romanesque sculpture, Gothic cathedrals and Auguste Rodin's *Gates of Hell*. As a result, his sculptural imagery of the 1950s is often based on ideas derived from literature and past art. A new series of *Cities* begun at this time expressed a greater violence than before (*Three Figures, II*, 1955–6, New York, Whitney Museum of American Art), and in the late 1950s a series of *Mephistopheles* was suggested by Goethe's *Faust* (*Mephistopheles, 2,* 1958, New York, Nordness Gallery).

Peter Grippe. 'Enter Mephistopheles, With Images', *Art News* LIX, October 1960.
Wayne V. Andersen. 'American Sculpture: The Situation in the Fifties', *Artforum* V, No. 10, 1967.

Gris, Juan (José Victoriano Gonzalès). Spanish painter, b. 1887 in Madrid; d. 1927 in Boulogne-sur-Seine, France. In 1906, like so many of his contemporaries, Gris was drawn to Paris, where he joined his fellow countryman Pablo Picasso and the Frenchman Georges Braque as the third great representative of the French Cubist movement. But unlike Picasso and Braque, who were both a little older, Gris was a relative latecomer to Cubism. It was not until 1911 that he began to paint his first pictures in this mode, by which time the fundamental discoveries of analytical Cubism had already been made. But even in these early works he made a completely individual contribution to Cubist composition. Gris was less interested in the reduction of objects to their geometric or stereometric components than either Braque or Picasso. He proceeded quite differently, starting with fragments of objects and organizing them into a compact and rhythmical pictorial structure. This is not to say that Cubist reduction was not a feature of his work. It was. But, in spite of this reduction, his pictures retained a distinctly tangible quality. The way in which he consistently incorporated objective elements—e.g. pieces of newspaper, carpets, imitation woodwork—into his works establishes him as one of the principal exponents of collage, a technique which had been discovered by the early Cubists. Here, too, his object was to impart a more tangible sense of reality to his paintings.

When he had finished his studies at the School of Industrial and Fine Arts and began working as a draughtsman for satirical magazines in Madrid, Gris was still an ardent adherent of the *Jugendstil,* to which he had been introduced primarily by *Simplicissimus* and *Jugend.* When he moved to Paris in 1906 he joined the circle grouped around Picasso and the poets Max Jacob and Guillaume Apollinaire, and lived in the Bateau-Lavoir, a complex of artists' studios in Montmartre, along with Picasso, Kees van Dongen and the poet André Salmon. At first he continued to earn his living as a satirical draughtsman. Then, in 1911, he started to paint in oils and in the following year the art dealer Daniel Henry Kahnweiler placed him under contract. His first pictures were still lifes and portraits of his friends, which were executed in the analytic Cubist style evolved by Braque and Picasso but which also revealed a vigorous and decorative trend. During the next five years Gris produced his most important works. These consist of the 'bright' pictures of 1912 with their strict diagonal rhythm, the richly coloured,

luminous still lifes of 1913 (which are constructed on a rigid framework of horizontal, perpendicular and diagonal planes made up of fragmentary objects), the rich collages of 1914 and the 'architectonic' pictures of 1916, with their contrasting *motifs* and enamel-like texture. During this period Gris worked on numerous occasions with Braque, Derain and Picasso and with the sculptors Manolo and Lipchitz in the South of France and in the Pyrenees. He also created a large number of book illustrations for publications by Pierre Réverdy, Max Jacob, Armand Salacrou, Gertrude Stein and Tristan Tzara, and various stage sets and costumes for Diaghilev's *Ballets Russes.* In fact, these illustrative and decorative works made up a large part of his output. In the later paintings the contours are softer and there is a greater emphasis on colour. For example, in the harlequin and pierrot compositions, which reflect the milieu of the travelling artiste, the whole mood is set by the melancholy colouring. In the closing years of his life, Gris was a very sick man. His writings—such as *Esprit Nouveau* (1921) and *Sorbonne Lecture* (1924)—should not go unmentioned. They afford a unique insight into the theory of Cubism.

Maurice Raynal. *Juan Gris*, Paris 1920.
Daniel-Henry Kahnweiler. *Juan Gris*, London and New York 1947.
Juan Gris. *Letters*, ed. Douglas Cooper, London 1956.
James Thrall Soby. Exhibition catalogue, *Juan Gris*, Museum of Modern Art, New York 1958.

Grochowiak, Thomas. German painter and gallery director, b. 1914 in Recklinghausen. In 1932 Grochowiak embarked on a course of training in commercial design. He did not begin to exhibit until 1945. Three years later he founded the *Junger Westen* group. Grochowiak paints in a Tachist, informal style. He is director of the Ruhr festival and of the Kunsthalle in Recklinghausen, where he founded the Icon Museum in 1957.

Gromaire, Marcel. French painter, b. 1892 in Noyelles-sur-Sambre; d. 1971. Gromaire was a self-taught artist. He moved to Paris at an early age. In 1914 he joined the French forces, and in 1916 was wounded on the Somme. After the war he visited Belgium, Holland, Germany and England. From 1921 onwards he exhibited in the Salon d'Automne, and from 1924 in the Salon des Tuileries. In 1937 he decorated the Sèvres Pavilion at the International Exhibition in Paris, and produced designs for Gobelins. In 1939 he collaborated with Jean Lurçat in the Aubusson factory, and so helped to revive the traditional art of tapestry. In 1952 he won the Carnegie prize.

During the early period Gromaire was influenced by Cézanne and the Fauvists. After the First World

War he took his lead from F. Léger, and by c. 1920 had evolved a new expressive style. In the large-format works which he created at that time he achieved a remarkable synthesis of decorative, human and sculptural elements. He was not interested in the picturesque character of events but in their quintessential significance. He had a great love for the French and Flemish primitives. In his early period Gromaire had made himself fully proficient in the painterly aspect of his craft, and from then onwards he gradually developed a full rich palette consisting of dark luminous colours: ruby red, emerald green and sea blue. His oeuvre is made up of landscapes, nudes and scenes from peasant and working-class life. Gromaire had a natural gift for fresco, which is reflected in his use of bold outlines, and in his flat figures and objects.

M. Zahar. *Gromaire*, Geneva 1961.
G. Besson. *Marcel Gromaire*, Paris n.d.

Gropper, William. American painter, b. 1897 in New York. He trained with Robert Henri and George Bellows in San Francisco, and also studied in New York. He began his career as a cartoonist and had soon established his reputation in this field. He also painted scenes which reflect his concern with politics and society. He produced murals, and exhibited in New York (at the ACA Gallery, from 1936) and in various European cities.

Gross, Chaim. American sculptor, b. 1904 in Kolomea, Austria. Gross's art education began in Budapest and Vienna after the First World War. In 1921 he went to New York, where he studied first at the Educational Alliance Art School, then with Elie Nadelman at the Beaux-Arts Institute of Design (1922–6) and in 1927 with Robert Laurent (b. 1890) at the Art Students' League. He gave his first one-man exhibition in New York in 1932.

Gross's major and almost sole subject was the human figure in action or play, most often used in rhythmical, vertically balanced compositions of circus performers or of a mother playing with her children (*Handlebar Riders*, 1935, New York, Museum of Modern Art; *Family of Three*, 1948, New York, Coll. Joseph H. Hirshhorn). Gross was mainly concerned with form rather than subject and, because of his preference for direct carving and his respect for the inherent qualities of his medium—primarily wood—the forms of his figures are dictated by the cylindrical shape of the block; they are thus generally thicker, rounder and more massive than they would be in reality, and project very little from the central columnar mass. In 1958, however, Gross also began to model in clay for casting in bronze, a method that allowed for more open and angular forms and rougher surfaces than in his carved wood sculpture.

Josef V. Lombardo. *Chaim Gross, Sculptor*, New York 1949.
Chaim Gross. *Fantasy Drawings*, New York 1956 (with introduction by A. L. Chanin and analytical essay by Samuel Atkin); *The Technique of Wood Sculpture*, New York 1964.

Gross, František. Czech painter and graphic artist, b. 1909 in Nová Paka. He was a pupil at the Prague Art School from 1928 to 1931. At the beginning of his career he worked in a Cubist and Surrealist manner, but his later output was nearer Realism. He illustrates aspects of city life. He has had major exhibitions in Prague, where he now lives, in 1942, 1944 and 1954. In 1950 he undertook a journey to Bulgaria in order to study further.

Grosz, George. German-American draughtsman and painter, b. 1893 in Berlin; d. 1959 in Berlin. Grosz studied for two years under R. Müller at the Royal Saxon Academy of the Fine Arts in Dresden and then at the Royal Arts and Crafts School in Berlin. He started to paint in 1911, but he is best known as a caricaturist. He began drawing for satirical reviews such as *Ulk* and *Lustige Blätter*, savagely depicting the social corruption of Germany. After serving in the forces during the First World War, he joined the Berlin Dada movement (1918–20) and later the *Neue Sachlichkeit* movement (1925). He published several books of satirical drawings, including *Ecce Homo* (1920), and was frequently prosecuted for insulting public morals and for blasphemy. In 1933 he went to New York to teach at the Art Students' League, and he became an American citizen in 1938. In America, he exhibited a number of oil paintings, in which his style had become more romantic and lyrical (*Approaching Storm*, 1940, New York, Whitney Museum of American Art), but he continued to wield his satirical pen against bourgeois materialism. After the Second World War, his caricatures covered a wider field and he produced alarming spectres like gaunt figures of *The Stickmen* series (1947–8). He revisited Germany in 1951 and returned there to live in 1959, but he died soon after his arrival in Berlin.

George Grosz. *A Little Yes and a Big No: Autobiography*, New York 1946; *Ecce Homo*, New York 1966.
Herbert Bittner. *George Grosz*, Boston 1960.
Exhibition catalogue, *George Grosz, 1893–1959*, Akademie der Künste, Berlin 1962.

Groupe de Recherche d'Art Visuel. This group was founded in Paris in July 1960 by eleven artists. Subsequently these were reduced to six: Garcia-Rossi, Julio Le Parc, François Morellet, Francisco Sobrino, Joel Stein and Yvaral. The object of the group was to provide a centre for research into visual art in general and into the artistic significance of light, movement and time in particular. The first group exhibition was staged in 1960 in the group's own *atelier* at 9 Rue Beautreillis, Paris, and was followed by further exhibitions in many different countries. Apart from producing individual works these six artists also collaborated on joint projects, such as their *Labyrinth*, which was shown at the Paris Biennale in 1963. All six adopt a basically scientific approach to art. Their declared intention is to produce works which involve the viewer in a new and direct relationship, that is, which liberate him from the purely receptive role that he had previously fulfilled by calling for a positive response. An essential aspect of this development has been the incorporation of new industrial materials which reflect the technological world in which we live.

GRAV pamphlets, Paris 1960–5.
J. Claus. *Kunst Heute*, Reinbek 1965.
Exhibition catalogue, *Groupe de Recherche d'Art Visuel*, Museum am Ostwall, Dortmund 1968.

Groupe Espace. The *Groupe Espace* was a Neo-Constructivist artists' association that was founded in Paris in 1951 by artists connected with the periodical *Art d'Aujourd'hui*. Its members included André Bloc, Del Marle, Pillet, Béothy, Nicholas Schöffer and Gorin. Their conception of art as simply one aspect of space, of architecture, or urban life—in other words, as a social and not an individualistic act—was derived from Neo-Plasticism and Constructivism and closely linked with other contemporary trends (*Spazialismo, Zero* group and *Groupe de Recherche d'Art Visuel*).

Group of Seven. This circle of twentieth-century Canadian painters instituted the first important national movement in Canadian painting. The leaders, both of whom were in Toronto by 1913, were the English-born J. E. H. MacDonald (1873–1932), a graphic designer in the *art nouveau* tradition who had turned to landscape painting (*Spring Breezes, High Park*, 1912, Ottawa, National Gallery of Canada), and Tom Thomson. In 1910 Lawren Harris (1885–1970), who had studied in Berlin, was painting the shabbier streets of Toronto in what was called a 'socialistic' style. Arthur Lismer (1885–1969) and Frederick Varley (1881–1969), who had emigrated from Sheffield in 1912, joined the ranks of the commercial artists, who by now also included Franklin Carmichael (1890–1945) and Frank H. Johnston (1888–1949). The group was complete when Alexander Young Jackson (1882–1974) arrived in 1913, bringing with him the Whistlerian-Fauvist influence of James Wilson Morrice. In the winter of 1912–13 MacDonald and Harris had seen an exhibition of Scandinavian painting in Buffalo, and both were influenced by the Scandinavian version of *art nouveau*.

The group became acquainted with the North Country of Ontario while on sketching trips to Georgian Bay and Algonquin Park (a nature reserve in Ontario) in 1912–13. In Algonquin Park in 1914, Jackson and Thomson arrived at a new method of painting the wild forested country by using bold colours and emphatic flat designs. Examples of this style are Jackson's *Red Maple* (1914, Ottawa, National Gallery of Canada) and Thomson's *Pointers* (1916–17, Toronto, Hart House, University of Toronto). The First World War scattered the group, and Thomson was drowned in Algonquin Park in 1917. The survivors reassembled in Toronto in 1919, and in 1920 held their first joint exhibition, calling themselves for the first time the Group of Seven. For these early group shows they painted large exhibition pieces in which they employed the common *motif* of a tree set against sky and water, as in Varley's *Georgian Bay* (1920), Lismer's *September Gale* (1921) and Harris' *Lake Superior* (1924)—all in the National Gallery of Canada. The austere, simplified forms and unsubtle colours of these works earned the artists critical abuse, which continued throughout the 1920s. MacDonald, Harris, Jackson and Lismer extended their field of work very widely throughout Canada during the 1920s and 1930s, and their undeniable love of their country eventually won them recognition. Varley eventually turned to figure painting (*Vera*, 1930, Ottawa, National Gallery of Canada); Johnston dropped out of the Group in 1922, and MacDonald died in 1932. Three new members joined: Alfred Joseph Casson of Toronto (1898–1976) in 1926, Edwin Holgate of Montreal (b. 1892) in 1931 and L. L. (Lionel Lemoine) FitzGerald of Winnipeg (1890–1956) in 1932, thus widening the Group's representation geographically, and increasing their number to eight. In 1933 the Group of Seven changed its name to the Canadian Group of Painters. The original members, however, continued their development along more individual lines. Lawren Harris, in particular, carried his already simplified landscape style into the realm of pure abstraction.

F. Housser. *A Canadian Art Movement: The Story of the Group of Seven*, Toronto 1926.
Exhibition catalogue, *Retrospective Exhibition of Painting by Members of the Group of Seven, 1919–1933*, National Gallery of Canada, Ottawa 1936.
Thoreau MacDonald. *Group of Seven*, Toronto 1944.
Russell J. Harper. 'Nationalism and Internationalism After 1910', *Painting in Canada*, Toronto 1966.

Gruber, Francis. French painter, b. 1912 in Nancy; d. 1948 in Paris. Ill-health prevented him from having a normal schooling, but he studied first under his father, who was a stained-glass artist, and then, from 1929 to 1932, at the Académie Scandinave with Dufresne, Friesz and Waroquier. At the age of 18 his success at the Salon d'Automne and the Salon des Tuileries exhibitions made him famous in the artists' quarter of Montparnasse. At first he had a rather Surrealist style, but later he became a precursor of Realism. All his paintings, whether enormous, like the mural he produced for the Lycée

Lakanal (*Homage to Le Nôtre*, 1936), or tiny, as some of his still lifes, were conceived on a monumental basis. In 1942–3, he taught at the Académie Ranson and he won the Prix National in 1947, a year before his death.

Catalogue, *François Gruber*, Tate Gallery, London 1959.

Grünewald, Isaac. Swedish painter, b. 1889 in Stockholm; d. 1946 in Oslo. Grünewald studied at the school run by the Swedish Artists' Association (*Konstnärsförbundet*) from 1905 to 1908 and under Matisse in Paris from 1908 to 1911. He made his début in 1909 with the *1909 års män* (The men of 1909), a group composed of young Swedish artists who shared the same approach to art. After coming to terms with Cézanne Grünewald evolved a vital and essentially Fauvist style between 1910 and 1920, which he subsequently abandoned in favour of a much more precise type of composition in which the pictorial objects acquired greater plasticity and the colours were applied by an impasted technique. At the same time Grünewald created a number of delicate *grisailles*, such as the portrait of his wife—the painter Sigrid Hjertén (1931)—and watercolours of the South of France, Spain and Lapland, which provided a perfect vehicle for his spontaneous technique. He also illustrated books by Swedish authors such as Levertin and Heidenstam. Grünewald's early works provoked considerable opposition from the Swedish establishment. Although he was awarded first prize in the competition for the decoration of the Registry Office in the Town Hall at Stockholm, he was not allowed to execute his design, which was uncompromisingly Fauvist. Later monumental projects were more successful. In 1926, for example, Grünewald decorated the small auditorium in the Stockholm Concert Hall. But it was in the theatre that he really made his mark as a decorative artist. His stage set for *Samson and Delilah* in 1921, which marked the beginning of a new anti-naturalistic phase in Swedish theatrical design, was the first of many such projects.

S. Strömbom. *Isaac Grünewald*, Stockholm 1934.
J. P. Hodin. *Isaac Grünewald*, Stockholm 1949.

Grupa Krakowska—*see* **Cracow Group**

Gubler, Max. Swiss painter, b. 1898 in Zürich. Gubler was the son of a painter and decorator. From 1914 to 1918 he attended the Teachers' Training College in Küssnacht. He then taught himself to paint and made the acquaintance of Hugo Ball, Tzara, Arp and Richter. The most influential figures in his early years were Picasso, Derain, Hodler and Karl Hofer. In 1921 Gubler visited Hofer in Berlin, in 1922 he was in Florence and from 1923 to 1927 he lived on the island of Lipari, off Sicily. The works of this period, which were painted in bright but delicate colours, reveal the influence of Cézanne. From 1930 to 1937 Gubler lived in Paris. In 1952 he was represented at the Biennale in Venice. His later landscapes and figure compositions are a synthesis of Late Impressionism, Cubism and Expressionism. They have a powerful, abstract line and are executed in Fauvist colours. Gubler has painted numerous murals. He is now living in Préfarguier, Marin, Switzerland.

M. Vogt. *Max Gubler*, Neuchâtel 1952.
Exhibition catalogue, *Max Gubler*, Museum Schaffhausen 1962–4.

Guderna, Ladislav. Slovak painter and graphic artist, b. 1921 in Nitra. He studied in Bratislava, where he now lives. He paints mainly portraits and landscapes. He is a member of the *Mánes-Union* group in Prague.

Gudnason, Svavar. Icelandic painter, b. 1909 in Hafu, Iceland. Gudnason studied in Copenhagen and under Léger in Paris. He now works in Reykjavik and Copenhagen. Gudnason was one of the pioneers of non-figurative art in Denmark and Iceland. With their bright, clear colours and their rhythmical composition his paintings are extremely powerful.

Guerrini, Lorenzo. Italian sculptor, b. 1914 in Milan. After studying at the Academies in Rome (1930) and Berlin Guerrini made working visits to Paris, Austria, Czechoslovakia, Poland, Germany and Brazil. He now lives in Rome. In 1949 Guerrini produced his first abstract medallions, which constitute a new approach to this art form within the Italian tradition. Since 1950 he has been sculpting monumental works in stone, bronze and copper, whose abstract structures are sometimes reminiscent of Wotruba.

Guggenheim, Willy (Varlin). Swiss painter, b. 1900 in Zürich. He was at first a lithographer, then studied painting in Berlin. From 1922 on he has lived in France, at Cros de Cagnes, Alpes Maritimes.

Guglielmi, O. Louis. American painter, b. 1906 in Cairo, Egypt; d. 1956. Guglielmi arrived in New York in 1914 after touring Europe with his father who was an orchestral musician. Although he studied at the National Academy of Design for five years and worked as an assistant to a mural painter, he was unable to paint seriously until about 1932. Before this time he supported himself by doing drawings for newspapers and other commercial art work. His early paintings are strongly rooted in the realm of Social Realism (*Sisters of Charity*, 1936, New York, Nordness Gallery) and it was while working in this vein that he received his first one-man show at the Downtown Gallery, New York (1938). As early as 1946, the influence of C. Demuth, C. Sheeler and especially S. Davis can be seen in such works as *Solitudes* (New York, Nordness Gallery), an influence which continued into the early 1950s. The use of abstract patterns, letters and familiar everyday objects in *Memo from Baton Rouge* (1950–1, New York, Nordness Gallery) certainly points back to Davis. Just before his death, he advanced to pure abstraction, often using a textured background recalling manuscript tessellation over which he superimposed a fragile linearity.

D. C. Miller and A. H. Barr Jr. Exhibition catalogue, *American Realists and Magic Realists*, Museum of Modern Art, New York 1943.

Guidi, Virgilio. Italian painter, b. 1891 in Rome. Guidi's father was a sculptor and poet. As a young man Guidi worked on the restoration of old frescoes in Rome and was able to study the paintings in the Villa Borghese. Later he attended the Rome Academy, where he was a contemporary of Sartorino. He became friendly with the artists in the *Gruppo Romano* and joined both the *Gruppo Moderno di Opere e Melli* and the *Valori Plastici*. In 1927 he was appointed to the teaching staff of the Venice Academy, transferring to the Academy of Bologna in 1935. He was a member of the *Movimento Spaziale*. Apart from his activities as a painter, Guido has also worked as a book illustrator and art critic. He is now living in Venice. After an early Neo-Impressionist phase Guidi adapted his style to meet the requirements of the new Neo-Classical trend in c. 1920. Since then he has produced works whose colouring is clearly derived from Matisse but whose rhythmical organization and plastic structure are specifically Italian.

B. Silvio. *Guidi*, Ancona 1966.

Guiette, René. Belgian painter, b. 1893 in Antwerp. After completing his university studies Guiette became a painter in 1919. At first he was influenced by Expressionism, but subsequently, between 1930 and 1946, he painted in a variety of styles, although during this second phase Picasso was the dominant influence. From 1950 onwards he produced works similar to the *pâtes* of Dubuffet. In these pieces he first built up a thick, relief-like ground and then scratched his design in the surface. More recently he has been painting lyrical abstracts. Guiette is now living in Brussels.

Robert Guiette. *René Guiette*, Antwerp 1950.

Gulbransson, Olaf. Norwegian draughtsman and painter, b. 1873 in Oslo; d. 1958 in Schererhof, Tegernsee. Gulbransson was already working as a caricaturist for newspapers and humorous magazines in 1889 when he was only sixteen. Then, in 1892, he attended the School of Art and Crafts in Oslo. In 1900 he went to Paris to study at the Académie Colarossi, returning to Oslo in the following year, where he made his name with an album of twenty-four caricatures of famous Norwegians. In 1902 A. Langen invited him to work for *Simplicissimus* in Munich and Gulbransson soon established himself as the most gifted of the contributors to this magazine. In 1916 he was elected to the Prussian Academy of Arts, and in 1924 he was made an honorary member of the Munich Academy where, in 1929, he was appointed Professor of Painting and Drawing. From 1923 to 1927 Gulbransson lived in Norway and subsequently visited Paris, Egypt and Italy. In 1951 he was elected to the Bavarian Academy of Fine Arts. Apart from his caricatures Gulbransson also produced portrait drawings, book illustrations and graphic works. But it was as a caricaturist that he acquired an international reputation. In this sphere he developed an incomparable technique based on highly simplified and economical outlines which he used to lay bare the foibles of public figures and pour ridicule on the narrow-minded attitudes of the *petit-bourgeois*. At no time did Gulbransson strive after cheap effects in his caricatures. His portraits are extremely delicate compositions executed in exquisite colours. He also produced many finely observed flower and animal studies, which reveal his aesthetic leanings and stand in marked contrast to his political work.

Exhibition catalogue, *Olaf Gulbransson*, Oslo and Munich 1962.

Gundersen, Gunnar S. Norwegian painter, b. 1921. After attending the School of Arts and Crafts in Oslo Gundersen completed his training by visiting Paris, Portugal, Belgium, Holland, Denmark and Sweden. When he returned to Norway he collaborated with Ludwig Eikaas on the decoration of various buildings, including the Kemiske Factory and the Kunstforbundets House in Oslo. Later he taught at the Academy of Art and the Technical College in Oslo. Gundersen's abstract paintings are based on Constructivist principles. With their distinctive forms and clear colours they are a spur to meditation.

Guston, Philip. American painter, b. 1913 in Montreal, Canada. He grew up in Los Angeles where, in 1930, he began his studies at the Otis Art Institute. In 1934 a journey to Mexico introduced Guston to the Social Realist murals there. This acquaintance was to serve him well when he worked as a muralist for the WPA Federal Arts Project in New York from 1936 to 1940. Guston achieved his initial success working as a figurative painter, and his first one-man show took place in 1944 at the Midtown Gallery, New York. He taught in many universities and art schools, such as Pratt Institute and Yale University, and travelled in Spain, France and Italy. He received the Prix de Rome in 1948 and a Guggenheim Fellowship in 1968.

Like many other artists of his generation who painted in New York, Guston eliminated representative or figurative references from his work around 1947–50 and began to paint abstractly. Along with Jackson Pollock, Willem de Kooning and Franz Kline, he chose to concentrate particularly on the existential and pictorial importance of gesture. His own version of Abstract Expressionism, often termed Abstract Impressionism, fluctuated between a characteristically sensuous, lyrical and subtly tinted manner and a more sober, discordant, less elegant style. In a typical painting from the mid-1950s, such as *Altar* (1953, New York, Coll. Morton Feldman), with its small, hatched brushstrokes of pale peach on a white ground, one observes the artist's more lyrical bent. Roughened patches of pastel colours hovering slightly off-centre on the canvas are frequent during this period and refer to Guston's interest in Mondrian's horizontal and vertical definition of the picture plane (*Painting*, 1954, New York, Museum of Modern Art). After 1954 organic forces predominated over this geometric tendency, while colour became rawer and more Expressionistic, with paint applied in bold and forceful strokes—a break from his habitually subdued and nuanced colour schemes, which are painted with a refined, rhythmic feeling, as in *Passage* (1957–8, Beverly Hills, Coll. David E. Bright). This increasing density is also indicative of Guston's study of Andrea Mantegna and Piero della Francesca while in Italy (1960), and his admiration for the assertive forms and dignified mood of works by these Renaissance masters. Although his style altered from year to year Guston, like his colleagues in the New York School, maintained his commitment to the personally expressive and subjective content of his paintings.

Irving Sandler. 'Guston: A Long Voyage Home', *Art News* LVIII, New York, December 1959.
H. H. Arnason. Exhibition catalogue, *Philip Guston*, Solomon R. Guggenheim Museum, New York 1962.

Gutfreund, Otto. Czech sculptor, b. 1889; d. 1927. One of a group of Czech *avant-garde* artists that included Filla, Kubišta and Procházka, he began to sculpt in the Cubist idiom from about 1911, after he had studied in Paris (1909–10) under Bourdelle. Also in 1911 he joined the Group of Avant-Garde Artists in Prague. His Cubist period lasted until about 1919, and he made an important contribution to Cubism in Czechoslovakia. Later his work grew more figurative.

Guttuso, Renato. Italian painter, b. 1912 in Bagheria, Palermo. Guttuso is the son of a land surveyor. He himself started to read law but gave up his studies in order to become a painter. In 1931, when he was only nineteen, he was represented at the Quadriennale in Rome. In the following year he was employed as a restorer by the Galleria di

Perugia and the Borghese in Rome. In 1933 he became friendly with Cagli, Fazzini and Manzù. He then returned to Sicily, remaining there until 1935, when he went to live in Milan. In 1937 he was in Rome, where he collaborated with Colacicchi and Scialoja. From 1940 to 1942 he was a member of the *Corrente* association and from 1943 to 1945 worked for the Italian resistance. After the war, in 1947, he became a founder member of the *Fronte Nuovo delle Arti*. In 1950 he won the Marzotto prize. He is now living in Rome.

Guttuso is the leading Italian representative of Social Realism. His artistic personality was stamped at an early age by the landscape of his native Sicily, which he experienced both *in natura* and in the works of earlier painters; his youthful works, in which he practised a descriptive, Impressionistic form of Realism, reveal marked national characteristics. Later, under the influence of C. Levi, Mafai and Scipione, he turned towards Expressionism. He then joined forces with the young Roman School in order to oppose Neo-Classicism and the programme put forward by the *Novecento*. For a while he was influenced by the archaic style of C. Cagli. But in the 1930s he became deeply involved with the works of Goya and Picasso—especially the latter's *Guernica*—and his subsequent artistic development was largely determined by his reactions to these two painters. Since then he has been a committed artist, quick to oppose social injustice and political abuse. His protests have found expression in Realistic paintings in which the pictorial objects are either indicated by a few brief strokes of the brush or are broken down and condensed in the Neo-Cubist manner. In either case the hard, simplifying outlines encompass dynamic volumes, whose luminous colours are carefully modulated to create an impression of expansion. Certain of the objects depicted in these works are set out in a graduated sequence based on diagonal lines, which structures the pictorial space and creates a sense of direction. The plasticity of the volumes is heightened by the harsh light, which usually falls on them from an oblique angle. The dynamism of the individual objects and the brutal way in which they are aligned reflects the sensitive, dialectical relationship between the artist and the world.

Giuseppe Marchiori. *Renato Guttuso*, Milan 1952.
Exhibition catalogue, *Renato Guttuso*, Kunstverein, Darmstadt 1967.

Gwathmey, Robert. American painter, b. 1903 in Richmond, Va. Upon high school graduation he worked for two years in a railroad office before entering North Carolina State College in 1924. The following year he attended the Maryland Institute of Design, Baltimore, and then transferred to the Pennsylvania Academy of Fine Arts, where he studied under George Harding and Daniel Garber.

In the summers of 1929 and 1930 he was awarded Cresson Scholarships from the Academy, which enabled him to travel abroad, sketching and visiting galleries and museums. After his graduation in 1930 he taught at Bever College, Jenkintown, Pa. (1931–8). After this position he destroyed everything he had previously painted because, in the words of the artist, 'it takes about ten years to wash yourself of academic dogma'. In 1939, when he became an Instructor in the Department of Painting and Design at Carnegie Institute of Technology, Pittsburgh, he exhibited *Land of Cotton*. On the basis of this work he was offered his first one-man show at the American Contemporary Art Gallery, an exhibition which did not take place until 1941. It took that amount of time for the artist, with his slow working methods, to produce a sufficient number of canvases for such an exhibition. A work such as *Hoeing* (1941, New York, Coll. Edgar Kaufmann Jr.) is representative of his style at this time. He employs strong colour contrasts, bold patterns and incisive lines while negating three-dimensionality and contrasts of light and shadow in order to emphasize definitively the design elements. His subject matter most often centres on social commentary—negro injustice, desolation, poverty, toil—although he also turns at times to caricature and satire. His social conscience parallels his work for the WPA, among which figures his mural for the Eutaw, Alabama Post Office. He has taught at Cooper Union, New York City, since 1942.

Paul Robeson. Exhibition catalogue, *Robert Gwathmey*, A.C.A. Gallery, New York 1946.

H

Haber, Shamai. Polish sculptor, b. 1922 in Lodz. After emigrating to Palestine in 1935 Haber studied at the Academy of Art in Tel Aviv from 1943 to 1947, and subsequently served an apprenticeship with a stonemason. In 1948 he moved to Marseilles, and in 1949 to Paris.

During his early period Haber was influenced by the works of Despiau, and by the monumental sculpture of the Hittites and Assyrians. In 1953 he made contact with the Parisian *avant-garde*, and exhibited in the Salon de la Jeune Sculpture in Paris. In 1959 he won the Prix Bourdelle. He is now living in Paris. Haber is an abstract artist.

Hadzi, Dimitri. American sculptor, b. 1921 in New York. Hadzi attended the Brooklyn Technical High School, Cooper Union, and the Brooklyn Museum Art School (1946–50). In 1950–1 he studied as a Fulbright Fellow at the Athens Polytechneion and at the Museo Artistico Industriale in Rome, where he eventually settled permanently. Hadzi received several major prizes and important commissions, including one for Philharmonic Hall, Lincoln Center for the Performing Arts, New York. His first one-man exhibition was held at the Galleria Schneider, Rome, in 1958, and this was followed by others there and in New York, Munich, Düsseldorf and the Massachusetts Institute of Technology in Cambridge (retrospective, 1963); in 1956 and 1958 his sculpture was included in the Venice Biennale.

Hadzi's imagery is generally derived from Classical *motifs*, battles and armour. His earliest sculptures are fairly literal allusions to mythological figures, but after 1958 his work became more abstract in a series based on shields and helmets (*Elmo-M.I.T.*, 1963, bronze, Cambridge, Massachusetts Institute of Technology). Although he also carved, Hadzi worked primarily in bronze, making his models in specially prepared wax. His sculpture is generally massive, made of heavy slabs and thick plates, although it may rest on slender points, and has an aggressive, rugged, yet ultimately static quality.

'New Talent, U.S.A.—Sculpture', *Art in America* XLIX, No. 1, 1961.

Haese, Günther. German sculptor, b. 1924 in Kiel. After training as a decorative painter Haese studied first under Bruno Goller and then at the Düsseldorf Academy, where he entered Ewald Mataré's 'Masters' Class'. He then worked as Mataré's assistant until 1958. Haese has made his name with delicate, imaginative montages, which he constructs from fragile, vibrating parts of clocks and whose poetic charm recalls the pictorial world of Paul Klee. Haese's work was specially commended at the Venice Biennale in 1966.

Exhibition catalogue, *Günther Haese*, Marlborough Gallery, London 1965.

Haese, Reinhoud d'. Belgian sculptor, b. 1928 in Grammont. D'Haese is the brother of Roel d'Haese. After studying at the École Supérieure des Arts Décoratifs in Brussels he made contact with the *Cobra* group. Since 1959 he has been living in Paris. After first working in plaster and terra-cotta d'Haese went over to metal sculptures, most of which are constructed from sheets of copper and brass. His informal constructions, which are full of Baroque movement, are reminiscent of works by R. Müller, but are more aggressive.

Haese, Roel d'. Belgian sculptor, b. 1921 in Grammont. After training at the Académie d'Alost and the École Supérieure de la Cambre, where he studied under Oscar Jespers, d'Haese concentrated on direct carving, producing works which reveal an early preoccupation with questions of sculptural form. This seems surprising in view of the fact that d'Haese was to make his reputation with Expressionist works, for which he employed quite different methods. In 1953 he began to use the cast-iron technique and in 1957 the lost-wax process. He was one of the first artists to create assemblages, and one of the first to produce informal sculptures. His Expressionism soon developed fantastic and Surrealistic characteristics. These, together with his grim sense of humour, indicate an affinity with Hieronymus Bosch. D'Haese is also an extremely gifted draughtsman.

Hague, Raoul. American sculptor, b. 1905 in Istanbul, Turkey. Hague arrived in the United States in 1921 and studied at Iowa State College (1921), at the Chicago Art Institute (1922–5), and at the Beaux-Arts Institute of Design in New York (1925–7). During the late 1920s he was influenced by the current sculptural concepts of direct carving and truth to materials through studies with William Zorach (1927–8) and through his acquaintance with John Flannagan. Hague began direct stone carving in the early 1930s and exhibited this early work in a group exhibition at the Museum of Modern Art (1932) and at the New York World's Fair (1939). By around 1947, however, his interest had shifted to wood, which had become his most satisfying medium; his first one-man show of carved wood sculpture in New York was held in 1962. Hague's mature style, after a development towards increasingly simplified forms, is characterized by massive and monolithic asymmetric forms that sometimes suggest the human torso, but tend to be abstract; the natural character of the grain and the surface of the wood remain evident and essentially unaltered in the sculpture (*Angel Millbrook Walnut*, 1964, New York, Egan Gallery).

Thomas B. Hess. 'Introducing the Sculpture of Raoul Hague', *Art News* LIII, New York, January 1955.
Gerald Nordland. Exhibition catalogue, *Raoul Hague*, Gallery of Modern Art, Washington (D.C.) 1964.

Hahn, Hermann. German sculptor, b. 1868 in Kloster-Veilsdorf; d. 1942 in Pullach. He studied at the Academy in Munich, then spent some years in Italy. He was greatly influenced by the academic sculptor Adolf von Hildebrand, and this influence was transmitted to many of the younger sculptors who trained with him. He created monumental and portrait sculpture.

Hains, Raymond. French photographer and affichiste, b. 1926 in Saint Brienc, Northern France. In 1946 Hains began working as a photographer for *France-Illustration*. It was then that he produced his first abstract photographs. In 1949 he and Jacques de la Villeglé made a number of films together, including *Loi du 29 Juillet 1881, Saint-German des*

Près-Colombiens and *Étude aux Allures*. These two also developed an interest in the late 1940s in *'affiches lacérées'* (torn posters). But Hains' poster work differed from his colleague's. De la Villeglé worked on his posters to produce an artistic or aesthetic effect. Hains did not. He left them as they were, using them to pinpoint the threadbare values of the advertising world. He also pursued a polemical purpose in his montages, which feature ambiguous advertising texts.

Hajdu, Étienne. French sculptor, b. 1907 in Turda, Transylvania. After leaving grammar school Hajdu turned to sculpture and in 1927 entered the Academy of Fine Arts in Vienna. Later the same year he went to Paris where he studied, first at the École des Beaux-Arts under Paul Niclausse, and subsequently at the Académie de la Grande Chaumière under Antoine Bourdelle. Eventually, however, he decided to complete his studies on his own. In 1930 Hajdu acquired French nationality. Meanwhile, he earned his living in a variety of ways, and made long visits to Greece, Crete and the Netherlands. In 1939 he established contact with the Galerie Jeanne Bucher in Paris but moved almost immediately to the Pyrenees, where he spent the war years. Since 1949 he has exhibited regularly in the Salon de la Jeune Sculpture, and since 1951 has also taken part in the Open Air Biennale in Antwerp-Middelheim. In 1955 Hajdu exhibited in the USA. He now lives and works in Paris.

During his early period Hajdu was influenced by Rodin and by the Romanesque sculptures of Moissac and Vézelay. In 1934 he turned abstract, using essentially passive components to create free-standing sculptures, which from 1940 onwards acquired pierced forms with jagged edges. Hajdu has also produced bas-reliefs. He works in marble, lead, copper and aluminium. From 1958 onwards he created a series of 'prints'. These are free adaptations in metal, some of them enlarged, of stamped designs. The general austerity of his work stems from the long years of isolation during the war.

Roberto Ganzo. *Hajdu*, Paris 1957.

Hajek, Otto Herbert. Russian-German sculptor, b. 1927 in Kaltenbach, Russia. Hajek studied from 1947 to 1954 at the Academy in Stuttgart, where he is now living. He first made a name for himself as a result of the commissions which he executed for the Catholic Church. His early sculptures were simple pierced forms, but from 1957 onwards he developed his 'Raumknoten' (Spatial Concentrates) and his 'Räumliche Wände' (Spatial Walls) and in 1963 produced his first 'traversable sculptures'. It was then that he introduced his system of coloured bands, which were spread over his works and extended into the surrounding space. These bands serve to disrupt the sculpture and also effectively incorporate the environment into the artistic ensemble. Hajek has been commissioned to execute numerous works for official bodies. Between 1961 and 1963 he created the *Way of the Cross* for the Church of the Regina Martyrum in Berlin-Plötzensee; in 1962 he produced a *Leitwand* (a wall designed to arrest and channel the viewer's gaze) for a memorial hall in Frankfurt am Main; and in 1968–9 he executed a wall relief for the University of Saarbrücken.

Exhibition catalogue, *O. H. Hajek*, Galerie Abels, Cologne 1964.

Haller, Hermann. Swiss sculptor, b. 1880 in Berne; d. 1950 in Zürich. He studied in Munich, Stuttgart, Rome and Paris. His work consists mainly of portraits and young slender female figures. He gained the Zürich Grand Prix in 1949.

Halpert, Samuel. American painter, b. 1884 in Russia; d. 1930 in Detroit, Michigan. He went to the United States as a boy and studied at the National Academy of Design. In Paris during the first decade of the twentieth century he studied with Bonnat and at the École des Beaux-Arts. Most strongly influenced by the Fauves, he became an imitator of Braque's Fauvist pictures in such works as *Brooklyn Bridge* (1913, New York, Whitney Museum of American Art). Halpert was vice-president and director of the Society of Independent Artists and a member of the faculty of the Master Institute of United Arts, New York, and the Detroit Society of Arts and Crafts.

B. D. Saklatwalla. 'L'Art contemporain des États-Unis', *Formes* No. 21, January 1932.

Hamaguchi, Yozo. Japanese printmaker, b. 1909. Hamaguchi works primarily with etchings. He attended the sculpture division of the Imperial School of Fine Arts, then in 1930 left for Paris, where he has lived ever since. A few of the numerous prizes which he has won are: first prize for prints at the São Paulo Bienal, 1957; second prize at the International Prints Biennale at Lugano, 1958; first prize at the International Prints Biennale, Ljubljana, 1961. His etchings are a marvellous example of the uniting of the Japanese sensibility with the logical system of European printmaking. His works are largely still lifes and landscapes to which he has given more and more depth as the years have gone by. His meticulously worked etchings have a smooth, velvety texture. His wife, Keiko Minami, is also a gifted printmaker.

Hamilton, Richard. British painter, b. 1922 in London. Hamilton studied at the Royal Academy Schools from 1938 to 1940 and from 1946 to 1947. He then attended the Slade School from 1948 to 1951. He helped to organize two exhibitions: *Growth and Form* (1951) and *Man, Machine and Motion* (1955). Meanwhile he had become a founder member of the Independent Group in 1952 and obtained a teaching post at the University of Newcastle in 1953. In 1960 he was represented in the *Situation* exhibition. He is now living in London. Hamilton is a friend and pupil of Marcel Duchamp. He has made a major contribution to the emergence of the New Realist movement in England and also plays an important part in the Independent Group and in the sphere of Pop Art. His pictures are montages constructed from significant fragments of real objects, which reflect the industrial culture of the big city. He treats subjects such as the gun, the woman driver, part of a washing machine, etc. His object is to raise the banal to the level of art.

Exhibition catalogue, *Richard Hamilton*, Hanover Gallery, London 1964.

Hamilton Fraser, Donald. British painter, b. 1929 in London. Hamilton Fraser trained at St. Martin's School of Art from 1949 to 1952 and then went to Paris with a French Government scholarship. He was greatly influenced by the work of de Staël in his last, most figurative phase.

Hanak, Anton. Austrian sculptor, b. 1875 in Brünn; d. 1934 in Vienna. After serving an apprenticeship as a cabinet-maker Hanak studied sculpture at the Viennese Academy. He was a friend of Gustav Klimt and Josef Hoffmann and a member of the Viennese Secession. He held a professorial post at the Viennese Academy from 1932 onwards. During his formative years Hanak was influenced by Michelangelo and Rodin. In his subsequent quest for a new block-like monumentality, for expressive emphasis and for a technique that would do justice to his materials he created numerous figurative sculptures. The writhing forms of these are charged with pathos and their texture seems almost to have anticipated the techniques of informal art. Hanak exerted considerable influence on his pupils, one of whom was Wotruba.

M. Eisler, *Anton Hanak*, Vienna 1921.
H. Steiner, *Anton Hanak*, Munich 1969.

Hantai, Simon. Hungarian painter, b. 1922 in Bia, Hungary. He studied at the École des Beaux-Arts, Budapest, and then travelled to Italy in 1948 and settled in Paris in 1949. Here he became friendly with André Breton and took part in the Surrealist movement (1953–4). His works often have the simplicity, delicacy and calligraphic emphasis of Oriental art, which has led to the characterization of his canvases as the graphic side of Action Painting. These qualities can be seen in *Homage to G. M. Hopkins* (1958, Paris, Galerie Kléber) with its flame-like arabesques creating a chiaroscuro juxtaposition of red-orange against a dark background.

Jean Yves Mock. 'Hantai at the Galerie Kléber', *Apollo* 69, London 1959.

Happening. The happening is a participational art form initiated in America and practised in Europe and Japan. It consists of a synthesis of environmental situations, composed and unplanned theatre events, the visual arts, and extra-artistic materials. Its origins are multiple, although its development as a viable form of 'total theatre' dates from the period around 1957–9 in New York. At that time a number of painters and artists affiliated with the Reuben Gallery were experimenting with perishable urban subject matter (termed 'gutter art' by some) and were concerned with extending the possibilities for the performance and exhibition of new art forms. Happenings actually grew out of painting, and might be seen historically as the theatrical counterpart of the kinaesthetic 'action' notions inherent in Abstract Expressionist painting. In fact, pictorial and painterly effects are still retained in many of the overall settings for happenings. The painters Allan Kaprow, Claes Oldenburg, Jim Dine, Red Grooms, Robert Whitman and Al Hansen all helped to originate the earliest happenings—the name of which derives from Kaprow's *18 Happenings in 6 Parts*, performed at the Reuben Gallery in October 1959. Assemblage, collage, junk sculpture and such combine-constructions as Robert Rauschenberg's early work or even Kurt Schwitters' *Merz* theatre serve as sources for the happenings as well. Found environments and perishable media that stress notions of change, obsolescence and a view of reality as a constant metamorphosis are also the common materials and subject matter of the performances. Everyday items and surroundings—objects from the home, the street, junk yards or from popular culture—are united in a large-scale time-space continuum that aims to eliminate the customary barriers that exist between audience and performer in traditional theatre. Artfulness is combined with anything drawn from outside the world of what is normally identified as art, although the happenings as they were first developed were not completely extemporaneous or disorganized events. The composer John Cage, who had been one of Kaprow's teachers, was a crusader for chance methods of arrangement and composition, and also contributed to the theoretical and practical background of these first happenings, in which nonverbal sounds, random noises and acausally related musical fragments or sequences were frequently employed.

Happenings challenge and revise our assumptions about the accepted identities of the plastic and performing arts. Although their general structuring is non-rational, predetermined or self-contained units

may be partially set up before the actual performance. The physical relation between diverse spatial situations or alogically combined materials, the environment and the spectator-performers is manipulated in such a way as to treat the 'performers' as things or effects and the props as 'performers', thereby increasing both the immediacy and the intimacy of the presentation. Unprogrammed occurrences are absorbed and combined with prepared effects in situations that attempt to expand the confines of the art experience beyond gallery, museum or stage display. Thus many happenings are presented in unorthodox places, such as lofts, stores, gymnasiums, parking lots (Oldenburg's *Autobodies* in Los Angeles, 1964), backyards (Kaprow's *Yard*, 1961), and make use of such materials as ice-cubes, cars and crowds, heaps of rubber tyres, water, food, trees, costumes, furniture, paint and plaster. The purposefully timed or compartmented unit may be thrown together with indeterminate acts, sounds, smells or sights that are improvised. Conscious subversiveness and primitivism are working assumptions for the happenings, which abandon plot or story structure in an attempt to break down the distinctions between art and life.

Michael Kirby. *Happenings: An Illustrated Anthology*, New York 1965.
Allan Kaprow. *Assemblage, Environments and Happenings*, New York 1966.

Hard edge. This is a type of abstract painting based on simple geometric or organic forms and executed in cool flat colours, which are separated from one another by 'hard edges' that constitute the dominant feature of this style. The pictures of Barnett Newman, Ad Reinhardt and Mark Rothko paved the way for the emergence of hard edge. So too did the pictures and writings of Josef Albers, who drew attention to the interaction of complementary colours and of colours placed in juxtaposition to one another. Another important source is to be found in the late collages of Matisse, whilst the development of acrylic paint provided the technical basis for this new technique. The actual concept was formulated by the late American critic Jules Langsner in 1958. It is largely synonymous with Michael Sandler's 'Cool Art', Max Bill's 'kalte Kunst' (Cold Art) and the generic term 'New Abstraction', which was used for an exhibition staged at the Jewish Museum in New York in 1963.

Catalogue, *New Abstraction*, Jewish Museum, New York 1963.
'Neue Abstraktion', *Das Kunstwerk* 10–12 1965.

Hare, David. American sculptor, b. 1917 in New York. Hare spent most of his early life in the South-West. With no formal training in art, he first worked in colour photography, publishing a portfolio of colour photographs on the American Indian for the American Museum of Natural History (1940), and exhibiting his work in New York (1940–1). From 1942 to 1944 he was editor of the Surrealist magazine *VVV*. Hare's interest shifted seriously to sculpture around 1943, and he began exhibiting in New York soon after. He has been included in international exhibitions, and is represented in major American museums.

Although Hare worked in other media, he is known primarily for his sculptures in metal, a material he has found suitable for its ease of manipulation since he first used it in 1949. As his style emerged in the 1940s, it was marked by an emphasis on line and open form, as well as Surrealist qualities in treatment and subject matter. Hare's sculptures often juxtapose prominent structural rods with smaller, weblike or spiky forms. Their roughly textured and mottled, multicoloured surfaces result from the welding process and the oxidization that takes place as the metals cool. Hare used figurative elements in such pieces as *The Eaters* (1952, New York, Kootz Gallery); *Juggler* (1950–1, steel, New York, Whitney Museum of American Art); and *Man Running* (1954, welded steel and bronze, New York, Museum of Modern Art). In the 1950s *motifs* of natural and celestial phenomena were also explored: *Sunrise* (1955, steel, bronze and alabaster, Buffalo, Albright–Knox Gallery) and *Sunset I* (1953, stone and painted wire, New York, Museum of Modern Art). Hare's sculpture is rich with associations, but he did not consider it symbolic. On the contrary, he was concerned with developing a 'mental space', a plastic art of directly expressed emotion 'stripped of its symbols'.

E. C. Goosen, Robert Goldwater and Irving Sandler. *Three American Sculptors: Ferber, Hare, Lassaw*, New York 1959.
David Hare. 'The Myth of Originality', *College Art Journal* XXIV, 1964–5.

Harth, Philipp. German sculptor and art writer, b. 1887 in Mainz. He was an apprentice in his father's workshop, then studied at art school in Mainz; in 1908 he went to Karlsruhe for further study, and in 1912 to Berlin. He works mainly in stone and wood, and the majority of his works are animals. He carves the figures of animals direct from the block, without first making models or sketches. He has also written theoretical studies.

Hartigan, Grace. American painter, b. 1922 in Newark, N.J. She held various jobs in New York City after her graduation from Millburn High School, New Jersey, in 1940. A period of concentrated effort and production in painting came in 1949 when she spent a year painting in San Miguel de Allende, Mexico. When she returned to New York she met Albert Leslie and Robert Goodnough. With them, she organized a show at the Kootz Gallery, exhibiting works by new artists. Clement Greenberg and Meyer Schapiro, who were selecting pictures for

an exhibition entitled *Talent—1950*, chose one of her Mexican paintings from the Kootz show. During this time, when she was given her first one-man show at the Tibor de Nagy Gallery, New York (1951), the two most important influences on her style were J. Pollock and W. de Kooning. This influence can be seen in her *Persian Jacket* which was acquired by the Museum of Modern Art, New York, in 1953. Up to this time she had been signing her works 'George Hartigan'. It was also in 1953 that she turned to a new form of artistic production, designing sets for Kenneth Koch's *Red Riding Hood* for the Artist's Theater, New York. In the mid-1950s her style temporarily changed from abstraction to figurative (*Grand Street Bride*), but by 1957 she was again executing abstract works such as *Billboard* (1957, Minneapolis, Minn., Institute of Arts). Here she creates a brightly coloured, freely handled arrangement of rectangular shapes which are interspersed with other less geometrical abstract designs and some recognizable forms such as figures and faces. Her work has been included in the Fourth Bienal at São Paulo (1957) and Documenta II, Kassel, Germany (1959), as well as many group and one-man shows in the United States and abroad.

Emily Dennis. *Grace Hartigan*, New York 1959.

Hartley, Marsden Edmund. American painter, b. 1877 in Lewiston, Maine; d. 1943 in Ellworth, Maine. The youngest of nine children, he moved with his family from New England to Cleveland in 1890. At this early age he was already interested in drawing and painting, and in 1892 he won a scholarship to the Cleveland School of Art, where he studied with Cullen Yates (1866–1915) and Nina Waldeck (1868–1916). In 1898 he moved to New York, where he was first a pupil of William Merritt Chase (1849–1916), and shortly afterwards a student at the National Academy of Design. In 1909 Hartley held his first one-man show at Stieglitz's Photo-Secession Gallery, 291 Fifth Avenue. At this time, his canvases had an affinity with the work of Albert Ryder and with the late works of the Impressionists (*Maine Snowstorm*, 1911?, Ferargil Galleries).

Following his early association with the 291 group (which lasted throughout his life), Hartley went abroad (1912–13). He experimented with Cubism and exhibited with the *Blauer Reiter* group in Munich. He was back in New York in time to participate in the Armory Show, but returned to Europe (1915–16), where his paintings took a decided turn towards abstract patternization (stripes, zigzags, checks). However, by 1919 he had become dissatisfied with abstract art and had resumed more representational work.

Hartley's literary interests were demonstrated with the publication in Paris of his *Twenty-Five Poems* (1922). It was also in the 1920s that the artist made a definite break with the abstractionist tendencies gleaned from his German associations and turned mainly to landscape painting, particularly to the depiction of the land, sea and sky of New England. His canvases from this period are characterized by massive volumes accentuated with strong, dark outlines, as in his *Mt. Katahdin, Autumn, No. 1* (1939–40, Lincoln, Nebraska, University of Nebraska Art Galleries, Coll. Hall). Hartley's still lifes and figures have these same stylistic qualities, combined with a rigidity of forms that seem to be suspended in a flat, two-dimensional space.

Elizabeth McCausland. *Marsden Hartley*, Minneapolis (Minn.) 1952.
Catalogue, *Lyonel Feininger—Marsden Hartley*, Museum of Modern Art, New York 1944, 1966.

Hartung, Hans. French painter, b. 1904 in Leipzig. After studying at the Academies in Dresden and Leipzig in 1924–5, Hartung went to France for the first time in 1927 and remained there until 1931. The following year he left Germany for good. In 1932 he went to Minorca for two years, then visited Stockholm in 1934–5 before settling in Paris in 1935–6. In 1939 he married the daughter of the Spanish sculptor Julio González. In 1939–40 he joined the Foreign Legion in North Africa as a volunteer and in 1944 had a leg amputated after being wounded at Belfort. In 1945 he returned to Paris and became a French citizen in the following year. In 1960 he won the Grand Prix at the Venice Biennale. He is now living in the South of France and is married to the painter Anna-Eva Bergmann.

During his formative years Hartung was greatly influenced by the Expressionists of the *Brücke* and by the early improvisations of Wassily Kandinsky and Paul Klee. After the Second World War he was one of the most stimulating artists in the *École de Paris*. Like Wols, Fautrier, Mathieu and Riopelle, he helped to initiate the new trends which came to be known as *art autre* or informal art. Through his experience of French Cubism and the paintings of Cézanne and through his encounter with González, Hartung found his way to an individual style, in which free, coloured forms are bonded together by the subtle rhythm of the composition. In 1933–4 Hartung's early block-like forms gave way to a new calligraphic technique and he began to paint pictures consisting of dark areas of colour built up with nervous, violent strokes of the brush, which in c. 1940 were condensed into an interlocking but transparent mesh of coloured lines. Hartung always took the monochrome ground as the point of departure for his pictures, regulating its depth by the direction of his coloured signs and his spontaneous but controlled brushwork. In his 'psychic improvisations' he writes calligraphic signs, which are drawn together to form dense but transparent coils of interlacing lines on the pictorial ground, which is usually perfectly smooth.

The power of this linear structure and the dynamism of the composition enables the viewer to assess the artist's experience of reality and the energy of his handling with unusual accuracy.

R. Gindertael. *Hans Hartung*, Paris 1960.
J. Tardieu. *Hans Hartung*, Paris 1962.
Exhibition catalogue, *Hans Hartung*, Vienna and Düsseldorf 1963.
Will Grohmann. *Hans Hartung: Aquarelle 1922*, St. Gallen (Switzerland) 1966.

Hartung, Karl. German sculptor, b. 1908 in Hamburg; d. 1967 in Berlin. After training at the School of Art and Crafts in Hamburg Hartung lived in Paris from 1929 to 1932. In 1933 he visited Florence, then returned to Hamburg, where he produced his first abstract sculptures. In 1936 he moved to Berlin. From 1939 to 1945 he served with the German forces. In 1951 he was given a professorial post at the College of Fine Arts in Berlin. During his early period Hartung produced objective, figurative sculptures, which bear the imprint of Bourdelle and Maillol. Later, due to the influence of the Hamburg abstract sculptor Haizmann and, subsequently, of Arp and Brancusi, he turned to abstract sculpture. During the postwar period, when Hartung's versatile and mature oeuvre became better known, he won recognition as one of Germany's first abstract sculptors. In addition to geometrical Cubist structures, he also produced abstract figurative compositions up to c. 1950. Hartung had a marked preference for beautiful, high-quality materials such as marble, granite, smooth hard wood and polished bronze. His sculptural forms, which are evolved with great precision, create firm and powerful structures, which appear as dynamic configurations in space. Hartung animated the surface texture of his works by means of delicate linear patterns or folds but without weakening the block-like outline of the total sculpture. Even his most dramatic formations are subordinated to the overall importance of the simple, monumental sign.

W. Grzimek. *Deutsche Bildhauer des 20. Jahrhunderts*, Munich 1969.

Hasior, Vladislav. Polish sculptor, b. 1928 in Novy Sacz, Poland. Hasior studied at the Academy of Art in Warsaw. He is now living in Zakopane. Since 1960 he has created sculptures and assemblages in a variety of materials, frequently using fire and water in the process and incorporating fragments of craft products. In these works Hasior has recourse to the quasi-primitive associations which are the essential characteristic of *art brut*.

Exhibition catalogue, *Vladislav Hasior*, Moderna Museet, Stockholm 1969.
Peinture moderne polonaise: Sources et recherches, Musée Galliera, Paris 1969.

Hassam, Childe. American painter and illustrator, b. 1859 in Dorchester, Massachusetts; d. 1935 in

East Hampton, New York. He studied in Boston and later spent some time in Paris. His style was that of the Impressionists, in particular Monet, and he produced some delightful cityscapes and landscapes in this mode (*Washington Arch in Spring*, 1890, Phillips Collection, Washington). He was a founder member of The Ten group in 1898, with J. Alden Weir.

Haukeland, Arnold. Norwegian sculptor, b. 1920. In 1944 Haukeland gave up his studies at the Technical College in Trondheim in order to train as an artist. He spent the following year as a pupil of Frederiksen and P. P. Storm, and in 1945 attended the Académie Colarossi in Paris. He established his reputation with an equestrian monument which he created for the town of Sandvika to commemorate the liberation, and in 1966 he produced sculptures for the west façade of Trondheim Cathedral. During his early period Haukeland used traditional realistic forms. Later, after coming into contact with the modern trends in European sculpture whilst travelling abroad, he produced abstract works of monumental power. One such expressive sculpture is his *Air*, which stands in front of the University in Blindern, near Oslo.

Hauser, Erich. German sculptor, b. 1930 in Rietheim, near Tuttlingen, Germany. Hauser served an apprenticeship as a steel engraver from 1945 to 1948. He then learnt sculpture at evening classes at the Freie Kunstschule in Stuttgart from 1949 to 1951. He is now living in Dunningen near Rottweil. Hauser's sculptures are abstract constructions consisting of triangular steel plates welded together into a closed, crystalline form.

Hausmann, Raoul. Austrian painter, writer and photographer, b. 1886 in Vienna. Hausmann was one of the leading members of the Berlin Dada movement. During the early part of his career he produced photo-montages, collages, Dadaist sculptures and photographs. He also contributed to various *avant-garde* journals (e.g. *Sturm* and *Aktion*) and composed several Dada manifestos. His 'optophonic poem' was the inspiration for Schwitters' 'original sonatas'. In 1921 Hausmann took part in the Dada festival in Prague together with Schwitters and Kurt Hoech. Then, in 1923, he stopped painting and did not start again until he settled in France in 1941. He is now living in Limoges, France.

Hausner, Rudolf. Austrian painter, b. 1914 in Vienna. After studying at the Viennese Academy from 1931 to 1935 Hausner painted Expressionist pictures. In 1938 he was classified as a 'degenerate artist' and forbidden to exhibit. In 1946, when he became a founder member of the 'arts club', he turned towards Surrealism. In 1960 he won a travel-ling scholarship which brought him to Rome. In 1965 he was visiting lecturer at the Hamburg College of Fine Art. He is now living in Vienna. Hausner is the most important artist in the Viennese School of Fantastic Realism. His work is centred on the Magical Realism of the young Otto Dix, the *Pittura Metafisica* of de Chirico and the Surrealism of Dali and Magritte. With immense care and Classical precision he paints dream-like scenes backed by deep perspectives. Highly analytical self-portraits frequently form the focal point of these paintings, whilst the surrounding areas are given over to Bosch-like fantasy creatures and symbolic figures of Freudian provenance.

W. Schmied. *Die Wiener Schule des Phantastischen Realismus*, Kestner Gesellschaft, Hanover 1964–5.

Havinden, Ashley. British commercial artist and painter, b. 1903. His work as a commercial artist and typographer was important in the 1920s and 1930s, but he also took up textile design and painting, holding an exhibition of the latter in 1937. His painting was abstract and closely related to his textile design.

Hawthorne, Charles Webster. American painter, b. 1872 in Lodi, Illinois; d. 1930. His first artistic training came in 1890 when he moved to New York City and attended evening classes at the Art Students' League. In 1893 he studied at Frank V. Du Mond's evening classes and then worked under George de Forest Brush and Siddons Mowbray at the Art Students' League (1894–5). He studied with William M. Chase in 1896 and helped his teacher to organize a new art school at that time. Two years later Hawthorne travelled to Holland to study. His letters home indicate the strong influence made upon him by the works of Frans Hals. After this year abroad he opened his own summer art school in Provincetown, Mass.—the Cape Cod School of Art—which flourished for the rest of his life. *Cleaning Fish* (1899, Provincetown, Mass., Town Hall) portrays the figure types and scenes that were to occupy the artist throughout his career—New England genre scenes handled with a Riberesque approach to the figure and a similar seventeenth-century use of brushwork and chiaroscuro. In addition to genre scenes, Hawthorne was interested in portraiture, an aspect which was given added impetus by a trip to Europe in 1906–7. His portrait of *Sir William Richmond* (1907, Maplewood, N.J., Coll. Mr. and Mrs. Stanley S. Ross) clearly reflects his debt to Tintoretto and especially to Titian. It exhibits the psychological penetration, placement and figural bulk of the latter Venetian. Both genre subject matter and the psychological interest seen in his portraits are combined in two later works: *Three Women of Provincetown* (c. 1921, Amherst, Mass., Coll. Amherst College), which seems to owe something to Frans Hals' *Lady Governors of the Old Men's Home of Haarlem*, and *The First Voyage* (1915, Provincetown, Mass., Provincetown Art Association). The psychic penetration and sense of isolation in the earlier work, each figure seemingly existing in his own world, is revealed partially, if not wholly, through the sad 'Hawthorne stare', for which the artist was unjustly criticized.

Marvin S. Sadik. Catalogue, *The Paintings of Charles Hawthorne*, University of Connecticut Museum of Art, Storrs (Conn.) 1968.

Hayden, Henri. Polish-French painter, b. 1883 in Warsaw; d. 1970. He studied first at Warsaw, then moved to Paris in 1907 and lived in France for the rest of his life. At first he worked in Pont-Aven, then in 1911 he was influenced by Cézanne and shortly afterwards embraced Cubism. In 1922 he began to paint in a more directly representational manner. Around 1949 his style developed further, and he blended Realism and Cubist principles in a pure, vigorous art.

Catalogue, *Henri Hayden*, Waddington Galleries, London 1962.

Hayter, Stanley William. British graphic artist and painter, b. 1901 in London. After studying the natural sciences at King's College, London, Hayter produced his first graphic works in 1921. From 1922 to 1925 he worked for the Anglo-Iranian Oil Company in Abadan. In 1926 he settled in Paris and took up painting. In 1927 he opened a studio at Rue Campagne-Première 17 which, from 1933 onwards, was known as the 'Atelier 17'; there he developed his new graphic techniques. Whilst in Paris, Hayter joined the Surrealists (1933–40). In 1940 he went to the USA and opened Atelier 17 in New York. He also continued his graphic work at the New York School for Social Research from 1940 to 1945. In 1950 he returned to Paris and reopened his Atelier 17 there, closing the New York branch in 1955.

Hayter owes his reputation primarily to his Atelier, where many important young artists have chosen to work and where he himself has evolved numerous graphic refinements, including a technique for producing multi-coloured prints from a single plate. By simplifying his pictorial models Hayter created a calligraphic style in which informal *motifs* acquire a dynamic function.

G. Limbour. *Hayter*, Paris 1962.
Catalogue, *S. W. Hayter: Paintings, Drawings and Engravings from 1927 to 1957*, Whitechapel Gallery, London 1957.
Graham Reynolds. *The Engravings of S. W. Hayter*, London 1967.

Heartfield, John (Helmut Herzfelde). German painter, designer and journalist, b. 1891 in Berlin; d. 1968. Heartfield's father was the poet Franz Held. His brother was Wieland Herzfelde. In conjunction with his brother and George Grosz, he founded the Malik-Verlag and launched the anti-militarist journal *Neue Jugend*, both in 1916–17. He was also a founder member of the Berlin Dada group. Heartfield worked as a painter, a poster designer, a décor artist and a journalist. But he is best known for his satirical photo-montages, which he executed in a Dadaist style and with which he conducted a lifelong struggle against capitalism, war and Nazism. Heartfield emigrated in 1933, returning to East Berlin in 1950.

Wieland Herzfelde. *John Heartfield, Leben und Werk*, Dresden 1962.

Heath, Adrian. British painter, b. 1920 in Burma. He studied painting first in Cornwall with Stanhope Forbes (1938) and then at the Slade School in Oxford. In 1940 he went into the RAF and was a prisoner of war from 1942 to 1945. After the war he spent two years at the Slade School in London. He exhibited his first abstract painting in 1949. His early works were composed of simple abstract shapes executed in impasto. These gradually became increasingly free and dynamic, concerned with movement expressed through free, open handling and light colour.

L. Alloway. *Nine Abstract Artists, Their Work and Theory*, London 1954.

Heaton Cooper, William. British painter, b. 1903 in Coniston, Lancashire. Heaton Cooper is a dedicated painter of the English Lake District. With his home, studio and gallery at Grasmere, he eschews London. He was elected a member of the Royal Institute of Painters in Water-Colours, Royal Institution, in 1953, and he has also exhibited at the Royal Academy and at the Royal Society of British Artists.

Hebald, Milton. American sculptor, b. 1917 in New York. After studying in New York at the Art Students' League and the Beaux-Arts Institute, he taught at a number of institutions including Cooper Union, the American Artist School and the Brooklyn Museum School of Art, all in New York, as well as the University of Minnesota and the Skowhegan (Maine) School of Painting and Sculpture. Though Hebald is best known for his relief at the Pan American Terminal (designed by the architectural firm of Tippetts, Abbett, McCarthy and Stratton) at John F. Kennedy International Airport, New York, this was by no means his only important architectural commission. Among his previous works are the façade of the Ecuador Pavilion for the 1939 New York World's Fair, a 16-foot bronze group for the East Bronx (New York) TB Hospital (1954) and a sculptural piece for the Isla Verdi Aeroport, San Juan, Puerto Rico (1954). The Pan American commission of 1957 was completed in 1959. Using a glass screen 210 feet wide and 23 feet high, the work is

studded with bronze conceptions of the twelve signs
of the zodiac. The work is constructed so as to be
seen from both sides, using double-faced, deep bas-
reliefs, so that it is conceived both as sculpture in
the round and as relief. All of the signs, such as
Sagittarius, are based on curvilinear forms punctured
with holes, expressing a variegated silhouette and an
interest in rough, tactile surface.

Exhibition catalogue, *Milton Hebald: Sculpture at Idlewild, N.Y.*,
    Nordness Gallery, New York 1960.

Heckel, Erich. German painter, b. 1883 in Döbeln,
Saxony. Heckel started to study architecture at the
Technical College in Dresden in 1904 and in the
following year joined with his fellow students Kirchner, Bleyl and Schmidt-Rottluff in founding the
Brücke association. From 1907 onwards he earned
his living as a draughtsman in Kreis' studio. Then
in 1911, after travelling with his friends to the
Moritzburg lakes, to Italy and to Dangast on the
Baltic coast, he settled in Berlin. In 1913 the *Brücke*
was dissolved and from 1914 onwards Heckel served
as a Red Cross orderly in Flanders, where he met
Beckmann and became friendly with Ensor, who influenced him for a while. In 1918 he returned to
Berlin and in the postwar years undertook numerous
journeys which greatly benefited his landscape
painting. In 1937, 729 of his works were removed
from German museums and confiscated as 'degenerate
art'. In 1944, when his Berlin studio was gutted by
fire, he lost all of his printing blocks and a large
number of paintings. He then moved to Hemmenhofen on Lake Constance, where he is still living
today. From 1949 to 1955 he taught at the Academy
in Karlsruhe. The pure colour of the Neo-Impressionists, the dynamic handling of van Gogh and the
psychological approach of Edvard Munch acted as
catalysts for the *Brücke* artists, whose revolutionary
early works set the tone of German painting at the
beginning of the twentieth century. But, although
Heckel also used extremely powerful colours and was
quite prepared to sacrifice formal considerations for
the sake of increased expressiveness during his early
phase, he was not really an emotional artist in an
absolute sense. On the contrary, his intellectual
powers and his lyrical gifts invariably exercised a
restraining influence. The anguished figures featured
in Heckel's pyschological figure compositions owe
much to his abiding interest in Russian literature.
His extremely personal brand of Expressionism,
which sometimes reveals Cubist traces, achieved its
maximum impact from 1911 onwards. The landscape,
to which Heckel was attracted at an early stage in
his career, eventually dominated his output. From
c. 1920 onwards Heckel's compositions became progressively more restrained. His approach grew more
Classical and more abstract, as is readily apparent
from his celebrated townscapes and views of mountains, fiords and harbours. During this period he

produced relatively few figure compositions, although
he has continued to paint circus pictures throughout
the whole of his life. He has also produced an impressive body of graphic work, including watercolours, drawings and art prints.

H. Kohn. *Erich Heckel: Aquarelle und Zeichnungen*, Munich 1959.
P. Vogt. *Erich Heckel*, Recklinghausen 1965.

Heemskerk van Baes, Jacoba. Dutch painter, b.
1876 in The Hague, Holland; d. 1923 in Domburg,
Holland. Heemskerk van Baes studied first at the
Academy in The Hague and then, in 1904, under
Eugène Carrière in Paris. Subsequently she worked
in Jan Toorop's circle and was introduced to
Cubism by Mondrian. She made her name largely as
a result of her contacts with H. Walden and the
Sturm. In 1924 the *Sturm* published an Heemskerk
van Baes monograph (*Sturm Picture-book* No. VII).
Heemskerk van Baes' paintings are a synthesis of
Expressionism and Constructivism.

Catalogue, *Jacoba van Heemskerk*, Stedelijk Museum, Amsterdam
    1960.

Heerup, Henry. Danish sculptor and painter, b.
1907 in Copenhagen. Heerup studied sculpture and
painting at the Copenhagen Academy from 1927 to
1932. Inspired by the art of primitive tribes and by
Romanesque sculpture, Heerup carves monolithic
granite sculptures with coarse textures and simplified
forms representing human beings, animals and plants
in a mystical and primitive light. The finished works
are then painted, which gives them a fetishistic
quality. Heerup's paintings reveal the same combination of formal simplification and symbolic expression. Heerup was represented at the Venice
Biennale in 1962. He is now living in Copenhagen.

H. Wilman. *Henry Heerup*, Copenhagen n.d.

Hegedušić, Krsto. Yugoslav painter and graphic
artist, b. 1901 in Petrinja, Croatia. After attending
the Academy of Art in Zagreb from 1920 to 1926
Hegedušić continued his studies in Paris for a number of years. He then returned to Zagreb, where he
and a number of fellow Croatian artists founded the
Zenlja (Earth) group with the object of reviving
popular interest in art but without reverting to the
outmoded forms of Naturalism. In 1929 he met
Ivan Generalić, who was then a fifteen-year-old
peasant, and helped him to develop his talent as a
draughtsman. This meeting eventually led to the
formation of the *Hlebine* association of peasant
painters.

  After the First World War Hegedušić was influenced, both as a painter and as a graphic artist, by
the verism and social criticism of Grosz and Dix. As
a countryman (from the district of Podravina) he also
drew on the peasant genre scenes of Pieter Bruegel.
But essentially his works are an authentic expression

of his own social and artistic conscience. From the banalities of everyday life, from the macabre and sordid scenes which he was obliged to witness, he has fashioned a pictorial reality that is both highly critical and artistically transfigured. His expressive, Surrealist paintings are the symbolic products of an aesthetic and ethical mind. Hegedušić is extremely well informed and highly imaginative, and these qualities have stood him in good stead, not only as an artist, but also as a pedagogue, for he is a member of the teaching staff at the Zagreb Academy, where he now runs a 'masters' class'.

M. Krleža. Introduction to *Motifs from Podravina*, Zagreb 1933.
O. Bihalji-Merin. *Krsto Hegedušić*, Prague 1965.

Hegenbarth, Josef. German painter and illustrator, b. 1884 in Böhmisch-Kamnitz; d. 1962 in Dresden. After studying in Dresden he went to Prague and there joined the Secession. Returning to Dresden in 1921, he worked on a number of magazines, including *Jugend* and *Simplicissimus*. For ten years (1930–40) he devoted himself to painting, but after the war again took up book and magazine illustration. His imagination was fired by fairy tales and legends. In his paintings he depicted circus and theatre scenes.

Fritz Löffler. *Josef Hegenbarth*, Dresden 1959.

Heiberg, Jean. Norwegian painter, b. 1884 in Oslo. Heiberg studied under Matisse from 1908 to 1910 and was one of the first Scandinavians to do so. With their clear composition and fresh colours, his early, essentially decorative works were obviously derived from Matisse. During his second stay in Paris— from 1919 to 1929—Heiberg developed a new, strictly constructive style and acquired an ascetic approach to the use of colour, which owed much to the Danish painter Georg Jacobsen. From 1935 to 1955 Heiberg taught at the Oslo Academy of Art, where he exerted a considerable influence on the younger generation of Norwegian painters.

H. Grevenor. *Jean Heiberg*, Oslo 1933.
B. Rise. *Jean Heiberg*, Oslo 1955.

Heiliger, Bernhard. German sculptor, b. 1915 in Stettin, Germany. Heiliger trained in Stettin and at the Berlin Academy (under Richard Scheibe). He visited Paris in 1937–8 and was deeply impressed by the works of Maillol, Despiau and Brancusi. Since 1949 he has taught at the Berlin Academy of Art. In the course of his career Heiliger has executed numerous public commissions, working in collaboration with architects. He created a *Ferryman* (1956) to go on the bridge over the Neckar near Esslingen. In 1958 he produced the *Figurenbaum* for the German pavilion at the International Exhibition in Brussels. A film was made at the time showing the genesis of this work. He is now living in Berlin. After producing figurative works in his early phase—which were strongly influenced by Moore until the mid-1950s— Heiliger moved towards an abstract style based on organic, vegetal forms. His abstract portraits have been highly commended.

H. T. Flemming. *Bernhard Heiliger*, Berlin 1962.

Heine, Thomas Theodor. German painter, b. 1867 in Leipzig; d. 1948 in Stockholm. Having studied in Düsseldorf, he went to Munich in 1889 and worked on the magazines *Fliegende Blätter*, *Jugend* and *Simplicissimus*. In 1933 he had to leave Germany and moved first to Prague, then to Oslo and finally Sweden. His illustrations were renowned for their satirical quality, and they ranged in style from a Beardsley-like linearity to naturalistically shaded drawings. He directed his caricatures against the social abuses of the time. He was also a painter of considerable skill, as shown by his self-portrait in the Nationalmuseum, Stockholm.

Held, Al. American painter, b. 1928 in New York. After attending New York public schools (1933–45) and serving in the United States Navy (1945–7), he studied at the Art Students' League for one year and then went to Paris (1949). Before going abroad his work was figurative, often in the genre of social commentary. Then he saw and was impressed by the work of J. Pollock, and while in Paris, where he studied painting at the Académie de la Grande Chaumière and sculpture with Zadkine, he tried to synthesize Pollock and P. Mondrian into a Classic-Expressive art. A series of paintings which attempted to realize this synthesis were exhibited in 1951 at the Galerie 8. Since he felt his aim had not been achieved in these works, he gave up painting for a year, confining himself to drawing rock forms. Just before he left Paris in 1951 he executed some of these forms on canvas and painted some ribbon-like compositions in which the pigment, applied with a palette knife in a thick impasto, moves horizontally across the canvas. In 1952–3 he was in New York where he continued painting heavily pigmented canvases, under the influence of Pollock, W. de Kooning, F. Kline, M. Rothko and other members of the New York School. After a couple of years in San Francisco, he returned East and was given his first one-man show in New York at the Poindexter Gallery (1959). By 1959 he began turning away from thickly painted canvases towards cleaner edges and more simplified forms. Scale became central to his conceptions, as seen in the tripartite *Greek Garden* (1964–6, New York, André Emmerich Gallery). The huge work (12 feet by 56 feet) employs three large forms—triangular, rectangular and circular—which avoid any lateral interaction or overlapping. Any one section of this work could singly retain its own integrity and totality. In 1967 an important change was seen in his painting entitled *Mao* (New York, André Emmerich Gallery). For the first time in many years, he superimposed one form over another, typing them together in a multi-layered space. This creates an aggressive pushing out towards the spectator, creating a tension of the two concentric forms advancing forward, while at the same time held in place by the rectangle behind. The same type of spatial agitation is seen in the 1967 mural commission for 'Architect's Collaborative', Tower East, Cleveland, Ohio. Held has been a visiting professor at Yale University (1962) and is currently teaching there. In 1966 he was the recipient of a Guggenheim Fellowship.

Exhibition catalogue, *Al Held*, San Francisco Museum of Art and Corcoran Gallery of Art, Washington (D.C.) 1968.

Heldt, Werner. German painter, b. 1904 in Berlin; d. 1954 in Ischia. He studied in Berlin from 1923 to 1930 and spent two years in Majorca, 1933–5. After the war, during which he was imprisoned, he settled in West Berlin; he used to spend the winters on Ischia, where he joined the 'Ischia painters', Werner Gilles and Eduard Bargheer.

Heldt painted Berlin scenes—streets, taverns— usually at night. Later his street scenes became unreal, more sparsely populated, and dramatized by a deep perspective treatment, as a result of the influence of Metaphysical painting and the *Neue Sachlichkeit*. After 1930, however, due to Maurice Utrillo's influence, Heldt began to use brighter colours. During the Third Reich he did mostly drawings, but in 1946 he began the long series of street scenes for which he is best known. The streets in these pictures are nearly always deserted, though occasionally a lone figure may be seen outlined against the peeling walls of the courtyards. The paintings became more and more abstract until eventually they came to resemble the architectonic works of Juan Gris' late period.

Heliker, John. American painter, b. 1909 in Yonkers, New York. Brought up on a farm in Stormville, New York, he left high school in his third year in order to pursue his interest in art. His first self-instruction came from copying paintings at the Metropolitan Museum of Art, New York. Here he met A. Gorky who was occupying himself with the same activity. From 1927 to 1929 he studied at the Art Students' League under Kimon Nicolaides, Boardman Robinson and Thomas Hart Benton. He was given his first one-man show at Walker's in October 1936. His works at this time, often with a Bruegel-like quality, express his life as a youth on a farm (*Pig Sticking*, 1936, ink drawing, University of Nebraska Art Galleries). After a short period working for the WPA (1938–9) on easel projects under Philip Evergood, he left New York for New

England where he concentrated on still lifes and landscapes. *Maine Coast* (1944, Atlanta, Ga., Atlanta University) reveals the artist's basic underlying sense of line and drawing. The stark forms, dramatic shapes of cliffs and clouds, and the solid Cubistic approach to rocks recall Marsden Hartley, another painter of the New England coast. After 1940 he exhibited widely and since 1947 has taught painting at Columbia University. He won the Prix de Rome from the American Academy in Rome in 1948 and 1949. In 1951 he was the recipient of a Guggenheim Fellowship. His style of the 1950s is less representational, though still basically emphasizing line (*Monreale*, 1950, Philadelphia, Pa., Museum of Art). His harmony of rectilinear forms was reinforced by and related to the architectural beauty of Italy, where he returned every summer from 1949 to 1953. In the mid-1950s his compositions became looser and more fluid with a new sense of movement and rhythm. The greater importance and variety of colour emphasize recognizable forms which have been translated into semi-abstract images (*Still Life*, 1956, Hartford, Conn., Wadsworth Atheneum). In the 1960s his style became more representational, often revealing the deep space of an interior but still approached in a linear manner, stemming back to the architectonic interests gleaned from his Italian experience (*Interior*, 1961, New York, Coll. Mr. and Mrs. Jack J. Katz).

L. Goodrich and P. Mandel. *John Heliker*, Whitney Museum of American Art, New York 1968.

Hélion, Jean. French painter, b. 1904 in Couterne, France. Hélion started out in life as an engineer and architect. In 1926 he made contact with Mondrian and from 1930 onwards collaborated with van Doesburg. From 1931 to 1934 he was a member of the *Abstraction-Création* association. In 1936 Hélion went to live in the USA but returned to France in 1940 to join the French army, only to be taken prisoner by the Germans. In 1942 he escaped, first to Marseilles, then to the USA, returning to France in 1946 and settling in Paris, where he has lived ever since. During his early phase, which lasted from 1929 to 1939, Hélion was influenced by Cubism and also by Léger and Mondrian. It was then that he created the mechanistic and modelled abstracts on which his reputation largely rests. In 1940 he began to paint objective pictures based on strictly geometrical designs. Later he turned towards a mannered form of Realism, whilst of recent years his work has revealed the influence of Frans Hals.

Exhibition catalogue, *Paintings of Jean Hélion*, Gallery of Modern Art, New York 1964.

Henri, Robert. American painter, b. 1865 in Cincinnati; d. 1929 in New York. Henri is notable less for his own art than for his spirit as a teacher and crusader against academic conservatism, in favour of a new democratic humanism in both art and life. His liberal attitudes, which fostered the development of modern painting in America, inspired a whole generation of young painters, including William Glackens, George Luks, John Sloan, Everett Shinn, George Bellows, Yasuo Kuniyoshi and Stuart Davis. These artists were encouraged to break away from the stifling aesthetic formulas of such establishment art organizations as the National Academy. Henri himself received a traditional training in art through studies at the Pennsylvania Academy of the Fine Arts in Philadelphia, as well as the Académie Julian and the École des Beaux-Arts in Paris. In 1891 he settled in Philadelphia, where he became acquainted with the newspaper illustrators Glackens, Shinn, Luks and Sloan, introducing them to the works of such European masters as Manet, Goya, Hals and Velasquez. When he returned from a trip to Europe in 1901, Henri was particularly concerned with the new values being explored by Gustave Courbet and Manet (*Storm Tide*, 1903, New York, Whitney Museum of American Art). He began teaching at the Chase School in New York, where he was joined by his four Philadelphia friends. But Henri soon became disenchanted with the stuffy attitudes encouraged by the Academy in the art schools and started his own school, where Edward Hopper, Rockwell Kent, Morgan Russell, Bellows, Kuniyoshi and Davis came to study. When this school was established, American taste favoured insipid and sentimental landscapes, stiff studio Realism and academic salon formulas. Henri, however, battled for an art that appealed more directly to life. Although his own work did not fulfil the radical implications of his principles, his teaching inspired independence and aesthetic progress, opening new and formerly unacceptable areas of life as subjects for art. In 1908, after being rejected by the Academy, Henri and his friends staged the now-famous independent exhibition of The Eight at the Macbeth Gallery in New York. In 1910 he also helped organize the first Independents Show; although it was an unjuried forum with no prizes, it gave young American painters a chance to show their work.

Henri's earliest paintings were sober scenes of Paris and New York. His travels in Europe influenced him to paint portraits in a style emulating the rapid and brilliant brushwork of Manet, Hals and Velasquez (*Laughing Child*, 1907, New York, Whitney Museum). With sharp observation, but rather facile surface effects, Henri painted Irish peasants, society ladies, young girls and Spanish dancers (*Dancer with Castanets*, 1904, New York, coll. of artist's estate). This superficiality is particularly apparent in his commissioned portraits, in which his lack of enthusiasm for the subject resulted in merely virtuoso demonstrations.

Exhibition catalogue, *Robert Henri: An Exhibition Held in Observance of the Centennial of the Artist's Birth*, University of Nebraska, Lincoln (Nebr.) 1965.
William Inness Homer. *Robert Henri and His Circle*, Ithaca (N.Y.) 1969.

Hepworth, Barbara. British sculptress, b. 1903 in Wakefield, Yorkshire; d. 1975. She began training as a sculptress at the Leeds School of Art in 1920. The following year she won a scholarship to the Royal College of Art in London, where she studied until 1924. She then spent a further two years training in Florence and Rome (1924–6), where she was engaged primarily on practical work (stone carving). Upon her return to England she and her first husband, the sculptor John Skeaping, staged a joint exhibition in London (1928). From 1928 to 1939 she lived and worked in Hampstead. During the 1920s and 1930s she was in constant touch with a large number of artists, including H. Moore (a fellow student), H. Arp, C. Brancusi, P. Picasso, N. Gabo and P. Mondrian. In 1931 she met the painter Ben Nicholson, who later became her second husband and from whom she was divorced in 1951. In 1933 she joined the French *Abstraction-Création* association and in 1934 the Unit One group (London). In 1939 she moved to St. Ives in Cornwall, where she lived until her death. She had numerous exhibitions and enjoyed an international reputation. She also received many distinctions, including the Grand Prix at the Fifth Bienal in São Paulo (1959) and honorary doctorates of the Universities of Birmingham (1960) and Leeds (1961). In 1965 she was made a Dame of the British Empire. Of her larger compositions, perhaps the most distinctive are the sculptures for State House, London (*Meridian*, 1959), and the Hammarskjöld Memorial for the UNO Building in New York (1963).

After carving a number of objective but highly simplified sculptures in marble or local English stone, which reflected a Classical view of art, Hepworth turned increasingly towards abstraction until, by c. 1933, she was creating free organic forms. In c. 1932—at much the same time as Henry Moore—she had begun to produce pierced forms. In 1934 she turned to geometric forms, heightening their spatial effect by the incorporation of strings and colour. Since 1955 Hepworth has also been producing models for subsequent casting in bronze, and her monumental commissions have all been executed in this way. Landscape is one of the central elements of Hepworth's work, but for her landscape is not just a structural form, it is also man's living environment. Time and again she has taken man's relations to nature, to light, to the seasons, as a point of departure for the realization of her sculptural ideas. Recently Hepworth's works have demonstrated the full breadth of her artistic range, which extends from geometric constructions (*Square Forms with*

Circles, 1963) to organic figures. These figures—which are represented both individually and in groups—are not, of course, based on objective forms. On the contrary, they assume the elemental forms created by Hepworth in order to express the spiritualization of the human figure.

J. P. Hodin. *Barbara Hepworth*, London 1961.
Michael Shepheard. *Barbara Hepworth*, London 1963.
Barbara Hepworth: Drawings from a Sculptor's Landscape, London and New York 1967.

Herbin, Auguste. French painter, b. 1882 in Quiévy, Cambrai; d. 1960 in Paris. In 1898 Herbin became a student at the École des Beaux-Arts in Lille. Three years later he moved to Paris, where he took an *atelier* in the Bateau-Lavoir in 1909. Like Vantongerloo, he was a founder member of the *Abstraction-Création* association and became editor of the magazine *Abstraction-Création, Art Non-Figuratif*. After passing through Impressionist and Post-Impressionist phases prior to 1905, Herbin turned to Fauvism. In c. 1912 he introduced Cubist structures into his expressive landscapes and, between then and 1915, gradually made his rhythmical, stereometric forms and dynamic colours more and more abstract until eventually the colour and form merged in an integrated composition. His brushwork then lost its rhythmical quality and became more even and uniform whilst his Cubist structures were replaced by a flat type of composition that was similar to Delaunay's Orphism. Herbin's first pure abstracts date from 1917–18. Between 1919 and 1921 he produced strictly geometrical and completely symmetrical compositions organized around a central axis. At that time he also created symmetrical reliefs in wood, cement and concrete which were broken down into small, coloured areas constructed at different heights. The planimetric sketches which he made between 1921 and 1924 were suddenly discarded in favour of works executed in the mode of the *Neue Sachlichkeit* which, by 1926, had degenerated into rigidly constructive, architectonic landscapes. These were followed, between 1926 and 1930, by organic and mechanistic abstracts. The strictly geometrical paintings which he began to produce in 1939 paved the way for the works of his late period, in which he represented basic geometrical shapes such as the square, the circle and the triangle in pure, unbroken colours and expansive and completely two-dimensional compositions.

Auguste Herbin. *L'Art non-figuratif et non-objectif*, Paris 1949.
R. Massat. *Herbin*, Paris 1953.
Exhibition catalogue, *Auguste Herbin*, Kestner-Gesellschaft, Hanover 1967.

Herman, Josef. Polish-British painter, b. 1911 in Warsaw. Herman studied at the Warsaw School of Art 1930–2, and held his first exhibition in Warsaw in 1932. He left Poland and went to Brussels in 1938, and in 1940 settled in Glasgow, where he was an important influence on the Glasgow School. In 1943 he went to London where, with L. S. Lowry, he held an exhibition at the Lefevre Gallery. In 1944 he moved to the Welsh mining village of Ystradgynlais and became a naturalized British subject in 1948. He joined the London Group in 1952 and the following year settled in London, where he is now living.

Herman's early works are Expressionist, and he generally concentrated on studies of Jewish life in Warsaw. In Wales he turned to the paintings of miners for which he is best known. These, and the French peasant subjects of the 1950s, recall Millet and, like that artist, his simple, monumental figures express his feeling for the dignity of labour.

Retrospective exhibition catalogue, *Josef Herman*, Whitechapel Art Gallery, London 1956.

Hernández, Mateo. Spanish sculptor, b. 1885 in Bejár; d. 1949 in Meudon, France. His sculptures were all of animals and birds, taken mainly from those in the private zoo he kept at his house in Meudon.

Herold, Jacques. Rumanian-French painter, b. 1910 in Piatra, Rumania. Herold went to Paris in 1930, where he joined the Surrealist movement in 1934. At first he painted semi-objective pictures based on crystalline designs, but later he went completely abstract, creating works which incorporated 'involuntary' shapes, i.e. shapes produced by spontaneous movements of the brush or palette knife. The colouring of these later works is clear and bright; the brushwork is uniform.

J. Charpier. *Jacques Hérold, le cristal et le vent*, Paris 1961.

Heron, Patrick. British painter, b. 1920 in Leeds. He studied in Cornwall and then at the Slade School (1937–9). He gave his first one-man exhibition at the Redfern Gallery, London, in 1947. He was art critic for the *New Statesman and Nation*, 1947–50, and London correspondent to *Arts*, New York, 1955–8. He exhibited twelve paintings in the São Paulo Bienal, 1953–4. He now lives and works in Cornwall. Influenced by the New York School, and especially by Rothko, his work has developed from abstraction based on landscape to pure abstraction that exploits the spatial effects of colour relations. Large simple shapes of strong colour float on plain grounds of equally strong but contrasting colour. The consequent relationship between shape and ground creates a shifting and ambiguous sense of space, in which the flatness of the picture surface seems simultaneously asserted and denied.

Exhibition catalogue, *Patrick Heron*, Wakefield City Art Gallery, Wakefield 1952.

Heyboer, Anton. Dutch graphic artist, b. 1924 in Sabang, Indonesia. In his graphic works, especially his etchings, Heyboer achieves a lyrical synthesis of objective, geometrical and calligraphic elements.

Higgins, Eugene. American painter and etcher, b. 1874 in Kansas City, Missouri; d. 1958. First a student in St. Louis art schools, Higgins went to Paris in 1897, where he studied for two years at the Académie Julian and under Gérôme at the École des Beaux-Arts. While in Paris, an entire issue of *Assiette au beurre* (9 January 1904), a militant journal of social satire in art, was devoted to his work—sixteen pages of pictures called *Les Pauvres* illustrated a poetic text by Jehan Rictos. In these drawings he reflects the influence of the French tradition of social satire, from Daumier to Toulouse-Lautrec, Forain and Steinlen, though Higgins' bitterness was unbearably sentimental and is tempered by the noble humility of Millet—an influence which had been manifest since his youth. He returned to the United States in 1905, after having exhibited at the American Art Club and the Paris Salons. In 1913 he exhibited several works in the Armory Show, including *Hunger under a Bridge* (New York, Coll. Mrs. Anita Higgins Cole), *Convicts and Guard* (New York, Coll. Mr. and Mrs. Irving Kaufman) and *Weary*, which was purchased from the show by G. W. Curtis. As the titles suggest, these works also portray poverty and types of dissolute and ruined humanity. His later works are of a similar genre. *The Black Cloud* (c. 1930, Williamsburg, Virginia, Coll. College of William and Mary), which won the Altman Prize at the National Academy of Design in 1931, is painted with thick, heavy impastos and dark tonalities, giving the feel of the earth. The bold masses of the bent figures are silhouetted against a luminous sky, all handled with little detail and a breadth and simplicity of colour, again recalling Millet.

American Artists Group Yearbook, New York 1935.

Higgins, (George) Edward. American sculptor, b. 1930 in Gaffney, South Carolina. He received a BA degree from the University of North Carolina in 1954 and worked only part-time as a sculptor until 1960, when he had his first one-man show at the Leo Castelli Gallery, New York. Before this time he was a labourer in a furniture factory in Long Island City, New York, where he had moved in the late 1950s. His works, created of steel and plaster, prompted his move from the South so that he could be near junk yards, the source of his raw materials. *Outside of a Soldier* (1959) and *Double Portrait— Torsos* (1961), both of steel and plaster and both in the Museum of Modern Art, New York, are representative of his style. The former was acquired after its inclusion in the Museum's 1959 exhibition,

Recent Sculpture, USA. The spherical form with projecting rod-like elements is lighter than his later work, whose solid, weighty forms are of a completely different aesthetic from two other contemporary sculptural trends: metallic flights of fancy and the 'nut and bolt school'. Contrasts of light and dark areas are created through the material itself in this simple, monolithic, volumetric piece. In addition to his activities as a sculptor, Higgins has taught sculpture at the Parsons School of Design, New York.

James A. Michener. Exhibition catalogue, *Edward Higgins*, Lafayette College, Easton (Pa.) 1966.

Hill, Anthony. British painter and sculptor, b. 1930 in London. He attended art schools in London but was largely self-taught. He first exhibited at the ICA in *Aspects of British Art*, 1950. His work developed from a rather free abstraction towards increasingly austere and rigorous compositions of geometric shapes. In the 1960s he turned to making constructions of perspex, vinyl, aluminium, etc., impersonal and very formal three-dimensional abstracts which depend for their effect upon the qualities of the materials used.

L. Alloway. *Nine Abstract Artists, Their Work and Theory*, London 1954.

Hill, Carl Fredrik. Swedish painter and draughtsman, b. 1849; d. 1911. After studying at the Academy of Art in Stockholm Hill went to Paris in 1873 and subsequently became a member of the Barbizon School. In 1876 he came under the influence of the French Impressionists and isolated himself from his compatriots in order to devote himself wholeheartedly to his painting. In 1878 he suffered a schizophrenic breakdown and in 1880 returned home to Sweden, where he was cared for by his sisters. Despite his illness, Hill was still able to draw during this final period of his life. The significance of his work, in which he sought to reconcile the new techniques evolved by the Impressionists with emotional expressiveness and compositional precision, was not recognized until after his death. Both as a colourist and as an innovator Hill was the equal of his compatriot Ernst Josephson.

E. Blomberg (ed.). *C. F. Hill: Drawings*, Geneva 1950.
A. Anderberg. *Carl Hill*, Stockholm 1951.

Hiller, Anton. German sculptor, b. 1893 in Munich. From 1913 to 1914 and from 1918 to 1923 Hiller studied at the Munich Academy, where he has held a professorial post since 1947. In his sculptures Hiller reduces the human body to basic forms.

Hiller, Karol. Polish painter, b. 1891 in Lodz; d. 1939 in Lodz. Hiller studied chemistry in Darmstadt, architecture in Moscow and painting in Kiev, and he also conducted research into the techniques of old Russian painting. He was one of the outstanding Polish representatives of the artistic *avant-garde*. After collaborating with the 'Workers' Theatre' he became editor of the *Forma* magazine for modern artists, in which his theoretical and critical works were published. From 1928 onwards he produced abstract compositions which bring out the stereoscopic quality of his geometric forms. Subsequently, from 1932 onwards, he painted pictures containing allusions to organic forms and biological structures which anticipate informal art. Meanwhile, in about 1930, he had begun to experiment with a heliographic process, transferring abstract compositions from translucent plates to sensitive paper and incorporating into his work random elements arising out of specific reactions. Some of these heliogravures are reminiscent of the abstract works of late Cubism.

Exhibition catalogue, *Karol Hiller*, Lodz Museum of Art, Lodz 1967.
Peinture moderne polonaise: Sources et recherches, Musée Galliera, Paris 1969.

Hillier, Tristram. British painter, b. 1905 in Peking. Hillier was educated at Downside and Christ's College, Cambridge (1922–4). In 1926 he went for two years to the Slade School, London. He then moved to Paris, where he studied under André Lhôte and at the Atelier Colarossi. He gave his first one-man exhibition at the Lefevre Gallery, London, in 1931, and became a member of Unit One in 1933. His early work is abstract Surrealist, but since 1937 he has painted landscapes. However, these are executed with a clarity and precision that still recalls de Chirico and the Surrealists.

Tristram Hillier. *Leda and the Goose*, autobiography, London 1954.

Hiltmann, Jochen. German sculptor, b. 1935 in Hamburg. Hiltmann studied at the Landeskunstschule in Hamburg, the Werkkunstschule in Krefeld and the Academy of Art in Düsseldorf. He is now living in Düsseldorf. Hiltmann made his name with his spherical and hemispherical sculptures, which he textures to resemble geological formations by placing smooth, roughened, and mass-produced sections in juxtaposition.

Hilton, Roger. British painter, b. 1911 in Northwood, Middlesex; d. 1975. He was a student at the Slade School, London, under Tonks (1929–31), and at the Académie Ranson in Paris under Roger Bissière (1932–9). From 1946 he visited Paris regularly. From 1954 to 1956 he taught at the Central School of Arts and Crafts in London, where he made his home. Hilton was one of the 'St. Ives painters'. His lyrical abstracts, which are based on highly simplified, two-dimensional colour designs and reveal a sensitive and restrained use of line, are still faintly reminiscent of the landscapes which prompted them. In the late 1950s Hilton was influenced by the American Abstract Expressionists.

A. Bowness. *Exhibition Catalogue No. 32*, Venice Biennale 1964.

Hiquily, Philippe. French sculptor, b. 1925 in Paris. Hiquily spent his youth in Mont-de-Marsan and Orléans, where he trained as a sculptor at the École des Beaux-Arts. Just before the end of the Second World War he volunteered for military service and fought in Indo-China. In 1947 he was released, and from 1949 to 1952 studied at the École Nationale Supérieure des Beaux-Arts in Paris. But at the end of his first year at the school he turned away from the academic style of sculpture, and began to work in iron. His subsequent abstract development was decisively influenced by G. Richier and R. Müller. Since 1956 Hiquily has exhibited regularly in the Salon de Mai and the Salon de la Jeune Sculpture in Paris. He works in brass, copper, aluminium and stainless steel. He is now living in Paris.

Hirschfeld-Mack, Ludwig. German painter, b. 1893 in Frankfurt am Main; d. 1965 in Sydney, Australia. After first training under Hölzel, Hirschfeld-Mack studied at the Bauhaus from 1920 to 1925. Whilst there he developed his 'light reflections' and 'colour projections'. He was one of the precursors of kinetic art.

Exhibition catalogue, *Hirschfeld-Mack*, Bauhaus Archives, Darmstadt 1963.

Hirshfield, Morris. American painter, b. 1872 in Poland; d. 1946 in New York. Although showing an interest in wood carving as a boy, Hirshfield did not turn to painting until he was sixty-five. Going to the United States in 1890, he first manufactured clothing and then became a successful manufacturer of bedroom slippers. When he retired owing to ill-health in 1937, he turned to painting. For three years he worked on two paintings, *Beach Girl* and *Angora Cat*, both works showing an interest in patternization and texture which stems from his years dealing with fabrics and designs. The former work is painted on an old canvas over which the artist created his own figure and space while incorporating the female face of the original painted surface. The emphasis on curvilinear rhythms of sky, sea and beach is echoed in the textural handling of the paint. In his later works, the interest in painterly texture is reduced in favour of the arrangement of simple forms on a flat surface, as seen in *Girl in the Mirror* (1940, New York, Museum of Modern Art). The geometrical quality of the forms and their parts is emphasized by their strong outlines which also stress the primitivism of the work. This is particularly evident in the small proportions of the hands and arms in relation to the body and the lack of a true reflection in the mirror. Due to his slow working methods and the short span of his career, the size of his oeuvre is small.

Sidney Janis. *They Taught Themselves: American Primitive Painters of the Twentieth Century*, New York 1942.

Hitchens, Ivon. British painter, b. 1893 in London. Hitchens trained at the St. John's Wood School of Art and the Royal Academy Schools. He held his first one-man exhibition at the Mayor Gallery in 1925 and became a member of the London Group in 1931. He held retrospective exhibitions at Temple Newsam, Leeds, in 1945, and at the Tate Gallery in 1963. Hitchens painted murals for Cecil Sharp House, Regent's Park, London, in 1954, and the University of Sussex, Brighton, in 1963. He is represented at the Tate Gallery, and now lives in Sussex.

Like Kandinsky, whose work he admires, Hitchens did not see his way ahead until the age of about 40, but already in the late 1920s he had painted a number of beautiful small interiors which showed an understanding of the spatial compression of Matisse. In the early 1930s Hitchens, like Ben Nicholson, was exploring still life as a source of forms of self-sufficient shape that could be arranged at will in an abstract manner, but which were still readily recognizable and had comfortable associations. These pictures are complex and reveal the influence of Braque. Hitchens soon stepped over the line into non-figuration, and in his important picture *Coronation* (1937) produced a painting in pure fields of colour which attempts an abstract synthesis of visual impressions of flags and pageantry. Although this painting is laid out in a regular, nearly rectilinear way, it foreshadows his later landscape synthesis.

Hitchens' typical long canvas had already appeared and in course of time he came to use it almost exclusively. This shape encourages the eye to scan the picture more easily and allows a more rhythmical articulation than the conventional proportions. Early in the war, Hitchens moved from bombed London to a very wooded spot in Sussex and from that time the relationships of foliage, branches, water and sky became his principal theme. These paintings rank as a great contribution to the English landscape tradition but are without any topographical content. They convey the verdant air of southern English woodlands but are designed like abstract works. Even during the war years, when so many artists showed a romantic veneration for the British land, Hitchens retained a more objective attitude.

P. Heron. *Ivon Hitchens*, London 1955.

Hjorth, Bror. Swedish sculptor and painter, b. 1894; d. 1968. Hjorth was a pupil of Bourdelle. From 1949 onwards he taught at the Stockholm College of Art. Although he incorporated Cubist and Primitive features into his work, it remained firmly rooted in Swedish folk art. His block-like sculptures are remarkable for their great strength and originality, and for their primitive and often brutal composition, which is alleviated to some extent by a certain lyrical component. For his paintings, and for his numerous polychrome wooden reliefs, Hjorth restricted his palette to simple basic colours, which gives these works a primitive and highly expressive quality.

Hlito, Alfredo. Argentinian painter, b. 1923 in Buenos Aires. Hlito studied at the Academy in Buenos Aires. After an early Expressionist phase he turned to abstract painting in 1944. Together with Maldonado and other abstract artists, he helped to found the Group of Concrete Artists and became co-editor of the magazines *Arte Concreto-Invención* (1946) and *Nueva Visione* (1951). With their clear open areas and pure colours, his pictures are true products of Concrete Art.

S. Presta. *Arte Argentino Actual*, Buenos Aires 1960.

Hockney, David. British painter, etcher and draughtsman, b. 1937 in Bradford, Yorkshire. After studying at the Bradford School of Art (1953–7), and at the Royal College of Art (1959–62), Hockney won a Gold Medal and the Guinness Award for Etching in 1961; he was awarded a prize in the Junior Section of the John Moores Liverpool Exhibition in 1961, and in the Graphics Section of the Paris Biennale in 1963. He had his first one-man exhibition at the Kasmin Gallery in 1963. A retrospective exhibition of *Paintings, Prints and Drawings 1960–1970* was mounted at the Whitechapel Art Gallery in 1970.

One of the best known of younger British painters, Hockney first gained attention with his highly personal essays in the Pop Art idiom. In a painting like *Flight into Italy—Swiss Landscape* (1962, London, Dufferin and Ava Collection), many of his characteristics are already apparent: the strong feeling for design and visual rhythm, the deliberately 'naïve' representational formulae (recalling Rousseau), and a light, teasing, allusive tone in the imagery that in his successful works can amount to wit, but which in less happy ventures appears merely coy.

A strong sense of pattern and a delight in rendering difficult visual phenomena (moving water and reflecting glass, for example) are evident in his work throughout the 1960s. Towards the end of the decade, however, Hockney became more interested in the problems of straightforward, naturalistic painting. The large double portrait of Celia Birtwell and Ossie Clark (1970, London, Tate Gallery) is typical of this trend, though even here 'naturalism' is a very relative term, the strong sense of pattern, high colour key and flat, acrylic textures adding an almost Surrealist aura to a quiet domestic scene.

Some of Hockney's best work has been done in black and white. Many of his portrait drawings, with their sparing but sure sense of line, are excellent; likewise the etched illustrations to the translations of Cavafy's poems (1966) and a selection of Grimm's Fairy Tales (1969)—the latter a perfect opportunity for his skill, wit and strong sense of fantasy, here without the latent sentimentality that runs through so many of the paintings.

Catalogue, *David Hockney: Paintings, Prints and Drawings 1960–1970*, Whitechapel Gallery, London 1970.

Hodgkins, Frances. New Zealand painter, b. 1869 in Dunedin, New Zealand; d. 1947 in Dorchester, Dorset. Hodgkins left New Zealand in 1900 and travelled in England, France, Holland, Italy and Morocco. She held her first one-man exhibition of North African watercolours in London in 1907 and the following year she settled in Paris. There she gained recognition as a watercolourist in a *plein-air* manner. She had a triumphant tour of New Zealand and Australia, where she exhibited her European works, and then moved from Paris to Cornwall just before the outbreak of the First World War. On her return to France in 1920, she was influenced by Matisse and adopted a more modern style of painting. In 1925–7 Hodgkins lived and worked in Manchester and in 1928 she began to exhibit with the London Group. She was also a member of the Seven and Five Society from 1929 to 1934. Hodgkins' work developed from the Impressionist influence of the early years, through later contact with Post-Impressionism, to the very personal and poetic landscapes of the last decades of her life.

Arthur R. Howell. *Frances Hodgkins, Four Vital Years*, London 1951.
Arts Council. *Ethel Walker, Frances Hodgkins, Gwen John*, Tate Gallery, London 1952.
John Rothenstein. *Modern English Painters: Sickert to Smith*, London 1952.

Hodler, Ferdinand. Swiss painter, b. 1853 in Berne; d. 1918 in Geneva. Hodler's artistic development is unlike that of many of his contemporaries; one might have thought that, coming from a country comparatively poor in artistic tradition, he would steep himself in the art of other countries—such as France. But on the contrary, throughout his life Hodler's art remained highly individual, while he himself was never associated with any artistic movement.

In 1867 Hodler was apprenticed to the *vedute* painter Ferdinand Sommer, and in 1872 became the pupil of the painter Barthélémy Menn. During this time, the influence of Holbein's work may be seen from pictures such as *Boy with a Feather*, 1875 (Basle, Öffentliche Kunstsammlung). In 1880, Hodler experienced a religious crisis, attending meetings of

the *Stündler* sect—encounters reflected in such paintings as *At Prayer* (Heerbrugg, Coll. Dr. Max Schmidheiny). His work of the 1890s has a highly mystical tone, Symbolist in content, and shows the influence of *art nouveau* in the treatment of its forms (as is also the case in much of his later work), e.g. *Night*, 1890 (Berne, Kunstmuseum), one of his most successful paintings of the period. His other work at this time, which is much influenced by the Parisian Rosicrucian movement, is, however, somewhat lacking in force. In 1900, Hodler was awarded the *médaille d'or* at the Exposition Universelle in Paris for his painting *Day*, 1899 (Berne, Kunstmuseum).

Very different from these contemplative works are those such as *The Battle of Näfels*, 1896–7 (Öffentliche Kunstsammlung), one of a series of murals for the external walls of the Zürich Landesmuseum. Many of his pictures of this period were either competition entries or direct commissions, are overtly historical in content, and may be in part explained in terms of the contemporary popularity of Swiss national history.

Hodler's landscapes form another important part of his oeuvre. Those dating from before the turn of the century were also normally intended as competition entries, e.g. *The Beechwood*, 1885 (Solothurn, Museum der Stadt), important as marking the beginnings of Hodler's 'parallelism', a structural theory which he derived from the study of nature. The later, more important landscapes date from his trips to the mountains, and are characterized by their bold, luminous colours and coloured shadows (e.g. *Eiger, Mönch and Jungfrau above a Sea of Mist*, 1908, Arlesheim, Coll. Prof. Arthur Stoll).

Hodler also produced many portraits (including more than thirty self-portraits); his series of works depicting the illness and death of his mistress, Valentine Darel (e.g. *Madame Valentine Darel and her Child*, 1913, Switzerland, private coll.), are some of his most profoundly human and most successful paintings.

After the showing of *Day* in Paris, Hodler became less popular with the French, although his popularity grew rapidly both in his own country and in Austria, where in 1904 he was given the main room at the Vienna Secession exhibition, for which he also designed the exhibition poster. In 1910 he received an honorary doctorate from Basle University, and in 1916 was awarded an honorary Professorship at the École des Beaux-Arts in Geneva.

Ewald Bender. *Die Kunst Ferdinand Hodlers*, Zürich 1923–41.
C. A. Loosli. *Hodler*, Paris 1931.
Hans Mühlestein. *Ferdinand Hodler, 1853–1918*, Zürich 1942.

Hoech, Hannah. German painter, b. 1889 in Gotha, Germany. Hoech was a pupil of Emil Orlik. She belonged to the Berlin Dada movement and was a friend of Raoul Hausmann and Schwitters. Her output consists of Dadaist photomontages and Surrealist and non-objective pictures. She is now living in Berlin.

Exhibition catalogue, *Hannah Hoech*, Galerie Rosen, Berlin 1946.

Hoehme, Gerhard. German painter, b. 1920 in Greppin, near Dessau. In 1948–9 Hoehme studied at Burg Giebichenstein, near Halle, and from 1950 at the Düsseldorf Academy, where he has been a teacher since 1960. In 1957–8, following the vital Tachist colour compositions of his early period, Hoehme produced painted wooden columns and works with irregular borders. His interest in monochromes and serial structures dates from 1959. In 1960 he created his *Schrift und Schreibe-bilder*, a series of calligraphic works which are reminiscent of Klee and Twombly. In 1964 he began to paint pictures on pattern paper, from which he then developed the idea for his Plexiglass boxes, which he first paints and then covers with nylon threads. Hoehme is one of the best-known representatives of informal art working in Germany today.

Exhibition catalogue, *Gerhard Hoehme*, Ulm Museum, Ulm 1967.

Hoerle, Heinrich. German painter, b. 1895 in Cologne; d. 1936 in Cologne. In 1919–20 Hoerle joined Max Ernst's Dada movement in Cologne. He also became a member of the Progressive Artists' association and helped to edit their magazine *a–z*. Hoerle's pictures are essays in social criticism after the manner of Georg Grosz. Technically, they are a development of Purism and the early Léger.

H. Schmitt-Rost. *Hoerle*, Cologne 1952.

Hoetger, Bernhard. German sculptor and architect, b. 1874 in Dortmund-Hörde, Germany; d. 1949 in Interlaken, Switzerland. After serving his apprenticeship as a stonemason in Detmold, Hoetger became head of a workshop for Christian art in Wiedenbrück in 1895. Meanwhile, in 1892, he had joined C. Janssen's 'Masters' Class' in Düsseldorf, which he attended up to 1900. He spent the next seven years in Paris, where he became a founder member of the Salon d'Automne. In 1911 he joined the Artists' Colony in Darmstadt and became one of its leading representatives. In 1919 he moved to Worpswede, where he lived in the 'Brunnenhof', which he had designed and built. From 1933 onwards he lived primarily in Switzerland. Hoetger belonged to the same generation as Lehmbruck, Haller and Kolbe. Like them, he tried to evolve sculptural forms that would enable him to give expression to his Nietzschian conception of the unspoilt, 'higher' human being. But the clear, simple forms of his early period became distorted in his subsequent quest for Expressionist values. Hoetger was a gifted eclectic, who successfully integrated Far Eastern, Gothic, *Jugendstil*, Cubist and Expressionist elements. When he came to design the buildings and sculptures for the Böttcherstrasse in Bremen he tried to create a synthesis reflecting every movement in German art. He also produced dynamic and Realistic sculptures depicting themes of Romantic misery.

Hoeydonck, Paul van. Belgian painter and sculptor, b. 1925 in Antwerp. From 1952 to 1956 Hoeydonck studied at the Institute of Archaeology and the Academy of Art in Antwerp. During his student years he helped to launch three magazines: *Formes*, *G 58 Hessenhuis* and *Art Construit*. In 1956 he began to produce kinetic works and in 1958 kinetic monochromes, Plexiglass reliefs and *tableaux ombres* (shade pictures). The strange, figurative works of more recent years are assemblages for what Hoeydonck calls an 'archaeology of the future'. They represent a world of spacemen, robots, meteorites, etc. On wooden reliefs painted white and entitled *Space-capes*, Hoeydonck depicts hovering, headless figures enveloped in loose drapery. Some of these figures are two-dimensional; others are modelled and project beyond the edge of the relief like prehistoric fossils. Hoeydonck is now living in Wihjnegem, near Antwerp.

Hofer, Karl. German painter, b. 1878 in Karlsruhe; d. 1955 in Berlin. After serving an apprenticeship in a bookshop in Karlsruhe (1892–6), Hofer studied at the Karlsruhe Academy of Fine Arts under Poetzelberger, Kalckreuth and Thoma (1896–1900). He first went to Paris in 1900. In 1902–3 he studied at the Stuttgart Academy under L. V. Kalckreuth. In 1903 he went to live in Rome and remained there for five years before going on to Paris in 1908. He then visited India from 1909 to 1911. When war broke out in 1914 he was again living in France and was interned by the French authorities until 1917, when he was allowed to go to Switzerland. In 1919 he returned to Berlin, where he obtained a teaching post at the Vereinigte Staatsschulen für Freie und Angewandte Kunst in the following year. In 1923 he was elected to the Prussian Academy. In 1934 he was dismissed from his post and banned from the teaching profession. In 1943 his Berlin studio was destroyed in an air raid. In 1945 he was appointed Director of the College of Fine Arts in Berlin.

Hofer's early works reveal the influence of his teacher Hans Thoma, a realistic artist with an academic style derived from the old masters. Later, whilst living in Rome (1903–8), Hofer was greatly impressed by the ideal art of Hans von Marées and began to paint lyrical, idealistic figure compositions of Classical simplicity. During his stay in Paris he learnt a great deal about colour values and 'colour modelling' from Cézanne's late works, whose technical composition he studied in detail. When he visited India—in the middle of his Paris period—he came back with a new and visionary conception of life, in which human beings played a completely passive role. He continued to hold this pacific view until it was finally shattered by the postwar social developments in Germany. During this period, in addition to portraits and still lifes, he painted pictures of phantoms, masks and groups of people sleeping in forests, using dry, fresco-like colours and firm, dark contours. Gradually his style matured until, in 1925, he produced his first major works: the Ticino landscapes. In 1930 he boldly experimented with non-objective art but in the following year reverted to his Classical, idealistic style. When his studio was burnt out in 1943 Hofer repainted the pictures that had been destroyed.

Karl Hofer. *Aus Leben und Kunst*, Berlin 1925; *Erinnerungen eines Malers*, Berlin 1953.
A. Jannasch. *Karl Hofer*, Potsdam 1948.
Exhibition catalogue, *Karl Hofer*, Akademie der Künste, Berlin 1966.

Hoflehner, Rudolf. Austrian sculptor, b. 1916 in Linz. After studying mechanical engineering in Linz (1932–6) and architecture in Graz (1936–8), Hoflehner trained at the Academy of Art in Vienna (1938–40). After the war he joined the staff of the School of Arts and Crafts in Linz, where he taught until 1951. He then went to live in Vienna and worked in F. Wotruba's studio until 1954, when he visited Greece for a period of six months. Since 1962 he has held a professorial post at the Academy of Fine Art in Stuttgart. He now lives in Vienna and Stuttgart.

Hoflehner has had numerous exhibitions and now enjoys an international reputation. His works are constructed from massive blocks of iron and steel. Although initially influenced by Wotruba he soon evolved a powerful style of his own. Up to 1963 he was producing upright figures from steel components. Due partly to the vertical and diagonal lines of force, partly to the rough jointing of the various components, these works possess an active and aggressive character. This has now been offset by the passivity of the more smoothly jointed reclining figures of recent years. But Hoflehner's artistic aims are not purely formal. What interests him is the symbolic character of his figures which, he says', are meant to express a 'mental attitude to the world'.

Werner Hofmann. *Hoflehner*, New York 1967.

Hofmann, Hans. German-American painter, b. 1880 in Weissenberg, Bavaria; d. 1966 in New York. As a young man he followed a scientific profession (1896–8), during which time he invented an electromagnetic comptometer. In the late 1890s he enrolled in an art school where he was primarily exposed to Post-Impressionism, as revealed in his pointillistic *Self-Portrait* of 1902 (coll. of artist). He was soon sent to Paris by his patron Freudenberg. Until 1914 he spent most of his time in France where he met Matisse, Picasso, Braque and Delaunay. He received his basic teaching in colour from Delaunay, while the Cubists of the group influenced many of his still lifes and landscapes. He was caught in Munich during the First World War and opened his own art school there in 1915. The Hans Hofmann School of Fine Arts was immediately successful and the artist remained primarily a teacher for the next twenty-five years. He first went to the United States in 1930, to teach at the University of California. Two years later he closed his school in Munich and moved to New York where he taught at the Art Students' League. The following year he opened his own school. Between 1930 and 1935 his work was mainly confined to drawing and only c. 1935 did he return to painting. From this time onwards his canvases became increasingly abstract. The Matisse-inspired *Pink Table with Flowers* (1935–6), still relying on external reality, reflects his use of brilliant colour and repeated geometrical shapes. By 1940 only a psychic awareness of subject is present (*Spring*, oil, Cos Cob, Conn., Coll. Mr. and Mrs. Peter A. Rübel); the canvas becomes a torrent of painterly drips of calligraphic colour. In the 1950s many modes of expression exist side by side. Clearly identifiable still lifes (*Magenta and Blue*, 1949–50, oil, New York, Whitney Museum of American Art) with a strong sense of geometry and linearity contrast with the pure love of paint texture and hue in *Blue Rhythm* (1950, oil, Chicago, Art Institute) with its few large strokes defining generalized shapes. His art theories concerning such concepts as the act of creation, the expressiveness of colour and the analysis of composition are set down in several manuscripts (*A Grammar of Vision, The Painter and His Problems*) which are as yet unpublished.

Frederick S. Wight. *Hans Hofmann*, Berkeley and Los Angeles 1957.
Sam Hunter. *Hans Hofmann*, New York 1963.
William C. Seitz. *Hans Hofmann*, Museum of Modern Art, New York 1963.

Hollegha, Wolfgang. Austrian painter, b. 1929 in Klagenfurt, Austria. Hollegha moved to Vienna in 1947 and attended the Vienna Academy of Art from 1948 to 1954. Many of his essentially calligraphic and informal works were prompted in the first instance by impressions of nature.

Holmgren, Martin. Swedish sculptor and draughtsman, b. 1921. As an artist Holmgren is interested primarily in the problems posed by movement. He has produced sensitive drawings of ballet *motifs* and executed a number of these as statuettes. He has also created experimental sculptures—such as his *Trafikmiljö (Traffic Environment*, 1953)—in which he has tried to reproduce the movement of traffic. Some of his reliefs—for example, the *Vertikalmiljö (Perpendi-*

cular Environment) which he made for the Post Office building in Landskrona (1955)—are almost completely non-figurative.

Hölzel, Adolf. German painter, b. 1853 in Olmütz, Czechoslovakia; d. 1934 in Stuttgart. After training in a lithographic workshop Hölzel began an apprenticeship as a typesetter in 1868, taking regular drawing and painting lessons in his spare time. In 1871 his family moved to Vienna and the following year he entered the Vienna Academy, going on from there to the Munich Academy in 1876, where he studied under W. Diez. In 1882 Hölzel visited Paris. He then married Emmy Karlowa and in 1888 settled in Dachau. Three years later he founded a private school of painting, where Nolde and I. Kerkovius both studied. In 1894 Hölzel, L. Dill and A. Langhammer founded the New Dachau Circle. In 1905 he visited Venice and in the following year was asked to join the staff of the Stuttgart Academy as head of a 'school of composition'. He accepted and was soon surrounded by a group of highly gifted students, including I. Kerkovius, H. Stenner, O. Meyer-Amden, W. Baumeister, O. Schlemmer and J. Itten. From 1916 to 1918 Hölzel was director of the Stuttgart Academy. In 1919 he was retired.

During his early period Hölzel painted genre scenes in the realistic style of the Diez school. Subsequently he came to terms with French and German Impressionism and made an intensive study of the new colour theories. Then, in 1895, he began to develop his own colour system. Between 1905 and 1907 he moved towards non-objective art, although he did not completely abandon objective forms. Most of the works which he produced at that time were religious compositions executed in powerful colours. Over the next ten years—from 1907 to 1917—Hölzel made his real breakthrough. In 1913 his work became still more abstract and by c. 1917 he had begun to produce his 'coloured sounds', which constituted the peak of this particular development. During his late period, when he started to work in stained glass, Hölzel's composition became more refined. As a result of his theoretical and—subsequently—his practical insight into the essential character of painting, Hölzel moved gradually further away from objective themes. He is now regarded as one of the precursors of the modern period and one of its greatest teachers.

Exhibition catalogue, *Adolf Hölzel 1853–1934*, Aargau House of Art, Aargau 1964.

Honneger, Gottfried. Swiss painter and graphic artist, b. 1917 in Zürich. From 1931 to 1935 Honneger was a scene-painter. He then ran a graphic workshop in Zürich from 1937 to 1958, when he went to live in New York, remaining there for two years. Since 1961 he has been living in Paris and Zürich. Honneger paints abstract reliefs based on geometrical designs, many of them white monochromes. He also produces collages and *biseautages*. The latter consist of cardboard patterns with angled edges, which are laid on top of one another to produce an impression of fine shading and relief work at the edges.

Hopper, Edward. American painter, b. 1882 in Nyack, New York; d. 1967 in New York. Thoroughly American in both his training and choice of subject, he remained practically untouched by his three trips to Europe (1906–10). His student years (1900–6) at the New York School of Art, where he studied with Robert Henri, were of far greater importance. Although included in the Armory Show (1913), he had little opportunity to exhibit for the next seven years and therefore worked as a commercial artist. He was given his first one-man show (of oils painted in Paris) in 1920. As early as 1909 his *Le Pavillon de Flore* (Coll. Mrs. Edward Hopper), although slightly Impressionistic, embodies the principles of later canvases. His intuitive sense of the architectonic and a focusing on large, solid masses and volumes dominated his style throughout his life. By 1913 a mood of quiet melancholy pervades; this too remains and is intensified in later years. *House by the Railroad* (1925, oil, New York, Museum of Modern Art) has become a landmark in American painting, capturing both a specific scene and synthesizing an entire concept of America. The play of light and shadow over the planes of the house and the emphasis on shapes and angles is in rapport with Hopper's sense of simplicity and grandeur. An enveloping loneliness and eerie quietude is the real subject of this canvas. Even his representations of city life have a desolate quality, often emphasized by the inclusion of anonymous, non-communicating figures (*Nighthawks*, 1942, oil, Chicago, Art Institute). As in his early works, stillness and loneliness are the subject. The harsh artificial light, petrified movement and vacuum-like environment convey a Surreal atmosphere reminiscent of de Chirico. Although figures are never present in his watercolours, these paintings are of the same spirit as the oils. The works in this medium most often depict a variety of New England architectural styles; the primary interest is the play of light and shadow on simple geometrical forms and the patterns that they create (*Methodist Church*, 1930, watercolour, Hartford, Conn., Wadsworth Atheneum).

Carl Zigrosser. *The Complete Graphic Work of Edward Hopper*, Museum of Art, Philadelphia 1962.
Lloyd Goodrich. Catalogue, *Edward Hopper*, Whitney Museum of American Art, New York 1964.

Horiuchi, Masakazu. Japanese sculptor, b. 1911 in Kyoto. Horiuchi studied at the Polytechnic Institute in Tokyo. From 1947 to 1966 he was a member of the *Nika* Group. He is now living in Tokyō. He creates optical structures in space. In his more recent work he has tried to achieve a synthesis of biomorphous forms and geometrical patterns.

Hosiasson, Philippe. Russian-French painter, b. 1898 in Odessa, Russia. Hosiasson settled in France in 1924 and became a French citizen in 1928. He was a founder member of the *Salon des Surindépendants*. He is now living in Boulogne-sur-Seine. Hosiasson was one of the pioneers of Neo-Classicism and continued to paint Neo-Classical pictures up to 1947. Since then he has produced informal works.

Hoskin, John. British sculptor, b. 1921 in Cheltenham, Gloucestershire. Hoskin was trained as an architectural draughtsman, but in 1950 he turned to sculpture; he had his first exhibition in 1954. Like other British sculptors, his work in the 1950s, although abstract, used shapes and modelled textures that were suggestive of animal and organic forms. By the mid-1960s he was using simpler welded shapes that were still in a sense organic, but which exploited their abstract qualities rather than their power of suggestion.

Howard, Charles. American painter, b. 1899 in Montclair, New Jersey. Howard was brought up in California and graduated from the University of California in 1921. He first travelled to Europe in 1922 and it was his experience of Italian art that, in 1924, turned him to painting. When he returned to the USA in 1925 he worked as a mural painter for a New York decorating firm. He moved to London via Paris in 1933 and remained in England until 1940, when he was obliged to return to the USA. During his years in England he was for a time associated with the English Surrealists. He passed the war years in San Francisco, but returned to Europe in 1946 and settled in London. His work since the 1930s, although abstract, has remained essentially Surrealist, reflecting perhaps the work of Miró and Picasso. In this it is comparable to the work of the New York school of the 1940s.

Hoyland, John. British painter, b. 1934 in Sheffield. Hoyland studied first at the Sheffield College of Art (1951–60) and then at the Royal Academy Schools in London. He now teaches at the Chelsea School of Art. In 1964 he visited New York, where he came into contact with such artists as Morris Louis, Noland and Olitski. The same year he also held his first one-man exhibition in London and he is now represented at the Tate Gallery and in other British, German and American public collections. Hoyland is a hard-edge painter. His pictures are made up of large bands of colour and just a few pictorial forms.

Bryan Robertson. Catalogue, *John Hoyland*, Whitechapel Gallery, London 1967.

Hrdlicka, Alfred. Austrian sculptor and graphic artist, b. 1928 in Vienna. Hrdlicka attended the Viennese Academy from 1946 onwards, studying painting under Gütersloh and Dobrowsky, and sculpture under Wotruba. In 1963 he was asked to teach at the Summer School in Salzburg. In 1968 he won the Austrian State Prize for Sculpture. He is now living in Vienna. In his graphic works, many of which are arranged in cycles, Hrdlicka depicts the world of the outsider. Suffering humanity is also the principal theme of his stone and marble sculptures, where, however, it is set against a mythical background.

J. Muschik. 'Alfred Hrdlicka', *Das Kunstwerk* XXI, 1967–8.

Hulewicz, Jerzy. Polish painter, graphic artist and writer, b. 1886 in Kościanki Wiel Kopolskie; d. 1940. He studied art at the university and academy in Cracow, and later in Paris and Munich. He exhibited in Paris from 1907 at the Salon des Indépendants, and in Posen from 1909. He was a leading member of the Posen Expressionist group. He was a member of the *Kolo art. Wielkopolskich* group in 1914, and a founder member of *Bunt* in 1917. He also exhibited with the *Formisci*. His works consist of oils, etchings, woodcuts, illustrations and designs for glass.

Hultberg, John Phillip. American painter, b. 1922 in Berkeley, California. After receiving a BA from Fresno State College, California, in 1943, he served in the United States Navy (1943–6) and then resumed studies first at the California School of Fine Arts and later at the Art Students' League (1949–51) under Morris Kantor and Byron Browne. Just before moving to New York, he had his first one-man show at the Contemporary Gallery, Sausalito, California (1949). He was given his first show in New York in 1953 at the Korman Gallery. His early works of the 1950s employ multiple squares forming a grid, often tilting this grid to gain the illusion of deep space, while maintaining the principles of two-dimensional space which he learned from C. Still and M. Rothko during his student days. The influence of the Abstract Expressionists can clearly be seen in *Silhouette* (1954, New York, Martha Jackson Gallery). *The Trap* of 1955 (New York, Martha Jackson Gallery) clearly advances in a new direction. Here he shows his ability to convey kinaesthetic movement. The grid, set in a deep vertigo-like perspective, and the idea of suspension grew out of his earlier success in *Silhouette*. 1956 was an important year for Hultberg: he received a Guggenheim Fellowship, participated in the Venice Biennale and started to hold a large number of one-man shows both in the United States and Europe. By 1957 his variety of style is truly manifest in *White Façade* (1957, New York, Martha Jackson Gallery). Here he combines free form and hard edge. Various geometric forms and vague but suggestive shapes are combined with typical Hultberg additions—a wing, animal horn, colour scale, flag—which float in a monochromatic space, and are handled with a virtuosity of brushwork. His search for form incorporates the lessons of Cézanne (kinaesthetic movement), Mondrian (two-dimensional space), Kline (impact painting) and Hofmann (geometric in combination with free-form abstraction) together with original contributions, including upright and tilted grid paintings, constructions, suspension as an art form, situation and environmental paintings. In addition to his painting he has taught at the Brooklyn Museum School of Art (1958), the Art Students' League (1960) and the San Francisco Art Institute (1964).

Exhibition catalogue, *Hultberg, White Paintings*, Martha Jackson Gallery, New York.

Humblot, Robert. French painter, b. 1907 in Fontenay-sous-Bois; d. 1962 in Paris. A scientist at first, he turned to painting and attempted to revitalize Classicism, forming a group with Georges Rohner for this purpose—*Forces Nouvelles*. He painted landscapes, whiich were less successful than his still lifes and allegories. He also made portraits and figure paintings.

Hundertwasser, Fritz (Fritz Stowasser). Austrian painter, b. 1928 in Vienna. After studying for a brief period at the Vienna Academy in 1948, Hundertwasser travelled through Tuscany in 1949 and visited Paris in 1950 and 1953. In 1951 he was in Morocco and Tunis and became a member of the Art Club in Vienna. In 1954 he went to Rome and settled there in 1957. In 1959 he was visiting lecturer at the College of Art in Hamburg and in 1961 he visited Japan. He now lives in Venice, Vienna and Normandy. In his early phase Hundertwasser was deeply impressed by the voluptuous tradition of the Austrian Baroque and by the rich ornamentation of the *Jugendstil*. Later he found fresh stimuli in Persian and Indian miniatures, the paintings of Giotto and Uccello, the woodcuts of Hokusai and the pictorial world of Paul Klee and the Douanier Rousseau. But Klimt and Schiele remained his two great mentors. Not surprisingly, in view of these multiple influences, Hundertwasser's paintings reveal a wide range of different styles, culminating in the decorative-abstract style which he adopted in 1952. The principal *motif* in the pictures of this period is the spiral, which Hundertwasser first discovered in 1953 and which he has treated ever since in numerous highly inventive variations: buildings and landscapes, human figures and fantastic abstract shapes all appear as exuberant spirals. Another remarkable feature of Hundertwasser's painting is his marked predilection for strange, Oriental colours. Phosphorescent greens and reds appear in an infinite number of variations, and

Hundertwasser also makes extensive use of gold and silver.

Catalogue, *Hundertwasser*, Kestner Gesellschaft, Hanover 1964.
Catalogue, *Hundertwasser*, Moos Galerie, Geneva 1967.

Huszar, Vilmos. Hungarian painter, b. 1884 in Budapest. In 1905, after he had completed his studies in Munich and Budapest, Huszar settled in Holland, where he met van Doesburg. In 1917 he joined the *de Stijl* group and for the next six years created interior decorations and designed stained-glass windows based on the *de Stijl* theory. In 1923, when he left the group, he turned to painting, evolving the figurative style in which he has worked ever since. He is now living in Hierden-Harderwijk, Holland.

Hutter, Wolfgang. Austrian painter, b. 1928 in Vienna. Hutter studied under his father, Gütersloh. He belongs to the Viennese School of Fantastic Realism and lives in Vienna. Hutter paints decorative, fairy-tale scenes set in jungle forests. There is a dream-like quality about these works, which are reminiscent of Rousseau. Hutter has also created numerous stage sets.

W. Schmied. *Malerei des Phantastischen Realismus—Die Wiener Schule*, Vienna 1964.

Huxley, Paul. British painter, b. 1938 in London. He went to the Harrow School of Art in 1953 and then studied at the Royal College of Art from 1956 to 1960. He held his first one-man show in 1963, and was represented at the New Generation exhibition in 1964. The following year he went to America with a Harkness Fellowship and remained there until 1967. Huxley's work has always been entirely non-figurative. It is large in scale, simple and clearly organized. Coloured shapes that flowed across a plain ground have recently given way to basic geometrical forms: squares, circles and triangles. His work is exclusively concerned with the abstract relation of figure to ground and their joint affinity to the shape of the canvas itself.

Hynckes, Raoul. Belgian painter, b. 1893 in Brussels. After studying at the Academies in Brussels and Malines, Hynckes went to Holland in 1914, living first in Amsterdam and later in Blaricum. During his early period, Hynckes painted stylized Cubist compositions. Then, in c. 1933, he moved towards a kind of Magical Realism, producing works which underline the vanity of human existence. His favourite subject is the still life. In 1967 Hynckes had a large retrospective exhibition in the Arnheim Museum.

H. Redeker. *In mijn ogen: Raoul Hynckes als schilder en schrijver*, Amsterdam 1964.
Exhibition catalogue, *Raoul Hynckes*, Arnheim Museum, Arnheim 1967.

I

Ikeda, Masuo. Japanese etcher, b. 1934 in Shenyan, Manchuria (China). He is self-taught. Will Grohmann evaluated him positively at the Tokyo International Exhibition of Prints in 1960, and he gained recognition as a prize-winner. He has had a number of exhibitions, including a one-man show at the Museum of Modern Art, New York, in 1965. His work, whose underlying subject matter is eroticism, composed of the figure of a woman, is made effective by abstract patterns. He lives in Tokyo.

Imai, Toshimitsu. Japanese painter, b. 1928 in Kyoto. He studied in Tokyo, where he won a municipal prize; since 1952 he has been living in Paris. He is an abstract artist who has contributed to the Salon d'Art Sacré. He has had one-man shows in Turin (1958); Paris, at the Galerie Stadler (1959); and Rome, at the Galleria L'Attico (1960).

Independent Group. Based on the Institute of Contemporary Art, London, the Independent Group was an informal non-exhibiting group of the radical van in British art in the 1950s. The original purpose was to discuss themes and speakers for ICA public lectures. Peter Reyner Banham (writer on architecture) organized the first programme in the winter of 1952–3.

After a year's interval the Independent Group was reconvened by John McHale and Lawrence Alloway. The latter, a critic who became the ICA's Assistant Director in 1955, remained a prime mover of the group which now also included Eduardo Paolozzi, Frank Cordell, Alison and Peter Smithson (architects), Nigel Henderson and Richard Hamilton (both interested in photography). Ideas exchanged and worked upon were seminal for British Pop (this term was invented by Alloway).

The Independent Group held in common a real appreciation for the mass media of modern urban society—cinema, advertising, SF, pop music—and assiduously drew upon their images. US-inspired commercialism presented British artists with new dimensions, a vivid multi-evocative iconography of products and packaging, new norms for Man and Brand, and new ideals—including expendability. The impact of the changing environment was more dramatic in Britain than in America where it had grown indigenously.

Pop Art works became inventories of popular culture. Built of the images and materials of mass media like visual/verbal crosswords, their meaning was also, so to speak, their construction (there are antecedents in Synthetic Cubism). Formally thrown forward, persuasively graphic—image and pictorial space came close to those of advertising. There is a vein of sociological awareness, the response, for example, of the knowing artist/consumer to the real motivation behind commercial blandishments, which is expressed with great subtlety in the best art of these years.

Lucy R. Lippard. *Pop Art* (Chapter 1), London 1966.
ICA bulletins from 1953.

Indiana (Clark), Robert. American painter, sculptor and graphic artist, b. 1928 in New Castle, Indiana, USA. In 1942, the year he graduated from Arsenal Technical High School, Indianapolis, he had his first one-man show of watercolours, works which betray the influence of R. Marsh, E. Hopper, C. Demuth and C. Sheeler. In 1945 he attended Saturday classes at the John Herron Art Institute, studying under Edwin Fulwinder. Though he received a scholarship to this institution in 1946, he entered the Army Air Corps instead. While serving in the Army he attended classes at Syracuse University and studied under Oscar Weissbuch at the Munson-Williams-Proctor Institute. From 1949 to 1953 he attended the School of the Art Institute, Chicago, completing his BFA requirements at the University of Edinburgh while on a travel fellowship, and then moved to New York. Along with his painting he had also been interested in writing, but he gave up poetry and considerations of a literary career after meeting e. e. cummings in 1955. In the mid-1950s he was living near Ellsworth Kelly, Jack Youngerman, James Rosenquist, Charles Hinman and other artists on Coenties Slip in New York. It was at this time that he began doing hard-edge paintings, the first ones based on the doubled form of the ginkgo leaf, a *motif* which continued for several years. *The Sweet Mystery* (1960–1, coll. of artist) represents a double leaf silhouetted on a dark rectangle, with the title of the painting stencilled below and diagonal stripes at the top and bottom. In 1958–9 he began the *Crucifix* mural, a rambling work of forty-four joined pieces of paper which incorporated the forms of the ginkgo and avocado and initiated his preoccupation with the circle. Soon after the completion of this work, he did his first constructions of junk wood and weathered iron. These works, at first severely geometric, combine metal and wood with gesso. Of this genre is *French Atomic Bomb* (1960, New York, Museum of Modern Art) which was included in the exhibition 'New Forms, New Media' at the Martha Jackson Gallery, New York. In the early 1960s several of his works were purchased by major museums and collectors and his pieces were included in many exhibitions, including his first one-man show in 1962 at the Stable Gallery, New York. In 1964 he collaborated with Andy Warhol on the film *EAT* and in the same year received his first public commission, a work for the exterior of the New York State Pavilion at the New York World's Fair—a 20-foot *EAT Sign*. In 1966 his third one-man show at the Stable Gallery was composed of *LOVE* paintings and *LOVE Sculpture*, the latter done with Herbert Feuerlicht in carved solid aluminium. The combination of these four letters was later further developed in *LOVE Wall* (1966, Pittsburgh, Pa., Carnegie Institute) and *LOVE Cross* (1968, Houston, Texas, University of St. Thomas). 1967 saw a further elaboration of his use of letters and numbers, this time for the American Pavilion at Montreal's 'Expo '67' for which he created a vertical declension of the ten *Cardinal Numbers*, hung in countdown to a height of over 50 feet. This pre-occupation stems back to 1962–3 when his interest in numbers was aroused by C. Demuth's *I Saw the Figure Five in Gold* (1928, New York, Metropolitan Museum of Art) and is manifest in such works as *X-5* (1963, New York, Whitney Museum of American Art) and *The Demuth American Dream No. 5* (1963, Toronto, Canada, Art Gallery of Ontario). In 1967 he exhibited one of his few figurative works, *Mother and Father* (1963–7, coll. of artist), at the Ninth São Paulo Bienal, Brazil. He was represented at Documenta IV, Kassel, Germany by some fifteen pieces and did a serigraph, *Die Deutsche Vier*, for this exhibition.

Exhibition catalogue, *Robert Indiana*, Institute of Contemporary Art, University of Pennsylvania, Philadelphia; Marion Koogler McNay Art Institute, San Antonio (Texas) and Herron Museum of Art, Indianapolis (Indiana) 1968.

Industrial design. The major trends in industrial design during the first half of the twentieth century have derived mainly from *art nouveau*, at the beginning of the century, *de Stijl*, beginning in the second decade of the century, and the Bauhaus, first developed in Europe from 1919 to 1933. In all three cases, there was an emphasis on establishing a principle or style which would unify all art forms—painting, sculpture, architecture—as well as link the industrial and fine arts. *Art nouveau* was decorative and ornate, rooted in recognizable organic forms, but with the development of *de Stijl* and the Bauhaus, the principles of design became increasingly focused on omission of extraneous detail, on basic simplicity in form and colour (for instance, the use of the circle and the square, the primary colours, and a precise, smooth finish) and on functionalism. These principles were of course in accord with modern machine production, which also established the concept of standard, mass production and of the disposability of objects, thus undermining the tradition of the unique and permanent object. The same industrial-design principles have, to a great extent, also been important and influential in modern architecture, painting and sculpture.

Herbert Read. *Art and Industry, the Principles of Industrial Design*, London 1934.
Nikolaus Pevsner. *Pioneers of Modern Design from William Morris to Walter Gropius*, 1st ed., London 1936.

Laszlo Moholy-Nagy. 'New Method of Approach—Design for Life', *Vision in Motion*, 1947.
Arthur Drexler. *Introduction to Twentieth-Century Design . . .*, Museum of Modern Art, New York 1959.

Informal art. This concept has been used in Europe from the early 1950s onwards to describe a new form of art based on 'psychic improvisation'. In this the artist abandons all geometrical and objective forms and employs completely spontaneous techniques, thus producing unconscious works of art. Informal art is therefore largely synonymous with Action Painting, *Art Autre, Abstraction Lyrique* and *Tachisme*. The two writers who have done most to popularize this concept are Michel Tapié and Georges Mathieu. Mathieu has commented on the nature of the artistic process: 'We have been dealing with the "non-form" and with what I have called the "not-yet-form", not simply for the pleasure of opposing traditional and current formalism, but also because we wish to leave the door open for any possibility of developing new and as yet unknown structures.' From this it is clear that Informal art is meant to embrace two extremes: on the one hand non-form or, to be more precise, not-yet-form, and on the other potential new structures. The structuring process was found to be necessary for, without it, this unconscious and hence purely fortuitous technique tended to be too arbitrary and to produce stereotyped and repetitive forms. The artists who have helped to establish Informal art include Wols, Jackson Pollock, Jean Fautrier, Jean Dubuffet, Mark Tobey, Georges Mathieu and Jean Paul Riopelle.

M. Tapié. *Un art autre*, Paris 1952.
H. Platschek. *Neue Figurationen*, Munich 1959.
G. Mathieu. *Au-delà du Tachisme*, Paris 1963.
J. Claus. *Theorien zeitgenössischer Malerei*, Reinbek 1963.

Iommi, Ennio. Argentinian sculptor, b. 1926 in Rosario. Iommi is Claudio Girola's brother. In 1964 he became a founder member of the *Arte Concreto-Invención* movement. In his works, which are completely abstract and testify to his constant quest for the integration of space and form, he uses a wide variety of materials. In 1958 he won a gold medal at the International Exhibition in Brussels.

Salvador Presta. *Arte argentino actual*, Buenos Aires 1960.
Romualdo Brughetti. *Historia del arte en la Argentina*, Mexico 1965.

Ipoustéguy, Jean. French sculptor, b. 1920 in Dau-sur-Meuse, France. In 1938 Ipoustéguy attended evening classes given by the sculptor R. Lesbounit in Paris. Later, in 1947–8, Lesbounit and A. Auclair commissioned him to paint a number of frescoes. At about this time he also executed some stained-glass windows, which had been designed by Sutter and J. Leduc, for the Church of St. Jacques in Montrouge. In 1949 Ipoustéguy settled in Choisy. He then began to concentrate on sculpture and since 1954 has worked exclusively in this medium. In 1964 he won the Bright Award at the Biennale in Venice. At present he is living in Choisy.

In the 1950s Ipoustéguy made only small sculptures—some abstract, some figurative—but since 1960 he has gone over to larger works in which he creates 'sculptural landscapes'. These include his *Discours sous Mistra* of 1964, a work made in three parts as a concrete casting in which the sculptural forms are joined together like the words in a sentence, and his *Alexander in Front of Ecbatana* of 1965 in which he treats the human figure against an architectural background. In these large-scale works Ipoustéguy places man in a cosmic context. Commenting on this aspect of his art, he once wrote: 'My source is the whole world', and then: 'to devour, to be nothing if not cannibals.'

Catalogue, *Ipoustéguy*, Städtisches Museum, Leverkusen 1965–6.
Catalogue, *Ipoustéguy*, Claude Bernard Galerie, Paris 1966.

Ironside, Robin. British painter and designer, b. 1912 in London. He is self-taught as a painter. His first one-man show was in 1944 at the Redfern Gallery, London; he had his first one-man show in the US in 1952, at the Durlacher Gallery, New York. He has designed sets and costumes for the theatre (*Sylvia* for the Royal Ballet, or Sadler's Wells as it then was, in 1952, together with his brother Christopher). He also writes on art.

Irwin, Gwyther. British painter, b. 1931 in Basingstoke, Hants. Irwin studied at Goldsmiths' College, 1951–2, and at the Central School of Arts and Crafts from 1952 to 1955, where he did textile design. His first one-man show was at Gallery One, London, in 1957.

Isakson, Karl. Swedish painter, b. 1878; d. 1922. After attending the Academy of Art in Stockholm from 1897 to 1901 Isakson went to Civita d'Antino in 1902 to study under Zahrtmann, and when this Danish artist returned home, he followed him to Copenhagen, where he remained for the rest of his life. Isakson was one of the foremost Scandinavian colourists of his generation and played an important part in the development of modern painting in both Denmark and Sweden. During his initial period he painted morphological *motifs*, but when he visited Paris between 1905 and 1907 he became interested in problems of colour and form. After revisiting Paris between 1911 and 1914 this interest was reinforced by his need to come to terms with the Cubists, with Matisse and, above all, with Cézanne. In his early still lifes, portraits, interiors and nudes Isakson placed large areas of complementary and contrasting colours in juxtaposition

whilst at the same time producing subtle colour and tone values. Later he revealed a growing preference for pure spectral colours. During his final period he executed a group of biblical compositions in visionary colours. Isakson lived a very secluded life and refused to exhibit. His works were unknown in Sweden until 1922, when a posthumous exhibition was staged in Stockholm.

G. Engwall. *Karl Isakson*, Stockholm 1944.

Israëls, Isaac. Dutch painter, b. 1865; d. 1934. He was the son of the painter Jozef Israëls, but his style differed greatly from that of his father. His Impressionistic manner was influenced by Breitner. He painted pictures of social life.

Istrati, Alexandre. Rumanian painter, b. 1915 in Dorohai, Rumania. After attending the Academy of Art in Budapest Istrati went to live in Paris in 1947 and completed his studies at the École des Beaux-Arts and in the *atelier* of André Lhôte. He paints harmonious colour compositions in the Lyrical Abstract manner. Istrati is married to the painter Natalia Dumitresco.

Itten, Johannes. Swiss painter, b. 1888 in Südern-Linden, Thun, Switzerland; d. 1967 in Zürich. After studying mathematics, science and the history of art, Itten trained under Adolf Hölzel at the Stuttgart Academy from 1913 to 1916. He then spent the next three years in Vienna, where he founded his own school of art. From 1919 to 1923 he taught at the Bauhaus in Weimar; from 1926 to 1931 he ran a private school of art in Berlin, and in 1932 he joined the staff of the Krefeld School of Textile Design. In 1938 he emigrated, going first to Amsterdam, then to Zürich, where he was appointed Director of the School of Arts and Crafts, the Museum of Arts and Crafts, the Rietberg Museum and the School of Textile Design. He relinquished the first three of these posts in 1953 and the fourth in 1961.

Itten's real significance in the sphere of modern art lies in his pedagogical work, which was quite outstanding. It was he who set up the 'Introductory Course' at the Bauhaus, which has since become a standard feature of art instruction, and it was he who suggested that Klee and Schlemmer should be appointed as teachers in Weimar. Since then he has published numerous treatises on the theory of art, e.g. *Kunst der Farbe* (1961). In his colour compositions, which were derived in the first instance from Hölzel and Delaunay, he came to terms with all the artistic movements of his day, from Futurism to Concrete Art.

Catalogue, *Johannes Itten*, Stedelijk Museum, Amsterdam 1957.
Catalogue, *Johannes Itten*, Bauhaus Archives, Darmstadt 1967.

J

Jack of Diamonds—*see* **Bubonovgi Valet**

Jackson, Arthur. British painter, b. 1911 in Rother-ham, Yorkshire. From 1929 to 1932 Jackson studied at the St. Martin's School of Art, London. Following this, during the period from 1932 to 1936, he was a pupil of, and was greatly influenced by, Ben Nicholson. In 1934 he exhibited with Nicholson in the Seven and Five Society, to which he had been elected a member. This exhibition of the Seven and Five (founded in 1920 of seven painters and five sculptors, developing from figurative beginnings) was the first of purely abstract art in England. Jackson has been a practising architect since 1947.

Jasia Reichardt. Catalogue, *Art in Britain 1930–40*, Marlborough Gallery, London 1965.

Jacobsen, Egill. Danish painter, b. 1910 in Copen-hagen. Jacobsen's expressive abstract painting, which took its initial orientation from Danish folk art and the works of Paul Klee, became well known in the late 1930s when he created his 'Masks'. Jacobsen's early pictures were executed in intense, luminous colours, which produced extremely drama-tic contrasts. Later he achieved a quieter, more lyrical expression by using a brighter and more richly modulated palette.

Jacobsen, Robert. Danish sculptor, b. 1912 in Copenhagen. Jacobsen started out in life as a sailor. In 1931 he went to live in America, where he taught himself to sculpt. He had admired the work of Rodin and H. Laurens since boyhood, but it was an exhibition of the work of German Expressionists in 1929 that persuaded him to become a sculptor. In the 1930s he produced wood carvings, which clearly reveal the influence of German Expressionism. Then, in 1940, Jacobsen adopted a rather more poetic view of reality, and in 1941 became a member of the Danish *Host*, a group with Surrealist leanings. In the same year he produced his first completely abstract pieces, and shortly afterwards had a meeting with Jean Arp which confirmed him in this new departure. Next Jacobsen produced stone carvings, and after the war he began to paint his sculptures. In 1947 he moved to Paris, where he was deeply impressed by the wide range of contemporary artistic expression. In Paris he opted definitively for metal sculpture, and established contact with the Galerie Denise René. In 1949 he made an experimental film with *musique concrète* entitled *Réalité A*. Since 1949 his sculptures have been concerned with the problems posed by the representation of movement and the incorporation of external space. Since 1949 he has shown his work regularly in the Salon de Mai and the Salon de la Jeune Sculpture in Paris; later he also began to exhibit in the Salon des Réalités Nouvelles in Paris. In 1952 Jacobsen won a prize awarded by the Danish newspaper *Politikon*. In the course of the 1960s he produced both large-format works and imaginative figurines made from scrap metal. At the same time he made an even more intensive study of mechanical movement and sought to create sculptures with a sense of inner dynamism. His welded sheet-iron constructions were followed by sculptures with open curved forms. These are also made of sheet iron, but are worked in a cold state and reveal clear traces of the working process. Jacobsen is now living in Montfermeil, Seine-et-Oise.

Catalogue, *Jacobsen*, Galerie de France, Paris 1963.
Catalogue, *Robert Jacobsen*, Galerie Anne Abels, Cologne 1965.

Jacquet, Alain George Frank. French painter, b. 1939 in Neuilly-sur-Seine, France. After studying architecture in Grenoble and Paris, Jacquet worked as an actor before becoming a painter. He is now living in Paris.

Jacquet is a Pop artist and employs the serigraphic technique that has come into vogue since the advent of Pop Art. In his portraits and monumental figura-tive pictures, he uses the dots of colour forced through the screen as a means of alienating perfect reproductions of human figures.

Jaeckel, Willy. German painter, b. 1888 in Breslau; d. 1944 in Berlin. After studying under O. Gussmann at the Academy in Dresden Jaeckel moved to Berlin in 1913. From 1919 onwards he taught at the State Academy of Art in Berlin until dismissed by the Nazis.

Jaeckel painted large two-dimensional monu-mental figure compositions, female nudes, portraits, landscapes and still lifes. In 1916–17 he executed murals for H. Bahlsen in Hanover. He also produced a large graphic oeuvre, in which he expressed a visionary and ecstatic view of life.

Jaenisch, Hans. German painter, b. 1907 in Eilenstedt. Jaenisch studied under Otto Nebel at the Bauhaus in Weimar. He joined the *Sturm* association in 1927 and later the *Künstlerbund* in 1950, both of which were centred on Berlin. During the Nazi period he was forbidden to exhibit his work. He is now living in Berlin, where he teaches at the Academy of Art. Jaenisch is an abstract artist.

Jakopič, Rihard. Yugoslav painter, b. 1869 in Ljubljana; d. 1943 in Ljubljana. He studied in Vienna and Munich, and later became the leader of the Slovene Impressionists, whose avowed object was to paint light. Others in the movement were Ivan Grohar (1867–1911), Matej Sternen (1870–1949) and Matija Jama (1872–1947).

Jančić, Olga. Yugoslav sculptress, b. 1929 in Bitolj, Macedonia. Jančić completed her training at the Academy of Art in Belgrade in 1950. By using elemental forms to simplify and control the sculptural volumes, she produces exciting tensions between the sheer mass of her material and the basic instinctuality of her theme.

Miodrag B. Protić. 'The Sculptures of Olga Jančić', *NIN*, Belgrade 29 March 1959.
Katarina Ambrozic. Catalogue, *Jančić*, Modern Gallery, Belgrade 1964.

Janco, Marcel. Rumanian architect and painter, b. 1895 in Bucharest. After completing his training as an architect in 1915 Janco went to Zürich, where he joined Hugo Ball's recently founded *Cabaret Voltaire* in February 1916. From then until 1921 he belonged to the inner cadre of the Zürich Dada movement. During this period he designed posters, decorations and a number of impressive abstract masks for the *Cabaret*, but his best-known Dadaist works were the abstract, architectonic reliefs which he fashioned in plaster. Some of these were left entirely plain; others were either painted or decorated with small pieces of wood or glass. In 1921 Janco withdrew from the Dada movement and in 1922 returned to Rumania where he worked as an architect and contributed to the development of *avant-garde* trends as editor of the Rumanian art magazine *Contimporanul*. In 1940 he emigrated to Israel, where he founded an artists' community in the village of Eyn Hod.

W. Verkauf and M. Janco (eds). *Dada*, Teufen (Switzerland) 1957.

Janssen, Horst. German draughtsman and graphic artist, b. 1929 in Hamburg. Janssen studied at the Landeskunstschule (State School of Art) in Hamburg under the draughtsman Alfred Mahlau. In 1968 he was represented at the Biennale in Venice. He is now living in Hamburg.

Janssen produces scurrilous drawings and art prints, in which he depicts macabre human figures in various stages of disintegration. These works, which reveal wit, irony and a penchant for obscenity and ugliness, are built up from delicate networks of lines and transparent shaded areas.

Exhibition catalogue, *Horst Janssen*, Kestner Gesellschaft, Hanover 1965–6.

Jaray, Tess. British painter, b. 1937. She studied at the St. Martin's and the Slade Schools. She has had one-man shows at the Grabowski Galleries, London, 1963; Hamilton Galleries, London, 1965 and 1967. She has participated in exhibitions throughout the world, and she is represented in many public collections in Britain and elsewhere. Her work is allied with Post-Painterly Abstraction, an essentially American movement which has had considerable influence in Britain; in it she experiments with perspective.

Jarema, Maria. Polish sculptress and painter, b. 1908 in Stary Samber; d. 1958 in Cracow. Jarema studied at the Academy of Art in Cracow from 1929 to 1935. From 1930 onwards she was a member of the revolutionary artistic movement in Poland. She also joined the Surrealistically oriented Cracow Group in 1930. From 1933 to 1939 she worked for the *avant-garde* Painters' Theatre 'Cricot'. After the war she again joined the Cracow Group when it was re-formed in 1957, produced stage and costume designs for Kantor's experimental theatre ('Cricot 2') and also acted under Kantor's direction. The sculptures which Jarema produced before the Second World War—virtually the whole of her output in this medium—reveal part-geometric, part-organic forms. After the war she concentrated almost entirely on her painting. Following an initial phase chiefly remarkable for its Surrealist allusions, Jarema turned to organic forms and, finally, to non-objective compositions in which the contours of the transparent patches of colour—which are built up one above the other—create a sense of movement and space.

Catalogue, *Maria Jarema*, National Museum, Cracow.
Peinture moderne polonaise: Sources et recherches, Musée Galliera, Paris 1969.

Jarnuskiewicz, Jerzy. Polish sculptor, b. 1919 in Kalisz. Jarnuskiewicz trained as a sculptor at the Cracow and Warsaw academies. He is now living in Warsaw, where he holds a professorial post at the academy.

Jarnuskiewicz has created a number of public monuments, including the one at Auschwitz-Birkenau. He creates metal constructions which produce marked spatial and optical effects.

Jawlensky, Alexei von (Aleksei Georgevich Yavlensky). Russian painter, b. 1864 in Kuslovo; d. 1941 in Wiesbaden. His early education was to have led to a military career; he was, however, able even in the first years of his military service to combine a profound enthusiasm for and, subsequently, practice of art with his other duties. In 1889 a transfer to St. Petersburg brought him into contact with Repin's circle, which included artists of the Russian Realist school such as Shishkin and Kuindzhi, as well as the future Impressionists Korovin and Serov. This period also saw the beginning of a prolonged intimacy with Repin's pupil Marianne von Werefkin (Mariamne Verefkina). From 1889 to 1896 Jawlensky studied at the St. Petersburg Academy, but dissatisfaction with academic instruction led him, upon leaving the army, to seek a more revolutionary form of art education in Munich, whither he was accompanied not only by Werefkin, but also by two other disillusioned students of the Academy, Igor Grabar and Dmitri Kardovsky (the latter was subsequently to occupy in post-Revolutionary Russia an administrative post in the artistic section of the Commissariat of the Enlightenment). On arrival in Munich, Jawlensky and his companions entered the art school of the well-known Anton Azbé, who was also the teacher of Dobuzhinsky, Bilibin and Kandinsky, although there is no evidence of Jawlensky's own personal contacts at this date.

As for Kandinsky, the early years of the twentieth century were for Jawlensky years of travel (Holland, Brittany). In 1905 he met Diaghilev in Paris in connection with the Russian exhibition at the Salon d'Automne. He also met Hodler. From 1906 to 1907 he was in contact with the Beuron artist Jan (Willibrord) Verkade, who transmitted via Jawlensky elements of *Nabi* doctrines and Synthetist theories of art to the subsequent Munich group. In 1907 the 'arch-*Nabi*', Sérusier, visited Munich. From 1908, Jawlensky's friendship with Kandinsky and Münter led to the formation of the *Neue Künstlervereinigung München* (1909). At the break-up of this association, caused by dispute on the part of the jury over the hanging of Kandinsky's *Composition V*, Jawlensky and Werefkin sided with the conservative elements ranged against Kandinsky, and hence were not invited by Kandinsky and Marc to participate in their new organization, the *Blauer Reiter*. In 1912 Jawlensky made the acquaintance of Nolde. At the outbreak of war, he went into exile at St-Prex (Lake Geneva).

Jawlensky's early painting is eclectic in character; above all, the influence of Post-Impressionism, of Cézanne and the modern French masters makes itself clearly felt. From 1908 onwards, however, a more personal style emerged, utilizing sharp contrasts of colour, with represented objects frequently displaying a heavy, black outline—a stylistic trait which appears to have influenced Kandinsky's work of this period. Gradually, two related themes began to dominate Jawlensky's painting: portraits, and an extended series of 'heads', the elements of which the artist, in his later work, was to reduce to the very brink of total abstraction.

The years in Switzerland were broken by the renewal of old and the creation of new friendships: Stravinsky, Nijinsky, Hodler, Amiet. In 1920 he participated in the Venice Biennale (*Variations, Heads*). He also separated from Werefkin. In 1922 he moved with his family to Wiesbaden. In 1924 he, together with Kandinsky, Klee and Feininger, formed *Die Blaue Vier*. From 1929 onwards, increasingly severe arthritis crippled Jawlensky's hands. From 1933 his work was officially rejected by the Nazi authorities; at the same time interest in his painting grew abroad.

Will Grohmann. *Alexej von Jawlensky*, Paris 1934.
Clemens Weiler. *Alexej Jawlensky*, Cologne 1959.

Jenkins, William Paul. American painter, b. 1923 in Kansas City, Missouri. At first he studied at the Kansas City Art Institute (1938–41) and served as an apprentice in a ceramic factory. Between 1948 and 1951 he worked at the Art Students' League in New York under Morris Kantor and Yasuo Kuniyoshi. Jenkins went to Paris in 1953 to live and work, feeling that he needed to resist the intellectual influence of Jackson Pollock, one of the leading contemporary New York Abstract Expressionists. Nevertheless, he continued to maintain residence in New York, where his first one-man show was held in 1956 at the Martha Jackson Gallery.

From 1953 Jenkins painted with a liquid medium in order to obtain an effect of colour in motion. Perhaps his early experience with ceramic glazes inspired the jewel-like range of colour that is characteristic of his work. His pictures trace his own emotional and aesethetic interaction with both the chance and the controlled method of painting with a fluid material. In 1956 he returned to New York, where he first saw paintings by Helen Frankenthaler, Morris Louis and Kenneth Noland, who had been working with poured, stained and spilled paint on unprimed canvas. Three years later a voyage to Spain, during which he worked in watercolour, led Jenkins to a further involvement with transparent, flowing colour. Alternately he used oil or the thinner, more versatile acrylic paints, with which he flooded white primed canvas. Avoiding the mark of the hand or brush, Jenkins worked by pouring paint from corner to corner, often pulling the canvas back on itself to create broadly flaring or tapering channels that blend with an abstract but mysterious suggestiveness, a feeling that distinguished the work of an earlier American painter of natural forms and phenomena, Georgia O'Keeffe. Pictures such as *Phenomena Nearing Isthmus* (1962–3, Los Angeles, Coll. C. Martin) or *Phenomena Red Wing* (1962, New York, Coll. David Kluger), with its rich purple, pure red and brilliant yellow forming a wing-like configuration, often evoke—without describing—shapes or processes in the midst of flux and growth.

Kenneth B. Sawyer. *The Paintings of Paul Jenkins*, Paris 1961.
Jean Cassou. *Jenkins*, London 1963.

Jensen, Alfred. American painter, b. 1903 in Guatemala City. After spending his childhood in Denmark Jensen studied in San Diego, California (1925–6), in Munich (1927–8 under Hans Hofmann) and in Paris (at the Académie Scandinave). In 1958 he taught at the Maryland Institute in Baltimore. He is now living in New York.

Jensen paints geometrical abstracts in pure spectral colours. His designs are the product of computations based on natural laws, arithmetic and harmonics.

Exhibition catalogue, *Jensen*, Stedelijk Museum, Amsterdam 1964.

Jespers, Floris. Belgian painter, b. 1889 in Antwerp. Jespers studied in Antwerp. His early paintings reveal the influence of Rik Wouters and the Fauves. Subsequently he embraced a wide variety of styles, ranging from Flemish Expressionism to the *École de Paris*, from Picasso and Klee to pure abstract art. His ability to assimilate these widely differing trends gives some hint of his artistic talent.

G. Burssens. *Floris Jespers*, Antwerp 1955.

Jespers, Oscar. Belgian sculptor, b. 1887 in Antwerp. Jespers studied in Antwerp. In 1927 he settled in Brussels, where he taught at the College of Architecture and Applied Arts. He joined various groups, including *Les Neuf*, and received many public commissions. He is now living in Brussels.

Jespers passed through three phases. He started as an Impressionist, then produced block-like figures in the Cubist mode before turning to Expressionism in the 1920s. His works are executed in stone or terracotta. They are all figurative, although his natural inclination towards stylized and archaic forms has led to a marked simplification of the human figure.

A. de Ridder. *Oscar Jespers*, Antwerp 1948.

Jeune Peinture belge. The *Jeune Peinture belge* was a Belgian artists' group that was founded in July 1945. Its leading members were Louis van Lint, Gaston Bertrand, Anne Bonnet and Marc Mendelson. Others associated with the group included the sculptor Anthoons and the painters Jan Cox, Luc Peire, Antoine Mortier, Jean Milo, Pierre Alechinsky, Pol Bury and Jo Delahaut. Although these artists pursued widely different goals, they were all basically abstract. The lyrical abstraction of the *École de Paris*, especially of Bazaine, and the works of the Flemish Expressionists exerted a strong influence on the members of the *Jeune Peinture belge*. Renée Lust, the president of the group, arranged exhibitions all over Europe. But when he died the *Jeune Peinture belge* quickly disintegrated, although its name has been preserved in the annual prize awarded for painters under the age of 40, the *Prix de la Jeune Peinture belge*.

Jevrić, Olga. Yugoslav sculptress, b. 1922 in Belgrade. Jevrić trained at the Academy of Art in Belgrade. The portraits and reliefs of her early period are based on condensed masses and simplified forms, which reveal an archaic trend. Later, when she went over to pure abstracts, she used ascetic materials, namely cement and scaffold pins, and from them constructed asymmetrical, sloping sculptures, which pinpoint the moment of transition from a static to a falling state.

Vera Horvat-Pintarić. Catalogue, Gallery of Contemporary Art, Zagreb 1964.
Ch. F. de Delloye. 'La Sculpture à la XXIX Biennale de Venise 1958', *Aujourd'hui* 19, 1958.

Jochims, Reimer. German painter, b. 1935 in Kiel, Germany. Jochims is a self-taught painter who uses no formal design. His works are based on subtle gradations and transitions of colour, and his handling is so fine that the paint merges imperceptibly with the picture plane. His output to date includes folding pictures (1955), chromatic planes (from 1961) and chromatic reliefs (from 1963).

John, Augustus. British painter and draughtsman, b. 1878 in Wales; d. 1961. John studied at the Slade School, 1896–9; he developed his talent as a draughtsman early there, rebelling against nineteenth-century traditions to produce a style of drawing which is immensely appealing for its brilliance and spontaneity and for which he has been famous ever since. John is perhaps best known for these drawings, but his work as a painter is also of some importance. In the years around 1910 he flirted with Post-Impressionism, but later settled into a fairly straightforward style best seen in his once celebrated portraits of such well-known figures as Dylan Thomas and W. B. Yeats. He entertained ambitions, never really fulfilled, of producing large decorative works for which his talent would, no doubt, have been admirably suited; yet some of his most attractive paintings are small, informal landscapes.

T. Earp. *John*, London 1934.
J. Rothenstein. *Augustus John*, London and New York 1944.

John, Gwen. British painter, b. 1876 in Haverfordwest, Wales; d. 1939 in Dieppe. From 1895 she was a Slade student with her brother Augustus, under Tonks. There was some influence from Ambrose McEvoy, a fellow student then interested in glazing techniques. Comparatively little is known about her life. In 1898 she left for Paris, where she attended Whistler's school. She left France in 1900 to resume life in England, exhibited regularly with the NEAC —gaining some favourable notices—and in 1903 exhibited jointly with her brother at the Carfax Gallery. From 1913 she lived in poverty in Meudon, where the theologian and art critic Jacques Maritain was a neighbour. The extent of his influence is debated (Wyndham Lewis gives it prominence). A further powerful factor in her life was an intimate friendship with Rodin—ultimately not sustained by the sculptor.

Unpretentious in art as in her life, Gwen John was sixty at the time of her only major exhibition (Chenil Galleries, 1936). Her brother described her as 'the greatest woman artist of her age, or, as I think, of any other'—an opinion finding support since the Matthiesen Gallery memorial exhibition of 1946.

Her principal theme is the single, youthful, feminine three-quarter or half-length figure whose introspective gaze expresses Gwen John's own quietism.

These pensive figures in oil and numerous drawings, often repeated in very similar variations, comprise a unified oeuvre of great sensitivity. With no English parallels, they sometimes recall Gauguin's Post-Impressionism or the paintings of her Parisian contemporary, Modigliani.

J. Rothenstein. *Modern English Painters, Sickert to Smith*, London 1952.
M. Taubman. Exhibition catalogue, Arts Council of Great Britain, London 1968.

Johns, Jasper. American painter, b. 1930 in Allendale, South Carolina. He studied at the University of South Carolina and came to New York to paint in 1952. The year 1955 marks the beginning of his mature work, a radical departure from the Abstract Expressionist painting then current. Johns began painting flags, targets, numbers and alphabets—an iconography of predetermined common imagery treated in such a way that familiar meanings and specific identities were confused by such devices as painterly facture, neutralization of colour and violation of flatness. Likeness became confusing, and the relation between the real and painted image challenged accepted associations and ways of seeing. Johns was interested in forcing the viewer to re-adjust his responses, and in works such as *Three Flags* (1958, Madison, Conn., Coll. Mr. and Mrs. Burton Tremaine) or *Target with Four Faces* (1955, New York, Museum of Modern Art) the flatness and focus of the image is equivocated by apparent spatial levels within the painting, or by the addition of three-dimensional compartments containing plaster casts of facial fragments. Gradually (1956–62) he shifted from the earlier emblematic images and subaesthetic common objects (beer cans, light bulbs and flashlights were cast in bronze and sculpmetal) to more Expressionistically painted works, but he was still concerned with this notion of ambiguity. Maps, words and the act of painting itself became the subjects for his new pictures (*Gray Alphabets*, 1956, New York, Coll. Ben Heller). In his early objects and pictures, the known qualities of his repetitive, iconographic subject matter were suppressed and masked by a painterly surface or a coating of pasty metal or encaustic. In 1961 (like his friend Robert Rauschenberg with his combine paintings) Johns began to attach real objects to the surface of his canvases, seeking an expanded vocabulary as he juxtaposed unexpected found materials, studio debris or collaged fragments against painted fields. The series of works called the *Devices* contained the rulers, compasses and measuring instruments with which parts of the forms within these pictures had been made. *False Start* (1959, New York, Coll. Mr. and Mrs. Robert C. Scull), one of his major works, is a web of visual (and even literary) puns and contradictions: stencilled labels are painted with the names of colours they are not, while bursts of bright red, blue, orange or yellow are falsely identified by the names of the hues printed over them. Space is neither three-dimensional nor flat, and the structuring is neither loose nor tight. What is read is not what is seen and vice versa. In many lithographs and drawings Johns has explored the collage and imprint methods suggested in such a painting.

Like his theoretical forebear, Marcel Duchamp, whose visual, philosophical and aesthetic puns and speculations defied the categories of art for half a century, Johns dissociates his art from artistic personality and self-expression, asking vital questions about the nature of seeing and conceiving. Although unlike Duchamp he never renounced painting, Johns maintained his art in a context of its own, peculiar to the ambivalent conditions and reflexive necessities of its own creation.

Leo Steinberg. *Jasper Johns*, New York 1963.
Alan R. Solomon and John Cage. Catalogue, *Jasper Johns*, Jewish Museum, New York 1964.
Max Kozloff. *Jasper Johns*, New York 1968.

Jolin, Einar. Swedish painter, b. 1890. After attending the school run by the Konstnärsförbundet (the Swedish Artists' Association) in Stockholm Jolin was a pupil of Matisse in Paris from 1908 to 1914 and during this period also made a study of eastern art. In 1912 he joined the *De åtta* (*The Eight*) group and in the 1920s the *Phalanges*. Jolin developed a style of painting which was both spiritual and ornate at one and the same time in which he combined Fauvist ideas with the decorative purity of Japanese coloured woodcuts and Persian miniatures. His oeuvre consists primarily of townscapes, highly stylized portraits and still lifes.

N. Palmgren. *Einar Jolin*, Stockholm 1947.

Jones, Allen. British painter, b. 1937 in Southampton. Jones studied at Hornsey College of Art, 1956–9 and 1960–1, and at the Royal College, 1959–60. Since 1964 he has taught at the Chelsea School of Art, but between 1964 and 1965 he lived in New York. He visited America again in 1966, going to Los Angeles. Jones was one of the British Pop artists of the 1964 New Generation. From the beginning of his career his work has been distinguished by its scale, its bold and simple design, and strong clear colour with the *motif* often set against a light ground. Elements of his painting are often figurative, but by his own account the literary element is secondary to the purely visual. Nevertheless the figurative part is important, and his pictures have come increasingly to be about the ambiguous relation between the reality of the details and the apparent unreality of the picture space in which they exist.

Jones, Arne. Swedish sculptor, b. 1914. Jones worked as a stonemason in various workshops from

1934 to 1944 and trained under Erik Grate at the Stockholm College of Art from 1941 to 1947. Jones is remarkable among Swedish sculptors in that he regards sculpture as an extension of architecture and an integral part of the environment. He made his name in 1947 with his *Katedralen* (*The Cathedral*), a 'Gothic' construction, whose slender ribs and arches incorporate areas of external space and also trigger mental associations with human forms. Most of Jones' monumental sculptures, whose composition changes each time the viewer changes his position, combine extreme lyricism with a sense of organic growth. In the 1950s Jones designed fountains, in which he used the water as an additional sculptural element. His *Spiral åtbörd* (*Spiral Gesture*), which he designed for Norrköping and in which the water ascends in a slender spiral, is a good example. Recently Jones has also treated artificial lighting as a sculptural element. Inspired by Daumier's caricatures, Jones has created a series of grotesque terra-cotta heads depicting Swedish writers.

Jones, David. British painter, engraver and writer, b. 1895 in Brockley, Kent. Jones trained at Camberwell School of Art, 1909–15, and after active service in France, at Westminster School of Art, 1919–22. He worked with Eric Gill at Ditchling and Capel-y-Ffin, 1922–7, and published *In Parenthesis*, 1937, *The Anathemata*, 1952, *Epoch and Artist*, a collection of shorter writings, 1959. He is represented in the Tate Gallery and in many public collections.

David Jones' most prolific period as a painter was from 1928 to 1932. During these years he moved from a certain primitivism, also to be found in Christopher Wood, towards a more elaborate and attenuated style with half-hidden lines and shimmering colour. Though never to be confused with Paul Nash, he shared with him a gently visionary, sometimes hallucinatory style and the strong suggestion of hidden meanings. Jones' output, most of it in pencil and watercolour, included portraits, landscapes, gardens and interiors, with the superb animal drawings which are his most objective works. From about 1940 his work in painting, much smaller in quantity, was more openly symbolic and concerned with his interest in the Arthurian legends and in early Christian Britain, while in style it tended towards Late Gothic linear complexity. In the last twenty years David Jones has also produced many inscriptions in pencil and watercolour.

David Jones, like Wyndham Lewis, has an equal mastery of painting and writing. *In Parenthesis*, one of the greatest works of art inspired by trench warfare, has for its secondary theme the continuance of the most ancient aspects of Britain into modern times. His poetic insight into the birth of the language and central traditions of the nation is Jones' third claim to greatness. The continuity of

past and present is inherent in all his activities, and so is the unity of the arts under a single principle: that all art is sign. Both these deeply held beliefs derive from his understanding of the Catholic faith.

David Jones. *Epoch and Artist*, London 1959.

Jorn, Asger. Danish painter, b. 1914 in Veyrun, Jutland; d. 1973. After moving to Silkeborg in 1929 Jorn began to paint in 1930, and to write in 1932. In 1936 he studied under F. Léger and Le Corbusier in Paris, and in the following year painted a large mural for the staircase of Le Corbusier's *Pavillon des Pays Nouveaux* at the International Exhibition. From 1939 to 1940 he completed his military service in Denmark, and from 1942 to 1943, when Denmark was occupied by the Germans, printed the underground magazine *Land og Folk*. He also helped to launch the *Helhesten* magazine, and produced an annotated Kafka translation. In 1944–5 he executed a series of twenty-three etchings, which were later exhibited under the title *Occupations 1939/1945*. In 1948 he joined with Christian Dotremont, Appel, Constant, Noiret and Corneille in founding the *Cobra* association. Subsequently, he organized *Cobra* exhibitions, and published the *Petit Cobra* magazine and monographs of the *Cobra* artists. In 1951 Jorn contracted tuberculosis and became a patient in a hospital in Silkeborg. In 1953 he visited Switzerland, Italy and France. Whilst in Switzerland he produced a series of twenty-three etchings which were later published as a *Swiss Suite*. Jorn became a founder member of *International situationniste*. In 1962 he collaborated with Dubuffet on a series of experimental atonal recordings. Jorn also became a founder member of the Scandinavian Institute for Comparative Vandalism. From 1954 onwards he lived primarily in Paris and Albissola Marina (Savona). During his early period Jorn's paintings were based on Neo-Impressionism, Scandinavian Expressionism and the Nature Lyricism of the 'Christiana-Bohème'. Later, between 1936 and 1939, he was influenced by Le Corbusier's 'Purist' doctrine. He also came to terms with Surrealism and in doing so produced a number of collages in which Surrealistic forms appear against monochrome grounds. Then, in 1939–40, the monochrome grounds were replaced by labyrinthine patterns of lines, which eventually led on to the development of an autonomous calligraphic technique. From 1953 onwards Jorn gradually abandoned this linear composition in favour of broad bands of glowing colour which summon up images of mythical heads and figures. Between 1956 and 1959 Jorn reached the peak of his career as a painter. During this period his automatism and his psychic improvisation were combined with a pictorial vision of immense power which found expression in highly luminous colour compositions that are remarkable for their furious, almost savage brushwork. Unlike Pollock, Jorn did not create linear patterns in his drip paintings, concentrating instead on Pointillist effects. In addition to paintings, Jorn's artistic oeuvre embraces sculptures, graphic works, pottery and weaving. But this oeuvre reflects only one aspect of his wide-ranging interests, for he has enquired into virtually every sphere of human activity. His writings include numerous publications dealing with different aspects of philosophy and art theory.

Asger Jorn. *Pour la forme. Image et forme. Contre l'empirisme éclectique*, Paris 1958.
Guy Atkins and Erik Schmidt. *Bibliographie over Asger Jorns Skrifter til 1963*, Copenhagen 1964.
Guy Atkins. *Jorn in Scandinavia: 1930–1953*, London 1968.

Josephson, Ernst. Swedish painter, b. 1851 in Stockholm; d. 1906 in Stockholm. Josephson studied at the Stockholm Academy of Art from 1867 to 1876. During his student years he made frequent visits to Norway and Paris, and the sensitive portraits which he painted in this period reveal the influence of Courbet and Renoir. From 1877 to 1879 he visited Holland and Italy, where he worked in the public museums, copying works by old masters such as Rembrandt, Raphael and Titian. In 1879 he settled in Paris and began to paint portraits of his friends. These pictures, which were Josephson's first masterpieces, were quickly followed by a series of powerful Realistic works, including the *Gosse med skottkärra* (*Boy with a Wheelbarrow*) of 1880 and the *Spanska smeder* (*Spanish Smithy*) of 1882, in which Josephson came to terms with *plein-air* painting. At the same time, however, he produced a second series of pictures, which gave expression to the passionate and Romantic side of his nature. The *Leitmotif* of this series was the Norwegian water-sprite, which symbolized the artist's longing for redemption and for union with nature. Thus, Josephson was able to incorporate an extremely moving statement of his personal philosophy into a series of landscapes, in which the magic of the northern summer nights is expressed in deep dark colours. This series exists in two versions. The first of these, which dates from 1882–3, is in the National Museum in Stockholm; the second, dating from 1882–4, is in Gothenburg. In 1884 Josephson painted a picture called *Strömkarlen* in which he portrayed this water-sprite in a daytime setting. The emotional power and psychological integrity of this work were quite overpowering, and it made a very considerable impact on Josephson's contemporaries. But it was in the mid-1880s, when he painted his penetrating portraits of women, that Josephson reached the peak of his career. These portraits are remarkable, both for their psychological insight and for the richly orchestrated colouring of the interiors in which they are set and which are reminiscent of Manet and Delacroix. As the principal member of

the Swedish artists' colony in Paris, Josephson was for a while the head of the Konstnärsförbundet, the Swedish artists' association, whose Naturalistic programme had been evolved as a reaction against the Neo-Classical tradition of the Swedish Academy. But Josephson was essentially a Romantic and idealistic artist, and in 1887 he withdrew from the association because he found its artistic programme too restrictive. In the following year he became schizophrenic, and was obliged to return to Sweden, where he lived the rest of his life in seclusion. During this tragic period he produced some two hundred paintings and two thousand drawings, whose themes were taken from myths, fairy tales, poems and historical narratives. In these works, in which Josephson gave free rein to his fantasies, gentle lyrical *motifs* alternate with *motifs* of volcanic ferocity. With its structural deformation, this mad art of Josephson's final period anticipated some of the stylistic innovations of twentieth-century painting. An exhibition of his late drawings, which was staged in Berlin in 1909, influenced the German Expressionists and a number of contemporary French artists.

P. O. Zennström. *Ernst Josephson*, Stockholm 1946.
E. Blomberg. *Ernst Josephson*, 3 vols., Stockholm 1951, 1956, 1959.

Judd, Donald (Don). American sculptor, b. 1928 in Excelsior Springs, Missouri. In 1964 he was prominent in introducing 'object sculpture' to New York: very large, simple straight-sided constructions of plain industrial fabrication, placed on the floor and not reaching above eye-level. Judd's work is static and makes no emotive appeal, but by its assertive dimensions it attempts to force the viewer into a more acute observation of the relations between it, him and the space in which they exist.

Jugendstil. The name by which *art nouveau* is known in Germany and Austria (*see* **Art Nouveau**).

Junk art. Based on the premise that any material is suitable for art and on the use of the found object—especially from the debris of urban culture—junk art is ultimately rooted in Cubist collage and construction, but was first most strongly manifested in the work of Kurt Schwitters. A widespread resurgence of junk art occurred both in Europe and the United States during the 1950s. Among the earliest American work in this development are the 'combines' of Robert Rauschenberg. Other important assemblagists include Richard Stankiewicz, working primarily with discarded industrial parts; John Chamberlain, using polychromed, smashed automobile parts; Mark di Suvero, making huge constructions of scrapped metal, wood, tyres and other materials; Lee Bontecou, making shaped canvas constructions from weathered tarpaulin and metal parts; and Louise Nevelson, creating large wall reliefs with pieces of wood and furniture from destroyed houses, though disguising her materials by painting them uniformly black, white or gold. The use of junk quite naturally also appeared in environmental tableaux, thus in a sense returning the material to their original settings, as in the work of Edward Kienholz. Junk materials also played a prominent role in the environments and happenings of the late 1950s and early 1960s, for instance in those by Allan Kaprow. A unique and isolated example of junk art is Watts Towers in Los Angeles, constructed single-handedly from 1921 to 1954 by an Italian tilesetter, Simon Rodia, from various discarded fragments.

Catalogue, *New Forms—New Media*, Martha Jackson Gallery, New York 1960 (with essay 'Junk Culture as a Tradition' by Lawrence Alloway).
William C. Seitz. *The Art of Assemblage*, Museum of Modern Art, New York 1961.

Jürgen-Fischer, Klaus. German painter and publicist, b. 1930 in Krefeld, Germany. Jürgen-Fischer studied at the Academies of Art in Düsseldorf and Stuttgart from 1949 to 1952. He is now living in Baden-Baden. In 1955 he joined the editorial staff of the magazine *Das Kunstwerk*; between 1960 and 1963 he edited the magazine *Vernissage*, and in 1965 began to edit the magazine *Syn*, in which he examines the feasibility of 'an integral art form . . . based exclusively on pictorial principles'. *Syn* is also the name of a group of contemporary painters, who include—apart from Jürgen-Fischer —Bernd Berner, Rolf-Gunter Dienst and Eduard Micus. In his paintings Jürgen-Fischer is trying to create a 'complex art' based on reconciliation and synthesis.

K

Kalinowski, Horst Egon. German sculptor, b. 1924 in Düsseldorf. Kalinowski attended the Academy of Art in Düsseldorf from 1945 to 1948. From 1949 to 1950 he was in Italy, where he studied mosaic techniques in Rome and Venice. He then spent two years in Paris, working under J. Dewasne and E. Pillet in the *Atelier d'art abstrait* at the Académie de la Grande Chaumière. From 1950 to 1954 he produced abstract paintings constructed from geometrical elements. In 1956 he progressed from paintings to collages (*tableaux-objets*), which later grew more complex. From 1960 onwards he made caissons (wood and iron constructions covered with leather). In the 1960s Kalinowski also produced art prints,

primarily etchings, and in 1964 a set of books appeared, which contained twelve etchings of his illustrating Japanese *Haikus*. In 1964 he also adapted his caissons to produce pulsations (by introducing electro-magnetic equipment). In the following year he again modified his caissons, turning them into stelae. In the course of his career he has created numerous designs for theatrical décors and costumes.

Kalinowski is not trying to re-establish mythical concepts but to establish new, living symbols. With his caissons he has proved that problems which first arose in a specific period in the past can also be tackled today without modish speculation. Kalinowski is now living in Paris and New York.

Kampmann, Rüdiger Utz. German sculptor, b. 1935 in Berlin. Kampmann studied from 1957 to 1963 at the Academy of Art in Berlin, where he was a pupil of K. Hartung. Prior to 1964, when he visited the Villa Romana in Florence, Kampmann had created totemistic sculptures and reliefs in clay and cement. At the instigation of W. Gaul he then produced 'coloured objects' in wood or aluminium, according the same degree of importance to the colour as to the sculptural form. The actual 'objects' consist of assemblages of boxes, combinations of cubes arranged at different levels, segments of cubes, parts of engines, radiators, etc. The strong colouring of these works denotes Kampmann as a member of the 'New Abstract' movement. His most recent work includes a wall design which was commissioned for the new Berlin satellite town, Märkisches Viertel, and which he executed in conjunction with the architect W. Poreinke.

Kandelin, Ole. Finnish painter, b. 1920; d. 1947. Kandelin was one of the best-known representatives of abstract art in Finland. He took his lead from the Surrealists of the Swedish *Halmstad* group and evolved a non-figurative style of painting with vigorous expressive forms.

Kandinsky, Vassily. Russian painter, b. 1866 in Moscow; d. 1944 in Neuilly-sur-Seine. He is generally regarded as one of the pioneers of abstract painting. Only at the age of 30 was Kandinsky, who had studied law and political economy at Moscow University, able to decide to abandon an academic career and devote himself to painting. Arriving in Munich at the end of 1896, he subjected himself for several years to an academic training as an artist, first under Anton Azbé, who was the teacher of a number of Russian painters, including Jawlensky, Bilibin and Dobuzhinsky, and later under the noted academician Franz von Stuck. However, convinced ultimately that his path to artistic maturity could only lie alone, Kandinsky dissociated himself from the Academy, began himself to practise as a teacher of art, and in 1901 founded the association *Phalanx*, devoted largely to arranging exhibitions of the work not only of its members but also of contemporary European artists. In 1902, he began a liaison with the young German painter Gabriele Münter, which lasted until the First World War. From 1903 to 1908 he undertook extensive travels in the company of Münter, including visits to Italy, Holland, Tunis, and an extended stay in Paris, 1906–7, where he exhibited at the Salon d'Automne. From 1908 to 1914, Kandinsky and Münter divided their time between Munich and the Bavarian village of Murnau, where during the period 1909–13 there developed a summer colony which also included, at various times, Jawlensky, Werefkin and (later) the younger German artists Franz Marc and August Macke. In 1909 Kandinsky became the first president of a new association, the *Neue Künstlervereinigung München* (New Artists' Union). Increasing differences between members of the association led, however, in December 1911 to the secession of Kandinsky and Marc, their organization of two exhibitions of contemporary art under the title *Der Blaue Reiter* (The Blue Rider), and the publication of an 'Almanac', also entitled *Der Blaue Reiter*—a publication which was to unite the productions of artists working in different domains, and which included a notable 'musical supplement' consisting of short compositions by Schoenberg, Berg and Webern. During this period Kandinsky's own pictorial work, despite its increasingly 'abstract' appearance, retained a specific (although largely concealed) thematic and motive content, often of an apocalyptic or eschatological nature, as for example his *Composition VII* of 1913 (Moscow, Tretyakov Gallery). His treatise *On the Spiritual in Art* raises, however, the question of the possibility of totally non-representational painting.

In 1914 Kandinsky, leaving many of his works in Münter's custody, returned by a circuitous route to Russia, where after the Revolution he played a leading role for some three years in cultural policy, helping to reorganize the provincial museums, and proposing a detailed programme of art instruction for *Inkhuk* (the Institute of Artistic Culture), a programme which was in part to provide the model for subsequent teaching at the Bauhaus. These projected reforms were, however, met with increasing hostility, and in 1921 Kandinsky accepted a call to the Bauhaus as Professor, a post which he continued to hold from 1922 until the closure of that institution in 1933. This period sees the increasing elaboration of his now geometrical, for the most part wholly non-representational compositions (e.g. *Composition VIII*, 1923, New York, Guggenheim Museum). In 1924 Kandinsky, together with Jawlensky, Feininger and Klee, formed a new association, the *Blaue Vier* (Blue Four); in 1926, his perhaps most influential theoretical treatise, *Point and Line to Plane*, appeared as a Bauhaus publication. From 1933 onwards he was resident in Neuilly. In his pictorial work of this last

period, the influence of Constructivism, which had been noticeable during the early twenties, gave way to a less harshly geometrical element almost of fantasy, reminiscent at times of the work of Miró.

In addition to his numerous oils and watercolours, Kandinsky is, as an artist, notable for his remarkable graphic works (e.g. the collections *Klänge* of 1913 and *Kleine Welten* of 1922); as a writer, he is of considerable significance not only for his theoretical publications, but also for his poems and his extraordinary stage compositions, only two of which have to date been published: *Der Gelbe Klang* (in collaboration with the composer Thomas von Hartmann) and *Violett*.

Will Grohmann. *Kandinsky, Life and Work*, New York 1958; London 1960.
H. K. Röthel. *Kandinsky, Das Graphische Werk*, Cologne 1970.
Paul Overy. *Kandinsky: the Language of the Eye*, London and New York 1970.

Kane, John. American primitive painter, b. 1860 in West Calder, Scotland; d. 1934 in Pittsburgh, Pa. He first worked on railroad construction and then at the Bessemer blast furnaces in Pittsburgh. Between 1884 and 1890 he mined coal at Alabama, Tennessee, Kentucky and Pennsylvania. He first began sketching at this time. After losing a leg in 1891, he was forced to do less strenuous work, taking employment as a railroad watchman until 1899 when he went to work for the Pressed Steel Car Co. When he lost this job in 1907 and a son died at birth, he took to drinking heavily, which eventually forced his wife to leave him in despair. His first paintings date from about 1910 when he was working as a house painter and carpenter in Ohio. One of several versions of *The Steel Farm* (Los Angeles, Coll. Steven L. Rose), done before 1910, was the first painting he sold. In the 1920s he worked for the Steel and Tin Plate Works of the National Tube Co., painting offices and decorating them to his own taste. He first received public notice when *Scene in the Scottish Highlands* (Pittsburgh, Carnegie Institute Museum of Art) was accepted for the 1927 Carnegie International Exhibition. From then until 1934 he was included in every Carnegie International. Around 1930 he devoted himself exclusively to painting and was given his first one-man show in 1931 at the Contemporary Art Galleries, New York. Many of his primitivistic works recall his boyhood Scotland (*Highland Hollow*, Pittsburgh, Pa., Carnegie Institute Museum of Art; *Scot's Day at Kennywood Park*, Los Angeles, Coll. Steven L. Rose). Surely his finest work is a *Self-Portrait* (1929, New York, Museum of Modern Art). His self-portraits can also be seen in *Touching-Up* (1931–2, private coll.), where he is situated in his studio, and also in the 1933 *Pietà* (New York, Harold Diamond, Inc.) which is based on the School of Avignon *Pietà* in the Louvre. Here he painted himself as the patron and included a 'portrait' of St. Paul's Cathedral, Pittsburgh, in the background. This cityscape detail is typical of the works he produced. They are executed in minute detail with stylized trees and clouds, but display convincing perspective and a sense of the breadth and expanse of the view. In such works he often freely rearranged elements of the land- or cityscape as in *Panther Hollow, Pittsburgh* (c. 1933–4, Pittsburgh, Carnegie Institute Museum of Art).

Sky Hooks, The Autobiography of John Kane, with foreword by Frank Crowninshield. New York, Philadelphia, London and Toronto 1938.

Kano, Mitsuo. Japanese etcher, b. 1933 in Tokyo. Kano is self-taught and started with an interest in Surrealism like most other Japanese artists. Late in the 1950s he acquired his own morphology as a metaphorical image from nature. He was represented at the São Paulo Bienal in 1957 and 1961. He now lives in Kamakura.

Kanoldt, Alexander. German painter, b. 1881 in Karlsruhe; d. 1939 in Berlin. Kanoldt studied in Karlsruhe and Munich from 1899. From 1901 to 1911 he was a member of the New Artists' Association in Munich, and from 1913 to 1920 of the Munich Secession. After the war he met Georg Schrimpf and Carlo Mense (b. 1889), developing the ideas advanced by the *Neue Sachlichkeit*. He started to teach at the Breslau Academy, 1925, and at the Berlin Academy in 1932, where he was one of the *Neue Sachlichkeit*'s leading representatives. After experimenting with Cubism, Kanoldt's natural inclination for Classical art brought him into contact with the works of André Derain and Carlo Carrà, and with the ideas of the *Valori Plastici*. He evolved a hard, plastic style of Realistic representation, but he seldom achieved the poetic quality of the Italians' work.

Kantor, Tadeusz. Polish painter and theatre director, b. 1915 in Wielopole, near Cracow. After studying at the Academy of Art in Cracow up to 1939 Kantor founded a secret experimental theatre during the war, which was revived in 1956 under the name 'Cricot 2'. In this theatre, which Kantor has described as an 'informal' or 'zero' theatre, the actors had to integrate with 'finished objects', authors' texts were torn to shreds, and the stage presentations consisted of extremely simple situations taken from real life. Since 1945 Kantor has been one of the chief advocates of modern art in Poland and has been largely responsible for the revival of the Cracow Group (*Grupa Krakowska*). In 1961 he was visiting professor at the College of Fine Arts in Hamburg. He is now living in Cracow.

After an early metaphorical phase Kantor moved towards Surrealism between 1948 and 1956 and subsequently towards Tachism. During his informal period, which lasted for several years, he incorpora-ted chance incidents into both his paintings and his theatrical presentations. In 1963 he began to design stage sets and 'emballage costumes'. His pictorial assemblages often incorporate *motifs* derived from packaging or clothing.

Peinture moderne polonaise: Sources et Recherches, Musée Galliera, Paris 1969.

Kaprow, Allan. American painter, assemblagist, creator of happenings and theorist, b. 1927 in Atlantic City, New Jersey. Within a brief and intense early career, Kaprow progressed from an interest in Abstract Expressionism and many-levelled paintings incorporating collage to assemblage. He then moved away from the single art object or picture frame to environments and to a new art form called Happenings. The paintings he showed at the Hansa Gallery in New York (1952) revealed an attempt to use many types of images and orientations within one work. Some rudimentary assembled constructions were also exhibited, and from these Kaprow developed an 'action-collage' technique in which he employed such materials as straw, wadded newspaper, twine and flashing lights. Influenced by the kinaesthetic paint-dripping methods of Jackson Pollock, as well as by the Abstract Expressionists' emphasis on the act of painting itself, Kaprow became a crusader for artist-spectator involvement over an extended field of operation. While he still made assemblages and painted such constructions as *Grandma's Boy* (1956, Pasadena, Calif., Museum), between 1956 and 1958 Kaprow was studying musical composition with the *avant-garde* composer John Cage. The notions of chance and indeterminacy as valid means of aesthetic organization (and disorganization) that Cage advocated were instrumental to Kaprow's subsequent thinking and artistic activity. In 1957–8 he began to create environmental works that demanded audience participation (an idea also stemming from Cage's experiments), and this integration of space, materials, time and people eventually led to the more experimental pieces. The first such work was called '18 Happenings in 6 Parts' —presented in October 1959 at the Reuben Gallery on Fourth Avenue in New York. It is from this performance that the now-famous term 'happening' is derived: used originally to indicate a very determined, rehearsed and heterogeneous production, the word has picked up the connotation of a spontaneous undirected occurrence—a meaning not altogether intended by Kaprow's entitling of the original event.

After 1960 he devoted himself to publicizing, creating and establishing the happening as a viable form of art in America. His concern, like that of such early Pop artists as Robert Rauschenberg, Robert Whitman, Claes Oldenburg and Red Grooms, with whom he originated this all-encompassing form of environmental theatre, has been to break down the traditional distinctions between life and the categories of art. In this attempt to enlarge the realm of art beyond gallery display and museum situations, many of the happenings have been performed in such untraditional settings as lofts, stores, gymnasiums and parking lots. *Yard* (1961), for example, consisted of a backyard full of rubber auto tyres heaped randomly for viewers to climb in and around. The happening, as Kaprow developed it, is a non-verbal, theatrical production that abandons stage-audience structure as well as the usual plot or narrative line of traditional theatre. Although a compartmented organization may be used, the performers are considered as objects—often kinaesthetically involved—within an overall design of environment, timing, sound, colour and light. Found environments are often used and built upon, but the events are not casually arrived at, nor are they entirely accidental and spontaneous. Performers are encouraged to capitalize upon unplanned occurrences while acting out fantasies based on real life within a certain roughly pre-ordained structure that suggests symbolic and universally basic themes and meanings. A field of aesthetic operation is thus created in relation to life, combining artfully determined materials with strong associational properties, and dimensions with events and things from the sphere 'outside' of customary definitions for art.

Allan Kaprow. *Assemblage, Environments, and Happenings*, New York 1966.
Catalogue, *Allan Kaprow*, Pasadena Art Museum, Pasadena 1967.

Karfiol, Bernard. American painter, b. 1886; d. 1952. Though born in Budapest, Karfiol was the son of American parents and spent his youth on Long Island, New York. In 1899 he attended Saturday watercolour classes at Pratt Institute and the following year studied at the National Academy of Design. In 1901 he travelled to Paris where he studied under J.-P. Laurens at the Académie Julian. He exhibited at the 1903 Grand Salon and the 1904 Salon d'Automne before returning to the United States in 1906. While in Paris he was friendly with Leo and Gertrude Stein and through them met Picasso and Matisse. Back in New York he taught at Mrs. Harry Payne Whitney's 8th Street Studio from 1908 to 1913. In the latter year he exhibited two paintings and several drawings at the Armory Show. He mounted his first one-man show in 1923 at the Brummer Galleries and from the mid-1920s was exhibiting in a great number of group and one-man shows. At this time he was practising a melancholic style reminiscent of Picasso's Blue and Rose periods with their hard, elongated forms, seen, for example, in Karfiol's *Boy* of 1924 (Washington, D.C., Phillips Collection). By the late 1920s he turned to the heavier, fuller, more phlegmatic types of Renoir, though his use of colour, brushwork and sense of composition owes more to Cézanne (*Seated Nude*, 1929, New York, Museum of Modern Art). By the

mid-1930s his style deteriorated. He was unable to handle large compositions and could not relate his figures to their environments. He therefore leaned more and more heavily on academic design, his large canvases becoming increasingly formal and contrived. His smaller canvases, especially his nudes, reverted back to his earlier hardness, but without the previous psychological penetration (*Christina*, 1937, Pittsburgh, Pa., Carnegie Institute Museum of Art).

Jean Paul Slosser. *Bernard Karfiol*, New York 1931.

Karsch, Joachim. German sculptor, b. 1897 in Breslau; d. 1945 in Gandern. Karsch studied in Breslau and Berlin from 1911 to 1916. In 1919 he was awarded a travelling scholarship by the Prussian Academy of Art to visit Rome. Karsch led a wandering life, settling for various lengths of time in Berlin, Silesia, the South of France and on the Baltic coast. He also made several visits to Italy. These frequent changes of domicile reflect the essential restlessness of a sensitive artist in search of an individual style. In his sculptures, most of which are smaller than life-size, he depicted vulnerable, introverted, suffering people. Stylistically, his work occupies a position between Barlach and Lehmbruck although temperamentally he was closer to the young G. Marcks. Despite his Realistic technique and his genre *motifs* Karsch fell foul of the Nazi doctrine on art, and in 1938 a number of his sculptures were confiscated as 'degenerate works'. The destruction of further works in the war, physical illness and the threat of deportation eventually drove him to suicide.

Briefe des Bildhauers Joachim Karsch aus den Jahren 1935–1945, Berlin 1948.

Karsten, Ludwig. Norwegian painter, b. 1876 in Oslo; d. 1926 in Paris. He studied in Oslo and Paris, where he worked with Carrière and Matisse. His painting was strongly Expressionist in character, with an admixture of Impressionist influences, and the result is a powerful and vivid art that reveals his turbulent personality.

Kaspar, Ludwig. German sculptor, b. 1893; d. 1945. He was trained in the Neo-Classical tradition, but sought to break away from it by trying to find new forms of expression in his work.

Kassak, Lajos. Hungarian poet, painter and linocutter, b. 1887. He was connected with the Constructivists, and was a great advocate of their movement. He works in harsh, gloomy colours. He has published books on art, one written with Moholy-Nagy.

Kaus, Max. German painter, b. 1891 in Berlin. Kaus attended the School of Art and Crafts in Berlin-Charlottenburg up to 1913.

The crucial factor in Kaus' development was his friendship with Erich Heckel. His output consisted largely of graphic works up to about 1925, when he began to produce paintings in an Expressionist style derived from the *Brücke*. Although he moved towards abstract art after the Second World War his pictures are still prompted by visual experiences. Since 1945 he has held a professorial post at the College of Fine Arts in Berlin.

Kawara, On. Japanese painter, b. 1933 in Kariya. Kawara is self-taught. He made his début with a series called *Bathroom* which depicted an enclosed situation. Recently he has been engaged in conceptual art, with only a description of date and place. He now lives in New York.

Keinbusch, William Austin (von). American painter, b. 1914 in New York City. From 1920 to 1932 he attended the Buckley School, New York, and the Hotchkiss School, Lakeville, Conn. In 1936 he graduated *magna cum laude* and Phi Beta Kappa from Princeton University, where he majored in Fine Arts. He then studied at the Art Students' League and the Colorado Springs Fine Arts Center under Henry Varnum Poor (1936–7). In 1937 he went to Paris, where he studied with Abraham Rattner and at the Académie Colarossi (1937–8). Back in New York he studied with Anton Refregier (1940–1) and Stuart Davis at the New School for Social Research (1941–2). He did service in the United States Army (1942–6), and from then on he spent his summers in Maine and the rest of the year in New York, teaching at the Art School of the Brooklyn Museum. His scenes deal principally with Maine and particularly with its coast. Using sketches and photographs, he paints in his studio rather than in front of his subject. He works mainly in casein, a water medium which can be used either opaquely or transparently. All his work has a strong linear quality, as in *Gong Buoy* (1948, Fort Worth, Texas, Coll. Bill Bomar) which is dominated by trapezoidal forms and interlaced with a series of directionally oriented fine lines. *From Dirigo to Eagle Island* (1953, New York, Krauschaar Galleries), with its multi-layered horizontal landscape elements, is tied together by criss-crossing diagonals. While Marsden Hartley may be the source of his use of dark tones to isolate elements of the composition, his later works, such as *Maine, Winter* (1964, New York, Kraushaar Galleries), perhaps owes to the Abstract Expressionists its impetuous handling of paint and colour. The composition, with no fixed edges and its concentration towards the centre of elements bursting out from the core, seems very close in spirit to another artist of Maine scenes, John Marin.

D. Judd. 'Exhibition at Kraushaar Gallery', *Arts* 37, March 1963.

Kelder, Toon (Antonius Bernardus). Dutch painter and sculptor, b. 1894 in Rotterdam. After attending the Academy of Art in Rotterdam Kelder moved first to The Hague and then to Paris, where he continued his studies privately. During his early period he painted landscapes, figurative compositions and still lifes in a quasi-Romantic style but later went over to a more abstract type of composition. Then, when he was fifty years of age, he suddenly turned to sculpture, producing stylized wire constructions and —subsequently—solid, abstract sculptures derived from organic forms, which reveal the influence of Brancusi.

Exhibition catalogue, *Toon Kelder*, Stedelijk Museum, Amsterdam, 1960.

Kelly, Ellsworth. American painter, b. 1923 in Newburgh, New York. He studied first at the Boston School of Fine Arts, then at the École des Beaux-Arts, Paris (1948–54). In 1954 Kelly returned to New York, but the mark of his Paris years was strong on the development of his sensibility and style. In the late 1940s Kelly made low-relief wood constructions laced with string, based on actual representational forms abstracted into formal relationships. These indicated familiarity with both Jean Arp's reliefs and the Surrealistic-biomorphic shapes developed by Joan Miró. Matisse's late *papiers collés* (cut-outs) also helped form Kelly's hard-edge abstract manner. Although in his earliest paintings monochromatic colour was used only to define form, a concern with the strength and intensity of simple colour relationships increasingly informed his discrete abstract shapes. Kelly continued to draw his forms from nature, although their origins were finally obscured in unified and brilliant coloured surfaces (*Blue on White*, 1961, Racine, Wis., Coll. Johnson).

Because of his relative isolation from New York during the crucial early years of Abstract Expressionism, Kelly was able to sustain an independent and vital body of work based on different pictorial and personal premises. When he encountered problems with figure-ground interaction in some of his bright two-dimensional images, he resolved them through a highly original form of curved planar sculpture. This brilliantly coloured sculpture, characterized by strong silhouettes, developed both from a sculptural screen commission for the Philadelphia Transportation Building (1956) and from his own monochrome paintings composed of joined sections (1966–7). Their uninflected contiguous panels, painted in a spectrum sequence or in flat primary colours, avoided the suggestions of internal space or positive-negative relations produced by shapes painted on neutral backgrounds. The sculptures themselves often seem more two- than three-dimensional (reminiscent of Alexander Calder's painted metal stabiles), since they usually consist of only two thin bent or flapped aluminium planes (*Pony*, 1969, New York, Janis Gallery).

Kelly later moved beyond these problematic figure-ground relationships in a series of separate but joined panel paintings shaped to suggest volumetric structures seen in perspective. By carefully balancing intensely saturated colours of equal value against the orthogonal illusionism and depth suggested by the format, Kelly secured both the flatness of surface and the identity of the image with its physical support.

William Rubin. 'Ellsworth Kelly: The Big Form', *Art News* LXII, New York, November 1963.
Barbara Rose. 'The Sculpture of Ellsworth Kelly', *Artforum* V, No. 10, New York 1967.

Kelly, Sir Gerald. British painter, b. 1879 in London; d. 1972. He studied in Paris from 1901, and exhibited regularly in the Salon d'Automne. From 1909 he took part in the Royal Academy exhibitions. He became an Associate of the RA in 1922, and a full member in 1930. He was a member of the Modern Society of Portrait Painters (from 1907), the Royal Society of Portrait Painters (1904–9) and the National Portrait Society (1909–14). He was knighted in 1945, and in 1949 was elected President of the Royal Academy. In 1957 he had a large exhibition there.

Kelly, Harold Osman. American primitive painter, b. 1884 in Bucyrus, Ohio; d. 1955 in Blanket, Texas. Kelly left school at the age of 16 and went to work on a Pennsylvania farm. During his youth he worked in thirty states, as a muleskinner, farmer, logger, bull-whacker, mill hand, sheepherder, freighter and rancher. In 1921 he and his wife moved to Texas where he remained for the rest of his life. His career as a painter began when he painted water-colours to give as Christmas gifts. He began painting in oils in 1949, a year before his first one-man show at the Dallas Museum of Fine Arts. Like other primitive painters such as Grandma Moses, John Kane and Joseph Pickett, he was untrained and painted from memory. His scenes are mainly western, but approached via a folk tradition rather than in the boisterous manner of Remington. Handled in bright, lively colours, his compositions are relatively flat, often with a tilted plane. His figures are most often represented in silhouette with little interest in modelling (*Eagle Wagon Yard*, Lubbock, Texas, Coll. Mrs. L. T. Patton). In addition to such western scenes he also reverted to the days of his adventurous, travelling youth (*Ohio River Sidewheeler*, Fort Worth, Texas, Coll. Fred C. Cutter) and his childhood, as in the snow scene depicted in *Ohio Farm—The Monnett Place* (Dallas, Texas, Coll. Mr. and Mrs. Frederick M. Mayer).

Retrospective exhibition catalogue, *H. O. Kelly (1884–1955)*, Dallas Museum of Fine Arts, Dallas 1960.
W. W. Johnson. *Kelly Blue*, New York 1960.

Kemeny, Zoltan. Hungarian-Swiss sculptor, b. 1907 in Banica, Transylvania; d. 1965 in Zürich. Kemeny studied architecture from 1924 to 1927 and painting from 1927 to 1930, both in Budapest. From 1930 to 1940 he was in Paris, where he pursued a number of occupations. He then lived for two years in Marseilles before moving to Switzerland and spending the rest of his life in Zürich, where he acquired Swiss citizenship in 1957.

In 1946 Kemeny began to incorporate a number of different materials into his work. In 1951 he produced his 'Translucent Reliefs', which were set up in front of electric lights. Then, in 1954, came the metal reliefs which brought him public recognition. In the course of time he introduced mass-produced articles into these reliefs on an ever increasing scale. The first of these industrial products were made of lead, zinc or iron, but later the majority were copper or aluminium. Despite the informal appearance of his reliefs Kemeny always worked according to a well-defined plan. He also had frequent recourse to archaeological, mineralogical and electronic models. In his *Images en Relief* Kemeny translated rhythmical problems and problems arising out of the grouping of individual standardized components into a genuinely poetic style, which is never mannered and never dogmatic.

Exhibition catalogue, *Zoltan Kemeny*, Musée National d'Art Moderne, Paris 1966.

Kennington, Eric. British painter and sculptor, b. 1888 in London; d. 1960. He studied at the Lambeth School of Art, 1905–7, and also at the City and Guilds School, Kennington. He enlisted in the army as a private in 1915 and was invalided out in 1916. From 1916 to 1919 he was an official war artist. Between the wars he worked mainly as a portrait painter, but he also did illustrations to T. E. Lawrence's *Seven Pillars of Wisdom*, travelling to Arabia for this purpose in 1920. It was at this time also that he did his most important sculptures, the *Monument to the 24th Division*, Battersea Park, 1924, the *Memorial to the Missing*, Soissons, and the sculptures on the Shakespeare Memorial Theatre, Stratford, 1930. In the Second World War he was again an official war artist. It is for his works in this capacity that he is best known, especially for his drawings of individual soldiers and for his studies of the ordinary daily life of soldiers. He was elected to the Royal Academy in 1959.

C. Dodgson and C. E. Montagu. *Artists at the Front IV*, London 1918.
Eric Kennington. *Drawing the RAF*, London 1942.

Kent, Adaline. American sculptress, b. 1900 in Kentfield, California; d. 1957 in Marin County. She studied in San Francisco, and with Bourdelle in Paris, then travelled around Europe and Central America until her marriage in 1930. She then settled in San Francisco, and had several one-man shows there and in New York and Paris. In 1939 she made a colossal *Musician* for the San Francisco World's Fair; she was represented at the São Paulo Bienal in 1956.

Kent, Rockwell. American painter and illustrator, b. 1882 in Tarrytown Heights, New York; d. 1971 in New York. Kent was a graduate of the Horace Mann School in New York and a student of architecture at Columbia University. Kent's artistic training came under the aegis of William Merritt Chase, Abbott Thayer and—most significantly—Robert Henri. He first exhibited in 1905 at the National Academy of Design in New York, and was given a one-man show the following year. Kent and Henri organized an independent show to run concurrently with the more traditional exhibition held at the National Academy in the spring of 1910. His style at this time reveals an innate love of nature and an interest in light and shadow over broad planes (*Toilers of the Sea*, 1907, New Britain, Conn., Art Museum of the New Britain Institute). These works are close to the conceptions of Winslow Homer, although handled more freely and with a more loaded brush. Kent's early works are mainly landscapes and marine paintings, in which he employed the dark palette used by The Eight and by his fellow students George Bellows and Guy Pène du Bois. With these artists, as well as with Pop Hart and John Steuart Curry, he exhibited in New York at the Whitney Studio Club before 1920. Kent's admiration for William Blake is revealed in some of his later paintings (*North Wind*, 1919, Washington, D.C., Phillips Gallery), and especially in his book illustrations. Unlike Blake, however, are his emphatic contrasts of strong darks and lights and his solid geometricizing forms—two key features of his paintings after about 1920 (*Wake Up, America!*, c. 1942, Au Sable Forks, N.Y., coll. of artist). He was a wanderer and adventurer, living in Maine, Newfoundland and Alaska. Among the published records of his life, work, travels and philosophy are *Wilderness: A Journal of Quiet Adventure in Alaska* (1920), *Rockwellkentiana* (1933), *This Is My Own* (1940), *It's Me, O Lord* (1955) and *Of Men and Mountains* (1959). Kent also published works expressing his political and social philosophy. In 1962 he was elected an honorary member of the Academy of Art of the USSR.

Rockwellkentiana: Few Works and Many Pictures by Rockwell Kent and Carl Zigrosser, New York 1933.
Rockwell Kent. *This Is My Own*, New York 1940.

Kerkovius, Ida. German painter, b. 1879 in Riga. Kerkovius is a German from the Russian part of the Baltic. In 1903 she met Hölzel in Dachau. Subsequently, after attending a school of art in Berlin for a brief period in 1908, she studied under him at the Academy of Art in Stuttgart, entering the 'masters' class' in 1910, which also included Baumeister, Schlemmer and Itten. From 1920 to 1923 she attended the Bauhaus during the winter terms, where she worked in the weaving shop and was taught by Klee, Kandinsky and Itten. In 1933 when the Nazis came to power, she was forbidden to exhibit and in the following year she left Germany, spending the next five years on educational visits to Norway, Belgium, France and Bulgaria. She is now living in Stuttgart.

Kerkovius' lively and gay colour compositions, in which a spontaneous, almost primitive quality is combined with great technical precision, reveal the influence of Hölzel (who became a lifelong friend), the Bauhaus (especially Klee) and Jawlensky (another friend and one whom Kerkovius greatly admired). There is also a rich vein of fantasy running through her works, an attribute that is doubtless of Baltic provenance. But the really dominant feature of her paintings is their colour. During her early period she used simple signs painted in intense, luminous colours to depict the objective world, working first in oils and subsequently in pastels. Then, in 1933, she entered on a second phase, in which she produced both pure abstract and objective compositions. From the mid-1950s onwards she also worked in stained glass, designing windows for various buildings including the Stuttgart *Rathaus* (1955). Another technique, which Kerkovius put to excellent use, is that of weaving; in the course of her career she has produced numerous extremely attractive picture tapestries.

K. Leonhard. *Ida Kerkovius: Leben und Werk*, Cologne 1967.

Kermadec, Eugène de. French painter and sculptor, b. 1899 in Paris. After spending his youth on the island of Guadeloupe in the Antilles Kermadec returned to Paris in 1920. During his early period he was influenced by the Cubists, but in 1927 began to evolve a personal style, which is best illustrated by the landscapes and female nudes of 1930. After the Second World War Kermadec came under the influence of the *École de Paris*, and since 1956 has been painting abstracts. He is now living in Paris.

Exhibition catalogue, *Kermadec*, Kunsthalle, Berne 1958.

Ket, Dick Hendrik (Dick). Dutch painter, b. 1902 in Den Helder; d. 1940 in Bennekom. Ket was a pupil at the *Kunstoefening* in Arnheim from 1922 to 1925. Unable to venture far from home due to a heart condition, he concentrated on self-portraits and still lifes. Like the Magic Realists Koch, Willink and Hynckes, Ket was very much preoccupied with textural qualities and fine detail.

Dick Ket: 1902–1940, Gemeentemuseum, Arnheim 1962.

Khnopff, Fernand. Belgian painter, b. 1858; d. 1921. He studied under Gustave Moreau, and was influenced by the English Pre-Raphaelites. One of the favourite painters of the Decadence, he did many pictures of sphinxes and other monsters of legend. He was also inspired by Symbolist writers such as Maeterlinck, Mallarmé and Verhaeren.

Kienholz, Edward. American painter and tableau maker, b. 1927. He produces tableaux, situations which envelop the onlooker and involve him physically. Often he creates realistic 'environments', exact reproductions of the everyday world. He is a 'funk' artist, using tawdry, shoddy material and depicting the warped nature of some events and situations of today.

Kiesler, Frederick. American sculptor and architect, b. 1896 in Vienna; d. 1965 in New York. While in Vienna Kiesler studied at a technical school and then at the Academy of Fine Arts. After around 1921 he began experimenting in architecture. He was also actively interested in theatre and, in addition to designing theatre buildings, worked extensively as a set designer, both in Europe and the United States. His earliest one-man exhibitions of sculpture in New York were given at the Museum of Modern Art (1951, 1960) and at the Leo Castelli Gallery (1961, 1962); in 1964 a retrospective exhibition was presented at the Guggenheim Museum.

Around 1923 Kiesler became associated with the Dutch *de Stijl* group, and in the late 1930s and the 1940s with the Surrealists. Primarily, however, he worked independently, developing his own theories, both in writing and in practice, under the general heading of Correalism—a concept emphasizing space-time continuity and the inclusion of an environmental context in art. One of Kiesler's main concerns was the expression of infinity, both in relation to natural and man-made forms. The first important example of this tendency was the architectural model for the 'Endless House' (1923), which was originally intended for a 'Space Theater', but was later gradually modified into a more sculptural form and was exhibited by the Museum of Modern Art, New York, in 1960. Kiesler's preoccupation with space and endlessness is also reflected in his sculpture, which is generally based on *motifs* from nature and the cosmos, such as the environmental *Galaxy* (c. 1950) and *Marriage of Heaven and Earth* (1961–4), both in the Martha Jackson Gallery in New York. The latter work was part of a landscape series of 1961–4. Closely connected with the concepts expressed in these sculptures was Kiesler's insistence that no object, either of art or nature, can exist without environment and that a work of art must include its context. Kiesler's art, then, is strongly environmental and is, moreover, a fusion of different media—sculpture, painting, architecture and theatre. It is also a highly Romantic art, resulting from his theories about the importance of time and space, as well as from his concept of creativity as a spontaneous, searching and instinctive process.

Catalogue, *Frederick Kiesler: Environmental Sculpture*, Solomon R. Guggenheim Museum, New York 1964.
Frederick J. Kiesler. *Inside the Endless House*, New York 1966.

Kinetic art. This concept, which comes from the scientific sphere, was introduced into art criticism in 1920. It refers to all forms of art in which movement appears to take place or actually does take place. This movement may have its origin either in the work of art or in the eye of the viewer. Often it is induced by the effect of light. Kinetic art calls for a new kind of perception: firm statuary forms are constantly dissolved by the force of the movement; the changing optical perspectives irritate and deceive the eye, forcing it to change its focus again and again. The sources of kinetic art are to be found in automatic machines, mechanical marionettes, motion pictures, etc. The introduction of real movement into sculpture was postulated by Boccioni as early as 1912 in his *Technical Manifesto of Futuristic Sculpture*, and in 1920 Duchamp began work on his 'optical precision instruments', which incorporate time sequences as structural components. In the same year the brothers Gabo and Pevsner called for a new art form based on movement. In their *Realistic Manifesto* they rejected the traditional view that only static rhythms were admissible as elements of art, insisting that, on the contrary, the most important components for twentieth-century artists were kinetic rhythms. In 1922 Moholy-Nagy and Alfred Kemény composed a further manifesto, in which they advocated a 'dynamic-constructive art form'. Seven years later, in 1929, Moholy-Nagy reformulated this concept when he spoke of a 'kinetic-constructive system of forces'. He saw the new painter as a co-ordinator of 'light-relations' and the new sculptor as a co-ordinator of 'voluminal and kinetic relations'. For Moholy-Nagy kinetic sculpture constituted the maximum sublimation of volume. Other precursors of contemporary kinetic art include: Thomas Wilfred, who exhibited his 'Clavilux' light apparatus in New York in 1922; Ludwig Hirschfeld-Mack and Kurt Schwertfeger, who both sought to create a 'synthesis of movement, light, colour and form'. In the 1950s these ideas were taken up and further developed all over the world. The Brazilian artist Abraham Palatnik exhibited his cinechromatic apparatuses from 1950 onwards; Frank Malina showed his 'Lunidyne' and 'Reflectodyne', while Nicolas Schöffer subjected rotating sculptures to the effects of light and, from 1954 onwards, created large-format kinetic sculptures governed by electronic mechanisms. Other artists have concentrated on sculptures which produce an impression of movement. Victor Vasarély's *cinétisme plastique* is a case in point. Various associations of kinetic artists have been formed including *Zero* (1958), *Gruppo T*, *Gruppo N* (1959), *Groupe de Recherche d'Art Visuel* (1961) and *EAT* (1966).

M. Compton. *Optical and Kinetic Art*, London 1947.
Exhibition catalogue, *Bewogen Beweging*, Amsterdam 1961.
Exhibition catalogue, *Nouvelle Tendance*, Paris 1964.
Exhibition catalogue, *Kinetic and Optic Art Today*, Buffalo 1965.
Exhibition catalogue, *Kunstlichkunst*, Eindhoven 1966.
F. Popper. *Naissance de l'art cinétique*, Paris 1967.

King, Philip. British sculptor, b. 1934 in Tunis. King came to England in 1945. From 1954 to 1957 he read languages at the University of Cambridge. In 1957–8 he studied under the sculptor Anthony Caro at the St. Martin's School of Art in London. In 1958–9 he was one of Henry Moore's assistants. Since 1959 he has been teaching at the St. Martin's School. He is now living in London.

King is the first English sculptor to work in polyester and glass fibre. He uses an 'additive' system, that is, he adds one component to the other until the sculpture is complete. Some of his works are painted in poster-type colours, others are left in the neutral colour of the synthetic material. In 1968 a considerable number of King's works were shown at the Biennale in Venice.

J. Russell. *Art in America* 55, No. 3, 1967.

Kinley, Peter. British painter, b. 1926 in Vienna. Kinley came to Britain in 1938. He studied at Düsseldorf Academy, 1948–9, and at the St. Martin's School of Art in London from 1949 to 1953. Like Keith Vaughan and several other painters of the 1950s, he was influenced by the de Staël exhibition of 1953. His work is basically representational (figures and landscapes). Like de Staël he works with the palette knife in flat areas of strong and textured colour which compose the figure and *motif* without disturbing the plane surface of the canvas, relying entirely on colour for depth and recession.

Kirchner, Ernst Ludwig. German painter, b. 1880 in Aschaffenburg; d. 1938 in Davos. In 1903–4 Kirchner attended the art school run by Debschitz and Obrist in Munich, and in 1905, when he had completed his architectural studies, he became a full-time painter. In the same year he joined with Bleyl, Heckel and Schmidt-Rottluff in founding the *Brücke* association. In 1911, after visiting Switzerland, Kirchner settled in Berlin, where he and Pechstein founded the *MUIM* Institute (Moderner Unterricht im Malen—Modern Training in Painting). In 1912 he was with Otto Müller in Bohemia and also painted murals for the *Sonderausstellung* in Cologne. From 1912 to 1914 Kirchner was in Fehmarn, and in 1914–15 he joined the German

forces but suffered a complete physical and mental breakdown in the following year which necessitated treatment in a sanatorium in Königstein (Taunus). From there he moved to Staffelalp, near Davos, but in 1917–18 was again obliged to seek treatment, on this occasion in Dr. Binswanger's sanatorium in Kreuzlingen on Lake Constance. After his release in 1918 Kirchner settled in Längmatt, near Frauenkirch. In 1922 he collaborated with the weaver Lise Gujer and in 1923 rented a house in the Sertig valley. In 1927 he became friendly with Dr. Bauer of Davos. From 1929 to 1932 Kirchner designed murals for the Folkwang Museum in Essen, but in 1933 he was deprived of his membership of the Academy of Fine Arts in Berlin. In 1936 he visited Klee in Berne. In 1937, 639 of his works were removed from German museums and confiscated by the National Socialists. The next year Kirchner committed suicide.

Kirchner exemplifies more clearly than any other artist of his generation the dichotomy implicit in German Expressionist painting. On the one hand the German Expressionists sought to establish strict formal structures, whilst on the other they tried to use their paintings as a means of expressing their innermost personality, a process that might quite conceivably lead to the total destruction of the artist's ego. Kirchner was the most gifted, the most sensitive and the most vulnerable of the *Brücke* artists. Driven onwards by his missionary zeal, by his illness and by drugs, he became the most biting chronicler of his day. Kirchner's development is clearly demonstrated by his extensive oeuvre, which includes both paintings and graphic works. Inspired in the first instance by the French Neo-Impressionists, by the frenzied brushwork of van Gogh, the psychological subtleties of Munch and the originality of the South Sea Island primitives, he evolved a revolutionary early style (by 1910–11) based on tortuous, flame-like forms. Subsequently, when Kirchner saw works by the Fauves (especially Matisse), he heightened his colours and between 1911 and 1913, i.e. during his Berlin period, produced a series of psychological portraits and scenes of big city life which are amongst the most perfect examples of Expressionist art. The tremendous tension in the work which he produced at that time was a pointer to his impending breakdown. When it came, he moved to the Swiss mountains in the hope that, by communing with nature, he might find his way back to his own inner self. Certainly the mountains had a far-reaching effect on him, for during his Swiss period he became more and more engrossed in purely artistic problems. Although Kirchner never abandoned natural forms he certainly modified them and in doing so produced what he himself described as a 'completely new form'. He also tried to express temporal sequences in spatial terms, thus creating simultaneous structures that are reminiscent of certain aspects of Picasso's work: formative elements are replaced by rhythmical and ornamental factors whilst natural forms are simplified to arabesques. But Kirchner suffered from a depressive condition which was exacerbated by the cultural policies pursued by the National Socialists and, not long after setting out on this new departure, he took his own life.

Will Grohmann. *E. L. Kirchner*, New York 1961.
Donald E. Gordon. *E. L. Kirchner*, New York and Munich 1968.

Kisling, Moïse. French painter and graphic artist, b. 1891 in Cracow; d. 1953 near Lyons. After studying under J. Pankiewicz at the Academy of Art in Cracow Kisling enrolled at the École des Beaux-Arts in Paris in 1910.

During his early period Kisling was influenced by the French Impressionists and, above all, by Cézanne. Later he passed through brief Cubist and Constructivist phases before adopting a more Realistic approach in the 1920s. The works of this period were executed in a smooth, polished style with gentle contours and soft, delicately modulated colours. In 1913 Kisling met Picasso and Gris in the Pyrenees. In 1914 he exhibited with the Indépendants. In 1916 he visited Spain, and in 1918–19 Marseilles and St. Tropez. In 1919 he had his first representative exhibition in Paris.

Carl Einstein. *Moïse Kisling*, Leipzig 1922.
Georges Charensol. *Moïse Kisling*, Paris 1948.

Kitaj, R. B. American painter, b. 1932 in Ohio. In 1950 Kitaj studied at the Cooper Union Art Institute, New York, then in 1951 at the Academy of Fine Arts, Vienna. He lived in various parts of Europe, and also worked as a seaman between 1951 and 1955 when he was called up for service in France and Germany. Leaving the army he went to the Ruskin School of Art, Oxford, and then the Royal College until 1961. From 1961 to 1967 he taught at the Camberwell and the Slade Schools. In 1967 he returned to America to work at the Berkeley campus of the University of California. Although an American Kitaj's work has closer affinities with the work of the younger generation of British painters than with that of his contemporaries in the States. He was one of the leaders of the movement in Britain away from the abstraction of the fifties towards a kind of painting which endeavoured to reconcile the lessons of Cubism and Matisse with complex subject matter. The catalogues of his one-man shows in London in 1963 and 1965 included lengthy quotations explaining the subjects of the pictures, but he endeavours also to express this complex subject matter through a single compact visual image. If the result is sometimes a little overloaded, it has also been at times very successful.

Kjarval, Johannes Sveinsson. Icelandic painter, b. 1885 in Reykjavik. After starting out in life as a fisherman Kjarval went to England, where he studied the works of Turner, and then to Denmark, where he attended the Academy of Art in Copenhagen. He returned to Iceland in the early 1920s. His oeuvre consists for the most part of landscapes, which depict the rockstrewn mountains and moors of his native land. He paints in a Lyrical Expressionist style, using rich broken colours and rapid brushwork that is reminiscent of van Gogh. There is a visionary quality about his landscapes, many of which recall the kind of magical world portrayed by primitive artists.

H. K. Laxness. *Johannes Sveinsson Kjarval*, 1950 (in English).

Klapheck, Konrad. German painter, b. 1935 in Düsseldorf, Germany. Klapheck was a student at the Academy of Art in Düsseldorf from 1954 to 1958. In 1955 he painted his first *Typewriter*. This marked the beginning of his campaign to create 'a prosaic superobjectivity', i.e. an art form capable of precise definition, with which to counter the Tachist and Lyrical Abstract creeds. He has continued in this vein, painting functional objects such as typewriters, sewing machines, water taps, telephones, shoes, keys, flatirons, bicycle bells, etc., and frequently running one object into the other. In c. 1959 the constructive element gained a temporary ascendancy and for a while Klapheck's machines were radically simplified. Subsequently, however, he reverted to his former, more detailed presentation. Klapheck uses both new and old advertisements as models, reproducing the illustrations with extremely delicate brushwork. He is now living in Düsseldorf.

Klee, Paul. German-Swiss painter, watercolourist and etcher, b. 1879 in Münchenbuchsee, near Berne; d. 1940 in Muralto, near Locarno. His father was a German musician, and music was always to mean a great deal to Klee. He learned to play the violin as a child and he married a musician in 1906. 'Klee the painter', his friend Lyonel Feininger remarked, 'is unthinkable without Klee the musician.' From 1898 to 1900, Klee was in Munich to study painting: first with Knirr and later at the Academy of Fine Arts under Stuck. In 1901–2, he visited Italy with the sculptor Hermann Haller; they visited Genoa, Pisa, Rome and Naples, where Klee was more interested in the Aquarium than the traditional tourist attractions.

Klee's first significant works were etchings; he worked mainly in black and white until 1912. Prints such as the *Virgin in a Tree* (1903), *Two Men Meet, Each Supposing the Other to be of Higher Rank* (1903) or the *Hero with a Wing* (1905) belong to an Expressionist style, half fantastic, half satirical, nourished by a wide variety of influences: Goya, Blake, Fuseli,

Böcklin, Redon and Ensor—and, among writers, Poe, Hoffmann, Gogol and Baudelaire.

In 1906, Klee married Lily Stumpf, a pianist and music teacher, and they settled in Munich, which was to be their home until 1920. During this same period, Klee's artistic allegiances and his own art broadened and changed. He came to admire van Gogh, Cézanne and Matisse (1908–10), and friendship with Kandinsky and Marc involved him in the foundation of the *Blauer Reiter* (Blue Rider) group in 1912. In 1913, Klee visited Paris, where he came into contact with Apollinaire, Picasso and Delaunay. In 1914 he visited Tunis and Kairouan with Macke, a trip that brought out in him a new and intense awareness of colour. From this time he concentrated on painting in watercolour.

In 1910, fifty-six of his works had been shown at the Berne Museum, and subsequently in Basle, Zürich and Winterthur; in the following year there was a one-man show at the Thannhauser Gallery in Munich. From 1916 to 1918, he served in the army. 1920 was a particularly auspicious year for Klee: 362 works were shown at the Goltz Gallery in Munich; two monographs on him were published; while on 25 November he was appointed to the faculty of the Weimar Bauhaus by Gropius (in 1926 he followed the institution to Dessau). With Jawlensky, Feininger and Kandinsky, he founded the group known as *Die Blaue Vier* (The Blue Four) in 1924, the year of his first exhibition in the United States. In 1925, he published the *Pädagogische Skizzenbuch* (*Pedagogical Sketchbook*) and was given his first one-man show in Paris. A visit to Egypt took place in the winter of 1928–9. By 1 April 1931 he was on the faculty of the Düsseldorf Academy. Dismissed by the Nazis in 1933 (seventeen of his pictures were included in the 1937 exhibition of 'Degenerate Art'), he left Germany and settled in Berne. The first signs of serious illness appeared in 1935, five years before his death.

Klee's art, among the most remarkable achievements of twentieth-century painting, is exceptionally difficult to describe and categorize. His elusive and seemingly frail idiom has a way of making ordinary style analysis seem both clumsy and irrelevant. At the same time, he was a man of his age, influenced by Expressionism, Cubism and Surrealism, and by the enhanced, post-Freudian interest in dreams and the subconscious. One of his artistic intentions, he once remarked, was 'to make memories abstract'; and many of his paintings seem like imaginative dreamscapes (*Dance of the Red Skirts*, 1924, Berne, private collection). He once defined his stylistic method as 'taking a line for a walk', a phrase that neatly underlines the deceptive simplicity of his art, with its ambiguous aura of sophistication and child-like innocence. It is hardly surprising that his work should have been compared to the unselfconscious productions of young children and to the no less

personal creations of the insane. But with Klee's work it is particularly important *not* to try and pin down his images. He created a hieroglyphic language, which is sometimes representational, sometimes not, and whose beauty, meaning and association—which are indivisible—lie in the visual appearance of the hieroglyphs themselves: *Battle-Scene from the Comic Operatic Fantasy 'The Seafarer'* (1923, Basle, private collection) is in a very strict sense indescribable.

Klee's art makes great demands on the spectator, who must be able to combine an adult response to colour harmony and abstraction (which grew stronger in his work in the 1930s), influenced by primitive art, with a child's simple sense of wonder and capacity to believe in the slenderest links between ordinary life and extraordinary pictorial form. Klee's style has been much imitated by illustrators and cartoonists, but it remains unique.

C. Giedion-Welcker. *Paul Klee*, New York 1952.
Werner Haftmann. *The Mind and Work of Paul Klee*, London and New York 1954.
Will Grohmann. *Paul Klee*, New York 1957.

Klein, Cesar. German painter and theatrical designer, b. 1876 in Hamburg; d. 1954 in Pansdorf. Klein studied in Hamburg, Düsseldorf and Berlin. In 1914 he was appointed Director of the Werkbund and in 1918 became a founder member of the *Novembergruppe*. From 1919 to 1933 he taught at the institute attached to the Museum of Arts and Crafts in Berlin. In 1937 he settled in Pansdorf, near Lübeck.

After coming to terms with Cubism, Expressionism and Surrealism Klein evolved an abstract style based on objective forms.

Klein, Yves. French painter, b. 1928 in Nice; d. 1962 in Paris. Yves Klein began his short, spectacular career in 1946. He seems to have avoided any significant academic training, though both his parents were painters. Since he was obviously possessed of a strong, individual personality, some measure of parent rejection very probably helped his rapid adoption of methods which were at that time considered highly unorthodox.

By the end of the first half of the twentieth century the battles of the pioneering anti-traditionalists were virtually won. The choice of the artist in subject matter, range and type of expression was practically limitless. It still remained, however, to question effectively the traditional form of the painter's expression, which was the easel painting or picture. By his work, and his actions, Klein proceeded to attack this standpoint, and in his subsequent development set many precedents which have been eagerly and widely followed.

Among his early work was a series of monochromatic panels. These performed two functions. On the one hand, since they were trowelled-on textured pastes of single colour, they were virtually sections of the wall where the painting was, thus denying its existence; on the other hand, they demonstrated his esoteric thinking (he was a Rosicrucian) of the cosmic energy of colour. In the final stages he used blue only, as in his view it was the most significant colour. In 1958 he held an exhibition which was simply the bare walls of the Galerie Iris Clert, in Paris. As a gesture, this was an exhibition of the 'Void'; at the same time it was the demonstrated end of the easel-painted, gallery painting.

His interest in judo, and the importance he attached to ceremonial procedure, led to a visit to Japan in 1952–3. His use of ceremony is exampled in his *Anthropometries* produced during 1958–60. These were performances, with an audience, of nude blue-painted models imprinting themselves on to the canvases, under his direction, with the accompaniment of instrumental musicians. In the *Cosmogonies* of 1960 his esoteric thinking led to producing works aided by natural weathering by exposure (air and water) followed by his *Fire-Paintings* (fire) which used the destructive effects of a blow-lamp.

Since his ideas seriously challenged the attitudes of the School of Paris, it is understandable that he was not popular in France. It was in Germany and Italy that he was sponsored. He did extensive mural decorations in the opera house in Gelsenkirchen, Germany. Somewhat surprisingly he was not well received in America, where he exhibited just before he died in 1961. The critic Pierre Restany issued a manifesto in 1960 extolling what he called the 'New Realism', a movement against abstract painting. He includes Klein, with Christo, Armand, Tinguely and others, in this group of artists.

Klimt, Gustav. Austrian painter, b. 1862 in Baumgarten; d. 1918 in Vienna. The eldest son of the engraver Ernst Klimt, he attended the School of Arts and Crafts of the Austrian Museum in Vienna. From 1883 to 1892 he worked with his brother Ernst and the painter Franz Matsch on large, allegorical paintings characterized by their intense colour, derived from Makart, and by the ornamental influence of Laufberger. Of his work of this period, Klimt's spandrels for the Kunsthistorisches Museum in Vienna appear a conscious recreation of Egyptian, Hellenic and ancient Italian styles. In 1892 his brother died. In 1897 Klimt became the first president of a newly formed, independent artistic organization, the *Vereinigung Bildender Künstler Österreichs* (Vienna Secession); he contributed regularly to the early numbers of *Ver Sacrum*, the organ of the Secession. This was the beginning of a new style, both Symbolistic (*Pallas Athene*, 1898, Historisches Museum der Stadt Wien) and decorative (*Die Musik II*, 1898, destroyed) in character, and revealing the decisive influence of *Jugendstil* decoration (poster for the first Secession exhibition). The antithesis between naturalism and stylization remained characteristic of all his later work. In 1902 he created his Beethoven frieze, conceived as part of the decorative setting for the showing of Max Klinger's statue of Beethoven at the fourteenth exhibition of the Secession; it reveals the influence of Mackintosh and perhaps Beardsley. During this period, Klimt worked on the designs for the ceiling of the great hall of Vienna University (*Philosophy*, 1899–1907, *Medicine*, 1900–7, *Jurisprudence*, 1903–7, formerly Österreichische Staatsgalerie; destroyed). These paintings were bitterly attacked by conservative elements within the university and the government, and were finally returned to the artist after a prolonged scandal; these works have now become recognized as Klimt's most important essays in the field of monumental art. *Jurisprudence*, in particular, looks forward to the mature style of the frieze which Klimt was commissioned to design for the dining room of Hoffmann's Palais Stoclet in Brussels (cartoons 1905–9; frieze executed 1909–11). This work is characteristic of Klimt's later painting in its use of geometrical shapes, decorative function of colour and, in particular, in its erotic subject matter.

E. Pirchan. *Gustav Klimt*, Vienna 1956.
Fritz Novotny and Johannes Dobai. *Gustav Klimt*, London and New York 1968.

Kline, Franz. American painter, b. 1910 in Wilkes-Barre, Pa.; d. 1962. His early training in painting was received at Boston University (1931–5) under Frank Durkee, John Grosman and Henry Hensche. Setting out for Paris, he settled instead in London, studying with Bernard Adams, Steven Spurrier and Frederick Whiting. While in London he married Elizabeth Parsons, a dancer with the Sadler's Wells Ballet. When he returned to New York in 1939, he was executing rather traditional canvases (*Palmerton, Pa.*, 1941, Coll. Dr. and Mrs. Theodore J. Edlich, Jr.) which developed into a bolder, more painterly approach and a style based wholly on traditional principles of abstract art (*The Dancer*, 1946, Coll. Dr. and Mrs. Theodore J. Edlich, Jr.). In the late 1940s and early 1950s this abstraction pervaded even in works of specific subject. *Rocker* (1951, Coll. Dr. and Mrs. Theodore J. Edlich, Jr.) reveals a great freedom of handling and stroke as well as a certain eastern quality of calligraphy. In 1950 he was given his first one-man show at the Egan Gallery, New York. At this time he executed *Chief* (New York, Museum of Modern Art), a canvas of tremendous boldness with its strong black strokes against a white background. Named for a famous train, this well-known work echoes Kline's fascination with railroads which can be seen throughout his oeuvre, from his early works of the 1940s until the very end of his career (*Caboose*, 1961, New York, Marlborough Gerson Gallery). Throughout the 1950s his painting career was coupled with one of teaching (Black Mountain

College, N.C.; Pratt Institute, Brooklyn, N.Y.; Philadelphia Museum School of Art). His works were included in the Fourth São Paulo Bienal, Brazil (1957), and the 30th Venice Biennale (1960). Towards the end of his career he continued the same virile approach seen in *Chief*, though incorporating vibrant colour which determines the relative positions of areas of canvas (*Provincetown II*, 1959, New York, Marlborough-Gerson Gallery). A great simplicity of form, often revealing a large dark area placed against a plain background, with a decreased sense of the painterly and a growing awareness of mass, are seen in his large late canvas entitled *Caboose*.

John Gordon. Exhibition catalogue, *Franz Kline 1910–1962*, Whitney Museum of American Art, New York 1968.

Klinger, Max. German painter, graphic artist and sculptor, b. 1857 in Leipzig; d. 1920 at Groszjena, near Naumburg. Klinger enrolled at the Karlsruhe Academy in 1874, where he studied under Gussow. In the following year, when Gussow moved to Berlin, he accompanied him, and it was there that he received his first large commission when he was asked to decorate the Villa Albers in the late 1870s. From 1883 to 1886 he was in Paris, where he laid the foundations of his monumental style of painting. From Paris Klinger went to Berlin. Then, from 1888 to 1893, he lived in Rome with the painter Stauffer-Bern. There he became still more deeply imbued with the spirit of Classical art and also received a further stimulus from the Italian landscape. After his return to Germany he settled in Leipzig; his house became the focal point of the artistic life of the city.

Klinger was one of the best known of the German *Jugendstil* painters. But his work suffered from his inability to decide between the rival attractions of idealism and naturalism. This is particularly true of his large-format paintings, but it also applies to his sculptures. His polychrome sculpture of *Beethoven* (1886–1902) is a case in point. This work, which formed the basis of Klinger's reputation during his lifetime, no longer meets with the same unqualified approval. But Klinger's greatest and most influential achievement was his graphic oeuvre. Like Stauffer-Bern, he insisted that graphic art must be regarded as a discipline in its own right and, by doing so, helped to raise its status. His etchings are his most sensitive works in this medium and include many well-known prints such as the series *Intermezzi* and *A Life*, the *Love* cycle dedicated to Böcklin and the Surrealist *Paraphrase on the Discovery of a Glove* of 1881. These symbolistic and fantastic graphic works, which reveal the influence of both Goya and Menzel, were extremely influential in their turn. Such widely differing artists as Kokoschka and de Chirico, Käthe Kollwitz and Otto Dix were all affected by them.

H. W. Singer. *Max Klinger: Radierungen, Stiche und Steindrucke*, Berlin 1909.
Zeichnung von Max Klinger, Leipzig 1912.
Willy Pastor. *Max Klinger*, Berlin 1918.

Knaths, Karl. American painter, b. 1891 in Wisconsin; d. 1971. He grew up in Milwaukee and never saw an original painting until he went to Chicago at the age of 20, where he began his studies at the Chicago Art Institute in 1912. Naturally conversant with the outdoors (the love of his early years), Knaths was initially drawn to the work of the Impressionists, but soon felt that their colouristic exaggerations were overly sensual and superficial. Even after the impact of the 1913 Armory Show (which travelled to Chicago), in which Matisse's and Cézanne's paintings appeared, Knaths still preferred a certain subdued and remote quality in the works of artists such as Millet, or in some rural scenes by van Gogh. He later admitted that he did not at first appreciate the paintings by Matisse, but was strongly attracted to the work of Cézanne. The latter's paintings revealed to him a method of rendering form concisely, although Knaths' version of abstraction always remained aloof from direct association with particular movements and schools. Abstract design and the poetic and spiritual possibilities of the simplest restructuring of nature were his primary concerns, and he tried to combine a deeply felt mystical attitude with an economical, though inventive, visual imagery. In 1919 Knaths settled in Provincetown, Cape Cod, often painting the seascapes around him (*Maritime*, 1931, Washington, D.C., Phillips Collection) in fresh, pure colours. His paintings are never literal translations of objects or scenes, for his interest is in the dynamics of space and pictorial design as metaphors in themselves. Knaths strongly believed in the correspondences between musical intervals, colour harmonies, and proportions, claiming they all arose from a common source. His art clearly reveals an awareness of Cubism, especially of the work of Georges Braque and of the American Abstractionists with whom he exhibited in the 1930s —Balcomb Greene (b. 1904), Ad Reinhardt, Giorgio Cavallon (b. 1904), Carl Holty (b. 1900) and others —yet it retains a particularly serene sensitivity to materials and subject matter throughout its range of forms and design. Many of Knaths' paintings are in the Phillips Collection in Washington, D.C., such as *Harvest* (1932–33) and *The Sun* (1950). Paintings in other collections include *Eliphaz* (1948, Philadelphia, Pennsylvania Academy of the Fine Arts) and *Lilac and Books* (1955, Rochester, Memorial Art Gallery).

Paul Mocsanyi. *Karl Knaths*, Washington (D.C.) 1957.
Catalogue, *Four American Expressionists: Doris Caesar, Chaim Gross, Karl Knaths, Abraham Rattner*, Whitney Museum of American Art, New York 1959.

Kneale, Bryan. British sculptor, b. 1930 in the Isle of Man. He studied at the Douglas School of Art and at the RA schools from 1948 to 1952. He held a painting exhibition in 1954, but in 1959 he stopped painting, and in 1960 he learned to weld and took up sculpture. He held his first sculpture show in that year. He moved into a forge and from 1960 until about 1966 he worked directly in steel, often using preformed parts, steel tubes, etc. His earlier work was not entirely non-figurative, recalling Picasso to some extent, but it became increasingly an expression of the qualities of the actual material itself, the forms dictated by the tensile strength and the load-bearing qualities of the steel. From this he turned, around 1966, to the use of materials like aluminium, brass, perspex, etc., but the sculpture continues to be about the materials, playing the peculiar properties of each against the other in a way that distinguishes him from the more orthodox Constructivists.

Knight, Dame Laura. British painter, b. 1877 in Long Eaton, Derbyshire; d. 1971. She studied at Nottingham School of Art, and her work first appeared in the Royal Academy in 1903. She is best known for her studies of the circus and the ballet. The Upper Grosvenor Galleries, London, held a retrospective exhibition of her paintings in 1963.

Kobro, Katarzyna. Polish sculptress, b. 1898 in Riga; d. 1950 in Lodz. Kobro studied in Moscow. During the revolutionary period she was a member of the artistic *avant-garde* in the USSR. In 1922 she left Russia with her husband, Vladyslav Strzeminski, to settle in Poland. From 1931 onwards she lived in Lodz. She joined three Constructivist groups: *Blok* in 1924, *Praesens* in 1926 and *a.r.* (Revolutionary Artists) in 1930. During her early period Kobro created Suprematistic compositions in space and experimental works, in which she investigated the effect of directional tensions and forces in a specific arrangement of geometrical forms. Subsequently, from the late 1920s to the mid-1930s, she went over to geometrical, multi-coloured compositions in space, which she constructed from curved sheets of metal and which were based on precise calculations of specific numerical relationships. The theoretical premises underlying these works were set out by Kobro and Strzeminski in 'Spatial Compositions: Calculations of the Time-Space Rhythm' (*a.r.* Archives, 1931). During her final period, from 1935 onwards, Kobro produced 'biological' works.

Catalogue, *Katarzyna Kobro*, Lodz and Warsaw 1956–7.
Peinture moderne polonaise: Sources et recherches, Musée Galliera, Paris 1969.

Kobzdej, Alexander. Polish painter, b. 1920 in Olesko (Zloczow). After studying architecture, sculpture and painting at the Polytechnic in Lwow and at the Academy in Cracow Kobzdej obtained a professorial post at the Warsaw Academy. In 1965–6 he was visiting lecturer at the College of Fine Arts in Hamburg.

After an early Realist period Kobzdej turned ab-

stract in 1955, painting works in which foreign influences vied with elements of the Polish Baroque and folklore traditions. From polyptychs he went on to constructions with movable components and, from 1968 onwards, to material structures painted in violent colours.

Catalogue, *Alexander Kobzdej*, National Museum, Posen 1968.

Koch, Pyke (Pieter Frans Christian). Dutch painter, b. 1901 in Beek, near Nijmegen. Koch is a self-taught artist. After studying law in Utrecht he began to paint in 1926. He made repeated visits to Italy. His oeuvre includes numerous portraits and figure compositions. Like Ket, Hynckes and Willink, Koch is a Magic (or Neo-) Realist.

Koenig, Fritz. German sculptor, b. 1924 in Würzburg. From 1946 to 1952 Koenig studied at the Munich Academy, where he was a member of Hiller's 'masters' class'. He has been teaching at the Technical College in Munich since 1964, and is now living in Ganslberg near Landshut.

In his early period Koenig sculpted individual figures and groups (both animal and human) with flat, simplified forms after the manner of the Munich School (Heinrich Kirchner). But in 1959 he began his series of *Votives*. These were then followed by the *Caryatids*, which are abstract representations of human figures set up on pedestals or pillars.

Kogan, Moissey. Russian sculptor, graphic artist and designer, b. 1879 in Orgyeyev, Bessarabia; d. 1943 in Germany. Between 1903 and 1910, when he was working in Munich as a medallist and potter, Kogan joined the New Artists' Association for a short while. From 1910 onwards he lived and worked in Paris, where he was helped by both Maillol and Rodin. He died in a concentration camp.

Kogan's constant theme was the female nude, which he portrayed in plain and simple forms.

Kohn, Gabriel. American sculptor, b. 1910 in Philadelphia; d. 1975. After studying in New York at Cooper Union and the Beaux-Arts Institute (1929–34), Kohn worked as a studio assistant to Herman MacNeil (1866–1947) and other sculptors, and from 1934 to 1942 as a sculptor and as a designer for the theatre and films. In 1946–7 he studied with Ossip Zadkine in Paris and until the late 1950s worked primarily in France and Italy. In 1961 he moved to California, where he established a studio and taught in La Jolla and San Francisco.

Kohn's mature style emerged in the early 1950s, when he began to explore carved, and, later, constructed wood sculpture. His own attitude towards his sculpture was that neither his medium nor his technique were important, but only the arrangement of forms. He was also much concerned with the relationships between architecture and sculpture and in fact conceived of his work as architecture-sculpture. Kohn's forms—clean-cut, relatively simple, and massive—are juxtaposed and balanced in oblique, projecting arrangements, with the weight distributed at unexpected points; the nature of the material and the process of construction remain visible in the laminations, the dowels and the naturally finished, unstained, and unpainted surfaces (*Long Beach Contract, No. 1*, 1965, laminated redwood, Long Beach, California State College).

Catalogue, *Cohen, Kohn, Schapiro . . . New Talent Exhibition*, Museum of Modern Art, New York 1950.
Valerie Petersen. 'Gabriel Kohn Makes a Sculpture', *Art News* LX, October 1961.

Kokoschka, Oskar. Austrian painter, b. 1886 in Pochlarn, on the Danube. Kokoschka attended the School of Arts and Crafts in Vienna from 1904 onwards. In 1908, when he was still only twenty-two, his exhibits in the *Kunstschau* and his series of postcards, *Dreaming Boys*, caused a considerable stir in the art world. His earliest pictures were painted in 1907 and consisted for the most part of portraits which were executed in a strange and completely novel style. Both the people and the objects portrayed in these works seem to radiate an inner light. Instead of using colour to depict surface texture as his predecessors had done, Kokoschka used it—in conjunction with a nervous, linear composition in which the lines are sometimes incised into the picture surface—in order to express the psychic make-up of his subjects. These early works were rooted in the intellectual atmosphere of contemporary Vienna, which had been determined by three principal factors: Freud's psychoanalysis, French Symbolism and the Munich *Jugendstil* (which assumed a morbid character in Vienna due to the influence of English *art nouveau*). This new climate of opinion had actually existed in Vienna since the early 1890s, which had seen the emergence of the Viennese Secession (1892) and the founding of the *Wiener Werkstätte*. Like Klimt Kokoschka drew on both Beardsley and Hodler. Then, in 1910, Herwarth Walden invited him to Berlin, where his portrait drawings were shown by the *Sturm*. As it happens, this was the *Sturm*'s first venture into the sphere of the fine arts. It was during this phase of his career that Kokoschka produced his great graphic cycles. These included the illustrations for Ehrenstein's *Tubutsch* (1910), Karl Kraus' *Chinese Wall* (1914) and the Bach cantata *O Ewigkeit—Du Donnerwort*. At the same time his paintings became more intense and more expressive. Until then the psychic forces underlying the physical phenomena in Kokoschka's pictures had been concealed from view. Now he tried to make them manifest. In other words, he tried to express the deepest layers of his artistic vision in pictorial

terms. The climax of this process was reached when he painted his *Bride of the Wind*. After the First World War Kokoschka moved to Dresden, where he was appointed to the teaching staff of the Academy in 1920. During the early part of his Dresden period he continued to paint pictures similar to his *Bride of the Wind*. But then, due no doubt to the turbulent atmosphere obtaining in postwar Germany, his works grew so exalted that they threatened to become entirely formless. With the onset of the 1920s, however, he took stock of his artistic position and changed his style accordingly: his colours became bright and luminous (somewhat after the manner of Nolde) and were concentrated in specific areas, a development which would hardly have been feasible but for the great example of Gauguin. In 1924 Kokoschka unexpectedly left Dresden and travelled via Switzerland and Vienna to Paris, where he was stimulated by the Impressionists and acquired new ideas which were of great importance for his future development. They enabled him to resolve the tormenting psychological problems which had been a prominent feature of his early works and to proceed to the portrayal of exuberant and colourful visual impressions. From Paris he travelled to Bordeaux, Biarritz, Marseilles, Toledo, Madrid and Lisbon. In 1926 he visited London. Then, after a further period in France, he went to Tunisia in 1928, going on from there to Constantinople. In 1931 he returned to Vienna and remained there until 1934, when he left for Prague to escape the Nazi terror. In Prague his paintings acquired symbolical overtones and after his flight to London in 1935 he produced many political allegories. In 1953 Kokoschka founded the International Summer School for Fine Arts and in 1955 the School of Perception, both in Salzburg. He is now living in Villeneuve, Switzerland.

Edith Hoffmann. *Kokoschka: Life and Work*, London 1947.
J. Russell. *Oskar Kokoschka: Watercolors, Drawings, Writings*, New York 1958.
H. M. Wingler. *Oskar Kokoschka: The Work of the Painter*, New York and Salzburg 1958.
Bernard Bultman. *Oskar Kokoschka*, New York 1960.

Kolbe, Georg. German sculptor, b. 1877 in Waldheim; d. 1947 in Berlin. Kolbe studied in Dresden, Munich and Paris, at the Académie Julian (1898). With the sculptor Richard Scheibe (b. 1879), he went to Rome in 1898 and stayed there for two years, during which time he met Louis Tuaillon and developed an interest in sculpture. From 1903 onwards he lived in Berlin, then returned to Paris in 1909 and met Rodin. Although Tuaillon had already aroused Kolbe's interest in sculpture, it was Rodin and later Maillol who were the decisive influences on him. His early figures are highly expressive—particularly the *Dancing Girl* of 1912 (Berlin, Nationalgalerie). Later, during the Third Reich, he indulged in the kind of monumental figures whose cheap pathos corresponded largely to the popular image of the 'master race'.

R. G. Binding. *Vom Leben der Plastik*, Berlin 1933.

Kollwitz, Käthe. German graphic artist and sculptress, b. 1867 in Königsberg; d. 1945 in Moritzburg. The work of Käthe Kollwitz is remarkable in that, although contemporary with the radical changes in ideas about art during the early part of the twentieth century, it remained very largely unaffected by them. Though sometimes classed with the German Expressionists, she had no use for 'studio art'. She obtained recognition as an artist in 1897, and subsequently her work continued unchanged in outlook and subject matter. She portrayed the wretched lot of those oppressed in life, whether by poverty, politics or war.

Fundamentally a graphic artist, she spent her life developing her great power of expressive drawing. Her early success was as an etcher, when she became known by her *Weavers' Revolt* series, based on Hauptmann's play on that theme. She followed this with a second series, the *Peasants' Revolt*. She extended her range of drawing into lithography and woodcuts. Losing a son in the First World War, and suffering the full rigours of war's aftermath in Berlin, she met these experiences by producing a powerful series of woodcuts entitled *The War* in 1923. Later, she produced bronzes, still with the same subject matter, mostly in relief. These sensitive drawings in the clay have little of the fierce Expressionism and sculptural force of her contemporary Barlach, whom it many ways she closely resembles.

The subject matter of her work she affirmed was her choice of themes 'which I felt as beauty'. Certainly in her best work she avoided sentimentality, and the banal propaganda of Social Realism. Her background was politically towards the left; her husband was a doctor with a practice in the poorer part of Berlin and Kollwitz herself spent much time in social relief work. She belongs in art with those artists, such as van Gogh and Daumier, who believe in 'involvement', but with mankind at the deepest human level, not with any sectarian or political creed. For herself this passionate concern for the sufferings of humanity seemed to be assuaged by the endeavour to portray the dignity of man under affliction, to elevate in art what life had cast down. Symbolic of her involvement is her life-long series of self-portraits.

Drawn to Communism by its interest in the workers, she was apparently not a member of the Communist Party. She did visit Russia in 1927. Under the National Socialist regime she was asked to resign from the Academy in 1933. She stayed in Germany and produced a powerful lithographic series, *Concerning Death*, as if to face openly a figure often implied in her lifetime's subject. She experienced a second time the suffering and bereavement of war. Her work remains as a kind of monument to all who are compassionate before all else, and to those who believe in the essentiality of serious purpose in art.

Kooning, Willem de. Dutch-American painter, b. 1904 in Rotterdam. He early gravitated towards an artistic career in Rotterdam, where he served an apprenticeship in a firm of commercial artists and decorators (Jan and Jaap Gidding). While so employed, he attended the Academie voor Beeldende Kunsten in Technische, a school which emphasized classical disciplines and 'accepted methods'. In 1920 he left the Giddings to work under Bernard Romein, an artist fully conversant with such *avant-garde* movements as the *de Stijl* group, the Paris School and the architecture of F. L. Wright. In spite of his teacher's interests, de Kooning was at this time more concerned with conservative trends— Dutch *art nouveau*, the Barbizon School, and the paintings of Toorop and the Italian Segantini. Before going to America in 1926, he attended Academy classes in Brussels, Antwerp and Rotterdam. Almost immediately upon his arrival in the United States he began experimenting with abstraction under the influence of Kandinsky. In 1927 he met A. Gorky, with whom he became close friends— the work of these two men often forms very close stylistic relationships. In the 1930s he was employed by the Federal Arts Project. This was the first time he had been able to devote all his energies to painting, and from this time on he was a full-time painter. During his associations with the Federal agency he produced murals for the Williamsburg Federal Housing Project and the Hall of Pharmacy at the New York World's Fair. In the 1930s his abstractions in greyed colours with pink or green accents existed side by side with meticulous figural works. Not until 1946 did his style coalesce, when the fruition of previous ideas was seen in his first one-man show at the Egan Gallery—black and white abstractions executed in commercial enamel paints. From this moment he became a leader in the field of postwar painters, among whom were R. Motherwell, C. Still, J. Pollock, M. Rothko and A. Gottlieb. His next important stylistic change occurred in the early 1950s when he was working on *Woman I*. In the first two years of the decade he worked continuously on it, scraping away one version after another. Completed in 1952, this canvas (New York, Museum of Modern Art) with its slashing lines, sense of the grotesque and use of visceral colours (greens, red-orange, yellow) represents a figure with no defining contours—existent in and for itself. The absence of space creates a oneness of figure and environment, one flowing freely into the other. This painting led to a series based on the female form. By 1955 this series turned into large abstractions which in fact relinquished their relationship to the human figure; colours became bolder, brushstrokes broader. In the 1960s de Kooning returned to the theme of the woman, executed in the bright tonalities employed in the late fifties. His strokes became less structured than those of *Woman I*, while the sense of amorphous flux and flow and a sense of palpable flesh replaced the dynamic energy of his 1952 picture (*Woman Sag Harbor*, 1964, New York, Joseph H. Hirshhorn Collection).

Thomas B. Hess. *Willem de Kooning*, New York 1959.
Harold Rosenberg. *The Anxious Object: Art Today and Its Audience*, New York 1964.
De Kooning Drawings, New York 1967.

Kósice, Gyula. Argentinian sculptor, b. 1924 in Kósice, Hungary. When he was four years old Kósice was taken to Buenos Aires, where he later trained as a sculptor. He took an early interest in the Bauhaus ideas and in the work of Moholy-Nagy, Gabo and Pevsner. In 1944 he helped to launch the *avant-garde* magazine *Arturo*, in 1945 he became a founder member of the *Arte Concreto-Invención* movement and in 1946 leader of the *Arte Madi* movement. In 1947 Kósice began to use Plexiglass for his kinetic light objects. In 1947 he settled in Paris, where he created most of his hydraulic sculptures and several wall pictures, for which he used transparent materials combined with jets of water and lighting effects. Kósice is also a poet and aesthetician. He has investigated the problems of hydro-light, hydro-space and hydro-movement and evolved a form of 'hydraulic architecture' (houses with transparent walls which have water flowing between them).

Guy Habasque. *Kósice*, Paris 1965.

Kostka, Josef. Czechoslovak sculptor, b. 1912. Kostka was one of the most important Slovak sculptors of the middle twentieth century. He was concerned to show his conception of the human condition by creating turbulent, passionate works of great drama.

Kowalski, Emanuel. Chilean draughtsman and graphic artist, b. 1943 in Santiago, Chile. Kowalski studied interior decoration in Jerusalem from 1960 to 1963. He had his first exhibition in 1965 at the Galería Edwards in Santiago. In his earlier crayon drawings, which are basically representational, Kowalski produced tortured figures in sombre colours, revealing a profound sense of *angst*, but latterly—under the influence of the vitalist philosophy of C. E. Gandarillas—he has abandoned formal design and adopted an increasingly abstract style, working almost exclusively in charcoal. Compositions such as *PICO 1968* (Madrid, private collection) are characterized by broad, sweeping strokes and suggestively erotic forms. He has had exhibitions at the Galería Edwards in Santiago (1965), the Museo de Arte Contemporáneo in Santiago (1967) and Beit Ha' Omanim in Jerusalem (1968).

Carlos Eastman. *Cinco artistas sudamericanos*, Buenos Aires 1969.

Kowarski, Felicjan. Polish painter, b. 1890; d. 1948. He studied in Odessa and St. Petersburg, then taught in Cracow (from 1923) and Warsaw (from 1929). The theme of his work is the plight of man in the modern world, and his love for his fellow human beings is revealed in sad depictions of Jewish persecution; his social conscience is also given expression in portraits and groups.

Krajcberg, Franz. Brazilian painter, b. 1921 in Kozienice, Poland. After studying in Vitebsk, Leningrad and Stuttgart (under Baumeister) from 1945 to 1947 Krajcberg went to Paris in 1948 before settling in São Paulo, where he remained until his return to Europe in 1958. In 1957 he won the first prize for painting at the Bienal in São Paulo. Krajcberg is an informal artist. He creates frottages and compositions of stones.

Kraljević, Miroslav. Yugoslav painter, b. 1885 in Gospic, Croatia; d. 1913 in Zagreb. He was a leading figure among Croatian painters. He studied in Munich and spent some time in Paris, where he came under the influence of Impressionism, but his style was closer to that of Courbet or Manet.

Kramer, Harry. German sculptor, b. 1925 in Lingen. In 1952, after training as an actor, dancer and choreographer, Kramer made his first marionettes: puppets with movable limbs and figures mounted on wheels, which moved in circles without the use of strings. He also drew up the plans for a 'mechanical theatre'. In the following year he constructed the prototype machines for the *sculptures automobiles* of 1958 (articulating wheels, cog-wheels, etc., made from wood and metal). The figures which Kramer created during the 1950s all bore the stamp of their mechanical origin, but in 1961, when he began to fashion mobile or ringing spheres, towers and columns from wire, he freed himself from the constraint imposed by the absolute precision of mechanical movement and rigid construction. In 1965 Kramer evolved a system for producing sculptures industrially. In the same year he lectured in the Kinetics Department at the Academy of Art in Hamburg and also visited Las Vegas. After his return from America in 1966 he produced sculptures and building components for incorporation into architectural schemes. Whilst working as a sculptor Kramer has also produced a number of short films in collaboration with W. Ramsbott. These include *Die Stadt* (1956), *Défense 58–24* (1957), *Die Schleuse* (1961), *Die Aufzeichnungen* (1965).

Kregar, Stane. Yugoslav painter, b. 1905 in Šentvid, Slovenia. After training at the Academy of Art in Prague from 1930 to 1935 Kregar completed his studies in Paris. He is now living in Ljubljana.

The Cubism of Kregar's early period was followed by a modified form of Surrealism. In 1952 this too was superseded by the Lyrical Abstract style in which he is still painting today. But Kregar is not a completely abstract artist, since his inner vision is still derived in the first instance from his optical impressions of reality.

Kricke, Norbert. German sculptor, b. 1922 in Düsseldorf. After attending the College of Fine Arts in Berlin from 1946 to 1947 Kricke settled in Düsseldorf, where he was given a teaching post at the Academy. In 1958 he won a prize from the Graham Foundation for Advanced Studies in the Fine Arts, Chicago, and since then has made several trips to the USA.

Kricke produced the first of his non-objective sculptures in space in 1949. His early works in this genre consist of tubes and wires bent into acute and right-angled shapes. In 1953–4 these were supplemented by curved shapes fashioned from bundles of wires made of tin, copper, nickel or steel. In 1954 Kricke began to arrange metal tubes in parallel rows. In 1962 Gropius invited him to Harvard University, Cambridge, Mass., to work out new forms of industrial sculpture and to design a fountain for the University of Baghdad. By then he had already produced a Plexiglass fountain for Bad Salzuflen (1958). In these fountains, which he calls *Wasserwälder* (water forests), the water slowly rises within vertical Plexiglass tubes and then runs down the outside of the tubes, where it forms a gleaming, vibrating film. In 1962 Kricke had sculptures erected in front of the Mannesmann building in Düsseldorf and in the park of the Château de Reux in Normandy.

E. Trier. *Norbert Kricke*, Recklinghausen 1963.
Exhibition catalogue, *Norbert Kricke*, Venice Biennale No. 32, 1964.

Kriwet, Ferdinand. German experimental artist, b. 1942 in Düsseldorf. Kriwet is a letterist. He arranges letters, words and fragments of words in purely formal sequences and without regard to their linguistic meaning on different grounds: paper, plastic, flags, transparent revolving discs, advertisement pillars, etc. Kriwet first made his name with 'mixed media demonstrations', experimental plays, *Hörtexte* (auditory texts), *Textfilme* (text films) and book publications (*Leserattenfänge*, 1965, and *Mixed Media*, 1969). He is now living in Düsseldorf.

Krohg, Per. Norwegian painter, stage designer and sculptor, b. 1889 in Asgardstrand, Norway. Krohg is the son of the painter Christian Krohg. He was brought up in Paris and studied, first in his father's atelier at the Académie Colarossi, and subsequently, from 1907 to 1909, under Matisse. From 1934 to 1945 he taught at the School of Arts and Crafts in Oslo and from 1946 onwards at the Oslo Academy.

Krohg, who came into contact with the modern trends in twentieth-century art at an early age, developed into a versatile, sophisticated and occasionally bizarre artist. The ironical and slightly theatrical pictures of modern big city life, which he painted in his early period, are characterized by exaggerated gestures bordering on caricature, intense Fauvist colours and Cubist composition. Later he adopted a more realistic style. But his major achievements were in the sphere of monumental painting. Amongst other things he created frescoes for the university and the town hall in Oslo and, in 1952, for the UN Building in New York. As a teacher Krohg exerted considerable influence on the younger generation of Scandinavian painters.

J. H. Langaard. *Per Krohg*, Oslo 1947.

Kroll, Leon. American painter, b. 1884 in New York; d. 1974. At 15 Kroll began to earn his own living, working his way through the Art Students' League where he was studying under John H. Twachtman (1900–2). At 18 he transferred to the National Academy of Design where he received sound academic training—an influence that can be seen throughout his oeuvre. After further study at the Académie Julian under J.-P. Laurens, he returned to the United States (1919) and became an instructor at the National Academy where he had his first one-man show in 1911. Best known for his academic nudes, all of his works become drier and less personal as his career unfolds. His early canvases, such as *The Bridge* (1910–11, Baltimore, Md., Union Memorial Hospital), give one a sense of the vibrancy of the city, revealing the same spirit as the artists of the Ashcan School, with whom his name is often linked. His earlier portraits also have a greater warmth, humanity and life (*Mary at Breakfast*, 1926, Minneapolis, Minn., Museum of Art) than his later more stilted and confining ones. While studying in Paris, Kroll's great idol was Poussin. This fact is revealed even in his later works and especially in his landscapes, such as *Road through Willows* (1933, New York, Whitney Museum of American Art). In addition to canvases he has also been active as a mural painter. He was one of eleven artists commissioned in 1936 to decorate the new Department of Justice Building, Washington, D.C., and from 1938 to 1941 he worked on murals for the Memorial Chamber of the Worcester (Mass.) War Memorial. Other murals are at the State Capitol, Indiana, the Omaha Beach Chapel in Normandy and Shriver Hall Auditorium, Johns Hopkins University, Baltimore (completed in 1956). In the 1950s he was especially active as a book illustrator, producing engravings for *Les Causes célèbres* by Jean

Paulhan (1951), *Hommage à l'écriture* (1954) and *XXIV Fables de la Fontaine* (1958) among many others. An extremely popular artist for many years, Kroll had 'a consummate knack for mixing sentimentality, voluptuousness and academic formulae' which made him a great prize-winner.

Leon Kroll, American Artists Group, New York 1946.

Krushenick, Nicolas. American painter, b. 1929 in New York City. When studying at the Art Students' League (1948–50) he was mainly involved with figurative imagery. This was followed by work at the Hans Hofman School of Art (1950–1) which influenced his work in the 1950s. During this decade he passed through a number of Abstract Expressionist idioms, executing his canvases with a soft brushwork which persisted until his hard-edge style took hold in 1962. He was given his first one-man show at the Camino Gallery, New York, in 1956 and has had one-man shows in Stuttgart and Paris. Since 1959 he has been included in many group exhibitions both in the United States and abroad. His hard-edge style is characterized by black lines that stripe the canvas, interspersed with vivid primary and secondary colours, creating overlapping forms resembling enlarged camera shutters, exotic plants and basketweave patterns (*Moon Maid*, 1966, Paris, Galerie Ileana Sonnabend). He has also used shaped canvases enabling him to complete contoured forms which would otherwise be cut by the edge of a rectangular canvas. In addition to his paintings he designed sets and costumes for the Center Opera Company's production of *The Man in the Moon* (1967–8). Krushenick has been the recipient of a Guggenheim Fellowship and a Tamarind Lithography Workshop grant.

Kubin, Alfred. Austrian author, draughtsman and illustrator, b. 1877 in Leitmeritz, Bohemia; d. 1959 in Zwickledt. After living in Salzburg from 1879 to 1882 Kubin's family moved to Zell am See. Five years later, on 8 May 1887, Kubin lost his mother, to whom he was deeply attached. Kubin attended the Gymnasium in Salzburg, 1877–8, the church school in Zell am See, 1888–91, and the School of Industrial Art in Salzburg, 1891–2. From 1892 to 1896 he was apprenticed to a photographer (Beer) in Klagenfurt. In October 1896 he made a suicide attempt at his mother's grave. In 1897 he enrolled for his national service, but suffered a nervous breakdown and was invalided out. From 1898 to 1901 Kubin studied at a private school of art run by Schmidz-Reute, then joined Gysis's class at the Munich Academy. In 1902 he had his first exhibition (in Bruno Cassirer's gallery in Berlin), and in 1903 Hans von Weber of Munich published a group of his drawings. On 1 December 1903 Kubin's fiancée Emmy Bayr died, and this triggered a psychological crisis. In late March 1904 Kubin married Hedwig Gründler (née Schmitz). In the autumn of 1905 he visited the South of France and Italy, and in 1906 he made his first visit to Paris; he also bought the small castle of Zwickledt near Wernstein in Upper Austria, and moved there from Munich. In 1907 he visited Bosnia and Dalmatia; on 2 November 1907 his father died; in the autumn of 1908 he completed his novel *Die andere Seite*; in 1909 he visited the Balkans with Karl Wolfskehl, and joined the New Artists' Association, Munich; in 1911 he visited Prague, and in 1912 joined the *Blauer Reiter*. In 1914 he revisited Paris. Two years later he passed through a further inner crisis, and started to perform Buddhist exercises. In 1921 Goltz of Munich staged the first retrospective exhibition of his work. In 1924 Kubin visited Switzerland, and from 1930 to 1940 he spent his summer holidays in the Bohemian forests. In 1930 he was elected to the Prussian Academy of Arts in Berlin; in 1937 he obtained a professorial post. In the same year a major Kubin exhibition was staged in the Albertina in Vienna. In 1947 Kubin was given the freedom of the city of Linz; on 15 August 1948 his wife died. In 1949 he was elected to the Bavarian Academy of Fine Arts; in 1951 he was awarded the Austrian national prize for the fine arts, in 1952 the Ulisse prize at the Venice Biennale, and in 1955 the international prize for drawing at the São Paulo Bienal.

After completing his illustrated novel *Die andere Seite*, Kubin produced illustrations for over two hundred books. He also made thousands of drawings, often in cycles, in which he depicted his own fantastic visions. His draughtsmanship remained virtually unchanged throughout his career. Using a combination of bold and spidery strokes he created a dense and extremely delicate network of lines, which provided a perfect vehicle for his mythical, dreamlike pictorial world.

P. Raabe (ed.). *Alfred Kubin: Leben, Werk, Wirkung,* Hamburg 1957.
Catalogue, *Alfred Kubin,* Kestner Gesellschaft, Hanover 1964.
Wieland Schmied. *Alfred Kubin,* London and New York 1969.

Kubišta, Bohumil. Czech painter, b. 1884; d. 1918. He was one of the leading *avant-garde* artists in Prague in the early years of the century. After seeing Expressionist and Impressionist works at exhibitions in 1905 and 1907, Kubišta, Filla and Procházka, with other young artists, formed *The Eight* (1907–8), a group whose aim was to foster a modern Czech art derived from the stylistic innovations that had impressed them so much. In 1909 he and Filla went to Paris and were deeply influenced by the Cubist discoveries. By 1913 he had developed his own Cubist style, and went on to Futurism in the following year.

Küchenmeister, Rainer. German painter, b. 1926 in Ahlen, Westphalia. Küchenmeister studied at the

Meisterschule für das deutsche Handwerk (Masters' School for German Arts and Crafts) in Bielefeld and at the College of Applied Arts in Berlin-Weissensee from 1946 to 1950. He now lives primarily in Paris.

Most of Küchenmeister's pictures are painted in earthy colours and depict monolithic, corporeal forms executed as silhouettes on monochrome grounds. He usually calls these works *figure* or *personnage*.

Kudo, Tetsumi. Japanese sculptor, b. 1935 in Aomori. Kudo graduated from Tokyo University of Art in 1958. He participated in the Yomiuri Independent Show in 1958–62, where he exhibited *Limitless Propagation*, a sculpture like a coral tree composed of thousands of knots twined around iron frameworks. He began to build boxes in Paris, where he went in 1962 and has been living ever since (the first prize which he won at the Pan-Pacific Exhibition for Young Artists supported his trip). He has remained in Europe as one of the extraordinary figures in such trends as 'Objecteurs' and 'Nouveaux Réalistes', and participated in a number of evocative experimental shows. His now-famous 'Philosophy of Impotence' is perhaps exemplified by a series called *Your Portrait*, which gives the feeling of raucous blasting jukeboxes of sensual images. Closed, the boxes look like dice with dots on the sides. Opened, sirens begin to wail, huge eyeballs peer out, open mouths gape, sets of injection needles, condoms, roulette wheels, etc., twitch fitfully, or rows of rubber dolls, compressed hideously in jars, confront the viewer. The strength of Kudo's images turns on the fact that their violence and hatred is directed at himself as well as at the stagnant *petit-bourgeois* society he inhabits. He does not purify or abstract his rage and fear, but displays it as much as an aspect of himself as of those to whom the malicious title, *Your Portrait*, is dedicated.

Kuhn, Walt. American painter, b. 1880 in New York; d. 1949 in New York. While still in his teens, Kuhn worked as a newspaper cartoonist in San Francisco. Then, for about a decade, he supported himself by executing drawings and cartoons for magazines and newspapers, as did many other American artists in the early part of the twentieth century. Kuhn studied art in Paris and Munich, then travelled through Holland, Spain, Germany and Italy, experimenting with the media and the many styles with which he came into contact. This easy susceptibility to outside influences served him well after 1913, for he was one of the few American Realists able to absorb and adapt the new modernistic modes of painting that were introduced to America at the New York Armory Show of 1913. The show marked a turning point in Kuhn's artistic life. In 1912 he had helped organize the Association of American Painters and Sculptors, a group that formulated plans for the Armory exhibition. Along with his friend Arthur B. Davies, who was president of the Association, Kuhn was sent to Europe by John Quinn—a lawyer and collector whom he served as secretary and who was backing the Armory Show—to collect *avant-garde* paintings. The works of the Fauvists Henri Matisse and André Derain, of Pablo Picasso, Paul Gauguin and others had a decisive influence on the stylistic aspects of the painting he did upon his return. Kuhn's favourite subjects were clowns, acrobats and jugglers, through whom he expressed his notions of universal moods and feelings. *Lavender Plumes* (1938, New York, Kennedy Galleries) is characteristic of the half-length, stoic, frontal portraits of circus figures in make-up and garish costumes that he produced throughout his artistic career. From Matisse he borrowed the boldly distorted forms and the bright, almost gaudy colours typical of his mature work of the mid-1920s, while the influences of Derain and Picasso are evident in the circus performers he loved to portray (*Blue Clown*, 1931, New York, Whitney Museum). In the 1920s Kuhn painted single figures on neutral backgrounds, deliberately limiting his focus to the starkly expressive human representation; during the 1930s he widened his repertoire to include flower studies, landscapes and still lifes. Kuhn's friendship with Jules Pascin during the 1940s had a strong effect on the graphic work he produced at that time. In later years he continued to paint circus subjects with great relish, but often with an overly sentimental, somewhat nostalgic facility.

Philip R. Adams. Catalogue, *Walt Kuhn—A Memorial Exhibition*, Cincinnati Art Museum, Cincinnati 1960.

Kujawski, Jerzy. Polish painter, b. 1921 in Ostrow Wielkopolski. Kujawski belonged to the Cracow *avant-garde* until 1947, when he moved to Paris. There he joined the Surrealist movement and at the end of the 1950s began to incorporate 'automatic writing' into his large-format Tachist compositions. From 1966 onwards he evolved new techniques, for which he used ready-made images, although he still continued to produce Surrealist works grounded in random dream associations.

Kulisiewicz, Tadeusz. Polish graphic artist and draughtsman, b. 1899 in Kalisz. Kulisiewicz studied at the College of Fine Arts in Warsaw from 1926 to 1929. He has held a professorial post at the College since 1946.

Prior to 1939 practically the whole of Kulisiewicz's oeuvre consisted of woodcuts, which he executed in what was essentially an Expressionist style. After the Second World War he produced cycles of drawings, either in black and white or in colours, in which he recalled visits to China, India, Mexico, Brazil and the

Carpathian Mountains. The principal features of Kulisiewicz's drawings are their synthetic structure, the multiplicity of the linear elements, the richness of the surface texture and the combination of necessary and contingent components.

J. Guze. *Tadeusz Kulisiewicz*, Warsaw 1956.

Kuniyoshi, Yasuo. Japanese-American painter, b. 1893 in Okayama; d. 1953 in New York. He went to Seattle in 1906 and worked for a long time at odd jobs before becoming interested in art. Kuniyoshi began his art studies in Los Angeles and continued them in 1916 at the Art Students' League in New York, where he studied with the Urban Realist painter Kenneth Hayes Miller (1876–1952). Kuniyoshi's early paintings of the 1920s often combined landscapes, figures (particularly children) and flowers in dreamlike compositions, humorously evocative and whimsical in expression (*Child*, 1923, and *Landscape*, 1924, both New York, Whitney Museum). Ink drawings of the 1920s and 1930s showed more freely associated combinations in this fantastic idiom, often related, however distantly, to Oriental aesthetic concepts (*Damp Place*, 1923, Whitney Museum). While in Europe in 1925 and 1928 Kuniyoshi was greatly impressed by the works of Chaim Soutine, Maurice Utrillo, Pablo Picasso and especially Jules Pascin, whose style had particular bearing on his later work. Like Pascin, Kuniyoshi concentrated on women and still lifes during the 1930s, delighting in the physicality of bodies and objects, which he often arranged in incongruous relations. *I'm Tired* (1938, Whitney Museum) shows a pensive female—half reading her newspaper, half dreaming—recalling Picasso's Blue Period figures as well as Pascin's special regard for women's moods. Surrealism also seems to have influenced his production at this time, and sexual connotations prevailed in the paintings of the 1940s, in which he combined studio realism with a richly imaginative world of fancy (*Upside Down Table and Mask*, 1940, New York, Museum of Modern Art). After 1948 the pictures of ruin and lonely desperation done during the Second World War in muted grey and earth tones (*Desert Woman*, 1943, Whitney Museum) were replaced by fresco-like gayer scenes of carnivals and costumes, brighter in colour and often more ironic than any of his earlier work (*Juggler*, 1952, Whitney Museum).

Kuniyoshi began teaching at the Art Students' League in 1933. In the mid-1930s he took part in many artists' organizations, and in 1947 was the first president of the Artists' Equity Association. The next year he was given a retrospective at the Whitney Museum of American Art in New York.

Yasuo Kuniyoshi. 'East to West', *Magazine of Art* XXXIII, Paris and New York, February 1940.
Lloyd Goodrich. *Yasuo Kuniyoshi*, New York 1948.

Kupka, Frank (Frantisek). Czech painter, b. 1871 in Opočno, Bohemia; d. 1957 in Puteaux, near Paris. After studying at the Prague Academy from 1887 to 1891 and at the Viennese Academy from 1891 to 1895 Kupka went to live in Paris, where he contributed to various satirical anarchist magazines such as *Canard Sauvage* and *Cocorico* from 1900 onwards. From 1902 to 1909 he worked as a book illustrator. In 1904 he settled in Puteaux and subsequently made contact with Villon and the painters of the *Section d'Or*, with whom he exhibited in 1912 in the Galerie la Boétie in Paris. It was during this period that he produced his *Newton-Disques*, a series of experimental abstract colour compositions which reveal the influence of Delaunay's Orphism. From 1918 to 1920 Kupka was visiting professor at the Prague Academy. In 1931 he became one of the leading members of the Parisian *Abstraction-Création* association. From 1940 to 1944 he lived in Beaugency, then returned to spend the rest of his life in Puteaux.

After an early period, in which he was influenced first by *art nouveau* and then by the Expressionists and Fauves, Kupka investigated the colour theories of Newton, Chevreul and the Neo-Impressionists (especially Seurat) and as a result gravitated towards abstract art. His works in this genre are of two main types: those based on lyrical, curvilinear, 'Baroque' forms and those grounded in strictly architectonic, geometrical structures. In this abstract development Kupka revealed a marked penchant for mystical and symbolical features, which are similar to those found in the works of Ciurlionis and the young Kandinsky and which derived in the first instance from his youthful preoccupation with occult and spiritualist ideas. The titles of his abstract works, many of which have musical or cosmic associations, also bear witness to his interest in such matters. Kupka was one of the pioneers of abstract art. His *Plans par couleur*, in which he sought to depict movement by breaking down objective images into vertical bands of colour, go back to 1910. In the following year—at roughly the same time as Delaunay was embarking on his abstract colour experiments—he began to evolve his *Plans verticaux*, in which he completely dispensed with objective forms. From then onwards he remained a true adherent of abstract art, which he once defined in the following terms: 'The work of art, which is itself an abstract reality, must be formed from invented elements. Its concrete significance arises out of a combination of morphological archetypes and the architectonic conditions appropriate to its own intrinsic organism.' It was only in the 1960s that Kupka's significance for the development of modern art was fully realized.

J. Cassou and D. Fédit. *Kupka*, Paris and Stuttgart 1964; New York 1965.
Exhibition catalogue, *Kupka*, Musée Nationale d'Art Moderne,

Paris 1966; Kunstverein, Cologne 1967; Museum des XX. Jahrhunderts, Vienna 1967.
Ludmila Vachtova. *Frank Kupka*, London 1968; New York 1969.

Kutter, Joseph. Luxembourg painter, b. 1894; d. 1941. He was born and died in the city of Luxembourg, and it was there that some of his finest work was done. He had links with Expressionism, but was more refined and painted with greater control. As well as some moving clowns (a series done in 1936–8), he painted landscapes with a sombre, desolate quality.

Kuwayama, Tadaaki. Japanese painter, b. 1931 in Nagoya. After graduating from Tokyo University of Arts, he went to the United States in 1958. He has consistently pursued stoic expression in a form of abstraction based on an anti-spiritual attitude. His preoccupation is to establish an estrangement between subject and object; to make a work a thing independent from the artist's mind.

Kylberg, Carl. Swedish painter, b. 1878; d. 1952. After first studying architecture Kylberg switched to painting in 1900 and became a pupil of Wilhelmson in Gothenburg, where he joined the group of artists led by Ivar Arosenius and Ole Kruse. For over thirty years Kylberg was obliged to earn his living as a commercial artist, cartoonist and book illustrator (*Lejonet Leo*, which was published in 1930, contains typical illustrations). Eventually, in the course of the 1930s, he managed to establish himself as a serious artist. After an early period, in which he progressed from Synthetist paintings to landscapes executed in the Pointillist technique favoured by Wilhelmson, Kylberg came under the influence of Isakson in the 1920s. From then onwards he concentrated on views of the open Danish countryside. But in these landscapes Kylberg reduced his original impressions of nature to highly emotive images, simplifying individual objects so that they appear as pantheistic symbols of cosmic processes. The colour scheme—which consists of a few dark colours applied with broad strokes of the brush offset by violent yellows, reds and blues—strengthens the general impression of a fluid world. In his mature period Kylberg was one of the most radical colourists working in Sweden. His major works include: *Inför en ny dag* (*A New Day is Dawning*, 1933, Paris Musée d'Art Moderne), *Uppbrottet* (*The Departure*, 1935, Stockholm, Moderna Museet) and *Vägen* (*The Way*, 1936, Copenhagen Statens Museum for Kunst). Kylberg also executed a painting in five parts—*Frid på jorden* (*Peace on Earth*, 1939–40) for the Community Centre in Västerås.

G. Näsström. *Carl Kylberg*, Stockholm 1952.

L

Labisse, Felix. French painter, b. 1905 in Douai. In 1927 Labisse went to live in Ostend, where he made the acquaintance of Ensor and Permeke. In 1930 he and M. Jacob founded the magazine *Tribord*. Between 1932 and 1935 Labisse lived partly in Paris. In 1938 he met Magritte and Delvaux. In 1939 he was in Cambrai, Montauban, Cannes and Paris, and in 1950 visited Brazil, Uruguay and Argentina. Since 1951 he has been living at Neuilly-sur-Seine.

Labisse, who is a self-taught painter, decided on an artistic career following his meeting with Ensor in 1927. In his paintings he represents fantastic visions, which are prompted by the daemonic and magical power of female eroticism. He uses smooth handling, which is reminiscent of Magritte and Dali, to produce a *trompe l'oeil* brand of Surrealism.

Exhibition catalogue, *Felix Labisse*, Ostend and Antwerp 1968.

Lacasse, Joseph. Belgian painter, b. 1894 in Tournai. Lacasse started out in life as a quarryman. From 1909 to 1911 he attended evening classes in drawing; in 1912 he studied at the Academy in Tournai and in 1919–20 at the Academy in Brussels. In 1925 he moved to Paris, where he is still living today. From 1939 onwards he was in close contact with Brancusi, and in 1931 he met Delaunay. During the Second World War he lived in England. From 1946 onwards he was in contact with Poliakoff. Lacasse was carrying out abstract Cubist experiments as early as 1910. Subsequently he reverted to figurative painting until he met Delaunay in 1931, when he again turned to abstract art. His later compositions, which consist of flat, interlocking, angular forms and are often painted in glowing colours that give them a mystical quality, are said to have influenced Poliakoff.

Catalogue, *Joseph Lacasse*, Drian Gallery, London 1962.
M. Seuphor. *Die abstrakte Kunst in Flandern*, Brussels 1963.

Lacey, Bruce. British sculptor, b. 1927 in Catford, London. He began to study art at the age of 21 after varied experience, including naval service as an electric mechanic. This is reflected in the animated constructions with Dada connections he exhibited in London in the mid-1960s and in his continuing interest in the entertainment value of robots and the like.

Lachaise, Gaston. French-American sculptor, b. 1882 in Paris; d. 1935. Educated in France, first at the École Bernard Palissy (1895–8) and then the Académie Nationale des Beaux-Arts, Lachaise went to the United States in January 1906. The provocation for the trip was Isabel Dutaud Nagle (later

Mme Lachaise), a Canadian-American whom he met in about 1901 in Paris. On arriving in Boston he first worked for the jeweller René Lalique and later for the sculptor Henry Hudson Kitson. When the latter moved to New York (1912), Lachaise followed but soon left Kitson's studio for an assistantship with Paul Manship. The academic leanings of both these sculptors were to be reflected later in the high degree of finish typical of much of the artist's independent work. A rough, spontaneous approach is, however, not absent from his work and can especially be noted in his portraits. This Impressionistic technique produces both a strong sense of immediacy and psychological revelation in the bust of *John Marin* (1928, painted plaster, Lachaise Foundation). His preoccupation with the female figure often provokes comparisons with the painting of Renoir. Both men revered the female form, though Lachaise's attitude is one of clear sexuality in which woman is regarded as a symbol of fertility, rather than Renoir's more discreet emphasis on femininity. The sculptor's wife was often his model and the *Standing Woman* (*Elevation*) of 1912–27 (New York, Whitney Museum of American Art) expresses both the physical and spiritual effect she must have had on him. The central principles of his art, 'simplification and amplification', are clearly embodied here. The large, simple forms emphasizing massive volumes, smooth transitions of planes and an elegant, almost mannered quality (in the delicacy of the small feet supporting a ponderous weight and attenuated hands flowing into massive arms and shoulders) are typical of much of his oeuvre. The affected elegance and refined technique seen here are often employed by Lachaise, e.g. in the *Dolphin Fountain* (1924, New York, Whitney Museum of American Art), while his love of the female form and his undaunted tribute to sexuality are blatantly revealed in his anatomical fragments (*Torso with Pendulous Breasts*, 1930–2, Estate of Isabel Lachaise).

Catalogue, *Gaston Lachaise, 1882–1935*, Los Angeles County Museum of Art and Whitney Museum of American Art, New York 1964.
Hilton Kramer *et al. The Sculpture of Gaston Lachaise*, New York 1967.

Laermans, Eugène. Belgian painter, b. 1864 in Brussels; d. 1940 in Brussels. Laermans was a deaf-mute who responded to the solitude of his personal situation by trying to create a socially significant oeuvre. Both in his early Realist period and in the Expressionist period which followed (and in which he revealed his affinity with Permeke) Laermans depicted the wretched living conditions of the working and agricultural classes at the beginning of the twentieth century. In fact, he drew his inspiration from the same source as the Social Realists of a later date.

Laethem-St-Martin. From c. 1890 to 1914 the remote village of Laethem-St-Martin (near Ghent, Belgium) housed an artists' colony, which was visited at one time or another by some fifty painters, sculptors, musicians and poets. Like the members of the artists' colonies in Barbizon, Pont-Aven and Worpswede they hoped to rediscover the lost unity of life and nature. In the course of its existence the colony at Laethem-St-Martin produced two important groups. The first of these, which emerged before 1900 and numbered de Saedeleer, Gustave and Karel van de Woestijne and Georg Minne amongst its members, established a symbolistic and meditative style of painting with religious overtones. This style —a development of the work of Pieter Bruegel the Elder and of Flemish folk art—constituted a reaction against the 'superficial' Impressionism of painters like Rik Wouters. The second group of Laethem-St-Martin painters, which was formed c. 1905, was in complete contrast. It reverted to the Impressionist mode, producing scenes from peasant life, in which the colour was accentuated at the expense of the graphic line. The founders of Flemish Expressionism —Constant Permeke, Gustave de Smet, Albert Servaes and Fritz van den Berghe—were all members of this group. Although the artists' colony at Laethem-St-Martin broke up following the declaration of war in 1914, the movements which had been initiated there continued to exercise a widespread influence on the development of Belgian art.

Paul Haesaerts. *L'École de Laethem-St. Martin*, Brussels 1945.
André de Ridder. *Laethem-Saint-Martin, Colonie d'Artistes*, Brussels 1945.

La Fresnaye, Roger de. French painter and sculptor, b. 1885 in Le Mans; d. 1925 in Grasse. La Fresnaye was the son of an officer. He spent the first eight years of his life in Cannes and Beauvernay, near Saint-Nizier-sous-Charlieu on the Loire. Long before he left school he was a virtuoso draughtsman. His parents made no attempt to discourage him from an artistic career, insisting only that he acquire a good general education. This he did, and continued to live with his parents, who had moved meanwhile to Paris, until he had completed his schooling. Then, in 1903, he entered the Académie Julian, where he studied under John Lefebre and Tony Robert-Fleury, and became friendly with Boussingault, Lotiron, L. A. Moreau and Dunoyer de Segonzac. In 1904, when he enrolled at the École des Beaux-Arts, he met Paul Vera, and developed a great admiration for the work of Puvis de Chavannes and Gustave Moreau. In 1905 he did his military service, and in 1906 left the Académie Julian. In 1908, thanks to Paul Vera, he saw works by Maurice Denis, and was so impressed that he decided to continue his studies at the Académie Ranson, where he worked under Denis and P. Sérusier and was introduced to the paintings of Gauguin and Cézanne. In 1908–9 he stayed in

Châteauneuf-du-Faon with Sérusier and painted a series of Breton landscapes in the manner of Gauguin. In 1909 he took part in a competition at the Académie Ranson and painted his *Après-midi d'un Faune*, an act of homage to Mallarmé and Debussy, whose works he greatly admired. The year 1910, when he visited Germany, saw the completion of a set of illustrations for a novel by Francis Jammes. This was followed by paintings which were shown in the Salon des Indépendants and the Salon d'Automne. Between 1919 and 1921 La Fresnaye became friendly with Maillol, Bourdelle and Duchamp-Villon, and began to work as a sculptor. In 1912 he visited Meuland. The landscapes of this period reveal the influence of both Gauguin and Cézanne. From 1912 onwards La Fresnaye was in regular contact with the Parisian Cubists, and became particularly interested in the work of R. Delaunay. He also joined the *Artistes de Passy* association. In 1913 he became co-editor of the *Montjoie* magazine, to which he contributed as an illustrator. In the same year he was elected to the jury of the Salon d'Automne, and produced a series of still lifes which, although not entirely geometrical, were essentially Cubist. In 1914 he made preliminary sketches for his *Quatorze Juillet* before joining the colours. In 1918 he was taken ill and spent some time in hospital. The following year he visited Cambo and Durtol in Clermont-Ferrand, and then went on to Grasse. In 1920 he made a brief visit to Paris, and also began to write for *Esprit Nouveau* and *L'Amour de l'Art*. In 1921, the year in which his father died, La Fresnaye entered the sanatorium in Belligneux, where he painted his last picture, a landscape of Belligneux. In 1922 he returned to Grasse but by 1923 was totally paralysed. In 1923 he also had a large exhibition in the Salon des Tuileries in Paris. La Fresnaye exerted considerable influence on the younger generation of Parisian artists.

Germain Seligman. *Roger de La Fresnaye*, New York 1945.
R. Cogniat and W. George. *Oeuvre complète de Roger de La Fresnaye*, Paris 1950.

Lagar, Celso. Spanish painter and sculptor, b. 1891 in Ciudad Rodrigo; d. 1966 in Seville. He first studied sculpture, in Madrid, and later painting. He went to Paris in 1916 and there came to know members of the Cubist circle. His best works, both painting and sculpture, show the life of the circus.

Lam, Wifredo. Cuban painter, b. 1902 in Sagua la Grande. Lam's father was a Chinese émigré, his mother a Cuban. After attending the academy at San Alejandro, Havana, he studied in Madrid from 1924 to 1938 together with Fernando Alvarez de Sotomayor. In 1928 Lam had his first exhibition in Madrid. In 1931 his wife and son died of tuberculosis. In 1936 Lam saw his first Picassos. In 1936–7 he studied at the Quatres Gates Academy in Barcelona and remained in Spain, apart from brief visits to Cuba, until the fall of the Republic in the following year, when he went to Paris. There he established close contact with the members of the Surrealist circle: A. Breton, V. Brauner, O. Dominguez, P. Éluard, M. Ernst, A. Masson, Y. Tanguy and T. Tzara. In 1941, accompanied by Breton, Masson and the ethnologist Claude Levi-Strauss, Lam left Paris for Martinique. From there he went to Havana, where he met B. Péret in 1942 and Breton in 1945. Between 1941 and 1950 he had exhibitions in the Galerie Pierre Matisse in New York. In 1946 he met A. Gorky, M. Duchamp and N. Calas in New York before returning to Paris later the same year. Between 1947 and 1952 he lived in Cuba, New York and Paris, and subsequently made several visits to Italy. In 1951 he won the first prize at the Salone Nazionale, Havana. In 1952 he left Cuba to live in Paris. In 1953 he won the Prix Lissone. In 1957–8 he joined the Graham Foundation for Advanced Study in Fine Arts, Chicago, and in 1958 took a studio in Albisola. In 1961 he married Lou Laurin in New York, and in 1961–2 visited Zürich. In 1962 Carlo Grosetti published his *Images*, a series of coloured prints.

During his early period Lam was influenced by the native art of Cuba. His themes were taken from the religious cults of the islanders and reflected the mythical presence of their jungle gods. Subsequently —in the late 1930s—his art received a further crucial impetus from the works of Picasso, especially his *Guernica* of 1937. From the analytical approach to pictorial form established by the Cubists Lam evolved a highly expressive monumental style, and from their colour techniques he developed a new range of pure, warm shades. It was Picasso who introduced Lam to the Parisian Surrealists, and his constant contact with them also exerted a crucial influence on his work. (In fact, this was reciprocal, for between 1939 and 1945 the Surrealists also received an important stimulus from Lam.) Finally, when he met Gorky in the mid-1940s, Lam was able to free himself from the rigid adherence to established models that had been such a marked feature of *avant-garde* art in Europe. After a brief excursion into Abstract Expressionism his linear composition acquired a new precision, and his palette became brighter and more varied. It was then that he created his great series of mythical jungle pictures, in which the dangerous world of the forest, with its mysterious intertwining forms, acquires a Surrealist aura from the threatening presence of savage gods and their macabre attendants. Lam breaks down contexts and concentrates on individual forms, then reduces the forms to their component elements, which interact in the most remarkable way. Thus, the knotted joints of the sugar and bamboo canes reflect the joints in the prancing limbs of the daemonic creatures. Because of their common properties, these human and vegetable forms merge to produce a new pictorial order: the demons and gods, the animals and ancestral statues, the ritual masks and the instruments of magic, the plants and the trees appear as symbols of a new and dangerous reality. The awesomeness of this apocalyptic jungle chronicle is heightened by the incandescent reds, lilacs and yellows, which erupt from the dark grey-brown of the pictorial ground. With his remarkable imaginative powers Lam has been able to reconcile the artistic forces of Latin America with the European tradition.

Jacques Charpentier. *Lam*, Paris 1960.
J. J. Sweeney. Catalogue, *Wifredo Lam*, University of Notre Dame Art Gallery, South Bend (Ind.) 1961.
Catalogue, *Wifredo Lam Travelling Exhibition*, Palais des Beaux-Arts, Paris; Moderna Museet, Stockholm 1967.

Lamb, Henry. British painter, b. 1883 in Australia; d. 1960. Lamb was brought up in Manchester, where his father was Professor of Mathematics at the University. He studied medicine in Manchester before he took up painting, first in London, then, in 1907–8, in Paris at the Atelier la Palette. In 1910 and 1911 he worked in Brittany. He was a member of the Camden Town Group, 1911–12, and exhibited a portrait of Lytton Strachey at the first Post-Impressionist Exhibition in 1912. At the outbreak of war he returned to medicine, and in 1916 joined up as a medical officer, serving in Macedonia, Palestine and France. He was also an official war artist. *Bombardment in the Judaean Hills* is his best-known war picture (Imperial War Museum). He was an official war artist again from 1940 to 1945, but after the First World War worked mostly as a portrait painter. His style remained throughout his life a variant of Camden Town Post-Impressionism, though becoming a little freer in his later years. His portrait style is comparable to that of Augustus John. He was made a member of the Royal Academy in 1949 and won the Military Cross in the First World War.

Lamberechts, Franz. Belgian sculptor, b. 1909 in Brussels. After training as a mason and becoming fully proficient in the technique of carving marble, Lamberechts studied at the Academy in Brussels from 1930 to 1933. During his early period he produced figurative sculptures, but from 1950 onwards his work grew more and more abstract. In 1958 he became interested in polyester, and in the same year produced a polyester sculpture which formed part of a programmed spectacle, for which Louis de Meester created the music and J. Baré the lighting.

Lamónica, Robert de. Brazilian graphic artist, b. 1933 in Ponta Porá, Brazil. After training at the School of Fine Arts in São Paulo Lamónica travelled in Europe and Asia in 1957–8. In 1959 he went to Rio de Janeiro to study graphic art under Friedlaender, and in 1961 he enrolled at the School of Graphic Art in Lima.

Lancaster, Osbert. British painter, designer and cartoonist, b. 1908 in London. He studied in Oxford and at the Slade School. He has designed stage sets for the theatre—opera and ballet—and has illustrated his own books. He is best known for his regular cartoon in the *Daily Express*.

Land art (earth works). Since about 1967 a number of American artists, including Walter de Maria, Michael Heizer, Denis Oppenheim, Carl Andre and Robert Smithson, have been engaged on this new form of art. In remote, uninhabited districts like the Sahara, the Mojave desert or the dried-up Lake Mirage in California they dig trenches or furrows, draw lines on the earth by spreading lime and make mounds of rocks. This romantic and highly ephemeral record of man's presence in what Heizer has called a 'religious setting', namely a completely uninhabited territory, is clearly intended as a protest against the artificiality of big city life. These artists object to the 'utilitarianism' of contemporary art, by which they mean the smooth perfection of present-day metal and synthetic constructions and the advertising or industrial connotations of Pop and Minimal Art. In fact, the land artists' quest for elemental experience, their cosmic approach to the earth and their longing for a timeless world stamp their work as a modern variant of the 'Back to Nature' movement.

Landuyt, Octave. Belgian painter, potter, stage and industrial designer, b. 1922 in Ghent. After studying at the Academy in Courtrai, Landuyt became a professor at the École Normale in Ghent and head of the Design Bureau MEWAF in Courtrai. In 1958 he won the Belgian Guggenheim Prize.

Landuyt is a Surrealist. During his early period he painted macabre pictures of repellent human bodies, masks and macrocephalous organisms. Then, in c. 1960, he turned to a more abstract form of Surrealism, depicting amorphous, half vegetable and half organic tissues in dark, glowing colours similar to those produced by Max Ernst with his *clichés*.

H. Torczyner. *Octave Landuyt*, Ghent 1962.

Lanskoy, André. Russian-French painter, b. 1902 in Moscow; d. 1976. After spending his childhood in St. Petersburg, Lanskoy fled to Kiev in 1919 and subsequently served with the White Russian army. In 1921 he settled in Paris, where he studied at the Académie de la Grande Chaumière and began to paint fantastic scenes and landscapes. After an early period, in which he took his orientation from van Gogh and Matisse, he came under the influence of Klee and Kandinsky in 1937 and gradually turned away from objective art. By 1941 he had evolved a new spontaneous painting technique. In the works of this period rhythmical forms executed in pale pink, yellow and green and frequently offset by black grounds are linked by linear patterns. In producing these forms Lanskoy uses a palette knife, like de Staël, but creates a more dynamic and 'impressionistic' effect. In the *École de Paris* in the 1950s Lanskoy occupied a position between de Staël on the one hand and Bazaine and Manessier on the other.

J. Grenier. *André Lanskoy*, Paris 1960.
Catalogue, *André Lanskoy*, Musée Galliera, Paris 1966.

Lanyon, Peter. British painter, b. 1918 in St. Ives, Cornwall; d. 1964. In 1938 Lanyon attended the Euston Road Art School in London and from 1939 studied under Ben Nicholson and Naum Gabo in St. Ives. From 1950 to 1957 he taught at the Bath Academy in London. In 1964 he was killed in a gliding accident.

Lanyon was one of the 'St. Ives painters'. The subject matter of his pictures was his native Cornish landscape, which he first painted in a traditional, lyrical style after the manner of Ivon Hitchens. Subsequently, under the influence of Ben Nicholson (1939–40) and Naum Gabo (1940–6), he began to paint in a more abstract style. In c. 1940 he adopted a Constructivist technique but abandoned it shortly afterwards. From 1946 onwards he introduced nudes into his landscapes and began to move towards de Kooning and Rothko.

La Patellière, Amédée de. French painter and graphic artist, b. 1890 in Vallet; d. 1932 in Paris. La Patellière exhibited regularly in the Salon des Indépendants from 1922 onwards. In 1934 the Salon d'Automne staged a retrospective exhibition of his work. Although contemporaneous with the French Cubists, La Patellière did not break down his pictorial forms in any way. On the contrary, he painted his objects in full perspective, arranging them in clear, three-dimensional patterns. But by concentrating on strictly limited views he was at the same time able to focus attention on the two-dimensional nature of the picture surface. For the most part La Patellière preferred dark colours, which he used *en masse*, distinguishing between them by means of light reflections. His works are conducive to contemplation.

Lapicque, Charles. French painter and scientist, b. 1898 in Theizé, Rhône. Lapicque began to study civil engineering and architecture in 1919 and in 1924 obtained an engineering degree at Lisieux. In 1925 he took up painting as a hobby. In 1937 he created the interior decorations for the Palais de la Découverte. In the following year he published his doctor's dissertation, 'On Optics and the Perception of Contours'. In 1939 he made contact with Villon and the *Peintres de la Tradition Française*, e.g. Bazaine, Manessier, Estève, and exhibited with them in 1941. He is now living in Paris.

Lapicque has been a member of the French *avant-garde* since 1940. Like the *Peintres de la Tradition Française* he has tried to take the abstract techniques evolved by the Cubists, Fauvists and Orphists and combine them with objective reality. As a result we find a fusion of subject—horse race, regatta, seascape, etc.—and composition in the works of his final period. In painting these cheerful, rhythmical and exuberant colour compositions Lapicque tries to make a direct emotional appeal. He wants to move the public in the same way as it is moved by a piece of music.

J. Lescure. *Lapicque*, Paris 1956.
Exhibition catalogue, *Charles Lapicque*, Galerie Jacques Dubourg, Paris 1966.

Laprade, Pierre (Coffinhal-Laprade). French painter, b. 1875 in Narbonne; d. 1932 in Fontenay-aux-Roses. Laprade studied under Bourdelle in Montauban and under Carrière in Paris. In Carrière's *atelier* he met Matisse, Derain and Puy (who subsequently founded the Fauvist movement), but was not really influenced by them. During that period he spent most of his time copying works in the Louvre. In 1901 he had his first exhibition with the Indépendants and in 1903 joined with Vuillard and Rouault in founding the Salon d'Automne. From 1907 onwards he made frequent visits to Italy. After the First World War he created stage sets for the Swedish Ballet and the Théâtre des Arts and also produced a large number of book illustrations (*Manon Lescaut, Les fêtes galantes*, etc.).

Although Laprade made his name as a Fauvist, he did not remain a member of this group for very long. He belonged to the same generation as Vuillard and Bonnard and was essentially a Late Impressionist painter. His artistic development was firmly grounded in the work of Signac, Cézanne and—above all—Renoir, whose influence is readily apparent in Laprade's pictures. These consist of gentle poetic interiors, landscapes and flower paintings that are executed in silvery tones and are pervaded by the same bright, magical atmosphere that is so characteristic of Renoir.

L. Gebhard. *Pierre Laprade*, Paris 1930.

Lardera, Berto. French-Italian sculptor, b. 1911 in La Spezia. After completing his studies at the University of Florence Lardera took classes at a school of drawing before embarking on an artistic career. He then taught himself to sculpt and produced his first works in this medium in 1941–2. In 1947 he settled in Paris. In 1950 he created the sculpture for Mies van der Rohe's *Haus Lange* in Krefeld and in 1968 the *Île de France* for the French Pavilion at the Montreal Expo. He is now living in Paris.

Lardera works exclusively in metal in a severe, archaic and completely individual style that lies between González and Calder. Like Hartung, Schneider and Soulages he was one of the artists of the *École de Paris* who came to the fore after the Second World War. Initially Lardera constructed two-dimensional sculptures from sheets of iron, copper and aluminium but soon progressed to three-dimensional forms by means of rectangular alignment. The Constructivistic severity of Lardera's black or copper-coloured forms acquires a poetic quality from the subdued drama of his subject matter. His mythical leanings are revealed by titles such as *Antique Deity* and *Heroic Rhythm*.

M. Seuphor. *Berto Lardera*, Neuchâtel 1960.
I. Jianou. *Lardera*, Paris 1968.
Werner Haftmann. *Lardera: La Rose des vents*, M. Knoedler Gallery, New York 1969.

Larionov, Mikhail. Russian painter, b. 1881 in Tiraspol, Bessarabia; d. 1964 in Fontenay-aux-Roses. Larionov, the creator of Rayonnism, is now also remembered principally for his early (including Neo-Primitivist) work, and his collaboration with Diaghilev's *Ballets Russes* during and immediately after the First World War. Larionov received his art education at the Moscow College of Architecture, Sculpture and Painting where, during his early years as a student, he met the artist Natalia Sergeevna Gontcharova, who was to become his lifelong companion, and whom he eventually married many years later. The early work of both Larionov and Gontcharova is Impressionistic or Post-Impressionistic in manner, and it was with work of this kind that they were represented at the Russian Exhibition in Paris, organized by Diaghilev in 1906 (for the opening of which both artists travelled to Paris at Diaghilev's invitation). From 1908 to 1909 onwards Larionov worked in a Primitivist manner, much influenced by Russian peasant carvings and folk prints (*lubki*). His *Soldiers* series of 1909–10 included, in addition to their 'crudeness' of imagery, also verbal jokes and obscenities; these paintings recall the Futurist poetry of writers such as Kruchenykh and Khlebnikov, for whose works (often hand-printed in very small editions) both Larionov and Gontcharova on occasion provided illustrations (*A Game in Hell*; *Half-Alive*). Larionov's earliest Rayonnist works, the subject of some controversy, would appear to date from the end of 1911 onwards; the influence of Italian Futurism upon both the theory and practice of Rayonnism is noticeable.

Also during this period, Larionov was active as an organizer of exhibitions of the Russian *avant-garde* (*Jack of Diamonds*, 1910–11; *Donkey's Tail*, 1912; *The Target*, 1913). During the summer of 1914, Larionov and Gontcharova travelled to Paris; the Galerie Paul Guillaume organized an important exhibition of their work, for the catalogue of which Apollinaire provided an introduction. Returning to Russia at the outbreak of war, Larionov was shortly afterwards invalided out of the army and, together with Gontcharova, rejoined Diaghilev in Switzerland; their work for the *Ballets Russes* opened up a 'second career' in the theatre, of which one of the high points was Diaghilev's production of the ballet *Chout* given in Paris in 1921, with designs by Larionov. This collaboration with Diaghilev continued until the latter's death. During his later years resident in France, Larionov at this period frequently returned to representations of early subjects, posing the present-day art historian—at least in certain cases—considerable problems of chronology.

Camilla Gray. *The Great Experiment: Russian Art 1863–1922*, London and New York 1962.
Waldemar George. *Larionov*, Paris 1966.

Lassaw, Ibram. Egyptian-American sculptor, b. 1913 in Alexandria. After living in Marseilles, Naples, Tunis, the Crimea and Constantinople, Lassaw went to the United States in 1921 and acquired citizenship in 1928 through his father's naturalization. From 1926 to 1930 he studied with Dorothea H. Denslow and at the Beaux-Arts Institute of Design in New York and attended the City College of New York, 1931–2. Lassaw was one of the first American artists to execute abstract sculpture, as early as 1933. His working method of using bent and welded iron wire, combined with irregular surfaces of welded bronze and further applications of steel, nickel or copper, creates a fluidity of form and texture in an otherwise rigid maze. In addition to sculpture, Lassaw studied painting with A. Ozenfant (1947–9) and has been a serious student of Zen under D. T. Suzuki of Columbia University, New York. Since his first one-man show at the Kootz Gallery, New York (1951), he has been represented at the Venice Biennale (1954) and the São Paulo Bienal (1957). By the early 1960s his sculptures became less geometrical, with a greater relation to forms in nature (*Sui Shih*, 1962, New York, Kootz Gallery). Lassaw was a founding member of American Abstract Artists (1936) and was its president 1946–9.

E. C. Goosen, R. Goldwater and I. Sandler. *Three American Sculptors: Ferber, Hare, Lassaw*, New York 1959.

Lataster, Ger (Gerard). Dutch painter and graphic artist, b. 1920 in Schaesberg, Province of Limburg. After studying at the School of Arts and Crafts in Maestricht and at the Amsterdam Academy, Lataster toured Brittany before settling in Paris, where he is still living today.

During his early period, Lataster was an objective artist. Later he became an action painter, creating large-format works, in which the powerful colouring produces highly emotional effects.

A. Maisonneuve. *Ger Lataster*, Paris 1966.

Lattanzi, Luciano. Italian painter and art theorist, b. 1925 in Carrara. After studying philology in Naples, Lattanzi began to paint in 1956 and in the following year he published his *Manifesto of Semantic Painting.*

In both his paintings and his graphic works Lattanzi draws on a corpus of basic *motifs* (circle, serpentine, zigzag, cross, etc.), which he superimposes one upon the other. In 1962 he published his book *La Peinture Sémantique.*

Laurencin, Marie. French painter, b. 1885 in Paris; d. 1956 in Paris. Apart from the drawing lessons which she received at the School of Art in Sèvres, where she attended evening classes in arts and crafts, Laurencin was a self-taught artist. In 1907, when she made contact with the *avant-garde* circle of painters and poets centred on Picasso and Apollinaire, she had already published a volume of poems. From then until 1912 she lived with Apollinaire and moved in the Cubist milieu of the *Groupe du Bateau-Lavoir.*

Laurencin painted delicate, idyllic pictures of graceful young girls in pastel shades. Prior to her association with the Cubists these had been influenced by Carrière. Subsequently, however, they became more stylized, more simple and revealed a number of Cubist techniques. Later still Laurencin moved towards Cézanne. But these changes were only superficial. The basic lyrical quality of her work remained unaltered.

H. von Wedderkop. *Marie Laurencin*, Leipzig 1921.

Laurens, Henri. French sculptor, b. 1885 in Paris; d. 1954 in Paris. Laurens, who came from a working-class family, started out in life as an apprentice paint-hand. His only formal training was a course in drawing taken at evening classes. His first experiments as a sculptor bore the stamp of Rodin. But then, in 1911, he became friendly with G. Braque and was introduced by him to the other Cubists grouped around Apollinaire. In their company Laurens quickly developed and was soon the foremost Cubist sculptor. During his early period he made constructions from wood, plaster and sheet iron and also experimented with polychrome sculptures. The still lifes which he executed between 1915 and 1918 were influenced by the Cubist paintings of Picasso and Braque. In 1920 he produced a series of reliefs in terra-cotta, wood and stone, many of which he coloured. From 1921 onwards D. H. Kahnweiler acted as his agent and the commissions which he then received for stage sets for the Russian Ballet, for sepulchral monuments and other decorative works provided him with a livelihood. In 1925 he reached a turning point in his career: slowly but surely he abandoned his Cubist compositions and moved towards an organic style based on volume;

his still lifes were then replaced by female nudes and personifications of myths and the elements. From 1932 onwards Laurens spent part of his time in Étang-la-Ville, although Paris remained his principal residence. In 1936 he was asked to execute several large works for the International Exhibition in Paris. In the following year, when he made his first visit to the seaside, he discovered a whole new range of subjects: bathers, nereids, sirens, oceanids and undines, which frequently appeared in his subsequent work. In 1936 and 1937 Laurens had exhibitions in New York. During and immediately following the Second World War he made illustrations for works by Éluard, Theocritus, Tzara, Lucian and other writers. Starting in 1947 a series of large Laurens exhibitions was held all over the world. In 1951 the Musée National d'Art Moderne staged a retrospective exhibition in his honour, and in 1953 he was awarded the *Grand Prix* at the Bienal in São Paulo; in the same year the large version of *Anthion,* one of his celebrated metamorphoses, was erected in Caracas. Laurens bequeathed his unsold works to the Musée National d'Art Moderne in Paris.

Laurens progressed from craftsman to artist in the best French tradition. Not surprisingly, the nature and handling of the raw material remained the cornerstone of his art at all times. He was highly inventive and his new stylistic discoveries once brought him into close contact, not only with Cubist painting but also with Constructivism. He also made an important technical contribution with his polychrome experiments, which were designed to render sculptors impervious to the effects of light, to strengthen them and make them more durable. But it was not until 1925, when he went over to figurative sculpture, that Laurens began to produce his really great works. At first he created silhouettes with superb rhythmical contours, then progressed to figures in the round. With their convex, organic forms these figures—especially the later ones—are so charged with vitality that the skin is drawn taut like the skin on a ripe fruit. Laurens allowed his figures to grow to their full stature, to the point where—as he himself once said—he was unable to add anything to them. But his ultimate aim was to ensure the inner unity of his statues, i.e. the unity of volume and space, for in his works the figures enter into a dialogue with external and internal space. In 1951 Laurens said: 'In a sculpture the spaces must be just as significant as the volume. Essentially sculpture is the seizure of space, space circumscribed by forms.' Kahnweiler considers Laurens to be the greatest French sculptor of our age.

Marthe Laurens. *Henri Laurens, Sculpteur*, Paris 1955.
Cécile Goldschneider. *Laurens*, Cologne and Berlin 1956.

Laurent, Robert. French-American sculptor, b. 1890 in Finistère; d. 1970. Laurent went to the United States in 1902 after spending his formative years studying and living in France and Italy. His first exhibition in the United States in 1915 was followed by others in both America and Europe. From the 1920s to 1960 Laurent taught successively at the Art Students' League, New York, the Corcoran School of Art, Washington, D.C.; Vassar College, Poughkeepsie, New York; Goucher College, Baltimore, Maryland; and Indiana University.

Laurent was fundamentally a carve-direct sculptor with a strong regard for the nature of his materials— primarily alabaster, stone and wood (which he exhibited as early as 1915, when it was considered a relatively unusual medium). Like his contemporaries at the beginning of the twentieth century, Laurent was influenced by Negro and Oriental art, and developed a style of massive, swelling forms that were both simplified and stylized. His most frequent subject was the female figure (*Kneeling Figure*, 1935, New York, Whitney Museum), which was sometimes incorporated within a mother-child *motif*. Laurent also created numerous portrait heads (*Mimi*, 1928, Cape Neddick, Maine, Coll. Mrs. Robert Laurent) and received a number of public commissions (for the New York World's Fair, 1939; Fairmount Park, Philadelphia; and Indiana University). In 1961 Indiana University held a retrospective exhibition of Laurent's sculpture.

Rosamund Frost. 'Laurent: Frames to Figures, Brittany to Brooklyn', *Art News* XL, April 1941.
N. Kent. 'Robert Laurent, Master Carver', *American Artist* XXIX, May 1965.

Lausen, Jens. German painter, b. 1937 in Hamburg. After serving an apprenticeship in a graphic workshop from 1955 to 1957, Lausen attended the State College of Fine Arts in Hamburg from 1957 to 1961. From then until 1963 he worked as an industrial designer. He is now living in Hamburg.

From his study of the German Romantic landscapist C. D. Friedrich and of Op and Pop Art Lausen arrived at a new conception of spatiality. With their transparent, essentially Romantic colouring and their precise three-dimensional structures his *Sign Pictures*—which are really fantasy landscapes— create an aura of metaphysical stillness.

Exhibition catalogue, *Jens Lausen*, Marlborough Gallery, London 1969.

Lausen, Uwe. German painter, b. 1941 in Stuttgart. Lausen started to read philosophy and law at university but broke off his studies to become a painter. He is now living in Munich.

Lausen combines Neo-Expressionism with American Pop Art. His extremely realistic paintings, in which he deliberately sets out to shock the viewer, are conceived as a protest against the depravity of the world and the corruption of the establishment.

Lavery, Sir John. British painter, b. 1856 in Belfast; d. 1941 in County Kilkenny, Eire. He studied in Glasgow, London and the Académie Julian and Atelier Colarossi, Paris. His first one-man show was at the Goupil Gallery, London, in 1891. He was knighted in 1918. He was primarily a portrait and figure painter, but produced some naval scenes during the First World War. A memorial exhibition was held at the Leicester Galleries, London, in the year of his death.

Lawrence, Jacob. American painter, b. 1917 in Atlantic City. Lawrence, a Negro, moved to Harlem in 1930 and began to work with Charles Alston (b. 1907) from about 1932. He developed a keen interest in Negro history, and depicted various episodes from it in several series of paintings: the immigration scenes of 1940–1, the Harlem series of 1943 and the John Brown series of 1946.

Lawson, Ernest. American painter, b. 1873 in San Francisco; d. 1939 in Miami Beach. He went to New York in 1890 and became one of the members of The Eight, a group of Realist painters who included Robert Henri, William Glackens, George Luks and John Sloan, and with whom he exhibited at the Macbeth Gallery in 1908. Lawson's academic training was a solid one, and included attendance at the Art Students' League in New York—where his teachers were the Impressionist masters John Twachtman and J. Alden Weir—and the Académie Julian in Paris. In 1913 he exhibited works in the controversial Armory Show.

Lawson travelled in Europe, Mexico and to various parts of the United States, yet in his paintings confined himself almost exclusively to portraying urban realistic scenes of Manhattan. Although an exponent of the Impressionist style, he sought to preserve a greater degree of naturalism in his images than did some of his French counterparts; he accomplished this by imparting to his forms a fundamentally solid and stable outline, unlike that of the French Impressionists. Lawson was also partial to heavily impasted surfaces with deeply glowing colours, thick pigmentation and strong chiaroscuro contrasts. He did not, like the other members of the Eight, create figure paintings but rather specialized in landscapes of a serene nature. These include several paintings in the Whitney Museum of American Art in New York (*Winter on the River*, 1907; *Fishermen*, 1911; *High Bridge*, 1934) and the Metropolitan Museum of Art, also in New York (*Winter*, 1914). Other works by Lawson are in the Barnes Foundation in Philadelphia, the Brooklyn Museum in New York and the Art Institute of Chicago.

Guy Pène Du Bois. Catalogue, *Ernest Lawson*, Whitney Museum of American Art, New York 1932.

Lebel, Jean-Jacques. French painter, art theorist and organizer of happenings, b. 1936 in Paris. Lebel spent his childhood in New York and studied painting in Florence. From 1959 onwards he has arranged numerous international exhibitions and manifestations, e.g. *Workshop de la libre Expression* (Paris, 1964). From 1960 onwards he has organized happenings. Lebel frequently incorporates political themes into his collages. He also writes on art. At present he is living in Paris.

Lebenstein, Jan. Polish painter, b. 1930 in Brest-Litovsk. Lebenstein studied at the Academy of Art in Warsaw. Since 1959 he has been living in Paris.

   In 1956 Lebenstein began to paint his 'axial figures', which he depicted with sacerdotal expressions and with a rich, painterly texture that gives them a symbolic character. In the early 1960s, when the Expressionistic and biological elements in Lebenstein's work became more pronounced, he began to incorporate allusions to petrified or fantastic fauna. Later he went on to create allegorical compositions, depicting human and animal figures in dramatic situations. Lebenstein has also produced an impressive body of lithographs and drawings which owe their inspiration to Goya.

Exhibition catalogue, *Jan Lebenstein*, Musée d'Art Moderne, Paris 1961.

Leblanc, Walter. Belgian painter and sculptor, b. 1932 in Antwerp. Leblanc studied at the local Academies in Antwerp, where he is now living. He was one of the founder members of the *G 58* group and he also organized the *Anti-Peinture* exhibition in the Hessenhuis in Antwerp. His *Mobilo-Statics* (reliefs which vibrate in the light) were developed from monochromes.

Le Brocquy, Louis. Irish painter, b. 1916 in Dublin. From 1934 to 1938 he worked in the family business, and then left Ireland for the first time, travelled in England, Italy, Spain and France, and settled in 1939 in Menton where he began to paint. In 1940 he returned to Ireland and worked there until 1946, when he moved to London. Between 1942 and 1956 he produced a number of mosaic, mural and textile designs and he was visiting tutor in textile design to the RCA in 1954. In 1956 he won the International Prize at the Venice Biennale, and in 1960 he moved to the South of France. His earliest works are figurative and recall Degas and Manet, but in the forties he developed a Cubist idiom influenced perhaps by Picasso (*Travelling Woman with a Newspaper*, 1947). By the mid-fifties this had given way to a more painterly manner. The canvases are light in tone, often with a single feature (*Nude Studies*, 1957). These become the isolated ghost-like skulls and portrait heads of the

sixties: the features are blurred and ambiguous and reminiscent of Giacometti or Bacon, but they have their own very personal poetry of suggestion.

Lebrun, Rico (Federico). Italian-American painter, sculptor and graphic artist, b. 1900 in Naples; d. 1964 in Malibu. Before going to the United States in 1924, Lebrun had attended the National Technical School (1910–14), the National Technical Institute (1915–17) and the Industrial Institute, Naples. He also attended drawing classes at the Naples Academy of Fine Arts and learned the technique of fresco from the painters Cambi and Albino (1918–22). From 1917 to 1920 he served in the Italian army and navy. He worked as a designer for a stained-glass factory in Italy, a branch of which prompted his trip to the United States. In 1925 he moved to New York and became a commercial artist, doing advertising illustration for *Vogue*, *Harper's Bazaar* and *The New Yorker*. He lived in Italy from 1930 to 1933, studying fresco with Galimberti in Rome. When he returned to the United States he executed a fresco with Louis Rubinstein at the Fogg Art Museum, Cambridge, Mass., which has since been walled over. After winning a Guggenheim Fellowship and teaching at the Art Students' League (1934–5) he worked on a WPA project for the Pennsylvania Station Post Office Annex, New York, with G. Barrows and C. Peake. After a good deal of conflict, the project was abandoned and later walled over. After moving to California in 1938 he taught at the Chouinard Art Institute and the Walt Disney Studio in Los Angeles. He first exhibited in 1941 at the Faulkner Memorial Art Gallery, Santa Barbara, California, and held his first one-man show in New York in 1944–5 at the Julien Levey Gallery. In many respects his work might be thought of as a twentieth-century version of the Baroque, a quality which seems especially evident in his drawings. While *Night* (1942, pencil, Santa Barbara, California, Coll. Mrs. Donald Bear) recalls Guercino, *Woman Leaning on a Staff* (1941, ink and chalk, Los Angeles, Coll. Thomas A. Freiberg) calls to mind the soldiers and brigands of S. Rosa. In 1947 he began working on his *Crucifixion* series, a theme which came to an end in 1950 with the completion of the large *Crucifixion Triptych* (Syracuse, New York, Coll. Syracuse University). In 1951 he became director of the Jepson Art Institute, Los Angeles, where he had been teaching since 1947. The following year he taught at the Instituto Allende in San Miguel de Allende, Mexico. In the 1950s many of his works seem close in spirit to Goya. *The Magdalen* (1950, tempera on board, Santa Barbara, Museum of Art) recalls Goya's black Bordeaux figures, and *Portrait of a Spanish Nobleman* (1958, Oakland, N.J., Coll. Selden Rodman) seems a gruesome version of Goya's *Duke of Wellington*. Lebrun's *Buchenwald* series also seems to owe much to the horror and gore of Goya (*Floor of Buchenwald, 2,*

1958, casein and ink on board, Dayton, Ohio, Coll. Mr. and Mrs. Leslie L. Johnson). In 1959 he received a commission for a mural at Pomona College, Claremont, California. Preliminary sketches and cartoons for this work were completed in Rome while he was Artist-in-Residence at the American Academy. The conception is in a realm between abstraction and realism, between geometry and life. Carried out in black, white and brown, the work was completed in 1961 with the aid of William Ptaszynski and James Pinto. In 1961 he began a series of drawings illustrating Dante's *Inferno*, later executed as prints at the Tamarind Lithographic Workshop, where he also did prints illustrating Brecht's *Threepenny Opera* and a *Crucifixion* after Grünewald. In the year before his death he began working on a series of sculptures with the assistance of George Goyer.

Henry J. Seldes and Peter Selz. Catalogue, *Rico Lebrun (1900– 1964)*, County Museum of Art, Los Angeles 1967.

Leck, Barth Anthony van der. Dutch painter, b. 1876 in Utrecht; d. 1958 in Blaricum, Holland. After serving an apprenticeship as a craftsman in stained glass, Leck attended the School of Applied Arts and the Academy of Art in Amsterdam from 1898 onwards. In 1917 he became a founder member of the *de Stijl* group but withdrew from it after 1918. He was interested primarily in the applied arts, such as wall decorations, stained-glass windows and pottery.

During his early period Leck worked in a style which was a cross between those of Israëls and Toorop. Then, from 1910 onwards, he tried to establish a new synthesis between architecture and painting by reducing natural forms to their linear components and using the vertical, horizontal and diagonal lines to create geometric shapes, i.e. right angles, triangles and their derivatives. At the same time he reduced his range of colours to red, blue, yellow, black and white. Leck's theoretical concepts exerted a powerful influence on the *de Stijl* artists, especially Mondrian. At one point during his brief association with the *de Stijl* Leck went over to pure abstracts but soon reverted to his former, basically objective style.

Catalogue, *Barth van der Leck*, Stedelijk Museum, Amsterdam 1959.

Le Fauconnier, Henri. French painter, b. 1881 in Hesdin, Pas de Calais; d. 1945 in Paris. Le Fauconnier moved to Paris in 1901, and in 1905 he entered the Académie Julian, where he studied under J. P. Laurens, and met Segonzac, Luc-Albert Moreau, Boussingault and La Fresnaye. In 1905 he also exhibited in the Salon des Indépendants in Paris. In 1906, 1907 and 1908 he made repeated visits to Brittany. Between 1909 and 1913 he was in close contact with the Cubist artists of Montparnasse,

especially Léger, Metzinger, Gleizes, Delaunay and Archipenko. During this period he also met the Italian Futurists. In 1910 he joined the New Artists' Association, Munich; in 1911 he exhibited with R. Delaunay in the Salon des Indépendants in Paris, and visited Italy; and in 1912 he had a special exhibition in the Folkwang Museum in Hagen. In the period prior to 1914 he also showed works in a number of important exhibitions in Munich, Berlin and Zürich. Between 1914 and 1919 he lived in Veere and Amsterdam, then returned to Paris. Between 1915 and 1923 he showed works in exhibitions throughout Europe. In 1933 he visited London, Madrid and Italy. In 1949 he had a retrospective exhibition in the J. B. Neumann Gallery in New York.

Although Le Fauconnier was one of the leading protagonists of French Cubism during its early phase, his Cubist structures never achieved the same significance as those of Picasso, Braque or J. Gris. Around 1914 he turned away from Cubism and developed an expressive, figurative style of painting. Le Fauconnier exerted a powerful influence on the younger generation of painters in his day.

J. Romain. *Le Fauconnier*, Paris 1922.
Catalogue, *Le Fauconnier*, Stedelijk Museum, Amsterdam 1959.

Léger, Fernand. French painter, b. 1881 in Argentan, Normandy; d. 1955 in Gif-sur-Yvette. The son of a farmer, he was first (1897–9) apprenticed to an architect in Caen. From 1900 to 1902 he was a draughtsman in an architect's office in Paris. He did his military service from 1902 to 1903 in Versailles. From 1903 on he studied in Paris—at the École des Arts Décoratifs; the Académie Julian; in the studios of Gérome and Ferrier and at the Louvre. From 1903 to 1904 he was a photographic retoucher in an architect's office in Paris. He met André Mare at this time. In 1907 he saw the Cézanne memorial exhibition at the Salon d'Automne, and formed a friendship with Delaunay and Cendrars. From 1909 on he was in close contact with Cubist circles, and met the Douanier Rousseau; the following year he met Picasso and Braque. He was a member of the *Section d'Or* group from 1911 to 1912. In 1913 he signed a contract with Daniel-Henri Kahnweiler. At the outbreak of war he enlisted in the engineers, and suffered gas poisoning, after which he was discharged. He married in 1919. In 1919–20 he was in contact with *de Stijl* and Purism. Around this time he began his friendship with Le Corbusier. From the 1920s on he was active as a designer of theatre sets and films (*Le Ballet Mécanique*, 1923–4), and produced mural decoration, mosaics, stained glass and illustrations. In 1924 he visited Ravenna; he also opened an *atelier libre* with Ozenfant in Paris. In 1925 his work was exhibited in Le Corbusier's *Pavillon de l'Esprit Nouveau* in Paris. He paid his first visit to America in 1931. Two years later he went to Greece with Le Corbusier. From 1940 to 1945 he lived in America, where he taught at Yale and in California. He returned to Paris in 1945 and joined the French Communist Party. For three years (1946–9) he worked on a mosaic for the church at Assy. In 1948 he attended the Peace Congress in Poland. He set up a ceramics studio in Biot in 1950; in 1951 he produced stained-glass windows for the church at Audincourt. He married again in 1952, and settled at Gif-sur-Yvette. He also created a mural for the UN Building in New York. In 1955 he won the Grand Prix at the São Paulo Bienal. After his death the Musée Fernand Léger was inaugurated at Biot in 1960.

Considered by many contemporaries as one of the giants of Cubism, Léger always stood slightly outside Cubism's central concerns. As for most of his contemporaries, full recognition of Cézanne in 1907 came as a revelatory conclusion to Léger's experiments with Post-Impressionist techniques. For him Cézanne's art was one of plastic contrasts and although, in the course of his Cubist paintings of 1909–13, this led to an art of near-abstraction (*Contrasts of Forms*, 1913, Philadelphia, Museum of Art), ultimately it was the basis for a modern Realism. Paintings like *Woman in Blue*, 1912 (Basle, Kunstmuseum), rank among the major analytical Cubist figure paintings: lines, overlapping coloured planes and modelled forms are reconciled to the rigidity of the flat surface.

Most of Léger's art was less exclusively concerned with the inbred means of painting. He shared the Futurists' faith in the modern world and their Romantic vision of an art to give it proper expression. He was an early enthusiast of the cinema and large-scale advertising. These feelings for the modern machine age deepened during his war-time service with the engineers (see *The Card Players*, 1917, Otterlo, Rijksmuseum Kröller-Müller), and after the war he became a leading spokesman for a 'machine aesthetic'.

In the 1920s the influences of the like-minded Purists and of contemporary abstract art were assimilated in a series of monumental figure paintings and still lifes—*Le Grand Déjeuner*, 1921 (New York, Museum of Modern Art); *L'Accordéon*, 1926 (Eindhoven, Stedelijk van Abbe Museum). The regularized forms and strong simple colours express an heroic modern ideal, combining hieratic dignity with elements of everyday informality and the vernacular.

The tight order of the mid-twenties still lifes gave way in the thirties and forties to a looser, more curvilinear manner, which bears clear relationships to contemporary Parisian Surrealism (*Composition on Blue Ground*, 1938, Basle, Galerie Beyeler). Objects and forms are juxtaposed almost randomly against flat, coloured grounds.

Les Loisirs, Hommage à David, 1948–9 (Paris, Musée d'Art Moderne), marks his postwar return to a tradition-conscious monumental Realism. His late subjects are explicitly 'of the people'—popular entertainers, workers, etc. The paintings are very large, using clear flat colours and thick black contours and laying great stress on a simple opposition of rectangular and curvilinear elements. In most (e.g. *The Builders*, 1950, Biot, Musée Léger) the colours are contained within the contours, but in the late *La Grande Parade* (1953–4, New York, Guggenheim Museum), the coloured bands are independent and cut right across the massive drawing.

Léger's considerable reputation and influence, in Europe and America (where he taught during the Second World War), stems mainly from the figure paintings of 1917–25 and 1945–55.

Katherine Kuh. *Fernand Léger*, Urbana (Ill.) 1953.
P. Descargues. *Fernand Léger*, Paris 1955.
R. L. Delevoy. *Léger*, Lausanne 1962.

Lehmann, Kurt. German sculptor, b. 1905 in Koblenz, Germany. After studying at the Academy of Art in Kassel, Lehmann lived in Berlin from 1931 to 1933. He then returned to Kassel and remained there until 1948, when he moved to Hanover to teach at the technical college there. He is now living in Hanover.

Although basically figurative—like the work of Blumenthal and Marcks—Lehmann's sculptures reveal an abstract trend.

W. Passarge. *Kurt Lehmann*, Kassel 1957.

Lehmbruck, Wilhelm. German sculptor and graphic artist, b. 1881 in Meiderich near Duisburg; d. 1919 in Berlin. Lehmbruck was the son of a miner. After training at the School of Arts and Crafts in Düsseldorf from 1895 to 1899, he worked as a sculptor's assistant until 1901. Then, from 1901 to 1908, he continued his studies at the Academy of Art in Düsseldorf, where he entered Karl Janssen's masters' class. During this long apprenticeship he visited Italy in 1905–6 and Paris in 1908, having been represented at an exhibition there in the previous year. Paris attracted him more than the Italian cities because Rodin and Maillol, the two great masters of contemporary sculpture, were both living there. In 1910 Lehmbruck moved to Paris with his family and during the following four years, in Montparnasse, he produced the highly individual, larger than life-size statues in artificial stone and bronze, on which his reputation chiefly rests: *The Standing Female Figure* of 1910; *The Kneeling Woman* of 1911; *The Young Man Rising* of 1913; and *The Thinker* of 1913–14. Whilst in Paris Lehmbruck also made a number of line engravings. But in 1914, when war broke out, he was obliged to return to Germany. He spent the next three years in Berlin, where he created the *Beaten Man* in 1915–16. In 1918, whilst he was staying in Zürich, he modelled his *Young Man Seated*.

Two other works date from 1918–19: his *Head of a Thinker* and his *Mother and Child*. At the end of March 1919, just a few days after his election to the Academy, Lehmbruck committed suicide in Berlin.

As a student in Düsseldorf, Lehmbruck took his lead from the Realist Meunier, although he was also an admirer of Rodin and must by then have been acquainted with G. Minne's Symbolism. The heavy, voluminous forms of his *Standing Female Figure*—which was the first of his Paris works—seem to reflect the ideal conception of Maillol. But, despite the air of inner contemplation which is a feature of his work, Lehmbruck did not really favour a static art form. Like the painter Hans von Marées, with whom he had a certain mental affinity, he attached great value to movement as a means of expression. And so he abandoned the Classical canon. He then reduced the volume of his works, elongated the limbs of his figures and gave them expressive gestures. His *Kneeling Woman* was the first example of the 'limb architecture', which was considered by many of his contemporaries to be the epitome of Expressionist sculpture. At that time, of course, Lehmbruck found himself in the company of a number of artists, e.g. C. Brancusi, A. Modigliani, A. Archipenko and H. Matisse, whose views were similar to his own and whose sculptures revealed comparable trends towards dematerialization and idealization. But the fact that he was—and felt himself to be—a member of this Parisian group does not in any way detract from his individual achievement, for which he was rightly honoured in his lifetime (one-man show in Paris, represented at the Armory Show in New York, 1913, and the *Werkbund* Exhibition in Cologne, 1914). The depth of feeling and clarity of form which he achieved in the *Kneeling Woman* also informs his later works. In fact, it grew more pronounced over the years. The architectonic principle is plainly discernible in the *Young Man Rising*, whilst in the *Beaten Man* it produces a structure that is not far removed from an abstract sculpture in space. But then, in the *Young Man Seated*, which is really a study in melancholy, Lehmbruck reverted to a more closed and highly diverse sculptural form. Perhaps he had realized that 'sculpture as such was threatened with dissolution' (A. Kuhn). At all events, Lehmbruck's latest works were studies in psychology rather than experiments in the sphere of expressive Constructivism which he had made his own.

Werner Hofmann. *Wilhelm Lehmbruck*, London 1958; New York 1959.
August Hoff. *Wilhelm Lehmbruck, Leben und Werk*, Berlin 1961.

Lehmden, Anton. Austrian painter, b. 1929 in Nyitra, Hungary. Lehmden studied under Gütersloh at the Vienna Academy. He has been living in Vienna since 1945.

Lehmden belongs to the Viennese School of Fantastic Realism. Using a Classical technique, which he derived from Bruegel, Altdorfer and the Italian Quattrocento artists, he paints pictures of people engaged in fearsome battles which are set against an equally fearsome and completely desolate background.

W. Schmied. *Die Malerei des Phantastischen Realismus—Die Wiener Schule*, Vienna 1964.

Leinfellner, Heinz. Austrian sculptor, b. 1911 in Steinbrück, Lower Styria. After attending the School of Industrial Art in Graz Leinfellner trained at the Academy of Fine Arts in Vienna from 1933 to 1939. He also studied under Hanak. In 1939 he won the Prix de Rome. From 1947 to 1951 he worked as an assistant to Wotruba. Since 1959 he has taught pottery at the Academy for Applied Arts in Vienna. He is a founder member of the International Art Club of Vienna.

During his early phase Leinfellner was influenced by Cubism. Subsequently, thanks to his thorough training and his considerable powers of empathy, he was able to experiment with various techniques. He produced numerous sculptures composed of large flat areas with rectilinear forms, which were designed as an integral part of new building developments. Of recent years he has abandoned these clearly defined structures in favour of flowing contours and rounded forms.

Catalogue, *Heinz Leinfellner*, Kunsthalle, Baden-Baden 1959.

Leissler, Arnold. German painter, b. 1939 in Hanover. Leissler studied from 1958 onwards at the Werkkunstschule in Hanover and the Academy of Art in Nuremberg. He is now living in Isernhagen. He paints geometrical compositions and tightly organized arrangements of organic forms, using a technique that is reminiscent of the old masters.

Lemieux, Jean-Paul. Canadian painter, b. 1904 in Quebec. He studied at the École des Beaux-Arts, Montreal, and in Paris. After a brief period in Montreal, 1935–6, he began in 1937 a long period of teaching at the École des Beaux-Arts, Quebec. About 1938 he abandoned his early, conventional style to begin a series of subjects inspired by French Canadian folklore and pageantry in a Surrealist style recalling that of Stanley Spencer (*Lazare*, 1941, Toronto, Art Gallery of Ontario). After a period spent in France, 1954–5, he adopted his present Symbolist style, characterized by soft colours and forms evocative of Canadian life and its landscape setting (*Le Visiteur du soir*, 1956, Ottawa, National Gallery of Canada). He lives in Quebec and spends summers on the Île-aux-Coudres in the St. Lawrence. He has formed a notable private collection of the early arts of French Canada. He was appointed Companion of the Order of Canada in 1968.

Catalogue, *Jean-Paul Lemieux*, Montreal Museum of Fine Arts, Montreal 1967.
Guy Robert. *Jean-Paul Lemieux, le poétique de la souvenance*, Quebec 1968.

Le Moal, Jean. French painter, b. 1909 in Authon-du-Perche. After studying in Lyons and Paris, Le Moal attended the Académie Ranson from 1934 to 1938, working under Bissière, who influenced him considerably. Later, due to his close contact with Manessier, Le Moal turned abstract and in 1939 collaborated on a monumental abstract ceiling painting for the International Exhibition in New York. From 1940 onwards he produced numerous designs for stage sets and in 1941, together with Manessier, Bazaine, Pignon, Gischia and others, became a founder member of the *Jeunes Peintres de la Tradition Française*. After the Second World War he belonged to the *École de Paris* and was a member of the successful group led by Bazaine, Manessier, Singier and Estève, which sought to translate real-life experiences into Lyrical Abstract art forms. Le Moal's dotted pictures, which he executes in blue, green, yellow and mauve, have much in common with Bazaine's Abstract Impressionist works.

Lenk, Kaspar-Thomas. German sculptor and graphic artist, b. 1933 in Berlin. In 1944 Lenk moved to Württemberg and has lived in Fellbach, near Stuttgart, ever since. After attending the Academy of Art in Stuttgart for a short while he set up as a freelance sculptor in 1944.

In recent years Lenk has been producing constructions. These are made of identical wooden or metal geometrical sections—mostly prefabricated—which he arranges either in juxtaposition or in layers. These works are all coloured, some partially, others completely.

Leoncillo, Leonardo. Italian potter and sculptor, b. 1915 in Spoleto. After training at the Art Institute in Perugia Leoncillo settled in Umbertide, Umbria, where he ran a pottery workshop. In 1942 he moved to Rome and in 1946 became a founder member of the *Nuova Secessione Artistica*, which later developed into the *Fronte Nuovo delle Arti*. He now gives pottery classes at the Art Institute in Rome.

In his early period Leoncillo experimented with Expressionist structures. He then progressed by way of Cubism to geometrical Constructivism. But in 1955 he abandoned the stylized presentation of reality, which had characterized his previous work, and developed a completely abstract technique. From his preoccupation with the intrinsic qualities of his material on the one hand and his own formal conceptions on the other, he has created a whole repertoire of new iconographic forms with which to express contemporary reality.

Le Parc, Julio. Argentinian kinetic artist, b. 1928 in Mendoza. After studying at the Academy of Art in Buenos Aires Le Parc won a French Government scholarship in 1958 and went to Paris, where he worked with Victor Vasarély. Later, in 1960, he joined with Sobrino, Garcia-Rossi and others in founding the *Groupe de Recherche d'Art Visuel*. In the course of their enquiries into dynamic and volatile art forms the members of this group created kinetic objects, which were executed in a wide range of materials—including iron, aluminium, wood and Plexiglass—and consisted of glossy or transparent surfaces, on to which rays of white or coloured light were projected, thus producing an impression of constant movement. Le Parc calls his mobiles *Continuel-Mobiles* or *Continuel-Lumière-Mobiles*. He also enables the viewer to participate in the artistic process by incorporating into his mobiles adjustable elements, which can be moved at will. At the Thirty-third Biennale in Venice, at which he was the only Argentinian artist, Le Parc was awarded the Grand Prix International. He is one of the leading exponents of kinetic art.

F. Popper. *Le Parc et le problème de groupe*, Paris 1966.
J. Romero Brest *et al. Le Parc*, Buenos Aires 1967.

Leslie, Alfred. American painter, b. 1927 in New York City. Leslie studied at New York University and with Tony Smith, W. Baziotes, H. Woodruff and J. McPherson. An artist of the second generation of New York painters, his works, such as *Four Panel Green* (1957, New York, Martha Jackson Gallery), stem from the art of W. de Kooning with its broad areas of colour, free, painterly strokes, drips and sense of impetuosity. He first exhibited in the Kootz Gallery's 'New Talent' show, in which the works were selected by Clement Greenberg and Meyer Schapiro. He had his first one-man show at the Tibor De Nagy Gallery, New York, in 1951 and was included in the Fifth Bienal, São Paulo, Brazil (1959). He was the editor of *The Hasty Papers* (1960) and was a co-director-producer of the film *Pull My Daisy*. In 1964 he taught at the San Francisco Art Institute.

Leufert, Gerd. Venezuelan painter and art historian, b. 1914 in Wilna, Lithuania. After studying in Europe and the USA Leufert went to live in Caracas, where he became editor of the magazine *El Farol* and curator of the Museum of Fine Arts. Leufert is a concrete artist.

Levi, Carlo. Italian writer, politician and painter, b. 1902 in Turin. After studying medicine Levi turned to painting in 1923. He first made contact with Casorati's followers and the early *Novecento* artists, then studied Neo-Impressionism and the works of Braque and Modigliani before finally evolving a light and extremely colourful form of Expressionism. Levi was the leader of the *Sei di Torino* group, which opposed the official academic art of the *Novecento*. His major literary work is his *Cristo si è fermato ad Eboli*, which he wrote in 1943–4. At that time he also produced a series of pictures, in which he portrayed *motifs* taken from the lives of the Lucanian peasants. Until 1942 Levi lived in France as an exile. He then returned to Italy, but in May 1943 he was rearrested. Following the liberation of Florence he became editor of *La Nazione de Popolo* and, subsequently, of *L'Italia Libera*. He then worked as a writer and politician for a number of years, but in the 1950s resumed his painting. Apart from Guttuso, he is now considered to be the foremost exponent of Social Realism in Italy.

G. L. Ragghianti. *Carlo Levi*, Florence 1948.

Levine, Jack. American painter, b. 1915 in Boston. Levine grew up in the slums of South Boston, and first studied art under Harold Zimmerman. Dr. Denman Ross of Harvard University acquainted the precocious Levine with the study of art history and with the paintings in local museums. Although he studied Ross's mathematically derived systems of colour and pictorial composition during the early 1930s, Levine never relied on them in his art. Influences at first came from such artists as Degas, Daumier and Rembrandt, while work subsidized by the WPA Federal Arts Project in 1935 encouraged Levine's moralistic orientation. Stylistic affinities were found in the more Expressionistic painters— El Greco, Rubens, Rembrandt, Chaim Soutine and Georges Rouault, whose strong emotional sensibilities, expressive chiaroscuro and figurative distortions particularly impressed Levine. He was consistently concerned with the dehumanization and corruption in modern life, and such paintings as *The Trial* (1953–4, Chicago, Art Institute) and the *Gangster Funeral* (1952–3, New York, Whitney Museum) reflect this concern by means of biting satire directed against the stereotyped men of a capitalist society. Social protest of this order links Levine not only to his nineteenth-century European prototypes—Daumier, Goya and Toulouse-Lautrec—but also to the whole twentieth-century tradition of radical protest art in America, from the Ashcan School of the early 1900s to George Grosz's cartoons and the Social Realists of the 1930s.

Levine's first one-man show was in 1939, and in 1955 a retrospective was held at the Whitney Museum in New York. He received Guggenheim Fellowships in 1945 and 1946, and his work is included in such major collections as the Museum of Modern Art and the Metropolitan Museum in New York, and the Phillips Gallery in Washington, D.C.

Frederick S. Wight. *Jack Levine*, New York 1955.
Frank Getlein. *Jack Levine*, New York 1966.

Levy, Rudolf. German painter, b. 1875 in Stettin (Szczecin), Poland; d. 1944/5 in Dachau or Auschwitz. Levy came from an orthodox Jewish family. After training in arts and crafts in Berlin and Karlsruhe, he went to Munich to study painting. In 1903 he went to Paris, and helped to form the nucleus of the Café du Dôme group, together with Friedrich Ahlers-Hestermann, Alfred Weissman, Hans Purrmann and Oskar Moll. He met Matisse, and worked in his studio for many years from 1907. In 1931 he went back to Berlin and lived alternately there and in Paris until 1933, when he left Germany and eventually (1937) settled in Italy. In 1943 he was seized by the Gestapo in Rome and deported to a concentration camp.

A member of the 'German Matisse' school, his work developed from a Cézannesque treatment of form to a Matisse-like emphasis on colour and pattern. He was one of the most exciting of Matisse's followers, though relatively little known.

Genia Levy. *Rudolf Levy*, 1961.

Lewis, Wyndham. British painter and writer, b. 1882 in Nova Scotia; d. 1957 in London. From 1898 to 1901 he studied at the Slade School. From 1902 to 1909 he travelled extensively in Europe, living in Paris. He first exhibited in London in 1911 with the Camden Town Group and in 1912 at the second Post-Impressionist exhibition. In 1913 he was a founder member of the Omega Workshops, but shortly afterwards quarrelled with Roger Fry and seceded to found the Rebel Art Centre. He was at this time in contact with Futurism, by which he was greatly influenced, though he repudiated it in his short-lived periodical *Blast*, 'a review of the great British vortex' (1914). Adapting this title, Ezra Pound christened the movement Vorticism. Lewis's painting of these years was dynamic Cubist in manner and closely related to Futurism and the work of the French Orphists, Duchamp, Delaunay, etc. In 1916 Lewis enlisted, working as official war artist to the Canadian Corps from 1917 to 1919. Returning to London at the end of the war, he held his first one-man show. In 1920 he organized Group X and in 1921 edited the *Tyro*, another short-lived review; both were part of an attempt to continue pre-war Vorticism. Still influenced by Cubism in his drawing, though vigorously rejecting abstraction, his style from this time on remained basically figurative, and some of his best-known and most controversial works are portraits (*Edith Sitwell*, 1923–35, and *T. S. Eliot*, 1938). In 1927 he launched yet another periodical, *The Enemy*, which ran for three numbers. During the Second World War he was in America. On his return to Britain he continued to be active even after the loss of his sight in 1951. In the end Lewis is perhaps more important as an agitator and propagandist than as a painter, although through

Vorticism he was responsible for provoking the first serious response to Cubism in Britain.

Wyndham Lewis. *Wyndham Lewis the Artist: from 'Blast' to Burlington House*, London 1939.
Charles Handley-Read (ed.). *The Art of Wyndham Lewis*, London and Toronto 1951.
Catalogue, *Wyndham Lewis and Vorticism*, Tate Gallery, London 1956.

LeWitt, Sol. American sculptor, b. 1928 in Hartford, Connecticut. A contemporary of Don Judd, LeWitt came into prominence at the same time with work that shared the same basic premises as 'object sculpture', but was distinguished from it by its open-frame structure as opposed to the slab-sided constructions of Judd and of Robert Morris (b. 1931).

Lhôte, André. French painter and writer on art, b. 1885 in Bordeaux; d. 1962 in Paris. In accordance with his father's wishes Lhôte went to work in a furniture factory and began to train as a wood carver in 1892. From 1893 to 1895 he studied sculpture in an *atelier* attached to the École des Beaux-Arts in Bordeaux. During this period he painted in his spare time and in 1905 gave up sculpture to become a full-time painter. In 1906 he made contact with the *Indépendants* and in 1907 became a member of the Salon d'Automne. In 1908 he moved to Paris. Two years later, in 1910, he saw works by Paul Cézanne and was deeply impressed by them. In 1911 he made contact with the Cubists and in 1912 became a founder member of the *Section d'Or* and one of the joint editors of its magazine. From 1917 onwards he contributed to the *Nouvelle Revue Française*. He taught at the Académie Notre-Dame des Champs from 1918 to 1920, at the Académie du Boulevard Raspail in 1920 and at the Académie Anderson from 1922 to 1926. In 1952 he visited Rio de Janeiro, where he opened a South American branch of the Académie Montparnasse, which he had founded in 1922.

After working as a wood carver for a brief period Lhôte taught himself to paint. Although he was certainly influenced by Cézanne and the Cubists between 1908 and 1910, he was far from dogmatic in the application of Cubist principles to his portraits, landscapes and figurative compositions. In fact, these extremely subtle works, in which the pictorial objects are arranged with great care and the various planes are distinguished from one another by the use of firm contours and pure colours, are virtually Constructivist. In many of his paintings, however, Lhôte was clearly more concerned with demonstrating his artistic theories than with the creation of works of art. As a teacher he had considerable influence on the younger generation. In his theoretical writings he broached important artistic issues and dealt in detail with the technical aspects of painting.

André Lhôte. Critical articles in *Nouvelle Revue Française* from 1917 onwards; *La Peinture, le Coeur et l'Esprit*, Paris 1933; *Écrits des Artistes*, Paris 1941.
A. Jakovsky. *André Lhôte*, Paris 1947.
Catalogue, *André Lhôte*, Musée de Lyons, Lyons 1966.

Lichtenstein, Roy. American painter and sculptor, b. 1923 in New York. He studied under Reginald Marsh at the Art Students' League (1939), served in the Army, then completed an MFA degree at Ohio State University in 1949. While painting in Cleveland (1951–7) he worked as a freelance designer, then taught at the State College in Oswego after moving to New York. Later he instructed at Rutgers University in New Jersey. Lichtenstein worked in a non-figurative Abstract Expressionist mode before 1957; then he began to use loosely handled cartoon images from bubble-gum wrappers, also reinterpreting paintings of the old West by Frederick Remington and others. His changeover to stylistic preoccupations with vulgar cartoon or pulp-magazine images, and to commercial subject matter and techniques, was complete by 1961. Conscious of the 'happenings' initiated in the early 1960s by Claes Oldenburg, Jim Dine and his Rutgers colleague Allan Kaprow, Lichtenstein shared their concern with making art from the materials and products of the industrial environment. He was particularly interested in the lack of sensitivity in mass-produced, often perishable images and merchandizing art, which prompted him to mimic such aspects of the public landscape in his own work. Rejecting the personal and romantic subjectivism of the Abstract Expressionists, Lichtenstein substituted the conventions of a crass contemporary art form, creating a kind of instant nostalgia. Comic-strip characters are extracted from their narrative context, blown up in size and reproduced with the same typographic screen techniques (Ben Day dots) with which they were printed, thus becoming an emblematic parody of the original (*Good Morning, Darling*, 1964, New York, Leo Castelli Gallery). But the simulation is not meant to bear a message of social commentary, ironic as it may seem. Just as the Pop subject matter dictates the use of a commercial technique for an aesthetic end, the message itself becomes an aesthetic one.

In his reproductions of corny popular romance characters, travel-poster vulgarizations of Classical ruins (*Temple of Apollo*, 1964, Pasadena, California, Coll. Mr. and Mrs. Robert A. Rowan), comic-book war heroes, advertising fragments (*Girl with Ball*, 1961, New York, Coll. Philip Johnson) or stylized landscapes, Lichtenstein contrasts what is already a travesty of emotion, scene or object with his unemotionally banal rendition. He oversimplifies and extracts from the artefacts of mass culture, creating new psychological overtones that reveal, but do not directly comment upon, the sensibility of an era. Lichtenstein also uses the discredited styles and mannerisms of earlier periods, such as his paintings and sculptures (1967–8) based on the once popular 1930s 'modern', a corrupt and ornamental version of Cubism. *Modern Painting With Yellow Interweave* (1968, Leo Castelli Gallery) and the curved brass or chrome, tinted glass and marble slabs of his elegant sculptures evoke the taste and style of that period. The subjects of Lichtenstein's 'Pop' paintings, ceramics, sculptures and posters are quoted from an anonymous idiom; with selective mechanical methods he transforms this source material into a personal style offering new sensations and terms for viewing and understanding art.

Lawrence Alloway. 'Roy Lichtenstein's Period Style: From the Thirties to the Sixties and Back', *Arts* XLII, September 1967.
Catalogue, *Roy Lichtenstein*, Art Museum, Pasadena 1967.
R. Morphet, G. R. Swenson and J. Coplans. Catalogue, *Roy Lichtenstein*, Tate Gallery, London 1968.

Licini, Osvaldo. Italian painter, b. 1894 in Monte Vidon Corrado; d. 1958 in Monte Vidon Corrado. Licini studied at the Academy in Bologna, where he became friendly with G. Morandi, whose painterly visions he occasionally incorporated into his pictures. In c. 1920 Licini began to paint objective portraits and figure compositions. Then, from c. 1930 onwards, he produced constructive improvisations consisting of integrated pictorial forms executed in harmonious colours. Like the objective pictures of the 1920s, these works—which were doubtless inspired by Malevich and Kupka—are remarkable for their technical virtuosity. In 1935 Licini exhibited at the Quadriennale in Rome, together with Magnelli and Soldati. He made numerous visits to Sweden and France, and frequently stayed in Paris. In c. 1950 he abandoned his constructive forms and developed an essentially animistic type of Surrealistic automatism. At the 1950 Biennale in Venice the significance of his Constructivist painting received public recognition, and at the 1958 Biennale in Venice Licini was awarded the Italian national prize for painting. In 1959 a large retrospective exhibition of his works was staged in Leghorn.

G. Marchiori. *Licini con 21 lettere del pittore*, Rome 1960.

Lie, Jonas. Norwegian-American painter, b. 1880 in Norway; d. 1940 in New York City. As a child he studied the fundamentals of drawing under Christian Skredsvig. He moved from Norway to Paris in 1892, staying with his uncle, the author Jonas Lie. The following year he went to the United States and attended the Ethical Culture School, from which he graduated in 1897. Upon completion of his basic education, Lie went to work as a designer of cotton fabric patterns and attended classes at the Art Students' League and the National Academy of Design. He became a full-time painter around 1903. Three years later he returned to Europe and was most strongly influenced by Monet. When he returned to the United States, his work took on a new

breadth and clarity of vision. The flickering coloured light and a sense of airy space which he inherited from Monet can be seen in the canvases of his entire oeuvre (*Out to Sea*, Cleveland, Ohio, Museum of Art). In 1912 he became an associate member of the National Academy. The next year he made a trip to Central America where he recorded the construction of the Panama Canal in a series of fifteen large paintings, thirteen of which are now at the United States Military Academy, West Point, New York. 1919 was particularly important for both Lie and the National Academy. In that year he led a revolt with G. Bellows, P. Manship and J. Pennell protesting the Academy's selection procedures. As an alternative to the Academy, they established a group called The American Painters, Sculptors and Gravers and accepted the artists who had been rejected by the Academy. Among those not accepted by the older organization but taken in by Lie and his associates were B. Robinson, J. Sloan, G. Luks and R. Kent. Ironically, Lie continued to be associated with the Academy. He was made a full member in 1925 and from 1934 to 1939 served as the Academy's president.

Liebermann, Max. German painter and graphic artist, b. 1847 in Berlin; d. 1935 in Berlin. After studying at Berlin University and working in Karl Steffeck's studio from 1866 to 1868 Liebermann attended the Weimar School of Art from 1868 to 1873. The year 1871 was a turning point, for it was then that Liebermann made his first trip to Holland and met the painter Munkácsy in Düsseldorf. Munkácsy exerted a considerable influence on him at that time, as is evident from Liebermann's *Goose Pluckers*. The impressions Liebermann received in Holland, where he studied the work of Frans Hals, opened up a new world that was very different from the academic world of his student years. His new-found sense of freedom was reinforced in 1872—when he paid a second visit to Holland, where he made a close study of nature and executed his first *plein-air* paintings—and 1874, when he visited Paris and Barbizon, where he was greatly impressed by the paintings of Millet. In 1878 Liebermann moved to Munich, remaining there until 1884, when he settled permanently in Berlin. Subsequently, he made many more trips to Holland, and during the late 1880s was strongly influenced by the Dutch *plein-air* painter Israëls. His *Women Mending Nets* is a typical example of his work at that time. It was not until 1890 that Liebermann discovered Manet, when his palette became brighter and his brushwork more relaxed. Subsequently, he turned more and more to Impressionism, and successfully promoted this style within the Berlin Secession, which he helped to found in 1908 and of which he was president until 1911. Together with Slevogt and Corinth, Liebermann was one of the foremost representatives of German Impressionism. Although his work continued to reflect the Realism of Menzel and the nature-lyricism of the Barbizon School, he none the less contrived to break away from the historicizing and idealizing style of contemporary academic painting; and with his objective and unsentimental attitude to nature he succeeded in establishing within German art the modern trends that had been developed in other parts of Europe. Liebermann remained the dominant figure in the Berlin art world for several decades. In 1897 he became a professor, in 1912 he was awarded an honorary doctorate, and in 1920 he was appointed President of the Berlin Academy of Fine Arts. In 1933 his work was proscribed on account of his non-Aryan origins. He died, abandoned by his former friends, two years later.

E. Hancke. *Max Liebermann: Sein Leben und seine Werke*, Berlin 1914.
K. Scheffler. *Max Liebermann*, Wiesbaden 1953.
F. Stuttmann. *Max Liebermann*, Hanover 1961.

Lin, Richard (Lin Show Yu). Chinese-British abstract painter, b. 1933 in Formosa. Lin was educated in Japan and at Millfield School, Somerset. From 1954 to 1957 he studied architecture in London, then turned to art. He produces Constructivist reliefs, often of metal (bronze or aluminium), of an austere rectilinear design reminiscent of Nicholson and Mondrian. They play different qualities of surface against each other in very shallow depth and are impressive through their sheer refinement and elegance.

Catalogues, *Richard Lin*, Gimpel Fils, London 1964; Marlborough Galleries, London 1966.

Linck, Walter. Swiss sculptor, b. 1903. Linck creates mobiles and stabiles, which explore the problems of movement in space.

Lindell, Lage. Swedish painter, b. 1920. Lindell studied under Grünewald and Erixson at the College of Art in Stockholm from 1941 to 1946. During his early period he painted scenes from the suburbs of Hagalund, in which the houses and people are transformed into ethereal objects reminiscent of Gothic structures. A typical example is his *Vår i Hagalund* (*Spring in Hagalund*) of 1947, which is now in the Nasjonalgalleriet in Oslo. These early townscapes were followed by landscapes executed in fresh soft colours and depicting scenes from the Island of Ven and Spain. It was in these works that Lindell began to move towards abstract art. Later he produced compositions consisting of black and white geometrical forms offset by touches of yellow, green and blue and so arranged that the different shapes seem to hover in space. Lindell's oeuvre also includes an earthenware mosaic executed in the courthouse in Sundsvall in 1955. In 1965 he collaborated on the decoration of the dining room at the Astra Factory in Södertalje.

Lindner, Richard. German-American painter, b. 1901 in Hamburg, Germany. After studying music in Bavaria and pursuing a career as a concert pianist (1919–23), Lindner turned to painting in 1922. His first training was at the Kunstgewerbeschule in Nuremberg, and then in 1924 he studied at the Academy of Fine Arts in Munich. After a year in Berlin (1927–8) he returned to Munich and worked as an art adviser for the publishing house of Knorr and Hirth. In 1933 he fled the Nazi regime, settling in Paris where he met Picasso and Gertrude Stein. He joined the French army (c. 1939) and was later attached to the British army. He moved to the United States in 1941 and became a successful illustrator for such magazines as *Fortune*, *Vogue* and *Harper's Bazaar*. In addition to his work on periodicals, he was also active as a book illustrator, doing designs for *Madame Bovary* (1944), *Tales of Hoffmann* (1946) and *Continental Tales of Longfellow* (1948) among others. In 1951 he gave up illustration, devoting all of his time to painting and teaching at the Pratt Institute, Brooklyn, New York. Though he had been painting in Paris, he found it difficult to break away from the commercial and the illustrative. The real beginnings of his artistic production came about 1953 (*The Meeting*, New York, Museum of Modern Art). By 1954, the year of his first one-man show at the Betty Parsons Gallery, New York, his mnemonic imagery is mainly concerned with childhood. These militant, over-fed pre-adolescents are the cruellest of all his subjects (*Boy with Machine*, 1954, New York, Coll. Judge Henry Epstein). His hyper-fastidious approach to the figure, modelled with a hard, plastic solidity in vivid clarity and colouration, is the keynote of his style. His approach has become increasingly abstract, invoking post-Cubist Léger, Futurism and ultimately the phantasmagoria of Dada and Surrealism. His sadistic children and inventive forms have developed into a highly sexual, symbolically erotic art which can be seen as early as *The Meeting* and has continued more overtly in *N.Y.C. II* (Turin, Italy, Galleria Galatea), a work of 1946, the year he was included in Documenta III at Kassel, Germany.

Sidney Tillim. *Lindner*, Chicago (n.d.).

Lindström, Bengt. Swedish painter, b. 1925 in Storsjökapell. After studying under Grünewald in Stockholm in 1944 and under Aksel Jörgensen at the Academy of Art in Copenhagen in 1945–6, Lindström attended the Art Institute in Chicago for a brief period late in 1946. In 1947 he went to Paris, where he studied under André Lhôte and Léger, and where he is still living today. Since 1958 Lindström has built up a considerable reputation. Using pure and strongly contrasting colours, which he applies with broad strokes of the brush to zinc oxide grounds, he portrays daemonic figures engaged in dramatic actions.

Anders Lidén (ed.). *Bengt Lindström: Un souffle frais de vie*, Uddevalla 1968.

Linnqvist, Hilding. Swedish painter, b. 1891. After studying at the College of Art in Stockholm from 1910 to 1912 Linnqvist turned his back on the academic tradition and went his own way. Between 1917 and 1920 he produced numerous highly individual primitive paintings, many of them executed in a small format and in dark colours with an enamel-like glaze. Typical examples are his *Militärbegravning* (*Military Funeral*, 1918, Modern Museum, Stockholm), *Stadsbild vid Klara sjö* (*Stockholm Townscape*, 1918, Modern Museum, Stockholm) and *Passionsblommor* (*Passion Flowers*, 1918). On journeys to France and Italy Linnqvist evolved a lighter and more controlled style, which can be seen in his *Torgbild, fransk smastad* (*Market Scene in a Small French Town*, 1921–5, Modern Museum, Stockholm). Linnqvist also visited Morocco and Spain (in 1928), Greece (in 1937) and Egypt. In 1934 he joined the *Färg och Form* (*Colour and Form*) group, and from 1939 to 1941 held a professorial post at the College of Art in Stockholm. Linnqvist received numerous monumental commissions and produced large-format works for various public buildings including the Stockholm City Library (in 1927–8) and the Marabou Chocolate Factory in Sundbyberg, near Stockholm (in 1938–9). These public commissions appear to have influenced Linnqvist's studio paintings, which have become more realistic and more decorative in the course of his career. Linnqvist has also created stage sets, and published biographical and critical writings. His *Grekisk resa* (*Greek Journey*) appeared in 1946 and his *Tankar om konst* (*Reflections on Art*) in 1949.

F. Holmér. *Hilding Linnqvist*, Stockholm 1955.

Lint, Louis van. Belgian painter, b. 1909 in Brussels. From 1945–6 onwards Lint's figurative paintings revealed a new and original sensitivity, and were executed in a style similar to that evolved by the *Cobra* group, which Lint subsequently joined. Shortly afterwards he moved towards abstract art, and was influenced for a while by Jean Bazaine. Lint also took part in the exhibitions staged by the *Jeune Peinture belge* association, of which he was a founder member. His first abstract works tended to be rather formalistic but, as his technique improved, his composition and draughtsmanship regained the personal quality that had characterized his figurative work during the postwar period. Of recent years Lint has been working in a new figurative style, which has benefited from his abstract experiments. In 1958 he was awarded the Grand Prix de la Critique at Charleroi.

L. L. Sosset. *Louis van Lint*, Antwerp 1951.

Lipchitz, Jacques. French sculptor of Polish-Jewish origin, b. 1891 in Druskininkai, Lithuania; d. 1973. He was the son of a building contractor. In October 1909 he went to Paris, where he studied at various academies up to 1911. In 1925, when he became a French citizen, he commissioned Le Corbusier to build him a house and studio in Boulogne-sur-Seine. In 1930, following a large restrospective exhibition, he became internationally famous. In 1940 he fled from Paris and in 1941 went to America, where he first worked in New York. In 1952 he settled in Hastings on Hudson, New York, where he is still living today. When he was first introduced to Cubism by D. Rivera, A. Modigliani and J. Gris, Lipchitz resisted the new movement and continued to create realistic sculptures. In 1914, when he visited Spain, he was greatly impressed by the works of El Greco. In 1915, however, he began to construct Cubist sculptures from prismatic forms, although even then the Mannerist movement, which remained a feature of his works, still distinguished them from the products of orthodox Cubism. In 1925 the heavy, angular forms, which had characterized Lipchitz's output during the previous decade, were replaced by the more abstract forms of his openwork sculptures (*sculptures transparentes*). This new style lent itself even less to categorizing: not only did Lipchitz continue to respond to the world around him in a completely spontaneous manner, he also frequently drew on past experience, which he adapted to meet his present need; and, no less important, he sought inspiration in archaic and primitive works with which he, as a collector, was well acquainted. His monumental sculptures such as the *Joie de Vivre* 1927, the totemistic *Figure* of 1930, the *Chant des Voyelles* of 1931 and the *Prometheus* of 1936, which also reveal traces of Surrealism, provide the link between the block-like forms of his Cubist work and the openwork style of his *sculptures transparentes*.

After the Second World War Lipchitz tried to give artistic expression to the turbulence and suffering of the preceding decade by modelling a number of mythological and biblical groups that are characterized by Baroque pathos and highly expressive gestures. From these it was but a step to his *Semi-Automatics* and to the series of highly complex wax compositions entitled *À la limite du possible*, in which he incorporated ready-mades.

Henry R. Hope. *The Sculpture of Jacques Lipchitz*, Museum of Modern Art, New York 1954.
Robert Goldwater. *Jacques Lipchitz*, New York 1959.
A. M. Hammacher. *Jacques Lipchitz*, Cologne 1961.

Lippold, Richard. American sculptor, b. 1915 in Milwaukee, Wisconsin. The son of a mechanical engineer, Lippold's schooling echoed the interests of his father. He attended the University of Chicago and the Art Institute of Chicago (1933–7), majoring in industrial design. While teaching at the University of Michigan (1941–4) he became interested in wire sculpture. Largely self-taught as an artist, his work is derived ultimately from the Constructivist tradition and his training in industrial design. From 1945 to 1947 he taught at Goddard College, Vermont, and gave his first one-man show in the latter year at the Willard Gallery, New York. The following year he was artist-in-residence at Black Mountain College, N.C., that outpost of *avant-garde* art in America, fathered by Joseph Albers. In 1950 he was commissioned by Walter Gropius to create an outdoor construction for the Graduate Law School Center at Harvard University, Cambridge, Mass. His most significant commission, however, came in 1953 from the Metropolitan Museum of Art, New York, for whom he executed *Variation within a Sphere, No. 10: The Sun*, completed in 1956. A sculptural ensemble of gold wires creating a variety of simple geometric forms: the relationships of ellipses, circles, triangles, cubes and cones change drastically with the slightest movement of the spectator in this work based on the tension of stretched wire.

Lipsi, Morice. Polish-French sculptor, b. 1898 in Lodz, Poland. After settling in Paris in 1912, Lipsi learnt ivory and wood carving from his brother. In 1916 he studied at the Paris Academy for a short while. In 1933 he acquired French nationality. In 1942 he fled, first to the South of France, then to Switzerland. Whilst in Geneva he created his series of *Masks, Snails* and *Leaves*. In 1945 he returned to France. In the course of his career Lipsi has gradually moved towards pure abstract art. His mature works consist of passive, block-like forms with coarse-grained, relief-like surfaces. Apart from the war years Lipsi has been living in Chevilly-Larne, near Paris, since 1933.

R. V. Gindertael (ed.). *Morice Lipsi*, Neuchâtel 1965.

Lipton, Seymour. American sculptor, b. 1903 in New York City. Graduating from high school in 1921, Lipton attended the College of the City of New York for one year and then entered Columbia University, from which he received a Doctor of Dental Surgery degree in 1927. He began working seriously as a sculptor in 1932, first developing his pieces through the use of clay models and later from drawings. He first exhibited in 1933–4 and had his first one-man show, mostly of wood carvings, at the American Contemporary Artists' Gallery in 1938. For many years he supported his family as a dentist and worked part-time as a sculptor. During these years he also taught sculpture at the New School for Social Research (1940–58), Cooper Union Art School

(1943–4), and New Jersey State Teachers' College, Newark (1944–5). In the mid-1940s he switched from wood and stone to lead and bronze in order better to express man's tragic experience of the Second World War. His working procedure begins with drawings which are then worked up into a small model in metal. This is produced as a full-scale piece made of thin, malleable sheet-metal that is cut and bent into the desired shapes; the edges of the pieces are then welded together. Over this armature he often uses a covering of melted nickel-silver or bronze. In the early 1950s Lipton temporarily stopped dealing with the human figure, turning instead to metaphorical expression drawn from botanical imagery. He returned to the human form again just before his inclusion in the 1957 São Paulo Bienal and the 1958 Venice Biennale. His human images are often merely suggested rather than explicit as in *Sentinel* (1959, New Haven, Conn., Yale Art Gallery). In his 1964 *Archangel* for the Philharmonic Hall at Lincoln Center, New York, the form can be thought of in musical terms—as bells, horns, cymbals or the heralding in of the Archangel —as well as in a physically figurative context.

Albert Elsen. 'Seymour Lipton; Odyssey of the Unquiet Metaphor', *Art International* V, February 1961.

Lismonde, Jules. Belgian draughtsman and painter, b. 1908 in Anderlecht, near Brussels. Lismonde studied at the Academies in Brussels and Saint-Josse. In 1943 he gave up painting in order to concentrate on his drawings. He then began to specialize in psychological portraits and, under the influence of Seurat and Villon, moved towards abstract art, becoming a member of the *Jeune Peinture belge* in 1946. He is now living in Linkebeek, near Brussels.

Lismonde produces extremely poetic drawings by building up linear designs with delicate strokes of the pen. Most of these compositions are based on landscapes which—as in the works of Bazaine—are still recognizable as such.

L. Lebeer. *Lismonde*, Brussels 1956.

Lissitzky, El (Eleazar). Russian painter and draughtsman, b. 1890 in Poshinok, Smolensk; d. 1941 in Moscow. After spending his childhood and early youth in Vitebsk and Smolensk, Lissitzky studied architecture in Darmstadt from 1909 to 1914. He then returned to Russia, working as an architect in Moscow and, from 1916 onwards, contributing to art exhibitions. Between 1917 and 1920 he produced woodcuts after the manner of Chagall, in which he represented scenes taken from Jewish literature. When he was invited to teach in Vitebsk Lissitzky made contact with Malevich, who was also teaching there. From 1919 onwards he produced his *Prouns* which, although undoubtedly inspired by Malevich's Suprematism, were essentially designs for spatial constructions based on geometric-*cum*-stereo-metric forms. At that time Lissitzky produced a number of daring architectonic designs, which proved impracticable since they called for far greater technical and economic resources than were then available in the USSR. His design for the 'sculptural organization' of an 'electro-mechanical display'—which was modelled on A. Krutscheny's opera *Victory over the Sun*—was one of these. In 1921, after a brief period as Director of the Department of Architecture at the Vchutemas Institute in Moscow, Lissitzky went to Berlin. Both there and in Hanover, which he also visited before returning to the USSR, he mediated between the revolutionary and 'industrial' artists in the USSR and the West. Whilst in Berlin he joined with Ilya Ehrenburg in editing a Constructivist magazine entitled *Veshch/Objet/Gegenstand*. He also contributed to the *G*, *Merz* and *de Stijl* magazines and in 1924 he and Hans Arp published *Die Kunstismen*. In 1923 an exhibition hall was built in Berlin in accordance with Lissitzky's *Proun* theory. It was followed by further exhibition halls in Dresden (1926) and Hanover (1927–8). Lissitzky also designed various Soviet propaganda and trade exhibitions, the first being that held in Cologne in 1928. These exhibition designs enabled him to incorporate new visual techniques into his highly dynamic Constructivist method (by means of photomontage, lettering, light and movement). Although the outbreak of the Second World War led to the cancellation of various exhibitions designed by Lissitzky in the late 1930s, it also inspired a series of propaganda posters which were published both as placards and in illustrated magazines.

Camilla Gray. *The Great Experiment: Russian Art 1863–1922*, London and New York 1962.
Sophie Lissitzky-Kuppers. *El Lissitzky*, Dresden 1967; Greenwich (Conn.) and London 1968.

Lohse, Richard P. Swiss painter, graphic artist and publicist, b. 1902 in Zürich. Lohse studied at the School of Arts and Crafts in Zürich. In 1933 he made contact with Paul Klee and in 1937 became a founder member of *Allianz*, the association of modern Swiss painters. From 1948 to 1955 he was editor of the journal *Bauen und Wohnen* (*Building and Living*). In 1959 he became joint editor of the journal *Neue Grafik* (*New Graphics*). He is now living in Zürich.

Like Bill and Bodmer, Lohse is one of the senior representatives of Concrete Art in Switzerland. In his paintings he endeavours to group the formal elements according to type and to organize these groups in rhythmical patterns.

Loiseau, Gustave. French painter, b. 1865 in Paris; d. 1935 in Paris. He was self-taught. He knew the Impressionists, and used their method in his work, adapting it to his own style. He had a feeling for

depth in landscape that differentiated him from the Impressionist school, and he was also aware of the geometric shapes in townscapes, which he used in such pictures as *View of Rouen* (1927).

London Group. Founded in 1913, the first exhibition of the group was held in the Goupil Gallery in 1914. The London Group was formed by the amalgamation of various small groups on the initiative of the Camden Town Group. The first president was Harold Gilman. The purpose of the group was to provide organized exhibitions for *avant-garde* artists of all persuasions. Its foundation was a protest against the conservatism of the Royal Academy on the one hand and the New English Art Club on the other, and its independence was stressed. Its strength lay in its range, and practically every *avant-garde* artist from Sickert to Wyndham Lewis was included in its exhibitions, either as a member or as a guest. Among early members were Jacob Epstein, David Bomberg, Vanessa Bell, Duncan Grant and Mark Gertler. The exhibitions were originally biennial. Roger Fry became a member in 1917 and played an important part in the heyday of the Group, the 1920s. Though the circumstances in which it was founded have long since changed, the group continues to hold its exhibitions and preserves its tradition of open-mindedness.

Gene Baro. 'The London Group's Jubilee Exhibition at the Tate', *Arts* XXXVIII, New York, September 1964.
G. S. Whitter. 'The Jubilee Exhibition of the London Group at the Tate Gallery', *The Studio* CLXVIII, London, September 1964.

Lörcher, Alfred. German sculptor, b. 1875 in Stuttgart; d. 1962 in Stuttgart. After completing a course of training in arts and crafts, Lörcher studied at the Academy of Art in Munich from 1898 onwards. He then made a lengthy visit to Italy before settling in Berlin, where he lived from 1908 to 1915. In 1918 he was appointed head of the pottery workshop at the School of Arts and Crafts attached to the Academy of Fine Arts in Stuttgart.

Lörcher's sculptures are figurative works based on a simplified conception of form and revealing a fundamentally Classical outlook. In his late period he also produced rhythmically organized groups.

Lorjou, Bernard. French painter, b. 1908 in Blois, Touraine. Lorjou is a self-taught painter who firmly believes that all painting must be grounded in reality. His *Miracle of Lourdes*, which he exhibited in the Salon d'Automne in 1947, was hailed at the time as a turning point in the quest for a new realism. In 1948 he joined with Buffet and Minaux in organizing the exhibition *L'Homme-Témoin* (*Man as Witness*). At the International Exhibition in Brussels in 1950 he showed his Late Expressionist pictures in a wooden hut, which he had erected himself, as a protest against non-objective art. Since then, however, little has been heard of him. He is now living in Paris.

Loth, Wilhelm. German sculptor, b. 1920 in Darmstadt. Loth became a sculptor in 1938, having been urged to do so by Käthe Kollwitz. He invariably works in bronze, and his favourite subject is the female body. In these works his principal object is to forge a bond between the 'sculptural sensations' created by the female form and 'human situations'. Over the years his bodies have become more abstract and more flat; some are virtually relief torsos consisting of a single undulating surface. Since 1958 Loth has been teaching at the Academy of Art in Karlsruhe.

Exhibition catalogue, *Wilhelm Loth*, Kölnischer Kunstverein, Cologne 1965.

Louis, Morris (Louis Bernstein). American painter, b. 1912 in Baltimore; d. 1962 in Washington, D.C. He first studied painting at the Maryland Institute of Art (1929–33), then worked under the WPA easel painting project (1937–40). Louis' work developed in a Late Cubist manner until 1953, when he became influenced also by the current mode of painterly Expressionism. His work was to become a bridge from this Cubist-based Expressionistic abstraction to a kind of painting that, employing new techniques, became free from tactile associations and aimed for an independent and open colour expression. His work changed abruptly after 1952, when Louis was introduced to Jackson Pollock's large 'drip' paintings of 1947–50 and after an important meeting with the painter Helen Frankenthaler, who showed him how to paint without brushes by staining unsized canvas with poured acrylic paint. The linear overall patterning of his earlier works (*Charred Journal, Firewritten II*, 1951, Chevy Chase, Md., Coll. Mrs. Marcella Brenner) was transformed into successive vertical waves, stained like translucent curtains into the fabric of the canvas in a series known as the *Veils*, done in 1954 and again in 1958 (*Tet*, 1958, New York, Whitney Museum). With these ambiguous veils of colour Louis returned to a visual approach that recalled Monet and the Impressionists, but created a new, more disembodied concept of coloured figuration. Because his methods allowed no changes or revisions, many paintings were destroyed, especially between 1955 and 1957—a period of considerable reorientation for the artist. Just as Pollock was able to free line from its traditional role of defining plastic contour, Louis divorced his painted configurations from a sense of tangibility, influencing a whole generation of younger 'colour field' painters in the decade after his death. The large plumes and crests of the *Veils* were released into more haphazard floral petals and ribbons in 1960–1 (the *Florals* or *Aleph* series) and into columns and

clusters of interweaving colour. After 1961, partly in response to the work of his friend Kenneth Noland, Louis painted his *Unfurled* series (*Sigma*, 1961, New York, private collection), in which brilliant rivulets of colour in parallel streams flow across the lower corners of otherwise blank fields. A further development of this approach appeared in the *Stripe* or *Pillar* paintings from late 1961–2 (*Third Element*, 1962, New York, Museum of Modern Art). In these last works, brilliant and intensely coloured bands were stacked or striped in groups parallel to, but not touching, the sides of the unprimed canvas.

Clement Greenberg. 'Louis and Noland', *Art International* IV, Zürich 1960.
Lawrence Alloway. Catalogue, *Morris Louis—Memorial Exhibition: Paintings from 1954–60*, Solomon R. Guggenheim Museum, New York 1963.

Lowry, L. S. (Laurence Stephen). British painter, b. 1887 in Manchester; d. 1976. His father was an estate agent. He was educated at Victoria Park School in Manchester, 1895–1904, and he also attended private painting classes. In 1909 his family moved to an industrial part of Salford. From 1905 to 1915 he attended the Manchester Municipal Art College, and thereafter he continued to attend occasional classes at Salford School of Art. Between 1915 and 1920 his own highly personal idiom developed as he became increasingly fascinated by the industrial scene around him in Salford. For the next twenty years his work was dominated by the apparently childish, urban industrial landscapes with countless factory chimneys, populated by black, jerky, ant-like figures, for which he is best known. During this period he exhibited in Manchester and at the Paris Salon. *An Accident* (1926) was bought by the City Art Gallery, Manchester. He became a member of the Royal Society of British Artists in 1936, and exhibited in a mixed show in London in 1938, but he received little real public recognition until his own first one-man show in London in 1939. At that show a painting was bought for the Tate Gallery, and since then his fame and popularity have steadily increased. He has received two honorary degrees from Manchester University and became an ARA in 1955 and RA in 1962. The figures in his paintings are often set against an almost white ground that recalls the skating and winter scenes of Peter Bruegel and his followers. This connection with the Bruegel tradition is very important in Lowry and is often direct (*Cripples*, 1949). Like Breugel he is fascinated with the grotesque, and his work is basically satirical, but it is also poetic and highly personal. As well as the teeming landscapes, there are in his work strange, desolate landscapes and seascapes; these perhaps complement each other, for in both there is a strange feeling of the isolation of the artist. The apparent naïveté of his style, like that of Stanley Spencer, is in fact the chosen vehicle for the expression of a complex and involved personality. He has created out of decaying industrial society a peculiar and inimitable poetry. Like Spencer, however, he is an eccentric in the history of twentieth-century painting.

Maurice Collis. *The Discovery of L. S. Lowry*, London 1951.
Mervyn Levy. *L. S. Lowry, A.R.A.*, London and Toronto 1961.
Retrospective exhibition catalogue, *L. S. Lowry, R.A.*, Arts Council, London 1966.

Lubarda, Petar. Yugoslav painter, b. 1907 in Ljubotinje, Montenegro. In 1925 Lubarda attended an art school in Belgrade but left after a few months in order to study at the Académie des Beaux-Arts in Paris. But he also left the Academy after a short while and from then on was a self-taught artist. He remained in Paris until 1932, during which time he exhibited his dramatic and highly metaphorical pictures of the visible world at the Salon des Indépendants. After returning to Yugoslavia he first worked in Belgrade, then in Cetinje, where he founded an art school.

After painting Expressionist colour compositions during his early phase, Lubarda later developed a highly personal way of looking at nature, disregarding everything except its substantial elements. He then created works, in which forms of men and animals, of mountain rocks and the sky, intertwine, dissolve and reunite to produce the structures of an abstract, Orphic world. His luminous colours strive for emancipation from natural forms. Instinct and vital expression lead to a new alignment in which a sensitive and intuitive conception of the modern world is permeated by more primitive layers of being. This convergence between the power of patriarchal myth and the forces of twentieth-century civilization has prompted works which reflect both the barbaric landscapes of Lubarda's native Yugoslavia and the universal spirit of our times. Although Lubarda has never completely abandoned figurative associations, his dynamic colour compositions have exerted a crucial influence on the development of abstract painting in Yugoslavia.

O. Bihalji-Merin. *Lubarda: The Battle of Kossovo*, Belgrade 1956.
Lazar Trifunović. 'Petar Lubarda', *Painters and Sculptors*, Belgrade 1964.
Miodrag B. Protić. Retrospective exhibition catalogue, *Lubarda*, Museum of Contemporary Art, Belgrade 1967.

Luce, Maximilien. French painter, b. 1858 in Paris; d. 1941 in Paris. He began his career working for a London newspaper, the *Graphic*. In 1887 he met Signac, and was included in the Salon des Indépendants; thereafter he worked with the Neo-Impressionists and also joined *Les Vingt* in Brussels. A friend of Signac, he spread the idea of Divisionism outside France, although his version of it was less rigid than his friend's. He produced landscapes and townscapes, portraits and a number of important drawings.

Lucebert (L. G. Swanswijk). Dutch painter, graphic artist and poet, b. 1924 in Amsterdam. Lucebert studied at the School of Arts and Crafts in Amsterdam from 1938 onwards. In 1948 he joined both the Experimental Group and the *Cobra* group and showed his *Poèmes-Peintures* at the first *Cobra* exhibition, which was held in the following year. In 1955 he accepted an invitation from Berthold Brecht to visit East Berlin. He is now living in Bergen, Holland. Lucebert is one of the best known of contemporary Dutch poets and has had numerous volumes of lyrics published in Holland. He is also a highly inventive artist. His works—most of them drawings—are grounded in the *Cobra* tradition. Using informal calligraphic techniques Lucebert creates phantom figures, some cheerful, others distinctly menacing.

Catalogue, *Lucebert*, Museum Boymans-van-Beuningen, Rotterdam 1964.

Luchian, Stefan. Rumanian painter, b. 1868 in Stefanesti; d. 1916 in Bucharest. Luchian studied in Bucharest and Paris, then returned to Rumania, where he helped to found the Salon of Independent Artists in 1896, and the Association of Young Artists in 1902. He became gradually paralysed after an illness in 1901, and could paint only with great difficulty. His work is a tribute to his determination to overcome pain, and an expression of his deep enjoyment of life in spite of his serious handicap.

Luginbühl, Bernard. Swiss sculptor, b. 1929. He prefers to use metal for his work, which has evolved from figurative to abstract art.

Luks, George. American painter, b. 1867 in Williamsport, Pennsylvania; d. 1933 in New York. Although his early childhood was passed in the coal-mining regions of eastern Pennsylvania, Luks' artistic education took place at the Pennsylvania Academy of the Fine Arts, as well as in Düsseldorf and Paris. While in Europe, where he remained for ten years, Luks often concentrated on drawing rather than painting, and this experience served him well on his return to America in 1895, when he became an illustrator for the *Philadelphia Press*. As a result of this position, he made the acquaintance of William Glackens, Everett Shinn and John Sloan, who introduced him to Robert Henri. This meeting had a decisive influence on Luks' art and thinking. Luks and Glackens were both sent to cover the Spanish-American War in Cuba, illustrating for the *Evening Bulletin*. In New York, Luks drew a cartoon strip for the *New York World*, and later created the cartoon *Hogan's Alley* for the same newspaper. In 1895 he began to paint scenes of New York's lower classes and street life with a certain vitality and humour. The rhetorical guidance of Henri, as well as Luks' love for Dutch seventeenth-century masters, especially for the work of Frans Hals, is evident in these paintings. With broad and quick brushstrokes, Luks depicted street urchins, wrestlers and coal miners, in such paintings as *Spielers* (1905, Andover, Mass., Addison Gallery) and *Wrestlers* (1905, Boston, Museum of Fine Arts).

Luks' work clearly reveals the artist's flamboyant personality and robust love of life. Although much of his stance was mere pose or fabrication (including his entirely fictitious career as a coal miner), he did actually work as a wrestler and journalist before turning to painting. Indeed, his temperament and personality typified the dynamism and optimism of early twentieth-century America, and his struggles against academicism with his Philadelphian friends, who formed the group known as The Eight, demonstrated a new spirit in American art. Its essence was defiance against the stultifying influence of the art establishment, combined with the desire to create a genuine American painting, as opposed to a second-rate imitation of European academic styles.

Elisabeth L. Cary. *George Luks*, Whitney Museum of American Art, New York 1931.
Catalogue, *The Work of George B. Luks*, Newark Museum, Newark (N.J.) 1934.

Lundqvist, Evert. Swedish painter, b. 1904. After studying at the College of Art in Stockholm from 1925 to 1931 and visiting Germany and France, Lundqvist began to paint Realistic-Impressionistic pictures which are remarkable for their dynamic composition and their impasted colours. In the 1940s he became a leading figure in the *Saltsjö-Duvnäs* association. Meanwhile, his painting grew more and more powerful, due partly to the highly expressive nature of his later pictorial forms and partly to the use of an even more heavily impasted technique. At this time Lundqvist also began to suppress the individual character of his *motifs* (landscapes, still lifes and figures) so as to focus attention on the general composition, which became more abstract and more emotive as a result. Lundqvist has painted numerous monochromes, and reveals a preference for reds, browns and blue-greys. In 1955 he created a stained-glass mosaic for the Town Hall in Skellefteå, and of recent years has produced a number of graphic works. Since 1960 Lundqvist has held a professorial post at the College of Art in Stockholm.

R. Söderberg. *Evert Lundqvist*, 1962.

Lundstrøm, Wilhelm. Danish painter, b. 1893 in Sundbyerne; d. 1950 in Copenhagen. Lundstrøm started his artistic career in 1916, when he began to carve Cubist relief sculptures. But he soon abandoned sculpture and by 1923 was painting in the South of France under the influence of Picasso and Braque. After an early Cubist phase he went over to

a Neo-Classical style incorporating highly simplified forms, which he used in his wall paintings. Subsequently, he developed a purist technique with bright luminous colours. Since 1944 Lundstrøm has held a professorial post at the Copenhagen Academy.

P. Uttenreitter. *Wilhelm Lundstrøm*, Copenhagen 1933.

Lurçat, Jean. French painter and tapestry designer, b. 1892 in Bruyères, Vosges; d. 1966 in Paris. After training as a scientist Lurçat turned to painting and studied under V. Prouvé in Nancy up to 1912. He then moved to Paris, where he attended the Académie Colarossi and worked under the graphic artist B. Naudin. In 1913 he helped launch the magazine *Feuilles de Mai* and made the acquaintance of Hodler during a visit to Switzerland. In 1914 he visited Marseilles and Italy, then joined the French forces, was wounded in 1914 and released in 1917. In 1923 he was in Spain and from 1924 to 1929 visited North Africa, the Sahara, Greece and the countries of the Near East. In 1931 he settled in Switzerland and from 1936 onwards undertook numerous journeys. In 1955 he was in China, after which he lived in Paris until his death.

After an early Impressionist phase Lurçat was strongly influenced by Cubism, due largely to his friendship with Picasso and Marcoussis. Later he also joined the Surrealist movement for a while. But it was the impressions of the desert landscapes of the Sahara and of Greek and Spanish architecture, which he received on his travels in the 1920s, that really determined his artistic development. Lurçat was one of the most important tapestry designers of the century and contributed greatly to the revival of this art form, whose techniques he first began to study in 1915. By transforming the naturalistic animals and plants of traditional tapestry design he created Surrealistic fables in glittering Byzantine colours. Amongst the many important works which he produced in this sphere, the most celebrated are perhaps the tapestries for the choir of the church in Assy. From 1921 onwards Lurçat also designed stage sets and theatrical costumes and from 1948 onwards he produced numerous book illustrations.

C. Roy. *Jean Lurçat*, Geneva 1961.
Catalogue, *Lurçat*, Kunstverein Düsseldorf, Düsseldorf 1962.

M

Maas, Paul. Belgian painter, b. 1890 in Brussels; d. 1962 in Brussels. After an early period in which he used a rather sombre palette, Maas developed an

Expressionist style based partly on Fauvist elements, which he had successfully integrated, and partly on a caricatural form of draughtsmanship closely allied to Grosz. His violent colour contrasts, which evoke seething crowds or writhing landscapes, were prompted by a highly personal conception of the Mediterranean coastline that reflects his deep-rooted sense of isolation.

Mabe, Manabú. Japanese-Brazilian painter, b. 1910 in Japan. He emigrated to Brazil and now lives in São Paulo. He began his art studies at the age of 23. He has exhibited each year since 1952 at the São Paulo Bienal, the Salão de Arte Moderna and the Salão de Arte Nacional Moderna. He is an abstract artist who has won various prizes, including the Leirner Prize in 1959 and the Fiat Prize in Turin, 1960. He participated in the 1956 International Exhibition in Tokyo.

MAC (Movimento per l'Arte Concreta). The *MAC* was founded in 1948 in Milan by Gillo Dorfles, Gianni Monnet, Bruno Munari and Atanasio Soldati in order to promote a non-figurative type of painting and sculpture within the general framework of 'concrete art'. The movement, which existed up to 1958, staged numerous exhibitions.

G. Dorfles. *Ultime tendenze nell'arte d'oggi*, Milan 1961.

MacBryde, Robert. British painter, b. 1913 in Ayrshire; d. 1966. MacBryde worked for five years in a factory as an engineer before taking up painting and going to the Glasgow School of Art (1932–7). From 1937 to 1939 he studied in France and Italy. In London during the war he was associated with Colquhoun, Craxton, Minton and others of the younger generation of artists influenced by Surrealism, and also with Jankel Adler. After the war the main influence on his work was Picasso. Together with Colquhoun he designed sets for Massine's Scottish ballet, *Donald of the Burthens*, in 1951.

Macdonald-Wright, Stanton. American painter, b. 1890 in Virginia; d. 1973. While attending and being expelled from several private and public schools in California, he was studying at the Art Students' League of Los Angeles under Warren Hedges and also with Joseph Greenbaum. From 1907 to 1913 he was in Europe. He studied for eighteen months at the Sorbonne and also briefly at the Académie Colarossi, Académie Julian and the École des Beaux-Arts. Among his teachers were J. E. Blanche, Albert Besnard and J.-P. Laurens. While in Paris he exhibited at the 1910 Salon d'Automne and the Salon des Indépendants of 1912. At this time he and Morgan Russell were studying colour under

Tudor-Hart and reading the colour theories of Chevreul. In 1912 he painted a *Synchromy* whose forms were based on a Michelangelo *Slave*. He sold this picture the same year to the collector Jean Dracopoli. He returned briefly to New York in 1913–14 and then moved back to Paris. At the outbreak of the First World War he and his brother Willard Huntington Wright moved to London where they published *Modern Art, Its Tendency and Meaning, The Creative Will* and *The Future of Painting*. In 1916 he returned to the United States, moving to California in 1919. It was not until about 1920 that he became dissatisfied with the orientation of modern painting and with the personal academicism of his own Synchromism, which he was still producing in the late 1910s (*Synchromy*, 1917, New York, Museum of Modern Art). On the West Coast he produced the first full-length, stop-motion film ever made in full colour, doing at least 5,000 pastel pictures for it. He also did colour film experimentations, developing an additive colour process for motion pictures, and made discoveries that formed the basis of projection for the kinetic colour machine which he perfected forty years later—the *Synchrome Kineidoscope*. Between 1922 and 1930 he was director of the Art Students' League, Los Angeles, and in 1924 wrote *A Treatise on Color* for his students. In the late 1920s and 1930s he was exhibiting with Morgan Russell. In 1932 he had a one-man show at A. Stieglitz's 'An American Place'. From the time he worked on the large mural for the Santa Monica (California) Library (1933–5) he was associated with the WPA. This mural, now in the Smithsonian Institution, Washington, D.C., was done in eight parts in oil on panel. Carried out in a variety of styles ranging from the Oriental with a synchromy basis as seen in *Prologue, Primitive Man* to the precisionism of *A Motion Picture Studio*, the work represents the technical and imaginative paths of man's development. After completing the mural he became director of the WPA Art Project for Southern California and later Technical Adviser of the WPA for seven Western states. During this affiliation (1935–42) he became interested in architectural decoration—especially mosaics—and invented the medium called *Petrachrome* for the decoration of walls. He also collaborated with Albert Knight on the book *The History of Mosaics*. From 1942 to 1952 he taught art history, Oriental aesthetics and iconography at UCLA. In the early 1950s he gave up teaching in order to devote all of his time to painting, executing both abstract and non-objective paintings (*Embarkation*, 1962, New York, Museum of Modern Art). From 1958 he spent five months of every year at a Zen monastery at Kenninji, Japan, pursuing a philosophy with which he was occupied for the last thirty years of his life.

David W. Scott. *The Art of Stanton Macdonald-Wright*, Smithsonian Institution, Washington (D.C.) 1967.

McEvoy, Ambrose. British painter, b. 1878 in Crudwell, Wilts; d. 1927 in London. He studied at the Slade School, and spent some time with Sickert in France. At first he painted landscapes and figure compositions, and later turned to portrait painting. He was a member of the New English Art Club from 1902, and a founder member of the National Portrait Society, 1911. During the First World War he was in the Royal Naval Division, and the portraits he made during this time can be seen in the Imperial War Museum. In 1933 there was a memorial exhibition in Manchester of his work together with that of Sir William Orpen and Charles Ricketts.

McEwen, Jean. Canadian painter, b. 1923 in Montreal. A graduate in pharmacy from the University of Montreal (1947), he is a self-taught painter and pursued this field intensively only after 1951 when he had his first one-man show at the Agnes Lefort Gallery, Montreal. In the same year he moved to Paris. When he began painting around 1943 his works were representational, but by the early 1950s he was doing abstract works with a palette knife. These canvases reflect his early preoccupation with individual strokes, which revealed a similarity to the style of van Gogh. In 1963 he had his first one-man show in New York at the Martha Jackson Gallery. The thick pigment of his primarily atmospheric abstractions is often applied with his fingers and then varnished, giving his works a relief quality. The dense colours of the somewhat scumbled technique pulsate with a continuous sense of change (*Violet Rainbow*, 1962, New York, Martha Jackson Gallery).

Evan H. Turner. 'McEwen', *Canadian Art* XIX, March–April 1962.

McFee, Henry Lee. American painter, b. 1886 in St. Louis, Missouri; d. 1953. He began his study of painting in 1907 at the Stevenson Art School, Pittsburgh, Pa. In 1908 he entered summer classes at the Art Students' League in Woodstock, New York, studying under Birge Harrison, and in 1910 made his home in Woodstock. He exhibited with the Post-Impressionist Group in 1912 at the McDowell Club, New York, his works conveying his debt to Cézanne, Picasso and the aesthetics of C. Bell, R. Fry and W. Kandinsky. Certain Cubist elements can be seen in his *Glass Jar and Summer Squash* (1919, New York, Coll. Dr. Alfred Braun), though this work still has more to do with Cézanne than Picasso. In the slightly later *Glass Jar with Glass* (1922–3, New York, Coll. Miss Jane Heap) he is more successful in producing a flat two-dimensionality and in creating a varied textural surface than he is in fragmenting pictorial elements. In his later works he turns toward a closer observation of nature, emphasizing the plasticity and existence of the objects in space (*Crow with Peaches*, 1928, New York, Whitney Museum of American Art). McFee was primarily a still-life painter. Even his portraits are approached as still lifes, with the emphasis on composition and form rather than on the psychological reaction and penetration of the sitter (*Man in a High Hat*, 1925, Buffalo, New York, Albright-Knox Art Gallery). McFee also served as Associate Professor of Art at Scripps College and Claremont Graduate School, both in Claremont, California.

Virgil Barker. *Henry Lee McFee*, New York 1931.

McGarrell, James. American painter, b. 1930 in Indianapolis, Indiana. He received an AB degree from Indiana University (1953) where he studied with Alton Picken and Leo Steppat and an MA degree from UCLA, studying under John Paul Jones and Gordon Nunes. He has also studied at the Skowhegan (Maine) School of Painting and Sculpture (1953) and the Academy of Fine Arts, Stuttgart (1955–6). In 1955 he was the recipient of a Fulbright Fellowship and in the same year held his first one-man show at the Frank Perls Gallery, Beverley Hills, California. The following year he took a position at Reed College, Oregon, and since 1959 has taught at Indiana University. A figurative painter, he was represented in the Museum of Modern Art's 1959 exhibition *New Images of Man*. He approaches his canvases in a loose, painterly manner, usually representing nude figures placed in a small section of an interior, though a greater sense of space is often conveyed to the viewer through the artist's inclusion of a background landscape as he does in *Crux* (1963, New York, Allan Frunkin Gallery). In portraying his interiors he often depicts a corner of the room, creating an interest in depth as well as a sense of spatial tension (*Interior with Tipped over Table*, 1967, and *Double Corner*, 1966, Paris, Coll. Claude Bernard). In all but his *Model Studies*, the use of a patterned background— landscape, wallpaper, picture within a picture— activates the design and creates further compositional unrest. McGarrell received a National Institute of Arts and Letters Grant in 1963 and a Guggenheim Fellowship in 1964. In the latter year he was included in Documenta III, Kassel, Germany.

Giovanni Testori. Exhibition catalogue, *James McGarrell*, Galleria Il Fante di Spade, Rome 1968.

MacIver, Loren. American painter, b. 1909 in New York. With the exception of a few childhood lessons at the Art Students' League, she was a largely self-taught artist who developed while working under the Federal Arts Project during the Depression (*Carey's Backyard*, 1939, New York, Metropolitan Museum), then turned to a decorative abstract style after 1939. Working as an illustrator, Loren MacIver designed magazine and book covers, illustrations for *Fortune* and *Town and Country* magazines, shop windows, murals for homes and ships, Christmas cards and posters. She especially admired John Marin, but Paul Klee has also been indicated as a source of influence in her work, which ranges in style from Realism to figurative and non-figurative abstraction. What interested her was the quiet drama of the familiar, the discovery that the simplest things can often project a universal significance: oil stains on a pavement, leaves, ashcans, the patterns on a sidewalk left by children's chalk games (*Hopscotch*, 1940, New York, Museum of Modern Art), transitory objects and markings made permanent through her vision in paint. Her pictures are always lyrical in feeling, delicately glowing with pastel hues. *Oil Splinters and Leaves* (1950, New York, Coll. Mrs. G. MacCulloch Miller) is notable in this sense for its stylized patterns and atmospherically greyed colour harmonies. These delicate harmonies also characterize several paintings that capture her impressions of European cities (*Venice*, 1949, New York, Whitney Museum; *Paris*, 1949, New York, Metropolitan Museum).

MacIver's first one-man show took place in 1940, and in 1957 she received first prize at the Corcoran Gallery of Art Biennial. She began her work of the 1960s under a Ford Foundation grant.

John I. H. Baur. *Loren MacIver and I. Rice Pereira: Retrospective Exhibition*, Whitney Museum of American Art, New York 1953.

Mack, Heinz. German sculptor, b. 1931 in Lollar, Rhineland. Mack studied at the Academy of Art in Düsseldorf from 1950 to 1953 and took the State Examination in Philosophy at Cologne in 1956. In the course of the next two years he evolved his 'light reliefs', which he constructs from polished metals. In 1958 he joined with O. Piene in founding the *Zero* group and was joint editor of the three *Zero* publications issued under its auspices. In the same year he began experimenting with vibrating columns of light and also started work on his *Sahara Project*. In 1961–2 he increased the size of his 'light dynamos'. These consist of metal plates with relief surfaces which are made to execute irregular movements behind sheets of curved glass by means of an electromotor. In 1965 Mack was awarded the first prize for sculpture at the Fourth Biennale in Paris. He is now living in Münchengladbach.

Macke, August. German painter, b. 1887 in Meschede a. d. Ruhr; d. 1914 in Perthes, France. From 1904 he studied at the Düsseldorf Academy; subsequently (1905–6) at the Kunstgewerbeschule in Düsseldorf under Ehmke. In 1907 he visited Paris for the first time; in the winter of that year he studied in Berlin with the German Impressionist painter Corinth. In 1908 he made a second visit to Paris; these years of study were eased financially by the generosity of Bernhard Koehler, who was subsequently to become one of the foremost collectors of modern German painting, and who was the uncle of Macke's future wife. The years 1909–10 he spent on the Tegernsee in Bavaria. During this period, he began an intimate friendship with the painter Franz Marc, which was to last till Macke's death; through Marc, Macke was introduced to Kandinsky's circle. After the split within the *Neue Künstlervereinigung* and the formation of the *Blauer Reiter*, Macke was won over to the new group (despite initial reservations) largely through Marc's influence. He contributed an essay, *The Masks*, to the *Blauer Reiter Almanac* of 1912, an essay which underlines the fascination of the *Blauer Reiter* artists with all forms of 'primitive' and 'non-Classical' art. From 1912 he lived in Bonn; this was also the period of his friendship with Campendonk and Delaunay. The influence of Orphism appears to triumph over that of Expressionism in his later work. In 1914 he visited Tunis in the company of Klee and Moilliet; this visit was to produce a group of colouristically superb landscape watercolours which won the admiration of Klee. His tragically early death, in the first German offensive in Champagne, leaves the future development of his work problematic, although even in his early work the transition from the influences of Cubism and Expressionism to an intensely personal style is clearly marked. In a moving peroration for his dead friend, Franz Marc (himself to encounter the same fate) wrote: 'Those of us who worked with him, his friends, we knew what secret future this man of genius bore within him. With his death, one of the most beautiful and most daring curves in the development of modern German art is abruptly broken off; none of us is in a position to continue it . . . This greedy war is richer, but German art is poorer by his heroic death.'

Gustav Vriesen. *August Macke*, Stuttgart 1957.

Mackintosh, Charles Rennie. Scottish architect and designer, b. 1868 in Glasgow; d. 1928 in London. He served his apprenticeship as an architect with John Hutchison, then in 1889 moved to the firm of Honeyman & Keppie as a draughtsman. In 1891 he won a travelling scholarship that took him to Italy, France and Belgium. In the early 1890s he attended evening classes at the Glasgow School of Art. There he became associated with Herbert MacNair, and Frances and Margaret Macdonald. He married Margaret in 1900. Together this group were known as the Four, and from about 1893 they created the Glasgow style of *art nouveau*. Mackintosh's own work is, however, distinct from that of the other three. He continued his practice as an architect up until 1914, when he left Glasgow. His most famous work is the Glasgow School of Art, 1897–1909, and his approach to design was the same as his approach to architecture. In fact he made no distinction between the two, designing a whole building in the same operation down to the knives and forks. His style is characterized by a kind of decorative simplicity that is unique within the *art nouveau* movement. He became internationally known and influential before he received any recognition in Britain, and after leaving Glasgow and moving to England he did little that was of importance. Living in London he designed textiles, some of striking originality, and he built one important house, at Northampton, for W. J. Basset-Lowke. In 1923 he and his wife went to live in south-west France, but because of his health they went back to England, where he died in 1928.

Thomas Howarth. *C. Rennie Mackintosh and the Modern Movement*, London 1952.

D. P. Bliss. *Charles Rennie Mackintosh and the Glasgow School of Art*, Glasgow 1961.

MacTaggart, Sir William. Scottish painter, b. 1903 in Loanhead, Midlothian. MacTaggart is the grandson of William McTaggart (1835–1910). He studied at Edinburgh Art College from 1917 to 1920. His first one-man show took place in 1924 in Cannes. He is now President of the Royal Scottish Academy, and sits on the committees of the Arts Council in Scotland and the Edinburgh Festival.

McWilliam, F. E. British sculptor, b. 1909 in Bainbridge, Ireland. He lived in Ireland until 1928 when he went to the Slade School (1928–31). From 1931 to 1932 he was in Paris and in 1936 he exhibited with the British Surrealists. During the Second World War he served in the RAF. In 1951 he was commissioned to do the *Four Seasons* for the Festival of Britain. His work has followed fairly closely the development of other British sculptors, from carved abstracts in the thirties when he took up sculpture, through the influence of Picasso in the forties, to the semi-figurative highly modelled rough-cast bronzes of the fifties. In the sixties he has turned increasingly to angular-carving the cast rather than modelling it, in variations on Henry Moore's theme of the reclining figure.

Catalogue, *F. E. McWilliam*, Arts Council, London 1961.
R. Penrose. *F. E. McWilliam*, London 1964.

Maes, Karel. Belgian painter, b. 1900 in Mol. After an early period, in which he produced experimental Neo-Impressionist, Fauvist and Cubist works, Maes painted his first abstract pictures between 1918 and 1920. He was co-editor of *Sept Arts*. Like *Der Sturm*, *De Stijl* and *Het Overzicht*, this magazine reproduced a number of quite remarkable linoleum cuts by Maes. Later Maes turned to a purely decorative form of art.

Mafai, Mario. Italian painter, b. 1902 in Rome; d. 1965 in Rome. Due primarily to the influence of Kandinsky, Mafai became an abstract painter at an early age. During this initial period, he produced Lyrical Abstract colour compositions prompted by impressions of landscapes and executed with agitated brushwork. This hectic element was reinforced by his encounter in about 1930 with the works of Kokoschka, Soutine and Ensor. It was then that he and Scipione founded the 'Roman School', which was greatly influenced by Soutine's exalted brand of Expressionism. With their tragic, ecstatic import and their pictorial expressiveness, Mafai's *Phantasies*—the series of pictures which he produced in the Second World War—vie with Ensor's macabre vision of a world carnival. In these works naked, mutilated bodies writhe in torment against a background of masked, lemuroid figures. In the course of his later development, Mafai painted a large number of townscapes, mostly of Rome. After 1945 his impassioned handling yielded to a more moderate style and the powerful, interlacing colours of his Expressionist phase were toned down and carefully harmonized. The strange beauty of these townscapes, which acquire a magical aura from their unrealistic lighting, is the product of an extremely subtle and lyrical approach. Mafai's subdued, melancholy and poetic view of reality has won him disciples amongst the younger generation of artists in Rome, e.g. Scialoja and Tamburi.

L. Venturi. *Pittori Italiani d'oggi*, Rome 1958.

Magnelli, Alberto. Italian painter, b. 1888 in Florence. Magnelli is a self-taught artist who began to paint in 1910–11, the year in which he first made contact with the Futurists and Cubists in Paris. In 1913 he saw works by the artists of the Italian Renaissance which made a profound impression on him. In the same year he met the Florentine Futurists in Marinetti's circle. In 1914–15 he revisited Paris, where he associated with the leading French artists of the day, who were grouped around Apollinaire, Max Jacob, Léger, Matisse and Picasso. From 1915 to 1931 he lived in Florence, where he worked consistently on his pictures (with the exception of 1929–30, when he stopped painting for a short period). In 1931 he moved to Bellevue-Meudon and in 1933 joined the *Abstraction-Création* association. During the German occupation, when he was living in Grasse, he was in close touch with Arp, Sophie Taeuber-Arp and Sonia Delaunay and tried to form an artists' colony (Lithos). In 1950 Magnelli had a one-man exhibition at the Biennale in Venice. He is now living in Meudon.

After an early naturalist phase, Magnelli came under the influence of Delaunay's Orphism and Kandinsky's Abstract Expressionism and in c. 1915 painted his first strictly abstract works, in which he used dynamic shades of colour, Futuristic perspective and Cubist composition. Between 1918 and 1928, when he was influenced by the *Pittura Metafisica*, he reverted to naturalistic paintings, which were extremely formal. Both the figure compositions and the landscapes which he produced between 1920 and 1930 were constructed in strict accordance with the principles of architectonic composition and were executed in cool colours. But when Magnelli visited the marble quarries in Carrara he was so impressed that he moved away from naturalism yet again and painted the near-abstract series *Le Pietre* (The Stones). Shortly afterwards, when he joined the *Abstraction-Création* association in 1933, he went completely abstract. The works of this period are constructed from clear-cut, geometric forms, which are set out in a choreographic arrangement and with a strong sense of order against light monochrome grounds. The severity of the geometric design is softened by the earthy, fresco-like tone values, which create an impression of intimacy and give many of Magnelli's abstract compositions a kind of still-life quality. Magnelli exerted considerable influence on the development of concrete painting in Italy.

Catalogue, *Magnelli*, Musée Nationale d'Art Moderne, Paris 1968.

Magritte, René. Belgian painter, b. 1898 in Lessines; d. 1967 in Brussels. It was not until some forty years after Magritte's first exhibition in 1927 that the significance and size of his oeuvre were universally recognized, and even this belated acclaim might well have been withheld but for the advent of Pop Art. Magritte's youth was marred by a personal tragedy. In 1912, when he was fourteen, his mother committed suicide. Magritte's sense of vocation came early, and was very strong. From the age of ten he took private lessons in painting, and in 1916, when he was eighteen, he enrolled at the Academy of Fine Arts in Brussels, which he attended for two years. Whilst there he pursued his own line of enquiry, and by 1919—the year in which he met the poet Pierre Bourgeois and E. L. T. Mesens—he had developed an active interest in Futurism and Orphic Cubism, and was executing automatist works in the sphere of poster and commercial design. At that time he was working in a studio that had been decorated in a near-abstract style by the painter and poet Pierre-Louis Flouquet. In 1922, when he was employed as a designer in a wallpaper factory, Magritte met the painter Victor Servranckx, who had already turned to non-figurative art. But it was when he met the poet Marcel Lecomte—also in 1922—that Magritte discovered his future path. Lecomte showed him a painting by Giorgio de Chirico, *Le Chant d'Amour*, which had a tremendous impact. Magritte himself said that the influence of this one work was 'more decisive than that exerted by my discovery of the Futurist painters: they introduced me to a style of painting. Chirico showed me that the most important thing was to know *what to paint.*' Louis Scutenaire tells us that Magritte conceived a 'new vision, in which the viewer rediscovers

his isolation and hears the silence of the world'. But it was not until 1925 that Magritte turned definitively to Surrealism. One of his earliest Surrealist paintings was *Les Deux Soeurs* (1925). This was actually a double portrait of a young girl seen by day and by night. The girl in question was Georgette Berger, whom Magritte had first met in 1913 when they were both adolescents, and who became his wife in 1922. She modelled for him throughout her life. In 1927 Magritte had his first exhibition, which was staged in the Galerie Le Centaure. In August 1927 he moved to Perreux-sur-Marne, near Paris, where his dealer Camille Goemanns was already living. From then onwards he was in personal contact with the members of the Surrealist group in Paris, especially André Breton and Paul Éluard, with whom he felt a strong affinity. During this period Magritte's output was prolific and his work was of exceptionally high quality. Mesens considers that his most brilliant 'ideas' were conceived at Perreux-sur-Marne. In 1930 Magritte settled permanently in Brussels. In 1938 he took part in the International Surrealist Exhibition in Paris. Magritte's style remained virtually unchanged, apart from an Impressionist period immediately after the Second World War, which critics have called his 'Renoir period', and a further period in 1948, which has been dubbed '*vache*' and which is chiefly remarkable for its thematic and structural aggression. At all other times Magritte deliberately disregarded technical innovations in order, as he himself said, to concentrate on the representation of ideas which reflect the visible world. Magritte regarded poetry as 'the representation of inspired thought' and, in referring to his work, André Breton spoke of 'Surrealism in the full light of day'. Magritte exerted a considerable influence on many of his contemporaries (including, according to E. L. T. Mesens, Salvador Dali), and also on the younger generation of European and Anglo-Saxon painters. Jim Dine, Rosenquist and Claes Oldenburg are obvious examples.

Catalogue, *L'Oeuvre de René Magritte*, Brussels 1962.
P. Waldberg. *René Magritte*, Brussels 1965.
J. T. Soby. *René Magritte*, New York 1966.

Maillol, Aristide. French sculptor, b. 1861 in Banyuls-sur-Mer; d. 1944 in Banyuls-sur-Mer. When Maillol came to Paris in 1881 he applied to enter the École des Beaux-Arts as a student of painting but was rejected. It was not until 1885 that he was able to begin his studies (under Gérome and Cabanel). In 1892 he came under the spell of Gauguin. He then lost interest in academic painting and turned to tapestry work, which he conceived as a two-dimensional art form that was firmly rooted in the craft tradition. During this early period his friends and artistic companions were the *Nabis*. He was especially close to M. Denis. In 1895 he began to sculpt whilst still continuing with his tapestry work. Then, in

1900, when he found that the close work on the tapestries was beginning to impair his eyesight, he gave it up and became a full-time sculptor. He had already exhibited some wooden sculptures in 1896. These were soon followed by a number of terracotta pieces, which not only demonstrated his interest in archaic and primitive cultures but also introduced to the French art public the firm, well-rounded forms which were to become the hallmark of *la femme Maillol*. In 1902 Maillol had his first one-man show with Vollard in Paris. This brought him the approbation of Rodin, who was quick to recognize a kindred spirit despite the obvious differences between them. The poet-critics of the day also entered the lists on Maillol's behalf, but despite their efforts he received no recognition from official bodies and no public commissions. Meanwhile, in 1903, he settled in Marly-le-Roi near Paris. In 1905, when he exhibited in the Salon d'Automne, he found a patron in Graf Kessler, who bought *La Méditerranée*, his first real masterpiece, and commissioned him to execute other works including *Le Désir*. In the same year Maillol was asked to create a monument to the Socialist L.-A. Blanqui and, although the finished work—*L'Action enchaînée* of 1908—caused a scandal, Maillol was now beginning to make his way. He also made two new friends in H. Matisse and A. Renoir. Then in 1908 he visited Greece in the company of Graf Kessler and the poet Hugo von Hofmannsthal and discovered in Olympia an art form that was closely akin to his own essentially Mediterranean conception. In 1910, at the request of his patron, he started work on a series of woodcuts illustrating Virgil's *Eclogues*. By the time the First World War was over Maillol enjoyed an international reputation, and he was asked to create monuments to commemorate the victims by a number of towns in his native province of Roussillon. In 1929 he saw his Cézanne memorial, which had originally been commissioned for Aix-en-Provence in 1912, erected in the Tuileries. In the second half of the 1930s he illustrated a number of books: Ovid's *Ars amatoria* in 1935; Longus' *Daphnis and Chloë* in 1937; Verlaine's *Chansons pour Elle* in 1939; and Ronsard's *Livre des Folastries* in 1940. Meanwhile Maillol had been working—often for years on end—on various large statues, e.g. *Pomona*, *La Nuit*, *Vénus au Collier*, *Les trois Nymphes*, *Île de France*, *L'Air* and *L'Harmonie*.

During his early period as a tapestry designer Maillol had been influenced by Puvis de Chavannes, P. Gauguin and the *Nabis*. As soon as he turned to sculpture, however, he developed a highly individual style, whose powerful forms appeared a-naturalistic to his contemporaries. From the very outset he sought to establish a condition of objectivity and monumentality based on formal simplification and static rhythms. He himself said that he was not interested in 'particular' conditions but only in a 'universal idea'. This is why he did not treat a wide range of subjects. There was no need. And so—apart from a few male nudes such as *Le Cycliste*—he modelled and drew the same passive, powerful female type over a period of forty years. André Gide described her in 1905: 'This woman is quite simply beautiful. She has no message. She is silent. I believe you would have to go a long way back in time before you found a work of art which so completely disregarded everything that is alien to the simple representation of beauty.' Maillol wanted to create a physical form that would remain essentially the same in all lights and from all angles. Hence his preference for massive volume, architectonic clarity and formal synthesis.

Judith Cladel. *Maillol, sa vie, son oeuvre, ses idées*, Paris 1937. John Rewald. *Maillol*, Paris, London, New York 1939. Rolf Linnenkampf. *Maillol. Die grossen Plastiken*, Munich 1960. Waldemar George. *Aristide Maillol*, Berlin 1964.

Maistre, Roy de. British painter, b. 1894 in New South Wales; d. 1968. He studied at the Royal Art Society and Art School, Sydney. In 1923 he went to London and then Paris on a travelling scholarship, working for two years in Europe (Paris and St-Jean-de-Luz). In 1926 he returned to Australia, but in 1930 he was back in London; from then until 1938 he lived in France and Britain. Before he left Australia he had already been experimenting with colour theory and the relationship between musical and colour harmony, producing abstract paintings in demonstration of his theories, but his first European works are in a restrained style derived from Camden Town Post-Impressionism. On his return to Europe he became increasingly interested in Cézanne, Picasso and Matisse, and turned to a purely Cubist idiom. He has remained interested in problems of the relation of colour to structure and expression. This is particularly apparent in his religious paintings, for example the *Stations of the Cross* (Westminster Cathedral), which are amongst his most striking and personal works.

Mäkilä, Otto. Finnish painter, b. 1904 in Turku; d. 1955. Mäkilä studied in Turku, Stockholm, Paris and Holland. During his early period he painted Surrealist pictures, which were something of a rarity in Finland. Later he went over to abstract art. Mäkilä's Surrealist works have a strange and typically Nordic fairytale quality.

Makowski, Tadeusz. Polish painter, b. 1882 in Oswiecim; d. 1932 in Paris. After studying at the Academy of Art in Cracow from 1903 to 1908, Makowski went to live in Paris, where he met Le Fauconnier, Gleizes, Metzinger and Léger. Between 1911 and 1913 he passed through a brief Cubist period before evolving a more robust style derived from the realism of the primitives and from

Expressionism. In 1923 he established close contact with a number of like-minded artists including M. Gromaire, E. Goerg and Per Krohg, with whom he exhibited in the Galerie Berthe Weil. Subsequently, in his mature period, Makowski painted in a style compounded of elements of Cubism, Polish folk art and the early Flemish and Dutch masters, especially P. Bruegel, whom he greatly admired. Makowski kept a diary in which he recorded his artistic ideas and which was published in Warsaw in 1962.

Exhibition catalogue, *Tadeusz Makowski*, National Museum, Warsaw 1963.

Makowski, Zbigniev. Polish painter, b. 1930 in Warsaw. Makowski is now living in Warsaw, where he studied at the Academy of Art.

In his early period Makowski was influenced by the semi- and non-objective Expressionism of Malevich and Strzeminski and by the automatic writing of the Surrealists. But by c. 1960 he had evolved his own personal style. Since then he has been painting highly cryptic pictures, in which he uses ideograms and ciphers, archetypal symbols, magical signs and tables, poetic glosses and notes.

Peinture moderne polonaise: Sources et recherches, Musée Galliera, Paris 1969.

Malczewski, Rafael. Polish painter and writer, b. 1892 in Cracow. He studied in Cracow and Vienna, and became a member of the *Rytm* group in Poland. He paints oil and watercolour landscapes, mountain scenes and sporting events. He lives in the USA.

Maldarelli, Oronzio. American sculptor of Italian origin, b. 1892 in Naples. His first artistic efforts were in the field of jewellery design, but he turned to sculpture when studying at the National Academy of Design, the Beaux-Arts Institute of Design and Cooper Union, all in New York. His early sculptures were of a highly realistic and objective nature, though this penchant changed after a two-year residence abroad as a Guggenheim Fellow (1931–3). His style became far more simplified and less detailed, as in *Caress* (1945, New York, Whitney Museum of American Art). Here the simple planes and swelling forms converge, disclosing a rhythmic play of light and shade. Among his many commissioned works are *Air-Mail Carrier* for the Post Office Building, Washington, D.C. (1936), *Fra Angelico* and *The Weaver* for the 1939 New York World's Fair and sculptural decoration for the Orange, Massachusetts, Post Office. He also won a competition for the *Madonna Altarpiece* at St. Patrick's Cathedral, New York. Maldarelli taught sculpture at Columbia University for many years.

'Modern Classicist', *Life* XXII, 24 March 1947.

Maldonado, Tomás. Argentinian painter, art theorist and designer, b. 1922 in Buenos Aires. Maldonado became one of the founder members of the *Arte Concreto-Invención* movement in Buenos Aires in 1945 and helped to launch the magazine *Nueva Visión* in 1951. He has exerted a major influence on the development of Concrete Art in Argentina. He also made contact with Vantongerloo and Max Bill and wrote a monograph on Bill in 1955, the year in which he became a professor at the Hochschule für Gestaltung in Ulm. Later he was appointed rector of the Hochschule. Maldonado's paintings are based on a rational, mathematical conception of art. He is primarily interested in industrial design.

Michel Seuphor. *Dictionnaire de la Peinture Abstraite*, Paris 1957.

Malevich, Kasimir. Russian painter, b. 1878 near Kiev; d. 1935 in Leningrad. Malevich was the inventor of Suprematism. From 1903 he studied at the School of Painting, Sculpture and Architecture in Moscow; from 1904 he painted mostly Post-Impressionistic pictures, such as *The Flower Girl*, 1904–5 (Leningrad, Russian Museum). In 1908 he began his gouache 'peasant' series, which appeared to show the influence of the 'peasant' themes of Larionov and Gontcharova. In 1911 he contributed five of these paintings to the second *Union of Youth* exhibition. In 1912 he showed a number of works at Larionov's *Donkey's Tail* exhibition, including *Chiropodist in the Bathroom*, 1908–9 (Amsterdam, Stedelijk Museum), which shows the influence of Cézanne's *Card Players* of 1890–2, and *Taking in the Harvest*, 1911, the tubular forms and bright, metallic colours of which recall much of Léger's work of this period. This and the *Woodcutter* (Amsterdam, Stedelijk Museum) are mature Cubo-Futurist works, leading directly to mechanical figures such as the man in the *Knife Grinder*, 1912 (New Haven, Conn., Yale Art Gallery).

In 1913 Malevich, Matyushin and Kruchenykh drew up the manifesto for the First Futurist Congress. Malevich designed costumes and scenery for the Futurist opera *Victory over the Sun*, with libretto by Kruchenykh and music by Matyushin. In 1914–15 he exhibited his first 'alogical' pictures in which totally unrelated objects are combined. These pictorial experiments parallel the ideas put forward in poetry by Khlebnikov and Kruchenykh, although 'Alogism' was developed by Malevich himself.

In December 1915, Malevich showed his first Suprematist works at the exhibition *0.10*, including his famous *Black Square* (Leningrad, Russian Museum). The origins of Suprematism have been traced to the backcloth designs for *Victory over the Sun*, which employ pure geometrical forms. Of his Suprematist paintings, Malevich declared that, 'Real forms were approached in many cases as the ground for formless, painterly masses from which a painterly picture was created, quite unrelated to nature.'

Also in 1915, Malevich began to experiment with three-dimensional architectural drawings showing a kind of idealized construction which he called *Planits* or *The Contemporary Environment*. In 1917, he joined the Federation of Leftist Artists; during 1918 he wrote in the daily papers against those artists who refused to join the Revolution. He became involved with the Commissariat of the Enlightenment (*Narkompros*), taking up posts in the Committee for Artistic Organization, the International Bureau, and as a teacher in the Free State Workshops. He designed costumes and scenery for Mayakovsky's *Mystery Bouffe*, produced by Meyerhold in Petrograd. In 1919 there was a State exhibition of Suprematism and Non-Objective Art in Moscow. Malevich wrote *On New Systems in Art* in that year; he also taught at the art school in Vitebsk at the invitation of Chagall, who subsequently retired as a result of his disagreements with Malevich and his pupils. In 1920 Malevich founded the group *Unovis* from among his supporters in Vitebsk, who decorated the town with their emblem, the Black Square (the sign of Suprematism), on the anniversary of the Revolution. When the group was ousted from the Vitebsk school, Malevich joined the Petrograd branch of the Institute of Art Culture, together with five of his pupils; in 1923, he became head of the Formal Theory department of the Institute. From 1924 to 1926 he worked with his pupils on architectural models; for the most part, he abandoned painting in favour of theoretical writing. In 1927 he visited Europe with a one-man exhibition of his work, and met Arp, Schwitters, Richter and others. His treatise *The Non-Objective World* was published as a Bauhaus book. In 1930 he was arrested on account of his connections with Germany; his papers were destroyed and he was unable to publish his writings. In his last period, Malevich painted mainly representational works, abandoning total non-objectivity.

Kasimir Malevich. *The Non-Objective World*, Chicago 1959.
Camilla Gray. Catalogue, *Kasimir Malevich, 1878–1935*, Whitechapel Gallery, London 1959; *The Great Experiment: Russian Art 1863–1922*, London and New York 1962.

Malharro, Martín. Argentinian painter, b. 1865 in Azul; d. 1911 in Buenos Aires. Malharro pioneered Impressionism in Argentina. After studying at the Academy of the Sociedad Estímulo in Buenos Aires he earned a meagre living by working as a lithographer and producing illustrations for newspapers. In 1896 he visited Paris, where he also earned his living as a lithographer. Whilst in Paris he saw works by the French Impressionists, and himself became an Impressionist. In 1902 he returned to Argentina, where his *plein-air* pictures revolutionized Argentinian painting, which until then had been completely

academic. Although he was attacked by the art establishment, Malharro received the enthusiastic support of the younger generation. He gave drawing classes, he held lectures and he became a passionate polemicist. But, above all, he created a series of quite remarkable watercolours and oil paintings, in which he reproduced the natural colouring and light of different parts of the Argentinian countryside. Shortly before he died Malharro published a book on the teaching of drawing in schools which was far ahead of its time.

Julio E. Payro. *Veintitres pintores de la Argentina*, Buenos Aires 1962.
Romualdo Brughetti. *Historia del arte en la Argentina*, Mexico 1965.

Malina, Frank Joseph. American kinetic and light artist, b. 1912 in Brenham, Texas. Malina is a scientist; he is a pioneer of jet propulsion and astronautical research. Since 1953 he has become increasingly involved with art works based on movement, light and colour; he has evolved sophisticated methods of projecting moving colour fields on a two-dimensional screen. An objective search for a synthesis of art and science is constant in Malina's work.

Mallary, Robert. American painter and sculptor, b. 1917 in Toledo, Ohio. He spent his youth in California and received his artistic training at La Escuela de los Artes del Libro in Mexico city (1938–9) and also studied graphics with Koloman Sokol in the same city. He had his first one-man show in San Francisco in 1944 and participated in two São Paulo Bienals (1955 and 1963). In 1962 he received a Tamarind Workshop Fellowship and two years later a Guggenheim Grant for Creative Sculpture. Mallary has taught at Pratt Institute, Brooklyn, since 1959 and has conducted seminars at Yale University. He is best known for his tremendous inventiveness of technique. In the 1950s he was creating sculptures from sheets of acetate which were cut and bent and then sprayed with luminous colour which can only be seen when under ultra-violet 'black' light. With this device he produces forms that seem to float from the ceiling. The stroboplane, a machine that creates an actual space picture, is another product of Mallary's fertile creativity. The device rotates eight transparencies at 1,000 rpm, causing the illusion of a static, deep-space picture resulting in a tiny four-by-five-inch world of galactic space.

'A Self-Interview', *Location* I, Spring 1963.

Mané-Katz. Jewish-French painter and sculptor, b. 1894 in Ukraine; d. 1962 in Tel Aviv. He studied in Paris before the First World War; in 1921 he went back and eventually became a naturalized French citizen. His travels in the Middle East, 1927–37, gave him inspiration for his many pictures of

Jewish history and lore, painted in glowing colours and with a child-like quality reminiscent of Chagall.

Manessier, Alfred. French painter and stained-glass artist, b. 1911 in Saint-Ouen, Somme. After studying architecture at the École des Beaux-Arts in Amiens from 1922 to 1929 Manessier went to live in Paris, where he attended the Academies in Montparnasse and exhibited at the Salon des Indépendants before returning to Amiens in 1936. In 1937 he was back in Paris and remained there until 1939, when he joined the French forces. In 1940–1 he studied under Bissière, whom he had first met in 1935. In 1941—together with Bazaine, Estève, Lapicque and Le Moal—he joined the *Peintres de la tradition française.* In 1955 he visited Holland. Since then he has been living in Paris.

After an early figurative and objective phase, Manessier turned to Surrealism in the 1930s. Then, in 1940, largely as a result of his preoccupation with Orphism, medieval stained glass and the emblematic art of Paul Klee, he joined the *École de Paris*, whose ideas on the indivisibility of form and colour greatly appealed to him. The central theme of Manessier's art is the effect of colour when permeated by light. By meditating on abstract forms he produced signs and symbols which illustrate the organization of nature and of natural phenomena within a deeply religious context. Manessier's art has found its most perfect expression in his stained-glass windows.

J. Cayrol. *Manessier,* Paris 1955.
Retrospective exhibition catalogue, *A. Manessier,* Kunsthalle, Bremen 1968.

Manguin, Henri Charles. French painter, b. 1874 in Paris; d. 1949 in St-Tropez. Manguin studied in Paris with Gustave Moreau and met Matisse and many of the other Fauvist painters, with whom he exhibited in 1905. He moved to St-Tropez in that year, delighting in the warm southern landscape and the brilliant light, a delight reflected in a great many of his paintings. His early Fauvist contacts gave him his sense of colour; he was also concerned with form and structure in nature, and his love of life and of the countryside around him is plainly seen in his warm, joyous painting.

Mannucci, Edgardo. Italian sculptor, b. 1904 in Fabriano. In 1930 Mannucci moved to Rome, where he became friendly with the sculptor A. Martini. He now teaches at the Academy of Art in Rome.

After executing archaistic and Expressionist works during his early period Mannucci came under the influence of A. Burri, and from c. 1950 onwards produced abstract constructions from bronze and silver wire.

Manolo (Manuel Martinez Hugué). Spanish sculptor, b. 1872 in Barcelona; d. 1945 in Caldas de Mombúy, near Barcelona. Manolo was a self-taught artist. In c. 1900 he went to Paris, where he associated with the artists grouped around Picasso and Moréas, the poet of the *École romance*, and led an impoverished Bohemian existence until the art dealer Kahnweiler placed him under contract, thus enabling him to concentrate on his sculpture. From 1910 to 1916 he worked in Céret, a village in the Pyrenees which was a favourite Cubist haunt. He then went back to Spain, remaining there until 1919, when he returned to Céret and devoted himself to painting. From 1927 onwards he lived in Caldas, near Barcelona.

There is something very Spanish about Manolo's powerful, squat, highly simplified statues of peasant women, mothers and children, *toreros* and female nudes. Although he was undoubtedly influenced by the sculptures of Gauguin, by Cubism, by the Classical statuary of Picasso and, above all, by Maillol, his works retained a highly individual quality which has far more in common with the Mediterranean tradition than with the new developments of twentieth-century art.

R. Benet. *El escultor Manolo Hugué*, Barcelona 1942.

Manship, Paul. American sculptor, b. 1885 in St. Paul, Minnesota; d. 1966 in New York. He studied in New York, Philadelphia and Rome, then lived in Paris, 1922–6. He was chairman of the Smithsonian Art Commission for twenty years, having first become a member in 1938. He taught at the Pennsylvania Academy of Fine Arts for three years from 1943. His work consisted mainly of mythological groups, and portraits.

Manzoni, Piero. Italian experimental artist, b. 1933 in Soncino; d. 1963 in Milan. Manzoni studied at the University of Milan. In 1957 he showed his first *Acromes.* These are white monochromes which he produced by dipping the canvas in lime and kaolin. He then experimented with glass wool, cotton wool and polystrol before going on to Neo-Dadaist experiments such as his 'sealed lines', the longest of which measures 7,200 metres. In 1959 Manzoni became a founder member of the Galerie Azimuth in Milan and helped launch its magazine.

Manzù, Giacomo. Italian sculptor, b. 1908 in Bergamo. After serving an apprenticeship as an engraver and stucco worker, Manzù trained as a sculptor at the Accademia Cicognini in Verona. In 1930 he settled in Milan. In 1933 and 1936 he visited Paris. In 1941 he joined the staff of the Accademia Albertinia in Turin and from 1943 to 1954 taught at the Brera in Milan. After returning briefly to Bergamo he settled in Milan, remaining there until he moved to his present home on the outskirts of Rome. In 1948 Manzù won the prize for sculpture at the Biennale in Venice. In 1950 he was asked to execute the bronze doors for St. Peter's in Rome.

After an early academic period, in which he based

his work on antique sculpture and on Donatello, Manzù was profoundly influenced by the Impressionists, especially Rodin and the Italian Medardo Rosso. Much later, in the 1940s, he reverted to the Classical canon, employing natural and intrinsically beautiful forms of great sculptural simplicity. The general sense of calm that pervades his works is offset by their texture, which is animated by slight irregularities. Manzù's portraits testify to his acute powers of observation. His freestanding sculptures are distinguished by the flowing movement and gentle lyricism of their component forms and by the simplicity and compactness of their overall structure. Manzù has also created reliefs, most of which deal with religious themes. With their fluid, rounded contours, which are modelled with great delicacy, these extremely restrained and technically perfect works provide the clearest possible illustration of his attitude to life and art. Manzù's religious works are the outcome of profound meditation of a mystical order. In the sculptural realization of these mystical visions he has never lapsed into a florid or excessively anecdotal style.

C. L. Ragghianti. *Giacomo Manzù, scultore*, Milan 1957.

Mara, Pol. Belgian painter, b. 1920 in Antwerp. After training at the Academy of Art and the Institut Supérieur des Beaux-Arts in Antwerp, Mara developed a Surrealistic style of painting, producing subtle and lyrical figurative works which evoke the lost innocence of the Garden of Eden. Even in these early paintings Mara revealed a predilection for spherical forms. Later, when he turned abstract, this became so pronounced that the works of this later period are quite literally like a saraband of colour. Their whirling forms summon up an organic and physiological universe composed of drifting galaxies, which establish secret links with the unconscious mind. After visiting Greece, Mara organized his abstract forms into more rigid patterns and eventually introduced figurative *motifs* which, although clearly derived from Pop Art and the sexual symbols of the mass media, also reflect a personal and an extremely acute conception of modern eroticism.

Marc, Franz. German painter, b. 1880 in Munich; d. 1916 near Verdun. Marc started his studies in 1900 at the Munich Academy under Hackl and Diez. In 1903 he visited Paris and Brittany and came into contact with Impressionism. In 1907 he paid a further visit to Paris and began an intensive investigation of animals (anatomical studies, studies of movement, etc.). In 1908 (in Lengries) he painted his celebrated series of horses, in which he first started to fuse constructive forms with colour nuances, and also produced his first animal sculptures. He then met Macke and Kandinsky and in 1910 joined the New Artists' Association in Munich, from which the *Blauer Reiter* evolved in the following year when the progressive faction split away under the leadership of Marc and Kandinsky. In 1911 the first *Blauer Reiter* exhibition was staged in the Galerie Thannhauser in Munich and from then onwards Marc's colouring became much freer and much more expressive. In combination with his earlier penchant for *Jugendstil* ideas this new development led him away from naturalistic painting and towards abstraction. Shortly afterwards he was also influenced by Delaunay's Orphism and by the Cubists. In 1913 he produced his first abstract compositions.

After emerging from the colourful world of the Impressionists, Marc espoused the linear harmony of the *Jugendstil* artists before evolving his highly personal and non-academic conception of art, in which he sought to establish his vision of a unified world. In his mature works animal and natural forms interact in complete harmony, thus making a view of creation that is perfect in every respect. Early on in his career, in Munich, Marc came into contact with a group of like-minded young artists who were then evolving their own highly personal conceptions, which ran parallel to but were quite separate from those of the North German Expressionists. Kandinsky, with whom Marc soon became friendly, exerted a powerful influence on all the members of the group, causing them to move away from objective and towards abstract forms. Marc was particularly receptive to such ideas. Subsequently he also acquired a number of structural ideas from the French Cubists whilst his friend Delaunay opened his eyes to simultaneous colour contrasts. But, despite its overall clarity, Marc's work reveals certain Romantic traits which lend a deeper significance to his compositions and which might almost be described as the German aspect of his painting. Marc's attitude to art and life was so profound as to be almost religious. During the final phase of his career he moved away from the objective world and entered a world of pure colour composition. This late development is well illustrated by two paintings, *Tyrol* and *Animal Destinies*, in which vibrant transparent colours form crystalline designs that are reminiscent of stained glass. True, Marc still incorporated simplified animal and natural forms into these works. But, although these undoubtedly continued to exercise their old symbolic function, they were not the sole means of artistic expression. By then Marc was already using colour composition as a vehicle for his ideas. Later still he painted pure abstracts. But then his development was suddenly cut short when he was killed while on active service near Verdun.

A Schardt. *Franz Marc*, Berlin 1936.
H. Bünemann. *Franz Marc*, Munich 1948.
K. Lankheit. *Franz Marc*, Berlin 1950.
Max Robinson. *Franz Marc*, Paris 1963.

Marca-Relli, Conrad. American painter, b. 1913 in Boston. He began drawing when he was in Italy with his journalist father, then studied at the Cooper Union, New York, and worked occasionally as an illustrator for periodicals. He taught in the mural and easel divisions of the WPA Federal Arts Project, where he made the acquaintance of many artists who were important to his later development, including Franz Kline, Willem de Kooning and John Graham, who introduced him to the principles of European modernism and to the work of Picasso, Miró and Matisse. After military service during the Second World War, Marca-Relli resumed painting, working with *motifs* from circus life and Italian Renaissance architecture. These subjects were organized in a Surrealistic manner suggesting influences from the Italian Metaphysical painter Giorgio de Chirico and the French primitive Henri Rousseau. In 1951 Marca-Relli began to paint organic, semi-abstract shapes derived from Surrealist notions of automation, which formally reflected the work of both Miró and Arshile Gorky. The formal order and topographical effects of ancient and Renaissance buildings were a continuing attraction, sustained through travels in France and Italy. The polish and spare elegance of Marca-Relli's paintings, collages and sculptures suggest a refined European taste in work that lacks the crude, unfinished treatment associated with some of his Abstract Expressionist contemporaries. In 1952 he began to introduce raw canvas into his paintings through a collage technique, attempting to approximate the textures and volumes of the Classical structures that inspired him with a plastic equivalent for their colours and forms, and enlarging the medium of collage in a series of restrained and monumental works. Contacts with de Kooning and Pollock in 1953 provided Marca-Relli with a loosened biomorphic vocabulary and balanced his urge for Classical harmony with a freer, more expressive abstraction. His semi-figurative series of *Sleeping Figures* (1953–4) and *Seated Figures* (1962–6), abstract vinyl and metal collages, aluminium reliefs (1962–4) and simplified metal sculptures (whose dense intersecting forms are interlocked with rivets or industrial springs) reflect his characteristic vacillation between an Expressionistic mode and a strictly ordered Classical equilibrium.

Marca-Relli's mural-size collages mark an ambitious high-point in his career, with such works as *Trial* (1956, Minneapolis, Institute of Arts) or *The Battle* (1956, New York, Metropolitan Museum), which include tautly composed canvas swatches in biomorphic shapes, energetically brushed with black or coloured areas of paint. After attempts to oppose the materiality of collage with more fully painted passages, Marca-Relli returned to the clarity of a cubic vocabulary, in which broader forms were 'pegged' into an increasingly spaceless field with actual or painted rivets (1961). Shallow aluminium reliefs and free-standing sculptures, as well as isolated painted shapes filling a bare field, followed his collages of the early 1960s.

H. H. Arnason. *Marca-Relli*, New York 1963.
William C. Agee. Catalogue, *Marca-Relli*, Whitney Museum of American Art, New York 1967.

Marchand, André. French painter, b. 1910 in Aix-en-Provence. In 1923 he started painting, and went to Paris in 1929 to study. In 1932 he exhibited for the first time at the Salon d'Automne. He visited Algeria in 1933. In 1937 he was awarded the Prix Paul Guillaume for painting. In the late thirties and the forties he developed a friendship with Gruber and Tal Coat. In 1941 he contributed to the *Young Painters in the French Tradition* exhibition in Paris. He now lives and works in Paris and Aix. His other activities include tapestry design for the Aubusson factory, theatre design, and book illustration, including Gide's *Les Nourritures Terrestres*. He has had major retrospective exhibitions in 1951 (Holland), 1952 (Belgium) and 1956 (Paris, Galerie Charpentier).

Like several other younger French painters in the late 1930s and early postwar years, Marchand objected to the apolitical character of 'pure' abstract art, in the belief that art should have an explicit social commitment. What emerged from it was a mannered style of figurative painting heavily influenced by Picasso.

G. P. Brabant. *André Marchand*, Paris 1954.

Marcks, Gerhard. German sculptor, b. 1889 in Berlin. Marcks is a self-taught artist. After being advised to take up sculpture by both Gaul and Kolbe, he worked in Richard Scheibe's studio from 1907 onwards. From 1914 to 1919 he served with the forces. He then taught at the School of Arts and Crafts in Berlin for a year before joining the Bauhaus as a 'master of form' in 1919. He remained with Gropius until 1925, running the pottery workshop in Dornburg. Whilst he was there, the Bauhaus-Presse published his first series of woodcuts. From Dornburg he went to the School of Arts and Crafts at Burg Giebichtenstein, near Halle, where he first taught pottery and was subsequently appointed Director of the School. After relinquishing this post in 1933, he eventually settled in Berlin (1937). After the war he was given a teaching post at the Landeskunstschule (State School of Art) in Hamburg. Since 1950 he has been living in Cologne. Whilst he was still learning his craft, Marcks took his orientation from Gaul, Kolbe and Scheibe. Subsequently Expressionism also made its presence felt. But these were not the really important factors. The influence of Ancient Greek sculpture, which is evident throughout his whole career, and of Romanesque sculpture, which becomes more prominent in his later works, is of far greater significance. His life-size statues of women, whose formal severity is offset by a sense of inner animation, his statues of Arcadian youths and animals, and his many small sculptures, all reveal the same basic trend towards an ideal art based on a rigorous and, in many instances, stylized simplification of sculptural form. In the course of his career, Marcks has executed numerous public commissions.

A. Rieth. *Gerhard Marcks*, Recklinghausen 1959.
Exhibition catalogue, *Gerhard Marcks*, Wallraf-Richartz Museum, Cologne 1964.

Marcoussis, Louis (Ludwig Markus). Polish-French painter, b. 1883 in Warsaw; d. 1941 in Cusset, near Vichy. He first studied at the school of fine arts in Cracow. In 1903 he moved to Paris, where he studied in the studio of J. Lefebvre and met Roger de la Fresnaye. From about 1907 to 1910 he worked as a cartoonist. In 1910 he met Braque, and was drawn by his influence back into painting. In 1911 he met Picasso and Apollinaire (who recommended his French pseudonym). In 1911 and 1912 he met other Cubists and exhibited in the *Section d'Or* exhibition in 1912. During the war he volunteered for service in the French Army. In 1919 he returned to Paris, where in 1920 he contributed to the *Section d'Or* exhibition. He was also active as an illustrator (notably in etchings), and the books on which he worked include *L'Indicateur des Chemins de Coeur* (1928) and *Planches de Salut* (1931), both by Tzara. In 1933 he visited America.

Marcoussis was a minor Cubist painter of considerable facility and sensitivity. His sympathy for Braque's painting is manifestly understandable from the painterly sensuality of much of his own work (*Still Life with Draughtsboard*, 1912, Paris, Musée d'Art Moderne). His activity within Cubism never aspired to extreme radicalism, but his understanding of Picasso's and Braque's concepts was perhaps uniquely perceptive among the lesser artists (e.g. *Portrait of Apollinaire*, etching, 1912, Chicago, Art Institute). His Synthetic Cubist paintings of 1913–14 have a tighter, more schematic character, probably inspired by Gris. After the war he continued to work within the terms of Synthetic Cubism (*Rain No 1*, 1927, London, Tate Gallery).

Jean Lafranchis. *Marcoussis, Sa Vie, Son Oeuvre*, Paris 1961.

Marczyński, Adam. Polish painter, graphic artist and stage designer, b. 1908 in Cracow. He studied in Cracow, then in Paris (in 1930 and 1936), and from 1939 to 1940 in Lemberg. He became a professor at the Cracow Academy. He has also won a gold medal at the Olympia Competition in London.

Marfaing, André. French painter, b. 1925 in Toulouse. Marfaing turned to painting after studying law. He paints informal pictures, which are remarkable for their powerful chiaroscuro. Commenting on this style of painting Marfaing has pointed out that it 'is not meant to solve problems but to create a whole new poetic world'.

Mari, Enzo. Italian sculptor and designer, b. 1932 in Novara. Mari studied at the Accademia Brera in Milan, where he is now living. Since leaving the Academy he has been enquiring into problems bearing on the reproduction of perceptible structures and also into certain aspects of design. His work on design has been carried out on behalf of the Associazione per il Disegno industriale, where he is employed as a researcher. He is also investigating the feasibility of producing works of art on an industrial basis. Mari's approach to art is similar to Munari's.

Marin, John. American painter, b. 1870 in Rutherford, New Jersey; d. 1953 in Cape Split, Maine. After an unsuccessful attempt at an architectural career, Marin entered the Pennsylvania Academy of the Fine Arts at the age of 29. Following his two-year stay there and another five aimless years, the artist travelled to Europe in 1905, remaining there until 1910, when he returned to New York. During his European years Marin was strongly influenced by Whistler's art, especially by the latter's etchings, with which he felt a spiritual kinship, as evidenced by Marin's own graphic works. Although he had not been overly influenced by European artists, his friendship with Edward Steichen (an American then living in Normandy) had a life-long effect. It was through Steichen, an intimate of Alfred Stieglitz, that Marin first exhibited at Stieglitz' *avant-garde* 291 Gallery in New York (1909).

After his return to the United States, Marin started painting cityscapes of New York; then in 1914 he was drawn to the state of Maine, living first at Small Point and then at Deer Isle. It was here that he began using dark slashing lines around the edges of his compositions to accentuate various areas of his land and seascapes (*Maine Islands*, 1922, Washington, D.C., Phillips Collection). These seemingly random short strokes were the key to his balance of composition; balance and life's movement were, for Marin, the two crucial elements in a work of art. These two features share much with two of painting's sister arts—the structure of architecture and the lyricism of music. Marin's primary medium was watercolour, although in the 1930s—after moving to Cape Split, Maine, in 1933—he began to work more and more in oils. These oil paintings grew generically from the watercolours, maintaining a respect for the flat surface and the bare canvas (previously the whiteness of the watercolour paper) and a commitment to the outdoors.

Catalogue, *John Marin, a Retrospective Exhibition*, Institute of Modern Art, Boston 1947.
Mackinley Helm. *John Marin*, Boston 1948.
Dorothy Norman (ed.). *The Selected Writings of John Marin*, New York 1949.

Marini, Marino. Italian painter and sculptor, b. 1901 in Pistoia. He studied painting and sculpture at the Academy of Art in Florence under the naturalistic artist Trentacosta. From 1928 to 1929 he was in Paris, and from 1929 to 1940 taught at the School of Art at the Villa Reale in Monza. In 1935 he won a Grand Prix for sculpture, and in 1940 was made Professor of Sculpture at the Brera in Milan. He was often in France, especially Paris, and also visited the USA, Germany and most other European countries. From 1942 to 1946 he lived in Switzerland. In 1952 he won the Prize for Sculpture at the Biennale in Venice, in 1954 the Grand Prix for Sculpture at the Accademia dei Lincei in Rome, and in 1963 the Prize for Sculpture awarded by the city of Milan. He now lives and works in Milan and Forte dei Marmi. He has been represented in all major exhibitions from 1923, and has had numerous one-man shows in Europe and the USA from 1932 onwards.

Marini is one of those rare artists with a genuine gift for both painting and sculpture. After an initial period, in which he concentrated primarily on painting and graphic art, he turned to sculpture in 1930, and for nearly twenty years worked almost exclusively in this medium. Marini's early paintings were influenced both by the Tuscan environment in which he had grown up and by Renaissance and Antique models. When he came to produce his sculptures, these influences continued to make themselves felt, but were further reinforced by the Impressionist techniques evolved by Medardo Rosso, A. Rodin and A. Renoir, and by the powerful Neo-Classical structures introduced by A. Maillol and A. Martini. The subject matter of Marini's sculpture is relatively restricted. In the early 1930s he depicted individual human figures, choosing representative and highly expressive types. Such were his mythological women: matriarchal figures with broad hips, firm breasts and powerful limbs. Such too were his fairground tumblers and boxers with their hard, bony bodies. During this period Marini also produced a large number of portraits of his contemporaries: gaunt creatures with sharp, watchful eyes, hollow cheeks, taut coarse skin and bare hunched backs. Then, in 1935, Marini discovered the age-old theme of the horse and rider, which he was to make so peculiarly his own. In the first works of this kind the horse and rider are represented as distinct creatures. Each exists independently of the other, and is composed of clearly discernible articulating limbs. Later they were completely fused, and the rider seemed like a rigid column set astride the tense elongated body of the horse, like a power pack mounted on the solid and earthbound pyramid formed by the animal. The growing intensity of this theme was accompanied by greater formal precision. Thus, the loose organization of the *Waiting Rider* of 1937 was followed in 1953 by the inexorable tension of the *Falling Horse and Rider*, in which elements of time, space and movement are combined in a completely integrated

composition, and the relationship between static and dynamic forces is made manifest in the sculptural form. Between 1953 and 1963, when the dramatic intensity of this *motif* reached its peak, the fleeting moment of the fall was expressed by tetrahedral structures with acute-angled directional axes.

Marini is essentially a modeller. True, he attaches great importance to a clear architectural structure. But having created it, he then goes to infinite pains to obtain a perfect finish. He works with a chisel on his bronze casts, opening up the surface to produce the correct epidermal texture. He also applies acids in certain places, thus creating a chemical reaction which colours the affected parts. Blemishes and joints produced during the casting introduce an element of chance. The colouring is added in the course of the sculpting or modelling process; consequently, it forms an integral part of the finished work, thus ensuring optimum functional efficacy.

As a painter Marini also portrayed metaphorical figures as individual and isolated *motifs*. After his middle period, in which he concentrated on sculpture, he began to paint again in 1948–9. Many of his pictures are near-abstracts in the formal sense, and although they allow spatial movement in the Cubist manner, this is really no more than a modulation of the picture surface.

In addition to sculptures and paintings, Marini has also produced a large body of drawings and graphic works.

Pietro Maria Bardi. *Marino Marini: Graphic Work and Paintings*, London and New York 1960.
Eduard Trier. *The Sculpture of Marino Marini*, London and New York 1961.

Marisol (Marisol Escobar). American sculptress, b. 1930 in Paris. Born of Venezuelan parents, Marisol spent her youth mainly in Los Angeles, where she attended high school, and in Paris, where she studied art at the École des Beaux-Arts and the Académie Julian. In 1950 she settled in New York and continued her studies at the Hans Hofmann School and the Art Students' League; from 1958 to 1960 she worked in Rome. Her first one-man exhibition was held at the Leo Castelli Gallery, New York, in 1957; her work was also shown in group exhibitions in the United States and Europe.

Marisol began to work primarily in sculpture around 1953. Her early efforts include small, playful and erotic terra-cotta figures, sometimes placed behind glass in boxes, and roughly carved wood figures of human beings and animals. Her mature work, from the late 1950s and the 1960s, consists of mixed-media assemblages that include juxtapositions of all media—painting, carving, drawing, plaster casts and found objects. The mixture of two- and three-dimensional effects characteristic of Marisol's sculpture provides an ambiguity and irony that underscores the witty, satirical commentary on society implied by her subject matter. Her skilfully crafted pieces are usually larger than life-size, sometimes conceived as single units, at other times as groups. Although they suggest an anonymous style, they are at the same time curious references to the artist herself, as they nearly always include such elements as plaster casts of her face, hands or feet. Characteristic examples of Marisol's work are the *Blacks* (1961–2, Coll. Mrs. Eleanor Ward), *Women and Dog* (1964, New York, Whitney Museum) and *Dealers* (1965–6, New York, Sidney Janis Gallery).

Dorothy C. Miller (ed.). Catalogue, *Americans 1963*, Museum of Modern Art, New York 1963.
Georgione Oeri. 'Marisol', *Quadrum* 16, Brussels 1964.

Marquet, Albert. French painter, b. 1875 in Bordeaux; d. 1947 in Paris. In 1890 Marquet enrolled at the École National des Arts Décoratifs, in 1892 he met Matisse for the first time, and in 1897 he went to work in Gustave Moreau's studio. In 1900 Marquet collaborated with Matisse on a series of decorations for the Grand Palais, and in 1904 became a founder member of the Salon d'Automne. In 1905 he was in Trouville and St-Tropez, in 1906 in Le Havre (with Raoul Dufy), and in 1907 in London and St-Jean-de-Luz (with Camoin and Friesz). In 1908 he took over Matisse's studio on the Rue St-Michel. He travelled extensively both in France and abroad. From 1915 to 1919 he lived partly in La Varenne and partly in Marseilles; in 1921–2 he was in Algiers, in 1923 in Sidi-Bou-Said, in 1924 Sète and Bordeaux, in 1925 Bougie and Norway. He visited Egypt in 1928. In 1931 he took a flat and studio on the rue Dauphine, where it joins the Quai des Grands Augustins. From 1932 to 1938 he visited Spain, Rumania, Russia, North Africa, Switzerland and Holland. During the German occupation he lived in Algiers. On 5 May 1946 he returned to Paris, and later the same year made his last journey—to Les Grisons in Switzerland.

Like Matisse, Marquet was a pupil of Moreau, and benefited from his intelligent and non-doctrinaire teaching. Other important factors in Marquet's early development were his studies in the Louvre and his investigations into contemporary trends of French painting. These are reflected in the nudes which he painted between 1898 and 1900 and which show him moving away from Impressionism towards the Divisionism of Georges Seurat. Marquet also resembled Matisse in his use of powerful expressive colours as a means of heightening the visual impact of his paintings. But despite its expressiveness Marquet's palette was composed entirely of cool colours. It is quite evident from his work that by c. 1905 he had already abandoned Fauvist principles. His luminous compositions were then superseded by paintings executed in rich, atmospheric tones, mostly in different shades of grey. This muted colouring was accompanied by a Classical composition based on contrasting areas of movement and passivity. Subsequently, Marquet revealed a growing preference for hazy settings, which found expression in numerous rain- and snowscapes.

Georges Besson. *Marquet*, Paris 1929.
M. Marquet. *Marquet*, Paris 1955.
F. Jourdain. *Marquet*, Paris 1959.

Marsh, Reginald. American painter, b. 1898 in Paris; d. 1954 in New York. Both of his parents were artists, and Marsh learned to draw while still a child, at which time he was also influenced by the drawings of his father's friend Boardman Robinson (1876–1952). The Realist tradition of illustration claimed his professional interest for a decade before he turned to painting, and Marsh worked as an illustrator for *Vanity Fair, Harper's Bazaar* and the *New York Daily News*. He also did drawings for some of the more radical political journals. Marsh himself was especially attracted by the circus and by the more perverse or lowly aspects of city life; burlesque queens, derelicts, shopgirls and prostitutes were among his favourite subjects. He is well known for his paintings of the crowds and amusement arcades in Times Square and Coney Island, and his careful and loving record of these spots is often quite accurate in detail (*Twenty-Cent Movie*, 1936, New York, Whitney Museum). In 1929 the artist Kenneth Hayes Miller prompted him to turn increasingly to urban scenes, and in keeping with his earlier interests, Marsh painted poor areas like the *Bowery* (1930, New York, Metropolitan Museum), with its rows of cheap hotels under the 'El' (elevated railway) and its embittered old drunkards. The 'El', a typically New York phenomenon, figured in several of his paintings (*Why Not Use the El?*, 1930, New York, Whitney Museum). Miller interested Marsh in Renaissance drawing and composition, but already Marsh's draughtsmanly training had made it clear that colour was less important to him than design. Indeed his use of colour in thin glazed layers often appears as a superfluous or later addition to the paintings, although this in no way detracts from their formal or narrative interest.

Lloyd Goodrich. *Reginald Marsh*, Whitney Museum of American Art, New York 1955.
Norman Sasowsky. *Reginald Marsh: Etchings, Engravings, Lithographs*, New York 1956.

Martin, Kenneth. British painter and sculptor, b. 1905 in Sheffield. Martin studied at the Sheffield School of Art and the Royal College of Art in London from 1929 to 1932.

After painting landscapes in the 1930s and early 1940s Martin turned abstract in the mid-1940s. Since 1951 he has been producing wire mobiles, which depict 'fields of force' and whose movements constantly create new spatial forms. His constructions express the beauty of logic rather than that of imagination. His *Mobile Spiral* of 1956 (bronze and steel, Calouste Gulbenkian Foundation) is a typical example.

Martin, Mary (Mary Balmford). British painter and sculptress, b. 1907 in Folkestone. In 1925, when she was eighteen, she moved to London, where she attended Goldsmith's School of Art and the Royal College of Art. In 1930 she married Kenneth Martin.

Martin paints still lifes and landscapes and—since 1950—has also constructed reliefs, most of which are based on simple sequences of numbers.

Martini, Arturo. Italian sculptor and painter, b. 1889 in Treviso; d. 1947 in Milan. After serving an apprenticeship, first as a goldsmith, then as a potter, Martini turned to sculpture in 1906. In 1909 he went to Munich to study under Adolf von Hildebrand, who influenced him greatly. In 1911 and 1914 he visited Paris but did not make contact with any modern groups. Martini was not opposed to Classical art, he merely wished to recast it in a modern mould. And so, in 1921, he joined the Neo-Classical movement propagated by the *Valori Plastici* magazine. Frequent changes of style produced works in the manner of Late Roman Antiquity, the Trecento and the Baroque and also led to the assimilation of certain abstract forms. During this period Martini seized on both historical and current events as themes for his terra-cotta sculptures. Then in 1945 he suddenly decided to give up sculpture and become a painter. He justified this act of desperation, which he performed shortly before his death, in a publication entitled *Scultura—lingua morta* (Sculpture—a dead language) (Venice, 1945).

Martini's central quality, which is present in all of his work, has only been recognized and properly assessed since his death: it is curiosity. But this curiosity is not restricted to the objective world. On the contrary, it is the sculptural counterpart to Surrealism and Magic Realism.

A. Martini. *Scultura—lingua morta,* Venice 1945; reprinted Verona 1948.
M. Bontempelli. *Arturo Martini,* Milan 1948.
R. Franchi. *Arturo Martini,* Milan and Florence 1951.

Martins, Aldemir. Brazilian draughtsman, graphic artist and painter, b. 1922 in Ceará, Brazil. Martins is a self-taught artist, who started to work as a newspaper illustrator in 1942. In 1946 he went to live in São Paulo, where he studied graphic art. Martins uses Indian and coloured inks for his figurative compositions, which are executed in a dynamic and economical style. He is at present Professor of Graphic Art at the Museum of Art in São Paulo. In 1956 he received first prize in the international competition for drawing at the Venice Biennale.

Martins, Maria. Brazilian sculptress, b. 1900 in Campanha. She first studied music, but became interested in sculpture in 1926 and eventually (1939) decided to work at it full-time. She had an exhibition in 1946 at the Museum of Modern Art, New York, and won first prize for sculpture at the 1957 São Paulo Bienal. Her bronze work is lush and rich, like the Amazon jungle from which she takes many of her subjects.

Marussig, Piero. Italian painter, b. 1879 in Trieste; d. 1937 in Pavia. Marussig studied in Vienna, Munich, Rome and Paris. In 1922 he became a founder member of the *Sette Pittori moderni* group, from which the *Novecento Italiano* later emerged.

After successfully integrating the influences exerted on him by van Gogh and Gauguin during his youthful period Marussig was faced with a difficult choice between the formal structures of the Post-Cubists and the Italian ideal of the *Novecento*. He solved the problem by compromising between the two, and this compromise continued to dictate the form of his paintings for years to come. It was only in his late works, which consist of landscapes, portraits and still lifes, that he finally placed his trust in the luminous power of pure colour composition.

V. Constantini. *Piero Marussig,* Milan n.d.
R. Carrieri. *12 opere di Piero Marussig,* Milan 1942.

Maryan (Pinchas Burstein). Polish-French painter and graphic artist, b. 1927 in Nowy-Sacz, Poland. Maryan lived in Israel from 1947 to 1950 and then studied at the École Nationale des Beaux-Arts in Paris from 1950 to 1953. He has been living in New York since 1962.

Maryan paints figurative pictures in an expressive style. He has adopted a number of the techniques evolved by the action painters.

Mascherini, Marcello. Italian sculptor, b. 1906 in Udine. Mascherini studied in Trieste. The major influences in his work stem from A. Martini on the one hand and Etruscan and Italian Quattrocento art on the other. In his female figures, which are notable for their Mannerist elegance, Mascherini—like Fazzini and El Greco—has tried to establish an abstract sculptural technique by stylizing and deforming the Classical canon. He also works as a theatrical and costume designer. He is now living in Trieste.

Masereel, Frans. Belgian painter and graphic artist, b. 1889 in Blankenberghe; d. 1972 in Avignon. After studying at the Academy of Art in Ghent Masereel moved to Geneva in 1915, where he worked for various periodicals including *Les Tablettes* and *La Feuille*. His woodcut series *Die Toten erwachen* (The Dead Awake), which appeared from 1917 onwards, brought him early fame. From 1920 to 1940

Masereel lived in Paris; from 1947 to 1951 he taught in Saarbrücken, and in 1949 he made his permanent home in Nice. In 1950 he won the International Prize for graphics at the Venice Biennale.

Masereel is a committed artist. Using simple, pictorial techniques—which reveal the influence of primitive art, folk art and Expressionism during his early period but become progressively more traditional—he depicts the sufferings of his fellow-men both in times of war and in the hectic conditions of big city life. He has also portrayed the milieu of the fishermen, sailors, workers and prostitutes in the great European ports and harbours and created stage sets for a wide range of dramatists, including Brecht and Lorca.

L. Lebeer. *Frans Masereel*, Antwerp 1950.
H. v. d. Gabelentz. *Frans Masereel*, Dresden 1959.

Masson, André. French painter, b. 1896 in Balagny. The work of André Masson has an important place in the development of Surrealism. He began his studies before 1914, at the Académie Royale des Beaux-Arts, Brussels, and the École des Beaux-Arts in Paris. He served in the Great War in the fighting lines, and was severely wounded. The war experience of Masson affected him very deeply. The abnormal realities of trench warfare, with its domination by extreme violence, its immediate contiguity of life and death, presented questions of the motivation of human behaviour. His work has been an essay in confronting life at that level of experience.

Masson went to Paris in 1922, and associated with Miró and with the poets Armand Salacrou, Michel Leiris and Georges Limbour. His interest in the deeper reality of man's behaviour drew him to Surrealism. In 1924 he met André Breton, joined the Surrealist group, and exhibited with them for some years. He became very involved with non-rational purpose in art, in developing drawing and painting as nearly as possible as direct thought transference. With Miró he produced 'automatic' drawings. These allowed the free movement of the pen line, without pre-thought or condition of any kind. To obtain the same effect in painting, Masson used drawn continuous lines of glue on the canvas, adding the colour by coating with different coloured sands.

Very early in his career Masson relinquished any desire to construct paintings on Cubist or any other lines. For him painting has not been a contrived art, a matter of developing a style. It had to be a part of life itself, a 'way of knowing' simultaneous with a way of action; admitting the violent, the erotic, the chaotic, spurning any rationally formulated order.

In 1940 he exiled himself to America. Masson's Surrealist ideas found the new soil productive, and his influence on American painting was strong. In particular Arshile Gorky drew on it, as did Jackson Pollock and Mark Rothko. Pollock's Action Painting has much in common with Masson's early sandpaintings, and with his automatism of method.

He returned to Paris in 1945. He designed the scenery for a production of *Hamlet* in 1946, and for Berg's opera *Wozzeck* in 1963. He had before the war been concerned in a similar way with various productions.

Masson's life work represents a series of periods of exploration, for his personal purpose, of various techniques, varying from full, rich polychrome to monochrome and purely linear work. On occasions involving closely defined biomorphic images, his work is characterized by extreme speed of execution and complex personal imagery.

M. Leiris and G. Limbour. *André Masson et son univers*, Geneva and Paris 1947.
Otto Hahn. *André Masson*, London and New York 1965.

Mastroianni, Umberto. Italian sculptor, b. 1910 in Fontana Lisi, near Rome. Mastroianni moved to Turin in 1926 and later studied in Rome. Like Spazzapan, he quickly made a name for himself, and after the Second World War was acknowledged as one of the most important abstract artists working in Turin. Since 1957 he has taught at the Turin Academy.

During his early period Mastroianni was influenced by the Futurists, especially Boccioni. His powerful, pointed and aggressive sculptural forms set up a dynamic relationship with their environment. His best-known works are the monument to the Italian partisans in Turin and the sculpture in the entrance to Rotterdam railway station. In 1958 Mastroianni won the Grand Prix for sculpture at the 29th Biennale in Venice.

N. Ponente. *Mastroianni*, Rome 1963.

Masurovsky, Gregory. American painter and graphic artist, b. 1929 in Bronx, New York. After graduating from New York's High School of Music and Art, Masurovsky attended the Parsons School of Design, Black Mountain College and the Art Students' League. In 1954 he moved to Paris and studied at the Sorbonne. It was in that city that he had his first one-man show at the Galerie du Haut Pavé (1955). He is best known for pen and ink drawings of tiny strokes, commas, squiggles and granules (*Untitled*, pen and ink, 1964, Paris, Galerie Europe). These non-objective, free-form works which spread out from the centre of the page have a quality of impermanence and constant evolution.

Jérome Mellquist. 'Gregory Masurovsky', *Quadrum* 10, 1961.
Michel Conil La Coste. 'Masurovsky, An American in Paris', *Studio International* 169, March 1965.

Mataré, Ewald. German sculptor, b. 1887 in Aachen; d. 1965 in Cologne. He studied painting at Berlin under Lovis Corinth from 1907 to 1914, then turned to sculpture in 1920. He was a professor at the Düsseldorf Academy in 1932, but was dismissed the following year and declared a 'degenerate artist'. He then turned to applied art for a livelihood, until reinstated at Düsseldorf in 1946. Although he is well known in Germany for some large postwar commissions such as the bronze doors of the south portal of Cologne Cathedral, his general reputation rests on his animal carvings, especially of cattle. He carved them in fine-grained woods, placing the emphasis on the fullness of their bodies and not on their muscular dynamism. Mataré was in contact with the *Blauer Reiter* group, one of whose members, Franz Marc, may have inspired his interest in animals. In his formal simplification of their bodies Mataré appeared to follow the example of François Pompon (1855–1933), going beyond him in the stylized exaggeration of their volumes, but stopping short of the high degree of abstraction that Brancusi imposed on these subjects.

H. Peters. *Mataré: Das graphische Werk*, Cologne 1957–8.

Mathieu, Georges. French painter, b. 1921 in Boulogne-sur-Mer. After studying English, law and philosophy Mathieu began to paint in 1942. In 1944, after reading a book by E. Crankshaw on the novelist Conrad, he produced his first non-figurative pictures. In 1947 he moved to Paris, where he first saw paintings by Wols. In 1947 Mathieu also joined with Bryen in organizing *L'Imaginaire*, an exhibition of works by painters engaged in *Abstraction Lyrique* and *Art Nonfiguratif*. This was followed by a second exhibition under the title *H.W.P.S.M.T.B.* in the Galerie Allendy in 1948, and a third under the title *White and Black* at the Galerie Drouin. In 1950 he had his first one-man show, which was staged at the Galerie Drouin, and also exhibited individual works at the Salon des Réalités Nouvelles and the Salon des Surindépendants. In 1952 he had his first New York exhibition. In 1954 Mathieu and Robert Descharnes made a film, which was inspired by a picture in the Salon de Mai entitled *La Bataille de Bouvines*. In 1956 they also made a short film on the relationships between art and play. In 1955 Mathieu designed stage sets for the play *Saga de Lug Hallwynn* by E. Looten, which was put on at the Théâtre du Creuset d'Artel in Paris, and in 1956 he painted a large-format picture (12 metres by 4) entitled *Hommage aux poètes du monde entier* in the Sarah Bernhardt Theatre as part of the 'Festival International d'Art dramatique'. In 1957 he visited Tokyo for an exhibition of his work and fascinated the Japanese art public by painting several large-format works in the course of just a few days immediately prior to the opening. In 1966 and 1967 he produced tapestry designs. Since 1944 Mathieu has also been an extremely active publicist. In 1953 he founded and helped to edit a new magazine, *United States Lines Paris Review*. He is now living in Paris.

Mathieu, the originator of *Abstraction Lyrique*, was one of the first modern painters to protest against the geometrical forms of abstract art and to free himself from the restraints imposed by the Classical tradition. In his early period, which began in 1944, Mathieu painted in a style closely akin to Abstract Surrealism. The real turning point in his career came three years later when he saw pictures by Wols. Subsequently, he also studied works by Pollock and de Kooning, and was soon able to throw off the shackles of figurative Post-Cubism, thus acquiring greater freedom of expression. From c. 1948 onwards he developed his spontaneous calligraphy, a sophisticated form of Action Painting modelled in part on traditional eastern calligraphic methods. Since 1950 Mathieu has produced numerous large-format pictures with monochrome grounds on which he records traces of his highly imaginative ideas. He creates his pictorial forms quite spontaneously, without recourse to preliminary sketches. The speed of the actual working process is so great that it precludes all possibility of mental control or the reproduction of memories. Writing in 1967, W. Haftmann defined the prerequisites of this kind of painting as 'meditation, concentration, and improvisation'. The dominant colours in Mathieu's works, which appear against monochrome grounds, are blue, red, white and black. The interlacing calligraphic lines form dense networks of infinite complexity, whose rhythmical patterns are disrupted by the swirling arcs and loops of colour. Mathieu's titles, which he adds subsequently and which are often rather pompous, provide a commentary on his works.

Georges Mathieu. *Analogie de la Non-Figuration*, Paris 1949; *Au-delà du Tachisme*, Paris 1963; *Le Privilège d'être*, Paris 1967. Catalogue, *Mathieu*, Musée des Beaux-Arts de la Ville de Paris, Paris 1963. Jean Charpentier. *Georges Mathieu*, Paris 1965.

Matisse, Henri. French painter, b. 1869 at Le Cateau-Cambrésis; d. 1954 in Vence. The son of a grain merchant, he had a classical education at the Lycée in St-Quentin and, after studying law in Paris (1887–8), started work in a lawyer's office. He first started painting during convalescence from appendicitis, 1889–90, and in 1890 gave up law to study art in Paris: at the Académie Julian (under Bouguereau) and then, about 1892–8, under Gustave Moreau. Here he met Marquet, Rouault, Manguin and Camoin. He spent the summers of 1895–7 painting in Brittany with Émile Wéry. In 1896 he showed four paintings at the Société Nationale des Beaux-Arts: one was purchased by the state. He acquired two van Gogh drawings from the American painter Russell. In 1897 he saw the Caillebotte bequest of Impressionist paintings at the Luxembourg, and also met Pissarro. The following year he married Amélie Parayre: together they visited London, Corsica and

Toulouse (1898–9). In 1899 he met Derain while studying at the Académie Carrière; he started to study sculpture. From Vollard he purchased Cézanne's *Three Bathers* despite extreme financial hardship (in 1936 Matisse presented this painting to the Petit Palais, Paris). At this time he was working part-time as a decorator.

He first exhibited at the Salon des Indépendants in 1901 and in 1903 at the Salon d'Automne. He met Vlaminck and Signac. In 1904 he had his first one-man show at Vollard's and then spent the summer working with Signac and Cross at St-Tropez. In 1905 and 1906 he exhibited with other Fauve painters at the Salon d'Automne. He subsequently met Gertrude Stein, who became an important patron, and through her, Picasso. He spent the summer at Collioure with Derain; from this time on he spent most summers painting in the south of France. In 1906 he met his Russian patron Shchukin (who in 1909 commissioned the *Dance* and *Music* paintings). In 1908 his essay *Notes d'un Peintre* was published in *La Grande Revue*, Paris. The period 1907–14 was one of extensive travel abroad, including Italy (1907), Germany (1908), Spain (1910–11), Moscow (1911) and Morocco (1911–12, 1912–13). In 1910 he visited Munich for an exhibition of Islamic art. His own work was by now being widely shown in Europe and America (Armory Show, New York, 1913).

During the 1914–18 war he divided his time between Paris and the south of France: he was in frequent contact with Marquet, Gris, Renoir and Bonnard. In 1919 Diaghilev commissioned the sets and costumes for Stravinsky's *Le Chant du Rossignol* (Opéra, Paris; Covent Garden, London). From the 1920s on he lived in Paris and Nice with occasional visits abroad: to Italy (1923, 1933) and Tahiti (1930, via San Francisco and New York). In 1943 he moved to Vence.

He continued to make sculpture as well as painting and worked occasionally as an illustrator (e.g. *Mallarmé, Poésies*; Skira, 1932). From 1948 on he worked extensively with cut-out coloured papers. His major commissions were for the *Dance* mural, Barnes Foundation, Pennsylvania (1930–2); designs for Massine's ballet *Rouge et Noir* (1937–9); and the entire decoration of the Chapelle du Rosaire, Vence (1948–51). He was made Chevalier (1925) and then Commander (1947) of the Légion d'Honneur and was awarded first prizes at the Carnegie International Exhibition, Pittsburgh (1927) and the Venice Biennale (1950). The Musée Matisse, Le Cateau-Cambrésis, was inaugurated in 1952.

Important retrospective exhibitions of his work include those at San Francisco (1936); New York (1943, 1951–2); Philadelphia (1948); Nice (1950); Los Angeles (1966); London (1968); Paris (1956, 1970).

Matisse wrote in his *Notes d'un Peintre* (1908):

'What I dream of is an art of balance, purity and serenity, devoid of troubling or depressing subject matter . . . which might be . . . like an appeasing influence, a mental soother, something like a good armchair in which to rest from physical fatigue.' The expressiveness of his art was distinct from the socio-political mission of early twentieth-century Expressionism, which he influenced artistically. It had more in common with the Arcadian hedonism of the European Classical tradition. On such grounds his art was often condemned as bourgeois decadence by subsequent *avant-gardistes*.

After the restrained Chardin-like early interiors and still lifes, 1890–1905 was a period of intensive experiment with Post-Impressionist techniques and theory. Neo-Impressionism was a major influence on his heightened palette, but Cézanne was the dominant early influence. From Cézanne, Matisse concluded that a painting was born from the relationships of its own internal energies and that through these the artist expressed his sensations in front of the *motif*. His ambition became 'to reach that state of condensation of my sensations that constitutes a picture'.

The bald, sometimes violent vigour with which he pursued his experiments (*Portrait with a Green Stripe*, 1905, Copenhagen, Museum of Fine Art; *Open Window, Collioure*, 1905, New York, J. H. Whitney Museum) established his leadership of the Fauves, 1905–6. The big figure compositions of the period— *Luxe, Calme et Volupté*, 1905 (Paris, private collection); *Joie de Vivre*, 1905–6 (Pennsylvania, Barnes Foundation); *Le Luxe*, 1907 (Copenhagen, Museum of Fine Art), etc.—are all poetic in mood, the titles often taken from Baudelaire. In form they became increasingly simple, eliminating modulation of colour and broken brushwork for an opposition of evenly saturated colours. This reached a climax in *La Desserte Rouge*, 1908, and in the great *Dance* and *Music* panels, 1909–10 (all in the Hermitage, Leningrad).

Although he maintained to the end that he painted nothing he had not seen, his art from this point on expressed a view of life more than of appearances and his anti-naturalistic treatment of space (he spoke of 'spiritual space') probably reflects current philosophical and scientific thought on the illusory nature of appearances. This tendency in his art was fed by his admiration for Near Eastern art which inspired an increase of textured decoration from 1910/11 onwards, and a new sense of the exotic. The influence of Cubism, 1914–16, encouraged a brief geometric period and subsequently a more complex ambivalence of space (*The Moroccans*, 1916, New York, Museum of Modern Art).

The great works of his maturity—the *Odalisques* (1920–5), the Barnes mural (1930–2), the Chapel at Vence (1949–51) and late cut-paper gouaches (*L'Escargot*, 1953, London, Tate Gallery)—all amplify his resolved ambition for an art of enriching expressive decoration. The sense of scale in his late work and the emancipation of pure colour oppositions have been responsible for a dramatic increase in his reputation among younger artists since the mid-1950s.

A. H. Barr Jr. *Matisse: His Art and His Public*, New York 1951.
G. Diehl. *Henri Matisse*, New York and Paris 1958.
J. Lassaigne. *Matisse: Biographical and Critical Study*, Geneva 1959.
R. Escholier. *Matisse: A Portrait of the Artist and the Man*, London and New York 1960.

Matta Echaurren, Roberto Sebastian. Chilean painter, b. 1911 in Santiago de Chile. Matta attended the Sacred Heart School and the Catholic University in Santiago de Chile. He completed his architectural studies in 1931, and went to live in Paris in 1933. Whilst there he visited Germany and Austria. From 1935 to 1937 he worked as a draughtsman in Le Corbusier's studio. In 1936 he met the poet Garcia Lorca in Madrid, and was introduced by him to Dali and the Surrealists. In 1937 he showed three drawings at the Surrealist Exhibition in the Galerie Wildenstein in Paris. In 1938 he painted his first picture, and published a pamphlet entitled 'Mathématique sensible—Architecture du temps' in *Minotaure*, the Surrealist magazine. In 1939 he went to live in the USA, and between 1941 and 1948 had regular exhibitions in the Pierre Matisse Gallery in New York. In 1948 he returned to Europe. From 1950 to 1954 he lived in Rome. In 1954 he visited Chile and Peru. From 1955 onwards he exhibited in the Salon de Mai. In 1956 he painted a mural for the UNESCO building in Paris. From 1961 he visited various South American countries, and made several trips to Cuba. In 1962 he won the Marzotto Prize.

During his initial period Matta used the kind of automatic writing developed by the European Surrealists in the 1920s. In his earliest paintings—the 'psychological morphologies' of c. 1938—he created agitated, psychologically motivated structures, and demonstrated their strange relationship to external reality. Matta's encounter with A. Gorky and the American Surrealists in 1939–40, and his discovery of the early Mexican cultures, paved the way for his large-format pictures. The structures and creatures depicted in these works were inspired by a mystical belief in the essential unity of all cosmic events, and it comes as no surprise, therefore, to find that in the mid-1940s Matta began to evolve a pictorial mythology for our own technological age. Fascinated by the mechanical precision and speed of automated processes, he painted spherical visions of a psycho-physical architecture in a style that went far beyond traditional Surrealism. His highly differentiated choreography of pictorial forms was the outcome of a bewildering symbiosis of organic limbs and mechanical components of cosmonaut

apparatuses: man was represented as a creature who had completely identified with his machines, and this 'man-machine' was placed in opposition to auto-generative apparatuses that are engaged in frenzied activity. This daemonic instrumentation and the unlimited extension of its functions in space were prompted in the first instance by the orgies of cruelty and destruction in the Second World War. Between 1950 and 1960 Matta's colouring acquired a shrill, vitriolic and luminous quality, and the sharply defined pictorial objects in the paintings of this period—cosmonaut apparatuses, astral configurations and strange hybrid creatures, half human and half insect—were depicted in the midst of endless space. Matta's fantastic and monumental portrayal of space is quite incommensurable. It expresses the limitless expansion of all human drives and constitutes a truly imaginative response to man's cosmic and cosmonaut ventures.

R. S. Matta Echaurren. 'Mathématique sensible—Architecture du Temps', *Minotaure*, Paris 1938.
Pierre Mabille. 'Matta and the New Reality', *Horizon XX*, London, September 1949.
William Rubin. 'Matta', *Museum of Modern Art Bulletin XXV*, No. 1, New York 1957.

Maurer, Alfred. American painter, b. 1868 in New York; d. 1932 in New York. The son of Louis Maurer (1832–1932)—a Currier and Ives lithographer who was opposed to his son's desire to be an artist—Alfred Maurer went to Paris at the age of 29 and began painting in a style reminiscent of J. A. M. Whistler (*Evening at the Club*, c. 1904, Andover, Massachusetts, Addison Gallery). During the next few years he gained recognition in both Europe and America. His earliest modernistic paintings (1906–14) are done in a style that broke away from traditional painting and that reveals his discovery of Henri Matisse and the Fauves; it is difficult to specify whether Maurer was, even then, an Expressionist or a Cubist—a duality that existed throughout his artistic career. In 1909 Alfred Stieglitz sponsored an exhibition of his works in New York, and Maurer later showed at Stieglitz' 291 Gallery in New York, along with Marsden Hartley, Max Weber and Arthur Dove. Maurer lived in Paris from 1897 until 1914, when the First World War necessitated his return to America. Financial considerations forced him to live with his family, who did not understand his style of painting. The stress caused by his family's lack of comprehension is reflected in his portraits of the 1920s—in the tortured and sad images of his self-portraits (*Self-Portrait with Hat*, 1922, Minneapolis, Walker Art Center), and in his double-headed portraits, a series that culminated in works such as *Twin Heads* (c. 1930, New York, Whitney Museum). In the 1920s he also produced semi-abstract Cubist still lifes of varied textures, composed with a restrained balance. Later he turned to a more Expressionistic, figurative manner.

247   MEIDNER

In 1924 the New York art dealer E. Weyhe bought all of Maurer's paintings and gave him several showings during the next few years. But the revival of interest in Americana that accompanied the Regionalist movement during the 1930s brought more attention to the lithographic works of his father than to his own. A deep depression, which became increasingly evident in his paintings, prevented Alfred from developing independently; shortly after his father's death in 1932, he hanged himself.

Elizabeth McCausland. Catalogue, *Alfred Maurer*, Whitney Museum of American Art, New York 1951.
James R. Mellow. 'Maurer Enigma', *Arts* XXXIV, January 1960.

Mavignier, Almir da Silva. Brazilian painter, b. 1925 in Rio de Janeiro. Mavignier trained as a painter in Rio de Janeiro, where he was a student of Arpad Szenes in 1947. In Brazil he was one of a group of abstract artists, which also included Ivan Serpa and Palatnik. In 1951 Mavignier moved to Europe. From 1953 to 1958 he taught 'Visual Communication' at the Hochschule für Gestaltung in Ulm. Since 1965 he has taught at the Hamburg Academy.

Due to the influence of Max Bill, Mavignier now paints monochromes in a Neo-Concrete or 'programmed' style.

Meadows, Bernard. British sculptor, b. 1915 in Norwich. Meadows studied at the Royal College of Art, and then worked as an assistant to Henry Moore (1936–9). He served in the RAF during the war, then returned to the RCA for two years in 1946. The most important formative influence on him was undoubtedly Moore, and it may perhaps still be traced in his work.

When he returned to sculpture after the war his work was mainly modelled, cast in bronze, and left unchased, in the style that was typical of British sculpture at that time. Although the images are basically abstract the richness of the modelling suggests animation and even particular animals or objects (*Cockerel*, 1955). In the early sixties he began to use actual objects in his casting, but the image remains suggestive rather than precise. More recently, like Moore he has taken to carving his model though still leaving his cast unchased. The forms he uses are jointed and interlocking like bones, but through their texture and compactness they recall rocks and stones, so identifying organic forms with the earth from which they come.

He is now Professor of Sculpture at the Royal College of Art.

Catalogues, Arts Council, London 1960; Gimpel Fils, London 1963 and 1967; Stedelijk Museum, Amsterdam 1965.

Medley, Robert. British painter, b. 1905 in London. In 1921 Medley went to the Byam Shaw School, London, and in 1923–4 to the Slade. From 1926 he worked in Paris. From around 1932 until 1938 a large part of his energies was taken up with the Group Theatre project in which he was involved with W. H. Auden, designing sets and costumes for Eliot's *Sweeney Agonistes*, Auden's and Isherwood's *Ascent of F6* and other plays. At this time he became interested in Surrealism and exhibited at the first Surrealist exhibition in London in 1937. In the war he first served in the ARP, then as a war artist to the ARP and finally as a camouflage officer in the Middle East. He is now head of the Department of Painting and Sculpture at Camberwell. In the thirties and forties his interest in form and structure dominated his work, which remained basically representational, even under the influence of Surrealism and abstraction. In the fifties his handling became looser and freer, and contact with American painting turned him away from direct representation. His painting became more concerned with the abstract relationships of paint and canvas, yet he never abandoned the sense of structure and precision learnt originally from his understanding of Cézanne.

Catalogue, *Robert Medley*, Whitechapel Gallery, London 1963.

Meidner, Ludwig. German painter and poet, b. 1884 in Bernstadt, Silesia; d. 1966 in Darmstadt. He started as a plasterer's apprentice and then studied art in Breslau (1903–5). He spent a year in Berlin working as a fashion designer. In 1906 he went to Paris and attended the Académies Julian and Cormon, where he met Modigliani. He returned to Berlin in 1908 and joined the *Novembergruppe*. His first exhibition took place in 1912 at the Sturm Gallery (connected with *Der Sturm* magazine). He served in the war and during that time wrote two books. He continued to concentrate on his literary work until the mid-thirties, when he taught for a while in a Jewish school in Cologne, then he moved to London in 1939. There he saw and was influenced by the work of William Blake. He returned to Germany in 1953 and finally settled in Darmstadt.

During the years prior to the First World War Meidner belonged to the Expressionist *avant-garde* of Berlin, centred on *Der Sturm*. He was something of a prophetic, visionary artist. After 1912 his most important work was produced—apocalyptic landscapes, burning towns and explosions (*I and the City*, 1915, Berlin-Lichterfelde, Coll. Steinhart). The strident tone of these pictures, their savage distortions and the sudden disruption of their perspective suggest a foreknowledge of the impending war. After 1918 the pictures grew less intense, and began to reflect Meidner's growing preoccupation with his Jewish faith. On his return to Germany he painted religious *motifs*, landscapes and portraits in a style that reverted to his early Expressionist period when he was influenced by van Gogh and the Fauves.

Lothar Brieger. *Ludwig Meidner*, Leipzig 1919.
T. Grochowiak. *Ludwig Meidner*, Recklinghausen 1965.

Meier-Denninghof, Brigitte. German sculptress, b. 1923 in Berlin. Meier-Denninghof trained as a sculptress at the Academies in Berlin and Munich from 1943 to 1946. In 1947 she joined the *Zen* group in Munich, and in 1948 became one of Henry Moore's assistants. From 1949 to 1950 she was with Antoine Pevsner in Paris. In 1955 she and her husband, Martin Matschinsky, executed a joint project, the first of many. In 1957–8 Meier-Denninghof was visiting lecturer at the Werkkunstschule in Kassel. In 1960 she settled in Paris, where she is now living.

In her early phase Meier-Denninghof produced abstract sculptures (*Mountains*) in wood, stone, clay and concrete. From 1955–6 onwards—due largely to the influence of Pevsner—she has been concentrating on constructions in space. These consist of metal rods welded together to form straight or curved surfaces or, alternatively, groups of perpendicular pipes rather like those on a church organ.

U. Kultermann. *Meier-Denninghof*, Cologne 1960.
Catalogue, *Meier-Denninghof*, Kestner Gesellschaft, Hanover 1966.

Meistermann, Georg. German painter, b. 1911 in Solingen. Meistermann studied at the Düsseldorf Academy under Nauen and Mataré from 1929 to 1933. In 1938 he produced his first stained-glass windows. In 1952 he joined the staff of the Städel Institute in Frankfurt, transferring to the Düsseldorf Academy in 1956. In 1960 he left Düsseldorf to teach at the Academy in Karlsruhe.

Meistermann is one of the best known of the German abstract painters of the immediate postwar period. The symbolic pictures which he produced at this time were inspired by the Late Cubists, especially Léger, and also by Miró. In c. 1958 he began to paint two-dimensional monochromes after the manner of Rothko. Meistermann has also created significant works in stained glass (*Rundfunkhaus* in Cologne and St. Kilian in Schweinfurth).

C. Linfert. *Georg Meistermann*, Recklinghausen 1958.

Melli, Roberto. Italian sculptor and painter, b. 1885 in Ferrara; d. 1958 in Rome. He went to Rome in 1911 and worked as a sculptor there until 1914, after which he turned to painting; he is better known for his sculpture, however. One of the finest is his portrait head of Vincenzo Costantini, done in 1913 (Rome, Galleria Nazionale). He belonged to the *Valori Plastici* group, and had large exhibitions in Rome: in 1947 at the Galleria La Cometa, and in 1957 at the Palazzo Barberini.

Mendelson, Marc. Anglo-Belgian painter, b. 1915 in London. Mendelson's mother was English, his father Belgian. After an early figurative period, in which he painted sensitive *Intimiste* works, Mendelson turned to abstract art, producing strictly organized colour compositions from 1948 onwards and, subsequently, simple 'material' pictures, which are conducive to meditation. Quite recently he reverted to a highly imaginative figurative style.

Mense, Carlo. German painter, b. 1889; d. 1965. He studied in Düsseldorf and Berlin (under Corinth). In the initial phase of his career he belonged to the Rhenish Expressionists but later joined the *Neue Sachlichkeit* movement, in which—together with Kanoldt and Schrimpf—he represented the Neo-Classical trend, whose ideas were based on the hard, sculptural portrayal of the object world established by the *Valori Plastici*. Later still he joined the *Novembergruppe*. From 1925 to 1932 he taught at the Breslau Academy. Since 1945 he has been living in Honnef, on the Rhine. He now paints flat, abstract compositions with figurative associations.

Mertz, Albert. Danish painter, b. 1920. Mertz has been living in France since 1963. In his painting, which incorporates elements of Dada, Schwitters, Delaunay and Dubuffet, he combines realistic *motifs* with an abstract and Constructivist type of composition, thus creating a strangely magical and illogical image of reality. He has also experimented with a wide variety of techniques such as photomontage, collage, linoleum cut and film strip.

Mesens, E. L. T. Belgian painter, b. 1903 in Brussels; d. 1971. Mesens started out in life as a poet and musician and worked as a composer up to 1923. Meanwhile, in Paris in 1921, he made the acquaintance of Tzara, Duchamp and Picabia and—under the influence of de Chirico—developed an interest in painting. In 1925 he and his friend Magritte published the magazine *Oesophage* and, subsequently, *Marie*. In 1928 he began to contribute to the Belgian Surrealist magazine *Variétés*. In 1938 Mesens moved to London, where he ran the London Gallery and edited its bulletin up to 1940. Apart from Magritte and Delvaux, Mesens is the foremost Belgian Expressionist painter. He is now living in London.

Messagier, Jean. French painter, b. 1920 in Paris. In 1942 Messagier attended the École des Arts Décoratifs in Paris, where he is still living today. In 1953 he discarded firm, formal structures and in 1958 began to evolve a highly individual, lyrical style, in which gesture predominates. The works of this period, which were prompted in the first instance by the artist's impressions of nature, are executed in a restricted colour range, which includes various greens, blue and ochre or red and ochre.

Messina, Salvatore. Italian sculptor, b. 1916 in Palermo, Sicily. Messina is the son of a sculptor. After training at the Academy of Art in Palermo he stayed in Trieste and, subsequently, Milan. In 1952–3 he was in the United States.

During his early, figurative period Messina was influenced by A. Martini. Then came the crucial encounter with the works of Arp and Brancusi, whose formal structures Messina—like his contemporary Viani—has reinterpreted in his dynamic and graceful sculptures.

Scultura italiana del XXe secolo, Rome 1957.

Meštrović, Ivan. Yugoslav-American sculptor, b. 1883 in Vrpolje, Croatia; d. 1962. Meštrović spent his childhood in the small mountain village of Otavica in Dalmatian Croatia. In 1898 he was apprenticed to Pavel Bilinić, a stonecutter in Split, and the next year studied in Vienna with Otto Koenig in preparation for the Academy of Art in Vienna where he was a student for four years (1900–4), working under Edmund Hellmer, Hans Bitterlich, Otto Wagner and others. By 1902 he was exhibiting with the Vienna Secession group. In their major exhibition of 1909 over fifty of his works were included, mainly pieces related to his Kossovo monument (1912 model in wood, Belgrade State Museum). Between 1914 and 1918 he was in Rome, London, Geneva and Cannes, returning to Yugoslavia in 1919. After a brief trip to the United States (1924–5), he executed his *Monument of Gregory, Bishop of Nin* as a gift to the city of Split—an elongated figure in bronze with large hands and spidery fingers encased in drapery of long tubular folds. In 1933 he was given a large one-man show which subsequently toured Prague, Berlin, Munich, Vienna and Graz. The next year King Alexander I commissioned him to do a *Monument to the Unknown Soldier* on Mount Avala, near Belgrade—a massive mausoleum raised on five 4-foot plinths, the roof supported at the front and rear entrances by four caryatids fashioned after Yugoslav peasant women dressed in regional costume. After completing this monument, he finished the decoration of a church and cloister, which houses a crucifix and thirty wood-panel reliefs depicting scenes from the life of Christ, on his property in Split. Here elongated, Cubistic figures swathed in drapery with patternized folds exist in stilted, formalized, almost hieratic compositions which vaguely recall Assyrian reliefs. During the Second World War Meštrović was imprisoned by the local Gestapo (1941–2). After his release he went to Rome, where he obtained a number of Vatican commissions. From 1943 to 1946 he was living in Switzerland. In the latter year he moved to the United States, where he became Professor of Sculpture at Syracuse University and assumed the same position in 1955 at the University of Notre

Dame. His late works, such as *Jacob's Well* (1957, bronze, South Bend, Indiana, Notre Dame University) still possess the monolithic, Cubistic quality of his early style, but his previous predilection for smooth surfaces is replaced by a rather rough, lumpy quality providing greater variety in textures and light and shade.

Laurence Schmeckebier. *Ivan Meštrović, Sculptor and Patriot,* Syracuse (New York) 1959.

Metaphysical painting—*see* **Pittura Metafisica**

Metcalf, James. American sculptor and graphic artist, b. 1925 in New York City. Metcalf studied at the Dayton Art Institute for one year and was then drafted into the United States Army in 1943. He was given a medical discharge after being wounded in 1944. From 1944 to 1946 he studied sculpture at the Pennsylvania Academy of Fine Arts. He then worked for four years in the studio of his father, Robert Marion Metcalf, a painter, designer of stained glass and Chairman of the Creative Arts Department of Antioch College, Yellow Springs, Ohio. James received his first important commission in 1948, executing a 10-foot male figure in hammered lead for the Middletown (Ohio) War Memorial. In 1950 he left for London where he studied blacksmithing, silversmithing and engraving at the Central School of Arts and Crafts (1950–3). On a grant from the Clark Foundation he spent the next two years doing research into ancient techniques of metalwork in Spain, Italy and Greece. While living in Majorca he did thirty-six wood carvings illustrating Robert Graves' *Adam's Rib*. He had his first one-man show in 1955 at the Galería Augusta in Barcelona and since 1956 has lived in Paris. The first piece he did there, *Falling Figure* (1956, Barcelona, Coll. Mme. Reid) is still figurative. Executed in welded iron, it has the rude strength of his primitive Majorcan works. He became friendly with Matta and occupied a studio next to Brancusi's—both factors aided to hasten his development towards greater aggressiveness and abstraction. The other forces which influenced his style—the vocabulary of the Surrealist bestiary, Matta's daemonic creatures and the enigmatic creations of Max Ernst—are revealed in his 1958 *Poet* (coll. of artist). Carefully handled polished surfaces appear first in 1959, the year he took part in the Fifth São Paulo Bienal. In *The Egg* (1959, bronze and ivory, Paris, Coll. Mr. and Mrs. B. Lee) and *Queen of Sheba* (1959, bronze, Vienna, Museum des 20. Jahrhunderts) contrasts of smooth and rough areas come into play. The dynamics of the latter work owe much to Duchamp-Villon's *The Great Horse* (1914, Chicago, Art Institute). In his late work, such as *Reflection in a Labyrinth* (1962, bronze, New York, Hilton Hotel), Metcalf continues to emphasize the contrast of smooth surfaces and rough welded edges and blows up his undulating forms, creating a greater density and solidity than that of his earlier works with their extending appendages.

Sam Hunter. *James Metcalf*, Chicago n.d.

Mettel, Hans. German sculptor, b. 1902 in Salzwedel; d. 1966 in Frankfurt am Main. Mettel served an apprenticeship as a stonemason and trained as a sculptor in Dresden from 1921 to 1923. He then went to Berlin, where he studied under Edwin Scharff in 1924 and Hugo Lederer from 1925 to 1929. In 1930 he won a travelling scholarship which took him to Rome and in 1931 received a Major State Award. In 1947 he joined the staff of the Städelsche Kunstschule in Frankfurt am Main and was director of the school from 1950 to 1956.

Under the influence of Lehmbruck, Barlach and Marcks, Mettel developed a severe, static style of sculpture based on simplified and compact masses, in which he portrayed human beings and horses. His work is similar to Blumenthal's.

Eduard Trier. *Junge Künstler 60/61*, Cologne 1961.

Metzinger, Jean. French painter, b. 1883 in Nantes; d. 1956 in Paris. In 1903 he moved to Paris, where he was influenced by Neo-Impressionism. He exhibited at the Salon des Indépendants. Around 1906 he met Delaunay, and in 1907 saw the Cézanne memorial exhibition. From 1906 to 1909 he was active as a writer, and published poetry in literary reviews. In about 1910 he met Picasso and Braque; he was a frequent visitor to Picasso's studio. He also became a friend of Mercereau. In 1910 he exhibited at the Salon des Indépendants and the Salon d'Automne with Gleizes and Le Fauconnier. From 1910 on he contributed articles on contemporary painting to various Paris journals. In 1911 he was represented in the Cubist group at the Salon des Indépendants. He was a founder member of the *Section d'Or* group in 1912, and showed in its exhibition. In that year the essay *Du Cubisme* (by Gleizes and Metzinger) was published. In 1913 he was represented in the *Der Sturm* exhibition in Berlin. When war broke out he enlisted and served in the army. In 1919 he returned to Paris, where he lived and worked until his death in 1956.

Highly literate, Metzinger played an articulate role in the building of the Cubist movement. One of the first artists to publish statements about the new art from 1910 on, his theoretical understanding of Cubism seems now to be more interesting than his own painting. *Cubist Landscape*, 1911 (New York, Janis Gallery) is typical of a lot of secondary Cubism. The influence of late Cézanne and some knowledge of the faceted geometric 1909–11 paintings of Picasso and Braque are clear, but these are expressed as stylistic mannerisms grafted on to traditional concepts. From 1912 on his flatter synthetic Cubist style

seems to owe a lot to Juan Gris—*Portrait of Gleizes*, 1912 (Rhode Island School of Design); *Still Life*, 1917 (New York, Metropolitan Museum). Similarly the brief period of Neo-Classical paintings in the 1920s followed in the wake of similar directions taken by the major Cubists. Like Gleizes, his main importance lies in his dissemination of Cubist ideas and, through his writing, in establishing a framework for later critical understanding of Cubist theory.

Catalogue, *Metzinger: Pre-Cubist and Cubist Works*, International Galleries, Chicago 1964.

Meyboden, Hans. German painter, b. 1901 in Verden on the Aller; d. 1965 in Freiburg im Breisgau. From 1920 to 1923 Meyboden was a member of Kokoschka's masters' class at the Dresden Academy. From 1929 to 1933 he taught at the Berlin Academy and then settled in Fischerhude, near Bremen. In 1956 he joined the staff of the Academy in Freiburg im Breisgau.

Meyboden was a Realist of the Post-Expressionist school. His lyrical paintings were influenced first by Kokoschka and subsequently by van Gogh, the Fauves and Paula Modersohn.

Exhibition catalogue, *Hans Meyboden*, Kunsthalle, Kiel 1967.

Meyer-Amden, Otto. Swiss painter, b. 1885; d. 1933. He was a pupil of Hahn in Munich, and in 1906 studied in Paris. From 1907 to 1912 he studied with Hölzel and Landenberger in Stuttgart. In 1928 he began to teach drawing at the Gewerbeschule in Zürich. His style was a reaction to Fauvism and had something of a kinship with Cézanne and early Cubism; it anticipated Surrealism. Memorial exhibitions of his work were held in Zürich (1933, 1953), Basle (1952), and Karlsruhe (1953).

Michaux, Henri. Belgian-French painter and poet, b. 1899 in Namur. After studying medicine, literature and music at Brussels University Michaux joined the merchant navy but resigned in 1921. He began to write in the following year. In 1924 he moved to Paris, and in 1925 saw works by Paul Klee, Giorgio de Chirico and Max Ernst, which exerted a crucial influence on him. In 1926–7 he produced his first oil paintings. In 1928 he visited Ecuador, and wrote about his visit in a book (*Ecuador*) published in the following year. In 1930–1 he visited Asia, and in 1935 Montevideo and Buenos Aires. From 1937 onwards he took a much more active interest in painting and had his first exhibition (1937) in the Galerie Pierre in Paris. From 1927 to 1939 he contributed to the *Hermès* review. In 1939 he visited Brazil, returning to Paris in 1940. He had an exhibition of drawings in the Galerie Rive Gauche, and in 1948 an exhibition of gouaches in the Galerie René Drouin in Paris. In 1956 he experimented with mescalin for the first time. In 1955 he acquired French citizenship. In 1960 he was awarded the Einaudi Prize at the Venice Biennale. In 1964 and 1965 he had large retrospective exhibitions in Amsterdam, Geneva and Paris. In 1965 he was also awarded the Grand Prix National des Lettres in recognition of his services to painting and literature, but refused to accept it. He is now living in Paris.

Michaux is not easy to classify, either as a painter or as a poet. His twin oeuvres are completely individual, and do not fit into any of the established artistic categories. For him painting began where poetry left off. In his early oil paintings—*Spots*—and drawings—*Alphabets*—of 1926–7 he tried to give pictorial expression to 'ideograms' and, in doing so, had recourse to the techniques of the earliest recorded civilizations. As a result he became one of the pioneers of recent pictorial developments. Michaux is a self-taught artist. Between 1927 and 1937 he made himself proficient in the techniques of drawing, watercolour, gouache and oil painting. From 1937 onwards he has worked without interruption both as a painter and as a draughtsman. Prior to 1939 he painted his *fonds noirs*, a series of gouaches in which figures, heads and, occasionally, landscapes emerge like apparitions from black grounds. From 1942 onwards he produced a series of watercolours of misty landscapes, in which he turned away from 'ideograms' in favour of free figuration. These were followed in 1944–5 by drawings and *frottages* depicting faces and heads, which merge with one another to produce macabre and frenzied compositions. In 1948, due to the shock caused by his wife's sudden death, Michaux produced hundreds of drawings within a few weeks. These visionary and Expressionistic works were executed in pen and ink, and finished in watercolour. In 1948–9 Michaux executed a series of lively watercolours in various shades of red, and in 1950–1 a large series of Indian ink drawings. These drawings, which Michaux called *Mouvements*, were a completely new departure. Using lively, dotted forms arranged like sequences of lines, he suggested the kind of gesture used in mime. In 1952–3 Michaux produced three further series of Indian ink drawings: *Mêlées*, *Foules* and *Préhistoire*. Then, in 1954, came his first large-format works, which were followed in 1955 by drawings inspired by mescalin experiments. These strange compositions are reminiscent of seismograms, for in them Michaux has recorded psychic disturbances with absolute precision. In 1956 he produced more Indian ink drawings, which express mental reactions in a completely personal, vibrant and lyrical pictorial style that is far more direct than any verbal style. From 1957 to 1959 Michaux continued to take mescalin. Since then he has produced numerous drawings and, from 1968 onwards, colour compositions executed in acrylic paints. Essentially, the reason why Michaux turned to abstract calligraphy was that he was no longer able to express in language the ecstatic sensations induced in him by his mescalin experiments.

Henri Michaux. *Épreuves, Exorcismes*, Paris 1945; *Peintures et Dessins*, Paris 1946; *Mouvements*, Paris 1951.
A. Jouffroy. *Henri Michaux*, Paris 1961.

Micus, Eduard. German painter, b. 1925 in Höxter. Micus started to paint in 1943–4 as a result of his contact with the group centred on R. Hamann, the art theorist. From 1948 to 1952 he studied under W. Baumeister. Since then he has worked as a typographer. Micus' pictures, which he calls *coudrages*, consist of different canvas grounds stitched together in accordance with precise architectonic principles. Since 1965 he has been introducing objective *motifs* into his work. Micus is now living in Munich.

Middleditch, Edward. British painter, b. 1923 in Chelmsford. Middleditch studied at the Regent Street Polytechnic and at the Royal College of Art. In the fifties he was painting still lifes and landscapes in a manner of fairly straightforward representation with elements derived from Cézanne. Since then, without abandoning entirely his subject matter, he has progressed towards abstraction through increasing freedom of technique.

Catalogue, Arts Council, London 1957.

Mihelić, France. Yugoslav painter and graphic artist, b. 1907 in Virmase, Slovenia. After studying at a Teachers' Training College (1923–7) and the Academy of Art in Zagreb, Mihelić taught at the Gymnasium in Kruševac and, subsequently, at Ptuj (1934–41). During the Second World War he joined the Resistance movement. He now holds a professorial post at the Academy of Art in Ljubljana.

Mihelić became a member of the *Zemlja* (Earth) artists' association in Zagreb. In both his paintings and his graphic works he treats fantastic themes, e.g. masked peasant dances (*Kurenti*), creating a Surrealist world of allegory, daydreams and unconscious manifestations. The figures in his works are products of mental derangement, of fear, of melancholy or of an hallucinatory world of peasant fantasy. Apart from working in oils, Mihelić also paints gouaches and, occasionally, frescoes. Since 1953 he has worked primarily as a graphic artist, although in 1958 he executed a series of panel paintings for the Slovene Parliament Building in Ljubljana.

G. Marchiori. Catalogue, *Mihelić*, Rome 1958.
Melita Stelé. Exhibition catalogue, *Mihelić*, Modern Gallery, Belgrade 1967.

Miki, Tomio. Japanese painter and sculptor, b. 1937 in Tokyo. Miki joined the Neo-Dada Organizer, a group which was the centre of activity for young artists involved in Pop-Junk-Happenings. At the time he produced a series of abstract paintings to be burned, and a series of junk sculptures composed of automobile parts. In 1963, he exhibited at the Yomiuri Independent Show the first series of *Ear* sculptures which made his name widely known nationally and later internationally. His *Ears*, which oddly enough are almost always left ones, range from actual size to 3 metres high. Cast in aluminium and also in Plexiglass with a metallic coating, his *Ears* suggest a solitude which has become frozen through the act of detachment. They symbolize in their sculptural elaboration the neutral realm between hearing and non-hearing, communication and the lack of it. 'I did not select the ear. The ear selected me.' And perhaps with these words in mind he insisted for a long time on applying himself to this subject matter alone, allowing only the single variation of extending the lobes. Recently he has constructed in painted wood large geometrical abstractions which continue to reflect the structure of the ear. He has participated in several international exhibitions such as the Paris Biennale, 1967, and the Venice Biennale, 1968. He was asked but refused for political reasons to participate in the São Paulo Bienal of 1969. He has constructed an enormous 'Ear Plaza' at Expo 70 in Osaka.

Mikl, Josef. Austrian painter, b. 1929 in Vienna. Mikl studied at the Vienna Academy from 1949 to 1956. From 1951 to 1955 he was also a member of the Art Club. He is now living in Vienna.

After developing an extremely sensitive objective approach to art Mikl progressed to Abstract Expressionism. He now paints abstract figures, using monumental blocks of colour and large, sweeping brush strokes.

Exhibition catalogue, *Josef Mikl*, Museum des 20. Jahrhunderts, Vienna 1964.

Mikulski, Kazimierz. Polish painter and poet, b. 1918 in Cracow. Mikulski trained at the Academy of Art in Cracow, where he worked as a scene painter and stage manager in the *Groteska* puppet theatre from 1945 onwards. In 1956 he became a founder member of the *Cricot 2* experimental theatre. Mikulski's painting, which developed in the Surrealistic climate of the postwar period, was influenced both by his theatrical work and by his poetry. Today he is searching for personal solutions in works which border on Pop and Op Art.

Millares, Manuel. Spanish painter, b. 1926 in Las Palmas; d. 1972. He first exhibited in 1945. Soon afterwards he moved towards Surrealism, and later to abstract art. He was a founder member of the El Paso Group in 1957. From 1959 his forms ripened and developed great dramatic impact, with red, white and black as his main colours.

Miller, Kenneth Hayes. American painter, b. 1876 in Oneida, New York; d. 1952 in New York. Miller's earliest influences included Arthur B. Davies and Albert Pinkham Ryder, both of whose styles prompted him to work in a Romantic and sentimental manner (*Landscape with Figures*, 1914, New York, Metropolitan Museum). He is best known as a teacher, one of the few to equal the stature and importance of Robert Henri, whose ideas foreshadowed Miller's own thinking. At his well-known school of 14th Street in New York, Miller was instrumental in reviving the Ashcan School's style and subject matter during the 1920s. Contemporary urban settings were used to express the counterpart of the rural American regionalism that was to dominate the country's painting throughout the 1930s. 14th Street was a centre for radical political activity, artistic production (many artists had their studios in the vicinity) and bargain shopping (*Fitting Room*, Metropolitan Museum), so that it was a fertile field for painters who were interested in representing typical urban scenes. In search of a methodological tradition (always a problem in the history of American art), Miller turned to Renaissance theories of composition and to academic techniques of representation that often drained his work of vividness and spirit. Precise detailing and careful composition were maintained in his work even after 1919, when Renoir's influence also became important. In *Shopper* (1928, New York, Whitney Museum), the meticulously defined, heavy-set woman in middle-class attire appears waxen and stiffly detached before the shop windows, isolated from the bustle of the street around her.

Among Miller's students were Isabel Bishop (b. 1902) and Edward Laning (b. 1906); he also encouraged Reginald Marsh to turn to city subjects during the early 1930s. Miller's viewpoint and methods were also perpetuated at the Art Students' League, where many former Henri pupils studied and where the ideology of regionalism was furthered by such teachers as Thomas Hart Benton.

Alan Burroughs. 'Kenneth Hayes Miller', *Arts* XIV, December 1928.
Lloyd Goodrich. *Kenneth Hayes Miller*, New York 1930.

Milles, Carl. Swedish sculptor, b. 1875; d. 1955. After training as a carpenter and studying at the Technical College in Stockholm Milles worked in Paris from 1897 to 1904. The sculptures of this early period were strongly influenced by Rodin; structurally diffuse, they are held together by the interplay of light and shade. From 1904 to 1906 Milles studied under Adolf von Hildebrand in Munich, where his sculpture became more powerful, with compact, block-like forms. Typical examples of his work at this time are his *Gustav Wasa* (now in the Nordic Museum, Stockholm) and his design for the *Sten Sture Monument* in Uppsala. In the years that followed Milles worked in a variety of styles; his statues of *Franzén* in Härnösand and *Scheele* in Köping are essentially Impressionist whilst the *Bronze Doors*, which he fashioned for the Church of Saltsjöbaden in 1911–12 and which were inspired by the Bernward door in Hildesheim, reveal clear traces of the *Jugendstil*, and his *Dancers*, which date from 1913–14, are a decorative variant of Archaic Greek sculpture. But from 1915 onwards Milles evolved his own highly personal style, producing works in which the sculptural figures seem to hover, as if completely weightless. Typical examples are the *Orpheus Fountain* in Stockholm, the *Resurrection Fountain* in Falls Church, USA, and *Människan och Pegasus* (*Man and Pegasus*). Milles revealed a marked preference for smooth rounded forms. In works such as his *Johannes Rudbeckius* in Västerås these are full of Baroque exuberance whilst in his fountains—*Solglitter* (*Gleam of the Sun*) in the Millesgården, Stockholm; *Europa och tjuren* (*Europa and the Bull*) in Halmstad; and *Flodernas möte* (*The Meeting of the Waters*) in St. Louis, USA—they appear light and insubstantial, due to the movement of the water. Milles also had a marked gift for fantasy and burlesque, which he demonstrated in his *Folke Filbyter* in Linköping (1927). In 1931 Milles went to live in the United States and remained there for the rest of his life. From 1920 to 1931 he had held a professorial post at the College of Art in Stockholm, and in America he taught at the Cranbrook Foundation from 1931 to 1945. In the numerous highly imaginative works which he created in the United States Milles continued to portray narrative themes. During this late period his sculptural forms became much harder and his contours more disrupted.

C. A. Arvidsson (ed.). *Milles berättar*, Stockholm 1954.
H. Cornell. *Carl Milles*, Stockholm 1963.

Milne, David. Canadian painter, b. 1882 in Paisley, Ontario; d. 1953 in Toronto. As a young man Milne taught at a country school, later going to New York (c. 1904) and studying briefly at the Art Students' League. After working for a time as a commercial artist, Milne remained in the New York area, and painted in a decorative style that was probably influenced by the Americans Maurice Prendergast and Ernest Lawson. He exhibited at the Armory Show in 1913. After painting a series of watercolours (*Arras Cathedral*, Ottawa, National Gallery) for the Canadian War Memorials in 1919, he returned to the United States and painted for several seasons (1921–3) in the Adirondacks, finally returning to Canada in 1928. His mature work in oils and watercolour is highly personal and sensitive, and often whimsical in expression (*Painting Place*, 1930, Ottawa, National Gallery).

Catalogue, *David Milne*, National Gallery of Canada, Ottawa 1955.
Alan Jarvis. *David Milne*, Toronto 1962.

Milosavljević, Pedrag (Pedja). Yugoslav painter and essayist, b. 1908 in Lužnice, Serbia. Milosavljević trained as a lawyer in Belgrade and studied painting under the Yugoslav artist Jovan Bijelić. In 1933 he entered the diplomatic service and served in Paris, Madrid and London. He has been living in Yugoslavia since the end of the Second World War. In 1958 he published a volume of essays on art and culture entitled *Between the Trumpet and the Silence* (Noalit Press, Belgrade).

The principal characteristics of Milosavljević's early, analytical style are his sensitive and restrained use of colour and his dynamic, rich handling. Using a lyrical and abstract technique to modify the objective world, he has drawn closer and closer to the sphere of Action Painting and informal art, although his work has never quite lost its realistic basis. His pictures would seem to indicate a constant preoccupation with the past. But the archaism underlying his painting of the ruins of the late antique city of Stobi or his townscapes of the cities on the Dalmatian coast, such as the city republic of Ragusa, is actually Fauvist in conception and, when combined with Milosavljević's technique, this produces a specifically Surrealist phantasmagoria.

Miodrag Kolarić. *Pedja Milosavljević*, Zagreb 1957.

Milunović, Milo. Yugoslav painter, b. 1897 in Cetinje, Montenegro; d. 1967 in Belgrade. After studying under A. Giacometti in Florence Milunović joined the Montenegran army at the beginning of the First World War. In 1921 he went to Paris, where he was influenced by Cézanne; when he returned to Yugoslavia in 1922 he introduced into the dramatic and passionate world of Slavonic art the clarity and the habit of creative thought which he had acquired in the French capital. As a result he has exerted a considerable influence on younger generations of Yugoslav painters. His early, Post-Cubist phase, which lasted until the mid-1920s, was followed by a decade of Neo-Classicism. Later he increased the structural definition in his works and adopted a more fluid and more transparent colour range based on an analysis which he carried out into the effects of light. From 1950 onwards his still lifes—fishing nets, lemons, sea rocks and naked youths—revealed a certain affinity with the lyrical, coloured wall-paintings in Pompeii. In his frescoes, his mosaics and his late panel pictures, Milunović combined the musicality of the antique with the reductive dissonance of modernity, striking a harmonious balance between soul and mind.

A. Celebonović. Catalogue, *Milunović Commemorative Exhibition*, The Cultural Centre, Belgrade 1967.

Minassian, Leone. Italian painter, b. 1905 in Constantinople. Minassian studied at the Academy in Naples from 1921 to 1923. He spent the next three years, from 1924 to 1927, in Venice and during this time became friendly with P. Semeghini. Apart from painting his own pictures, Minassian has copied works by old and new masters and has also taken a lively interest in architecture. He is now living in Venice.

It was in c. 1948 that Minassian first came to grips with Abstract Surrealism. During the next two years he executed paintings in heavy, dark colours which, although still objective, contained elements that were strangely reminiscent of the *Pittura Metafisica* and of Surrealism. Then, in 1950, he went over to abstract art. Minassian has also produced a large body of graphic works.

Minguzzi, Luciano. Italian sculptor, b. 1911 in Bologna. Minguzzi received his initial tuition from his father, who was also a sculptor. Later he attended the Academy of Art in Bologna. He now teaches at the Accademia di Brera in Milan.

During his early period Minguzzi was strongly influenced by the works of Picasso and Marini. Subsequently he created metal sculptures in a spirited and elegant semi-abstract style. In many of these works the dynamic tensions are reduced by the incorporation of wire frameworks similar to those in the works of Chadwick, Salvatore and Mannucci.

G. Marchiori. *Luciano Minguzzi*, Milan 1962.

Minimal art. Minimal art, primary structures, Post-Painterly Abstraction, and hard-edge all have in common a neutral and impersonal quality as opposed to the popular, often satirical aspect of their contemporary trend, Pop Art, and the Romantic Abstract Expressionist style of the preceding generation. The sources of the new aesthetic stem ultimately from Kasimir Malevich's work of c. 1913 (*Black Square on a White Ground*, 1913, Leningrad, State Russian Museum) and Marcel Duchamp's readymades, such as the *Fountain* (actually a urinal, 1917, Milan, Gallery Schwarz), the former working on the hypothesis that anything on canvas is a picture, and the latter allowing that any object is a work of art. The immediate predecessors of the Minimalists were Ad Reinhardt and Josef Albers, who brought to their canvases the 'exclusive, negative, absolute, and timeless' quality so desired by the Minimal artists. There are also roots of this new mode in Abstract Expressionism, particularly in the chromatic abstractions of Barnett Newman, Mark Rothko and Adolph Gottlieb. The Minimal artists rejected the painterliness and spontaneous emotionalism of their predecessors, but at the same time maintained the primacy of colour, all-over composition, scale and directness in works by the older generation. The optical impact of colour and shape supersedes the tactile qualities inherent in the works of the Abstract Expressionists, whose 'handwriting' and 'gestures' of the 1950s are dismissed and replaced by an anonymity of execution. Ellsworth Kelly's *Red Blue Green* (1963, New York, Sidney Janis Gallery)—with its immaculate surface, pure colour and simple geometric forms executed with razor-sharp precision—is typical of this new aesthetic, as are the shaped canvases of Frank Stella and Charles Hinman (b. 1932) and the pure abstractions of Larry Zox (b. 1936), Robert Huot (b. 1935) and Darby Bannard (b. 1931). Donald Judd's (b. 1928) 1965 untitled work of galvanized iron and painted aluminium (New York, Coll. Philip Johnson) is representative of Minimal sculpture. Also grouped with the Minimal artists are Jules Olitski, Kenneth Noland, Jack Youngerman, Larry Poons, Al Held and Morris Louis. The utmost restraint and understatement, mechanical precision, anonymity and lack of personal involvement characterize this art and indicate both its merits and its limitations.

Kynaston McShine. Catalogue, *Primary Structures: Younger American and British Sculptors*, Jewish Museum, New York 1966.

Gregory Battcock (ed.). *Minimal Art: A Critical Anthology*, New York 1968.

Minne, Georg. Belgian painter and sculptor, b. 1866 in Ghent; d. 1941 in Laethem-Saint-Martin. After entering the Academy at Ghent as a student of architecture, Minne transferred to the Fine Arts department in the middle of his course and in defiance of his father's wishes. The historical subjects and Classicistic forms of his early oil paintings and sculptures, which were conceived on the grand scale, reveal clear traces of an academic view of art. But in 1886 he reached a turning point in his career when he met Maurice Maeterlinck and a number of other Symbolist poets. He joined their ranks and began to illustrate their poems. At about the same time he started to draw on Rodin for his sculptural inspiration. He went to visit him in Paris in 1891 and was encouraged by him to continue in his monumental style. In c. 1895 Minne also incorporated a number of medieval *motifs* into his sculpture (*St. Jean Baptiste*, 1895; *Les Trois Saintes Femmes au Tombeau*, 1896). In 1898 he settled in Laethem-Saint-Martin, a small village on the Lys, where an artists' colony gradually developed, the members of which all subscribed to the Symbolist cause. Minne's major sculptures during this *Jugendstil* phase of his career were *Le Petit Porteur de Reliques* (1897) and the *Well with the Kneeling Boys* (1898). These works, in which the ecstatically religious, rather melancholy themes and the simplified, contoured designs suggested a Gothic Renaissance, exerted a considerable influence on many of the younger sculptors of the day, including W. Lehmbruck. From 1908 onwards Minne produced naturalistic works, entering into competition with his fellow-countryman C. Meunier. During the First

World War he was in England. In 1921, by which time he was a much lauded and highly influential sculptor, Minne began to produce monumental block-like works of variable quality.

L. van Puyvelde. *Georg Minne*, Brussels 1930.
A. de Ridder. *Georg Minne*, Antwerp 1947.

Minton, John. British painter and illustrator, b. 1917 in Cambridge; d. 1957 in London. Minton studied at the St. John's Wood Schools (1936–8). He taught at the Camberwell School of Art (1943–7), the Central School (1947–8) and the Royal College of Art (1948–56).

A reviewer of his American debut at the Durlacher Gallery (1948) noted: 'His intensely impressionable and uneven talent . . . capitalizes on English romantic tradition . . . (bringing together) pictorial and picturesque effects, description with romanticism and abstraction to achieve the desired combination of modernity and nostalgia.'

Minton gained prominence for barely ten years. Essentially an illustrator, he was indebted to a tradition from Samuel Palmer and including Paul Nash, Edward Bawden and John Piper. His graphic and topographic mannerisms were rife in postwar British art schools, until the vogue succumbed to Pasmore's neo-Bauhaus and other intellectually more viable formulations. Minton's oeuvre shows no marked development. He seemed unable to conceive of a future for figurative art (in fact it continued to throw out varied new shoots), and ended his increasingly disparaged position by suicide.

The scale and medium of watercolour suited him best. Books illustrated by Minton include: A. Fournier, *The Wanderer* (London 1948); J. Minton and A. Ross, *Time Was Away* (London 1948). Minton exhibited at the RA, RSA and smaller London galleries and in New York. His works can be found in the Victoria and Albert Museum, London, and in various other British and American public collections.

Michael Middleton. Exhibition catalogue, *John Minton*, Arts Council, London 1959.

Mir Iskusstva (World of Art). This was the name of both a movement and a magazine: the movement was founded by Serge Diaghilev in the 1890s, and the magazine which grew out of it was first published in 1898. The movement included among its members the principal designers for Diaghilev's *Ballets Russes*, Benois, Bakst, Golovin, Roerich; it became a focus of *avant-garde* painting in Russia and was in a sense the Russian equivalent of *art nouveau*. It also looked back to the heritage of the past, stimulating interest in the treasures of previous centuries.

Alexandre Benois. *Reminiscences of the Russian Ballet*, London 1941.

Mirko (Mirko Basaldella). Italian sculptor, b. 1910 in Udine. Mirko comes from an artistic family. After training in Venice, Florence and Monza with his brother, the painter Afro, he went to Milan, where he studied under A. Martini at the Brera from 1932 to 1934. He visited Rome in 1934, and Paris in 1937. In 1954 he had a special exhibition at the Biennale in Venice, and in 1955 won the Grand Prix for sculpture at the Bienal in São Paulo. In 1958 he was asked to teach at Harvard University, Cambridge, Mass. He is now living in Rome.

Mirko uses a wide range of materials. After an early period, in which he was influenced by Martini's Classical conception of sculpture, he sought his inspiration in Cubism and the art forms of primitive tribes. From 1940 onwards he subjected his sculptural forms to extreme simplification, and so developed a dramatic and Expressionistic abstract style. From 1950 onwards he was influenced by C. Cagli's Roman School. Many of Mirko's *motifs* are based on the totems found in primitive art. He has played a major part in the development of postwar Italian sculpture, and has executed numerous public commissions, including a cenotaph for Mauthausen.

Miró, Joan. Spanish painter, b. 1893 in Barcelona. In the twentieth century Spain has produced three painters whose works have made a major contribution to modern art: Joan Miró, Juan Gris and Pablo Picasso. All three became deeply involved with the city of Paris and the development of French art but, unlike his two older compatriots, Miró also maintained close links with his native land. He spent part of his time in Spain (Barcelona, Montroig and Palma de Mallorca), part in Paris, and his painting received its most powerful stimuli from the tensions set up by this constant exchange between the great French capital and the Catalan countryside. For Miró every painting has been a new adventure, a quest, in which he has sought to arrest his living experiences by a spontaneous, dreamlike act of creation: in his works artistic fantasy and reality are indissolubly fused in an enigmatic picture world. Miró is a Surrealist in so far as he has sought to destroy the supremacy of reason and logic in order to release the creative forces of the unconscious and a-logical mind, in so far as he has tried to fathom the secrets of the invisible as well as the visible world.

After overcoming considerable opposition from his father—a goldsmith by trade—Miró studied at Francesco Gali's School of Art in Barcelona from 1912 onwards. In his early pictures—landscapes and portraits—elements of Catalan folk art are combined with expressive, Fauvist-type gestures. Between 1918 and 1922, whilst he was coming to terms with Cubism, Miró developed the highly individual, primitive style which characterizes his 'detailed' landscapes (e.g. *Peasant Village*, 1922) and which is both objective and poetic at one and the same time. When he settled in Paris in 1920, Miró immediately made contact with the circle of *avant-garde* writers grouped around Max Jacob, Pierre Réverdy and Tristan Tzara and joined in the meetings of the Paris Dadaists. Then, towards the mid-1920s, he went over to the Surrealists, signing their manifesto in 1924. He also contributed to the first Surrealist exhibition, which was staged in the Galerie Pierre in 1926. It was then that he began producing his linear, dreamlike compositions. His visit to Holland in 1928 and his ensuing interest in the works of the old masters, especially Vermeer, gradually wrought a further stylistic change. In his mature period he combined impressions of the visible world with hallucinatory experiences in a body of highly figurative works. He also painted his *Dutch Interiors* and produced sculptures and collages during this period. When the Civil War broke out, Miró left Spain and began to paint the frightful visions which fill his 'wild' pictures.

With the *Constellations*—a series of luminous gouaches on paper which he created between 1940 and 1941 in Varengeville (Normandy), Palma and Montroig (Spain)—Miró entered on his late period. In these works he depicted man and nature, the earth and the cosmos, using magical and highly inventive pictorial images. From 1940 to 1948 Miró was in Spain, having left France to escape the Second World War. Whilst there he turned his hand to pottery, working in collaboration with the Spanish potter Llorens Artigas. Later, between 1954 and 1959, he devoted himself almost exclusively to this medium and in the monumental projects which he was asked to execute for the UNESCO Building in Paris and for Harvard University in Cambridge, Mass., he developed an entirely new style of ceramic wall design. Meanwhile, from the late 1920s onwards, he had been producing a wide range of graphic works, which reached their gripping climax in the *Barcelona* series of 1944. Ten years later, in 1954, Miró was awarded the Grand Prix for graphic art at the Biennale in Venice.

After the war Miró continued to translate the world of reality, which always impressed itself upon him in its harsher aspects, into magical images. The scurrilous humour and the frightening ambiguity of his work, which—as in the case of Klee—is a product of 'psychic improvisation', reflect the spirit of the twentieth century in terms which are valid and extremely forceful. Since 1956 Miró has been living and working in the large studio house built by the architect J. L. Sert in Palma, on the island of Majorca.

Clement Greenberg. *Joan Miró*, New York 1948.
Walter Erben. *Joan Miró*, Munich 1959.
Jacques Dupin. *Joan Miró, Life and Work*, London and New York 1962.
Yves Bonnefoy. *Miró*, London and New York 1967.

Mitchell, Joan. American painter, b. 1926 in Chicago. She studied at Smith College (1942–4) and received a BFA degree from the Chicago Art Institute in 1947 and an MFA from New York University in 1950. She had her first one-man show at the St. Paul (Minnesota) Gallery in 1952. Like M. Goldberg, A. Leslie and G. Hartigan, she is one of the second generation of New York artists whose style is based on that of W. de Kooning. Her variety of texture, vibrancy of colour and vivacity of stroke produce a depth and palpability of superimposed colour (*George Swimming at Barnes Hole, but It Got too Cold*, 1957, New York, Stable Gallery).

Irving Sandler. 'Mitchell Paints a Picture', *Art News* LVI, October 1957.
Eleanor C. Munro. 'The Found Generation', *Art News* LX, November 1961.

Mobiles and stabiles. The development of the mobile is most closely associated with Alexander Calder, who experimented in the late 1920s with constructions involving motion produced by manually operated cranks and in 1932 developed the first wind-driven mobiles. In its most commonly known form, the mobile is suspended from the ceiling, but Calder also created standing mobiles and wall mobiles; they may be moved either by wind or by mechanical means, they may be indoor or outdoor works, and they may vary in size from table mobiles to huge environmental or architectural constructions. The term 'stabile' suggests an antithesis to the concept of the mobile and seems best applied to Calder's own powerfully immobile sculptures developed from the late 1930s on. They are characteristically made of black metal sheets in abstract shapes bolted or welded together, and assumed their most monumental form in the 1960s, when Calder created a number of large-scale, open-form, outdoor environmental stabiles large enough to walk through.

Exhibition catalogue, *Alexander Calder—Retrospective Exhibition*, Solomon R. Guggenheim Museum, New York 1964.
H. H. Arnason. *Calder*, Princeton (New Jersey) 1966.

Modigliani, Amedeo. Italian painter, draughtsman and sculptor, b. 1884 in Leghorn; d. 1920 in Paris. Modigliani was the fourth son of a Jewish banker who at a later date lost his money. In 1895, the boy suffered a serious attack of pleurisy, which foreshadowed the tuberculosis that eventually killed him. In 1898 he left school (after an attack of phthisis) and began to study painting in the studio of Guglielmo Micheli, a landscape painter who had been a pupil of Fattori. After periods of study in Florence (1902) and Venice (1903), Modigliani settled in Paris (in 1906), where he quickly immersed himself in the exceptionally stimulating artistic life of the city, meeting people such as Picasso, Utrillo, Max Jacob, Soutine, Kisling, Lipchitz and Cocteau, and taking note of the stylistic developments of the time—notably Fauvism, Expressionism and Cubism. He was also tremendously impressed by the 1907 retrospective exhibition devoted to Cézanne, whose portraits certainly influenced the candid, frontal, three-quarter length presentation of so many of his own figure studies (*Oscar Miestchaninoff*, 1916, Berne, private collection).

In 1908, Modigliani (who was very poor) met Dr. Paul Alexandre, who became not only a friend but virtually his only patron, buying most of his output until the outbreak of war in August 1914; from 1916 until the artist's death in 1920, this position was held by the dealer Leopold Zborowski. In 1909 Dr. Alexandre introduced Modigliani to Brancusi, who quickened his interest in sculpture; and he remained actively interested in carving, in a linear style that reveals the influence—apart from Brancusi's—of Romanesque figures, African masks and Greek *kouroi* (e.g. limestone *Head*, c. 1912, in the Solomon R. Guggenheim Museum, New York).

Modigliani exhibited relatively little during his lifetime. He contributed six paintings to the Salon des Indépendants in 1910; and seven of his sculptures were included in the Salon d'Automne of 1912. More important, and more auspicious, was the larger showing of his works in London (at Heal's) in 1919, an exhibition partly organized by Osbert and Sacheverell Sitwell.

Modigliani has become a difficult artist to evaluate, partly because of the unevenness and occasional glibness of his art, but to an even greater extent because of the legends that have come to surround his 'Bohemian' life and which have, in turn, produced a hostile counter-reaction. He was an eclectic artist, who painted many of his finest pictures at the end of his life, and although he was profoundly influenced by Cubism (*Moïse Kisling*, 1915, Milan, private collection) and by Expressionism (especially by its elongation of form: see almost any of his more elaborate figure-studies or the nudes), he is in many ways atypical of his generation. All the influences that he absorbed were subservient to an overriding sense of linear design, which, in its emphasis on continuity and grace, suppleness and harmony, seems both to recall and still to express a much older tradition. To describe Modigliani as a 'Cubist Botticelli' might not be very scholarly; but it sums up some of the contradictions and ambiguities that are apparent in his work. At the same time, the linear qualities of his art can be over-emphasized, to the detriment of a very fine colour sense (his handling of reds is often masterly) and, in the portraits, of a strong feeling for individual character. The finest of the nudes, besides being graceful, are also memorably erotic.

A. Pfannstiel. *A. Modigliani et son oeuvre: Étude critique et catalogue raisonné*, Paris 1956.
J. Modigliani. *Modigliani: Man and Myth*, New York and Toronto 1958.
Giovanni Scheiwiller. *Modigliani*, Zürich 1958.
Franco Russoli. *Modigliani*, London and New York 1959.

Moholy-Nagy, Laszlo. Hungarian painter, sculptor and experimental artist, b. 1895 in Bàcs-Borsod; d. 1946 in Chicago. After studying as a lawyer and fighting in the First World War, Moholy-Nagy became a full-time artist in 1918. In the preceding year he had joined with a number of painters, who were friends of his, in founding the *avant-garde MA* group (*MA* = Today). At that stage in his career he was painting highly individual landscapes and portraits in a lively, decorative style. From 1919 to 1920 he was in Vienna. He then came under the influence of Malevich and El Lissitzky and in 1921 met Lissitzky in Düsseldorf before moving to Berlin, where he experimented with collages, photographs and photograms. In 1922 he exhibited in the Sturm Gallery. In the following year he was invited to join the Bauhaus staff as a 'master of form'. He accepted the offer and, whilst in Weimar and Dessau, continued to work on his paintings and sculptures and took an active interest in photography, typography, industrial design, films, theatre, ballet, architecture and light experiments. He also helped Gropius to edit and publish the series of *Bauhausbücher*. (No. 8 was his own publication *Malerei, Fotografie, Film*—Painting, Photography, Films.) In 1928, when Gropius left the Bauhaus, Moholy-Nagy also resigned. He then went to live in Berlin, where he designed stage sets and did experimental film work. In 1934 he emigrated to Amsterdam and in 1935 to London. It was in London that he created his first Space Modulators. These three-dimensional constructions, which are made of Plexiglass and perforated or polished metal discs, produce sophisticated optical effects due to the play of light on the component elements, which are capable of co-ordinated movement. In 1937 Moholy-Nagy settled in Chicago and took charge of the New Bauhaus. When this closed down he opened his own School of Design (1938). In America he continued to develop his Space Modulators and also worked as a designer. Shortly before his death he finished his book *Vision and Motion*, which appeared as a posthumous publication in New York in 1947.

As a Constructivist Moholy-Nagy was one of Malevich's successors. He was the prototype of the modern experimental artist and in his artistic works, which were concerned with problems of light, space and movement, utilized new materials and new processes taken from the world of technology. Moholy-Nagy once said that for him art was simply a part of the 'total work', in other words a part of living. And so he took the experiences which he made in the sphere of 'pure art' and applied them in all visual spheres of modern life. By doing so he identified himself with the functionalist conception in modern art and consequently with Mondrian and the *de Stijl* artists.

Laszlo Moholy-Nagy. *The New Vision and Abstract of an Artist,* New York 1947.
Sibyl Moholy-Nagy. *Moholy-Nagy, Experiment in Totality,* New York 1950.
Catalogue, *Moholy-Nagy Travelling Exhibition,* USA 1964.

Moilliet, Louis. Swiss painter, b. 1880 in Berne; d. 1962 in La Tour de Peilz, Lake Geneva. Between 1900 and 1907 Moilliet studied under Mackensen in Worpswede, von Olde in Weimar and Kalckreuth in Stuttgart. In 1910 he settled on the Thuner See, and his friendship with Macke dated from the following year. He then established close relations with the artists of the *Blauer Reiter* and subsequently introduced Paul Klee, whom he had known since early youth, into the group. In 1914 he accompanied Klee and Macke on a journey to Tunisia. Later he withdrew to La Tour de Peilz, where he lived a completely secluded life.

Outside Switzerland Moilliet is best known as the man who accompanied Klee and Macke on their famous trip to Tunisia. But he was also an artist in his own right. After early Neo-Impressionist and Fauvist phases he came under Macke's productive influence and created a synthesis of early Cubist composition and Orphist colour. His most successful pictures are the watercolours which resulted from the pictorial insights gained in Tunisia.

Catalogue, *Louis Moilliet,* Kunsthalle, Berne 1963.

Molfessis, Iasson. Greek painter, b. 1924 in Athens. He studied in Athens and in Paris, where he has been living since 1950. His work is an authentic expression of direct and dynamic brushwork as well as of the 'toning' of the surface. The same is true for his latest work, in which he uses mostly technological media.

Molinari, Guido. Canadian painter, b. 1933 in Montreal. He studied at the École des Beaux-Arts, Montreal (1948), and also at the school of the Montreal Museum of Fine Arts under the abstract painter Marian Scott. He began as an Abstract Expressionist but in 1956 was a founding member of a new group, *Les Plasticiens,* who reacted against this style. In 1956–7 he painted a series of black-and-white compositions which inaugurated his 'hard-edge' style. The latter evolved into the painting of large pictures painted in stripes of sonorous colours (*Mutation triviolet,* 1966, Ottawa, National Gallery of Canada). He is also a member of the *Association des Artistes non-figuratifs de Montréal.* In 1961 he won a prize for painting in the *Concours Artistiques* of the Province of Quebec. He painted in Rome in 1968 and has recently made 'light sculptures'. He lives in Montreal.

Moll, Oskar. German painter, b. 1875 in Brieg, Silesia; d. 1947 in Berlin. Moll was a pupil of Corinth and Leistikov. In 1907 he visited Paris, where he made friends with Purrmann and Levy and became a founder member of the German Matisse School. In 1908 he returned to Berlin but visited Paris annually up to the outbreak of war. In 1918 he became a founder member of the *Novembergruppe* and joined the staff of the Breslau Academy. In 1926 he was appointed Director of the Academy and subsequently invited Schlemmer, Otto Müller, Muche, Molzahn and Scharoun to teach there. In 1934, when he was dismissed as a 'degenerate artist', he settled in Berlin.

Moll painted landscapes, still lifes and interiors in a cultured, lyrical style, which reveals the influence of Matisse (in his Fauvist period) and, to a lesser extent, of Cézanne and the Cubists.

Exhibition catalogue, *Oskar Moll,* Wilhelm Lehmbruck Museum, Duisburg 1967.

Molzahn, Johannes. German painter, b. 1892 in Duisburg, Germany; d. 1965 in Munich. Molzahn was a self-taught painter. In the inter-war years he taught at the School of Arts and Crafts in Magdeburg and at the Academy in Breslau. In 1938 he emigrated to the USA, returning to Germany in 1959, when he settled in Munich.

From 1920 onwards Molzahn moved towards an ornamental, abstract style which reveals the influence of Cubism and Futurism. His late works are architectonic compositions in space, which incorporate Surrealist aerial perspectives and symbolic designs of antique or Christian provenance.

Exhibition catalogue, *Johannes Molzahn,* Wilhelm Lehmbruck Museum, Duisburg 1964.

Mondrian, Piet. Dutch painter, b. 1872 in Amersfoort; d. 1944 in New York. Mondrian was one of the principal artists behind the *de Stijl* movement, and one of the creators of non-objective painting. His first landscapes reveal his debt to the Dutch seventeenth-century tradition; much of his early work, however, also reveals the influence of Symbolist painting, of Impressionism and, subsequently, of Expressionism (Mondrian's *Red Tree* of 1908 is regarded as one of the masterpieces of Expressionist painting). From this point in his development, several narrowly circumscribed themes dominate his work: tree subjects, still lifes, beach and seascapes, and the façades of buildings. The influence of French Cubism, the development of which Mondrian witnessed at first hand during his stay in Paris (December 1911–July 1914), is noticeable in his later versions of certain of these subjects, for example, the *Still Life with Ginger Jar,* or his drawings of cathedral façades. Mondrian, nevertheless, soon concluded that 'Cubism did not accept the logical consequences of its own discoveries; it was not developing towards its own goal, the expression of pure plastics'. After his return to Holland from Paris, Mondrian was already moving away from Cubism, as his *Composition in Line and Colour*, 1913 (Otterlo, Kröller-Müller Museum) shows in its treatment of space. And in his various *Pier and Ocean* studies of 1913 onwards, Mondrian's reduction of natural forms to a series of elaborate, quasi-geometrical hieroglyphs takes painting to the very brink of total non-objectivity.

In 1916–17 Mondrian, Bart van der Leck and Theo van Doesburg formulated the principles of *de Stijl*. The fundamental elements of painting were seen as the square, the cube and thus also the right-angle, which were regarded as symbols both of the forces underlying nature and of nature itself. The mystical and symbolic elements in Mondrian's interpretation of the fundamentals of painting, and the transcendental colour symbolism of *de Stijl*, may be traced back to Mondrian's early interest in theosophy (he became a member of the Theosophical Society in 1909), and also to the influence of the writings of Dr. M. J. H. Schoenmaekers, particularly his book *Het Nieuwe Wereldbild* (*The New Image of the World*). It was precisely his desire to express in pictorial terms the new image of the world which led Mondrian, believing that 'particularities of form obscure pure reality', to choose the simple elements of *de Stijl* in an attempt to express a 'clear vision of reality'. In his work of the early twenties, the number of lines and rectangles decreases, grey is abandoned, primary colours are reduced to two or one and made much smaller in area, until by 1925, in pictures such as *Composition in Yellow and Blue* (Rotterdam, Boymans-van Beuningen Museum), he had created a distinctive personal style which was to remain with him almost until his death. Only in his last works, created during the period of his self-imposed exile, and which reflect above all Mondrian's experience of modern America, do the rhythms of jazz and the hubbub of urban living invade his tranquillity, as in his justly famous *Broadway Boogie-Woogie* (New York, Museum of Modern Art).

Michel Seuphor. *Piet Mondrian: Life and Work*, New York 1956.

Monet, Claude Oscar. French painter, b. 1840 in Paris; d. 1926 in Giverny. He was the son of a grocer. In 1845 his family moved to Le Havre and by 1855 he had made an early reputation there as a caricaturist. He met Boudin in Le Havre in 1858 and Pissarro in Paris in 1859 at the Académie Suisse. He admired the work of Delacroix. From 1860 to 1862 he did his military service in Algeria. Back in Le Havre in 1862, he worked with Boudin and met Jongkind. From 1862 to 1864 he studied in Paris at the École des Beaux-Arts, in the *atelier* of Gleyre, and met Renoir, Sisley and Bazille. They painted together in summer trips to the forest of Fontainebleau, where they met Daubigny and the Barbizon painters. He knew Manet by this time. In 1864 he met Courbet. In 1865, after disagreements with his family, his allowance was cut and he suffered a period of extreme hardship, alleviated only by occasional help from painters and collectors in the sixties and seventies. Two seascapes were well received at the 1865 Salon. He frequently worked on the coast with Boudin, Daubigny, Courbet, Jongkind and Whistler. In 1869 and 1870 his work was rejected at the Salon, whereupon Daubigny resigned from the jury. In 1870 he married Camille Doncieux, the mother of his son Jean (born 1867). He was in London during the Franco-Prussian War. In 1871 he started to collect Japanese prints. He visited Holland twice (1871 and 1872). He spent the 1870s working in Paris and its suburbs (Argenteuil, Vétheuil), with visits to the Normandy coast. He was much harassed by creditors.

In 1874 the First Impressionist Exhibition took place. (Monet contributed again in 1876, 1877, 1879, 1882; but not 1880, 1881, 1886.) His son Michel was born in 1878. The following year his wife Camille died. From about 1884 he began to work in the south of France (Menton, Antibes, Juan-les-Pins) and on the Italian coast (Bordighera, Ventimiglia). In 1885 he was commissioned by his dealer Durand-Ruel to decorate his apartment. In 1886 he met Geffroy and Mirbeau. He was represented in a large Impressionist exhibition in America. He paid visits to London in 1888 and 1891. In 1889 he mounted a subscription to purchase Manet's *Olympia* for the state. He also had a successful joint exhibition with Rodin at the Georges Petit Gallery, Paris. In 1890 he began his series paintings (these were exhibited periodically in groups at Durand-Ruel's). He bought a house and large plot of land at Giverny and started to construct the water-garden ('outdoor studios'). In 1892 he married Blanche Hoschédé, widow of a former patron. In 1895 he visited Norway.

He began the great series of water-lily paintings at Giverny in 1899; he also started the Thames series on visits to London (1899–1904). In 1900 he temporarily lost the sight of one eye. In 1903 he bought a car and drove to Madrid in 1904 to see Velasquez's paintings. His Venice paintings were done over the period 1908–12. In 1911 his second wife died. By 1912 his sight was deteriorating. His son Jean died in 1914.

From 1914 to 1916 Monet started to plan a large-scale mural cycle of water-lily paintings (encouraged by Clémenceau). He built a large new studio to accommodate them and started work. In 1918 he offered two of these canvases to the state to commemorate the Armistice: this became in 1920 a plan to donate twelve enormous canvases. The plan was formalized in 1921 and the reconstruction of the

Orangerie at the Palais du Louvre to house them was started. In 1922, almost blind from double cataracts, he abandoned work. An operation in 1923 restored partial sight to one eye and he continued work on the Orangerie murals, despite extreme depression and anxiety, until his death on 5 December 1926. Pallbearers at his funeral were Clémenceau, Bonnard, Vuillard and Roussel. The Orangerie murals (*Les Nymphéas*) were dedicated in 1927. Major exhibitions of his work include those in Paris (1931), Zürich (1952), London (1957) and New York (1960).

One of the founder members of Impressionism in the late 1860s and early 1870s, Monet alone sustained its disciplines and objectives until the end of his long working life. He was the only Impressionist to earn substantial public recognition in his lifetime. An anti-establishment radical by instinct, he was apolitical as an artist. The strength and stamina of his artistic faith carried him, and contemporaries like Renoir, through years of hostile opposition and acute hardship.

The astonishing facility to achieve a likeness in his adolescent caricatures remained the outstanding characteristic of his early Impressionist paintings (*La Grenouillère*, 1869, New York, Metropolitan Museum). This is what distinguishes them from the atmospheric generalizations of mid-nineteenth-century landscape painters (Corot, Daubigny). Inspired by them (especially Boudin and Jongkind, in the 1860s), he took nature rather than art as his criterion. Working in close partnership with Renoir at first (1865 on) and then independently, he directed landscape painting into an exclusively perceptual preoccupation with the visual sensations experienced in front of the *motif*. Traditional concepts (composition, subject matter, finish) were rejected or ignored in this pursuit (e.g. *Impression Sunrise*, 1872, Paris, Musée Marmottan—the painting which earned Impressionism its derisive name).

Monet advised, 'Try to forget what you have before you, a tree, a house, a field, whatever; merely think, here is a little square of blue, here an oblong of pink, here a streak of yellow, and paint it just as it looks to you . . .' His paintings of the 1870s presented these fragmentary raw materials of visual experience in very spontaneous terms: separate highly coloured brush-marks assault the eye simultaneously and fuse optically into a dazzling direct illusion.

The late series paintings (about 1890 onwards— *Poplars*, *Rouen Cathedral*, *Haystacks*, etc.) concentrated on the changing appearance of a single *motif* under different light and atmospheric conditions. They came to be less about the things seen than the process of seeing, recorded in paint. He worked on each canvas in turn (over a hundred for the *Thames* paintings) until conditions changed (as little as seven minutes at a time on the *Poplars*).

Water was an obsessive subject: like mist and fog, it created ready-made optical abstractions of the seen *motif*. The symmetry of reflected images (*Argenteuil*, 1874, London, Courtauld Institute Galleries; *Poplars*, 1891, New York, Metropolitan Museum) is a recurrent compositional device, emphasizing the flattening surface-qualities of the Impressionist technique. As well as his heightened perception (hence Cézanne's famous 'only an eye; but, my God, what an eye!' remark), Monet had a latent instinct for design, reflected in his taste for Japanese art.

The late water-lily canvases—mural in scale— create a vast decorative environment (l'Orangerie des Tuileries, Paris). Although they retain a sense of Impressionist spontaneity, they also express a semi-articulate nature-mysticism. (Other examples are in the Museum of Modern Art, New York, and the National Gallery, London.) Since Monet's death, it is the scale and painterly informality of these works that have been most influential: they were 'rediscovered' by American and European artists in the 1950s.

D. Rouart. *Claude Monet: Historical and Critical Study*, Lausanne 1958.

Y. Taillandier. *Monet*, Paris 1963.

Raymond Cogniat. *Monet and his World*, London and New York 1966.

C. M. Mount. *Monet: A Biography*, New York 1967.

Monory, Jacques. French painter, b. 1924. Monory paints scenes from modern urban life. He incorporates parts of advertisements cut out of colour supplements into his pictures in order to create theatrical or cinematic effects. He makes no attempt to distinguish between reality and fantasy in his work. Although not a Pop artist himself, Monory has profited from this movement, which has provided him with a challenge.

Moon, Jeremy. British painter, b. 1934; d. 1973. Like Tess Jaray, Moon followed the American Post-Painterly Abstraction but experimented with depth and perspective.

Moore, Henry. British draughtsman and sculptor, b. 1898 in Castleford, Yorkshire. Moore is the son of a miner. From 1919 to 1925 he studied at the Leeds School of Art and the Royal College of Art in London. He then visited Italy, prior to joining the staff of the Royal College in 1926. In 1931 he transferred to the Chelsea School of Art in London, where he continued to teach up to 1939. From 1940 to 1942 he worked as a war artist, making drawings of people in air raid shelters and miners at work. After the war he received public commissions from many different countries and had numerous exhibitions. As a result he soon became one of the best-known artists of his day. He has also received many honours, ranging from the doctorate conferred on him by the University of Leeds in 1945 to the Dutch Erasmus Prize of 1968. Moore is now living in St.

Ives, Cornwall. Moore received his earliest artistic stimulus from English medieval sculpture and the primitive, non-European works on view in the British Museum. At first he was greatly attracted by the Ancient Egyptian exhibits but later—from c. 1925 onwards—he was drawn more to the pre-Columbian art of Mexico. These archaic influences are revealed in many of his early works, such as the *Mother and Child* of 1924–5 and the *Reclining Figure* of 1929. The heavy, block-like forms which he created during this period testify to a vital conception of art that is far removed from the Classical canon. Like his fellow-sculptors Brancusi, Gaudier-Brzeska, Epstein and Archipenko and the painter-sculptors Picasso, Modigliani and Derain, Moore pursued what Sir Herbert Read has called a process of 'assimilation'. In his case this was completed by 1930 and was followed, from 1930 to c. 1936, by a phase in which he came to terms, first with Surrealism (*Composition*, 1931) and then with non-objective art (*Rectangular Form*, 1936). But his excursion into the realm of geometrical abstraction was of brief duration, and he soon reverted to the organic and, above all, the human forms which have dominated his sculptures. During his experimental period, Moore developed two important techniques which have played a central part in his later work: the hollowing out of solid volumes to reveal internal forms and the grouping together of different forms to make a composite work. His interest in the reclining figure also dates from his early period. This central theme, which he has since presented in a wide variety of forms, has been joined—from 1950 onwards—by the contrasting theme of the upright figure. But, important though these figures are, they constitute only one facet of Moore's wide range of subjects, whose archetypal significance has now been recognized and interpreted. Both formally and thematically he is a highly inventive artist and his works, which reached their full maturity after the Second World War, include such diverse products as the *Stringed Figures* (1936–40), the *Helmet Heads* (from 1939–40), the *Internal and External Forms* (from 1951), the *Family Groups*, the two- and three-piece *Reclining Figures* (of the present period), the *Locking Piece* (1962) and the *Atom Piece* (1964). During his early period, i.e. up to 1939, nearly all of Moore's works were carved in stone or wood. Since 1945 he has concentrated on bronzes. Moore himself has commented on the artistic problems posed by these different media in a number of important articles, in which he also explains his attitude to nature and early art and presents his view of the whole meaning and purpose of sculpture.

Moore received his first public commission in 1926, when he was asked to carve a relief for the headquarters of the London Passenger Transport Board. The result was his *Northwind*, the first of many large-scale works executed for official bodies by this artist, who has always regarded sculpture as a social art. These works include: a *Madonna and Child* for the city of Northampton (1943), a group of three standing figures for Battersea Park in London (1947), the screen for the Time-Life building in Bond Street, London (1952–3), a wall relief for the Building Centre in Rotterdam (1955), an enormous reclining figure for the UNESCO Headquarters in Paris (1957–8) and the monumental two-piece reclining figure for the Lincoln Art Center in New York (1963–5). Like all his other works these public commissions clearly indicate Moore's stature as a sculptor and his great insight into the human condition in our day.

Will Grohmann. *Henry Moore*, Berlin 1960.
Herbert Read. *Henry Moore*, London 1965.
Philip James (ed.). *Henry Moore on Sculpture*, London 1966.

Mooy, Jaap. Dutch sculptor and painter, b. 1915 in Bergen, North Holland. Mooy started out in life as a ship's boy and subsequently trained as a ship's engineer. His voyages brought him to Africa, America and many other parts of the world. In 1939, after meeting the painter Charley Toorop, Mooy taught himself to paint and in 1940 completed his first oil paintings. In 1950 he began to make photomontages and in 1956 produced his first sculptures: iron constructions made of scrap metal—parts of motor cars, bicycles, etc.—whose grotesque forms are reminiscent of works by Paolozzi. Of recent years Mooy has been painting in a geometrical, hard-edge style.

Morales, Armando. Nicaraguan painter, b. 1927 in Granada, Nicaragua. Morales trained at the School of Fine Arts in Managua from 1941 to 1945. Since then he has won awards at the Biennials in Madrid, in Houston, Texas (1956), in Guatemala (1956) and in São Paulo (1959).

Moralis, Yannis. Greek painter, b. 1916 in Arta. He studied in Athens and Paris. From 1947 he has been Professor of Painting at the School of Fine Arts, Athens. He has done excellent work in stage sets, and in murals. He is a Post-Cubist and Post-Fauvist painter, using with creative insight elements from Greek ancient vase painting as well as from the art of Byzantium. He has recently shown a preference for geometrical form.

Morandi, Giorgio. Italian painter, b. 1890 in Bologna; d. 1964 in Bologna. After working in his father's office in 1906 Morandi studied at the Accademia di Belle Arti in Bologna from 1907 to 1913. In 1909 he met G. Licini, and in 1910 went to the Biennale in Venice, where he saw his first Renoirs. He also visited Florence, and studied the works of Giotto, Masaccio and Uccello. In 1911 he visited Rome, where he saw originals by Monet. In

1913 he met Riccardo and Mario Bacchelli. In 1914 he attended the first Futurist exhibition in Florence, at which he met Carrà and Boccioni, and also visited Rome, Assisi and Padua. Subsequently (between 1914 and 1930) he gave drawing classes at various schools in Bologna. In 1915 he served with the Italian forces in Padua. In 1916 he visited Tolé di Vergata. In 1918 one of his works was reproduced in the magazine *Raccolta*. Shortly afterwards he met Mario Broglio, the originator of the *Valori Plastici* magazine, and visited Carrà. Whilst in Rome he met de Chirico. In 1920 he saw twenty-eight paintings by Cézanne at the Venice Biennale, and was greatly impressed. In 1926–7 he was Director of Schools for various districts in the provinces of Reggio Emilia and Modena. From 1927 to 1932 Morandi spent his summers in Grizzana. From 1930 to 1956 he was Professor of Graphic Art at the Accademia di Belle Arti in Bologna. From 1933 to 1938 he spent his summers in Roffeno. From 1939 to 1944 he lived in Grizzana. In 1948 he was made a member of the Accademia di San Luca in Rome, and in 1952 of the Swedish Academy. In 1956 he made his only trip abroad, when he visited Winterthur for the opening of an exhibition of his works. In 1962 he was awarded the Reubens Prize by the town of Siegen, and in 1963 the Archiginnasio d'Oro by the town of Bologna. From 1914 onwards Morandi was represented in all major exhibitions, and he also had many one-man shows. He died in Bologna in 1964 after a protracted illness.

The gentle humanity of Morandi's oeuvre owed much to his native town of Bologna, whose quiet seclusion and long creative tradition were major factors in his artistic development. Like Carrà, he took simple, everyday objects and depicted them in such a way that they acquired a new metaphysical reality. In his early period Morandi was influenced by the Cubists' visual approach and, more especially, by Cézanne's. It was Cézanne who taught him to concentrate on the plasticity of objects, and to transfer that plasticity to his picture surface by means of modelling. And it was from Cézanne, Corot and Chardin that he learned to appreciate the expressive power of simple object representation. The pictorial objects in Morandi's earliest works are full of surface movement in the Cubist manner and so seem to exist at many different levels. In c. 1918 Morandi became briefly involved with the *Pittura Metafisica*, although he never subscribed to its ideals. However, it was as a result of this involvement that he came to acquire a deeper understanding of Giotto's painting, and from 1918 onwards his pictorial objects possessed a strange, metaphysical air of unreality. It is as if they existed in a complete vacuum: illumined by harsh artificial lighting, they cast long, flat, black shadows. Unlike the Surrealists, who merely wished to make ironical or semi-literary statements, Morandi incorporated negative forms into his compositions, and took due

account of the relationships and tensions between his pictorial objects. In order to paint his pictures Morandi needed suitable objects; and, in fact, he arranged the objects in his still lifes to suit his own purposes; sometimes he even painted them so as to ensure that they reflected his vision of the object world. Then, when he came to paint his pictures, he simply reproduced the Cubist plasticity of the objects and their tonal values. In many cases he dulled the objects down by superimposing layers of fluff and dust. Morandi's gentle, lyrical pictures, which consist of still lifes with just a sprinkling of deserted landscapes, are purely visual works. They were the outcome of the artist's engrossment in objective and pictorial reality. By meditating on the nature of real-life objects Morandi slowly evolved pictorial analogies for them. Although his style did not undergo any sudden changes, Morandi progressively reduced his repertoire of objects until in the end his pictures consisted of just two containers. Invariably his banal objects are set out in accordance with strict, architectonic, pictorial principles, and are framed between a foreground area and the apparent background created by their own coloured volumes. Up to 1945 the objects in Morandi's still lifes were still spread out all over the table. But in the 1950s they gradually drew closer together until in the end they were perched on the edge of the table, as if on the brink of a precipice. Morandi also produced a large and significant graphic oeuvre.

F. Archangeli. *Giorgio Morandi*, Milan 1964.
Lamberto Vitali. *Giorgio Morandi: Pittore*, Milan 1965; *L'Opera grafica di Giorgio Morandi*, Turin 1965.
Catalogue, *Giorgio Morandi*, Palazzo dell'Archiginnasio, Bologna 1966.
Jean Leymarie. *Acquarelli di Morandi*, Bologna 1968.

Moreau, Gustave. French painter, b. 1826 in Paris; d. 1898 in Paris. Moreau studied painting under François Picot (1846) and Th. Chassériau (1848). Chassériau became a close personal friend, and he and Moreau lived together. In 1853 Moreau had his first picture hung in the Salon. In 1856 Chassériau died. From 1857 to 1859 Moreau was in Italy, where he copied works by Carpaccio, Gozzoli, Mantegna, Michelangelo, Leonardo and Titian, and met Degas and Puvis de Chavannes. In 1862 he painted the Stations of the Cross in the church at Decazzeville; in 1864 Prince Jerome Napoléon bought his painting of *Oedipus and the Sphinx*; in 1875 he was made a Knight of the Legion of Honour; and in 1880 he was represented in the Salon for the last time. In 1881 Moreau completed the first part of a series of illustrations of fables by La Fontaine for his friend Anthony Roux, the art collector, and in 1883 he was made an Officer of the Legion of Honour. In 1884, when his mother died, Moreau withdrew from the world and went into deep mourning; in 1885 he visited Holland, where he studied works by Rembrandt; and in 1886 he produced the remaining illustrations for the La Fontaine series. In 1888 Moreau became a member of the Académie des Beaux-Arts, and in 1892 took over the teaching post previously held by his friend Élie Delaunay. His pupils included the celebrated group led by Matisse, Rouault and Marquet. In his will Moreau left his pictures to the state. These were then housed in the Musée Gustave Moreau, which was opened in 1903.

Moreau soon discarded the painstaking detail of his early Realistic pictures, in which he had sought to express symbolic ideas through rather banal techniques. Subsequently, he produced two main types of paintings: those consisting of large-format scenic compositions, and those in which the paint was applied with thick, violent strokes of the brush or, in some cases, with the spatula. The pictorial forms scratched into the heavily impasted surfaces of these works convey what is really no more than an impression of metaphysical forms. Moreau also painted a vast number of watercolours, using rapid flowing brushwork and recording in a completely spontaneous manner pictorial conceptions that are almost non-objective. In these watercolours, which testify to a masterly sense of colour composition, Moreau anticipated structural features that were not fully developed until several decades later. Moreau's principal *motif* was the female figure. His women appeared in many different forms drawn from Greek or Eastern mythology and bore many different names, such as Salome, Delilah, Sulamith, Pasiphae, Helen, Leda and Circe. But the differences were more apparent than real, for these women were all sublimely beautiful, and they all radiated the same symbolic power. Despite the metaphorical complexities of his subject matter, Moreau remained a product of nineteenth-century positivism: his pictorial imagination was bound by contemporary ideas on the nature of the physical world and by certain academic conventions.

R. von Holten. *L'Art fantastique de Gustave Moreau*, Paris 1960.
Catalogue, *Gustave Moreau*, Musée du Louvre, Paris 1961.

Moreau, Luc Albert. French painter, b. 1882 in Paris; d. 1948 in Paris. Moreau studied under J. P. Laurens and J. E. Blanche at the École des Beaux-Arts in Paris. From 1920 to 1925 he was Vice-President of the Société des Artistes Indépendants, which he had first joined in 1907.

Moreau is best known for his lithographs. He produced illustrations for numerous books, including Fr. Carco, *Chansons Aigres-Douces* of 1913; Ch. Maurras, *Le Mystère d'Ulysse* of 1923; Émile Paul, *Tableaux de Zarès* of 1927; and Colette, *La Naissance du Jour* of 1931. As a painter he revealed a general preference for scenes from circus and sporting life, but he also produced portraits, landscapes and still lifes.

Moreni, Mattia. Italian painter, b. 1920 in Pavia. After living in various Italian cities, Moreni moved to Paris in 1956 and remained there for a period of ten years. He then returned to Italy and settled in Brisighella, near Russi. In 1953–4 he began to evolve a form of painting based on spontaneous gestures, in which he sometimes uses written words and slogans. Of more recent years he has also been treating landscape *motifs*.

Catalogue, *Sei Pittori Italiani*, Istituto Italo-Latino Americano, Rome 1967.

Morgenthaler, Ernst. Swiss painter, b. 1887; d. 1962. He was independent of particular movements, but helped to bring *avant-garde* thinking to Switzerland and contributed to her artistic development.

Morgner, Wilhelm. German painter, b. 1891 in Soest, Westphalia; d. 1917 near Langemark. Morgner studied under Georg Tappert in Worpswede in 1908 but returned to Soest in 1909. He visited Berlin in 1911 and joined the Berlin Secession. He then made contact with the *Blauer Reiter* group and in 1912 was represented at the *Sonderbund* Exhibition in Cologne.

Morgner was one of the Rhenish Expressionists. At first he was influenced by van Gogh but later turned to the *Blauer Reiter* painters, especially Kandinsky, for his inspiration. His paintings, although small in number, range from highly expressive works, which are full of movement, to ornamental abstracts. Like his drawings, they contain striking examples of German Expressionism.

H. Seiler. *Wilhelm Morgner*, Cologne 1956.

Mori, Camilo. Chilean painter, b. 1896 in Valparaiso. He was in Paris from 1921 to 1924, and while there his style underwent a change from Romantic Realism to a constructionist type of Realism rooted in Cubism. In 1940 he moved to New York, where his style altered again, becoming sensual and sweeping with elemental rhythms.

Morita, Shiryu. Japanese painter and calligrapher, b. 1912 in Toyooka, Hiogo. Morita occupies an important position in international culture as a mediator between Japanese and western art. In 1951 he brought out the first issue of the magazine *Bokubi*. In 1952 he became a founder member of the Japanese artists' association *Bokujin* and helped to produce its magazine. Morita has also devoted a great deal of time to re-thinking and revising the ancient Japanese art of calligraphy. In fact, this constitutes his principal contribution to the development of modern art in Japan. He himself has formulated the essential connection between the old and the new: 'Not only the calligraphy but also the

other arts of the Orient will acquire a living significance when—as a result of direct contact with
life—we rediscover the origin of art deep in man.'
Morita is now living in Kyoto, Japan.

Morlotti, Ennio. Italian painter, b. 1910 in Lecco,
Lombardy. Morlotti studied at the Academy in
Florence and the Brera in Milan. He was a pupil of
A. Funi. He made contact with the *Corrente* artists,
and after the war joined the *Fronte Nuovo delle Arti*
and the *Gruppo degli Otto*. He is now living in Milan.

Morlotti's favourite *motif* is the South Italian
landscape with its olive trees, cacti, sunflowers and
maize fields. During his early period he painted
objective landscapes in rich earthy colours, some
of which are reminiscent of Morandi. Then, after
the war, he developed a powerful abstract style that
was inspired by Picasso. Since 1953 he has painted
informal pictures. But even in this late period his
works reveal clear associations with original landscape or figurative *motifs*. From 1952 onwards
Morlotti has exhibited at the Biennale in Venice.

G. Testori. *Morlotti*, Ivrea 1957.

Morrice, James Wilson. Canadian painter, b. 1865
in Montreal; d. 1942 in Tunis. He moved to Paris in
1890, and stayed in France for most of his life. He
was friendly with Whistler and was influenced by
Henri Harpignies. He exhibited with the Salon
d'Automne from its inception in 1903. His work is
filled with bright colour, and he had the ability to
conjure up a scene with a few strokes of the brush.

Morris, George Lovett Kingsland. American painter
and critic, b. 1905 in New York City. A graduate of
the Groton School (1924) and Yale University
(1928), Morris studied at the Art Students' League
under John Sloan and Kenneth Hayes Miller and at
the Académie Moderne in Paris with F. Léger and
Amédée Ozenfant. He had his first one-man show in
1933 at Curt Valentine's, New York, and three years
later was a founding member of the American
Abstract Artists, serving as its president from 1948
until 1950. His painted essays have much in common
with the sculpture of Jean (Hans) Arp, his co-editor
of the Paris periodical *Plastique*. He has also been
an editor of *Partisan Review* (New York), contributing many articles on abstract art. Among his
articles in this periodical are: 'Hans Arp' (1937),
'Miró and the Spanish Civil War' (1938), 'On Critics
and Greenberg: A communication' (1948), 'On the
Mechanics of Abstract Painting' (1941), 'Picasso:
4,000 Years of His Art' (1940) and 'Relations of
Painting and Sculpture' (1943). He also published
American Abstract Artists (New York, 1946), a docu-
mentation of the members of that organization, and
was a contributor to 'What Abstract Art Means to
Me'—statements by leading artists recorded in the

Museum of Modern Art *Bulletin* of 1951. Morris
lectured on American Art throughout Europe in
1952, when he was the United States Painting
Delegate to the UNESCO conference in Venice. He
has taught at the Art Students' League (1940–1) and
was Artist-in-Residence at St. John's College, Anna-
polis, Maryland (1960–1).

George L. K. Morris. 'What Abstract Art Means to Me', *Museum
of Modern Art Bulletin* 18, No. 3, New York 1951.

Morris, Robert. American sculptor, b. 1931 in
Kansas City, Missouri. He studied at the University
of Kansas City and the Kansas City Art Institute
(1948–50) and then at the California School of Fine
Arts in 1951. From 1953 to 1955 he was at Reed
College, Oregon. He was given his first one-man
show at the Dilexi Gallery, San Francisco, in 1957.
Included in the exhibition *Primary Structures* at the
Jewish Museum, New York, in 1966, his works of
the early 1960s are just that. They range from his
1964 *Untitled* of painted rope and wood (New
Canaan, Conn., Coll. Philip Johnson) to large hard-
edge works such as the 1967 *Untitled* (New York,
Leo Castelli Gallery), an aluminium rectangular
frame supported by legs at two adjacent angles so
that one edge of the frame rests on the floor. 'Each
work embodies a single, relatively simple, plastic
idea; the variety amongst his works shows the
fertility of his mind.' His materials range from hard
steel to soft felt to moulded fibreglass. In his 1968
Earthwork, a temporary object, he used earth, peat,
steel, aluminium, copper, brass, zinc, felt, grease and
brick, all randomly combined in a pile. Morris has
written a number of important articles in *Artforum*
(1966–7) all entitled 'Notes on Sculpture', which
express his aesthetic attitudes. He was given an
important one-man show at the Stedelijk van
Abbemuseum in Eindhoven, Holland, in 1968.
Morris is an Assistant Professor of Art at Hunter
College, New York.

Robert Morris. 'Notes on Sculpture', *Artforum*, New York 1966–7.
Barbara Reise. '*Untitled 1969*: a footnote on art and minimal-
stylehood', *Studio International* 177, April 1969.

Mortensen, Richard. Danish painter, b. 1910 in
Copenhagen. Mortensen studied at the Royal
Academy in Copenhagen from 1931 to 1932. In his
final year as a student he saw works by Kandinsky
and was strongly influenced by them. In 1934 he
became a founder member of *Lines*, a Danish
artists' association, and in 1936–7 joined the
Groeninger group. In 1937 he also visited Paris,
where he made contact with French artists. His first
stage sets (for *The Soldier's Tale* by Stravinsky) date
from 1944. In 1947 he settled in Paris, where he is
still living today. In 1960 he had a special show in
the Danish Pavilion at the Biennale in Venice.

Apart from a brief Surrealist phase (under the
influence of Tanguy and Dali) Mortensen has been

producing abstract paintings, based partly on organic structures, partly on geometric forms, ever since 1932. In the 1950s and 1960s he has revealed a preference for triangular and rectangular forms and their derivatives. In many of these works he has created an irritating kind of perspective, which disrupts the impression of spatiality and forces the viewer to take note of the picture surface. In his use of clear, pure colours Mortensen has remained true to the tradition of concrete painting. Apart from Vasarély Mortensen is the most important painter in the group of geometrical abstract artists associated with the Galerie Denise René.

Exhibition catalogue, *Richard Mortensen*, Galerie Denise René, Paris 1962.

Mortier, Antoine. Belgian painter, b. 1908 in Brussels. Both as a student and during the initial phase of his career Mortier concentrated on drawing and sculpture, and it was not until he was thirty years old that he discovered his vocation as a painter. In 1946 he became an Abstract Expressionist, although most of his pictures still retained objective associations even after that date, and he has never been opposed to figurative themes on principle. In his political compositions he seems to be intent on reducing reality and then restoring its essence by a process of abstraction. Mortier is a member of the *Jeune Peinture belge* association. But he is also extremely aware of his own individuality, and has never failed to assert it, either in his work or in his private life.

Morton, Alastair. British designer and painter, b. 1910 in Carlisle; d. 1963 in Penrith. Morton studied at Edinburgh University and Oxford. He later became a director of Edinburgh Weavers Ltd. He designed fabrics and invented the means of reproducing as textiles the designs of such leading artists as Barbara Hepworth and Ben Nicholson (a Bauhaus established practice). He also painted and has had various exhibitions in London and other towns in Britain.

Jasia Reichardt. Catalogue, *Art in Britain 1930–40*, Marlborough Gallery, London 1965.

Moser, Koloman (Kolo). Austrian painter and graphic artist, b. 1868 in Vienna; d. 1918 in Vienna. He was one of the original members of the Vienna Secession, founded in 1897. He was also responsible, with Josef Hoffmann and Fritz Wärndorfer, for setting up the *Wiener Werkstätte*, an enterprise devoted to the production of *Jugendstil* arts and crafts. Moser and Hoffmann designed many of the products of the workshops in characteristic geometrical style: goods in leather, gold and silver, book bindings, and furniture. Moser also designed posters for some of the Secession exhibitions.

Moses, Anna Mary Robertson ('Grandma'). American painter, b. 1860 in Greenwich, New York; d. 1961 in Hoosick Falls, New York. The paintings of Grandma Moses attracted attention only in the late 1930s. Her first works were yarn pictures, mainly landscapes executed in bright colours copied from illustrations. She first 'exhibited' her efforts at the Woman's Exchange in Thomas' Drug Store in Hoosick Falls, N.Y., and also at the Cambridge Fair along with her canned fruit and jams. She won prizes for the latter, but not for her paintings. It was not until the art collector Luís Caldor bought three of her paintings which were exhibited at the Museum of Modern Art in New York that the public was made aware of her existence. She was given her first one-man show in 1940 at the Galerie St. Étienne and a second one in 1942 at the American-British Art Center where such works as *Black Horse* (whereabouts unknown) were exhibited. Its attempted sense of atmosphere, rather naïve use of *repoussoir* trees and interest in patternization seen in the fields of the background is characteristic of her style. Her choice of subject falls into four types corresponding to the four seasons. Her working method is highly structured and unique. The ground consists of masonite pressed wood treated with linseed oil topped with a base of three coats of flat white paint. The landscape is then painted—never done from nature but rather from imagination. Never omitting the minutest of details, to the completed landscape she then adds figures dressed in costumes from all eras of American history. The blatant naïveté of her work is saved by the intimate feeling for nature, animals and children, her decorative sense of design and the lustrous brilliance of colour all placed into a composition showing action arrested in a moment of time.

Otto Kallir (ed.). *Grandma Moses, American Primitive*, New York 1947.
Anna M. Moses. *Grandma Moses: My Life's History*, New York 1952.

Motherwell, Robert. American painter, b. 1915 in Aberdeen, Washington. His interest in art can be traced to as early as 1926 when he received a fellowship at Otis Art Institute in Los Angeles. He entered Stanford University in 1932, graduating in 1936. Though he was impressed by the Matisse collection at Stanford, he found the Art Department uninteresting and changed his major from art to philosophy, writing his thesis on O'Neill's relation to psychoanalytic theory. The following year he entered Harvard University where he combined his art and philosophy interests, concentrating in aesthetics with a thesis on Delacroix's journals. When he entered Columbia University's Department of Art History and Archaeology, he was encouraged by Meyer Schapiro to forfeit scholarship for painting. Through Schapiro he met and became friendly with European

Surrealists in exile and became interested in Surrealist theory, especially automatism, in accordance with his previous researches in psychoanalysis. At this point he also nurtured a fascination with French Symbolist poetry, which first intrigued him while he was in Europe in 1935. The 1940s were perhaps the most meaningful years of his artistic development as well as the period when he developed friendships with the leading *avant-garde* artists in New York. In 1940 he went to Mexico with Matta, producing such works as *Little Spanish Prison* (coll. of artist), which is a precursor of the aesthetics of the 1960s in its striped format and became a recurring theme in Motherwell's work, even when his major concern changed from painting to collage in 1943 (*Pancho Villa, Dead and Alive*, gouache and oil with collage on cardboard, New York, Museum of Modern Art). His interest in collage was fostered by Peggy Guggenheim's invitation to him (and to J. Pollock and W. Baziotes, both of whom he had met the previous year) to submit collages for an exhibition at her gallery. The following year Miss Guggenheim gave him his first one-man show. In 1948 he and Baziotes, C. Still, M. Rothko, B. Newman and D. Hare collaborated in forming a school called The Subjects of the Artist (to emphasize that abstract art has a subject matter). This school became a meeting place for discussions of *avant-garde* artists and writers. The same year he began his series *Elegy of the Spanish Republic*, a group of works which was continued through the early 1960s. *Elegy of the Spanish Republic LIV* (1957–61, New York, Museum of Modern Art) hearkens back to his nearly totally black pictures of 1943.

In 1951 he became an Associate Professor at Hunter College and remained with that institution for seven years. He has been engaged in writing ever since the early 1940s, his best-known work being his edition of *The Dada Painters and Poets: An Anthology*, for which he wrote the preface and introduction. Since the early 1940s he has been included in nearly every major exhibition of modern American art. His first retrospective exhibition was held in 1959 at Bennington College; another larger one was installed at the Museum of Modern Art, New York, in 1966.

Frank O'Hara. *Robert Motherwell*, Museum of Modern Art, New York 1965.

Movimento per l'Arte Concreta—*see* MAC

Moynihan, Rodrigo. British painter, b. 1910 in Tenerife. Moynihan lived in England and the United States, then studied painting in Rome in 1928 and at the Slade (1928–31). From 1948 to 1957 he was Professor of Painting at the RCA and since 1957 has lived in France. In the thirties he was a leading member of the Objective Abstraction Group and later was associated with the Euston Road School. After the war he was still painting in the Realist manner of Euston Road, but in 1956 he turned to abstraction, and since living in France, he has painted in a manner closely related to the *École de Paris* Abstract Expressionism.

Mucha, Alphonse. Czech painter and poster designer, b. 1860 in Ivancice; d. 1939 in Prague. He studied in Paris at the Académie Julian and Académie Colarossi, and became one of the prime exponents of *art nouveau*. Although he produced some notable paintings, including a cycle on the history of the Slav people (1910–28), Mucha is best known for his beautiful posters, of which one of the most famous is that for 'Job' cigarette papers, 1898. The flowing luxuriant lines of his art appealed to Sarah Bernhardt, the great actress, and she used Mucha as her poster designer during the height of her success in the 1890s. His posters are currently becoming fashionable again, and reproductions of them are widely available.

Muche, Georg. German painter, b. 1895 in Querfurt/ Halle an der Saale. Muche's father, Felix Ramholz, was a Sunday artist. After studying in Munich and Berlin from 1913 to 1915, Muche taught at the *Sturm* School of Art in Berlin from 1916 to 1919. From 1919 to 1927 he was a member of the Bauhaus staff. From 1927 to 1931 he taught at Itten's School of Art in Berlin and from 1931 to 1933 at the Breslau Academy. In 1939 he obtained a post at the School of Textile Engineering in Krefeld, where he remained until 1958. Since 1960 he has been living in Lindau on Lake Constance.

Up to 1922 Muche painted abstract pictures with mystical overtones, which reveal the influence of Kandinsky and Klee. Since then his works have become more and more figurative but without losing their mystical quality. Faces and plants standing out in relief against hazy, pastel-coloured grounds are typical of this later period.

Georg Muche: Bilder—Fresken—Zeichnungen, Tübingen 1950.
Georg Muche. *Blickpunkt*, Munich 1961.

Müller, Jan. German-American painter, b. 1922 in Hamburg; d. 1958 in New York City. After living in Hamburg, Nuremberg and Brandenburg, Müller moved with his family to Czechoslovakia in 1933 and then to Switzerland. In 1936 he was in Amsterdam and two years later in Paris. After being interned as a German refugee he escaped to Spain, Portugal and finally the United States in 1941. He began painting in 1945, when he studied at the Art Students' League for six months. From 1945 to 1950 he was at the Hans Hofmann School of Art. He first exhibited with Miles Forst, John Grillo, Lester Johnson, Felix Pasilis and Wolf Kahn in a show entitled *813 Broadway*—the rudiments of the Hansa Gallery. It was at this gallery (which opened in 1952) that Müller had his first one-man show in 1953. Among the founders of the Hansa Gallery were Jean Follett, Barbara and Miles Forst, Wolf Kahn, Allan Kaprow, Felix Pasilis and Richard Stankiewicz.

Müller's early works were in the abstract idiom of Hofmann, and he approached his compositions in a mosaic-like manner as seen in *The Robe* (c. 1952, Los Angeles, Coll. Mr. and Mrs. Conrad J. Moss). By 1953–4 he began introducing objective elements— landscape, still life and finally figures (*The Heraldic Ground*, 1953, New York, Coll. Mrs. Jan Müller). In his late works he turned to literary sources for his subjects—the Bible, Cervantes, Shakespeare and Goethe. These narrative scenes are often represented by grotesque, wildly gesticulating figures, painted a ghostly white or black and situated in bright, boldly coloured environments (*The Temptation of St. Anthony*, 1957, New York, Mrs. Jan Müller). The lack of articulation in the bodies and physiognomies recalls the stark nakedness and horror of medieval German sculpture (*The Virgins*, 1957, New York, Mrs. Jan Müller).

Long a sufferer from rheumatic fever, he succumbed to the disease at the age of thirty-five.

Exhibition catalogue, *Jan Müller*, Solomon R. Guggenheim Museum, New York 1962.

Müller, Otto. German painter, b. 1874 in Liebau, Silesia; d. 1930 in Breslau. After attending an elementary school in Görlitz, Müller served an apprenticeship as a lithographer, which stood him in good stead when he came to produce his graphic works. This was followed by a course of study at the Academy in Dresden, where he was influenced by the works of Ludwig von Hofmann and Arnold Böcklin. He spent the next ten years in Gerhard Hauptmann's circle, to which he was drawn partly for family reasons, his mother having passed her childhood in the dramatist's parental home. Then in 1907, Müller settled in Berlin, where he established a friendly relationship with the founder members of the *Brücke*, especially Heckel and Kirchner. Although he was very much their senior, the relationship flourished, and in 1910 he joined their association. It was at that time that he began to develop his own individual style, into which he subsequently incorporated certain aspects of Ancient Egyptian art. During his Berlin period he was also closely associated with the New Secession and made friends with Wilhelm Lehmbruck.

Müller's works, most of which are undated, are all rather similar, for he made no dramatic changes in the course of his development. Unlike Kirchner and Heckel, who reveal a preference for city scenes, he concentrated on landscapes with figures, producing poetic visions of the life of rural gypsies. In many of his paintings, in which young girls are portrayed bathing in forest pools, the solitude of the woodland scene is transformed into a latter-day Arcady by the nascent sensuality of their adolescent forms. Whereas the younger members of the *Brücke* favoured hectic if not indeed violent colour combinations, Müller preferred gentle, harmonizing shades of grey, brown, ochre, yellow and green, which he applied on coarse-grained canvas using a tempera technique. On the other hand, his highly expressive contours, which are particularly pronounced in his lithographs, are very much a product of *Brücke*-type Expressionism. Although Müller's artistic range was small, his work is distinguished by its dreamlike, musical quality and by the delicacy of its nuances. This sensitive and poetic painter added a note of melancholy and reserve to the forceful art of the *Brücke* association.

L.-G. Buchheim. *Otto Mueller: Leben und Werk*, Feldafing (Germany) 1963.

Müller, Robert. Swiss sculptor, b. 1920 in Zürich. He studied with Baenninger in Zürich, and with Germaine Richier. He moved to France in 1950, and four years later had his first one-man exhibition. He also exhibited at the Venice Biennale, 1956, and at the São Paulo Bienal, 1957. His sculptures are welded from scrap iron, often incorporating found objects. Some of his more sinister pieces include animals and fish, and barbaric instruments. His work is aggressive and powerful, springing up from the ground or extending horizontally in knotted masses. He has also produced water-driven 'mobiles' of unusual fascination.

Multiples. These are works of art produced by industrial or serigraphic processes and can therefore be supplied in any quantity or replaced at any time. Whereas traditional works of art are valued for their uniqueness, the value of multiples lies in their ability to transmit ideas in a particular artistic form. Multiples are not collectors' pieces but consumer articles which help to fashion social consciousness by transmitting visual images reflecting the attitudes and insights of specific individuals. In our scientific age they fulfil an integrating function by giving expression to new trends in aesthetics and social criticism.

Munari, Bruno. Italian sculptor, kinetic artist, designer and film-maker, b. 1907 in Milan. Ever since the early 1930s Munari has been making wire mobiles, which he calls *machines inutiles*. In 1938 he published the *Manifesto del mechanismo* and in 1949 became a founder member of the *MAC* group (*Movimenta per l'Arte Concreta*). He has been tackling the problem of the fragmentation of light in his *Projections* and has also constructed transparent and coloured collages from plastic materials. He has written numerous articles, in which he argues the case for 'programmed art' and design. In his search for an 'objective, visual language', which would take account of the dynamics of our age, he has also made a number of experimental films including *I colori della luce* (1963) and *Moiré* (1964). Munari is now living in Milan.

Bruno Munari. *Arte come mestiere*, Laterza 1966.

Munch, Edvard. Norwegian painter, b. 1863 in Loeiten; d. 1944 in Ekely, near Oslo. In 1883 he attended the Christiania school of drawing, run by the sculptor Midelthun. His first important works date from 1884 onwards, and are characterized by their dark colours and their choice of subject, 'interiors, people reading and women knitting'. In 1885 he visited Paris, where he first made contact with the work of the Impressionists and of Seurat, van Gogh and Gauguin. Although he worked in the studio of Léon Bonnat, it is not so much academic influences as rather the influence of Gauguin which manifests itself in Munch's later work of this Paris period. He was also impressed by the sombreness of Redon's lithographs, and by the monochrome palette of Carrière—influences which are combined in Munch's claustrophobic picture of 1895, *Puberty* (Oslo, Nasjonalgalleriet).

After his stay in Paris, and his discovery of the expressive properties of line and colour, Munch resolved to abandon his former style and subject matter, and instead to paint pictures of 'living people who breathe and feel and suffer and love', to attempt to express in his pictures the various states of the human mind. Hence the recurrence of themes of illness, death and depression, as, for example, in the *Death Bed* (Oslo, Nasjonalgalleriet). These themes, however, reflect not only the discoveries of contemporary science about the human psyche, but also contemporary trends in literature: the affinity between Munch's pictorial work and the subjects of Ibsen's plays has frequently been remarked. Munch, himself, had also come into personal contact with illness and depression from an early age. His mother and sister died of consumption when he was in his teens, and he himself suffered a nervous breakdown in the winter of 1908–9. Yet he was capable of observing dispassionately even his own state of mind, as in his self-portrait *In Hell*, 1895 (Oslo, Kommunes Kunstsamlinger, Munch Museet), in which the soul, with piercing eyes, looks out of the naked body; while in his famous *The Cry*, 1893 (Oslo, Munch Museet), the horror felt by the principal figure is expressed in the lurid reds and greens of the sky, the contrasting curved and straight lines, and in the reduction of the human body to a hieroglyph, whose curves are almost one with those of the landscape. In 1895, Munch described the picture as depicting the moment when 'alone, trembling with anguish, I became aware of the vast, infinite cry of nature'.

The last decade of the nineteenth century is re-garded as Munch's most successful period. In 1892 he exhibited in Berlin at the invitation of the Verein Berliner Künstler, but his work proved so disturbing that the show had to be prematurely closed, causing a split within official art circles which was ultimately to lead to the foundation of the Berlin Secession. His work also exercised a profound influence on the artists of the *Brücke*, especially Kirchner, although Munch himself is recorded as saying, on first seeing the work of Schmidt-Rottluff, 'Evil times are upon us!' On the other hand, his later work, as typified by his murals (*History* and *Alma Mater*) for the Aula of Oslo University, is calmer and more philosophical in character; Munch himself said of these murals that he wanted them to be 'at one and the same time peculiarly Norwegian and universal'. After 1909 there are in general more landscapes and scenes of everyday life, and far fewer penetrating insights into the nature of man's inner world; one might suggest that Munch's art created after his mental breakdown adopts a more optimistic and universal approach in accordance with the artist's new-found psychological well-being.

F. B. Deknatel. *Edvard Munch*, Boston 1950.
A. Moen. *Edvard Munch: Graphic Art and Paintings*, 3 vols., Oslo 1956–8.
J. H. Langaard and R. Revold. *Edvard Munch: Masterpieces from the Artist's Collection in the Munch Museum in Oslo*, New York and Toronto 1964.

Mundy, Henry. British painter, b. 1919 in Birkenhead. Mundy studied at Birkenhead Art School from 1937 to 1939, and then, after war service, at Camberwell from 1946 to 1950. In 1961 he won first prize in the John Moores Competition, Liverpool. From 1958 to 1966 he taught at Corsham and from 1966 he has taught at the St. Martin's School of Art in London. Since 1960 he has exhibited at the Hanover Gallery, London. Mundy's work of the fifties and early sixties developed from his earlier still-life painting, though his interest moved from the objects themselves to include the space in which they exist. In this process his art became increasingly abstract, though references to 'things' in the pictures still remain. His freedom of handling, often allowing the paint to run, intermingling line and colour area, and the preoccupation with the tension between depth and surface that this represents, reveal the influence of the New York School, especially Pollock and de Kooning. This interest in American painting Mundy held in common with other members of the Situation Group of 1960. More recently he has turned to popular imagery for inspiration (*Red Rover*, 1966, Stuyvesant, London), but in spite of the figurative element that this has introduced the same preoccupation with depth and surface persists.

Catalogues, Hanover Gallery, London, from 1960; Arts Council, London 1963.

Munich Secession—*see* **Secession**

Munnings, Sir Alfred. British painter, b. 1878 in Mendham, Suffolk; d. 1959 in Dedham, Essex. He began exhibiting at the Royal Academy in 1899 and in the same year went blind in one eye. He studied at the Académie Julian in Paris for a year, 1903–4. His first one-man show, at the Leicester Galleries, London, was in 1913. He was President of the Royal Academy from 1944 to 1949 and was knighted in 1944.

Muñoz, Godofredo Ortega. Spanish painter, b. 1905 in San Vicente de Alcantara, Caceres. He is a landscape painter, and owes much to the influences of both naturalism and Expressionism. He paints the lonely bleak country of his native Estremadura, using harsh earth colours.

Münter, Gabriele. German painter, b. 1877 in Berlin; d. 1962 in Murnau. Münter studied under Kandinsky at the Phalanx School in Munich in 1902 and then lived with him until 1915. In 1908 they settled in Murnau and were visited by Jawlensky, who worked with them there. From 1909 to 1911 Münter was a member of the New Artists' Association and in 1912 she joined the *Blauer Reiter* group. When Kandinsky returned to Russia in 1915 she went to live in Scandinavia, remaining there until 1920. In 1931 she again settled in Murnau. Münter had preserved Kandinsky's early works and in 1958 she presented them to the Städtische Galerie in Munich.

Münter's fresh and delicate paintings are derived from the early Fauvist works executed by Jawlensky and Kandinsky during their Murnau period.

K. H. Röthel. *Gabriele Münter*, Munich 1957.

Munthe, Gerhard. Norwegian painter, b. 1849 in Elverum; d. 1929 in Oslo. He studied in Oslo, Düsseldorf and Munich. He was associated with Christian Krohg (father of Per) and Erik Werenskiold, and was considered a Symbolist painter. Many of his paintings and watercolours were inspired by the myths and legends of his native country.

Murtić, Edo. Yugoslav painter and graphic artist, b. 1921 in Velika Pisanica, Croatia. Murtić studied at the academies in Zagreb and Belgrade. In the course of his career he has designed posters, stage sets and interiors for factories and public buildings. He has also produced a number of ceramic compositions.

In the immediate postwar years Murtić integrated the dramatic drawings and sketches, which he had made whilst fighting with the partisans, into the Post-Cubist style that characterized his early period. Later, when he was visiting America in 1952, his desire for greater simplification and for a more abstract representation of reality, which had always been a feature of his work, became more pronounced. The gigantic townscape of New York, which forms part of his American cycle and in which the teeming life of the city is organized into a rhythmical structure built up from a whole labyrinth of verticals, horizontals and diagonals, was created at that time. In c. 1960 he began to translate his Mediterranean experiences into fluorescent arabesques and lively signs, which create an impression of an eternal but inanimate world. Subsequently Murtić adopted a completely abstract outlook. Of recent years his interest in screen processing and in the presentation of inner structures has become more marked. So too have his Orphist tendencies.

Bozo Bek. *Edo Murtić*, Zagreb 1958.

Music, Zoran Antonio. Italian painter and graphic artist, b. 1909 in Gorizia (Görz), then in Austria. After studying at the Academy of Art in Zagreb Music visited Dalmatia in 1935, where the limestone hills made a deep impression on him and permanently influenced his work. He returned to Italy in the following year, settling in Venice. He then painted numerous frescoes in Italian churches. In 1943 he was sent to Dachau by the Germans. After the war he won an award for graphic art at the Biennale in Venice (1956).

The themes of Music's early works were closely linked with nature and his handling at that time was extremely economical. The shadowy forms in his cycle *Scorched Earth* (c. 1960–1) are built up from blobs of paint and organized in a rhythmical structure. Of recent years he has used rich colours and inventive designs (e.g. in the pictures and prints executed in Cortina in 1963–4) which stand in marked contrast to the ascetic rigour that was the characteristic feature of his early period. Music now lives primarily in Paris.

Myers, Jerome. American painter, b. 1867 in Petersburg, Virginia; d. 1941 in New York. Although poor himself, he was attracted to the slums of New York's Lower East Side, which he began to romanticize in his paintings as early as 1887. Instead of the grim and rigorous existence that the inhabitants of this section were forced to confront, Myers found in their raggedness and toil a rare poetry, as well as dignity in their effort and spirit (*Night Mission*, 1906, New York, Metropolitan Museum). Along with that of The Eight (the Ashcan School) and his friend John Sloan, Myers' work had been rejected for exhibition by the National Academy in 1907. He then helped to form the Association of American Painters in 1911, and along with Walt Kuhn, the gallery director Henry Fitch Taylor and the painter Elmer

Macrae (1875–1955), Myers helped lay the foundations for the 1913 Armory Show. Myers was patriotic in his attitude towards American art, and later regretted his suggestion that Arthur B. Davies be appointed head of the Association of American Painters, since Davies expanded the Armory Show to include the European moderns, whose work greatly eclipsed that of the American exhibitors.

Myers' work is both sentimental and romanticizing in its treatment of urban street life (*Street Group*, Metropolitan Museum). He thought of New York as a 'tapestry of romance' and discovered a world of almost abstract fantasy through his study of the labourers, children and merchants who populate the slum districts. *The Tambourine* (Washington, D.C., Phillips Collection), with its gay children dancing around an organ-grinder, is characteristic of Myers' view of the poor but happy urchins who manage a few joyful moments in their otherwise bleak lives.

After 1914 Myers resigned from the Association of American Painters and Sculptors and was honoured by acceptance into the National Academy. He maintained his old style even after the First World War.

Jerome Myers. *The Artist in Manhattan*, New York 1940.
Harry Wickey. Catalogue, *Jerome Myers Memorial Exhibition*, Whitney Museum of American Art, New York 1941.

N

Nabis, The. A group of young artists who came together in 1888 in Paris and exhibited as a group from 1891 to 1899. They form a coherent body within the wider context of the Symbolist movement. The name *Nabis* is derived from the Hebrew word for 'prophets'. The principal members of the *Nabis* were Paul Sérusier, Pierre Bonnard, Paul Ranson, Maurice Denis and Édouard Vuillard.

In the summer of 1888 Paul Sérusier, a student at the Académie Julian, visited Pont-Aven where he met Gauguin and painted a small picture under his direct guidance, in the wood known as the 'Bois d'Amour'. Gauguin's instructions to Sérusier on this occasion are celebrated: 'How do you see those trees? They are yellow. Well, put down yellow. And that shadow is rather blue so render it with pure ultramarine. Those red leaves. Use vermilion.' Sérusier named his picture *Le Talisman* and took it back to Paris where he showed it to the other students at the Académie Julian: Bonnard, Vuillard and Denis among them. This small but daring painting was instrumental in introducing these young men to Gauguin's influence and he remained the chief inspirer of the *Nabis*. The group met regularly at a number of places: the restaurant L'Os à Moelle, Ranson's studio, the art shop of Père Tanguy (where they could see works by Cézanne and van Gogh), their own art dealer, Le Barc de Bouteville (who gave them several exhibitions from 1891 to 1897), the *Revue Blanche* (where they made friends with Toulouse-Lautrec) and at the *avant-garde* Théâtre de l'Oeuvre founded by their friend Lugné-Poë, for whom they designed sets.

The *Nabis*' doctrine was summed up by Denis in his Theory of Two Distortions: 'The Objective Distortion based upon a purely aesthetic and decorative concept, upon the technical principles of colour and composition, and the Subjective Distortion, which brings into play the artist's own perception.'

This doctrine the *Nabis* applied not only to easel painting but to the decorative arts, and they were important contributors to the development of *art nouveau*. Perhaps the most characteristic *Nabi* products are their lithographic posters and prints such as Bonnard's highly original *France Champagne* of 1889 or his poster for the *Revue Blanche* of 1894.

The group exhibited together for the last time in 1899 at the Durand-Ruel Gallery, but by then they had already begun to go their separate ways.

Agnès Humbert. *Les Nabis et leur époque 1888–1900*, Geneva 1954; Paris 1955.
Charles Chassé. *The Nabis and their Period*, London and New York 1969.

Nadelman, Elie. Polish-born American sculptor, b. 1882 in Warsaw; d. 1946 in New York. After leaving Warsaw around 1901, Nadelman went to Munich where he became familiar with the drawings of Aubrey Beardsley. From 1903 to 1914 he worked and exhibited in Paris, where he gained recognition as a modernist sculptor; during his Paris years he had an especially successful and famous one-man show at the Galerie Druet (1909), and also exhibited in Barcelona, London and Berlin. In 1914 he went to New York, and by 1918 he had established himself there as a popular sculptor especially in demand for portrait busts. After the Great Depression of the 1930s, however, in which he suffered severe financial losses and the inadvertent destruction by workmen of much of his sculpture, Nadelman withdrew from the New York art world and stopped exhibiting his works.

Nadelman's major and persistent interest was in relationships of form, which he expressed primarily in simplified curvilinear and balanced human and animal figures. Some of his early work also shows a more Cubistic orientation to form (*Standing Bull* and *Wounded Bull*, both 1915, New York, Museum of Modern Art). The major groupings of Nadelman's work are simplified, Impressionistic marble portrait heads, female figures of dancers and circus performers (*Circus Woman*, c. 1924, Riverdale, New

York, Coll. Mrs. Elie Nadelman), and small figures caricaturing members of high society.

William Murrell. *Elie Nadelman*, Woodstock (N.Y.) 1924.
Lincoln Kirstein. Catalogue, *The Sculpture of Elie Nadelman*, Museum of Modern Art, New York 1948; *Elie Nadelman Drawings*, New York 1949.

Naïve art. The work of modern primitive painters has a distinctive, unmistakable style. Their subjects are depicted in minute detail and, generally, with a tendency to disregard the classical laws of perspective, which gives the paintings their great charm. Bright colours are used in compositions which very often show everyday events in the life of the community, or views copied from picture postcards. Primitive artists often come to light only late in life, since they are not attached to any particular school of painting, nor do they follow the mainstream development of art. Among the best known are: in France, Le Douanier Rousseau, Séraphine, Louis Vivin, Camille Bombois, Dominique Peyronnet and André Bauchant; in Belgium, Léon Greffe; in Greece, Theophilos; in America, Grandma Moses, Morris Hirschfeld, Joseph Pickett and Israel Litwak; in Yugoslavia, Ivan Generalić.

Nakian, Reuben. American sculptor, b. 1897 in College Point, New York. Nakian began studying sculpture by copying plaster casts in the Metropolitan Museum of Art (1906–11), and later studied at the Art Students' League (1912), the Independent Art School and the Beaux-Arts Institute of Design (1915). In 1916 he became a studio apprentice to Paul Manship, and from 1920 to 1923 shared a studio with Gaston Lachaise. He began exhibiting in 1923 and held his first one-man show in New York in 1926. Nakian received an important commission in 1961 for decorating the façade of New York University's Loeb Student Center in Washington Square. He taught at the Newark School of Fine and Industrial Arts (1946–51) and at Pratt Institute, Brooklyn (1952–4).

Nakian believed that the grandeur and elegance of past European art, especially painting, should be an important source of inspiration for the modern sculptor. He sought to express these qualities, often on a monumental scale, in his own work, emphasizing mass and form. In the early 1930s Nakian did a series of portraits of artists and government officials, and in 1934 made an 8-foot sculpture of the baseball hero Babe Ruth. Later in the thirties, and through the next decade, Nakian worked little on sculpture and exhibited rarely, concentrating instead on drawings. He returned to sculpture around 1947, with a series of small works in terra-cotta based on mythological themes, which he first exhibited in 1949 and continued developing into the sixties. With their spontaneity, expressive tactility and sensuousness, these sculptures are among his most successful works (*Voyage to Crete*, 1949, New York, Coll. Mr. and Mrs.

Thomas B. Hess). Nakian also explored mythological themes in both small and monumental bronzes, and in large welded steel constructions; some of the larger works were conceived as group sculptures (*Rape of Lucrece*, 1955–8, welded steel, New York, Museum of Modern Art; and *Goddess of the Gold Thighs*, 1964–5, bronze, New York, Egan Gallery).

Robert Goldwater. 'Reuben Nakian', *Quadrum* 11, Brussels 1961.
H. H. Arnason. 'Nakian', *Art International* VII, Zürich, April 1963.
Frank O'Hara. Catalogue, *Nakian*, Museum of Modern Art, New York 1966.

Nanninga, Jaap (Jacob). Dutch painter, b. 1904 in Winschoten; d. 1962 in The Hague. After first studying in Groningen, with Werkmann and Wiegers, and Amsterdam, Nanninga attended the Academy of Art in The Hague from 1939 to 1943. Between 1945 and 1948, while living in the South of France, he made a number of visits to North Africa. He also made several working trips to Paris. During this period Nanninga came under the influence of Geer van Velde and, from 1917 onwards, moved towards an Expressionistic type of abstract painting. Much of his work reflects landscape *motifs* and in some instances reveals an affinity to Corneille. His palette is made up of dull whites, greys, blues and greens. In 1951 and 1953 Nanninga won the Jacob-Maris Prize. His death in 1962 was the result of a road accident.

Exhibition catalogue, *Jaap Nanninga*, Rotterdam Museum, Rotterdam 1963.
G. Lampe. *Jaap Nanninga*, Amsterdam 1964.

Nash, John. British painter and illustrator, b. 1893 in London. He is the younger brother of Paul Nash, with whom he had an exhibition in 1913. He was a member of the London Group and the New English Art Club. He was a war artist in 1918. He has taught at the Ruskin School, Oxford (1922–7) and the Royal College of Art, London (1934–57, with a break in the war years). There was a retrospective of his work at the Leicester Galleries, London, in 1954.

Nash, Paul. British landscape painter, b. 1889 in London; d. 1946 in Boscombe, near Bournemouth. Nash studied at the Slade School. In 1914 he enlisted in the Artists' Rifles, and in 1917 he was appointed an official war artist. In 1918 he exhibited his war pictures, and these powerful images of shattered landscapes are his first important works. Although they show an awareness of Post-Impressionism, they are essentially individual and they already demonstrate his power of transcending what is prosaic in landscape without ignoring it, in a way that is truly poetic. In the next ten years he produced a series of landscapes, often lyrical, sometimes ominous, that seem to be influenced by Cézanne. In 1928 his painting changed through his first contact with Surrealism, and from this time onwards he frequently exploited the haunting irrationalities that look back to de Chirico; but this influence really only reinforced his own sense of the mysterious poetry of landscape. In 1940 he was again appointed a war artist, this time to the Air Ministry, and some of his best-known paintings are of the war in the air (*Totes Meer*). The extraordinary landscapes painted towards the end of his life (*Vernal Equinox*, 1943) and the unfinished sunflower series, however, will perhaps remain the most remarkable of all his works and will take their place in the tradition of visionary landscape that goes back to Palmer and Blake.

Herbert Read. *Paul Nash*, London 1944.
A. Bertram. *Paul Nash: The Portrait of an Artist*, London 1955.

Nauen, Heinrich, German painter, b. 1880 in Krefeld; d. 1941 in Kalkar. He studied in Düsseldorf and Stuttgart, then settled in Laethem-St-Martin for several years (1902–5). In 1911 he moved to Dillborn, in the Rhineland. There he joined the circle of Campendonk and Macke, and contributed to the 1913 Rhenish Expressionists' exhibition. He was one of the movement's leading representatives, and the luminous effects and strong colours of his early landscapes are reminiscent of van Gogh and Matisse.

Nay, Ernst Wilhelm. German painter, b. 1902 in Berlin; d. 1968. He worked in Berlin, then Paris and Rome. In 1937, at the invitation of Munch, he went to Norway. There he painted Realist pictures, until in about 1948 his work grew more abstract. His works are elemental, suggesting the original chaos and the revolutions of the heavenly bodies. In 1951 Nay joined the Cologne *Zen* group, the aim of which was to bring mysticism and spiritual ideas into art. Nay's work covered a wide range, but a unifying spirit pervaded it all, as could be seen from the two big retrospectives held in Düsseldorf (1959) and Essen (1962).

W. Haftmann. *Ernst Wilhelm Nay*, Cologne 1960.

Nebel, Otto. German painter and poet, b. 1892 in Berlin. He studied architecture and, later, painting (under Kandinsky). By the time of his first exhibition, in 1921, he was developing towards abstraction, but it was not until 1924 that he found his own style in a series of paintings of lines, curved and straight, against a white ground. He also published caricatures. His work was influenced throughout his life by Kandinsky, Klee and in fact the whole spirit of the Bauhaus.

Negret Duenas, Edgar. Colombian sculptor, b. 1920 in Popayán. After training at the Academy in Cali from 1938 to 1943, Negret worked in Popayán until 1948. In 1949 he moved to New York, where he studied metal techniques at the Sculpture Center, and in 1951 he went on to Paris. In 1952 he travelled through Spain and was deeply impressed by the work of Antonio Gaudí. During a visit to Palma de Mallorca in 1953, he created a series of objects which he called *Magical Apparatuses*. In 1955 he was given a grant to enable him to continue his studies at the New School of Social Research in New York. His most recent works are constructed from curved or folded sheets of aluminium which are screwed together and painted. The *Masks* and *Navigators*, which were shown at the Fourth Documenta exhibition in Kassel, are typical of this phase. Negret is now living in Bogotá.

Carmen Ortega Ricaurte. *Diccionario de artistas en Colombia*, Bogotá 1965.

Nemes, Endre. Hungarian painter and graphic artist, b. 1909. After working in Czechoslovakia until 1940 Nemes moved to Sweden, where he taught at Valand's School of Art in Gothenburg from 1947 to 1955. During his formative years Nemes was impressed by Cubism, Surrealism and the Bohemian Baroque, and on this basis he evolved a highly personal and imaginative art form involving an intricate system of symbols and splendid luminous colour schemes. The macabre and visionary *Harlequin* and *Clown* pictures of the 1940s were followed by works in which brightly coloured geometrical or organic forms are arranged in a more spontaneous manner to produce Expressionistic compositions. The luminosity of Nemes' colours is seen to its best advantage in enamel paintings such as the clock in Västertorp, Stockholm, which he decorated with the signs of the zodiac in 1951. Four years later Nemes decorated the façade of the Burgher's House at Högbrotorp, Gothenburg, with marble intarsia. His graphic oeuvre consists of aquatints, lithographs and monotypes; he has also designed a number of important stage sets.

A. Oldenburg (ed.). *Endre Nemes*, Stockholm 1955.

Neo-Dada Organizer. This Tokyo-based group was formed in 1960 by Genpei Akasegawa, Shusaku Arakawa, Ushio Shinohara, Masunobu Yoshimura *et al.* It presented a Dadaistic rebellion, as its tag indicates. It was mainly active at the 'Independent' shows and sometimes made demonstrations on the street or the beach. In 1963 it dispersed when the 'Independent' was discontinued because it was considered too drastic.

Zenei no Michi (*The Road to the Avant-Garde*), including a brief history of Japanese *avant-garde* by Yusuke Nakahara, Tokyo 1967.

Neo-Impressionism. In his book *From Eugène Delacroix to Neo-Impressionism* (1899), Paul Signac defined the Neo-Impressionist painters as 'those who have revived and since 1886 developed the technique called Divisionism in employing the optic mixture of tones and colours as a means of expression'. The aim of the Divisionist technique, in which pure colours are put down on the canvas side by side in small dabs, was to achieve greater luminosity than could be got by the mixture of tones on the palette: in Divisionist painting the mixture of tones is optical and there is therefore no loss of luminosity. Divisionism was based on the scientific theories of colour described by M. E. Chevreul in his *De la Loi Simultane des Couleurs*, 1839, and by the American physicist O. N. Rood, whose *Modern Chromatics* was published in 1880. Neo-Impressionism can thus be seen as an extension and rationalization of the Impressionists' preoccupation with light and it can even be seen as an attempt to put painting on a scientific basis.

The leading figures in Neo-Impressionism were Paul Signac and Georges Seurat, and the start of the movement can be dated to the foundation in 1884 of the Salon des Indépendants (reconstituted the next year as the Société des Artistes Indépendants) as a result of the exclusion of many of the *avant-garde* artists from the official Salon that year. At the Indépendants in 1884 Seurat showed his huge painting *Une Baignade* (London, National Gallery); Signac saw it there and was struck by its dull colouring, the result of Seurat's retention of earth colours in his palette. But apart from this, Signac was immensely impressed and later wrote, 'The understanding of the law of contrast, the methodical separation of elements: light, shade, local colours and the interaction of colours . . . give this canvas its perfect harmony.'

Signac introduced Seurat to the works of the Impressionists and the two of them soon developed the Divisionist technique described above. From this time, too, their paintings were carried out according to the laws of simultaneous contrast of tones (light and dark), of colours (warm and cold), of line (rising or descending), and in 1890 Seurat summarized his aesthetic theories in a letter to the writer Maurice Beaubourg: 'Aesthetic: Art is harmony. Harmony is the analogy of contraries, the analogy of similarities in tone (*ton*), colour (*teinte*), and line considered under the aspect of the dominant one and under the influence of lighting in gay, calm, or sad combinations. The contraries are: in tone, a lighter, more luminous one in place of a darker; in colour, complementaries, that is, a certain red opposed to its complementary, red-green, orange-blue, yellow-violet etc.; in line, those making a right-angle. Gaiety, in tone is obtained through the use of dominant luminosity; in colour, of prevailing warmth; in line, through those above the horizontal. Calmness, in tone is the equality of light and dark; in colour, of warm and cool; and the horizontal for line. Sadness, in tone is prevailing dark; in colour, a prevailing cool one; and in line, directions downward from the horizontal. Technique: When we admit the phenomena of the duration of luminous impressions on the retina, synthesis imposes itself as a result. The means for expression is the optic mixture of tones and colours (according to the placing and the way the colours are lighted, by sun, oil lamp, gas, etc.), that is to say, the mixture of lights and their reactions (shadows) following the laws of contrast, diminution, and irradiation. The frame is in harmony opposed to that of the tones, colours, and lines of the picture.'

Following these theories, Seurat and Signac produced some of the great masterpieces of late nineteenth-century painting and, perhaps surprisingly in view of their scientific approach, works like *La Cirque* by Seurat (1890–1) or the amazing portrait of *Félix Fénéon* (1890) by Signac are vibrant, expressive and pulsing with life as well as possessing an imposing monumentality.

François Maret. *Les Peintres Luministes*, Brussels 1944.
John Rewald. *Post-Impressionism: from van Gogh to Gauguin*, New York 1962.

Neon sculpture. Art involving the use of light increased in the 1950s and 1960s after a dormant period following early experiments in the first decades of the twentieth century. It functions in a variety of contexts—kinetic art, Pop Art and formal, abstract structures. Neon and fluorescent light, based on similar principles of illumination, are comparable in being shaped by relatively thin tubes, having numerous colour possibilities, and carrying commercial associations. In Pop Art, neon has been used for commercial imagery and environmental effects by such artists as George Segal and Robert Indiana. In a more sculptural mode, it has been notably developed by Chryssa, whose work was stimulated by an interest in the commercial lighting and advertising of Times Square, New York, and in letters and words. Her use of neon, dating from 1962, presents both monochrome and polychrome illumination, subtle lighting sequences, repeated forms usually boxed in Plexiglass, and an interest in the process by exposed electrical parts. More non-objective and environmental effects exist in the fluorescent light arrangements of Dan Flavin, who began using light in 1962 and works with unaltered standard and commercially available fluorescent tubes. Other neon artists residing in the United States include Stephen Antonakos, Ben Berns and Billy Apple.

Elizabeth C. Baker. 'The Light Brigade', *Art News* LXVI, New York, March 1967.
Athena T. Spear. 'Sculptured Light', *Art International* XI, December 1967.

Neri, Manuel. American sculptor, b. 1930 in Sanger, California. He studied in San Francisco and became a prominent West Coast figure in the arts. He started as an Abstract Expressionist painter, but then turned to sculpture. From a few pieces of funk art, his work developed into figure sculpture of a disturbingly morbid tenor. He used plaster which he left somewhat rough, but which he coloured attractively. In about 1966 Neri's work underwent an abrupt change:

he abandoned his Expressionistic style and produced geometric constructions.

Nesch, Rolf. German-Norwegian graphic and experimental artist, b. 1893 in Oberesslingen, Württemberg. In 1907 Nesch embarked on an apprenticeship in Heidesheim to train as a decorative painter. From 1909 to 1912 he attended the School of Arts and Crafts in Stuttgart and, upon completion of his studies, went to Dresden as a painter's assistant. In 1913–14 he studied at the Dresden Academy and made contact with E. L. Kirchner and the other members of the *Brücke*. From 1914 to 1918 he served with the German forces. After the war he met Kokoschka and in 1924 studied the art of printing under Kirchner in Frauenkirch/Davos. In 1929 he went to live in Hamburg, where he joined the Hamburg Secession, and in 1933 emigrated to Norway, where he visited E. Munch. In 1943 Nesch was involved in a street accident, which left his left side paralysed. In 1946 he became a Norwegian citizen and since 1951 has been living in Aal in Hallingdal, Norway.

In the course of his career Nesch has progressed from Expressionism to a highly individual style based on extremely simple pictorial structures. Throughout his career he has revealed a marked preference for cycles. Thus, the aquatints, which he produced between 1931 and 1936, were all executed in groups. Shortly after 1937 Nesch created his first material pictures by soldering copper wires to the printing plates which he used for his metal prints. Later he varied this technique by working coloured glass, different kinds of stone, stamped metal, wire mesh and nails into the plates. With this new technique, which constitutes a definite advance on the collage, Nesch overcame the limitations of the traditional painting and art print, which merely produce an illusion of reality. The reality which he has created is entirely new.

Alfred Hentzen. *Rolf Nesch: Graphik. Materialbilder*, Stuttgart 1960.
Exhibition catalogue, *Rolf Nesch*, Akademie der Künste, Berlin 1966.

Nesjar, Carl. Norwegian painter, b. 1920. From 1927 to 1948 Nesjar lived primarily in the United States. From 1936 to 1938 he was a student at the Pratt Institute in Brooklyn and from 1940 to 1943 at the School of Arts and Crafts in Oslo. In 1947 he studied the history of art under Meyer Shapiro at Columbia University, New York. Nesjar has paid frequent visits to France, where he made contact with Picasso in 1957.

For his landscapes, which have become progressively more abstract, Nesjar uses dark colours; he has also produced a number of coloured graphic works. Nesjar is extremely versatile. Apart from painting, he works as a lecturer and journalist, and

makes cultural films. Between 1956 and 1958 he created decorations in aerated concrete for the new government building in Oslo. In 1961 he created similar decorations in Barcelona, where he worked from designs made by Picasso.

Neue Sachlichkeit (New Objectivity). In 1923 G. F. Hartlaub, the director of the Kunsthalle in Mannheim, arranged an exhibition whose purpose was to show the development of postwar painting. He himself gave the exhibition the title *Neue Sachlichkeit*, explaining that the expression 'ought really to apply as a label for the new realism bearing a socialist flavour. It is related to the general contemporary feeling in Germany of resignation and cynicism after a period of exuberant hopes . . . Cynicism and resignation are the negative side of *Neue Sachlichkeit*; the positive side expresses itself in the enthusiasm for immediate reality as a result of a desire to take things entirely objectively, on a material basis, without immediately investing them with ideal implications.'

The characteristics of this new Realism are an exact and straightforward three-dimensional depiction of the subject matter, very unlike the Expressionists' destruction of form, and a return to the small easel picture, in accordance with the new conception of the minuteness of reality.

The most important exponents of the New Objectivity were Otto Dix and Georg Grosz. Grosz (1893–1959) was primarily a draughtsman; even before the war his drawings expressed what he described as his 'profound disgust for life', a disgust made even stronger by his experience both of military service and of civilian life during the war years. His drawings, with their nervous, thin and childlike lines, of the corrupt officers, the mutilated soldiers and the greedy civilians indulging in debauchery while others suffered, appeared in *Die Neue Jugend* and the *Second Grosz Portfolio* in 1916–17.

Otto Dix (b. 1891) was, unlike Grosz, primarily a painter. His disgust with postwar society also found its outlet in Dada. The clarity of his paintings is achieved through the use of tempera, while their brilliance of colour is strangely at odds with the 'ugliness' of their subject matter.

The problem of evil, and of man's existence in a postwar world, first described by Dix and Grosz, was later treated in a more philosophical fashion by Carl Hofer and Max Beckmann. Lesser artists who may also be considered adherents of the New Objectivity included Heinrich Davringhausen, Kurt Günther, Alexander Kanoldt (a former member of the Munich *Neue Künstlervereinigung*) and Georg Schrimpf.

Nevelson, Louise. Russian-American sculptress, b. 1900 in Kiev. She left Russia with her family in 1905, settling in Rockland, Maine. After she married in 1920 she moved to New York where she studied painting and drawing as well as voice and drama. It was not until the end of the decade that she began to pursue her career in the visual arts more seriously, studying at the Art Students' League and in 1931 with Hans Hofmann in Munich. When she returned to the United States, she and Ben Shahn assisted Diego Rivera on his mural for the New Workers' School. The following year she started exhibiting in various galleries but was not given a one-man show until 1941. During this period her works show various influences ranging from the Futurist dynamics of Boccioni to the simple pure forms of Brancusi. Her works were not actively sought after until the mid-1950s when the Whitney Museum of American Art acquired *Black Majesty* (1955), a large horizontal arrangement of geometric forms in wood. This purchase was succeeded in the following two years by the Brooklyn Museum's acquisition of *First Personage* and the Museum of Modern Art's of *Sky Cathedral*. In the late 1950s she began her 'sculptured walls'—large arrangements of boxes filled with geometric forms or elements inspired by everyday or industrial objects and painted in a single hue (*Homage to 6,000,000*, 1964, painted wood, New York, Jewish Museum). By 1966 the sculptress began working in a greater variety of materials—plastic, Plexiglass, lucite, magnesium, aluminium—arranging her simple geometric forms in more open, less compact compositions, with none of the *horror vacui* seen in her works of 1955–65 (*Offering* 1966, aluminium and black epoxy enamel, New York, Pace Gallery).

Colette Roberts. *Nevelson*, Paris 1964.
John Gordon. *Louise Nevelson*, New York 1967.

Nevinson, Christopher Richard Wynne. British painter, etcher and lithographer, b. 1889 in London; d. 1946 in London. Nevinson was the son of the author and war correspondent H. W. Nevinson. He studied painting at the St. John's Wood School of Art and the Slade School, where he was discouraged by Henry Tonks, and in Paris. While in Paris, 1912–13, he shared a studio with Modigliani. He was included in the 'Post-Impressionist and Futurist' exhibition at the Doré Galleries in 1913. He met and became friendly with the Futurist Severini, and through him with other Futurist painters. When the author of the *Futurist Manifesto*, Marinetti, came to England in 1913, Nevinson spoke in French at a dinner in his honour. The association with Marinetti continued in 1914 when the latter visited England again. With Nevinson, he published a statement headed 'Vital English Art' which became known as the *English Futurist Manifesto*.

The original *Futurist Manifesto* of 1909 had attacked aspects of traditionalism important in an Italian context. The English manifesto undertook to do the same for England, but the objects attacked, which must have been specified by Nevinson, were already of little consequence. Marinetti and Nevinson appended the names of Wyndham Lewis and seven other artists to the manifesto without permission and were denounced by them for doing so. In consequence Nevinson was left in an isolated position.

In 1914 Nevinson, who was unfit for active service, joined the Red Cross and was attached to the French Army at Dunkirk. Later he became an RAMC orderly and was invalided out in January 1916. In September–October 1916 he held a one-man exhibition at the Leicester Galleries of pictures painted as a direct result of his experiences in 1914–15. It was a success. The hard and simple faceted style seemed to all serious observers to be exactly adapted to the subject.

In these works painted in 1915–16 Nevinson was certainly using some generalized ideas drawn from Futurism and Cubism, but simultaneous representation was not among them. His knowledge of the angles and facets of Cubist pictures merely helped him to evolve a steely manner of painting (though not without sensitivity and mellowness in the actual handling) the grim events he had observed. These pictures represent Nevinson's greatest contribution to English art. Although he became an official war artist, his drawings of 1917–18 are more conventional. It might be said that in his 1915–16 paintings, Nevinson had not only discharged the burden of what he had seen of war but, with it, all that he had seen of modern art. He was never again to be considered as an advanced artist.

O. Sitwell. *C. R. W. Nevinson*, London 1925.

New Artists' Association. When it came into being in 1909 this association reflected the artistic ideas of Vassily Kandinsky, Alexei Jawlensky and Kandinsky's pupil Gabriele Münter. But their ideas were not static and, when these three artists continued to develop, the association was unable to keep pace. Faced with Kandinsky's new abstract phase, which set in in 1910, the majority of members fell back on a form of art compounded of Munich *Jugendstil* and expressive Fauvism. The ensuing dispute led to the secession of the *Blauer Reiter* group in 1911. Marianne von Werefkin, Adolf Erbslöh, Alexander Kanoldt and Alfred Kubin were also founder members of the association. Paul Baum, Carl Hofer, Vladimir von Bechtejeff, Erna Bossi, Moissey Kogan and the dancer Sacharoff joined for a brief period in 1909. In 1910 two French artists, Pierre Girieud and Henri Le Fauconnier, became members and were followed in 1911 by Franz Marc and Otto Fischer. After Kandinsky's departure, Fischer became the spokesman for the association. The first exhibition to be held under the auspices of the New Artists' Association was staged in 1909, the second in 1910. Both were housed in H. Thannhauser's Moderne

Galerie before being sent on a tour of German cities. The second exhibition included works by various guest artists: David and Vladimir Burljuk, Wassili Denisoff and Alexander Mogilewsky from Russia; Braque, Picasso, Rouault, Derain, Vlaminck and van Dongen from Paris; the sculptors Scharf and Hoetger from Germany.

New English Art Club. This was an exhibition society founded by artists acquainted with French art and institutions, and out of sympathy with the Royal Academy. Their style was Impressionist and they favoured the elective system of the French Salon. The first exhibition took place in 1886: the rules were drawn up by Fred Brown. Wilson Steer was a founder member. During the first ten years Sickert and Whistler joined; later members included Beer-bohm, D. S. McColl, G. Moore, McEvoy, Orpen, L. Pissarro, Augustus and Gwen John, Conder, Shannon, W. Rothenstein, Fry and Paul Nash. It was agreed by contemporary critics that the club played a vital role in English painting from about 1886 to 1910. According to Sickert the style was a method of 'painting with a clear and solid mosaic of thick paint in a light key': the vision he thought derived from Impressionism, but the subject matter was more traditional to England—more of the 'august site' *motif* and the 'smartened-up young person' *motif*. Monet, Morisot and Degas exhibited as guests. Selection of all works at the annual exhibition was by a jury elected by all intending exhibitors from a list of the members and others who had shown the previous year. The style did change over the years (Fry notes 'draughtsmanship' rather than 'Impressionism' in 1906). However, the change was not rapid enough: Frank Rutter founded the Allied Artists' Association (without jury) in 1908, Fry's Post-Impressionist exhibitions (1910 and 1912) were without New English Art Club co-operation, and the Camden Town Group formed round Sickert, Gilman and Gore in 1910, which soon led to the foundation of the dominant London Group. The London Group still exists.

Newman, Barnett. American painter, b. 1905 in New York; d. 1970 in New York. Newman studied in New York at the Art Students' League (1922–6) with Duncan Smith (1877–1934), John Sloan and William von Schlegel (1877–1950), went to City College, New York, then did graduate work at Cornell University. In 1947, along with William Baziotes, Mark Rothko and Robert Motherwell, he helped found a school on Eighth Street, New York, called 'Subjects of the Artist', from which the famous 'Club' meetings of the Abstract Expressionists developed during the early 1950s. Newman was an associate editor of *Tiger's Eye* (1947–8), a magazine published by these New York painters and dealing

with the mythological and aesthetic themes that preoccupied them. With Adolph Gottlieb and Mark Rothko, Newman rebelled against both American regionalism and European geometric abstraction early in the 1940s. Both were held to be academic solutions to the problem of finding a viable contemporary subject matter for painting. Without turning to European models, Newman sought inspiration in the archetypal creative force and vitality of North-West Coast Indians and in pre-Columbian art. He maintained this interest in the basic absolutes of feeling and form, and always avoided an associative use of symbols.

Although Newman's approach to subject matter was, therefore, always reductive, early in his career (1944–6) he was involved in the emotional content of the act of painting itself, avoiding prior mechanical or logical structuring. The destruction of the void concerned him at first (*Pagan Void*, 1946, and *Genetic Moment*, 1947, both New York, Coll. Mrs. Annalee Newman), and his works were full of darkly eclipsed circular forms and streaks of scrubbed light, with titles evoking, but not illustrating, the myth of primordial creation. Evidence of Newman's concern for declaring a space and for establishing a presence appears, for example, in the seminal *Onement I* (1948, New York, coll. of artist). In this painting a band of cadmium red, running vertically down the centre of a rectangular plum-coloured field, is seen not as a line but as an area where edges meet, declaring a vital space that excludes all forms of representation or symbolism. Newman's characteristically grand, empty fields, often saturated with intense colour and inflected with one or several vertical stripes of other colours, developed out of this small early work. His compositions were not organized hierarchically, but deductively, with the thin bands echoing only the framing edges, rather than being related internally. These bands not only acknowledge the shape of the support, but also help to define a broad field of colour by their varied phasing of contrasting hues and values in the areas around them. This forces the viewer to concentrate on the *spatial* experience of sheer colour, perceived in purely optical terms. A picture such as *Adam* (1951–2, New York, Coll. Ben Heller), with its close-valued areas of brown-maroon and scarlet, or *Cathedra* (1951, Pasadena, California, Museum) demonstrates this notion of powerfully affecting colour space. This new attitude towards composition and forms exerted an important influence on such younger painters as Larry Poons and Frank Stella.

The artist's hand remains evident in Newman's paintings, where, through a highly reduced formal vocabulary, an effect of great spiritual impact is achieved, with a heroic, universalistic conception still the basis for his work.

Harold Rosenberg. 'Barnett Newman: The Living Rectangle', *The Anxious Object: Art Today and Its Audience*, New York 1964.

Lawrence Alloway. Catalogue, *Bernard Newman: The Stations of the Cross, Lema Sabachthani*, Solomon R. Guggenheim Museum, New York 1966.
Thomas Hess. *Barnett Newman*, New York 1969.

New materials. During the first half of the twentieth century, the principle was firmly established that any material is suitable for art, including discarded junk materials, industrial materials, and plant and animal life, which have brought corresponding changes in style and technique. Sculpture and constructions have been particularly affected by the availability and acceptance of new materials. The beginnings of the use of discarded materials, or materials taken from another, pre-existing context, are in Cubist collage, which eventually developed into assemblages of all sorts, including so-called junk art, and blurred the traditional distinctions between painting and sculpture. Among industrial products, probably the most significant new materials have been various metals, synthetics such as plastics, and electrical media. The use of these materials has led to such new possibilities as welded metal sculpture, in contrast to traditional cast or carved forms; to polychrome, transparent or soft plastic sculpture; and to electric-light art, much of which has been integral to the development of kinetic art. In painting, a notable new medium has been acrylic, or plastic, paint, which, beginning with the late 1950s, has allowed stained-canvas painting, in which the paint can be stained directly into the canvas rather than applied to the surface, as in oil painting. As the art of the mid-century has increasingly moved away from both representational and traditional abstract art, towards environmental and systems art, the incorporation of such natural media as earth and plant or animal life has appeared in works where processes and temporal effects dominate and in which rigid boundaries—of materials, time or space —no longer exist.

Hubert M. Percy. *New Materials in Sculpture*, London 1965.

New Objectivity—*see* **Neue Sachlichkeit**

New Realism (*Nouveau Réalisme*). The art of the twentieth century is characterized by its conscious defiance of traditional forms. This has been supported by critical activity challenging the basic concepts of art itself. As a result, since the Second World War a very wide sanction has been granted in matters of art, and various forms have been presented as of superior importance, deeper realism, or greater contemporary significance. Though presented as positive in outlook, there is usually an undercurrent of rejection of other modes considered to be exhausted.

One such movement which has been identified by name was put forward by the critic Pierre Restany. In 1960 he published a manifesto in Milan under the title of *The New Realism*. This was a grouping, from a critical point of view, of a number of artists who were rejecting, in their various ways, the 'painting', and particularly the detached and more pointless abstracts, of the time. In its place they endeavoured to make use of real material and existing artefacts assembled directly into the art object. With Dada as an acknowledged precedent, these objects were chosen mainly from contemporary manufactures, often in a broken or scrap-heap condition.

In 1961 Restany organized an exhibition at his Galerie J in Paris, called *40 Degrees Above Dada*, which included among others the work of Armand, Tinguely, César and Christo. Loosely united in a common outlook, these artists did not become an organized group, though each continued to develop the various possibilities of the method. Armand produced 'accumulations' of industrial artefacts repeated in orderly patterns. César produced 'sculpture' using power presses to crush scrap metal into solid forms. Tinguely gave mechanical scrap a rebirth by reuniting it into working engines of fascinating complexity. Christo worked on his real objects by concealment, making packages by wrapping them up in polythene sheeting laced together with metal wire. His scope developed to include buildings, and later a large area (one million square feet) of rocky coastline in Australia.

The influence of these rather spectacular works has been extensive, sanctioning the use of anything as material for art. The use of rubbish, particularly scrap metal in a kind of collage Constructivism, has given rise to the term 'Junk art'.

New York School. The New York School encompasses a broad and diverse group of artists who are often also variously grouped under the headings of Abstract Expressionism, Abstract Impressionism and Action Painting. The difficulty of classification, in fact, reflects a principal characteristic of the artists of the New York School: strong and innovative individualistic expression, resulting in independent styles rather than a single group style. The artists were unified only loosely—by such circumstances as their common urban environment of New York, personal interchange and communication, and a sense of solidarity in rejecting many past traditions and creating a strong, original, American *avant-garde* painting that eventually had broad international effects.

The development of the New York School began in the early 1940s. It was stimulated by a number of contemporary occurrences, including the opening of Hans Hofmann's art school in New York, the exhibition of *avant-garde* European art by Peggy Guggenheim, and especially the introduction of Surrealism to the United States, both from exhibitions and from the immigration of many of the artists themselves from Europe during the Second World War. The Surrealists especially influential for the New York

School were Miró, Masson and Matta, whose work inspired a reliance on the unconscious, spontaneity and chance in many of the New York painters. At the same time, other European art was also an important stimulation—especially Cubism and the painting of Kandinsky—although the New York artists transformed all these sources into forceful, individual statements. Particularly important among the artists beginning their major work in the early 1940s were Hans Hofmann, Arshile Gorky, Robert Motherwell, Willem de Kooning, Mark Rothko, Clyfford Still and Jackson Pollock—who probably provided the most marked impact of the New York *avant-garde*. After around 1947 came a turn in the development of the New York School, with the addition of such painters as Philip Guston, Bradley Walker Tomlin and Franz Kline, and with a trend towards the huge canvas and black-and-white painting. Other artists often included in the New York School are William Baziotes, Adolph Gottlieb, Barnett Newman, Jack Tworkow and Ad Reinhardt. Sometimes the artists are roughly divided into two groups: those who were 'action painters', such as Pollock, de Kooning and Kline, interested mainly in the gestural effect and the qualities of the brush and of paint, and those, such as Rothko, Motherwell, Reinhardt and Still, who were more interested in colour fields and a quieter suggestiveness. None the less, the artists shared an interest in largely rejecting representational images, in working with a large, environmental canvas and in presenting the act of painting itself as the essential aspect of their work. Although in the 1950s a second generation of the New York School emerged, much of the newer work seemed derivative, and the movement was largely spent by the late 1950s.

Harold Rosenberg. 'The American Action Painters', *Art News* LI, New York, December 1952.

Clement Greenberg. 'American Type Painting', *Partisan Review* XXII, No. 2, New York 1955.

Catalogue, *American Abstract Expressionists and Imagists*, Solomon R. Guggenheim Museum, New York 1961.

Artforum IV, No. 1, New York, September 1965. Special issue on Abstract Expressionism.

Maurice Tuchman (ed.). Catalogue, *The New York School: The First Generation; Paintings of the 1940s and 1950s*, Los Angeles County Museum of Art, Los Angeles 1965.

Nicholson, Ben. British painter, b. 1894 in Denham, Buckinghamshire. Nicholson is the son of Sir William Nicholson, whose delicate refinement of tone he has inherited. He spent one term at the Slade in 1911, but otherwise had no formal art education. Before the war he was briefly connected with Vorticism. He held his first one-man show in 1922, by which time his work was already showing a sophisticated understanding of modern French painting, and, though perfectly individual, it is perhaps closest in spirit to the formal Cubism of Juan Gris or the Purists Corbusier and Ozenfant. He produced his first abstract painting in 1923–4, but his work has never been exclusively abstract, and throughout the twenties he continued to produce a series of semi-Cubist still lifes of a kind that have remained the basis of much of his painting ever since. In 1927 and 1928 his discovery with Christopher Wood of the Cornish naïve painter Alfred Wallis turned his interest to landscape. In these Cornish and Cumbrian landscapes the sophistication of his understanding of Cubist picture arrangement is disguised but given new freedom by the assumed roughness of the naïve painter. In the thirties he returned to pure abstraction and produced in 1933 his first painted relief. He also continued to produce still lifes, sometimes very formal and of great elegance. He was at this time a member of the *7 & 5 Group* and of *Unit One*. From 1933 to 1935 he was also a member of the French *Abstraction-Création* group and had contact with most of the leading Continental abstract artists, especially Mondrian and Gabo, both of whom spent some time in England before the war. With Gabo and J. L. Martin, he produced *Circle* in 1937. The contact with Mondrian was most important, and through his influence the Cubist still lifes developed into the great series of formal abstracts of the late thirties (*Painting*, 1937, London, Tate Gallery). His reliefs took on a new formality and austerity at this time. There are also a number of paintings in which line, sometimes incised on a dark ground, is almost entirely liberated of descriptive purpose and runs in free arabesque over the picture's surface. In 1939 he moved to Cornwall. There he began a new series of landscapes, and throughout the forties landscape occasionally appears in his work. Basically, however, his style was formed in the thirties. Since that time his main works have been reliefs with simple circular or rectangular *motifs*, or else highly formal semi-abstract paintings which are in their arrangement essentially Cubist, shapes arranged in overlapping planes to create a shallow space. In the fifties he began to introduce into this arrangement the wandering arabesque line that had first appeared in the thirties. Sometimes descriptive or sometimes there for its own sake, it asserts the presence of the picture plane against the shallow space of the picture, and it displays his marvellous draughtsmanship. In the sixties the reliefs and the paintings have come together. The shallow space of the paintings is expressed by the actual depth of the reliefs. These works are of quite exquisite refinement, and refinement is perhaps the keynote of all Nicholson's work: refinement upon a basically Cubist pictorial structure to a point of formal elegance and precision perhaps reached by no other twentieth-century painter.

Herbert Read. *Ben Nicholson*, London 1956.
R. Alley. *Ben Nicholson*, London 1963.

Nicholson, Winifred. British painter, b. 1893 in Oxford. The first wife of Ben Nicholson, from 1931 to 1935 she was a member of the *7 & 5 Group*; in Paris from 1934 on her friends in the *avant-garde* included Gabo and Giacometti (whose sculptures she photographed for *Circle*). Reminiscences of Mondrian, with whom she fled France, provide valuable insights. From 1934 to 1937 her work was largely abstract; otherwise characteristic are freely formalized landscapes and flower pieces close to the moods and light of nature.

Jasia Reichardt. Catalogue, *Art in Britain 1930–1940*, Marlborough Gallery, London 1965.

Nikos (Nikos Kessanlis). Greek painter, b. 1930 in Thessaloniki. He studied in Athens and spent some time in Rome; since 1959 he has lived in Paris. An energetic and inventive painter, he has passed through a successful Informal period, during which he made intense use of the relief. During recent years he has mainly used the technique and impressions of photography.

Nivola, Constantino. American sculptor, b. 1911 in Orani, Sardinia. As a boy Nivola learned the crafts of plastering, masonry and woodcutting. He studied art at the Istituto Superiore d'Arte in Monza, Italy (1930–6), where his teacher was Marino Marini, who was the first to interest him seriously in sculpture. From 1936 to 1939 Nivola was art director of the Olivetti Company, and during these years he also held several exhibitions of painting and sculpture in Milan. In 1939 he went to New York, where he held his first one-man exhibition of sculpture in 1950. From 1953 to 1957 he was director of the Design Workshop at Harvard University in Cambridge, Massachusetts, and from 1961 to 1963 he taught at Columbia University in New York.

Nivola's primary interest and achievement was in relief sculpture, although he also made free-standing pieces. He executed a number of commissions for large architectural reliefs, including one for the Olivetti Company showroom (1953–4) in New York, but also worked on a much smaller and more intimate scale, as in a series of small terra-cottas of landscapes and seascapes in the early 1960s. He used nature imagery in a spontaneous, free style, frequently fusing it with figural suggestions (*Summer Day*, 1965, bronze, New York, Byron Gallery). Nivola was especially known for his reliefs in reinforced plaster; these had rich textural surfaces formed with sand and were often painted in bright colours (*Isposso*, 1953, reinforced plaster with sand, New York, Peridot Gallery).

Sam Hunter. 'Constantino Nivola', *Art in America* XLIII, February 1955.
'Nivola Between Sculpture and Architecture', *Zodiac* No. 4, Milan 1959.

Noël, Georges. French painter, b. 1924 in Béziers. After completing his classical and technological studies Noël carried out research into turboreactors up to 1955. He then became a full-time painter.

Noël is an informal artist and uses a calligraphic technique. In many of his compositions the pictorial lines and forms appear against grounds that are virtually monochrome.

Noguchi, Isamu. American sculptor, b. 1904 in Los Angeles. He spent his childhood in Japan (1906–17). His early artistic training came from Onorio Ruotolo at the Leonardo da Vinci Art School in New York (1924), but he received his most significant direction from Brancusi, with whom he studied while a Guggenheim Fellow in Paris (1927). This influence can be seen as early as 1928 in *Foot-Tree* (brass, coll. of artist) and continued through the 1930s, as revealed in his 1932 *Miss Expanding Universe* (aluminium, Toledo, Museum of Art). In the 1930s he worked for the WPA; his experience with this project led to his sculptured mural of coloured cement on carved brick, *History of Mexico* (1936, Mexico City). Two years later he won his first competition—reliefs for the Associated Press Building at Rockefeller Plaza. These bronze sculptures, basically Cubistic in form, reveal certain affinities to Picasso's work, though Noguchi worked with heavier, broader, less faceted planes. In the 1940s he re-affirmed his preference for working with stone and again returned to a Brancusi-like fluidity of form (*Leda*, 1942, alabaster, coll. of artist). Since he was working in New York, the most readily available marble was in slab form. The given material therefore imposed itself on works such as *Kouros* (1945, New York, Museum of Modern Art) which was exhibited in the Museum of Modern Art's exhibition of 1946, *Fourteen Americans*. The interconnecting slabs of abstract shapes existing in and creating areas around space exemplify for Noguchi the essence of sculpture which is for him 'the perception of space, the continuum of our existence'. In addition to his sculptures he concerned himself with, among other creative occupations, theatre and costume designs, garden plans and playground facilities. He became involved with theatre and ballet as early as 1935 and throughout the 1940s and 1950s created designs for Martha Graham, George Balanchine, Merce Cunningham and Sir John Gielgud. His playground and garden plans include a memorial at Keio University in Japan, two memorial bridges at Hiroshima, the United Nations Playground, the UNESCO Gardens in Paris and the 5-acre sculpture gardens for the National Museum in Jerusalem. In the late 1950s his sculptures fall into two classes—those of anodised aluminium which deny weight and substance, as *The Kite* (1958, coll. of artist) and such monolithic works in stone as *Integral* (1957–8, marble, New York, Whitney Museum of American Art)—a piece which was produced for an exhibition at the Stable Gallery in 1959, a show which, in the words of the artist, 'was in the nature of a homage to Brancusi, and recapitulated sculptural values I associated with him'. Both affinities, for weight and weightlessness, are combined in works of the 1960s. His *Vertical Man* (1964, New York, Cordier & Estrom, Inc.) employs a large Cubistic block of stone hanging over and seemingly suspended upon a vertical plank of wood.

I. Noguchi and R. Buckminster Fuller. *Isamu Noguchi: A Sculptor's World*, New York 1968.

Nolan, Sidney. Australian painter, b. 1917 in Melbourne. Nolan took up painting full-time in 1938. His earliest works reflect at a distance *avant-garde* European painting of the thirties. At his first exhibition, held in Melbourne in 1940, one of the viewers was so outraged that he threw green paint over the exhibits. In 1942, while in the army, Nolan painted his first backwoods landscapes, exhibited in Melbourne in 1943, and in 1946 he began the first *Ned Kelly* series by which he really made his name. The *Fraser and Bracefell* series was exhibited in 1948, and the *Explorer* paintings of Burke and Wills in 1950, together with his first desert landscapes. He himself travelled to Europe for the first time in that year. His pictures had preceded him, as the *Ned Kelly* series was shown in Paris the year before. He went back to Australia and painted the extraordinary pictures of drought in the hinterland, then finally returned to Europe in 1953. He worked first in Italy, then in Greece, and has travelled in Africa and Abyssinia, but as well as subjects drawn from those countries he has continued to paint Australian subjects, though in an increasingly personal and poetic way. His fame will probably ultimately rest on the Australian paintings of 1947–53, for in these he deliberately set out to produce an Australian mythology and was peculiarly successful in creating a pictorial idiom to express it.

Catalogue, *Sidney Nolan: Paintings from 1947 to 1957*, Whitechapel Gallery, London 1957.
Colin MacInnes and Bryan Robertson. *Sidney Nolan*, London 1961.
Catalogue, *Sidney Nolan, African Journey*, Marlborough Fine Art, London 1963.
Elwyn Lynn. *Sidney Nolan: Myth and Imagery*, London 1967.

Noland, Kenneth. American painter, b. 1924 in Ashville, North Carolina. He studied art with Ilya Bolotowsky (b. 1907) at Black Mountain College in North Carolina (1946), and with Ossip Zadkine at the Zadkine School of Sculpture in Paris (1948–9). He taught at the Institute of Contemporary Art and at Catholic University, both in Washington, D.C., as well as at Emma Lake University in Saskatchewan, Canada. Noland's first one-man exhibition was held in 1949 at the Galerie Creuze in Paris, and his work was subsequently shown widely in the United States and in such international exhibitions as the Seattle World's Fair (1962) and the Venice Biennale (1964).

Noland's painting marked a significant departure from the dominating Abstract Expressionist movement in American art by its emphasis on colour, untextured surface and geometric form. An important catalyst for the development of Noland's major style was his introduction, in the early 1950s, to acrylic paints and to the particular way in which they were used by Helen Frankenthaler to stain the canvas. Through this technique, the paint becomes part of the actual picture surface, and if part of the raw canvas is juxtaposed with the painted areas, a visual ambiguity is created between the painted image and its physical support. Like his friend Morris Louis, who began using acrylics at the same time, Noland often made large areas of bare canvas part of the total visual image. Central to the development of his art was the relationship between the image and the size and shape of the canvas. In the late 1950s and early 1960s Noland used the *motif* of concentric, hard-edged rings, precisely centred on a square canvas. Sometimes these rings were ellipsoid and appeared either centred (*Hover*, 1963, Cambridge, Mass., Fogg Art Museum), or above or below centre, creating a laterally symmetrical organization of the canvas. Lateral symmetry was at first retained in Noland's next important structural *motif*, the chevron, which he began to use in 1962. By 1964, however, he had moved the chevrons off centre to create an asymmetrical image. With this *motif* Noland also established a closer relationship between the painted image and the specific size, shape and edge of the canvas. This was accomplished through giving the canvas a diamond shape and having the legs of the chevron paralleling, and sometimes forming, the edges of its two sides (*Away*, 1964, Chicago, Coll. Walter A. Netsch, Jr.). The same fusion of canvas shape and image characterizes the elongated, diamond-shaped canvases of about 1966. In these paintings parallel stripes that rush diagonally across the surface were aligned with two edges of the parallelogram. In about 1967 these stripes lengthened into horizontal bands on extremely long and thin rectangular canvases (*Via Blues*, 1967, New York, André Emmerich Gallery). Although Noland's work is limited formally to few *motifs*, developed in a series, a considerable amount of variation occurs within each. The essentially dynamic configurations of targets, chevrons or extended stripes produce a sense of movement along the bands themselves, while another apparent movement, backward and forward in space, is produced by juxtapositions of the colour. Since the formal structure is relatively simple and repetitive, colour can emerge as dominant, whether juxtaposed with bare canvas or contrasted in adjacent colour bands of the same or different widths.

This emphasis has caused Noland to be categorized as a 'colour painter'. In this respect, as well as for his experiments with the relation of image to canvas, his art was significant in shaping the post-Abstract Expressionist period.

Michael Fried. Catalogue, *Three American Painters: Noland, Olitski, Stella*, Fogg Art Museum, Cambridge (Mass.) 1965.

Nolde, Emil (Emil Hansen). German painter, b. 1867 in Nolde, Schleswig; d. 1956 in Seebüll. Nolde, the son of a farmer, became one of the foremost German Expressionists. During his formative years he did not join any artistic group, and his work is very much a product of his own passionate nature, which always took precedence over considerations of intellectual precision. Although his pictures grew more profound in the course of time, his style remained essentially the same throughout his whole career. There was no real development in the customary sense of the word, and Nolde made no attempt to adapt to changing social conditions. In fact, he remained at all times a dedicated exponent of Expressionism.

After serving an apprenticeship as a furniture designer and cabinet-maker Nolde taught in St. Gallen from 1892 to 1899. In the watercolours which he produced during this period he was already trying to express his impressions of nature in terms of colour. But these were early days, and he had yet to acquire the necessary technique with which to achieve this transformation.

After leaving St. Gallen he joined Stuck's circle in Munich, then went to Dachau to work under Hölzel before visiting Paris in 1900, where he attended the Académie Julian for a short period. The next few years were crucial, for it was in the early 1900s that Nolde evolved his visionary art. Like all the Expressionists he used the system of optical mixtures developed by the Neo-Impressionists. His most important mentors were Munch, van Gogh and Ensor. In 1906 Nolde joined the *Brücke* but left again in the following year without having been influenced to any significant extent. He caused a considerable stir with his religious pictures, e.g. his *Whitsun Picture* and *The Last Supper* of 1909 and his *Life of Christ* of 1911. In 1910, in Berlin, he discovered the pleasures of big city life and began to paint sensuous figure compositions and rowdy low-life scenes. By this time Nolde was using colour to express layers of being which are inaccessible to the intellect alone. Like most other Expressionists he was fascinated by primitive art, which he discovered on a voyage to New Guinea and which he integrated into numerous drawings and watercolours.

The human being provided Nolde with one of his major themes. The other was furnished by the countryside, especially that of his native Schleswig-Holstein, which he conceived as a daemonic and mythical phenomenon and translated into symbolical compositions of universal import. But, although he undoubtedly elaborated on his original impressions and intensified his colours to a very considerable degree, Nolde never entirely abandoned objectivity. Even his late *Faces* and his *Unpainted Pictures*—a series of highly Expressionistic small prints produced when he was forbidden to paint by the Nazis —retain links with the visible world. Apart from paintings and watercolours Nolde also created a large body of graphic works. Like the graphic works produced by the *Brücke* artists these constitute one of the peaks of Expressionist art.

Max Sauerlandt. *Emil Nolde*, Berlin 1922.
Werner Haftmann. *Emil Nolde*, London and New York 1960.

Nonell y Monturiol, Isidro. Spanish painter, b. 1873 in Barcelona; d. 1911. At first he was influenced by Rusiñol, as is shown by the lyrical Realism of his early work. He later began to illustrate street scenes and incidents from the life of the poorer classes. He visited Paris in 1897. Two years later he exhibited at the dealer Vollard's there, when his pictures showed mainly gypsy girls. In about 1900 he had a 'dark green' period similar to the blue period of Picasso. Because of his subject matter (scenes of poverty) and his left-wing sympathies he had little success until the end of his life.

Nordström, Lars-Gunnar. Finnish painter and sculptor, b. 1924. Nordström is one of the most important exponents of Concrete Art working in Finland today. In his two-dimensional paintings he creates contrasting areas of clear, pure colour. During his early period his pictorial forms were gently modulated, but later his composition became progressively bolder and more simplified. Nordström's sculptures are structurally similar to his paintings.

Nouveau, Henri (Henrik Neugeboren). Painter, musician and writer, b. 1901 in Brasov-Kronstadt, Rumania (formerly Hungary). Nouveau was extremely versatile. After studying music in Berlin (1921–5) and Paris (1925–7), he not only worked as a composer and painter but also took an active interest in geology, psychoanalysis and poetry. After a brief Surrealist period Nouveau evolved a poetic form of geometrical abstract art, which he consistently developed throughout the rest of his life. He produced nearly 700 small-format paintings.

Catalogue, *Henri Nouveau*, Galerie Michel Couturier, Paris 1961.

Nouveau Réalisme—*see* **New Realism**

Novecento Italiano. In 1922 Funi, Marussig, Sironi, Carrà, Rosai, Campigli, Semeghini and Tosi joined together to form the *Novecento Italiano* association, which was officially launched at an assembly held in the Pesaro Gallery in Milan in the following year; Mussolini was one of the speakers. In 1924 after being represented at the Biennale (for which it published a special programme), the association broke up as a result of internal tensions. One of the dissident factions then regrouped to form the *Comitato Direttivo del Novecento Italiano*, whose members included Funi, Marussig, Sironi, Tosi, Salietti and the sculptor A. Wildt. The principal aim of the new committee was the creation of a national artists' association capable of organizing its annual exhibitions. This aim was realized in 1926 when the new *Novecento Italiano* staged its first exhibition in Milan.

The *Novecento Italiano* association set out to revive the large-format, figurative composition of Classical art. It failed to do so. Instead, it produced a purely decorative form of Neo-Classicism. In the course of its development the *Novecento Italiano* also helped to promote official Fascist ideology, and its works were soon identified with the sentimental products of the state propaganda department and with the worst kind of provincial eclecticism.

Novelli, Gastone. Italian painter, b. 1925 in Vienna. Novelli studied politics and the social sciences at the University of Florence up to 1947. He then met Max Bill and began to draw. From 1948 to 1955 he was in Brazil and from 1951 to 1954 taught at the Institute attached to the Art Museum in São Paulo. In 1955 he settled in Rome, and in 1956–7 he and Perilli launched the magazine *L'Esperienza Moderna*. In 1961 Novelli joined the *Continuità* group. He is now living in Rome.

Novelli's works, which reveal the influence of Cy Twombley, come under the general heading of 'calligraphic' painting. They incorporate words, letters, signs and geometric forms and arrangements in a pseudo-infantile manner.

Novembergruppe. This German group was formed around 1918 in Berlin by the leaders of German Expressionism, who were joined by the Berlin Dadaists. The aims of this group and of the Workers' Council were eventually united and incorporated into the Weimar Bauhaus movement. Through the *Novembergruppe* there was a great deal of contact with the artistic developments in France, and Cubism, abstraction, Constructivism and Dada were all represented in exhibitions put on by them. They also embraced the work of modern architects. The group's members were strongly leftist, with socialist ideals; however, by about 1924 the general mood of the public was shifting to the right, and disillusionment began to set in. With public support withdrawn, the group broke up. Its ideals, and the style it had fostered, manifested by a fascination with mechanical progress and the representation of the human figure in the form of a machine, were

to make some impression on the *Neue Sachlichkeit* movement and the development of Social Realism.

Nowosielski, Jerzy. Polish painter, b. 1923 in Cracow. Nowosielski studied at the Academy of Art in Cracow, where he now holds a professorial post. His art was formed partly by the knowledge of philosophical problems which he acquired during the Second World War in a Greek Orthodox monastery and partly by the Polish icon painters, who still exercise their craft in various provincial centres. Later Nowosielski was also influenced by Surrealism and by geometrical abstraction. In his highly individual paintings Nowosielski has applied the intellectual and emotional premises of the Byzantine-Slavonic tradition to the problems posed by the autonomous painterly object and the new figuration of our own day. He has also produced a number of religious polychromes, in which formal experiment is combined with a profound knowledge of the liturgical and dogmatic peculiarities of various rites.

Peinture moderne polonaise: Sources et recherches, Musée Galliera, Paris 1969.

Nul. This is a Dutch artists' association that evolved in 1961 from the *Nederlandse informele groep*, which was itself founded in 1958. Its members include Henk Peeters (b. 1925), Armando (b. 1929) and J. J. Schoonhoven (b. 1914). The aims of the association are similar to those of the *Zero* group, with which it is in close contact. From 1961 to 1965 the association published a magazine, which also appeared under the title *Nul*.

O

Objective Abstractionists. *Objective Abstractions* was the title of an exhibition held in Zwemmer's London Gallery in 1934. Seven artists participated, but in fact only three of them, Roderigo Moynihan, Geoffrey Tibble and Graham Bell, together with Edgar Hubert, who was a member of the group though he did not exhibit, were really abstract painters at the time. The other four, Victor Pasmore, Ceri Richards, Thomas Carr and Ivon Hitchens, were represented by work that was more or less figurative. All the painters were, however, united by their rejection of contemporary European abstract art and in their wish to replace it with something that would be, in their own word, objective. Their aims are put forward in the catalogue through the answers given by each artist to a series of questions. They were fairly unanimous in maintaining that their art had to begin with nature, but that thereafter a picture might develop independently of this initial point of reference and according to an internal logic of its own. The abstract paintings that they produced in 1933 and 1934 (apparently Tibble was the first to turn to this kind of painting, followed by the other three) were freely and openly painted, and quite strikingly resemble British abstract painting of twenty years later. After 1934 Tibble and Moynihan turned to a tighter, more careful style, then in 1926–7 moved away from abstraction. The Euston Road school was in fact the true successor of this movement.

Catalogues: Zwemmer's Gallery, London 1934; Arts Council of Wales, 1962.

Objet Trouvé (found object). *Objets trouvés* were first used in works of art by the German Dadaist painter and author Kurt Schwitters (1887–1948). Schwitters took articles of refuse such as labels, used stamps, old tram tickets, jam-jar lids and worn-out metal utensils, and incorporated them into his collages. By doing so, he transformed these discarded objects into a new pictorial medium. Although worthless as consumer articles, they acquired a new value in pictorial compositions, where they expressed the multifarious aspects of their own existential reality. The exponents of various modern trends—such as Neo-Dada, Surrealism, Pop Art and *Nouveau Réalisme*—have all exploited the associative qualities of the *objet trouvé* in their accumulations and assemblages.

Obrist, Hermann. Swiss sculptor, b. 1863 in Zürich; d. 1927. He was one of the leading members of the applied art movement. He studied in Karlsruhe, Weimar and Paris. In 1892 he started an embroidery workshop in Florence. Later he went to Munich. He was a keen promoter of *art nouveau*.

Ocampo, Miguel. Argentinian painter, architect and diplomat, b. 1922 in Buenos Aires. Although Ocampo studied architecture in Buenos Aires until 1947, he had already begun to paint in 1944. During a visit to France in 1948, he attended the classes given by André Lhôte and developed a style based on French Cubism. Later he turned to *Tachisme*. In 1953 he contributed to the group exhibition in the Stedelijk Museum in Amsterdam: *Eight Argentinian Abstract Artists*. Of recent years Ocampo has reverted to a figurative style, which reveals Divisionist features.

C. Córdova Iturburu. *La pintura argentina del siglo XX*, Buenos Aires 1958.

O'Conor, Roderic. Irish painter and engraver, b. 1860 in Roscommon; d. 1940 in Neuil-sur-Layon, Maine-et-Loire. O'Conor studied in London, Antwerp and Paris; he settled in France in 1883. He was one of the Pont-Aven Group from 1892, and exhibited with the Salon des Indépendants, the Salon d'Automne and *Les Vingt* in Brussels. He was influenced by Gauguin and the Symbolists.

Oelze, Richard. German painter, b. 1900 in Magdeburg. From 1921 to 1925 he attended the Bauhaus in Weimar; then he moved to Dresden, Berlin and, in 1933, Paris. There he came to know the Surrealist group—Breton, Éluard, Ernst and Dali. In 1936 he went to Switzerland, and in the same year took part in the International Surrealist Exhibition in London and the exhibition of Fantastic Art, Dada, Surrealism at the Museum of Modern Art, New York. He returned to Germany in 1939 and fought in the war. He emerged from obscurity in 1959, and showed some work in the 1968 Venice Biennale.

His art is Surrealistic and stylized, originating from the *Neue Sachlichkeit* of the 1920s and influenced in its early days by both Magritte and Ernst. Since then, however, it has remained untouched by the subsequent development of art. Oelze has used earth colours (ochre, umber, sienna) to create a strange world of petrified forests, with grotesque shapes and curious, almost human vegetable forms.

O'Gorman, Juan. Mexican painter and architect, b. 1905. Apart from designing a number of houses, including one for Diego Rivera, O'Gorman created some murals for the airport in Mexico City (1937–8) which met with the disapproval of the government and were destroyed. He has created many other mural decorations for public buildings.

Okada, Kenzo. Japanese painter, b. 1902 in Yokohama. He graduated from the Meijigakuin Middle School in 1920 and studied at the Tokyo Fine Arts University from 1922 to 1924. He studied in Paris with Foujita, 1924–7, and exhibited in the Salons there. He returned to Japan in 1927 and two years later had his first one-man show at the Nichido Gallery in Tokyo. In Japan Okada taught at Nippon University School of Fine Arts (1940–2), Musashino Art Institute (1947–50) and Tama Fine Arts College (1949–50). It was not until he came to the United States in 1950 that he truly grasped the Japanese aesthetic, interpreting it and Japan itself from a distance. He received his first one-man show in the United States in 1953 at the Betty Parsons Gallery, New York. His early abstractions tend to be hazy and amorphous, executed in soft pastel tones as in *Dynasty* (1956, Buffalo, New York, Albright-Knox Art Gallery). By the late 1950s his forms crystallized slightly, accompanied by a greater interior painterliness and sharper outlines to the forms (*Gate*, 1959, Hartford, Conn., Wadsworth Atheneum). In such late works as *Vertical* (1946, coll. of artist) he reduces the number of shapes or areas in the canvas, applies his pigment more thinly and uses localized, unmodulated colour. In addition to a number of one-man shows, Okada participated in the 1955 São Paulo Bienal and the Twenty-ninth Venice Biennale (1958).

Gordon B. Washburn. Exhibition catalogue, *Kenzo Okada: Paintings, 1952–65*, Asshi-Shimbun Press, Tokyo; National Museum of Modern Art, Kyoto; Honolulu Academy of Arts; M. H. de Young Memorial Museum, San Francisco; University of Texas Art Museum, Austin 1966–7.

Okamoto, Taro. Japanese painter, b. 1911 in Tokyo. He paints in the western idiom. He first studied in Tokyo, then went to Paris, where he contributed to the Salon des Surindépendants from 1932. He worked at the Sorbonne from 1933 to 1939. He was a member of the *Abstraction-Création* group from 1933 to 1937. In 1940 he returned to Japan, and in 1947 became a member of the *Nikakai* group there. He visited Europe in 1952/3. He has had work shown in the Contemporary Art Exhibition of Japan in 1954, the International Art Exhibitions in Japan, 1952 and 1953, and an exhibition of selected masterpieces in 1954.

O'Keeffe, Georgia. American painter, b. 1887 in Sun Prairie, Wisconsin. She received her early schooling in Sun Prairie and Madison, Wisconsin, and Chatham, Virginia, and then studied at the Chicago Art Institute (1905–6) under John Vanderpoel and at the Art Students' League with William M. Chase, F. L. Mora and K. Cox. She had further training between 1912 and 1916 under Arthur Dow and Alan Bement. In the second decade of the century she held teaching positions in Amarillo, Texas, the University of Virginia and West Texas State Normal College, Canyon. She gave up her teaching career in 1918 and became a member of the group sponsored by A. Stieglitz at his 291 Gallery. Though she had exhibited at Stieglitz's as early as 1916 her first one-man show was held at the Anderson Galleries, New York, in 1923. She was married to Stieglitz, the organizer of this show, the following year. An early Precisionist, she produced close-up views of flowers and plants from the beginning of her career (*Abstraction, White Rose*, 1927, coll. of artist). Her Precisionism is displayed in such works as *Ranchos Church. Front* (1929, New York, Coll. Jack Lawrence), a canvas which also reveals her long connections with the South-West. The same relation to such subjects can be seen in the bleached bones of *Summer Days* (1936, Newport, R.I., Coll. Mrs. Robert R. Young) which is rendered in the abstracted Precisionist manner always connected with O'Keeffe. In the 1940s her works display a greater abstraction

and reduction of forms, often using a single element to fill the entire canvas as in *Pelvis Series, Red with Yellow* (1945, Fort Worth, Texas, Coll. Mrs. A. B. Windfohr) or using a large space containing little in the way of identifiable objects (*Wall with Green Door*, 1952, coll. of artist).

Mitchell A. Wilder. Catalogue, *Georgia O'Keeffe. An Exhibition of the Work of the Artist from 1915 to 1966*, Amon Carter Museum of Western Art, Fort Worth (Texas) 1966.

Oldenburg, Claes. American sculptor and environmentalist, b. 1929 in Stockholm, Sweden. His father was a diplomat, and Oldenburg spent much of his early childhood shuttling between the United States, Sweden and Norway. This itinerant life and the consequent difficulty with the language produced an introverted child with a rich fantasy life, augmented by images from magazine advertisements contained in scrapbooks sent by a Swedish aunt. Oldenburg graduated from Yale University in 1950, worked as a Chicago reporter on the police beat, then attended the city's Art Institute for two years (1953–4). By 1956 he was doing loosely brushed figurative paintings and had moved to New York. There he became involved with poetry and drawing as well as painting, but his art was difficult to sell at that period. Around 1960 he became involved with a group of New York artists, including Robert Whitman (b. 1935), Jim Dine, Red Grooms (b. 1937) and Allan Kaprow, who initiated a new form of participational art called 'happenings'. Between 1960 and 1965 Oldenburg conducted many happenings, beginning with *Snapshots from the City* (1960) and *Store Days* (1962), and concluding with such ambitious enterprises as the Los Angeles *Autobodies* (1964), which involved ice cubes, automobiles and crowds of people as the material for art. The crude costumes and roughly painted cardboard props used in the happenings formed the basis for many of his later sculptures and objects. During the same year Oldenburg opened a small storefront on New York's Lower East Side called 'The Store', where he sold painted plaster replicas of food (*Dual Hamburger*, 1962, New York, Museum of Modern Art) and other commodities. With these objects Oldenburg created one of his now characteristically tragicomic statements on the cultural environment and became one of the initiators of Pop Art. The images he used derive from the street, home, daily functions and commerce (*Bedroom Ensemble*, 1963, New York, Sidney Janis Gallery; and *Soft Toilet*, 1966, New York, Coll. Mr. and Mrs. Victor Ganz), and point out the fetishistic nature of common objects (*Giant Light Switches*, 1964, New York, Sidney Janis Gallery and Coll. Leon Kraushar). Oldenburg's interest in the tactile quality of these objects relates him to Abstract Expressionism, as does the messy, loose application of enamel paints on his earlier food replicas. His oversize, stitched-together pieces in such soft materials as vinyl or canvas, stuffed with kapok, were important sculptured innovations. Reversing the expectations of hard sculpture, these huge collapsing objects rely on gravity and chance for their final form. The evocation of the human and of the erotic in his ghostly models of fans, typewriters and sauce bottles, whose deflated forms flounder like hybrid scarecrows, works to soften the potential irony of their inflated scale. Sensual pleasure rather than hard-core social comment is the primary aim of much of Oldenburg's executed work, although his drawings and models for giant imaginary monuments to be located on actual urban sites indicate greater social and political involvement.

Michael Kirby. *Happenings: An Illustrated Anthology*, New York 1965.
Barbara Rose. *Claes Oldenburg*, New York 1968.

Olitski, Jules. American painter, b. 1922 in Gomel, Russia. Olitski studied in New York at the National Academy of Design (1939–42), then in Paris, first at the Académie de la Grande Chaumière (1949–50), then at the Ossip Zadkine School. He taught for many years in New York at C. W. Post College and New York University, as well as at Bennington College, Vermont. Olitski's work between 1952 and 1959 was characterized by densely encrusted surfaces built up from rough smears and trails reminiscent of Hans Hofmann (*Diane de Poitiers*, c. 1959, Shaftsbury, Vermont, coll. of artist). Beginning in 1960 he moved to a stained canvas technique to create a more flexible picture surface. More precise biomorphic and geometric shapes were defined, such as ovals ringing each other or clustering in one area of the field (*The Julius Dmikhovsky Image*, 1961, coll. of artist). Olitski's interest in the primacy of colour and paint rather than in the importance of drawing led him to abandon compositional devices in his later work in order to establish the independent value of sensuous colour situations.

By 1963 Olitski was working to obliterate the drawn contours of his shapes through the sheer impact of rich, saturated colours. In a progressive effort to renounce sculptural space and tactile sensations he became more and more antagonistic to the notion of local colour and began to spray tiny particles of paint on to soaked, unprimed canvas, masking all linear boundaries (*Prince Patutsky Command*, 1965, New York, Coll. Henry Geldzahler). Later even these faint internal edges disappeared, as defined shape was displaced to the peripheries of the canvas, where thickly brushed bands contrast with the illusory clouds of paint sprayed across the rest of the field. Soft greens, sweet pinks and ingratiating oranges and purples (*Beyond Bounds*, 1966, Jewett Art Center, Wellesley College, Mass.) delicately sprayed into broad rectangles resist a frontal reading and create an illusory, dissolving

space, while the thickly painted bands establish the literal existence of the canvas.

Kermit Champa. 'Olitski: Nothing but Color', *Art News* LXVI, New York, May 1966.
Michael Fried. Catalogue, *Jules Olitski: Paintings, 1963–67*, Corcoran Gallery of Art, Washington (D.C.) 1967.

Oliveira, Nathan. American painter and graphic artist, b. 1928 in Oakland, California. He studied under Leon Goldman, Otis Oldfield and Hamilton Wolf and was with Max Beckmann at Mills College in 1950. In 1952 he received an MFA degree from the California College of Arts and Crafts. After serving in the United States Army, 1953–5, he taught at Mills College. In 1956 he received a Louis Comfort Tiffany Grant in print-making and the following two years saw his first one-man shows—the first of prints at the Eric Locke Gallery, San Francisco, and the second of paintings at the Alan Gallery, New York. In the latter year he received a Guggenheim Fellowship. His works of the late 1950s recall Giacometti's painted figures—roughly handled in scruffy paint, often small in size in relation to the area of the canvas and set in a non-specific space (*Standing Man with Hands in Belt*, 1960, Minneapolis, Minn., Walker Art Center). By the early 1960s his figures exist in a real space and are executed with a slightly greater amount of detail (*Nude Stepping from Carpet*, 1962, Beverly Hills, California, Coll. Mr. and Mrs. Burt Kleiner). His late style exhibits a vast change in orientation. The previous painterliness is excluded; the figure becomes either non-existent or of little importance while the greatest emphasis is placed on stage, an item which actually exists in his studio, an abandoned theatre (*Stage No. 2 with Bed*, 1967, Los Angeles, Felix Landau Gallery). Since 1961 Oliveira has taught at the University of Illinois, UCLA and Stamford University.

Frederick S. Wight. *Nathan Oliveira*, Los Angeles 1963–4.

Olofsson, Pierre. Swedish painter and graphic artist, b. 1921. In 1947 Olofsson began to paint Cubist pictures, in which he represented impressions of Paul Klee in a semi-figurative primitivistic style. Subsequently, he turned completely non-figurative, arranging ellipsoids and other gently rounded shapes in overlapping patterns to produce rich, intricate pictures composed of interacting pictorial forms and planes. In 1950 he was appointed artistic adviser on residential and industrial developments in the mining districts of Kiruna, Narvik and Malmberget, and since then has concentrated on environmental works. He collaborated with Arne Jones on mosaics for the Västerås waterworks (1953) and the Luleå power station (1955), and on wall paintings for the dining-room at the Astra factory in Södertälje (1956) and the entrance vestibule of the Hammar pump station near Kramfors (*Sgraffito*, 1964).

Omega Workshops. Founded in July 1913 by Roger Fry, the Omega Workshops were really a continuation of the Arts and Crafts tradition. According to Fry in the Workshops brochure, 'The Omega Workshops is a group of artists who are working with the object of allowing free play to the delight in making objects for common life.' The workshop was intended to be a community enterprise in which artists who were paid a retainer of seven shillings and sixpence a day co-operated anonymously on the design of household objects, especially rugs, fabrics, pottery and painted furniture. The more elaborate objects were not manufactured on the premises, but all the smaller ones were. The most important artists involved were Fry himself, Duncan Grant, Vanessa Bell and, initially, Wyndham Lewis, Frederick Etchells and Edward Wadsworth. These last four left in the autumn of 1913 to form the Rebel Art Centre, objecting to a situation in which everybody was anonymous except Fry. Fry, Grant, Etchells and three others had already worked on a co-operative venture in 1911, one which recalls strongly Rossetti and Morris decorating the Oxford Union and the decoration of the Borough Polytechnic Refectory. The Omega differed from the Arts and Crafts, however, in that it was a direct attempt to marry painting and applied design, and its style was based on the almost contemporary works of Matisse and the Cubists. In this Omega was ten years ahead of its time, but, somewhat paradoxically, together with this super-modernity Fry quite explicitly rejected the machine. There was therefore an element of Romantic anachronism built in to the movement. Whether this would have proved fatal time did not show, as the First World War put an end to the experiment; though it remained vigorous until 1916, in 1919 it had to be sold up. During the three main active years the workshops had considerable success, however. Apart from household objects they also executed whole interiors. They exhibited one at the Ideal Home Exhibition in 1913 and did the lounge of the Allied Artists' Exhibition in 1914. Amongst other commissions they did the Cadena Café, Westbourne Grove (now destroyed), mosaics at No. 1 Hyde Park Gardens, and mural paintings at 4 Berkeley Street.

Roger Fry. *Omega Brochure*, London 1913.
Niklaus Pevsner. *Architectural Review*, London 1941.

Onosato, Toshinobu. Japanese painter, b. 1912 in Nagano. Onosato studied painting under Seifu Tsuda in 1931. Subsequently he became one of the best-known Japanese artists of his generation. From 1938 to 1956 he was a member of the *Jiyu Bijutsa Kyokai* artists' association. In 1955 he joined the Art Club of Japan.

Onosato's works, which were on show at the Biennale in Venice in 1964 and 1966, reveal a certain affinity with Neo-Plasticism. By and large he uses only three colours: yellow, red and blue. His compositions consist of arrangements of tiny rectangular shapes which are almost invariably superimposed on one or more large circular shapes.

Onslow-Ford, Gordon Max. British-American painter, b. 1912 in Wendover, England. Having studied at the Royal Naval Colleges at Dartmouth and Greenwich, he spent some ten years in the Royal Navy. While in Paris from 1936 to 1939, he was a frequent visitor at the studios of Léger and Lhôte. Self-taught as an artist, his greatest cultural growth came from his associations with Matta and members of the Surrealist group. His early works owe most to Matta, as seen in *Birth Transcontinental* (1939, coll. of artist) with its rectilinear geometric elements and free-form, amoeba-like shapes floating in space. When he moved to the United States in 1940, he was given his first one-man show at the Karl Nierendorf Gallery, New York, and taught at the New School for Social Research. From 1941 to 1947 he was in retreat in Mexico. By the 1940s his Surreal world was approached with a Pointillistic technique, though it had a greater solidity of forms than that of the Post-Impressionists. Coupled with this handling was the dynamic power of Futurism, as seen in *A Present for the Past* (1942, coll. of artist). The dynamism of the stroke, its directional force and its relation to the larger forms became increasingly important in the later years (*Migrations with Birds*, 1948, casein, coll. of artist). Though he had begun to withdraw from Surrealism in 1943 ('during the war I found it impossible to be a Surrealist'), it was not until 1951 that his work lost all of its Surrealist connections, in favour of a new lyrical, personal calligraphy.

Gordon Onslow-Ford. *Towards a New Subject in Painting*, Museum of Art, San Francisco 1948.

Op Art. This, which is synonymous with the earlier French concept of *art visuel*, embraces all works of art in which special importance is attached to the purely visual rapport between the viewer and the work. The object of Op Art is to effect a change in the viewer's physiological perception by means of contrasting or overlapping colours, forms and structures. K. J. Fischer defined this process in 1961: 'Because of the equivalence between the component elements, which remain virtually unaccented, the individual forms acquire structural significance. Such a picture is organized as a cellular structure and its unity is of a cellular order. It is possible to disturb the regularity of such a structure by the rhythmical transposition of individual parts, by introducing disruptive elements or creating gaps, i.e. by effecting insignificant alterations, without distracting the viewer to such an extent that he loses sight of the whole. By using graphs, facets, screens and similar graphic devices the artist is able to bring the fore- and back-ground into close alignment, so much so that in many cases they form a single surface or, alternatively, two corresponding surfaces—one positive, the other negative—which are inseparable from one another. The slight disruption of the component elements within the overall structure gives rise to an optical aberration whereby the work appears to pulsate, flicker, vibrate etc.' By means of such apparent movement the artist contrives to create a situation in which the viewer is required to concentrate on the unstable aspects of visual phenomena. In doing so he suppresses his personal handwriting, adopting instead a completely anonymous, mechanical style and frequently employing materials taken from the new industrial sphere. On the one hand Op Art derives from the concrete, Constructivist tradition of European art such as was evolved at the Bauhaus, whilst on the other hand it exploits the scientific and technical processes of the modern world. Op Art, which frequently runs over into kinetic art, is represented both by its 'old masters', i.e. men like Vasarély and Josef Albers, and also by a large number of younger artists. Although they vary considerably in their approach, Richard Anuskiewicz, Almir Mavignier, Larry Poons, Agam, de Soto and Bridget Riley all work in an Op Art style. Of the many exhibitions which helped to popularize this movement the most influential was *The Responsive Eye*, which was organized by William G. Seitz and staged in the New York Museum of Modern Art in 1965.

William G. Seitz. Catalogue, *The Responsive Eye*, Museum of Modern Art, New York 1965.
Lucy Lippard. 'Perverse Perspectives', *Art International* XI, Zürich, March 1967.

Oppenheim, Maeret. German-Swiss painter and sculptress, b. 1913 in Berlin. Oppenheim made contact with the Surrealists in 1913. From 1937 to 1939 she studied at the Industrial School of Art in Basle. She is now living in Thun.

In her lyrically composed ready-mades Oppenheim emphasizes the Surrealistic aspect of commonplace objects by subjecting them to a process of alienation. Her 'fur objects' are well known.

Orloff, Chana. Russian-French sculptress, b. 1888 in Konstantinovka, Ukraine; d. 1968 in Tel Aviv. She moved to Palestine in 1904, then six years later went to Paris, where she studied, and met Modigliani and Apollinaire. Some of her early works were done in a Cubist style. Later she made nude sculptures and portraits; after 1945 she used mainly bronze and made a large number of bird figures.

Orozco, José Clemente. Mexican painter, b. 1883 in Zapotlán, Jalisco; d. 1949 in Mexico City. Orozco studied at the San Carlos Academy of Art, Mexico City, from 1908 to 1914. Like Diego Rivera and David Siqueiros, he was a politically committed artist, and during the social revolution in Mexico promoted the cause of the peasants and workers by painting large poster-like murals depicting scenes from the life and history of the Mexican people. Using bold outlines and strong colours Orozco developed a highly dramatic and Realistic form of Expressionism, which was a perfect medium for his simple allegories and symbolic figures. He began his career as a painter of murals in 1922, when he decorated the Mexican National Training School. This was followed by frescoes for the Casa de los Azulejos and the Industrial School in Orizaba. From 1929 to 1934 he was in the United States, where he also painted murals (for Pomona College in Claremont, California; the New School of Social Research in New York; and the Baker Library at Dartmouth College in Hanover, New Hampshire), and exerted a powerful influence on the development of the new American Realist school. After his return to Mexico in 1934 he painted the pacifist frescoes for the Palace of Fine Arts in Mexico City and murals for the National Palace, and for the University and the Cabanas Hospital in Guadalajara. Throughout his career Orozco treated the same basic themes: the misery, hunger, rebellion and suppression of the common people; and he lent added significance to these themes by relating them to actual incidents around the world. After completing his mural in the Museum of Modern Art, New York, in 1940 Orozco spent the closing years of his life decorating the Mexican Palace of Justice and the church in the Jesuit Hospital.

J. Fernandez. *José Clemente Orozco*, Mexico 1942.
L. Cardoza y Aragón. *José Clemente Orozco*, Buenos Aires 1944.
MacKinley Helm. *Man of Fire: J. C. Orozco*, Boston and New York 1953.
A. Read. *José Clemente Orozco*, New York 1956.
J. C. Orozco. *An Autobiography*, Austin (Texas) and London 1962.

Orpen, Sir William. Irish painter, b. 1878 in Stillorgan, near Dublin; d. 1931 in London. He studied in Dublin and London, and became a member of the New English Art Club in 1900. He was a founder member of the National Portrait Society in 1911, and was elected to the Royal Academy in 1921. He was an official war artist and was knighted in 1918. His work, together with that of McEvoy and Ricketts, was shown in Manchester in 1933.

Orphism. 'Orphism' or 'Orphic Cubism' was the term coined in 1912/13 by the poet Apollinaire principally to describe the work of Robert Delaunay and his wife Sonia Delaunay-Terk and to distinguish it from Cubism generally. In some respects it is synonymous with the contemporary term '*Simultanéisme*'. It was coined at a time when Apollinaire was in close contact with Delaunay and may also have served to separate his painting from the work of the Italian Futurists, with whom he was later in heated dispute over the origins of 'simultaneity'. The first public distinction of Orphist painters from the Cubists was at the 1913 Salon des Indépendants, Paris; they were treated separately in the hanging of the exhibition and in much of the critical writing.

Like many of Apollinaire's art terms, Orphism is loose, imaginative and open to confused misinterpretation. For him the literary and musical analogies were obviously important: his poetry cycle *La Bestiaire au Cortège d'Orphée* had only recently been completed. He described Orphism as 'the art of painting new structures out of elements which have not been borrowed from the visual sphere, but have been created entirely by the artist, and been endowed by him with the fullness of reality. . . . This is pure painting' (*Les Peintres Cubistes*, Paris, 1913). The abstractness of Delaunay's art of 1912–13 was its main point of departure from Cubism, and other artists that Apollinaire associated with Orphism (Léger, Kupka, Picabia, Duchamp) were at the time reaching similar—if only temporary—conclusions. Discussion of the possibility of painting attaining a 'pure' condition, analogous to music, was at its height. But for Apollinaire the new lyrical sensuality of colour that Delaunay brought to Cubist painting and a more poetic use of free associations were at least as important.

The series of paintings through which Delaunay moved to abstraction, *Les Fenêtres* (1912–13), inspired a poem of the same name in which Apollinaire wrote 'the window opens like an orange, the beautiful fruit of light' (published in the Delaunay exhibition catalogue, *Der Sturm*, Berlin, 1913). This Romantic concept of Orphism, embodying a free, lyrical interchangeability of word, image, colour, mood and medium, and seeing light almost as the new 'muse', enjoyed wide currency at the time. It accounts for the presence within Parisian Orphist circles of several poets including Canudo, the editor of the Orphist review *Montjoie* from 1913 on, and Cendrars, who in 1913 published the first *simultanéiste* book, over six feet in length, its type printed in varied sizes and colours against an abstract design by Sonia Delaunay. It also accounts for the association with Orphism of artists as different as Chagall, Picabia and Kupka and for Orphism's influence on Romantic Expressionist art in Germany (Klee, Macke, Marc).

In his own later writings (*Du Cubisme à l'Art Abstrait*, Paris, 1957) Delaunay tightened the definition to apply more exclusively to himself and his immediate followers in Paris (Sonia Delaunay, Bruce, Frost and the American Synchromist painters Russell and Macdonald-Wright). Delaunay saw Orphism as an abstract art of colour that retained a non-Expressionist connection with nature through its analysis of light. He acknowledged Orphism's ancestry in Impressionism, Cézanne and Neo-Impressionism: Cubism was merely 'a transition'. He was familiar with some of Seurat's theoretical sources (Chevreul). While the main emphasis of his writing describes abstract art as the ultimate end, his paintings show that Orphist painting could also embody explicit contemporary images (the Eiffel Tower, a Cardiff rugby team, Blériot's historic aircraft). Thus while Orphism was the first abstract art movement in Paris, it did not totally deny the Cubist ambition for a new language of representation.

Werner Haftmann. 'Orphism', *Painting in the Twentieth Century*, Vol. 1, London and New York 1960.

Ortman, George Earle. American painter and graphic artist, b. 1926 in Oakland, California. After serving in the United States Naval Air Corps, 1945–7, he attended the California College of Arts and Crafts (1947–8), S. W. Hayter's Atelier 17 in New York (1949), the Académie André Lhôte, Paris (1950), and the Hans Hofmann School of Fine Arts (1950–1). He received his first one-man show in 1953 at the Tanager Gallery, New York. Ortman has also been included in such important exhibitions as *New Media—New Forms*, I (1960, New York, Martha Jackson Gallery) and *Toward a New Abstraction* (1963, New York, Jewish Museum). His works, executed in primary colours and employing geometrical and other highly regularized forms—circles, squares, diamonds, crosses, arrows—applied with a fastidiousness of execution, seem a rebellion against the Abstract Expressionism of his student days (*Dyce Head*, 1964, New York, Howard Wise Gallery). Ortman was the recipient of a Guggenheim Fellowship in 1965 and a Tamarind Lithography Workshop Grant (1966). While at Tamarind he produced a series of fourteen lithographs entitled *Oaxaca*, executed in a less formalized manner than his earlier painting style, in which a cross-hatching technique is employed. He taught at the School of Visual Arts, New York, from 1957 to 1965 and was Artist-in-Residence at Princeton University, 1966–7.

Ossorio, Alfonso. American painter, b. 1916 in Manila, Philippine Islands. First going to England (1924), he moved to the United States in 1929 and attended Harvard University in 1938, followed by a year at the Rhode Island School of Design (1938–9). He received his first one-man show at the Wakefield Gallery, New York, in 1941. From 1943 to 1946 he served in the United States Army. His early canvases are drip paintings with some broadly painted areas. The drip style continued into the mid-1950s, but these later brightly coloured works include flame-like forms which lend a quality of the fantastic to the earlier style (*Warrior, Owl and Dove*, 1954–5, coll. of artist). This fantastic aspect was replaced by the bizarre in his works of the late 1950s and 1960s. Into a rich impasto of considerable thickness the artist pressed gems, rope, shells, feathers, fake eyeballs, wood and other objects which give the works a bright jewel-like quality with a surprising variety of colour, texture, shape and light (*Sum*, 1959, New York, Museum of Modern Art).

Jean Dubuffet. *Peintures Initiatiques d'Alfonso Ossorio*, Paris 1957.
B. H. Friedman. *Art International* VI, Zürich, April 1962.
Michel Tapié. *Ossorio*, Turin 1962.

Ostrower, Fayga. Polish-Brazilian graphic artist, b. 1920 in Lodz, Poland. Ostrower lived in Germany until 1933, and settled in Brazil in 1934. Later she studied graphic art in Rio de Janeiro. In 1955 she visited the United States, and in 1958 won the Grand Prix for graphic art at the Venice Biennale. Ostrower produces sensitive abstract etchings, aquatints and coloured woodcuts. Of recent years she has also worked on textile designs. She now teaches at the Museum of Modern Art in Rio de Janeiro.

Oteiza Embil, Jorge de. Spanish sculptor and ceramicist, b. 1908 in Orio, Basque Province. He is self-taught, and has been exhibiting since 1931. From 1941 he taught ceramics at the Escuela Nacional de Cerámica in Buenos Aires, and in 1942 he went to Bogotá. He now lives in Irún.

He was a figurative sculptor at first, but gradually turned to an Expressionist abstraction. He has considerable influence through his ideas.

Ouborg, Piet (Pieter). Dutch painter and draughtsman, b. 1893 in Dordrecht; d. 1956 in The Hague. After training as a draughtsman, Ouborg taught drawing in the Dutch East Indies from 1916 to 1938. During this period he visited Holland twice, in 1923–4 and 1931. In 1939 he returned home for good and settled in The Hague.

After an early derivative period, in which he was influenced primarily by Tanguy and Max Ernst, Ouborg evolved his own personal form of Surrealism during the 1930s. The abstract paintings which he produced from 1945 onwards are light, expressive and spontaneous works executed in bright, clear colours. His automatistic drawings are reminiscent of the work of Henri Michaux. Ouborg was a member of the *Vrij Beelden* group in Amsterdam.

Exhibition catalogue, *Piet Ouborg*, Stedelijk van Abbemuseum, Eindhoven 1965.

Oudot, Roland. French painter and designer of tapestries, stage sets and costumes, b. 1897 in Paris. He studied at the École Nationale des Arts Décoratifs. His work was first shown at the 1919 Salon. At first he hesitated whether to follow the Fauves or Cubism, but later the influence of Corot became apparent in his style. He painted figures, portraits and landscapes, and did mural decorations for the Palais de Chaillot. He has designed tapestries for the Gobelins and Aubusson factories, and has illustrated books by such writers as Gérard de Nerval, François Mauriac and Jean Giraudoux. Oudot has exhibited in Holland, Zürich and the USA.

Ozenfant, Amédée. French painter and writer on art, b. 1886 in Saint-Quentin; d. 1966 in Cannes. After passing his childhood in Spain, Ozenfant returned to Saint-Quentin, where he attended the local school of drawing before going on to study with Segonzac and La Fresnaye at the Académie de la Palette under Cottet, Desvallières and Blanche. In 1915 he launched the magazine *L'Élan*, which continued to appear up to 1917. He then visited Holland, Italy and Russia and in 1917 met Ch.-E. Jeanneret, to whom he later gave the name 'Le Corbusier' and with whom he published the Purist manifesto *L'Esprit Nouveau* (1920–5). In 1931 Ozenfant established the Foundation of Modern Art, where he taught from 1935 to 1938. He then went to Washington and in the following year settled in New York, where he taught at the Ozenfant School of Fine Art until 1955, when he returned to Paris.

Ozenfant's first pictures date from c. 1903. They are paintings of human figures and landscapes executed in a dark, almost a black, monochrome. From then onwards his work—which was influenced in both composition and colour by Cézanne and the Cubists—developed with absolute consistency to the point where his pictorial objects were almost completely dematerialized. The series of still lifes of bottles, guitars and pipes which he painted from 1925 onwards illustrates his transition from vegetal to crystalline forms, in other words to the clarity and highly organized structural world of Purism. Ozenfant's treatment of the human form underwent a similar development: the all too stylized figures of his early period were replaced from c. 1930 onwards by massive, powerful figures, which usually appear against a bright ground and whose coarse texture creates an impression of relief-like compactness. In its final phase Ozenfant's Purism led to the production of contrapuntal compositions consisting of simple forms, which seem to be almost transparent.

Ozenfant was also an important author and art theorist. In c. 1918 he protested bitterly against the reduction of Cubism to mere decoration, and in his *Après le Cubisme* he praised the beauty of the machine and its products. Theoretically Ozenfant had much in common with the *de Stijl* movement. In practice, however, he differed from Mondrian and his followers by his insistence on objective representation, which always remained an important feature of Purist painting.

K. Nierendorf. *Amédée Ozenfant*, Berlin 1931.
Amédée Ozenfant. *Foundations of Modern Art*, New York 1952.

P

Paalen, Wolfgang. Austrian-Mexican painter, b.1907 in Vienna; d. 1959 in Mexico. After studying in France, Germany and Italy Paalen settled in Paris in the late 1920s. Between 1931 and 1935 he was in contact with the *Abstraction-Création* association and, subsequently, with the Surrealist movement. In 1936 he was represented at the Surrealist exhibition in London. In 1939 he emigrated to Mexico, where he and Breton organized an international Surrealist exhibition in 1940. But in the following year Paalen broke away from the Surrealist movement. From 1942 to 1943 he edited the *DYN* magazine and in 1951 took part in the *DYNATON* exhibition in San Francisco. In 1959 Paalen committed suicide.

Paalen made his name as a member of the Surrealist movement and is generally acknowledged to have been the inventor of the *fumage* technique (blackening the canvas with candle smoke). After an early period, in which he painted geometrical abstracts, Paalen developed a phantasmagoric form of Surrealism, which placed him in the company of Max Ernst, Tanguy, Masson and, occasionally, Victor Brauner. He also produced Surrealist objects. After turning away from Surrealism, he painted Expressionist and, subsequently, Tachist pictures.

Wolfgang Paalen. *Form and Sense*, New York 1945.
Gustav Regler. *Wolfgang Paalen*, New York 1946.
Homage to Wolfgang Paalen, Museo de Arte Moderno, Mexico 1967.

Pace, Achille. Italian painter, b. 1923 in Termoli. Pace came to live in Rome in 1935 when he was still a child. Up to 1964 he exhibited with *Gruppo 1*, an Italian artists' association founded in the previous year. He first made his name with monochromes, in which the outlines provide the only structural element. Pace's paintings, which are largely dematerialized, constitute a further development of informal art.

Paciurea, Dimitrie. Rumanian sculptor, b. 1875 in Craiova; d. 1932 in Bucharest. He went to Paris in 1895, and there learned much from the work of Rodin. He made portraits of great writers and musicians (Beethoven, Shakespeare) which convey admirably his idea of the subject's personality. Later on he created a series of *Chimeras*—strange creatures of his imagination. His earlier sculpture, however, was his best work.

Palazuelo, Pablo. Spanish painter, graphic artist and poster designer, b. 1918 in Madrid. He studied architecture in Oxford, and painting at the Central School of Arts and Crafts in London. Since 1948 he has been living in Paris, where he took part in the Salon de Mai (1951) and exhibited at the Galerie Maeght in 1955 and 1958. He is an abstract artist.

Palencia, Benjamin. Spanish painter, b. 1902 at Barrax, Albacete. He is a great landscapist, and paints with poetic vision. He is able to express emotion through colour. The School of Madrid has tended to focus round him.

Pallady, Theodor. Rumanian painter, b. 1871 in Iassy; d. 1956 in Bucharest. He attended the École des Beaux-Arts in Paris from 1891 to 1900, and continued to live in that city until 1939. He knew Matisse, whose influence is visible in some of his work. He was awarded the Grand Prix for painting in 1926.

Pan, Marta. Hungarian-French sculptress, b. 1923 in Budapest. She studied first in Budapest, then in Paris (from 1947), and from 1950 began showing her work in the Salon des Réalités Nouvelles. She used organic shapes in her early sculpture, and went on to make adaptable works that could be viewed from many angles; some had moving parts with which their forms could be altered. She also made a beautiful sculpture in polyester (1961) which floats on a lake in the Kröller-Müller Museum, Otterlo.

Pankok, Bernhard. German designer and illustrator, b. 1872 in Münster; d. 1943 in Baierbrunn, Bavaria. He studied in Düsseldorf and Berlin, then moved to Munich (1892–1902). During this time he contributed to the magazines *Jugend* and *Pan* and was a founder member of the *Vereinigte Werkstätte* (1897). From 1913 to 1917 he was director of the Industrial School of Art in Stuttgart.

Pankok is best known for his interior decoration, such as the *Gentleman's Study* he designed for the 1900 Paris International Exhibition. This was made to resemble the wardroom of an old sailing ship. He made great efforts to integrate all areas of design— furniture, interior decoration and graphics—and the furniture he created is of considerable interest.

In his book illustrations, Pankok made extensive use of ornamental borders, which consisted of abstract patterns derived from organic forms. He designed the official German catalogue for the 1900 Paris exhibition, and gained widespread recognition for it.

Pankok, Otto. German painter, graphic artist, sculptor and writer, b. 1893 in Mulheim/Ruhr. He studied in Düsseldorf and Weimar, and was a professor at the Staatliche Kunstacademie in Düsseldorf from 1945. His work is Expressionist in essence, and consists largely of landscapes, figures, animals and portraits.

Paolozzi, Eduardo. Scots-Italian sculptor, b. 1924 in Edinburgh. Paolozzi studied at Edinburgh College of Art and the Slade School, then served in the army during the Second World War. After the war he held his first one-man show, an exhibition of drawings, in London in 1947, then from 1947 to 1950 he worked in Paris. In 1949 he exhibited in London a series of bas-reliefs and in 1951 carried out his first major sculptural commission, a fountain for the Festival of Britain. His drawings and reliefs show the inspiration of the Surrealism of artists like Miró. They are semi-abstract and semi-figurative, relying rather on suggestion than direct statement, and though the images have changed radically this exploitation of the power of suggestion of half-familiar forms has persisted in his work. In the fifties, like most British sculptors, he used heavily modelled, rough-cast bronze. His work, though not directly figurative, often comes close enough to representation to suggest a title (thus *Chinese Dog*, 1956). At this period, however, the solemn free-standing figures with square boxy forms (like the *Icarus* series of 1957) look forward to his later work, and in spite of the use of modelling already have mechanistic overtones. These figures develop into the mechanical men of the early sixties. Great ominous totem figures, they are often brilliantly coloured and are composed entirely from casts of pieces of machinery, car engines, ventilator shafts, etc. They are assertively mechanistic, yet the bright colour underlines the paradox of their non-function as machines and so emphasizes the unsettling suggestion of their humanity. More recently, he has turned away from this semi-figurative work to pure abstraction, though he still uses manufactured parts or shapes that suggest a mechanical function. He has also recently produced several series of prints (for example, *Moonship Empire News*, 1967) which in their elaborate literary references recall his earlier association with Kitaj.

Catalogue, *Eduardo Paolozzi: Sculpture and Graphics*, Hanover Gallery, London 1967.

Paris, Harold. American sculptor, b. 1925 in Edgemire, New York. He studied in Europe, in Madrid and Munich; he moved to France in 1956 and taught there. On his return to the United States he continued to teach, and worked in association with other sculptors of the West Coast, where he had settled. He used a variety of materials—terracotta, bronze and other metals, rubber and plastic; the range of his work is extremely wide.

Paris, School of—*see* **École de Paris**

Park, David. American painter, b. 1911 in Boston, Massachusetts; d. 1960 in Berkeley, California. After moving to Los Angeles, he began his art studies at the Otis Art Institute (1928). The following year he moved to San Francisco; he lived in the Bay Area for the rest of his life save the years 1936–41 when he was head of the Art Department at the Winsor School in Boston. From 1931 to 1935 he taught in private schools and was active in the WPA art project. In the latter year he had his first one-man show at the San Francisco Museum of Art. He came deeply under the influence of Picasso around 1938 and broke from his rather boring WPA style. At this time he gravitated towards a European form of *avant-garde* abstraction which he pursued for about six years. He became so dissatisfied with this mode of expression, however, that he burned most of the paintings handled in this manner. Another stylistic change came about 1945. He was one of the first West Coast artists to abandon abstraction and return to the figure. In *Ethiopia* (1959, Coral Gables, Florida, University of Miami, J. and E. Lowe Art Gallery) the figures exist alone and for themselves. Close to the picture plane, with no real ambience, they are handled with a free, lively brush in powerful colours. Park taught at the California School of Fine Arts from 1943 to 1952 and from 1955 was a member of the Art Department at the University of California, Berkeley. In 1955 he exhibited in the Third Bienal at São Paulo, Brazil.

Paul Mills. *David Park (1911–1960) Retrospective Exhibition*, Staempfli Gallery, New York 1965–6.

Parker, Raymond (Ray). American painter, b. 1922 in Beresford, South Dakota. He studied at the State University of Iowa and during the 1940s worked as a merchant seaman and as a professional jazz trumpeter for eight years. In 1950 he became acquainted with several New York Abstract Expressionist painters and moved there the following year. Parker's early paintings still manifest Cubist concerns—the internal balancing of forms and colours in relation to the picture's size and rectangular shape. After 1950 he increasingly explored the possibilities and limitations of colour (variations in density, value and texture) in abstract paintings whose colour planes edged each other actively. Subsequent larger canvases became more painterly in treatment and the wide, scrubbed brush-strokes characterized an Abstract-Impressionist phase.

Around 1958 Parker was one of several younger painters who reacted against the 'academic' imitators of Willem de Kooning and Jackson Pollock. The brush-strokes took on a new discipline, defining legible shapes from the inside out (so that drawing and painting were simultaneous), and ordering the structure of the pictures more coherently. *Stack* (1958, New York, coll. of artist), with its three cloud-or loaf-like forms suspended one above the other in a vertical rectangular field, is typical of this period. The muted colours—deep musky lavender, ochre, earthy brown or plum—are also characteristic of the subtle harmonies Parker chose to explore, as the shapes seem to float in a shallow region in front of the white grounds. By 1962 four or five roughly square or rectangular forms replaced these earlier clouds, now crowding the picture space in parallel vertical or horizontal rows (*No. 120*, 1963, Washington, D.C., Coll. Dr. and Mrs. Julian Eisenstein). These clusters were superseded by squares in grid arrangements (*No. 132*, 1964, New York, Kootz Gallery), until the regularity was broken in 1965 by freely cut-out shapes in more intense hues, scattered randomly across a neutral ground (*No. 171*, 1966, New York, coll. of artist). Coloured fields of Matisse-like brilliance were contrasted with bending mobile strands in equally bright hues in Parker's paintings of 1967–8.

Raymond Parker. 'Student, Teacher, Artist', *College Art Journal* XIII, No. 1, 1953.
Gerald Nordland. Catalogue, *Ray Parker*, Gallery of Modern Art, Washington (D.C.) 1966.

Pascali, Pino. Italian experimental artist, b. 1935 in Bari; d. 1968. Pascali worked in Rome. After an early informal phase he went on to experiment with Neo-Dadaist works and play pieces that make demands on the viewer's imagination. His *Fictitious Sculptures* of 1966 and his *Water Pieces* of 1967 are typical examples. The *Water Pieces* consist of aluminium containers holding water that has been dyed with aniline to create an illusion of the sea.

Catalogue, *Pino Pascali*, Galleria nazionale d'arte moderna, Rome 1969.

Pascin, Jules (Julius Pincas). American draughtsman and painter, b. 1885 in Vidin, Bulgaria; d. 1930 in Paris. Pascin's father was a Spanish Jew and his mother an Italian. He studied painting in Vienna and Munich and had already made a name for himself by 1903 through the drawings which he executed for *Simplicissimus*. As a young man Pascin led a Bohemian life and travelled widely until he eventually settled in Paris in 1905. From 1914 to 1920 he lived in the United States and became an American citizen. In 1922 he returned to Paris, where he belonged to the intimate circle of artists grouped around Chagall, Soutine, Modigliani and Foujita. In 1930, on the day on which his first major exhibition was due to open in the Galerie Georges Petit, he hanged himself in his studio.

In his sensitive drawings Pascin depicted young girls in graceful, sensuous poses and gallant scenes from the life of a decadent social class. His paintings are characterized by clear colours, which gleam like mother-of-pearl, and nervous flickering brushwork, whose expressive, searching rhythms hint at the artist's underlying melancholy. Although the sensuous charm of these works is often reminiscent of the gallant painting of the French rococo, to which Pascin was greatly attached, and although their stylistic qualities have more in common with an exalted form of Impressionism than with Expressionism, behind these surface qualities we sense a sensitive, endangered and harassed personality, richly endowed with an apocalyptic fantasy that places Pascin on a level with Soutine, Meidner or Scipione. This inner quality lends a melancholy and poetic magic to even the most gallant scene and transforms it into a legendary setting. But it also led to a gradual diminution of Pascin's artistic power and, finally, to his tragic death.

A. Warnod. *Pascin*, Monte Carlo 1954.
Exhibition catalogue, *Jules Pascin*, Haus der Kunst, Munich 1969; Paris 1969.

Pasmore, Victor. British painter, b. 1908 in Chelsham. Pasmore studied at the Central School from 1927 to 1931 under A. S. Hartrick. In 1937 he was a co-founder of the Euston Road School. Initially a figurative painter, Pasmore is now best known for his later abstract art and for the pedagogic method rationalizing it (deriving from Bauhaus teaching) which he introduced into Durham University from the mid-1950s. As 'basic design', this method permeated all British art schools.

Pasmore's Neo-*de Stijl* paintings and constructions seldom have the rigour of absolutist Constructive art. Generally they remain allusively figurative. Well supported officially, Pasmore has achieved international status. In 1959 he was awarded the CBE. He has exhibited at the Thirtieth Venice Biennale (1960), in São Paulo (1965) and widely elsewhere. Examples of his work are to be found in the Tate, London, and at major US and Dutch galleries.

A. Bowness. 'The Paintings and Constructions of Victor Pasmore', *Burlington Magazine*, London, May 1960.
H. Read. Introduction to the 1965 São Paulo exhibition catalogue.

Pasternak, Leonid. Russian painter, b. 1862 in Odessa; d. 1945 in Oxford. He was the father of the great writer Boris Pasternak. He became a member of the St. Petersburg Academy in 1905, but in 1921 moved to Berlin. The advent of the Nazi regime caused him to move to London, and he lived in England for the rest of his life. He was influenced by the *Nabis* in his early years. Many of his works are portraits, and the sitters include Tolstoy and Einstein.

Paulucci, Enrico. Italian painter, b. 1901 in Genoa. Paulucci studied in Turin. In 1928 he joined the *Gruppo dei Sei*, which was the guiding spirit behind the Turin school of painting. He now teaches at the Academy in Turin.

Paulucci was influenced, first by Cézanne and subsequently by R. Dufy and H. Matisse. His strictly Neo-Cubist compositions tend to suffer from an undue insistence on elegant colour combinations and mechanical, albeit sophisticated designs.

Pavia, Phillip. American sculptor, b. 1912 in Bridgeport, Connecticut. He studied in New York, Paris and Florence. In the late thirties he was influenced by the direct carving fashion then current. He made figurative sculptures at first, then began to use bronze and to work in an abstract style. In the 1960s he turned to using stone and made some abstract compositions consisting of piles of cube shapes in various marbles.

Pearlstein, Philip. American painter, b. 1924. Pearlstein is a Realist painter who sometimes works from photographs.

Pechstein, Max. German painter, b. 1881 in Eckersbach, near Zwickau; d. 1955 in Berlin. Pechstein became a member of the *Brücke* group in Dresden in 1906, and enjoyed greater popularity than many of his fellow Expressionists. His paintings were more comprehensible to the public than the more profound work of his colleagues, but ultimately they had less value and indeed were regarded as purely imitative by Kirchner. He was in fact greatly influenced by Matisse, which is apparent from some of his nudes in a landscape of around 1912.

In 1908 he moved to Berlin, and two years later founded the New Secession there, in an attempt to provide a focus for German Expressionism. He, like his fellow painters, developed an interest in the primitive art of the South Seas, and after a trip to the Caroline Islands in 1914 he produced a number of exotic, brightly coloured works in the flat primitive manner. Later he painted portraits and landscapes, and his Expressionist origin became less apparent.

Konrad Lemmer. *Max Pechstein und der Beginn des Expressionismus,* Berlin 1949.

Pedersen, Carl-Henning. Danish painter, b. 1913 in Copenhagen. Pedersen is a self-taught painter. In 1939 he visited Paris. He was a member of the *Helhesten* (the Horse of Hell), an association of Danish abstract artists, from 1940 to 1949, when he became a founder member of the *Cobra* group. In 1958 he won the Danish Guggenheim Prize and in 1962 was represented at the Biennale in Venice.

Pedersen started as an abstract artist, painting symbolic linear works based on Klee and Miró. Later, when he embraced the Nordic Expressionism of the *Cobra* artists, he portrayed a fantastic world of dwarfs, daemonic animal-beings, phantoms, suns and castles.

Exhibition catalogue, *Malningar, Skulpturer, Grafik av Henry Heerup, Carl-Henning Pedersen, Palle Nielsen,* Moderna Museet, Stockholm 1967.

Peeters, Josef. Belgian painter, b. 1895 in Antwerp; d. 1960 in Antwerp. After training at the Academy of Art in Antwerp Peeters passed through a phase in which he was influenced by the Futurists before turning abstract. In 1918 he founded the *Moderne Kunst* association, and in 1920 organized the First Congress of Modern Art in Antwerp. In 1921 he met Mondrian and Vantongerloo in Paris, in 1922 he joined the editorial board of *Het Overzicht,* and in 1925 and 1926 published the review *De Driehoek.* In 1927 Peeters gave up painting, and did not resume until 1956, when he reverted to figurative compositions. But in the following year he again took up his abstract experiments. In 1960, the year of his death, a large retrospective exhibition of Peeters' works was staged in Antwerp as an act of homage on the part of the younger generation of Belgian artists to a man who had been neglected for too long.

Pellan, Alfred. Canadian painter, b. 1906 in Quebec. He was precocious in his development, having had a painting purchased by the National Gallery, Ottawa, by 1923, while he was still at the École des Beaux-Arts, Quebec. In 1926 he won a Province of Quebec prize and studied in Paris with Lucien Simon. Remaining in Paris, he won first prize at the Salon d'Art Mural in 1936, by which time he was associated with Picasso, Léger and Miró. His style was a light-hearted Surrealism (*Au clair de la lune,* 1937, Ottawa, National Gallery of Canada). On his return to Canada in 1940, he became a central figure in the new art movement in Montreal and leader of the short-lived *Prisme d'yeux* (1948). He began teaching at the École des Beaux-Arts, Montreal, in 1943 and soon ousted its conservative director and revolutionized its teaching. His painting at this point involved the use of a complex symbolism including Canadian folklore, sex, science fiction, sport and Surrealist poetry (*Floraison,* 1945, Ottawa, National Gallery of Canada). In 1955 a one-man exhibition of his work was held by the Musée d'Art Moderne, Paris, and in 1960 a retrospective exhibition was organized by the National Gallery of Canada. He has painted murals in the National Library, Ottawa (1965), and other buildings. His series of *Jardins* is typical of the more lyric vein of his recent painting (*Jardin jaune,* 1958, Ottawa, Coll. Harold Shenkman). Besides painting, he is a pioneer of theatre design in Canada.

Catalogue, *Alfred Pellan,* National Gallery of Canada, Ottawa 1960.
Guy Robert. *Pellan, sa vie et son oeuvre,* Montreal 1963.

Penalba, Alicia. Argentinian sculptress and painter, b. 1918 in San Pedro. She studied painting in Buenos Aires, then went to Paris in 1948 and concentrated on sculpture. She learnt from Ossip Zadkine and Arp. Her work is organic in form, sometimes vertical in structure, sometimes spreading out horizontally.

Peploe, S. J. (Samuel John). Scottish painter, b. 1871 in Edinburgh; d. 1935 in Edinburgh. Peploe was one of the 'Scottish Colourists', together with Leslie Hunter (1879–1931) and F. C. B. Cadell (1883–1937). He studied at Edinburgh and in Paris, at the Académies Julian and Colarossi. His first one-man show was in Edinburgh in 1903. He spent three years in Paris, 1910–13, and was impressed by Manet. Later he taught at Edinburgh Art College (from 1933). Peploe's work is notable for its powerful but subtle colour and its purity of line.

Pereira, I. (Irene) Rice. American painter, b. 1907 in Massachusetts; d. 1971. When her father died in 1922, she became the wage-earner for the family. Working as a stenographer, she attended night classes at the Art Students' League, studying under R. Lahey and J. Matulka. She travelled to Europe in 1931–2, and upon her return to the United States she began to paint full-time. Her first one-man show came the following year at the American Contemporary Art Gallery, New York. At first she painted scenes dealing with the sea or the machine age (*Anchor*, 1932, coll. of artist). In 1936 when she began to teach painting, composition and design synthesis at the Design Laboratory—a WPA Federal Arts Project enterprise—she turned more decidedly towards abstract art, producing her first pure abstractions in 1937. Before this time her works showed traces of Cubism, Surrealism and abstraction (*Man and Machine*, 1936, Durlacher Bros., New York). Among her first abstractions was *White Rectangle, No. 1* (1938, Durlacher Bros.). In this wholly rectilinear work, she varied texture through patterning, scraping, incising and palette-knife work which created light vibrations and changes of speed and intensity of light, producing pure luminosity. Her work with the WPA also led to the use of varied materials as seen in *Transverse Parallels* (1946, mixed media, Durlacher Bros.). Constructed of two planes of corrugated glass, the front plane sandblasted and the back plane oil on gesso panel, wavy lines are created which change with the movements of the viewer. The effect of the piece also relies strongly on the light and reflections of the environment. The artist has taught at Pratt Institute (1943–4) and Ball State Teachers' College, Indiana (1951).

John I. H. Baur. Catalogue, *Loren MacIver, I. Rice Pereira*, Whitney Museum of American Art, New York 1953.

Perilli, Achille. Italian painter, b. 1927 in Rome. After becoming a founder member of the *Forma I* group in 1947, Perilli helped to launch three magazines: *Arti Visive* in 1952, *L'Esperienza Moderna* in 1957 and *Grammatica* in 1964. During his early period he produced paintings based on gestures. By 1960 these had developed into what he called *Picture-Stories*, i.e. comic-strip compositions, in which insect-like figures are arranged in sequence and contrasted with coloured zones, bands and right angles, the whole being set against a monochrome ground. Of more recent years Perilli has also been working for the theatre. In 1961, for example, he created his *Collage* (a stage setting involving mobile sculptures, projections and film strips, for which Aldo Clementini provided the music) and in 1967 his *Grammatica No Stop Teatro 12 Ore* (in which he collaborated with Nanni Balestrini). Perilli is now living in Rome.

Exhibition catalogue, *Achille Perilli*, Marlborough Galleria d'Arte, Rome 1967.

Perlin, Bernard. American painter, b. 1918 in Richmond, Virginia. Perlin is of Russian descent. He studied in New York, and produced some excellent murals. During the Second World War he was attached to the Office of War Information, in the graphics division, and was also war artist for *Life* magazine. From 1948 he spent most of his time in Italy, but is now back in the United States.

Permeke, Constant. Belgian painter, b. 1886 in Antwerp; d. 1952 in Ostend. Permeke was the son of the marine painter H. Permeke. After studying at the academies in Brussels, Bruges and Ghent (under J. Delvius), he went to live in Laethem-St-Martin from 1906 to 1914. Like Servaes, van den Berghe and the brothers de Smet, he belonged to the second school of Flemish Expressionism and is generally regarded as its most important representative. In 1914 he enlisted in the Belgian forces but was seriously wounded later the same year and spent the remainder of the war in England. In 1918 he returned to Belgium, where he worked first in Antwerp and subsequently in Ostend. In 1951 he visited Brittany.

After an early Impressionist period, Permeke turned to the kind of expressive Realism that was characteristic of Belgian art at that time. But even in the early 1920s his still lifes were already remarkable for their heavy colours and powerful ornamental contours and for the way in which the pictorial objects stood out from the background. Permeke's understanding of the essential contingency and vanity of all living things enabled him to see man and his working environment in a fresh light. In his painting the social element became a new pictorial *motif*. But his pictures of peasants in the fields and villages, of fishermen at sea and of travelling circus artists are not works of social criticism. On the contrary, they give expression to Permeke's sense of a magical reality. In his search for simpler and more condensed structures, Permeke adhered to the stringent conception of form advanced by the Cubists, which kept his Realistic tendencies in check. Thus, the heavy pathos of his pictorial conceptions was offset by the simple, archaic attitudes of his figures. By using powerful brushwork and dark earthy colours, Permeke was able to give full plasticity to the ponderous gestures of his human and animal figures. The glowing colours interlaced with rich shades of gold in which he painted his objects have the effect of distinguishing them from one another whilst allowing them to merge into the dark tones of the general colour scheme. Throughout his life Permeke remained a faithful adherent of Flemish Expressionism in its original form, to which he gave a fresh impetus by incorporating the pathos of man's working environment into the realm of Magic Realism. Permeke's obsession with plasticity prompted him to carry out sculptural experiments. In 1935–6 he created a number of expressive figurative sculptures in clay, plaster of Paris and cement. Like his paintings, these illustrate his preference for monumental forms and his use of light and shade to produce an impression of plasticity.

P. Fierens. *Permeke*, Brussels 1959.
Exhibition catalogue, *Constant Permeke*, Antwerp 1959.

Petrasco, Gheorghe. Rumanian painter, b. 1872 in Tecuci, Moldavia; d. 1949 in Bucharest. Petrasco studied in Bucharest, Munich and Paris (at the Académie Julian, 1898–1902). He travelled in France, Italy and Spain and therafter painted some marvellous landscapes in rich glowing colours.

Petrović, Nadežda. Yugoslav painter, b. 1873 in Cacak, Serbia; d. 1915 in Valjevo. She trained in Belgrade and Munich and spent two years in Paris. She worked in an Impressionist manner, but incorporated the warm colours of the Fauves. She was a major figure in Yugoslavian art of the modern era.

Pettoruti, Emilio. Argentinian painter, b. 1892 in La Plata; d. 1971. Pettoruti, a self-taught artist, pioneered Cubism, Futurism and abstract art in Argentina. He lived in Europe—chiefly in Florence, Rome, Milan and Paris—from 1913 to 1924. In 1914 he painted his first pure abstracts, whose highly dynamic geometrical forms reflect an entirely personal attitude to Cubo-Futurist techniques. Whilst in Europe Pettoruti made contact with de Chirico, Prampolini and the Cubists, and exhibited with them in the Sturm Gallery in Berlin in 1923. He was also on friendly terms with Juan Gris and Severini. In 1924, when he returned to Buenos Aires, his *avant-garde* paintings provoked a violent controversy, which led to a renewal of Argentinian art. From 1930 to 1947 he was curator of the museum in La Plata. In 1953 he went to live in Paris, where he passed through what was essentially a Cubist phase before reverting to pure abstracts. In his late period he produced series of abstract landscapes, birds and butterflies. In 1967–8 his work was shown in a travelling exhibition, which visited numerous European art centres, including Berlin, Brussels and Basle.

J. Payró. *Emilio Pettoruti*, Buenos Aires 1948.
Emilio Pettoruti. *Un pintor ante el espejo*, Buenos Aires 1968.

Peverelli, Cesare. Italian painter, b. 1922 in Milan. Peverelli studied at the Brera in Milan under Carrà from 1940 to 1942. Since 1957 he has been living in Paris. After coming to terms with Cézanne, Matisse, Cubism and Futurism during his early period Peverelli was influenced by Wols in c. 1949 and for the next nine years created informal works. Then, after meeting Matta and Bacon, he began to paint imaginary settings whose calligraphic rhythms and mist-coloured fields of force project a Surrealistic and hallucinatory image of the world.

J. Selz and E. Tadini. *Peverelli*, Paris 1961.

Pevsner, Antoine. French painter and sculptor of Russian origin, b. 1886 in Orel; d. 1962 in Paris. Pevsner was the brother of Naum Gabo. After training at the School of Art in Kiev from 1902 to 1909, he entered the Academy of Art in St. Petersburg as a student but was asked to leave at the end of his three-month probationary period. As a result of this setback Pevsner completely lost faith in the academic world. At that time he was greatly impressed by the medieval Russian icons and the modern French paintings which he had seen in various Moscow collections. In 1911 he visited Paris where he saw Cubist pictures in the Salon des Indépendants. On a second visit, which he made in 1913, he was introduced to the Cubist painters by Archipenko and Modigliani. These meetings, together with his impressions of the Futurist constructions of Boccioni, which he also saw in 1913, encouraged him during his hesitant transition from figurative to abstract art. After returning to Russia in 1914 Pevsner lived in Moscow but then, at his parents' instigation, joined his younger brother Naum Gabo in Oslo in the following year. By that time Gabo was already producing Constructivist sculptures, and it was these which finally prompted Pevsner to renounce figurative art and become a Constructivist painter. When the Revolution broke out in 1917 the two brothers returned to Russia, where Pevsner worked as a professor of painting. In 1920 he and Gabo both signed the *Realistic Manifesto*, in which they denied the primacy of volume in sculpture and questioned its figurative and imitative role. In place of volume they advanced space and time as the fundamental bases of a new, non-imitative art form. In 1923 when Pevsner left Russia, he began to work as a sculptor. After spending several months in Berlin where he met Marcel Duchamp and Katherine Dreier, he went on to Paris, arriving there in 1924. In 1930 he became a French citizen and spent the rest of his life in Paris. In 1931 he joined the *Abstraction-Création* association together with Gabo, Herbin, Kupka and Mondrian. Although he contributed to various international exhibitions in Europe and the United States in the 1930s, it was not until after the Second World War that he was recognized and honoured as one of the pioneers of Constructivist sculpture.

Like his brother Gabo, Pevsner first produced abstract figurations. His *Portrait of Marcel Duchamp* of 1926, which consists of zinc and celluloid discs on a wooden ground, is typical of his output during this early phase, which reached its peak in the *Construction for an Airport* of 1934. But this work was not only a peak, it was also a turning point, for it gave the first hint of the new formative principles which were to govern the second phase of Pevsner's career. These were demonstrated more clearly in the *Construction for an Airport* of 1935, in which the theme—dynamic surfaces evolved from linear elements—is expressed with far greater force. The new trend was carried still further in the *Developable Surface* of 1936, a work of great beauty which was to become the *leitmotiv* of Pevsner's subsequent artistic career. This developable surface, which consists of thin sections of oxidized copper or bronze soldered together to form a single continuous structure, extends into space in great, sweeping curves. Pevsner subsequently created a number of variations on this basic theme, to which he gave the generic name of *Projections in Space*. In certain cases he also provided a metaphorical title (e.g. *Bird Ascending* for the projection erected in front of the Technical Center of General Motors in Detroit) to ensure that his works were regarded, not only as sculptural parallels to certain technological processes, but also as poetic creations in their own right.

Carola Giedion-Welcker. *Antoine Pevsner*, Neuchâtel 1961.
Alexei Pevsner. *Naum Gabo and Antoine Pevsner*, Amsterdam 1964.

Pfahler, Georg Karl. German painter, b. 1926 in Emetzheim, Bavaria. Pfahler attended the Academy of Art in Stuttgart from 1950 to 1954 and founded the *Gruppe 11* in 1955.

Pfahler's works have been placed in the general category of 'signal' painting. He combines elements of Op and Pop Art with rich colours and clear, geometric shapes in designs which are subjected to subtle, spatial distortion. The net result is a highly poetic art form which transcends the normal sphere of poster art.

Philipson, Robin. British painter, b. 1916 in Broughton-in-Furness. Philipson studied at Edinburgh College of Art, and joined the staff in 1947. In 1960 he became head of the School of Drawing and Painting. He was elected to the Royal Scottish Academy in 1962, and in 1966 became a Fellow of the Royal Society of Arts and a member of the Royal Fine Art Commission for Scotland. Philipson

has had many one-man exhibitions in London and Edinburgh, and has featured in some important group exhibitions—*Seven Scottish Painters* at the IBM Gallery, New York, 1965; the *First Edinburgh Open Hundred*, 1967; *Three Centuries of Scottish Painting*, Canada, 1968. In 1966 he produced a mural for the airport at Glasgow.

Phillips, Peter. British painter, b. 1939 in Birmingham. Phillips attended Birmingham College of Art (1955–9). He was one of the Pop artists in the 1964 *New Generation* exhibition which launched Pop Art on the British scene. Popular imagery provides the main compositional elements in his work, but it is apparently not chosen for any particular significance that it might have. The result is a slightly pointless marriage of comic book image and Post-Cubist composition. In 1964 Phillips was one of the young artists employed on the Shakespeare Memorial exhibition.

Piaubert, Jean. French painter, b. 1900 in Feydieu, Gironde. After studying at the École des Beaux-Arts in Bordeaux, Piaubert went to Paris in 1922 and attended the academies of Montparnasse. In order to earn a living, he executed theatre décor and costumes on the instructions of Paul Poiret, as well as fabric designs. His first exhibition took place at the Galerie Zack in 1932. Since the war his painting has resolutely crossed the bounds of figuration, his style being marked by its austerity: rigid forms, sombre colours, rigorous composition. Piaubert is one of those abstract painters who even in his boldest interpretations does not lose the precious qualities of clarity, proportion and zest which are the privilege of artists in the French tradition (*Delphi*, 1955, New York, Solomon R. Guggenheim Museum). His work is characterized by the precision and elegance of the drawing, the sensual colour, and the sense of order and organization which nevertheless allows some leeway in the picture for fantasy and the unexpected.

Picabia, Francis. French painter, b. 1878 in Paris; d. 1953 in Paris. His father was Cuban, his mother French. He studied at the École des Beaux-Arts, the École des Arts Décoratifs and, from 1898, under Pissarro. In 1905 he had his first one-man exhibition. In 1908 he met and the following year married Gabrielle Buffet. In 1909/10 he met the Duchamp brothers and joined the Puteaux group of Cubist artists. In 1911 he was a founder member of the *Section d'Or* group: he was in close contact with Apollinaire and Marcel Duchamp. In 1913 he contributed to the Armory Show, and visited New York for its opening. He also met the publisher-photographer Alfred Stieglitz and contributed to *291* (1914–16) and other journals. He was called up at the outbreak of war and was posted to New York; he was discharged there in 1915 after a 'serious illness'. He spent 1916 and 1917 travelling between America and Europe, contributing to and founding various Dada publications and exhibitions, mainly statements, poems and drawings. His pamphlet *391* was first published in Barcelona in 1917. In 1918 he joined the Zürich Dadaists at the invitation of Tzara. Around 1918 or 1919 he returned to Paris, where he was active in Dada and Surrealist circles. In 1924 he collaborated on a ballet, *Relâche*, with Erik Satie and a film, *Entr'acte*, with René Clair. Around 1925 he was comparatively withdrawn from *avant-garde* activities, living mainly in the south of France. He was, however, still represented in Surrealist exhibitions, etc. In 1945 he returned to Paris and took up abstract painting again.

Picabia enjoyed a prodigious early success as an Impressionist painter in the 1900s: the same facility of assimilation and invention marked each phase of his contacts with new ideas. From his first close friendship with Marcel Duchamp in about 1911 until the mid-1920s, he remained at the forefront of Cubist, Dada and Surrealist activities. His role in them was that of publicist and improvisator more than inventor, but on the whole the exuberantly experimental nature of his work compensates for his eclecticism. This applies equally to his post-Cubist abstractions (*Udnie*, 1913, Paris, Musée d'Art Moderne), his collages and mechanistic images of 1914–22 and the stream of aphorisms he produced for his own and other journals ('Our heads are round to allow thought to change direction', c. 1925). He believed in the constant questioning of accepted values and in the value of a dandified, blasphemous sense of humour, but was never nihilistically anti-art and only obliquely political. Some of his *Transparencies*, painting done in the twenties and thirties, collages using cellophane sheets and thin colour washes, are delicately lyrical. His importance lies in the infectious influence of Dada ideas that he generated wherever he went.

M. Sanouillet. *Picabia*, Paris 1964.
R. Hunt. Catalogue, *Picabia*, Institute of Contemporary Arts, London 1964.

Picasso, Pablo. Spanish-French painter and sculptor, b. 1881 in Malaga; d. 1973. The son of an art teacher, he had a prodigious success as a student. The years 1895–1904 were spent in Barcelona, where he had his first contact with *avant-garde* ideas. His 'Blue Period' evolved from around 1901 to 1904. He visited Paris in 1900 and 1901 (when Vollard gave him an exhibition), and again from 1902 until 1903. In 1904 he settled in Montmartre, where he lived on and off until 1945. There he attracted a circle of artist and writer friends, Jacob, Jarry, Apollinaire, the Douanier Rousseau, Derain, as well as his early patrons—Leo and Gertrude Stein, Uhde, Shchukin. From 1904 to 1906 his 'Rose Period' developed.

About 1906 he met Matisse, Kahnweiler and Gris. The Cézanne memorial exhibition took place in 1907, the year he met Braque. His close partnership with the latter in Paris lasted from 1909 to 1914. During this time he made frequent summer trips to Spain and the south of France, sometimes with Braque, Gris or Derain. In 1912 he created his first collages. In 1917 he visited Italy, and worked with Cocteau and Diaghilev on the ballet *Parade*. In 1918 he married the ballerina Olga Koklova, and their son was born in 1921. He met Miró in 1919, and from 1920 to 1925 he produced his 'Neo-Classical' paintings. From about 1925 on he was in contact with the Surrealists, a contact which was mutually influential; he met Breton, and developed a friendship with Éluard. In 1932 he bought a château at Boisgeloup: there he made large iron sculptures (with González) and plaster heads. In 1933 came the etchings of *The Sculptor's Studio*. In 1935 his daughter Maïa was born to Marie-Thérèse Walter, his model since the early thirties. At this time he was active as an illustrator (Balzac's *Chef d'Oeuvre Inconnu*, Ovid's *Metamorphosis*, Bouffon's *Histoire Naturelle*) and contributed to Surrealist periodicals. For about two years (1936–8) he lived with Dora Maar, his model for many paintings and drawings. In 1936 he was appointed Director of the Prado Museum at the outbreak of the Spanish Civil War. After 1937, when he exhibited *Guernica* in the Spanish Pavilion of the Paris World's Fair, he never went back to Spain. Later in 1937 he visited Klee in Switzerland. He remained working in Paris throughout the German occupation, though deeply distressed by the war. In 1941 he wrote a short play, *Desire Caught by the Tail*. From 1946 to 1948 he lived in Antibes with Françoise Gilot. Their son Claude was born in 1947, their daughter Paloma in 1949; they separated in 1953. In 1948 he settled in Vallauris, where he set up a ceramics workshop. From 1948 to 1951 he took an active part in various Peace Congresses throughout Europe. In 1953 Clouzot's film, *Le Mystère Picasso*, was made about him. In 1955 he moved to Cannes and then, in 1958, bought the Château de Vauvenargues, near Aix. In that year he did the mural decoration for the UNESCO building in Paris. In 1961 he married Jacqueline Roque and moved to a large house near Mougins. Major exhibitions of his work have been seen in Paris (1955), London (1960), New York (1962) and again in Paris (1966–7).

The prodigious facility and invention with which Picasso established a reputation in Paris over the period 1900–6 has marked each subsequent phase of his career. This early period was one of radical enquiry, experiment and assimilation of new ideas (Neo-Impressionism, *art nouveau*, Symbolism) as well as more traditional forms. The Blue Period paintings, soaked in a melancholic, *fin-de-siècle* mysticism (*The Old Guitarist*, 1903, Chicago, Art Institute), and the Rose Period, lighter in mood and palette (*Boy with Horse*, 1905, London, Tate Gallery), were complete and accomplished and made his name. The preoccupation with life-and-death allegories and the brooding Expressionism recur constantly in his later work.

This refined resolution was abandoned about 1906 or 1907 in a renewed questioning of the process of image-making. Looking first at the stylization of medieval art and then at non-naturalistic African masks and carvings, he painted *Les Demoiselles d'Avignon* (New York, Museum of Modern Art). The savageness of its technique and alterations symbolizes its revolutionary gesture against European traditions of naturalistic illusion. It was Picasso's more conceptual approach that enabled him and Braque to see Cézanne's late work objectively as a means of putting an image together, rather than as Neo-Impressionist landscape painting. Although in his analytical Cubist paintings he was drawn by Braque into the Parisian traditions of painterliness and visual analysis, Picasso stretched them to new limits. Works like *Portrait of Kahnweiler*, 1910 (Chicago, Art Institute) combine illusionistic and graphic references to the sitter in a refined manipulation of paint, colour and tone that creates form-space relationships without compromising the canvas's flat surface.

The invention of collage (from '*coller*', to paste) in 1912 was another channel for Picasso's irreverent gestures against High Art inhibitions. His sharp, opportunist improvisation with materials and ready-made images came to the fore, as did the fundamentally Expressionist nature of his art. From 1913 on he made a succession of paintings (*Green Still Life*, 1914, New York, Museum of Modern Art), reliefs (*Still Life with Upholstery Fringe*, 1914, London, Tate Gallery) and sculptures (*Absinthe Glass*, painted bronze, 1914; edition of 6) which not only provide the framework for his own later oeuvre, but also anticipate generations of later painting and assemblage.

His visit to Italy in 1917 perhaps encouraged the strongly classical flavour of the figure paintings of 1919–25 (*Seated Woman*, 1923, London, Tate Gallery; *Three Musicians*, 1921, Philadelphia, Museum of Art). This gave way to a ritualistic violence and fantasy in the mid-1920s (*Three Dancers*, 1925, London, Tate Gallery). The subsequent series of invented anatomies (in paintings, sculpture and drawings) were influential for Surrealism. He exhibited with the Surrealists and shared their political aspirations. The political protest of *Guernica* (New York, Museum of Modern Art) was anticipated in the *Dream and Lie of Franco* etchings of 1936–7 and has occasionally surfaced in his work since.

His work since the Second World War has in general been more relaxed and less prolifically inventive, including numerous family portraits, sets of variations on *motifs* from other artists (Velasquez,

Poussin, Delacroix) and an enormous output in graphic media and ceramics.

Probably the most influential and controversial figure of modern art, Picasso was at the forefront of the European *avant-garde* from the early 1900s until the Second World War. His prolific oeuvre seems uneven not only in achievement but also in the seriousness of its premises; embracing a radical intellectualism, serious political commitment, a playful wit and whimsicality and the showmanship of his life style. None of this can qualify his importance in twentieth-century art history: very little that has happened since does not demand to be seen in some relationship to the work of his early maturity.

Christian Zervos. *Picasso*, 19 vols., Paris 1932 on.
Maurice Raynal. *Picasso: Biographical and Critical Studies*, Geneva 1953.
A. H. Barr Jr. Catalogue, *Picasso: Seventy-Fifth Anniversary Exhibition*, Museum of Modern Art, New York 1957.
Roland Penrose. *Picasso: His Life and Work*, London 1958.
H. L. C. Jaffe. *Picasso*, London and New York 1964.

Picelj, Ivan. Yugoslav painter and graphic artist, b. 1924 in Okučani, Croatia. Picelj trained at the Academy of Art in Zagreb from 1943 to 1946. Since 1948 he has been responsible, together with V. Richter and Alexander Srnec, for the artistic preparation of Yugoslav exhibitions abroad. In 1951, when he went completely abstract, he and a group of friends founded the *EXAT 51* group, the first abstract artists' association in Yugoslavia.

Picelj is a highly intellectual artist with a great yen for clarity, which he achieves by restricting the formal range of his works to a group of absolutely basic elements of a technological and architectonic order. The principal feature of his silhouette-like compositions—which consist of combinations of right angles, gradients, curves and segments of circles and are executed in quiet colours—is the sense of harmony and balance that exists between the component elements. The total figuration that emerges from these rhythmical relations has something of the coolness of Bauhaus work and of the Neo-Plasticist trend within the *Abstraction-Création* movement. Picelj's completely unemotional approach to art and the scientific rigour with which he has pursued his objective are something quite new in Yugoslavia, where the Slavonic race and the Mediterranean climate have always combined to oppose any such development.

Michel Seuphor. 'Ivan Picelj', in Th. Knaur (ed.), *Lexikon abstrakter Malerei*, Munich 1957.
R. Putar. 'The Designer Ivan Picelj', *Architektura*, Belgrade 1962.

Pickett, Joseph. American painter, b. 1848 in New Hope, Pennsylvania; d. 1918 in New Hope. He worked for many years on carnival routes, running various types of concessions, most often shooting galleries. When he married in the last decade of the nineteenth century and opened a modest grocery store, he devoted much of his leisure time to painting. He at first used house paint but later changed to regular artist's materials. He worked for years on a single painting, continuously adding colour, thereby giving his surfaces a raised texture. His works were first discovered and purchased by another artist, Lloyd Ney, who later sold the paintings in exchange for picture frames. Pickett's works were finally seen in the framer's shop by Holger Cahill, who brought the paintings to the attention of the public. One of Pickett's best-known paintings is the large *Manchester Valley* (New York, Museum of Modern Art). The tactility of the surface is increased here not merely through repeated applications of pigment but also by the addition of sand, shells and other gritty substances to the paint. Perspective is less significant in this work than the personal experiences of the artist and the importance he placed on various elements regardless of their distance from the viewer. Executed in fresh, vibrant colours, the scene has the quality of a pristine and carefully planned toy village.

S. Janis. *They Taught Themselves*, New York 1942.

Piene, Otto. German painter, sculptor and kinetic artist, b. 1928 in Leasphe, Westphalia. Piene studied at the Munich Academy (1948–50) and Cologne University (1953–7). In 1955 when he was still a student he became interested in screen processing. In 1959 he worked on light reflectors, photogravures and heliographs and also produced his first *Light Ballet*. In 1960 he made 'smoke pictures' (with candle black) and created a *Mechanical Light Ballet* in which machines took the place of dancers. Whilst continuing to paint pictures—most of them simple colour contrasts in red and black—Piene has also been working on freestanding kinetic compositions (light spheres) since 1967. He is evidently fascinated by light, for it enters into every branch of his work. Piene now lives in Düsseldorf and New York.

Exhibition catalogue, *Zero*, Kestner Gesellschaft, Hanover 1965.

Pierluca (Pierluca degli Innocenti). Italian sculptor, b. 1926 in Florence. After studying at the Florence Academy from 1948 to 1951, Pierluca worked as a restorer of ancient Italian stained glass up to 1958. He then began to produce his abstract sculptures. These consist of peeling layers of smooth metal with jagged edges and are formed by a modelling process under heat. Pierluca has been living in Bois d'Arcy, Paris, since 1960.

Pignon, Edouard. French painter, b. 1905 in Bully, Pas-de-Calais. A miner first of all, then a metalworker in Paris from 1927, he was to take up various occupations before he was able, in 1936, to devote himself entirely to painting. Two canvases, sixteen years apart, on the same subject (*Dead Worker*) sum up his realistic approach. From the one to the other,

from 1936 to 1952, the formulation of the theme becomes suppler and evolves from a hieratic composition to a method of outlining which links and separates forms in the space it defines. Between these two works there are rigorous still lifes, serious *Catalans* (1945–6), *Maternities* (1948–51) with broader features, and lastly the visions of *Ostend* (1947–9) with its wintry overtones, its broad flat tints with their slow rhythms. But in 1953, with the first *Olive Trees* and the great nudes in a landscape, Pignon's creative work was to rise to new heights. A natural radiance sparkles from the canvas (the *Olive Tree*, 1958, Paris, Galerie de France; the *Furrowed Hillside*, 1958). Several summers spent in Italy (1958–62) resulted in the *Threshing*, the stormy assaults of the *Corn Gatherers*, then the menacing *Battles* (1963–5).

Pillet, Edgard. French painter and publicist, b. 1912 in Saint-Christoly-de-Medoc (Gironde). After studying at the academies in Bordeaux and Paris from 1927 onwards, Pillet began to sculpt but went over to painting in 1939. In 1945 he joined the *École de Paris* and became a founder member of the Atelier d'Art Abstrait. He also works as a publicist (for *Art aujourd'hui* and other publications) and as a film producer.

Most of Pillet's paintings are concerned with dualistic problems of form. Up to 1955 his work was strictly geometrical, but since then he has moved towards a more spontaneous and informal style. He was responsible for developing the *creusets* (concave pictures).

Piper, John. British painter, b. 1903 in Epsom. After five years' legal training and practice, Piper studied at the RCA. Early influenced by French painters, particularly Braque, his Parisian contacts in the 1930s included Arp, Brancusi and Giacometti. Piper graphically recorded the London *Blitz* (1940–1). His subsequent achievements range from theatre design, stained glass (figurative for Eton College, abstract for Coventry Cathedral), to topographic and architectural illustration of a creative kind (some in cooperation with John Betjeman) and writings for various books and periodicals.

Underrated by purists, Piper's sheer fecundity and technical ability, the intense preoccupation with *matière* and Romantic imagery in strange lighting, place him at the extreme of twentieth-century English picturesque, painterly art—meriting him an historical niche similar to Piranesi's. Examples of his work are in the Tate, the Victoria and Albert Museum, the New York Museum of Modern Art, etc.

J. Betjeman. *John Piper*, London 1944.
J. Woods. *John Piper*, London 1955.

Pirandello, Fausto. Italian painter, b. 1899 in Rome. Pirandello is the son of the playwright Luigi Pirandello. After travelling a great deal he settled down to work in Paris, Berlin and Rome. Although Pirandello was deeply impressed by Cézanne and the Cubists in 1928, their influence was short-lived, for in 1930 he reverted to a descriptive form of naturalism. Subsequently, however—from c. 1940 onwards —he began to reduce the density of his colours and the plasticity of his pictorial forms in accordance with Neo-Cubist practice.

Pirandello's colours, which look as if they had been applied with a palette knife, are organized into dense, crystalline designs, which produce an overall rhythmical effect that is greatly enhanced by his architectonic use of light. At the same time his pictorial objects, which are set out in horizontal and perpendicular rows, are rendered insubstantial by the luminosity of certain of his colours and so transformed into transparent schemas. Pirandello has also shown a preference for bold outlines, and by c. 1950 this had brought him close to abstract art.

Pisis, Filippo de. Italian painter, b. 1896 in Ferrara; d. 1956 in Milan. After reading literature at the University of Bologna Pisis turned to painting and studied under O. Domenichini and G. Longanesi. From 1919 to 1925 he lived in Rome, and between 1920 and 1940 made frequent visits to Paris, where he became the leading figure in the Italian artists' colony. In 1926 he was represented at the first *Novecento* exhibition, in 1942 he visited Florence, and in 1951 had a large retrospective exhibition in the Castelle Extense in Ferrara. Pisis also worked as a poet and critic. He spent the final period of his life, from 1950 onwards, in Paris and Venice.

Initially, Pisis was influenced by the *Pittura Metafisica* of Carrà and de Chirico. But the plasticity and structural precision of their work was not really compatible with his own Expressionistic leanings, nor was he interested in their metaphysical interpretations of everyday objects, or their theatrical Surrealistic settings. Consequently, he was unable to develop a personal style during this early phase. In c. 1919 Pisis tried to free himself from the problems of pictorial form by joining the Dadaists. But he soon abandoned this new venture, for the idea of an essentially arbitrary and absurd art form was alien to him. In fact, it was as a result of this brief excursion into Dadaism that Pisis came to realize the importance of a firm structural framework for his pictorial conceptions. This realization was strengthened both during Pisis' six-year stay in Rome, where he had his crucial meeting with Spandini, and during his repeated visits to Paris. In Paris Pisis was influenced briefly by the French Cubists, and subsequently made an intensive study of Impressionist colouring. But although the landscapes produced between 1918 and 1925 were inspired by Manet, Sisley, Pissarro and Utrillo, they are executed in a very personal and highly expressive style. Gradually, Pisis' luminous colours grew brighter. Using powerful

brushwork, he painted pictures that were full of movement and vibrant light. Traces of the style of Matisse, Derain and Soutine also began to appear in Pisis' work. But, above all, his preoccupation with French Impressionist colouring led him back to the eighteenth-century Venetians, especially Guardi. After living in Milan, London and Rome, he finally settled in Venice, whose colourful and lyrical atmosphere was admirably suited to his artistic temperament. From 1927 onwards Pisis produced numerous Venetian still lifes, landscapes and coastal views in a highly lyrical style. In these essentially melancholy works he identified completely with his subject, so that his Venetian scenes are not so much objective reproductions of actual settings as his own emotional response to those settings. With powerful, almost staccato strokes of the brush Pisis created firm spatial structures which he then diffused by his use of colour and light. The vibrant atmosphere that is one of the principal characteristics of his work is due to his highly differentiated palette, which embraced a wide range of colours, from grey, green, pink and pale blue to brown and a smooth black. This diversity made for extremely subtle colouring, which was enhanced by the fineness of Pisis' tonal values. Pisis takes isolated objects and macabre metaphysical scenes, and invests them with an intensely lyrical and visionary quality, thus transforming the objective world into a mass of colour and light.

Filippo de Pisis. *Prose e articoli*, Milan 1947.
Waldemar George. *Filippo de Pisis: Castello Estense*, Ferrara 1951.
G. Raimondi. *Filippo de Pisis*, Florence 1952.

Pissarro, Lucien. British-French painter, b. 1863 in Paris; d. 1944 in Hewood, Somerset. He was the eldest son of the Impressionist Camille Pissarro. He moved to London in 1890; he became a member of the New English Art Club in 1906 and of the Camden Town Group in 1911, when it was founded. His first one-man show took place at the Carfax Gallery, London, in 1913. He was also a designer and printer of books. There was a centenary exhibition of his work at the Arts Council in 1963.

Pistoletto, Michelangelo. Italian painter, b. 1933 in Biella. Up to 1957 Pistoletto worked as a restorer of picture frames. In 1968 he moved from Turín to Rome, where he is still living today.

Pistoletto is a member of the New Realist school. In 1962 he began to incorporate photographs into his paintings. In the works of this period the pictorial objects, which seem to be completely absorbed by the light, appear as rigid structures within an infinite and intangible spatial schema. He has also produced *Mirror Pictures*. These works, which consist of photocollages mounted on polished steel grounds, constitute an attempt to involve the viewer in the life of the picture, namely by incorporating his mirror image.

S. Simon. 'Michelangelo Pistoletto', *Art International* X, Zürich 1966.

Pittura Metafisica. The brief period of Italian 'metaphysical painting' set in at the beginning of 1917. It was then that Carlo Carrà and Giorgio de Chirico met in the military hospital in Ferrara, and for the next six months, whilst they were convalescing in the local monastery, these two Italian artists painted together. The dreamy atmosphere of this north Italian town with its large deserted squares, archaic statues, monumental walls and frozen Quattrocento frescoes provided the physical framework within which Carrà finally broke away from the dynamic and essentially metropolitan doctrine of Futurism, to which he had subscribed since its inception in 1910 but whose functionalism he had found more and more objectionable. It was partly because of his aversion to this functionalist trend, and partly because he had been so impressed by Giotto's archaic forms in 1915, that Carrà rejected Futurism. Having done so, he joined with de Chirico in searching for the inner aspect of the object world, which the Futurists with their abstract, functionalist and psychologically oriented forms of expression had completely disregarded. The magical quality that pervades de Chirico's early mythological works stemmed partly from his childhood experiences in Greece and partly from his preoccupation with the sombre and fantastic paintings of Böcklin and Klinger, the *Jugendstil* artists. When he met Carrà in Ferrara, de Chirico was also reunited with his brother Alberto Savinio, whose oversensitive, febrile poems exerted a crucial influence on both artists, encouraging them in their quest for magical intensity and in their study of the great Italian masters Giotto and Masaccio, who had regarded nobility of soul as the one quality that could raise human beings above the purely functional level of daily life. Unlike the Futurists, who wanted to represent 'universal dynamism . . . as a dynamic sensation', Giotto had used his naturalistic but highly imaginative technique to portray essentially passive scenes, in which the object world acquired an aura of noble simplicity. As for the *Pittura Metafisica*, its aim was defined by de Chirico as 'constructing a new metaphysical psychology of objects by means of painting'. This involved a process of alienation: functional objects were removed from their normal environment and painted as isolated phenomena. As a result of this isolation, they acquired a magical quality, an enigmatic and mythical aura, which became one of the principal characteristics of the *Pittura Metafisica*. With their lyrical individuality, these banal isolated objects often achieve a quite remarkable degree of pathos that makes them extremely moving. By the end of 1917 the *Pittura Metafisica* movement as such had come to an end, but the ideas on which it was based were still being applied by Morandi after 1918. Although short-lived, the *Pittura Metafisica* was highly significant, since it helped to pave the way for French Surrealism and German Magic Realism.

Giorgio de Chirico. 'Sull'arte metafisica', *Valori Plastici* I, Nos. 4 and 5, 1919.
Carlo Carrà. *Pittura metafisica*, Milan 1945.
U. Apollonio. *Pittura metafisica*, Venice 1950.

Pizzinato, Armando. Italian painter, b. 1910 in Maniago, Udine. In 1946 Pizzinato became a founder member of the *Fronte Nuovo delle Arti*. Since 1952 he has been a contributor to the magazine *Realismus*. He is now living in Venice.

After passing through Futurist and Cubist phases Pizzinato turned to Neo-Realism. But by 1950 his propagandist paintings, which were executed in a poster style and were aimed at the masses, had grown top-heavy. The outmoded poster technique was no longer able to encompass the thematic requirements to which it was subjected, and Pizzinato's work lost all significance.

G. Ghiringhelli. *Pittura moderna italiana*, Turin 1949.

Plumb, John. British painter, b. 1927 in Bedford. Plumb studied at the Central School of Art in London, 1954–7. He held his first one-man show in 1957 at Gallery One and in 1960 took part in the *Situation* exhibition. The American hard-edge painters, such as Barnett Newman and Ellsworth Kelly, form a point of departure for his work. He is interested in the tension between shape, colour and surface, stretching taut bands of colour over a ground of black and white interlocking shapes. He plays the linear tension of the strong colour against the tension between the areas of black separated by white.

Pointillism is virtually equivalent to Divisionism (*see* **Neo-Impressionism**).

Polesello, Rogelio. Argentinian painter and draughtsman, b. 1939 in Buenos Aires. Polesello studied at the School for Visual Art in Buenos Aires. He has works in museums in Argentina and New York, and also in Washington, where he won the first prize in the Salon of Young Latin American Artists in 1965.

Poliakoff, Serge. Russian-French painter, b. 1906 in Moscow; d. 1969 in Paris. Serge Poliakoff was a Russian who lived and worked in Paris from 1923 onwards. A gifted musician, he went with his aunt, the singer Nadia Poliakoff, to Constantinople in 1919, when forced to leave Russia by the Revolution. After various European tours with her, he settled in Paris in 1923. For the next twenty years or so he earned his living as a cabaret guitarist. At the age of 24 he began painting, and for the next few years received instruction from various sources, including the Slade School in London. His early works are figurative in content, but after meeting

Kandinsky in 1937, and becoming a close friend of Sonia and Robert Delaunay, he began to work in the abstract style.

His first one-man show was in 1945 in Paris, and he was awarded the Kandinsky Prize in 1947, from which time he progressed steadily towards his foremost position among the abstract painters of the *École de Paris* in the 1950s. He approached his work from an attitude of 'constant search', believing it to be essential that each artist find his own appropriate technique for complete fulfilment. He was essentially a colourist, and his works have little trace of conventional picture space or geometric linear construction. He seems to have been free from any leanings towards the representational elements which concerned his friend de Staël. In his method of application of paint, in his own formulated manufacture of his colours, and in his concern with technique he produced as a craftsman paintings which were objects in themselves. His work could be taken as a fulfilment of the prediction of the Neo-Impressionist H.-E. Cross, who had perceived the possibility of paintings 'as chromatic harmonies completely invented and established so to speak without reference to Nature as a point of departure'. Poliakoff also produced lithographs which were in the same style of carefully positioned areas of intuitional, brilliant colour.

Poliakoff appears more as a culminator than an initiator in respect of ideas in twentieth-century abstract painting. He seems to have been little affected by the growing ideas of the time which were questioning the validity of paintings as art-objects. His very acceptable work was given a retrospective exhibition at Berne in 1960, and after his death in 1969 an exhibition of his work was held at the Whitechapel Art Gallery, London.

Pollock, Jackson. American painter, b. 1912 in Cody, Wyoming; d. 1956. Pollock moved with his family to Southern California in 1925. He was at first interested in sculpture but soon shifted his concentration to painting. By 1929 he and his brother Charles were studying with Thomas Benton at the Art Students' League. His work shows both the influence of his teacher and that of the American Romantic painter, A. Ryder (*Seascape*, 1934, New York, Coll. Lee Krasner Pollock). The late 1930s and early 1940s were both personally and professionally significant for Pollock. During these years he worked for the Federal Arts Project (1938–42), had his first exhibition at the McMillan Gallery with Willem de Kooning and Lee Krasner (1940), and was given his first one-man show at Peggy Guggenheim's Art of This Century Gallery (1943). Throughout the 1940s his work was championed by the critic Clement Greenberg, whose writings led to both praise and castigation by the art world. In 1946 Pollock was simultaneously painting in two styles,

one characterized by an elegant linearity (*The Blue Unconscious*, Coll. Mr. and Mrs. Saul Schwamm), the other an all-over, rich, impasto style (*Eyes in the Heat*, Venice, Coll. Peggy Guggenheim). The following year his approach changed completely, ushering in the free, seemingly random drip paintings for which he is best known (*Full Fathom Five*, oil and aluminium paint on canvas, New York, Museum of Modern Art). In 1950 he was given his first one-man show in Europe—an exhibition held in Venice and Milan, organized by Peggy Guggenheim. In the same year he was included in the Venice Biennale along with A. Gorky and W. de Kooning. Throughout the 1950s he produced works with amazing fecundity. His canvases ranged from black and white figurative works such as *Black and White, Number 5* (1952, New York, coll. Lee Krasner Pollock, Sidney Janis Gallery) which chronologically parallel the black and white paintings of F. Kline, W. de Kooning and R. Motherwell, to all-over drip paintings (*Convergence*, 1952, Buffalo, New York, Albright Art Gallery) and impasto works (*Scent*, 1955, New York, Coll. Mrs. Leo Castelli) in which he returned to the vitality, delicacy and joyful chromatic harmonies of the late 1940s. Though he was given one-man shows, included in most major exhibitions of contemporary painting and sold his works to major museums, Pollock was often severely criticized, especially for his working methods, a phenomenon which is only recently waning.

Frank O'Hara. *Jackson Pollock*, New York 1959.
Bryan Robertson. *Jackson Pollock*, New York 1960.

Polychrome sculpture. Colour in sculpture may be inherent in the material or may be added; both kinds have been revived in the twentieth century, after a long post-Renaissance tradition of uncoloured or, at the most, tonal sculpture. In the early twentieth century, colour was used by sculptors working in a Cubist style, notably by Alexander Archipenko. Other major sculptors in America using colour, from the 1930s on, were Alexander Calder and David Smith. A distinct new movement in polychrome sculpture began in the late 1950s, continuing through the 1960s. Some of the reasons for this development were the contemporary importance of colour in painting (e.g. in Op Art), the increasing fusion of sculpture and painting, and the new sculptural materials—those with inherent colour (some plastics and neon light) creating polychrome effects directly, and those with neutral or unfinished surfaces requiring treatment with paint, often with a strongly coloured and slick, industrial kind of finish. An early example from this period of a special kind of polychrome sculpture is the work of John Chamberlain, assemblages of coloured metal sheets from destroyed automobiles. Other artists in whose work colour is a major consideration include

Chryssa, who works with coloured neon; David Weinrib, who uses translucent and clear coloured plastics; George Sugarman, who utilizes colours to dissociate the separated, variously grouped elements of his sculpture; Robert Hudson, who creates illusory spatial relationships with added surface patterns and forms; Peter Voulkos, John Mason and Kenneth Price, who produce polychrome clay sculpture; and Sidney Geist and Ronald Bladen.

Sidney Geist. 'Color It Sculpture', *Arts Yearbook Number 8: Contemporary Sculpture*, New York 1964.
Jasia Reichardt. 'Color in Sculpture', *Quadrum* XVIII, 1965.

Pomodoro, Arnaldo. Italian sculptor, b. 1926 in Morciano di Romagna. Before turning to sculpture Pomodoro studied architecture and theatrical décor and served an apprenticeship as a goldsmith. In 1954 he settled in Milan, where he is still living. In 1955 he had his first exhibition, in Milan; in 1963 he won the prize for sculpture at the Bienal in São Paulo and in 1964 the prize for Italian sculpture at the Biennale in Venice.

During his early period Pomodoro was closely associated with Informal art. Since then, however, he has produced works in bronze or combinations of different materials, in which he has been investigating organic and technological structures. His *Grande Omaggio alla Civiltà Tecnologica* (Great Homage to Technological Culture), a large relief which he created for the College of Further Education in Cologne, is typical of these later works.

Pomodoro, Giò. Italian sculptor, b. 1930 in Orciano di Pesaro. Pomodoro is the brother of A. Pomodoro. He is a self-taught artist and has been living in Milan since 1953. In 1954 (in Florence) he had the first of many exhibitions of his sculptures and in 1959 was awarded the prize for sculpture at the Biennale in Paris.

Pomodoro produces single- and double-sided reliefs in cast bronze and—of more recent years—porcelain. By strictly limiting the volume of these works and modulating the surfaces, which are virtually porous, he creates an impression of continuous movement in space.

Poons, Larry. American painter, b. 1937 in Tokyo. Poons first studied at the New England Conservatory of Music before attending the Boston Museum School of Fine Arts (1955–7). A musical composition class with the *avant-garde* composer John Cage at the New School for Social Research in New York introduced Poons to methods of random composition that were to affect his later paintings considerably. His earliest pictures also involved certain musically rhythmic progressions of geometric forms, recalling the moving syncopated relationship in Mondrian's late work (e.g. *Broadway Boogie-Woogie*). Other important influences on his development include the concept of all-over pictorial composition that he found in Jackson Pollock's 'drip' paintings, and the broad fields of intense colour in Barnett Newman's canvases. Absorbing these influences, Poons added optically activating combinations of colour, a distinguishing feature of the paintings he produced between 1963 and 1965. These contain fields of saturated colour perforated with discs and ovals that seem to recede, spin, project, or create ghost-like or subliminal after-images (*Nixes' Mate*, 1964, New York, Museum of Modern Art), while a seemingly random yet controlled distribution of elements on invisible grids was combined with an intuitive choice of colours. In 1966 Poons began to work with close-valued combinations of hues that suggested both a great spatial and atmospheric depth, and a seemingly disembodied suspension of the small coloured units (*Wildcat Arrival*, 1966, New York, Coll. Albert List). Even though the surface tension of his earlier paintings was neutralized in these later works, the possibility of the field's lateral extension became more apparent and suggestive. In 1967 the influence of such painters as Jules Olitski (b. 1922) could be seen in Poons' loosening of the spatial field and in the increasing range and richness of the colour in his work.

Kermit S. Champa. 'New Paintings by Larry Poons', *Artforum* VI, No. 10, 1968.
Lucy Lippard. 'Larry Poons: The Illusion of Disorder', *Art International* XI, Zürich, April 1967.

Pop Art. This style, which first emerged in the mid-1950s, had its origins in the mass media (comic strips, advertisements and advertising slogans), the consumer sphere (supermarkets), traffic scenes (street hoardings) and industrial products (motor cars and television sets), the image of youth and the image of the star (the Monroe cult). One group of Pop artists uses these *motifs* as themes; another treats them simply as structural devices; whilst a third group exploits both their thematic and their formal potential. Some Pop artists adopt a critical attitude to the commercial world, which finds expression in their work. Others simply reproduce the *motifs* and forms which they observe in that world, sometimes enlarging or multiplying them but otherwise leaving them completely unchanged. The concepts of Pop Art and Pop culture ('pop' = 'popular') came into vogue in the mid-1950s as a result of a meeting which was held in the Institute of Contemporary Arts in London to discuss fashion, the mass media, industrial design, science fiction and allied subjects and which was attended by artists and architects and by the writers of the *Independent Group*. Laurence Alloway, Reyner Banham, Richard Hamilton, Eduardo Paolozzi and Alison and Peter Smithson were amongst those present. This group formed the original cadre of English Pop Art. Various important exhibitions were staged, including *Parallel of Life* and *Art* of 1953, *Man, Machine and Motion* of 1955 and *This is Tomorrow* of 1956. There have been three distinct phases in the development of English Pop Art. The first of these, which lasted from 1953 to 1958 and was concerned with technology, was represented by artists like Hamilton and Paolozzi; the second, which was essentially a product of the Royal College of Art and saw the incorporation into Pop Art of abstract techniques, produced artists like Richard Smith and Peter Blake; and the third, which commenced in 1961 and attached major importance to painterly qualities and figuration, was represented by painters like David Hockney, Allen Jones and Peter Phillips. Meanwhile, in New York, from the mid-1950s onwards Jasper Johns and Robert Rauschenberg had been using abstract techniques in works depicting objects from everyday life. Subsequently Roy Lichtenstein, Claes Oldenburg, James Rosenquist, Andy Warhol and Tom Wesselmann began to paint 'popular images' by reproducing commercial techniques. The Hansa, Green, Reuben and Judson galleries specialized in this 'new' art form. Oldenburg's *Ray Gun Manufacturing Company of 1961* was an important milestone in the development of New York Pop Art. So too were the two exhibitions staged in the Martha Jackson Gallery: *New Forms, New Media* of 1960 and *Environments, Situations, Spaces* of 1961.

California was also an important centre of American Pop Art. Al Bengston, Edward Kienholz, Mel Ramos, Edward Ruscha and Wayne Thibaud all worked on the West Coast, where the general approach was less rigid than in New York, with less emphasis on the reproduction of commercial techniques. Whilst Pop Art was establishing itself in England and America, a new art form was emerging in Central and Western Europe under the name of *Nouveau Réalisme* which incorporated elements from each of the various phases of Pop Art. These are to be found in the works of Valerio Adami, Winfred Gaul, Peter Klasen, Bernard Rancillac, Martial Raysse and others. Pop Art had its origins in the commercial arts and, once it was established, it exerted an immediate and enduring influence on them. And so we find numerous elements of Pop Art in television, films, theatre, literature and magazines. No artistic movement has had such far-reaching effects since the days of the Bauhaus.

John Coplans. Catalogue, *Pop Art USA*, Oakland Art Museum, Oakland (Calif.) 1963.
G. R. Swenson. 'What Is Pop Art?', *Art News* LXII, November 1963; February 1964.
R. G. Dienst. *Pop Art*, Wiesbaden 1965.
J. Becker and W. Vostell. *Happenings, Fluxus, Pop Art, Nouveau Réalisme*, Reinbek 1965.
Lucy R. Lippard. *Pop Art*, London and New York 1966.

Popova, Liubov. Russian painter, b. 1889; d. 1924. After studying in Moscow she went to Paris in 1912 with Nadezhda Udaltsova, and there worked with Le Fauconnier and Metzinger. The language of Cubism was adapted by her to produce original work that was representational to begin with but which later approached abstraction.

Porter, Fairfield. American painter, b. 1907 in Winnetka, Illinois. He studied in New York, and was influenced by such diverse figures as Manet, Winslow Homer, Thomas Eakins, Vermeer and Bonnard. Some of his early works are social commentary; after the war he painted everyday scenes, both interior and exterior, in light but rich colours and with a masterly technique.

Portinari, Cándido. Brazilian painter, b. 1903 in Brodosque, near São Paulo; d. 1962 in Rio de Janeiro. After studying at the Academy in Rio de Janeiro Portinari lived in Europe from 1928 to 1930. He spent most of this period in Paris, but also visited the museums of art in the French provinces, Spain, Italy and England before returning to Brazil. Although he was not influenced to any real extent by the modern trends that he encountered in Europe, he none the less turned to modern art after meeting Foujita in Rio in 1932. The first picture that he painted in his new style (which he himself refers to as his 'brown style') was his *Café*, which won a special commendation in the Carnegie Competition of 1935. From the mid-1930s onwards, due no doubt to the influence of the new school of Mexican fresco painting, Portinari began to paint pictures portraying the life of the poor Brazilian peasants, the cowherds and coffee-bean pickers. From 1936 onwards he executed numerous wall paintings for public buildings, including the Ministry of Education. In 1939 he had large retrospective exhibitions in the Museum in Rio de Janeiro and the Museum of Modern Art in New York. In 1941–2, when he created wall paintings for the Library of Congress in Washington, he adopted an entirely new and passionate style, which reveals the influence of Picasso and the Expressionists and which came to dominate the work of his final period. Of his late wall paintings the most important were the monumental compositions on the subjects of *War* and *Peace*, which he executed between 1950 and 1956 for the UNO building in New York. Portinari won several awards, including the Guggenheim Prize.

R. Kent. *Portinari: His Life and His Art*, Chicago 1940.
F. de Aquino. *Cándido Portinari*, Buenos Aires 1965.

Post-Painterly Abstraction. This term was invented by the American critic Clement Greenberg when he organized an exhibition of contemporary painting at the Los Angeles County Museum of Art in 1964. He used it to describe the generation of artists (Ellsworth Kelly, Friedel Dzubas, Ray Parker, Kenneth Noland, Frank Stella, Jules Olitski, Edward

Avedesian, Darby Bannard, Al Held, Helen Franken-thaler, Sam Francis, Paul Feeley, Gene Davis) who had matured in the decade after the peak years of the Abstract Expressionist movement—artists who had learned from that style and who were reacting to it in various ways. The phrase thus refers to a broad diversity of personal styles, in which many of the artists who rejected the more extreme painterliness of Abstract Expressionism still retained some of its features, while also absorbing the influences of its less Expressionistic practitioners (Ad Reinhardt, Mark Rothko, Barnett Newman).

Some of the salient features of this art produced during the early 1960s are described by Greenberg in his catalogue essay for the exhibition and in his previous criticism. According to Greenberg, modernist painting is defined by the way in which it calls attention to its own limitations as positive factors of that art. Thus the two-dimensional flatness of the picture support, its specific shape and its material aspects (e.g. fabric stretched tautly over wooden bars) are openly acknowledged instead of being concealed by illusionistic devices or tricks. Sculptural and tactile illusion are frequently denied or suppressed, while pictorial organization no longer relies on hierarchical elements or on tradi-tional part-to-part compositional relationships. In-stead, the painting is presented as an instantly appre-hensible unity. Its hard discrete edges, liquefied and stained or sprayed colour fields, definitively structured supports, and repetitive or serialized forms are per-ceived as a direct and holistic experience. Lucid con-trasts of pure hue rather than light and dark tonalities are favoured, while anonymous brush-strokes that avoid the personalized mark of the painter's hand are also frequently employed. The primacy and pure opticality of colour—often appear-ing in wide saturated expanses (Olitski, Morris Louis, Kelly, Frankenthaler, Larry Poons)—or the literal establishment and assertion of the properties of the canvas and its armature (Louis, Olitski, Stella, Noland, Ronald Davis, Bush), are particularly characteristic of the paintings done during the first half of the 1960s. Much of this also reflects the important influence of the Abstract Expressionist painter Jackson Pollock, who in his 'drip' paintings of 1947–50 had attempted to divorce line from its customary role of drawing and defining plastic con-tours. Freed from such tangibility and from three-dimensional connotations, high-keyed colour and overall configuration could now be made to function more independently, relying on their own clarity of image for the impact and freshness of the pictorial expression.

In the late 1960s many of those artists who had earlier rejected illusionism *per se* began to emphasize a particularly artificial kind of illusionism in their paintings. Stressing the abstract quality of that illusionism through the use of contradictory perspec-tive devices or patently artificial, man-made surfaces that vary in glossiness, reflectivity and materials (plastics, metallic pigments, fluorescent colours, etc.), artists such as Stella, Davis, Bannard and Olitski continued to point out the viability and extensi-bility of the medium while concentrating on its own limitations.

Clement Greenberg. Catalogue, *Post-Painterly Abstraction*, Los Angeles County Museum of Art, Los Angeles 1964.
Bruce Glaser. 'The New Abstraction: A Discussion Conducted by Bruce Glaser', *Art International* X, Zürich, 20 February 1966.

Potworowski, Pjotr. Polish painter, b. 1898; d. 1960. His work derived from Post-Impressionism, and is of some importance in the recent development of Polish art.

Pougny, Jean (Ivan Puni). French painter of Russian origin, b. 1894 in Konokkala, St. Petersburg; d. 1956 in Paris. Pougny first came to Paris in 1910 and during the next two years attended various Parisian schools of art before returning to St. Petersburg in 1912. There he established contact and exhibited with Malevich, Tatlin and Larionov. In 1913–14 he again visited Paris, where he came to grips with Cubism. In 1916 he signed the Suprematist manifesto in St. Petersburg and in 1918 was appointed to the teaching staff of the Leningrad Academy of Art. But in 1919 he left Russia and settled in Berlin in the following year. He then had an exhibition in the Sturm Gallery, joined the *Novembergruppe* and made friends of Schwitters, Richter and Eggeling. After moving to Paris in 1923 he met Léger, Ozenfant, Marcoussis, Severini and others. In 1932 he shared an exhibition with Lanskoy and de Pisis. In 1946 he acquired French citizenship.

After passing through Constructivist, Cubist and Dadaist phases in the 1910s, Pougny unexpectedly developed what was virtually an Impressionist tech-nique from c. 1920 onwards. The cheerful, brightly lit pictures of this final period, which are almost invariably small-format works and frequently depict Paris street scenes, are reminiscent of paintings by Vuillard, Bonnard and occasionally de Pisis.

R. W. Gindertael. *Jean Pougny*, Geneva 1957.

Pousette-Dart, Richard. American painter, b. 1916 in St. Paul, Minnesota. The son of Nathaniel Pousette-Dart, a painter, art writer and lecturer, and of a poet mother, he most naturally gravitated towards an artistic career. He studied at the Scar-borough School, Scarborough-on-Hudson, New York, and then attended Bard College (1936) but left academic life almost immediately in order to live and paint in New York. From 1936 to 1941 he worked as a secretary by day and painted at night. In the latter year he had his first one-man show at the Artists' Gallery. He painted in an abstract idiom almost from the beginning, though such works as *Head* (1939, coll. of artist) show a certain affinity to Surrealism and primitive art. By 1940 he was working out his own calligraphy, a form which calls to mind Arabic characters and design (*Fugue*, 1940, coll. of artist) and by 1942 was working in his heavy impasto manner, a style which he practised through the 1950s (*Symphony Number 1, The Transcendental*, 1942, New York, Betty Parsons Gallery). Often using totem-like elements or geometric forms handled with rich pigments of brilliant colour, his works produce the quality of a tapestry in their form, colour and tactility. His latest works are of an overall design of dots and squiggles in one or two dominant colours. He often places a single circular form within this bed of restive colour, as in *Ramapo Night* (1962, New York, Betty Parsons Gallery). The artist has been awarded a Guggenheim Fellowship (1951) and a Ford Foundation Grant (1959) and has taught at the New School for Social Research.

John Gordon. *Richard Pousette-Dart*, Whitney Museum of American Art, New York 1963.

Poynter, Sir Edward. British painter, b. 1836 in Paris; d. 1919 in London. Poynter studied in London and Paris. He was a painter of historical subjects, which he researched with great care and attention to detail. He also designed stained glass, mosaics, pottery and tiles. He was Slade Professor at University College, London (1871–5), Director of the National Gallery (1894–1904) and President of the Royal Academy (1896–1918).

Prachensky, Markus. Austrian painter, b. 1932 in Innsbruck. After studying architecture, Prachensky became an action painter. His works are composed of simple signs and are executed in a small range of colours, in which red predominates.

Prampolini, Enrico. Italian painter, b. 1894 in Modena; d. 1956 in Rome. Prampolini made contact with Balla in 1911 when he was still a student at the Academy in Rome, and in the following year he joined the Futurist movement. From 1914 onwards he came to terms with 'material' pictures; in 1916 he made contact with the Zürich Dadaists and began to take part in Dada manifestations, becoming editor of the Dadaist magazine *No. 1* in the following year; in 1919 he joined the *Novembergruppe*. From 1925 to 1937 Prampolini lived in Paris. During this period he signed the *Aeropittura* manifesto (1929) and joined both the *Cercle et Carré* and the *Abstraction-Création* associations. It was in Paris that he produced his *Cosmic Pictures* and his *Interviste con la Materia*, in which he employed a wide range of components such as sponge, cork, tinfoil and synthetic materials. After leaving Paris he returned to Rome and remained there for the rest of his life.

Like Magnelli and Soldati, Prampolini was one of the great pioneers of abstract art in Italy and was well versed in international developments in this sphere. After an early Futurist period he progressed by way of his *Cosmic Pictures*—which continued the tradition established by Max Ernst and Jean Arp—to a dynamic kind of abstract art based on concrete forms. From 1914 onwards he was concerned with *arte polimaterico*. Prampolini's 'polymaterial' compositions were conceived as a counterpart to modern functional architecture and were intended as a substitute for wall paintings.

P. Courthion. *Enrico Prampolini*, Rome 1957.
F. Menna. *Enrico Prampolini*, Rome 1967.

Prantl, Karl. Austrian sculptor, b. 1923 in Pöttsching, Burgenland. After studying painting under Gütersloh at the Vienna Academy, Prantl turned to sculpture in c. 1950. He was one of those responsible for the Symposium of European Sculptors in St. Margarethen. He is now living in Vienna.

Prantl carves abstract, block-like, monolithic sculptures, usually in polished granite, which he calls *Stones of Meditation*. The indentations on these pieces, which are set out in a regular pattern, make them look like menhirs.

Prassinos, Mario. French painter, b. 1916 in Constantinople. From 1932 to 1936 Prassinos studied languages at the Sorbonne and, whilst there, made contact with the Paris Surrealists. In 1940 he acquired French citizenship. He now lives in Paris.

After an early Surrealist phase Prassinos progressed via *Tachisme* to a personal form of Abstract Expressionism. Apart from paintings, he also produces graphic works, stage sets and illustrations.

Exhibition catalogue, *Mario Prassinos*, Marseilles 1968.

Precisionist Painters (The Immaculates). The Precisionist group of painters, although never a unified school, developed during the 1920s and formed part of the contemporary abstractionist trend in American art. Their painting style is characterized by clean-cut contours, simplification of form, large flat areas of colour, a smooth finish and a general sense of fixed precision and order. Their subject matter most often consisted of American industrial and architectural *motifs*, but is presented analytically and formally, without social or human references. The most prominent artists of the group were Charles Sheeler, Niles Spencer, Charles Demuth and Georgia O'Keeffe.

John I. H. Baur. *Revolution and Tradition in Modern Art*, Cambridge (Mass.) 1951.
Martin L. Friedman. Catalogue, *The Precisionist View in American Art*, Minneapolis 1960.

Pregelj, Marij. Yugoslav painter and graphic artist, b. 1913 in Kranj, Slovenia; d. 1967 in Ljubljana.

After studying at the Academy of Art in Zagreb from 1932 to 1936 Pregelj taught at the *Gymnasium* in Ljubljana from 1938 to 1941. He spent the next two years in prisoner-of-war camps in Italy and Germany before returning to the *Gymnasium* in 1943. In 1946 he gave up his post there to become a professor at the School of Arts and Crafts in Ljubljana. In 1948 he transferred to the neighbouring Academy of Art, where he worked first as a lecturer and subsequently, from 1962 onwards, as a professor of painting. In the course of his career Pregelj illustrated the literary writings of his father I. Pregelj, as well as works by Hemingway and Jack London. He also created a cycle of illustrations for Homer's *Iliad* and *Odyssey* in 1950–1. Eleven years later, in 1961–2, he painted a series of mosaics in Ljubljana, Kampor (on the island of Rab), Trbovlje (Workers' House of Culture) and Belgrade (Parliament Building for Slovenia and the Palace of the Federal Administrator).

Pregelj painted in oils on canvas, using a variety of techniques. In his early phase, which continued until after the Second World War, he was a Realist. Subsequently he developed a visionary style. In his late works he often presented the human figure in the form of a cross, thus creating a grotesque but humane symbol that is evocative of the great masses of men and women incarcerated in the concentration camps and prisons of modern civilization. Pregelj's graphic output is made up of woodcuts and monochrome and multicoloured lithographs.

F. Šijanec. *Contemporary Slovene Art*, Maribor 1961.
Melita Stelè. 'Marij Pregelj', *Umetnoost Magazine* II, 1965.

Prendergast, Maurice Brazil. American painter, b. 1859 in St. John's, Newfoundland; d. 1924 in New York. Though born in Canada, Prendergast lived in Boston from infancy. His initiation into the career of art came at the age of 14 when he was apprenticed to a painter of show cards; even after a visit to England in the summer of 1886 he maintained this commercial occupation. It was not until his second trip abroad in 1891, when he studied at the Académie Julian in Paris and became friendly with the Canadian painter James Wilson Morrice (who introduced him to Walter Sickert, Aubrey Beardsley and Somerset Maugham), that he seriously pursued painting. His earliest influences in Paris were Manet and Whistler, but his interest was soon captured by the work of the *Nabis*. He returned to the United States (1894–5) an accomplished watercolourist and established a studio in Boston while working in his brother's frame shop. His exhibit of rather diffuse watercolours at the Chase Gallery (1897), Boston, attracted the patronage of Mr. and Mrs. Montgomery Sears, who sent him to Venice in 1898. Prendergast felt an affinity for the pageantry of Venice, which is reflected in his paintings of Boston and New York (*Merry-Go-Round*, 1900, pencil and

watercolour, Springfield, Massachusetts, Museum of Fine Arts). In 1908 he exhibited with The Eight but was poorly received. After two more trips abroad, he began to experiment with new subject matter, principally nudes and still lifes. He also attempted a new technique, characterized by a rather divisional brush-stroke, as in *The Rider* (c. 1914, pencil and watercolour, Coll. Mr. and Mrs. John G. Pierce), and he took part in the 1913 Armory Show. However, he soon returned to his former style, in which he applied daubs or spots of colour, as opposed to the structured strokes he had briefly worked with, and to the subjects he so loved—outings, promenades and carnivals. In his last years (1918–24) he abandoned the use of merging spots of paint for a broad, sweeping stroke (*Four Girls in Meadow*, c. 1919–20, pencil, watercolour and pastel, Coll. Mrs Charles Prendergast). Though he employed oils at times, he is best known for his watercolours and monotypes.

Margaret Breuing. *Maurice Prendergast*, New York 1931.
Hedley Howell Rhys. *Maurice Prendergast, 1859–1924*, Cambridge (Mass.) 1960.

Previati, Gaetano. Italian painter, b. 1852 in Ferrara; d. 1920 in Lavagna, Liguria. He trained in Ferrara, Florence and Milan, and became an exponent of Divisionism about 1889. He created large decorative panels in the fluid *art nouveau* style.

Prica, Zlatko. Yugoslav painter and graphic artist, b. 1916 in Pečuh, Hungary. Prica studied at the Academy of Art in Zagreb from 1937 to 1940. As a painter he has achieved an elaborate and highly individual synthesis of abstract and objective trends. In his works, the linear elements are organized into lively and expressive rhythmical structures whilst the pure, elemental colours are arranged in dissonant combinations. Prica's paintings have been influenced by the Indian art which he saw on his travels. In conjunction with Edo Murtić Prica has illustrated various books, including the poems of Goran Kovačić. He has also painted a number of murals.

D. Sepić. *Zlatko Prica*, Zagreb 1958.
Hans Neuberg. Catalogue, *Prica*, Zagreb 1961.

Price, Clayton S. American painter, b. 1874 in Bedford, Iowa; d. 1950 in Portland, Oregon. After living on a cattle ranch for twenty-one years, Price received his first and only lessons in art at the St. Louis School of Fine Arts (1905–6). He then returned to ranching for a few years, only to give it up again in order to take a position as an illustrator for the *Pacific Monthly* (*Running Bucking Horse*, c. 1908–10, Portland, Oregon, Coll. Maurice A. Price). He later moved to San Francisco where in 1915 he saw an exhibition of modern French painters. This event prompted him to give up illustration and devote himself entirely to personal artistic expression. He was given his first one-man show in San

Francisco at the Beaux-Arts Gallery in 1927. Price moved back to Portland in the 1930s where he worked on the WPA Federal Art Project. It was due to the funds of this project that he was able, for the first time, to paint large pictures. The influence of the French painters can be seen as late as the mid-1930s in *Landscape with Horns* (c. 1934, Portland, Oregon, Coll. Maurice A. Price) with its free brush-work and slight Cubistic tendency in composition and form which calls to mind the very earliest of Braque's Cubist landscapes. In his late works, forms are relatively indistinct. The keynote of the works, such as *Cow with Calf* (1949, C. S. Price estate), is the boldness of stroke which reminds one of the works being done by W. de Kooning and F. Kline in the late 1940s and early 1950s. Price was awarded an Honorary Master of Arts degree from Reed College in 1948.

Catalogue, *C. S. Price: The Man; the Artist (1874–1950)*, Oregon Journal, Portland (Oregon) 1950.

Primitive art—*see* **Naïve art**

Primitivism. This was a Russian form of Expressionism, which evolved between 1905 and 1920 under the influence of Fauvism and Cubism. It also received a powerful impetus from Russian folk art. The type of subject favoured by the Russian primitives—scenes from working-class life—reveals their social sympathies. Technically, they used highly simplified, block-like forms and powerful, undifferentiated colours. The members of the Moscow *Blue Rose* group—Larionov, Gontcharova and Burljuk—were typical primitives. So too was Malevich in his early phase.

Camilla Gray. *The Great Experiment: Russian Art 1863–1922*, London and New York 1962.

Procházka, Antonín. Czech painter, b. 1882; d. 1945. A member of the *avant-garde* circle in Prague around 1910, which included Filla, Kubišta and Gutfreund, Procházka was influenced by Cubism and responded to it in his work. With Filla and Kubišta he had helped form The Eight in 1907–8, a group dedicated to fostering a modern Czech art drawn from both the Expressionist and Impressionist movements that had been revealed to them in recent exhibitions. In 1911, with Filla, Procházka formed the Group of Avant-Garde Artists, which combined Expressionist and Cubist elements in an original Czech art. Procházka's Cubist phase was fairly brief, and eventually his work became more formalized.

Programmed art—*see* **Computer art**

Pronaszko, Andrzej. Polish painter, b. 1889. Pronaszko's art derived from Cubism and Expressionism. Both of these influences were apparent in the work of the *Zdroj* and *Formisci* groups of which he was a member, together with Chwistek and Czyzewski.

Protić, Miodrag B. Yugoslav painter and art critic, b. 1922 in Vrujačka Banja, Serbia. Protić studied first under M. Josić, then under Jovan Bijelió and Zora Petrović. Subsequently he was appointed Director of the Museum of Contemporary Art in Belgrade.

Protić's early works, which were derived from his impressions of Cézanne and André Lhôte, have something of the purity and the rational approach of Classical art. His experimental works, in which he investigates the relationship between picture plane and surface, between colour and form, have a lyrical and pictorial quality which is reflected in the soft, restrained tonal values. These paintings are almost pure abstracts. The basic qualities underlying all of Protić's work—both as an artist and as a critic—are his extreme sophistication and his broadly based culture.

Pedja Milosaljević. Catalogue, *Miodag Protić*, Modern Gallery, Belgrade 1963.
Zoran Pavlović. 'The Painting of Miodrag Protić', *Umetnost Magazine* X, Belgrade 1967.

Prouvé, Victor. French painter, b. 1858; d. 1943. Prouvé was one of the leading figures in the School of Nancy, which was an important centre of the *art nouveau* movement and included such designers as Émile Gallé (1846–1904) and Louis Majorelle (1859–1926).

Puig, Augusto. Spanish painter, b. 1929 in Barcelona. He is self-taught. In 1947 he gained a French government grant which enabled him to study in Paris, where he lived until 1953. He has exhibited in Barcelona, Berne, Stockholm, Frankfurt, etc. Puig is an abstract artist.

Purism. The theoretical premises of Purism were set out by Amédée Ozenfant and Édouard Jeanneret (Le Corbusier) in *Après le Cubisme*, which they published in 1918. Ozenfant and Jeanneret criticized the Cubists for turning to mere decoration, and insisted that fantasy and individuality must be excluded from art. They then advocated an entirely new kind of artistic discipline, in which objects would be depicted in their architectonic simplicity. This conception was inspired by the machine, whose perfect forms were only made possible by the exclusion of all non-functional properties. Purism remained a theory. As far as painting was concerned it exerted no influence of any significance.

Purrmann, Hans. German painter, b. 1880 in Speyer; d. 1966 in Basle. He studied in Karlsruhe and moved to Berlin, where he became a member of the Secession. In 1906 he went to Paris and met Matisse. He returned to Berlin in 1914, and remained there until 1935, going to Italy or the South of France for the summers. His works were declared 'degenerate' by the Nazis, and he did not go back to Germany after 1935, settling in Switzerland from 1944 and remaining there for the rest of his life.

The turning point of Purrmann's career was his meeting with Matisse in 1906; shortly afterwards he took over the development and direction of the Académie Matisse, where he soon proved that he was more independent and had a more powerful personality than the other German disciples of Matisse. He built up his charming and almost Classical landscapes, still lifes and figure compositions with close-set, chromatic brushwork. In his late period he moved away from the decorative brightness of the Fauves, producing vibrant tones with a richness and depth that recall the late Renoir.

Erhard Göpel. *Leben und Meinung des Malers Hans Purrmann*, Wiesbaden 1961.

Puvrez, Henri. Belgian sculptor, b. 1893 in Brussels. He started to sculpt in 1914, and within about eight years had begun producing massive stone figures of monumental simplicity. Both Expressionism and Negro art made an impact on him. Later he turned to modelling his figures instead of direct carving. He settled in Antwerp, and taught there for some years.

Puy, Jean. French painter, b. 1876 in Roanne, Loire; d. 1960 in Roanne. He studied in Paris and knew Matisse there. Although he was closely associated with the Fauvist circle he was not a convinced member of the movement, and preferred to work in the country rather than be in the centre of Parisian artistic development. His nudes, still lifes and landscapes were executed in clear, bright colours with great vitality. Design was always a primary consideration, which he was able to exercise in the murals and ceramics that he produced.

Q

Quinte, Lothar. German painter and graphic artist, b. 1923. Quinte was visiting lecturer at the Werkkunstschule in Krefeld, 1959–60. He is now living in Karlsruhe.

Quinte's paintings, which are a lyrical form of new abstract art, consist of bands of luminous colour set against monochrome grounds, which are normally dark.

Quizet, Alphonse. French painter, b. 1885 in Paris; d. 1955 in Paris. He was a close friend of Maurice Utrillo and often worked in company with him, painting townscapes of Montmartre. Other suburban areas of Paris also interested him, and he was able to capture the peace and charm of these less fashionable areas. He had considerable skill in the use of colour.

R

Räderscheidt, Anton. German painter, b. 1892 in Cologne; d. 1970 in Cologne. After studying at the Düsseldorf Academy Räderscheidt joined the *Progressive Künstler* association in Cologne. In the 1920s he painted extremely precise pictures in the style of the *Neue Sachlichkeit*. In 1933 he emigrated, but returned to Germany in 1950, when he settled in Cologne. Since then he has developed an informal style of painting.

Catalogue, *Anton Räderscheidt*, Kunstverein, Cologne 1962.

Radice, Mario. Italian painter, b. 1900 in Como. Radice is a self-taught artist. After an early Futurist period he went over to abstract art in Milan in the 1930s. Like M. Rho, he was one of the pioneers of the abstract movement in Italy and did much to promote its growth.

Radice also edited two magazines: *Quadrante* and *Valori Primordiali*. He is now living in Como.

The severe, abstract compositions of Radice's late period, which are executed in cool, dispassionate colours, were prompted by his impressions of the objective architecture of recent years.

Radziwill, Franz. German painter, b. 1895 in Strohhausen, Oldenburg. After serving an apprenticeship as a plasterer and training as an architect Radziwill visited Berlin (1920–1), where he made contact with Grosz's circle. He then joined the Secession and the *Novembergruppe*. In 1927 he was in Dresden and whilst there met Otto Dix. From 1933 to 1935 he taught at the Düsseldorf Academy. He is now living in Dangast, Oldenburg, where he first settled in 1921.

Radziwill turned towards Magic Realism in 1924. Since then he has painted landscapes in a veristic style based on Classical techniques. In many of these works—which reveal the influence of Dix—he has incorporated aircraft, thus producing a Surrealist effect.

W. Augustiny. *Franz Radziwill*, Göttingen 1964.

Rainer, Arnulf. Austrian painter, b. 1929 in Baden, Austria. After studying at the Academy of Art in Vienna Rainer began painting black monochromes in 1953. These were followed in 1959 by 'overpaintings' (of his own and other artists' works). In 1959 he also began to publish the *Pintorarium* in conjunction with Hundertwasser and Ernst Fuchs. Rainer has been living in Vienna since 1950.

Ramseyer, André. Swiss sculptor, b. 1914 in Tramelan, Berne. He studied under Zadkine in Paris, 1935–6, and went to Italy in 1938; then he returned to Switzerland. His first works were figurative and classically inclined; these developed into freely expressed, stylized shapes adapted from natural forms. Eventually his work became completely abstract, and principally expressed themes of growth or of the sea.

Rancillac, Bernard. French painter and designer, b. 1931 in Paris. During the 1950s Rancillac painted cartoons in a style based on trick film techniques. Subsequently, under the influence of Roy Lichtenstein, he evolved a new style compounded of science fiction and comic strip. In the works of this period, which incorporate elements of Pop Art in a Surrealistic form, he has always treated the same theme: the star cult of the mass society. Since 1960 Rancillac has also designed stage sets and environmental works. He is now living in Paris.

Ranson, Paul. French painter, b. 1864 in Limoges; d. 1909 in Paris. Ranson was the son of a cloth merchant. After studying at the Académie des Beaux-Arts in Limoges he enrolled at the Académie Julian in Paris in 1888, where he met Sérusier, Denis, Bonnard and Vuillard, with whom he was shortly to found the *Nabis* group. He also collaborated with Bonnard, Vuillard and Sérusier on the decorations for the Théâtre de l'Art. In 1893–4 he produced lithographs for the *Revue Blanche* and in 1895 designed his first tapestries.

Ranson made his name as a member of the *Nabis* group and as the founder of the celebrated Académie Ranson. In his paintings he adhered to the *Nabis* doctrine, which was prompted in the first instance by Gauguin's ideas on colour and was subsequently reinforced by Sérusier's theories. With their mysterious, solemn light Ranson's fantastic landscapes reveal a marked inclination towards a Romantic form of occultism. His pictorial objects are enclosed by dark contours with the result that the areas between them, which are executed as abstract, decorative designs, seem to lead an independent existence.

A. Humbert. *Les Nabis et leur Époque*, Geneva 1954.
Charles Chassé. *The Nabis and Their Period*, London and New York 1969.

Rattner, Abraham. American painter, b. 1895 in Poughkeepsie, New York. First interested in architecture and city planning, he attended George Washington University's School of Architecture before entering the Corcoran School in Washington, D.C. In 1916 he won a scholarship to the Pennsylvania Academy of Fine Arts. Between 1917 and 1919 he served in the United States Army's camouflage section in France. When discharged, he returned to the Academy and won a Cresson Travelling Fellowship. He went to Paris and there studied with M. Denis, E. Berman and C. Bérard at the Académie des Beaux-Arts as well as at the Académies Ranson, Colarossi, Julian and la Grande Chaumière, and at the Sorbonne. By 1923–4 he was exhibiting in many Parisian exhibitions, including the Salon National, Salon d'Automne, Salon des Tuileries, Salon des Indépendants and Salon des Sur-Indépendants. His style at this time showed echoes of Cubism and Futurism as seen in the undulating forms of *Flying Trapeze* (1926, New York, Downtown Galleries). He received his first one-man show in 1934 at the Bonjean Gallery, Paris, and his first American one-man the following year at the Julien Levy Gallery. After returning to the United States in 1939, he spent the next decade developing a wholly personal style characterized by its bright colour, recalling jewels, mosaics or enamel, very often depicting biblical subjects (*Composition, Head and Flowers,* 1949, New York, Coll. Joseph H. Hirshhorn). His *Last Judgement Triptych* of 1954–6 (New York, Downtown Gallery) is representative of his works of the 1950s in which the gesture of the brush, textural variation, free use of colour and the force obtainable through sheer size are the most important features. The increasing abstraction of the 1950s is coupled with a greater sense of movement and dynamism which perhaps stems back to his early Futurist influences. In addition to painting, Rattner has taught at many schools and universities including the New School for Social Research, Yale University, the University of Illinois, the Art Students' League, Michigan State University and the Brooklyn Museum School.

Frank Getlein. *Abraham Rattner,* New York 1960.

Rauschenberg, Robert. American painter, b. 1925 in Port Arthur, Texas. He had studied pharmacy at the University of Texas and had served in the Second World War before taking up studies at the Kansas City Art Institute. He furthered his studies at the Académie Julian, Paris (1947), and Black Mountain College, North Carolina (1948), where his desire for discipline was answered while studying with J. Albers. His final training was received at the Art Students' League (1949) under Vaclav Vytacil and Morris Kantor. Two years later he was given a one-man show at the Betty Parsons Gallery, exhibiting white paintings with black numbers or figurative symbols. In the 1950s his paintings became increasingly allied with collage and assemblage (*Rebus*, 1955, coll. of artist) and even entered the realm of sculpture (*Odalisk*, 1955, New York, Coll. Mr. and Mrs. Victor Ganz). In the early 1960s he made use of the process of *frottage* to transfer newspaper and magazine pictures in his thirty-four drawings illustrating Dante's *Inferno*, and reproduced photographs by a silk-screen stencilling technique in *Tracer* (1964, coll. of artist). This process was also used in *Axle*, exhibited at the Documenta, Kassel, Germany (1964). In the same year he won first prize at the Venice Biennale. Rauschenberg has been connected with dance companies since the mid-1950s, designing sets and costumes for Merce Cunningham. He has danced with the Surplus Dance Theater and performed on roller skates in his own choreographed work, *Pelican*.

Alan R. Solomon. Catalogue, *Robert Rauschenberg*, Jewish Museum, New York 1963.

Ray, Man. American painter, sculptor and filmmaker, b. 1890 in Philadelphia; d. 1976. Interested in art from childhood, he attended life drawing classes in his early twenties at the Ferrer Center in New York. In 1913 he married and moved with his wife and the poet Alfred Kreymborg to Ridgefield, New Jersey, where they hoped to establish a community of artists. In this crucial year in American art, he, like most of his contemporaries, was strongly influenced by the current European trends exhibited at the Armory Show. He was one of the few American artists to produce genuine Synthetic Cubist works directly after this exhibition (*The Rope Dancer Accompanies Herself with Her Shadow*, 1916, New York, Museum of Modern Art). The year 1915 was also an important one for him—he was given his first one-man show, launched his experiments in photography and began a life-long friendship with Marcel Duchamp. His literary interests began to develop at this time and he, Duchamp and Francis Picabia prompted the publication of two magazines—*The Blind Man* and *Rongwrong* (1917). In 1918 he began his aerograph series—paintings executed with a spray gun whose softness of form emulates photographic effects (*First Object Aerated*, 1918, Paris, Coll. Mr. and Mrs. Man Ray). In 1921 he went to Paris where he was warmly received by the Dadaists and was given a one-man show. In 1922 he published a collection of photographs entitled *Les Champs délicieux* and was included in the first international Dada exhibition: *Salon Dada*. In 1923 film-making became his chief outlet of artistic expression (*Le Retour à la raison* was his first film) and the next year he appeared with Duchamp, Picabia and Erik Satie in René Clair's *Entr'acte*. Throughout the 1920s he participated in a number of films (*Anaemic*

Cinema, Emak Bakia, L'Étoile de mer, Les Mystères du Château de dé). In the 1930s he published several albums of photographs and rayographs (photographic impressions made on a sensitized plate) accompanied by essays and poems by André Breton, Duchamp, Tristan Tzara and himself. His painting style of the 1930s was overtly Surrealistic, giving rise to a variety of psychological interpretations (*The Misunderstood One*, 1938, Paris, Coll. Mr. and Mrs. Man Ray), but periodically he returned to a vaguely Cubistic aesthetic (*Diamond Cactus*, 1948, Paris, Coll. Mr. and Mrs. Man Ray). In 1940 he fled the Nazi occupation of Paris and eventually made his way to Hollywood. In the 1940s he was included in many exhibitions and was given almost annual one-man shows. His interest in collage and mixed media objects extends from the second decade of the century to the present. The former were done as early as 1916: *Theatr* (Stockholm, Moderna Museet); while the objects continue even today. His *Indestructible Object* (1958, Coll. Mr. and Mrs. Morton G. Neumann) is a replica of the 1923 original *Object to be Destroyed* which was destroyed by a group of students in 1957 at a Paris exhibition, in response to its title.

Man Ray. *Self-Portrait*, Boston 1963.
Catalogue, *Man Ray*, County Museum of Art, Los Angeles 1966.

Raynaud, Jean Pierre. French painter and sculptor, b. 1939 in Colombes, Paris. Between 1957 and 1959, when he was serving his apprenticeship at the School of Horticulture in Versailles, Raynaud attended painting courses in Paris in his leisure time. He has been living in Paris since 1961.

Raynaud is an 'object artist'. By arranging objects in Neo-Dadaist combinations he draws attention to the psychic forces which they bring into play.

Rayonnism. A style of painting (*Luchizm* in Russian) 'invented' by the painter Mikhail Larionov and employed by him and the artist N. Gontcharova in their work of around 1912–14 (the dates given by Larionov to certain of his 'early' Rayonnist paintings must be regarded as questionable). A 'manifesto' of Rayonnism, entitled *Rayonnists and Futurists* and signed by a number of Russian *avant-garde* artists, appeared in the anthology of 1913, *Oslinyi Khvost i Mishen* (the *Donkey's Tail* and *The Target*); there can, however, be little doubt of Larionov's authorship. Here, the author explains that 'the style of Rayonnist painting . . . denotes spatial forms arising from the intersection of reflected rays of various objects, forms chosen by the will of the artist', an idea which has much in common with the perceptual notions which determined Italian Futurism. The influence of contemporary Italian painting is particularly noticeable in Gontcharova's Rayonnist paintings, especially her treatment of mechanical and industrial themes.

Larionov's Rayonnist work is, on the other hand, characterized by a higher degree of abstraction. However, despite his assertion (in his article *Rayonnist Painting*) that 'painting is self-sufficient . . . has its own forms, colour and timbre', few of his pictures of this period may be considered wholly non-representational.

Camilla Gray. *The Great Experiment: Russian Art 1863–1922*, London and New York 1962.
Catalogue, *Two Decades of Experiment in Russian Art, 1902–1922*, Grosvenor Gallery, London 1962.

Raysse, Martial. French painter and maker of mixed media and collages, b. 1936 in Golfe Juan, Nice. A young member of the French *Nouveaux Réalistes*, among whose members are Jean Tinguely, Yves Klein and Arman, his works have an affinity to the production of British and American Pop artists. His first one-man show was held at the Galerie Longchamp, Nice, in 1957 and in 1960 he first presented assemblages of pop items, such as *L'Étalage Hygiène de la Vision* (1960, Paris, Galerie Schwarz) in which everyday objects such as sponges, mops and toy boats are gathered together in a display-rack manner. For Raysse beauty is above all neatness and health—clean, sparkling, pure. In the artist's words, 'I wanted my works to possess the serene self-evidence of mass-produced refrigerators.' His *Raysse Beach* (1962, New York, Alexandre Iolas Gallery) uses cheap store items around an inflatable children's swimming pool with large photos of girls in bathing suits on the walls and a neon sign which reads 'Raysse Beach'. In his garishly 'awful paintings' such as *Made in Japan* (1964, Los Angeles, Dwan Gallery), which employs Ingres' *Odalisque* (1814, Paris, Louvre), he strives, in his manner, to depict life. 'To track life down in the realm of colour, I tried using plastics, fluorescence, relationships that were untrue, out of key, or paintings with errors . . . flawed and faulty . . . or (in) bad taste, . . . the hideous and the horrible. And now, especially by using neon and artificial lighting, I seek in transcendental colour a substitute for life.' In addition to this type of work he has done designs for stage decorations (sets for the 1967 production of the Royal Ballet's *Paradise Lost*, Covent Garden) which are in fact an extension of his interest in environments.

Otto Hahn. *Martial Raysse ou l'Obsession solaire*, Paris 1965.
Catalogue, *Martial Raysse*, Stedelijk Museum, Amsterdam 1965.
Catalogue, *Martial Raysse*, Dwan Gallery, Los Angeles 1967.

Ready-made. Marcel Duchamp used this name for certain prefabricated, everyday objects which he came across by accident and, without exercising his aesthetic faculty in any way, isolated from their normal environment, placed on a pedestal and exhibited as 'works of art'. By this act Duchamp demonstrated his firm belief in the absurdity and the fortuitousness of life and its so-called 'values', thus rejecting the aesthetic, the meaningful and the 'sacred' character of art. In his view the only factor which determined whether an object was a work of art or not was the act of perception. Thus, the ready-made was the ultimate, the most caustic and the most 'cynical' consequence that could be drawn from the Dadaist 'principle of chance'. The first ready-mades date from the first half of the 1910s when Duchamp was working on his *Bachelor Machine*. In 1913 he 'found' the bicycle and in 1914 the bottle drier. But these finds of his were strictly limited. He himself has written on them at some length: 'My Ready-Mades have nothing to do with the Found Object, which is a matter of personal taste. It is personal taste that decides whether this so-called 'Found Object' is a beautiful and unique object. Most of my Ready-Mades were mass-produced articles and could have been duplicated, which is also an important distinction. . . . Where my Ready-Mades were concerned I tried to keep away from personal taste and to concentrate on the problem.' Of recent years the ready-made has been incorporated into both Pop Art and *Nouveau Réalisme*. Various contemporary artists, including Arman, Spoerri, Oldenburg and Rauschenberg, are now working with prefabricated objects, many of which are mass-produced, although, unlike Duchamp, most of these artists attach great importance to the organization of their pictorial objects. However, the original idea for the ready-made—which has been one of the most influential concepts in the whole of twentieth-century art—was Duchamp's.

Rebeyrolle, Paul. French painter, b. 1926 in Eymoutiers, Haute-Vienne. He went to Paris in 1944 and met Bernard Lorjou. He began painting crude and vital pictures of day-to-day life and events. These extended to landscapes, and scenes of country life. He won the Prix de la Jeune Peinture in 1950, and had an exhibition in London in 1964 at the Marlborough Gallery.

Recalcati, Antonio. Italian painter, b. 1938 in Bresso, Milan. Recalcati's artistic development was crucially influenced by the Surrealism of M. Ernst and R. Magritte, and by the works of Matta and F. Bacon. His pictorial figures and objects, which are presented in collage form, illustrate political and ideological themes. Recalcati is now living in Milan.

Reder, Bernard. Austrian-American sculptor, architect and graphic artist, b. 1897 in Czernowitz, Bukowina, Austria. After his early education in Czernowitz and service in the Austrian Army (1914–18) he entered the Academy of Fine Arts, Prague, where he studied graphics with Peter Bromse for a year and then studied sculpture under Jan Stursa. In the 1920s he worked as a stonemason in Czernowitz, doing sculpture in his spare time. At the end of the decade he won a prize in an international architectural competition (1927) which included his designs for a structure to house a monument to Columbus in Santo Domingo (now Ciudad Trujillo, Dominican Republic). The following year he had a one-man show of watercolours at the Rudolphinum, Prague. It was not until 1935 that he had his first one-man exhibition of sculpture at the Mánes Gallery, Prague. Two years later he moved to France at the encouragement of A. Maillol. His works of the 1930s were mainly female figures of large volume which emphasize contour and density of the form (*Bather, I*, 1933, sandstone, Uniontown, Pennsylvania, Coll. Jay C. Leff). Remaining in France during the Second World War, he came to the United States in 1943. In the 1950s his theme was still the female form, as well as animals. *Bull Captured by the Amazons* (1956, bronze, Haverford, Pennsylvania, Coll. Mr. and Mrs. William P. Wood) was produced while living in Italy (1954–8). By this time his interest changed from one of volume to one of surface qualities. Here he is most concerned with the flicker of light over the rough metallic forms (which initially have the properties of a terra-cotta *bozzetto*), and the inter-relation of the forms to each other and their space. Among his series of woodcuts are: *Bust and Torso* (1934), *Apocalypse* (1940), *Legends of Noah* (1948) and three series from 1954—*The Seven Deadly Sins, Song of Songs* and *Susanna and the Elders*. In 1960 Reder was awarded a grant for sculpture from the Ford Foundation Program in Humanities and the Arts.

John I. H. Baur. Catalogue, *Bernard Reder*, Whitney Museum of American Art, New York 1961.

Redon, Odilon. French painter and lithographer, b. 1840 in Bordeaux; d. 1916 in Paris. He spent a solitary childhood on the family estate at Peyrelebade, Gironde. He developed a deep interest in music and from 1855 studied drawing: his first paintings were done in 1862. Around 1862/3 he met and became a close friend of the botanist Armand Clavaud and the graphic artist Rodolphe Bresdin in Bordeaux. Bresdin taught him etching and engraving techniques and they shared an admiration for the work of Rembrandt and Goya. Redon also studied briefly at the École des Beaux-Arts in Paris during the 1860s. In 1867 he exhibited an etching at the Salon, Paris, and started keeping a journal. In 1868 and 1869 he wrote very perceptive Salon Reviews for *La Gironde* (Bordeaux). He did his army service in the Loire Valley during the Franco-Prussian War, 1870–1. In 1871 he settled in Paris, making occasional trips to Brittany. He developed a friendship with Fantin-Latour, who taught him lithographic techniques. In 1878 he made the first of many trips to Holland. In 1879 his lithographs *Dans le Rêve* were published.

In 1880 he married Camille Falte. He exhibited charcoal drawings at *La Vie Moderne*, Paris, in 1881 and at the first Salon des Indépendants in 1884: he was subsequently elected its President. In 1886 he exhibited with *Les Vingt* in Brussels and at the last Impressionist exhibition. From 1889 on he exhibited regularly with Durand-Ruel and/or Vollard. In 1889 his son Arï was born. Around 1890 he became a close friend of Mallarmé and met other Symbolist poets: at around the same time he also met Gauguin and the younger painters around him. After Gauguin's departure for Tahiti in 1891, Redon replaced him in the respect of these artists (the *Nabis*, Bernard, etc.).

In 1894/5 he went through a period of religious crisis. In 1897 he sold the family estate at Peyrelebade. His *The Apocalypse of St. John* lithographs were published by Vollard in 1899 and in the same year an exhibition of younger painters at Durand-Ruel's gallery was dedicated to Redon. In 1900 he visited Italy. The following year he undertook two decorative commissions, in Burgundy and Paris. In 1903 he was nominated for the Légion d'Honneur. In 1904 a special exhibition of his work (over sixty exhibits) was held at the Salon d'Automne. *Les Yeux Clos* was purchased by the Musée du Luxembourg, Paris. In 1907 he visited Switzerland. He made tapestry cartoons for Gobelins in 1908.

From 1909 he lived mainly in Bièvres, outside Paris. His work was becoming widely known outside France—he was represented in the 1910 Post-Impressionist exhibition in London and had over seventy paintings, drawings and prints in the 1913 Armory Show in New York.

The first major retrospective exhibition was held in Paris in 1920. His Journal of 1867–1915, *À Soi-Même*, was published in Paris in 1922 and his *Letters 1878–1916* in Paris the following year.

Most of Redon's early work was in black-and-white media. The subject matter of his drawings and prints was a private, imaginative hybrid world of floating eyes and half-human plants and insects, stemming in part from the idyllic but haunted solitude of his childhood and in part from his religious introspection. Their black mood and metamorphic fantasy (he called them '*les Noirs*') made them ideal material for the taste of Huysmans' decadent hero in the novel *À Rebours* (published in Paris, 1884) and ancestor-images for the Surrealists.

The strength of Redon's solitary stand against naturalism in art from the late 1860s on and his belief in an enchanted inner vision made him a father-figure for the younger Symbolists in the 1890s. Redon's ideas acted as a direct stimulus and endorsement for Gauguin. He remained highly admired by the *avant-garde* until his death: Matisse, Bonnard and Marcel Duchamp were among those who felt in his debt.

He believed in the suggestive power of the

materials he used (particularly charcoal) and saw the first marks made on a surface as crucial stimulants to the imagination. Intense and particularized study of natural phenomena served the same function. From the later 1890s he worked more in colour —small pastels and paintings—which suggests that his religious crisis exorcised the macabre obsessions of his early life and work. Although many were simple flower pieces, strong colour is used evocatively. Bonnard commented on 'the blending of two almost opposite features: a very pure plastic substance and a mysterious expression' (1912).

The small scale of Redon's art and his personal reticence have led to an under-rating of his very considerable influence on the direction of Post-Impressionist art.

R. Bavou. *Odilon Redon*, Geneva 1956.
K. Berger. *Odilon Redon: Fantasy and Colour*, London and New York 1965.

Redpath, Anne. Scottish painter, b. 1895 in Galashiels; d. 1965 in Edinburgh. Redpath trained at the Edinburgh School of Art. After her marriage and a period of residence in France, she resumed painting in 1934. She is represented at the Tate Gallery, London, and in many public collections. She was elected to the RSA in 1952, and was made an ARA in 1960. She was given an honorary doctorate of law by Edinburgh University and the OBE in 1955. She was a founder of the modern school of painting centred in Edinburgh.

Reggiani, Mauro. Italian painter, b. 1897 in Monantola, Modena. Reggiani studied at the academies in Modena and Florence. He has been living in Milan since 1925.

Reggiani was a member of the first abstract group formed in Italy. He painted a number of objective landscapes and still lifes in 1940, when he came under the influence of G. Morandi, but soon reverted to abstract compositions, which he has produced ever since.

Regionalism. Although generally applicable to any artist's portrayal of a particular environment, the term is usually reserved for a small group of American artists whose work became popular during the 1930s and early 1940s. Their works are often considered to be closely allied to the production of many artists involved with the WPA. The paintings of the regionalists, however, were the result of a conscious reaction to the expatriatism of the 1920s, whereas the products of the WPA artists were concerned with Americana primarily because of the dictates of the project. The protagonists of regionalism—Thomas Hart Benton, Grant Wood, John Steuart Curry and sometimes Charles Burchfield—were all from the Mid-West and all extolled the virtues of life in the small Mid-Western rural communities. Their work is often seen in terms of the fanatical patriotism of the American critic Thomas Craven, who crusaded against contemporary European artists, American expatriates and the New York School. Craven's chauvinistic approach, however, influenced these artists less than has generally been believed; for much of their work had been produced before he initiated his programme, and much of his writing was concerned with criticism of non-regionalists rather than the advocacy of the Mid-Westerners. The regionalists' success eventually succumbed to the spirit of internationalism that prevailed in American art during and after the Second World War.

Catalogue, *Painting and Sculpture from 16 American Cities,* Museum of Modern Art, New York 1933.
Merrill Jensen (ed.). *Regionalism in America*, Madison (Wisc.) 1951.

Reichel, Hans. German painter, b. 1892 in Würzburg; d. 1958 in Paris. In 1918 Reichel attended the Hoffmann School in Munich and met R. M. Rilke; in 1919 he met P. Klee and in 1924 was in Weimar with V. Kandinsky. In 1927–8 he accompanied the painter C. Holty on journeys to Switzerland and Italy prior to settling in Paris. In 1930 he met Jeanne Bucher and subsequently became friendly with R. Bissière. In 1939–40 he was interned.

After a brief early phase, in which he was influenced by Delaunay's Orphism, Reichel became engrossed in the imaginative world of P. Klee. During this period, which lasted from 1920 to 1930, he took over certain of Klee's formal and thematic *motifs*, due more to a sense of genuine affinity than to plagiarism. In c. 1950 Reichel adopted a Lyrical Abstract style. He then produced small-format works, in which he portrayed dream-like, poetic themes, using transparent colouring and a rhythmical composition.

Catalogue, *Hans Reichel*, Kestner Gesellschaft, Hanover 1960–1.
Hans Reichel, Galerie Jeanne Bucher, Paris 1962.

Reichert, Josua. German draughtsman and printer, b. 1937 in Stuttgart. Reichert was apprenticed to a Stuttgart book printer from 1956 to 1957. In 1959 he began to study at the Academy in Karlsruhe under H. Grieshaber. He has been living in Munich since 1961.

Due partly to the influence of the Dutch printer H. Werkman and partly to his teacher Grieshaber, Reichert began to produce 'pictorial texts' in 1960. He uses wooden letters, arranging them so as to form typographical designs. Some of these are purely pictorial, others incorporate a verbal statement.

Reinhardt, Ad. American painter, b. 1913 in Buffalo; d. 1967 in New York. He studied at Columbia University with the art historian Meyer Schapiro (1931–5). After graduation he studied both at the National Academy of Design and at the

American Artists' School with Francis Criss (b. 1901) and Carl Robert Holty (b. 1900), then at New York University's Institute of Fine Arts with the Orientalist Alfred Salmony (1945–51). In 1937 Reinhardt joined the American Abstract Artists group, at that time an exciting and important influence on his work. Before and after serving as a Navy photographer during the Second World War, Reinhardt was a part-time staff artist and art critic for the New York newspaper *PM* (1944–6), and was noted for his sharp, satirical cartoons and articles. He taught at Brooklyn College (from 1947), the California School of Fine Arts (1950), the University of Wyoming (1951), Yale University (1952–3), Syracuse University (1957) and Hunter College, New York (from 1959). He had his first one-man exhibition at New York's Columbia University in 1943, from 1946 exhibited at the Betty Parsons Gallery in New York, and appeared in group exhibitions at the Museum of Modern Art, as well as at the World Fairs held in New York, Brussels and Seattle.

Reinhardt's painting was a very conscious and conceptual process, about which he wrote frequently and dogmatically. His main premise was to separate the areas of life and art: 'Art is art-as-art and everything else is everything else. Art-as-art is nothing but art' (1962). Only abstract art, he believed, could express this pure standard—'no other art or painting is detached or empty or immaterial enough' (1962).

Reinhardt was consistently an abstract painter; his earlier work reflected several influences, including late Cubism as well as the painting of Stuart Davis and Piet Mondrian, but in the last two decades of his life he attained individualistic solutions that he considered ultimate. Reinhardt's geometric abstractions of the late 1930s (*Untitled*, 1938, New York, Museum of Modern Art) were predominantly bold compositions with hard-edged forms and bright hues, which in the 1940s gave way to a more detailed, softer, overall style that Reinhardt at first explored in abstract collages, then in oils. Despite his later rejection of Abstract Expressionism, his work was affected by it during the late 1940s; he was close to many of the major exponents of that style and participated, with Robert Motherwell, in editing the publication *Modern Artists in America* (1950), based on discussions among contemporary artists. Reinhardt worked in an increasingly rejective mode towards pure and essential painting, and began to achieve considerable originality in the early 1950s, although he continued to work in several styles. In 1951 he began to grey his colours and to de-emphasize contrasts; the first geometric, closely valued, red-and-blue paintings developed from 1951 to 1953 (*Abstract Painting, Blue*, 1952, Pittsburgh, Carnegie Institute, Museum of Modern Art); and the first symmetrically trisected paintings, which later became standard for him, appeared around 1952. The first 'all black' paintings, with barely distinguishable tonal varia-

tions from one rectilinear division to the next, were shown in 1953, and by 1960 Reinhardt had developed his 'ultimate' painting: a black, 5-foot square, symmetrically trisected and evenly painted canvas (*Abstract Painting*, 1960–2, New York, Museum of Modern Art), which he repeated from then on, and which in its exactitude, purity and impersonality was a herald of the Minimal Art of the 1960s.

Maurice Tuchman (ed.). Catalogue, *New School, The First Generation: Paintings of the 1940s and 1950s*, County Museum of Art, Los Angeles 1965.
Ad Reinhardt. 'Ad Reinhardt on His Art', *The Studio* CLXXIV, London, December 1967.

Reinhoud—*see* **Haese,** Reinhoud d'

Renoir, Pierre-Auguste. French painter, b. 1841 in Limoges; d. 1919 in Cagnes. Renoir was the son of a tailor. In 1845 his family moved to Paris. Between 1856 and 1859 he took an apprenticeship and then worked as a porcelain painter, also taking evening classes in drawing. He then studied at the École des Beaux-Arts, Paris, in the *atelier* of Gleyre. He was a fellow student of Monet, Sisley and Bazille; he went on summer painting trips with them to Chailly and Fontainebleau. He studied the eighteenth-century paintings in the Louvre, and also met Corot, Millet and Diaz. In 1864 his work was first accepted at the Salon. From 1865 to 1870 he worked with Monet and Sisley in the Paris suburbs. In 1870 he did his military service in Bordeaux and the Pyrenees. He then returned to Paris: during the 1870s he painted with Monet at Argenteuil and elsewhere, and came to know Cézanne, Degas, Pissarro, etc. In 1874 his work was included in the first Impressionist exhibition (and in three of the subsequent seven: 1876, 1877, 1882). He also exhibited intermittently at the Salon. He had little public success but was patronized by Caillebotte, Chocquet and others. From the late 1870s on he enjoyed increased success at the Salons, especially with portraiture. In 1881 he married Aline Charigot: together they visited Algeria and Italy (Rome, Venice, Naples). He became dissatisfied with Impressionism and felt renewed admiration for Ingres, Raphael and eighteenth-century art. During the 1880s he worked increasingly in the south of France (occasionally with Cézanne in Provence). His son Pierre was born in 1885, and Jean (later the film director) in 1893. In 1892 he had a large one-man show in Paris. In 1894 he was executor to the Caillebotte bequest of paintings to the nation. In the same year he met Vollard, dealer and publisher, and suffered his first serious arthritic attacks. In 1897 six of his paintings were accepted into the Musée du Luxembourg, Paris. From the 1890s on he lived mainly in the south, at Cagnes. In 1900 he was made Chevalier de la Légion d'Honneur. In 1901 his son Claude was born. Around 1907 he started clay modelling. From 1910 on his severe arthritic attacks increased: he was sometimes paralysed and confined to a wheelchair. In 1915 his wife died, only four years before his own death.

Renoir's early work as a porcelain painter reflects two constant characteristics of his art: an enormous natural facility and a dedication to eighteenth-century standards of decoration and craftsmanship. At the École des Beaux-Arts, he passed examinations with ease. Among his early paintings there are works of considerable academic accomplishment (*Diana*, 1867, Washington, National Gallery). His landscapes of the 1860s were painted under Monet's influence (sometimes at his side: *La Grenouillère*, 1869, Stockholm, National Museum) in their extreme concentration on first visual impressions. He was also encouraged in this respect by Corot and Diaz. The character of Impressionism emerged from their paintings of 1867–70: the gentle sensitivity of Renoir's eye, his muted colour and feathery touch complemented the more audacious and clean execution of Monet. Like Monet, he experimented with complementary colour and coloured shadow (*Lise*, 1867, Stockholm, Folkwang Museum; *Nude in Sunlight*, c. 1875, Paris, Louvre).

Apart from the personality of his brushwork, the main distinction of his 1870s Impressionism was his preoccupation with the figure as subject matter and particularly with the gay vitality of Parisian life. In *Le Moulin de la Galette* and *The Swing* (both 1876, Paris, Louvre), the broken brushwork and colour express not only the shifting fall of light through leaves, but also the transience and exuberance of urban relaxation. In the same way Renoir's landscapes have a sense of charmed escape from the town to the country, related to his son's early films.

Less rigorously introspective than Monet ('If painting were not a pleasure to me, I should certainly not do it'), he made his reputation at the Salons from the late 1870s with a series of fashionable portraits (*Mme Charpentier and Daughters*, 1878, New York, Metropolitan Museum). Here his dexterity was combined with an anecdotal charm.

In the 1880s he felt he had exhausted Impressionism and in a period of change and uncertainty ('I didn't know either how to paint or to draw') he turned to traditional art for support—French Renaissance sculpture, Raphael, Ingres. In *Les Parapluies*, c. 1883 (London, National Gallery), there is a tight sense of drawing and a new hard contour. The ambitious *Baigneuses*, 1884–7 (Philadelphia, Tyson Collection), was preceded by a series of drawn studies dependent on Renaissance sources and attempted, like Cézanne's late *Bathers* paintings, to reconcile Impressionism's visual spontaneity to a sense of the monumental. When, in his late work, this linearity gave way again to a more painterly style, he retained a sense of massive plasticity (*Seated Bather*, 1914, Chicago, Art Institute; *Bathers*, 1918,

Paris, Louvre). Many of the sculptures he made at the end of his life are direct transpositions of painted *motifs* (*Mother and Child*, 1914, London, Tate Gallery). These were largely made by an assistant (a pupil of Maillol), Renoir's own hands being almost crippled with arthritis.

J. Baudot. *Renoir: Ses Amis, ses Modèles*, Paris 1949.
W. Pach. *Pierre-Auguste Renoir*, New York 1950.
John Rewald (ed.). *Renoir, Drawings*, New York 1958.
Jean Renoir. *Renoir, my Father*, Boston 1962.

Renqvist, Torsten. Swedish painter, draughtsman and graphic artist, b. 1924. Following in the path of English artists like Nash and Sutherland, Renqvist paints highly Expressionistic pictures, using startling and sometimes brutal colour contrasts. With his original and stimulating conception of reality, and his personal and often symbolic style, he paved the way for the Neo-Expressionism which developed in Sweden in the 1950s. Renqvist's graphic work reveals a close interest in nature and a deep sense of social commitment. Typical works are: *Djur* (*Animals*, 1952, a portfolio of woodcuts); *Upplopp* (*Insurrection*, 1957, a series of etchings inspired by the crisis in Hungary); *Klot* (*Sphere*, 1959, a series of etchings presenting an imaginative account of the Creation); and *Fragment i jorden* (*Fragments in the Earth*, 1960, a series of etchings). Renqvist has also executed a number of monumental works; his decorations for the Folkets Hus in Västerås (1959) are representative. From 1955 to 1958 Renqvist taught at Valand's Art School in Gothenburg.

A. Ellenius. *Torsten Renqvist*, Stockholm 1964.

Repin, Ilya. Russian painter, b. 1844; d. 1930. He studied in St. Petersburg, then joined the *Wanderers* group, who started the Russian Realism movement. He gained great prominence with his social commentaries and his portraits. Repin was a forerunner of Social Realism, the Soviet movement introduced in 1932.

Requichot, Bernard. French painter, b. 1929 in Saint Gilles, Sarthe; d. 1961. Requichot received his practical training at the Atelier d'Art Sacré and the Atelier Charpentier from 1945 to 1948, when he joined the Paris Academy and studied under Souverbie and Brianchon. In 1952 he was painting Cubist works. Then, from 1956 onwards, he produced his *papiers choisis* (collages made of colour photographs taken from illustrated magazines). In 1958 he created his first big sculpture and in the following year settled in Apt in the Vaucluse, where he wrote his first poems. In 1960 he produced a cycle entitled *La Guerre des Nerfs* (*The War of Nerves*). In 1961 he committed suicide. His 'Letters' were published posthumously.

In the mid-1950s, when informal art was at its

peak, Requichot took the crucial step from abstraction to representation by incorporating real objects or photographs into his paintings. And so, like Yves Klein and Armand, he helped pave the way for the *Nouveau Réalisme* of the 1960s.

Catalogue, *Bernard Requichot*, Galerie Daniel Cadier, Paris 1964.

Resnick, Milton. Russian-American painter, b. 1917 in Bratslov, Russia. After studying in Paris in the mid-1940s he went to the United States. In the mid-1950s, while teaching at Pratt Institute (1954–5) and the University of California, Berkeley (1955–6), he was given one-man shows on the East and West Coasts, at the De Young Museum in San Francisco (1955) and at the Poindexter Gallery, New York (1955). Many of his works are done on a monumental scale, some as large as 10 by 16 feet. His 1960 *Capricorn* (New York, Howard Wise Gallery) initially seems to be a drip painting due to the freedom of handling and the size of the canvas. It is in fact composed of freely applied squiggles of paint interspaced with blotches of colour—blues, reds, greens and yellows. An exhibitor in the 1957 and 1959 Whitney Annuals, he was given a major retrospective at the Madison Art Center, Madison, Wisconsin, in 1967.

Reth, Alfred. Hungarian-French painter, b. 1884 in Budapest; d. 1966 in Paris. In 1905 Reth settled in Paris, where he joined the Cubists and exhibited with them from 1908 onwards. In 1931 he became a member of the *Abstraction-Création* association.

Reth has used various experimental materials in his pictures, including sand, egg shells and cement. Basically, the simple, abstract compositions which make up his output are refinements of Cubist techniques.

W. George. *Alfred Reth*, Paris 1955.

Reuterswärd, Carl-Fredrik. Swedish painter, filmmaker and poet, b. 1934. Reuterswärd is much given to sophisticated material effects and technical experiments. His paintings, which are dominated by blacks and whites, are executed in a spontaneous process and closely resemble calligraphic pictures. His *images plexiques* are painted on the back of Plexiglass. In some of his paintings, and also in his poems, Reuterswärd works in a completely nonsensical style that is essentially Dadaist. In 1955 he joined the Parisian *Phases* group. In 1965 he created the décor for a modern opera in Stockholm and joined the teaching staff at the College of Art in Stockholm. Recently Reuterswärd has also engaged in kinetic art, experimenting with laser beams in darkened rooms.

Reverón, Armando. Venezuelan painter, b. 1889 in Caracas; d. 1954 in Caracas. Reverón spent his childhood in Valencia (Spain), returning to Venezuela in 1904. He studied at the Academy in Caracas, then continued his training in Europe, where he worked in Madrid, Barcelona and Paris, and was greatly influenced by Spanish painting. In 1921 he went back to Venezuela and settled in Macute, where he and his wife—who acted as his model—lived in almost total seclusion. But Reverón suffered from a deep-seated neurosis which became progressively more severe, and in 1945 he was obliged to enter a sanatorium. In 1931 and 1954 retrospective exhibitions of his works were staged in Caracas, and in 1956 in various North American cities. Reverón painted Impressionist landscapes which are remarkable for their powerful colours and their chiaroscuro.

Revold, Axel. Norwegian painter, b. 1887 in Alesund; d. 1962. After studying in Oslo and Paris (under Matisse) Revold held a professorial post at the Oslo Academy from 1925 to 1946.

Revold is generally considered to have been one of the most important twentieth-century monumental artists in Norway. His frescoes for the Stock Exchange in Bergen, which date from 1921–3 and whose highly simplified forms reveal Revold's indebtedness to Matisse and his preoccupation with Cubism, mark the beginning of the modern period of Norwegian architectonic painting. In his clear, powerful works Revold usually depicted the Norwegian landscape and scenes from everyday life. He produced numerous wall paintings for public buildings.

Rezvani, Serge. Persian-French painter and lithographer, b. 1928 in Teheran. He moved to France in 1931. He studied with Othon Friesz at the Académie de la Grande Chaumière in Paris, and was first shown at the 1951 Salon de Mai. He joined the group of young artists called *Les Mains Éblouies*. His work is abstract. He has illustrated volumes of poetry by Paul Éluard.

Richards, Ceri. British painter, b. 1903 in Dunvant, Wales; d. 1971. Richards studied at Swansea and at the RCA, where he later taught. His association with Surrealism in the 1930s was productive of several fully 'European' assemblages, such as can be seen in the Tate Gallery, London.

From 1944 to 1957 Richards held nine one-man exhibitions at the Redfern Gallery, London, and in 1960 a Whitechapel Gallery retrospective. His middle period works are of an abstracted Romanticism conveying Welsh qualities of mood and place. They accord with the spirit of emotional release prevalent in postwar British art. Richards has stated: 'Temperamentally I feel attuned to the movement and dynamism that lie in nature and events. . . .' Contemporary criticism has stressed the influence of Picasso, Miró, Ernst and Richards' musical correspondences with, for example, Debussy's *La Cathédrale Engloutie*.

He won the Einaudi Prize at the 1962 Venice Biennale. He also produced murals for the Shakespeare Exhibition, Stratford (1964), and subsequently certain interior features for Liverpool Catholic Cathedral.

J. Russell. Introduction to the Catalogue of the 1962 Venice Biennale.
D. Thompson. *Ceri Richards*, London 1963.
A. Bowness. *Recent British Painting*, London 1968.

Richier, Germaine. French sculptress, b. 1904 in Grans, near Arles; d. 1959 in Montpellier. Richier trained at the École des Beaux-Arts in Montpellier under Guiges, who had been an assistant of Rodin's and was then Director of the Academy in Montpellier. In 1925 she moved to Paris, where Henri Xaver and de Rudier persuaded Bourdelle to accept her as a private pupil. In 1929 she left Bourdelle and took a studio in the Avenue du Maine. In 1934 she had her first exhibition (in the Galerie Kaganowitsch in Paris), in 1936 she won the Blumenthal Prize for Sculpture, and in 1937 was awarded a Diploma for Sculpture at the International Exhibition in Paris. From 1939 to 1945 she lived in Switzerland and the South of France, and in 1944–5 had exhibitions in Switzerland. In 1945 Richier returned to Paris, and in 1951 won a prize for sculpture at the Bienal in São Paulo. On 15 September 1955 she married the writer René de Solier.

After a thorough training embracing every aspect of sculpture Richier produced busts, torsos, and male and female figures with an Impressionistic texture that was reminiscent of Rodin and with Neo-Classical forms that revealed the influence of Bourdelle. This early period came to an end in c. 1940, when she abandoned the organic structures of Classical art and tried to evolve an alternative mode of expression that would do justice to the new kinds of experience with which she was forced to contend. She then sought her inspiration in weird insects and daemonic nocturnal fauna. In her hard but determined struggle to achieve a new sculptural synthesis, Richier was greatly influenced by the works of A. Giacometti. With the creation of her *Women-Insects* of 1945 she turned away from the physical forms of traditional Mediterranean statuary and developed a sculptural style in which new compact physical forms were combined with sinister groping limbs that have more in common with insects than men. With their fearsome gestures, the bloated bodies and distorted forms and the pierced, torn and rigid surfaces of the human figures which Richier created in 1947–8 also reflect the disintegration of natural forces. In *L'Orage*, which dates from the same year, man is represented as the daemonic carrier and interpreter of apocalyptic catastrophes, whilst in *La Grande Sauterelle* of 1946–7 he appears as a hybrid creature (half human,

half insect) of monumental and macabre proportions. It soon became apparent that metamorphosis was to be the central theme of Richier's art, and by 1953–4 we find human, animal, vegetable and mineral forms in bizarre, grotesque or frightening combinations. In *La Fourmi* of 1953 Richier attached the solid compact body of the ant to a network of diagonal wires whilst allowing its slender groping extremities to extend into space. The wire framework served a dual purpose, for it effectively indicated the third dimension and also created the prison in which the figure of the ant is hopelessly enmeshed. The really marvellous thing about this and similar sculptures is the way in which the lemuroid creatures are incorporated into three-dimensional space frames, and the way in which observed reality is translated into mythical, pictorial reality.

Richier's general preoccupation with ugliness was interrupted in c. 1956 by a brief abstract period, in which she produced a series of Cubist constructions consisting of blocks of stone laid one on top of the other. In 1955–6 she also created a number of extremely moving portraits, in which man is depicted as a wounded and suffering creature.

Richier's sculptures are mounted on irregular flat bases, and are often placed in front of painted or tiled wall panels. These establish a firm spatial framework, which enhances the plasticity of the sculptural objects.

Jean Cassou. *Germaine Richier*, Cologne and Berlin 1961.
Enrico Crispolti. *Germaine Richier*, Milan 1968.

Richter, Gerd. German painter, b. 1932 in Dresden. Richter studied in Dresden from 1951 to 1956. Since 1961 he has been living in Düsseldorf, where he and Konrad Lueg organized the exhibition *Eine Demonstration für den kapitalistischen Realismus* (A Demonstration for Capitalist Realism) in 1963.

Richter paints realistic pictures in the Pop Art manner, using photographs as models. By means of a 'blurring technique' he creates an impression similar to that produced by an out-of-focus snapshot.

Richter, Hans. German painter, sculptor and filmmaker, b. 1888 in Berlin; d. 1976. His early training was in carpentry in Berlin—a craft which was obligatory for the study of architecture. He then studied at the Hochschule für Bildende Künste, Berlin (1908), and in 1909 entered the Academy of Art in Weimar. At this time he was most influenced by the Fauves, the *Blauer Reiter* and Cubism, the latter style manifesting itself in his 1914 portrait of *Dr. Udo Rukser* (Quillota, Chile, Coll. Rukser). In 1914 he was a collaborator on the review *Die Aktion*, a whole issue of which was devoted to Richter. Two years later he had his first one-man show at the Galerie Hanns Goltz, Munich. After being invalided out of the Army he joined the Dada group in Zürich. The complete freedom available in this association led to his 'visionary portraits' of 1917, his black and white abstractions and Dada heads (*Dada Head I*, 1918, Chicago, Coll. Mies van der Rohe). In 1919 he and W. Eggeling created their first scrolls, Richter's based on the positive-negative interplay of planes (*Preludium*, 1919, pencil, New Haven, Conn., Yale University Art Gallery). Two years later he made his first abstract film: *Rhythm 21*, now a classic in *avant-garde* film-making. In 1940–1 he went to the United States where he was appointed a professor at the College of the City of New York and Director of the Film Institute. Still producing scrolls, the works became less rectilinear and incorporated collage elements (*Liberation of Paris*, 1945–6, oil and collage, Paris, Musée de l'Art Moderne). He had his first one-man show in America in 1946 at the Art of This Century Gallery, New York. In the 1960s he painted both horizontal and vertical scrolls, with an emphasis on the free flow of colour rather than on form (*Motorhythm I*, 1960, coll. of artist). Among his most memorable films are *Dreams that Money can buy* (1944–7), *8 × 8* (1955–8), and *Dadascope* (1956–61), which were produced with such men as Jean Arp, Marcel Duchamp, Man Ray, Max Ernst and Alexander Calder. He has written many articles on film and art; among his books are: *Filmfeinde von Heute, Filmfreunde von Morgen* (Berlin, 1929), *Film gesteren, heden, morgen* (Amsterdam, 1935), *The Political Film* (New York, 1941), *Dada Profile* (Zürich, 1961) and *Dada Kunst und Anti-Kunst* (Cologne, 1964).

Hans Richter, Autobiography; introduction by Sir Herbert Read, Neuchâtel (Switzerland) 1965.

Richter, Heinrich (Henryk Rychter). Polish-German painter, b. 1920 in Inowroclaw, Posen. After spending his childhood and youth in Poland Richter became a displaced person as a result of the war and in 1945 found himself in Berlin, where he is still living today. In 1952 he made a working visit to Paris. In 1965 he met Günther Grass.

Like his friend Bellmer, Richter paints erotic, Surrealist pictures of the female body, portraying the anatomical detail in highly civilized colours and with sensitive, swirling brushwork that is reminiscent of Baroque technique. Dissolved contours merge with monochrome grounds to produce ambiguous compositions, which reveal an affinity with the work of Francis Bacon, although they lack the Englishman's aggressive sense of commitment. Richter made his name in 1965 when he illustrated Günther Grass's *Blechtrommel* (*Tin Drum*).

Catalogue, *Heinrich Richter*, Städtisches Museum Schloss Morsbroich, Leverkusen.

Richter, Vjenceslav. Yugoslav architect, sculptor and designer, b. 1917 in Zagreb. After completing his architectural studies at the Technical College in Zagreb Richter became a member of the *EXTAT 51*

group and obtained a post on the staff of the Centre for Industrial Design. In 1963 he joined the New Trends association.

Richter is one of the most important young architects working in Yugoslavia today. He designed the Yugoslav Pavilion for the International Exhibition in Brussels in 1958, for the Industrial Exhibition in Turin in 1961 and for the Triennale in Milan in 1964. He is one of those concerned with the concept of 'synthetic urbanism'. In his architectural projects he moulds sculptural and visual elements into an aesthetic whole, whilst in his statuary and reliefs he carries out sculptural experiments in space. Richter's ultimate objective is to adapt the individual work of art so as to be able to reproduce its unique quality on an industrial scale as a consumer product.

V. Richter. *Sinturbanizam*, Zagreb 1964.
O. Bihalji-Merin. Introduction to the *Profile VI* exhibition catalogue, Bochum 1966.

Ricketts, Charles. British painter and designer, b. 1866 in Geneva; d. 1931 in London. In 1882 he attended the Lambeth School of Art, and there got to know Charles Shannon, with whom he ran a magazine, *The Dial*. He designed stage sets, and exhibited at the International Society from 1906 and the Grosvenor Gallery from 1921. He wrote several critical art studies. His work was included in the exhibition of late members' work at the Royal Academy in 1933.

Rickey, George. American sculptor and painter, b. 1907 in South Bend, Indiana. Rickey spent his childhood and youth in Scotland. His extensive education in history, art and art history included studies at Balliol College, Oxford (1929, BA; 1941, MA with honours); the Ruskin School of Drawing and Fine Art, Oxford (1928–9); the Académie André Lhôte and Académie Moderne, Paris (1929–30); New York University (1945–6); and the Institute of Design, Chicago (1948–9). From 1930 on, Rickey taught at various schools in the United States, including Indiana University, Bloomington (1949–55), Tulane University, New Orleans (1955–62), and Rensselaer Polytechnic Institute, Troy, New York (from 1961). His first one-man exhibition of paintings was held at the Caz-Delbo Gallery, New York, in 1933, and of sculpture, at the John Herron Art Institute, Indianapolis, in 1953.

Rickey's development began with painting; in the 1930s and 1940s he worked particularly with murals in tempera, for which he received numerous commissions (United States Post Office, Selinsgrove, Pennsylvania, 1938; Knox College, Galesburg, Illinois, 1940–1). He made his first mobile in 1945, and began to work extensively in kinetic sculpture around 1950. Rickey's sculptures are usually intended for the outdoors, and their movements generally depend on natural air currents; thus they are neither predictable nor exactly repetitive, their slowly moving parts creating an effect of subtlety and calmness. Rickey's early kinetic constructions are fairly complicated and agitated and depend strongly on natural imagery, as indicated by titles such as *Silverplume, II* (1951, Ghent, New York, Coll. Mr. and Mrs. Larry Gelbart) and *Waterplant* (1959–61, Andover, Mass., Addison Gallery of American Art). His later work, though still sometimes suggestive of natural phenomena, tends to be simpler and more geometrical and abstract (*Sedge II*, 1961, stainless steel, Hanover, New Hampshire, Dartmouth College; *Two Red Lines*, 1966, painted stainless steel, coll. of artist).

George Rickey. 'The Metier', *Arts Yearbook 8: Contemporary Sculpture*, New York 1964.
Peter Selz. Catalogue, *George Rickey: Sixteen Years of Kinetic Sculpture*, Corcoran Gallery of Art, Washington (D.C.) 1966.

Riley, Bridget. British painter, b. 1931 in London. She studied at Goldsmith's, 1949–52, and at the RCA, 1952–5. She held her first one-man show in 1963 at Gallery One. She worked almost entirely in black and white at first, and her painting is in a strict sense optical in that it uses interference and other optical effects to dazzle and confuse. She is inspired by Vasarély, but her work differs from his in its exclusive preoccupation with optical effect. She does not use composition in any conventional sense but designs patterns that cover the whole surface of the painting and appear to the eye constantly to shift and vibrate. Her painting is in a sense therefore purely mechanical, but because of its positive and unqualified assertion of the subjective relation of the spectator to the painting, it is not without significance in the history of twentieth-century painting.

Riopelle, Jean-Paul. Canadian painter and sculptor, b. 1922 in Montreal, Quebec. He studied with Paul-Émile Borduas and first exhibited in 1945 with his teacher, and the other artists of the Borduas group, who were known as the Automatists. Soon after this exhibition he left for Paris where he exhibited with Ozias Leduc and met Bryen, Wols and Malespine—artists involved with *Tachisme* and Informal Painting. He returned to Canada in 1948 and signed the *Refus Global* Manifesto, a statement which was as important for French-Canadian *avant-garde* painting as were the manifestos of the Surrealists in their time. He soon returned to Paris and rejected his Surrealist leanings, concentrating instead on a form of 'non-figurative pantheism' which is rooted to his love of landscape and still life, a concern which dates back to the early years of his career. By the 1950s his works show a more pronounced concern for texture, often applying the paint with heavy impasto in a fragmented, tesserae-like manner (*Festival*, 1953, Paris, Galerie Jacques Dubourg). In the 1960s his concern for texture is manifest in sculptural experi-

ments. His large glyptic forms are hard and rough, of great weight, density and mass, echoing the more powerful manner of his later painting style as opposed to his earlier, more lyrical manner. The entire issue of *Derrière le miroir*, June 1966, was devoted to Riopelle.

G. Duthuit. Catalogue, *Riopelle*, Galerie Rive Droit, Paris 1954.
Jean Cathelin. 'Jean-Paul Riopelle', *Cimaise* X, November–December 1963.
J. Russell Harper. *Painting in Canada*, Toronto 1966.

Ris, Günter Ferdinand. German painter and sculptor, b. 1928 in Leverkusen. Ris studied painting at the Academies in Karlsruhe, Düsseldorf and Freiburg im Breisgau between 1947 and 1950. He became a sculptor in 1960–1.

Ris produces abstract sculptures with smooth, polished surfaces in marble or bronze. The component sections of these works, which are concave in shape, articulate with one another like human limbs or the sections of a suit of armour and so create a figurative impression.

Catalogue, *Günter Ferdinand Ris*, Galerie Thomas, Munich 1967.

Rissanen, Juho. Finnish painter, b. 1873 in Kuopio; d. 1950 in Miami, Florida. After studying in Helsinki, Turkey and St. Petersburg (under Repin) Rissanen became a founder member of the *Septem* group in 1914. In 1918 he settled in France, remaining there until 1939, when he emigrated to the United States. Rissanen was a powerful and highly individual painter, whose most original works date from his early period. Until he moved to France Rissanen painted large-format pictures, in which he portrayed the poor peasants of his native Finland. With their simplified forms and colours, these deeply felt monumental works have something of the quality of archaic art.

Ritschl, Otto. German painter and writer, b. 1885 in Erfurt. At first he was active as a writer. In 1918 he began to paint, and was self-taught as a painter. He was closely associated with Jawlensky. His work is abstract, and consists of close-set rows of coloured dots arranged in strict geometrical order. In 1955 he had a major exhibition in Wiesbaden, where he settled. He has exhibited widely in Germany.

Rivera, Diego Maria. Mexican painter, b. 1886 in Guanajuato; d. 1957 in Mexico City. Rivera pioneered the monumental painting of the new Mexican school. After studying at the Academy of San Carlos in Mexico and, from 1907 to 1908, in Madrid, he visited France, England, Belgium and Holland between 1908 and 1910 before settling in Paris in 1911. There he made contact with Derain, Braque, Picasso and Gris and turned to Cubism. But after returning to Mexico in 1921 he rediscovered his native folklore, especially the art of the Mayas and the Aztecs, and so gradually freed himself from European influences. At the same time he was drawn into the Mexican revolution, became a member of the artists' commune and joined the revolutionary movement led by Orozco and Siqueiros. The wall paintings which he executed for the National Preparatory School in Mexico and for the Ministry of Education between 1923 and 1928 and in which he depicted scenes from the social and political history of his native country were the first of his great series of monumental works. The popular, expressive Realism of these paintings with their simplified flat forms and their powerful decorative colours exerted an enduring influence on Mexican art and also made a considerable impression in Europe and, more especially, the USA.

In 1927 Rivera visited Soviet Russia. In 1929 he was put in charge of the Central School of Fine Arts in Mexico. Like Orozco, Rivera also worked in the United States, where he created frescoes for the Rockefeller Center in New York in 1933. Between 1930 and 1944 he worked on the decorations for the Mexican Government Building. Rivera also engaged in politics, wrote and illustrated books and, in addition to his wall-paintings, executed a wide range of studio pictures, including portraits, figurative works, histories and erotic compositions. But his major achievement was undoubtedly his monumental painting. In this sphere Rivera created a simple, popular but none the less 'modern' style which paved the way for a completely new kind of Realism.

B. Wolfe. *D. Rivera: His Life and Times*, New York and London 1939.

H. F. Secker. *D. Rivera*, Dresden 1957.

E. F. Gual. *D. Rivera*, Buenos Aires 1966.

Rivera, José de. American sculptor, b. 1904 in West Baton Rouge, Louisiana. In 1924 de Rivera went to Chicago, where he worked in machine shops to earn his living and from 1928 to 1931 studied art at the Studio School. He began making sculpture in the early 1930s and received his first major commission in 1938 for Newark Airport in New Jersey (*Flight*, aluminium, now owned by the Newark Museum). His first one-man show was held in New York in 1946. He taught at Brooklyn College (1953), Yale University (1954–5), and the North Carolina School of Design (1957–60).

De Rivera began to work in a modernist direction in the early 1930s with simplified, stylized and highly polished metal sculptures; at the same time he was still exploring, in several granite pieces, the current movement of carve-direct sculpture. In the late 1930s he became familiar with the work of Piet Mondrian and Constantin Brancusi, whose emphasis on elemental form and colour was influential on his own style, as were the Constructivists' principles of movement, space and time. From the beginning de Rivera was interested in using rotation in his sculpture to produce a slow, controlled movement and a changing relationship of forms in space, and to increase and complicate the play of light on the polished metal surfaces. Around 1939 he began making constructions of abstract and simply shaped aluminium sheets painted in primary colours (*Blue and Black*, 1951, New York, Whitney Museum). The other, but related, line of development in de Rivera's work is found in the series of highly polished stainless steel constructions of curvilinear and continuous forms, which are usually, though not always, alternately thickened and attenuated (*Homage to the World of Herman Minkowski*, c. 1955, New York, Metropolitan Museum; *Construction 34*, 1954, New York, Grace Borgenicht Gallery; and *Construction 29*, 1956, forged square steel rod, Coll. Gustav P. Heller).

Dore Ashton. 'The Sculpture of José de Rivera', *Arts* XXX, April 1956.

John Gordon. *José de Rivera*, American Federation of Arts, New York 1961.

Rivera, Manuel. Spanish painter and sculptor, b. 1927 in Granada. He studied art in Seville, and since 1951 has been living in Madrid. He is an abstract artist. He exhibited at the 1957 São Paulo Bienal and at the twenty-ninth Venice Biennale in 1958. His works are on show in Madrid, The Hague and New York. He has had major exhibitions in 1959 at the Sala del Prado des Ateneo, Madrid, and at the Matisse Gallery in New York, 1961. He makes abstract constructions from molten iron which give the impression of pictures. He is a member of the *El Paso* group.

Rivers, Larry. American painter and sculptor, b. 1923 in New York. He first began a career in music, studying at the Juillard School of Music in New York, and later working professionally as a jazz saxophonist. Rivers is also known for his poetry, stage design, graphics and illustrations. He began painting seriously while studying for two years with Hans Hofmann in Provincetown, Massachusetts, experimenting there with the dynamics of abstraction. A year in Europe (1950), where he carefully observed the work of Bonnard and Soutine, convinced him that the modern painter could still work creatively in a realistic, figurative mode. As an early admirer of Willem de Kooning's Abstract Expressionist style, Rivers was to adapt the latter's spontaneous brushwork and subjective focus to a montage-like combination of images taken from the urban and commercial environment. Indirect suggestions of socio-political themes were combined with painterly execution and accomplished draughtsmanship in such works as *Washington Crossing the Delaware* (1953, New York, Museum of Modern Art) and the *Dutch Masters Series* (1963, New York, Dwan Gallery), which refer to reproductions of other paintings or commercial trademark images. Rivers, always inspired by realistic subject matter, constantly shifted from semi-abstract to more figurative works during his career as a painter and sculptor. Portraits of his mother-in-law are notable for their unabashed realism and candidness (*Double Portrait of Birdie*, 1955, New York, Whitney Museum), while works containing popular images and insignia (1954–5 and after 1961) are treated in out-of-focus, multiple views.

By giving banal themes and materials a tactile surface treatment, Rivers—among other artists in the 'second generation' after Abstract Expressionism —offered an alternative to that first independently American style of the twentieth century. Since 1963 he has worked predominantly on constructions, collages, prints, shaped-canvas constructions and painted figural sculptures. Polemical as well as sentimental motivations remained apparent in his versatile work (*Throwaway Dress: New York to Nairobi*, 1967, New York, Marlborough-Gerson Gallery).

Larry Rivers. 'Discussion of the Work of Larry Rivers', *Art News* LX, March 1961.
Catalogue, *Larry Rivers*, Brandeis University, Rose Art Museum, Waltham (Mass.) 1965.

Roberts, Tom. Australian painter, b. 1856 in England; d. 1931. He studied in Melbourne and in London at the Royal Academy Schools. He went back to Melbourne and in 1885 founded the Heidelberg School, a group of Impressionist-oriented painters. His works are largely portraits and scenes of the countryside. He was instrumental in the development of a purely Australian art.

Roberts, William. British painter, b. 1895 in London. He was apprenticed to a commercial artist in 1909, but also attended evening classes at the St. Martin's School and in 1910 went to the Slade, until 1913, on an LCC scholarship. Already interested in Cubism, he travelled in France and Italy in 1913 and on his return was associated with the Omega Workshop. Although he did not actually join the Rebel Art Centre he was in touch with Wyndham Lewis, and in 1914 he signed the Vorticist manifesto in *Blast*, where two of his drawings were reproduced. He exhibited with the Vorticists and in 1920 with Group X. In 1917 he became an official war artist, and in 1922 he did illustrations for the *Seven Pillars of Wisdom*. His earliest works are in a hard and angular form of Cubism (*Toe-Dancer*, 1914), but his war pictures are softer and a little more atmospheric. In the later twenties and the thirties the influence of Léger and Picasso led him to an imposing figure style of clear forms and simple gestures (*Routiers*, 1933). In his later works, however, this became a little wooden and heavy, and the Cubist elements still present in his work tended to become a rather doll-like formality (*Trooping the Colour*, 1958–9).

John Rothenstein. *Modern English Painters*, London and New York 1956.
William Roberts. *Paintings, 1917–1958*, London 1960.
Catalogue, *William Roberts, ARA: Retrospective Exhibition*, Tate Gallery, London 1965.

Robus, Hugo. American painter and sculptor, b. 1885 in Cleveland, Ohio. A graduate of Cleveland's Central High School (1903), he studied at the Cleveland School of Art (1904–8) and the National Academy of Design (1910–11) before going to Paris (1912–14). In France he studied sculpture with Antoine Bourdelle at the Académie de la Grande Chaumière and was friendly with Gertrude Stein, Marsden Hartley and Jacob Epstein. Though mainly studying sculpture in Paris, he was strongly influenced by Impressionism and the Futurists in his painting. By 1920 he devoted himself entirely to sculpture. The influence of Paris, and more precisely of Brancusi, can be seen in his early *Despair* (1927, New York, Whitney Museum of American Art) with its smooth forms and flowing contours. In the 1940s he gave up his lithe, delicate figures in favour of bulkier shapes handled in a quasi-Cubist style reminiscent of J. Lipchitz. The rough-hewn, abstract quality of *Reunion* (1945, Cleveland, Museum of Art) reveals a new sense of weight and strength. It was during this period that he had his first one-man show at the Grand Central Galleries in New York (1946). This bold approach to form was short-lived, however. By the 1950s he returned to a very smooth volumetric approach. In many of the works of this period the artist's sense of humour is revealed, as in the three headless and legless female figures entitled *Three Caryatides Without a Portico* (1954, coll. of artist). Robus has taught at Columbia University Summer School (intermittently from 1942 to 1956), Hunter College (1950–8), the Brooklyn Museum Art School (1955–6) and the Munson-Williams-Proctor Institute (1948).

Lincoln Rothschild. *Hugo Robus*, New York 1960.

Rocklin, Raymond. American sculptor, b. 1922 in Moodus, Connecticut. He studied in New York and Italy, and had his first one-man show in 1956 in New York (Tanager Gallery). He adhered to the Abstract Expressionist movement, and made curious but attractive assemblies of thin leaves of metal—brass or copper.

Rodchenko, Aleksandr. Russian painter, b. 1891 in St. Petersburg; d. 1956 in Moscow. Rodchenko was one of the leading Russian Constructivists. His first works, done for the theatre, were executed while still studying, first at the Kazan School of Art, subsequently at the Stroganov College in Moscow. In 1915–16 he produced his first abstract designs, five of which were sent to Tatlin's exhibition *The Store* in Moscow (March 1916). From 1916 to 1917 he made studies of surface texture, e.g. *Abstract Painting*, 1918 (Moscow, Tretyakov Gallery), which shows the influence of Tatlin; 1917 also saw the beginning of his 'line constructions'. In 1918 Rodchenko was appointed to the directorship of the Moscow Museum of Artistic Culture; in 1919 he replied to Malevich's *White on White* series with his famous *Black on Black*. In 1920 he joined the *Institute of Art Culture*. Tatlin, Rodchenko and his wife Stepanova represented the principal 'productivist' artists within the Constructivist movement. In that year he also became dean of *Vkutemas*. In 1921 Rodchenko sent five works to the $5 \times 5 = 25$ exhibition in Moscow, including three canvases painted yellow, red and blue respectively. He advocated the 'absoluteness of industrial art and Constructivism as its sole form of expression'. In 1922 he entered the First Textile Factory, Moscow, as a designer; he also took up photography. In 1925 he designed the workers' club for the Soviet Pavilion at the Paris exhibition of decorative arts; from this period onwards he was active in the field of typography and journalistic photography. His collaboration with Stepanova on various journalistic and literary projects continued until his death.

Camilla Gray. *The Great Experiment: Russian Art 1863–1922*, London and New York 1962.

Rodhe, Lennart. Swedish painter, b. 1916. During his early period, when he was influenced by Picasso, Rodhe painted Cubist works made up of interrelating two-dimensional elements and executed in powerful colours. In 1947 Rodhe turned completely abstract and became one of the foremost representatives of the Swedish *art concrète* group. He then sought to give expression to his conception of 'intangible space' by arranging angular forms in spiral formations. Typical examples of this kind of composition are his tile relief in the Post Office at Östersund (1948–52) and his tempera wall painting at the new elementary school in Stockholm (1948–53). Shortly afterwards, in 1955–7, Rodhe created a stained-glass window for the main counter section of the Swedish Commercial Bank in Stockholm which was based on a strictly stereometric design composed of luminous circular shapes. Later, he abandoned this geometrical approach in favour of a more spontaneous style, and since then has produced works composed of freely arranged areas of colour linked by interrelating *motifs* of lines and dots. His enamel painting in the Limnological Institute at the University of Uppsala, which dates from 1961–3, is a typical example. Rodhe has designed tapestry cartoons and stage sets, and has also produced graphic works, primarily lithographs. The drawings which he made on journeys to Southern Europe and North Africa, and which have provided the point of departure for his non-figurative painting, show him to be a keen observer of objective reality. Rodhe has held a professorial post at the Stockholm College of Art since 1958.

Rodin, Auguste. French sculptor, b. 1840 in Paris; d. 1917 in Meudon. He was educated at Beauvais, 1851–4, and then at the Petite École in Paris, 1854–7, a fellow student of Dalou: he was taught by Lecoq de Boisbaudran. He also studied at the Louvre and the Collège de France. In 1857/8, working on decorative carvings for a living, he started making sculpture in his spare time. He failed the entrance examination to the École des Beaux-Arts. In 1862/3 he underwent a religious crisis following his sister's death: he entered the Order of the Holy Sacrament for a brief period. In 1864 his first entry to the Salon (*Man with the Broken Nose*) was rejected. He worked as an assistant to Belleuse. At around this time he first met Rose Beuret, his lifelong mistress and, eventually, wife. He served in the National Guard during the Franco-Prussian War, 1870–1. In the early 1870s he continued working on ornamental carvings in Paris, Brussels, Antwerp, Nice and Marseilles. From 1875 to 1876 he visited Italy and was impressed by Renaissance sculpture, particularly that of Michelangelo. From this point on he devoted more time to his sculpture. In 1877 his *Age of Bronze* was exhibited in Brussels and Paris: in 1880 it was purchased by the State.

In 1880 he was commissioned to make an ornamental doorway for the Musée des Arts Décoratifs, Paris (the *Gates of Hell*), and later allocated studios in Paris to work on it. In 1882 he met Camille Claudel, who studied with him and modelled for him, as well as becoming his mistress. He received an increasing number of portrait commissions. He made frequent visits to London, and often exhibited there.

In 1884 he was commissioned to do *The Burghers of Calais* (originally the commission was for a single figure). It was first erected in Calais in 1895, and moved to its present site there in 1924. The cast in Parliament Square, London, was erected in 1913. He illustrated Baudelaire's *Fleurs du Mal*, 1886–8. In 1887 the State commissioned a large marble of *The Kiss* (copy in the Tate Gallery, London). In 1888 he was appointed Chevalier de la Légion d'Honneur. He held a successful joint exhibition with Monet at the Georges Petit Gallery, Paris, in 1889. The State also commissioned the *Monument to Victor Hugo* (bronze, now on the Ave. Victor Hugo, Paris). In 1891 he was given a State commission for the *Monument to Balzac*. In 1893 he moved to Bellevue, Meudon, and bought a villa there in 1895. When he exhibited the plaster *Balzac* in 1898–9, it was criticized and refused by the committee. The bronze version is now on the Boulevard Raspail, Paris. In 1899 he separated from Camille Claudel.

In 1900/1 he organized a highly successful large retrospective exhibition of his own work at the Place de l'Alma, Paris, to coincide with the Exposition Universelle. In 1902 his correspondence with Rilke began. From 1902 he received a succession of public honours in England: *John the Baptist* was bought by public subscription in 1902 (Victoria and Albert Museum); he was made President of the Society of Sculptors and Painters in 1903; he was given honorary degrees from Glasgow (1906) and Oxford (1907).

In 1905 he formed an association with the American Duchesse de Choiseul, which lasted until 1910. In 1908 he rented the Hôtel Biron, Paris, to work in. In 1910 he was appointed Grand Officier de la Légion d'Honneur. He was in England at the outbreak of war, and then visited Rome. In 1916 he suffered a stroke. In that year he offered all of his work to the French government on condition that it remained in the Hôtel Biron (by then State-owned) as a museum. This is now the Musée Rodin, the principal collection of his work. In January 1917 he married Rose Beuret, two weeks before her death. After contracting pneumonia, Rodin died himself on 17 November the same year.

Of the same generation as the Impressionists (he knew them and collected their work), Rodin was the only major sculptor of the late nineteenth century. Painting was becoming an increasingly small-scale and private activity and some sculptors (Daumier, Rosso, Degas, Gauguin) were moving the same way. Rodin attempted to meet the public scale of monumental sculpture in a modern idiom. He had a deep sense of tradition—both the Classical Renaissance of Italy and the French Gothic tradition (see his essay, *Cathédrales de France*, Paris, 1914). He also saw the study of nature as a criterion.

His long experience as a craftsman bred a thoroughly professional attitude to his work. Often condemned now as reactionary for the mechanical insensitivity of his marble works (made by an army of assistants and pupils from his small plaster maquettes), his modern reputation rests chiefly on the bravura of his modelling, his extraordinary use and re-use of images and part-images and the psychological realism of major works like *The Burghers of Calais*.

The string of incomplete commissions and dissatisfied patrons is evidence of his nonconformism and of the difficulty of his ambition. *The Gates of Hell* (Musée Rodin), still incomplete at his death, absorbed him during the 1880s and provided the genesis for many later works (*The Kiss, Le Penseur, Three Shades, The Prodigal Son*, etc.).

A lot of these compositions were improvised re-compositions of the same or similar figures, or even of different parts of them—torsos, limbs, even hands —usually with very different titles. His use of partial images may have sprung from seeing fragmentary antiques or from the unfinished work of Michelangelo (whose double-finish he consciously imitated in the marbles), but it became for Rodin a uniquely uninhibited and dispassionate process of assemblage, using ready-made plaster parts which were then cast in bronze.

He dominated the field of portraiture from the 1880s on, and in general contemporary sculptors (including the young Brancusi) felt overshadowed by his reputation. His pupils included Bourdelle and Despiau.

His late drawings and small plasters had the masterly control and economy of all great 'late styles'. The drawings of Cambodian dancers (1906) and the small bronze *Dance Movement* series (1910–11) are vital, fluid and relentlessly inventive.

Judith Cladel. *Rodin*, New York and Toronto 1937.
Bernard Champigneuile. *Rodin*, London and New York 1967.
Robert Descharnes and Jean-François Chabrun. *Auguste Rodin*, Paris and Geneva 1967.

Roeder, Emy. German sculptress, b. 1890 in Würzburg. After studying under Hoetger in Darmstadt from 1912 to 1914 Roeder settled in Berlin. In 1918 she joined the *Novembergruppe*. From 1920 to 1925 she studied at the Berlin Academy under Lederer. During this period she formed friendships with Belling, Philipp Harth, Heckel and Schmidt-Rottluff. From 1937 to 1949 she lived in Italy and from 1950 to 1953 taught at the Landeskunstschule (State School of Art) in Mainz, where she is now living. In her early period Roeder produced Expressionistic sculptures after the manner of Barlach and Hoetger, but later she developed an abstract technique, which was slightly stylized and austere. Although she carved animals as well as figures, portraits were her speciality.

F. Gerke. *Emy Roeder*, Wiesbaden 1963.

Roerich, Nicholas. Russian painter and designer, b. 1874 in St. Petersburg; d. 1947 in Kulu, India. Roerich was a member of the *Mir Iskusstva*, the movement founded by Diaghilev in the 1890s. He contributed designs for Diaghilev's *Ballets Russes*, among them the sets for the Polovtsian Dances from *Prince Igor* (Borodin) and the *Rite of Spring* (Stravinsky). He was inspired by the legends and folklore of Oriental Russia, and his work reflects the brilliance and barbarism of the East.

Rogers, Claude. British painter, b. 1907 in London. Rogers was brought up partly in the Argentine. He studied at the Slade from 1925 to 1929. A convinced Realist, he was one of the founders of the Euston Road School in 1937, and since then he has continued to work in a directly representational manner. He still paints landscape, portraits and genre in a style which, though much looser, is developed from his Euston Road painting. He is now Professor of Fine Art at Reading University.

Rohlfs, Christian. German painter, b. 1849 in Niendorfner Leezen, Kreis Segeberg; d. 1938 in Hagen, Westphalia. Rohlfs was the son of a small farmer. In 1870 he entered the Academy of Art in Weimar as a student of painting. After completing his studies he joined with Buchholz, Hagen and Brendel in embracing German Realism, a movement which had emerged during the second half of the nineteenth century and which crystallized into a specific style in the course of the 1890s due to the impact of French Impressionism. In 1901, when he was over fifty, Rohlfs was asked to teach in Hagen, where he saw works by Daumier, Renoir, Signac, Seurat, Cézanne, van Gogh, Gauguin, Hodler, Minne, Maillol and Rodin and embarked on a new phase of development. He then discovered the revolutionary art of Matisse and Braque, of the *Brücke* and the *Blauer Reiter*, and he established a firm friendship with Nolde. At first he was influenced by the Neo-Impressionists and van Gogh, but by 1910 his work —which was contemporaneous in its origins with the paintings of Uhde, Trübner, Liebermann, Monet, van Gogh and Gauguin—had entered the general sphere of Expressionist art. During the First World War he produced his impressive series of religious paintings and also treated religious themes in his graphic work. In 1919, when he was seventy, he began to travel. This led to the Upper Bavarian landscapes of 1920–1, the pictures of his native Holstein of 1922 and the views of Sooden and Erfurt of 1924. The works of this postwar period had grown progressively more profound and internationalized and this process reached its peak in 1927, when Rohlfs went to live in Ascona on Lake Maggiore. The individual colours in his paintings then became quite insubstantial; their material values were replaced by a spiritual quality which radiates from the delicate network of interlacing patterns like an inner light. These late works are nearly all executed in tempera, which Rohlfs used more and more from 1922 onwards. Under the Nazis Rohlfs was classified as a 'degenerate artist'. His works were then removed from public museums and many were destroyed.

Paul Vogt. *Christian Rohlfs: Aquarelle und Zeichnungen*, Recklinghausen 1958–60.

Rolfsen, Alf. Norwegian painter, b. 1895 in Oslo. Rolfsen is one of the most important modern exponents of monumental painting in Norway. His work is in the European tradition and reveals the influence of both the Italian Renaissance and French Cubism. Rolfsen has shown a preference for large, fully modelled pictorial forms, clear linear structures and a rhythmical, constructive type of composition, which has the effect of integrating the painting and the surrounding space into a corporate entity. From 1922 onwards Rolfsen created wall paintings in numerous public buildings, including the town hall in Oslo.

J. H. Langaard. *Alf Rolfsen*, Oslo 1932.

Romagnoni, Giuseppe. Italian painter, b. 1930 in Milan; d. 1964. Romagnoni studied at the School of Applied Art and the Accademia Brera in Milan. He packed his visionary pictures with isolated Realistic phenomena (bodies, faces, mechanical and industrial components) which he arranged in a narrative sequence. He also used photomontages to heighten the realism.

E. Crispoti *et al.* Catalogue, *Alternative Attuali 2*, Milan 1965.

Romiti, Sergio. Italian painter, b. 1928 in Bologna. Romiti studied under G. Morandi. He is now living in Bologna.

Romiti's early period was dominated by his encounter with Morandi. But in 1940, due to the influence exerted on him by the *École de Paris*, he moved away from objective art. He now produces large-format, dynamic colour compositions, which were originally inspired by M. Rothko's light walls.

V. Rubin. *Sergio Romiti*, Milan 1967.

Ronald, William. Canadian-American painter, b. 1926 in Stratford, Ontario. He studied painting at the Ontario College of Art, Toronto, under Jock Macdonald and had his first one-man show at Hart House, University of Toronto, in 1954. Two years later he received the Guggenheim Museum Award for Canadian Painting. His works of the late 1950s seem to owe to the Abstract Expressionists, particularly Motherwell and de Kooning, in his use of large, scrubby, forceful forms in space and in the freedom of stroke and scratching of the pigment into the canvas. His works of the 1960s are more delicate, often with greater emphasis on design, with stark contrasts of brightly coloured severe forms placed against a solid background. In 1958 he exhibited at the Brussels World's Fair and in 1959 at the Whitney Annual and the Fifth Bienal, São Paulo.

Rooskens, Anton. Dutch painter, b. 1906 in Griendsveen/Hort, Limburg. Rooskens is a self-taught artist. During his early period, when he worked as a landscapist, he was influenced by Permeke and the Belgian Expressionists. But after the Second World War he was deeply impressed by Picasso and the Mexican Primitives and evolved a new, more spontaneous and more abstract style. Rooskens has also produced wall paintings and pottery. In 1948 he became a founder member of the Experimental Group and also joined the *Cobra* association.

Cobra exhibition catalogue, 1948–51, Boymans–van Beuningen Museum, Rotterdam 1966.

Rosai, Ottone. Italian painter, b. 1895 in Florence; d. 1957 in Ivrea. Rosai left school when he was sixteen to set up his own *atelier*, having studied briefly at the Istituto d'Arti Decorative and the Accademia di Belle Arti in Florence in 1906. In 1911 he had his first exhibition of graphic works in Pistoia, which was followed by an exhibition of paintings in Florence in 1913. Later the same year he met the Futurist artists grouped around Marinelli, Boccioni and Carrà at the *Mostra di Lacerba* in the Galleria Gonnelli, Florence. In 1914, at Soffici's instigation, he began to contribute to the magazine *Lacerba*. From 1915 to 1918 he served with the forces. After the war Rosai lived in Rome for a while before returning to Florence. From 1930 onwards he contributed to important exhibitions.

By 1919 Rosai had integrated the Futurist influences to which he had been subjected in 1915–16 and evolved a plain, neo-primitive style of painting; the intense colours, the macabre isolation of the pictorial objects and the exaggerated perspective in the works of this period are a legacy of the *Pittura Metafisica*. In c. 1920 he began to attach particular importance to colour as a means of establishing the mood of his extremely painterly compositions, in which he depicted extremely popular scenes from the streets and inns of Florence. From c. 1930 onwards he painted clear, large-format pictures, in which houses, trees and walls are arranged in simple Cubist designs. Rosai was never sentimental. Even the monumental townscapes of his late period were highly sensitive and poetical works.

P. C. Santini. *Ottone Rosai*, Florence 1960.

Rosati, James. American sculptor, b. 1912 in Washington, Pennsylvania. Self-taught as a sculptor, he worked with Frank Vittor in Pittsburgh after having been a violinist with the Pittsburgh Symphony Orchestra for two years. He was given his first one-man show in 1954 at the Peridot Gallery, New York, and has exhibited in many Whitney Annuals. His heavy, block-like abstractions, such as the 1961 bronze *Head* (New York, Otto Gerson Gallery), are often given a degree of lightness through the surface handling of his pieces, which give the impression of being made of fresh, slightly wet clay; the build-up of layers of primary material is clearly visible. Rosati has taught at Cooper Union, Pratt Institute, Yale University and Dartmouth College (Visiting Critic). He was the recipient of a Guggenheim Foundation Fellowship in 1964.

Rosenquist, James. American painter, b. 1933 in Grand Forks, North Dakota. He studied art at the Art Students' League and at the University of Minnesota in 1952, first showing his work in New York at the *avant-garde* Green Gallery in 1962 and 1964.

Influenced in spirit by the Surrealists Salvador Dali and René Magritte, as well as by his fellow Pop artists Jasper Johns and Robert Rauschenberg, Rosenquist traces his stylistic origins to the billboard painting by which he supported himself during his first years in New York (1955–60). The technique of photographic enlargement used in this trade served Rosenquist in his own art: he developed a method of splicing and combining fragmentary blown-up images taken from commercial advertising along with the *motifs* of our industrial culture so that the effect is often as abstract and disconcerting as cinemascope movie close-ups. Like his Pop Art colleagues, he took a mechanical, commercial process and transformed it into the material for fine art, dislocating the banal and familiar from its expected context.

Rosenquist's iconography of the recognizable includes images that are used for their specific contemporary associations as well as for their more abstract qualities: big swirls of canned spaghetti, rubber tyres, atom-bomb clouds, automobile parts, human faces, food, clothing and light bulbs. In his largest three-panel mural *F-III* (1955, New York, Coll. Mr. and Mrs. Robert Scull) he interweaves these images with the fuselage of a giant aeroplane, painted in luridly harsh billboard colour. Although designed as a mural, the painting was not commissioned for a particular space, and thus lacks the traditional decorative function of the mural mode, while it demonstrates the contemporary issue of monumental scale in its attempt to take psychological advantage of its huge proportions. By 1962 Rosenquist had also extended this montage-enlargement method to single-panel paintings, so that the fragmentary images (more collage-like in earlier work, but single cut-outs in the later canvases) were almost beyond recognition due to their scaling (*Above the Square*, 1963, Coll. Mr. and Mrs. Robert Scull). Current methods used in advertising account for what Rosenquist terms his interest in 'visual inflation' and his use of image juxtaposition. He incorporates familiar aspects of our environmental exposure—sublimation, hard sell, pictorial bombardment—into his own work. He had abandoned his early experiments with an Abstract Expressionist style because he found greater potential in these factors of his former trade and his urban surroundings. Rosenquist uses the materials of our modern industrial complex inventively in many of his works—plastic sheeting, Plexiglass, neon light, simulated metal. Free-standing constructions have also occupied the artist for several years (*Capillary Action II*, 1963, New York, Leo Castelli Gallery). His trademark continues to be his quasi-photographic method of reproducing images from a commercial context on a projectively large scale.

Lucy Lippard. 'James Rosenquist: Aspects of a Multiple Art', *Artforum* IV, No. 4, 1965.
Ivan C. Karp. Catalogue, *James Rosenquist*, National Gallery of Canada, Ottawa 1968.

Rossi, Gino. Italian painter, b. 1884 in Venice; d. 1947 in Venice. He went to Paris in 1907 and there was fired with the love of painting; over the rest of his brief working life (cut short by insanity at the age of 42) he produced landscapes, still lifes and figure groups of considerable importance. He was influenced to a certain extent by Gauguin, Cézanne and the Cubists, but his work nevertheless shows great originality and ensured him recognition as an important Italian painter of this century. A retrospective show of his pictures was mounted at the Venice Biennale in 1948.

N. Barbantini. *Gino Rossi*, Venice 1942.

Rosso, Medardo. Italian sculptor, b. 1858 in Turin; d. 1928 in Milan. Rosso entered the Accademia Brera in Milan to train as a sculptor in 1881, but was sent down in 1883 for going against the academic curriculum. From the sculptures which he produced in 1881–2 it is easy to see why he fell out with the academicians: Rosso evidently had little liking for marble monuments; he wanted to portray the daily life around him in spontaneous, Impressionistic statuettes and busts. His *Impressione d'Omnibus*, which he made in 1883 but which has since been destroyed, was typical of the style and content of his works at that time. It was virtually a sculptural 'snapshot', which had its parallels both in Impressionist paintings and in the sphere of photography. In 1884 Rosso paid his first visit to Paris, where he worked under Dalou, whose delicate modelling of genre *motifs* appealed to him. At that time Rosso was producing sculptures in wax—a material which he liked because of its malleability and which he frequently coloured—and in 1886 he was able to exhibit a number of these works in the Salon de Paris. He then left Paris for Milan, where he lived for three years before returning to the French capital in 1889, when he took part in the International Exhibition. Although his economic situation at that time was bad he enjoyed a considerable reputation in artistic circles, which was greatly increased when his *Conversation in a Garden* of 1893 and his *Boulevard Impression, Paris at Night* of 1895 became known. What excited the art public about these sculptures was the conscious lack of detail and the hint of flowing movement which, coupled with the effects of light and atmosphere, created an impression of 'pictorial sculpture'. By then Rosso was on friendly terms with both Degas and Rodin. But—although Rodin is said to have owed the inspiration for his Balzac monument to him—their friendship came to an abrupt end when they quarrelled over which of them was the originator of Impressionist sculpture. Rosso was also acclaimed in Vienna and in London (where he was greatly admired by the Pre-Raphaelites) but remained relatively unknown in Italy until the Futurists acknowledged their debt to him for his opposition to academic sculpture and his appreciation of the importance of movement. Rosso has also exerted an influence on later sculptors.

Ardengo Soffici. *Medardo Rosso*, Florence 1929.
Giovanni Papini. *Medardo Rosso*, Milan 1945.

Roszak, Theodore. American painter and sculptor, b. 1907 in Poznan, Poland. He arrived in the United States in 1909. While still in high school he attended classes at the Art Institute of Chicago and enrolled as a full-time student in 1924. The next year he moved to New York where he studied at the National Academy of Design under Charles Hawthorne as well as studying with George Luks. He returned to Chicago in 1927 and served as a part-time instructor at the Art Institute. Two years later he travelled to Europe on a fellowship and set up a studio in Prague. At this time he came under the influence of the Surrealists, especially G. de Chirico. Though as late as 1935 he was still producing many paintings and lithographs (first one-man show in New York in this year) Roszak first turned to sculpture in 1931, a medium which was his increasing concern from this time on. He taught at the Design Laboratory in New York (1938–40) under the guidance of Laszlo Moholy-Nagy. This school was a WPA project intending to transplant Bauhaus techniques and principles into the United States. At this time he saturated himself in Constructivist ideas and until 1945 his work shows a concentration on this type of geometric abstraction. His first one-man show of metal sculpture was held at the Pierre Matisse Gallery in 1951. His spire and bell tower for Eero Saarinen's chapel at the Massachusetts Institute of Technology, Cambridge, Mass. (1953, aluminium), reveals a combination of earlier Constructivist principles as well as a greater interest in texture, movement and the relationships of a work of art to its environment. *Whaler of Nantucket* (1952–3, steel, Chicago, Art Institute), a far smaller, non-commissioned work, displays his departure from Constructivism and the personal attempt of the artist to ally his work with society, literature, personal experience and introspection.

H. H. Arnason. Catalogue, *Theodore Roszak*, Walker Art Center, Minneapolis (Minn.) 1956.

Rot, Diter. German painter, b. 1930 in Hanover. Rot uses the *décollage* technique in order to combat the coercive forces brought to bear on the modern consumer. His mould pictures, his overpaintings (with paint and chocolate) and his ironical and lyrical pictorial formulae are all designed to make the viewer aware of the determination underlying our consumer society whilst at the same time revealing the aesthetic appeal of consumer articles when considered simply as articles, i.e. without their consumer connotations. Rot has also engaged in Dadaistic actions in conjunction with Wolf Vostell and Stefan

Wewerka. In 1968 he was represented at the Documenta IV exhibition in Kassel. He lives in Hanover and Reykjavik.

Rotella, Mimmo. Italian affichiste, b. 1918 in Catanzaro, Calabria. Rotella studied at the Academy of Art in Naples and, subsequently, at the University of Kansas (on a Fulbright scholarship). In 1954 he exhibited his *Manifesti lacerati* (torn posters). Commenting on these, he once said: 'The search which I am conducting is not concerned with aesthetics but with an unforeseen element and even with the moods of the material.' In 1960 Rotella joined the *Nouveaux Réalistes*. Like the three Frenchmen—de la Villeglé, Dufrêne and Hains—he is one of the leading affichistes of the day. He lives partly in Rome, partly in Paris.

Rothenstein, Sir William. British painter, lithographer and draughtsman, b. 1872 in Bradford; d. 1945. He studied at the Slade School under Legros, 1888–9, and in Paris at the Académie Julian from 1889 to 1893. His first exhibition, with Charles Conder, was at the Galerie Thomas in Paris in 1891. He became a member of the New English Art Club in 1894. He travelled to Spain, Morocco, India and the United States, and his first American exhibition took place in Chicago in 1912, at the Art Institute. From 1920 to 1935 he was the Principal of the Royal College of Art, and received his knighthood in 1931. He was an official war artist in both world wars. A memorial exhibition of his work was put on at the Tate Gallery in 1950.

Rothko, Mark. American painter, b. 1903 in Dvinsk, Russia; d. 1970. This largely self-taught artist moved with his family to Portland, Oregon, at the age of ten. From 1921 to 1923 he attended Yale University and furthered his artistic education at the Art Students' League where he attended Max Weber's drawing classes. He first exhibited in 1929 at the Opportunity Gallery and was given his first one-man show in 1933 at the Contemporary Arts Gallery. In 1935 he was co-founder of The Ten, a group of artists with Expressionistic tendencies that held annual shows for almost a decade. In 1945 he had another one-man show at the Art of This Century Gallery, his paintings of this period expressing strong Surrealistic affinities with the biomorphic compositions of Gorky and Baziotes (*Baptismal Scene*, 1945, watercolour, New York, Whitney Museum of American Art). In 1947 his style became formulated into the characteristic rectangular shapes floating in space by which he is best known. The constant repetition of this theme is illustrated by his 1956 *The Black and the Red* (New York, Coll. Dr. and Mrs. Frank Stanton), where soft-edged rectangles of black and white are suspended before a red background. Throughout his life Rothko has pursued an active

teaching career, ranging from teaching children at the Center Academy in Brooklyn to positions at Brooklyn College and Tulane University.

Peter Selz. Catalogue, *Mark Rothko*, Museum of Modern Art, New York 1961.

Rouault, Georges. French painter, b. 1871 in Paris; d. 1958 in Paris. Rouault occupies a special position amongst twentieth-century French painters on various counts. In the first place he continued the French Romantic and Baroque tradition as represented by Géricault, Delacroix, Daumier and Moreau, carrying it far forward into the twentieth century and refusing to abandon the expressive and objective pictorial form of these earlier masters despite the ascendancy acquired by the Cubist, Constructivist and Surrealist movements during his lifetime. And then, of course, he was one of the great religious artists of our day, reviving biblical subjects and reinterpreting them within a modern context. Moreover, although Rouault's links with the Fauves were extremely tenuous in the historical sense, he was essentially the most powerful artist to paint in the Fauvist manner and he continued to do so long after Fauvism as such had disappeared from the scene. In one sense, therefore, his astonishing and highly individual works, with their great intensity and power of expression and their uncompromising integrity, form an integral part of the broad historical spectrum of French art. In another sense, however, they stand quite alone.

Rouault, the son of a craftsman, served an apprenticeship as a worker in stained glass and was subsequently employed by a master engaged in the restoration of stained-glass windows in French churches. During this time he also attended evening classes at the École des Arts Décoratifs. His great love of the strictly hierarchical style and the luminous colours of stained glass and his predilection for dark contours and religious themes were to exercise a crucial and lasting influence on his later paintings. It was not until 1890 that Rouault definitely decided to become a painter. In the following year he joined the École des Beaux Arts and studied under Gustave Moreau, who then became a close friend. In Moreau's *atelier* he met Matisse in 1893 and—subsequently—Marquet, Manguin and Camoin, i.e. the later Fauves. Like Matisse, Rouault was very interested in the expressiveness of colour, although never at the expense of the subject. He insisted—far more than Matisse—on the fusion of colour and thematic expression. The turn of the century was a critical time for Rouault, due partly to Moreau's death, and partly to material and family difficulties. He often called at the abbey of Ligugé, near Poitiers, during this period and it was there that he met the poet Huysmans. Later, in 1904, he was greatly impressed by the new form of moral theology evolved by the Catholic writer Léon Bloy (1846–1917). In 1903–4 he also made a vital break-through in his work when he painted his series of whores, clowns, acrobats and pierrots. With these 'dark' gouaches, which were executed in sombre blues and blacks with short, sharp strokes of the brush, Rouault created a shattering symbol of the profane, which stood in complete contrast to the religious themes of his early period.

In 1905, when the Fauves showed their explosive works in the Salon d'Automne, Rouault exhibited in the same salon but not in the same room. Three years later, in 1908, he discovered a new and fascinating pictorial world when he began to paint his studies of judges and law courts. He also met the art dealer Vollard at that time, and this was to have far-reaching repercussions. Although initially Vollard was interested only in the painted pottery which Rouault had produced in 1906–7, in 1913 he bought every picture in his studio and in 1917 fitted out a room in his own house for him to work in. It was during this period of collaboration with Vollard that Rouault began to produce his extensive range of graphic and illustrative works. The most striking examples in this genre are *The Miserere* (51st Psalm), *The Passion* and *Les Fleurs du Mal*.

In 1918 Rouault gave up watercolours and gouaches in order to concentrate on oil paintings. Apart from portraits and landscapes most of the works produced during this late period were on religious themes. But Rouault also ventured into two completely new spheres when he created the décor and costumes for Diaghilev's production of Proko-fiev's ballet *Le Fils prodigue* (1929) and when he drew the cartoons for five stained-glass windows for the Church of Assy in the Haute Savoie. After the Second World War Rouault received many public honours.

Lionello Venturi. *Georges Rouault*, Lausanne 1959.
Pierre Courthion. *Georges Rouault*, New York 1962.

Rousseau, Henri (Le Douanier). French painter, b. 1844 in Laval; d. 1910 in Paris. In the history of European art the work of Henri Rousseau is unique. It is so personal that it eludes classification of style. In retrospect he seems to have arrived as a visitor from one of his own dream worlds, into a circle of artists whose thinking was bent on destroy-ing the myth which supported him, but whom he forced in one way or another to accept him.

He was born into the class of provincial bourge-oisie, a mode of life that he does not seem to have rejected, for he remained at home in it in spite of the intellectual contacts of his later years. He saw some service in the army, stationed at Caen as a clarinet-tist in the regimental band. His claim to have served in Mexico is unsupported by evidence. In 1869, after leaving the army, he went to Paris, where he married his first wife. Eventually he obtained employment in the customs-house at the city gate. This gave rise to his nickname 'Le Douanier', though this in fact elevates his office. He was simply the gatekeeper who inspected the in-going waggons for dutiable goods.

In 1885 he retired from this employment even though it was very undemanding, choosing instead to support himself in various odd employments, such as teaching and the painting of inn-signs and portraits. It is from this time that his painting career is deemed to begin, and when his desire to become a famous artist materialized. Typical of his origin, this, in his mind, meant rivalling the famous Salon idols of the day, such as the now forgotten Bouguereau and Gérôme.

From about 1886 he began to exhibit in the Salon des Indépendants. Suffering the derision of all such primitive painting, his work did none the less attract the serious attention of some artists, for example Redon and Toulouse-Lautrec, and the critic Gustave Coquiot. Alfred Jarry was also interested in him. He became more and more accepted by the *avant-garde*, helped by his initiative in holding *soirées* to which they were invited, and came. Apollinaire supported him, and Picasso's group adopted him as a serious artist, even if also as an amusing clown. His work was given an exhibition in America in 1910.

His personality and life-story are full of contradic-tions. His recorded utterances are naïve, but they contain a ring of clear truth. He has been labelled amateur and 'Sunday painter', but as an artist he lived to paint, meanwhile supporting himself in any way possible, like countless professionals. He appears simple and gullible, but no one could be completely so and survive as he did in the circle of ambitious artists in which he moved. Undeniable, however, is his utter confidence in himself. Possessing an un-shakeable belief in the inevitable and justified glory of great artists, in the face of everything he had no doubt that he was one himself.

His known works all date from after 1880. His first subjects are the scenes and people of local life, child-like in their perception and their descriptive statement of detail. Though believing himself con-cerned with the description of nature in art, it was his strong imagination aided by his unbounded self-confidence which gives the true reality of his inven-tion. In his famous *Exotic Landscapes* and *Jungle Scenes*, painted during 1900–7, he has given full rein to this imagination, for they derive from picture-books and notes made at the Jardin des Plantes. The strength, scale and conviction of these pictures are remarkable. His figures and animals anticipate Pop Art, and their strength of image in such genre cannot be surpassed. One of his last works, *Le Rêve*, painted in 1910, does more. It is a memory figure of his first love reclining on a sofa in one of his dream jungles. Here is the dream made most convincingly real, a generation before the Surrealists developed the same idea.

He was told that his work 'is not of this century', and he agreed. Such imagination is not in any case the prerogative of a particular historical period. His success and popularity have stimulated appreciation of children's art, and encouraged many amateurs. Proper valuation puts him, as he did himself, among the great artists of all time.

J. Bouret. *Henri Rousseau*, Greenwich (Conn.) 1961.
D. Vallier. *Henri Rousseau*, New York 1964.

Roussel, Ker-Xavier. French painter, b. 1867 in Lorry-lès-Metz; d. 1944 in L'Étang-la-Ville. He trained at the Académie Julian in Paris in 1888 and then became a member of the *Nabis*. He was friendly with Édouard Vuillard, who later became his brother-in-law. He was influenced by Gauguin and later by the Impressionists. He painted landscapes, very often with a mythological subject. His early work was flat and rather subdued in tone; learning from the Impressionists he lightened his colours but kept the decorative elements of the *Nabis* group.

L. Werth. *Ker-Xavier Roussel*, Paris 1930.

Roy, Pierre. French painter, b. 1880 in Nantes; d. 1950 in Milan. After serving an apprenticeship in an architect's office Roy studied painting at various schools of art in Paris. In 1908 he made contact with Savinio and de Chirico and was greatly influenced by the latter. From 1925 to 1931 he associated with the Surrealists and took part in their exhibitions. Roy made several visits to the United States and also visited Hawaii in 1939.

Within the Surrealist movement Roy represented a specifically French form of the *Neue Sachlichkeit*. After starting as a Neo-Impressionist he began moving towards Surrealism from 1920 onwards, due primarily to the influence of de Chirico. In his pictures Roy employed three specific techniques. In the first place, he painted with a degree of precision and an eye for detail which is reminiscent of the old Dutch masters and which gave his works a sort of still-life quality; secondly, he alienated the objects represented in his pictures (stones, mussels, technical instruments, wine glasses, ribbons, etc.) by placing them in unusual combinations and making them stand out in relief against a perspective background (usually a landscape); thirdly, he created veristic *trompe l'oeil* effects. The interaction of these three techniques produced an illusory pictorial world which is very similar to that of de Chirico and Magritte.

Catalogue, *Pierre Roy*, Kestner Gesellschaft, Hanover 1967.

Rude, Olaf. Danish painter, b. 1886; d. 1957. Rude visited Paris in 1911 and was greatly impressed by Gauguin, van Gogh, Matisse and Picasso. In 1918 he turned to Cubism and from then onwards produced landscapes, interiors, still lifes and portraits in this style. Rude is the most important representative of the Bornholm school. In 1953 he was given a professorial post at the Academy of Art in Copenhagen.

Rusiñol, Santiago. Spanish painter and writer, b. 1861 in Barcelona; d. 1931 in Aranjuez. He spent some time in Paris, but for most of his life was a leading member of the Catalan group, painting landscapes and figure compositions. He also wrote poetry, plays and novels.

Russell, Morgan. American painter, b. 1886 in New York City; d. 1953 in Ardmore, Pennsylvania. He first studied with Robert Henri and, after going to Paris in 1906, with Henri Matisse. His most important artistic moment came around 1912 when he and Stanton Macdonald-Wright formulated the concept of Synchromism. His first Synchromist canvases were exhibited at the Salon des Indépendants in 1913. In the same year he was represented in the Armory Show by some pictures sent from Paris. Though the forms he used in these canvases were more precise ones than those used by Macdonald-Wright, the geometric forms were secondary to the colour theory they represented (*Four-Part Synchromy, No. 7*, 1914–15, New York, Whitney Museum of American Art). From 1919 on, Russell mainly confined himself to representational painting. After the death of his first wife he lived in relative seclusion at Aigremont in Burgundy and his growing religiosity was reflected in a number of large biblical works (*Resurrection*, 1942–50, New York, Rose Fried Gallery). He returned to live permanently in the United States in 1946.

Russolo, Luigi. Italian painter, b. 1885 in Pontogruaro, Venice; d. 1947 in Cerro di Laveno. Russolo started out in life as a musician and it was not until 1910, when he had completed his musical studies and settled in Milan, that he began to paint. In Milan he became an active member of the literary *avant-garde* centred on Marinetti and contributed articles to the magazine *Poesia*. He also met Boccioni and Carrà and signed the *Manifesto of Futuristic Painting* and the *Technical Manifesto of Futuristic Painting*, which were both published in 1910. He then exhibited with the Futurists in their collective exhibitions. But between 1910 and 1913 Russolo reverted to music. He was the inventor of 'bruitism' or 'Noise Music' and in 1913 he issued the manifesto of 'Noise Music'. In 1913 and 1914 he gave concerts both in Italy and abroad, using special instruments which he made himself. When war broke out Russolo joined the forces, serving until he was wounded in 1917. From 1918 to 1930 he lived in Paris, where he became interested in yoga and the occult. He then returned to Italy, settling in Cerro on Lake Maggiore, where he began to paint again. The works of this late period are extremely poetic and contain numerous Surrealist traits. But Russolo's major work dates from his early years. He was one of the most active and most polemical members of the Futurist movement.

M. Z. Russolo. *Russolo, l'uomo, l'artista*, Milan 1958. *Archivi del Futurismo*, Rome 1958.

Rysselberghe, Théo van. Belgian painter, b. 1862 in Ghent; d. 1926 in St-Clair, France. He was a founder (1883) of *Les Vingt*, the group formed in Brussels to encourage the creation and acceptance of contemporary art, largely by contact with the current developments in France. Thereafter Rysselberghe travelled a great deal and met Seurat in Paris; he adopted the theory of Divisionism and used it in his landscapes and portraits. He also worked in the field of the decorative arts, designing posters, jewellery, etc. He moved to Paris in 1898 and became friendly with the Symbolist writers and their circle. Some time later he moved to Provence and relaxed his theoretical approach to his painting, which now became brighter and more free-flowing.

G. Pogu. *Théo van Rysselberghe*, Paris 1963.

S

Sachinis, Nicos. Greek painter, b. 1924 in Thessaloniki. He studied law in Thessaloniki but is self-taught in painting. He has done a considerable amount of stage designing. A Post-Cubist painter with strong sensual feelings, he uses pieces of junk with notable success, as well as the technique of children's drawings.

Saedeleer, Valerius de. Belgian painter, b. 1867; d. 1941. De Saedeleer, Minne and van de Woestijne were the first artists to live in Laethem-St-Martin, which later became a flourishing artistic colony. They aimed at a primitive art through communion with nature; their work, with its warmth and simplicity, was completely opposed to the Expressionism of other Belgian artists, notably Ensor, then current.

Sage, Kay. American painter, b. 1898 in Albany, New York; d. 1963 in Woodbury, Connecticut. Aside from the war years, she lived in Italy until 1937 when she moved to Paris for two years. She had her first one-man show while still in Italy, at the Galleria del Milione, Milan (1936). In France, her works showed a strong affinity to those of Italy's leading modern artist, G. de Chirico. This is manifest in the geometric forms and emphatic cast shadows placed in an expansive space, as seen in *Sempre* (1938, estate of artist). While living in Paris she participated in several exhibitions, including the Salon des Surindépendants (1938). When she went back to the United States in 1940 her surreal works showed greater interest in architectural forms. The scenes are inhabited by non-figurative elements—pieces of waving drapery—which act figuratively (*Mother of Time*, 1948, New York, Coll. Catherine Viviano). Architecture and draperies continued to figure significantly throughout her career, though in the later paintings they are brought closer to the picture plane and are placed in exaggerated perspective (*Day Without Name*, 1955, New York, Coll. Mr. and Mrs. Lee A. Ault). The presentation to the spectator is thus an even more psychologically disturbing view of her world than her previous works had revealed.

Catalogue, *Kay Sage Retrospective Exhibition, 1937–1958*, Catherine Viviano Gallery, New York 1960.

St. Ives painters. The term 'St. Ives School' was formerly applied to a group of Victorian naturalist painters. The modern St. Ives school originated with the presence there during the war of Ben Nicholson and Barbara Hepworth. Peter Lanyon, a native of St. Ives, lived there until his death. Among others more or less continuously associated with the place are W. Barnes-Graham (b. 1912), Terry Frost, Patrick Heron, Alexander MacKenzie (b. 1923), John Wells and Bryan Wynter. Whatever the influences upon and within this group of highly individual artists, a St. Ives style can be detected and has been a formative influence on the development of British art in the fifties and early sixties. If there is a common factor it is in the adoption of gestural painting to create a near-abstract synthesis of landscape impressions.

Saint Phalle, Niki de. French sculptress, b. 1930 in Neuilly. Saint Phalle made her name in the early 1960s with assemblages incorporating small bags of paint which the artist burst by shooting at them with a pistol so that the paint splattered the sculptures. The assemblages were soon followed by *Nanas* (grotesque female figures painted in glaring colours) and the *Hon* (a gigantic sculpture on which she collaborated with P. O. Ultvedt and J. Tinguely and which was erected in the Moderna Museet in Stockholm). These works created a considerable stir, especially the *Hon*, which was so big that the viewers were able to walk on it. Saint Phalle is now living in Paris.

Saint-Saëns, Marc. French painter and tapestry designer, b. 1903 in Toulouse. He studied in Toulouse and Paris, then became concerned with the challenge of painting murals, of which he did several for various public buildings. After making the acquaintance of Jean Lurçat he began to design tapestries. His designs were successful in bringing this ancient art to the attention of the public. The subjects were generally mythological.

Saito, Yoshishige. Japanese painter, b. 1904 in Tokyo. Saito was self-taught in painting and later in literature. He began his adult life as a painter, left it abruptly to make serious efforts at writing under the influence of Surrealism, and only returned to painting once again in 1933. During 1939 and 1940 he participated in the *Bijussu-Bunka*, one of the groups which tended to deal with the anti-war feeling in terms of Surrealism. After the war, during the period in which the art world was regrouping and re-forming, Saito remained completely remote from the scene. After years of secret dedication to his highly personal art, he was brought suddenly to the public view in 1958 with a series of *Oni* (Ogre) paintings which received immediate acclaim. These represented an original combination of Surrealistic feeling with abstract composition. Since then, the figures have gradually disappeared and a Lyrical Abstraction predominates. His technique at that time was to make scars and lines on a monochromatic ground applied to plywood. To achieve this and in a deliberate effort to negate his skilful hands he chose the electric drill for the execution of these controlled yet random abstractions. It was with these works that he achieved international recognition (i.e. the International Prize at the Guggenheim). As a professor of art at Tama University he has lent his support to many young artists and has been of tremendous influence.

Sallinen, Tyko. Finnish painter, b. 1879 in Nurmes; d. 1955 in Helsinki. Sallinen was the foremost Finnish representative of Expressionism. After studying in Paris from 1909 to 1912 he returned to Finland, where his radical Expressionistic paintings caused a considerable stir. Essentially, Sallinen drew his inspiration from the people and countryside of his native land. But the coarseness and emotional power which were a feature of his early work were subsequently brought under control by a new sense of discipline acquired from his study of Cézanne. His late landscapes, portraits and figure compositions are remarkable for their subdued colouring which, on occasions, acquires a strange luminous quality. Sallinen became a founder member of the Finnish *Novembergruppe* in 1916.

Samaras, Lucas. American painter and sculptor, b. 1936 in Kastoria, Macedonia, Greece. In 1955 he became a United States citizen and the same year entered Rutgers University on a State Scholarship, studying under Allan Kaprow. At Rutgers he had his first one-man show, also in 1955. He then studied Art History at Columbia University on a Woodrow Wilson Fellowship under Meyer Schapiro (1959–62). In the late 1950s and early 1960s he was making sculptural figures of rags dipped in plaster which were then moulded into shape. At this time he also executed a large number of pastels ranging in subject

from Pop Art ice-cream sodas to Surrealistic fantasies. In the early 1960s he already showed his interest in a tremendous variety of materials. *Book No. 4* of 1962 (mixed media, New Canaan, Conn., Coll. Philip Johnson) makes use of pins and ready-mades —a book covered by hundreds of pins, with a knife, razor blade and scissors protruding from its pages. The combination of pins and yarn can be seen in his 1965 *Untitled* work (Minneapolis, Walker Art Center) in which two chairs, both slanting in the same direction, face each other—one haphazardly covered with pins, the other with carefully laid pieces of yarn either parallel to each other or forming concentric rectangles. His highly inventive use of materials—pins, yarn, nails, pencils, kitchen utensils, liquid aluminium, stuffed birds, photographs, nuts, bolts, string, sand, plastic, mirrors, etc.—makes his work fall into the realm of many exhibitions held in the first half of the 1960s including *New Forms, New Media II* (1960, New York, Martha Jackson Gallery), *The Art of Assemblage* (1961, New York, Albright-Knox Gallery) and *Pop and Op* (1965, New York, Sidney Janis Gallery).

L. Alloway. *Samaras, Selected Works 1960–66,* Pace Gallery, New York 1966.

Sandels, Gösta. Swedish painter, draughtsman and graphic artist, b. 1887; d. 1919. Sandels attended the school of painting run by the Swedish artists' association in 1905–6 and in the following year became a founder member of the *De Unga* (The Young) group in Paris. But unlike the other members of this group, he did not study under Matisse. Instead he went his own way, which brought him to Spain, Copenhagen and Oslo. Sandels was impressed by the works of Cézanne, Delacroix, Edvard Munch and Hendrik Sørensen. But it was van Gogh whose influence proved really crucial. After seeing works by this artist he developed a highly personal style of painting based on a type of brushwork that closely resembled van Gogh's. When he joined the artists' colony in Kungälv Sandels painted a series of Romantic works, in which he portrayed his extremely vivid impressions of nature, using vital and intense colour combinations. Typical examples are his *Strandfynd* (Flotsam, 1914, Gothenburg Museum of Art) and *Skeppsbrott* (*Shipwreck*, 1914, National Museum, Stockholm). During this period Sandels also produced drawings and lithographs. In 1916, when he moved to Stockholm, he began to paint more placid pictures, whose clear colours and decorative brushwork are reminiscent of Matisse. But Sandels reached the peak of his development on his last visit to Spain in 1919. In that year he produced a body of work, including a series of watercolours, which is remarkable for the charm of its colouring and the ease and spontaneity of its brushwork. Sandels' mature period was very brief. But the quality of the work which he produced in that period was unsurpassed by any other Swedish artist of his day.

G. Serner. *Gösta Sandels*, Stockholm 1941.
C. Nordenfalk. *Konstnäru i Kungälv*, Gothenburg 1946.

Sandig, Armin. German painter and draughtsman, b. 1929 in Hof. Sandig paints lyrical abstracts in subtle gradations of colour. His drawings are finely structured diagrams whilst certain of his *motifs* bear a resemblance to vegetal forms. He is now living in Hamburg.

Santomaso, Giuseppe. Italian painter, b. 1907 in Venice. Santomaso studied at the Academy of Art in Venice. In 1937 he visited Amsterdam, where he discovered van Gogh, and then went on to Paris, where Braque made a powerful impression on him. He was also influenced by the Late Cubists and, as a result, developed a more constructive type of composition. At this point he made an intensive study of the Byzantine mosaics in San Marco. In 1946, together with Birolli, Vedova and others, he became a founder member of the *Nuova Secessione artistica italiana* (which later developed into the *Fronte Nuovo delle Arti*). From 1953 onwards Santomaso was influenced by Hartung and his 'psychic improvisation'. In 1954 he won the first prize for Italian Painting at the Biennale in Venice. He is now living in Venice and teaches at the Venice Academy.

Santomaso is a landscape artist who translates his experiences of nature into lyrical, hermetic, abstract compositions which are sometimes reminiscent of Estève and Afro. His Venetian origin is revealed by his bright and cheerful palette.

P. Francastel. *Cicale e Cattedrali*, Amriswil 1962.

Sargent, John Singer. Anglo-American painter and watercolourist, b. 1856 in Florence; d. 1925 in London. After a short spell as a student at the Accademia delle Belle Arti in Florence (1868–9), Sargent entered the studio of Carolus-Duran in Paris (1874). His precocious talent soon became evident. In 1876 he met Monet; and in 1878 his *Oyster Gatherers of Cancale* (Washington, Corcoran Gallery of Art) was favourably received at the Paris Salon. It was about this time that Sargent embarked on his career as a portrait painter; of his early portraits, the full-length of *Madame Pierre Gautreau* (New York, Metropolitan Museum) is probably the most famous. When it was exhibited at the Salon of 1884, it caused a scandal, and this episode was one of the reasons why, in 1885, Sargent moved to England, where in the course of the next fifteen years he became the most widely admired portraitist in the world.

The secret of his success, which has cast its shadow over conventional portraiture throughout the twentieth century, perhaps lay in his capacity to reconcile seemingly contradictory artistic impulses. On the one hand, Sargent was a great admirer of the old masters, notably Hals and Velasquez (of whose paintings he made brilliant informal copies), and this sense of tradition permeates nearly all his portraits. On the other hand, he knew the Impressionists and was alive to all the developments in *avant-garde* French painting, expressed in portraiture by a whole range of novel, informal poses and a contrived casualness of effect. With an exceedingly sharp eye for a likeness and a brilliant technique, Sargent was able to combine these tendencies, and produce a brand of portraiture that was both aesthetically reassuring and piquantly up to date. If the best of Sargent's society portraits—such as *Lady Sassoon* (1907, private collection)—carry complete conviction it is probably because his style ultimately represents not the calculated adjustments of a cynical face-painter, but the conflicting tendencies of an intelligent, exceptionally gifted but rather unimaginative artist who was perhaps too well aware of the conflicts inherent in painting in the last quarter of the nineteenth century.

Sargent came to hate portraiture, which he practised less and less after 1907. What absorbed him were scenes from ordinary life (which he had always painted) in watercolours and oil on a small scale, and a series of ambitious murals that he was preparing for the Museum of Fine Arts and the Public Library in Boston. Well researched and high-minded though they may be, these decorations are feeble and unconvincing; the paintings and drawings inspired by the First World War, culminating in the large canvas, *Gassed* (1918–19, London, Imperial War Museum), are only marginally better from the imaginative point of view.

In a series of unforgettable canvases and drawings, Sargent captured and pinned down the opulence and assurance, the arrogance and vulgarity of Edwardian society. It was inevitable that after his death—in 1925—his reputation would be severely devalued, along with everything else that people resented about an age and a governing class that had precipitated the war. But Sargent deserves a better fate: within his own limitations, he was always an interesting and often a brilliant painter.

Richard Ormond. *Sargent: Paintings, Drawings, Watercolours*, London and New York 1970.

Sassu, Aligi. Italian painter, b. 1912 in Milan. Sassu became a founder member of the *Corrente* association in 1939. He now lives in Milan.

After passing through Impressionistic and Futuristic phases Sassu joined the Milanese *avant-garde*. His uninhibited fantasy is reflected in the furious brushwork and powerful colours which are characteristic of his work.

Sato, Key. Japanese painter, b. 1906 in Oita. Sato first made his name as a figurative painter in Japan.

Later, in Paris, he produced Lyrical Abstract works, in which the textural quality of the pigment plays an important part. It is quite evident from his work that he has made a detailed study of minerals. He uses subdued, mostly earthy colours.

Saura, Antonio. Spanish painter, b. 1930 in Huesca. He went to Paris in 1953, and spent two years there, during which he became involved in the Surrealist movement. Disillusioned with it, he moved to Madrid and in 1957 became a founder member of *El Paso*, a group that included Millares, Canogar and Feitó, and which was highly critical of the dictatorship. His work now became intensely Expressionistic, and he painted only figures—imaginary portraits, nudes, crucifixions and crowd scenes, done as abstractions and executed in a harsh, brutal style, intended as protests against the regime that dominated his country.

Marc Berkowitz. 'Five Spanish Painters', *The Studio* CLXX, London, August 1965.

Savinio, Alberto. Italian painter, composer and author, b. 1891 in Athens; d. 1952 in Rome. Savinio was the brother of the painter Giorgio de Chirico. He studied music at the Athens Conservatory and, later, in Munich, where he was a contemporary of Max Reger. From 1911 to 1915, when he was in Paris, he devoted himself to literary activities, took part in the *Soirées de Paris* organized by Apollinaire and published *Les Chants de la Mi-Mort* (1914). In 1915 he returned to Italy to join the forces. In 1918 he published his first book, *Hermaphrodite*. From 1926 to 1934 he was again living in Paris. Between 1924 and 1952 he composed a great deal of music, including several operas and ballet suites. Meanwhile, in 1927, he had begun to paint. With his great artistic versatility Savinio soon showed himself to be one of the most stimulating artists in the French and Italian Surrealist movements. Most of his pictures were painted in the Surrealist mode and many of them incorporate Classical *motifs* taken from his brother's work. The pathos of his pictorial themes is offset by bold, firm, painterly brushwork and, in many instances, by Manneristic colouring. Savinio also designed stage sets and theatrical costumes.

Catalogue, *Alberto Savinio*, Gissi Galleria d'Arte, Turin 1967.

Scanavino, Emilio. Italian painter, b. 1922 in Genoa. After studying at the Liceo Artistico in Genoa Scanavino was in contact with the Milanese *Spazialismo* from 1947 onwards. He visited Paris in 1947, and London in 1951. In the early 1950s he produced pottery in Albissola, and also worked briefly as a sculptor. Subsequently, he exhibited with the *Phases* group. In 1958 Scanavino settled in Milan, where he is still living today. In 1960 he had a special exhibition at the Biennale in Venice.

Scanavino works in an Informal style that is often reminiscent of Mathieu. But for all his spontaneity, he is a highly conscious artist. Thus, the dynamic bands of colour, which are the principal feature of his paintings, are clearly distinguished from one another by linear *motifs*. Scanavino tends to use subdued colours such as brown, blue and black.

Schamberg, Morton Livingstone. American painter, b. 1881 in Philadelphia; d. 1918. He studied in Philadelphia, then went to Paris in 1906. Back in Philadelphia he became friendly with Charles Sheeler, and returned to Paris with him a few years later. He derived ideas from Cubism and Matisse, and later got to know the Dada circle, Duchamp and Picabia. He was interested in American folk history, and collected artefacts in Pennsylvania for some years. This interest extended to machines, which were excellent subjects for his modified Cubist style and which he depicted a great deal. Unlike his Dada acquaintances he did not see any black humour in the advent of the machine age, but rather looked upon it as a hopeful development for humanity, and expressed his optimistic attitude in his representations of machines.

Scharff, Edwin. German sculptor, b. 1887 in Neu-Ulm; d. 1955 in Hamburg. He studied painting in Munich, and turned to sculpture during a two-year stay in Paris from 1911. In 1913 he returned to Munich and became a founding member of the New Secession. He taught at the Berlin Academy (1923–33), the Düsseldorf Academy (1933–47) and the State School of Art, Hamburg (from 1946). Scharff's early sculptures were rhythmically structured, block-like figures in the Cubist mode. After 1920 he developed a distinctly representative, monumental style, derived primarily from Aristide Maillol. In these later works the surfaces of his figures, often mythological and accompanied by horses, were highly polished, with their constituent planes modulated by the interplay of light and shade.

Gottfried Sello. *Edwin Scharff*, Hamburg 1956.

Scharff, William. Danish painter, b. 1886; d. 1959. Scharff was influenced in c. 1910 by the Cubists and Kandinsky and in 1920 by Uccello's feeling for abstraction. Using constructive, refracted forms and luminous colours Scharff painted romantically toned pictures of the animals, woods and legends of his native Denmark. A characteristic feature of Scharff's painting is his diagonal brushwork.

Scharl, Josef. German-American painter, b. 1896 in Munich; d. 1954 in New York. After serving an apprenticeship as a decorative painter Scharl attended the Munich Academy from 1919 to 1921 and became a member of the Munich Secession. In 1938 he emigrated to the United States.

In the 1920s and 1930s Scharl was a well-known Post-Expressionist artist. He painted simple figures and objects in familiar and completely unsentimental settings, creating powerful and decorative colour compositions, which bear a marked affinity to the work of van Gogh. Later, when he came under the influence of Picasso, his pictorial forms became virtually abstract. In America Scharl was almost unknown as a painter, although the illustrations which he produced for Grimm's *Fairy Tales* were extremely successful.

A. Neumeyer (ed.). *Joseph Scharl*, New York 1945.
Joseph Scharl, Galerie Nierendorf, Berlin 1967.

Scheibe, Richard. German sculptor, b. 1879 in Chemnitz; d. 1964 in Berlin. After studying painting in Munich under Knirr Scheibe spent two years in Rome, where he became friendly with Kolbe, who was still working as a painter at that time. It was not until 1907, when he was living in Berlin, that Scheibe turned to sculpture, largely as a result of the influence of Maillol. During his early period, in which he made contact with Marcks and Gropius, he produced small bronzes, mostly of animals. From 1925 to 1933 he held a professorial post at the Städelschule in Frankfurt am Main. In 1936 he joined the staff of the Berlin Academy.

Scheibe was a contemporary of Lehmbruck, Haller and Hoetger. Like them, he was influenced by Maillol and tried to create a harmonious and Classical but none the less animated image of man. Unfortunately, his close personal ties with Kolbe also affected his work. Like Kolbe, Scheibe succumbed to the heroizing trend of National Socialist art, producing academic sculptures that were essentially meaningless. The many public monuments which he created are particularly inane.

E. Redslob. *Richard Scheibe*, Berlin 1955.

Schiele, Egon. Austrian painter, b. 1890 in Tulln a. d. Donau; d. 1918 in Vienna. In 1901 he attended high school at Krems, and later at Klosterneuberg. In 1905, on the death of his father, his uncle became Schiele's guardian. From 1906 he studied under Griepenkerl at the Vienna Academy of Art. His first works were Impressionistic in style (e.g. *Orchard in Spring*, 1907, New York, Private coll.). At this point he joined the Wiener Werkstätte; the influence of Klimt, which is reflected in his works of this period, incurred his teacher's displeasure, and Schiele therefore left the Academy in 1909. He showed four large paintings at the *Kunstschau* exhibition, where van Gogh's work was also shown; in the same year he joined the *Neukunstgruppe*, which held exhibitions at the Pisko Gallery in Vienna, and also in Prague and Budapest. His work was consistently attacked during these years. The year 1910 saw the beginnings of his mature style, which was Expressionist in its distor-

tion and emaciation of the human form (*Seated Male Nude*, 1910, Vienna, Coll. Dr. R. Leopold) and his depiction of the inner man, although Schiele was never personally to identify himself with the Expressionist movement.

In 1911, Schiele moved to his mother's former home, Krumau on the Moldau, which he depicted in *Picture of a City (Krumau)*, 1911. The erotic element in his work led to his arrest for 'making immoral drawings', and his detention for a period of twenty-seven days. In 1912 he moved into a studio in Vienna, Hietzinger Hauptstrasse 101. In June 1913 he married Edith Harms; he was called up four days after his marriage. He spent part of the war working as a war artist; in 1917 he was commissioned to make drawings of military establishments in the Tyrol. In 1918 he took part in the forty-ninth exhibition of the Vienna Secession in which he showed nineteen of his most recent paintings, many watercolours and drawings; he also designed an exhibition poster, *The Friends (Round Table)*. This exhibition, held so shortly before Schiele's tragically early death from Spanish influenza, was, ironically, the first to bring him international acclaim.

Otto Benesch. *Egon Schiele as Draughtsman*, Vienna 1951.
O. Kallir. *Egon Schiele*, New York 1966.

Schifano, Mario. Italian painter and film-maker, b. 1934 in Homs, Libya. In the pictures which he produced in 1961–2 Schifano introduced enlarged reproductions of fragments of advertisements. This subsequently led to a form of art in which he has commented on aspects of our commercialized world. From 1964 onwards, especially in his *Hommages* to the Futurists, he has used historical documents, e.g. photographs. Schifano has also made a number of short experimental films. He is now living in Rome.

M. Fagiolo. *Rapporto 60*, Rome 1966.

Schippers, Willem Theodoor. Dutch graphic designer, b. 1942 in Groningen. Schippers trained at the Institute for Arts and Crafts in Amsterdam. He has been active in many different spheres but is best known for his *Groten Stoel (Big Chair)*, which was installed in the Vondelpark in Amsterdam in 1966, for his TV programme *Hoepla* and for his 'sad movies' (which he produced in collaboration with the filmmaker Wim van der Linden). Schippers is now living in Amsterdam.

Schjerfbeck, Helene. Finnish painter, b. 1862 in Helsinki; d. 1946 in Saltsjöbaden, Sweden. Schjerfbeck studied, first in Helsinki, and then in Paris, where she worked under Bastien-Lepage and Puvis de Chavannes. She made her mark in the 1880s with *plein-air* paintings which are chiefly remarkable for the freshness of their colouring. In 1900 her health began to fail and from then onwards she lived in almost total isolation. During this late period Schjerfbeck developed a completely independent and extremely simplified style, producing still lifes, landscapes, figurative compositions and self-portraits. With their highly sophisticated colouring and their ethereal import, these works constitute Schjerfbeck's major achievement. They did not receive public recognition until late in the day, for the first exhibition of Schjerfbeck's mature oeuvre was delayed until 1937. She is now generally recognized as one of the leading Scandinavian painters and as a pioneer of modern art in Finland.

G. Johansson (ed.). *Helene Schjerfbeck*, 1945.

Schlemmer, Oskar. German painter and sculptor, b. 1888 in Stuttgart; d. 1943 in Baden-Baden. After starting out in life as a commercial artist in 1909 Schlemmer attended the Stuttgart Academy, where he studied under Landenberger and Hölzel. In 1914 he volunteered and fought at the front until 1916. In 1920 he was offered a teaching post by Gropius. He accepted and remained with the Bauhaus until 1929. He then taught at the Breslau Academy until 1932, when he joined the staff of the Vereinigte Staatsschulen in Berlin-Charlottenburg. In 1933 he was dismissed by the National Socialists and sought refuge in Eichberg near the Swiss frontier. In 1937 he moved to Sehringen near Badenweiler and in the same year pictures of his were shown in the National Socialist exhibition of 'Degenerate Art'. During the late 1930s he supported himself by producing decorative paintings for a studio in Stuttgart and from 1941 onwards by his work for the Institut für Malstoffkunde (Institute for Research into Paint) run by the paint manufacturer Kurt Herberts in Wuppertal. In 1942 Schlemmer contracted a serious illness, to which he succumbed in the following year.

After starting as an Impressionist Schlemmer passed through a Cubist phase which ended in c. 1915. He then evolved his own personal style, in which he abstracted natural forms by reducing them to static and fundamentally geometrical concentrates but without eliminating their organic appearance. This new style, which was dominated by straight lines and curvatures, emerged at the same time as Schlemmer's new theme, 'man in space', which was to occupy him for the rest of his life. In his endless search for a pure artistic form Schlemmer was very sparing in his use of pictorial *motifs* and, in exercising such strict self-control, he will doubtless have been inspired by the late works of Cézanne and Marées. Schlemmer's Bauhaus period was undoubtedly his most productive. Whilst working with Gropius he extended his ideas from the sphere of painting to that of the theatre: he composed ballets, designed costumes and stage sets and tried to evolve a new synthesis which would embrace all the arts. But, although he was passing through what might almost be called his 'Baroque' period, he still observed the strict

formal canon which he had set up for himself. The human form remained the criterion for everything: in it organic and geometrical structures were fused into a balanced whole, into a pure artistic form. Action, in the traditional sense of the word, had no part in Schlemmer's pictures. The reduction of the human figure to a two-dimensional shape and the concentration of human existence within a flat imaginary space precluded the possibility of powerful movement and dramatic composition. Schlemmer's figures are always portrayed in full view—from the front, the side or the rear—and he avoided foreshortening because this would have distorted his geometrical components. And yet his works are not at all Constructive. In fact, they have a timeless quality, which stems partly from their formal severity and partly from Schlemmer's predilection for the Classical mode. His paintings show only what is strictly necessary and so constitute a quintessence of formal experience. A painter who 'abstracts natural forms' is well on the way to becoming an abstract artist. On two occasions—once during his early phase in his *Bild K (Picture K)* and once towards the end of his life in his symmetrical compositions—Schlemmer actually produced concrete works of art. Basically, however, he was an abstracting but not an abstract artist. His sculptures reveal a similar approach. He created a number of reliefs, for which he freely adapted his pictorial ideas, but he was not attracted by free-standing sculptures. Although hard pressed to earn a living during the later years of his life Schlemmer did not lose heart and, from an artistic point of view, this proved a productive period. After settling in South-West Germany he began to paint landscapes but later destroyed most of these. The major works of this late period include the *Window Pictures*, a series of nocturnal townscapes featuring houses seen from the window of his Wuppertal studio, in which the visual impression and the tectonic structure are perfectly fused. These pictures were a new departure, one that might well have proved extremely fruitful had it not been cut short by Schlemmer's sudden and untimely death.

H. Hildebrandt. *Oskar Schlemmer*, Munich 1951.
Oskar Schlemmer. *The Theatre of the Bauhaus*, Middletown (Conn.) 1961.

Schlichter, Rudolf. German painter, b. 1890 in Calw, Württemberg; d. 1955 in Munich. Schlichter made his name as a member of the *Neue Sachlichkeit*. After completing his studies in Stuttgart and Karlsruhe he went to Berlin, where he joined both the Dada and *Neue Sachlichkeit* movements. The veristic pictures which he painted at that time, and which were conceived as acts of social criticism, reveal the influence of Grosz and Dix. In 1939 Schlichter went to live in Munich, where he founded the *Neue Gruppe* together with Edgar Ende and Geitlinger in 1947.

Rudolf Schlichter. *Das Abenteuer der Kunst*, Hamburg 1949.

Schlotter, Eberhard. German painter and graphic artist, b. 1921 in Hildesheim. Schlotter studied at the Munich Academy from 1939 to 1941. Since 1945 he has been living in Darmstadt. He paints technically sophisticated pictures in an eclectic style, which combines realism with fantasy.

Schmidt-Rottluff, Karl (Karl Schmidt). German painter, b. 1884 in Rottluff, near Chemnitz, Saxony. Schmidt-Rottluff was the son of a mill-owner. After taking his *Abitur* at a humanist *Gymnasium* he went to Dresden to study architecture. In 1905, whilst he was in Dresden, an artists' association was formed there which was destined to become the foremost Expressionist group in Germany. Schmidt-Rottluff was its youngest member and it was he who suggested its name: *Die Brücke.* Although in the early days of their association the members of the *Brücke* used a communal style there were none the less marked differences between them. Kirchner was a sensitive and extremely percipient artist, Heckel had a decidedly lyrical temperament whilst Schmidt-Rottluff was given to bold and powerful compositions. He created a monumental style by simplifying natural forms. Like the other German Expressionists he was influenced, first by the Post-Impressionists and the expressive form of Post-Impressionism evolved by van Gogh, and subsequently by the works of Toulouse-Lautrec, Vuillard and—above all— Munch. In 1906 he produced his first lithographs, which marked the beginning of a powerful body of graphic work. In the same year he worked with Nolde on the island of Alsen, where he used pure colours for the first time. Between 1907 and 1910 he and Heckel painted together in Dangast on the Jade Busen. In 1911 he created his famous series of Norwegian landscapes before settling in Berlin together with Heckel and Kirchner. Whilst there he discovered the block-like forms of Negro art, which are a feature of his subsequent work. In 1912 he produced bronze reliefs of the four apostles for the chapel at the *Sonderbund* exhibition in Cologne. In the same year he made friends with Feininger. In 1914, in the March issue of *Kunst und Künstler (Art and Artists),* Schmidt-Rottluff published the only public statement he has ever made on his art. In it he rejected all theoretical discussion as meaningless. After serving in the German forces in the First World War he made wood carvings and woodcuts up to 1918, most of them on religious themes. Up to 1922 his style remained unaltered: Expressionism based on block-like signs. But since then he has evinced a growing interest in natural phenomena. Under the National Socialists he was classified as a 'degenerate artist': 608 of his pictures were removed from public museums in Germany and in 1941 he was forbidden to paint. After the Second World War the old-style compositions with their lapidary signs were replaced by a new conception of art. Schmidt-Rottluff then began to paint monumental studies of nature. His colours retained their intensity but were no longer as violent; his forms became softer and more fluent.

Rosa Schapire. *Karl Schmidt-Rottluffs Graphisches Werk bis 1923,* Berlin 1924.
Will Grohmann. *Karl Schmidt-Rottluff,* Stuttgart 1956.
Schmidt-Rottluff, Aquarelle und Zeichnungen, Munich 1963.

Schnabel, Day N. Austrian-American sculptress and painter, b. 1905 in Vienna. She first studied painting at the Vienna Art School and then pursued both painting and architecture in Amsterdam under Berend Jordaens. In Paris she studied at the Académie Colarossi under Marcel Gimond and at the Académie Ranson with Malfray. While living in Paris she participated in several exhibitions, including the last Salon des Tuileries, before the Occupation in 1941. During the war she was in the United States, where she worked under Zadkine. Producing sculptures in bronze, wood, clay and cast stone, her works of the mid-1940s are solid and crude in form, often relatively flat with little detail, as in *Eternal Mother* (c. 1946, bronze, New York, Mortimer Brandt Gallery) which has the simplicity of a Cycladic figure and the hieratic quality of a cult image. At the same time she produced some highly faceted, rather *retardataire* Cubistic pieces. She returned to France in 1947 and, after a long period of solitude at Megève, turned towards abstraction. At first concerned with contrasts of horizontals and verticals, she later concerned herself with the spherical form. By the late 1950s her works took on a wholly abstract quality, as in the convoluted, complex play of rhythms and lights seen in *The Wall* (1959, welded bronze, coll. of artist).

Herta Wescher. 'Day Schnabel', *Cimaise* 2, December 1953.

Schneider, Gérard. French-Swiss painter, b. 1896 in Ste-Croix, Switzerland. He trained in Neuchâtel and in Paris, at the École des Arts Décoratifs (1916–18) and the École des Beaux-Arts (1918–20). His first one-man show took place in 1920 in Neuchâtel, and he settled in Paris in 1924. He had work exhibited in the Salon d'Automne in 1926 and the Salon des Surindépendants in 1936 and 1939. He inclined towards abstraction, and after experimentation with Cubism and Surrealism arrived at the full development of his art around 1944. His work then was a continually inventive examination of shape and colour; he would rough in a starting-point on the canvas and from there explore the endless possibilities inherent in it. He was unwilling to title his paintings, believing that it was unnecessary to hint at the nature of his theme: he considered abstraction to be pure painting expressive of the mental state, a state indefinable except through the painting itself. In 1967 there was an exhibition of his work at the Galerie Arnaud, Paris.

Marcel Brion. Catalogue, *Gérard Schneider,* Kootz Gallery, New York 1958.

Schöffer, Nicolas. Hungarian-French sculptor, b. 1912 in Kolocsa. He trained at the Budapest Art School, then at the École des Beaux-Arts in Paris, where he settled in 1937 and took French nationality. He began his career as a painter, but after the war he turned to sculpting in the Constructivist tradition of Gabo and Moholy-Nagy (a fellow countryman). The essence of this tradition was the notion expressed by Gabo in his *Realist Manifesto* of 1920 and Moholy-Nagy in his manifesto *The System of Dynamo-Construction Forces* of 1922, that art should cease to be static and become dynamic and that in sculpture the most important plastic value besides dynamism was space.

In 1948 Schöffer began to make 'spatiodynamic' constructions: slender, vertical, very open towers consisting of a basic skeleton to which was applied plates of Plexiglass or thin metal from which light was reflected or refracted. They were, as he said, open, airy and penetrable. In 1950 he introduced actual movement into his works, using electric motors and giving them elaborate programmes directed by an electronic brain. Schöffer has always felt that his spatiodynamic towers should be carried out on a very large scale and in 1955 he constructed a 50-metre tower at St. Cloud in Paris which broadcast its own music from six tape recorders programmed by an electronic brain.

G. Habasque and J. Ménétrier. *Nicolas Schöffer*, Neuchâtel 1963.

Scholz, Georg. German painter, b. 1890 in Wolfenbüttel; d. 1945 in Waldkirch. After studying under Corinth in Berlin Scholz joined the *Novembergruppe*. Subsequently he obtained a post at the Academy in Karlsruhe, which he retained until 1933.

Scholz was a representative of the *Neue Sachlichkeit* and his veristic paintings, in which he depicted man at the mercy of the machine age, were intended as acts of social criticism.

Scholz, Werner. German painter, b. 1898 in Berlin. Scholz was wounded in the First World War and lost an arm and an eye. In 1919 he studied art in Berlin, where he met Emil Nolde. In 1933 his work was classified as 'degenerate'. In the Second World War his Berlin studio was destroyed in an air raid. Scholz then moved to Alpbach in the Tyrol, where he is still living today.

Scholz is a Late Expressionist. During his formative years he was influenced by the *Brücke*, the *Blauer Reiter* and, more particularly, Nolde. As a result he evolved a sombre style of painting dominated by black and white colour contrasts. During this early period, which lasted up to 1945, Scholz's constant theme was suffering humanity. After the Second World War he widened his range and began to paint religious and mythological scenes, large-format pastels (such as his *Apocalypse*) and mountain landscapes, for which he used a brighter palette.

H. G. Gadamer. *Werner Scholz*, Recklinghausen 1968.

School of Paris—see École de Paris

Schoonhoven, Johannes Jacobus (Jan). Dutch painter and sculptor, b. 1914 in Hof van Delft. Schoonhoven has produced numerous paintings and drawings but is best known for his white reliefs and *papier mâché* objects, which are made up of congruent panels. Like Armando and Henk Peeters, he is a member of the *Nul/Zero Nederland* association. Schoonhoven was represented at the Bienal in São Paulo in 1967. He lives and works in Delft.

Schrag, Karl. German-American painter and graphic artist, b. 1912 in Karlsruhe. He graduated from the Humanistische Gymnasium, Karlsruhe, in 1931 and then studied briefly at the École des Beaux-Arts in Geneva before going to Paris in 1932. In the French capital he studied at the École Nationale Supérieure des Beaux-Arts, the Atelier Lucien Simon, the Académie Ranson under Roger Bissière, and the Académie de la Grande Chaumière. From 1936 to 1938 he was in Belgium and had his first one-man show in Brussels at the Galerie Arenberg before moving to the United States. In New York he studied print-making at the Art Students' League under Harry Sternberg. In 1945 he worked at Atelier 17 with Stanley William Hayter and became its director in 1950. His early works were rather academic and traditional, but by the time he had his first American one-man exhibition of prints at the Smithsonian Institution, which was followed by a one-man show of watercolours two years later (1947, Kraushaar Galleries, New York), his style became livelier; he produced turbulent works full of energy, movement and vitality (*Trees Against the Sky*, watercolour, 1946, Brooklyn, Museum of Art). By the 1950s his work combined an energetic, staccato stroke or draughtsmanship with a joyous, lyrical airiness and colouration (*Garden of the Alcazar*, 1959, etching; *Wild Iris*, 1956, watercolour, Hartford, Conn., Wadsworth Atheneum). Schrag has taught at Brooklyn College and, since 1954, at Cooper Union.

John Gordon. *Karl Schrag*, New York 1960.

Schreib, Werner. German painter and graphic artist, b. 1925 in Berlin. After studying engineering Schreib attended the Werkkunstschulen in Kiel and Wiesbaden. He then spent lengthy periods in Spain, North Africa, France, Italy and England (1950 to 1958). In 1959 he was a student at the Académie Ranson and Atelier 17 (under Hayter) in Paris.

The basic components of Schreib's work are forms and signs, e.g. verticals, horizontals, circles and crosses. The picture surfaces (which are composed of an artificial resinous compound) are structured by impressions of *objets trouvés* (*cachetage*), of destructive scenes (*grattage*, *découpage*), of explosions and pyrogravures, which are superimposed by stamping. In 1959 Schreib was awarded the *Grand Prix International de Gravure* at the First Biennale in Paris and in 1966 he won the *Prix ex Aequo* at the First Biennale in Cracow. In 1961 he and the Italian painter L. Lattanzi published a joint manifesto entitled *On the Semantic Picture*. In 1967 he published a second manifesto on his own account under the title *On Semi-Mechanical Production*. Schreib has been living in Frankfurt am Main since 1960.

Schrimpf, Georg. German painter, b. 1898 in Munich; d. 1938 in Berlin. Schrimpf began to paint in 1915, when he was working as a labourer. His first works, executed in a clumsy, Expressionist style, were shown at the *Sturm* Gallery. About 1920 he began to take up the Neo-Classical ideas of the *Valori Plastici*. From 1926 to 1933 he taught at the Technical School of Art in Munich, then transferred to the Academy in Berlin-Schöneberg. Schrimpf is one of the best-known members of the *Neue Sachlichkeit*. Together with Kanoldt and Mense he represented the slightly Romantic trend, which was influenced by Derain, Carrà, and the ideas of the *Valori Plastici*, and which tried to establish a simple, clear, plastic definition of the objective world. His simple compositions have something of the naïve force and magical quality of amateur painting.

M. Pfortner. *Georg Schrimpf*, Berlin 1940.

Schroeder-Sonnenstern, Friedrich. German painter, b. 1892 in Tilsit, Lithuania. In his time Schroeder-Sonnenstern has worked as a gardener, a bible preacher, an astrologer and a faith healer. He first began to paint during a brief period spent as a patient in a mental hospital, but it was not until 1949 that he was able to become a full-time artist. He is now living in Berlin.

It is scarcely possible to place Schroeder-Sonnenstern's work in any specific category. Although his heraldic fantasy figures with their daemonic eroticism and their air of Oriental enchantment contain elements of both primitive art and Surrealism, they are also indicative of hallucinatory schizophrenia. Schroeder-Sonnenstern's compositions have a certain affinity with the pictorial world of Victor Brauner.

Schultze, Bernhard. German painter, b. 1915 in Schneidemühl, West Prussia. Schultze studied at the academies in Berlin and Düsseldorf from 1934 to 1939, when he was conscripted for army service. He was demobilized in 1945 and went to live in Frankfurt in 1947. From 1951 onwards he made regular

visits to Paris. His first Tachist pictures reveal the influence of Riopelle, Lanskoy and Wols. In 1951–2 he joined with Götz, Greis and Kreutz in forming the Frankfurt Group. In 1956 he began to produce relief paintings, in which he used straw, cloths, artificial resin, etc. These were followed in 1961 by the *Migofs*, which Schultze has described as 'coloured sculptures'. They are made from wire mesh swathed with resin-impregnated cloths, painted in garish, venomous-looking colours, and resemble webs. Later versions of these *Migofs* incorporate objects.

Following an early phase, in which he produced figurative but fantastic Surrealist works, Schultze evolved a Romantic form of *Tachisme* based on morbid Rococo-style colours. Of more recent years he has assimilated Neo-Dadaist influences and, as a result, has incorporated colour photographs into his works, which now have something of the quality of a picture puzzle.

Catalogue, *Bernhard Schultze*, Kestner Gesellschaft, Hanover 1966.

Schumacher, Emil. German painter, b. 1912 in Hagen, Westphalia. Schumacher studied at the School of Arts and Crafts in Dortmund from 1923 to 1925. In 1937 he met Rohlfs. From 1939 to 1945 he worked as a technical draughtsman. In 1947 he became a founder member of the *Young West* group. Later he joined the *Zen 49* group and, in 1958, the *Zero* group. From 1958 to 1960 he taught at the Hamburg Academy and in 1966 at the Karlsruhe Academy. In 1967–8 he was visiting lecturer at the Minneapolis School of Art in the United States. He is now living in Hagen, Westphalia.

Schumacher is one of the best-known representatives of Informal art in Germany. He went abstract in 1951 and at first was strongly influenced by Wols. Subsequently, however, he began to attach far greater importance to colour. He then used a more earthy palette and applied his paint by the *pastosa* technique, thus creating a heavy, encrusted picture surface. By 1957 this process had reached a point where his paintings were virtually reliefs and since then he has been producing what he calls 'tactile objects'. These are abstract compositions painted primarily in red, brown, grey and black. The designs are reminiscent of old weathered walls that are full of scars and cracks.

E. Sylvanus. *Emil Schumacher*, Recklinghausen 1959.
Catalogue, *Emil Schumacher*, Westfälischer Kunstverein, Münster 1962.

Schwitters, Kurt. German painter, b. 1887 in Hanover; d. 1948 in Ambleside, England. He lived and was educated in Hanover until 1909, when he went to study at the Kunst-Akademie in Dresden until 1914. The following year he married. He did his military service in Hanover as a clerk and draughtsman, 1917–18. In 1918 he produced his first collages; he also visited Zürich and met Arp and

Hausmann. In 1919 he was a founder member of the Dada group in Hanover, when he invented 'Merz'. He had exhibitions at the Sturm Gallery in Berlin; his articles and prose-poems were also published in *Der Sturm* magazine. From 1921 on he contributed enthusiastically to Dada performances in Prague, Holland, France, Switzerland and Germany and to many Dada periodicals. In 1922 he attended the famous Dada conference at Weimar. In 1923 he founded the magazine *Merz*, and from that year he worked on his first *Merzbau* ('The Cathedral of Erotic Misery') in Hanover; it was destroyed by bombs in 1943. The first of his many visits to Norway took place in 1931. The following year he joined the *Abstraction-Création* group. In 1937 he moved to Norway, after his works had been shown in 'Degenerate Art' exhibitions in Germany and removed from German museums. He began work on his second *Merzbau* in Lysaker in that year; it was destroyed by fire in 1951. In 1940 he fled from the Nazis to England, where he was held in various internment camps, 1940–1. When he was released he moved to London, and then in 1945 to Ambleside, in the Lake District. In 1947 he started work on his third *Merzbau*, which was unfinished at his death the following January.

Schwitters was one of the most original and poetic of German Dadaists. His conversion from a pedestrian early style of figurative painting to *avant-garde* art about 1917 or 1918 relates first to his discovery of the Cubist tradition of collage constructions and second to his contact with Zürich Dadaists, particularly Arp. The name *Merz*, a word fragment taken from a random scrap of newspaper, was as meaningless as Dada, but served as a symbolic distinction of the apolitical nature of his own art. After 1921 he was ostracized as a bourgeois reactionary by the political extremists of the Berlin Dada. He defined *Merz* as 'freedom' and the emancipation of nonsense ('I play off sense against nonsense. I prefer nonsense, but that's a purely personal matter'). From 1919 on he produced a prolific output of *Merzplastik* (paintings and collages), *Merzbilder* (constructions) and the three *Merzbau* (in effect housefuls of *Merz*—a continuous fabric of grottoes and structures running throughout his house, occasionally extending through windows, etc.). He wrote and performed a great deal of *merz*-poetry (at times purely phonetic, at others a collection of word and phrase fragments), influenced by Hausmann's work in Zürich, but developed into a very original and powerful personal performance. He also had projects for *merz*-theatre.

In the sense that much of his material was rubbish (a random collection of found objects and scraps) he subscribed to the anti-aesthetic credo of Dada. Nevertheless he produced works of substantial artistic qualities and occasionally of a very delicate aesthetic sensitivity (*Cherry Picture*, 1921, New York, Museum of Modern Art; *Opened by Customs*, 1937–9, London, Tate Gallery). Similarly the wit and humour that he valued so highly in art was not anti-social, but a positive, generous source of energy. The simple, almost Classical, abstract reliefs with which he responded to the influence of van Doesburg and *de Stijl* in the 1920s exemplify his antipathy to the anti-art concept. He wrote, 'Art is an arch-principle, as sublime as the godhead, as inexplicable as life, indefinable and without purpose' (*Merz*, 1921). Most of his work combines a wide range of media—assorted papers and cloths, wood, wire, ready-made objects, print, paint, drawing. In some, the elements are glued flat to the wood or canvas surface like a Cubist collage; others are more aggressively three-dimensional either in coarse relief or, occasionally, free-standing.

Although highly respected by most of his fellow artists, he enjoyed almost no public recognition in his lifetime. He has since been recognized as one of the great pioneers of the art of assemblage and has remained highly influential.

H. Bergruen. *Kurt Schwitters*, Paris 1954.
Werner Schmalenbach. *Kurt Schwitters: Leben und Werk*, Cologne 1967.

Scialoja, Toti. Italian painter, b. 1914 in Rome. Scialoja worked as a critic and journalist and then studied law before deciding, in 1937, to become a painter. During the war he worked for the Italian Resistance. Between 1943 and 1945 he created theatre décors. In 1947–8 he visited Paris. In 1953 he was appointed to the teaching staff of the Academy in Rome. In 1956 and again in 1959–60 he visited New York. He is now living in Rome.

During his early period Scialoja was influenced by the Roman Expressionists, especially Scipione. In c. 1950, following a probing investigation of French Cubism, he began to paint pictures which closely resemble Afro's compositions and in which the large areas of dark colour create a distinctly melancholy effect. In 1960, when Scialoja encountered American art, he again changed his style, producing paintings which, although not quite so clearly defined as the original American works in this genre, are none the less based on the new hard-edge technique.

G. Dorfles. *Scialoja*, Rome 1959.

Science Fiction. H. Szemann has described Science Fiction as a 'sociological phenomenon that is already operative in various spheres of human activity and is capable of appearing in any given form'. Certainly Science Fiction has acquired growing significance of recent years. Up to the early 1920s it was largely restricted to works of literature, whose authors described hypothetical situations based on innovations or new conceptions in science, genetics, technology, etc. Since then Science Fiction themes have also been treated in a number of predominantly visual spheres such as photography, films, posters, book illustrations and children's toys. J. Protozanow's *Aelita* of 1924 and F. Lang's *Metropolis* of 1926 were early Science Fiction films. A more recent example is Jean-Luc Godard's *Alphaville* of 1965. Science Fiction has been one of the dominant themes of contemporary art, where it frequently appears in combination with the comic strip. In the second half of the 1960s several large Science Fiction exhibitions were staged: *Science Fiction*, Berne, 1967, Paris and Düsseldorf, 1968; *Cybernetic Serendipity*, London, 1968; *Some More Beginnings*, New York, 1968. Some contemporary artists (Matta, Fahlström, Rancillac) have incorporated Science Fiction *motifs* into their works; others (Tsai, Castro-Cid, Schöffer, Takis, Kudo) have used special techniques which produce Science Fiction associations.

Catalogue, *Science Fiction*, Berne 1967, Paris and Düsseldorf 1968.
Jasia Reichardt. Catalogue, *Cybernetic Serendipity*, London 1968.

Scipione, Gino Bonichi. Italian painter, b. 1904 in Macerata; d. 1933 in Arco. Scipione studied at the Academy of Art in Rome, where he was a contemporary of Mafai and Mazzacurati, with whom he founded the *Roman School* in 1928. In 1932 he was obliged to stop work due to the accumulated effect of a progressive tubercular disease, to which he succumbed in the following year.

During his early period Scipione was influenced by El Greco, the Italian Mannerists and the European Baroque artists on the one hand and by Soutine, Rouault and Ensor on the other. His Baroque-like paintings reflect the morbidity of modern Rome: using dark colours to create mystical effects he portrayed and caricatured the erotic sinfulness and *joie de vivre* of the Italian capital. The specific forms of his basic designs are obliterated by the furious brushwork so that in his finished works light, line and colour appear to merge into a single pictorial structure. Because of their complete lack of formal definition his paintings acquire a Neo-Baroque dimension. The greens, reds and violets intertwine to form finely shaded, rhythmically organized arabesques whilst the highlights, which are applied with a view to a plastic effect, impart a hovering sense of restlessness. Any firm spatial constructions which may have existed in the original design are virtually destroyed by the diagonal rhythms of the colour composition; all that is left of them in the finished work is the merest hint of dissonance. Scipione's fantasy was sparked off by chance incidents and it enabled him to produce works of burning intensity. His complete dedication, which was tantamount to an obsession, would seem to have been an outward sign of the fear and frenzy triggered off in him by a consuming sense of guilt, which he felt obliged to confess. These artistic confessions, which were prompted by apocalyptic necessity, acquired a visionary quality from the pictorial techniques employed in their execution. Scipione's

Expressionism has exerted a lasting influence on later Italian painters.

G. B. Scipione. *Carte Segrete*, Florence 1943.
U. Apollonio. *Scipione*, Venice 1945.
Catalogue, *Scipione*, Galleria d'Arte Moderna, Rome 1954.

Scott, William. British painter, b. 1913 in Greenock, Scotland. Scott studied at Belfast College of Art (1928–31) and the Royal Academy Schools (1931–5), where he was receptive to the aesthetics of Clive Bell and Roger Fry, which underpin his later development. He lived in Cornwall with Dylan Thomas (1936). Scott and his wife left England to work mainly in Pont Aven, Brittany (1937–9). His paintings from these years recall Gauguin and Cézanne. He taught at Bath Academy (1946–56). He had a retrospective at the Venice Biennale (1958), and won the John Moores Prize in 1959.

Scott's first-hand contact with American painters in 1953 was significant for the development of British mainstream art towards abstraction. 'I have no theory,' he has said, 'what matters to me in a picture is the indefinable.' His recent work is remarkable in being abstract, non-formal and also expressionless—the artist's ultimate abnegation of traditional roles. Scott has been given considerable official support in Britain and abroad.

A. Bowness. *William Scott*, London 1964.

Scottish painting. In the early twentieth century the dealer Alexander Reid was selling Impressionist pictures to Glasgow industrialists. The best days of the Glasgow School were over, but Scotland's ancient connections with France were to be briefly revived by the 'Scottish Colourists'—S. J. Peploe, Leslie Hunter (1877–1931) and F. C. B. Cadell (1883–1937), with J. D. Fergusson (1874–1961). These artists were French in outlook and prepared to learn from Manet, the Fauves and Cézanne, among others. They painted sometimes brilliantly but were pure empiricists uninterested in modern art theory. The more important and thoughtful contribution of Scotland to *art nouveau* had little good effect in painting.

After 1918 a painful recession impoverished Glasgow and brought bad times to Scotland. The 'Colourists', in or out of the country, sold what they could. No artists attempted a radical re-appraisal such as Unit One stood for in England. Instead a cautious, un-English renewal took place with the emergence of the leaders of the Edinburgh School in the 1930s—Anne Redpath, W. G. Gillies (b. 1898), the younger William MacTaggart and John Maxwell (1905–62). These artists quietly asserted the necessity for a personal vision on a plane where photographic representation is irrelevant; hardly a radical programme, but one that established the continuity of the best Scots painting in the next thirty years.

After the Second World War émigré Scots did

much to establish modern British art as a recognized force (Colquhoun, MacBryde, Gear, Davie). At home the Edinburgh School attracted many adherents and became the face that Scottish art presented to England, resulting possibly in unfairness to some original artists such as James Cowie (1886–1956). Its sensuous evocative art of rich colour and *matière*, with elements of Chagall-like fantasy, was very unlike the prevailing mood of English painting at that time. Younger adherents brought in Expressionist (e.g. Robin Philipson), Tachist and other elements, and loosely included the unique, single-minded Joan Eardley. The Edinburgh School lost cohesion by about 1960 and good painting is now more evenly distributed among the four big cities.

A group of sound painters born in the 1930s, who are now (1972) assuming places of authority in practice and teaching or other ways, came from all four art schools—for example, John Houston (b. 1930; Edinburgh), John Knox (b. 1936; Glasgow), Ian McKenzie Smith (b. 1935; Aberdeen)—and quietly transformed the scene from the early 1960s. As elsewhere the 1960s was a time of uncertainty and disaffection. But still the tight organization of art teaching and the conditions of the country hindered the emergence of an effective youthful *avant-garde*. To-day it seems impossible to define a collective character. If the most interesting artists in Scotland now are mavericks (e.g. Patricia Douthwaite, Ian Hamilton Finlay—see Concrete Poetry—Gerald Laing, Tam McPhail, of whom only the first is a painter) Scotland may be thus true to an earlier individualist nonconformity.

Secession. A term used to denote the breaking-away of a group of (often) younger or more radical artists from an older artistic institution and, usually, the formation of a new organization and exhibiting society. In modern German art, the most famous of the Secessions were those of Munich, Berlin and Vienna. Of these, the oldest and most conservative was the Munich *Sezession* (1892), the semi-official character of which may be judged from the leading role played by the famous academician Franz von Stuck (1863–1928). Of a more revolutionary character, the *Berliner Sezession* came into being as the indirect result of a dispute within the *Verein Berliner Künstler* caused by the showing of the works of Edvard Munch in Berlin in 1892, although it was not until 1899 that the association, under the leadership of the German Impressionist painter Max Liebermann, was able to launch its first exhibition in its own building. During the early years of the twentieth century, both the Berlin and Munich associations were active in exhibiting the work of contemporary German and European artists, although often of a rather conservative variety: it was, for example, not until 1908 that a small exhibition of graphic works by the *Brücke* artists was mounted by

the Berlin Secession—an exhibition which, in the eyes of the more reactionary members, marked the 'downfall' of the movement. In 1910 the measure of control over the association exercised by those conservative elements associated principally with the German Impressionist school of painting led to the founding of a new Secession—the *Neue Sezession*—under the leadership of Max Pechstein, with the intention of exhibiting the works of those more *avant-garde* artists who had been rejected by the members of the old *Sezession*. The older association was itself split once again in 1913 by the appearance of yet another breakaway movement, the *Freie Sezession* (Free Secession), in which the Expressionist artists Ernst Barlach and Max Beckmann were also involved.

The Vienna Secession (*Vereinigung bildender Künstler Österreichs*) represents, on the other hand, a far more radical and self-contained movement within the development of modern art—a movement, moreover, with a distinctive personality and *Weltanschauung*. Founded in 1897 under the presidency of Gustav Klimt, its avowed aim was to raise the level of artistic production in Austria to that of other European nations, as well as encouraging the work of native Austrian artists, craftsmen and designers. Exhibiting members of the society included such figures as Gerstl, Roller, Boehm, Kokoschka and, later, Schiele. The close personal contact maintained between a number of members of the Secession and the leading artists of the *Jugendstil* movement, as well as international *art nouveau*, may be remarked. Symbolism and *art nouveau* represent the two principal influences upon the formation of the *Sezession*-style, while the interest of the Austrian designers, especially, in contemporary Scottish art—above all the work of Charles Rennie Mackintosh—is also significant. The Secession rapidly achieved both popular success and a measure of official recognition, influencing, through a series of major international exhibitions, almost every aspect of contemporary artistic life in Vienna (the *Sezession* building, designed by Josef Maria Olbrich, in which the exhibitions of the society were held, remains one of the architectural landmarks of present-day Vienna). The influence of the Secession was also strongly felt in the fields of applied art and design through the work of the Vienna Workshops (*Wiener Werkstätten*), under the leadership of Josef Hoffmann and Kolo Moser: the execution of the Palais Stoclet in Brussels (1905–9) was to unite the architecture of Hoffmann, the productions of the *Wiener Werkstätten*, to whom were entrusted all details of the interior design, and the pictorial art of Klimt, who created, in the *Frieze of Life* for the dining-room of the house, one of the landmarks of twentieth-century art.

Charles Holme (ed.). *The Art Revival in Austria*, New York 1906.
Erich Haenel. *Die Wohnung der Neuzeit*, Leipzig 1908.

Section d'Or. In 1912, during the transition from the Analytical to the Synthetic phase of Cubism, a group of young artists who had previously been members of this movement broke away to form the *Section d'Or*. This group—which included Metzinger and Gleizes (the theorists of Synthetic Cubism), La Fresnaye, Léger, Picabia, Marcel Duchamp and Frank Kupka—met in the *atelier* of the brothers Jacques Villon (alias Gaston Duchamp-Villon) and Raymond Duchamp-Villon in Puteaux, Paris. There they discussed the *Nabis* theories of ideal proportions, the Golden Mean and the beauty of geometric forms. Their spokesman was Jacques Villon, who was well versed in the theoretical aspects of art and had studied, amongst other things, Leonardo da Vinci's 'Theory of the Pyramids'. In their approach to Cubism Picasso and Braque were completely objective, which is to say that they derived their pictorial structures from the objects which they portrayed. Villon and his friends proceeded quite differently. They presupposed a specific aesthetic canon, which they then tried to express in pictorial terms. Their criticism of the static and colourless character of 'Classical' Cubism was doubtless prompted in some measure by the impact of Fauvism and Futurism. Other Cubist features to which the *Section d'Or* artists took exception were its rejection of perspective and its exclusion of all but still-life themes. They wanted to portray life in all its richness and dynamism and hoped to solve the problem of perspective by drawing on the harmonious proportions of the Golden Mean. Cézanne was their great mentor. The results of these deliberations were works of crystalline clarity and harmonious colouring, whose fragmented three-dimensional structures provide a cryptic setting for the pictorial objects and figures. The *Section d'Or* group was formed in September 1912 and had its first exhibition in October of the same year in the Galerie la Boètie in Paris. Apart from the artists mentioned above the thirty contributors to this exhibition included André Lhôte, Marie Laurencin, Archipenko, Segonzac, Gris, Herbin and Marcoussis. At the same time the group published the first—and last—issue of its magazine. With the outbreak of hostilities in 1914 the *Section d'Or* broke up and, although an attempt was made to revive it after the war, this proved abortive.

H. E. Timerding. *Der goldene Schnitt*, Leipzig 1919.
Élisa Maillard. *Du nombre d'or: Diagrammes de chefs-d'oeuvre*, Paris 1943.
Michael Ayrton. *Golden Sections*, London 1957.
Pierre Cabanne. *L'Épopée du Cubisme*, Paris 1963.

Sedgley, Peter. British painter, b. 1930. His work comes into the category of Op Art. Like Bridget Riley, Sedgley attempts to confuse the focus of the spectator in order to effect new optical experiences.

Seehaus, Paul Adolf. German painter and graphic artist, b. 1891 in Bonn; d. 1919 in Hamburg. Seehaus was one of the Rhenish Expressionists, a group led by Macke, Campendonk and Nauen. In 1913 he exhibited with this group under the pseudonym of Barnett. In little more than six years Seehaus produced a large collection of etchings in the Expressionist style of the *Brücke* group, and a number of prismatically organized, imaginary landscapes in a somewhat stylized form, which reveal the influence of Cubism, Futurism and Orphism.

Segal, George. American sculptor, b. 1924 in New York City. He grew up in the Bronx and moved in 1940–1 to South Brunswick, N.J., where he worked part-time on his father's poultry farm while attending Rutgers University (1941–6). He briefly studied at Pratt Institute in 1947 but transferred to New York University in 1948 where he received a BS degree in Art Education (1949). In 1956 he had his first one-man show of figurative paintings at the Hansa Gallery, New York. Two years later he began experimenting with plaster sculpture made with chicken wire and burlap, later changing to direct casting sculpture. The first piece made in this manner, which has become the main characteristic of his art, was a self-portrait: *Man at a Table* (1961, coll. of artist). Since 1956 he has had at least one one-man show every year and has been included in every major contemporary exhibition dealing with sculpture, Pop Art, environments, the figure or new media. Among these exhibitions was the 1962 *New Realists* show at the Sidney Janis Gallery, New York, where his sculptures received high critical acclaim. His works are often of one figure but sometimes more, placed into a specific context which may range from a chair (*Vera List*, 1965, plaster and metal, New York, Coll. Mr. and Mrs. Albert A. List) to something more complex such as *Woman Shaving her Leg* (1963, plaster, porcelain, shaver and metal; Winnetka, Ill., Coll. Mr. and Mrs. Robert B. Mayer) which includes a tub, bathroom hardware and tiled walls, to a whole environment as in *The Diner* (1964–6, plaster, wood, chrome, formica, masonite; New York, Sidney Janis Gallery). In 1963 Segal received an MFA degree from Rutgers University. He exhibited in the Seventh and Ninth Bienals at São Paulo, Brazil in 1963 and 1967.

Catalogue, *George Segal. 12 Human Situations*, Museum of Contemporary Art, Chicago 1968.

Segall, Lasar. Russian-Brazilian painter and sculptor, b. 1891 in Vilna, Lithuania; d. 1957 in São Paulo. Segall is generally regarded as one of the foremost pioneers of modern art in Brazil. After studying in Vilna and at the Academy of Art in Berlin (from 1906 to 1909) he joined the Berlin Secession. In 1910 he moved to Leipzig and in 1912–13 visited Brazil for the first time. In 1919 he joined the Dresden Secession and made contact with Dix and Grosz, who both influenced him. In 1920 he had an exhibition in the Folkwang Museum. Then, in 1923, he emigrated to Brazil, where he subsequently became a Brazilian citizen. In 1929 he visited Paris and created his first sculptures. In 1932 he settled in São Paulo, where he founded the *Sociedad Paulista Pro Arte Moderno (SPAM)* and where a Segall Museum has now been opened.

After being proscribed in Germany in the 1930s as a 'degenerate artist', Segall revived the Expressionist *motifs* of his early period in his celebrated paintings *War, Pogrom* and *Emigrant Ship*. After the Second World War he produced the two great series of paintings *Erradias* and *Favellas*, in which he depicted the misery of the poor, and a third—*Florestas*—which is a hymn of praise to the beauty of the Brazilian countryside. In his paintings Segall combined the artistic experiences of his Russian period with German Expressionism and *motifs* culled from Brazilian folklore. He had a special show at the Twenty-ninth Biennale in Venice.

P. Fierens. *Lasar Segall*, Paris 1938.
Mario de Andrade. Catalogue, *Lasar Segall*, Museo Nacional de Belas Artes, Rio de Janeiro 1943.
P. M. Bardi. *Lasar Segall*, São Paulo 1952.
G. Ferraz. *Lasar Segall*, Buenos Aires 1966.

Segonzac, André Dunoyer de—*see* **Dunoyer de Segonzac,** André

Segui, Antonio. Argentinian painter, b. 1934 in Córdoba. After reading for the bar Segui became an art student in 1951, training in Spain and France. From 1957 to 1961 he lived in Mexico, then visited the United States before settling in Paris in 1963. In 1964 he was represented at the Biennale in Venice. At present he is living in Buenos Aires.

In his expressive, figurative and macabre portraits Segui pillories the upper classes (generals, judges, etc.) of his native land for their unscrupulous exploitation of the poor. The early paintings in this genre are reminiscent of Daumier and Dubuffet, but more recently Segui has been moving towards English Pop Art.

Catalogue, *Antonio Segui*, Galerie Claude Bernard, Paris 1964.

Seitz, Gustav. German sculptor and draughtsman, b. 1906 in Neckarau, near Mannheim. From 1922 to 1924 he trained in sculpture in Ludwigshafen, at the same time studying drawing in Mannheim. He later studied in Karlsruhe and Berlin. In 1927 he went to Florence, where he was impressed by the Etruscan sculpture. The following year he went to Paris and came under the influence of Maillol and Despiau. His first one-man show was in 1932 in Mannheim, and consisted of sculpture and drawings. In 1934 he went to Greece and Egypt. From 1937 he collabora-

ted with the architect Heinrich Tessenow. He was taken prisoner during the war, and in 1943 all the works in his Berlin studio were destroyed by bombing. From 1947 he was a professor at the art school in Berlin-Charlottenburg, and in 1950 he moved to the academy at Berlin-Weissensee. In 1949 he won the national prize in Weimar. He then travelled in China and Russia. In 1957 he was awarded the Cornelius Prize by the town of Düsseldorf. His work consists largely of nudes, especially female figures, and portraits.

Seiwert, Franz-Wilhelm. German painter, b. 1894 in Cologne; d. 1933 in Cologne. Seiwert belonged to the Progressive Artists' Association in Cologne and was a friend of Hoerle, Max Ernst and Otto Freundlich. From 1929 to 1933 he helped to edit the magazine *a–z*.

Technically, his pictures are strictly geometrical compositions. Thematically, they are studies of 'working-class types' and are intended as social criticism.

C. O. Jatho. *Franz-Wilhelm Seiwert*, Recklinghausen 1964.

Sekine, Nobuo. Japanese painter and sculptor, b. 1942 in Omiya. He graduated from the Graduate School of Tama University, Tokyo. He at first painted mathematical *trompe l'oeil* pictures. Afterwards he made structures of soil and modelling-clay. He now lives in Tokyo.

Seley, Jason. American sculptor, b. 1919 in Newark, New Jersey. He first studied architecture at Cornell University (1936–40) and then worked under O. Zadkine at the Art Students' League (1943–5). He received a United States Office of Education and Department of State Travel and Maintenance Grant for creative sculpture in Haiti, 1947–9. It was while he was in Haiti that he had his first one-man show at Le Centre d'Art, Port-au-Prince. His first one-man show in the United States came the following year at the American-British Art Center, New York (1947). In 1950 he studied at the École des Beaux-Arts, Paris, on a Fulbright Scholarship. His early works were semi-abstract; only in the mid-1950s did he find the technique with which his name is associated. Since that time he has used automobile bumpers, first as armatures for plaster which was then cast in bronze or aluminium, and then around 1959 he began to use welded bumpers and bumper guards by themselves, creating shiny, convoluted masses of compact, curvilinear forms (*Masculine Presence*, c. 1961, chrome, New York, Museum of Modern Art). Seley has exhibited in several Whitney Annuals (1952, 1953, 1962) and Documenta III, Kassel, Germany (1964). He has taught at Hofstra College (1953) and was Artist-in-Residence at Dartmouth

College. He has been Chairman of the Art Department, College of Architecture, Cornell University, since 1967.

'Jason Seley '40', *Cornell Alumni News*, September 1965.
'Taped Dialogue', *Ikon* I, No. 2, 5 April 1967.

Seligmann, Kurt. Swiss painter and graphic artist, b. 1900 in Basle; d. 1961 in Middletown, New York. After studying at the Academy of Art in Geneva Seligmann lived in Paris from 1929 to 1938. Whilst there he was in contact with the Surrealists and the members of the *Abstraction-Création* association. His early work was influenced by Arp and Miró. In 1939 Seligmann went to the United States and lived on a farm in Sugar Loaf, where he painted his *Cyclonic Forms*, a series of visionary works reflecting his reaction to the American landscape and American geology. Seligmann's Surrealism is remarkable for its magical, apocalyptic metamorphoses of man and nature. He had a profound interest in the occult and wrote a book on this subject entitled *The Mirror of Magic* (1948). Seligmann also produced numerous book illustrations.

Catalogue, *Kurt Seligmann*, D'Arcy Galleries, New York 1961.

Semantic Painting. The term Semantic Painting (Greek *sēmantikos* = significant) has been used since the late 1950s to denote a style of painting in which fundamental gestures or movements are built up to form a pictorial whole. In Semantic Painting verticals, horizontals, circles, zigzag lines, serpentines and spirals—which occur quite spontaneously in Informal art—are systematically and rationally organized. The principal representatives of Semantic Painting are Luciano Lattanzi and Werner Schreib.

L. Lattanzi. *Semantic Paintings*, London 1957.
L. Lattanzi and W. Schreib. *Über das semantische Bild*, Frankfurt 1961.

Seoane, Luis. Argentinian painter, graphic artist, potter, illustrator and author, b. 1910 in Buenos Aires. Seoane spent his youth in Galicia, where he trained as a lawyer and developed an early interest in art. In 1936 he returned to Argentina. He then founded his own presses and worked as a journalist, painter and illustrator. Between 1937 and 1958 he published more than twenty books and portfolios of drawings. From 1942 onwards he produced woodcut illustrations for works by various authors, including García Lorca and Franz Kafka. He has visited England, France, Switzerland, Germany and Spain. Seoane has also created large-format wall paintings, mosaics, metal reliefs, pottery designs and tapestries. His style reveals monumental characteristics; his palette is made up of pure luminous colours.

S. García Sabell. *Seoane*, Vigo 1954.

Séraphine (Séraphine Louis). French painter, b. 1864 in Assy, Oise; d. 1934 in Senlis. She did not start painting until she was about forty, and it was not until 1912 that she came to the attention of the critic Wilhelm Uhde, who encouraged her. A primitive painter, in the sense that she belonged to no definite school and was ignorant of the developments in art of that period, she produced marvellous imaginary flower and tree pictures filled with colour and with a rich variety of forms. Her approach to painting was almost religious, with elements of the erotic —eyes and lips hidden among the flowers of her bouquets.

Serpan, Jaroslav. French painter, b. 1922 in Prague. Serpan comes of Russian stock. In 1927, when he was still a child, he was brought to France. In 1948 he moved to Paris, where he studied mathematics and biology at the Sorbonne, obtaining his doctorate there in 1953. He started painting in 1940. From 1946 to 1948 he was a member of the Surrealist movement but left it to become a follower of Michel Tapié, the author of the book *Art autre* and the spokesman for Informal art. In 1950 Serpan helped to launch the magazine *Rixes*. He is now living in Le Pecq.

Serpan's paintings are products of Informal art or 'psychic improvisation'. He has been influenced primarily by Masson and Wols. Using a spontaneous drawing technique Serpan creates vortiginous designs with tiny, thorn-like strokes of his pen. The overall impression is reminiscent of drawings of magnetic fields of force.

Catalogue, *Jaroslav Serpan*, Galerie Staedler, Paris 1963.
Serpan 1945–65, Paris 1965.

Serra Guell, Eudaldo. Spanish sculptor, b. 1911 in Barcelona. He was a pupil of Angel Ferrant in Barcelona. From 1935 to 1938 he was in Japan. He returned to Spain in 1948 via the USA. He now teaches in Barcelona.

Serrano, Pablo. Spanish sculptor, b. 1910 in Crivillén. He studied in Barcelona, then in 1930 went to Argentina and in 1933 to Uruguay. He spent some years teaching at the University of Montevideo. He now lives in Madrid. He is a member of the *Nouvelle École Européenne* group.

Sert y Badía, José Maria. Spanish painter, b. 1876 in Barcelona; d. 1945 in Barcelona. In 1900 he moved to Paris. He painted murals and decorations for public and private buildings all over Europe and America, including the Waldorf-Astoria Hotel in New York (1930–1), the League of Nations Assembly Hall in Geneva (1936) and the cathedral at Vich, near Barcelona (1926–30). The latter murals were destroyed in the Civil War, and Sert created new ones for the rebuilt cathedral (1941–5).

Alberto del Castillo. *José Maria Sert: Su Vida y Su Obra*, Barcelona 1947.

Sérusier, Paul. French painter, b. 1863 in Paris; d. 1927 in Moarlaix. From 1886 onwards Sérusier was a student at the Académie Julian, where he met Maurice Denis, Bonnard, Vuillard, Vallotton, Ranson, Roussel and Ibels. In 1888 he was introduced by Émile Bernard to Gauguin and accompanied him to Pont-Aven, where he painted his first 'synthetist' picture under Gauguin's guidance. This work, *Bois d'Amour*, was hailed by his fellow students at the Academy as a revelation and was subsequently adopted by them as a sort of talisman for the *Nabis* association, which was formed in the following year, Sérusier being a founder member. In 1889 Sérusier went to paint in Brittany, again with Gauguin, and in 1891 contributed to the famous exhibition of Impressionist and Symbolist painters staged in the Galerie Le Barc de Boutteville. In 1891 he also began to create theatre décors. Sérusier visited Italy on several occasions—in 1893 with Bernard, in 1895 and 1899 with Maurice Denis. In 1895 he met Verkade in Prague and in 1897 and 1899 visited him in the Benedictine monastery at Beuron in Germany. In 1903 he went to live at Châteauneuf-du-Faon in Brittany but returned to Paris in 1908 to teach at the Académie Ranson. Then, in 1914, he retired to Brittany for good and spent the rest of his life in the seclusion of the countryside. In 1921 he published his *ABC de la Peinture*, a book on art theory.

Apart from Maurice Denis, Sérusier was the only real theorist amongst the *Nabis* and it was he who introduced them to the synthetism of the Gauguin School. This penchant for theoretical and philosophical speculation gave him a very conscious attitude to art, which made itself felt in his paintings. Sérusier combined a simplified line, which served to heighten the decorative effect, with ornate arabesques and pure, flat colours. True to his synthetist leanings he made little attempt to depict inner form.

M. Denis. *Sérusier, sa vie, son oeuvre*, Paris 1943.
A. Humbert. *Les Nabis et leur époque*, Geneva 1954.

Servaes, Albert. Belgian painter, b. 1883 in Ghent; d. 1966 in Lucerne. He studied in Ghent, then joined the artists' community at Laethem-St-Martin. His fellow artists there included Saedeleer, Minne and Woestijne. He developed an Expressionist style, and his paintings of peasants and their daily life were remarkable for their tortured, tragic spirit. He also did religious paintings which combine Expressionist with Byzantine influences. He moved to Switzerland in 1945.

Servranckx, Victor. Belgian painter, sculptor, art critic and designer, b. 1897 in Diegem; d. 1965 in Vilvoorde. Servranckx became a student at the Brussels Academy in 1913. Upon completion of his studies (in 1917) he had an exhibition of abstract paintings, the first of its kind in Belgium. From 1921 onwards he produced numerous abstract sculptures and up to 1925 was employed as a designer in a carpet factory. During this period he also designed furniture and worked as an interior decorator. In 1932 he joined the staff of the School of Arts and Crafts in Ixelles. In 1945 he became a member of the *Réalités Nouvelles* association in Paris.

Servranckx was the pioneer of abstract art in Belgium, which he promoted with great zeal both as an artist and as a publicist. Although Servranckx followed a wide variety of trends, including Cubism, Dadaism, Kandinsky-type Expressionism, Constructivism and Surrealism, these all proved transitory. After each new phase he always reverted to strictly geometrical compositions.

M. Bilcke. *Servranckx*, Brussels 1964.
Catalogue, *Victor Servranckx Retrospective Exhibition*, Musée d'Ixelles, Brussels 1965.

Seuphor, Michel. Belgian-French painter, graphic artist and art critic, b. 1901 in Antwerp. Seuphor has been living in Paris since 1925. He is an abstract artist who works primarily with graphic techniques, producing pictures in which geometrically and organically based structures are contrasted with one another. Seuphor played an active part in the founding of the *Cercle et Carré* and *Abstraction-Création* associations. He has published important writings on modern art including *L'Art abstrait: Ses origines, ses premiers maîtres* (*Abstract Art: Its Origins and First Masters*), 1949, and *La Sculpture de ce siècle* (*Sculpture in This Century*), 1959. He also wrote a monograph on Piet Mondrian and compiled a dictionary of abstract painting, both in 1957.

Seurat, Georges. French painter, b. 1859 in Paris; d. 1891 in Paris. Though cut short by his early death the work of Seurat had a profound effect on subsequent developments in painting. The influence of the unique method of painting—'Pointillism'—which he found necessary to develop was very powerful, and in greater or less degree it affected all those who came into contact with it. An equally powerful influence came from his concern with the process of creation itself. He affirmed that order, logic and intellect are as important as intuition and imagination. Significant also as regards his influence on the twentieth century was his demonstration of the use of non-art factors in the very fibres of art itself.

Born of well-to-do parents, he was not distracted by financial worries. His career began with his enrolment at the École des Beaux-Arts. The training was Ingres-based, and Seurat's drawings of this time show a marked competence of the traditional kind, and evidence of his perseverance towards completion which characterizes his later works. During his National Service in 1879–80 he seems to have spent his time in developing drawn studies from close observation of nature. He returned to Paris in 1881. From the beginning he found his own mentors: Delacroix for luminosity of colour; Puvis de Chavannes for pictorial organization; Millet for Classical form in contemporary genre. Like all original thinkers he took and assimilated all that helped his own single purpose. Seurat, however, as a painter, is remarkable in that his sources of inspiration included non-aesthetic ideas; he came to give a very dominant consideration to optics as presented in the writings of scientists of the time.

Though apparently he had not come into contact with the works of the Impressionists before about 1882, it is in the context of their outlook that he later proceeded to work. Neither he nor his supporters considered themselves as innovators. Rather than replacing Impressionism they hoped to extend it by introducing order in the Classical sense into its predominantly transient effects, to give light and colour the orderly basis of logic to strengthen the direct, unmodified observation.

Among the scientific works which Seurat first studied were those of Charles Blanc and Eugène Chevreul. Later he read Ogden Rood's *Modern Chromatics*. Briefly, he took from Chevreul the theory of contrast, the optical effect implicit in juxtaposition of colour and tone; and from Rood the perception of colour by optical mixing, with its different base of primaries from that of pigment mixing. These were the basis of the development by Seurat and his friends of the style called 'Neo-Impressionism', though Seurat did not like the term.

The culmination of this assiduous study came in 1884, when Seurat exhibited his first large work. This, the famous *Baignade à Asnières*, had been refused by the Salon. However, Seurat, with Signac, Henri Cross and others, formed a 'Groupe des Artistes Indépendants' holding their own Salon, at which the work was shown with immediate success.

This painting set the pattern for Seurat's subsequent career. The first of a series of masterworks, it was followed by *Un Dimanche d'Été à la Grande Jatte* (1886), *La Parade* (1887), *Les Poseuses* (1888), *Le Chahut* (1890), *Le Cirque* (1891). Each of these works was developed from large numbers of sketches, in the studio and out of doors, with many drawn studies of great quality of figures and details. These supported the grand plan of the major painting, which was worked out to the last detail of overall organization. At the same time he produced many smaller paintings very largely involving the sea or the river, which demonstrate his ideas of representation.

Following Rood's theories, it was necessary to avoid pigment mixing to obtain colours and tone before application to the canvas. As the alternative,

pure colour, pre-toned with white or black, was applied in small dots side by side methodically, which at the proper distance fused optically into the required effect. For Seurat it was simply the way of ordering colour and tone; he was equally concerned with order in line, and predominantly with the 'hollowness' of the picture, the proper representation of space. This 'dot' method became known as 'Pointillism' or 'Divisionism'.

In 1886, Seurat met Charles Henry, author of the treatise *Une Esthètique Scientifique*. This work greatly impressed him and he began a closer study of the theories of expression in painting, with concern for the proper correlation of colour and line for indicating mood. This was cut short by his death, but in a letter to his friend Charles Beauberg he left a statement of his theory. It began with the affirmation that 'Art is harmony. Harmony is the analogy of contrary and similar elements of tone, of colour and of line, considered according to their dominants and under the influence of light, in gay, calm or sad combinations.'

Pointillism or Divisionism continued to influence other painters, but each eventually modified its use. Signac and Henri Cross remained true to Seurat's theories and ideas, and with his friend, the critic Fénéon, did much to propagate his influence into the early twentieth century.

J. Rewald. *Georges Seurat*, New York 1946.
H. Dorra and J. Rewald. *Seurat: L'Oeuvre peint, biographie, et catalogue critique*, Paris 1959.
W. I. Homer. *Seurat and the Science of Painting*, Cambridge (Mass.) 1964.
J. Russell. *Seurat*, London and New York 1965.

Seven and Five Society—7 and 5 Abstract Group. When it was founded in 1920 this association of English artists was composed of seven painters and five sculptors, all of whom worked in a figurative, lyrical style. By the rules of the Society these twelve members were required to seek re-election annually, which meant, of course, that there was a built-in bias in favour of change. This greatly facilitated the transition—which took place in the early 1930s and was largely due to Ben Nicholson's influence—from an objective to an abstract association. The most prominent artists in the group in 1934 were Barbara Hepworth, Henry Moore, Ben Nicholson, John Piper and Ivon Hitchens. By then there were very few of the older members left and in the following year, when they were eliminated entirely, the association was renamed the '7 and 5 Abstract Group' (or just the '7 and 5'). The exhibition held by the group in 1935 was the first completely abstract exhibition of art ever put on in England.

Severini, Gino. Italian painter, b. 1883 in Cortona; d. 1966 in Paris. Severini left Tuscany to settle in

Rome in 1899 and in the following year met Umberto Boccioni in G. Balla's *atelier*. It was then that Severini finally decided to become a painter and in 1904–5 he worked as a copyist, reproducing works by Botticelli and Fra Filippo Lippi. In 1906 he went to Paris, where he met Modigliani and Max Jacob, Suzanne Valadon, Utrillo, Dufy and the artists grouped around Picasso and Braque. In 1910 he signed both the *Manifesto of Futurist Painting* and the *Technical Manifesto of Futurist Painting*. In 1911 he introduced his Milanese Futurist friends into the Parisian art world and from 1912 onwards took part in the international Futurist exhibitions and collaborated with A. Soffici and G. Paini in the magazine *Lacerba*. In 1918 he became friendly with J. Gris, who introduced him to Léonce Rosenberg. He also contributed to the *de Stijl* magazine. In 1921 he published his book *Du Cubisme au Classicisme* and in 1930 joined the Salon des Indépendants. In 1935 he won the first prize for painting at the Quadriennale in Rome and in 1950 the first prize for painting at the Biennale in Venice. During his early period Severini was influenced by Divisionism, especially Seurat's original theory, and produced large-format Pointillist works. He then went over to Futurism and, from 1916 onwards, to Cubism. His Cubist works are composed of large areas of vibrant colour —mostly silver-grey—which are clearly distinguished from one another. In 1920–1, following the lead given by Picasso and the *Valori Plastici*, he reverted to a Neo-Classical, objective style. In his harlequin pictures, still lifes and interiors, the pictorial objects, which are fully modelled, are removed from a naturalistic to a metaphysical level of reality by the cool uniform light. The dry, fresco-like technique lends a peculiarly Italian quality to this Manneristic style. In c. 1930, again following Picasso's lead, Severini reverted to a decorative form of Cubism. Later he moved towards the French *Abstraction-Création*. Severini's decorative talent, which is apparent in every phase of his development, his sense of proportion and his rich repertoire of pictorial techniques gave him the necessary confidence to tackle numerous monumental frescoes and mosaics.

Gino Severini. *Du Cubisme au Classicisme*, Paris 1921; *Tutta la vita di un pittore*, Milan 1946.
B. Wall. *Gino Severini*, London 1946.
L. Venturi. *Gino Severini*, Rome 1961.
P. Paccini. *Gino Severini*, Florence 1966.

Shadbolt, Jack. Canadian painter, b. 1909 in Shoeburyness, Essex. After moving to Canada as a child, he lived at Victoria, British Columbia, where he was influenced by Emily Carr and by West Coast Indian art. He worked for a time with F. H. Varley, a member of the Group of Seven, in Vancouver and was later influenced to some extent by Mark Tobey and Morris Graves. In 1937–8 he studied in London with Victor Pasmore and Sir William Coldstream, in Paris with André Lhôte, and in New York. After the Second World War, during which he painted for the army, he developed his characteristic 'animist' style of the forties: details of nature painted in tangled compositions and sombre colours. A more abstract manner accompanied by the use of glowing colours appeared at about the time of a painting trip to the Côte d'Azur in 1956–7 (*Autumn Tokens*, 1958, Vancouver, Coll. Dr. John Parnell). He won a Guggenheim International Awards prize in 1958. In 1961 he painted in Greece; and his style at this point became considerably bolder in design, though still based on nature. He has painted a number of murals, mainly in British Columbia. Until 1966 he was head of the painting section of the Vancouver School of Art.

Jack Shadbolt. *In Search of Form*, Toronto 1968.

Shahn, Ben. American painter, b. 1898 in Lithuania; d. 1969. A resident of the United States since 1906, he was apprenticed to a lithographer for four years (1913–17), where he learned some of the rudiments of the graphic arts. Between 1919 and 1922 he attended New York University and the City College of New York, which he left in the latter year to study at the National Academy of Design. In 1925 and 1927 he travelled in Europe and North Africa, the latter serving as subject matter for many of the works exhibited in his first one-man show at the Downtown Gallery in 1930. In the following two years he produced some of his best-known works, a series of twenty-three gouaches and two mural panels illustrating the Sacco-Vanzetti trials (*Bartolomeo Vanzetti and Nicola Sacco*, 1931–2, gouache, New York, Museum of Modern Art). From this point on his subjects take on a decided penchant for scenes from American life and social protest. This is illustrated by his production of the next three years—fifteen gouaches and tempera panels depicting the case of Tom Mooney (1932–3) and eight temperas concerning prohibition for a mural to decorate the Central Park Casino, done under the auspices of the New York City Public Works of Art Project. For the next ten years he was producing various mural projects, especially for public buildings (fresco mural in the Social Security Building, Washington, D.C., 1940–2). His preparation for work in this field was provided by his assistance on Diego Rivera's ill-fated fresco for the RCA Building, New York: *Man at the Crossroads*. In the 1940s his interest shifted to poster illustration as exemplified in his 1946 *Hunger* (US Department of State). In addition to various forms of painting he has been actively interested in book illustration for many years.

James T. Soby. *Ben Shahn, His Graphic Art*, New York 1957; *Ben Shahn: Paintings*, New York 1963.
Ben Shahn, *The Shape of Content*, Cambridge (Mass.) 1957; *The Biography of a Painting*, New York 1966.

Shannon, Charles. British painter, b. 1863 in Warrington, Lancs; d. 1937 at Kew, Surrey. He went to the Lambeth School of Art in 1882 and there met Charles Ricketts, with whom he became close friends. His first one-man exhibition was at the Leicester Galleries in 1907. He was a member of the New English Art Club and the International Society.

Shaped canvases. The development of the shaped, or three-dimensionally formed, canvas over hidden supports was largely a development of the 1960s. One early precursor was Lee Bontecou, who began making shaped canvases from weathered tarpaulin and wires in 1959, but who can also be linked with the earlier tradition of assemblage from discarded materials; another was Frank Stella, who in the early 1960s began cutting out portions of a flat canvas or creating non-rectilinear forms, paralleled by painted bands on the canvas, that produced an illusionistic three-dimensionality. Stella's intent is more closely related to that of the later artists of the shaped canvas, whose work emphasizes formal qualities, the concept of the canvas as an independent three-dimensional object rather than a surface for illusionistic representation, and the recently increasing lack of clear distinction between painting and sculpture. The major English artist of the shaped canvas is Richard Smith; additional American artists include Sven Lukin, Charles Hinman and Neil Williams.

Lawrence Alloway. Catalogue, *The Shaped Canvas*, Solomon R. Guggenheim Museum, New York 1964.

Sharrer, Honoré Desmond. American painter, b. 1920. The daughter of an army officer, she attended schools in various parts of the United States, Europe and the Far East. She received some basic artistic guidance from her artist mother and attended the Yale School of Fine Arts for one year (1939–40). She then went to California, where she was associated with the WPA Federal Art Project. While affiliated with this agency she unsuccessfully entered several mural competitions. Her work falls into the general trend of Social Realism, but contains no propagandistic overtones. Best known for the polyptych *A Tribute to the American People* (1946–51, New York, Knoedler Galleries), which includes scenes of a county fair, a parlour, a farm and a school with an industrial scene as the central panel, the work is executed with the minute preciseness and naïveté of a folk artist. One of her works, *Workers and Paintings* (1943), is owned by the Museum of Modern Art, New York.

Seckler, Dorothy. 'Sharrer Paints a Picture', *Art News* 50, April 1951.

Sheeler, Charles R., Jr. American painter and photographer, b. 1883 in Philadelphia, Pennsylvania; d. 1965. His first artistic training at the School of Industrial Art, Philadelphia (1900–3), was primarily in the field of applied design. The next three years were devoted to painting under the tutelage of William M. Chase at the Pennsylvania Academy of Fine Arts. At this time he emulated Chase's painterly manner. During the time he was sharing a studio with Morton Schamberg (1907–9), he travelled to Italy, London and Paris, where he was introduced to analytical Cubism and the work of Cézanne, Matisse, Picasso and Braque. His return to the United States heralded a major shift in style—such a diversion from his previous mode that his former dealer in Philadelphia was no longer willing to show his work. *The Mandarin* (1912, Utica, N.Y., Munson-Williams-Proctor Institute), with its planes, its geometric cast and its use of strong shadows, is typical of his style in these years and especially reflects the influence of Cézanne, an influence which was reinforced by the Armory Show (1913), where Sheeler exhibited six paintings. He took up photography in 1912, but used this merely as a means of income. By 1917 both he and Schamberg were using photography for expressive ends. When Schamberg died (October 1918) Sheeler moved to New York and was practising a style completely free of the Chase influence, as can be seen in his basically architectural painting of 1920, *Church Street El* (Philadelphia, Coll. Mrs. Earle Horter), with its dominant simple geometric forms stressing the structural essentials. In 1923 he became a photographer for Condé Nast's *Vogue* and *Vanity Fair* magazines. It was also in the early 1920s that Sheeler first published art criticism and began showing in a great number of exhibitions, in addition to those at the De Zayas Gallery, where he was a staff member. His thirty-two photographs of the Ford Motor Company's River Rouge Plant (1927) brought him international acclaim as a photographer and fostered his preoccupation with the machine. *Upper Deck* (1929, Cambridge, Mass., Fogg Art Museum) displays this new concern. The first oil painting he produced in two years, it reveals a new working method of gradually building up a mental image rather than executing a loosely woven composition done in three or four sittings without preliminary planning, as was true of his previous oil painting of 1927, *Spring Interior* (Leominster, Mass., Lane Coll.). In the 1930s his interest in photography dissipated, as did his previous concern for cityscapes. He now concentrated on interiors and farm buildings. In the 1940s the theme of rural architecture continued, as a fascination with industrial architecture and machinery increased (*Water*, 1945, New York Metropolitan Museum of Art). In the last decade of his production, cityscapes again came to the fore, as revealed in his studies of Rockefeller Center and the United Nations complex. *New York No. 2* (1951, Utica, N.Y., Munson-Williams-Proctor Institute) is typical of the period and also displays his use of superimposed images which he often worked out through a technique of tempera on Plexiglass. Known as a Precisionist along with Stuart Davis, Charles Demuth, Georgia O'Keeffe and others, Sheeler reveals in his work a pristine, static, unpopulated approach to the American environment, executed in styles ranging from photographic Realism to abstraction. The artist suffered a stroke in October 1959 and was from then on unable to paint or use a camera.

Catalogue, *Charles Sheeler*, Smithsonian Institution, Washington (D.C.) 1968.

Shinn, Everett. American painter, b. 1876 in Woodstown, New Jersey; d. 1953 in New York City. After studying at the Pennsylvania Academy of Fine Arts he joined the staff of the *Philadelphia Press*. In 1896 he moved to New York City where he worked for the *New York World*, *New York Herald* and *New York Journal* as well as doing illustrations for *Harper's Magazine, Harper's Bazaar, Puck, La France, Critic, Arts and Decoration, Depictor* and *Everybody's Magazine*. He was later art editor of *Ainslee's Magazine* and art director of *Cosmopolitan Studios*. The success of his first one-man show in 1902 led to a commission for ceiling and panel decorations in the home of playwright Clyde Fitch as well as portrait commissions, including Mark Twain and Ethel Barrymore. In 1908 he exhibited as a member of The Eight at the Macbeth Gallery. One of the paintings included in that show was *London Hippodrome* (Chicago, Art Institute) which, though not colouristically, recalls works of the French Impressionists in its fresh, spirited handling of pigment and in its subject, representing a slice of life of a contemporary scene. His 1911 decorations for the Trenton (N.J.) City Hall display the first use of murals representing a contemporary subject in a Realist style. This idiom, however, only came into the mainstream of American painting in the 1930s. In addition to the previously mentioned designs, he decorated the interior of the Belasco Theatre, New York, in a rather banal version of French Rococo. Shinn also did illustrations for *The Christmas Carol, Rip Van Winkle, The Sermon on the Mount* and numerous children's books.

N. Kent. 'The Versatile Art of Everett Shinn', *American Artist* IX, October 1945.

Shinohara, Ushio. Japanese painter, b. 1933 in Tokyo. He attended the Tokyo University of Arts and was a founding member of the Neo-Dada Organizer group, where he demonstrated an anti-artistic manifestation. In 1964 he advocated 'Imitation Art' that deliberately abandoned creation and plagiarized works, as for example of Jasper Johns and Robert Rauschenberg. Then, affected by Pop Art, he executed an *Oiran* (courtesan of Edo period) series according to the icons of Ukiyo-e. He lives in New York.

Sibellino, Antonio Silvestre. Argentinian sculptor, b. 1891 in Buenos Aires; d. 1960 in Buenos Aires. Sibellino studied at the academies in Buenos Aires, Turin and Paris. In 1924 he exhibited his *Girl Walking Down Florida Street* and became the acknowledged leader of the sculptural *avant-garde* in Argentina. Two years later he created the first abstract relief in Argentinian sculpture, which he called *Sunset*. The Spanish Civil War and the Second World War inspired a number of dramatic works which, although abstract, are charged with humanitarian feeling. In 1942 Sibellino won the Argentinian national prize for sculpture, and in 1952 he represented Argentina at the Venice Biennale.

J. M. Taverna Irigoyen. *Escultura argentina de este siglo*, Santa Fé (Argentina) 1967.

Sickert, Walter Richard. British painter, b. 1860 in Munich; d. 1942 in Bath. Sickert was of Danish parentage. For a brief time he was an actor in minor roles. He studied at the Slade under Legros before apprenticing himself to Whistler, from whom he gained experience in etching. Sickert was later to move away from the Whistlerian anti-literary theory of drawing.

He met Degas in 1883. At a time when English painting had become insular, this link is important. Sickert's style shows the continuing influence of Degas's themes, artificial light, *contrejour* effects and an attitude to colour summed up by Degas's observation that: 'The art of painting is so to surround a patch of, say, Venetian red, that it appears . . . vermilion.'

In 1888 Sickert joined the New English Art Club, which was subsequently to show Degas, Monet and Morisot in London. Sickert exhibited with this group until 1914. From the 1890s he began to spend much of his time in Dieppe. He also made prolonged visits to Venice. From both there are numerous architectural themes, some figure compositions and portraits. In England the Camden Town pictures date from c. 1907. In these Sickert expresses uniquely well the *moeurs* of the unfashionable suburb dweller, the *ennui*, the shabby world of Mornington Crescent and Granby Street.

In 1911 Sickert was a founder of the Camden Town Group (renamed the London Group in 1913). After the war and a further three years in Dieppe, when he executed the *Baccarat* pictures, Sickert settled in England. The *Echoes*, dating from c. 1927, were based on Victorian illustrations ('It's such a good arrangement, Cruikshank and Gilbert do all the work and I get all the money,' said Sickert). Other late works drawn direct from press photographs are now regarded as some of the most interesting and original in Sickert's entire oeuvre.

Sickert's writings are published as *A Free House!*

Unstructured, fluent and witty, they provide the best insights for his art and ideas. A trenchant if biased critic, Sickert's own enthusiasms are reflected in the advice he gave his students—to study Rowlandson and Cruikshank, Keene, Ingres, Millet and Degas. But Sickert was unable to see the stature of many contemporaries. Cézanne he felt to be overrated, and when Roger Fry presented two exhibitions of Post-Impressionism in London (1910 and 1912) Sickert dismissed Monet's *Haystacks* and other series, so seminal for twentieth-century art at this time, as banal.

In Sickert's case this hardening of the aesthetic arteries was both strength and weakness, for simultaneously he was producing some of his most memorable paintings. The music halls, now an indelibly Sickertian memory, still preoccupied him when European mainstream art was concerned with Cubism.

Robert Emmons. *The Life of Walter Sickert*, London 1941.
W. Sickert. *A Free House!* (ed. Osbert Sitwell), London 1947.
L. Browse. *Sickert*, London 1960.
Marjorie Lilly. *Sickert*, London 1971.

Signac, Paul. French painter, b. 1863 in Paris; d. 1935 in Paris. After starting to study architecture at the Collège Rollin Signac decided to become a painter and enrolled at the Atelier Libre de Bin in 1883. He then met Guillaumin and, after being introduced by him to the Impressionists, began to copy works by Degas and Manet. But it was not until he met Seurat at the exhibition staged by the Salon des Artistes Indépendants—where two of his own canvases were on show—that he really began to understand the Neo-Impressionist movement, whose principal theorist he himself was shortly to become. In 1886 he painted his first Divisionist picture and in 1896 his first watercolours. Later, from 1910 onwards, he was to paint a large number of watercolours. Meanwhile, in 1899, he wrote a book entitled *De Delacroix au Néo-Impressionnisme*, in which he expounded the Neo-Impressionist theory. From 1882 onwards Signac had spent as much time as he could in various ports on the Mediterranean and French Atlantic coasts: Collioure, Marseilles, Venice, La Rochelle and Constantinople. In 1886 he exhibited at the eighth Impressionist exhibition. In 1888 he joined the *Salon des XX* in Antwerp. From 1905 until his death he was president of the Société des Artistes Indépendants.

After a brief Impressionist phase Signac, who was impressed by the work of his friend Seurat, evolved the theoretical premises of Neo-Impressionism, which were based on the concept of optical mixtures (Divisionism) and from which Pointillism subsequently emerged. According to Seurat Divisionism enabled the artist to exploit all the benefits of luminosity, colour and harmony: by the optical mixture of pure pigments; by the separation of different elements; by the balancing of those elements and their proportions; by the selection of a type of brushwork proportionate in size to the size of the picture.

Of all Seurat's disciples Signac was the one who adhered most rigorously to the Neo-Impressionist system following the master's untimely death. The object of the system was to obtain brighter and clearer secondary colours by making a series of small, regular blobs of two primaries. When viewed from a certain distance these blobs merged optically, thus forming an 'optical' or 'additive' mixture and producing a much cleaner colour than could be obtained by mixing the actual pigments.

Watercolours form an important part of Signac's oeuvre. The greater freedom which this medium affords was particularly beneficial in his case and his watercolours are generally less encumbered by demands of theory and reveal more fluid handling than the majority of his paintings. The later paintings are an exception. Here too—due in no small measure to the influence exerted by his watercolour technique—Signac relaxed his insistence on the strict application of Divisionist theory. None the less, Signac always was and always remained a convinced Neo-Impressionist. As a result his colours produced a marked ornamental effect which, amongst other things, was well suited to the requirements of the formal two-dimensional art to which he subscribed.

Lucie Coustourier. *Paul Signac*, Paris 1922.
George Besson. *Paul Signac*, Paris 1934.
M.-T. Lemoyne de Forges. Catalogue, *Signac*, Louvre, Paris 1963.

Signori, Carlo. Italian sculptor, b. 1906 in Milan. He studied in Paris with André Lhôte (painting) and Charles Malfray (sculpture), then began to produce somewhat Expressionist work. He won a competition for a monument to the Rosselli brothers in 1948, and went to Carrara to work on it, returning there over and over again. His light, smooth shapes have a certain affinity with Brancusi's work.

Silva, Maria Vieira da—*see* **Vieira da Silva,** Maria

Simonsson, Birger. Swedish painter, b. 1883; d. 1938. Simonsson studied from 1906 to 1913 in Paris, where he became a founder member of the *De unga* (The Young) group. From 1916 to 1919 he taught at Valand's School of Painting in Gothenburg, and from 1931 onwards at the College of Art in Stockholm. During his early period Simonsson was influenced by Cézanne, Bonnard and Hendrik Sørensen, and developed an impressionistic style of painting, producing landscapes and portraits of women and children, which are remarkable for their personal warmth and harmony. In his early works Simonsson used a combination of warm and cool colours, but later in his career bright yellows tended to predominate. Simonsson was also a gifted organizer and propagandist, and it was thanks to him and Gösta Sandels that modern painting was able to establish itself in the cities of western Sweden.

S. Ullman. *Birger Simonsson*, Stockholm 1933.

Singier, Gustave. Belgian-French painter, b. 1909 in Warneton. In 1919 Singier moved to Paris, where he served an apprenticeship as a decorative painter from 1933 to 1936. He then earned his living as a decorator, and painted in his spare time from nature and in the Louvre. He first exhibited with the Indépendants, then in the Salon d'Automne (1937 to 1949) and the Salon des Tuileries, of which he was a founder member (from 1943). In 1941 he joined with Bazaine, Estève, Lapicque, Le Moal and Manessier in founding the *Peintres de la Tradition Française* association. He is now living in Paris.

After an early period, in which he was influenced by the Cubist conception of pictorial space, the colouring of the Fauves and the structural deformation of the Expressionists, Singier developed an abstract style based on a rigidly Constructive type of composition and the use of bright colours.

Georges Charbonnier. *Singier*, Paris 1957.

Sintenis, Renée (Renée Weiss). German sculptress, b. 1888 in Glatz, Silesia; d. 1965 in Berlin. After attending the Stuttgart Academy Sintenis studied at the School of Arts and Crafts in Berlin from 1908 to 1911. Subsequently she was promoted by Rilke and her work quickly gained currency. She specialized in small sculptures, which she executed in a lively Impressionist style, working entirely from her imagination. Her favourite subjects were children, animals and ethereal young girls. She was particularly attracted by the ungainly movements and awkward stances of baby foals, fawns, etc. In the course of her career Sintenis also produced many portraits and illustrations. Although she taught at the Berlin Academy from 1947 to 1955 her works— like those of Kolbe, who closely resembled her— were forgotten by the art world following the Second World War.

H. Kiel. *Renée Sintenis*, Berlin 1956.

Siqueiros, David Alfaro. Mexican painter, b. 1896 in Chihuahua. Apart from Rivera and Orozco Siqueiros is the best-known representative of the new Social Realist movement in Mexico. From 1911 onwards he studied at the Academy of San Carlo, the Open Air School in Santa Anita and the Mexican Academy, where he made the acquaintance of Orozco. When the revolution broke out in 1914 Siqueiros joined the army and was promoted to the general staff. In 1919 he was appointed military attaché to the Mexican Embassy in Madrid and, whilst there, toured Europe and became friendly with Rivera. After returning to Mexico in 1922 he collaborated with Rivera on the first revolutionary murals (in the National Preparatory School). Since then Siqueiros has worked both as a politician and as an artist, with the exception of the five-year period from 1925 to 1930, when he gave up painting to help the workers in their struggle. Eventually he was forced to flee the country and went to the United States. Later he made several visits to South America, where he painted and gave lectures on art. In 1937 he went to Spain to fight on the Republican side in the civil war, returning to the United States in 1939. In 1942 he was painting in Chile and later in Cuba. In 1960 he was arrested for his political activities and sentenced to four years in prison, where he produced a number of landscapes and woodcuts.

By incorporating elements of folklore and Surrealism into his Social Realism Siqueiros was able to create a symbolic style of painting that is both highly expressive and very simple. Apart from his murals, which are to be found in various public buildings in Mexico, Cuba and Chile and which are works of social criticism, Siqueiros has produced still lifes, landscapes, self-portraits and historical portraits. He was also a pioneer in the technical sphere in so far as he drew his inspiration from photographs, used synthetic paints and employed an aerograph instead of a brush.

Alma M. Reed. 'David Alfaro Siqueiros', *The Mexican Muralists*, New York 1960.
R. Tibel. *David Alfaro Siqueiros*, Buenos Aires 1966.

Sironi, Mario. Italian painter, b. 1885 in Sassari, Sardinia; d. 1961 in Milan. After enrolling as a student of mathematics at the Technical College in Rome Sironi decided to become a painter and went to work in Balla's *atelier*, where he met Boccioni and Severini. In 1914 he accompanied Boccioni on a visit to Germany and France and, after his return to Milan, joined the Futurist circle centred on Marinetti. In August 1914, like his Futurist friends, he volunteered for military service. From 1915 to 1917 he contributed to the magazine *Gli Avennimenti* and in 1918 returned to Milan. In 1926 he staged the first and in 1929 the second *Novecento* exhibition. Between 1936 and 1940 he created his great wall paintings and mosaics.

Although Sironi was certainly influenced by the Futurists during his early period, he did not fully embrace their Neo-Impressionist style of painting, nor did he try to exploit the dynamic and mechanical elements of Futurist art after the manner of Boccioni. Sironi was more interested in the portrayal of modern life in metaphysical terms. Using a Cubist technique and rich, heavy colours he analysed the sad beauty of the industrial townscape. Not surprisingly, he responded readily to the *Pittura Metafisica*, depicting the robot character and the lifelessness of the modern industrial age in splendid visionary works. Often his vision was greater than his art, for many of these paintings remained unfinished. His great figurative compositions of 1919 were conceived in the Neo-Classical style of the *Novecento*: the pictorial objects, enclosed by soft, dark contours, stand out from the background as fully modelled forms. In his 'pictorial diagrams' Sironi combined various separate themes, linking them together by purely formal devices. These works continue the ancient tradition of Italian wall painting.

A. Pica. *Mario Sironi, Painter*, Milan 1955.
M. Valsecchi. *Mario Sironi*, Rome 1962.
Catalogue, *Mario Sironi Retrospective Exhibition*, Brescia 1963.

Sitter, Inger. Norwegian painter, b. 1929. Sitter studied under André Lhôte and in Hayter's Atelier 17. She is an abstract artist and produces pictures composed of interrelating areas of subdued colour which are remarkable for their delicate brushwork. In her works spontaneity and calculation are present in equal measure.

Situation Group. *Situation* was the title of an exhibition held in the RBA Galleries, London, in September 1960, and the term has been extended to describe the group of artists exhibiting. The exhibition was organized by the artists themselves, stimulated originally by the practical difficulty they were finding in exhibiting large pictures. Eighteen artists participated: Robyn Denny, Harold and Bernard Cohen, Peter Stroud, John Plumb, Gordon House, John Hoyland, William Turnbull, Peter Coviello, Marc Vaux, Gillian Ayres, Henry Mundy, Anthony Green, Richard Smith, Peter Hobbs, John Epstein, Robert Law and Brian Young. The conditions by which a picture was eligible were that it should be wholly abstract and at least thirty feet square in size. Scale and abstraction were the features of British painting responding to the influence of American painting of the fifties, and so effectively these conditions defined a group of painters with common aims, if they lacked a common style. The title *Situation* expresses the idea that with this large-scale painting where the canvas fills the whole of his field of vision the spectator is directly involved in the event that the canvas portrays—in short, he is drawn by the painting into a situation.

Catalogues, *Situation*, RBA Galleries, London 1960; *New Situation*, Marlborough Fine Art Ltd., London 1961; Arts Council, London 1962.

Sköld, Otte. Swedish painter, graphic artist, scenic artist and museum director, b. 1894; d. 1958. From 1914 to 1918 Sköld was in Copenhagen, where he was able to acquaint himself with recent developments in European art. During this period he experimented with Futurist and Cubist techniques, painting *motifs* taken from vaudeville shows, military parades and similar public displays in matt colours, and producing sophisticated woodcuts, both monochrome and coloured. From 1919 to 1928 he lived in Paris and visited Italy, Spain and North Africa. In c. 1920 he passed through a brief primitive phase before embracing the *Neue Sachlichkeit* and becoming the leading exponent of this movement in Sweden. The works of this period include town views with picturesque gables observed through open windows, still lifes executed with extremely delicate brushwork to reproduce the highly glazed texture used by the old masters, and a group of imaginative genre scenes depicting the atmosphere of bars and dance halls. Sköld also executed numerous commissions for decorative works including *Folkvisan* (*Folksong*, 1937), a fresco for the concert hall in Gothenburg; mosaics for the Chapel of Rest at Skogskyrkogården in Stockholm (1938) and the Crematorium in Malmö (1943); and *Vindens saga* (*The Tale of the Wind*), a painting for the Västertorp School in Stockholm (1951). In addition, Sköld designed stained-glass windows and stage sets, and as a teacher and propagandist did much to improve working conditions for his fellow artists. He held a professorial post at the College of Art in Stockholm from 1932 to 1942, was Director of the College from 1941 to 1950, and Director of the National Museum in Stockholm from 1950 to 1958. In this last capacity he watched over and promoted the project for a Modern Museum of Art, which he opened in 1958, just before he died.

G. Paulsson. *Otte Sköld*, Stockholm 1935.
U. Hård af Segerstad. *Otte Sköld*, Stockholm 1945.
F. Holmér (ed.). *Otte Sköld*, 1957.

Skúlason, Thorvaldur. Icelandic painter, b. 1906 in Bordeyri. Skúlason was one of the pioneers of abstract art in Iceland. After studying at the School of Art in Oslo he visited Paris from 1931 to 1933 and again from 1938 to 1940.

With their dark colouring and modelled forms Skúlason's early figurative compositions and still lifes reveal the influence of his teacher Gromaire. But in c. 1945 Skúlason evolved a type of abstract painting with highly simplified, flat shapes and bright colours.

Slevogt, Max. German painter and graphic artist, b. 1868 in Landshut; d. 1932 in Neukastel. Slevogt studied at the Academy of Fine Arts in Munich from 1885 to 1889. Like many of his contemporaries, he spent a term at the Académie Julian in Paris (1889). Then, in 1890, he made a working visit to Italy. Whilst the graphic work which Slevogt produced for *Jugend* amd *Simplicissimus* from 1896 onwards remained essentially traditional, his pictures revealed the growing influence of the new school of *plein-air* painting and also reflected the impact of the Rembrandt exhibition which he had seen in Amsterdam in 1898. Slevogt's Impressionist technique, with which he sought to capture the magic of the passing moment, is clearly demonstrated both by his paintings of the singer d'Andrade (whom he first met in 1902) and by the Egyptian landscapes which he painted in 1913–14. In 1901 Slevogt had settled in Berlin, where he was given a professorial post later the same year. In 1915 he was made a member of the Academy of Fine Arts in Dresden and from 1917 onwards was in charge of a 'Masters' Atelier' at the Academy of Fine Arts in Berlin. The graphic works which Slevogt produced during this period were extremely significant. The expressiveness of his etchings and lithographs was quite remarkable and their spontaneity something entirely novel. Many of these have become famous in the form of illustrations for books such as *Ali Baba and the Forty Thieves* (1903), *The Iliad* (1907), *Lederstrumpf* (1909), *Benvenuto Cellini* (1913), *Achilles* (1916) and *Die Insel Wak-Wak* (1922). Slevogt also created splendid illustrations in the margin of a printed score of Mozart's *Die Zauberflöte* (1920). Slevogt was an extremely versatile artist. Quite apart from his paintings and graphic works he also executed murals and designs for stage sets, which lent themselves particularly well to his highly imaginative narrative style. Together with Liebermann and Corinth, he was one of the foremost representatives of German Impressionism. After an early period, in which he painted naturalistic works after the manner of Leibl and Trübner, Slevogt evolved an Impressionistic *plein-air* style of painting, using light, rapid brushwork (dabbing rather than brushing the paint on to the canvas so as to produce the effect of a spontaneous sketch) and bright clear colours which create a flickering atmosphere.

J. Sievers and E. Waldmann. *Max Slevogt: das druckgraphische Werk 1890–1914*, Heidelberg 1962.
H. Imiela. *Max Slevogt*, Karlsruhe 1968.

Sloan, John. American painter, b. 1871 in Loch Haven, Pennsylvania; d. 1951 in Hanover, New Hampshire. He studied at the Spring Garden Institute in Philadelphia and the Pennsylvania Academy of Fine Arts under Thomas Anshutz in the 1890s. He was first in commercial art and then became an artist for the *Philadelphia Inquirer* (1892–5) and the *Philadelphia Press* (1895–1903). He began to paint seriously in 1897 at the encouragement of Robert Henri, the leader of a group of young Philadelphia Realists who were revolting against academic idealism. Sloan later moved to New York where he supported himself doing magazine illustration. In 1908 he organized a loosely constructed group called The Eight (Everett Shinn, William Glackens, George Luks, Arthur B. Davies, Ernest Lawson, Maurice Prendergast, Robert Henri and Sloan) who exhibited together in that year. His early works, such as *The Rathskeller* (1901, Cleveland, Museum of Art), show the influence of Henri in the quick, facile, painterly approach, suppression of detail and interest in scenes depicting daily life. This style and content continued for many years with little or no significant change. After The Eight exhibited together he organized the Exhibition of Independent Artists (1910) and was the President of the Society of Independent Artists from 1918 to 1944. Sloan had his first one-man show in 1916 at the Whitney Studio Club, New York. In the 1930s his style changed radically from the quick, impetuous stroke and interest in flickering light of his genre scenes (*Hairdresser's Window*, 1907, Hartford, Conn., Wadsworth Atheneum) to a preoccupation with the female nude, in which the rather sculptural forms are handled in a complex technique of underpainting, glazing and linework (*Nude with Nine Apples*, 1937, New York, Whitney Museum of American Art). Sloan taught for many years at the Art Students' League as well as at the George Luks School and the Archipenko School of Art. Based on his teaching experience, he wrote *The Gist of Art* (New York, 1939) with Helen Farr, who was to become his second wife in 1944. Sloan also had publishing experience when he served as art editor of the magazine *The Masses*.

Lloyd Goodrich and Rosalind Irvine. *John Sloan (1871–1951)*, Whitney Museum of American Art, New York 1952.
Van Wyck Brooks. *John Sloan, A Painter's Life*, New York 1955.
Bruce St. John (ed.). *John Sloan's New York Scene*, New York 1965.

Sluyters, Jan (Johannes Carolus Bernardus). Dutch painter, b. 1881 in 's Hertogenbosch; d. 1957 in Amsterdam. After attending the School of Drawing in 's Hertogenbosch Sluyters studied at the Teachers' Training College (1897–1900) and the Academy of Art (1901–4) in Amsterdam. In 1904 he won the Prix de Rome and between 1904 and 1906 visited Italy, Spain, Portugal and Paris. From 1906 to 1916 he worked in Amsterdam, Laren and Staphorst. From 1916 onwards he worked primarily in Amsterdam.

After experimenting in a variety of different styles —ranging from *art nouveau* to Fauvism and from van Gogh to the Cubists—Sluyters evolved his own form of Expressionism, which he called 'Colourism'. He was one of the best-known Dutch painters of the interwar period and revealed a preference for portraits, paintings of children and female nudes.

J. N. van Wessem. *Jan Sluyters*, Amsterdam 1966.

Smet, Gustave de. Belgian painter, b. 1877 in Ghent; d. 1943 in Deurle. After serving an apprenticeship as a paint-hand with his father and studying at the Academy in Ghent Smet went to live in Laethem-St-Martin in 1901. There, together with van den Berghe, Servaes, Permeke and his brother Léon, he founded the Second Laethem Group, from which the Flemish Expressionists later emerged. During the First World War he lived in Holland with Frits van den Berghe. Whilst there he met Le Fauconnier, Sluyters and Toorop and was introduced to the work of the German Expressionists. In 1920 he became a founder member of the *Sélection* association, which actually triggered off the Expressionist movement in Belgium. Other groups to which he belonged include: *Les Neuf, L'Art contemporain, L'Art vivant* and *Compagnons de l'Art*. In 1927 he settled in Deurle on the Scheldt, where he died after a long illness.

Smet was one of the leading representatives of Flemish Expressionism. Like Permeke, he exercised a crucial influence on the development of Belgian art in the interwar years. After an early Impressionist period he came under the influence of Le Fauconnier and the German Expressionists, especially Campendonk and Marc, and developed his own powerful brand of Expressionism, which was based on a scale of colours running from ochre through brown to black and in which a rational, Cubist element is discernible in the strictly schematic treatment of form. There is also a trace of Léger's Realism in his peasant portraits. Later the formal precision of Smet's composition was somewhat relaxed. His last landscapes, which are executed in dark colours applied by means of a *pastosa* technique, have a clearly defined and perfectly simple linear structure.

P. G. van Hecke. *Gustave de Smet: sa vie et son oeuvre*, Brussels and Paris 1945.

Catalogue, *Gustave de Smet Retrospective Exhibition*, Koninklijk Museum, Antwerp 1961.

Smith, David. American sculptor, b. 1906 in Decatur, Indiana; d. 1965 near Bennington, Vermont. He first studied art in 1924 at Athens, Ohio, University. More beneficial to him than his brief college career, however, was the experience that he gained while working at the Studebaker plant in South Bend, Indiana, during the summer of 1925. It was there that he first acquired the skill in metal working that was to give him his absolute mastery of the medium in later years.

In 1926, while working for a finance company in New York, Smith enrolled at the Art Students' League, where he studied painting first under Richard Lahey (b. 1893), and in 1927 under John Sloan and later Jan Matulka (b. 1890). Matulka introduced Smith to the modern European painters, particularly the Cubists, and thus had an important influence on the development of his career. Smith's enthusiasm for the contemporary European masters led him to the discovery of certain iron sculptures by Pablo Picasso reproduced in a French art publication, and in 1933 to the construction of his own steel sculpture. Smith wrote that Picasso's sculptural work was 'a liberating factor', which permitted him to

make use of a skill he had originally gained simply for the purpose of supporting himself while pursuing the study of painting.

Smith's first steel constructions were fashioned from parts of agricultural machinery and 'found objects'. In 1938 he had his first one-man show in New York. Two years later he exhibited his series of fifteen reliefs entitled *Medals of Dishonor*, in which he used Picassoesque elements drawn from such works as *Guernica* to express not only his dismay at the war raging in Europe, but also his concern for the violence, hate and greed present in the United States. The medal depicting *Private Law and Order Leagues*, for example, has a relevance that clearly transcends the particular time and events for which it was created. Indeed, there is a universality about much of Smith's work, for his themes are truly universal. His recurring *motifs* of human violence and greed are expressed metaphorically in the gaunt, skeletal and tortured configurations of such works as *Pillar of Sunday* (1945), the *Royal Bird* (1947–8, Minneapolis, Walker Art Center) and *Australia* (1951, New York, Coll. William S. Rubin).

In the late 1940s and early 1950s, some of Smith's sculpture takes the form of open and linear 'drawing' in metal, a kind of Constructivist calligraphy that is two-dimensional in its effect (*Star Cage*, 1950, Minneapolis, University of Minnesota Gallery).

During the late 1950s and 1960s, until his death, Smith concentrated upon simpler, less troubled and more monumental imagery. He filled the grounds of his Bolton Landing farm, purchased in the 1930s, with large, monolithic works of sculpture, such as the *Tank Totems*, *Sentinels* and *Cubis*. The *Cubi* series is especially noteworthy, and consists of great block-like, polished and abraded or 'textured' shapes made of stainless steel. These last works are apt expressions of Smith's deep affection for the structure and material of machines. Furthermore, they evoke 'the great quiet of stopped machines', which Smith found more fascinating and more beautiful than all the remnants of bygone ages in the museums or ancient cities of Europe.

H. Arnason. *History of Modern Art*, New York 1968.

David Smith by David Smith, ed. Cleve Gray. New York 1968.

Hilton Kramer. 'David Smith', *New York Times Magazine*, 16 February 1969; 'The Poetic Vein of David Smith', *New York Times* review, 9 June 1968.

Smith, Jack. British painter, b. 1928 in Sheffield. Smith attended Sheffield College of Art (1944–6), St. Martin's School (1948–50) and the Royal College of Art (1950–3). In the fifties his name was associated with Bratby's in the so-called 'Neo-Realist' style (*Child Walking*). His subject matter was, however, comparatively unimportant and his interest was already in more formal problems. This led in the later fifties to a series of still lifes in which the pattern of light made by the objects in the picture was elaborated into increasingly abstract compositions in which, in 1959, heavy impasto became actual relief. In these works the influence of the *École de Paris* is very apparent. Recently he has turned to more hard-edged abstraction, using overall patterns of clear drawn symbol shapes against plain grounds, the variation of the shapes and their relation to each other, the ground, and the margins of the canvas forming a kind of visual narrative, not unlike the work of Harold Cohen.

Smith, Kimber. American painter, b. 1922 in Boston, Massachusetts. He moved to New York City in 1939 and from 1942 to 1945 served in the United States Marines. After the war he returned to New York, where he studied at the Art Students' League and worked as a typographer. He moved to Paris in 1954 and received his first one-man show at Klipstein and Kornfeld, Berne, Switzerland, in 1959. Strongly influenced by the Abstract Expressionists, his canvases exhibit bold slashing strokes which execute simple patterns and forms in broad, flat, bright areas of colour with stark contrasts of light and dark areas and startling juxtapositions of hue (*Le Jardin de Joan*, 1961, Paris, Galerie Lawrence). He was given his first one-man show in the United States at the Peridot Gallery, New York, in 1960. Smith currently teaches at the Dayton Art Institute.

Catalogue, *Kimber Smith*, Galerie Lawrence, Paris 1962.

Smith, Sir Matthew. British painter, b. 1879 in Halifax, Yorks; d. 1959. He worked first in his father's business, and then eventually was allowed to study design at Manchester from 1900 to 1904, his father meanwhile strongly resisting his wish to become a painter. In 1905, however, he went to the Slade, where he remained until 1907. He then travelled to France on his doctor's advice, though his father forbade him to go to Paris. He visited Pont-Aven and Étaples and finally went to Paris in 1910. There he attended Matisse's painting school briefly, seeing Matisse himself only three times, though he remembered the experience vividly. In 1912 he moved to London, settling in 1913 in Fitzroy Street where he was friendly with Sickert and Epstein. He first exhibited in London only in 1916, and in the same year his two *Fitzroy Street Nudes*, in which the influence of Matisse was very clear, were rejected by the London Group. These were his first important paintings. The first pictures in which he really found his own style, however, were perhaps the series of Cornish landscapes painted in 1920. It was in the next year at the age of 42 that he sold his first picture. He held his first one-man show in 1926. It was a success, and thereafter his reputation was assured. In the twenties and thirties he worked a great deal in France, in Paris

and in the south, especially Aix, and he was in France when the Second World War broke out.

Smith's style was formed by 1920. It is distinguished by its explosive colour. This stems from his experience of Gauguin and Matisse, but in his work colour is sometimes used with a reckless violence that reveals an Expressionist purpose foreign to either of those artists. This is sometimes apparent in the handling and drawing as well, but in the end his sense of discipline and the unity of a painting prevail, creating at times a powerful tension in his work, though he was capable also of a more lyrical mood. He was perhaps the only British artist to create an individual, powerful and consistent style from the inspiration of Post-Impressionism. His work has an energy and conviction beside which his contemporaries seem a little pale.

John Rothenstein. Catalogue, *Matthew Smith*, Tate Gallery, London 1953; *Matthew Smith*, London 1962.
Catalogue, *Matthew Smith Memorial Exhibition*, Royal Academy, London 1960.
P. Hendy, F. Halliday and J. Russell. *Matthew Smith*, London 1962.

Smith, Richard. British painter, b. 1931 in Letchworth. From 1948 to 1950 he attended Luton School of Art, from 1952 to 1954 St. Alban's School of Art, and from 1954 to 1957 the Royal College of Art. In 1959 he went to America on a Harkness Fellowship. He stayed there until 1961 and returned in 1963; since 1965 he has spent some time there. He held his first one-man show in New York. In 1960 he exhibited with the Situation Group. His experience in America meant that he was one of the first of the younger generation of British painters to react directly to modern American painting and its preoccupation with the abstract mechanics of colour and surface. In the late fifties his work was essentially Abstract Expressionist. In the early sixties he was doing big, freely painted shapes in strong colours and on large canvases. About 1963 the logic of the consideration of paint and canvas as a single unitary object led him to experiment with canvases that were actually extended into three-dimensional shapes. A good example of this kind of work is *Spread* (1965, Tate Gallery, London). This would be sculpture if the artist were not so exclusively concerned with surface and still, in a curious way, with pictorial space.

Smith, Tony. American sculptor, b. 1912 in South Orange, New Jersey. Following studies at the Art Students' League in New York (1933–6) and the New Bauhaus in Chicago (1937–8), Smith worked from about 1938 to 1960 as an architect, assisting Frank Lloyd Wright during the first two years. He began working in sculpture around 1940, although it was not until 1960 that he devoted himself exclusively to this medium. Smith emerged then as one of the most prominent sculptors of the 1960s, and the forerunner and chief influence on the Minimal sculpture of this period. He was influential not only through his work and participation in major group and one-man exhibitions (first one-man show in 1967 at the Wadsworth Atheneum, Hartford, Connecticut), but also through his teaching (New York University, Cooper Union, Pratt Institute, Bennington College and Hunter College). Smith's aesthetic derives in part from his architectural sensibilities, particularly a long-time interest in the primitive geometric architecture of the Pueblos. 'Presence' is the word that he prefers to describe the quality of his work, and he has expressed his concern with the 'inscrutability and mysteriousness of the thing'. Although his work often begins from modular units (model for the *Maze*, 1967, two modules 6 ft. 8 in.×10 in.×30 in., and two modules 6 ft. 8 in.×5 in.×30 in., New York, Finch College Museum of Art), his sculptures rarely preserve the symmetry evident in other Minimal sculpture (*Night*, 1966, plywood mock-up painted black to be executed in steel, New York, Fischbach Gallery). Like that of his contemporaries, however, Smith's work is often large in scale, severe (usually painted black) and geometrical (*Die II*, 1967, steel, 6-foot cube, Fischbach Gallery). Occasionally allusions are made to objects or persons (*Cigarette*, 1967, plywood mock-up to be executed in steel, Fischbach Gallery; and *Willy*, 1962, blackened plywood).

Catalogue, *Tony Smith—Two Exhibitions of Sculpture*, Wadsworth Atheneum and the Institute of Contemporary Art, Hartford (Conn.) and Philadelphia 1966.
Gene Baro. 'Tony Smith: Toward Speculation in Pure Form', *Art International* XI, Zürich, Summer 1967.

Smits, Jakob. Dutch-Belgian painter, b. 1856 in Rotterdam; d. 1928 in Mol, near Antwerp. After some years in Haarlem, he settled in 1889 at Mol, which touched him by its poverty and desolation. He regarded the human figure with warm fellow-feeling—which explains his admiration for Rembrandt—and he painted religious scenes and landscapes, remarkable portraits as well as rustic interiors. The portraits done before 1910, especially those of his second wife Malvina, are notable for their gravity and spiritual depth as much as for the glowing freshness of their colours. Later on he sought to embody light, using white paint thickly laid on, but rather than making it shimmer he succeeded only in dulling it. At the end of his life he changed his style again and replaced the heavy outlines by a rapid sketchy line, using lighter colours, which nevertheless still gave the impression of seriousness and contemplation.

Sobrino, Francisco. Spanish sculptor, b. 1932 in Guadalajara. In 1960 Sobrino helped to found the *Groupe de Recherche d'Art Visuel* in Paris. His most important works are geometric sculptures constructed from delicately coloured Plexiglass components, which are identical in shape. The transparency, reflective-

ness and multiplicity of the component forms are the principal features of these works. Sobrino is now living in Paris.

Social Realism. This movement in American painting has been associated with the 1930s Works Progress Administration (WPA), and many of the artists involved had in fact worked on that federal project, often influenced in their protests by artists of the Mexican Revolution. Nevertheless, many works with socio-political content, such as Ben Shahn's gouaches recording the Sacco and Vanzetti trials (*Passion of Sacco and Vanzetti*, 1931–2, New York, Whitney Museum), were done before the WPA had come into existence. The use of distortion for expressive purposes in the *Sacco and Vanzetti* series is tempered somewhat in Shahn's eight *Prohibition* designs done for but rejected by the WPA (*W.C.T.U. Parade*, 1933–4, New York, Museum of the City of New York), while his project portraying penal reform for Rikers Island Penitentiary (1934–5) is yet more conservative, expressing the lack of real significance this project had for the realm of protest. The Depression years turned many American painters to the consideration of such social problems as labour–management struggles, the miseries of poverty and unemployment, middle-class materialism, lawmakers and law enforcers, and racial discrimination. Pictures of poverty and the underworld by such artists as Jack Levine (*Feast of Pure Reason*, 1937, New York, Museum of Modern Art) and George Biddle (b. 1885; *Sweatshop*, study for fresco, c. 1935, College Park, Md., University of Maryland) made treatments of similar themes by The Eight seem relatively romantic. Along with these artists and such other Americans as Philip Evergood (*Railroad Men*, c. 1935, present location unknown) and William Gropper (*Old Tree and Old People*, 1939, New York, Whitney Museum), many European artists who fled to America in the 1930s produced socially oriented, often satirical art. Most significant among the foreigners of this persuasion was George Grosz, whose angry protestations during his German years became less violent in the 1930s but veered ahead again at the outbreak of the Second World War (*Peace II*, 1946, Whitney Museum).

Milton W. Brown. *American Painting from the Armory Show to the Depression*, Princeton (N.J.) 1955.
Donald D. Egbert. *Socialism and American Art*, Princeton (N.J.) 1967.

Société Anonyme, Inc. The Société Anonyme, Inc., subtitled A Museum of Modern Art, opened on 30 April 1920 at 19 East 47th Street, New York. The major founders were Katherine S. Dreier and Marcel Duchamp, who continued to function officially as President and Secretary for the duration of the Société's existence until 1950. The Société fulfilled a need for the promotion and exhibition of contemporary art in the United States that was occasioned not only by the closing of Alfred Stieglitz's 291 Gallery in 1917, but also by the general unwillingness of the major existing museums to exhibit contemporary art and by recent art movements such as the American Immaculatism and the European Futurism, Suprematism and *de Stijl*, which had no public outlet in America. The Société Anonyme, which declared its purpose as the exhibition of exclusively contemporary art on an objective and primarily educational basis, thus became the first museum devoted totally to contemporary art in the United States and even preceded the major contemporary art museums in Europe. Although it fell short of its aim to establish a chain of subsidiary galleries across the country, the Société Anonyme was remarkably prolific, especially in its early years, in the number of its exhibitions, publications and lectures, and the development of a permanent collection of modern art. Between 1920 and 1940 the Société organized eighty-four exhibitions that represented the most outstanding European and American artists, many never before seen in the United States (e.g. Campendonk, Klee, Malevich, Miró, Vantongerloo). The largest and most significant exhibition of its kind since the Armory Show was the international exhibition of 1926 at the Brooklyn Museum, which was organized by the Société Anonyme and was subsequently circulated to the Anderson Galleries in Manhattan and to the Albright Art Gallery in Buffalo, thus realizing the concept of a travelling loan exhibition in the United States. The publications of the Société Anonyme included primarily catalogues and monographs, which continued until 1944; the lectures, held from 1920 to 1940, often at educational institutions, were subsumed under the heading 'New Forms in Art' and included not only lectures and symposia on all the visual arts, but radio programmes, literature readings of contemporary writers, modern dance performances, and recitals of contemporary music. The final legacy of the Société Anonyme was its superb international collection containing over 600 works in all media executed from 1909 to 1950; formed largely by Katherine Dreier and Marcel Duchamp and bequeathed to the Yale University Art Gallery in 1941, it indicates well the scope of the vision of the Société Anonyme.

Catalogue, *Collection of the Société Anonyme: Museum of Modern Art, 1920*, New Haven (Conn.) 1950.
Rudi Blesh. *Modern Art, U.S.A.—Men, Rebellion, Conquest, 1900–1956*, New York 1956.

Society of Independent Artists, Inc. The organization of the Society of Independent Artists in 1916 provided a replacement for the Association of American Painters and Sculptors, which had been dissolved after the Armory Show. The new organization planned to hold annual spring exhibitions as a counter-gesture to the National Academy of Design, which would give unknown contemporary artists an opportunity to show their work (the Society planned to include also literature, music, drama and film). The right to exhibit was extended to anyone paying a minimal membership fee, and the exhibitions were based on the principle of no juries and no prizes that had been made famous by the Society's French predecessor of 1884, the Salon des Indépendants. For the first few years, the Society comprised both the radically modernist as well as the more conservative representatives of American art: the first administrative officers were William Glackens, President (followed a year later by John Sloan); Maurice Prendergast, Vice-President; Walter Pach, Treasurer; John Covert, Secretary; and Walter Arensberg, Managing Director. The directors of the Society during the first year included Marcel Duchamp.

The first exhibition organized by the Society, held from 6 March to 6 April 1916, was its largest and most important one; it included 2007 entries representing more than 1,000 artists from both Europe and the United States (e.g. Joseph Stella, Charles Demuth, Marsden Hartley, Man Ray, Georgia O'Keeffe, Max Weber, Arthur G. Dove, Picasso, Albert Gleizes, Paul Signac, Duchamp-Villon, Constantin Brancusi, Maurice de Vlaminck). Although the Society continued to hold annual exhibitions into the mid-1940s, the scope and quality of the later exhibitions were diminished. In 1917 the *avant-garde* leaders Duchamp and Arensberg resigned from the Society after Duchamp's attempt to exhibit his notorious ready-made, *Fountain by R. Mutt*; by 1919 the number of entries had dropped to about one third of that for the first exhibition; and the number of foreign artists represented showed the greatest decrease, especially during the 1920s, when America had generally adopted an isolationist policy, and the first phase of modernist American art had passed.

An Exhibition of Painting and Sculpture, Commemorating the Armory Show of 1913 and the First Exhibition of the Society of Independent Artists . . ., American Academy of Arts and Letters, New York 1955.
Rudi Blesh. *Modern Art, U.S.A.—Men, Rebellion, Conquest, 1900–1956*, New York 1956.

Soest, Pierre Gerardus Cornelis van. Dutch painter, b. 1930 in Venlo. Soest trained at the State Academy in Amsterdam. His oeuvre includes paintings, drawings, etchings, lithographs and monumental works. During his early period Soest was strongly influenced by the *Cobra* movement, but of recent years his style has become less violent. Many of his *motifs* are fragmentary (parts of the human body, insects' legs, eyes, etc.).

Soffici, Ardengo. Italian painter, b. 1879 in Rignano; d. 1964 in Forte dei Marmi. After attending the Academy of Art in Florence for a short while Soffici went to live in Paris from 1900 to 1907.

Whilst there he made contact with the *avant-garde*. After his return to Italy he contributed to the magazine *La Voce* from 1908 to 1916. In 1913, in Florence, he joined with G. Paini in founding *Lacerba*. He also made contact with the Futurists and in 1913–14 took part in their meetings and exhibitions. But in 1915, together with Papini and Palezzeschi, he broke away from the Futurists. From 1919 onwards he collaborated with the *Valori Plastici*. He was also attracted by the Neo-Classical tendencies of the *Novecento* movement, with their strong nationalistic overtones, which found expression in his *Periplo dell'Arte* (which had the subtitle *Call to Order*).

Like Rosai and Sironi, Soffici was a latecomer to Futurism, which impinged on his style only to a limited extent. His best works were produced when he was contributing to *La Voce* and *Lacerba*. Whilst his landscapes, which date from c. 1913, are still reminiscent of Cézanne, his rhythmical still lifes, which he executed in clear, bold colours, reveal the influence of Futurism. But with his secession from the Futurist movement in 1915 Soffici reverted to a traditional, Classical type of composition, using local colours and schematic chiaroscuro and attaching particular importance to thematic considerations. The landscapes of his late period are simply exercises in bravura. In fact Soffici's real significance lay in his role as art critic and as a source of inspiration for the younger generation.

Ardengo Soffici. *Ricordi di Vita Artistica e Letteraria*, Florence 1930.
G. Papini. *Ardengo Soffici*, Milan 1933.
A. Lugli. 'Ardengo Soffici', *I Contemporanei* I, Milan 1963.

Solana, José Gutiérrez. Spanish painter, b. 1885 in Madrid; d. 1945 in Madrid. He was untaught and came of a poor but proud family. His painting was largely concerned with the life of Madrid and its surrounding districts, and the flea market in the town inspired many remarkable pictures. He also painted figure compositions of various classes of townspeople about their business or at leisure. Solana was one of the greatest Expressionist painters in Spain.

Soldati, Atanasio. Italian painter, b. 1896 in Parma; d. 1953 in Parma. Soldati began training as an architect before the First World War but was obliged to interrupt his studies to serve with the forces. He finally obtained his architect's diploma in 1920. Two years later he started to paint. In 1925 he taught drawing in Langhirano, near Parma, but moved later the same year to Milan, where he joined the staff of the Scuola di Libro dell'Umanitaria. In 1946, together with Dorfles, Monnet and Munari, he became a founder member of the *Movimento Arte Concreta* (*MAC*). Until 1950 he was one of its most important representatives.

During his early period, when he was teaching himself to paint, Soldati's work was influenced by his architectural studies. In c. 1925 Soldati espoused the pictorial principles of Cézanne and Analytical Cubism. Later, he moved on to Synthetic Cubism and, in the course of the 1930s, received a further powerful stimulus from the *Pittura Metafisica*. Up to 1935 Soldati concentrated on still lifes, but subsequently he also painted geometrical abstracts which reveal the influence of the Bauhaus and *de Stijl*. After the Second World War he executed compositions of immense precision and great plasticity in luminous colours.

L. Venturi. *Soldati*, Milan 1954.

Soldi, Raúl. Argentinian painter, b. 1905 in Buenos Aires. Soldi studied in Buenos Aires and, from 1923 onwards, at the Brera in Milan, where he joined the *Avanguardici artistica* and *Il Milione*. After returning to Argentina in 1933 he worked as a painter and book illustrator, and also designed film sets. His oeuvre consists primarily of landscapes and figure compositions, although he has also executed several large murals, including one for the Opera in Buenos Aires.

Eduardo Baliari. *Raúl Soldi*, Buenos Aires 1966.

Somaini, Francesco. Italian sculptor, b. 1926 near Lomazzo, Como. Somaini began to sculpt in 1935 when he was only nine years old. Later, after reading law in Milan, he trained at the Accademia Brera. Between 1944 and 1948 he travelled abroad and met many leading artists. He is now living in Lomazzo.

After studying the works of Arp, Somaini abandoned the Classical, figurative style of his early period and began to produce dynamic sculptures in space, which create an impression of monumentality. The elegance which is a characteristic feature of so many of these twisted and fissured structures stands in marked contrast to their coarse-grained surface texture.

Léon Dégand. *Francesco Somaini*, 1956 (private publication).

Sonderborg, Kurt R. Hoffmann. German-Danish painter, b. 1923 in Sonderborg, Denmark. Sonderborg is the son of a German jazz musician. After growing up in Hamburg and training for a commercial career he began to paint in 1946. From 1947 to 1949 he attended the Landeskunstschule (State School of Art) in Hamburg. He then joined the Hamburg Group of concrete artists and also the *Zen* group, but did not stay long with either. Sonderborg received his first really important stimuli in 1951 from a lengthy stay which he made on the volcanic island of Stromboli. At about the same time he also came under the influence of Julius Bissier.

Then, in 1953–4, he studied graphic techniques under Hayter in Paris, after which he visited England, Paris and New York, before settling in Stuttgart in 1966. He now teaches at the Academy of Art in Stuttgart.

In producing his calligraphic paintings Sonderborg first applies black ink or oil paint by means of an automatic writing technique, then scratches, scrapes or makes impressions in this basic design. Although his method is in fact similar to that employed by Mathieu, Kline and Vedova, Sonderborg attaches greater importance to speed and movement. The titles of his extremely dynamic paintings contain both the date and the time of day at which they were created.

O. Hahn. *Sonderborg*, Stuttgart and Paris 1964.

Sørensen, Hendrik. Swedish-Norwegian painter, b. 1882 in Fryksaüde, Sweden; d. 1962 in Oslo. Sørensen studied under Zahrtmann in Copenhagen from 1904 to 1905 and under Matisse in Paris from 1909 to 1910. Although he incorporated certain features of modern French painting and German Expressionism into his work, basically he painted in the Norwegian tradition established by Dahl, Werenskiold and Munch. With their highly expressive, contrasting colours and angular forms Sørensen's lyrical, sensitive and ecstatic works, which consist for the most part of landscapes, portraits and religious compositions, present a Romantic view of the Norwegian character. Sørensen also produced numerous monumental paintings for public buildings, including the Town Hall in Oslo.

Soria, Salvador. Spanish painter, b. 1915 in Valencia. In 1939 he produced the murals for the Mairie of Septfonds in France. He contributed to the 1940 and 1952 International Exhibitions in France, and returned to Spain in 1953, when he exhibited at the Second Salon of Modern Mediterranean Art in Valencia. He then contributed to the 1956 Spanish-American Biennale in Barcelona, and with the *Parpalló* group exhibited in the Ateneo in Madrid. In 1957 he won the first prize at the Autumn Salon in Valencia, and in 1960 exhibited in the Venice Biennale. He is an abstract artist, in whose work traces of *Tachisme* and Expressionism can be seen. He is a member of the *Nouvelle École Européenne.*

Soto, Jesus Raphael. Venezuelan painter, b. 1923 in Ciudad Bolivar. Soto studied at the Academy of Art in Caracas from 1942 to 1947. From 1947 to 1950 he was Director of the School of Art in Maracaibo, Venezuela. In 1950 he settled in Paris, where he is still living. He has won numerous international awards, including the David Bright Prize at the Biennale in Venice in 1964.

Soto calls his pictures *Vibrations*. They are divided into two separate structural areas, which are distinguished from one another in terms of both texture and space. The lower area consists of a linear or two-dimensional painting executed on a wooden or hard fibre panel and surmounted by wire sculptures, wrought iron and nylon cords. However, the components are not important in themselves. What matters is their relationship to one another and the viewer's relationship to them. The materials are in fact dematerialized, i.e. transformed into energy. Soto's paintings are also kinetic in so far as the relations between the various components change each time the viewer changes his position. The colours used in these works are very restrained and their range is small. Soto has also executed a number of murals, including those for the University of Caracas (1957) and the University of Rennes (1968).

Catalogue, *Jesus Raphael Soto*, Kestner Gesellschaft, Hanover 1968 (and elsewhere).

Souček, Karel. Czech painter and graphic artist, b. 1915 in Kročehlavy. He studied in Prague from 1934 to 1937. He received the second prize in the competition for the decorations for the National Theatre, Prague, in 1953. Major exhibitions of his work were held in Prague in 1957, and Brno in 1956. His work consists largely of figures and portraits.

Soulages, Pierre. French painter, b. 1919 in Rodez, Aveyron. Soulages became interested in the prehistoric and Romanesque art of his native district at an early age. In 1938–9 he spent several months in Paris. Whilst there he visited the Louvre and saw exhibitions of works by Cézanne and Picasso, whereupon he decided not to attend an academy of art. In 1940 he joined the French forces. From 1941 to 1946 he worked as a farm labourer near Montpellier, then returned to Paris, where he had exhibitions in the Salon des Surindépendants and subsequently in the Salon de Mai (until c. 1958). From 1948 onwards he also showed his work in individual and group exhibitions both at home and abroad. In 1949 he designed stage sets for Graham Greene's *Héloise et Abélard* in the Théâtre de l'Athénée in Paris, and in 1952 for *Geste pour un Génie*, the ballet produced to commemorate the five hundredth anniversary of Leonardo da Vinci's birth. In 1957–8 Soulages visited the United States, Japan and India. In 1959 he won the Grand Prix for Graphic Art at the Biennale in Ljubljana.

Soulages is one of the most important representatives of the *École de Paris*. Ever since he started to paint he has consistently rejected all imitative techniques. His compositions consist of broad black bands, which intersect and overlay one another to form latticed structures against bright grounds. At no time in Soulages' career have these structures had any connection with extra-pictorial reality. They are completely independent and self-sufficient configurations, which exist at three different levels: first, the pictorial ground is covered with a framework of intersecting bands; then a vertical organization is established; and finally horizontal and diagonal elements are superimposed, creating a dynamic upper stratum, whose intersecting rectilinear forms generate spatial rhythms. The active elements in Soulages' pictures are almost invariably black. The effectiveness of Soulages' colouring is achieved by the transitions from extremely dark to extremely bright values. He also has occasional recourse to blues, browns and reds.

H. Juin. *Pierre Soulages*, Paris 1959.
Catalogue, *Pierre Soulages*, Gimpel/Hanover Galleries, Zürich and London 1967.

Soutine, Chaim. Russian painter, b. 1893 near Minsk, Lithuanian Russia; d. 1943 in Paris. He was the tenth of eleven children of a Jewish tailor. In his youth, he took art lessons from a teacher in Minsk; in 1910 he attempted, but failed, the entrance examination of the School of Fine Arts in Vilna, and was finally admitted after taking private tuition from a member of the staff. In 1913 he arrived in Paris, studying for a short time at the École des Beaux-Arts. Chagall and Léger occupied neighbouring studios at La Ruche, rue Dantzig; he also befriended Laurens, Pascin, Lipchitz, Zadkine and Modigliani. In 1916, Modigliani introduced Soutine to the poet and dealer Zborowski, whose interest in Soutine's work helped to alleviate the latter's extreme poverty. From 1918 to 1922 he travelled between Paris, Céret and Cagnes, returning to Paris with over 200 paintings, mostly landscapes, many of which were bought in 1923 by the American collector Albert Barnes. This purchase, and the article which Barnes wrote about Soutine, both aided the popularity of Soutine's work and gave him a measure of financial stability.

After 1925, Soutine turned increasingly from landscape to still life, installing the carcass of an ox and dead fowl in his studio (*Fowl*, 1926, Paris, Coll. M. Pierre Wertheimer). In 1928 a monograph on Soutine by Waldemar George, and in 1929 another by Élie Faure, were published; in 1935 Soutine had his first major exhibition at the Arts Club of Chicago. In 1940, although in danger during the German occupation of France on account of his Jewish origins, Soutine refused an invitation to emigrate to America. In 1941 he began to suffer badly from stomach ulcers, and died two years later after an operation.

In art, Soutine admired particularly Cézanne, Bonnard and Corot—Cézanne's art in particular may have influenced Soutine's landscapes and helped to bring about the breaking up of objects. But Soutine was also influenced by Tintoretto, El Greco and—to the extent that he made reconstructions of their work—by Rembrandt and Courbet.

Soutine's work is characterized by its distortions both of space and of subject matter, violence of colour and brush-stroke, making the painting a whirlwind of movement. Modigliani once compared Soutine's work to his own drug-induced hallucinations: 'Everything dances around me, as in a landscape by Soutine.'

Raymond Cogniat. *Soutine*, Paris 1945.
D. Sylvester. Catalogue, *Chaim Soutine, 1894–1943*, The Arts Council, London 1963.
M. Castaing and J. Leymarie. *Soutine*, New York 1964.
Andrew Forge. *Soutine*, London 1965.

Soutter, Louis. Swiss painter and draughtsman, b. 1871; d. 1943. He was outstanding as a draughtsman, and his work, which only began to be appreciated some twenty years after he died, assures him a place in the history of Swiss art.

Soyer, Raphael. American painter, b. 1899 in Borisoglebsk, Russia. In his early teens, Raphael Soyer moved with his family to the United States and settled in New York City. After attending Cooper Union, he entered the National Academy of Design, where he studied until 1922. Then, forced to take odd jobs to support himself, he painted only in his spare time. In 1926 he began to exhibit and sell his work, and in 1929 he had his first one-man show. Encouraged by the success of this exhibition, he rented a studio and began to devote himself fully to his painting.

During the 1930s and 1940s, Raphael Soyer painted such subjects as tramps and derelicts standing about drab streets in the Bowery, shop girls crowding the sidewalks around Union Square, or bored travellers waiting in Pennsylvania Station (*Waiting Room*, c. 1940, Washington, D.C., Corcoran Gallery).

Soyer completely ignored the various trends and movements that dominated the art world in the 1950s and 1960s, and continued to paint in a Realistic style. His paintings became brighter and took on a kind of youthful affirmation, as he turned to such subjects as groups of young people in the East Village (*Village East Street Scene*, 1965–6, Coll. Avnet) or flower children gathered in Central Park (*À Watteau*, 1967; coll. of artist).

Lloyd Goodrich. *Raphael Soyer*, New York 1967.

Špála, Václav. Czech painter, b. 1885; d. 1946. Špála was a representative of Fauvism in Czechoslovakia; then in 1911 he joined the *Group of Avant-Garde Artists*, organized by Filla and Procházka, and with them developed a Cubo-Expressionism of some importance. However, his concern with Cubism later gave way to formalization.

Spazialismo (Movimento Spaziale). The *Spazialismo* movement in modern art has been propagated by Lucio Fontana, who first defined its aims in his *Manifesto blanco* in Buenos Aires in 1964. *Spazialismo* combines many of the ideas of Concrete Art with the experimental and provocative processes of Dadaism. Amongst other things the members of this movement reject the time-honoured conception of the 'easel painting' and insist on the free development of colour and form in space, the adoption of new techniques based on recent development in technology and the incorporation into their pictures of movement and time. After his return to Italy Fontana worked in Milan, where he became the central figure in a group of like-minded artists. This group, which included painters such as Dova, Crippa, Donati and Bacci, published its new theories in the *Manifesto Spaziale*. In practice, however, these artists tended to revert to *Tachisme* or Informal art. In 1954 Fontana also published a further manifesto entitled *Manifesto Tecnico dello Spazialismo*. His ideas aroused considerable interest. Amongst those influenced by them were the members of the *Zero* group.

G. Giani. *Spazialismo*, Milan 1956.

Spazzapan, Luigi. Italian painter, b. 1890 in Gradisca, Friuli; d. 1958 in Turin. After studying in Vienna and Paris Spazzapan worked in Görz until 1928, when he settled in Turin. There he joined the Turin School, which had been influenced by Casorati. After 1945 Spazzapan, Moreni and Mastroianni became the leaders of the Turin *avant-garde* movement.

Following an early Fauvist period Spazzapan evolved a visionary form of Expressionism. Because of his insistence an abstract structures many of his landscapes, still lifes and figure compositions appear somewhat contrived and tend to resemble posters. His best paintings are the landscapes which he produced in 1950. In these works the vibrant colour values do not encroach on the calligraphic outlines, which means that their inner rhythms are not dissipated. Spazzapan also produced a significant body of drawings, which are executed in an elegant, decorative and—in the best sense of the word—illustrative style.

L. Venturi. *Luigi Spazzapan*, Rome 1960.

Spear, Ruskin. British painter, b. 1911 in London. Spear is a painter of plebeian Realism (*Strawberry Mousse*, 1959) and straight portraits (*Carel Weight*, 1962). He has had exhibitions at the Royal Academy (of which he is a member), the London Group (of which he was President 1949–50) and the Leicester Galleries, among others. Examples of his work are in the Tate Gallery, London, and he did the reredos in St. Clement Danes Church, London.

Speicher, Eugene (Edward). American painter, b. 1883 in Buffalo, New York; d. 1962. After high school he attended evening classes at the Buffalo Art School, where he studied with Lucius Hitchcock and Urquhart Wilcox (1902–6). From 1906 to 1908 he studied under William M. Chase and Frank V. Du Mond at the Art Students' League. He then attended the Henri School of Art for one year before his year's residence abroad (1910–11). As soon as he returned to the United States, his list of prizes began to grow. He had his first one-man show in 1918 at the Montross Gallery, New York, and by 1920 was among the country's leading portraitists. His early portrait of *Georgia O'Keeffe* (1908, New York, Art Students' League) reflects the dark, painterly manner of Chase. For several years in the 1920s he devoted himself entirely to portraiture and limited himself to six or eight clients a year. *Katherine* (1923, Boston, Museum of Fine Arts) is typical of the period—generally handled in a soft, painterly manner, the strong light seems to harden the contours of the face into a schematization. The dark oval eyes are a prominent feature of Speicher's portraits, which also tend to formularize his sitters. *Katharine Cornell as 'Candida'* (1926, Buffalo, New York, Albright-Knox Art Gallery) is saved from these conventions through the lighting of the face and a negation of his usual stereometry of contour, eyebrow and eye. In the late 1930s and 1940s he increasingly concentrated on landscape and casual portraits of his friends and neighbours. His less formal handling of men, such as in *Farm News* (1944, estate of artist), is more satisfying, with little of the dependence on formulae seen in his female portraits. In 1945 Speicher was appointed Director of the American Academy of Arts and Letters.

Eugene Speicher, American Artists Group, New York 1945.
Eugene Speicher. *A Retrospective Exhibition of Oils and Drawings ... 1908–1949*, Albright-Knox Art Gallery, Buffalo (New York) 1950.

Spencer, Niles. American painter, b. 1893 in Pawtucket, Rhode Island; d. 1952 in Dingman's Ferry, Pennsylvania. He received his first training at the Rhode Island School of Design (1913) and in the summers of 1914 and 1915 painted with Charles Woodbury in Ogunquit, Maine. In 1915, while still a student, he became an instructor at Rhode Island. The same year he spent one month studying with R. Henri and G. Bellows at the Ferrer School. When he tried to institute some of the new ideas he had learned in New York, he was asked to leave Rhode Island. He returned to New York in 1916 and continued his studies with Henri. After living for four years at the Hamilton Easter Field colony in Ogunquit he spent a year in Europe (1921–2) and then settled in New York in 1923. He was given his first one-man show in 1925 at the Daniel Gallery, New York. His early works are Realistic with some affinities to Cézanne, particularly in his still lifes (*The Green Table*, 1930, New York, Whitney Museum of American Art). In the 1930s his works fell into the mainstream of the Precisionists. At this time he revealed the essential surfaces and volumes of objects but did not as yet reduce these forms to their elemental qualities of plane (*Across the Tracks*, 1935, Allentown, Pa., Art Museum). By the 1940s he had taken a close-up view of his cityscapes and machines, rendering them in a few large areas of flat colour and concentrating on basic geometric forms, as in *City Shapes* (1946, Tempe, Arizona, Arizona State University). It was during the 1940s that he participated in many exhibitions including *A New Realism* (1941, Cincinnati Modern Art Society) where his works appeared with those of Charles Demuth and Charles Sheeler. By 1950 his scenes became abstractions of forms seen from a very close vantage point so that the subjects are not immediately recognizable (*Above the Excavation, 2*, Ithaca, New York, Cornell University, White Art Museum).

Richard B. Freeman. *Niles Spencer*, University of Kentucky Art Gallery, 1965.

Spencer, Stanley. British painter, b. 1891 in Cookham, Berks; d. 1959 in Taplow, Bucks. After a scanty general education Spencer enrolled at the Slade School (1908–12), gaining a scholarship and other awards.

He joined the Medical Corps in the First World War, later serving as an infantryman in Macedonia. These experiences provided themes for subsequent compositions. After the war Spencer exhibited for a few years with the New English Art Club (by then institutionalized). He married Hilda Carline in 1925; she and her two daughters figure in Spencer's paintings. The six *Beatitudes of Love* date from the 1930s and were originally intended for a proposed Chapel of Peace complementing the War Chapel, Burghclere, near Newbury. Officially appointed to record the Second World War, Spencer drew themes from the Clyde shipyards. He painted a further *Resurrection* as a series of interrelated pictures in 1945–50. However, most of Spencer's art is intimately connected with his home, the Berkshire village of Cookham. His most ambitious undertakings remain the *Resurrection* (the stage being set in Cookham churchyard; Tate Gallery, finished 1926) and the nineteen canvases of the War Memorial Chapel, Burghclere (finished 1932).

An eccentric figure in British art, Spencer's minuteness of observation is in line with the Pre-Raphaelite Brotherhood, but his own brand of evangelical primitivism is unique. The strong narrative and didactic intention is sometimes obscured by what Elizabeth Rothenstein has called 'pictorial garrulity'. With rare exceptions, such as *Christ in the Wilderness, Scorpions* (1939), Spencer's inner vision lacks the power of Blake, with whom he has been compared. His remarkable talent is most immediately felt in the *Scrapbook Drawings* (many annotated on the reverse), which should be studied to appreciate Spencer's full stature and visual innocence.

G. Spencer. *Stanley Spencer by His Brother Gilbert*, London 1961.
G. Hayes (ed.). *Scrapbook Drawings of Stanley Spencer*, London 1964.
E. Rothenstein. *Stanley Spencer*, London 1967.

Spilimbergo, Lino Enea. Argentinian painter and graphic artist, b. 1896 in Buenos Aires; d. 1964 in Unquillo. Spilimbergo trained in Buenos Aires and Paris (under André Lhôte). After an early naturalistic period he evolved a type of composition based on Post-Cubist forms and when he returned to Argentina in 1930 painted numerous landscapes in a basically geometrical style. As a professor at the Institute of Fine Arts in Tucumán Spilimbergo taught many young artists who have since become well known. In 1932 he collaborated with Siqueiros on the decoration of a private residence, and in 1946 painted a dome in the Galería Pacífico in Buenos Aires. The still lifes, landscapes and figure compositions of Spilimbergo's mature period reflect both his admiration for Piero della Francesca and Giovanni Bellini and his highly individual attitude to modern art.

Alberto Prebisch. *Spilimbergo*, Buenos Aires 1967.

Spilliaert, Léon. Belgian painter, b. 1881 in Ostend; d. 1946 in Brussels. Like James Ensor—and despite the fact that he passed part of his life in Brussels—Spilliaert remained faithful to his native town of Ostend, portraying its sights in a highly personal style, in which he combined Realism with vision. Spilliaert was a self-taught artist; he studied composition at an early age and soon acquired a virtuoso technique, which he employed primarily in gouaches, watercolours and Indian-ink drawings. Although he joined various artists' associations, including *Sélection, Les Compagnons de l'Art* and *Le Sillon*, he was careful to preserve his independence and individuality. He was on friendly terms with the Belgian poets of his day, especially Émile Verhaeren. He also knew Maurice Maeterlinck, and produced a series of illustrations for his *Les Serres chaudes*. Spilliaert's oeuvre, which occupies a position midway between Symbolism and Expressionism, introduces us to a world that already contained many of the dream *motifs* which were to play such a dominant role in Surrealism. This world, which is also a place of solitude, helplessness and existential anguish, is placed in sharp relief by the extreme simplicity of Spilliaert's draughtsmanship, and by the economy and significance of his palette.

Frank Edebau. *Léon Spilliaert*, Antwerp 1950.

Spoerri, Daniel. Swiss sculptor, b. 1930 in Galati, Rumania. Spoerri settled in Switzerland in 1942.

After training as a ballet dancer in Zürich and Paris from 1950 to 1954 he was engaged as lead dancer by the State Opera Company in Berne from 1954 to 1957. Whilst in Berne he also produced plays by Ionesco, Tardieu and Picasso. Between 1955 and 1961 he published five issues of the magazine *Matérial* to help 'preserve concrete poetry and ideography'. Meanwhile, in 1959, Spoerri went to live in Paris, where he published the first edition of *MAT (Multiplication d'Art transformable)* in the same year. This publication, in which he dealt with the reproduction of 'transformable' works of art, i.e. works which are capable of modification within themselves, was subsequently revised by Spoerri and Karl Gerstner and reprinted in 1964. Prior to this, in 1960, Spoerri had produced his first *tableaux pièges* ('trap pictures'). In these constructions functional objects and consumer goods were glued to tables, chairs, etc., which were then turned on their side and hung on the wall. From 1960 onward Spoerri also contributed to the exhibitions and shows organized by the New Realists in Paris, where he now lives most of the time.

Spruce, Everett. American painter, b. 1908 near Conway, Arkansas. After graduating from Mulberry High School in Mulberry, Arkansas (1925), he was a scholarship student at the Dallas (Texas) Art Institute, working under Olin H. Travis and Thomas M. Sell, Jr. (1925–8). One year after his first association with the Dallas Museum of Fine Arts, he was given his first one-man show there (1932). During the years of affiliation with this institution, serving both as teacher and Assistant Director, his works revealed connections with Surrealism, particularly in the eerie desolation seen in his landscapes (*Arkansas Landscape*, 1936, Washington, D.C., Phillips Collection) and in the heavy volumetric figures rendered with tight, precise brushwork and modelling as in *Mending Fence* (1937, Southern Methodist University). In 1940 he joined the faculty of the University of Texas, Austin, and became a full professor in 1954. In the late 1940s and early 1950s his style employed a heavy impasto overwritten with a delicate calligraphy. His landscapes, figures and animals were often executed through the use of schematic forms, emphasizing the decorative quality of the subjects (*Yellow Rooster*, 1951, coll. of artist). In the late 1950s his work became more lyrical and even mystical, giving the viewer the impression that he is looking at the subject through a gossamer veil. Throughout his career he has favoured subjects which portray elements indigenous to his native South-West.

John Palmer Leeper. *Everett Spruce*, New York 1959.

Spur Group. This group was founded in Munich in 1957 by the painters Heimrach Prem (b. 1934),

Helmut Sturm (b. 1932) and Hans-Peter Zimmer (b. 1936) and the sculptor Lothar Fischer. Between 1959 and 1962 the group gradually aligned itself with the International Situationists and during this period (1960–1) published seven issues of the *Spur* magazine. For a while the style of the group was strongly influenced by Asger Jorn, with whom the members came into close contact, but subsequently it veered towards *art brut* and Pop Art.

Srbinović, Mladen. Yugoslav painter and graphic artist, b. 1925 in Sušica, near Gostivar, Macedonia. Srbinović completed his studies at the College of Art in Belgrade in 1950. From 1957 onwards he moved away from the concrete and towards the ornamental representation of objects. None the less, his works remained basically objective in the formal sense, although the objects depicted in them acquired a new, symbolic significance, which reflects the human situation.

In his paintings Srbinović combines the solemnity of the Byzantine and Slavonic tradition with the new spirit of Cubist composition and Orphist colouring. Spontaneity and reflection are both present in these works, in which rhythm and chaos, the real and the inscrutable, are dramatically fused. In Srbinović's philosophy man is surrounded by opposing forces: he soars, dies and is transformed into a light wave of knowledge and suffering.

Katarina Ambrozić. 'Mladen Srbinović', *Umetnost Magazine I*, Belgrade 1965.
A. Celebonović. Catalogue, Salon of Modern Art, Belgrade 1968.

Stackpole, Ralph. American sculptor, b. 1885 in Williams, Oregon. He studied in San Francisco and Paris, then with Robert Henri. In 1921 he returned to Paris and took part in the Salon des Indépendants exhibition. He moved to California two years later, and taught in San Francisco until 1941, when he was appointed to the Fine Arts Commission. In 1949 he returned to France for good. Ten years later he had his first one-man show in Paris. His work consisted of monuments as well as portraits.

Stadler, Toni. German sculptor, b. 1888 in Munich. Stadler is the son of the painter Toni Stadler. After studying under August Gaul in Berlin and Hermann Hahn in Munich he made friends with Wrampe and Ludwig Kasper. In 1925 came the crucial meeting with Maillol in Paris. In 1934 he won a travelling scholarship which brought him to Rome. From 1942 to 1945 he taught at the Städelschule in Frankfurt am Main and from 1946 to 1958 at the Munich Academy. He is now living in Munich.

Although Stadler developed his lyrical conception of the human form partly from early Greek and Etruscan art and partly from Hildebrand and Maillol, his figures are not monumental and they reveal no sign of pathos. In their expression his nymphs and youths approach the Classical ideal.

But the deliberate choice of 'open form' structures and the sensitive, vital handling of the surfaces are contemporary features, which stem from Moore, Giacometti and Marini.

W. Haftmann. *Toni Stadler*, Munich 1961.
Catalogue, *Toni Stadler*, Kunstverein, Hanover 1965.

Staël, Nicholas de. Russian-French painter, b. 1914 in St. Petersburg; d. 1955 in Antibes. Nicholas de Staël was born into an aristocratic family, and was forced into exile in Poland in 1919. Left an orphan in 1922, he was sent to school in Brussels, where he excelled in Classical studies. He became interested in painting, and began serious study at the Royal Academy of Fine Art in Brussels in 1933. He became a prize-winning student after a year there, but left to begin travels through Europe, Morocco and Algeria, which lasted until 1938 when he returned to Paris. At the outbreak of war he joined the Foreign Legion, and served until demobilization in 1940. He went to live in Nice, but returned to Paris in 1943, suffering continued poverty and privation. In 1944 he became a close friend of Braque, and began to paint in an abstract style. He took part in that year in an exhibition of *Peintures Abstraites* with Domela, Kandinsky and Magnelli. During the last years of the 1940s abstract painting was gaining ground. De Staël followed this lead, producing 'compositions' in paint, of restricted colour at first, later becoming more fully polychromatic. Jeanne Bucher, who had befriended him for some years, gave him a one-man show at her gallery in 1945, and his work began to receive notice. By 1947 this interest had spread to American dealers, leading to an exhibition in New York in 1950. He visited England, exhibiting at the Mathieson Gallery in 1952.

De Staël appears never to have accepted the necessity, among abstract painters, of the complete denial of subject. He made no secret of his great regard for traditional painting of the past, and seems to have struggled to evolve a method of valid synthesis between representation and abstract modes of presentation. Concerned deeply with problems of developing 'ways of seeing', the presence of the landscape, and the objects, were essential to him. Stimulated by the colourful effects of the flood-lighting of sporting events he produced some remarkable paintings which were openly figurative. He continued to develop his personal style of painting derived from the observed subject, mainly landscape and still life, until his death, by his own hand, in 1955.

De Staël's personal vision, his particular formalization in the rendering of light, colour and space, produced paintings of great quality, with supreme taste and sensitivity. After his death they became well known and had considerable influence, and much success in the popular estimation.

Douglas Cooper. *Nicholas de Staël*, London 1961.

Stahly, François. French sculptor, b. 1911 in Constance, Germany. In 1912, Stahly was taken to Switzerland, where he remained until 1931 and completed the first stage of his artistic training at the School of Arts and Crafts in Zürich. Subsequently, from 1931 to 1938, he studied under C. Mafray at the Académie Ranson in Paris. In 1940 he acquired French nationality. In 1945 he settled in Mortagne (Orne), moving to Meudon in 1949, where he opened an *atelier*. From 1958 onwards Stahly has collaborated with various young sculptors and architects in Meudon. From 1960 onwards he has taught at numerous American universities and institutes, including the Aspen School of Contemporary Art in Colorado, Washington University in Seattle and Stanford University in California. In 1957 he won the *Grand Prix* at the Bienal in São Paulo and in 1965 the prize for sculpture at the Biennale in Tokyo. When he is not abroad Stahly lives in Meudon.

Stahly employs a wide variety of sculptural styles: his works incorporate organic forms at one end of the scale and geometric forms at the other. The influence of totemistic sculpture is also quite marked, especially in his larger projects. Of the works executed for public bodies the *Fountain of the Four Seasons* in the Golden Gateway in San Francisco (1961–5) is perhaps the best known. Since 1965 Stahly has been working on a *Labyrinth* for the Faculty of Sciences at the University of Paris.

Catalogue, *François Stahly*, Musée des Arts Décoratifs, Paris 1966.
C. Giedion-Welcker. *François Stahly*, Zürich (n.d.).

Stajuda, Jerzy. Polish painter and art critic, b. 1936 in Warsaw. Stajuda turned to painting and criticism after completing his architectural studies. He is a non-objective painter and his works reveal the influence of late nineteenth-century Romanticism, modernism and Symbolism.

Stamos, Theodoros. American painter, b. 1922 in New York. The son of Greek immigrants, Stamos was educated in New York, where he attended the American Artists' School on a scholarship at the age of 14, specializing in sculpture. Encouraged by his instructor Joseph Solman (b. 1909), he began to paint at home in 1937, and at the age of 22 had his first one-man show of oils and pastels at the Wakefield Gallery in New York (1943). After this he began to evolve a more distinctive style, at first realistic, then abstracting and distorting from such subjects as beach debris, shells, driftwood or starfish forms arranged in broad symbolic patterns. This early work was done in a deliberately primitivizing manner, suggesting imaginary Greek landscapes or based on scenes of the New Jersey Palisades. The influence of the painter Milton Avery was evident in Stamos's choice of thinly painted pattern-like shapes. Like his older colleagues Adolph Gottlieb and William

Baziotes, Stamos has been called a 'poetic symbolist' because of his preference for lyrically abstract biomorphic forms, and for the subtle moods and tones that are both the content and the characteristic look of his paintings.

In 1948–9 a European tour that included France, Italy and Greece was perhaps responsible for the more Classical basis of Stamos's painterly reveries with their floral or altar-like forms in earth–sky landscapes, floating moons and evocations of the infinite. He shared this interest in the symbolic forms of ancient mythical themes and primordial *motifs* with such other New York painters as Barnett Newman, Gottlieb, Jackson Pollock and Clyfford Still, all of whom also sought a universally meaningful, though still personal and subjective basis for content in their art. By 1952 a more consolidated abstract structure began to replace the earlier allusive imagery; references to the womb or to biological and geological formations were abandoned in favour of a spare, lightly textured surface within a generally more abstract pictorial enterprise. Stamos often works in series, and by 1958 had embarked on a group of pictures such as *High Snow, Low Sun, No. 3* (1957, New York, André Emmerich Gallery), which established cosmically radiant colour presences, suggesting without describing the kinetic effects of atmosphere and weather. Later works continued this intention of gently evoking climatic moods and effects through colour: *Day of Two Suns* (1963, Minneapolis, Minn., Walker Art Center), with its tilted dark mass drifting above a roughly scrubbed 'horizon' and a pale 'sea', or *Aegean Sun Box No. 2* (1965, André Emmerich Gallery), a more precisely geometric organization of a thin horizontal bar of colour over an off-centre rectangle on a light ground, still find their sources in the colours, air and light of nature. Stamos retains a Classical directness in his cohesive compositions, delicately modulating earth or marine colours with great clarity and refinement. In 1959 the Corcoran Gallery in Washington, D.C., held a retrospective exhibition of his work.

Kenneth B. Sawyer. *Stamos*, Paris 1960.
Ralph Pomeroy. 'Stamos' Sun-Boxes', *Art News* LXVII, March 1968.

Stančić, Miljenko. Yugoslav painter, b. 1926 in Varaždin, Croatia. After studying at the Academy of Art in Zagreb from 1945 to 1952 Stančić became a lecturer there in 1961. Apart from paintings he also produces graphic works and designs books and theatrical décors.

In his paintings Stančić creates a phantom company which is half human, half creature and which he sets against a dream background compounded of shadows, premonitions and desires. His colouring—a cross between Vermeer and the Neo-Surrealists—produces hallucinatory effects which are well suited to his themes: panic and death,

compulsive ideas and Freudian libido dreams. Any anecdotal tendencies are transformed into a genuine pictorial reality by the refulgence and sensuality of the colour. It is the radiant power of the colour which lends artistic permanence to these compositions, many of which might otherwise produce a sweet and soporific effect.

Miroslav Krleza. M. *Stančić*, Zagreb 1964.

Stankiewicz, Richard. American painter and sculptor, b. 1922 in Philadelphia, Pennsylvania. He began working as a naturalistic painter, though this mode of expression changed (after serving in the Second World War) when he studied at the Hans Hofmann School of Fine Arts, New York (1948–50). The next two years he studied in Paris, first at the Atelier Fernand Léger; later he turned to sculpture, working under Ossip Zadkine. With the latter he began carving and modelling and then produced terracotta pieces, later turning to wire and finally welding. In welding he renewed a contact of his youth, having lived next to a foundry dump in Detroit. Stankiewicz employs the discarded object—pipes, nuts, bolts, screws, wheels, springs and other machine parts—materials which seem an extension of the Dadaists' found objects. His works have a sense of the force, energy and thrust of machinery; with crude elements he creates a relationship of parts which produces coherence, cohesiveness and direction (*Diving to the Ocean Bed*, 1958, steel, New York, Coll. William Rubin). Though his early works often contain a strong degree of humour and wit, in the 1960s he concerned himself less with the parody of human and animal figures and more with non-objective design, creating lighter, more lyrical abstract forms (*Untitled: 1961—24*, steel, New York, Stable Gallery). His sculpture was included in the Twenty-ninth Biennale, Venice (1958), and the Sixth Bienal, São Paulo (1961). He was given a large one-man show at the Jewish Museum, New York, in 1964.

Fairfield Porter. 'Stankiewicz Makes a Sculpture: Soldier', *Art News* LIV, September 1955.
Richard Stankiewicz. 'An Open Situation', *Arts Yearbook 8: Contemporary Sculpture*, New York 1964.

Stázewski, Henryk. Polish painter, b. 1894 in Warsaw. After studying at the Warsaw Academy from 1914 to 1919 Stázewski became a founder member of the *Blok* Constructivist group and editor of its magazine, which appeared under the same name. From 1924 onwards he was in contact with the Polish exponents of Neo-Plasticism and in 1926 became a founder member of the *Praesens* group. In the early 1930s he went to Paris, where he was in close contact with Mondrian and Seuphor. He also joined the *Cercle et Carré* group and, in 1932, the *Abstraction-Création* association. After returning to

Poland he became a member of the *a.r.* (Revolutionary Artists) group in Lodz. He is now living in Warsaw.

Apart from Strzeminski, Stázewski is the most important of the early exponents of geometrical abstraction in Poland. During his early period he dealt with Constructivist problems in compositions executed, for the most part, either in black and white or as white monochromes. Then, towards the end of the 1950s, he began to come to terms with spatial and kinetic problems in white and coloured reliefs. Of recent years he has also created works in which gradations of colour are arranged in series within a rhythmical framework of simple, relief-like geometrical forms.

Catalogue, *Henryk Stázewski*, Lodz Museum of Art, Lodz 1969.
Peinture moderne polonaise: Sources et recherches, Musée Galliera, Paris 1969.

Steer, Philip Wilson. British painter, b. 1860 in Birkenhead, Cheshire; d. 1942 in London. Steer was an exact contemporary and close friend of Sickert. He studied in Paris (1882) under the academics Bouguereau and Cabanel, returning to England in 1884. He was a founder member in 1886 of the New English Art Club—a radical group in which *plein-air* Impressionism, established twelve years earlier in France, now also found support in England.

Steer's four main themes were: compositions (characteristically beach scenes with children), in a decorative form of late Impressionism, using high-keyed colour; oil and watercolour landscapes, recalling Constable; decorously erotic nudes harking back to eighteenth-century France; and portraits (including some of Steer's best works, e.g. *Mrs. Cyprian Williams and Her Children*, 1890–1; Tate Gallery, London). His inventive exhaustion after c. 1910 and decline to tasteful, repetitive picture production was partly due to the deadening effect of English society patronage.

R. Ironside. *Wilson Steer*, London and Toronto 1943.
D. S. MacColl. *Philip Wilson Steer*, London 1945.

Steinberg, Saul. American painter and cartoonist, b. 1914 in Râmnicul-Sărat, Rumania. After attending schools in Bucharest, he lived for several years in Milan, where he attended the Reggio Politecnico, studying psychology, sociology and architecture. He received a degree of Dottore d'Architettura in 1940 from this institution. From 1939 to 1941 he practised architecture in Milan and in the latter year escaped to the Dominican Republic and then to New York (1942) in the course of the Second World War. He held his first one-man show in 1943 at the Wakefield Gallery, New York, and in the same year entered the United States Navy. Since the war his work has been published on a regular basis in *The New Yorker* and other magazines. His drawings,

cartoons and border decorations have much in common with the child-like quality of Klee, though Steinberg has denied any direct influence. The dominant force upon his style has been the discipline of his architectural training, in which he combines a technological orientation of precision, draughtsmanship and reason with ambiguity, violence and joy. Throughout his career he has reduced his repertory so that he comes ever closer to pure geometry (*Ariadne*, 1966, ink and pastel, New York, Sidney Janis Gallery). Among the publications of his drawings are *All in Line* (1945), *The Art of Living* (1949), *The Passport* (1954), *The Labyrinth* (1959) and *The New World* (1965).

Pierre Baudson. Catalogue, *Steinberg*, Museum Boymans–van Beuningen, Rotterdam 1967.

Steinlen, Alexandre. Swiss-French painter and illustrator, b. 1859 in Lausanne; d. 1923 in Paris. He went to Paris in 1882 and there produced lithographs for various magazines and journals. He also did posters, including one of Yvette Guilbert. His paintings have a certain affinity with Daumier's in their depiction of the lower classes.

Stella, Frank. American painter, b. 1935 in Malden, Massachusetts. He studied painting at Phillips Academy, then at Princeton University under Stephen Greene (b. 1918) and the art historian William Seitz. Although his earliest work was oriented towards Abstract Expressionism, the first paintings shown publicly were a rigorous group of black canvases (1958–9) in which parallel stripes, outlined by bare canvas, reiterated or inverted the pattern of their framing edges. The austerity of this work was a denial of over-indulgent Abstract Expressionist gesturing, while the organization responded to the non-relational compositions of Barnett Newman. By means of the stripes 'generated' by the edges of the canvas, structure was deduced from the literal format rather than depicted within a field, thus emphasizing the painting's existence as an object. Stella's choice of particularly artificial metallic or fluorescent colours also heightened the man-made, artificial quality of the painting. Stella, always a prolific painter, tended to work in series, varying the solutions to particular problems of structure, colour or shape while extending the range and variables of his work as a whole.

Between 1960 and 1963 Stella worked on three series of metallic aluminium, copper and magenta paintings in multiple geometric shapes (including trapezoids with cut-out centres, octagons, pentagons and parallelograms) with concentric parallel striations. The choice of which edge or edges would generate the stripes (some of the canvas borders might cut obliquely across them) was determined only by the painter's will. In 1962 a group of multicoloured paintings, in which concentric bands of graded values created depth illusions like camera bellows, served as a kind of antidote to the monochrome and formal rigour of the other series. Between 1964 and 1965 Stella worked simultaneously on two series, one of zigzags and irregular V-shaped stripes in metallic polychrome (*Empress of India*, 1965, Los Angeles, Coll. Irving Blum) and another of pinwheels in brilliant fluorescent stripes. These two groups advanced the notion of literalness and enlarged the vocabulary of his painting. At the same time he departed from the stripe technique in a series of eccentrically shaped paintings whose internal shapes coincided only partially with the silhouette of the canvas. Triangles were made to wedge into rectangles and squares, or trapezoids seemed to be superimposed over banded rectilinear elements (*Moultonboro III*, 1966, New York, Leo Castelli Gallery). Later an intricate sequence of interlacing circles, arcs and fanning protractor shapes became Stella's concern (1966–7). In a wide range of searing, Day-Glo fluorescent colours he explored many formats (including the tondo, joined half and quarter circles, and squares within hemispheres), all filled with radial strokes and ambiguously juxtaposed arcs and bands (*Sabra II*, 1967, Leo Castelli Gallery). Although still concerned with formal problems, Stella's notion of structure became increasingly complex through the interaction of shapes and synthetic but sensuous colours.

Michael Fried. 'Shape as Form: Frank Stella's New Paintings', *Artforum* V, No. 3, 1966; Catalogue, *Three American Painters: Noland, Olitski, Stella*, Fogg Art Museum, Cambridge (Mass.) 1965.

Stella, Joseph. American painter, b. 1877 near Naples, Italy; d. 1946 in New York. Educated in Italy, he arrived in the United States in 1896 and immediately began studies in medicine and pharmacology. He withdrew from these subjects in 1897 and enrolled at the Art Students' League. The following year he entered the New York School of Art where he attracted the attention of William M. Chase and won a scholarship for the following academic year. In the decade 1900–10 Stella was constantly sketching scenes of his neighbourhood, the Lower East Side of New York (*Italian Immigrant*, c. 1907, pencil, New York, Coll. Edgar Kaufmann, Jr.). His first drawing was published in *Outlook* in 1905 for an article entitled 'Americans in the Rough', depicting immigrants at Ellis Island. This published work was followed by illustrations for Ernest Poole's novel *The Voice of the Street* (1906) and drawings of mining disasters and the mining environment of West Virginia (1907) and Pittsburgh (1909) for the publication *Survey*. In 1909–10 he went to Europe, staying mainly in Italy, and in 1911–12 he was in Paris where he met Matisse, Modigliani, Carrà and probably Boccioni and Severini. In 1913 he had his first

one-man show, as well as participating in the Armory Show. By 1917–18 his relationship to Futurism was already manifest in *Madonna of Coney Island* (New York, Metropolitan Museum of Art) and in 1919 he first exhibited a major industrial painting, *The Gas Tank*, under the title *American Landscape* (1918, New York, Coll. Mr. and Mrs. Roy R. Neuberger). His first version of *Brooklyn Bridge* (1919–20, New Haven, Conn., Yale University Art Gallery), with its architectonic angularity and emphasis on deep perspective, was exhibited at a one-man show at the Bourgeois Galleries in 1920. At this time he joined the Société Anonyme with Marcel Duchamp and Man Ray and exhibited with them throughout the 1920s. This style continued through the 1930s with such works as *American Landscape* (1929, Minneapolis, Walker Art Center). Though known as America's first and leading Futurist, not all of his works are purely Futurist and his connections with the Italian Futurist movement are tenuous at best. In the 1930s and 1940s he sometimes concentrated on a few elements, made prominent through the use of dark outlines as in the 1944 *Still Life* (Plainfield, N.J., Coll. Dr. and Mrs. Leonard M. Weinstock) and at other times employed a style reminiscent of the Immaculates, a mode of expression dating back to his early career (*Sunflower*, c. 1919, crayon, Glen Head, N.Y., Coll. Sergio Stella).

John I. H. Baur. *Joseph Stella*, New York 1963.

Stenvert, Curt. Austrian painter, sculptor and filmmaker, b. 1920 in Vienna. Stenvert studied at the Academy of Art in Vienna under Gutersloh and Wotruba from 1945 to 1949. He is now living in Vienna.

In 1951 Stenvert gave up sculpture and painting to make experimental and documentary films. It was not until 1962 that he began to sculpt again and, even then, it remained a part-time occupation until 1966, when he completed his last film. His sculptures are 'functional constructions' made up of trivial objects. They are meant to portray 'human situations' and tend to be both anecdotal and macabre.

Stephenson, Ian. British painter, b. 1934 in Browney, Co. Durham. Stephenson studied fine art at King's College, Newcastle (1951–6). His work has developed from the inspiration of American Abstract Expressionism, especially that of Pollock, and is concerned with that reconciliation of unity and variety within the canvas that Pollock stands for. He achieves this by building up a stipple pattern of strong colour sprayed on to the surface and sometimes including a rectangle or some other feature within the colour area. More recently he has been experimenting with multiple canvases. His work is represented in the Tate Gallery.

Stephenson, John Cecil. British painter, goldsmith and designer, b. 1889 in Co. Durham. From 1908 to 1914 he attended Leeds School of Art, from 1914 to 1918 the Royal College of Art and in 1918 the Slade School. In 1932 he turned from straightforward representation to abstract painting, exhibiting with the *7 & 5 Group*, and was a member of *Circle*. His work at that time was inspired by Mondrian and Moholy-Nagy. In 1951 he was commissioned to do a mural for the Festival of Britain, and since that time he has done a number of mural designs.

Stern, Jonasz. Polish painter, graphic artist and book illustrator, b. 1904 in Kalusz. He studied in Lemberg, and from 1929 to 1934 at the academy in Cracow. He is a member of the *Grupa Krakowska*, which sought to divorce itself from the academy. From 1939 to 1942 he was in Lemberg; he was imprisoned in a concentration camp and only escaped death by a fluke, when 600 other Jews were shot.

Sterne, Maurice. American painter and sculptor, b. 1878 in Libau, on the Baltic; d. 1957 in New York City. Between 1891 and 1899 he received both formal and practical training in art, first working as a designer's helper in a map-engraving firm, then studying mechanical drawing at Cooper Union and finally spending five years at the National Academy of Design. He received his first one-man show at the Old Country Sketch Club, New York, two years before he left for Europe on a scholarship from the Academy. He was in Europe from 1904 to 1908 and then went to Greece, where he began doing sculpture under the inspiration of ancient marbles. From 1911 to 1914 he travelled to Egypt, India, Burma, Java and Bali. His early style reflects both the European artistic influence of Cubism and the cultural and ecological impressions made by the East (*Dance of the Elements*, 1913, Raleigh, N.C., North Carolina Museum of Art). He returned to the United States in 1915. In the 1920s the Cubistic elements vanished from his paintings in favour of a more realistic approach. Such canvases as *Girl in Blue Chair* (1928, New York, Coll. Mr. and Mrs. Samuel A. Lewisohn) is typical of the less interesting subject, psychological effect and paint surface seen in these years. This bland style can also be seen in his heavy-handed, block-like sculpture (*Monument to Early Settlers*, 1926–9, Worcester, Mass., Rogers-Kennedy Memorial). While teaching at the California School of Fine Arts, San Francisco (1934–6), he was working on another monument, *Welcoming the People*, for Fairmount Park, Philadelphia, and murals for the library of the Department of Justice Building, Washington, D.C. These murals were not installed until 1941, because of opposition to the panel *Ordeal* which portrayed a victim of the Inquisition with his torturer

and a churchman. Sterne's late style is one of a light, airy, lyrical spirit, more the work of a young man than an ageing artist (*After the Rain*, 1948, New York, Museum of Modern Art).

Catalogue, *Maurice Sterne. Retrospective Exhibition 1902–1932*, Museum of Modern Art, New York 1933.
C. L. Mayerson (ed.). *Shadow and Light—The Life, Friends and Opinions of Maurice Sterne*, New York 1965.

Stieglitz, Alfred—*see* **291 Gallery**

Stijl, de. *De Stijl* was the name given to an artistic movement and magazine which were both founded in Leiden, Holland, in 1917 by Theo van Doesburg and Piet Mondrian. Other members of the movement included Vilmos Huszár, Antonie Kok, Bart van der Leck, Gerrit Rietveld, J. J. P. Oud, Robert van't Hoff, Georges Vantongerloo, Gino Severini and Hans Richter. The *de Stijl* movement was completely abstract and its followers all rejected the use of sense data or of any aspect of visual reality. They also reduced the pictorial, plastic and architectonic elements in their work to a basic canon. The thinking underlying this movement stemmed in part from the ideas evolved by the Dutch philosopher Shoenmaeker in his *Het nieuve werdbeeld* (*The New Image of the World*) of 1915 and his *Beginselen der beeldende Wiskunde* (*Principles of Plastic Mathematics*) of 1916. Schoenmaeker postulated a universal consciousness, which naturally gave rise to a supra-personal, collective style. Mondrian regarded this 'universal consciousness' as the source of all art which, he considered, should be dedicated to the representation of 'universal harmony'. This universality, which was necessarily 'anti-subjective', was to be achieved by the abstraction of forms and colour. Consequently, the *de Stijl* artists reduced their colour range to the primary colours red, blue and yellow and the contrasting colours white, black and grey and also simplified their linear composition by using only rectangular structures. This was the technical arsenal with which they sought to establish their *nieuwe beelding* or 'Neo-Plasticism', which was the alternative name given to *de Stijl* from 1920 onwards following the publication of Mondrian's book under the same title. Mondrian, who had made a major contribution to the ideological development of the group, left in 1925. The year before van Doesburg had evolved his 'Elementalism', a new type of composition based on contrasts, which modified the original *de Stijl* conception. From the very outset the *de Stijl* had gravitated towards other artistic spheres, especially architecture. Oud, Wils and van't Hoff developed a type of architecture based on Cubist structures. From 1923 onwards van Doesburg also contributed to *de Stijl* architecture, which exerted a considerable influence on Functionalism and the International Modern Style. The *de Stijl* movement came to an end in 1931 following van Doesburg's death. The *de Stijl* magazine ceased publication in the same year.

Catalogue, *De Stijl*, Museum of Modern Art, New York 1953.
H. L. C. Jaffé. *De Stijl: 1917–1931*, London 1956.
Catalogue, *Mondrian, De Stijl, and Their Impact*, Marlborough-Gerson Gallery, New York 1964.

Still, Clyfford. American painter, b. 1904 in Grandin, North Dakota. He received his art training at Spokane University, where he was a scholarship student and earned a Master's degree in 1935 from Washington State University. He remained at this institution for the next six years as an instructor and assistant professor. During this period he passed through many phases and styles—Bauhaus, Dada, Surrealism, Cubism—but did not remain with any of them. Between 1941 and 1943 artistic production was curtailed, as he was working in the war industries in Oakland and San Francisco, California. The number of works he executed at this time was significant enough, however, to assemble a sufficient number of canvases for his first one-man show at the San Francisco Museum of Art (1943). For the next two years he taught at the Richmond Professional Institute, turning out a great many works, some of which were incorporated in an exhibition in 1945 at Peggy Guggenheim's Art of This Century Gallery. Included in this show was *Jamais* (1944, Venice, Coll. Peggy Guggenheim), a boldly executed composition with vaguely Surrealistic overtones and a certain dark Romanticism of flame-like or bold forms. He returned to the West Coast for the next four years, teaching at the California School of Fine Arts in San Francisco, and then returned to New York, where he stayed from 1950 to 1961. In New York he arrived simultaneously with J. Pollock, B. Newman and M. Rothko at oil on canvas painting of mural scale. He very often introduced contrasts of sharp-edged claw-like forms against broad areas of colour, executed in extremely thick impasto as opposed to the thinly applied pigment of Rothko and Newman (*1948-D*, 1948, New York, Coll. Prof. William Rubin). Since 1961 Still has lived and worked in seclusion in Westminster, Maryland.

Catalogue, *Clyfford Still*, Institute of Contemporary Art, University of Pennsylvania, Philadelphia 1963.
Clyfford Still. Thirty-three Paintings in the Albright-Knox Art Gallery, Buffalo 1966.

Storrs, John Bradley. American sculptor, b. 1885 in Chicago; d. 1956 in Mer, France. He studied in Germany, Chicago, Pennsylvania and Paris. He also travelled a great deal, and after 1920 lived mainly in France. During the war he was imprisoned in a concentration camp. He worked in a Cubist manner, making abstract sculptures in stone, wood, bronze and other metals, and coloured terra-cotta.

Strindberg, August. Swedish dramatist and painter, b. 1849 in Stockholm; d. 1912 in Stockholm. Strind-berg's activity as a painter, although little known and little appreciated outside Scandinavia, occupies an important place not only within his own oeuvre, but also within the pre-history of non-objective painting. The *motifs* of his paintings, for the most part landscapes and seascapes, are recognizable only with difficulty. The artist himself termed his work 'symbolist'; his contemporaries, however, saw an organic link between his pictures and his interest in the occult—above all, his alchemical experiments. This judgement may appear less implausible in view of the following description, by the writer K. O. Strombäck, of the genesis of Strindberg's pictures: 'Streams of colour are slapped on to the canvas with the brush. From there, the work proceeds with the bare hands, and by this unusual means he rubs and kneads this dough of colours into an even greater confusion.'

The majority of Strindberg's paintings are in private collections; the national museums in Stockholm and Copenhagen possess examples of his work.

Karl Jaspers. *Strindberg et van Gogh*, Paris 1953.

Struycken, Peter. Dutch painter and sculptor, b. 1939 in The Hague. Struycken trained at the Academy of Fine Arts in The Hague and now teaches at the Arnhem Academy. In his work he investigates the interaction of form and colour and the properties revealed by each of these in the course of their interaction. Of recent years Struycken has made use of a computer in order to eliminate the element of chance.

Strzeminski, Vladislav. Polish painter and art theorist, b. 1893 in Minsk, Russia; d. 1952 in Lodz. After attending the Military School of Engineering in St. Petersburg Strzeminski studied art in Moscow, 1918–19. He was an active member of the artistic *avant-garde* in Russia; he collaborated with Malevich in Vitebsk and worked as a revolutionary activist in Smolensk. In 1922 he and his wife, the sculptress Katarzyna Kobro, left Russia to live in Poland. In 1923 he organized the 'New Art' exhibition in Vilno, which marked the beginning of the Polish Constructivist movement. He also became a founder member of *Blok*, the Constructivist artists' association, in 1924. In 1926 he worked with the *Praesens* group and in 1930 joined with H. Stázewski, K. Kobro and others in founding the *a.r.* (Revolutionary Artists) group. From 1931 onwards he lived in Lodz and between 1945 and 1950 taught at the Lodz Academy.

Strzeminski was one of the pioneers and one of the leading representatives of modern art in Poland. In 1928 he formulated his own artistic theory—unism—which he arrived at from an analysis of the implications of Cubism and Suprematism and which sought to establish the organic 'unity' of texture, colour and composition. The pictures which Strzeminski painted from 1930 to 1934, in which the whole of the picture surface is covered with vibrant colour, anticipate certain departures. His late pictures, in which the colouring is very powerful, are the outcome of his research into the phenomenon of the 'after-image' (*powidok*). Strzeminski published numerous writings on the theory of art, including *Unism in Painting*, 1928, *Spatial Compositions: Calculations of the Time-Space Rhythm*, 1931 (joint production with K. Kobro), and *The Theory of Perception*, 1957 (posthumous publication).

Catalogue, *K. Kobro and V. Strzeminski*, Warsaw 1956–7.
Peinture moderne polonaise: Sources et recherches, Musée Galliera, Paris 1969.

Stuck, Franz von. German painter, graphic artist and sculptor, b. 1863 in Tettweis, Lower Bavaria; d. 1928 in Tetschen (Decin). After studying at the School of Arts and Crafts and the Polytechnic in Munich from 1882 to 1884 Stuck enrolled at the Munich Academy in 1885. But he did not attend regularly, preferring to model himself on Böcklin and Leubach, whom he greatly admired. During this period Stuck also contributed to the *Fliegende Blätter*. Meanwhile, his work grew more and more original and in 1889 he won the second prize at the Munich annual exhibition. Although Stuck continued to paint mythological and symbolistic scenes and representative portraits, by the turn of the century his style contained features which revealed his preoccupation with the *Jugendstil*. Meanwhile, in 1893, he had become a founder member of the Munich Secession and in 1895 obtained a professorial post at the Munich Academy, where his pupils included Kandinsky, Klee, Purrmann and Levy. In 1906 he was elevated to the nobility. He was also made an honorary member of the academies in Berlin, Dresden, Milan and Stockholm. In later life Stuck worked as a sculptor. His best-known work in this medium is his *Amazone*. When he came to build and decorate his Munich town house—the *Stuck-Villa*—he tried to realize the *Jugendstil* conception of the 'total work of art'. Stuck was one of the celebrated Munich 'painter princes' of the turn of the century, whose reputations soon dimmed once they had died. But, although Stuck was greatly overrated during his lifetime, his contribution to the *Jugendstil* is not to be denied. With their simple decorative composition and their flat colours Stuck's symbolistic scenes, which revolve around mythological or erotic *motifs* and in which the form and colouring no longer fulfil a purely descriptive function but also set the mood of the picture, helped to pave the way for a new approach to painting, which was subsequently explained and developed by Stuck's pupils, especially Kandinsky.

F. v. Ostini. *Das Gesamtwerk Franz von Stucks*, Munich 1909.
H. W. Singer (ed.). *Zeichnungen von Franz von Stuck*, Leipzig 1912.

Stupica, Gabrijel. Yugoslav painter, b. 1913 in Dragoše, Gorensko, Slovenia. Stupica studied at the Academy of Art in Zagreb. Since 1946 he has held a professorial post at the Academy of Art in Ljubljana.

In the periods immediately preceding and following the Second World War Stupica was painting Realistic colour compositions. From these he went on to psychological studies executed in a modified form of Expressionism. Between 1943 and 1946 he had been using a dark range of colours. This too was abandoned in favour of a brighter palette, thus reducing and eventually eliminating the plasticity of his works, so that in the end he was producing flat, linear compositions. At this point he began to incorporate collage and mock collage into his works, using them as elements in his pessimistic image of man. Because he himself was full of doubts as to the nature of reality the dividing line between reality and illusion was also indistinct in his paintings. Fragmentation and dissonance, inscrutability and illusion became the vehicles for his sensitivity. With his growing alienation from the tangible world he gradually evolved an ascetic pictorial world based on a system of relations which virtually defy both conceptual and visual definition and which have their being in the shadowy zone which separates abstract from figurative art. In these late works the mock collages, which are painted with exaggerated precision and are intended to represent indefinable toy phantoms and banal objects, are illuminated by the lonely light of intuition.

Luc Menaše. *Gabrijel Stupica*, Ljubljana 1959.
O. Bihalji-Merin. *Gabrijel Stupica: Seine Brautbilder und Selbstporträts*, Brussels 1964.
Vera Horvat-Pintarić. *Gabrijel Stupica*, Zagreb 1966.

Sturm, der. The *Sturm* was a magazine founded by Herwarth Walden in Berlin in 1910. Like Karl Kraus's *Fackel* in Vienna and Papini's *Voce* in Florence, it was a polemical publication designed to promote *avant-garde* developments, and, as such, it marked the beginning of Early Expressionism in the German literary sphere. Very soon, however, Walden extended the scope of his magazine to include the fine arts. Thus, in its first year of publication, the *Sturm* presented Oskar Kokoschka's *Portrait of the Week*, a remarkable series of portrait drawings which foreshadowed the Expressionist portrait proper. In the second year of publication works by the *Brücke* artists were reproduced and in the third year works by the *Blauer Reiter* artists. The critical writings published by the *Sturm* included contributions from Marc, Kandinsky, Delaunay and Léger. The Futurist manifesto was also printed.

In March 1912 the Sturm Gallery was opened and in the monthly exhibitions which followed the Berlin art public was introduced to the work of many of the most important artists of the century. In retrospect

Walden's instinct seems quite phenomenal, for at the time these artists were virtually unknown. From these modest beginnings Walden quickly built up a whole network of *avant-garde* exhibitions, which covered all of Europe and even extended as far as Tokyo and Canada. But the really crucial exhibitions were held in 1912: the *Blauer Reiter* and their associates exhibited in March and the Futurists in April. In May there was an exhibition of recent French graphic art, including a large number of Picassos. Then came the German Expressionists, who were represented by Kandinsky, Marc, Jawlensky, Campendonk and others. They were followed by the French Expressionists: Braque, Derain, Vlaminck, Friesz, Laurencin and Herbin. Other artists shown in the Sturm Gallery at that time included Ensor, Delaunay, Soffici, Severini, Archipenko and the members of the Swiss *Modern Association*. From this wide range of contemporary artists Walden was able to select the contributors to the First German Autumn Salon, which he staged in 1913 and which was representative of the whole of the European *avant-garde*. Later, in 1914, Chagall also exhibited in the Sturm Gallery. So too did Léger, Gleizes, Metzinger, Molzahn, Muche and the leading Czech artists.

After the First World War Walden founded the Sturm School, where Muche taught from 1916 to 1920, the Sturm Theatre and the Sturm Bookshop. But the whole *Sturm* movement was essentially a product of early Expressionism and in the course of the 1920s its importance greatly diminished. Then Herwarth Walden went to Russia and in 1928 the *Sturm* magazine ceased publication.

Edith Hoffmann. 'Der Sturm', *Signature* 18, London 1954.
Nell Walden and Lothar Schreyer (eds.). *Der Sturm*, Baden-Baden 1954.
H. Bolliger. Catalogue, *Der Sturm*, Kunstgewerbemuseum, Zürich 1955.
Lothar Schreyer. *Erinnerung an Sturm und Bauhaus*, Munich 1956.
Catalogue, *Der Sturm: Herwarth Walden und die europäische Avantgarde, Berlin 1912–1932*, Nationalgalerie, Berlin 1961.
Nell Walden. *Herwarth Walden: Ein Lebensbild*, Berlin 1963.

Stursa, Jan. Czech sculptor, b. 1880; d. 1925. He was deeply influenced by Rodin and Bourdelle, whose work was exhibited in Prague in 1902 and 1909.

Subirachs, José Maria. Spanish sculptor, b. 1927 in Barcelona. He works mainly in metal. He studied in Barcelona, and worked in the studio of Enrique Casanova, 1948–9. In 1951 he went to Paris and then on to Belgium. He had a one-man exhibition in 1951 at the Casa del Libro, Barcelona, and again in Madrid, in the open air, in 1957. His work consists of reliefs, latterly made of iron. In 1958 he won the Julio González Prize in Barcelona.

Sugai, Kumi. Japanese painter, b. 1919 in Kobe. Sugai studied at the School of Art in Osaka from 1927 to 1932. Until 1952 he had an *atelier* in Kobe. In 1952 he moved to Paris, where he is still living today.

Little is known about Sugai's artistic development before 1952, when he began to make tentative experiments in Surrealism and the abstract style of the *École de Paris*. In 1954 he changed his palette, using dark, powerful and luminous colours to portray pictorial signs developed from eastern forms. In 1956 he abandoned atmospheric colouring and evolved new large-format pictorial forms. In the works of this period Sugai expressed his relationship to the world by means of beam shapes, intertwining spirals, circles, triangles and squares, the tensions set up by these signs being offset by harmonic colour contrasts which exert an exotic appeal. The theme of these pictures is pure, isolated form. Since 1963 Sugai has enlarged his pictorial symbols to monumental proportions and given greater plasticity to his pictorial objects by his use of colour whilst at the same time veiling their symbolic import.

André de Mandiargues. *Sugaï*, Paris 1960.
Jean-Clarence Lambert. 'Sugaï, peintre érotique', *XX Siècle* 25, May 1963.
Catalogue, *Kumi Sugai*, Kestner Gesellschaft, Hanover 1963.

Sugarman, George. American sculptor, b. 1912 in New York. He studied in New York at Hunter College. He held his first one-man show in 1958. At first his sculpture was abstract and Cubist in style; later he became concerned with form and the use of space, and produced groups of separate pieces spread out over a wide area. He made striking use of colour, mainly on wood.

Sullivan, Patrick J. American painter, b. 1894 in Braddock, Pennsylvania. He first worked as a playground manager in Wheeling, West Virginia, and after the First World War for the American Railway Express Co. in the same city. He began painting during his many hours of free time in the Depression years. His first 'all-original canvas' was painted in 1936—*Man's Procrastinating Pastime* (New York, Coll. Sidney Janis). Like all his works, this painting is firmly rooted in the folk tradition but with a certain relationship to Surrealism in its grotesque figures and highly symbolic subject matter. Most of his works have some hidden meaning, a factor which places Dali high on Sullivan's list of modern masters, while he admires Rousseau for his Realism. He uses pure colours ground in oil, and when dry he sandpapers the built-up pigments, which are then covered with a flat varnish. Sullivan was included in the Museum of Modern Art's 1938 exhibition *Masters of Popular Painting*.

Sidney Janis. *They Taught Themselves*, New York 1942.

Sunyer, Joaquin. Spanish painter and etcher, b. 1875 in Sitges; d. 1956. From 1893 onwards he studied with Steinlen and Willette in Paris, and lived there until 1911, when he moved to Sitges. His figures, nudes, portraits and landscapes show the influence of Cézanne. He has also done book illustrations.

Suprematism. A non-objective type of art invented by Kasimir Malevich. In his book, *The Non-Objective World*, Malevich states that 'the Suprematists have . . . abandoned the representation of the human face (and of natural objects in general) and have found new symbols with which to render direct feelings (rather than externalized reflections of feelings), for the Suprematist does not observe and does not touch—he feels'.

The 'new symbols' employed by Malevich were the square, the triangle and the circle: 'The Suprematist square and the forms proceeding out of it can be likened to the primitive marks (symbols) of aboriginal man which represented, in their combinations, not ornament but a feeling of rhythm.'

Malevich traced the beginnings of Suprematism to the back-cloth designs he made for *Victory over the Sun*, a Futurist opera by Kruchenykh, with music by Matyushin, first performed in December 1913 in St. Petersburg. One of Malevich's designs does indeed use a purely geometric design of two triangles, one white, one black, placed so as to form a square. However, Malevich did not actually proclaim his Suprematist system until December 1915, at the exhibition *0.10*, where he showed thirty-five non-objective works, none of which was actually described as Suprematist, but of which Malevich said 'real forms were approached in many cases as the ground for formless, painterly masses from which a painterly picture was created, quite unrelated to nature'.

The paintings at *0.10* were mostly simple, geometrical compositions, such as *Black Square* (Leningrad, Russian Museum). Other paintings of this period gradually introduced colour; in *Suprematist Composition* (1914, New York, Museum of Modern Art), a 'dynamic axis' was employed, and the balancing geometrical forms were played off one against the other, suggesting space by means of gradations of colour. After 1916, Malevich's Suprematist works became more complex, and as a result more three-dimensional. Shades of colour were now used—greys, browns and pinks, which threw into relief the delicate shapes juxtaposed against them, as for example in *Dynamic Suprematism* of 1916 (Moscow, Tretyakov Gallery). This and paintings like it mark the beginning of a new mystical phase in Malevich's work: his paintings were to give the spectator a sense of infinity. To this end, Malevich created in his *White on White* series of 1917–18, his most radical paintings of 'pure sensation', writing, in an essay published in the catalogue of the *Tenth State Exhibition, Abstract Creation and*

Suprematism (Moscow 1919), 'Swim! The free white sea, infinity, stretches before you.'

The graphic artist and draughtsman El Lissitzky was also a great exponent of Suprematism, and took with him the ideas behind it when he went to Germany in 1922. Through Laszlo Moholy-Nagy these ideas were passed on to the Bauhaus, on which they had considerable influence.

Surrealism. Together with Cubism, the most important movement in modern art. It transformed, not only painting and sculpture, but the theatre, the cinema, literature and revolutionary politics.

Surrealism received its name from the poet Guillaume Apollinaire, who designated as *surréaliste* a drama which he wrote in 1916 called *Les Mamelles de Tirésias*. André Breton, the founder of Surrealism (sometimes called the Pope of Surrealism), later adopted the word: 'I believe in the future resolution of these two states which in appearance are so contradictory, that of the dream, and that of reality, into a kind of absolute reality, a *surreality* if one may call it such.'

Surrealism is continuous with the Dada movement founded by Hugo Ball in Zürich in 1916 to 'draw attention, across the barriers of war and nationalism, to the few independent spirits who live for their ideals' (Hugo Ball, May 1916). The Dadaists did indeed draw attention to themselves and Dada quickly spread to Berlin, Cologne, Hanover, New York and Paris. It was a nihilistic, anti-art movement in that it was concerned to dump the inheritance of the past and enable artists to make a new start, and this attitude is exemplified in Marcel Duchamp's *Mona Lisa* to which he added a moustache and an obscene caption. But it should not be forgotten that, at the same time, Duchamp and other Dadaists were making some of the fundamental innovations in twentieth-century art.

Dada arrived in Paris in 1919 where André Breton, Louis Aragon and Philippe Soupault were already publishing the review *Littérature* which became a focus for the Paris Dada group. However, André Breton did not share the Dadaists' nihilism and in 1922 he took sole control of *Littérature*. Two years later he published that crucial document, the *First Manifesto of Surrealism*, which we can say gave Dada a programme and a sense of direction. In it he defined Surrealism, as he said, 'once and for all': 'SURREALISM, noun, masc. Pure psychic automatism by which it is intended to express either verbally or in writing the true function of thought. Thought dictated in the absence of all control exerted by reason, and outside all aesthetic or moral preoccupations.

'ENCYCL. Philos. Surrealism is based on the belief in the superior reality of certain forms of association heretofore neglected, in the omnipotence of the dream, and in the disinterested play of thought. It leads to the permanent destruction of all other psychic mechanisms and to its substitution for them in the solution of the principal problems of life.'

In the field of painting and sculpture Surrealism was a reaction against the rationalism of Cubist and Post-Cubist art. The Surrealists felt that in the postwar world it was no longer enough for artists to pursue exclusively formal ends, or to base their work ultimately on their perceptions of the world around them. As Breton wrote in *Surrealism and Painting*: 'A very strict conception of *imitation*, which has been given as the purpose of art, is the root of a grave misunderstanding. . . . The plastic work, in order to respond to the necessity for the absolute revision of real values which all minds today agree is necessary, will *refer to a purely interior model or cease to exist*.' Breton's interior model was of course the human subconscious as defined by Freud (without whom Surrealism could not have existed) and the problem for the Surrealist artist was to gain access to the subconscious and to translate the flow of thought into terms of art. In painting, Giorgio de Chirico had already produced remarkable paintings in which objects, often very ordinary, were given an intense visionary quality by being associated in unexpected contexts. The influence of de Chirico was crucial for the development of one kind of Surrealist painting. To his free associations, the Surrealists added the imagery of the dream, the only subconscious activity which is sometimes made available to the conscious mind. Thus a kind of painting developed in which traditional figurative means were used to create visions of an alternative reality. The first major work of this kind was Max Ernst's masterpiece *Les Hommes n'en Sauront Rien* of 1923, which has a dedication to Breton on the back, and this type of Surrealist painting is exemplified by the work of René Magritte, Paul Delvaux and Salvador Dali, who took it to hallucinatory extremes by using his 'paranoiac-critical' method.

Almost simultaneously, however, an alternative method of Surrealist painting was created by Picasso and Miró who, while they remained somewhat aloof from the Surrealist group, were hugely admired by Breton. In a sense they created a more authentic Surrealist art in that they used improvisatory techniques and images that were suggestive or ambiguous rather than figurative, and thus came closer to Breton's definition of Surrealism as 'pure psychic automatism': impulses were allowed to flow from the mind and embody themselves in the mark left by the gesture of the brush on the canvas. Picasso's *Three Dancers* (1925, London, Tate Gallery) is the first masterpiece of this kind of painting, and within the Surrealist group André Masson and Roberto Matta became its principal exponents.

Although Surrealism ended as a coherent movement with the outbreak of the Second World War, it was a major influence in western art in the 1940s and 1950s and its ideas have become a vital part of our political and cultural baggage.

Herbert Read (ed.). *Surrealism*, London and New York 1936.
J. L. Bédouin. *Vingt ans de surréalisme, 1939–1959*, Paris 1961.
Patrick Waldberg. *Surrealism*, New York 1965; London 1966.
José Pierre. *Le Surréalisme*, Lausanne 1966.
Marcel Jean. *The History of Surrealist Painting*, New York 1967.
William S. Rubin. Catalogue, *Dada, Surrealism and Their Heritage*, Museum of Modern Art, New York 1968.

Survage, Leopold (Sturzwasgh, Leopoldij). Finnish-French painter, b. 1879 in Willmanstrand, Finland. Survage studied at Moscow Academy from 1901 onwards. Whilst he was there he saw pictures by Matisse in the Stchukin Collection and in 1908 he went to Paris to establish contact with the Matisse school. In Paris he was greatly impressed by Cézanne. He then joined the Cubists and exhibited with them in 1912 in the Salon des Indépendants. Towards the end of the same year he painted the first of his *rythmes colorées*. A little later he created the décor for Diaghilev's production of the ballet *Mavra*. In 1937 he executed a series of murals for the International Exhibition.

After an early Fauvist phase Survage embraced a modified form of Cubism which was derived from Gleizes. During this period he produced works which, although basically Cubist, retained a lyrical and spontaneous quality not normally associated with this movement. He also placed greater stress on the figurative and spatial aspects of painting than his more orthodox companions. In 1921 he turned away from Cubism and began to paint objective signs against imaginary backgrounds after the manner of Masson. But for Survage Surrealism was always more of a decorative device. Of more recent years he has been painting abstract visions of cosmic phenomena.

Catalogue, *Leopold Survage*, Yale University Art Gallery, New Haven (Conn.) 1950.

Šutej, Miroslav. Yugoslav painter and graphic artist, b. 1936 in Duga Resa, Croatia. Šutej studied at the Academy of Art in Zagreb. In 1964–5 he worked in Paris.

In his drawings and paintings Šutej deals with the transformation processes involved in geometrical configurations. He uses the circle—the one symbol to have survived all stylistic changes from neolithic times onwards—to represent both the sun and the vulva, i.e. both the macrocosm and the microcosm. In his works this symbol is transformed into a microstructure of light, a microstructure of the linear and plastic manifestation of decorative tensions. Šutej formulates his themes, which have their being in the borderland of human perception, in linear terms. The result is an interlacing, two-dimensional network of internal structures.

Vera Horvat-Pintarić. 'Icons and Optics in the Works of Miroslav Šutej', *Umetnost Magazine* II, Belgrade 1965.

Sutherland, Graham. British painter, b. 1903 in London. Sutherland studied engraving at Goldsmiths' School of Art (1921–6). His early etchings recall Samuel Palmer. He became a Catholic in 1926 and married Kathleen Barry in 1927. He taught at the Chelsea School of Art (1928–39). During the 1930s Sutherland turned to oil and watercolour whilst retaining an etcher's linearity and the ability to translate minuscule objects into greater scale, thus resignifying them. The early *Welsh Landscapes*, some measuring only a few inches, are among his strongest works. Anthropomorphized trees occur by 1939. Sutherland's attempt to express essence beyond sensible form is in line with the mystical Romanticism of Blake, Palmer and Calvert. Particularly significant is his view of found objects—for Sutherland not dead things: 'Their sap may have gone out of them but their form remains . . . I am fascinated by the whole problem of the tensions produced by the power of growth.'

As a war artist (1940–5) Sutherland painted armaments factories and the devastation of shattered masonry and twisted iron in blitzed cities. The stylistic change to subjects for which he is now best known coincides with the first of his *Crucifixions* (1946, St. Matthew's Church, Northampton). Plant and insect themes of the late 1940s are characterized by what Ruskin precisely termed in another age 'the pathetic fallacy', and this period reflects the influence of some of Picasso's more Expressionistic pictures (e.g. *Guernica*). In contradistinction to the Grünewald/Belsen-inspired *Crucifixions*, the main figure of the Coventry Cathedral tapestry *Christ in Glory* (completed 1962) rests on Byzantine prototypes.

Future critics may come to regard Sutherland's portraits as his best works. The unambiguous demands of what he termed 'pinning down a person's essence' enabled him to achieve through *Somerset Maugham* (1949), *Churchill* (1954), *Madame Rubinstein* (1957) and certain other sitters, standards of pictorial stability and clarity in an increasingly fragmented oeuvre.

G. Sutherland. Catalogue, *On Painting*, Tate Gallery, London 1953.
D. Cooper. *Graham Sutherland*, London 1961.

Suvero, Mark di. American sculptor, b. 1933 in Shanghai, China. In 1941 di Suvero's family emigrated to California, where he later studied at San Francisco City College and the University of California at Berkeley, majoring in philosophy. He moved to New York City in 1957, and three years later had his first one-man show there.

Di Suvero's early sculpture showed a violent Expressionism, but in the early 1960s he began making small constructions that developed into his major, giant constructions of old wooden beams and planks, tyres, chains and other scrap materials from junkyards and demolished buildings (*Hank Champion*,

1960, New York, Coll. Mr. and Mrs. Robert C. Scull). Thus, like John Chamberlain and Richard Stankiewicz, di Suvero drew upon the environment for his materials, and was much more interested in the formal possibilities of his assemblages than in social comment based on the origins of his found objects, despite the Romanticism inherent in his monumental restitutions of the ruined. Di Suvero's work is on a colossal scale, and in the long, energetic strokes that the beams of his constructions cut through space, it resembles the Abstract Expressionist paintings of Franz Kline. His constructions are generally characterized by oblique, centrifugal lines of force and by a tension that holds the various suspended elements in a seemingly precarious balance. In some of di Suvero's works there are mobile seats—usually old rubber tyres—in which the viewer is invited to sit and thereby become directly involved in the space of the construction by moving around and through it.

Sidney Geist. 'New Sculptor: Mark di Suvero', *Arts* XXXV, December 1960.
Max Kozloff. 'Mark di Suvero: Leviathan', *Artforum* V, No. 10, 1967.

Svanberg, Max Walter. Swedish painter, b. 1921. He was the leader of the Imaginist group which was formed at Lund, Sweden, and which developed a form of Surrealism from 1953.

Sveinsson, Ásmundur. Icelandic sculptor, b. 1893. Sveinsson studied from 1920 to 1926 under Carl Milles in Stockholm and from 1926 to 1929 under Despiau and Bourdelle. After working in a Cubo-Expressionist style in the 1920s he began to create stylized monumental figures in cement from 1930 onwards. Since 1949 his sculptures have acquired a rhythmical quality, and he has occasionally produced pure abstracts. During his late period he has worked in terra-cotta, wood and metal.

Symbolism. 'The art of painting', wrote Gustave Courbet in 1861, 'should consist solely of the representation of objects visible and tangible to the artist.' This Realist aesthetic dominated *avant-garde* art in France in the 1860s, and in the 1870s reached a climax in the work of the Impressionist group. However, from about 1880 artists began to react in favour of a more idealizing, imaginative or abstract approach and by the end of that decade this reaction had developed into a widespread movement which became known as Symbolism. It was a literary as well as an artistic phenomenon and it was a poet, Jean Moréas, who in 1886 published a manifesto, *Le Symbolisme* (*Figaro Littéraire*, 18 September 1886), in which he said that Symbolism was 'the only word capable of adequately describing the current tendency of the creative spirit in art'. He defined its aim as being 'to clothe the idea in a sensitive form'.

The implications of this are crucially important: the Symbolist artist should seek forms in words or paint which would render an idea, rather than seeking simply to describe or imitate the visible world.

There are two tendencies in Symbolist painting. The first, and perhaps the most important historically, stems from Paul Gauguin and Émile Bernard and dates from Gauguin's second visit to Pont-Aven in Brittany in 1888. This style became known as Synthetism or *Cloisonnisme* and involved simplifying and distorting figures and objects and treating them as flat shapes with a strong outline enclosing a flat area of colour. Colour was used with great freedom: it could be strong, crude and, if necessary, non-naturalistic. Gauguin took the view that in painting colour and form and the internal relationships of the picture speak directly to the spectator: 'There is an impression resulting from any particular arrangement of colour, light and shade. It is what is called the music of the picture. Even before knowing what the picture represents . . . frequently you are seized with this magic accord. Here is the true superiority of painting over other forms of art for this emotion addresses itself to the most intimate part of the soul.' And, he says, colour should be used, not descriptively, but for 'giving the musical sensations which proceed out of its own nature, its own interior, mysterious, enigmatic force'. The ultimate implications of all this quickly became obvious and in 1891 Gauguin's follower, Maurice Denis, published his manifesto *Définition du Néo-traditionnisme* (his word for Symbolism), the much quoted first sentence of which says, 'It must be recalled that a painting, before it is a war-horse, a nude woman or some anecdote, is essentially a flat surface covered by colours assembled in a certain order.' This was a blueprint for abstract art, although complete abstraction was still twenty years in the future. Gauguin left Paris for Tahiti in 1891, but his pupil, Paul Sérusier, passed his ideas to Pierre Bonnard and the group surrounding him in Paris. They called themselves the *Nabis* and played a major role in the development of Symbolism in the 1890s.

The second tendency in Symbolism was less concerned with formal innovation. Like Gauguin, the Symbolists of this second tendency were reacting against Realism, but their reaction took the form of a retreat into the past and into an exploration of religious, historical and mythological themes, using the existing means of the European tradition of painting. The chief originators of this style were the English Pre-Raphaelites, especially Rossetti and Burne-Jones, and the French painters Gustave Moreau, Pierre Puvis de Chavannes and Odilon Redon. In the 1890s this tendency manifested itself in Paris in the annual 'Salons de la Rose-Croix' organized by the amazing figure of Joséphin Péladan from 1892 to 1897.

It is difficult to summarize the overall significance of Symbolism: on the one hand it contributed as much as Impressionism to the ultimate development of abstract art, on the other it created a great body of imaginative painting which foreshadowed the Freudian dream paintings of the twentieth-century Surrealists.

E. Raynaud. *La Mêlée Symboliste*, Paris 1918–22.

Maurice Denis. *Théories 1890–1910: Du Symbolisme et de Gauguin vers un nouvel ordre classique*, Paris 1920.

Charles Chassé. *Le Mouvement Symboliste dans l'art du XIXe siècle*, Paris 1947.

Philippe Jullian. *Dreamers of Decadence*, London and New York 1971.

Synchromism. This was a movement in which pure colour was the all-important element. It was originated in Paris in 1912 by the Americans Stanton Macdonald-Wright and Morgan Russell, and was drawn from a number of sources including Impressionism, Cézanne and Matisse. Later the Orphism of Delaunay also contributed. The theories of colour incorporated in Synchromism were based on the creation of shapes through colour and the juxtaposition of colours from different points of the spectrum to produce interesting effects.

The first American movement to arise in modern painting, it was joined by the painters Patrick Bruce and Arthur Frost, also Americans. The group took part in the Armory Show in 1913, and first came to international notice then.

William C. Agee. Catalogue, *Synchromism and Related Color Principles in American Painting, 1910–30*, M. Knoedler & Co., New York 1965.

Szapocznikow, Alina. Polish sculptress, b. 1926. Szapocznikow studied in Prague from 1945 to 1946 and in Paris from 1946 to 1951. She has been living in Paris since 1963.

Szapocznikow's sculptures are a variant of 'Expressionistic Biologism'. In 1966 she began to use new synthetic materials.

Szczuka, Mieczyslav. Polish painter, b. 1898 in Warsaw; d. 1927 in Zakopane. Szczuka was one of the pioneers of the Polish *avant-garde*. After studying at the Academy of Art in Warsaw from 1915 to 1918 he became a founder member of the Warsaw Constructivist group *Blok* in 1924 and helped to launch its magazine, which appeared under the same name. During his early period Szczuka was influenced by the Expressionists, but from 1920 onwards he became a firm advocate of applied art, which he practised in various spheres: scenography, typography, applied graphic art and architecture. He regarded architecture as a synthesis of all the arts. During his final period he turned to Constructivist painting. He also experimented with photomontages.

M. Berman and Anatol Stern. *M. Szczuka*, Warsaw 1965.

Szenes, Arpad. Hungarian-French painter, b. 1900 in Budapest. Szenes moved to Paris in 1925 and worked there with Lhôte, Léger and Bissière. In 1939 he went with his wife to Brazil but returned to Paris in 1947, where he is still living today.

Szenes paints Lyrical Abstract pictures in subdued greys and whites. Many of these works were prompted by visual impressions of landscapes.

Szymanski, Rolf. German sculptor, b. 1928 in Leipzig. Szymanski studied at the School of Arts and Crafts in Leipzig and the Academy in Berlin (under Heiliger and Scheibe). He is now living in Berlin. His essentially Informal sculptures contain veiled allusions to the human figure.

Catalogue, *Rolf Szymanski*, Kunstverein, Brunswick 1966.

T

Tabuchi, Yasse. Japanese painter, b. 1921. After studying at Tokyo University Tabuchi painted pictures which contained Surrealistic features. Since then he has developed a new style, in which linear composition combines with sensitive, restrained colouring to produce a gentle expressive effect.

Tachisme. This concept is derived from the French word *tache* (blob). In 1889 the writer Félix Fénéon used the expression *tachistes* to describe the Impressionist techniques, and in 1909 Maurice Denis suggested that the things that had 'misled the young Tachists' (presumably the Fauves) and had persuaded them 'to be content with puddles of pure colour or a few zebra stripes' were all to be found in van Gogh. These statements clearly refer to certain early forms of *Tachisme*, namely the Impressionism of Monet's *Water Lilies* and the Expressionistic elements of Fauvism. Meanwhile, in the early 1950s, this word acquired a more precise meaning. Thus, a modern Tachist work is one in which, far from planning the composition in advance, the artist applies his paint in a completely spontaneous and highly dynamic manner. The texture of the picture refers back to the actual handling, it expresses the whole 'ritual' of the painting process. Consequently, the physical quality of the paint is of great importance and we often find it applied by means of an impasted technique. In 1951 Pierre Guéguen spoke of 'Tachist painting', and he was probably the first person to use this concept after the Second World War. Commenting on this new expression Georges Mathieu pointed out that the adjective Tachist 'at least has the virtue of referring directly to the [act of] painting. It is', he suggested, 'interesting to note that the artist does not make his blot [*tache*] for the sake of the blot but because he needs a certain kind of texture in a specific area and because this is the most direct way of applying his brush to the canvas, with a greater or lesser degree of force, and without first delineating the space that he wishes to cover with paint.' Tachist painting has been influenced by certain aspects of the calligraphic art of Eastern Asia. The concept of *Tachisme* has established itself in Europe but is less popular in the United States, where the terms Abstract Impressionism, Action Painting and Drip Painting are more commonly used. The following artists have worked in the Tachist manner: Jean Dubuffet, Pollock, Wols, Mathieu, Bryen, Fautrier, Ossorio, Toshimitsu Imai, Henri Michaux, Riopelle and Sam Francis.

Pierre Guéguen. 'Tachisme et désintégration', *Aujourd'hui* V, Seine (France) and New York, April 1960.
G. Mathieu. *Au-delà du Tachisme*, Paris 1963.
J. Claus. *Theorien zeitgenössischer Malerei*, Reinbek 1963.

Taeuber-Arp, Sophie. Swiss painter and sculptress, b. 1889 in Davos; d. 1943 in Zürich. After training as a textile designer at the School of Art in St. Gallen from 1908 to 1910 Taeuber-Arp studied in Munich in 1911, at the School of Arts and Crafts in Hamburg in 1912 and again in Munich in 1913. In 1915 she became a member of the Swiss *Werkbund* and from 1916 to 1929 taught at the School of Arts and Crafts in Zürich. From 1916 to 1920 she was a member of the Dada movement. In 1921 she married Jean Arp. In 1927–8 she collaborated with Arp and van Doesburg on the decoration of a restaurant in Strasbourg. In 1928 she went to live in Meudon, remaining there until 1940. In 1930 she joined the *Cercle et Carré* association and from 1931 to 1936 was a member of the *Abstraction-Création* and *Die Allianz* associations. From 1937 to 1939 she was chief editor of the magazine *Plastique*. From 1941 to 1943, when she was living in Grasse, she collaborated with Arp, Sonia Delaunay and Magnelli.

The crucial early influences in Taeuber-Arp's artistic development came from Zürich Dadaism, Neo-Plasticism and Constructivism. Her earliest works were rhythmical colour compositions made up of pure geometrical forms. The combination of rhythmical forms and 'melodic' colours remained the basis of Taeuber-Arp's future work, in which rhythmical elements evolved from synthetic Cubism merged with melodic elements derived from pure colours after the manner of Delaunay. This is true of both her paintings and her sculptures.

G. Schmidt. *Sophie Taeuber-Arp*, Basle 1948.
E. Scheidegger (ed.). *Zweiklang: Sophie Taeuber-Arp, Hans Arp*, Zürich 1960.
Catalogue, *Sophie Taeuber-Arp*, Musée National d'Art Moderne, Paris 1964.

Tajiri, Shinkichi. American sculptor, b. 1923 in Los Angeles. Tajiri is of Japanese extraction. After attending the Art Institute of Chicago he studied in Paris under Ossip Zadkine (1948) and Fernand Léger (1949). He then made contact with the *Cobra* group. In 1955 he worked on a number of short, experimental films including *The Snakes* and *Ferdi.* From 1956 onwards he had his studio in Amsterdam, from 1962 onwards in Baarlo, Holland.

Tajiri constructed his first sculptures from scrap metal in 1950. Many of these metal figures of his are derived from vegetable forms and their surfaces are eaten away by acid. In the 1960s his style has grown progressively more severe and he now works with ready-made technical apparatuses. He himself has defined his subjects: speed, eroticism and force.

Catalogue, *Shinkichi Tajiri*, Biennale, Venice 1968.

Takamatsu, Jiro. Japanese painter, sculptor and designer, b. 1936 in Tokyo. He graduated from Tokyo University of Art in 1958. His first works were a series of *Points* and *Threads* (1961–2) which revealed his involvement with the problem of distance. These were mainly shown in conjunction with the *High Red Centre*, a group which he organized along with Akasegawa and Nakanishi. In 1964, he began a series of *Shadow* paintings in which he experimented with the elongation and reduction of the object through its shadow. In 1966 he showed his first attempts at 'solidified perspective', a term used to indicate the sculpting into three dimensions of the illusory perspective of two. *Table* looked at from the appropriate distance in line with the built-in perspective appears to the viewer as any ordinary table would; when it is approached, the perspective, in the closer position, no longer corresponds to the logic of seeing and thus one is presented with two opposing points of view in the same place. With this series he won the Carlo Cardozzo Prize at the Venice Biennale in 1968. His recent works, shown at the Paris Biennale of 1969 as a member of the *4 Bossots*, are a series of *Wrinkles* and *Nets*. The huge wrinkled cloth, which cannot be stretched because the woven squares get larger towards the inside, develops the idea of 'solidified perspective' into the tactile two-dimensional realm. He has also worked on stage and film sets. He has constructed a *Mirror Plaza* at Expo 70 in Osaka.

Takis. Greek sculptor, b. 1925 in Athens. Apart from a few protracted visits to London Takis has been living in Paris since 1954. He is a self-taught sculptor.

Between 1955 and 1958 Takis constructed sculptures from steel wire. These works, which he called *Signals*, were weighted at the top and consequently were in a state of constant vibration. In 1959 he produced the first of the magnetic and telemagnetic sculptures with which he has made his name.

J. Clay. Catalogue, *Takis*, Galerie Iolas, Paris 1966.

Tal Coat, Pierre. French painter, b. 1905 in Clohars-Carnoët, Brittany. Tal Coat is the son of a fisherman and is a self-taught artist. He first went to Paris in 1924 but returned to Brittany in 1926. Five years later, in 1931, he was back in Paris again. From 1940 to 1944 he lived in Aix-en-Provence. In 1947 he became friendly with A. Masson. He now lives in Paris and Aix-en-Provence.

Tal Coat revealed a marked talent for drawing as a child, which was furthered by his early acquaintance with professional artists. His first important works were the result of his experiences in the Spanish civil war: between 1936 and 1939 he depicted the horrors of military massacres in an Expressive style. From 1940 to 1944 he analysed Cézanne's conception of artistic form, painting pictures of natural scenes and exploring the effects of light. In c. 1945 Tal Coat was influenced by Picasso and two years later A. Masson introduced him to Chinese landscape painting. As a result he produced an important series of lyrical landscapes in the 1950s and 1960s, in which he sought to reflect the atmospheric interplay of light and movement. These works are not concerned with specific settings but with the artist's general impressions of landscape. In fact, Tal Coat has never sought to reproduce nature as such. What interests him is abstracted forms of reality.

Catalogue, *Pierre Tal Coat*, Galerie Maeght, Paris 1956.

Tamayo, Rufino. Mexican painter, b. 1899 in Oaxaca. Tamayo was an orphan. In 1907, when still a child, he went to live in San Carlos, where he enrolled at the Academy of Art in 1917. But Tamayo did not respond to formal training, and soon left the Academy. He then taught himself, seeking his inspiration, first in Impressionism, then Expressionism, and finally Cubism. But in 1921, when he was appointed head of the department for ethnographic drawing in the Mexican Anthropological Museum, he reached a turning point in his career. In this department Tamayo came into close contact with the art of the indigenous Mexican tribes and was deeply impressed by them. He then evolved a new style of painting, in which he created a synthesis of these pre-Columbian traditions and the pictorial forms of modern art. In 1926 Tamayo had his first exhibition in Mexico, which made no impression on his compatriots, who were accustomed to the revolutionary art of Diego Rivera, Orozco and Siqueiros. From 1926 to 1928 Tamayo worked in New York, returning to Mexico in 1929, where he obtained a professorial post at the School of Fine Arts. In 1933 he created his first mural, which was commissioned by the Conservatory in Mexico City. From 1938 onwards he lived chiefly in New York, where he held a professorial post at the Dalton School, although he always returned to Mexico in the summer vacations. In 1950 Tamayo went to Europe and exhibited his pictures—which still reflected the same synthesis of Mexican folklore and modern European pictorial forms—in Paris, Brussels, Rome and Venice. In 1952–3 he created large murals for the Palace of Fine Arts in Mexico and in 1958 decorated the Conference Hall in the UNESCO building in Paris. In 1953 he won first prize at the Bienal in São Paulo.

R. Goldwater. *Tamayo*, New York 1947.
R. Cogniat. *Rufino Tamayo*, Paris 1951.
P. Westheim. *Tamayo*, Mexico 1957.

Tamburi, Orfeo. Italian painter, b. 1910 in Jesi. Tamburi began to study in Rome in 1928 and became a member of the *Roman School*, which was founded by Scipione and Mafai in the same year. He now lives in Rome and Paris.

Apart from Mafai Tamburi is the most important of the contemporary Roman townscapists. His dry colours, which are reminiscent of fresco, and his firm composition distinguish his work from the expressive tonality of other artists working in this genre.

Tanaka, Atsuko. Japanese painter, b. 1931 in Osaka. Tanaka studied at Kyoto University of Arts. He was a member of the *Gutai* group from 1955 to 1965. He was included in the Guggenheim International Award Exhibition in 1960 and 1963, and the *New Japanese Painting and Sculpture* show at the Museum of Modern Art, New York in 1966. He produces abstract painting of brilliant hues and irregular circular shapes, with great spontaneity. He lives in Osaka.

Tanaka, Shintaro. Japanese painter and sculptor, b. 1940 in Tokyo. Tanaka is self-taught. He joined the Neo-Dada Organizer group. Along with recent trends, he has made hard-edged painting and coloured sculpture, and he seeks non-emotional expression. He lives in Tokyo.

Tancredi (Parmeggiani). Italian painter, b. 1927 in Feltre; d. 1964 in Rome. Tancredi studied for a short period at the School of Art in Venice. In 1961 he became a member of the *Continuità* group.

In his paintings, which are executed in bright, transparent colours, Tancredi portrayed his experiences of Informal art.

Tandberg, Odd. Norwegian painter and sculptor, b. 1924. After training at the Academy of Art in Oslo, Tandberg showed his first paintings—strictly geometrical abstracts—in 1950. Later he exhibited abstract sculptures, many of them cast in concrete.

He has also produced sculptures composed of sawn blocks of concrete decorated with different coloured stones. One of these decorative works stands in the park before the principal building of the Norsk Hydro in Oslo.

Tanguy, Yves. French-American painter, b. 1900 in Paris; d. 1955 in Woodbury, Connecticut. Tanguy's father was a ship's captain, who later worked as an official in the French Admiralty. As a child Tanguy often spent his holidays in Brittany, whose landscapes, rock formations and menhirs created a lasting impression on him. From 1909 to 1918 he lived in Paris, then joined the merchant navy for two years as an officer cadet, sailing to Africa and South America as ship's boy. From 1920 to 1922 Tanguy did his national service, and during this time met Jacques Prévert, who shared his aversion to army life. After their release in 1922 Tanguy joined up with Prévert in Paris, where they led a Bohemian existence. Tanguy then executed his first drawings, which attracted the attention of Vlaminck, and discovered Lautréamont's *Maldoror* and a number of Surrealist tracts. Then, in 1923, he saw a picture by de Chirico in the Gallery Paul Guillaume, and decided to become a painter. He also met Marcel Duhamel, and in 1924 read the early issues of *La Révolution Surréaliste*. From then onwards he began to take a serious interest in Surrealism. In 1925 he met André Breton, who became a close friend. He then joined the Surrealist group, exhibited a number of drawings in the Salon de l'Araignée, and in 1926 had his first finished painting reproduced in *La Révolution Surréaliste*. In 1930 he visited Africa, where he was fascinated by the rock formations. In 1938 he was in England, and in 1939 met the American painter Kay Sage in Paris. He passed the summer of 1939 in the castle of Chemillieu in the company of Breton, Matta and Esteban Francés before emigrating to New York, accompanied by Kay Sage. In 1940 he toured the United States, and in 1941–2 Canada. In 1946 Tanguy settled in Woodbury, Connecticut, where he acquired American citizenship two years later. In 1951 he visited Sedona, Arizona, and had a meeting with Max Ernst. In 1953 he visited Europe.

Tanguy was a self-taught artist. When he saw the painting by de Chirico in 1923, it made a tremendous impact on him, firing his imagination and concentrating his mind on artistic problems. In 1924 he produced a number of humorous illustrations. These were followed in 1925–6 by landscapes and figure compositions which have much in common with the works of the great primitive painters but whose motionless figures and fantastic composition also reflect Tanguy's close affinity to the Paris Surrealists. In 1926 Tanguy painted his first Surrealist works: timeless dream landscapes with stimulative coloured grounds, in which abstract objects that are reminiscent of sea fauna float aimlessly about, emerging from behind unreal mountains and glowing cloud formations. From 1927 onwards these pictorial objects were accompanied by elongated shadows. Thus Tanguy created twin worlds which he effectively alienated by introducing delicately drawn fragments of geometrical patterns. The mushroom growths, the sculptural forms that are reminiscent of Arp, and the Surrealistic pictorial objects in these works stand in marked contrast to the lambent flames and the rootlike growths on the monumental rock formations. But it was after his visit to Africa in 1931 that Tanguy created his most significant pictures of rock formations (*The Amoire of Proteus*, 1931, Paris, Coll. André Breton). In the landscapes painted between 1931 and 1934 rugged cliffs and mountains rise up in terraced formations against hazy backgrounds executed in gentle colours which stretch away to distant horizons. Between 1934 and 1940 these landscapes, in which the pictorial objects emerge from the haze like gigantic menhirs, underwent a progressive metamorphosis. Instead of cliffs and mountains, Tanguy painted abstract forms which interlock like the pieces of a jigsaw puzzle and are reminiscent of bone or cartilage formations. The forms are set out in Surrealistic patterns against gentle atmospheric grounds. Between 1940 and 1951 these landscapes were transformed in their turn, and instead of a multiplicity of small interlocking forms we find in this late period much larger jointed forms, which are painted in cool metallic colours and are reminiscent of marionettes.

James Thrall Soby. Catalogue, *Yves Tanguy*, Museum of Modern Art, New York 1955.
Kay Sage, André Breton, Paul Éluard *et al. Yves Tanguy: Un recueil de ses oeuvres*, New York 1963.

Tanning, Dorothea. American painter and graphic artist, b. 1910 in Galesburg, Illinois. After a brief period at Knox College she left school for Chicago, where she attended the Chicago Academy of Arts for two weeks. Convinced that one cannot learn to be a painter, she moved to New York and immersed herself in literature and art—Faulkner, Joyce, Stendhal, Picasso, Braque, Matisse. Inspired by the Museum of Modern Art's 1937 exhibition, *Fantastic Art, Dada, Surrealism*, she went to Paris and Stockholm (1939–41). She first exhibited in the year she returned to the United States, at the Julien Levy Gallery. In 1944 she had her first one-man show there. Her early canvases are blatantly Surreal, rendered in a meticulous technique and filled with inexplicable elements and strange figural actions. A preoccupation with architecture, especially doors, windows and deep tunnelling spaces, as well as with crinkled drapery containing hidden images, is a keynote of her style (*Max in a Blue Boat*, 1946, Paris, Coll. Max Ernst; *Palaestra*, 1947, New York, Copley

Coll.). Before and after her marriage to Max Ernst, she was occupied with the design of costumes and stage decorations. For G. Balanchine she created designs for the ballets *Night Shadow* (1945), *Bayou* (1952) and *Will o' the Wisp* (1953) and for *La Sorcière* at Covent Garden. Living in Paris and Sedona, Arizona, she had as frequent guests Man Ray, Marcel Duchamp, Georges Balanchine, Dylan Thomas, Yves Tanguy, Kay Sage, Tristan Tzara, Jean Arp, André Breton and many others. Through the 1950s and especially in the 1960s her canvases became less objective, with a greater interest in colour, though the strange Surreal quality of the previously used faceted drapery still appeared, often with figures indistinctly emerging (*Aux Environs de Paris*, 1961–2, New York, Whitney Museum of American Art), as in the later works of P. Tchelitchew.

Catalogue, *Dorothea Tanning*, Arthur Jeffress Gallery, London 1955.
Alain Bosquet. *La Peinture de Dorothea Tanning*, Paris 1966.

Tàpies, Antonio. Spanish painter, b. 1923 in Barcelona. After reading law at the University of Barcelona from 1943 to 1946 Tàpies taught himself to paint and began to produce impasted pictures into which he incorporated materials such as string and paper. Between 1948 and 1951 he was a member of the group centred on the magazine *Dau al Set* and for a while adopted the group's Late-Surrealist style. In 1950–1 he went to Paris on a French government scholarship and in 1953 visited New York for his first American exhibition. It was in 1953 that Tàpies began to develop his own individual style, in which the material has been the determining factor. From a mixture of glue, plaster of Paris and sand he created relief-like pictures in rich, dark, earthy colours, into which he introduced mysterious signs and forms, some of them scratched into the surface after the manner of Dubuffet's graffiti, others simply painted on. In such works Tàpies is trying to establish a new conception of reality by 'forcing these inert materials to speak'. The severity of his works and the seriousness of his general attitude to life distinguish him from the majority of Informal artists, although he has a great deal in common with Alberto Burri, whose highly poetic and sombre material pictures were also prompted by a deep sense of commitment. For Tàpies painting has to have a 'moral substratum'. He himself has described his artistic aims: 'To remind man of what he really is, to give him a theme to think about, to set up a shock in him which will rouse him from his artificial world—that is what I am trying to do in my work.' In formal terms Tàpies alternates between pictures incorporating spontaneous gesture, blurring, *craquelure* and overpainting at one end of the scale and strictly symmetrical works at the other. Sometimes he combines both methods within a single work, thus creating dialectical compositions. Tàpies has won numerous prizes, including the prize for painting at the 1958 Venice Biennale.

M. Tàpies. *Tàpies*, Barcelona 1959.
Catalogue, *Antonio Tàpies*, Solomon R. Guggenheim Museum, New York 1962.
Joan Teixidos. *Antonio Tàpies*, Greenwich (Conn.) 1965.
Blai Bonet. *Tàpies*, New York 1969.

Tapper, Kain. Finnish sculptor, b. 1930. After training as an industrial designer Tapper was influenced by contemporary Italian art, and between 1955 and 1958 created Informal sculptures, mostly wood carvings, with extremely sophisticated textures. Subsequently, he experimented with different materials, producing composite works. In 1962 he created his Sibelius monument in the Tavastehus.

Tatlin, Vladimir. Russian painter and sculptor, b. 1885 in Kharkov; d. 1953 in Moscow. At the age of 18 he ran away to sea, and the subject of the sea figures occasionally in his later painting, for example *The Sailor*, 1911–12 (Leningrad, Russian Museum). In 1909 he enrolled at the School of Architecture, Sculpture and Painting in Moscow, where he shared a studio with Aleksandr Vesnin, the future Constructivist architect. After a year he left the school to become a free-lance painter. In 1911 he made his début with eleven works at the *Union of Youth* exhibition in Moscow; in 1912 he showed some fifty works—including a number of costume designs for the *Emperor Maximilian and his Son Adolf*—with Larionov's *The Donkey's Tail* group. In 1913 there was an exhibition of *Ancient Russian Painting* which revealed many previously unknown icons; their influence upon Tatlin is seen in the flatness, curved forms and decorative quality of his work of this period, e.g. *Composition from a Nude*, 1913 (Moscow, Tretyakov Gallery), which borrows the traditional seated form of a saint or the Virgin.

After breaking with Larionov, Tatlin exhibited with the *Union of Youth*, *World of Art* and *Knave of Diamonds* groups before leaving for Paris in an attempt to meet Picasso, whose collages provided the starting-point for Tatlin's own more radical constructions. In the winter of 1913–14 he created his first 'painting-reliefs'; in 1914 Malevich and Tatlin left the *Union of Youth*. In 1915 his *Reliefs*, made of wood, metal and other materials, were shown at the exhibition *Tramway V*. In 1916 he took part in the exhibition *The Store* in Moscow. He is thought to have collaborated with Yakulov in 1917 in the decoration of the Café Pittoresque in Moscow. In 1919 he was made head of the Moscow branch of *IZO* (the artistic section of the Commissariat of the Enlightenment); in 1920 he transferred to the Petrograd section. He worked on the model of a monument for the Third International, which was shown in Petrograd and Moscow on the occasion of the Eighth Party Congress. In 1921 or 1922 he was appointed professor in the Sculpture Department of the Museum of Artistic Culture in Petrograd. In 1923 his designs for Khlebnikov's *Zan-gezi* were produced at *Inkhuk* (the Research Institute for Artistic Culture). After the reorganization of *Inkhuk*, Tatlin was appointed head of the department of the 'culture of materials' (his own phrase). In 1925 he became head of the theatre and film department of the Kiev Art Institute. He returned to Moscow in 1927 as head of the department of wood and metal in the re-organized *Vkhutemas* (the former School of Architecture, Sculpture and Painting and the Stroganov College). From 1929 to 1931 he was occupied in building an air-bicycle, *Letatlin* (the name is formed from a combination of Tatlin's own name and the Russian verb 'to fly'), which was exhibited in Moscow in 1932.

From 1934 to 1952 he worked as a theatrical designer for more than twenty productions; his paintings of these years consist mostly of nudes and still lifes.

Camilla Gray. *The Great Experiment: Russian Art 1863–1922*, London and New York 1962.

Tchelitchew, Pavel. Russian-American painter, b. 1898 in Kaluga, near Moscow; d. 1957 in Grottaferrata, near Rome. He and his family fled to Kiev in 1918 at the outbreak of the Soviet Revolution. As a youth he did drawings after Gustave Doré illustrations and attended drawing classes at Kiev Academy, where his artistic proclivities were encouraged by his teacher Alexandra Exter, a pupil of Léger. By 1921 he was in Berlin where he was creating designs for theatre, ballet and opera. He moved to Paris in 1923. His interest in landscape painting and portraiture at this time indicates his reaction against the current mode of abstract art. He created a series of circus pictures throughout the 1920s, often employing exaggerated perspective and a variety of media (*Nude*, 1926, oil, sand and coffee, New York, Coll. Julien Levey). These pictures were, without doubt, inspired by his theatrical connections, though the series came to an end in the early 1930s with such works as *The Rose Necklace* (1931, London, Coll. Mrs. E. Maast), while he continued to create ballet designs throughout the 1930s and 1940s for productions of *Orfeo*, *L'Errante*, and *The Cave of Sleep* among others. His early interest in portraiture also continued through the thirties, when his friends Charles Henri Ford and Edith Sitwell sat for him on several occasions. He went to the United States in 1934 and the following year conceived his composition of *Phenomena* (Moscow, Tretyakov State Gallery) which was finished in 1938. The work displays a rather Surreal handling of space and subject matter, which comes to fruition in his best-known works, *Leaf Children* (1939) and *Hide and Seek* (1940–2), both in the

Museum of Modern Art, New York. Heads and bodies of children, translucent and transparent, are arranged in compositions which deny real space. The figures are placed over a visceral background of colour splotches, vein-like calligraphy and a pulsating light.

Lincoln Kirstein (ed.). *Drawings by Pavel Tchelitchew*, New York 1941.
Catalogue, *Tchelitchew: Paintings, Drawings*, Museum of Modern Art, New York 1942.
Catalogue, *Pavel Tchelitchew*, Gallery of Modern Art, New York 1964.
Parker Tyler. *The Divine Comedy of Pavel Tchelitchew*, New York 1967.

Tchorzewski, Jerzy. Polish painter, b. 1928 in Siedlce. Tchorzewski studied at the Academy of Art in Cracow and is now a lecturer at the Warsaw Academy. He became a member of the Polish *avant-garde* early on in his career and, after passing through Surrealist and Informal phases, evolved his own form of non-objective art which is remarkable for its rich, fluorescent, painterly texture, its unusual imagery and its massed contrasts. In 1968–9 Tchorzewski began to incorporate figurative allusions into his work.

Franco Russoli. *Avanguardia Internazionale*, Milan 1962.
Enrico Crispolti. *Ricerche dopo l'Informale*, Officina Edizione, Rome 1968.

Teana, Marino di. Italian sculptor, b. 1920 in Teana, Southern Italy. In 1936 Teana went to live in Argentina, where he studied at the Escuela Superior de Bellas Artes in Buenos Aires. In 1952 he visited Spain, and whilst there worked with the sculptor Jorge de Oteiza. In 1953 he settled in Paris, where he is still living.

During his Argentine period Teana produced portraits which reveal the influence of Etruscan art. In Paris he began to work in metal, producing constructions consisting of geometrical shapes set out in contrasting arrangements.

Telemaque, Hervé. French painter, b. 1937 in Port-au-Prince, Haiti. Telemaque studied at the Art Students' League in New York from 1957 to 1960. He has been living in Paris since 1962.

Telemaque's two-dimensional pictures are composed of writings, geometric patterns, objects from everyday life, objects from the world of advertising and parts of the human body. The colouring and drawing are based on the comic strip. L. R. Lippard has described Telemaque's style as 'a fusion of Anglo-American Pop Art and New Realism'.

Téréchkovitch, Kostia (Konstantin). Russian painter, b. 1902 in Metcherskoe, near Moscow. He studied in Moscow and then travelled to Paris, arriving in 1920. His first one-man show was in 1926. He painted portraits (including many of his

painter friends in Paris) and landscapes. He also designed tapestries and ceramics and produced book illustrations.

Teshigahara, Sofu. Japanese sculptor and calligrapher, b. 1900 in Tokyo. He was the founder and leader of the Sogetsu school of flower arrangement in Tokyo. He works in wood, terra-cotta and metal. He is an abstract artist. He has had many one-man shows in Tokyo, and also exhibited in 1959 at the Galerie Stadler, Paris, and the Jackson Gallery in New York.

Tharrats, Juan José. Spanish painter, b. 1918. He was a member of the *Dau al Set* group, set up in Barcelona in 1948 by Antonio Tàpies and others. The group aimed to overcome the artistic stagnation that had overtaken Catalonia, and to that end acclaimed the innovations of Gaudí and Miró. He was influenced by Klee. Around 1956 he started to paint Informal pictures in rich enamelled textures.

Thayer, Abbott. American painter, b. 1849 in Boston; d. 1921 in Monadnock, New Hampshire. He studied in New York and became well known as a painter of animals. In 1875 he spent some time studying in Paris, and thereafter painted mainly portraits and figures. He illustrated his own writings on the subject of animal camouflage, and also made many drawings. In his last years he turned more to landscapes.

Thévenet, Louis. Belgian painter, b. 1874 in Bruges; d. 1930 in Hal, near Brussels. He first started to exhibit in 1903, and showed some of his work with the Libre Esthétique. He retired in 1914 and moved to Hal, where he became a recluse. Most of his works are interiors and still lifes.

Thiebaud, Wayne. American painter, film-maker and graphic artist, b. 1920 in Mesa, Arizona. Before receiving a formal art education he worked in New York and Hollywood as a cartoonist, designer and advertising art director (1938–9) and served in the United States Army Air Force (1942–6). He obtained BA (1949) and MA (1951) degrees from San Jose State College and Sacramento State College respectively. Upon gaining the latter degree he taught in the Art Department of Sacramento City College until one year before his first one-man show at the Cooperative Gallery, Sacramento, California (1961). Since 1962 he has had many one-man shows and has been included in several important group shows, including *The New Realists* (1962, New York, Sidney Janis Gallery), *Mixed Media and Pop Art* (1963, Buffalo, New York, Albright-Knox Art Gallery) and the Ninth Bienal at São Paulo, Brazil (1967). Best known for his paintings of food, often handled with a thick, juicy pigment as seen in *Pies* (1961, Sacramento, Coll. Mr. and Mrs. Philip L. Ehlert), he usually repeats variations of a single object as though they are on display in an advertisement or cafeteria. Usually taken out of any specific context, placed against a solidly coloured background, the objects' colours are stark and overly bright, emphasizing their synthetic quality. Among his favourite subjects are pies, banana splits, yo-yos, hot dogs, ice-cream cones and lipsticks. He also does some figural work, most often a single figure, rendered in advertising-copy realism—bright colours, strong outlines, deep shadows created by a bright, spotlight illumination, placed against an unmodulated white background (*Girl with Ice Cream Cone*, 1963, New York, Allan Stone Gallery; *Girl in White Boots*, 1965, Villanova, Pa., Coll. Mr. and Mrs. Edwin M. Sabol). Thiebaud is currently Professor of Art, University of California, Davis, and has produced many educational motion pictures at Baily Films, Hollywood.

John Coplans. Catalogue, *Wayne Thiebaud*, Pasadena Art Museum, Pasadena (Calif.) 1968.

Thieler, Fred. German painter, b. 1916 in Königsberg, East Prussia. Thieler began painting in 1941 after qualifying as a doctor. From 1946 to 1948 he studied under Karl Caspar at the Munich Academy and from 1951 to 1952 under Hayter in Paris. He became a member of the *Zen* group and of the New Munich Group.

Thieler has developed a sophisticated style of Action Painting which, of recent years, has involved the use of collage techniques.

Thodoros (Thodoros Papadimitriou). Greek sculptor, b. 1931 in Agrinio. He studied in Athens and in Paris; he has been living in Paris since 1959, with intervals in Greece. He is an environmentalist oriented towards the organization of adaptable 'wholes'. The physical elements of his sculpture have a complex geometrical formation.

Thommesen, Erik. Danish sculptor and writer on art, b. 1916 in Copenhagen. Thommesen is a self-taught artist. The archaic simplicity of his abstract sculptures, most of which are carved from oak, is reminiscent of Brancusi. Thommesen is one of the best-known and most individual Danish sculptors of his generation. He has written numerous articles on artistic problems.

Thomson, Tom. Canadian painter, b. 1877 in Claremont, Ontario; d. 1917 in Canoe Lake, Algonquin Park, Ontario. He grew up near Owen Sound, on Georgian Bay, and became a machinist's apprentice in 1898. Thomson attended business school at Chatham, Ontario, before going to stay with a brother in Seattle, where he worked as a photo-engraver and began to sketch. On his return to Toronto in 1905, Thomson was employed as a

commercial designer and during this period met several of the painters who later formed the so-called Group of Seven. He made his first sketching trip in 1911 and exhibited his first canvas two years later. In 1914 the support of his patron, Dr. J. M. MacCallum, and the painter Lawren Harris (b. 1885) enabled him to paint full time. Thomson then spent the summers from 1914 to 1917 making sketches of scenes in Algonquin Park, a nature reserve in northern Ontario, and his winters in Toronto painting such canvases as the *Jack Pine* (1917, Ottawa, National Gallery). His brief career as a painter, marked by an extremely rapid attainment of skill, ended tragically when he was drowned in Canoe Lake in Algonquin Park. Thomson has since become the prototype of the Canadian woodsman-artist. Other works by him include the vivid *Pointers* (1916–17, Toronto, Hart House, University of Toronto) and *Northern River* (1915, Ottawa, National Gallery).

Robert Hamilton Hubbard. *Tom Thomson*, Toronto 1962.
Blodwen Davies. *Tom Thomson*, Vancouver 1967.

Thorn-Prikker, Jan. Dutch painter, b. 1868 in The Hague; d. 1932 in Cologne. After studying under Koelman at the Academy in The Hague Thorn-Prikker worked in Visée, where he produced batiks, furniture designs and sculptures. In 1904 he left Holland for Germany, where he taught at the Industrial School of Art in Krefeld from 1904 to 1910, the Folkwang School in Hagen and Essen from 1910 to 1919, and the Industrial School of Art in Munich from 1919 to 1923. He lived in Düsseldorf from 1923 to 1925, then taught at the Industrial School of Art in Cologne from 1925 to 1932.

Thorn-Prikker was a decorative artist, who specialized in stained-glass windows, for which he produced symbolic designs. The Dreikönigskirche in Neuss and the Liebfrauenkirche in Krefeld contain examples of his work.

Catalogue, *Thorn-Prikker*, Kaiser-Wilhelm-Museum, Krefeld 1949.
August Hoff. *Johan Thorn-Prikker*, Recklinghausen 1958.

Tiffany, Louis Comfort. American painter and craftsman, b. 1848 in New York; d. 1933 in New York. He studied in New York and Paris, and travelled around Europe, where he became interested in the revival of arts and crafts current at the time. Returning to the United States, he decided to establish (1878) a foundation encouraging the relation of architecture to interior design, and himself created beautiful glassware in the *art nouveau* idiom, of which he was one of America's first exponents, and which he made fashionable among the wealthy.

Tilson, Joe. British sculptor, b. 1928 in London. After working as a carpenter Tilson studied at the

St. Martin's School of Art and the Royal College of Art in London from 1949 to 1955. From 1958 onwards he has been teaching at various English art schools and also at the School of Visual Art in New York. He is now living in London.

Tilson is a Pop artist. He constructs relief pictures and sculptures from painted wood and metal, in which he depicts trivial objects of big city life, e.g. a keyhole, a watch, a number, an advertising slogan. In some of his works these objects are organized in diagrammatic compositions, in others (e.g. *Wristwatch*) they appear, reproduced on a gigantic scale, in complete isolation, thus acquiring symbolic force. Tilson also uses Op Art techniques (e.g. in his *Ziggurat Variations*).

Tinguely, Jean. Swiss sculptor, b. 1925 in Fribourg. In 1927, when Tinguely was two years old, his parents moved to Basle. Later, between 1941 and 1945, he attended the School of Art and Crafts there, but not on a regular basis. In 1945 he began to paint abstract pictures and subsequently produced constructions from wire, metal, etc., before settling in Paris in 1952. In 1954 he constructed a series of reliefs made up of layers of moving rods; these were his *Formes mouvementés*. They were followed (up to 1956) by 'meta-mechanical' reliefs and a number of free-standing sculptures. Between 1956 and 1959 Tinguely produced reliefs with rotating metal elements and then, from 1959 onwards, he began to exhibit his 'painting machines'. The one which he showed at the First Paris Biennale, the *Meta-matic-automobile odorante et sonore*, produced 40,000 multi-coloured pictures which were executed on paper. In 1960 Tinguely demonstrated his *Hommage à New York* in the Garden of the Museum of Modern Art in New York. This sculpture, which was specially constructed to batter itself to pieces, was the first of a series: in 1961 Tinguely's *Hommage à Dali* was set up in the arena in Figueras, Spain; in the same year his *Study for the Destruction of the World* was on view in the Louisiana Museum in Copenhagen; and in 1962 his *End of the World* was set up in the Nevada desert. In 1964 Tinguely created a monumental sculpture entitled *Eureka*, which he exhibited at the Swiss Provincial Exhibition in Lausanne. Two years later, working in collaboration with Niki de Saint-Phalle and Per-Olof Ultvedt, he built a gigantic sculpture in the Moderna Museet in Stockholm. This work, which was called *Hon*, was so big that viewers were able to walk on it.

In an assessment of Tinguely's work to date, which is based on the relative prominence accorded by the artist to movement on the one hand and materials on the other, the art critic J. C. Ammann has divided his career up into three principal periods. In the first of these, which lasted from 1954 to 1959 and which Ammann calls the constructive period, movement is simply a 'complementary factor'. In the second, which lasted from 1960 to 1962, Tinguely identified with his material. In the third, from 1963 onwards, he has redressed the balance of sculptural autonomy by stressing movement. The majority of Tinguely's sculptures have been welded together from ready-made sections of iron. The irony which dominated his early works has receded to an ever-increasing extent in the course of his development, although Tinguely has never entirely abandoned it. But the most striking aspect of his work is his insistence on 'viewer participation'. He wants people to become involved in the life of his sculptures.

Catalogue, *Jean Tinguely*, Alexander Iolus Gallery, New York 1964.
J. C. Ammann. 'Jean Tinguely', *Werk*, March 1966.
'*Hon*', *Catalogue News Sheet*, Moderna Museet, Stockholm 1966.

Tirronen, Esko Aulis. Finnish painter, b. 1934. In his early period Tirronen was an Informal artist but from 1965 onwards he evolved a neo-figurative style, producing paintings with Surrealistic features. Tirronen does not use a brush, preferring to spray the paint on to the picture surface.

Tobey, Mark. American painter, b. 1890 in Centerville, Wisconsin. Other than Saturday classes at the Art Institute of Chicago, he had no formal training. He left high school in 1909 and became a fashion illustrator, a career he pursued in Chicago and New York until 1917. In that year he had a one-man show at Knoedler's, New York, of charcoal portraits which he had been doing for about five years. He gave up fashion illustration at about this time for interior decorating. Around 1918 he became a convert to the Bahá'í World Faith, a creed of religious universalism with an optimistic outlook. Between 1922 and 1925 he taught at the Cornish School in Seattle, Washington, where he began painting ideographic pictures— 'unconventional and motivated by his love of art'. During this period on the West Coast he became interested in Japanese woodcuts, American Indian art and the techniques, calligraphy and composition of eastern painting, which he learned from a Chinese student at the University of Washington. After a trip to Europe and the Near East, Tobey taught at Dartington Hall (1930–8), the progressive school in Devonshire, England. Here he came in contact with Pearl S. Buck, Aldous Huxley and others who were, like himself, devoted to a cultural fusion of East and West. In 1934 he travelled to the Orient where he studied calligraphy and eastern poetry and spent a month in a Zen monastery. This trip strongly affected his new style of 'white writings', as seen in *Broadway* (1936, tempera, New York, Metropolitan Museum of Art), which he did while on a trip to the United States. It realizes his desire to 'smash' form through a negation of perspective, a goal unfulfilled since 1919–20. During the 1940s and 1950s he continued producing his 'white writings', which are often linked up with earlier influences, as seen in *Drums, Indians and the Word of God* (1944, tempera on wood, New York, Coll. Hermann Shulman) which displays his interest since the 1920s in American Indian art. *Multiple Voyages* (1957, tempera, coll. of artist) is a painting typical of Tobey's late style. Finely brushed white writing in a thread-like, labyrinthine manner over a reddish-brown ground at one and the same time creates a flat, two-dimensional image and a sense of an infinity of depth. In 1958 he won first prize at the Twenty-ninth Biennale, Venice.

William C. Seitz. *Mark Tobey*, Museum of Modern Art, New York 1962.
Mark Tobey. *The World of a Market*, Seattle 1964.
Wieland Schmied. *Mark Tobey*, New York 1966.

Tomasello, Luis R. Argentinian painter, b. 1915 in La Plata. Tomasello studied painting in Buenos Aires. In 1957 he settled in Paris, where he is still living today.

Tomasello belongs to the group centred on the Galerie Denise René. His optically bewildering pictures are flat, 'chromoplastic' compositions, which fall into the category of *Art Visuel* or Op Art. In 1956 Tomasello's works were shown in the important American exhibition, *The Responsive Eye*.

Tomlin, Bradley Walker. American painter, b. 1899 in Syracuse, New York; d. 1953 in New York City. While still attending the College of Fine Arts of Syracuse University (1917–21) he won a prize for poster design, illustrated the children's books *The Story of the Stork* by A. Bennett-Edwards and *Billee: The Story of a Little Boy and a Big Bear* by Isabel Hawley Scott, and painted two murals with Julian Mansfield at the Syracuse Memorial Hospital. From 1923 to 1924 he travelled to Paris on a scholarship and there worked at the Académie Colarossi and the Académie de la Grande Chaumière. He returned to New York in 1924 and the following year joined the Whitney Studio Club, where he became a regular exhibitor. Little of his early work survives, though some notion of his style is discernible through his magazine covers for *Vogue* and *House and Garden*. From about 1939 to 1944 he pursued a rather decorative Cubism. In *Burial* (1943, New York, Metropolitan Museum of Art) the symbolism seems more significant than the formal relations. He attached himself to A. Gottlieb after his close friend Frank London died in 1945; it was the former who seems to have turned him away from Cubism towards a more *avant-garde* mode. In the late 1940s he comes closest to Expressionism and displays a certain relation to Action Painting; both are coupled with a suggestion of symbolism which probably stems from Gottlieb's pictographs (*Maneuver for Position*, 1948, New York, Betty Parsons Gallery). He found a new and more personal expression only towards the end of his life in such works as *Number 20—1949* (New York, Museum of Modern Art) where he integrated the structural significance of every stroke with a spontaneity of approach.

J. I. H. Baur. Catalogue, *Bradley Walker Tomlin*, Whitney Museum of American Art, New York 1957.

Tonitza, Nicolae. Rumanian painter, b. 1886 in Birlad, Moldavia; d. 1940 in Bucharest. He studied in Jassy, Munich and Paris, and spent the First World War in a prison camp. He was director of the School of Fine Arts at Jassy from 1937. His work was concerned with city and suburban life and the wretched state of those in poverty.

Tonks, Henry. British painter and draughtsman, b. 1862 in Solihull; d. 1937 in London. He studied medicine and later painting. He joined the New English Art Club in 1895. He became Slade Professor in 1918. He was an official war artist. An exhibition of his work was held in 1936 at the Tate Gallery.

Tonnancour, Jacques de. Canadian painter, b. 1917 in Montreal. He studied at the École des Beaux-Arts, Montreal, and the school of the Montreal Museum of Fine Arts. His early landscapes show the influence of Goodridge Roberts (b. 1904), but a little later he was affected by Alfred Pellan and the works of Picasso and the *École de Paris*. In the forties he became one of the leading members of the Montreal School. In 1945 he painted in Rio de Janeiro (*Deux femmes assises*, 1945, Ottawa, National Gallery of Canada). After painting figures such as the latter, and landscapes (*Paysage de juin*, c. 1958, Ottawa, National Gallery of Canada), he turned to abstraction in 1959 and in 1963 to a Surrealist imagery. His public commissions include a mural in the Dow Planetarium, Montreal (1965). Retrospective exhibitions of his work were held in Vancouver and Montreal in 1966. He teaches at the École des Beaux-Arts, Montreal, and lives at Saint-Lambert, Quebec.

Catalogue, *De Tonnancour*, Vancouver Art Gallery, Vancouver 1966.

Tooker, George. American painter, b. 1920 in Brooklyn, New York. Tooker graduated with a BA in literature from Harvard in 1942, then served in the Marines before attending the Art Students' League. There, in the early 1940s, he worked under the New York Urban Realist Kenneth Hayes Miller, and later studied privately with the illustrator and painter Paul Cadmus, who taught him to use his favourite medium, egg tempera. Tooker's style, in which realistically drawn scenes of figures are defined with a polished and deliberate precision, has been termed 'Magic Realism'. The contrast between the careful execution and the unsettling psychological implications of his subject matter sets up a particularly compelling tension. Tooker deals with themes of alienation and dehumanization in contemporary settings. His manner also refers to early Italian painting—to the figurative renditions of Paolo Uccello or the early Sienese painters—and to the Surrealistic associations of works by René Magritte and Balthus, both of whom were important influences. In his well-known *Government Bureau* (1956, New York, Metropolitan Museum) Tooker comments upon the machine-like sterility of modern bureaucracy as he shows identical-looking people lined up in front of booths containing strange, staring and hostile officials. In *Box* (c. 1967, coll. of artist), he again emphasizes the concern with psychological discomfort that pervades his work. Its subject is a nude figure cramped into a shallow, illusionistic, box-like frame.

Frederic Taubes. 'Egg Tempera Painting; Selected Examples by Tooker', *American Artist* XXI, May 1957.
Ralph Pomeroy. 'George Tooker, Really', *Art and Artists* II, April 1967.

Toorop, Charley. Dutch painter, b. 1891 in Katwijk; d. 1955 in Bergen. Toorop was the daughter of Jan Toorop. After training as a musician and working in this sphere for a number of years she became a painter in 1914. She had already been teaching herself to paint, under her father's guidance, since 1905 and she continued to do so until 1916, when she studied under H. F. Bremmer. Subsequently, she explored Holland and spent working holidays in Paris, the South of France, Brussels, Berlin and Spain.

During her early phase Toorop was influenced by Dutch *art nouveau*. But it was the works of van Gogh that made the most profound impression on her. Later, between 1930 and 1940, she produced figurative compositions, still lifes, portraits and townscapes which are reminiscent of both the *Neue Sachlichkeit* and the Surrealism of Dali. In her works, in which she invariably treats *motifs* with philosophical and social implications, Toorop combines expressive power with formal precision. From 1940 onwards she strengthened her pictorial forms still further by her use of Neo-Cubist techniques. She also created designs for stage sets for the national Theatre in Amsterdam, a task for which her essentially monumental style was well suited.

Catalogue, *Charley Toorop*, Hammer Gallery, New York 1952.

Toorop, Jan. Dutch painter, b. 1858 in Poerworedjo, Java; d. 1928 in The Hague. After coming to Holland in 1869 Toorop studied at the Amsterdam Academy, 1880–1, and at the Brussels Academy from 1882 to 1885. He then joined the Belgian group *Les Vingt* and visited England. In 1890 he entered into a friendship with Maeterlinck and Verhaeren and in 1905 became a Catholic.

Toorop's childhood memories of Java were one of the crucial factors in his artistic development. In c. 1890, as a result of his contact with Maeterlinck and Verhaeren, he began to paint in a Symbolist style, combining both pagan and Christian symbols in compositions which reflect the desperate search of an atheist for religious reassurance. During this period he tried out all the different styles that were in vogue in the 1880s and finished up by adopting the kind of eclectic approach that was so popular in Europe at the turn of the century. From 1893 onwards he was in thrall to *art nouveau* and, in the figurative compositions and landscapes of that period, he tended to envelop his pictorial objects in a dense network of ornamental lines which are reminiscent of Beardsley. The atmospheric colour contrasts, the solemn gestures and the literary symbols in these works combine with the total isolation of the individual pictorial objects to create an air of numinous mystery. With his poetic intensity and his decorative but mannered linear structures Toorop carried Dutch *art nouveau* to its furthest point of development. He also made designs for tile paintings and stained-glass windows and produced Dutch tiles, enamel and clay ware and etchings.

Albert Plasschaert. *Jan Toorop*, Amsterdam 1925.
M. Jaussen. *Herinneringen an Jan Toorop*, Amsterdam 1933.
John B. Knipping. *Jan Toorop*, Amsterdam 1948.

Topolski, Feliks. Polish-British draughtsman and illustrator, b. 1907 in Warsaw. Topolski studied in Warsaw, Paris and Italy. He moved to Britain in 1935 and was a war artist from 1940 to 1945. In 1955 he was awarded a gold medal by the International Fine Arts Council. He has made portraits and caricatures of many famous faces and has illustrated a number of books.

Torres-García, Joaquín. Uruguayan painter, b. 1874 in Montevideo; d. 1949 in Montevideo. Torres-García was the founder of the Uruguayan Constructivist movement. In 1891 he went to Catalonia, where he studied painting and drawing at the academies in Mataró and Barcelona and where his fellow-students included Sunyer, Canals, Hugué and Nonell. Torres-García's early landscapes were Impressionist works. But by c. 1900 his style began to acquire something of the quality of Steinlen and Toulouse-Lautrec. At that time he was in contact with the modernists, who used to meet in the Quatre Gats Café, where Torres-García made the acquaintance of Picasso. In 1906 he collaborated with Antonio Gaudí on the stained-glass windows for the cathedral in Majorca. Immediately afterwards, between 1906 and 1909, he created his first important works. These were the murals which he painted for various secular and ecclesiastical buildings and which, although Neo-Classical in their general conception, incorporated modern forms. From 1900 to 1910 Torres-García lived in Brussels, then returned to Catalonia to teach painting at the Colegio Mont d'Or. Between 1913 and 1916 he painted some remarkable frescoes in the Palace of Deputies in Barcelona, but these were later destroyed during the rule of Primo de Rivera. In 1917 Torres-García finally abandoned his Neo-Classical leanings and opted definitively for the *avant-garde* mode of expression. From 1920 to 1922 he worked in New York, where he was hard pressed for money, in 1923 he was in Italy, and from 1924 to 1932 in France. For a number of years he earned his living as a toymaker. In Paris he made contact with Seuphor, van Doesburg, Vantongerloo, Kandinsky, Mondrian and other abstract artists, and he and Seuphor launched the *Cercle et Carré* magazine in order to oppose the Surrealist movement. But just as he was beginning to make a name for himself in France, the economic slump forced him to return to Spain. He arrived there in 1933 and subsequently went on from there to Uruguay. In Montevideo, where he lived from 1934 until his death in 1949, he was extremely active, both as a painter and as a teacher and propagandist. He ran a studio, where he introduced his pupils to Constructivist ideas and techniques; he published books and magazines, gave lectures, and played an important role in the artistic life of both Uruguay and Argentina. His output during this final period included a number of large murals and paintings for his four series: *Naturalism, Constructivism, Expressionism* and *Recollections*. He also erected a Cosmic Monument in the Rodó Park in Montevideo, a Constructivist work in the fullest sense, which provides what is virtually a synthesis of Torres-García's mature oeuvre. Most of the major European and American galleries possess works by Torres-García, and there are good collections in both the Torres-García Museum and the Museum of Fine Arts in Montevideo.

Joaquín Torres-García. *Historia de mi vida*, Montevideo 1931.
Claude Schaefer. *Joaquín Torres-García*, Buenos Aires 1945.
José Marí Podestá. *Joaquín Torres-García*, Buenos Aires 1946.
Julio E. Payró. *Torres-García*, Buenos Aires 1966.

Tosi, Arturo. Italian painter, b. 1871 in Busto Arsizio; d. 1956 in Milan. After attending the Accademia Brera at Milan in 1889 Tosi worked for two years in Ferraguti-Visconti's *atelier*. In c. 1900 he made contact with Cézanne and Bonnard. He was a member of the *Novecento Italiano*.

During his early period, from c. 1890 onwards, Tosi came to terms with Courbet's Realism and the new Impressionist approach to light and colour. Subsequently, in c. 1900, he was more profoundly influenced by Cézanne's use of colour as a medium for the representation of the inner forms of objects and by Bonnard's warm, glowing and subtle palette. It was in c. 1910 that he began his great cycle of lyrical landscapes of the Bergamo district. In these contrapuntal works Tosi used large, open and peaceful expanses of sky to offset the Cubist organization of the mountainous terrain. The freshness of his earthy colours contrasts with the atmospheric appearance of the air and the clouds. Between 1930 and 1935 Tosi painted pictures, primarily still lifes, in which the Expressionistic brushwork and the rich glowing colours seem almost to consume the pictorial objects (as in Ch. Soutine's works). Essentially, however, he remained the calm and completely unacademic interpreter of rustic scenes. Tosi made a major contribution to the modern revival of the traditional woodcut.

G. C. Argan. *Tosi*, Florence 1942.
G. Scheiwiller. *Arturo Tosi*, Milan 1942.

Toulouse-Lautrec, Henri de (Henri-Marie-Raymond de Toulouse-Lautrec Monfa). French painter, draughtsman and lithographer, b. 1864 in Albi; d. 1901 in Malromé. The child of aristocratic parents, he had a conventional boyhood, with plenty of riding and shooting. In 1878 and 1879, however, he broke his left leg and right femur, accidents that left him a dwarf, with a normal torso but stunted legs. In 1882, he enrolled in Bonnat's studio in Paris; when Bonnat gave up teaching, he went on to work under Cormon. In 1885 he settled in Montmartre, a raffish area that satisfied his need to find a milieu in which his physical appearance would be accepted without embarrassment. Montmartre also provided Lautrec with a series of dubious women, from one of whom he contracted the syphilis that contributed to his early death.

Montmartre was also the artistic centre of the *avant-garde*. Initially interested in a relatively conventional style of painting, and official honours, Lautrec soon changed both his attitude and his idiom under the impact of Impressionism and the first manifestations of Post-Impressionism (he met both Émile Bernard and van Gogh). From 1887, he began to exhibit regularly with the *Société des XX* in Paris and Brussels, and at the Salon des Indépendants, the *Cercle Volney* and with the *Arts Libéraux*. He also began to contribute to various periodicals: *Rire, Figaro Illustré, Paris Illustré* and *Courrier Français*.

In 1888, Lautrec produced his first really independent, mature work: *The Cirque Fernando* (Art Institute of Chicago), which reveals such characteristic Impressionist devices as the flattening of the picture space, the employment of a rather unusual viewpoint, and the cutting of the figures by the edge of the composition. Peculiar to Lautrec himself, however, is an ingredient of caricature (in the ringmaster, for example) and the use of bold, simplified, non-naturalistic colour. The painting already contains most of the elements that Lautrec was to exploit in his posters.

His first lithographic print, a poster for the Moulin Rouge, dates from 1891; in the remaining ten years of his life, he was to make nearly 400 prints in black and white and in colour, and produce thirty-one posters proper. Lautrec was among the first and, in many respects, the greatest of all poster designers. A man with a strong theatrical sense, interested in individual personality and fascinated by what was *outré* and extreme, he had the right kind of flair, panache and an appropriate, often sardonic sense of exaggeration. The *Divan Japonais* or *Jane Avril–Jardin de Paris* combine inventiveness and keen visual precision with a kind of careless, cynical elegance in a way that is quite breath-taking. Lautrec's influence on the development of the poster was enormous.

Like Degas—but unlike most of the Impressionists—Lautrec was not really interested in landscape; and the lighting in his pictures is often most convincing and effective when it is artificial. His favourite themes were the Parisian dance halls, cabarets and circuses (notably the Moulin Rouge and the Moulin de la Galette), and even life in the brothels, where he spent a great deal of his time—as an observer as well as a customer. His ordered and calculated pictures of the calculating but disordered world of the prostitute are neither lascivious nor coy; and in their unglamorized acceptance of the facts of real life, they were to be influential in the history of twentieth-century art. The young Picasso, for example, was obviously influenced by them.

Lautrec also painted relatively conventional nude studies, and he incorporated in his work in various ways many of the celebrities of the music-hall world: Jane Avril, 'La Goulue', Valentin-le-Désossé, Loïe Fuller and Yvette Guilbert. As the 1890s wore on, Lautrec's life became increasingly dissipated; and the quantity and quality of his work began to decline. In 1899 he suffered a complete physical and mental breakdown, and was confined to a sanatorium. While he was still an inmate he resumed work (partly to establish his sanity), and on his release he began painting again. His style, however, was now different. In the later works (*In a Private Room at the 'Rat Mort'*, 1899, London, Courtauld Gallery), the colouring is more sombre, the handling broader; the emphasis has become painterly rather than linear. His health broken, and worn out by his excesses, Lautrec died in September 1901, surrounded by his family. The contents of his studio were later presented to his native town of Albi.

Gerstle Mack. *Toulouse-Lautrec*, London and New York 1938.
D. C. Rich. *Henri de Toulouse-Lautrec 'Au Moulin Rouge'*, London 1949.
Douglas Cooper. *Toulouse-Lautrec*, New York 1956.

Town, Harold. Canadian painter, b. 1924 in Toronto. Harold Town has drawn from many sources for his paintings and prints, such as the *motifs* of Indian, Viking and Oriental artefacts, the Action Painting of the New York School (*St. Lawrence Seaway Mural*, 1958, Cornwall, Ontario), and

optical paintings (*Silent Light No. 3*, exhibited in 1969 in Montreal). Town's work also reveals a striking contrast between simple, precise forms (*Stretch No. 3*, exhibited in 1969 in Montreal) and brightly coloured and richly textured surfaces (*Festival*, 1965; exhibited at the Jerrold Morris International Gallery, Toronto). Town has won a prize at the São Paulo Bienal (1957) and a Guggenheim International Award (1960).

Catalogue, *Harold Town 1954/1959, Prints and Collages*, Jerrold Morris Gallery, Toronto.
J. Russell Harper. *Painting in Canada*, Toronto 1966.

Toyen (Marie Germinova). Czech painter, b. 1902 in Prague. From 1933 she adhered closely to Surrealism, and her paintings and drawings in this mode are often deeply disturbing. In 1947 she settled in Paris, and participated in the exhibitions that André Breton arranged for the Surrealists.

Tozzi, Mario. Italian painter, b. 1895 in Fossombrone, Umbria. Tozzi studied at the Academy of Art in Bologna. Later he joined the *Novecento Italiano*. He now lives partly in Paris, partly in Suna on Lake Maggiore.

Tozzi paints landscapes, still lifes and figure compositions. He uses a linear technique and tries to obtain a monumental effect.

L. Fiumi. *Mario Tozzi*, Paris n.d.

Trier, Hann. German painter, b. 1915 in Düsseldorf. After visiting France in 1933 and completing his *Arbeitsdienst* in 1934 Trier studied at the Düsseldorf Academy under Heuser from 1934 to 1938. During this period he visited Switzerland, Italy and Holland. From 1939 to 1941 he served with the German forces, and from 1941 to 1944 worked as a technical draughtsman in Berlin. In 1946 he settled just outside Bonn, where he later founded the *Donnerstaggesellschaft*. In 1952 he emigrated to Colombia, but remained there for only three years, during which time he visited Ecuador, Venezuela, Mexico and the United States. He then returned to Germany, where he was visiting lecturer in Hamburg from 1955 to 1960, and has been teaching at the College of Fine Arts in Berlin since 1957. He is an abstract artist.

Trökes, Heinz. German painter, b. 1913 in Duisburg-Hamborn. Trökes studied under Johannes Itten from 1933 to 1936. In the following year he visited Paris, where he met Kandinsky. In 1940 he studied under Georg Muche in Krefeld before settling, later in the same year, in Berlin, where he remained until 1950, apart from a brief period spent as a teacher at the Weimar Academy in 1947–8. From 1950 to 1952 he was in Paris, where he came to know Wols. In 1952 he settled in Ibiza. From 1956 to 1958 he gave drawing classes at the Hamburg Academy, then returned to Ibiza again, remaining there until 1961, when he joined the staff of the Stuttgart Academy. In 1966 he transferred to the Academy in Berlin.

Trökes is an abstract artist who translates his impressions of the world—especially those formed on his numerous and lengthy journeys—into poetic compositions, which reveal the influence of Klee and Muche. These paintings, which are reminiscent of hieroglyphic systems, are executed in delicate, transparent colours. The titles frequently testify to an exotic source, e.g. *African Tracks* and *Desert Places*.

Karl Linfert (ed.). *Tagenachtbuch*, Cologne 1963.

Tršar, Drago. Yugoslav sculptor, b. 1927 in Planina, near Rakeh, Slovenia. Tršar studied at the Academy of Art in Ljubljana, where he subsequently obtained a post as assistant lecturer in 1960 and as lecturer in 1965.

After producing sculptures in the round in his early period Tršar went on to deal with the problems posed by what he calls the 'sculpture of the mass'. His work reveals a sensitive approach to movement and great skill in the combination of horizontals and verticals. In 1963–4 he produced portraits and groups, e.g. *Demonstrators* (1960). In his later work he has integrated the rhythms of the crowd with the natural rhythms of the stalactites in the limestone caves of his native Slovenia, translating into lyrical and cosmic terms the phenomenon of an expanding society in search of new human dimensions.

It is not really possible to place Tršar's work in any given category. 'Figurative' and 'abstract' are terms which lose their validity when applied to him, for he is fashioning the collective beings of a social sphere that is only just beginning to emerge.

Miodrag Kolarić. *New Yugoslav Sculpture*, Belgrade 1961.

Tryggvadottir, Nina. Icelandic painter, b. 1913. Since 1952 Tryggvadottir has lived and worked in Paris and London. She is an abstract painter and from 1955 onwards has worked in an Abstract Expressionist style, painting massive Cubist forms in luminous colours. Tryggvadottir has also created collages and stained-glass windows.

Tsarouchis, Yannis. Greek painter, b. 1909 in Piraeus. He studied in Athens, and moved to Paris in 1968. He has done many stage sets. He is essentially a Post-Fauvist artist. He makes successful and clever use of the technique of ancient Greek vase painting and of Byzantine and folk art.

Tschumi, Otto. Swiss painter and graphic artist, b. 1904 in Bittwil, near Berne. Tschumi attended evening classes given by Ernst Link and also studied at the School of Art and Crafts in Berne. In 1920 he began to experiment with Expressionist and Cubist compositions. In 1925 he visited Paris. From 1926 to 1930 he worked primarily as a commercial artist. In 1934 he met Klee. Between 1936 and 1940, when he was again in Paris, he met Arp and Max Ernst. It was then that he turned to Surrealism. In 1960 he was represented at the Biennale in Venice. He is now living in Liebefeld, near Berne.

In his dream-like and frequently scurrilous Surrealist works Tschumi employs all known automatic techniques. Although he gives a free rein to fantasy and uses a great deal of distortion, both the concept of real space and the world of reality remain an integral part of his pictorial composition. In addition to his paintings Tschumi has produced numerous illustrations for texts by Kafka, Rimbaud, Poe, Melville and others.

Catalogue, *Otto Tschumi*, Gimpel and Hanover Galleries, Zürich 1968.

Tsoklis, Costas. Greek painter, b. 1930 in Athens. He studied in Athens and Rome, and from 1960 has been living in Paris with intervals in Greece. He is an environmentalist in many ways. He created pseudo-realities by using 'real' objects in perspective. He consistently shows an ironic and Surrealistic attitude.

Tucker, William. British sculptor, b. 1935 in Cairo. Tucker was brought to England in 1937. After reading history at university he trained as a sculptor at the St. Martin's School of Art (under Anthony Caro) and the Central School of Art in London from 1958 to 1960. He now teaches at the St. Martin's School and lives in London.

Like Philip King and many other young English artists, Tucker makes *Indoor Sculptures*. These are abstract, glass-fibre constructions, whose component forms—many of them identical—are produced by industrial methods, then painted and assembled.

Tumarkin, Ygael. Israeli painter and sculptor, b. 1933 in Dresden. Tumarkin was taken to Palestine as a child in arms in 1935. The component elements in his paintings and monumental sculptures have both a constructive and a symbolic value. His sculptures are conceived as a significant extension of the countryside and are intended to be permanently displayed there. Tumarkin has also worked as a theatrical designer, chiefly for the Berlin Ensemble.

Tunnard, John. British painter, b. 1900 in Bedfordshire; d. 1971. From 1919 to 1923 he studied at the Royal College of Art, and worked commercially from 1923 to 1929. From 1930 he worked in Cornwall, and painted in a manner close to that of Paul Nash in the thirties and of the London Surrealists. His works are mainly landscapes, painted with clarity and precision, but into which are introduced strange alien elements, often of a Cubist kind, which are bizarre in space and scale and which lend a peculiar mystery to the scene.

Turcato, Giulio. Italian painter, b. 1912 in Mantua. After studying in Venice Turcato helped to draw up the manifesto for the *Forma I* artists' association in 1947. He joined the *Fronte Nuovo delle Arti* in 1949, the *Gruppo degli Otto* in 1950 and the *Continuità* group in 1962. He is now living in Rome, where he teaches at the Liceo Artistico.

During his early period Turcato was influenced by Expressionism, Cubism, Futurism and the concrete art of Magnelli. But in 1952, with the active support of L. Venturi, he abandoned the expressive and polemical approach of the *Fronte Nuovo* and began to paint pictures based on the principle of rhythmical composition, which reflected his preoccupation with the Cubist conception of spatiality, and autonomous colouring, which was derived from Matisse. In the end he dropped the third dimension completely and began to introduce monochrome grounds. His interrelating linear structures, which often create a highly sophisticated decorative effect, are indicative of a sensitive lyrical temperament. Since 1960 Turcato has been producing meditative compositions of stellar design.

Catalogue, *Turcato*, Galleria Marlborough, Rome 1965.
G. de Marchis. *Giulio Turcato*, Venice 1968.

Turnbull, William. British painter and sculptor, b. 1922 in Dundee. From 1947 to 1948 he attended the Slade, then from 1948 to 1950 he worked in Paris. He held his first one-man show in London in 1950. American painting was the main formative influence on his work, and he was one of the first British painters to demonstrate a real understanding of the meaning and importance of the new large-scale painting of the New York School of the fifties. He took part in the *Situation* exhibition in 1960. In the forties his work was large in scale, with fairly open brushwork and simple softly defined shapes often interrupted by the edge of the canvas. In the early sixties it became more hard-edged and his interest became exclusively concerned with the actual presence of the surface of the canvas. This is often painted in a single unbroken colour, asserted only by a stripe across one corner or a border of bare canvas. His early sculpture was basically figurative. In the early sixties he produced abstract totem figures of wood and stone, solid and free-standing, but recently he has been working in painted steel, like Anthony Caro, and his sculpture now presents the same bare uncompromising abstraction as his painting. It is powerful in its simplicity.

Catalogues, Marlborough Gallery, London 1962; Kunsthalle, Basle 1963; Waddington Gallery, London 1967.

Twombly, Cy. American painter, b. 1929 in Lexington, Virginia. He received his artistic training at the Boston Museum School, the Art Students' League and, on the advice of Robert Rauschenberg, at Black Mountain College where he worked under F. Kline and R. Motherwell. Since his first one-man show at the Kootz Gallery, New York, in 1951 he has had many solo exhibitions both in the United States and Europe; he has lived in Rome since 1957. His style is based on the art of Klee and the Abstract Expressionists. His abstract canvases, known as 'writings', may be characterized as 'a kind of meandering and imprecise graphology'. In the mid-1950s his earlier abstractions were replaced by compositions of allover graffiti. By 1956 he rejected the use of superimposition of lines, his canvases growing more bare, with an increased amount of space given over to a solid background (*Olympia*, 1957, Rome, Coll. Baron Giorgio Franchetti). By the late 1950s he showed greater concern for the surface on which the lines, words and doodles were placed, giving it the effect of an abused, crumbling wall (*School of Athens*, 1961, Rome, Coll. Baron Giorgio Franchetti). His latest works most immediately bring to mind the doodles on a telephone book—spirals, wave designs, repeating parallel lines, as in the 1967 *Untitled* painting in the New York collection of artist Andy Warhol.

Gillo Dorfles. 'Le immagini scritte de Cy Twombly—Written Images of Cy Twombly', *Metro* VI, June 1962.
Catalogue, *Cy Twombly*, Milwaukee Art Center, Milwaukee (Wisc.) 1968.

291 Gallery. The Photo-Secession Gallery at 291 Fifth Avenue, New York—usually referred to simply as '291'—was opened by the American photographer Alfred Stieglitz in 1905. Although it was originally established for the exhibition of photography, beginning in 1907 Stieglitz broadened its scope to include also exhibitions of painting, sculpture and the graphic arts. In effect, he maintained a principle of the interrelationship of all the arts and for the first time exhibited photography on an equal level with the other visual arts. With Stieglitz as an indispensable and pervasive guiding spirit for experimentation and freedom of creativity, 291 soon became the most vital centre of *avant-garde* art in America, despite its smallness, air of intimacy, and total aversion to any commercialism.

Through 291 America was introduced to the major contemporary modernists, both European and American. Between 1908 and 1914 Stieglitz (with the advice of Edward Steichen, then living in Paris) gave the first American exhibitions for Auguste Rodin, Henri Matisse and Paul Cézanne, and the first one-man exhibitions anywhere for Pablo Picasso and Constantin Brancusi. From 1909 on Stieglitz also began exhibiting, perhaps even more avidly, the work of the first American modernists: John Marin, Alfred Maurer and Marsden Hartley were given their first exhibitions in 1909 and were followed by other artists, including Arthur B. Carles, Arthur G. Dove, Max Weber, Elie Nadelman, Georgia O'Keeffe and Stanton Macdonald-Wright. In addition, in 1912

Stieglitz organized the first exhibition of children's art, and in 1914, the first exhibition of African primitive sculpture as art rather than as anthropological material.

The official publication of 291 was *Camera Work*, published and edited by Stieglitz from 1903 to 1917. In its first years it emphasized photography—by Steichen, Stieglitz and others—but soon included articles on all the visual arts (including some by George Bernard Shaw and Maurice Maeterlinck), *avant-garde* literature (e.g. the first published writing of Gertrude Stein), and a record of the controversial, often hostile, contemporary criticism of 291.

The 291 Gallery was closed in 1917, when the building housing it was torn down. A degree of continuity was provided by two later galleries established by Stieglitz, the Intimate Gallery (a room in the Anderson Galleries), 1925–9, and An American Place (509 Madison Avenue), 1929–46, both of which emphasized the work of American artists, especially Marin, Hartley, Dove and O'Keeffe.

'What Is 291?' *Camera Work* 47, January 1915.
Waldo Frank *et al.* (eds). *America and Alfred Stieglitz, A Collective Portrait*, New York 1934.
Oliver Larkin. 'Alfred Stieglitz and 291', *Magazine of Art* XL, May 1947.

Tworkov, Jack. American painter, b. 1900 in Biala, Poland. He went to the United States in 1913, and studied at Columbia University (1920–3) and at the National Academy of Design (1923–5). He also worked at the Art Students' League under Guy Pène Du Bois and Boardman Robinson. During the Depression, like many of his New York artist colleagues, Tworkov worked for the Public Works Art Project (1934) and later for the WPA (1937–41), although he claims that his project paintings were the worst in his production, since aesthetics were subordinated to the needs of social message. Cézanne's work was a great and pervasive influence for Tworkov, and summer contacts at Provincetown with the painter Karl Knaths encouraged this interest, also introducing him to the work of Joan Miró, Paul Klee and Vassily Kandinsky. His early work included figurative paintings, landscapes and still lifes. He met Willem de Kooning while working for the government art project in 1934, and later banded together with him and other Abstract Expressionist painters to form the New York School in the 1940s and early 1950s. During the Second World War Tworkov worked as a tool designer, and when he returned to painting in 1946 he began to explore an abstract automatic method based on an interest in Surrealism's experiments with the unconscious. In 1947 he abandoned still lifes for the figure (*Figure*, 1948–9, Hartford, Conn., Wadsworth Atheneum) but the figuration was set into ambiguous layers of activated brushwork spontaneously applied. The Virginia landscape offered Tworkov the inspiration

for more painterly compositions while he taught at the American University in Washington, D.C. (1948–1949). He also taught at Black Mountain College, North Carolina, Queens College and Pratt Institute in New York, and at the University of Minnesota during the course of his career. For several years after his return to New York, Tworkov worked in the studio adjoining de Kooning's, and like his friend worked to synthesize remnants of configuration with fluid paint and colour that dissolved the edges and shapes of forms.

By 1954 the colour and flame-like diagonal strokes had become the components of a more subtle atmospheric style, creating shimmering, transparent fields of textured pigment as in *Watergame* (1955, New York, Coll. Mr. and Mrs. Lee V. Eastman). The process was increasingly one of obliterating specific references to the forms or scenes that initiated the paintings. In 1962 a series of red, white and blue canvases occupied Tworkov, as he dealt with balancing quantities of pure tube colour in gridlike arrangements, more taut than the flickering façades of his previous work, and without the chromatic modulations characteristic of the freer style. Although he was one of the exponents of an Expressionistic mode during the high point of Abstract Expressionism in the mid-1950s, the control he exercised distinguished his paintings from the rawness of a de Kooning (*Queen*, 1957, Southfield, Michigan, Coll. Mr. and Mrs. A. A. Taubman; and *Transverse*, 1957–8, New York, Coll. Ben Heller).

Edward Bryant. *Jack Tworkov*, New York 1964.

Tytgat, Edgard. Belgian painter, b. 1879 in Brussels; d. 1957 in Brussels. Tytgat began by painting Impressionist works, but after the First World War he joined the ranks of the Expressionists, bringing to the Belgian branch of the movement his own gentle humour and almost naïve approach. In contrast to the prevailing attitude of contempt for narrative work, Tytgat painted scenes from stories and legends which have a tender charm, with their formalized figures and delicate colouring. He also depicted the circus many times, and the simple, flat compositions are full of the warmth and understanding with which he viewed circus people and their way of life.

Jozef Muls. *Edgard Tytgat*, Brussels 1943.
Maurice Roelants. *Edgard Tytgat*, Antwerp 1948.

Tyzack, Michael. British painter, b. 1933 in Sheffield. Tyzack attended the Sheffield College of Art and the Slade School. In 1964 he became Lecturer in Fine Art at Cardiff Art College. In 1965 he won the main prize at the John Moores Exhibition, Liverpool. He has had exhibitions in London, Paris and Switzerland, and a one-man show in Amsterdam, 1967, and was in the Documenta IV exhibition at

Kassel in 1968. Tyzack has paintings in the Victoria and Albert Museum, the Arts Council, and the Contemporary Arts Society, London, and the São Paulo Museum, among others.

U

Ubac, Raoul. French painter, graphic artist and sculptor, b. 1910 in Malmédy, Belgium. Between 1928 and 1934 Ubac visited numerous European countries, and lived for a while in Cologne, where (as Rolf Ubach) he joined the *Progressive Künstler* association, which was headed by Freundlich, Max Ernst and Hoerle. In 1935, when he was in Paris, he made contact with André Breton's Surrealist group. Subsequently, he contributed photographs to the Surrealist magazine *Le Minotaure*, and studied in William Hayter's Atelier 17. In 1946 he discovered some unusual slates in Savoy, from which he created double-sided reliefs. Although his early works—trees, steles and landscapes—were virtually abstract, his more recent ones have revealed a much stronger figurative component, and also possess archaic associations. In addition to slate reliefs (*ardoises*) and sculptures Ubac has produced paintings, drawings, etchings, photographs, illustrations for books, and tapestries.

Udaltsova, Nadezhda. Russian painter, b. 1886; d. 1961. Like her friend Popova she left Moscow for Paris in 1912, and there studied Cubism as represented by Le Fauconnier and Metzinger. On her return to Moscow in 1914 she was able to incorporate the basic structure of Cubism into her work.

Uecker, Günther. German sculptor, b. 1930 in Wendorf, Mecklenburg. Uecker studied at the Academies of Art in Berlin-Weissensee and Düsseldorf. It was in 1957 that he first began working on his objects in space and his welded 'nail trees'. Since then nails have been his favourite material. In 1958–9 he began to arrange them in symmetrical patterns on sheets of metal and boards. Later works of this kind reveal a more fluid arrangement. From 1960 onwards Uecker has also incorporated light sources enclosed in light boxes and rotating discs. In late 1961 he began to move towards O. Piene and H. Mack and, until it was disbanded in 1966, these three formed the inner cadre of the *Zero* group. In 1964–5 they collaborated on 'light spaces' and 'light mills'. Of recent years Uecker has been making in-creasing use of artificial light—especially neon tubes —in his sculptures. He lives primarily in Düsseldorf.

Uhlmann, Hans. German sculptor, b. 1900 in Berlin. He studied in Berlin and had his first show there in 1930. He was unable to work during the Nazi rule, but in 1950 he was appointed professor at the School of Fine Art in West Berlin. In his sculpture he uses iron and other metals, and his works derive from Constructivism. They include reliefs and machine-like assemblies. In 1961 Uhlmann was commissioned to decorate the façade of the Opera House in Berlin.

Ultvedt, Per-Olof. Finnish sculptor, painter, graphic artist and film-maker, b. 1927. During his early period Ultvedt produced paintings and graphic works featuring animal *motifs*. Then, in the mid-1950s, he began to make mobiles from welded metal and from carved wood. Later he used articles of furniture and kitchen utensils as components, arranging them in such a way as to produce ironical impressions, and creating stimulative movements by mechanical means. Ultvedt has also produced rotating reliefs, and black collages on white grounds. The optical illusions set up by these extremely vital collages are so powerful that they induce feelings of vertigo. Ultvedt's black and white film *Nära ögat (Almost in the Eye)* is informed by this same vital rhythm.

S. Key-Aberg. *Per-Olof Ultvedt*, Konstrevy 1958.

Unit I. This association was formed in 1933 when a number of English artists, who represented a wide variety of trends ranging from Surrealism to Constructivism, gathered around the painter Paul Nash. These artists were: Henry Moore, Barbara Hepworth, Ben Nicholson, John Armstrong, John Bigge, Edward Burra, Tristram Hellier, Edward Wadsworth and the architects Wells Coates and Colin Lucas. The association's spokesman was Herbert Read, its secretary Douglas Cooper. In the introduction to the catalogue of the Unit I 1934 exhibition in the Mayer Gallery, London, the aims of the association were described in the following passage: '. . . these artists have not agreed that there is only one method of painting, sculpting or building, nor even that their art should express a common sentiment or even a conscious direction . . . each one stands for the expression of a truly contemporary spirit, for that thing which is recognized as peculiarly of today . . . The title then combines the idea of unity—*Unit*— with that of individuality—*One.*' In the mid-1930s a Constructivist trend emerged within the association, due largely to the influence brought to bear by the emigrant artists Gropius, Moholy-Nagy and Naum Gabo, who had entered into close contact with Unit I. This splinter group later subscribed to the manifesto issued by Ben Nicholson, Naum Gabo and the architect J. L. Martin in 1937. Meanwhile, thanks to the initiative displayed by the members of Unit I, the now famous International Surrealist Exhibition was staged in London in 1936. But with the outbreak of war in 1939 the artists grouped around both Unit I and the Circle went their separate ways.

Herbert Read. *Unit I*, London 1934.

Urban, Reva. American painter and graphic artist, b. 1925 in Coney Island, New York. She received her training at the Art Students' League, where she studied on a Carnegie Scholarship. She had her first one-man show at the Peridot Gallery, New York, in 1958. By 1959 she was working exclusively on shaped canvases and may perhaps be the innovator of this format. Her works are executed in bold colours, handled in broad, often billowing areas which extend beyond the straight edges of the canvas (*Seated Metamorphosis*, 1960, New York, Grippi and Waddell Galleries). At times she adds three-dimensional elements to her canvases, as in the 1963 *Grace and the Wheel* (New York, Grippi and Waddell Galleries) with its spoked wheel in the centre of large sensuous swells of colour. In 1960 she received a Yaddo Foundation Fellowship and in 1963 a Tamarind Lithography Workshop Fellowship. Her latest free-standing paintings, which employ several panels, have the quality of a large Constructivist relief, though she includes representational elements such as the torso and lips of *Hugo's Cabinet* (1965, New York, Grippi and Waddell Galleries) in this piece of vivid colour and varied tactility. The artist was married in 1949 to the late German-born painter Albert Urban.

Catalogue, *Reva Urban—5 years, 2 galleries*, Grippi and Waddell, and Jason Galleries, New York 1965.

Urteil, Andreas. Austrian sculptor, b. 1933 in Sombor, Yugoslavia; d. 1963 in Vienna. Urteil studied under Wotruba at the Academy of Art in Vienna from 1951 onwards.

There is something anthropomorphic about Urteil's abstract sculptures. These stone, wood or bronze pieces, which are full of movement after the manner of Baroque sculpture, are reminiscent of both Boccioni and Hanak.

Usami, Keiji. Japanese painter and light artist, b. 1940 in Osaka. He is self-taught in painting. At his first one-man show in the Minami Gallery in 1963, he exhibited almost white monochromatic abstractions with subtle microscopic drips. Starting in 1965, he developed an interest in cut-outs of human figures and various ways of combining them. His two recent shows, *Laser-Beam Joint* (Tokyo, 1968; The Jewish Museum, New York, 1969), mark an interesting attempt to bring yet another dimension to his idea of 'relation'. In this case, it is the laser beam which effects the combination of the cut-out figures, and which itself is influenced by the motion of the viewer. He designed the light system for the Concert Hall at Expo 70 under the directorship of Toru Takemitsu.

Utrillo, Maurice. French painter, b. 1883 in Paris; d. 1955 in Le Vésinet. He was the son of Suzanne Valadon. Neglected as a child and a failure at school, he early became an alcoholic and by the age of 18 had repeated need for curative treatment in hospital. He was introduced to painting to mitigate the effects of his alcoholism and to give him a reason to live. His work begins near Impressionism in subject matter, colour and handling. His paint was sometimes thickened with plaster: white dominated his palette during these years (c. 1910–15). Later his colours became brighter, his brushwork more calligraphic, and figures assume a more decided part of his compositions. The dealer Sagot became interested in his work in 1905. He exhibited at the Salon d'Automne in 1909: his first one-man show was in 1913. In 1950 he represented France at the Venice Biennale. Much of his early work was painted in Montmartre; he made two journeys to Corsica and Brittany, and often painted from postcards. He was practically self-taught, but once set towards painting he produced a large oeuvre—even under the influence of drink at the local police lock-up. During the latter part of his life he had the support of Lucie Pauwels, the widow of a rich Belgian banker, whom he married, and who acted partly as his mentor and business manager. This period was marked by a far greater sobriety; he would withdraw to pray in an oratory he had built at his villa at Le Vésinet. Taking into account his way of life, the paintings are surprisingly consistent in quality; the subjects are dominated by architecture—streets, parks and churches. The buildings are personified as acutely as portraits of living people, but the firmness of his pictorial structure and his feeling for colour harmony objectify his emotion. He has been called a primitive, but though his figures may be puppet-like, his feeling of place and his delineation of urban landscape is highly sophisticated. Also his work has been described as of little significance to modern art by critics intent on the description of the *avant-garde*. The use of Impressionism and certain aspects of van Gogh's and Gauguin's styles led Utrillo to a personal, consistent and communicable view of man's environment.

A. Tabarant. *Utrillo*, Paris 1926.
P. MacOrlan. *Utrillo*, Paris 1952.
P. Pétridès (ed.). *Maurice Utrillo: L'Oeuvre complète*, Paris 1959–62.
Waldemar George. *Utrillo*, New York 1960.

V

Vacchi, Sergio. Italian painter, b. 1925 in Castenaso, Bologna. Vacchi studied at the academies in Bologna and Rome. Since 1951 he has been associated with the *Il Milione* Gallery in Milan.

During his early period Vacchi was influenced by Cézanne and the Cubists. He then passed through an informal phase before evolving a somewhat contrived form of Neo-Surrealism, which he derived from the early works of Wols.

F. Arcangeli. *Sergio Vacchi*, Milan 1959.

Valadon, Suzanne (Marie-Clémentine Valadon). French painter, b. 1867 in Bessines; d. 1938 in Paris. Suzanne had a difficult relationship with her mother and a childhood of poverty. She was self-reliant and escaped from home at the age of 13 to work as a dish-washer and at other menial jobs. She joined a circus but fell from the trapeze. Convalescing from this, she became an artist's model. She also began to draw, 'to catch a moment of life in movement in all its intensity'. She sat for Puvis de Chavannes in 1882 and had a love affair with Renoir (who was indifferent to her drawing). She then became a kind of hostess to Toulouse-Lautrec, who was the first to buy her work. He introduced her to Degas; he became a life-long friend and her first engravings were printed on his press. He, in turn, introduced her to the dealer Vollard, who showed her graphic work in 1895. In 1889 she had become interested in Gauguin's work and, with much encouragement, began herself to paint in 1909. Her work has the unexpected perspective of Degas, the charged outline of Gauguin, and a hard vitality all her own. She left few written remains but could be easily persuaded to reminisce about life in Montmartre. Her son Maurice was born when she was 18. Miguel Utrillo y Molins later formally registered paternity, but she maintained that a man named Boissy was the father. Early on she left the child much to himself but later came to devote her life to his care. Her work consists of many drawings of the nude; the paintings are mostly of figure subjects.

A. Basler. *Suzanne Valadon*, Paris 1929.
M. Mermillion. *Suzanne Valadon*, Paris 1950.
J. Storm. *The Valadon Drama*, New York 1959.

Vallotton, Félix. Swiss-French painter, b. 1865 in Lausanne; d. 1925 in Paris. Félix Vallotton was of Swiss origin, but the whole of his career was spent in Paris, where he went at the age of 17 to start his training at the Académie Julian. Among his fellow students there were Vuillard, Bonnard, Denis and Ranson. Through them Vallotton had close contact with Sérusier and Gauguin, and he was further associated with them when their group, called the *Nabis*, was formed in 1890. His paintings at this time were free and spontaneous, street scenes and still lifes, full of wit in observation and manner. He also developed an interest in lithography and poster art. Vallotton was much concerned with drawing and the use of line. He had a great respect for Toulouse-Lautrec and van Gogh. He became a constant exhibitor at the Salon des Indépendants, for a time being influenced by the dominant style of Pointillism.

In 1890 he began to make woodcuts. In this medium his acute observation and wit were well exploited in a series of portraits for *La Revue Blanche*, mainly of those connected with this periodical. Vallotton came to excel in woodcut techniques. The direct, pungent representation in these, with the similar qualities in his painting, had some influence on the early Expressionists.

Vallotton seems to have been very independent by nature, always collaborating with but never fully accepting the ideas of his associates. After 1900 he grew even further apart from them in his choice of style. In almost deliberate defiance of Fauvist and Expressionist developments he adopted a cold, precise Realism. His later, austere paintings of nudes, portraits and still lifes seem a defiant revival of past attitudes, combined with an expression of his affirmed delight in 'the smoothness of the egg'.

H. Hahnloser. *Félix Vallotton et ses amis*, Paris 1936.
F. Jourdain. *Félix Vallotton*, Geneva 1953.

Valori Plastici. The *Valori Plastici* artists' association took its name from the *Valori Plastici* magazine which was launched in November 1918 in Rome by M. Broglio. Carrà, Severini and de Chirico, who were founder members of the new association, had attacked Cubism and Futurism, which they wished to see replaced by the aesthetics of the *Pittura Metafisica*. The *Valori Plastici* revered traditional Classical art which it interpreted in terms of *Italianità*—and called for the revival of academic training methods such as drawing and painting from plaster models. The long-term danger for the *Valori Plastici* lay in the ignorance and provincialism of the third-rate artists amongst its members, who eventually succumbed to the sentimental and nationalistic slogans of Fascism. Initially, however, the leading exponents of the new style found confirmation of their ideas in the Neo-Classical periods of Picasso and Derain. The principal characteristics of *Valori Plastici* paintings are their hard, linear composition, their plasticity and—in many cases—their Realistic and even Mannerist handling.

Valtat, Louis. French painter, b. 1869 in Dieppe; d. 1952 in Paris. He studied at the Académie Julian in Paris, and spent a great deal of time in the South of France. Early in his career he made the acquaintance of Bonnard and Vuillard; later he also met Renoir, Signac and Cross. His first works were Pointillist in character, but in about 1895 he began to use pure, strong colour to construct his shapes. He was one of the first painters to adopt this approach, which through Matisse and Marquet developed into the Fauvist movement. After 1913 Valtat settled in Paris and dropped out of the public gaze. His work is now being recognized as an important contribution to the development of modern art.

R. Cogniat. *Louis Valtat*, Neuchâtel 1963.

Vandercam, Serge. Danish painter, b. 1924 in Copenhagen. Vandercam is a self-taught artist. He began his career as a photographer, and it was whilst working in this medium that he discovered his highly personal abstract world. Not long afterwards he started to paint, and helped to found the Gallerie Taptoe. His first canvases were violent Expressionist colour compositions. These were followed in 1958 by an exhibition of more restrained, lyrical works, in which blue is the dominant colour. In the following year Vandercam showed his first terra-cottas, and in 1962 he reverted to an extremely free and extremely dynamic form of figurative painting, producing a series of works on the theme *Homme de Tollund*. Since then he has again adopted a richer palette, and his composition has tended to be rather more Realistic. Vandercam has also produced some highly imaginative and distinctive pottery, having studied this craft in Albissola. He is now living at Bierges-Lez-Wavre, near Brussels.

Vantongerloo, Georges. Belgian sculptor and painter, b. 1886 in Antwerp; d. 1965 in Paris. After studying at the academies in Antwerp and Brussels Vantongerloo was interned during the First World War in Holland, where he made the acquaintance of van Doesburg. In 1917 he joined the *de Stijl* movement and signed its manifesto, after which he became a contributor to the *de Stijl* magazine. But in 1921 Vantongerloo left the movement and went to live in Menton, remaining there until 1927, when he settled in Paris. In 1928–9 he produced his 'airfield designs', in 1930 he was represented at the *Cercle et Carré* exhibition and in 1931 became a founder member and vice-president of the *Abstraction-Création* association.

After making various early attempts to evolve an abstract style Vantongerloo finally adopted the Neo-Plastic principles of the *de Stijl* movement in 1917, which he then applied to the sphere of sculpture. Unlike Mondrian, however, he based his work on mathematical calculations. His sculptures from this period—which consist of simple cubic forms organized in spatial patterns based on contrasting horizontal and perpendicular elements—made a considerable impact on contemporary architecture. Several of the Bauhaus architects, including Mies van der Rohe, were influenced by this style. In the late 1930s Vantongerloo abandoned his rectilinear

forms in favour of curves. Later, in the closing years of his life, he worked with painted Plexiglass.

Georges Vantongerloo. *Paintings, Sculptures, Reflections*, New York 1948.
Max Bill. *Georges Vantongerloo*, Marlborough Galleries, London 1962.

Vasarély, Victor. French painter, sculptor and graphic artist, b. 1908 in Pecs, Hungary. After studying medicine, Vasarély attended the Poldini-Volkmann Academy in Budapest in 1927 and the Mühely Academy (the 'Bauhaus of Budapest') in 1928–9. In 1930 he moved to Paris. Since then he has won numerous international awards, including the Guggenheim Prize in New York (1964), the *Grand Prix* at the Bienal in São Paulo (1965) and the Foreign Ministers' Prize at the Eleventh Biennale in Tokyo (1967). He is now living in Annet-sur-Marne.

It was in 1947 that Vasarély finally opted for the constructive, geometrical medium in which he has made his major contribution to art. The basic formal characteristics of the works of this period are: the circle and its derivatives (ellipsoids), which appear both in isolation and in conjunction with other fundamental forms; the square and the right angle and their derivatives (rhomboids); triangular forms and segments of circles. These may be broken down into linear characteristics consisting of verticals, horizontals and sets of lines drawn at varying distances from one another which are 'disturbed' by sets of parallel undulations and circular forms and so given a spatial function. The ambiguity, which is one of the most striking qualities of Vasarély's work during his mature period, was later taken up by the adherents of Op Art. In fact, he exerted a very considerable influence on the younger generation of visual artists and was largely responsible for the development of the *Groupe de Recherche d'Art Visuel* in Paris. Commenting on his sculptures in 1958 Vasarély wrote: 'I believe that I am able to point to the existence in my works of an architectonic, abstract art form, a sort of universal folklore, whose language is readily adaptable to the highly developed techniques of urban construction.' This claim is borne out by his three-dimensional metal pillars, his pyramid-shaped metal reliefs and by all those projects in which he collaborated with architects, thus ensuring that his own contribution was integrated into a wider, sociological structure. This last group includes the ceramic mural and aluminium relief constructed for the University of Caracas in 1954, numerous works executed in Paris (*Rue Camou 6–8, Boulevard Lannes 59–65, Avenue de Versailles 54–56*, etc.), the Jerusalem Museum and the 1967 French Pavilion at the Expo in Montreal.

Jean Dewasne. *Vasarély*, Paris 1952.
M. Seuphor (intro.). Catalogue, *Vasarély*, Galerie Denise René, Paris 1955.

M. Joray. *Vasarély*, Neuchâtel 1965.
Catalogue, *Vasarély*, Sidney Janis Gallery, New York 1968.

Vaughan, Keith. British painter, b. 1912 in Selsey Bill. He was largely self-taught as a painter. He worked from 1931 to 1939 in the art department of an advertising agency and had little contact with the mainstream of British painting until the forties, when he met Graham Sutherland, John Minton, Colquhoun and other artists of similar inclination. During this period these artists, and especially Sutherland, were the chief influence on his work. He held his first one-man show in 1946 and in the same year the experience of the Picasso and Matisse exhibition helped him to move towards a style increasingly preoccupied with structure and form. Some of his figure compositions of this period are close to Matisse and Cézanne, showing a clear and firm understanding of their work. In the early fifties the example of de Staël turned him towards a flatter and more abstract composition, emphasizing surface but keeping the interest in contour that derives from Cézanne. Since then, though still related to figure and landscape composition, his style has become more abstract with free and broken handling of paint.

Catalogue, *Keith Vaughan*, Whitechapel Gallery, London 1962.

Vedova, Emilio. Italian painter, b. 1919 in Venice. He began painting at an early age, and joined the *Corrente* movement in Milan (1942). He was a founder member of the *Fronte Nuovo delle Arti* in 1946, and one of the Eight Italians grouped together in the 1952 Venice Biennale. His painting is preoccupied with claustrophobia, and many of his works, both figurative and abstract, suggest a feeling of oppression and an effort to break loose from a world grown too small for his vision.

Velde, Bram van. Dutch-French painter, b. 1895 in Zoeterwoude, near Leyden. Velde, who is the brother of the painter Geer van Velde and of the writer Jacob van Velde, was apprenticed to a decorative artist in 1907, when he was twelve years old. The pictures which he painted during his apprenticeship reveal the influence of the Dutch artist Breitner. In 1922 Velde's master sent him to Worpswede to complete his artistic training. In 1925 he went to Paris, where he began to paint flower pieces and landscapes, using Fauvist colours. From 1926 onwards he exhibited in the Salon des Indépendants and the Salon des Surindépendants. In 1930 he visited Corsica and between 1932 and 1936 lived on the island of Majorca. He then returned to Paris, where he is still living today.

After first painting in an Expressionist style Velde gradually introduced Cubist structures into his work. Subsequently—from the late 1930s onwards—he evolved an Abstract Expressionist style, incorporating flowing brush-strokes, which run through his pictures like veins, and transparent areas of colour, which are organized into cellular structures and whose triangular and oval forms trigger associations with living figures and masks. Velde's oil paintings are so dynamic that they seem quite spontaneous. In point of fact, however, he is a very slow and meticulous worker and many of his paintings took months to complete. Not surprisingly, his oeuvre is relatively small, comprising some 200 works in all.

J. Putman. *Bram van Velde*, Paris 1958; *Bram van Velde*, Turin and Paris 1962.
Catalogue, *Bram van Velde*, Knoedler and Co., New York 1968.

Velde, Geer van. Dutch painter, b. 1898 in Lisse. Velde, who is the brother of Bram van Velde, is a self-taught artist. After living in Paris from 1925 to 1939 he spent the war years in Cagnes-sur-Mer. He then returned to Paris in 1945 and eventually settled in Cachau, near Paris, where he is still living today.

Velde is a member of the *École de Paris*. Using subtle shades of delicate, transparent colour and harmonious geometrically based abstract forms he paints pictures which derive in the first instance from objective *motifs* and are reminiscent of abstract interiors or still lifes. It is almost as if the objects were concealed within the abstract forms. Between 1926 and 1930 Velde exhibited with the Indépendants. He also contributed to the Salon de Mai.

S. Beckett. 'Geer van Velde', *XXe Siècle* 4, 1954.

Velde, Henry van de. Belgian architect, industrial artist, painter and art critic, b. 1863 in Antwerp; d. 1957 in Zürich. After attending the Academy of Art in Antwerp from 1881 to 1883 Velde continued his studies in Paris in 1884–5. Whilst there he met various French Impressionists and Symbolists, including Monet, Signac, Pissarro, Verlaine and Debussy. In 1885 he returned to Belgium, where he lived in Antwerp and Brussels, and made contact with Socialist groups. He also continued to paint, and became a regular contributor to two magazines: *La Wallonie* (Liège) and *L'Art Moderne* (Brussels). During this period Velde wrote articles on painting, the theatre and music. In 1889 he joined the *Les Vingt* association in Brussels, and made contact with the painter and potter Willy Finch, who introduced the English craft movement into Belgium. The year 1889 was a fateful one for Velde: after suffering a nervous collapse brought on by his mother's death he decided to give up painting, and turned instead to purely decorative art forms. In 1893 he made his first furniture designs, and in 1894 had his first meeting with Meier-Graefe and Bing. Gradually he began to make a name for himself. In 1895 he designed the first of the private houses which he built for his own occupation: Bloemenwerf, in Uccle; and made interior designs for Bing's Maison Moderne in Paris. Subsequently, he exhibited a group of interior designs in Paris (1896) and Dresden (1897). He was extremely successful in Germany, where he designed the interior of the Folkwang Museum in Hagen (1900) and the interior fittings for the Kunstsalon Cassirer in Berlin. In 1901 he accepted the post of artistic adviser to Archduke Wilhelm Ernst of Saxe-Weimar. In 1904 he obtained a professorial post, and in 1906 designed the Industrial School of Art in Weimar, where completely new pedagogic methods were introduced. In 1917 Velde went to live in Switzerland, and during the next four years was in contact with E. L. Kirchner. In 1921 the art collector Kröller-Müller invited him to Holland, where Velde designed various buildings for him. He also produced plans for the Kröller-Müller Museum in Otterlo, which subsequently underwent considerable modification. In 1922 Velde built his second house (in Wassenaar, near The Hague), for which he used prefabricated components. In 1926 he moved to Brussels, and obtained a professorial post at the University in Ghent. In 1937 work started on the Kröller-Müller Museum. In 1947 Velde settled in Oberägerl in Switzerland, where he wrote his memoirs. In 1954 he visited Holland to supervise the construction of the entrance vestibule of the Museum in Otterlo. In 1957 he died in a clinic in Zürich.

Velde was a leading exponent of the *Jugendstil*, and one of its most important spokesmen, especially in the field of the applied arts. His research into the expressive function of pictorial means and their intrinsic coherence anticipated the abstract conclusions drawn by Kandinsky and Klee.

M. Casteels. *Henry van de Velde*, Brussels 1932.
Hermann Teirlinck. *Henry van de Velde*, Brussels 1959.
Henry van de Velde. *Geschichte meines Lebens*, Munich 1962.
A. M. Hammacher. *Le Monde de Henry van de Velde*, Antwerp and Cologne 1967.

Veličković, Vladimir. Yugoslav architect, painter and draughtsman, b. 1935 in Belgrade. After completing his architectural studies in 1960 Veličković attended Krsto Hegedusic's 'masters' class' in Zagreb in 1962–3. By then he had already been working as an artist for some considerable time, having had his first exhibition as early as 1951. During his early period he painted fantastic interiors, still lifes and landscapes in dark colours. These were followed by monumental compositions on tragic themes executed in various shades of pale grey. The poetic handling and aggressive intent of these apocalyptic visions of massive inhumanity contain a message and a warning. In his compositions, in which monsters and scarecrows are juxtaposed with crucifixes, Veličković employs an Illusionist modelling technique which dissolves stylistic boundaries. As a result Realism and Abstraction, Surrealism and Expressionism merge to form a new and powerful configuration.

Max Clarac-Séron (intro.). Catalogue, *Veličković*, Galerie du Dragon, Paris 1967.
J. Denegri. 'The Painting of Vladimir Veličković', *Izraz*, Sarajevo, June 1967.

Verheyen, Jef. Belgian painter, b. 1932 in Iteghem. Verheyen studied at the Academy of Art and the Institut des Beaux-Arts in Antwerp from 1948 to 1952. In 1958 he published a manifesto under the title *Essentialisme*, in which he argued against contrasting colour schemes and geometric symbols and stressed the need to experience 'existential colours'. In 1960 he became a founder member of the New Flemish School, which is trying to effect dematerialization of the picture surface.

Verheyen is one of the best-known representatives of monochrome painting in Belgium. He is now living in Antwerp.

Verlon, André (Willi Verkauf). Swiss painter, b. 1917 in Zürich. Verlon spent his childhood and early youth in Zürich and Vienna. In 1933 he emigrated and for the next thirteen years lived most of the time in Jerusalem, where he eventually worked as a publisher. In 1946 he returned to Europe and lived in Vienna and Switzerland until 1961, when he moved to Paris. He started to paint in 1946 and became a full-time artist in 1958.

In his pictures—most of which are a mixture of photo-collage and Action Painting—Verlon is protesting against the brutality of a world that has been dehumanized by technology, science and politics.

P. M. T. Sheldon-Williams. *Verlon*, London 1963.

Veronesi, Luigi. Italian painter and film-maker, b. 1908 in Milan. After studying in Milan and Paris Veronesi became a founder member of the *Abstraction-Création* association. Between 1937 and 1943 he produced stage sets. Since 1938 he has been making abstract films. He was one of the earliest abstract artists in Italy.

Vespignani, Renzo. Italian painter, b. 1924 in Rome. Vespignani is a self-taught painter. In 1949 he joined with G. Urbinati and A. Muccini in founding the *Pittori del Portonaccio* group. He is now living in Rome.

Vespignani portrays the social milieu of the Rome slums in extremely subtle drawings which reveal some Surrealist and Pop Art influences.

B. Degenhart. *Italienische Zeichner der Gegenwart*, Berlin 1956.

Vézelay, Paule. Franco-British painter and designer, b. 1893 in England. She spent the years 1926–39 in Paris, but then returned to London. Around 1927 she began to work in an abstract manner. She joined the *Abstraction-Création* group in Paris (1934), and was president of the British branch of the *Groupe Espace* from 1957. She illustrated books, designed carpets and fabrics, created sculptures and did some engraving, but her paintings are her most typical works. She is represented in many private collections in Britain and France and has exhibited in major shows throughout the world.

Viani, Alberto. Italian sculptor, b. 1906 in Quistello, Mantua. Viani trained at the Academy of Art in Venice under A. Martini, first as a student and then as an assistant. In 1946 he joined the *Fronte Nuovo delle Arti*. He now teaches at the Venice Academy.

After an early period, in which he produced works based on Martini's artistic ideas, Viani evolved a somewhat archaic style. Later, when he began moving towards abstract art, he came under the influence of Brancusi and Arp. But, despite their simplification, the rounded forms of Viani's elegant sculptures—most of which are executed in polished marble—remain firmly grounded in the basic three-dimensional concept of the human body.

Sculture di Alberto Viani, Milan 1964.

Vicente, Esteban. American painter, b. 1906 in Segovia, Spain. He left his schooling at a military academy when he was sixteen in order to study sculpture at the Real Academia de Bellas Artes de San Fernando in Madrid, and a few years later gave up sculpture for painting. In 1927 he moved to Paris where he worked for five years and where he received his first one-man show. He moved to the United States in 1936, had his first one-man show in New York the following year at the Kleeman Gallery and became associated with the Abstract Expressionists. His works of the late 1940s and early 1950s depend on a variety of shapes and colours placed across the surface of the canvas—a style which depends on the tradition of Late Cubism and his own construction of shifting planes (*Growth*, 1951, New York, Peridot Gallery). Some of his later works are black and white collages made with newsprint, while others are freer and more painterly, with a greater use of colour—an approach which seems to derive to a degree from Philip Guston. Vicente received a Ford Foundation Grant in 1961 and 1962 and was director of the Highfield Art Workshop, Falmouth, Mass. He has taught at Yale and Princeton Universities, Queens and Black Mountain Colleges, the University of California in Berkeley and Los Angeles and at the University of Puerto Rico. He has exhibited in many Whitney Annuals and at the 1963 Bienal, São Paulo.

Elaine De Kooning. 'Vicente Paints a Collage', *Art News*, September 1953.

Vieira da Silva, Maria Elena. Franco-Portuguese painter, b. 1908 in Lisbon. She studied sculpture in Paris under Bourdelle and Despiau, and later with Dufresne, Friesz and Léger. She first began to attract attention in the early thirties, with her abstract, linear compositions in neutral tones. She strove to express the relationship of shapes in space without resorting to the accepted rules of perspective, and the result was a fascinating mass of geometrical forms interacting with one another in lively fashion. Gentle colour and soft light characterize her work, which is often mysterious but never disturbing. From 1946 she has had many shows in New York, Paris and London, and is represented in many European and American public collections.

René de Solier. *Vieira da Silva*, Paris 1956.

Vienna Secession—*see* **Secession**

Vigeland, Gustav. Norwegian sculptor, b. 1869 in Mandal; d. 1943 in Oslo. Vigeland was the most celebrated and most controversial Norwegian sculptor of the first half of the twentieth century. In 1892, after training in Oslo and Copenhagen, he studied under Rodin and was influenced by him during the initial phase of his career. Eventually, after absorbing elements of the *Jugendstil*, he evolved an idealized, heroic and monumental style, producing symbolic works with erotic overtones based on the theme of man, woman and child.

Vigeland was the creator of the famous Frogner Park in Oslo. When he started work on this project in 1905 only a single fountain was planned, but subsequently Vigeland went on to sculpt a total of 150 different groups of figures arranged around a 17-metre-high monolith composed of innumerable intertwining bodies. This gigantic undertaking, which produced a whole park full of sculptures, became Vigeland's life's work.

Nathan C. Hale. *Embrace of Life: The Sculpture of Gustav Vigeland*, New York n.d.
Arne Breuna. *Guide to Gustav Vigeland's Sculpture Park in Oslo*, Oslo 1960.
R. T. Strang. *Gustav Vigeland*, Oslo 1965.

Villeglé, Jacques de la. French affichiste, b. 1926 in Quimper, Finistère. After studying architecture at the Paris Academy Villeglé began to collaborate with Raymond Hains in the early 1950s. Amongst other things they made a film, *Étude aux Allures*, and held an exhibition, *Affiches Lacérées* (Torn Posters) (Paris 1957). As an affichiste Villeglé seeks to create aesthetic effects by organizing the letters on his torn posters into rhythmical structures. In 1960 he became a founder member of the *Nouveaux Réalistes*. He is now living in Paris.

Villon, Jacques (Gaston Duchamp). French painter, b. 1875 in Damville; d. 1963 in Puteaux. Villon was the brother of Marcel Duchamp, Raymond Duchamp-Villon and Suzanne Duchamp. After studying law he settled in Paris in 1894, where he worked in Cormon's studio and earned his living as a draughtsman. During this period he contributed to the magazines *Le Chat noir, Gil Blas, L'Assiette au Beurre* and *Le Courrier français*. In 1904 he became a founder member of the Salon d'Automne, in which he regularly exhibited. In 1912 he helped to organize the *Section d'Or* exhibition, and in 1913 took part in the International Exhibition of Modern Art (the Armory Show) in New York, at which he sold nine pictures. Between 1921 and 1930 he produced thirty-four prints for *Architectures*. In 1937 he won an award for painting and graphic art at the International Exhibition of Art in Paris. In 1940–1 he was in Bernay with Mme André Mare. In 1944 he became friendly with Louis Carré and exhibited in his gallery. In 1949 he won the Grand Prix for graphic art in Lugano, and in 1950 took part in the Twenty-fifth Biennale in Venice, and won the Carnegie Prize in Pittsburgh. In 1954 he was made Commandeur de la Légion d'Honneur and Commandeur des Arts et Lettres. In 1956 he won the Grand Prix for painting at the Twenty-eighth Biennale in Venice and in 1958 the Grand Prix at the International Exhibition in Brussels. In 1961 he was made an honorary member of the American Academy of Arts and Letters and the National Institute of Arts and Letters in the United States.

During his early period, when he worked primarily as a draughtsman and etcher, Villon was influenced by Steinlen and Toulouse-Lautrec. In 1906 he became more interested in painting, and during the next five years took his lead from Degas and the Fauves. Then, in 1911, he embraced Analytical Cubism, which satisfied his need for order and discipline. Subsequently, he tried to develop a new style of painting based on mathematical proportions corresponding to the golden section. Later, between 1919 and 1929, he painted abstracts, in which he sought to represent the essence of objects by means of signs and not properties. During this period he restricted his palette to greys and browns. In 1930 he began to use colours from the prismatic sequence of tones. After this abstract phase Villon reverted, in 1933, to natural forms and pure colours. In c. 1950 he stopped painting landscapes and figure compositions, and evolved a new and carefully thought-out form of abstract painting, for which he used cool colours.

Jacques Lassaigne. *Jacques Villon*, Paris 1950.
William Liebermann. Catalogue, *Jacques Villon: His Graphic Art*, Museum of Modern Art, New York 1953.
François Stahly. *Jacques Villon: Son Oeuvre Gravé*, Zürich 1954.
Dora Vallier. *Jacques Villon: Oeuvres de 1897 à 1956*, Paris 1957.

Vingt, Les. In the 1880s a Belgian patron of the arts, Octave Maus, realized that there was no outlet for the new directions art was taking in Belgium, and after the work of some young artists had been officially rejected, he founded *Les Vingt* in 1883. The group of twenty painters and sculptors invited the best foreign artists to come to Brussels and exhibit with them. In this way the tremendous developments of art in Paris were brought to the notice of a much wider public. The organizers of the exhibitions showed great perspicacity in choosing often unknown artists who later vindicated their judgement—Rodin, Whistler, Monet, Renoir, Redon, Seurat, Toulouse-Lautrec, Signac, Cross, Gauguin, Cézanne, van Gogh were among the exhibitors between 1884 and 1892. *L'Art Moderne*, the magazine which was first published two years before the group's foundation and which became its mouthpiece, was adorned with articles by leading critics and writers, including Mirbeau, Huysmans and Fénéon; lectures on the annual exhibitions were delivered by Mallarmé, Verlaine and Catulle Mendès, among others.

The actual composition of the group varied. Some of the members who achieved widespread recognition were Ensor, Minne, Rops and van de Velde. The group was, sensibly, disbanded in 1893, before there could arise the danger of stagnation or decline.

Visser, Carel (Cornelis Nicolaas). Dutch sculptor and graphic artist, b. 1928 in Papendrecht. After studying at the Technical College in Delft (Department of Architecture) from 1948 to 1949 and at the Academy of Art in The Hague from 1949 to 1951 Visser visited London and Paris before settling in Amsterdam in 1952. His iron and steel constructions, which are built up from horizontal and vertical forms, are grounded in the principles of the *de Stijl* movement. He himself has acknowledged his debt to Brancusi and Giacometti. Visser is one of the most important of contemporary Dutch sculptors and has acquired an international reputation.

C. Blok. *Carel Visser*, Amsterdam 1968.

Vitullo, Sesostris. Argentinian sculptor, b. 1899 in Buenos Aires; d. 1953 in Paris. After studying in Buenos Aires he moved to Paris in 1925 and learned from the work of Rodin and Bourdelle. There he evoked his beloved country by creating images of Argentinian people and animals (gauchos, condors), and the sun and moon, subjects of so many legends. His sculptures, carved in wood or stone, have a harsh simplicity with their sharp planes and solid forms.

Viviani, Giuseppe. Italian painter, b. 1899 in Agnano. After an early phase in which he was influenced by Seurat and Morandi, Viviani turned to Surrealism. Using relatively undifferentiated colours Viviani paints large-format pictures, in which the nightmare *motifs* of the *Pittura Metafisica* are hinted at but never fully elaborated. A certain *naïveté* in Viviani's conception of reality and his rich poetic talent give his paintings and etchings an unreal, dreamlike quality. He has produced a significant body of graphic work and he won the prize for graphics at the Venice Biennale in 1950.

E. Carli. *Giuseppe Viviani*, Florence 1957.

Vivin, Louis. French painter, b. 1861 in Hadol, near Épinal; d. 1936 in Paris. Vivin, a postman by trade, started to paint at a very early age. He first showed his pictures at an exhibition for Post Office workers in Paris, when he was transferred there in 1889. After his retirement in 1922 he became a full-time painter and three years later was discovered by Wilhelm Uhde, who presented his works to the general public at the *Painters of the Sacred Heart* exhibition in 1928 together with those of Rousseau, Bombois, Bauchant and Séraphine. He was again associated with these artists at the *Maîtres populaires de la Réalité nouvelle* exhibition, which was staged in Paris and Zürich in 1937 and in New York in 1938. In the closing years of his life Vivin suffered from a partial paralysis and was unable to paint.

Vivin's primitive paintings were the most uninhibited and the gayest of these five amateur masters' work. He did not have the visionary power of a Rousseau or the inventiveness of a Bauchant. His quality was more personal. Vivin's small, silvery townscapes with their silky blue skies are poems dedicated to a much-loved environment: the streets and squares of Paris, the churches, the castles and the quays of the Seine, which he painted from postcards with loving care. With childlike persistence he set brick upon brick to create a sensitive linear composition which served as a background for his toy-like human beings, animals and vehicles. Vivin created a flat, transparent pictorial world, in which drama and tragedy had no part.

Catalogue, *Exposition des oeuvres de Louis Vivin*, Galerie Bing, Paris 1948.
W. Uhde. *Five Primitive Masters*, New York 1949.

Vlaminck, Maurice de. French painter, b. 1876 in Paris; d. 1958 in Rueil-la-Gadelière. Vlaminck said that what he had tried to express in paint would, in a social context, have entailed throwing a bomb. He derided Classical and Renaissance art, wished to burn the École des Beaux-Arts 'with my vermilions', and wanted to translate his feelings into paint without a thought of what had been painted before. Vlaminck's father was of Flemish stock, his mother a Lorrainer: they were both musicians. As a young man living in Chatou, Vlaminck was a racing cyclist (champion and professional). In these years he met Derain, who encouraged him to paint full-time: this he attempted, earning money by playing the violin in a theatre. Derain and he formed the *École de Chatou*. Even by 1900 his colour was violent and his brushwork turbulent: he was largely self-taught. Then in 1901 came the famous visit to Bernheim Jeune's van Gogh exhibition, where he declared that van Gogh meant more to him than his own father, and where he was introduced by Derain to Matisse. He exhibited perhaps as early as 1902. Then came the historic Salon d'Automne exhibition of 1905, when Vlaminck joined Derain, van Dongen, Manguin, Puy, Friesz, Marquet, Rouault and Matisse—the Fauves. Kandinsky invited him to exhibit at the second New Artists' Association exhibition at Munich and he was represented in Fry's second Post-Impressionist exhibition in London in 1912. Unlike Derain and Matisse, Vlaminck used colour straight from the tube in his Fauve years: it is more intense than Derain, the brush more fully loaded, the strokes less formally structural than Matisse; the spaces are emphatically evoked. After this initial period he became, like many, interested in Cézanne's art around 1906, and then in Cubism (he claims to have initiated Parisian interest in primitive art; this is disputed). In 1910 followed his first one-man show. His later work has pleased critics less. Bright colour is rejected in favour of sombre tones, the wide and deep perspectives are more traditional, the mood sombre. Motoring and racing cars rather than cycling became an interest. He left Paris, living first like van Gogh at Auvers, and then at Verneuil-sur-Avre. His works are mostly undated and their chronology, particularly from the Fauve years, still unsettled. He also wrote poetry, articles (he contributed to *Anarchie* c. 1900) and extended prose works (e.g. *D'un Lit à l'Autre*). He painted theatre scenery, made cartoons for tapestry and illustrated books.

K. G. Perls. *Vlaminck*, New York 1941.
J. Selz. *Vlaminck*, New York 1963.
Pierre Cabanne. *Vlaminck*, Paris 1966.

Volpi, Alfredo. Brazilian painter, b. 1896 in Lucca, Italy. Volpi was taken to Brazil as a child in arms in 1897. In 1939 he was deeply impressed by the exhibition of French painting *From Manet to the Present Day*. Encouraged by Lasar Segall he turned his attention to modern trends of painting and eventually produced pure abstract compositions. In 1953 he won the Grand Prix for Brazilian painting at the Bienal in São Paulo and in 1958 the Guggenheim Prize. He has executed wall paintings in São Paulo and Brasilia.

Volten, André (André Theo Aart). Dutch sculptor, b. 1925 in Andijk. After attending the School of Arts and Crafts in Amsterdam for one year in 1945 Volten spent four years abroad before settling in

Amsterdam in 1950, where he worked as a painter up to 1953 and, subsequently, as a sculptor. From 1954 to 1958 Volten was employed as a trainee by a shipbuilding firm. His sculptures are monumental, free-standing compositions constructed from perpendicular and horizontal elements. These works—most of which are in iron—are integrated into the architectural environment. They also reveal Volten's preoccupation with technology.

E. Hartsuyker. *André Volten*, Amsterdam 1966.

Volti (Volti Antoniucci). Italian-French sculptor, b. 1915 in Albano. He studied in Paris at the École des Beaux-Arts. From 1943, when he had to start work afresh because his previous output had been destroyed in the war, he made large sculptures of nudes as well as decorations for public buildings.

Vordemberge-Gildewart, Friedrich. German-Dutch painter, b. 1899 in Osnabrück; d. 1963 in Ulm. Vordemberge-Gildewart studied sculpture and architecture in Hanover from 1919 onwards and in 1924 founded the *Gruppe K*. He knew Schwitters, Arp, El Lissitzky and van Doesburg, he joined the *Sturm* and the *de Stijl* groups and the *Abstraction-Création* association. In 1937 he moved to Switzerland; in 1938 he settled in Holland, where he worked as painter, author and publisher and acquired Dutch citizenship. From 1954 onwards he taught 'Visuelle Gestaltung' (Visual Form) at the Hochschule für Gestaltung in Ulm.

Starting as a Suprematist Vordemberge-Gildewart moved towards the aesthetics of the *de Stijl* movement, after which he remained a Constructivist for the rest of his life. Of the *de Stijl* artists the one whose work is most closely related to his is van Doesburg. Vordemberge-Gildewart also published a large number of written works.

R. P. Lohse. *Vordemberge-Gildewart*, Ulm and Teufen (Switzerland) 1959.
Catalogue, *Vordemberge-Gildewart*, Ulm Museum, Ulm 1963.

Vorticism. Vorticism, an English *avant-garde* movement of short duration, arose from the impact of Futurist ideas on a group of disaffected English artists with fissive tendencies, which included one genius in Wyndham Lewis. In 1914 Marinetti on a visit to London had incited certain of these artists to publish a Futurist-inclined manifesto called *Vital English Art*, in the names of them all. This was repudiated by Lewis and some others who in June 1914 published a magazine called *Blast! A Review of the Great English Vortex*. A second issue appeared in July 1915.

In 1956 Wyndham Lewis claimed to be the only begetter of Vorticism. 'Vorticism, in fact, was what I, personally, did, and said, at a certain period.' His claims have been hotly disputed by William Roberts,

another Vorticist, in several private pamphlets. In Lewis's view, expressed forty years afterwards, the salient features of Vorticism were that 'it was dogmatically anti-real', and that it, or rather he himself, 'considered the world of machinery as real to us, or more so, as nature's forms'. Although much oversimplified by their context (the catalogue of the Wyndham Lewis retrospective exhibition, Tate Gallery 1956) and the artist's changed viewpoint, the words do echo those of the first *Blast*: 'This enormous, jangling, journalistic fairy desert of modern life serves him (the modern artist) as Nature did more technically primitive man.'

If Vorticism is in effect the work of Wyndham Lewis, these words accurately reflect the rather heartless cheerfulness and hard delineation of this self-styled 'fanatic for the externality of things'. But the preface to *Blast* was signed by ten other people. The only signatories whose reputations have survived were Henri Gaudier-Brzeska, William Roberts and Edward Wadsworth. Only one signatory, probably, understood the range of Lewis's views—the poet Ezra Pound. To most of them Vorticism was a protest movement against the extreme conservatism of British art. No movement can live on reaction alone and thus it was only Lewis's affirmative achievement that gave Vorticism the little enduring identity that it has. Although its visible traces are few, Vorticism actually anticipated Léger's ideas regarding urban and industrial landscape and drew attention in an original way to the blind unconscious forces in modern mechanistic life.

Dennis Farr. 'Wyndham Lewis and the Vorticists', *Burlington Magazine* XCVIII, London, August 1956.
Catalogue, *Wyndham Lewis and Vorticism*, Tate Gallery, London 1956.
William C. Lipke. 'The New Constructive Geometric Art in London 1910–15', *Art News Annual* XXXIV, 1969.

Voss, Jan. German painter, b. 1936 in Hamburg. After studying at the Munich Academy from 1955 to 1960 Voss settled in Paris, where he is still living today. In 1966–7 he was visiting lecturer at the College of Fine Arts in Hamburg.

Voss has evolved a lively Surrealist narrative style, which reveals the influence of the Comic Strip and Pop Art. Although basically similar to Bertholo, Voss has a more poetic and more complex fantasy. In his paintings countless tiny figures, objects or configurations are distributed evenly and without a true focal point on pale, pastel-coloured grounds which afford occasional perspective views of distant landscapes executed in the Surrealist mode.

B. Brock. 'Jan Voss', *Junge Künstler 1966/67*, Cologne 1967.

Vostell, Wolf. German painter and organizer of happenings, b. 1932 in Leverkusen. In 1956 Vostell began to produce torn posters. What interested him in this medium were the word fragments and over-printing created as a result of the tearing process. Later he overpainted and burnt these surfaces. He called his poster work *Décollage* and from 1962 on-wards he published a magazine under this name. In 1958 he began to produce *Décollage-Happenings*, the most celebrated of these being his *In Ulm, um Ulm und um Ulm herum* (*In Ulm, about Ulm and round about Ulm*) of 1964. Vostell's happenings frequently contain political allusions or references to actual situations and to this extent they differ from the happenings organized in America. Vostell is now living in Cologne.

J. Becker. *W. Vostell—Happenings: Fluxus, Pop Art, Nouveau Réalisme: Eine Dokumentation*, Hamburg 1965.

Voulkos, Peter. American sculptor, b. 1924 in Boze-man, Montana. His earliest major interest was in ceramics; in 1952 he received an MFA degree from the California College of Arts and Crafts in Oak-land, and rapidly gained an international reputation as an excellent ceramicist. He taught at several schools, including the Archie Bray Foundation, at Helena, Montana; the Otis Art Institute, in Los Angeles; and the University of California at Berkeley.

Voulkos's innovative approach enabled him to develop the clay medium in new directions that led to a renewal of clay sculpture. While in Los Angeles (1954–9), in response to the influence of Abstract Expressionist painting, he experimented freely with the form and surface of clay as expressive means in themselves and abandoned the concept of the pot as a vessel. During these years he created multipart forms, which he joined with epoxes, and began to use epoxy paints together with glazes. Around 1958 Voulkos made a definite shift, using boldly piled-up cylinders of clay as armatures for large-scale, massive ceramic sculptures (*Little Big Horn*, 1959, Oakland, Art Museum). With these sculptures, how-ever, Voulkos virtually exhausted the emotionally expressive possibilities of clay, and after moving to the San Francisco Bay area in 1959, he turned pri-marily to bronze. Together with other sculptors living in the vicinity, he built a foundry where he did his own casting. Working in a manner similar to his previous approach to clay, Voulkos cast separate slabs of bronze, bent or broke them up, and then welded or bolted them together in bold, rugged con-structions, sometimes contrasting geometric platform-like blocks with dynamic, Expressionistic forms (*Bad Day at Shattuck, II*, c. 1964, bronze and wood, Los Angeles, Coll. David Stuart Galleries). In the mid-1960s, however, Voulkos abandoned this style of juxtaposition and executed such harmonious, clear-cut, geometrical constructions as *Hiro* (1964–5, aluminium and bronze, Los Angeles, County Museum of Art), which is essentially a post and lintel

arrangement with spherical forms attached above and below the horizontal element.

Voulkos's importance in the development of American sculpture stems both from his own work, and from his influence on other West Coast sculptors. During his years in Los Angeles, he catalysed an important movement in clay and promoted trends towards unorthodox uses of materials and poly-chrome sculpture. John Mason (b. 1927) and Kenneth Price (b. 1935) worked in especially close association with him at this time. After moving to the Bay area, Voulkos, together with Harold Paris (b. 1925) and other sculptors, initiated extensive and experimental use of bronze on the West Coast.

'California Sculpture Today', *Artforum* II, No. 2, 1963.
Catalogue, *Peter Voulkos*, Los Angeles County Museum of Art, Los Angeles 1965.

Vuillard, Édouard. French painter, b. 1868 in Cuiseaux; d. 1940 in La Baule. His father died when he was young, forcing his mother to earn a liveli-hood. She worked in textile designing and manu-facturing, then at dressmaking. At school in Paris at the Lycée Condorcet, Vuillard, gifted academi-cally, met several people who proved important in his later life, i.e. Ker-Xavier Roussel (who encouraged him to take up art when he was about 19), Lugné-Poe and Maurice Denis. In 1886 he entered the École des Beaux-Arts, coming to know Ibels, Sérusier, Vallotton and Ranson through his boy-hood friends Roussel and Denis. Shortly after this he met Bonnard at the Académie Julian. His formative years were then spent in the *Nabis* circle and he was closely associated with the Natansons' *Revue Blanche*. He was also acquainted with H.-E. Cross and attended Mallarmé's 'Tuesdays'. He exhibited at the Salon from 1889, at the Barc de Boutteville Gallery from 1890. The dealer Bernheim Jeune gave him exhibi-tions from 1903. Later in life he exhibited little, having no one-man shows between 1912 and 1938. Much of his early work consisted of theatre scenery, decorative panels (in line with *Nabi* theories of the function of art) and engraving. His early work for the stage (Théâtre de l'Oeuvre) for Lugné-Poe is destroyed and undocumented. The 'interiors' for Dr. Vaquez (1896) are now in the Petit Palais: his decorations for the Comédie des Champs-Élysées (1913) are still *in situ*. He made important colour prints from c. 1896 to 1901 (Vollard published the series of colour lithographs *Paysages et Intérieurs* in 1899). From then on he made etchings and litho-graphs in black and white only. His works are mostly undated. Vuillard lived with his mother until her death in 1928. From 1900 he spent much time with the Hessels, a wealthy couple, who offered him the kind of environment he liked—quiet, cultivated gatherings in opulent, tasteful surroundings. His early work has affinities with Degas, Gauguin,

Japanese prints and with that of his friends Bonnard, Lautrec and Cross. Denis became critical of Vuillard's work in that he did not 'synthetize' and 'abstract' but observed and recorded. His paintings were closely related to his daily life (as were Bonnard's), giving rise to the description '*intimiste*'. He would stand aside from some social occasion to take a photograph: many of those appearing in his paintings are close friends (and his mother) recorded in these circumstances. In the 1890s his colour areas were flat, the picture area strongly patterned, the colour more adventurous than Bonnard's. By 1904–5 pattern, depth and quality of paint find a balance. Later in the 1930s perspective and paint became more conventional. His work differs from Bonnard's in its greater tonal contrast (as opposed to Bonnard's higher tonality and more saturated hues), his lesser attention to the female nude, the greater tenseness of his figures, the less complex spatial organization and the dominant note of middle-class drawing-room life. Vuillard wrote little on his art: his diaries are not to be published until 1990. There exists an important letter to Denis in 1897 where he stressed his desire to be personal and see the particular and not the general.

Claude Roger-Marx. *Vuillard*, London and New York 1946.
Andrew C. Ritchie. *Édouard Vuillard*, Museum of Modern Art, New York 1954.
J. Russell. *Vuillard*, London 1971.

Vujaklija, Lazar. Austrian-Yugoslav painter, graphic artist and tapestry designer, b. 1914 in Vienna. After training as a bookbinder Vujaklija studied painting under Petar Dobrović in Belgrade.

Vujaklija paints landscapes with figures, using dark colours and a linear structure. In these works, which are inspired by archaic folk traditions, he combines human figures with animals, plants and objects on a two-dimensional plane. Vujaklija is evolving an individual style.

O. Bihalji-Merin (intro.). Catalogue, *Vujaklija*, Belgrade 1960.

Vulliamy, Gérard. Swiss painter, b. 1909 in Paris. After training as a decorative painter Vulliamy attended various Parisian art schools, including the school run by André Lhôte. In 1932 he painted his first abstracts and joined the *Abstraction-Création* association. In 1935 he embarked on a brief Surrealist phase, painting fantastic apocalyptic pictures composed of vegetal forms, for which he used an Automatist technique. His *Trojan Horse* of 1936–7 is the best-known example of his Surrealist oeuvre. Shortly after completing this painting Vulliamy reverted to his abstract style, producing rhythmically organized compositions executed in diaphanous lyrical colours.

Catalogue, *Gérard Vulliamy*, Darmstadt 1962.

W

Wadsworth, Edward. British painter, b. 1889 in Yorkshire; d. 1949 in London. He studied engineering in Munich 1906–7, but at the same time he attended the Knirr Art School there, and in 1907 he gave up engineering and went to Bradford School of Art. There he won a scholarship to the Slade School, where he studied from 1908 to 1912. In 1912 he exhibited at the first Post-Impressionist exhibition and in 1913 he joined the Omega Workshop, but seceded with Wyndham Lewis to found the Rebel Art Centre. He published translations from Kandinsky in *Blast*, the Vorticist magazine, and in 1915 showed in the Vorticist exhibition. He was briefly associated with Lewis again in 1920 in Group X. During the war he served in the RNVR and from 1917 to 1918 worked on dazzle camouflage for ships. In the twenties the sea became increasingly important in his work and he moved away from Vorticism. For a period in the early thirties he turned to abstraction and was associated with Unit I and Circle; his interest in the sea remained dominant, however. Under the influence of Surrealism the marine still lifes which he had begun to paint about 1925 developed into the sort of paintings for which he is best known. In these, familiar seaside objects are given new meaning through oddities of scale and juxtaposition and by the dreamlike clarity of the light and handling. With the exception of a brief excursion into Pointillism around 1938–40 he continued to work in this manner for the rest of his life. In 1938 he carried out a large mural in the saloon of the liner *Queen Mary*.

O. R. Drey. *Edward Wadsworth*, London 1921.
T. W. Earp. 'Edward Wadsworth', *Apollo* IX, London, May 1929.
John Rothenstein. *Modern English Painters*, London and New York 1956.

Wagemaker, Jaap. Dutch painter, b. 1906 in Haarlem. After studying at the School of Arts and Crafts in Haarlem, Wagemaker taught himself to paint. He then worked alternately in France and Holland. In 1945 he finally settled in Amsterdam.

After painting landscapes and figurative compositions during his early period Wagemaker became interested in the evocative power of different materials in 1955 and is now one of the best-known Dutch artists working in the field of 'material pictures'. For these pictures he uses materials such as wood, slate, shells, iron shavings and sand in conjunction with thick, heavy paint. His palette consists primarily of earthy colours and his compositions, which have something of the quality of 'wall pictures', are reminiscent of works by Burri and Tàpies. In 1955 Wagemaker had his first one-man show in Amsterdam, which was followed by an exhibition in the Stedelijk Museum in 1957.

C. Doelman. *De informele kunst van Jaap Wagemaker*, Amsterdam 1963.

Walker, Dame Ethel. British painter, b. 1861 in Edinburgh; d. 1951 in London. She studied at several schools in London, including the Slade, to which she returned periodically until 1922. She also attended Walter Sickert's evening classes. Her first one-man show was at the Redfern Gallery, London, in 1927. She painted portraits, flowers and land- and seascapes. A memorial exhibition of her work, together with that of Gwen John and Frances Hodgkins, was held at the Tate Gallery in 1952.

Walker, Horatio. Canadian painter, b. 1858 in Listowel, Ontario; d. 1938. He studied in Toronto and New York, and spent some time in Europe, where he learned much from the Barbizon painters. His works depicted the daily life of the workers and the dignity of labour.

Walkowitz, Abraham. Russian-born American painter, b. 1880 in Tunen, Siberia; d. 1965 in Brooklyn, New York. He was taken to the United States during early childhood, and studied art first at the National Academy of Design in New York, and later at the Académie Julian in Paris. Walkowitz spent a number of years alternately travelling and studying between 1907 and 1914. The work done after his return to America in 1907 shows the influence of Henri Matisse, the Fauves and Vassily Kandinsky. Through contacts with Alfred Stieglitz's 291 Gallery in New York and its artists—John Marin, Marsden Hartley, Max Weber and Arthur Dove—he developed his own semi-abstract style. In an expressive personal manner, Walkowitz portrayed the industrial and urban phenomena that had been Robert Delaunay's inspiration in Paris (*New York*, 1917, New York, Whitney Museum). He first showed at Stieglitz's gallery between 1912 and 1917, and was included in the famous Forum Exhibition at the Anderson Gallery in New York, America's answer to the plight of native modernism in the 1913 Armory Show. Walkowitz, like Kandinsky and the Fauves, was especially interested in children's drawings, whose qualities of freshness and freedom were captured in his own watercolours. He did many sketches of figurative subjects (*Bathers*, 1910, New York, Coll. Mr. and Mrs. Lawrence B. Karter), as well as scenes of New York's buildings tangled in webs of abstract lines. During the 1920s he dropped from public attention but continued to work on figurative abstractions (*Dance Rhythms*, 1920, New York, Zabriskie Gallery) in which bodies in motion

are indicated by broken swirls and rhythmic brush-strokes.

Abraham Walkowitz. *One Hundred Drawings, From the Objective to Abstract*, New York 1925; *A Demonstration of Objective, Abstract, and Nonobjective Art*, Girard (Kans.) 1945.

Wallis, Alfred. British painter, b. 1855 in Devonport; d. 1942 near St. Ives. Discovered living in St. Ives in 1928, Wallis became the most influential British primitive through his effect on the St. Ives painters. His paintings are mainly of ships, coasts and harbours, not drawn from life, but re-enacted from a store of remembered or imagined experience of an almost atavistic kind. 'It is what I have seen Before', he wrote to H. S. Ede. Wallis usually worked on pieces of cardboard, frequently cut in irregular shapes, composing within the shape with an intuitive precision emulated by the sophisticated St. Ives painters. He is represented in the Tate Gallery.

Warhol, Andy (Andrew). American painter, graphic artist and film-maker, b. 1930 in Philadelphia, Pennsylvania. He attended the Carnegie Institute of Technology in Pittsburgh, Pa., and went to New York in the early 1950s where he worked as an advertising illustrator, winning the 1957 Art Director's Club Medal. His early works included stencilled pictures of row on row of dollar bills and Campbell's soup cans (*Dollar Bills*, 1962, acrylic on canvas, New York, Coll. Mr. and Mrs. Robert C. Scull). Like other Pop artists, he chose familiar images such as Jacqueline Kennedy, Elizabeth Taylor and Marilyn Monroe, as depicted in dehumanized newspaper photographs (*Gold Marilyn Monroe*, oil, acrylic and silkscreen enamel on canvas, 1962, New York, Museum of Modern Art). From newspapers too came his works depicting violent death—electric chairs, automobile accidents (*Saturday Disaster*, silkscreen enamel on canvas, 1964, Waltham, Mass., Coll. Brandeis University). By the mid-1960s he was producing his works of art like a manufacturer—clipping pictures from mass-media publications, ordering silkscreens and then producing any number of the work, with slight variations. These works were done in his studio, called the Factory, and reflect the artist's thoughts on art and society: 'The reason I'm painting this way is because I want to be a machine. Whatever I do, and do machine-like, is because it is what I want to do. I think it would be terrific if everybody was alike.' His 'sculptures' too are often produced in quantity and by means of manufacturing methods (*Brillo*, silkscreen enamel on wooden box, 1964, New York, Leo Castelli Gallery). Although he called himself a retired artist in 1965, stating that he planned to devote most of his time to film-making, in 1966 he created *Clouds (Silver Pillows)* (polyester and plastic, New York, Leo Castelli Gallery), inflated pillows which formed part of the staging for Merce Cunningham's ballet *Rainforest*. In 1964 he won the Independent Film Award of *Film Culture* magazine for his five films *Eat, Kiss, Haircut, Sleep* and *Empire*. The latter two films, six and eight hours long respectively, which portray little or no movement, reflect the artist's statement, 'I like boring things.' His 1966 *The Chelsea Girls* with Nico, Mario Montez and Ingrid Superstar is a seven-hour film which is run on a divided screen, thereby lasting only three and a half hours. It was the first 'underground' film shown in commercial theatres and was viewed at the 1967 Cannes Film Festival. Among his other films are: *I, A Man; My Hustler; More Milk, Yvette; Flesh; Lonesome Cowboy* and *Trash*. Warhol was also the manager and mind behind the rock music group The Velvet Underground and the Electric Circus discothèque. In June 1968 he was shot and severely wounded by one of his superstars, Valerie Solanas. In the spring of 1971 he had an exhibition at the Tate Gallery, London.

Alan Solomon. Catalogue, *Andy Warhol*, Institute of Contemporary Art, Boston 1966.
Andy Warhol, Stephen Shore, Paul Morrissey, Undine and Nico. *Andy Warhol's Index (Book)*, New York 1967.
Andy Warhol, Moderna Museet, Stockholm, February–March 1968.
Andy Warhol and Gerard Malanga. *Intrasit—the Andy Warhol–Gerard Malanga Issue*, Eugene (Oregon) 1968.

Washington Color Painters. The artists comprising the Washington Color Painters were first identified as a group in the single exhibition of that title organized by the Washington, D.C., Gallery of Modern Art in 1965, which included the work of Morris Louis, Kenneth Noland, Gene Davis, Thomas Downing, Howard Mehring and Paul Reed. Within the group, however, there is considerable variety of style and intent. Basically, the artists have only such broad similarities as their residence in Washington, where most of them met at the Washington Workshop, and their focus on the qualities of colour, especially through the medium of acrylic paints (thin, water-soluble paints that can be stained directly into an unsized, unprimed canvas). Louis and Noland were the first of the group to experiment with acrylics, after seeing Helen Frankenthaler's canvases with poured acrylic paint in New York in 1952. The lucidity and translucency inherent in the acrylics were valuable in helping the Washington artists to achieve expressive colour painting, although they explored different qualities of the medium.

Morris Louis was most interested in the effects of pouring the thin paint on to the canvas and forming colour images by tilting the canvas and letting the paint flow in certain directions. The resulting overlapping layers of different colours revealed their translucency, and the large areas of canvas left bare in juxtaposition with the painted areas, which bleed

at their edges, emphasize the fact of the stained, rather than the painted, canvas. The work of the other Washington Color Painters, when taken as a whole, emphasizes more the optical effects of colour through geometrical, essentially hard-edged, and repetitive patterns. Each artist used different forms (e.g. Noland is noted for target patterns, chevrons and horizontal stripes; Davis for thin vertical stripes, unvaried in width, which cover the entire canvas; and Downing for small circles in a colour field), but their approach was similar in that they usually repeated the forms within each canvas and, moreover, worked in a series, so that the constancy of a particular form serves to emphasize the variability and quality of the colour. This kind of colour painting readily led to predominantly optical effects, and several of the Washington artists (Davis, Noland, Downing and Louis) were occasionally represented by certain works in broader group exhibitions devoted to optical art, although the painting and approach of the Washington group seems generally more Romantic and intuitive than in most of the contemporary optical and hard-edged painting.

Elisabeth Stevens. 'The Washington Color Painters', *Arts* XL, November 1965.
Gerald Nordland (intro.). Catalogue, Washington Gallery of Modern Art, *The Washington Color Painters*, Washington, D.C., 1965.

Watkins, Franklin C. American painter, b. 1894 in New York City. After attending both the universities of Virginia and Pennsylvania, Watkins enrolled in the Pennsylvania Academy in Philadelphia, in 1913, where he began his formal training in art. In 1923, he went to Europe, where he studied Spanish and Italian Renaissance paintings. In 1931, while still in Europe, he submitted the painting *Suicide in Costume* (Philadelphia, Museum of Art) to the Carnegie International, winning first prize. The next year, he had his first one-man show in New York City. Examples of his work during this period include the expressive *Negro Spiritual* (c. 1932, Lynchburg, Virginia, Randolph-Macon Women's College) and the dramatic, narrative *The Fire Eater* (1934, Philadelphia, Museum of Art).

In 1936, Watkins visited Moscow, where he made a study of the paintings by Matisse then preserved in the former Shchukin mansion. Matisse's influence on Watkins can readily be seen in such later works as *Roman Garden* (1954, Philadelphia, Coll. Magill) and *Diana* (1957, Detroit, Coll. Fleischmann).

Weber, Max. Russian-American painter, b. 1881 in Bialystok, Russia; d. 1961 in Great Neck, New York. He went to New York at the age of ten. He obtained his artistic training at Pratt Institute (1898–1900) and for the next five years taught art in Virginia and Minnesota. In 1905 he went to Paris, studying at the Académie Julian and Académie Colarossi. During his four-year stay in Europe he made trips to Spain, Italy and the Lowlands. It was during this period that he met Matisse, Cézanne, Picasso, Flandrin, and became especially friendly with Henri Rousseau. He returned to New York in 1909 and in that year had his first one-man show. He exhibited regularly after this time, especially with the 291 Group, and organized the first show of works by his Parisian friend Rousseau in 1910. For many years Weber supported himself by teaching, first at the White School of Photography and later at the Art Students' League. The principal influences of the second decade were European—Fauvism, Cubism and Futurism. His 1911 *Figure Study* (Buffalo, N.Y., Albright-Knox Art Gallery) owes to Picasso and Cézanne in its Cubist composition and form, which distorts reality in favour of formal cohesiveness. More typical of his personal Cubism is *Chinese Restaurant* (1915, New York, Whitney Museum of American Art) which opposes the Cubists' monochromatics. The insistence of bright, glaring colour is derived rather from the Fauves, and specifically from Matisse, with whom he had briefly studied. Weber's sculptures were among the first Cubist pieces executed anywhere, such as his 1915 *Spiral Rhythm* (New York, Coll. Joseph H. Hirshhorn). His later style of the 1930s and 1940s shows greater variety of subject, particularly social themes and Jewish life, combined with an increasing sense of fantasy and wit. His colour becomes more intense in spots and the formal elements tend towards a spirited linearity (*Adoration of the Moon*, 1944, Whitney Museum of American Art). In addition to his paintings and sculptures, Weber was a prolific writer. *Primitives* (1926), *Essays on Art* (1916) and *Cubists' Poems* (1914) are among his principal works.

L. Goodrich and R. Irvine. *Max Weber Retrospective Exhibition*, Whitney Museum of American Art, New York 1944.

Weidemann, Jacob. Norwegian painter, b. 1923. Weidemann attended the School of Arts and Crafts in Oslo from 1938 to 1940 and studied at the Academy of Art in Stockholm from 1944 to 1945. In 1954 he visited Paris and Italy. In his early works, in which imagination took precedence over the need for objective reproduction, Weidemann used elements drawn from a wide variety of styles. But after an exhibition in Oslo in 1957, at which he had shown geometrical abstracts executed after the manner of the Swedish concrete artists, Weidemann withdrew from society for a while to make an intensive study of the forests of northern Norway, whose stones and mosses, branches and foliage provided the *motifs* for the works of his next period. These pictures were executed in heavy impasted colours, which gives them a special and extremely physical quality that is immensely powerful. Later Weidemann introduced a lyrical note into his landscapes, and his most recent works depict the creative wonder of spring. In 1960–1 Weidemann produced decorative works for the Norsk Hydro in Oslo, in 1965 he created stained-glass windows and a decorative mural for the church in Steinkjer, and in 1967 he decorated Sandvigske Samlinger's festival hall in Lillehammar. In 1966 Weidemann represented Norway at the Venice Biennale.

Weie, Edvard. Danish painter, b. 1879 in Copenhagen; d. 1943 in Copenhagen. Weie, who studied under Zahrtmann, was one of the most important Danish colourists of modern times. He was largely responsible for propagating the new pictorial ideas evolved by Cézanne, the Fauves and the Cubists in Denmark. In c. 1910, under the influence of Delacroix and Karl Isakson, Weie abandoned his early Realism in favour of a highly simplified pictorial style. Using pure luminous colours he produced paintings in which he sought to create the kind of lyrical and dramatic expression achieved by musicians. From the 1920s onwards Weie's figure compositions, still lifes and landscapes grew progressively more abstract.

L. Swane. *Edvard Weie*, 1932.

Weir, J. Alden. American painter, b. 1852 in West Point, New York; d. 1919 in New York. He studied in Paris from 1873, and on a trip to Spain was impressed by Velasquez's paintings. Although he saw the work of the Impressionists in Paris he was not at all taken with it and it had no effect on his own style, which was solidly conservative and which gained him election to the American National Academy in 1886.

He returned to Europe in 1883, and this time the Impressionists' achievement made an impact on him. His previous rather rigid taste opened up, and by about 1891 his work was reflecting a distinct Impressionism. Because of his status as an Academy member, his championship of the new movement carried a great deal of weight, and it was accepted by the public without demur. With John Twachtman, Childe Hassam and other artists Weir formed The Ten, a group dedicated to the promotion of Impressionism in America.

Dorothy W. Young. *The Life and Letters of J. Alden Weir*, New Haven (Conn.) 1960.

Weisgerber, Albert. German painter, b. 1878 in St. Ingbert, Palatinate; d. 1915 at Ypres. Whilst serving an apprenticeship as a paint-hand in Kaiserslautern and Munich Weisgerber attended art classes in his free time and from 1898 to 1900 was a pupil of Stuck. From 1904 onwards he designed posters for the magazine *Jugend*. In 1906–7 he visited Paris, where he made contact with the *Café du Dôme* group and was deeply impressed by Cézanne. In 1907 he settled in Munich and in 1909 joined the New Artists' Association. In 1913 he became a founder member and was later president of the New Secession in Munich.

The decorative, ecstatic compositions of Weisgerber's youthful period brought him early recognition. In most of these works, which bear the stamp of the *Jugendstil* movement and of German 'nature lyricism', he dealt with mythical or religious themes. But his major paintings were not produced until after 1912. They are figurative compositions with idealistic and Expressionistic overtones. Cézanne's influence is clearly discernible in the structure of these late works.

W. Hausenstein. *Albert Weisgerber*, Munich 1918.
Catalogue, *Albert Weisgerber*, Kurpfälzisches Museum, Heidelberg 1962.

Wells, John Clayworth Spencer. British painter, b. 1907 in London. Wells practised medicine in the Scilly Isles. His freely geometricizing abstractions with sensitive qualities of texture and restrained colour are closely akin to those of his friend Ben Nicholson (they met in 1928). Wells also has close ties with Barbara Hepworth and Naum Gabo. From 1945 he painted in Newlyn, Cornwall. He has had exhibitions at the Lefevre Gallery, London (1946); the Durlacher Gallery, New York (1952 and 1958); the Waddington Gallery, London (1960 and 1964). He has works in the collection of the British Council and various public collections in America and Sweden.

Wercollier, Lucien. Luxembourg sculptor, b. 1908 in Luxembourg. He studied in Brussels and Paris, and was at first influenced by Maillol and Laurens in his figure sculptures. In 1952, however, he turned to abstract work, and here he is more reminiscent of Arp and Brancusi with his smooth polished surfaces and sensuous curves.

Werefkin, Marianne von. Russian painter, b. 1860 in Tula, Russia; d. 1938 in Ascona, Switzerland. Werefkin studied under Ilya Repin in St. Petersburg from 1881 onwards. In 1891 she became friendly with Jawlensky and in 1896 they both settled in Munich. Werefkin also came into close contact with Kubin and exhibited with the *Blauer Reiter* group. In 1914 she left Germany for Switzerland, settling in Ascona in 1917, where she spent the rest of her life.

In her early period Werefkin produced Symbolistic pictures in the *Nabis* tradition. Later, as a result of her contact with German Expressionism and the Fauvism of Kandinsky and Jawlensky, she developed a flat-pattern, decorative and somewhat mystical style of painting based on powerful colours.

J. Hahl-Koch. *Marianne von Werefkin und der russische Symbolismus*, Munich 1967.
C. Weiler. Catalogue, *Marianne Werefkin*, Museo Marianne Werefkin, Ascona 1967.

Werenskiold, Erik. Norwegian painter, b. 1855; d. 1938. He painted landscapes in a straightforward, Realistic manner, and produced portraits and book illustrations.

Werkman, Hendrik Nicolaas. Dutch printer and painter, b. 1882 in Leens; d. 1945 in Groningen. After pursuing a variety of professions Werkman eventually opened a printing shop and in 1917, when he was thirty-five, he began to paint. But it was not until 1923, when an economic crisis brought his printing shop to a standstill, that he was really able to concentrate on his *Print Pictures*, for which he developed a highly individual technique. With the letters, figures and signs from his type case he created flat coloured forms, which he built up in layers by multiple—sometimes as much as fiftyfold—overprinting to produce both abstract and figurative compositions. By masking the letters with paper, by using a handstamp, by applying broad bands of colour with a roller and, above all, by his use of screens (from 1935 onwards) Werkman evolved a rich and varied printing style which reflected contemporary developments in the sphere of painting. His first pamphlet *The Next Call* brought him into contact with Michel Seuphor and the *Cercle et Carré* association, with which he exhibited in 1930. From 1940 onwards he created his celebrated series *De Blauwe Schnit*, in which he called for resistance to the German occupation. In 1945 Werkman was arrested by the Gestapo and shot as a hostage.

Catalogue, *Hendrik Nicolaas Werkman*, Städtische Kunstgalerie, Bochum 1961.

Werner, Theodor. German painter, b. 1886 in Jettenburg, Württemberg; d. 1969 in Munich. Werner studied at the Stuttgart Academy in 1908–9 and in Paris from 1909 to 1914. From 1919 to 1929 he lived near Stuttgart. During this period he made frequent trips to Paris and in 1920 went to live there, remaining for five years. In the early 1930s he made contact with the *Abstraction-Création* association and became friendly with Braque and Miró. From 1939 to 1945 he was in Potsdam, after which he lived in Berlin until 1960, when he moved to Munich. Werner was forbidden to exhibit in the Third Reich, but an exhibition in the Galerie Rosen in Berlin in 1947 made his reputation in Germany; it had long been established abroad.

After an early period, in which he painted landscapes and still lifes that reveal the influence of Post-Impressionism and, more particularly, of Cézanne, Werner passed through brief Cubist and near-abstract phases before evolving an individual style based on flat patterns and linear elements. It was not until 1944 that Werner abandoned objective forms. When he did so, he began to stress the 'developmental' aspect of his work by using open, i.e. incomplete, forms. By placing jagged, fragmented structural elements against flowing and painterly coloured grounds he sought to represent movement, vibration and tension. Werner himself often explained and justified his highly personal Informal style in metaphysical terms. Like Willi Baumeister, Fritz Winter and Julius Bissier, he belonged to the small group of twentieth-century German artists who have investigated calligraphic forms as a new pictorial category.

C. Zervos. 'Theodor Werner', *Cahiers d'Art*, 1956.
Catalogue, *Theodor Werner*, Marlborough Gallery, London 1959.
Catalogue, *Theodor Werner*, Galerien Franke und Möller, Cologne and Munich 1951–2.

Werthmann, Friedrich. German sculptor, b. 1927 in Barmen. Werthmann creates Informal sculptures by heating and welding together pieces of metal, usually steel. By changing the temper of the material he seeks to produce a lighter and more dynamic effect.

Catalogue, *Werthmann Sculptures*, Karl-Ernst-Orthaus-Museum, Hagen 1969.

Wessel, William. German painter, b. 1904 in Iserlohn. Between 1927 and 1931 Wessel studied at Berlin University (archaeology) and at the Berlin College of Fine Arts (under Hofer).

In his early period Wessel painted figurative works, but in 1953–4 he began to produce Informal compositions, using a collage technique and incorporating a wide variety of different materials. He is now living in Iserlohn.

Wesselmann, Tom. American painter, b. 1931 in Cincinnati, Ohio. While attending Hiram College, Ohio, and the University of Cincinnati he was not at all interested in art, but turned to drawing cartoons while in the army. He received his first art training at the Cincinnati Art Academy and then studied under Nicholas Marsicano at Cooper Union. Cartooning was eventually replaced by a desire to paint. He soon gave up his first attempts in the Abstract Expressionist idiom and turned to collage: 'It seemed completely hopeless because de Kooning had already painted all my paintings.' In his collages, paintings and assemblages illusion and reality come together, setting up a reverberation between the real world and the world of art often by combining a flatly painted nude and store-bought items. These same nudes, handled in clear colours with no modelling and an emphasis on broadly conceived areas, are also translated by Wesselmann into painted Plexiglass 'sculptures' (*Great American Nude*, London,

Coll. Allen Jones) and reduced to simplified anatomical fragments placed against a landscape as in the *Colour Study for Sea Scape* (1966, acrylic on corrugated paper, New York, Sidney Janis Gallery)—a leg set against a schematized sky. Though the artist has said that he has no interest in social comment, satire or humour, his art is inseparable from its subject and therefore difficult to view outside this context. Wesselmann received his first one-man show at the Tanager Gallery, New York, in 1961 and has been included in such important exhibitions as *The New Realists* (1962, Sidney Janis Gallery, New York) and *Mixed Media and Pop Art* (1963, Albright-Knox Art Gallery, Buffalo, New York).

G. R. Swenson. 'Wesselmann—The Honest Nude', *Art and Artists* I, May 1966.

Westerik, Co (Jacobus). Dutch painter, b. 1924 in The Hague. Westerik studied at The Hague Academy from 1942 to 1947. He was a lecturer at the Free Academy in The Hague from 1955 to 1958, when he transferred to the Royal Academy in The Hague. He has made numerous visits to the United States, France, England and Italy.

Westerik paints in an extremely detailed Realistic style which he evolved from the *Neue Sachlichkeit* of Grosz and Dix. His subjects are scenes and events from everyday life, which he portrays with such intensity that his work acquires a strange and magical aura. Humour, gravity, poetic and dream-like qualities are all combined in Westerik's pictures, which in many ways anticipated English Pop Art.

Catalogue, *Co Westerik*, The Hague Museum, 1964.

Westermann, Horace Clifford. American sculptor, b. 1922 in Los Angeles. Westermann studied at the Chicago Art Institute School from 1947 to 1954. After 1957 he exhibited frequently in the United States, especially in Chicago, New York and on the West Coast. He began to work in sculpture around 1953, and during the 1950s and the 1960s developed a highly individualistic style that is based on irony and paradox through unexpected uses of materials and the resulting ambiguous—or startlingly precise—meanings. Thus *A Rope Tree* (1964, wood, Milwaukee, Coll. Dr. and Mrs. A. Melamed) is a piece of wood carved into a twisted shape that simultaneously resembles a rope and a tree, while *Walnut Box* (1964, mixed media, Chicago, Coll. Mr. and Mrs. E. A. Bergman) is precisely what it is labelled—a walnut wood box filled with walnuts. Westermann's early work reflects a number of more humanistic, sometimes sinister or erotic, themes. In the early 1950s he dealt with the imagery of war and death; around 1956 he began a series of eccentric and ambiguous 'houses' and 'towers' with such titles as *Madhouse*, *Mysteriously Abandoned New House* and *Suicide Tower*; and in the late 1950s he produced a number of figurative architectural personages (*Angry Young Machine*, mixed media). In the early 1960s he became more interested in the paradoxical possibilities of materials themselves and in more abstract concepts. Although in some respects Westermann's work is related to Dadaism and Surrealism, it is not easily classifiable with any specific earlier movements; this is especially true of his work of the 1960s, in which the emphasis on the unusual use of materials, on craftsmanship and on the treatment of sculpture as an autonomous object (rather than representation) is original and contemporary.

Martin Friedman. Catalogue, 'H. C. Westermann', in *Eight Sculptors: The Ambiguous Image*, Walker Art Center, Minneapolis 1966.
Dennis Adrian. 'The Art of H. C. Westermann', *Artforum* VI, No. 1, 1967.

Whiteley, Brett. Australian painter, b. 1939 in Sydney. From 1957 to 1959 he was at the Julian Ashton Art School, Sydney. In 1960 he came to Europe on an Italian government scholarship. In 1961 he won the international prize at the Paris Biennale. He exhibited in London in 1962 and was represented in the *British Painting in the Sixties* show in 1963 and in the *New Generation* show in 1964. His work is semi-abstract, semi-figurative. Like Bacon he uses the devices of abstract painting to do violence to the figures that he draws, distorting and deforming. Violence is the recurrent theme of his painting: the series based on the murderer Christie for example; and recently the figures in his pictures have as it were burst out of the picture plane to spill their entrails at the spectator's feet.

Catalogues, Marlborough Galleries, London 1964, 1965, 1967.

Wiecek, Magdalena. Polish sculptress, b. 1924 in Katowice. Wiecek studied at the College of Fine Arts in Sopot and the Academy of Art in Warsaw. Later she became a lecturer at the College of Fine Arts in Poznan.

After an early Realist phase Wiecek turned to abstract art, producing constructions in space which are built up from amorphous and strangely dynamic components.

Wiegers, Jan. Dutch painter and graphic artist, b. 1893 in Kommerzijl; d. 1959 in Amsterdam. After completing his studies at the academies in Groningen, The Hague and Amsterdam, Wiegers became a founder member of *De Ploeg* (The Plough), an artists' association in Groningen, in 1918. In 1920–1 he was in Davos, where he met E. L. Kirchner and was greatly influenced by him. From 1934 onwards he lived in Amsterdam and in 1953 became a professor at the Amsterdam Academy.

Wiegers painted portraits, landscapes and figurative compositions. His style and colouring were closely allied to German Expressionism.

Catalogue, *Jan Wiegers*, Stedelijk Museum, Amsterdam 1960–1.

Wiemken, Walter. Swiss painter, b. 1907 in Basle; d. 1940 near Castel San Pietro. He studied in Munich and Paris, where his art developed considerably. He travelled a great deal throughout Europe—to Spain and the Balearics, Brittany, Belgium and France. His manner was at first somewhat naïve, but progressed through the influence of Picasso to a style containing elements of Surrealism, Constructivism and later Expressionism.

Wijckaert, Maurice. Belgian painter, b. 1923 in Brussels. Wijckaert studied at the Académie des Beaux-Arts in Brussels between 1940 and 1948. In the 1950s he was in close contact with the *Cobra* group and the Situationists. His paintings, which are executed in strong, rich colours, are Informal works derived from landscapes. Wijckaert is now living in Brussels.

Wilfred, Thomas. American kinetic artist, b. 1889 in Copenhagen. Wilfred studied art and music in Copenhagen, Paris and London between 1905 and 1911. In 1916 he settled in the United States, where he is still living today.

Wilfred began to conduct light experiments using simple apparatuses, as early as 1905. When he went to America he built his *Clavilux*, which he demonstrated for the first time in the Neighborhood Playhouse in New York in 1922. In this apparatus the light passed through an assembly of coloured glass slides and adjustable mirrors—which were controlled by various keyboards—before being projected on to a screen, where it produced subtle gradations of colour. Wilfred called these light projections *lumina* and he went on numerous tours with them in the United States, in Canada and—from 1925 onwards—in Europe. Then, in 1930, he founded the Art Institute of Light, which had laboratories and an auditorium for Clavilux projections, in the Grand Central Palace in New York. This institute existed up to 1943. In 1945 Wilfred made a new apparatus, which produced light compositions automatically. He has also made a number of light machines for use in the theatre. It is only of recent years that he has been recognized as one of the pioneers of kinetic art.

T. Wilfred. 'Light and the Artist', *Journal of Aesthetics and Art Criticism* 5, No. 4, June 1947; 7, No. 2, December 1948.
J. Claus. *Kunst heute*, Reinbek 1965.

Willink, Albert Carel. Dutch painter, b. 1900 in Amsterdam. After studying architecture in Delft from 1918 to 1920 Willink became a student of painting. He then attended the Amsterdam Academy before moving to Berlin, where he worked under H. Baluschek from 1920 to 1923. In 1926 he worked in Le Fauconnier's *atelier* in Paris. He is now living in Amsterdam.

Initially Willink painted abstract pictures and exhibited with the *Novembergruppe* in Berlin. The works of this period reveal the influence of Léger. But in 1926 Willink moved towards the *Neue Sachlichkeit* and, from then onwards, produced figurative compositions and landscapes with Classical sculptures or with animals and figures in architectural settings. The dominant feature of these works is their hard, unreal light. In his late period Willink has combined reality and fantasy, creating a style that is a variant of Magic Realism.

P. H. Dubois. *A. C. Willink*, Amsterdam 1950.
J. H. M. van der Marck. *Neo-realisme in de Schilderkunst*, Amsterdam 1960.
Catalogue, *A. C. Willink*, Arnheim Museum, Arnheim 1968.

Willumsen, Jens Ferdinand. Danish painter, sculptor, architect, graphic artist and potter, b. 1863 in Copenhagen; d. 1958 in France. Although he engaged in a wide range of artistic activities and was invariably in the forefront of affairs, Willumsen was very much the odd man out in the Danish art world. With revolutionary fervour he progressed from Naturalism via Symbolism to Expressionism. During two visits to Paris in the period 1888–94 Willumsen was in close contact with the Symbolists and the painters of Pont-Aven. Under the influence of Gauguin he produced pictures and polychrome wooden reliefs in a flat, highly simplified style. Then from 1890 onwards, as a result of his friendship with Odilon Redon, he began to incorporate fantastic elements into his work. Between 1897 and 1900, when he was artistic director at the Bing and Grøndahl Porcelain Factory in Copenhagen, he concentrated primarily on pottery and sculpture. His so-called *Great Relief*, which was conceived as a pottery design in 1893 and later executed as a sculpture in different kinds of marble and gilded bronze, perfectly illustrates his dualistic outlook. On journeys to Spain and Algeria undertaken between 1910 and 1915 he was deeply impressed by El Greco's Mannerism and began to paint highly expressive figures in a harsh flat light. Willumsen also created lithographs, etchings and woodcuts. His private collection of his own works is now housed in the Willumsen Museum in Fredriksund.

S. Schultz. *Jens Ferdinand Willumsen*, Copenhagen 1948.

Wilson, Scottie. British painter, b. 1889 in Glasgow; d. 1972. He did not begin painting until he was 45 years old, when he was employed as a commercial traveller. His work is the purest primitive art: it is concerned with the expression of the two forces of good and evil, the one conveyed by images of nature —animals, birds and plants—and the other by the curious carved faces of Indian art which he saw while working in Canada. He has also produced designs for ceramics and tapestry. His work can be seen in the Tate Gallery, London, as well as in the Museums of Modern Art in New York and Paris, and various other galleries throughout the world.

Wines, James. American sculptor, b. 1932 in Oak Park, Illinois. He worked under Ivan Mestrovic as a scholarship student at Syracuse University (1950–5) and had his first one-man show at the University's Museum of Art in 1954. He then moved to Rome where he worked from 1956 to 1963 after winning the Prix de Rome for sculpture in 1956. His bronzes of 1959–60 show the influences of Minguzzi and Giacometti, with their attenuated forms, variegated surfaces and sense of loneliness and melancholy (*Ritual Tower* and *Procession*, New York, Marlborough-Gerson Gallery). His style developed towards a greater solidity, employing large block-like forms and dense spheres in which iron or bronze were combined with cement (*Frontier Wall*, 1961, bronze and cement, New York, Marlborough-Gerson Gallery). In 1962 he won a Guggenheim Award and two years later received a Ford Foundation Grant. His later style concentrates on circular forms with a greater openness, coupled with the use of heavy metal elements creating a duality of lightness and weight, as in *Nautilus II* (1964, iron and cement, New York, Marlborough-Gerson Gallery) which employs the heavy chains and hooks of an ocean liner contained within the sweeping lightness and openness of a cement arc. In addition to many one-man shows he has participated in the Whitney Annuals of 1958, 1960, 1962 and 1963, the Museum of Modern Art's *Recent Sculpture* of 1959 and the 1963 São Paulo Bienal. Wines teaches at the School of Visual Arts, New York City.

David Sellin. Catalogue, *James Wines. Recent Sculpture, 1963–66*, Charles A. Dana Creative Arts Center, Colgate University, Utica (New York) 1966.

Winiarski, Ryszard. Polish painter, b. 1936 in Lwow. After studying at the Polytechnic in Warsaw and working as an engineer for two years Winiarski attended the Warsaw Academy of Art. He is now living in Warsaw. Winiarski's Neo-Constructivist pictures are composed of standardized components, which he fits together according partly to a preconceived design and partly to statistical chance (for example, by a throw of the dice).

Catalogue, *Konstruktive Kunst: Elemente und Prinzipien*, Biennale, Nuremberg 1969.

Winter, Fritz. German painter, b. 1905 in Altenbögge, Westphalia. Winter began to draw and paint in 1924, and made a study of the works of Paula Modersohn-Becker. In 1926–7 he worked as a miner, then made a tour of Holland, where he saw paintings by van Gogh. In October 1927 he joined the Bauhaus in Dessau, where he worked under Schlemmer, Kandinsky and Klee. From 1929 onwards he made frequent visits to Kirchner in Davos. In 1930 he visited Berlin and whilst there worked in Naum Gabo's studio. In the summer of 1930 he returned to Dessau; in 1933 he moved to Munich and visited

Paul Klee and Else Lasker-Schüler in Zürich; in 1935 he moved to Diessen; and in 1937 he was declared a 'degenerate artist' and forbidden to paint. From 1939 to 1944 he served with the German forces and was severely wounded; from 1945 to 1949 he was a prisoner of war in Russia. In 1949 he became a founder member of *Zen 49*; in 1950 he visited Hans Hartung in Paris, and won a prize for painting at the Twenty-fifth Biennale in Venice; in 1951 he visited Willi Baumeister and in 1952 E. W. Nay in Cologne. In 1953 he was visiting lecturer at the Landeskunstschule in Hamburg, and in 1955 joined the staff of the State College for Fine Arts in Kassel. In 1955 he won the Lissone Prize, and in 1958 the Marzotto Prize. In 1958 he also visited Italy. He is now living in Diessen in Upper Bavaria.

During his early period Winter was influenced by van Gogh and, subsequently, by Klee and Kandinsky. But in 1931 he turned away from the structural ideas that he had acquired at the Bauhaus and, taking his lead from Naum Gabo, evolved an extremely simple pictorial style. Using dark, matt, opaque colours, which he often mixed with cement, sand or plaster, Winter built up his finely textured layers of paint, as in bas-relief. In 1932, however, he abandoned this puritanical simplicity and painted highly inventive works rich in pictorial detail. From then onwards he treated pictorial space as if it were an infinite and brightly coloured realm. In 1932–3 he produced biomorphic configurations, and from 1932 to 1934 architectonic constructions. He then stopped painting for ten years, and when he resumed in 1944 he produced his *Triebkräfte der Erde* (*Forces of the Earth*), which were a direct development of these two trends. Later, after his meeting with Hans Hartung in Paris in 1950, the structural character of his works changed completely. Previously he had used pictorial forms that were closely allied to natural forms. He now abandoned these in favour of absolute forms that were far removed from natural models. In the so-called *Energetic Pictures* of this period free floating forms, or signs, appear against a background built up from contrasting colours, which create a three-dimensional pictorial space. The signs—which were executed as modulated bands of dense colour at first but subsequently acquired a streaky, spongy texture —create a vibrant effect. Since 1961 Winter has produced compositions in which the pictorial space is broken down into different colour zones. The accents in these colour and light walls, which contain no graphic detail, are determined by the vertical movement of the brush and the horizontal alignment of the layers of paint.

Catalogue, *Fritz Winter*, Kunstverein, Hanover 1966.

Winther, Richard. Danish painter and graphic artist, b. 1926. Winther trained at the Academy of

Art and the School of Graphic Art in Copenhagen. For a short period he belonged to the *Lines*, a group dedicated to Concrete Realism. Later, especially in his graphic works, he evolved a visionary form of Expressionism. Winther has also created occasional sculptures.

Witkiewicz, Stanislav Ignacy. Polish painter, author and dramatist, b. 1885 in Warsaw; d. 1939 in Wolyn. Witkiewicz was the son of the painter and art critic Stanislav Witkiewicz. After studying at the Academy of Art in Cracow he spent the war years in Russia, where he associated with the artistic *avant-garde*. In 1918 he returned to Poland and made contact with the 'formists' in Cracow. In 1919 he published a theoretical essay on 'New Forms in Painting and the Misunderstandings to which These Have Given Rise'. In this essay he argued that 'pure form' is a free manifestation of the existence of the individual, which enables the artist to advance to the general metaphysical 'secret of existence'. Between 1917 and 1923 his pictures revealed fantastic biological forms with symbolic implications, an extremely powerful and restless use of line and a marked deformation of figurative *motifs*, which underlines the intensity of Witkiewicz's artistic experience. But in 1924 Witkiewicz abandoned his search for 'pure form', which he had come to regard as a hopeless undertaking in view of the rapid growth of artistic perversion (which he had predicted). From then onwards he concentrated on portraits, which he painted under the influence of drugs and whose expressive power stemmed from a hallucinatory form of psychic Automatism. After the outbreak of the Second World War and the occupation of Poland Witkiewicz committed suicide. As a dramatist his principal quality was his clear understanding of social and political conditions. With his radical approach to dramatic rules he is closely allied to the dramatists of the modern theatre of the absurd.

Catalogue, *Stanislav Witkiewicz*, National Museum, Cracow 1965.
Peinture moderne polonaise: Sources et recherches, Musée Galliera, Paris 1969.

Witkowski, Kamil. Polish painter, b. 1876 in Skierniewice; d. 1950 in Milanówek, near Warsaw. He studied in Warsaw and also at Cracow. In 1920 he became a co-founder of the *Formisci* group in Warsaw; from 1922 he was a member of *Rytm*, and from 1933 of the *Plastycy Nowoczesni* and *Praesens*. He produced murals, and in 1922 stage sets for the Theatre Reduta in Warsaw. In 1930 there was an exhibition of his work in the Garlinski Salon there. Witkowski's work was Impressionist in tone to begin with, when he did mainly portraits and landscapes; later it became more Cubist, as is evident from the still lifes that he did at this period.

Woestijne, Gustave van de. Belgian painter, b. 1881 in Ghent; d. 1947 in Brussels. He studied in Ghent and then moved to Laethem-St-Martin in 1899. There he painted landscapes and portraits, the latter owing something to the peasants of Pieter Bruegel. He became Director of the Academy in Malines in 1925, and in 1938 moved to Brussels. His painting grew progressively more geometric in form and vivid in colouring.

Firmin van Hecke. *Gustave van de Woestijne*, Antwerp 1949.

Wolff, Gustav. German sculptor, painter, graphic artist and writer, b. 1886 in Zittau; d. 1934 in Berlin. He was self-taught. He spent the years 1900–5 in Rome, and 1906–14 in Paris. He was interned in France during the First World War, after which he moved to Berlin and taught there. In 1931 he went to the academy in Leningrad. He worked mainly in stone, wood and bronze. His forms are tense and concentrated, giving a somewhat pagan effect. Memorial exhibitions of his work have been seen in Hamburg in 1934–5 and in 1957.

Wols (Alfred Otto Wolfgang Schülze). German-French painter, b. 1913 in Berlin; d. 1951 in Paris. He was the son of well-to-do parents, his father being an important civil servant who was interested in the contemporary arts. Wols began to play the violin at the age of four, and developed this skill to a high professional level, playing in an orchestra in his youth. Though apparently he was producing drawings all his life, he seems not to have been concerned with becoming a painter. His first studies were in ethnology as a student at the Institute of African Studies at Frankfurt. He did spend a short period at the Bauhaus under Mies van der Rohe and Moholy-Nagy. He went to Paris in 1932, earning his living by photography and teaching German. He began to work in watercolour at this time. He also became interested in Surrealism, making the acquaintance of Miró, Ernst and others.

Wols next went on a long visit to Spain. The Spanish way of life appealed to him very strongly because of its freedom and spontaneity, particularly as expressed in flamenco music. The civil war forced his return to Paris in 1936. There he worked and exhibited successfully as a professional photographer. He was always drawing and painting, keeping a kind of diary of private images of his thoughts and dreams.

In 1939, at the outbreak of war, he was interned and detained in various camps for eighteen months. Here he began the type of drawing in thin, freely wandering line of strongly lyrical quality for which he later became very well known. Freed in 1940, he lived in great poverty in the south of France for the rest of the war, still maintaining the flow of his private drawings. The collector Henri Roché, his companion at this time, describes his work as 'drawing flowing from his fingers'. Wols himself affirmed that 'the movements of the hand and fingers suffice to express everything. The arm movements necessary in painting a canvas involve too much ambitious purpose and gymnastics. That is not what I want.' Nevertheless, when he returned to Paris at the end of the war he began to use canvases. In fact, he at last began to devote himself to painting, though he refused to regard it as a profession, and would have nothing to do with galleries. His refusal to exhibit was part of his maintenance of a mode of life which rejected normal social values.

His work attracted those who were proclaiming a new style, *Un Art Autre*. This painting claimed origins fundamentally different from traditional attitudes. It relied on semi-accidental Tachist effects to convey a lyrical, intuitional, abstract imagery. Wols used his art as a personal commentary, a gesture against the inhuman aspect of the times in which he had suffered. This gave his work a kind of involvement which appealed to many, including Sartre, who used him as an illustrator. Wols' *Art Autre* gave indication of the freedom of the new approach, a dream world of alternative possibilities. His work achieved a posthumous fame immediately after his death in 1951, and its influence over the next decade was very extensive.

Catalogue, *Wolfgang Schülze Wols*, Galerie Claude Bernard, Paris 1958.

Wolvens, Victor (Henri-Victor Wolvenspergens). Belgian painter, b. 1896 in Brussels. After studying painting Wolvens completed his training by taking lessons in sculpture. During his early period he was influenced by Ensor but subsequently veered towards the Animists before eventually adopting a bolder and essentially Expressionist style. His impasted technique and his bold colours earned him a certain reputation amongst a group of Belgian painters who, although lacking in originality themselves, had the wit to recognize and the ability to incorporate into their work recent developments in the sphere of figurative art.

Wood, Christopher. British painter, b. 1901 near Liverpool; d. 1930 at Salisbury. He took to painting in 1920 on leaving school. In 1921 he spent some time at the Académie Julian in Paris. Later that year he visited Italy, and from then until 1928 he lived an almost peripatetic life, travelling constantly around Europe and the Mediterranean, though he also spent several fairly long periods in Paris. In 1923 he met Picasso, through whose influence he was later (1926) associated with Diaghilev on designs for the ballet *Romeo and Juliet*, though they were never completed. He also met Cocteau in 1924. During this period his work is very variable, reflecting a variety of influences, those of the last two named artists especially but also, in 1925, Utrillo and Vlaminck. In 1926 he met Ben Nicholson and in 1927 he held his first exhibition with Nicholson and his wife at the Beaux-Arts Gallery, London. In 1928 he worked in Cumberland with the Nicholsons and also visited Cornwall, and it was at this time, through the influence of Nicholson and also Alfred Wallis, that his own style began to emerge. He worked in Brittany in the late summer of 1929, and also designed a ballet for C. B. Cochrane (produced in Manchester, 1930). In 1930 he worked through the spring in Cornwall. In May he showed in Paris at Bernheim's. He then worked in Brittany till he returned to England, where in August he was killed by a train.

Almost all his important paintings were produced in the last two years of his life, of Cornish and Breton subjects. They are small in scale and poetic in mood, sometimes with a quality of deliberate naïveté that suggests the Douanier Rousseau as well as Alfred Wallis. Colour harmonies are light with a beautiful balance of tone, recalling Utrillo and Nicholson but also, in moments of intensity, Vlaminck. Sometimes a curious poignancy is given by an unexplained and unexpected detail, like the parachute in the *Zebra and the Parachute*, his last picture. If it were not for his perfect taste his simplifications might seem coy and merely pretty, but instead he occasionally achieves effects of great intensity; his work, if it is not monumental, is certainly poetic; for example, *Nets at Treboul*, or the *Plage Hotel, Treboul*.

Eric Newton. *Christopher Wood*, London and Toronto 1938.

Wood, Grant. American painter, b. 1892 in Anamosa, Iowa; d. 1942 in Iowa City. In 1910 he enrolled at the Handicraft Guild of Minneapolis, where he took advanced courses in wood and metal work and studied design. After eighteen months there he returned to Cedar Rapids, Iowa, and opened a handicraft shop and attended the life class at the University of Iowa. In 1912 he went to Chicago and studied at the Art Institute. During the First World War he was with the camouflage division and later taught art in Cedar Rapids. Around 1920 he went to Paris, where he studied at the Académie Julian and painted in an Impressionistic manner (*Cottage, Brittany*, 1925, Cedar Rapids, Coll. Mrs. Grace Crager). When he returned to the United States he began painting seriously, concentrating on American scenes and becoming a leading figure in the Regionalist movement. He gained wide acclaim with his 1930 *American Gothic* (Chicago, Art Institute). The following year he combined decorative realism with humorous fantasy in *The Midnight Ride of Paul Revere* (1931, Memphis, Tenn., Coll. Mrs. C. M. Gooch). Though the former work has satirical overtones, the only overtly satirical painting in his oeuvre is *The*

Daughters of the American Revolution (1932, Beverly Hills, California, Coll. E. G. Robinson). In the 1930s he was supervisor of most of the Iowa projects of the Public Works Art Project and was himself one of the first artists to do decorations for the Post Office Department Building, Washington, D.C. He also did the murals at the Iowa State College Library, Ames, Iowa, entitled *When Tillage Begins, Other Arts Follow*. In 1935 he had his first two one-man shows (Ferargil Galleries, New York, and Lakeside Press Galleries, Chicago) and in 1959 a retrospective exhibition was held at the University of Kansas. Wood taught for many years at Iowa State University.

Catalogue, *Drawings and Paintings by Grant Wood*, Lakeside Press Galleries, Chicago 1935.
Darrell Garwood. *Artist in Iowa—A Life of Grant Wood*, New York 1944.

World of Art—*see* **Mir Iskusstva**

Wotruba, Fritz. Austrian sculptor, b. 1907 in Vienna. After serving an apprenticeship as a metal engraver Wotruba entered Anton Hanak's school as a student of sculpture but left shortly afterwards to continue his training alone. In 1928 he completed his first independent work and in 1931 had an exhibition at the Folkwang Museum in Essen. In 1934 he worked in Switzerland and in 1938 took up residence there to escape persecution. In 1945 he was offered a teaching post at the Vienna Academy and has lived in Vienna ever since. He has had numerous exhibitions in Europe and America and enjoys an international reputation.

Although Wotruba received a certain artistic stimulus from the writers and musicians amongst his personal friends, he owed nothing to the other sculptors of his own generation. He himself, however, has exerted a powerful influence on the younger European artists and was responsible for the emergence of the Viennese School, which includes a number of important sculptors such as Hoflehner, Avramidis and Urteil.

Wotruba's material is stone, his theme the human being. From the *Male Torso* of 1928 to the great *Marburg Relief* of 1965 he has always carved stone 'figures' whose basically organic forms are organized in Cyclopean structures. This one central theme— man conceived as an architectonic structure—has appeared in endless variations ranging from simple torsos to groups hewn from a solid block of stone, whose weight, density, solidity and resistance Wotruba always respects. But, although he undoubtedly enters into a dialogue with his material, his art is more than a technical exercise; it is also a response to the spirit of our age. Despite their rigidity Wotruba's figures are full of genuine pathos. Between them they make up a body of work which, although reminiscent of archaic cultures, is essentially a product of our own era. As such it stands in marked contrast to the modern trend towards movement, space and perishable, malleable material.

Elias Canetti. *Fritz Wotruba*, Vienna 1955.
Friedrich Heer (ed.). *Fritz Wotruba*, Neuchâtel 1961.
Otto Breicha (ed.). *Schriften zum Werk*, Vienna 1967.
Catalogue, *Fritz Wotruba*, Kestner Gesellschaft, Hanover 1967.

Woty (Woty Werner, *née* Rütgers). German painter and tapestry artist, b. 1903 in Berlin. Woty is the widow of the painter Theodor Werner. After studying in Berlin, Munich and Paris she lived in Paris and Berlin for many years before finally settling in Munich.

Early in her career Woty abandoned paintings in favour of tapestries, which she weaves without preliminary studies, creating abstract, evocative designs that are reminiscent of Klee and Miró.

Wouters, Rik. Belgian painter and sculptor, b. 1882 in Malines; d. 1916 in Amsterdam. Wouters first began to sculpt in his father's studio in 1894 when he was twelve. In 1899 he enrolled at the Academy of Art in Malines, where he was a pupil of Theo Blick, and in 1901 entered the Academy of Art in Brussels, where he studied under the sculptor van der Stappen. He married in 1905, and in 1907 won the Godecharle Prize for sculpture in Brussels. In 1909 he became friendly with the painter Simon Levy, and saw photographs of works by Cézanne. In 1912 he had an exhibition in the Galerie Giroux in Brussels. In the same year he visited Paris, where he saw originals by Cézanne, and visited Düsseldorf and Cologne. In 1913 he designed stage sets for the play *Le Petit Poucet*—which was produced in Brussels and Paris—won the Picard Prize, and had an exhibition in Antwerp. In 1914 he joined the Belgian forces, but was interned in the following year in the camp at Zeit, Holland. In 1915–16 he underwent three major operations, which left him so debilitated that he died shortly afterwards.

In 1916 a large retrospective exhibition of his works was staged in Amsterdam. Wouters' sculptures were conceived in the French Impressionist mould. His draped figures were completely conventional, but he did create a number of convincing portraits. One of his most celebrated sculptures, of which several casts were made, is the *Mad Girl* of 1912, a work inspired by the dancer Isadora Duncan.

Wouters was a self-taught painter. His first pictures date from 1908 and reveal the influence of J. Ensor. Subsequently, he changed his style completely, due to the impact of Cézanne. The harsh colours of his early period then became quite subdued, and he applied his paint with small careful strokes of the brush, using it as a means of modelling, and so creating an impression of plasticity. Later, from c. 1912 onwards, he incorporated Fauvist elements into his paintings. This was an important development, for it was Wouters who introduced Fauvism into Belgium, thus creating a Flemish school of Fauvism.

Catalogue, *Rik Wouters*, Musée National d'Art Moderne, Paris 1957.

WPA/FAP (Works Progress Administration/Federal Arts Project). The programme was established by the US Government in August 1935 and grew out of three previously existing New Deal projects that had been initiated to aid artists during the Depression. The first of these, the Public Works of Art Project (December 1933–June 1934), was established to aid unemployed artists through the winter of 1933–4. Approximately 2,500 artists, working at 'plumbers'' wages, were employed by the project, producing over 15,000 oil paintings, murals, sculptures, watercolours, etchings and drawings to decorate public buildings. The artists were given complete freedom of expression in their depictions of America. The Treasury Section of Painting and Sculpture (October 1934–June 1943) employed artists by contract rather than by weekly salary to produce paintings, murals and architectural sculpture for the embellishment of federal buildings. As with the former project, the themes dealt with American life, although the handling of the scenes tended to be more conservative, since artists were selected through competitions. Among the artists working on this project were Grant Wood, Reginald Marsh, Rockwell Kent, Guy Pène du Bois and William Zorach. The third division, the Treasury Relief Art Project (July 1935–June 1939), was a complement of the Treasury Section. Works of art were produced for both new and old buildings, while payments for the Treasury Section's projects came from the building funds—one per cent of the total budget of new edifices. The Federal Art Project (August 1935–April 1943), like the other projects, provided employment, encouraged the growth of artistic expression, promoted a broader interest in American art, and established centres for art education. Artists were hired to produce works of art in all media for distribution to tax-supported institutions.

Perhaps the most significant, and sometimes most disappointing, works of these projects were the murals. The artists were inspired by the Mexican muralists José Clemente Orozco and Diego Rivera, whose works were produced in a revolutionary milieu. The Americans lacked the daring of their Latin colleagues; in fact their murals tended to be more conservative than their pre-WPA paintings. The restraints and conservatism were fostered by the selection of competitors by non-artistic bureaucrats. The change in style is especially evident in the works of abstract artists such as Arshile Gorky and Karl Knaths. Stuart Davis was one of the few progressive artists whose style exhibits no such detrimental change, although Davis never decorated any federal buildings. Such a relatively traditional artist as George Biddle changed slightly if at all. Though atypical, works by such artists as Ben Shahn (*Worker with Electric Drill*, 1938, study for Bronx Central Post Office mural, College Park, Md., Coll. University of Maryland) and Kindred McLeary (*Lower East Side*, 1939, New York, Madison Square Post Office) reveal some of the fine achievements of the WPA murals. Nearly every known artist of the period, except those who were teaching, was in some way connected with the WPA. The project itself seems to have been far more significant to the development of painting in the 1940s and 1950s than has generally been thought, perhaps more important for American art than the immediately preceding artistic events on the Continent.

Holger Cahill (intro.). Catalogue, *New Horizons in American Art: Exhibition of W.P.A. Art*, Museum of Modern Art, New York 1936.
Francis V. O'Connor. *Federal Art Patronage, 1933 to 1943*, University of Maryland Art Gallery, College Park (Md.) 1966.

Wrampe, Fritz. German sculptor, b. 1893 in Munich; d. 1934 in Munich. Wrampe was a pupil of Hermann Hahn at the Munich Academy. His work consisted of animal sculptures. After his murder there was a memorial exhibition of his work in the Bibliothek der Deutschen Museen, and later (1951, 1959) in Cologne and Munich.

Wroblewski, Andrei. Polish painter and art historian, b. 1927 in Vilna; d. 1957 in the High Tatra. Wroblewski studied painting at the Cracow Academy and the history of art at Cracow University. In his dual capacity as painter and art historian he was fully integrated into the Cracow art world.

In 1948 Wroblewski began to paint abstract compositions incorporating symbolic elements, but in the following year he went over to figurative works. As one of the founders of the 'autodidactic group' at the Cracow Academy he helped to formulate, and contributed to, its programme of committed art. In his case the commitment took the form of an anti-aesthetic bias. In 1956–7 Wroblewski started to paint dramatic pictures fashioned from simple, symbolic signs.

Catalogue, *Andrei Wroblewski*, National Museum, Poznan 1968.
Peinture moderne polonaise: Sources et recherches, Musée Galliera, Paris 1969.

Wunderlich, Paul. German painter and graphic artist, b. 1927 in Berlin. After studying from 1947 to 1951 Wunderlich obtained a post at the Landes-kunstschule (State School of Art) in Hamburg, where he taught graphic techniques from 1951 to 1960. He then spent two years in Paris before joining the staff of the College of Fine Arts in Hamburg in 1963.

In his paintings, which are executed in a Neo-Surrealist style and incorporate elements of *Jugendstil* and veristic anatomical detail, Wunderlich tries to create aesthetic effects. Both his paintings and his art prints are technically extremely sophisticated.

Catalogue, *Paul Wunderlich*, Pfalzgalerie, Kaiserslautern 1965.

Wyeth, Andrew. American painter, b. 1917 in Chadds Ford, Pennsylvania. He was the pupil of his father, Newell Convers Wyeth, a noted illustrator and mural painter. His sister and brother-in-law, Henriette and Peter Hurd, as well as his sister Carolyn and son James are also painters. His sister Ann is a musician and composer. Wyeth had his first one-man show at the William Macbeth Gallery, New York, in 1937. From the beginning, he painted in a highly detailed, Realistic manner, most often in watercolour or tempera, his colour range centring on earth tones. His works often reflect a sense of melancholy and desolation, as in *Wind from the Sea* (1947, tempera, Amherst, Mass., Coll. Prof. and Mrs. Charles H. Morgan). The old lace curtains, cracked wall and ripped window blind betray his high degree of technical ability. The same psychological penetration in *Christina's World* (1948, tempera, New York, Museum of Modern Art) is emphasized by the vast space between the figure seen from behind and the distant houses. In juxtaposition to this psychic orientation are works of touching sentiment, such as *Faraway* (1952, Coll. Mrs. Andrew Wyeth), a portrait of the artist's son, a work which Wyeth considers one of his first really successful paintings in his dry-brush technique. An artist of tremendous popular appeal, he has been included in many exhibitions and has had many one-man and retrospective exhibitions.

Catalogue, *Andrew Wyeth. Temperas, Water Colors and Drawings*, Albright-Knox Art Gallery, Buffalo (New York) 1962.
Edgar P. Richardson. Catalogue, *Andrew Wyeth. Temperas, Water-colors, Dry Brush, Drawings—1938 into 1966*, Pennsylvania Academy of the Fine Arts, Philadelphia 1966.
Richard Meryman. *Andrew Wyeth*, Boston 1968.

Wynter, Bryan. British painter, b. 1915 in London; d. 1975. From 1938–40 he attended the Slade School. His first one-man show was held in 1947 at the Redfern Gallery. In common with other British painters, he moved from landscape to a British version of Abstract Expressionism which, unlike its American counterpart, still bears some tenuous relationship to things outside itself, if only through the artist's interest in the painting's power of suggestion of space and form to the spectator. In the sixties he has turned to producing mechanical light and colour constructions which really extend naturally from his work as a painter. These coloured shapes revolving before a concave mirror present to the spectator a constantly changing kaleidoscope.

X

Xceron, John. Greek-American painter, b. 1890 in Isari, Greece; d. 1967 in New York. Xceron went to America when he was 14, and studied in Washington and New York. He spent ten years in Paris from 1927, there acquiring a Cubist style which gradually became more abstract. He returned to New York in 1937, having had his first one-man show there two years before, and joined the Association of Abstract Artists.

Xenakis, Cosmas. Greek painter and architect, b. 1925 in Vraile, Rumania. He studied in Athens and spent some time in Paris. He makes long-range experiments on purely pictorial problems. He has an explicitly geometrical approach but without creating flat surfaces. He avoids all Expressionistic tendencies.

Y

Yamaguchi, Katsuhiro. Japanese sculptor, b. 1928 in Tokyo. Yamaguchi studied law at Nihon University, Tokyo. He has experimented with methods chiefly related to materials. In 1952 he invented a variable relief with translucent glass named *Vitrine*. Thereafter he made floating wire gauze and kite-shaped cloth constructions. Lately he has begun to work in light art. He was included in the Fifth Guggenheim International Exhibition in 1967, and the Venice Biennale in 1968. He lives in Tokyo.

Yamaguchi, Takeo. Japanese painter, b. 1902. He studied art in Paris from 1927 to 1931, and was influenced by Fernand Léger and Ossip Zadkine. He won first prize at the Tokyo Biennale in 1954, and has been invited to numerous international exhibitions. Beginning with Léger-like colourful semi-abstractions he arrived, after the Second World War, at a very simple geometric composition which reminds one at times of ancient Chinese hieroglyphics. His recent works are composed of neatly applied layers of paint forming monochromatic irregular rectangles which occupy most of the space. The surfaces give the feeling of a tilled field rooted in the traditional relationship of the labourer to nature.

Yeats, Jack Butler. Irish painter, writer and illustrator, b. 1871 in London; d. 1957 in London. Yeats was the son of J. B. Yeats and the brother of W. B. Yeats. He was brought up in Sligo, in the west of Ireland. He returned to London to attend the Westminster School of Art. He worked first as a graphic artist and illustrator. He had his first one-man show in Dublin in 1899, and settled there in 1900. He did not, however, finally take up painting until about 1905, though he had first worked in oils in 1897. His inspiration seems to have been French Impressionism, and his earliest works reflect particularly Degas, Manet and Toulouse-Lautrec, in subject (horse races, circuses, etc.) as well as in style. When he exhibited in the Armory Show in New York in 1913 his work still retained this style to some extent (*Dwarf at the Circus*), but it was also beginning to be more violent in colour and deliberately less elegant in drawing. From that time onwards his brushwork became increasingly free and Expressionistic and his drawing more broken. The Irish Troubles seem to have affected him very deeply and his pictures became in several senses increasingly Irish. They are not only about the external appearance of Ireland, but also about the actual experience of being Irish, especially the Civil War pictures (*Bachelor's Walk*, 1922). In this his approach to painting is in many ways like his brother's approach to poetry. He also began to develop a mysterious and poetic kind of symbolism (*The Blood of Abel*, 1941, with its allusion to the war, and its symbolism of the human journey expressed through the image of the tinkers). As this element grew in his work he developed for it an Expressionist freedom of handling that almost ignores drawing, a dazzling pattern of paint slashed on with the palette knife, the colour violent, sometimes almost lurid. In his handling and drawing the closest parallel to his work would be Kokoschka, who greatly admired him, but in his approach to his subject, though not its organization, he is more akin to Chagall. More than either of these two, however, he is a brilliant eccentric, and he is wholly Irish.

Thomas MacGreevy. *Jack B. Yeats: An Appreciation and an Interpretation*, Dublin 1945.
Catalogues, *Jack B. Yeats*, Waddington Galleries, London 1961 and 1963.

Yoshida, Minoru. Japanese painter and sculptor, b. 1935 in Osaka. He graduated from the Kyoto University of Arts. He is a member of the *Gutai* group. He developed colourful abstract painting with vegetal shapes and then turned to constructions of light and movement and sometimes of sound, which contrast the organic with the mechanical image. He now lives in Kyoto.

Yoshihara, Jiro. Japanese painter, b. 1905 in Osaka. In the 1930s his paintings marked the influence of the European movement. He has participated in the *Nika* group from 1934 to the present. He won the first prize at the Tokyo Biennale in 1967. He is also well known as the founder of the *Gutai* group, which is considered the fore-runner of 'happenings' and Action Paintings. After such collective experimentation, his own works developed into a simplified irregular circular form left blank on a painted ground. These paintings tend to remind foreign viewers of the free-hand paintings of the ancient Zen Buddhist masters.

Youngerman, Jack. American painter, b. 1926 in Louisville, Kentucky. He studied at the École des Beaux-Arts in Paris, and was influenced by the Constructivists' geometrical approach. He returned to the United States, where his work became recognizable from 1954 by its flowing lines and flat, vivid colours. By the 1960s he was experimenting with 'interchangeable' pictures, in which figure and background, being of complementary shape, could take each other's place. In addition to painting he made silk-screens and lithographs which with their brilliant colouring and sharp outlines recall Matisse's late work.

Yuhara, Kazuo. Japanese sculptor, b. 1930 in Tokyo. Yuhara graduated from the Tokyo University of Arts. In 1963 he went to Paris. He has shown at the Paris Biennale and the Salon de la Jeune Sculpture of the Rodin Museum in 1965, and the Fifth Guggenheim International Exhibition in 1967. Yuhara creates abstract sculpture as a substantial and internal expression. He lives in Paris.

Yunkers, Adja. Russian-American painter and graphic artist, b. 1900 in Riga, Latvia. The son of wealthy Russian parents, he lived in St. Petersburg until 1914, when he left home and lived with groups of poets and painters. In 1916 he joined the army and was in the cavalry of the Imperial Guard until the Revolution. In 1918 he went to Germany and first exhibited at Maria Kunde's Gallery in Hamburg. He spent the next few years travelling in Germany, Italy, Spain, the Canary Islands and West Africa. In 1923 he was in Paris and the following year moved to Havana, Cuba, where he became an advertising manager and interior decorator and also started an art review. He spent a brief period in Mexico before moving back to Europe and settling in Paris, where he remained until 1933 when he moved to Sweden. There he edited the art magazines *Creation* and *ARS* and started *Ars Konstserie*, a series of portfolios of modern Swedish graphic artists. In 1947 he moved to the United States, where he received a Guggenheim Fellowship (1949–50, renewed 1954–5) and a Ford Foundation Grant (1959). He is best known as a graphic artist of tremendous impact, revealing deepest emotions; a work such as *Crying Woman* (1944, coloured woodcut, Boston, Museum of Fine Arts), with its strongly executed dark lines and distortions for the sake of psychological effect, recalls the work of E. Munch. His later works, such as *The Birdlover* (1951, coloured woodcut), have the same emotive force but are less descriptive and more abstracted. The horror of this face seems like an image seen in a shattered mirror. His later pastels and oils are infinitely more delicate and more abstract. In works such as *Passage de la lune* (1961, pastel, New York, Coll. Dore Ashton) he combines the colourism of the Impressionists with the breadth of handling and forcefulness of execution associated with the Abstract Expressionists. Yunkers has taught at the New School for Social Research, New York (1947–56), and in summer sessions at the University of New Mexico (1948 and 1949).

John Palmer Leeper. 'Adja Yunkers', *New Mexico Quarterly* 20, No. 2, Summer 1950.
Catalogue, *Adja Yunkers*, Baltimore Museum of Art, Baltimore 1960.
Catalogue, *Adja Yunkers*, Stedelijk Museum, Amsterdam 1962.

Z

Zabaleta, Rafael. Spanish painter, b. 1907 in Quesada; d. 1960. He first studied at the Escuela de Bellas Artes in Madrid, and then in Paris. His first one-man show was in 1942 in Madrid. He visited France and Italy. He won the UNESCO prize at the Spanish-American Biennale, in Barcelona, and in 1961 a prize at the thirtieth Biennale in Venice.

Zack, Leon. Russian-French painter, b. 1892 in Nijni-Novgorod. After leaving Russia in 1920, he stayed first in Florence, then Berlin, before settling in Paris in 1923. He took part in various Salons, particularly the Salon des Surindépendants. Zack became known for his ballet décor and book illustrations, then he turned—successfully—to religious art. Thus he produced the *Way of the Cross* at Carsac in the Dordogne (1950), stained-glass windows for the chapel of St. Sulpice in Paris (1957) and the Sacré-Coeur at Mulhouse (1959). From 1954 his painting became non-figurative, first of all geometric in inspiration, before evolving towards a Tachist style, more lyrical and freer.

Zadkine, Ossip. Russian sculptor, b. 1890 in Smolensk; d. 1967 in Paris. On his mother's side Zadkine was descended from Scottish shipbuilders, who had emigrated to Russia. In 1905 he was sent to Northern England to learn languages and whilst there received his first lessons in art. In the following year he ran away to London, where he scraped a living by carving ornaments until his parents agreed to pay his way through art school. In 1908 he studied in London and in 1909 in Paris. In 1910 he fitted out a small studio in Paris and began to contribute to the exhibitions in the Salon des Indépendants and the Salon d'Automne. In 1915 he volunteered for the French Army. In 1919, after his demobilization, he began to exhibit again. His work soon gained widespread recognition and in 1929 the first Zadkine monograph was published. In 1941 Zadkine fled to New York to escape from the German occupation, but returned to Paris as soon as the war was over. From 1946 onwards he taught at the Académie de la Grande Chaumière. In 1950 he was honoured with a retrospective exhibition in the Musée National d'Art Moderne in Paris and in 1950 was awarded the prize for sculpture at the Biennale in Venice. His monument to *The Destroyed City*, which was erected in Rotterdam in 1953, brought him international fame. Subsequently he created other well-known monuments, including that to Vincent van Gogh. His works have been shown in numerous exhibitions staged in important international galleries.

Zadkine never joined a particular school or group. He went his own way, although in the course of his long development he made contacts with the representatives of the dominant artistic trends of his day. There are traces of Cubism in his work. But there are traces of Expressionism and Surrealism as well: severe, block-like forms are integrated into lively, Baroque compositions. The formal and thematic aspects of Zadkine's sculptures are welded together to produce a body of work which is immensely rich and full of poetry and humanity.

Maurice Raynal. *Ossip Zadkine*, Rome 1924.
Catalogue, *Ossip Zadkine*, National Gallery of Canada, Ottawa 1956.
A. M. Hammacher. *Zadkine*, New York 1959.
Ionel Jianou. *Zadkine*, New York 1965.

Zak, Eugène. Polish painter, b. 1884 in Molijino; d. 1926 in Paris. He studied in Paris and travelled to Italy and Munich. He was a member of the *École de Paris*, and was influenced by Pierre Puvis de Chavannes. He painted landscapes with figures at first, but later the setting disappeared and one figure would stand out against a neutral ground. His Slav origin imbued him with an intense imagination.

Zañartu, Enrique Antúnez. Chilean painter, b. 1921 in Paris. Zañartu is the brother of Nemesio Antúnez Zañartu. After beginning his artistic career in Santiago, Chile, Zañartu worked in New York from 1944 to 1949. Since then he has been living in Paris, where he has taught graphic art at Hayter's Atelier 17.

Zañartu is an Abstract Expressionist. He has illustrated books by numerous authors, including Michel Butor.

Catalogue, *Enrique Antúnez Zañartu*, Buenos Aires 1969.

Zañartu, Nemesio Antúnez. Chilean painter and graphic artist, b. 1918 in Santiago, Chile. After starting to train as an architect in Santiago Zañartu went to New York in 1943, where he stayed until 1949 and studied graphic art in Hayter's Atelier 17. From 1950 to 1953 he worked in Europe, then returned to Chile and founded his own Atelier 99 in Santiago, where he has since trained numerous students. At the 1957 Bienal in São Paulo he was honoured as the best Latin American painter. In his paintings Zañartu creates imaginary worlds after the manner of Matta.

Zao Wou-Ki. Chinese painter, b. 1921 in Peking. After studying (from 1935 to 1941) and teaching (from 1941 to 1947) at the Academy of Art in Hangchow Zao Wou-Ki went to Paris in 1948 and has remained there ever since. During a brief early period he produced figurative works which possess both the delicate colouring and the linear qualities that we associate with Paul Klee, but not his gentle irony. Subsequently, Zao Wou-Ki evolved an extremely precise and subtle abstract style based on his own eastern tradition, which calls for subjective contemplation and graphic spontaneity. In this essentially harmonious form of painting the artist seeks to evoke the changing face of nature, the different kinds of beauty found at different times of day and in different seasons of the year. In doing so, he inclines towards a kind of serene mysticism. Unlike his western counterpart, who often paints pictures of immense power, Zao Wou-Ki invariably produces reflective and extremely delicate works that are in perfect harmony with a universe whose tensions and placidity, gentleness and anger, constitute his sole theme.

Zaritsky, Yossef. Israeli painter, b. 1891 in Kiev. After studying painting in Kiev and Moscow Zaritsky settled in Palestine in 1923. For the next twenty-five years he painted watercolours. His landscapes, which at first revealed clear traces of *Intimisme*, gradually developed into pure and subtle abstracts. Zaritsky was largely responsible for founding the *Horizons Nouveaux* group in 1948. With their strict formal designs and their lyrical scenes his paintings are typical of post-war Israeli art, which still bore the imprint of the Jewish tradition of the *École de Paris*.

Zigaina, Giuseppe. Italian painter, b. 1924 in Cervignano, Friaul. Zigaina is a member of the *Pittori Realisti* group. He is now living in the Villa Vicentina (Udine).

Zigaina paints scenes from the life of the Udine peasants and tenant farmers in an expressive, Social Realist style which he derived from R. Guttuso.

R. Usiglio. *Zigaina*, Milan 1954.

Zille, Heinrich. German painter and draughtsman, b. 1858 in Redenburg; d. 1929 in Berlin. Zille studied both lithography and painting in Berlin. He created illustrations for magazines such as *Simplicissimus* and *Jugend*, and from 1901 exhibited in the Berlin Secession's graphics shows. His drawings showed his deep concern for social ills, expressed with a humorous Realism.

Zimmermann, Mac. German painter, b. 1912 in Stettin. Zimmermann studied in Stettin and Hamburg. In 1946 he began to teach, first at the Academy in Dessau, then at the Academy in Berlin. In 1958 he transferred to the Academy in Munich, where he is still teaching today.

Zimmermann's Surrealist scenes with their deep perspectives and Bacchanalian figures were inspired by Klee and the *Pittura Metafisica*.

B. Degenhart. *Mac Zimmermann*, Berlin 1955.

Živković, Bogosav. Yugoslav sculptor, b. 1920 in Leskovac, Serbia. Živković started out in life as a house porter in Belgrade. In 1957 he began to produce his wood carvings. These consist of two basic types: wooden posts with a row of carvings set one above the other as on totem poles, and sections of tree trunks with several parallel rows of carvings set one above the other. The forms used by this primitive sculptor are products of the collective unconscious.

O. Bihalji-Merin. *Bogosav Živković: The World of a Primitive Sculptor*, London 1962.

Zobel, Fernando. Spanish painter, b. 1924 in Manila, Philippines. He studied in Spain, Switzerland and the USA. His first one-man show was in Boston in 1950, and he has also exhibited in Madrid, where he now lives. He took part in the exhibition of modern Spanish painting at the Tate Gallery, London, in 1962. He has won first prize three times at the National Philippine Exhibition of Painting: in 1952, 1955, and 1956.

Zogbaum, Wilfred M. American painter and sculptor, b. 1915 in Newport, Rhode Island; d. 1965 in Upton, New York. The grandson of the mural painter and illustrator Rufus F. Zogbaum, he graduated from St. George's School, Newport, and attended the Yale School of Fine Arts (1933–4), the John Sloan Class in New York (1934–5) and the Hans Hofmann School of Fine Arts in New York and Provincetown, Mass. (1935–7). From 1937 to 1938 he was on a Guggenheim Foundation Scholarship. Though he worked mainly in Bavaria with Fritz Winter and other former Bauhaus artists, he spent some time in London and Paris, where he met Ben Nicholson, Gabo, Moholy-Nagy, Léger and Kandinsky. After serving in the United States Army Signal Corps (1941–6) he worked as a magazine and advertising photographer. He only turned to painting and sculpture as a full-time occupation in 1948, and in 1952 had his first one-man show at the Iolas Gallery, New York. His paintings, such as *Crowned with Glory* (1957, New York, Stable Gallery), falls into the tradition of Motherwell and the Abstract Expressionists, with their patches of colour juxtaposing each other in areas of light and dark, and woven together by a casual linearity. His sculpture ranges from light, Calder-like fanciful works with delicate linear appendages extending into space (*Green Hills*, 1959, Washington, D.C., Obelisk Gallery), to the solid rectangles and smooth, flat surfaces of *Coast Guard* (1964, San Francisco, Dilexi Gallery) which recall the late works of David Smith. Zogbaum was Visiting Associate Professor of Art, University of California, Berkeley (1957–8), and Visiting Artist, University of Minnesota (1958).

Zorach, William. American painter, sculptor and graphic artist, b. 1887 in Eurburg, Lithuania; d. 1966 in Bath, Maine. He left school in the eighth grade and went to work for a lithography company in Cleveland. He studied drawing and painting at evening classes of the Cleveland School of Art (1903–6) and studied for two winters at the National Academy of Design (1908–10). When he went to Paris in 1910 he enrolled at La Palette, where he studied under John D. Fergusson and met his future wife, Marguerite Thompson. At this time he was strongly influenced by the Fauves (1913, *Spring, 1*, Coll. Zorach Family) and several of these Fauvist works were accepted for the 1911 Salon d'Automne. In that year he returned to the United States and the following year he had his first one-man show at the Taylor Galleries, Cleveland. In the mid-1910s his style veered away from Fauvism towards Cubism, as reflected in *One Horse Farm* (1917, Coll. Zorach Family). In 1922 he abandoned painting for sculpture, a medium in which he was less affected by contemporary trends than in his paintings, as seen in the marble *Mother and Child* (1927–30, New York, Metropolitan Museum of Art) with its smooth flow of forms, suppression of detail, textural interest and emphasis on essential volumes. He also worked in various metals, as seen in the 1932 *Spirit of the Dance* (New York, Radio City Music Hall). Here too the heavy, solid contours and block-like bulk and weight are the salient characteristics. His sculptural style changed little throughout his career, as witnessed by his 1957 *The Family* (granite, New York, Coll. L. Arnold Weissberger). Among Zorach's important commissions are: *Benjamin Franklin* (1936–7, Washington, D.C., Benjamin Franklin Post Office), *Builders of the Future* (1939, New York World's Fair), *Man and Work* (1953, Rochester, Minn., Mayo Clinic) and a 1961 relief for the Municipal Court Building,

New York City. He taught in progressive schools in and around New York (1920–35) and at Columbia University summer sessions (1932–5) as well as at the Art Students' League (1929–60). The author of many articles, he also wrote the book *Zorach Explains Sculpture* (1947).

Paul S. Wingert. *The Sculpture of William Zorach*, New York 1938.
William Zorach. *Zorach Explains Sculpture*, New York 1947.
John I. H. Baur. Catalogue, *William Zorach*, Whitney Museum of American Art, New York 1959.
Donelson F. Hoopes. Catalogue, *William Zorach—Paintings, Watercolors and Drawings, 1911–22*, Brooklyn Museum, New York 1968.

Zuloaga y Zabaleta, Ignacio. Spanish painter, b. 1870 in Eibar; d. 1945 in Madrid. He trained in Paris, and on his return to Spain painted such subjects as episodes from daily life, the countryside, and the bullfight. He had to a certain extent absorbed the influence of Impressionism from his Paris period, when he had also been acquainted with Degas, Gauguin and Rodin. He painted powerful pictures with subdued colouring.

Zwobada, Jacques. French sculptor, b. 1900 in Neuilly-sur-Seine; d. 1967 in Paris. He learned much from Rodin, though later he turned from figurative to abstract sculpture. In 1948, after a fifteen-year break in which he taught drawing, he returned to an approximation of his early style. His last great work was a funerary monument of considerable extent.